D0759876

ENCYCLOPEDIA OF PSYCHOLOGY

EDITORS

Senior Editors

Edward B. Blanchard
Richard R. Bootzin
Gordon H. Bower
Jane Close Conoley
Kay Deaux
Ronald E. Fox

Lenore W. Harmon
William C. Howell
Anthony J. Marsella
Richard H. Price
Lauren B. Resnick
Henry L. Roediger III

Robert Rosenthal
Neil W. Schmitt
Jerome L. Singer
Larry R. Squire
Carolyn Zahn-Waxler

Consulting Editors

Paul B. Baltes
James N. Butcher
Patrick H. DeLeon

Herbert C. Kelman
A. David Mangelsdorff
Ronald B. Miller
Robert J. Sternberg

Warren R. Street
Richard M. Suinn
James Waller

Biography Editor

Ludy T. Benjamin, Jr.

Associate Editors

Mark I. Appelbaum
Margret M. Baltes*
Mahzarin R. Banaji
Larry E. Beutler
Edward B. Blanchard
Richard R. Bootzin
A. Kathleen Hoard Burlew
James N. Butcher
Elizabeth D. Capaldi
Laura Carstensen
Stephen J. Ceci
Deborah J. Coon
Kay Deaux
Patricia G. Devine

Donald A. Dewsbury
Shari S. Diamond
Thomas K. Fagan
Raymond E. Fancher
Donald K. Freedheim
Laurel Furumoto
Rochel Gelman
Morton Ann Gernsbacher
Maribeth Gettinger
William T. Greenough
Margaret G. Hermann
James G. Kelly
Eric Klinger
Gerald P. Koocher

Marianne LaFrance
Frederick T. L. Leong
Richard M. Lerner
Walter J. Lonner
A. David Mangelsdorff
Dan P. McAdams
Barbara G. Melamed
Ronald B. Miller
Raymond S. Nickerson
Michael J. Patton
Michael C. Roberts
Henry L. Roediger III
Ralph L. Rosnow
Caryl E. Rusbult

Peter Salovey
Neil W. Schmitt
Neil Schneiderman
Edward P. Shafranske
Marybeth Shinn
Edward J. Shoben
Laurence D. Smith
Larry R. Squire
Karen Callan Stoiber
Warren R. Street
Samuel M. Turner
Richard K. Wagner
Drew Westen
Jeremy M. Wolfe

International Advisory Board

Rubén Ardila
Michael Harris Bond
Schlomo Breznitz
Roland Diaz-Loving
Hans J. Eysenck*
M. Samir Farag
Hiroshi Imada

Susan D. Iversen
Cigdem Kagitcibasi
Ludmila Karpenko
Willem J. M. Levelt
Ingrid Lunt
David N. Magnusson
Leon Mann

Serge Moscovici
Dan Olweus
Kurt Pawlik
Jai B. P. Sinha
Jan Strelau
Endel Tulving
Zhong-Ming Wang

*Deceased

ENCYCLOPEDIA OF PSYCHOLOGY

Alan E. Kazdin
Editor in Chief

VOLUME 5

AMERICAN
PSYCHOLOGICAL
ASSOCIATION

OXFORD

UNIVERSITY PRESS

2000

AMERICAN
PSYCHOLOGICAL
ASSOCIATION

Washington, D.C.

OXFORD
UNIVERSITY PRESS

Oxford New York
Athens Auckland Bangkok Bogotá Buenos Aires Calcutta
Cape Town Chennai Dar es Salaam Delhi Florence Hong Kong Istanbul
Karachi Kuala Lumpur Madrid Melbourne Mexico City Mumbai
Nairobi Paris São Paulo Singapore Taipei Tokyo Toronto Warsaw

and associated companies in
Berlin Ibadan

Copyright © 2000 by American Psychological Association and Oxford University Press, Inc.

Published by American Psychological Association
750 First Street, NE, Washington, D.C. 20002-4242
www.apa.org
and
Oxford University Press, Inc.
198 Madison Avenue, New York, New York 10016
www.oup.com

Oxford is a registered trademark of Oxford University Press.

Library of Congress Cataloging-in-Publication Data
Encyclopedia of psychology / Alan E. Kazdin, editor in chief
p. cm.
Includes bibliographical references and index.
1. Psychology—Encyclopedias. I. Kazdin, Alan E.
BF31 .E52 2000 150'.3—dc21 99-055239
ISBN 1-55798-187-6 (set); ISBN 1-55798-654-1 (vol. 5)

AMERICAN PSYCHOLOGICAL ASSOCIATION STAFF

Gary R. VandenBos, Ph.D., *Publisher*
Julia Frank-McNeil, *Commissioning Editor*
Theodore J. Baroody, *Senior Development Editor*
Adrian Harris Forman, *Project Editor*

OXFORD UNIVERSITY PRESS STAFF

Karen Casey, *Publisher*
Claude Conyers, *Commissioning Editor*
Marion Osmun, *Senior Development Editor*
Matthew Giarratano, *Managing Editor*
Peri Zeenkov and Norina Frabotta, *Project Editors*
Nancy Hoagland, *Production Manager*
Jessica Ryan and Will Moore, *Production Editors*
AEIOU, Inc., *Index Editor*
AEIOU, Inc., Linda Berman, Denise McIntyre,
Space Coast Indexers, Inc., Linda Webster, *Indexers*
Suzanne Holt, *Book Design*
Joan Greenfield, *Cover Design*

3 5 7 9 8 6 4 2

Printed in the United States of America
on acid-free paper

L CONTINUED

LEARNING. [*This entry provides a broad survey of learning. It comprises five articles:*

An Overview
Molecular and Cellular Aspects
Conditioning Approach
Cognitive Approach for Humans
Cognitive Approach for Animals

Many independent entries related to learning are included in the encyclopedia: Animal Learning and Behavior; Artificial Intelligence; Avoidance Learning; College Teaching and Learning; Computer Learning; Emotional Learning; Informal Learning; Latent Learning; Learning, Transfer of; Learning and Memory; Learning and Motivation; Learning Disabilities; Learning Skills; Learning Technologies; Learning Theories; *and* Taste Aversion Learning.]

An Overview

Learning is said to have taken place if an organism's response to a particular situation or problem is shaped or determined by its earlier experiences with that type of situation. Learning is of great interest to psychologists because it is a pervasive feature of human behavior and is also evident in many nonhuman animals. People learn all sorts of things, ranging from complicated skills that require extensive and special training (such as calculus and heart surgery) to motor habits and emotional likes and dislikes that are learned with virtually no effort or instruction. Many obvious forms of human learning require some linguistic competence and involve conscious awareness. When something that has been learned is accessible to consciousness, it is called explicit or declarative knowledge. Learning can also occur in the absence of conscious awareness, resulting in the acquisition of procedural or implicit knowledge. Both declarative and procedural learning have been investigated in studies with people. In con-

trast, studies with animals have focused on procedural learning.

A comprehensive definition that encompasses all forms of learning and is compatible with all major theoretical approaches is difficult to formulate. However, all definitions include four fundamental features.

Learning as Distinct from Performance

Learning can be identified only by a change in the behavior or performance of an organism. However, not all instances of learning are immediately evident in what the organism does. Special test procedures or prompts may be required to reveal what an organism has learned. This is obviously true for implicit knowledge that is not accessible to consciousness. However, even evidence of declarative learning requires the presence of effective retrieval cues. To accommodate instances of learning that are not immediately evident in a change in behavior, in many definitions learning is said to involve a change in "behavioral potential" (e.g., Anderson, 1995; Bower & Hilgard, 1981). A related approach involves emphasizing that learning involves a change in the "mechanisms of behavior" rather than a change in behavior itself (Domjan, 1998).

Learning as an Enduring Change

Something is said to have been learned if the effects of the experience last for a considerable period of time. How long may be debated, but effects that are fleeting are not considered to reflect learning. Kimble (1961) addressed this issue by referring to learning as something that is "relatively permanent," a choice of wording that has been retained by more recent theorists (e.g., Anderson, 1995). A related characterization is that learning represents and "enduring" change (Domjan, 1998). The requirement that learning be "enduring" helps distinguish learning from more transient sources of behavior change such as fatigue or temporary changes in motivation. This requirement also makes learning inextricably related to memory. Learning and memory are like two sides of a coin: one cannot exist without the other.

Learning as Caused by Prior Experience

Learning is considered to result from prior experience with events that are related to the learned behavior. Changes in behavioral mechanisms that do not require prior experience with the particular task under investigation are not considered to involve learning. This requirement serves to distinguish learning from maturational changes that do not require exposure to specific stimuli.

Learning as Mediated by the Nervous System

Learning is assumed to reflect changes in the neural mechanisms of behavior. Leahey and Harris (1997), for example, noted that "to begin with, learning must involve some change in the nervous system of the organism" (p. 4). The assumption that learning is mediated by neural processes motivated Ivan Petrovich Pavlov's original studies of classical conditioning (Pavlov, 1927) and has provided major impetus for contemporary studies of neural function (e.g., Martinez & Kesner, 1991). This assumption also helps to distinguish learning from growth and maturation that do not depend on neural changes. To borrow an example from Walker (1996), practice in lifting weights improves one's ability to lift heavy objects, but this does not reflect learning because it is due primarily to the growth of muscle mass rather than changes in the nervous system.

Conceptual and Methodological Implications

The four defining features described have important conceptual and methodological implications for the study of learning. The primary conceptual implication is that learning is fundamentally a theoretical construct. It is not something that can be observed and measured directly. This is true in part because learning involves a change in the mechanisms of behavior. Since behavioral mechanisms are usually inferred rather than observed directly, learning also cannot be observed directly.

Learning is also a theoretical construct because it is presumed to result from prior experience. Thus to identify something as an instance of learning, one has to be sure that the behavior is caused by prior experience. Causes cannot be observed directly but have to be inferred from carefully designed experiments. Therefore, studies of learning can only be conducted with experimental methods. Because of this, investigations of learning have involved primarily laboratory experimentation. Naturalistic observations can provide useful suggestive evidence, but conclusive identification of instances of learning requires the use of experimental methods.

Varieties of Learning

The field of learning may be partitioned in different ways. One distinction of considerable interest concerns the type of organism whose learning is being investigated. A common distinction is between "animal learning" and "human learning." Studies with human participants can make use of verbal instructions that quickly define the learning task and tell the participant what aspect of the task he or she is expected to remember. Verbal instructions cannot be used with the rats, pigeons, and monkeys, which typically serve in studies of animal learning, or with human infants that lack verbal skills. Because of this, human and animal studies employ distinctively different methodologies.

The field of learning also may be partitioned in terms of the type of learning that is involved or the procedures used to produce the learning. The simplest learning procedures involve the repeated presentation of a single stimulus. Such procedures are used to study habituation, sensitization, and perceptual learning. Other basic procedures involve the presentation of two stimuli or events in various contingent relations (to study classical conditioning and the learning of causal inferences) and the presentation of a reinforcing stimulus contingent on a particular response (to study instrumental or operant conditioning). Investigators have also explored how more cognitively demanding skills such as reading, writing, and mathematics are learned.

In general, human beings show many of the forms of learning that are evident in nonhuman animals, but people also can learn various complex cognitive tasks that have not thus far been identified in animal subjects.

Bibliography

Anderson, J. R. (1995). *Learning and memory*. New York: Wiley. General textbook, with an emphasis on human learning and memory.

Bower, G. H., & Hilgard, E. R. (1981). *Theories of learning* (5th ed.). Englewood Cliffs, NJ: Prentice Hall. Classic textbook describing major theories of learning.

Domjan, M. (1998). *The principles of learning and behavior* (4th ed.). Monterey, CA: Brooks/Cole ITP. Describes recent research on animal learning and animal cognition.

Kimble, G. A. (1961). *Hilgard and Marquis' conditioning and learning*. New York: Appleton-Century-Crofts. A historically important book describing studies of animal learning.

Leahey, T. H., & Harris, R. J. (1997). *Human learning*. Englewood Cliffs, NJ: Prentice Hall.

Martinez, J. L. Jr., & Kesner, R. P. (Eds.). (1991). *Learning and memory.* San Diego: Academic Press. Describes research on the neural mechanisms of learning.

Pavlov, I. P. (1927). *Conditioned reflexes* (G. V. Anrep, Trans.). London: Oxford University Press. A historically important summary of Pavlov's research.

Walker, J. T. (1996). *The psychology of learning.* Upper Saddle River, NJ: Prentice Hall. General textbook, with an emphasis on human learning and memory.

Michael Domjan

Molecular and Cellular Aspects

Since the publication of D. O. Hebb's *Organization of Behavior* in 1949, psychologists and neuroscientists have viewed the synapses through which nerve cells communicate as likely sites of learning and memory. Hebb presented a plausible theory in which assemblies of interconnected neurons represented elementary aspects of memory, and interconnected assemblies of neurons represented syntheses of these elementary memories into more complex ones. Two related concepts have since dominated theorizing: (1) learning involves selective strengthening (and possibly weakening) of existing synapses, as Hebb specifically proposed; and (2) learning would involve the formation (and possibly elimination) of synapses. In either case, this would lastingly alter the pattern of flow of information in the neural network of the brain. This "synaptic plasticity" received increased attention after it was demonstrated in the 1960s that (1) experience during development regulated the number of synapses in the visual system, and (2) new synapses could "sprout" in the damaged brain. Shortly thereafter, studies indicated that synapses could also change in size, shape, and number as a result of behavioral experience and learning. Subsequently, both synapse formation and synapse alteration have received sufficient support to render them likely mechanisms, independently or in combination, in many aspects of learning and memory.

Synapse Number Changes in Learning and Memory

Synapse formation has been inferred both from studies using electron microscopy, which allows direct visualization of synapses, and indirectly from studies of stained or dye-injected nerve cells in which dendrites and spines (signal-receiving elements of synapses) can be quantified. A consistent finding is that rats reared in situations in which there are more learning opportunities (e.g., group housing in a large object-filled cage) have more synapses per neuron, more dendrites per neuron, and a higher density of dendritic spines on neurons compared with rats raised in barren laboratory cages. Presumably these changes reflect stored information. Similar changes have been found in visual cor-

tex, other cerebral cortical areas, parts of the hippocampus, basal ganglia regions, and cerebellar cortex. Where investigated, similar effects have also been seen in adult and aged rats housed in such environments, as well as in various brain regions following maze training, motor skill training, and other forms of learning in adult rodents. Although neural plasticity is associated with learning across the life span and across brain regions, the specific changes can vary. In cerebellar cortex, motor skill learning increases the number of synapses, whereas associative eyeblink conditioning or unpaired conditional stimulus and unconditional stimulus presentation is associated with loss of synapses. In one paradigm, motor skill learning was compared with motor activity in a treadmill or running wheel that did not involve learning; animals that learned showed synapse number increases, whereas animals that exercised increased the amount of capillaries but added no synapses. Thus, the synaptic changes appear to be specific to learning and not caused by mere neuronal activity.

Similar learning-associated changes have been described across a broad variety of species. Complex environment rearing increased dendritic material in cerebellar cortex of macaque monkeys and increased synapses per neuron in the visual cortex of cats. In birds, synapse formation (or sometimes loss) has been described in brain regions involved in various types of learning including song and other vocal learning, imprinting on a maternal substitute, and aversive learning. Synapse formation and loss also apparently mediate various kinds of learning in primitive invertebrates such as snails.

Synapse Structure Changes in Learning and Memory

The most commonly reported structural change in synapses in association with learning and memory is increased size of various parts of the synapse. The part most commonly studied has been the postsynaptic density (PSD), where the majority of the neurotransmitter receptors are believed to be located. PSDs are larger, for example, in visual cortical synapses of rats reared in a complex environment, and in motor cortical synapses of adult rats taught motor skills. Changes have also been described in the size of the presynaptic terminal, postsynaptic processes (e.g., the dendritic spine), and in various aspects of neurotransmitter-containing presynaptic vesicles (e.g., their number and position). Each of these size changes can be interpreted as underlying a change in the strength (or efficacy) of the synapse. A change that is more curious involves the tendency for PSDs either to contain perforations or to appear as separate, unconnected segments. The relative frequency of such irregular PSDs is increased following exposure to a complex environment (in visual cortex) and following motor skill training (in motor cortex) in rats. These irregular PSDs are also altered following induction of long-term potentiation (LTP). [*See* Long-Term Potentiation.]

Electrophysiological Analyses of Learning Effects on Synapses

Although most electrophysiological analyses of learning involve cellular activity related to performance of the learned task, a few studies have been directed at measuring the electrophysiological effect of synapses added as a result of learning. In cats reared in a complex environment, for example, enhanced visual cortex receptive field sensitivity was reported. In rats reared in a complex environment, altered hippocampal formation physiology was retained in tissue slices removed from the brain and studied in vitro. Aside from these examples, there are limited data indicating physiological alteration in association with altered synapse number or structure. However, there are a number of reports of altered cellular physiological relationships following learning (e.g., altered auditory receptive fields) that are compatible with altered synaptic inputs. [*See* Memory, *article on* Memory Systems; *and* Sensation and Perception.]

Cellular and Molecular Aspects of Learning

Changes in synapse number or structure are the manifestations of changes at the molecular level. In the late 1950s it was discovered that long-term memory took time to form following learning, and that memory could be both disrupted and facilitated during this labile period. Because different treatments were effective at different delays, it appeared that various cellular processes had to run their course to bring about complete long-term memory. A variety of "memory-modulating" substances have been identified, and this paradigm of drug treatment either immediately before or at intervals following learning has been adopted for studies of a broad range of memory mechanisms, as well as for clinical applications such as Alzheimer's disease.

In the early 1960s, behavioral neuroscientists began to examine the popular hypothesis that learning and memory may utilize the same general cellular mechanisms that neurons use to accomplish other goals. Thus it was suggested that learning and memory might involve gene expression through transcription of the gene into messenger ribonucleic acid (mRNA) followed by the synthesis of proteins, which in turn perform whatever cellular functions underlie memory, such as the formation of new synapses or changes in synapse strength. Early studies showed that inhibitors of RNA or protein synthesis, administered before or shortly after learning, typically abolished or impaired subsequent memory. Other studies found that new RNA and protein were often synthesized as a result of learning. Although many of these early studies were flawed in their design, the consensus argued that gene expression was involved, as did studies of the persistent form of long-term potentiation (LTP).

Subsequently, the central problem has become the identification of the genes/proteins that are involved in learning and memory formation, as well as a complete description of how the process occurs. If memory involves the formation (and possibly loss) of synapses, then the proteins involved may be similar or identical to those involved in synapse formation during development. There appear to be literally hundreds of proteins present at the synapse and in dendrites, and it is possible that a large number of them provide necessary support for learning and memory to occur because of their roles in synapse or other cellular functions, although they are not directly involved in the learning and memory process. Hence, the goal is to delineate which proteins are involved in learning and memory and to specify their roles. Given that there appears to be more than one form of plastic synaptic change, it seems likely that there may be multiple molecular processes involved in learning and memory. [*See* Brain Development.]

Whereas most of the proteins found at the synapse are probably produced in the neuron's cell body surrounding its nucleus and transported to dendritic or synaptic locations, it has recently become clear that at least some proteins are actually synthesized in distal dendrites or at synapses using mRNA that is present there. In addition, many proteins that might have actions that are manifest at synapses need not ever be present at synapses (e.g., transcription factors that regulate the expression of synaptic proteins). It should be clear that many, probably most, of the proteins involved in either the formation of synapses or the modification of synapses, may be synthesized in advance of performing this role. Hence, both proteins synthesized in advance and those synthesized in response to learning may be involved in learning and memory.

Although a number of candidate proteins have been proposed, both from research on animals undergoing learning and from research on LTP, there is little agreement at this point on a particular set of molecular processes that underlie learning and memory. Thus, it may be more illustrative to think about some categories into which proteins involved in learning and memory might fall.

The most obvious category is that of effectors, or fundamental changes, the proteins that actually implement memory-related changes. In the case of new synapse formation, synapse structural proteins, and particularly those involved in new synapse initiation, would fall into this class. In one case of synapse efficacy change, minor modification of the protein making up an ion channel that allows sodium to enter the cell, changes the sodium influx rate, and this changes the amount of neurotransmitter released by the presynaptic terminal.

A second category might be events that bring about fundamental changes. For example, the ion channel just mentioned is functionally modified when a protein called a *kinase* adds a phosphate group to its structure. There are many kinases and similar proteins that can alter the function of other proteins. Changes of this sort have been found to underlie, for example, a type of learning called *sensitization* in the sea snail *Aplysia californica*. Such modifications can change a synapse so that it operates more efficiently or less efficiently, depending upon the exact protein and how it is modified.

A third category contains regulators of gene expression. These often involve "cascades," in which one protein activates another, and this in turn activates a third, and so on until a change occurs that can cause one or more genes to be turned on (or off) so that its protein is expressed (or shut down). Regulators that bind to the gene and affect its readout into mRNA are *transcription factors*; some of these are rapidly produced or activated in response to learning. A transcription factor that appears to be involved in a number of different kinds of learning across a wide array of species is CREB (cAMP responsive element binding protein), of which there are several related forms. Changes occurring at synapses at large distances from the neuron's nucleus can be communicated to the nucleus through cascades, as appears to occur with CREB. The protein that results from the gene expression might be an effector protein that would have to be transported back only to the proper synapses, a difficult problem requiring that the synapses to be altered by learning be temporarily "tagged" in some manner. Local regulation of protein synthesis at the synapse provides an alternative mechanism to select only active synapses for modification.

An illustrative case has been made for differential involvement of genes in various stages of memory formation for avoidance learning in the fruit fly. The stages identified are learning (LRN), short-term memory (STM), middle-term memory (MTM), anesthesia-resistant memory (ARM), and long-term memory (LTM); the last two stages occur in parallel, following the first three in sequence. Both activation of CREB and protein synthesis appear to be necessary for LTM but not for the other stages. ARM is dependent on a gene named *radish*, and each of the other stages of the learning-memory process has been shown to depend on unique genes. This does not indicate that the genes are directly involved in the particular memory process for which they are required. Rather, it means that mutations in them can be used as tools both to dissect the components of the memory process at a behavioral level and to begin to tease apart the biochemical mechanisms underlying these components.

[*See also* Neuron; *and* Synapse.]

Bibliography

Davis, H. P., & Squire, L. R. (1984). Protein synthesis and memory: A review. *Psychological Bulletin, 96*, 518–559. Comprehensive and thoughtful review of the history of this field.

Dubnau, J., & Tully, T. (1998). Gene discovery in *Drosophila*: New insights for learning and memory. *Annual Review of Neuroscience, 21*, 407–444. Delineates both genes necessary for memory and genes that appear to be directly involved in various aspects of memory.

Greenough, W. T., Withers, G. S., & Wallace, C. S. (1990). Morphological changes in the nervous system arising from behavioral experience: What is the evidence that they are involved in learning and memory? In L. Squire & E. Lindenlaub (Eds.), *The biology of memory, Symposia Medica Hoechst 23, Stuttgart* (pp. 159–185). New York: Schattauer Verlag. Systematic evaluation of the evidence for involvement of plastic synaptic change in learning and memory.

Hebb, D. O. (1949). *The organization of behavior*. New York: Wiley. A classic work that transformed views of how memory might involve the activity of neurons.

McGaugh, J. L. (1966). Time-dependent processes in memory storage. *Science, 153*, 1351–1358. Classic article summarizing evidence for a memory-formation process that occurred over a substantial time period following learning.

Rosenzweig, M. R., Leiman, A. L., & Breedlove, S. M. (1999). *Biological psychology: An introduction to behavioral, cognitive and clinical neuroscience*. Sunderland, MA: Sinauer. This textbook contains a chapter on development and two well-conceived chapters on the neurobiology of learning and memory that expand on topics described here.

Silva, A. J., Kogan, J., Frankland, P. W., & Kida, S. (1998). CREB and memory. *Annual Review of Neuroscience, 21*, 127–148. Illustrative review of potential roles of transcription factors in molecular memory mechanisms.

Wallace, C. S., Hawrylak, N., & Greenough, W. T. (1991). Studies of synaptic structural modifications following LTP and kindling: Context for a molecular morphology. In M. Baudry & J. Davis (Eds.), *LTP: A debate of current issues* (pp. 189–232). Cambridge, MA: MIT Press. Comprehensive review of plastic synaptic structural changes.

William T. Greenough and James E. Black

Conditioning Approach

The classical and instrumental conditioning paradigms were discovered serendipitously during Ivan Petrovich Pavlov's (1897) investigations of digestive processes and Edward Lee Thorndike's (1898) studies of animal intelligence. After Pavlov's conditioning research became known in the Unites States (Pavlov, 1906; Yerkes & Morgulis, 1909), it was quickly recognized that he provided (1) an objective and highly controlled method for the study of learning; (2) an enumeration of the many conditions affecting the formation and retention of learned responses; and (3) a procedurally defined terminology (conditioning, conditioned and unconditioned stimuli, reinforcement, stimulus generalization, extinction, and so on). Thorndike (1898), in seeking to assess Darwin's (1871) assertion of mental continuity between man and animals, conducted a series of experiments designed to determine an animal's problem-solving ability. In the experiments, cats, dogs, or monkeys were placed inside a box from which they were required to learn to escape by pulling a looped string, turning a button, or lifting a latch to obtain food. Thorndike observed that over trials, erroneous responses dropped out and the correct response was made successively faster. Thorndike (1911) concluded that problem solving does not involve reasoning but a simpler trial-and-error (selective) learning process in which a hierarchy of alternative responses are elicited and the frequency of one of them is increased by reinforcement while all other responses decreased. From these selective learning experiments, Thorndike (1913) developed his famous law of effect, which asserts that the "satisfying" or "annoying" consequences of a response served to strengthen or weaken the degree of control stimuli would exert over the response.

At the time of Thorndike's investigations, the distinction between selective learning and instrumental conditioning had not been made. Nevertheless, Thorndike's analysis was widely applied to the conditioning paradigm (instrumental) in which only a single response is isolated for study under a reinforcement contingency. It was not until the 1930s that a theoretical controversy (Konorski & Miller, 1937, Skinner, 1937) laid the foundation for the operational distinction between classical and instrumental conditioning (Hilgard & Marquis, 1940).

In the basic Pavlovian conditioning paradigm, there is a set of operations involving an unconditioned stimulus (US) that reliably elicits an unconditioned response (UR) and a conditioned stimulus (CS) shown to not initially produce a response resembling the UR. The CS and US are then presented repeatedly to the organism in a specified order and temporal spacing, and a response similar to the UR develops to the CS, which is called the conditioned response (CR); that is, CS–CR functions are obtained. Control over the temporal conjunction of the CS, US, and UR makes classical conditioning preparations ideal vehicles for studying associative learning because they can uniquely specify stimulus antecedents to the UR and CR from the start of training. Various temporal arrangements of the CS and US give rise to different forms of classical conditioning (for example delay, trace, simultaneous). Classical conditioning is called classical reward and defense conditioning if the US is an appetitive or aversive stimulus, respectively. As is also true for instrumental con-

ditioning, the appetitive or aversive designation depends on the independent demonstration of the organism performing instrumental responses necessary to obtain or remove itself from the US. What distinguishes classical from instrumental conditioning is that (1) presentation or omission of the US is independent of CR occurrence and (2) the definition of a CR is restricted to a target response elicited as a UR. All instrumental conditioning procedures are characterized by a contingent relationship between the organism's response and a stimulus that is identified as positive, negative, or neutral if it increases, decreases, or leaves response probability unaffected, respectively.

Instrumental contingencies give rise to a variety of paradigms of which the five most extensively studied derive from responses producing a positive (reward) or negative (punishment) stimulus; preventing a positive (omission) or negative (avoidance) stimulus from occurring; and terminating a negative stimulus (escape). Commonly, operant conditioning is also designated as an instrumental conditioning paradigm. However, the operant is defined as having no causal stimulus antecedents (Coleman, 1981; Skinner, 1937); consequently, it lacks the stimulus antecedents that permits instrumental conditioning paradigms to studying associative learning (that is, learning resulting from the organism's exposure to the temporal conjunction of two or more events). Accordingly, the operant is restricted to the study of performance variables.

Nonassociative Controls

The associative nature of classical conditioning has come to be determined by the contiguous occurrence of the CS and US and a set of operations intended to estimate the contribution of other possible processes to CS responding. All response systems show some level of baseline activity, often raised by US presentations, which can produce an adventitious coincidence of the CS and target response. Moreover, the likelihood of a target response occurring to a CS may be systematically affected by alpha responses, which are URs to the CS in the same effector system as the target response, and pseudo-conditioned and sensitized responses established by prior US-alone presentations.

Detailing the latency, duration, amplitude, and course of habituation of the alpha response with a control group given CS-alone presentations can serve to eliminate alphas as CRs, since they are of shorter latency. In particular, if a sufficiently long CS–US interval is employed, alphas and CRs can be scored separately in the interval (Gormezano, 1966; Gormezano, Kehoe, & Marshall, 1983). The reinstatement or augmentation of alphas to the CS through US-alone or CS–US pairings is referred to as sensitization. After eliminating alphas from consideration, the contribution of pseudo-CRs to CR measurement can be assessed by giving one or more

US presentations prior to the CS. The procedure frequently results in responses to the CS, labeled pseudo-CRs, which are treated separately from CRs since they occur without CS–US pairings. However, the US-alone procedure precludes trial-by-trial assessment of pseudo-CRs with CRs. Accordingly, a single unpaired control has evolved in which CS-alone and US-alone trials are presented randomly the same number of times as the paired CS–US group, but at variable CS–US intervals exceeding those effective for CR acquisition. Therefore, responses (excluding short-latency alphas) on CS trials provide a summative measure of pseudo-CRs and baseline responses.

The unpaired control is based on two associative assumptions: Temporal contiguity of the CS and US is necessary for CR acquisition; and responding produced by the unpaired control is nonassociative, since the randomized sequencing of CSs and USs at exceedingly long, random intervals prevents CS–US contiguity effects. However, in the 1960s, use of the unpaired control was challenged by a contingency hypothesis (Prokasy, 1965; Rescorla, 1967), which asserts that associative learning is determined by the statistical relationship between the CS and US rather than their temporal contiguity. Thus if US probability is greater in the presence of the CS than in its absence, a positive contingency is said to prevail and excitatory associative effects accrue to the CS; and, conversely, if US probability is higher in the absence than in the presence of the CS, the negative contingency yields inhibitory associative effects.

The contingency hypothesis also assumes the unpaired control's perfectly negative contingency would lead the CS to acquire inhibitory associative effects. Accordingly, Rescorla (1967) proposed a "truly random" control as an associatively neutral condition for assessing excitatory and inhibitory conditioning. However, Rescorla's delineation of pairing and unpairing conditions cannot be specified a priori but only empirically. Specifically, CS–US pairings are determined by the CS–US intervals demonstrated to produce CR acquisition for a specific preparation, while "explicitly unpaired" refers to CS–US intervals outside the intervals for effective conditioning. Consequently, in the absence of an empirically derived metric (that is, effective CS–US conditioning intervals) to designate paired and unpaired conditions, it is virtually impossible to program an associatively neutral truly random control. Despite this profound deficiency and others that have been delineated (Gormezano & Kehoe, 1975; Papini & Bitterman, 1990; Wasserman, 1989), the truly random control is still widely employed, even though Rescorla and his associates (for example, Holland & Rescorla, 1975; Rescorla, 1973), by reverting to the use of the unpaired control, appear to have abandoned the truly random control shortly after it was proposed.

In instrumental conditioning, any occurrence of the target response without its prior conjunction with the reinforcing stimulus is designated as a nonassociative response attributable to base rate, independent presentations of the reinforcing stimulus, and presentations of the reinforcing stimulus independent of the target response. Implementing controls for the first two factors are self-evident. Achieving a control for the third factor has been essentially limited to the yoked-control design, where pairs of subjects are selected and one of them is randomly designated the experimental subject and the other the control. During conditioning, when the experimental subject performs the target response, the contingent event is received by both subjects. Accordingly, both members of the pair receive the same number and temporal distribution of stimulus events. The only difference between pairs is that the experimental subject always receives the reinforcing event after execution of the target response, whereas the yoked-partner receives the reinforcing event at that time, independent of the response.

The yoked-control design would appear to be admirably suited to testing the null hypothesis that the temporal relationship between the response and subsequent stimulus event is irrelevant to the observed change in the target response. Unfortunately, however, the design confounds within-subject sources of random error with the treatment effect. Specifically, the experimental subject's control of stimulus events allows for systematic differences in the number of experimental subjects that are more affected by the stimulus event than their yoked partners. Consequently the results of yoked-control designs are confounded (Church, 1964). A means for assessing the contribution of the third nonassociative factor to instrumental conditioning has not yet been determined.

Stimulus–Stimulus Paradigms

Over the last quarter of the twentieth century, the designation "classical conditioning" came to be applied to paradigms only requiring presentations of the CS and US independent of the target response while ignoring the second requirement of selection of the UR. As a consequence, the term "classical conditioning" has been extended from Pavlov's CS–CR paradigm to stimulus–stimulus (S–S) paradigms involving principally conditioned stimulus–instrumental response (CS–IR) and autoshaping procedures. The CS–IR paradigms include conditioned suppression and other classical-instrumental transfer procedures in which the stimulus-stimulus pairings of classical conditioning are conducted with a CS and a biologically significant event (such as shock) but without measurement of the UR or CR. The CS is then presented during ongoing instrumental behavior and its facilitory or disruptive effect on responding is measured; therefore, CS–IR functions are obtained. Autoshaping consists of response-independent presentations of a lighted manipulandum (for example, key pecking) as a CS and activation of a food supply as the US; the target response is contact with the manipulanda (key pecking). Key pecking is not an instrumental response, and it is not a UR to food in the mouth. Accordingly, autoshaping would be considered a new learning phenomenon arising only from the stimulus presentation procedure of classical conditioning, with the stimulus antecedent to the response remaining to be specified. Some discriminative approach procedures have also been designated as "Pavlovian" simply because an explicit cue (CS) is presented and food or water, designated the US, is made available at a fixed time following CS onset, and the approach behavior, by definition instrumental to receipt of the reinforcing event, is erroneously designated a CR. The S–S and discriminative approach paradigms have been extensively employed in the study of associative learning. Nevertheless, they lack the analytic power of CS–CR learning paradigms to exercise absolute control over the timing and sequencing of stimulus events and to identify the stimulus antecedents to the target response from the onset of training.

CS–CR Paradigms: Neural Substrates

Despite Pavlov's limited number of neural investigations, his CS–CR paradigm is ideally suited for the study of the biological substrates of associative learning because the elicitation of the UR permits identification of the CR's final common neural pathway(s) outside the conditioning situation, thereby affording the opportunity to observe changes in its activity from the start of conditioning. In contrast, the basic instrumental conditioning, CS–IR, and discriminative approach paradigms are inherently unsuitable for studying the biological basis of learning. In CS–IR paradigms, changes in the instrumental target response is not the result of its participation in the learning process but of its interaction with hypothetical CRs to CSs that are governed by prior CS–US pairings. Moreover, for instrumental conditioning and discriminative approach paradigms a wide variety of body movements can yield the required contingent outcome, hence it is virtually impossible to identify a final pathway for the response. This precludes their ability to be employed in the delineation of the neural substrates of learning.

Bibliography

Church, R. M. (1964). Systematic effects of random error in the yoked control design. *Psychological Bulletin, 62*, 122–131.

Coleman, S. R. (1981). Historical context and systematic functions of the concept of the operant. *Behaviorism, 9*, 207–226.

Gormezano, I. (1966). Classical conditioning. In J. B. Sidowski (Ed.), *Experimental methods and instrumentation in psychology* (pp. 385–420). New York: McGraw-Hill.

Gormezano, I., & Kehoe, E. J. (1975). Classical conditioning: Some methodological-conceptual issues. In W. K. Estes (Ed.), *Handbook of learning and cognitive processes, Vol. 2:* (pp. 143–179). *Conditioning and behavior theory* Hillsdale, NJ: Erlbaum.

Gormezano, I., Kehoe, E. J., & Marshall, B. S. (1983). Twenty years of classical conditioning research with the rabbit. In J. M. Sprague & A. N. Epstein (Eds.), *Progress in psychobiology and physiological psychology* (Vol. 10; pp. 197–275). New York: Academic Press.

Hilgard, E. R., & Marquis, D. G. (1940). *Conditioning and learning.* New York: Appleton-Century-Crofts.

Holland, P. C., & Rescorla, R. A. (1975). Second-order conditioning with food unconditioned stimulus. *Journal of Comparative and Physiological Psychology, 88*, 459–467.

Konorski, J., & Miller, S. (1937). On two types of conditioned reflex. *Journal of General Psychology, 16*, 264–272.

Papini, M. R., & Bitterman, M. E. (1990). The role of contingency in classical conditioning. *Psychological Review, 97*, 396–403.

Pavlov, I. P. (1906). The scientific investigation of the psychical faculties or processes in the higher animals. *Science, 24*, 613–619.

Prokasy, W. F. (1965). Classical eyelid conditioning: Experimenter operations, task demands, and response shaping. In W. F. Prokasy (Ed.), *Classical conditioning: A symposium* (pp. 208–225). New York: Appleton-Century-Crofts.

Rescorla, R. A. (1967). Pavlovian conditioning and its proper control procedures. *Psychological Review, 74*, 71–80.

Rescorla, R. A. (1973). Informational variables in Pavlovian conditioning. In G. H. Bower & J. T. Spence (Eds.), *Psychology of learning and motivation* (pp. 1–46). New York: Academic Press.

Skinner, B. F. (1937). Two types of conditioned reflex: A reply to Konorski and Miller. *Journal of General Psychology, 16*, 272–279.

Thorndike, E. L. (1898). Animal intelligence: An experimental study of the associative processes in animals. *Psychological Monograph, 2* (8).

Thorndike, E. L. (1911). *Animal intelligence.* New York: Macmillan.

Thorndike, E. L. (1913). Educational diagnosis. *Science, 142*, 248.

Wasserman, E. A. (1989). Pavlovian conditioning: Is contiguity irrelevant? *American Psychologist, 44*, 1550–1551.

Isidore Gormezano

Cognitive Approach for Humans

Of all species of animals, human beings display the most dazzling capacity for learning. At least from birth (and perhaps before), infants are rapidly learning about their environment, their caregivers, and how to manipulate both to receive satisfaction and to survive. Some evidence indicates that infants may learn about their mothers' voice characteristics even before birth. Language learning begins very early, at first passively, and then later, at around ages 2 to 4, very rapidly, with children learning to understand and to use many words a week for a period of years. Of course, humans learn many kinds of knowledge and skills: facts of all sorts, personal experiences dated in time, social skills, physical skills, and the myriad other types of knowledge that make us human. Newborns of all races or ethnicity are capable of learning any language, skill, and culture that exists on earth.

The cognitive approach to human learning began with pioneering studies of Hermann Ebbinghaus (1850–1909). Ebbinghaus was the first to study learning empirically and conducted numerous careful experiments, with himself as the only participant, asking how learning took place. He chose to use nonsense syllables (e.g., ZUK, BEP), hoping to minimize the influence of past experience in examining new learning, and he placed such syllables in long lists that he memorized to perfection. He measured the number of trials (or the amount of time) to learn lists to one perfect recitation and he examined the influence of numerous variables on the speed of learning and how much was later retained. For example, in one study, he showed that spaced practice at learning lists produced better retention of the lists on a later test than did massed presentation. That is, people are better able to retain information that they acquire over several study episodes (with space between each episode) than information acquired all at one time (as in a cramming session for an exam). This outcome has been replicated many times since its discovery. Although Ebbinghaus began the study of human learning, later scholars found his approach rather limiting. Today the cognitive study of learning occurs in many different forms. [See the biography of Ebbinghaus.]

Developmental psychologists study how learning develops over the early years of life, and also how it declines in old age. Infants and children are wonderful "preparations" in which to study learning, because they are so inquisitive in exploring and grasping the world around them. Some researchers study how newborns come to recognize faces, to reach for rewards, and to perceive the world around them. Many others study the fascinating topic of language learning. Just as other animals, such as birds, have critical periods in which they learn their songs from proper exposure, children learn language easily at early ages. All it takes is exposure. However, later in life (as most of us know) learning to understand and speak a new language is a very difficult process. Although children learn much

about the world around them, they usually cannot consciously remember this information. The years before ages three or four are blanketed by infantile (or childhood) amnesia, which is simply a term describing the fact that we remember practically nothing of the events occurring before age four or so.

Cognitive psychologists who study young adults examine learning in many forms. Following Ebbinghaus, some study the learning of verbal materials over repeated trials in laboratory settings. Others study learning from more complex materials such as prose passages. Educational psychologists study how students learn from text materials. However, not all learning is verbal in nature. Other cognitive scientists study the learning of visuospatial skills, such as the learning of maps or faces. Still others study the learning of complex cognitive skills, such as multiplication. Finally, the learning of both simple and complex motor skills consumes the attention of many researchers. In each domain, researchers have studied the topic for many years. Here we try to present a few basic facts that have been uncovered.

First and foremost is the learning curve. Learning in almost all of its forms follows a general law: Over repeated trials of practice at any skill, performance shows large gains at first and then smaller ones later on. Such findings are revealed in learning curves. A learning curve is simply a graph relating some measure of performance on the y-axis to the number of trials (or opportunities for learning) on the x-axis. The data shown in Figure 1 are typical of learning curves. Before we explain what these data show, however, first just notice the smooth and regular characteristics of the curves showing improvements in a task with practice. This form is quite general, occurring in almost all types of learning of large sets of information.

The data shown in Figure 1 came from an experiment on two methods of paired-associate learning, a task in which participants are asked to learn connections between two independent elements, the stimulus and the response. In this experiment, participants were asked to memorize the associations between nonsense shapes (the stimuli) and two-digit numbers (the responses). The participants' task was to try to recall the two-digit number when the nonsense shape was presented by itself. Two different methods of learning, the anticipation method and the recall or study/test method, were used in this experiment, with different groups of participants experiencing each method. In the anticipation method, each trial began with a viewing of the stimulus item for 5 seconds, followed by a viewing of the stimulus-response pair for 5 seconds. After viewing the entire list, the participant's task on each trial was to anticipate, or to provide the response during the 5-second interval when only the stimulus was presented. Whether or not the participant suc-

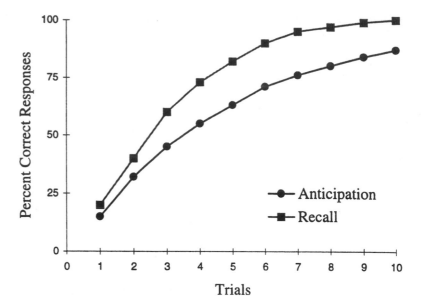

LEARNING: Cognitive Approach for Humans. Figure 1. Learning curves for the anticipation and recall methods over ten trials of a paired-associate learning procedure. (Adapted from Battig & Brackett, 1961.)

ceeded, the stimulus-response pair was then provided for 5 seconds. In the recall or study/test method, the list of pairs was presented in its entirety, with each stimulus-response pair occurring for five seconds. After the list was presented, the recall or test trials began, in which each stimulus was presented for 5 seconds and the participant tried to produce the response. If the participant could not produce the response for a particular stimulus, he or she did not get feedback until the next time the entire list was presented (i.e., there was no immediate feedback). The primary difference between the two methods of presentation was whether the test and study occurred close in time (the anticipation method) or were more distant in time (the recall or study/test method).

The results from the two methods are shown in Figure 1 and reveal several important facts. First, both learning curves are negatively accelerated, with large gains being made on the early trials and smaller ones on the later trials. For example, 50% performance was achieved after only three trials, but it took another seven trials to gain the other 50% (and the participants who learned by the anticipation method were not at 100% even after ten trials). This is the typical shape of the learning curve, with rapid learning at first, and slower learning later in training. A second point to be gleaned from Figure 1 is that the recall (or study/test) method produced better learning than did the anticipation method, although this finding has not always been obtained in other comparisons of the two techniques.

Many theories explain how learning occurs, but the fact that there are many theories indicates that none are generally agreed upon. At least two broad classes of ideas exist. One is that experiences leave traces in the nervous system—memory traces—and these become more strongly engrained with repeated practice. The stronger or deeper the memory traces, the better is performance. Another general idea is that experiences multiply memory traces; instead of the same trace becoming stronger or deeper or more resistant to forgetting, each experience might create a new trace. Therefore, with repeated similar experiences, many traces would exist that would cumulate to explain learning. Well-learned information or well-practiced tasks would be supported by numerous traces of past experience. It is difficult to decide among these general accounts of learning, despite the best efforts of psychologists focusing on the issue.

[*See also* Learning, *article on* Cognitive Approach for Animals.]

Bibliography

Battig, W. F., & Brackett, H. R. (1961). Comparison of anticipation and recall methods in paired-associate learning. *Psychological Reports, 9,* 59–65.

Bower, G. H., & Hilgard, E. R. (1981). *Theories of learning.* Englewood Cliffs, NJ: Prentice Hall.

Ebbinghaus, H. (1964). *Memory. A contribution to experimental psychology.* New York: Dover. (Original work published 1885)

Gleason, J. B. (Ed.). (1993). *The development of language.* New York: Macmillan.

Hall, J. F. (1971). *Verbal learning and retention.* Philadelphia: Lippincott.

Healy, A. F., & Bourne, L. E., Jr. (1995). *Learning and memory of knowledge and skills: Durability and specificity.* Thousand Oaks, CA: Sage.

Leahey, T. H., & Harris, R. J. (1997). *Learning and cognition.* Englewood Cliffs, NJ: Prentice Hall.

Schwartz, B., & Reisberg, D. (1991). *Learning and memory.* New York: Norton.

Henry L. Roediger III and Michelle L. Meade

Cognitive Approach for Animals

Questions about animal cognitive abilities are asked today that were all but taboo 25 years ago. Some examples: Do animals rehearse and is rehearsal necessary for events to become associated? Are animals aware of themselves as individuals and are they aware of the effects of their behavior on others? How developed is memory in animals and to what extent is it similar to human memory? Do animals possess various forms of numerical competence? Indeed, and perhaps ironically, the two great procedures employed in animal learning, classical and instrumental conditioning, which traditionally have been given associative interpretations (but see Tolman, 1932) are routinely interpreted today employing cognitive mechanisms.

To a significant extent, animal learning has been converted into animal learning and cognition. The major factor responsible for this transformation is the cognitive revolution which began around 1960. About that time there began to be an increase in the belief that animals form representations of events and that they process information. It should not be thought, however, that prior to 1960 concern with the cognitive capacities of animals was unknown. Far from it. In point of fact, historical speculation concerning the cognitive capacities of animals has encompassed the extremes; animals have been variously described as automatons at one extreme and as possessing almost human cognitive capacities at the other. Consider a few historical examples.

Aristotle wrote of the moral and intellectual capacities of animals, assigning wisdom and kindness to the elephant. In the Middle Ages, animals were held responsible for their actions and were even brought to trial for various crimes such as murder and destruction of crops. On the other hand, Descartes suggested that while people were possessed by volition and complex ideas such as self-awareness, nonhuman animals were incapable of voluntary action and were governed by reflexes.

With Darwin and the theory of evolution, awareness arose that in addition to continuity between the morphological characteristics of various animals there may also be continuity between their learning and cognitive processes. This belief led to a search for cognitive continuity between humans and nonhuman animals, one which emphasized anecdotal evidence. For example, Darwin in his *Descent of Man and Selection in Relation to Sex* (1871), on hearing from a zookeeper that a monkey with poor teeth hid a stone it used to break open nuts, suggested that the animal had the idea of property rights, a capacity which Darwin assigned also to dogs (they hide bones) and birds (they build their own nests). The use of anecdotes to advance the idea that animals possessed humanlike intelligence was advanced most persistently by George J. Romanes (1882), a close friend of Darwin's.

With the advent of behaviorism around 1915, animal learning became a dominant area in psychology and with some exceptions, such as the cognitive behaviorism of E. C. Tolman (1932), association formation, as between a stimulus and a response, was deemed to be the basis of all learning and indeed of all putative higher level cognitive processes such as insight. For example, novel solutions to unexperienced problems (insight) might be explained in terms of stimulus and response generalization. In the hands of radical behaviorists such as B. F. Skinner (1938), even association formation was considered to be mentalistic and thus inappropriate. However, the more widely accepted view in the behaviorist period was that expressed by Clark Hull (1943). Hull saw stimulus-response (S-R) association as the basis of all learning. from simple withdrawal responses to anticipatory or expectancy responses. Vertebrate animals were considered to learn according to the same basic equations. Differences between animals in learning abilities were ascribed to differences in the constants of the equations.

In the light of this history, three comparisons between certain historical and contemporary approaches to animal cognition are worth mentioning. First, anecdotal and other impressionistic approaches to animal cognition are frowned upon today. In their place are highly controlled and sophisticated experimental procedures, many of which had their origin in animal learning. Discussion and evaluation of these procedures, beyond that attempted here, is to be found in two excellent recent textbooks of animal cognition (Pearce, 1997; Roberts, 1998). Both texts are a rich source of data and theory in contemporary animal cognition. Second, today as in the past, animal cognition often is equivalent to comparative cognition, particularly comparing certain critical cognitive capacities of animals to those of people. Finally, it is to be expected that cognitive interpretation or phenomena will be closely scrutinized and possibly challenged, with an eye toward offering simpler associative interpretations of them. Indeed, many reported phenomena said to involve cognition, such as transitive inferences, have been given a competing associative interpretation. In a transitive inference experiment, an animal may learn, for example, that A is greater than B and B is greater than C. In a test, the animal is asked if A is greater than C.

As indicated, cognitive interpretations have been provided for Pavlovian and instrumental conditioning. Pavlovian conditioning is a procedure for presenting stimuli; for example, tone (conditioned stimulus) followed by food (unconditioned stimulus). Learning is manifested when the animal comes to salivate on presentation of the conditioned stimulus. This occurs, according to Hull's S-R view, because of an association between the conditioned stimulus and the response produced by the food, the unconditioned responses. Some newer interpretations, however, emphasize that learning in Pavlovian conditioning involves an association between a representation of the conditioned stimulus and a representation of the unconditioned stimulus. Too, Pavlovian conditioning has been seen as involving information processing and to be useful for understanding the acquisition of causal knowledge.

Instrumental conditioning, too, has been seen as useful for understanding the acquisition of causal knowledge. In instrumental conditioning a response in the presence of some stimulus may produce a reinforcer. It is not at all uncommon today to suggest that instrumental learning is mediated by representations of various kinds, such as for example, the memory of one or more prior reinforcement outcomes or the anticipation of one or more future reward outcomes (Capaldi, 1994).

Some specialized procedures employed to study animal cognition are relatively novel, whereas others have a longer history. Consider first some relatively novel procedures introduced to study aspects of animal awareness. As one example, when an animal behaves in a particular way, say it growls or begs for food, does it intend for this behavior to produce a predictable response in another animal or person? Examining the capacity of animals to deceive others has produced a positive answer to this question but not one that has gone unchallenged (Heyes, 1993). Self-awareness in animals has also been studied. A basic finding here is that chimpanzees and orangutans, but not other nonhuman animals, show self-recognition when looking into a mirror. Self-awareness is inferred when animals manifest interest in marks on their bodies affixed when they were unconscious and which can only be seen in the mirror.

Three areas of contemporary concern which received considerable experimental attention in the past employing humans, animals, or both are memory, serial learning, and concept learning. Areas receiving some attention, but less than those mentioned above, in the past include the ability of animals to enumerate events, to orient in space, and to employ language.

Questions about memory have been asked employing a variety of experimental procedures. A typical one, in general terms, is to provide animals with a stimulus which indicates which of two or more responses will be correct after a retention interval. Animals are capable of such memory over long temporal intervals. Forgetting in animals, as in people, is facilitated by proactive interferences (prior memories interfere with current memories) and retroactive interferences (current memories interfere with prior memories).

In one type of serial learning task, events are presented successively in predictable order, the animal's task being to anticipate each event prior to its occurrence. In another type, events are presented simultaneously and the animals must respond to them in a given order, that is, pick A before B, B before C, and so on. Human serial learning has been studied extensively, as has animal serial learning in recent years. Three interpretations which have been applied for human serial learning have been applied to animal serial learning. These are that associations are formed between and among the items of a series (between adjacent items, for example, items A and B and between remote items, for example, items A and C); that associations are formed between items and their position in the series (item 1 is A, item 2 is B); and that animals learn rules which may be built into series (numbers in the series 10-5-3-1-0 decrease monotonically). It may be that all three types of learning occur (Capaldi, 1994). Serial learning studies reveal that animals chunk, that is, forge items together into a new functional unit, as for example, when the individual letters *C*, *A*, and *T* are combined by people to form the word *CAT*. At least some kinds of chunks are concepts.

In concept learning, a common category name may be applied to a number of discriminable different stimuli. For example, roses and lilies may be categorized as flowers. Three views of categorization are classical feature theory which specifies the necessary and sufficient features of a concept; prototype theory which specifies the typical or common features possessed by the exemplars of a concept; and exemplar theory which suggest that concepts are names applied to individual events. The rich variety of concept studies reported to date suggest that concept learning found in people may also be found in animals.

It has been suggested that the ability of animals to time events and to enumerate events may be accomplished by a common mechanism. A variety of procedures have been employed to investigate animal timing. It has been suggested that animals possess an internal clock which can time continuously or which can be stopped and started without losing track of time during the stop period. The ability of animals to enumerate events has been examined in a number of different species ranging from birds to chimpanzees. Formal criteria of counting have been proposed such as the one-one principle, which states that one and only one tag is to be applied to each event. The ability of animals to count and to employ other numerical processes, for example to sum events, is considered to be established by some investigators, but is questioned by some others.

The ability of animals to encode spatial information is of considerable biological importance. Animals must find their way home, be able to find where food has been hoarded or stored, and so on. The ability of animals to form cognitive maps, that is learn relationships between locations in the environment, is of great concern using various apparatus such as the water maze, a large vat of water in which animals must learn to find a hidden submerged platform. Various means by which animals learn to navigate over short and long distances have been investigated.

There is, of course, no doubt that animals are able to communicate with each other by various means. Among issues in question are the extent to which animals are aware of what they are communicating and if animals possess language ability. No area in animal cognition has been as controversial as that concerned with animal language ability. Two major criticisms of early language studies in chimpanzees were that trainers were being mimicked by the animals and, besides, what the animals were doing was simply a variety of serial learning based on simple associations. According to a more recent view, the early studies were misguided because they involved production, that is, they asked the animals to make signs or select stimuli in a particular order. Work with a bonobo, emphasizing comprehension or understanding, has been said to produce much better evidence for language acquisition in animals than early studies employing production (Savage-Rumbaugh et al., 1993).

[See also Animal Learning and Behavior; Learning, article on Cognitive Approach for Humans.]

Bibliography

Capaldi, E. J. (1994). The sequential view: From rapidly fading stimulus traces to the organization of memory and abstract concept of number. *Psychonomic Bulletin & Review, 1,* 156–181.

Darwin, C. (1871). *The descent of man, and selection in relation to sex.* London: John Murray.

Heyes, C. M. (1993). Anecdotes, training, trapping and triangulating: Do animals attribute mental states? *Animal Behaviour, 46,* 177–188.

Hull, C. L. (1943). *Principles of behavior.* New York: Appleton-Century-Crofts.

Pearce, J. M. (1997). *Animal learning and cognition: An introduction* (2nd ed.). East Sussex, England: Psychology Press.

Roberts, W. A. (1998). *Principles of animal cognition.* Boston: McGraw-Hill.

Romanes, G. J. (1882). *Animal intelligence.* London: Kegan, Paul, Trench.

Savage-Rumbaugh, E. S., Murphy, J., Sevick, R. A., Brakke, K. E., Williams, S. L., & Rumbaugh, D. M. (1993). Language comprehension in ape and child. *Monographs of the Society for Research in Child Development, 58* (Nos. 3–4), Serial No. 233.

Skinner, B. F. (1938). *The behavior of organisms.* New York: Appleton-Century-Crofts.

Tolman, E. C. (1932). *Purposive behavior in animals and men.* New York: Appleton-Century-Crofts.

E. John Capaldi

LEARNING, TRANSFER OF. Transfer of learning implies that previously acquired skills or knowledge are used in a novel setting; transfer therefore presupposes prior learning and memory for what was learned, as clarified in the following definitions:

Learning: The acquisition of *new* skills, information, or thinking strategies.

Memory: The retention of those newly acquired skills or knowledges so that they are accessible later.

Transfer: The ability to use previously learned skills or knowledges in settings or on problems different from the original learning, including the capacity to distinguish when and where those learnings are appropriate.

Historical Conceptions

Research on transfer spans at least a century and, from the beginning, was both theoretical and applied. For example, as early as 1901, Edward Lee Thorndike and Robert Sessions Woodworth (*Psychological Review, 8,* 247–267, 384–395, 553–564) reported studies disputing the dominant theory of the day—known as the doctrine of "formal disciplines"—which held that mathematics, Latin, and the like, served to exercise and discipline the mind and therefore improve thinking in general. They found that mathematics or Latin had virtually no effect on performance or reasoning in other fields. Subsequent studies also showed that memorizing numbers had little relation to memorizing words, and even that learning algebraic procedures had limited transfer to many other algebraic procedures.

In contrast to formal discipline theory, Thorndike developed identical elements theory. As the name implies, amount of transfer was expected to vary directly as a function of the number of common elements between the learning task or environment and the transfer task or setting. Thus the acquisition of Latin may transfer to learning Spanish but not to Chinese or mathematics; learning geometry may transfer to advanced geometry or perhaps architecture but not to languages and likely not even to algebra.

Identical elements theory spawned its own critics. They questioned the degree of similarity needed between elements to promote transfer and whether an element had to be a single stimulus-response (SR) association or could be a larger cognitive unit, among other issues.

A 1908 study by Charles Hubbard Judd (*Educational Review, 36*, 28–42) focused the problem. Two groups of boys were taught to throw darts at an underwater target at a depth of 12 inches. Their ability to transfer their learning was then tested by changing the depth of the target to 4 inches. Before doing the transfer task, one of the groups received instruction on light refraction, while a control group had no such instruction. The instructed group easily outperformed the control group. They showed quick adaptation to the new task demands, presumably because they now understood the principle underlying both tasks. The noninstructed group, in contrast, had practiced a skill until it was habitual, but they had little or no understanding of the task or their skill.

This theme, emphasizing the difference between SR connections and meaningful whole-unit understandings, became the rallying cry for the Gestalt psychologists such as Max Wertheimer (1945, *Productive Thinking*, New York). Their studies on perception, problem solving, and transfer contrasted with Thorndike's emphasis on elements in suggesting that the whole—a meaningful principle—is greater than the sum of its parts.

By the 1960s, and 1970s, Gestalt principles as well as identical elements theory had both been incorporated into interference theory, which allowed a more complex analysis of transfer because it gave memory processes center stage. Any learning episode occurs in a continuous sequence, influenced by memories of previous experiences—what was called a proactive effect of previous experience (for example, the proactive interference of growing up with feet and inches and then having to learn the metric system). That same learning episode then affects subsequent learning, but it also affects recall of previously learned knowledge or skills—what was called a retroactive effect of subsequent experience (for example, the retroactive facilitation effect of learning a biological classification system on the random facts about cats, dogs, and dinosaurs learned previously).

To provide evidence for one or more of the foregoing effects required appropriate experimental and control groups, the logic of which is similar to that for proving drug effects in medical research. Hundreds of such studies were conducted, along with implications for properly sequencing curricula. Most notable were *learning hierarchies* (Gagné & Paradise, 1961, *Psychological Monographs, 75*, whole no. 518), the *spiral curriculum* (Bruner, 1966, *Toward a Theory of Instruction*, New York, and *advance organizers* (Ausubel, 1960, *Journal of Educational Psychology, 51*, 267–272). Educational psychologists were eager to draw on such research for rec-

ommendations to teachers, as described in the section on Educational Implications.

Current Conceptions

The 1980s and 1990s have seen the rise of cognitive constructivism, with its emphasis on the active, constructive, and socially mediated nature of learning as a search for meaning (e.g., Brown, 1994, *Educational Researcher, 23*(8), 4–12). The research agenda—clearly influenced by the "cognitive revolution," as well as by Jean Piaget and Lev Semenovich Vygotsky—emphasized studies of the differences between experts and novices, the organization and construction of knowledge, perception and automaticity, and memory processes. Metacognition has also emerged as a major field, including comprehension-monitoring strategies for reading text such as reciprocal teaching (see Brown, 1994). In addition, two major theories of transfer have emerged from this research: situated cognition theory and identical productions theory.

Situated cognition theory is based on three basic tenets. First, "knowledge" (what comes to be known) is largely determined by *how* it is learned. Second, learning occurs in a specific situation; what is learned is therefore not easily decontextualized to allow transfer to other situations. Third, knowledge is not only context-specific, but part of an enculturation process in which apprentices learn to use their tools and skills in authentic activities of the culture of real-world practitioners as mentors.

According to situated cognition theory, broad transfer of knowledge or skills is virtually impossible because all learning is so contextualized. To teach for transfer, then, one would have to develop curricula full of authentic activities, including on-the-job training if possible, so that learners can actively construct their own knowledge in social interaction with mentors and other learners in cultural context. Such educational experiences should produce more meaningful learning, better memory for what was learned, and increased transfer to that target situation, but likely not to others. Or, as Carl Bereiter (in McKeough, Lupart, & Marini, 1995) suggests, instead of teaching for transfer across situations, we can find ways to transfer the situation itself.

Perhaps the most theoretically encompassing theory of transfer is identical productions theory. Deduced from John Anderson's ACT* (act star) theory (*The Architecture of Cognition*, Cambridge, MA, 1983), predictions of transfer derive from the widely accepted distinction between *declarative* and *procedural* knowledge, where the former is factual or conceptual (knowing that . . .), whereas the latter involves skills or performances (knowing how . . .). A *production* is a set of condition-action rules, involving stimulus-response elements and/or cognitive/perceptual elements. For example, "If the figure has four right angles, then it is a rectangle" (a declarative production) or "If the light turns green and it is safe to go, smoothly release the clutch with your left foot while simultaneously pressing on the accelerator with your right foot" (a procedural production).

Matches or mismatches can occur between declarative or procedural learning and declarative or procedural transfer in four ways:

1. Procedural to procedural: learning to drive one car and assessing transfer on other cars (or trucks).
2. Declarative to declarative: learning the Pythagorean theorem and seeing how it applies to architectural design.
3. Procedural to declarative: learning to read with automaticity, which should facilitate subsequent learning of facts and concepts.
4. Declarative to procedural: learning the principles of light refraction and applying them to underwater target-shooting.

As Singley and Anderson (1989) specifically noted, theirs is a more cognitively complete version of Thorndike's identical elements theory: the more similar the knowledge or skills between the learning and transfer tasks, the greater the likelihood of transfer.

Educational Implications

The cognitive revolution in psychology has broadened without substantially altering our conceptions of transfer. Empirical studies still find much less spontaneous transfer than teachers would hope for, but teaching techniques that capitalize on the last century of research continue to be invented, leading to some optimism concerning teaching for transfer. Consider the following suggestions from the entire span of transfer research:

1. Learners must develop a rich knowledge base and master, to near automaticity, basic skills.
2. Learners must practice multiple methods and strategies to avoid a "one-best-way" mentality or perceptual set.
3. Prior relevant knowledge must be activated in the target situation.
4. Learners must be challenged to identify underlying principles and to find how seemingly diverse problems or tasks resemble one another.
5. Learners must learn comprehension-monitoring and other metacognitive strategies.
6. Learners need to negotiate the above in a social context, where ideas and explanations provide what Piaget called "cognitive conflicts" to motivate continual reorganization of their knowledge and skills, as well as improved metacognitive strategies.
7. Curricula need to be sequenced so that each new unit reinforces, reviews and incorporates what was learned in previous units and anticipates subsequent units.
8. If situations can be transferred, individual learnings that are contextualized to those situations may follow.

[*See also* Learning.]

Bibliography

Brown, J. S., Collins, A., & Duguid, P. (1989). Situated cognition and the culture of learning. *Educational Researcher, 18*(1), 32–42. The article that popularized the situated cognition movement, while also stimulating much debate in subsequent issues of the same journal.

Cormier, S. J., & Hagman, J. D. (Eds.). (1987). *Transfer of learning: Contemporary research and applications.* San Diego: Academic Press. Excellent summaries of various lines of empirical evidence about transfer in such domains as knowledge, motor skills, and cognitive strategies and in such environments as schools and the military.

Deese, J., & Hulse, S. H. (1967). *The psychology of learning* (2nd ed.). New York: McGraw-Hill. A general text on learning theory, with chapters on transfer of training and on retention and forgetting that provide clear accounts of the logic and experimental designs for transfer experiments, as well as for interference theory in general.

Detterman, D. K., & Sternberg, R. J. (Eds.). (1993). *Transfer on trial: Intelligence, cognition, and instruction.* Norwood, NJ: Ablex. A collection of essays debating interpretations of transfer, including the relation to intelligence, situated learning, and cognitive vs. behavioral approaches.

Ellis, H. C. (1965). *The transfer of learning.* New York: Macmillan. Perhaps the most influential textbook to date, with excellent discussions on the measurement of transfer, influential factors, and reprints of several significant empirical studies.

Gagné, R. M. (1985). *The conditions of learning* (4th ed.). New York: Holt, Rinehart and Winston. Gagné's influential typology of learning along with his theory of instruction, which includes structuring a curriculum according to learning hierarchies for maximum transfer.

McKeough, A., Lupart, J., & Marini, A. (Eds.). (1995). *Teaching for transfer.* Mahwah, NJ: Erlbaum. A collection of essays spanning the range of current approaches to the issue of transfer, including Carl Bereiter's dispositional approach, Ann Brown's reciprocal teaching, and Michael Pressley's cognitive strategies.

Perkins, D. N., & Salomon, G. (1989). Are cognitive skills context bound? *Educational Researchers, 18* (1), 16–25. An easily understandable history of transfer research, along with a conception of the complementary "low road" and "high road" strategies for teaching for transfer.

Singley, M. K., & Anderson, J. R. (1989). *The transfer of cognitive skill.* Cambridge, MA: Harvard University Press.

An analysis of transfer from the perspective of Anderson's theory of cognition. Although the reports of the empirical studies make difficult reading, the introduction and summary chapters are essential reading for current theory building in transfer.

J. Ronald Gentile

LEARNING AND MEMORY. [*This entry comprises two articles on learning and memory:* In Humans *and* In Animals. *For general discussions of learning and memory, see* Learning; *and* Memory.]

In Humans

Human learning and memory is often conceived as having three stages: encoding, storage, and retrieval (Melton, 1963). Encoding refers to the acquisition and initial processing of information; storage refers to the maintenance of the encoded information over time; and retrieval refers to the processes by which the stored information is accessed and used. Historically, the scientific study of human memory can be seen as progressing through four phases, the first three of which correspond to an emphasis on encoding, storage, and retrieval, respectively. The fourth phase, which reflects the current state of the field, emphasizes the dynamic interaction among the stages.

The earliest influential concept of memory, derived from Aristotle, was that of an association, a connection between two ideas, thoughts, or events. Associations are formed when two items occur close together in time or space, when two items are very similar, or when two items are very different. The presence of one of these, the cue, brings the other to mind. One point of disagreement was whether associations could be formed only between adjacent items (direct associations) or whether an association could be formed between items that were further removed (a remote association). For example, for three events that occur in a series, not only could there be a direct association between the first and second and between the second and third, but there could also be a remote association between the first and third. Although many early theorists devoted much thought and speculation to the nature of memory, their enthusiasm and insight were hampered by a lack of appropriate tools, methods, and procedures.

Convincing evidence on this issue was not available until 1885, when Hermann Ebbinghaus published the first scientific study on memory. Ebbinghaus was the first scientist to design, conduct, and report an experiment to distinguish between two competing theories of memory. In a series of studies, he reported evidence not only for direct and remote associations, but also for backward associations. Ebbinghaus is also noted for being among the first to use statistical procedures to analyze his data.

Until the 1950s, the verbal learning tradition dominated research on memory in the United States. Following the lead of Ebbinghaus (1885), the emphasis was on the encoding stage, especially on how associations were formed and acquired. One particularly influential line of research, for example, focused on measuring how well learning transferred to new situations (Osgood, 1953). Of course, some emphasis was placed on retrieval; in particular, the dominant theory of forgetting, interference theory, included both unlearning and response competition as factors. Nonetheless, even within this framework, principles of acquisition, such as the differential effectiveness of massed versus distributed rehearsal, dominated (Underwood, 1961).

Beginning in the 1950s, the so-called cognitive revolution ushered in a change of emphasis to storage. The dominant metaphor was the computer, with various buffers, registers, and other forms of storage that were linked to different hypothetical memory structures. The most common view of memory, called the modal model (after a statistical measure, the mode) had three such hypothetical memory structures: sensory register, short-term store, and long-term store (Atkinson & Shiffrin, 1968). Information was first briefly registered in a sensory buffer before being converted from its raw physical form into a more durable (usually verbal) code and deposited into short-term store. Short-term store had a limited capacity, around five to nine items, or "chunks," and was intended mainly as a buffer where information could be temporarily stored. Rehearsal was the process whereby an item was either maintained or copied into long-term store.

Despite the considerable success of this type of model (Glanzer, 1972), empirical and logical problems quickly became apparent (Neath, 1998). The most significant of these was trying to separate the contributions of short- and long-term store in a given situation. Two reactions followed. One was the development of the idea of working memory (Baddeley, 1986), an update of the short-term memory concept. Working memory viewed memory in a broader context, including an attentional and visuospatial system, and was fundamentally a place where cognitive work was performed. The other reaction was an increasing emphasis on processes rather than structures; this emphasis on processing also followed an intensive study of the retrieval stage in the late 1960s and early 1970s. Indeed, working memory can be seen as a hybrid model, containing both a structure (the phonological store) and a process (the articulatory loop).

According to the levels of processing framework (Craik & Lockhart, 1972), memory is the result of a successive series of analyses, each one at a deeper, more conceptual level than the previous, that are performed on the information. The deeper the level of analysis, the better the memory. Memory is therefore more of a by-product than anything else; it is the residue of the processing that was performed. This view offered an explanation for why intent to learn is not an important factor in subsequent tests of memory (Postman, 1964): if a person tries to memorize something but uses an inappropriate process, performance is poor. Indeed, most of the information that people do remember is not learned intentionally; rather, it is the residue of their processing of the original experience.

Levels of processing focused almost exclusively on encoding and said relatively little about retrieval. The second major processing view of the 1970s was developed as a way of rectifying this omission (Morris, Bransford, & Franks, 1977). The primary difference between levels of processing and transfer-appropriate processing is that the latter explicitly includes retrieval as a factor. According to this view, a particular encoding process leads to better performance not because it is necessarily deeper but rather because it is appropriate given the kind of processing that the test requires.

Currently, memory research is in the fourth phase, where the interaction between encoding and retrieval is emphasized. A good example is Tulving's (1983) encoding specificity principle. According to this principle, the recollection of an event, or a certain aspect of it, depends on the interaction between the properties of the encoded event and the properties of the encoded cues available at retrieval. Note that there is an explicit acknowledgment of two possible distortions: the representation of the original information may or may not be veridical, and the representation of the retrieval cues may or may not be veridical. Memory is the interaction of these two potentially distorted representations.

It follows from this type of interactive view that memory is inherently cue driven: Information cannot be recollected or otherwise used in processing unless an appropriate cue is present. A second implication is that slight changes in the cue constellation can easily disrupt memory performance. Even a good cue can lose its effectiveness if it is used too often, a phenomenon known as cue overload (Watkins, 1979). A third implication is that memory is a dynamic process, including the potential for multiple ongoing distortions of the event, both from processing that occurs at study and processing that occurs at test. These implications are inherent in most current theories.

It has already been noted that intention to learn is not necessarily an important factor in subsequent memory performance. One topic that has been of considerable interest in recent years concerns situations where both acquisition and retrieval of information is performed without conscious awareness. This area is typically referred to as implicit memory, although the terminology is quite confusing. The most clear terms separate the type of learning situation (intentional or incidental) and the type of test (direct or indirect). Traditional memory research focused on intentional learning ("Try to remember the following list of items") and direct tests ("Recall the list of items you just studied"). Implicit memory research uses incidental learning ("Rate these items for pleasantness") and indirect tests ("Complete these word fragments with the first word that comes to mind"). (Of course, all combinations are possible.) The interesting finding is that the information processed at study facilitates performance on a variety of tests even though the subject is unaware of this influence.

One ongoing controversy concerns how best to view memory, as either a set of multiple memory systems (Schacter & Tulving, 1994) or a set of processes (Crowder, 1993). The multiple memory systems view attributes memory performance to the underlying memory system. Although there is some disagreement about the number of memory systems, the most popular conception lists five. The procedural memory system is responsible for performance on tasks that involve motor skills (typing, bicycle riding), simple conditioning, and simple associative learning. The perceptual representation system is responsible for identifying and processing visual forms and in speech recognition. Primary memory (also known as working memory) is responsible for storing information that is to be held briefly, such as a telephone number for the time between looking it up and dialing. Semantic memory processes knowledge, and episodic memory is concerned with autobiographical information and events that have been personally experienced.

The major advantage of this view is that it is able to explain a large number of dissociations. A dissociation occurs when one variable, such as delay between study and test, affects one memory task differently than a second. Thus a typical explicit memory task shows worse performance after a long delay, whereas the typical implicit memory task shows almost no detrimental effect of delay. According to the multiple systems view, implicit memory is supported by the procedural representation system, whereas explicit memory depends on episodic memory. Because two different systems are used, two different results are seen. Similar explanations are offered to account for amnesia and the effects of normal aging: different systems can be affected and selectively impair some types of memory performance while leaving other memory abilities unimpaired.

The two major weaknesses of this approach are the lack of consensus on the number and type of systems and the lack of predictive dissociations. Although most multiple-system theorists subscribe to the divisions presented above, many offer additional systems (such as sensory memory systems reminiscent of the modal model), whereas others prefer fewer systems (such as combining episodic and semantic memory).

The inability of this view to formulate predictive dissociations is more problematical. For example, there is a phenomenon known as the fan effect: the time to respond to a given sentence increases as the number of facts known about the components in the sentence increases. The fact that this is true only for episodic tasks and not for semantic tasks is taken as evidence supporting the distinction between these two systems. However, the exact opposite finding—if the fan effect were seen only in semantic tasks and not episodic tasks—would also be taken as support for a distinction between the two systems. The problem is that the multiple-systems view cannot yet predict a priori the nature of the dissociations. Many researchers are currently working on addressing this problem.

The other major theoretical orientation is the processing (or proceduralist) view. Sometimes known as the monolithic view (due to the unwillingness to fractionate memory into multiple systems), this view arose out of and is related to the levels of processing and transfer-appropriate processing views. The main idea is that memory resides in the same neural units that originally processed the experience. When an event is initially experienced, it is processed by certain neural assemblies. Memory is what happens when the same or similar neural units are stimulated by a cue (either an external, bottom-up, or internal, top-down, cue) and similar processing results. As Craik (1994, p. 156) put it, "Encoding is simply the set of processes involved in the perception and interpretation of the original event . . . and retrieval is the attempted recapitulation of the original pattern of encoding activity."

Supporting research comes from many areas, including current research into the effects of normal aging on memory. Whenever a task requires a process that is initiated by an internally produced cue—regardless of whether the task is episodic, semantic, or whatever—performance will be less successful in the elderly than when the process can use an externally provided cue. Thus the type of processing is more predictive of memory performance than the presumed underlying memory system.

One criticism of the processing approach has been that it is vague about exactly how many processes are involved. The process dissociation framework (Jacoby, 1991) is one attempt to separate the contribution of different processes. The basic logic is to examine at least two situations. One test, an inclusion test, is designed so that all processes can contribute beneficially to recall; a second test, the exclusion test, is designed so that one response cannot contribute. In essence, the effect of one process can be subtracted out and its contribution assessed.

Several other areas of research highlight the view that memory is cue driven, dynamic, and reconstructive. The reality monitoring (or source monitoring) paradigm examines the ability of people to remember the source of an event. Subjects may be asked to imagine an episode, or may actually experience the episode. During the test phase, the question of interest is whether the subjects can determine the source. The data show that people are more likely to say that an imagined event was real than a real event was imagined. The study of eyewitness memory reinforces these findings. Unless there is objective evidence available, there is no way of assessing the accuracy of recollection of an eyewitness: They may be very accurate, very inaccurate, or somewhere in the middle. Among the factors that do not predict subsequent accuracy are the duration of the event; the emotional intensity of the event; the unusualness of the event; the number of details that can be recalled; the confidence expressed about the memory; and the delay between the event and the subsequent questioning.

Current interest focuses on what is unfortunately called false memory, recalling information that was not presented (Roediger & McDermott, 1995). The term is unfortunate because it implies a dichotomy between "true" and "false" memories; if these really were the only options, then all memories would have to be labeled false. The far more interesting and important question is the degree to which the current recollection departs from the original episode. With subsequent tests, the recollection may become more or less accurate, but it always contains some distortion and thus some false elements on the part of the rememberer.

Current formal models of memory are also reflective of the fourth phase, the emphasis on both encoding and retrieval. Indeed, a large number of models are termed global memory models because they address memory performance in a wide variety of paradigms (Raaijmakers & Shiffrin, 1992). The four most influential are ACT* (pronounced act star), SAM (search of associative memory), TODAM (theory of distributed associative memory), and MINERVA2 (after the Greek goddess of wisdom). Connectionist models of memory have not fared well and have had less impact on the field.

Memory, then, is a dynamic, fundamentally reconstructive set of processes that enable previously encoded information to affect current and future performance. The effects of memory need not be consciously available to the rememberer, and each successive recollection may further distort or reconstruct the memory.

[*See also* Learning, *article on* Cognitive Approach for Humans.]

Bibliography

Atkinson, R. C., & Shiffrin, R. M. (1968). Human memory: A proposed system and its control processes. In K. W. Spence & J. T. Spence (Eds.), *The psychology of learning and motivation* (Vol. 2, pp. 89–195). New York: Academic Press.

Baddeley, A. D. (1986). *Working memory*. New York: Oxford University Press.

Craik, F. I. M. (1994). Memory changes in normal aging. *Current Directions in Psychological Science, 3,* 155–158.

Craik, F. I. M., & Lockhart, R. S. (1972). Levels of processing: A framework for memory research. *Journal of Verbal Learning and Verbal Behavior, 11,* 671–684.

Crowder, R. G. (1993). Systems and principles in memory theory: Another critique of pure memory. In A. F. Collins, S. E. Gathercole, M. A. Conway, & P. E. Morris (Eds.), *Theories of memory* (pp. 139–161). Hove, UK: Erlbaum.

Ebbinghaus, H. (1885). *Über das Gedächtnis.* Leipzig: Duncker und Humboldt. (Available in English as *Memory: A contribution to experimental psychology,* H. A. Ruger, Trans., 1964, New York: Dover).

Glanzer, M. (1972). Storage mechanisms in recall. In G. H. Bower & J. T. Spence (Eds.), *The psychology of learning and motivation* (Vol. 5, pp. 129–193). New York: Academic Press.

Jacoby, L. L. (1991). A process dissociation framework: Separating automatic from intentional uses of memory. *Journal of Memory and Language, 30,* 513–541.

Melton, A. W. (1963). Implications of short-term memory for a general theory of memory. *Journal of Verbal Learning and Verbal Behavior, 2,* 1–21.

Morris, C. D., Bransford, J. D., & Franks, J. J. (1977). Levels of processing versus transfer appropriate processing. *Journal of Verbal Learning and Verbal Behavior, 16,* 519–533.

Neath, I. (1998). *Human memory: An introduction to research, theory, and data.* Pacific Grove, CA: Brooks/Cole.

Osgood, C. E. (1953). *Method and theory in experimental psychology.* New York: Oxford University Press.

Postman, L. (1964). Short-term memory and incidental learning. In A. W. Melton (Ed.), *Categories of human learning* (pp. 146–201). New York: Academic Press.

Raaijmakers, J. G. W., & Shiffrin, R. M. (1992). Models for recall and recognition. *Annual Review of Psychology, 43,* 205–234.

Roediger, H. L. III, & McDermott, K. B. (1995). Creating false memories: Remembering words not presented in lists. *Journal of Experimental Psychology: Learning, Memory, and Cognition, 21,* 803–814.

Schacter, D. L., & Tulving, E. (1994). What are the memory systems of 1994? In D. L. Schacter & E. Tulving (Eds.), *Memory systems 1994* (pp. 1–38). Cambridge: MIT Press.

Tulving, E. (1983). *Elements of episodic memory.* New York: Oxford University Press.

Underwood, B. J. (1961). Ten years of massed practice on distributed practice. *Psychological Review, 68,* 229–247.

Watkins, M. J. (1979). Engrams as cuegrams and forgetting as cue overload: A cueing approach to the structure of memory. In C. R. Puff (Ed.), *Memory organization and structure* (pp. 347–372). New York: Academic Press.

Ian Neath

In Animals

It is interesting to compare early laboratory studies of animal memory reported by Walter Samuel Hunter (1913) with the behavior in the wild of the Clark's nutcracker, a bird that lives in the western United States. Hunter devised the delayed-response procedure. Hungry animals restrained in a delay chamber were able to determine which of three doors led to food because a light was flashed in front of the correct door. Animals ran from the delay chamber to the doors varying times after the light was extinguished. Rats were not able to select the correct door following a delay of more than 10 seconds; raccoons could withstand a delay of 25 seconds; dogs could withstand a delay of as much as 5 minutes.

The nutcracker stores the seeds of pine cones in underground caches in the late summer and early autumn, recovering them in winter and spring when food is scarce. It is estimated that the bird may store as many as 33,000 seeds in caches of four or five seeds each. A high percentage of the seeds is recovered. That animals possess a complicated and well-developed memory system is, of course, more clearly indicated by the real-word findings for the Clark's nutcracker than the laboratory findings of W. S. Hunter.

Following Hunter, laboratory data indicating that animals, like people, are able to retain information over long periods were reported. Skinner (1950) trained pigeons to peck for food at a spot on an illuminated key. Following a 4-year retention interval the pigeons were tested and immediately pecked the key. Wendt (1937) trained a dog to withdraw its foot at the sound of a tone paired with shock. After a 30-month retention period, foot withdrawal to the tone occurred on 80% of the test trials, only a slight drop from the prior training session.

In the days of Hunter and for some time thereafter, animal memory was not a popular object of investigation in part because it did not fit well with behaviorism, the then dominant approach in animal learning. With the rise of the cognitive approach around 1960, animal memory became of increasing concern and its many similarities to human memory began to be recognized. As examples of these trends, consider that a textbook on animal cognition (Roberts, 1998) devoted 3 of its 12 chapters to animal memory, and many of the remaining 9 chapters refer frequently to memory. In a book that covers extensively many important topics in memory (Spear & Riccio, 1994), several chapters liberally intersperse findings from animal and human memory to demonstrate important points.

Whether memory is a single unitary system or is composed of two or more subsystems is a currently debated topic. Numerous systems are now postulated, some examples being procedural versus declarative memory, semantic versus episodic memory, and long-term versus short-term memory (Spear & Riccio, 1994). One of the popular distinctions in the animal area is that between working memory and reference memory. Working memory is concerned with keeping track of information that may change from one trial to the next. Reference memory is concerned with isolating important relationships in the situation that are stable over trials. As an example, rats rewarded for a running response on every other trial, a single alternation schedule of rewarded and nonrewarded trials, may eventually come to run faster on rewarded than on nonrewarded trials. In this situation working memory would be used to determine whether reward or nonreward occurred on the prior trial and thus whether reward or nonreward is to occur on the current trial. Reference memory would be employed to learn that rewards and nonrewards occur according to a particular rule or schedule, a single alternating one.

Working memory should not be confused with short-term memory, or memory which decays rapidly in a matter of seconds or minutes. For example, in the single-alternation situation described above, rats have responded appropriately even when trials were separated by a 24-hour interval (Capaldi, 1994). Thus working memory is capable of keeping track of changing trial information over long temporal intervals. The single-alternation situation is useful for understanding a second popular distinction between memories in the animal area as well as in human memory; that between retrospective and prospective memory. In the case of the single-alternation schedule, retrospective memory would consist of retaining the memory of prior reward or nonreward over the retention interval, utilizing that memory to determine whether responding on the current trial should be fast or slow. Employing prospective memory, the animal would determine at the time of reward or nonreward whether it should run fast or slow on the subsequent trial, thus making it unnecessary to retain the memory of reward or nonreward over the retention interval.

Items in memory are said to go through three stages. The first, encoding, is the stage in which the memory is formed. The second, retention, refers to the persistence of the memory over time. The third, retrieval,

refers to recall of the stored memory. In a seminal paper on memory, McGeoch (1932) identified three sources of forgetting. One is decay, the simple diminution or loss of the memory over time. McGeoch argued against decay with respect to long-term or reference memory, a position which has come to be generally accepted. However, decay is popularly invoked with respect to items in short-term memory both in the human and animal area, a position vigorously rejected by some—for example, by Capaldi (1994) with respect to animal memory and by Nairne (1996) with respect to human memory. According to this view, short- and long-term memory are governed by similar principles.

A second source of forgetting according to McGeoch is changed context. According to this view, a memory may be better recalled to the extent that cues present when the memory was stored are available at retrieval. Contextual change has received considerable experimental and theoretical attention in recent years. Investigation of internal context may concern a person who learns something when, inebriated (or in a given emotional state) that is then remembered poorly, if at all, in a sober state (or in another emotional state). This phenomenon is called state-dependent memory. Contextual changes may involve external context as when an animal or human that learns something in, say, a given room performs relatively poorly when tested in another room.

The third factor mentioned by McGeoch, interference, refers to one set of associations masking or interfering with another set of associations. Two major sources of interference have been identified. In retroactive interference, memory for material learned earlier may be interfered with by material learned later. In proactive interference, material learned earlier would interfere with the memory of material learned subsequently.

Of the various procedures employed to study working memory in animals, the most popular is delayed matching to sample (DMTS). In this procedure a pigeon is initially trained to peck each of three keys arranged in a horizontal row on the wall of an apparatus called an operant chamber. A typical trial begins by exposing a stimulus, the sample stimulus, on the center key, say, a horizontal line on a white background, the side keys being blank. After the pigeon has observed the horizontal line, or sample stimulus, for some period (or has pecked it), the center key goes blank. There then ensues the retention interval in which all three keys remain blank. When the appropriate retention interval has elapsed the side keys are illuminated, one with the horizontal line and the other with a vertical line. These are called the comparison stimuli. A correct response, which may produce food reward, consists of pecking the side key that contains the comparison stimulus matching the sample—in the present example, the horizontal line. The horizontal and vertical lines may be presented equally often as samples in an irregular fashion over trials. The positions of the comparison stimuli are varied irregularly over trials such that each may appear equally often on the right key and on the left key. There are many variations of the basic DMTS procedure described above (Roberts, 1998).

A controversy in the DMTS area in recent years is concerned with whether correct responding is based on retrospective memory, remembering the sample stimulus over the retentional interval, or prospective memory, an instruction at the time the sample is presented as to what response to make when the comparison stimuli are presented. Several experiments indicate that both sorts of process can direct correct responding (Tarpy, 1997).

Retroactive and proactive interference have been demonstrated in the DMTS situation. Consider first retroactive interference. Animals are typically kept in a dark operant chamber in the DMTS situation. If after the sample stimulus is removed the chamber is illuminated, correct responding decreases substantially. Retroactive interference of this sort has been demonstrated in both pigeons and monkeys. Roberts (1998) suggests that stimuli illuminated during the retention interval become the focus of attention, interfering with rehearsal processes the animal employs to select its choice of comparison stimuli.

A considerable number of experiments have isolated various sources of proactive interference in DMTS (Wright, Urcuioli, & Sands, 1986). As one example, performance is better when many sample and comparison stimuli are used because the frequency of conflicting choices at the time of retention is reduced. When unique stimuli only were employed, monkeys performed above chance accuracy with a retention interval of 24 hours. Proactive interference appears to be a major source of forgetting in animals and in people.

It is useful to think of a memory as being composed of a number of attributes. For example, a rat may remember a particular food item as being sweet, hard, brown, and so on. It appears that over a retention interval some of these attributes may be forgotten more rapidly than others. A good example is available from a study in which rats were trained to run in a black tunnel (called a runway) for food. When tested shortly after in a white runway the rats ran much more slowly than in the black runway. But after a longer retention interval running in the white runway was rapid. It appears that the rats forgot the color of the runway more rapidly than some of its other attributes, such as its enclosed space. Analogous findings have been obtained in a variety of situations (Spear & Riccio, 1994).

When attempting to remember say a phone number, it is helpful to repeat it over and over (rehearse it). A variety of studies concerned with rehearsal in animals

have been reported. Several individuals (e.g., Wagner, 1976) have suggested that surprising events are better rehearsed and thus better remembered than expected events. This proposition has a number of interesting implications, among them that the increments in learning (the additional amount learned) grow progressively smaller over successive trials because surprise progressively decreases trials. Thus when a tone is followed by shock, a considerable increment in fear may be acquired by the representation of the tone on the initial pairing because the shock is completely surprising or unsuspected. On the next trial the additional increment in fear acquired by the representation of the tone would be smaller to the extent that shock is expected.

All animals, including humans, must learn our way about the environment. Because it is so important, spatial memory, or memory for direction and places, has been extensively investigated in animals. A frequently employed apparatus for this purpose is the radial maze, which consists of a central platform with a number of paths or alleyways (usually 8 or 12) radiating from it. Each arm may be baited with a single food item and the arms may not be baited again until all arms are selected once. The rat is placed on the central platform and allowed to select freely among the paths. Following fairly minimal training, the rat learns to enter each path only once (that is, few errors are made). When rare errors are made, latencies in the arm are longer than usual, suggesting that the rat nevertheless has some memory of having entered the arm. In the radial maze rats rely extensively on the surrounding stimuli in the environment to guide choices: if the arms are covered, obscuring external cues, many more errors are made. A common interpretation of radial maze performance is that it depends on the rat forming a cognitive map, that is, learning relationships among stimuli in the environment.

Organizational processes in human and animal memories are of particular interest. For example, a person asked to remember a list of 16 randomly presented items, consisting of 4 each of flowers, fruits, animals, and utensils, will tend to output the items at recall in a particular order, for example, the 4 fruits, followed by the 4 animals, and so on. Similar results have been obtained for rats in the radial maze (Roberts, 1998). A 12-arm radial maze was baited with four each of three different types of food, always in the same arms over successive trials. For example, cheese might be placed in Arms 1, 3, 5, and 8 on successive trials. The rats learned to take the food items in a particular order, each of the four preferred foods first, the four least preferred foods last. As another example of organized memory in rats, consider the following. If rats trained in a runway are given four nonrewarded trials followed by a food-rewarded trial, they will come to run progressively faster over the nonrewarded trials and extremely fast on the rewarded trial, indicating that the five separate trials have been formed into a single unit that is called a chunk. Even more impressively, organizationally speaking, rats can use the memory of an entire series of reward events (say, two rewarded trials followed by a nonrewarded trial) to correctly predict some 20 minutes later another entire series of reward events, which may be identical to or different from the prior remembered series (Capaldi, 1994).

A particularly illuminating example of how animal and human data may be combined to advance our general understanding of memory is provided by Spear and Riccio (1994). Humans have great difficulty remembering events that occurred in infancy, a phenomenon called infantile amnesia. Freud's explanation of infantile amnesia was that infants deal with sexual ideas and behavior in a socially unacceptable manner and so these early memories are thrust from consciousness as the person becomes aware of what is or is not socially acceptable. Unfortunately for this idea, or so it would seem, infantile amnesia has been found in every altricial mammal so far tested, including rats, wolves, and monkeys. Repression of sexual memories would not seem to be a good explanation for infantile amnesia in these nonhuman species. Of course, it is possible that the cause of infantile amnesia is different for humans and animals. But this does not seem an attractive alternative in view of the similarities existing between animal and human memory, such as those considered here.

[*See also* Learning, *article on* Cognitive Approach for Animals.]

Bibliography

Capaldi, E. J. (1994). The sequential view: From rapidly fading stimulus traces to the organization of memory and abstract concept of number. *Psychonomic Bulletin and Review, 1,* 156–181.

Hunter, W. S. (1913). The delayed reaction in animals and children. *Behavior Monographs, 2,* 1–86.

McGeoch, J. A. (1932). Forgetting and the law of disuse. *Psychological Review, 39,* 353–370.

Nairne, J. S. (1996). Short-term/working memory. In E. L. Bjork & R. A. Bjork (Eds.), *Memory* (Vol. 10, pp. 101–126). New York: Academic Press.

Roberts, W. A. (1998). *Principles of animal cognition.* Boston: McGraw-Hill.

Skinner, B. F. (1950). Are theories of learning necessary? *Psychological Review, 57,* 193–216.

Spear, N. E., & Riccio, D. C. (1994). *Memory: Phenomena and principles.* Boston: Allyn and Bacon.

Tarpy, R. M. (1997). *Contemporary learning theory and research.* New York: McGraw-Hill.

Wagner, A. R. (1976). An information-processing mechanism for self-generated or retrieval-generated depression in performance. In T. J. Tighe & R. N. Leaton (Eds.), *Habituation: Perspectives from child development, animal behavior, and neurophysiology* (pp. 95–128). Hillsdale, NJ: Erlbaum.

Wendt, G. R. (1937). Two and one-half year retention of a conditioned response. *Journal of General Psychology, 17,* 178–180.

Wright, A. A., Urcuioli, P. J., & Sands, S. F. (1986). Proactive interference in animal memory. In D. F. Kendrick, M. E. Rilling, & M. R. Denny (Eds.), *Theories of animal memory* (pp. 101–125). Hillsdale, NJ: Erlbaum.

E. John Capaldi

LEARNING AND MOTIVATION. The role of motivation in psychological theory and research has had a long and checkered history. It was central to the field in the heydey of drive theories and then became barely peripheral to the mainstream of research on learning from a cognitive psychological or cognitive science perspective. However, since the 1970s psychologists have rediscovered the limitations of a purely cognitive science model for explaining adaptive human functioning (Searle, 1992). Or, to return to the roots of American psychology as represented by William James (1890), psychologists recognized that the assumption that individuals are just conscious automata is "an unwarrantable impertinence in the present state of psychology" (James, 1890, p. 138). Psychology has benefited greatly from cognitive and computer-based models, but it seems clear that these models do not capture all of the complexity and dynamic nature of an individual's learning and thinking. It seems necessary that motivational constructs such as goals, efficacy and control beliefs, values, and interest should be incorporated into models of learning. At the same time, these motivational constructs reflect the cognitive turn in motivational theory and research since the 1970s, and this general cognitive perspective has made it easier to develop theoretical and empirical linkages between motivation, cognition, and learning. Accordingly, from the 1980s on, much more research examined how different motivational constructs are related to cognition and learning.

There are a number of different definitions and theories of motivation, but for the purpose of this article, the focus is on general social-cognitive constructs that reflect individuals' self-perceptions of such capabilities as self-efficacy, attributions, competence, and self-concept, as well as their goals, interest, and value for the task. Although emotions, mood, and anxiety are clearly related to cognition, they are not discussed here.

The focus here is research that has most often linked motivation to cognition and learning. As such, cognition and learning are defined in terms of memory performance, learning and comprehension of text material, and use of various cognitive and self-regulatory strategies for learning. This definition includes performance on memory tasks in terms of items recalled or performance on text comprehension tasks in terms of recall of information, as well as comprehension of gist and meaning. It also includes the various strategies that learners might use on these tasks, including rehearsal, chunking, and mnemonic strategies for memory tasks, as well as learning strategies such as elaboration (i.e., paraphrasing, summarizing) or organizational strategies (i.e., outlining, networking, note-taking) that can be used in text comprehension tasks. Finally, there are more general metacognitive and self-regulatory strategies that learners can use to control and regulate their cognition, such as planning, monitoring their performance or comprehension, and changing their cognition to repair deficits in their performance or comprehension (Weinstein & Mayer, 1986).

Given these working definitions of motivation and cognition, there are four general positions that describe the relations between motivation and cognition:

1. Motivation and cognition are unrelated to one another.
2. Cognition precedes and influences motivation.
3. Motivation precedes and influences cognition.
4. Cognition and motivation are reciprocally related to one another.

The first position is well represented in basic cognitive psychology and cognitive science research. Most cognitive models of the structures and processes that individuals use to perceive, categorize, reason, think, problem solve, and learn have not included motivational constructs. Given that these models are *competence* models of cognition, they seek to describe the normative and basic cognitive operations that individuals use when involved in cognitive tasks. It is usually not a concern of these models to explain why some individuals might use some cognitive processes or strategies and others do not, a classic problem in *performance* models that are concerned with motivation and individual differences. Accordingly, general cognitive models are not concerned with motivational factors and, by default, seem to assume that motivation and cognition are separate systems and are basically unrelated to one another.

In contrast, more recent research in both laboratory and field settings suggests that motivational beliefs are correlated with cognition (see review by Pintrich & Schrauben, 1992). Most of this research has been conducted with the implicit or explicit assumption of position 3, that motivation precedes and influences cognition and learning. This position is in line with almost all traditional motivational models that assume that motivational constructs influence the instigation and direction (selection, choice) of behavior as well as the quality and quantity of engagement, persistence, and performance on the task. For example, individuals who are efficacious as well as interested in and value a task will be more likely to be cognitively engaged in the task and perform better. At the same time, it seems reasonable that as individuals learn and perform well, their cognition could influence their subsequent motivation for the task in line with position 2. Although there is a long history of debate between these two general positions in the research on the linkages between self-concept and achievement, as Wigfield and Karpathian (1991) suggest, it now seems relatively fruitless to continue this debate about the causal predominance of motivation and cognition. It seems very likely that motivation and cognition are reciprocally related to one another as suggested by position 4 and that future research should attempt to describe the nature of the reciprocal and functional relations between motivation and cognition.

The remainder of this article summarizes the research on the functional relations between various motivational constructs and individuals' cognition and learning. Although a general reciprocal model is assumed, most of the research that has explicitly linked motivation and cognition has followed position 3.

The Role of Expectancy Motivational Constructs in Cognition and Learning

In almost all motivational theories, there is a construct that concerns individuals' perceptions of their competence to perform the task, or, in more colloquial terms, an answer to the basic question, "Can I do this task?" (Pintrich & Schunk, 1996). The construct goes under various names including *self-efficacy, self-competence, self-perceptions of ability*, and *expectancy beliefs* or *judgments*, to name a few. The term *self-efficacy* will be used here and will refer to learners' beliefs about their capabilities to perform a task.

The Role of Self-Efficacy in Cognition. General motivational models assume that positive self-efficacy beliefs will lead to the *choice* to engage in challenging tasks (e.g., continue taking math courses when not required to do so), quantity or level of *engagement* in the task (e.g., trying hard, high levels of effort), and *persistence* at the task in the face of difficulties. The research that has linked self-efficacy to learning suggests that it is not just the quantity of engagement or effort in the task, but also the *quality* of the engagement in terms of the nature of the cognitive processing that leads to better performance and achievement.

The research that has linked self-efficacy beliefs to cognition and learning is fairly extensive and includes memory performance in experimental settings, the use of cognitive, metacognitive, and self-regulatory strategies in classroom studies, as well as reading and text comprehension, writing strategies, and mathematical problem solving in both laboratory and classroom settings. The main generalization from this research is that self-efficacy beliefs are positively related to better memory performance, the use of deeper processing strategies (e.g., elaboration in comparison to surface strategies such as rehearsal), the use of more metacognitive and self-regulatory strategies for learning and better text comprehension, writing, and mathematics performance (Bandura, 1997; Pintrich & Schrauben, 1992; Pintrich & Schunk, 1996). Although there are variations on this generalization as a function of individual and contextual factors (e.g., age, gender, ethnicity, type of task, classroom context, etc.), the basic finding holds across a large number of studies and suggests that positive self-efficacy beliefs do not just increase choice, effort, and persistence, but can also lead to qualitatively different and better types of cognition and learning.

The Role of Attributions in Cognition. Attribution, a related motivational construct but one that is distinct from efficacy, concerns the attributions individuals make as they perform a task and receive feedback. Attributions involve the individuals' perceptions of the reasons or causes for their success or failure on a task (Weiner, 1986). Although there are an infinite number of attributions for success or failure, there are some that are most commonly used such as ability (e.g., "I succeeded because I'm smart/good at this task.") and effort (e.g., "I failed because I did not try hard enough."). More importantly, attributional theory proposes that it is not the specific attribution per se that has motivational implications, but rather that the motivational "push" for attributions derives from their classification into three basic dimensions based on the causal structure of the attributions (Pintrich & Schunk, 1996; Weiner, 1986). These dimensions include *locus* (how internal to external the cause is perceived to be), *controllability* (how controllable to uncontrollable the cause is perceived to be), and *stability* (how stable to unstable the cause is perceived to be). These dimensions have been linked to self-efficacy and expectancy for success beliefs in numerous studies. The basic findings are that outcomes that are ascribed to a stable cause (e.g., success due to ability; failure due to lack of ability) will be expected to occur again, while those outcomes due to unstable causes (e.g., failure due to lack of effort) will be expected to be less likely to occur. Stability and controllability can also relate to the individual's feelings of helplessness or hopefulness as well as efficacy for future tasks (Pintrich & Schunk, 1996; Weiner, 1986).

In terms of the links between attributional patterns and cognition, research shows poor memory performance or poor reading comprehension that is attributed to lack of effort or to the use of poor strategies (both internal, controllable, and unstable attributions)

results in more adaptive cognition on future performance (Pintrich & Schrauben, 1992). In addition, the research on learned helplessness (Peterson, Maier, & Seligman, 1993) as well as self-determination theory (Deci & Ryan, 1985), which focus more on the dimension of controllability, not stability, suggests that individuals who perceive that they have some control over events in their lives, or are self-determining, have more adaptive cognition on learning tasks as well as more positive affect, effort, and persistence. Finally, research on attributional retraining suggests that changing the patterns of attributions for performance can have a positive influence on future performance, and when combined with cognitive strategy instruction this attributional retraining can have even more powerful effects on learning (Pintrich & Schunk, 1996; Schneider & Pressley, 1997).

The Role of Goals, Values, and Interest Constructs in Cognition and Learning

In traditional expectancy value models of motivation, perceptions of efficacy are only one half of the equation that predicts behavior. In these models, it is not enough that individuals feel competent to do the task, they must also "value" the task in terms of beliefs about its importance or interest to them. The other general component concerns the values the individual has for the task, or more colloquially, the answer to the question, "Why am I doing this task?" Again, there are a number of different motivational constructs that address the reasons for why an individual might engage in a task. The focus in the present article is on three general constructs—goal orientation, task value, and interest.

The Role of Goal Orientation in Cognition. Currently one of the most active areas of research on motivation and achievement is the different goal orientations that individuals adopt as they approach a task. The research has generally focused on two goal orientations to tasks, *mastery* and *performance goal* orientations (also called *learning, task involved* vs. *ability focused, ego involved*). A mastery orientation reflects a general purpose and focus on mastery, learning, challenge, and self-improvement, while a performance orientation reflects a focus on besting others, obtaining the highest score, and a concern for how one's ability or self will be evaluated. This distinction is somewhat similar to the distinction between intrinsic and extrinsic motivation, but goal-orientation models take a more situated, contextualized, and social-cognitive view of motivation as opposed to the more personality or traitlike view of motivation offered by some intrinsic motivation theories (Pintrich & Schunk, 1996).

In terms of the linkages between these two goal orientations and cognition, the evidence is fairly clear from both experimental and correlational studies about the positive benefits of adopting a mastery goal orientation to the learning task. Individuals who adopt a mastery goal and stay focused on their learning, not their performance, use deeper processing strategies, including metacognitive and self-regulatory strategies, and perform better in terms of their memory, learning, and achievement. They also use more adaptive attributions and report more interest and positive affect toward the task (Pintrich & Schunk, 1996). In contrast, some research has found that students who adopt a performance orientation do not engage in the tasks in such an adaptive manner, report less use of cognitive and metacognitive strategies, as well as poorer performance. Currently, however, there is some debate on whether there may be different types of performance orientation, including one focused on trying to achieve at high levels and do better than others, which can have positive effects (see Harackiewicz, Barron, & Elliot, 1998); one focused on avoiding looking dumb and protecting one's ability, which can lead to negative effects; or even a third orientation to grades and extrinsic rewards, which also seems to have negative consequences. It seems likely that future research will tease apart these different aspects of performance orientation, some having positive and others negative effects. For now it is clear that a general mastery orientation is propaedeutic for learning and cognition on a number of different cognitive tasks including memory, text comprehension, and school learning tasks.

The Role of Task Value and Interest in Cognition. In expectancy value models of motivation, task value is defined in terms of individuals' judgments of the utility, importance, and interest the task or content of the task has for them. *Utility* refers to perceptions that the task is useful for future goals (e.g., "Math is useful for me because I want to be an engineer"); *importance* refers to the general importance of doing well on the task for the individual; and *interest* refers to the general enjoyment or liking of the task and the content of the task (Pintrich & Schunk, 1996). In other research on personal and situational interest (Renninger, Hidi, & Krapp, 1992), *personal interest* is defined as a relatively enduring or stable personal disposition to enjoy or like a particular activity or task, while *situational interest* is more fleeting and a function of characteristics or features of the environment or task (e.g., novelty, surprise, complexity, ambiguity, etc.).

Research on these aspects of task value and personal interest and their links to cognition shows a positive relation, albeit less strong than those for efficacy and mastery goal orientation. Individuals who value the task in terms of its utility, importance, and interest are more likely to engage in deeper cognitive processing, use metacognitive and self-regulatory strategies, remember more information from texts, and perform better on school reading and mathematics learning tasks. Again, there may be some individual and contextual moderators of this basic relation, but the generalization is observed in both experimental and correlational studies across different types of tasks including memory, text comprehension, and academic subject area tasks such as mathematics and reading.

Summary and Future Directions

Although relatively recent, the research that has explicitly addressed the relations between motivation, cognition, and learning has generated some fairly consistent findings. There are various individual and contextual moderators of these relations, but the generalization that adaptive motivational beliefs facilitate not just more effort and persistence, but qualitatively better cognitive processing and learning, seems to be valid across different types of tasks, subject areas, and the life span. Adaptive motivational beliefs include positive self-efficacy beliefs, adaptive attributional patterns, a mastery orientation to the task, and high levels of value and interest in the task.

In terms of future research, there are a number of directions. First, there is a need for a more complete theoretical explication of the relations between motivational beliefs and cognition. This will include (1) clarification of the different motivational constructs including their situation-specificity versus traitlike nature; (2) the specific cognitive mechanisms that might underlie the well-documented linkages; (3) more specific theoretical descriptions and explanations for the reciprocal relations between motivation and cognition; (4) clarification of the operation of individual and contextual moderators of the relations between motivation and cognition. Second, there will be development of more ecologically valid measures of motivation and cognition at the psychological level, and there may be linkages to more physiological measures. Finally, there will be a focus on interventions that seek to improve both motivation and cognition in order to facilitate better learning and achievement.

[*See also* Motivation.]

Bibliography

Bandura, A. (1997). *Self-efficacy: The exercise of control.* New York: Freeman. Details role of self-efficacy in all aspects of human functioning including cognition.

Deci, E., & Ryan, R. (1985). *Intrinsic motivation and self-determination in human behavior.* New York: Plenum Press.

Harackiewicz, J., Barron, K., & Elliot, A. (1998). Rethinking achievement goals: When are they adaptive for college students and why? *Educational Psychologist, 33,* 1–21.

James, W. (1890). *Principles of psychology* (Vol. 2). New York: Holt.

Peterson, C., Maier, S., & Seligman, M. E. P. (1993). *Learned helplessness: A theory for the age of personal control*. New York: Oxford University Press. Explicates how personal control beliefs are related to both mental and physical health.

Pintrich, P. R., & Schrauben, B. (1992). Students' motivational beliefs and their cognitive engagement in classroom academic tasks. In D. Schunk & J. Meece (Eds.), *Student perceptions in the classroom* (pp. 149–183). Hillsdale, NJ: Erlbaum. Summarizes research on how different motivational beliefs are linked to student cognition in classroom contexts.

Pintrich, P. R., & Schunk, D. H. (1996). *Motivation in education: Theory, research and applications*. Englewood Cliffs, NJ: Prentice Hall/Merrill. Provides a review and evaluation of all major theories of motivation relevant to achievement and learning.

Renninger, K., Hidi, S., & Krapp, A. (Eds). (1992). *The role of interest in learning and development*. Hillsdale, NJ: Erlbaum. Edited volume that has the best overall representation of different perspectives and theories on personal and situational interest and their role in learning.

Schneider, W., & Pressley, M. (1997). *Memory development between two and twenty*. Mahwah, NJ: Erlbaum. The most comprehensive review of memory development research to date.

Searle, J. (1992). *The rediscovery of the mind*. Cambridge, MA: MIT Press.

Weiner, B. (1986). *An attributional theory of motivation and emotion*. New York: Springer-Verlag.

Weinstein, C. E., & Mayer, R. (1986). The teaching of learning strategies. In M. Wittrock, (Ed.), *Handbook of research on teaching* (pp. 315–327). New York: Macmillan.

Wigfield, A., & Karpathian, M. (1991). Who am I and what can I do? Children's self-concepts and motivation in achievement situations. *Educational Psychologist, 26,* 233–262.

Paul R. Pintrich

LEARNING DISABILITIES. A variety of practitioners use the phrase *learning disability* to describe a range of academic difficulties. The term was coined by the late special educator and psychologist Samuel Kirk, who in 1962 introduced it in his text on exceptional children:

> A learning disability refers to a retardation, disorder, or delayed development in one or more of the processes of speech, language, reading, writing, arithmetic, or other school subject resulting from a psychological handicap caused by a possible cerebral dysfunction and/or emotional or behavioral disturbances. It is not the result of mental retardation, sensory deprivation, or cultural and instructional factors. (p. 263)

Although the year 1962 marks the formal introduction of the modern term learning disabilities, the origin of the concept has at least a 100-year history. Gall's early nineteenth-century work on brain injury and subsequent spoken language disorders has been cited (Lyon, 1996) as the first research having significant implications for the modern conceptualizations of learning disabilities. Later in the nineteenth century, Paul Broca and Carl Wernicke were able to identify specific areas in the left hemisphere of the brain that control both expressive and receptive speech in adults with aphasia, that is speech and language learning disabilities (Hallahan, Kauffman, & Lloyd, 1996). In the 1920s and 1930s, Kurt Goldstein contributed to the emerging understanding of learning disabilities through his work with brain-injured World War I veterans. He identified various visual-perceptual problems such as an inability to identify figure-ground relationships, letter reversals, and copying errors in his subjects (Bender, 1995). Around this same time period, neurologist Samuel Orton studied reading disabilities, or "dyslexia," in children. He described the condition as "word blindness," or strephosymbolia. He postulated that reading problems resulted from mixed dominance of the hemispheres of the brain, that is, the left hemisphere which controls language is not in control of this function as it is in persons without reading difficulties. In accordance, Orton also offered treatment suggestions for these children, including systematic phonics instruction and kinesthetic methods such as letter tracing. During the 1940s, Alfred Strauss and Heinz Werner studied children with mental retardation that did not result from genetic causes. They coined the term "minimal brain damage" and observed that these children generally had characteristics of perceptual-motor problems, neurological impairment, and normal intelligence. Each of these theorists, as well as many others, contributed substantially to our current definitions of learning disabilities.

Definitions

Soon after Kirk introduced the term learning disabilities in 1962, much momentum was gained toward including this group in the special education movement. President John F. Kennedy (who had a sister with special needs) created the Division for Handicapped Children in the U.S. Office of Education to promote research interests in the field, and he appointed Samuel Kirk as director. Numerous learning disability advocacy groups also began to form at this time. As a result of these forces, the Specific Learning Disabilities Act of 1969 (Pub. L. No. 91–230) was enacted. The definition of specific learning disabilities as presented in this legislation was highly similar to Kirk's 1962 description (Hallahan, Kauffman, & Lloyd, 1996). Soon after, the Education for All Handicapped Children Act of 1975 (Pub. L. No. 94–142) was passed, stipulating that all school-age children, regardless of handicapping condition, are entitled to a free and appropriate public education. This law was renamed the Individuals with Disabilities Education Act, popularly known as IDEA (Pub. L. No. 101–476), in 1990 and was also reauthorized and amended in 1997 (Pub. L. No. 105–17). The 1997 *Federal Register* contains the regulations for identifying and defining students with specific learning disabilities under the current legislation so that they may receive special educational services. The definition is as follows:

> "Specific learning disability" means a disorder in one or more of the basic psychological processes involved in understanding or in using language, spoken or written, that may manifest itself in an imperfect ability to listen, think, speak, read, write, spell or to do mathematical calculations, including conditions such as perceptual disabilities, brain injury, minimal brain dysfunction, dyslexia, and developmental aphasia. The term does not include learning problems that are primarily the result of visual, hearing, or motor disabilities, of mental retardation, of emotional disturbance, or of environmental, cultural, or economic disadvantage. (U.S. Department of Education, 1999, p. 12422)

This definition serves as a guideline for states charged with determining eligibility for special education. The states, however, have some flexibility in interpreting this definition; therefore, some make slight changes to this federal guideline. Moreover, other definitions have been proposed by the Learning Disabilities Association of America, the Interagency Committee on Learning Disabilities, and the National Joint Committee on Learning Disabilities (Hallahan, Kauffman, & Lloyd, 1996). These definitions overlap considerably, yet some differ significantly from the federal definition.

In addition to defining specific learning disabilities, the 1999 *Federal Register* also outlines criteria that should be considered in identifying students with this disorder. The disability must result from a deficit in one or more basic learning behaviors such as memory, reasoning, organization, and perception; must manifest itself in the form of one or more significant learning difficulties in one or more of seven areas—oral expression, listening comprehension, written expression, basic reading skills, reading comprehension, mathematics calculation, and mathematical reasoning—compared with other children of the same age; must be evidenced by a severe discrepancy between intellectual ability and academic achievement in at least one of these seven areas; and must not be caused by mental retardation, hearing or vision impairment, motor impairment, emotional and behavioral disorder, or environmental disadvantage (U.S. Department of Education, 1999). As can be seen, the *Federal Register* offers a rather generic description of specific learning disabilities by encompassing a variety of possible characteristics.

In comparison, another major method of defining and characterizing learning disabilities is through the *Diagnostic and Statistical Manual of Mental Disorders* (*DSM–IV*; American Psychiatric Association, 1994). The *DSM–IV* outlines three major types of learning disorders: reading disorder, mathematics disorder, and disorder of written expression, in addition to learning disorder NOS (not otherwise specified), as opposed to offering one general definition. However, the descriptions of these disorders in the *DSM–IV* share one important similarity with that found in the *Federal Register*. Both stipulate that there must be a discrepancy between achievement in the area in question and intelligence. It is this requirement (one or more achievement deficits relative to measured intelligence) that has been the major point of debate in determining criteria for learning disabilities classification.

Ability-Achievement Discrepancy

According to Bender (1995), "Discrepancy criteria are used to indicate a substantial difference between intelligence, as measured on standardized IQ assessments, and achievement in a number of academic subject areas" (p. 21). Methods of determining such a discrepancy vary from state to state in the United States since no particular method is recommended in the federal guidelines. Four primary means have been used. First, discrepancy can be determined by deviation from grade level, meaning that a student performs below what is expected of his or her grade placement (a fifth grader reading at a first grade level would be considered learning disabled). However, this procedure ignores individual differences in intelligence. This approach is especially problematic for gifted children with superior intelligence who have difficulty keeping up with grade-level work, in that they would not necessarily be identified. Second, expectancy formulas can be used to calculate predicted grade level achievement, thus taking intelligence test scores into account. Although an improvement on the first method, expectancy formulas rely on the use of grade equivalents, an ordinal scale which varies from test to test, thus making comparisons untenable. Third, simple standard-score comparisons involve the comparison of standard scores on intelligence tests and achievement tests, where a discrepancy of about one to one and a half standard deviations (or 15 to 22 points) between achievement and intelligence scores is normally required. Among other problems, this method tends to overidentify those with higher levels of intelligence; for example, a child with an IQ of 130 would have a better chance of scoring 110 or below on reading achievement, whereas a child with an IQ of 90 would be less likely to have a score of 70 or below on reading, thus underidentifying those with lower intelligence test scores. Another problem with the standard-score comparison model is that it fails to take into account the fact that achievement and IQ scores tend to be moderately to highly correlated.

Thus a fourth method, regression-based discrepancy formula, was devised to control for this relationship between IQ and achievement. The regression approach controls the size of ability-achievement discrepancy regardless of ability level. However, this model has been criticized in that intelligence sets the upper limit for achievement, when this may not actually be the case (Berninger & Abbott, 1994). In terms of use, the simple standard score and regression methods predominate.

As can be inferred, no single method for determining ability-achievement discrepancy for the purpose of diagnosing learning disabilities has garnered sufficient scientific support. In fact, several researchers have questioned the overall validity and usefulness of the ability-achievement discrepancy concept. Stanovich (1991, 1993) has proposed the use of a more educationally applicable ability measure, such as listening comprehension or phonological skills as opposed to IQ, to compare with overall reading achievement in determining the presence of a reading disability. In a similar vein, Siegel (1992) found that "both these groups [reading disabled (dyslexic) and poor readers] deserve the label of reading disabled and have similar problems in reading and spelling and significant problems in phonological processing, memory, and language" (p. 627). Similarly, Fletcher, Francis, Rourke, Shaywitz, and Shaywitz (1992) tested the validity of discrepancy-based definitions of reading disabilities by comparing the performances of four groups of children classified as reading disabled according to four different methods with one group of nondisabled children on a battery of neuropsychological tests. They found no significant differences among the "disabled" children, thus calling into question the "validity of segregating children with reading deficiencies according to discrepancies with IQ scores" (p. 555). Stanovich and Siegel (1994) subsequently tested Stanovich's phonological-core variable-difference model of reading disability, again finding that "garden variety" poor readers did not differ from reading-disabled readers on measures of phonological, word recognition, and language skills. They concluded:

> If there is a special group of children with reading disabilities who are behaviorally, cognitively, genetically, or neurologically different, it is becoming increasingly unlikely that they can be easily identified by using IQ discrepancy as a proxy for the genetic and neurological differences themselves. Thus, the basic assumption that underlies decades of classification in research and educational practice regarding reading disabilities is becoming increasingly untenable. (p. 48)

Findings such as these portend substantial change in existing diagnostic methods.

Prevalence and Comorbidity

Recent reports estimate that the public schools have identified approximately 2.3 million students 6 to 21 years of age as learning disabled, or 4.09% of the general population in this age range (U.S. Department of Education, 1994). These figures may be underestimates as they do not include children being served in private facilities. Further, according to Hallahan, Kauffman, and Lloyd (1996), most research studies indicate that the number of males identified as learning disabled outnumbers females by about three or four to one. Possible reasons for this overrepresentation of males include increased biological vulnerability overall for boys or bias in referral and assessment procedures. With regard to race/ethnicity, the learning disability population includes 67.2% White, 21.6% Black, and 8.4% Hispanic individuals, whereas the general population is of 70% White, 12% Black, and 13% Hispanic (U.S. Department of Education, 1992).

Learning disabilities are also likely to exist concurrently with other disorders (that is, comorbidity) and symptoms. For instance, it has been estimated that 10 to 25% of persons with learning disorders as described in the *DSM–IV* also have disorders such as conduct disorder, oppositional defiant disorder, attention-deficit/hyperactivity disorder, major depressive disorder, and dysthymic disorder. In turn, persons with one type of learning disorder are likely to have other types of learning disorders. Also, persons with learning disorders often have difficulties in work settings and with social skills.

Subtypes

Three major subtypes of learning disabilities are described in the *DSM–IV*. The first learning disorder described in the *DSM–IV* is reading disorder (315.00). The diagnostic criteria are as follows: "Reading achievement, as measured by individually administered standardized tests of reading accuracy or comprehension, is substantially below that expected given the person's chronological age, measured intelligence, and age-appropriate education" (p. 50). Furthermore, this problem must interfere with academic achievement or daily living. The reading problems must also extend beyond those presented by a sensory deficit. Incidentally, these same caveats apply to all three learning disorder subtypes. According to the *DSM–IV*, the majority of those diagnosed with reading disorder are males, and the overall prevalence of the disorder is estimated to be 4% in school-age children. Further, reading disorder is rarely diagnosed before first grade, the time when intense reading instruction is begun.

Second, the diagnostic criteria for mathematics disorder (315.1) are: "Mathematical ability, as measured by individually administered standardized tests, is substantially below that expected given the person's chronological age, measured intelligence, and age-appropriate education" (p. 51). The prevalence rate for mathematics learning disabilities has been estimated as

6%. However, according to the *DSM–IV*, an estimated 1% of school-age children have been diagnosed with mathematics disorder. Like reading disorder, mathematics disorder is seldom detected before children reach the first grade. Mathematics disorder is also often found in conjunction with a disorder of written expression and/or reading disorder.

Third, the diagnostic criteria for disorder of written expression (315.2) are: "Writing skills, as measured by individually administered standardized tests (or functional assessments of writing skills), are substantially below those expected given the person's chronological age, measured intelligence, and age-appropriate education" (p. 53). The *DSM–IV* reports that the prevalence of disorder of written expression is thought to be quite small, but has not yet been adequately measured. Again, as with reading disorder and mathematics disorder, disorder of written expression is not often diagnosed before children reach first grade. Disorder of written expression is also usually found in combination with other learning disorders. The *DSM–IV* also includes a category for learning disorder not otherwise specified (315.9), to include those persons who do not meet criteria for a given specific learning disorder but who have difficulty in academic achievement.

Causes

Several hypotheses regarding the etiology of learning disabilities have been and are currently being investigated. An area that has received much attention is neurological dysfunction. Technologies such as magnetic resonance imaging (MRI) and positron emission tomography (PET) have contributed to a greater understanding of cerebral function. In summarizing some of this research, Hallahan, Kauffman and Lloyd (1996) state: "Several researchers have found that the brains of people with dyslexia, or severe reading disorders, are structurally and functionally different from the brains of people without disabilities" (p. 84). Specifically, it is thought that those with learning disabilities have deficits of the left cerebral hemisphere, the area primarily responsible for language. Heredity has also been implicated as a possible cause for learning disabilities on the basis of considerable evidence of family resemblance for learning disabilities. However, the specific contributions of genetic as well as environmental factors are yet to be determined. Moreover, alcohol, cigarette smoke, cocaine and other illegal drugs, among other teratogens, have been identified as possible causes for neurological problems that may lead to learning disabilities. Perinatal influences, such as premature birth and low birth weight and the use of forceps, have also been presented as possible causes of learning disabilities (Bender, 1995). Postnatal influences such as head injury, meningitis, diabetes, exposure to environmental toxins such as lead, and malnutrition also have been investigated as possible causes, although definitive findings are not yet available (Hallahan, Kauffman, & Lloyd, 1996).

Treatments

The primary mode of treatment for learning disabilities is through the provision of special education and other educational services. As mentioned earlier, federal legislation exists requiring that students with learning disabilities be provided with a free and appropriate public education. Students with learning disabilities can receive their education through a variety of service delivery models, depending upon which is deemed most appropriate. These options often include regular education, regular education with modifications, collaborative consultation with special education, coteaching, resource room (part-time special education), self-contained special education, special day school, or residential school (Hallahan, Kauffman, & Lloyd, 1996). Focus has been placed on the importance of early intervention in recent years (Kirk, Gallagher, & Anastasiow, 1997). Early intervention can be used not only to intervene with learning disabilities sooner, but also to possibly prevent disabilities in young children at risk for developing them.

Several specific instructional methods have been used with varying degrees of success with learning disabilities: applied behavior analysis and behavioral intervention, self-monitoring, metacognitive-strategy instruction, attribution training, cooperative learning, peer tutoring, and mnemonic devices (Bender, 1995; Kirk, Gallagher, & Anastasiow, 1997). Some educational researchers have found that coaching active reasoning skills appears to be a promising instructional method to use for students with learning disabilities (Sullivan, Mastropieri, & Scruggs, 1995). Other strategies have been proposed but have yielded mixed results: biofeedback, relaxation training, and multisensory instruction (VAKT, visual, auditory, kinesthetic, tactile). Some proposed treatments have shown no proven beneficial effects for the treatment of learning disabilities; these include Doman and Delacato's patterning method, the Feingold diet, megavitamins and minerals, and chiropractic care (Bender, 1995). However, it has been demonstrated that aggressive tutoring in reading may be beneficial for children with reading problems (Vellutino et al., 1996).

Future Directions

The field of learning disabilities is relatively young, and numerous research topics need to be addressed further. Issues of continuing research interest include the definition and diagnostic criteria for learning disabilities, the validity of the ability-achievement discrepancy model, longitudinal studies of course and outcome, and efficacious treatment methods.

[*See also* Developmental Disorders; *and* Dyslexia.]

Bibliography

American Psychiatric Association. (1994). *Diagnostic and statistical manual of mental disorders* (4th ed.). Washington, DC: Author.

Bender, W. N. (1995). *Learning disabilities: Characteristics, identification, and teaching strategies* (2nd ed.). Boston: Allyn and Bacon.

Berninger, V. W., & Abbott, R. D. (1994). Redefining learning disabilities: Moving beyond aptitude-achievement discrepancies to failure to respond to validated treatment protocols. In G. R. Lyon (Ed.), *Frames of reference for the assessment of learning disabilities: New views on measurement issues* (pp. 163–183). Baltimore: Paul H. Brookes Publishing Company.

Fletcher, J. M., Francis, D. J., Rourke, B. P., Shaywitz, S. E., & Shaywitz, B. A. (1992). The validity of discrepancy-based definitions of reading disabilities. *Journal of Learning Disabilities, 25* (9), 555–561.

Hallahan, D. P., Kauffman, J. M., & Lloyd, J. W. (1996). *Introduction to learning disabilities*. Boston: Allyn & Bacon.

Kirk, S. A. (1962). *Educating exceptional children*. New York: Houghton Mifflin.

Kirk, S. A., Gallagher, J. J., & Anastasiow, N. J. (1997). *Educating exceptional children* (8th ed.). New York: Houghton Mifflin.

Lyon, G. R. (1996). Learning disabilities. In E. J. Mash & R. A. Barkley (Eds.), *Child psychopathology* (pp. 390–435). New York: Guilford Press.

Lyon, G. R. (Ed.). (1994). *Frames of references for the assessment of learning disabilities: New views on measurement issues*. Baltimore: Paul H. Brookes Publishing Company.

Mash, E. J., & Barkley, R. A. (Eds.). (1996). *Child psychopathology*. New York: Guilford Press.

Siegel, L. (1992). An evaluation of the discrepancy definition of dyslexia. *Journal of Learning Disabilities, 25* (10), 618–629.

Stanovich, K. E. (1991). Discrepancy definitions of reading disability: Has intelligence led us astray? *Reading Research Quarterly, 26* (1), 7–29.

Stanovich, K. E. (1993). A model for studies of reading disability. *Developmental Review, 13* (3), 225–245.

Stanovich, K. E., & Siegel, L. S. (1994). Phenotypic performance profile of children with reading disabilities: A regression-based test of the phonological-core variable-difference model. *Journal of Educational Psychology, 86* (1), 24–53.

Sullivan, G. S., Mastropieri, M. A., & Scruggs, T. E. (1995). Reasoning and remembering: Coaching students with learning disabilities to think. *Journal of Special Education, 29* (3), 310–322.

U.S. Department of Education. (1992). *Fourteenth annual report to Congress on the implementation of the Individuals with Disabilities Education Act*. Washington, DC: Author.

U.S. Department of Education. (1994). *Sixteenth annual report to Congress on the implementation of the Individuals with Disabilities Education Act*. Washington, DC: Author.

U.S. Department of Education. (1999). Definition and criteria for defining students as learning disabled. *Federal Register, 64* (48).

Vellutino, F. R., Scanlon, D. M., Sipay, E. R., Small, S. G., Chen, R., Pratt, A., & Denckla, M. B. (1996). Cognitive profiles of difficult-to-remediate and readily remediated poor readers: Early intervention as a vehicle for distinguishing between cognitive and experiential deficits as basic causes of specific reading disability. *Journal of Educational Psychology, 88* (4), 601–638.

Randy W. Kamphaus and Cheryl N. Hendry

LEARNING SKILLS are activities engaged in by individuals for the purposes of facilitating the acquisition of knowledge or skill or advancing understanding. Contemporary interest in this topic is propelled by the general zeitgeist of constructivism, a notion used to contrast active learning with learning as a process of passive assimilation or accretion of information.

Prior to the 1970s, attention on learning skills focused less on the role of enabling learners and more on modifying the learning environment. Furthermore, it was typical to think that children did less well because they had less capacity per se. During the 1970s, the focus shifted from children's capacity to their ability to make strategic use of their innate capacity. The 1980s were perhaps most notable for the burgeoning of research in the area of metacognition that emerged in two distinct programs of research: *knowledge about cognition* and *regulation of cognition*. In the 1990s, self-regulation was broadened to include not only control of cognitions but also monitoring, controlling, and regulating additional factors that can influence learning, namely, motivation, volition, effort, and the self-system.

Assessing Learning Skills

Think-alouds are valued for the insight they provide into the specific strategies learners employ while engaged in learning activity. The protocols are analyzed for evidence of problem-identification and problem-solving strategies. In turn, these data can be used to inform the design of interventions for enabling less skilled learners to engage in the kinds of learning activities employed by more skilled learners. Pressley and Afflerbach (1995) have summarized the think-aloud research and report that (1) students who are better monitors of their reading show higher levels of comprehension and learning, and (2) there are numerous aspects of monitoring, including monitoring of text characteristics and comprehension problems.

Several self-report questionnaires have been designed to assess various aspects of self-regulation, including the Learning and Study Strategies Inventory (LASSI; Weinstein, Schulte, & Palmer, 1987), reflecting a domain-general perspective; the Motivated Strategies for Learning Questionnaire (MSLQ, Pintrich & De Groot, 1990), reflecting a domain-specific view; and the

Self-Regulated Learning Interview Schedule (SRLIS; Zimmerman & Martinez Pons, 1986), employing an individual interview format to ascertain how the respondent would behave in six different academic contexts.

Learning Skills for Self-Regulation

The goal of identifying strategies that can be used to promote learning across domains has spurred the design and conduct of numerous intervention studies: (1) *Cognitive* interventions focus on developing particular task-related skills such as underlining; (2) *Metacognitive* interventions focus on the self-management of learning; for example, on planning and monitoring one's learning efforts; (3) *Affective* interventions focus on those aspects of learning related to motivation and self-efficacy.

In their meta-analysis, Hattie, Biggs, and Purdie (1996) examined the relationship between effect size and attributes of the student participants in intervention research, determining that the effect sizes are greatest for those identified as underachieving, followed by those in the middle of the academic distribution. Low-ability students profited little from most intervention programs, while underachieving but capable students profited the most. The greatest effect for learning skills interventions is on performance, typically with tasks that are identical or closely related to the task used in the intervention. This is followed by effects on affect. The smallest effect is seen for reported use of study skills. Most positive outcomes occur for near-transfer tasks, or low-cognitive level tasks. Finally, it appears that the best results for learning skills instruction are derived when such instruction is conducted metacognitively (i.e., attending to the self-monitoring and self-management of the skills in question), with appropriate motivational and contextual support.

These modest findings, in hand with the increased interest in teaching for deep understanding of subject matter, explain why enthusiasm for domain-general strategies waned in the 1980s. Furthermore, researchers have suggested that skillful performance is not a function of strategy use but rather reflects richly organized knowledge of the problem space that enables the individual to represent the problem in such a manner that the solution becomes transparent.

Learning Skills for Domain-General Problem Representation

Research in this area assumes that in order for individuals to acquire knowledge, they must be actively involved in the construction and revision of their own existing and evolving mental representations, a process hypothesized to occur through self-explanation. A variation on self-explanation is engaging students in the process of self-questioning when reading a text as well as listening to class lectures. The rationale for this intervention is that in the process of trying to answer questions that have been generated using such question stems, students may experience feedback about what knowledge they fail to understand, and such feedback can help them resolve their lack of understanding (King, 1992).

The issue of domain and task generalizability is one of the unresolved issues in theories of metacognition and self-regulation. For example, we do not have empirical data speaking to such issues as the relationship between a student's metacognitive awareness on a reading comprehension task when compared with a mathematical problem task. The importance of this issue is largely a function of theoretical perspective; if one assumes that cognition is always situated, then one would not anticipate consistency across domains, tasks, or time. However, if one regards metacognition as a stable, personal characteristic, then one would expect a high level of consistency across time and activities.

Learning Skills for Domain-Specific Problem Representation

Science. One means of addressing the issue of the domain specific/general nature of subject matter learning is to examine the processes used by more and less successful learners within a subject. Schauble, Glaser, Raghavan, and Reiner (1991) demonstrated that good and poor learners engage in different strategies in solving electric circuit problems. Specifically, good learners were superior in planning and in controlling variables, generated a larger number of hypotheses, and were better at data management.

Linn and Songer (1993) explored the feasibility of facilitating scientific thinking and reasoning through a course that emphasized the integration of science concepts with everyday thinking. They observed that students' ideas regarding such concepts as scientific explanation and parsimony could be enhanced. Similarly, Rosebery, Warren, and Conant (1992) conducted research in elementary classrooms in which students designed investigations to explore questions they found compelling and found evidence of the generative nature of children's thinking in this context, and in particular, the deepening of their scientific thinking.

Mathematics. Researchers in mathematics have actually been more concerned with the negative effects that "strategy" instruction can play in mathematics learning than with its facilitative effect, to the extent that the teaching of skills detracts from building upon intuitive understandings in math, or enabling students to map their understanding of the nature of the mathematics problem to its solution. For example, strategy-based operations, such as means-ends analysis, place an additional load on working memory and provide little opportunity for schema acquisition; that is, learning to categorize problems and then apply particular rules.

Schoenfeld's (1991) research was motivated by an interest in students coming to understand mathematics as a tool for identifying and solving problems. He has demonstrated the importance of knowledge of one's own thought processes and the use of self-monitoring practices in enhancing achievement in mathematics. Similarly Lampert (1990), working in elementary classrooms, has demonstrated the value of teaching students to develop and defend strategies, state hypotheses, and question and defend assumptions in improving mathematics achievement.

Writing. Inquiry into the role of learning skills in writing has a relatively long history, one milestone of which was the think-aloud research conducted by Flower and Hayes (1977), who examined the writing processes used by competent writers. Several programs of research have been predicated on the assumption that the difficulties encountered by students in writing are a function of their failure to engage in executive control processes. Several researchers have documented the value of teaching students strategies that relate to planning, organizing, evaluating, and revising one's writing.

Reading. Teaching students learning skills designed to enhance their comprehension of text has a significant history. Interventions conducted in the early 1980s typically focused on the teaching of individual strategies (such as question generating, visualizing, and summarizing), thus paralleling components of the general study skills literature. As researchers came to appreciate the manner in which skilled readers orchestrate multiple cognitive processes, interventions involved the teaching of multiple strategies. The next "generation" of strategy instruction in reading is probably best represented in the interventions designed and studied by Pressley and his colleagues, which integrate the teaching of multiple strategies with teacher and student use of think-aloud to share their reasoning about the text, and takes place across the curriculum and across the school day.

Conclusion and Future Issues

Traditional learning skills research has been informed by cognitive perspectives from which learners are regarded as "bundles of knowledge structures that become increasingly sophisticated and hierarchical as they gain experience" (Gallagher, 1994, p. 172). In contrast, social constructivist perspectives on learning and teaching challenge this view and suggest that expertise is characterized not in terms of knowledge structures but rather in terms of facility with the discourse, norms, and practices that are associated with particular communities of practice.

Contemporary educational reform efforts, reflecting this perspective, assume that from the earliest grades, children should play a significant role in knowledge generation; they should be engaged in the processes of identifying their own learning goals, pursuing these goals in sustained ways, and experiencing learning as processes of problem finding and problem creation, interpretation, revision, and invention. Furthermore, from this perspective, learning is assumed to occur through processes of interacting, negotiating, and collaborating with others.

Concomitant with this reconceptualization of teaching and learning is the view that it is through these experiences that children come to develop metacognition. In essence, as children experience the processes of generating and examining claims, exploring evidence, and revising their thinking, they come to know a good deal about the learning process, about themselves as learners, and about the value of learning skills as tools that will enable them to achieve their goals. This notion is consistent with Winne's (1997) view that students do not learn to become self-regulating but rather that self-regulated learning is inherent in goal-directed engagement.

Future research is likely to address issues regarding the role that metacognition plays above and beyond the effects of domain-specific skills and knowledge. In addition, the merger of motivational and cognitive issues is likely to advance our understanding of how learner goals and values figure in the acquisition, use, and refinement of learning skills. Finally, as educators and psychologists continue to advance conceptions of situated learning in complex environments, it is interesting to speculate whether, in the future, an encyclopedia entry formerly entitled *learning skills* will give way to an entry entitled *learning activities*.

[*See also* Learning.]

Bibliography

Flower, L. S., & Hayes, J. R. (1977). Problem-solving strategies and the writing process. *College English, 39*, 449–461.

Gallagher, J. J. (1994). Teaching and learning: New models. *Annual Review of Psychology, 45*, 171–195.

Hattie, J., Biggs, J., & Purdie, N. (1996). Effects of learning skills interventions on student learning: A meta-analysis. *Review of Educational Research, 66*, 99–136.

King, A. (1992). Comparison of self-questioning, summarizing, and notetaking-review as strategies for learning from lectures. *American Educational Research Journal, 29*, 303–323.

Lampert, M. (1990). When the problem is not the question and the solution is not the answer: Mathematical knowing and teaching. *American Educational Research Journal, 27*, 29–63.

Linn, M. C., & Songer, N. B. (1993). How do students make sense of science? *Merrill-Palmer Quarterly, 39*, 47–73.

Pintrich, P. R., & De Groot, E. (1990). Motivational and self-regulated learning components of classroom academic performance. *Journal of Educational Psychology,* *82,* 33–40.

Pressley, M., & Afflerbach, P. (1995). *Verbal protocols of reading: The nature of constructively responsive reading.* Hillsdale, NJ: Erlbaum.

Rosebery, A., Warren, B., & Conant, F. (1992). Appropriating scientific discourse: Findings from minority classrooms. *Journal of Learning Science, 2,* 235–276.

Schauble, L., Glaser, R., Raghavan, K., & Reiner, M. (1991). Causal models and experimentation strategies in scientific reasoning. *Journal of Learning Science, 1,* 201–238.

Schoenfield, A. H. (1991). On mathematics as sensemaking: An informal attack on the unfortunate divorce of formal and informal mathematics. In J. F. Voss, D. N. Perkins, & J. W. Segal (Eds.), *Informal reasoning and education.* Hillsdale, NJ: Erlbaum.

Weinstein, C. E., Schulte, A., & Palmer, D. (1987). *LASSI: Learning and study strategies inventory.* Clearwater, FL: H & H.

Winne, P. H. (1997). Experimenting to bootstrap self-regulated learning. *Journal of Educational Psychology, 89,* 397–410.

Zimmerman, B. J., & Martinez-Pons, M. (1986). Development of a structured interview for assessing student use of self-regulated learning strategies. *American Educational Research Journal, 23,* 614–628.

Annemarie Palincsar and Kathleen Collins

LEARNING TECHNOLOGIES. During the past century, technologies such as radio, television, videotapes, videodiscs, computers (along with CD-ROMs and other forms of digital video such as DVD), and the Internet have become commonplace. Understanding their effects on learning—both positive and negative—is an important goal of psychological and educational research.

Modern technologies have the potential to be either helpful or harmful. Too much time spent watching television, playing video games, or surfing the Internet can be problematic. On the other hand, new technologies can help people acquire important skills by providing guided practice in areas such as reading, mathematics and other subjects; understand difficult concepts by providing dynamic visual models or allowing people to experiment with simulations that encourage the active exploration of complex systems; and access the world's libraries and museums, participate in exciting electronic field trips, and learn from one another by making connections electronically.

Bringing Important Problems into the Classroom

New technologies encourage problem finding and problem solving by introducing realistic, real-world problems. Interactive video-based technologies such as videodisc, CD-ROM, and DVD provide important advantages over radio, television, and videotape; the interactive technologies make it much easier to search and explore complex environments. Teachers can instantly access important events to use as illustrations; students can easily return to specific scenes in order to explore them more fully. This flexibility is very important for helping students achieve in-depth understanding of events.

Simulation environments can also introduce realistic problem situations. Simulations support a particularly active form of learning because students can manipulate the simulations and see the consequences. For example, they might specify important features for a fishpond (amount of oxygen, food, and bacteria) and see the effects on life in the pond.

Additional ways to introduce students to problems include electronic field trips, where students accompany experts on adventures such as underwater exploration or trips to the North Pole. Students can also be introduced to worldwide problems, such as global warming or acid rain, and can collaborate with other students who each collect data in their local area and share their results electronically.

Resources and Tools as Scaffolds for Learning

In addition to introducing students to complex problems, technology serves as a scaffold for solving these problems by enabling them to seek assistance from outside the classroom and by enhancing their work through the use of powerful tools.

Many traditional reference materials such as encyclopedias and magazines are now available on CD-ROM or on line. The World Wide Web brings an enormous database of information into the classroom. These resources make use of hypermedia, a method of organization in which students can move directly from one topic to other related topics. With hypermedia, dynamic images, sound, and text can be seamlessly woven together and flexibly organized. When compared with text-based resources, electronic references are easier to search and to update.

Online conferences provide opportunities for students to write about their work and discuss it with classmates, as well as with students and adults at remote locations. These discussions facilitate the solution of complex problems by capitalizing on the expertise distributed among members of the group.

Technology-based tools can help students organize the vast array of resources at their fingertips. Students planning a mission to Mars might use a customized database containing pointers to electronic materials appropriate for their topic and grade level. Additional tools include word processing, spreadsheets, and easy-to-use graphing calculators. Students can also learn to invent their own electronic-based tools and hence learn to "work smart."

Opportunities for Feedback, Reflection, and Revision

New technologies make it easier to provide the feedback that students need in order to revise and improve their thinking. Computer-based simulations and tutoring environments serve this function. They not only introduce problems and provide resources but also give detailed feedback. Simulations are particularly useful for modeling invisible processes or events that happen too quickly or infrequently to be easily studied.

Electronic Web-based "challenges" have been used to present interesting problems in science or mathematics. Students submit answers to the Web and see summaries of other classes' answers, as well as receive feedback about their choices. These challenges are motivating and increase student learning.

Teachers' opportunities to provide feedback can be increased with technology. For example, a computer-based tool for providing feedback on student-generated blueprints cut in half the time that teachers needed to help students improve their work.

Communication and Community Building

Communication technologies are vital in linking students inside and outside the classroom. Online conferences among classmates allow students to discuss both academic and social issues. Conferences can also be asynchronous, so students do not have to interact at the same time. Electronic conversations can create a permanent database that supplements the fleeting oral conversation of an in-class discussion. If absent from class, a student can find out what was talked about by looking at the database.

Technology also connects classrooms to the broader community. Students, teachers, parents, and community members can discuss problems that are mutually interesting. Unlike large-group face-to-face conversations, asynchronous conversations via e-mail or the World Wide Web allow everyone time to reflect on a problem and contribute their ideas.

Communication can be enhanced through the use of multiple media. The creation of multimedia presentations is highly motivating and provides an opportunity for learning grammar, writing, spelling, and so forth within a meaningful context.

New technologies have great potential for enhancing learning. A vigorous program of research is needed to ensure that we understand how to use them most effectively.

Bibliography

Cognition and Technology Group at Vanderbilt. (1997). Looking at technology in context: A framework for understanding technology and educational research. In D. C. Berliner & R. C. Calfee (Eds.), *The handbook of educational psychology* (pp. 807–840). New York: Macmillan.

Cognition and Technology Group at Vanderbilt. (1997). *The Jasper project: Lessons in curriculum, instruction, assessment, and professional development.* Mahwah, NJ: Erlbaum.

Dede, C. (1998). *Learning with technology.* Alexandria, VA: Association for Supervision and Curriculum Development.

Grabe, M., & Grabe, C. (1998). *Integrating technology for meaningful learning.* Boston: Houghton Mifflin.

Hmelo, C. E., & Williams, S. M. (Eds.). (1998). Learning through problem solving [Special issue]. *Journal of the Learning Sciences, 7*(3, 4).

Kafai, Y. B., & Resnick, M. (1996). *Constructionism in practice.* Mahwah, NJ: Erlbaum.

Koschman, T. (Ed.). (1996). *CSCL theory and practice of an emerging paradigm.* Mahwah, NJ: Erlbaum.

Lajoie, S. P., & Derry, S. J. (1993). *Computers as cognitive tools.* Hillsdale, NJ: Erlbaum.

Vosniadou, S., De Corte, E., Glaser, R., & Mandl, H. (Eds.), *International perspectives on the psychological foundations of technology-based learning environments.* Hillsdale, NJ: Erlbaum.

Susan M. Williams and John D. Bransford

LEARNING THEORIES. Theoretical issues in learning have captivated the attention of numerous prominent psychologists during the twentieth century.

The Era of Grand Theories

Early theoretical efforts were very ambitious and far-reaching. In the absence of much empirical data, theoreticians felt free to construct conceptual systems that sought to encompass virtually all major psychological phenomena. The era of grand theories sputtered to a close as the cognitive revolution took hold of much of psychology during the 1960s. What followed was the modern era of mini-theories that address more limited sets of empirical data.

Thorndike. The first major American learning theorist was Edward Lee Thorndike (1874–1949). Thorndike is remembered best for the law of effect and for the puzzle-box experiments, which he conducted for his Ph.D. dissertation. Thorndike tested animals in 15 different puzzle boxes. A learning trial began when the experimental subject (a young cat or chicken, for example) was placed in a puzzle box. There was a piece of food in plain view outside the box, and the animal's task was to get out and obtain the food. Some of the boxes required pressing a pedal or manipulating a latch. Others required self-directed responses such as yawning and grooming. Thorndike measured the latency to exit a given box. Escape latencies decreased as the animals learned what was required in their particular puzzle box.

To explain the basic result of the puzzle-box experiments, Thorndike formulated the law of effect. The law of effect is an associational mechanism that explains learning produced by reinforcement in the language of reflexive behavior. [See Law of Effect.] According to the law of effect, a response R that is followed by a satisfying state of affairs (or "reinforcer" in contemporary terminology) becomes more likely because the reinforcer strengthens an association between the response R and the stimuli S that were present when the response was made. Thus the law of effect explains learning in terms of the formation of an S-R association.

The law of effect was highly innovative because it claimed that associations are formed between stimuli and responses rather than between ideas, as had been considered by previous theoreticians. The law of effect was also innovative because it assumed that associations are established by a "satisfying state of affairs" rather than mere practice. The assumption that learning involves S-R associations was adopted by other major theorists (such as Clark Leonard Hull) and encouraged an emphasis on response learning even in studies of classical conditioning. The claim that associations are established by reinforcement was also adopted by subsequent investigators and even became incorporated into definitions of learning. However, neither of these theoretical claims survived to the end of the twentieth century.

Ironically, perhaps the most enduring of Thorndike's contributions was one that received little attention during the era of grand learning theories. Thorndike found that in general learning occurred more successfully in puzzle boxes that required some type of manipulative response than in boxes that required subjects to yawn or groom to get out. Thorndike explained these differences by postulating the concept of "belongingness." Yawning and grooming presumably could not be reinforced by escape from a box and access to food because these responses did not "belong" with food. The role of belongingness in learning was not addressed again until many years later when various additional "biological constraints on learning" were discovered. More recently, these phenomena have been incorporated into behavior systems theory, a biologically based approach to learning that incorporates functional and mechanistic considerations (see Timberlake & Lucas, 1989).

Pavlov. The second major scientist to lay the foundations of learning theory in the twentieth century was the Russian physiologist Ivan Petrovich Pavlov (1849–1936). Pavlov was a virtuoso experimentalist who developed innovative surgical techniques and was actively involved in empirical research for over 50 years (see Babkin, 1949). After a productive career studying digestive physiology (for which he was awarded the Nobel Prize in 1904), Pavlov turned his attention to studies of what has come to be called classical conditioning.

Pavlov is best remembered for his studies of the conditioning of the salivary reflex in dogs. However, he investigated the conditioning of other responses as well, and both Pavlov and the American behaviorists who learned about his work quickly became convinced that the principles of classical conditioning he was uncovering were applicable to a wide range of problems in psychology.

Pavlov's conditioned reflexes fit perfectly with the behaviorism that swept over American psychology during the first quarter of the twentieth century. At first, many of Pavlov's ideas were accepted in the West without replication or empirical extension. In fact, systematic research on Pavlovian conditioning did not begin in North America until the 1960s. However, by then, Pavlov's work had formed the basis for explanations of emotional learning and systematic desensitization, a widely used procedure for the treatment of fears and phobias.

Pavlov analyzed classical conditioning both at the behavioral level and at the neural level. Although his neural conjectures were short-lived, the behavioral procedures and terminology he used and the phenomena and issues he identified (conditioned excitation, conditioned inhibition, extinction, stimulus discrimination, stimulus generalization, and so on) continue to be highly relevant. Furthermore, the concepts of Pavlovian conditioning have been extended far beyond the glandular visceral responses Pavlov focused on and now include placebo effects, conditioned cardiovascular changes, conditioned drug responses, conditioned immunological responses, sign tracking, conditioning of sexual and aggressive behavior, and conditioning of maternal behavior and infant suckling (see Hollis, 1997; Turkkan, 1989).

Watson and Guthrie. The S-R concepts of Thorndike and Pavlov were subsequently adapted and elaborated in various ways by other major theorists. John Broadus Watson (1878–1958) accepted the idea that the occurrence of a response in the presence of a particular stimulus can lead to the formation of an association between the stimulus and the response. However, he rejected Thorndike's claim that a reinforcer following the response is necessary to establish an S-R association. For Watson, temporal contiguity between a stimulus and a response was sufficient for associative learning, and the strength of the S-R association was determined by repetition or practice.

Edwin Ray Guthrie (1886–1959) followed Watson in assuming that temporal contiguity is sufficient to produce learning and in believing that reinforcers and motivation were not required. However, unlike other theorists, Guthrie rejected any strengthening or practice rules. Guthrie maintained that learning occurs at full strength in a single trial. According to Guthrie, the incremental feature of learning curves does not represent the strengthening of an S-R association but the establishment of more associations. Guthrie arrived at this proposition from a molecular analysis of the sensory events that animals encounter in learning experiments. All environmental events consist of multiple stimulus elements depending on where the animal happens to be looking and what it hears, smells, or touches. Furthermore, the stimulus elements that are encountered on one trial are not likely to be identical to those that are encountered on subsequent trials. As learning proceeds, the response becomes associated with a greater number of the stimulus elements that are available in a particular situation. As more of these associations become established, the probability of the response in that situation gradually increases.

In principle, Guthrie's theory was very simple. However, use of the theory to explain learning phenomena required assumptions about variations in stimulus elements that were difficult to verify empirically. Other theorists adopted more complex systems. The most elaborate of these was the system developed by Hull and his students and collaborators.

Hull. Clarke Leonard Hull (1884–1952) was a dominant influence in the field from about 1930 to 1960. In addition to providing a theory of learning, Hull promoted a highly disciplined approach to theory construction. He was impressed with the power of the hypotheticodeductive method and with the precision afforded by quantitative expression of theoretical concepts. He sought to make all of his assumptions explicit and to state his theory in precise quantitative terms that made the ideas easily accessible to experimental verification. Although many of Hull's ideas eventually were abandoned, the research he stimulated provided numerous new insights into the mechanisms of learning. As Bolles (1979) commented, "Hull was a hero in the heroic age of learning theory."

Hull sought to provide a mechanistic account of how organisms engage in purposive or goal-directed behavior to meet biological needs. He accepted many of Thorndike's ideas and elaborated on them. Like Thorndike, Hull regarded reinforcement to be important for learning and considered learning to be an incremental process. He called the basic unit of learning a "habit" rather than an S-R association. However, to indicate that habits represent learned responses to specific stimuli, Hull symbolized habit strength as $_sH_R$.

Because he was primarily interested in how behavior is used to meet biological needs, Hull provided a framework in which learning was integrated with motivation to produce adaptive behavior. He assumed that a biological need (for food, water, or sex, for example) creates a drive state, D, which energizes behavior in a nondi-

rective fashion. The specific actions the organism takes when motivated by a drive state depend on its acquired habits. Thus Hull assumed that behavior is a function of drive and habit strength. He proposed, further, that these factors operated in a multiplicative fashion.

Hull also considered inhibitory influences on behavioral output. In particular, he proposed two sources of response inhibition, reactive inhibition I_R (which reflects fatigue) and conditioned inhibition $_sI_R$ (which is the opposite of $_sH_R$ and is produced by nonreinforcement of a response). Putting these concepts together, behavioral output was predicted by the expression

$$D \times {}_sH_R - (I_R + {}_sI_R)$$

To take into account results indicating that motivation also can be produced by the anticipation of a reinforcer, Hull later added an incentive motivation factor, K, to his equation. These various factors (K, D, $_sH_R$, I_R, and $_sI_R$) were presumed to have fixed values on each learning trial. Therefore, they were expected to produce a specific level of responding. Hull was intent on predicting exactly what an organism will do. However, he recognized that behavior is typically variable. Many theorists ignore this variability but Hull did not. To account for behavioral variability, he postulated the existence of an oscillator function $_sO_R$ that randomly varied the threshold of activation of behavior. Based on these ideas, he stated that behavioral output will equal

$$K \times D \times {}_sH_R - I_R - {}_sI_R - {}_sO_R$$

Hull's system was an intellectual masterpiece, but some of its fundamental assumptions turned out to be flawed. Emerging evidence cast doubt on the existence of a generalized drive state and the necessity of drive reduction for the occurrence of reinforcement. Investigators also came to question the reliance on implicit stimuli and responses in some of Hullian theory. With these developments, Hull's dominance gradually waned.

Tolman. A prominent exception to the S-R learning tradition was the theoretical work of Edward Chace Tolman (1886–1959). Tolman pointed out that the elaborate S-R mechanisms of Watson, Guthrie, and Hull were no more available to direct inspection and observation than more mentalistic intervening variables. For Tolman, stating intervening variables in S-R language did not make them less hypothetical or less "mentalistic" than other well-defined intervening variables stated in more cognitive language. Tolman rejected S-R explanations of complex behavior and sought instead to develop precise and testable characterizations of learning stated in unapologetic cognitive or "mentalistic" language. However, Tolman was careful to anchor his cognitive concepts in observable behavioral events.

Tolman was impressed with the variability, unpredictability, and flexibility of behavior and saw these features as incompatible with the strictly deterministic connotations of S-R mechanisms. He regarded animals as learning about the structure of their environment rather than learning specific response habits or S-R connections. In his terminology, animals acquire a "cognitive map" of how their environment is organized and where food is located. An organism's behavior was then based on its cognitive map. In one famous Tolmanian experiment, for example, rats were first trained to swim through a maze filled with water to reach a goal box where food could be obtained. After training, the maze was drained, and the rats were tested to see if they could find the food by running rather than swimming through the maze. Remarkably, the transfer of learning was quite good, even though the stimuli experienced in the dry maze were very different from those of the wet maze, and distinctly different responses were required. The transfer of learning was predicted by a cognitive map interpretation but not by S-R mechanisms of learning.

Tolman's ideas remained outside the mainstream of learning theory during his lifetime. However, his ideas regained currency with renewed interest in animal cognition and studies of spatial learning during the last quarter of the twentieth century.

Skinner. Another prominent iconoclast during the era of grand theories was Burrhus Frederic Skinner (1904–1990). Skinner remained faithful to Watson's call to restrict the study of psychology to publicly verifiable measurements of behavior. In fact, Skinner's behaviorism was absolutely pure in that he rejected the need for any theoretical constructs or intervening variables in the study of learning (Skinner, 1950). He was satisfied to investigate behavior for its own sake, and not as a way to understand the nervous system or the mind. He was impatient with even the simplest of theoretical constructs, such as the concept of an S-R association.

Like Thorndike, Hull, and Tolman, Skinner was primarily interested in goal-directed behavior. Unlike the other theorists, however, he advocated a science of behavior that consisted simply of empirical generalizations (preferably expressed in quantitative language) that described how contingencies of reinforcement controlled the rate of an instrumental response. Skinner's approach has come to be called *the experimental analysis of behavior*.

Because the Skinnerian approach was primarily empirical, it depended on methodological innovations. Two major innovations were the "Skinner box," more properly termed the operant conditioning chamber (in which an organism could repeatedly perform an instrumental or operant response so that the rate of that responding could be monitored over lengthy experimental sessions), and the cumulative recorder (which provided a graphic record of responding during the course of an entire session). Using these methods, Skinner and his associates conducted extensive investigations of how various schedules of reinforcement determine the pattern and rate of operant behavior (see, for example, Ferster & Skinner, 1957).

Skinner's analyses departed from the S-R tradition in two important respects. First, he did not consider goal-directed behavior to be elicited by an antecedent stimulus in the same way that classical or Pavlovian conditioned responses are elicited. In fact, Skinner made a strong distinction between elicited behavior, which was subject to classical conditioning, and goal-directed behavior, which he considered to be emitted rather than elicited. His second major departure was that he did not define behavior in terms of motor or muscular movements but in terms of the effects that the behavior had on the environment. To this end, Skinner introduced the concept of the "operant." An operant response is defined in terms of how the response alters a specified feature of the environment. Any motor movement that produces the specified environmental consequence is considered to be the same operant. A common operant in research involves pressing a response lever with sufficient force to close a microswitch. Any action, involving any body part, that effectively closes the microswitch is considered the same lever-press operant.

Skinner's operant conditioning stimulated a great deal of empirical research with both animal and human subjects (much of it reported in *The Journal of the Experimental Analysis of Behavior*). Skinnerian analyses and techniques also have been applied to the analysis of numerous aspects of human behavior and extended to numerous educational and other human settings (reported in journals such as *The Journal of Applied Behavioral Analysis*).

The Modern Era

The phenomena of classical and instrumental conditioning discovered during the era of the grand theories, and the investigative techniques that supported these phenomena, have withstood the test of time. However, the details of the theoretical positions have not survived, and much of the grandeur and scope of learning theories has been curtailed. The era of grand theories has been replaced by an era of limited theories—theories devised to explain restricted sets of phenomena.

The Rescorla–Wagner Model. Perhaps the most influential of the modern theories of learning is a model proposed by Rescorla and Wagner (1972). Before the Rescorla–Wagner model was introduced, organisms were thought to learn about a particular stimulus independently of what they had previously learned about other cues present during a conditioning trial. This independent-learning assumption was challenged by several striking phenomena discovered toward the end of the 1960s. The most influential of these was the blocking effect developed by Kamin (1969).

The blocking effect involves two phases of training. In the first phase, one cue S1 is paired with an unconditioned stimulus often enough to condition S1 to asymptote. In the second phase, another cue, S2, is added to S1, and the stimulus compound is paired with the same unconditioned stimulus. The purpose of the experiment is to see how the prior conditioning of S1 influences the conditioning of S2. The common finding is that the conditioning of S2 is disrupted by the presence of S1, with the degree of this interference or blocking directly related to the associative strength of S1.

The Rescorla–Wagner model assumes that the total amount of learning or associative value (V) that a stimulus can gain is limited by the unconditioned stimulus that is used. How much of the unconditioned stimulus is available to produce new learning on a particular trial is assumed to be determined by how much learning has already occurred to all of the cues that are present on that trial. The more associative value the various cues present on a particular trial have, the less of the unconditioned stimulus will be available to produce new learning. These ideas are captured in the equation $\Delta V = \alpha\beta\,(\lambda - V_T)$, where ΔV presents the change in the associative value of a particular stimulus, α and β represent learning rate parameters, λ represents the limit of learning set by the unconditioned stimulus, and V_T represents the total associative value of all of the cues present on a particular trial. Notice that how much new learning occurs (ΔV) is limited by how close V_T is to the asymptote λ. In the blocking effect, the presence of the previously conditioned stimulus S2 makes V_T equal to λ. This makes $\lambda - V_T$ equal to zero and prevents the new stimulus S1 from gaining associative value.

The Pearce–Hall Model. In the Rescorla–Wagner model, how much new learning occurs is determined by how much of the unconditioned stimulus remains available for new learning. In a sense, different conditioned stimuli compete for access to the unconditioned stimulus. Competition for learning also can be produced by changes in attention to the conditioned stimuli. A prominent attentional model was proposed by Pearce and Hall (1980).

In this model, learning is assumed to be directly related to the degree of attention a conditioned stimulus commands. Attention to the conditioned stimulus increases if the outcome of a trial is surprising. If the outcome of a trial is expected (because of prior learning), attention decreases. According to the model, the blocking effect occurs because the initial conditioning of S1 makes the trial outcome fully expected when S1 and S2 are subsequently presented together and paired with the same unconditioned stimulus. The expected

outcome decreases attention to S2, and thereby also decreases the likelihood that S2 will become conditioned.

Unlike the Rescorla–Wagner model, the Pearce–Hall model can explain the disruption of the blocking effect that is produced by a surprising decrease or omission of part of the unconditioned stimulus in the second phase of the blocking design. However, the Pearce–Hall model is limited by the fact that the surprisingness of the unconditioned stimulus alters attention to the conditioned stimulus only on the next trial. Therefore, the Pearce–Hall model cannot explain one-trial blocking—the blocking that occurs when there is only one conditioning trial in the second phase of the blocking design.

SOP and AESOP Models. The Rescorla–Wagner and the Pearce–Hall models both ignore temporal variables. They treat conditioning trials as discrete events but ignore the duration of conditioned and unconditioned stimuli, the interval between them, and the time between trials. Subsequent theories have been more cognizant of temporal variables. The most ambitious of these are the SOP and AESOP models proposed by Wagner and his collaborators (see, for example, Wagner & Brandon, 1989). In addition to being real-time models, these models also attempt to explain why the conditioned response is sometimes similar to, and sometimes different from, the unconditioned response. SOP refers to the standard operating procedures of memory and/ or sometimes opponent process, and AESOP is the affective extension of the SOP model.

SOP and AESOP assume that the presentation of a stimulus activates a corresponding node in memory. Features of the stimulus are represented as elements of the memory node. The presentation of the stimulus at first moves the elements from an inactive state to a state of primary activation, A1. The elements then gradually decay from the A1 state to a secondary state of activation A2, and then back down to inactivity. Two stimuli are assumed to become associated if both of them are in the A1 state at the same time. Thus a conditioned stimulus (CS) becomes associated with an unconditioned stimulus (US) to the extent that the elements of the CS and the US are both in the A1 state.

An important feature of the models is that the consequence of a CS–US association is that the CS comes to activate the A2 state of the US. This feature permits the models to explain the blocking effect. The blocking effect presumably occurs because presentation of the previously conditioned stimulus S1 moves most of the US elements into the A2 state during the S1/S2 trials of the second phase of the blocking design. As a consequence, not enough US elements remain inactive and able to enter the A1 state for association with the added stimulus S2.

With some unconditioned stimuli, the behavioral

manifestations of activating the US elements into the A_1 and A_2 states are similar. In these instances, the conditioned response (which reflects the A_2 state of the US) will be similar to the initial responses elicited by the unconditioned stimulus. In contrast, if the A_1 and A_2 states of activation for the US have opposite behavioral manifestations, the conditioned response will be opposite in form to the initial responses elicited by the US. Thus SOP and AESOP explain why the conditioned response is sometimes similar to and sometimes different from the unconditioned response.

AESOP was developed as an extension to SOP to acknowledge the fact that unconditioned stimuli are complex events that have both sensory and emotional properties. AESOP assumes that the sensory and emotional aspects of an unconditioned stimulus are represented in separate memory notes, each with its own A_1 and A_2 states of activation. Furthermore, because emotional effects tend to be more extended in time than sensory effects, the parameters of activation and decay of the A_1 and A_2 states are presumed to differ for the sensory and emotional US nodes.

Scalar Expectancy Theory. SOP and AESOP focus on the temporal events that occur within a conditioning trial. According to SOP and AESOP, once all stimulus elements activated during a trial have decayed back to the inactive state, the duration of the intertrial interval does not matter. However, this assumption is contrary to evidence. Studies with pigeons, for example, have shown that conditioned responding depends both on the duration of the conditioned stimulus (trial time, T) and the duration of the interval between successive food presentations (cycle time, C). Learning occurs more quickly as the ratio of cycle time to trial time (C/T) increases.

To explain the effects of variations in cycle time and trial time, Gibbon and Balsam (1981) formulated scalar expectancy theory. According to the theory, conditioned responding depends on expectancies of the unconditioned stimulus that develop during a conditioning trial and expectancies that develop as a result of having the unconditioned stimulus presented periodically in the experimental situation, irrespective of the target conditioned stimulus. These expectancies are assumed to become "spread" across the trial time and the cycle time, respectively. Conditioned responding develops if the ratio of US expectancies during the cycle time and US expectancies during the trial time exceeds a critical value.

Although scalar expectancy theory has been highly successful in describing the results of studies in which the intertrial interval is varied in relation to the trial time, it has not been applied to other learning phenomena.

The Comparator Hypothesis. All of the models considered so far except scalar expectancy theory were designed to explain not only conditioned excitatory responding, but also conditioned inhibitory responding. The comparator hypothesis, developed by Miller and his collaborators extended the approach introduced by scalar expectancy theory to conditioned inhibition (see Miller & Matzel, 1988). According to the comparator hypothesis, whether conditioned inhibition or conditioned excitation is observed depends on a comparison between the extent to which the target CS has become associated with the US and the extent to which the context in which the CS was presented became associated with the US. If CS excitation exceeds context excitation, excitatory conditioned responding will occur. In contrast, if context excitation exceeds CS excitation, inhibitory conditioned responding will occur. A provocative and unique prediction of the comparator hypothesis is that changes in the associative value of the context after conditioning of the target CS can alter conditioned responding to the target. Thus inhibitory responding to a CS can be reduced by reducing the associative value of the context in which the inhibitory CS was conditioned. Such predictions have been confirmed.

[*See also* Instructional Theories; Learning; Memory; *and* Social-Cognitive Theory.]

Bibliography

Amsel, A., & Rashotte, M. E. (1984). *Mechanisms of adaptive behavior; Clark L. Hull's theoretical papers, with commentary.* New York: Columbia University Press. Discusses Hull's major theoretical contributions from a modern perspective.

Babkin, B. P. (1949). *Pavlov: A biography.* Chicago: University of Chicago Press.

Bolles, R. C. (1979). *Learning theory.* New York: Holt, Rinehart and Winston. Lively summary of theories developed during the era of grand learning theories.

Bower, G. H., & Hilgard, E. R. (1981). *Theories of learning* (5th ed.). Englewood Cliffs, NJ: Prentice Hall. Detailed discussion of the status of learning theory during the first eight decades of the twentieth century.

Catania, A. C. (1980). Operant theory: Skinner. In G. M. Gazda & R. J. Corsini (Eds.), *Theories of learning: A comparative approach* (pp. 135–177). Itasca, IL: F. E. Peacock. Summarizes Skinner's approach to the analysis of learning and behavior.

Ferster, C. B., & Skinner, B. F. (1957). *Schedules of reinforcement.* New York: Appleton-Century-Crofts.

Gibbon, J., & Balsam, P. (1981). Spreading association in time. In C. M. Locurto, H. S. Terrace, & J. Gibbon (Eds.), *Autoshaping and conditioning theory* (pp. 219–253). New York: Academic Press.

Guthrie, E. R. (1952). *The psychology of learning* (2nd ed.). New York: Harper & Row. Summarizes Guthrie's views on learning.

Hollis, K. L. (1997). Contemporary research on Pavlovian

conditioning: A "new" functional analysis. *American Psychologist, 52*, 956–965.

Hull, C. L. (1943). *Principles of behavior.* New York: Appleton-Century-Crofts.

Hull, C. L. (1952). *A behavior system.* New Haven, CT: Yale University Press. With Hull (1943), presents Hull's theory at two different stages of development.

Kamin, L. J. (1969). Predictability, surprise, attention, and conditioning. In B. A. Campbell & R. M. Church (Eds.), *Punishment and aversive behavior* (pp. 279–296). New York: Appleton-Century-Crofts.

Miller, R. R., Barnet, R. C., & Grahame, N. J. (1995). Assessment of the Rescorla-Wagner model. *Psychological Bulletin, 117*, 363–386. Provides a detailed evaluation of the Rescorla-Wagner model in light of various phenomena obtained after the model was proposed.

Miller, R. R., & Matzel, L. D. (1988). The comparator hypothesis: A response rule for the expression of associations. In G. H. Bower (Ed.), *The psychology of learning and motivation* (Vol. 22, pp. 51–92). New York: Academic Press.

Pavlov, I. P. (1927). *Conditioned reflexes* (G. V. Anrep, Trans.). London: Oxford University Press. Summarizes Pavlov's work on classical conditioning.

Pearce, J. M., & Hall, G. (1980). A model for Pavlovian learning: Variations in the effectiveness of conditioned but not of unconditioned stimuli. *Psychological Review, 87*, 532–552.

Rescorla, R. A., & Wagner, A. R. (1972). A theory of Pavlovian conditioning: Variations in the effectiveness of reinforcement and nonreinforcement. In A. H. Black & W. F. Prokasy (Eds.), *Classical conditioning* (Vol. 2, pp. 64–99). New York: Appleton-Century-Crofts.

Sidman, M. (1960). *Tactics of scientific research.* New York: Basic Books. Describes the experimental methodology advocated by B. F. Skinner and others in the experimental analysis of behavior.

Skinner, B. F. (1950). Are theories of learning necessary? *Psychological Review, 57*, 193–216.

Skinner, B. F. (1953). *Science and human behavior.* New York: Macmillan. Describes Skinner's approach to the analysis of behavior and the applications of such an analysis to various aspects of human behavior.

Thorndike, E. L. (1911). *Animal intelligence: Experimental studies.* New York: Macmillan. Summarizes Thorndike's puzzle box experiments and his Law of Effect.

Timberlake, W., & Lucas, G. A. (1989). Behavior systems are learning: From misbehavior to general principles. In S. B. Klein & R. R. Mowrer (Eds.), *Contemporary learning theories: Instrumental conditioning and the impact of biological constraints on learning* (pp. 237–275). Hillsdale, NJ: Erlbaum, 1989.

Tolman, E. C. (1932). *Purposive behavior in animals and men.* New York: Century. Summarizes Tolman's approach to the analysis of learning and behavior.

Turkkan, J. S. (1989). Classical conditioning: The new hegemony. *Behavioral and Brain Sciences, 12*, 121–179.

Wagner, A. R., & Brandon, S. E. (1989). Evolution of a structured connectionist model of Pavlovian conditioning (AESOP). In S. B. Klein & R. R. Mowrer (Eds.), *Con-temporary learning theories: Pavlovian conditioning and the status of learning theory* (pp. 149–189). Hillsdale, NJ: Erlbaum.

Michael Domjan and Melissa Burns

LE BON, GUSTAVE (1841–1931), French social theorist. An important founder of the theory of the group mind, Le Bon was born in Nogent-le-rotrou, France. He lived for over 90 years, exerting an influence in a number of fields: anthropology and archaeology, history, the physical sciences, politics, and social science. Le Bon was an influential editor of popular scientific works at the publishing house of Flammarion. He also cut a broad swath in the political life of France's Third Republic through his friendships with important politicians and his numerous connections in the world of science and letters. His most significant contributions to the culture of prewar European culture were his writings on race and on collective phenomena, which he treated as a kind of applied racial psychology.

Le Bon was trained as a medical doctor, and although he never practiced medicine, he retained a medical outlook of pathology and norm in all his analyses of historical and contemporary social, political, and religious phenomena. This point of view predisposed him to a conservative position in the political spectrum of the day, in favor of order, state authority, nationalism, the integrity of the French "race" and against socialism, labor movements, liberal educational ideals, and immigration. For Le Bon, the ferment of rebellion was fueled by emotionally inspired social and political forces, but unlike many of the conservatives of his day, Le Bon chose to study the patterns of such social forces and their psychological underpinnings rather than simply condemn them as irrational. Virtually all Le Bon's social science writings investigate these phenomena.

In 1895, Le Bon published *La psychologie des foules* (The Psychology of Crowds), at the outset of the first popular stirrings of the Dreyfus affair. In this book Le Bon laid out his principal theories about the formation and behavior of crowds of different kinds, falling on a spectrum between heterogeneous street crowds and more homogeneous crowds composed of individuals from common social or occupational backgrounds. In all such groups, he claimed, individuals surrendered their individual reason in the "contagion" of ideas and sentiments common in collectivities and behaved subsequently as automata, blown this way and that by changing circumstances and leadership. Le Bon's work was an amalgam of contemporary ideas on hypnosis, notions of juridical nonresponsibility based on heightened emotional states, and the evolutionary theory of his day. Le Bon postulated that individuals in crowds descended the evolutionary ladder to the level of "savages, women, and children," and although they were capable of great acts of heroism and generosity, they were also capable of murderous and destructive activity, as in mob violence or revolutions.

Le Bon's work seems to have been written more in the spirit of a political tract for the times than as a foundation for social science theory. His work, however, was taken up by a number of social and psychological theorists precisely because it seemed to account so effectively for the social and political phenomena of modern democratic life. The unusual turbulence of electoral, labor, and revolutionary crowds in the period from 1900 to 1940 made theories of nonrational group mind attractive to political sociologists like Gaetano Mosca, Vilfredo Pareto, and Robert Michels, and to early writers in the field of social psychology such as the Americans Edward A. Ross, Robert Park, and Herbert Blumer, the British writer William McDougall, and the French jurist and social theorist Gabriel Tarde. Sigmund Freud's influential *Group Psychology and the Analysis of the Ego* (Vienna, 1922) was largely modeled on Le Bon's notions of the crowd mind.

Since World War II, the idea that crowds are nonrational and largely dangerous phenomena incapable of rational and purposeful behavior has been challenged by numerous empirical studies of crowd behavior, by metatheorists like Elias Canetti, and by historians of crowd phenomena like George Rudé, who have found ample evidence that crowds pursue limited and interested goals consistent with their social and political orientations. Although echoes of Le Bon's outlook may be found in the "deindividualization" model of group behavior of Leon Festinger and Paul Zimbardo, trends have stressed the studies of "emergent norms" in collective activity over any notion of a preexisting, or violent substratum. In short, the "social" has taken precedence over the "psychological" in the psychology of groups.

Bibliography

Le Bon, G. (1960). *The crowd.* New York: Viking. (Original work published 1895)

Nye, R. A. (1975). *The origins of crowd psychology: Gustave Le Bon and the crisis of mass democracy in the Third Republic.* London: Sage.

Robert A. Nye

LEHRMAN, DANIEL SANFORD (1919–1972), American comparative psychologist. Daniel S. Lehrman was an accomplished psychobiologist, noted for his teaching and lecturing, scientific administration, research, and writings on the science of animal behavior. He was a member of the National Academy of Sciences and a fellow of the American Academy of Arts and Sciences. Lehrman received the Howard Crosby Warren Medal of the Society of Experimental Psychologists and a Research Career Award from the National Institutes of Health.

Lehrman was born in New York City and attended the Townsend Harris High School for intellectually gifted pupils. Under the influence of a scoutmaster, he became an avid birdwatcher. He began research with scientists at the American Museum of Natural History and published his first article in 1938 while still in high school. He attended the City University of New York, receiving his bachelor of science degree in 1947 after 4 years of service as a cryptanalyst in World War II. Lehrman completed his Ph.D. degree at New York University under the supervision of T. C. Schneirla. He became an assistant professor of psychology at the Newark branch of Rutgers University in 1950. Lehrman was promoted to full professor in 1958 and served as director of the Institute of Animal Behavior at Rutgers, which he founded, from 1959 until his death. He was married to Dorothy Dinnerstein, a Newark professor of psychology, and had two daughters.

Lehrman conducted a variety of research projects, the most notable of which was a long program on the neuroendocrine correlates of reproductive behavior in ring doves. Reflecting Schneirla's integrative approach, he showed that the behavior not only was affected by hormones but alters the hormonal milieu. More remarkably, there is a mutual influence between male and female, so that the behavior of the male alters the behavior and hormonal milieu of the female and vice versa. There is thus a continuing, dynamic interaction between the behavioral and physiological systems of the two animals.

Lehrman's greatest impact came with his 1953 publication of "A Critique of Konrad Lorenz's Theory of Instinctive Behavior" in the *Quarterly Review of Biology.* This was a wide-ranging evaluation of some of the fundamental concepts of European ethology, especially the proposed dichotomy of the learned and innate. Lehrman viewed development as a dynamic epigenetic process that he believed was lost with the rigid categories of Lorenz's approach. He pointed out that there are many interacting influences on behavioral development, not just genes and learning. Not only did this article not further divide European ethologists and American comparative psychologists, but it helped bring them together. With the areas of disagreement clearly defined, discussions ensued and understandings were reached. Lehrman not only had the open personality needed for this but the credibility of a gifted naturalist whom the Europeans learned to both like and trust.

Declining various offers to move elsewhere, Lehrman preferred to remain in the New York City area. The Institute of Animal Behavior became the leading center for the study of neuroendocrine correlates of behavior. Lehrman hired a range of scientists with interests and approaches that complemented rather than duplicated his own, and thus created a unique intellectual environment. The many important scientists who were educated at the Institute provide testimony to the effectiveness of Lehrman's efforts.

Bibliography

Articles by Lehrman

Lehrman, D. S. (1953). A critique of Konrad Lorenz's theory of instinctive behavior. *Quarterly Review of Biology, 28*, 337–363.

Lehrman, D. S. (1961). Hormonal regulation of parental behavior in birds and infrahuman mammals. In W. C. Young (Ed.), *Sex and internal secretions* (pp. 1268–1282). Baltimore: Williams & Wilkins.

Lehrman, D. S. (1965). Interaction between internal and external environments in the regulation of the reproductive cycle of the ring dove. In F. A. Beach (Ed.), *Sex and behavior* (pp. 35–380). New York: Wiley.

Lehrman, D. S. (1971). Behavioral science, engineering and poetry. In E. Tobach, L. R. Aronson, & E. Shaw (Eds.), *Biopsychology and development* (pp. 459–471). New York: Academic Press.

Articles about Lehrman

Beach, F. A. (1973). Daniel S. Lehrman: 1919–1972. *American Journal of Psychology, 86*, 201–202.

Beer, C. G. (1973). Daniel Sanford Lehrman. *Auk, 90*, 485–486.

Beer, C. G. (1975). Was Professor Lehrman an ethologist? *Animal Behaviour, 23*, 957–964.

Rosenblatt, J. S. (1995). Daniel Sanford Lehrman June 1, 1919–August 27, 1972. In *Biographical Memoirs of the National Academy of Sciences of the United States of America* (Vol. 66, pp. 227–245). Washington, DC: National Academy Press.

Donald A. Dewsbury

LEIBNIZ, GOTTFRIED WILHELM (1646–1716), German philosopher. Leibniz was born in Leipzig, Germany, on 1 July 1646, the son of a philosophy professor at the city's university. A prodigy who could read Latin at the age of 6, he entered the university at 14 and by 19 completed all requirements for a doctorate in law, including a dissertation on combinatorial logic. Disdaining a university appointment, Leibniz became legal adviser to the elector of Mainz in 1667, thus beginning his lifelong career as a courtier. After demonstrating his usefulness in a variety of projects, he was sent to Paris in 1672 as a diplomat. There he met the mathematician Christian Huygens (1629–1695) and the Cartesian philosopher Nicolas de Malebranche (1638–1715), among others, and in the stimulating Parisian atmosphere he polished his philosophical and mathematical skills. He made two major mathematical discoveries. Binary arithmetic—the system of calculation with just ones and zeroes—seemed intellectually fascinating even though Leibniz could scarcely imagine its future practical implications for digital computers. Of much greater immediate practicality was the infinitesimal calculus, which Leibniz invented without knowing about Isaac Newton's similar earlier work, and which he published before Newton. Also while in Paris, Leibniz won international recognition by inventing a calculating machine far superior to anything previously available.

Following the death of the elector of Mainz in 1676, Leibniz reluctantly left Paris to become court councillor to the house of Hanover. En route to his new position, he visited Holland and met the microscopist Anton van Leeuwenhoek (1632–1723) and the philosopher Benedict Spinoza (1632–1677). Leeuwenhoek's demonstration of living microorganisms inspired a vision of the universe as consisting of hierarchical levels of organisms within organisms, and Spinoza's account of his monistic and parallellist alternative to Cartesian dualism reinforced certain doubts that Leibniz had already begun to entertain about Descartes's physical theories. Once at Hanover, the polymathic Leibniz devoted the rest of his life to an astonishing variety of activities both practical and intellectual, including mining engineering, historical research, the development of public health and safety services, silk production, and legal advising. He continued to involve himself deeply in philosophy, mathematics, and logic—maintaining an enormous correspondence with scholars from all over Europe and promoting the establishment of scientific societies and scholarly journals. Much of Leibniz's work remained hidden in partially completed manuscripts, which, along with his most important correspondence, were not published until long after his death in 1716. The true breadth and depth of his accomplishments were unappreciated during his lifetime and he was sometimes portrayed as a pedantic fool; Voltaire's satirical character Pangloss, from *Candide*, was modeled on Leibniz.

Leibniz contributed to psychology's development with his staunch defense of nativism—an emphasis on the innate properties of the mind as molders of human experience and knowledge. His posthumously published *New Essays on Human Understanding* (1765), composed as a response to the *empiricism* of John Locke's *An Essay*

Concerning Human Understanding (1690), took issue with Locke's image of the mind at birth as a "tabula rasa" or blank slate passively awaiting the imprints of experience. Leibniz proposed an alternative metaphor: a block of veined marble whose internal lines of cleavage predispose it to being sculpted into some shapes more than others. Summarizing Locke's position as, "there is nothing in the intellect that was not first in the senses," Leibniz proposed to add the crucial qualification, "except the mind itself." His general nativistic emphasis took particular hold in Germany and helped create an intellectual atmosphere receptive to the study of the mind's innate properties, which in due course fostered the development of scientific psychology.

Leibniz also contributed to psychology by hypothesizing differing levels of perception and awareness. At the lowest level were minute perceptions, which he likened to the impression created by a single drop of water in a crashing surf. Although individually imperceptible, minute perceptions may have profound effects when acting collectively. Anticipating later dynamic psychologies, Leibniz argued that aggregated minute perceptions provide the basis for one's sense of continuity as a self and provide an unconscious source of many motives. At the highest level of awareness, Leibniz proposed a process of apperception that goes beyond ordinary perception by entailing a concurrent, reflexive awareness of one's self as a thinking being and by organizing experiences in terms of certain innate, "necessary truths" such as the laws of mathematics and logic.

Leibniz energetically disputed the Cartesian and Lockean assumption that the most basic explanatory units of the physical universe must be extended, material particles in motion. Drawing on his work with the calculus, Leibniz argued that any extended particle, no matter how small, may still be subdivided infinitely and therefore cannot logically be an "ultimate" explanatory unit. Leibniz's fundamental unit was the monad— a concept he probably first encountered in the writing of the Englishwoman, Lady Anne Finch Conway (1631–1679). He described monads as essentially vitalistic entities, characterized by urges to fulfill tendencies innate within them and by varying capacities for perception. The simplest or "bare" monads, which aggregate to form the physical objects in the world (including the bodies and organs of living things) are capable only of minute perception. "Sentient" monads have the capacity for ordinary conscious perception and constitute the souls of living animals. When joined by a "rational monad," which can apperceive as well as perceive, the resulting aggregate is a human being. Although monads may join together in various combinations, they do not causally interact with each other like Cartesian particles but pursue their own independent courses.

Those courses, however, have a "preestablished harmony," analogous to the harmony of many individual clocks all set to the same time, which ensures that the universe operates according to apperceivable laws. Leibniz thus saw mind and body as inextricably conjoined in an ultimately harmonious psychophysical parallelism, as opposed to Descartes's interactive dualism.

In one of his most ambitious uncompleted projects, Leibniz strove to construct a universal language, understandable like mathematics to the members of all nationalities, that could directly express the degrees to which various concepts include or exclude each other (for example, the concept of "living thing" includes that of "animal"). With such a language, one could theoretically calculate the solutions to any logical or even ethical problem—a process that might ultimately be performed by a machine similar to Leibniz's calculator. Leibniz never succeeded in constructing his universal language, but his attempt to unite mathematics and logic anticipated the nineteenth-century invention of symbolic logic, and his general goal prefigured that of modern investigators of artificial intelligence.

[*Many of the people mentioned in this article are the subjects of independent biographical entries.*]

Bibliography

Works by Leibniz

Leibniz, G. (1956). *Philosophical papers and letters* (Translated, edited, and introduced by L. E. Loemker). Chicago: University of Chicago Press. The most complete selection of Leibniz's work in English.

Leibniz, G. (1962). *Discourse on metaphysics, Correspondence with Arnaud, and Monadology* (Edited by G. R. W. Montgomery). LaSalle, IL: Open Court.

Leibniz, G. (1982). *New essays on human understanding* (Translated and edited by P. Remnant and J. Bennet). Cambridge: Cambridge University Press.

Works about Leibniz

Aiton, E. J. (1985). *Leibniz: A biography.* Bristol, UK: Hilger.

Fancher, R. E. (1996). *Pioneers of psychology* (3rd ed.). New York: Norton. Chapter 3, "Philosophers of mind," describes and compares the psychological ideas of Locke and Leibniz; and Chapter 13, "Minds and machines," summarizes Leibniz's role in the history of artificial intelligence.

Jolley, N. (1984). *Leibniz and Locke: A study of the New Essays on Human Understanding.* Oxford: Clarendon Press.

Jolley, N. (1995). *The Cambridge companion to Leibniz.* New York: Cambridge University Press. Expositions of the many different aspects of Leibniz's thought.

Pratt, V. (1987). *Thinking machines: The evolution of artificial intelligence.* Oxford: Basil Blackwell. Provides details about Leibniz's calculating machine, as well as his visionary program to establish a universal language of logic.

Ross, G. M. (1984). *Leibniz*. New York: Oxford University Press. A concise and readable summary of Leibniz's life and thought.

Raymond E. Fancher

LESBIANISM. *See* Homosexuality; *and* Sexual Orientation.

LEWIN, KURT (1890–1947), German American psychologist. Born in Prussia, Lewin studied under Carl Stumpf at the Psychological Institute of the University of Berlin. He was influenced by the philosophy of Ernst Cassirer as well as the new Gestalt psychology, which had its beginnings at the Psychological Institute with the arrival of Max Wertheimer, Kurt Koffka, and Wolfgang Köhler. Although Lewin completed the requirements for his degree in 1914, it was not conferred until 1916. He served in the German army for most of World War I. In 1917 he married Maria Landsberg, with whom he had two children. He returned to the Psychological Institute and was appointed a *Privatdozent* (unpaid instructor) in 1921 and an *Ausserordentlicher Professor* (associate professor without tenure) in 1927. As a Jew, Lewin knew that further promotion was closed to him. In 1929 he attended the International Congress of Psychology at Yale University and, along with the publication of a translation by J. F. Brown of some of his earlier work, ensured an American audience for his work. He divorced and remarried that year, to Gertrud Weiss, with whom he also had two children.

Having visited the United States on several occasions, Lewin emigrated in 1933 after resigning his post in Berlin following the Nazi ascension to power. His first appointment was a temporary position in the School of Home Economics at Cornell University. In 1935, Lewin accepted an appointment at the Iowa Child Welfare Research Station at the University of Iowa. Here he and his research fellows and students conducted numerous studies in diverse areas of human psychology. In 1939, Lewin was appointed as full professor at the University of Iowa. During World War II, he was engaged in various projects for the Office of Strategic Services. He remained at Iowa until the launching of the Center for Group Dynamics at the Massachusetts Institute of Technology in 1944. That same year he was deeply involved in the founding and research of the Commission on Community Interrelations of the American Jewish Congress. With much of the research at the Center for Group Dynamics and the Commission on Community Interrelations still in embryonic form, Lewin died suddenly of a heart attack at his home on February 11, 1947.

Lewin's thought can be characterized roughly as encompassing three periods: the early Berlin studies, the Iowa years, and the beginnings of his work on group dynamics and action research at Iowa that was carried over to MIT. Although this division may obscure his unique understanding of the research process and the place of theory in his work throughout his life, it is sufficient to allow an overview of his contributions to the discipline. Often remembered as an important founding figure of modern experimental social psychology, Lewin in fact worked in many areas of psychology prior to the creation of more narrow subdisciplines that followed World War II. His early research was broadly developmental, and he contributed to such diverse areas of psychology as organizational/industrial, personality, motivational, clinical, as well as social psychology. In addition, most of his research was collaborative, and his many students often published work that had been completed with Lewin under their own names. His broader theoretical program, typically referred to as field theory, was intended to be of explanatory significance to all areas of human psychology, and in some of his writings he implied that it was as broadly explanatory as (and could replace) Clark Hull's behaviorism.

Lewin's early research program in Berlin was focused on the investigation of action and emotion. Critical of associationist psychology, he introduced a series of mechanical metaphors to describe human action. These included notions such as force, tension, systems, energies, dynamics, and field. In this period Lewin sought to find the causal laws of psychical structures based on a dynamic conception of the mind (*die Seele*) as a constellation of forces. His often quoted equation, $B=f(PE)$, that is, behavior is a function of the person and the environment, is less concerned with behavior than with the total "event." Tension systems exist in the whole person, and Lewin contrasted these to the structure of the psychological environment that is composed of topological relations (connections, barriers, and the like) and fields of force (the direction and strength of various forces). Lewin and his coworkers attempted to put these ideas into practice in a series of studies aimed at delineating the function of tension systems by, for example, examining the resumption of interrupted activities, forgetting an intention, and the retention of completed and uncompleted activities. (This latter study was conducted by Bluma Zeigarnik, whose name still refers to the effect found in the study.)

Two important features of the Berlin period are Lewin's reliance on conceptions initially consistent with the Gestalt psychology of his colleagues at the Psychological Institute, and the development of a comprehensive understanding of the relationship between the philosophy and history of science and its importance to psychology. On the question of Gestalt theory, Lewin frequently drew attention to its importance in his own work even if he was willing to use these concepts more metaphorically than realistically. His philosophy of science distinguished Aristotelian modes of thought from Galileian. Aristotelian lawfulness was ascribed to cases that occur regularly and frequently. Lewin felt this was a quasi-statistical notion of lawfulness and contrasted this to the Galileian mode of thought that emphasized: (a) homogenization (the unity of the physical universe); (b) a distinction between the phenotype and genotype of a case, wherein seemingly different events could have the same cause; and (c) the concreteness of the individual case and situation. Lewin argued that the last in particular was important for psychology, since it is only when we understand the particular case and concrete events that we have a scientific explanation. This is in contrast to the Aristotelian emphasis on functional generalities that could not differentiate properties from dynamic relations. For Lewin, the emphasis given to aggregate statistics in psychology was thoroughly Aristotelian, and hence a procedure that obscured the true nature of psychic phenomena by merely presenting averages.

When Lewin went to Cornell University, and two years later to the Iowa Child Welfare Research Station, he attempted to replicate the intense discussions and activities of the Berlin Psychological Institute. The students and colleagues who joined him at Iowa were to have a profound influence on the shape of postwar psychology, especially social psychology. His monograph entitled *Principles of Topological Psychology* (1936) and several subsequent publications continued his commitment to formalization and mathematization. Yet his concepts resisted strict formalization and numerical expression. He preferred to produce theory through a process of gradual approximation, avoiding elaborate models in favor of metaphorical and mathematical presentations of tensions, forces, topology, and so forth. In 1940, Lewin reiterated that his field theory was a theory of action, emotion, and personality that consisted of the two basic claims: "Behavior has to be derived from a totality of coexisting facts" and "these coexisting facts have the character of a 'dynamic field' in so far as the state of any part of this field depends on every other part of the field."

Despite his complex work on field theory, it was his large number of empirical studies that were responsible for the reputation of his active research group in the United States. These focused on such wide-ranging problems as frustration and regression in children, democratic versus autocratic leadership styles, conflict resolution in children, aggression in groups, the cohesiveness of groups, personal pressure and resistance, and related subjects. Subtle differences began to exert themselves in this research, reflecting the gradual influence of American psychology on Lewin's work. Some of the studies began to display the characteristics associated with the typical research studies conducted in North America, including a greater emphasis on operationalization and the occasional use of aggregate statistics.

By the time Lewin left Iowa for MIT, he had already turned to the problems of group processes and the resolution of social conflict. He was a founding member of the Society for the Psychological Study of Social Issues (and its president from 1942 to 1943). In 1939, he coined the term *group dynamics* to describe the positive and negative forces in a group, the study of which must always begin with the premise that a group is an organic whole. He conducted a number of studies in industrial settings with his associates, beginning in 1939 (a theme he had touched upon in an early left-wing, social-democrat–inspired paper published in Berlin in 1920 on Taylorism).

The Harwood Manufacturing Corporation in rural Virginia became the site for these studies, carried out over an 8-year period, on the nature of group processes, leadership, supervision, and management. Although these are now sometimes criticized for their manipulative tendencies, the studies proved influential in shaping the research that followed at the Center for Group Dynamics. The research at the center was divided into six major program areas: group productivity, communication and influence, social perception, intergroup relations, group membership and individual adjustment, and leadership training. Although conducted on different topics using varying methods, this work was inspired by Lewin's strong belief that scientific methods of studying group life and the elaboration of concepts of group dynamics had to be intimately intertwined with attempts to change those groups under investigation.

Lewin's interest in the Jewish community in America led not only to a series of papers (e.g., "Bringing up the Jewish Child," 1940) but to the efforts that created the Commission on Community Interrelations. This group was also concerned with community leadership and the betterment of intergroup relations, but it was immediately thrust into community problems that required more immediate intervention rather than study. Although it had varieties of research built into its mandate, Lewin was frustrated by administrative and political problems within the organization. Despite this, the commission continued to produce various forms of what Lewin had called "action research" long after his death in 1947. In addition, one of the tasks the commission accepted was the formation of a summer workshop in 1946 at Teachers' College, New Britain, Connecticut, led by Lewin, which proved to be the inspiration for the sensitivity training movement and the establishment of the National Training Laboratories that followed.

The large number and variety of studies and theoretical papers produced by Kurt Lewin during his lifetime defy easy classification. Although the chronological division presented here provides a rough overview, it does not do justice to his unique vision of theory and its place in psychology, nor to his unique form of experimentation and research. On the former, Lewin is often quoted for his aphorism that "there is nothing so practical as a good theory" (1944). This line was directed to the applied psychologist, and in the same paragraph Lewin exhorted the theorist not to be afraid of addressing social problems. He believed that the two should always inform each other, lest theory become sterile and abstract and research tend to the trivial. In the experimental social psychology produced after his death, many of his students gradually succumbed to the temptation to restrict their research activities to testing functional hypotheses via aggregate statistics, a form of research that Lewin himself had so clearly decried as a remnant of the Aristotelian mode of thought.

The form of experimentation and research professed by Lewin was entirely unique and contains a host of insights that have yet to be fully understood, historically or theoretically. A psychology of action and emotion that takes the entire context or field of that action into account has not quite failed in the second half of the twentieth century, as it has not been appropriated by the research community. Lewin's enduring reputation is due more to his status as a convenient founding figure of experimental social psychology than to a serious consideration of his impressive theoretical and empirical investigations. In this respect, Kurt Danziger's judgment of the Lewin legacy as "something of a buried treasure" (1990) is an apt judgment. Given the renewed interest in Lewin's work and influence by historians of psychology, this may yet change.

Bibliography

Works by Lewin

Lewin, K. (1935). *A dynamic theory of personality: Selected papers.* New York: McGraw-Hill. An important English-language introduction to Lewin's early work containing the paper on Aristotelian and Galilean modes of thought, published shortly after his immigration to the United States. Still available in many university libraries and from antiquarian booksellers.

Lewin, K. (1997). *Resolving social conflicts* (G. W. Lewin, Ed.) & *field theory in social science* (D. Cartwright, Ed.). Washington: American Psychological Association. (Originals published in 1948 and 1951, respectively.) A reissue in one volume of two important collections of papers by Lewin, published after his death. A good overview of Lewin's research papers in English from the mid-1930s to the time of his death.

Works about Lewin

Ash, M. G. (1992). Cultural contexts and scientific change in psychology: Kurt Lewin in Iowa. *American Psychologist, 47,* 198–207. Ash considers how Lewin's work was changed by the Iowa context, a good example of the new historical interest in Lewin.

De Rivera, J. (Ed.). (1976). *Field theory as human science: Contributions of Lewin's Berlin group.* New York: Gardner Press. Still the best source in English of the early papers of Lewin and his coworkers in Berlin.

Elteren, M. van (1993). From emancipating to domesticating the workers: Lewinian social psychology and the study of the work process till 1947. In H. J. Stam, L. P. Mos, W. Thorngate, & B. Kaplan (Eds.), *Recent trends in theoretical psychology* (Vol. 3, pp. 335–358). New York: Springer-Verlag. An example of the critical historical work recently undertaken on Lewin, particularly with respect to his involvement in industry.

Marrow, A. J. (1969). *The practical theorist: The life and work of Kurt Lewin.* New York: Basic Books. This is the standard (and only book-length) biography of Lewin. It is especially important for its details of the studies conducted by Lewin and his associates in different locations. However, it suffers from its entirely uncritical treatment of Lewin, and provides very little insight into his personal life and motives.

Patnoe, S. (1988). *A narrative history of experimental social psychology: The Lewin tradition.* New York: Springer-Verlag. An interesting and brief account in the form of interviews of Lewin's students and colleagues at the Center for Group Dynamics as well as interviews with subsequent generations of researchers, clearly (but unintentionally) showing how Lewin's influence gradually dissipated.

Henderikus J. Stam

LIBIDO. Like many key terms used by Freud, the term *libido* took various meanings during the 50 years in which he contributed to psychoanalysis. Libido chiefly refers to sexual appetites or sexual needs, and the adjective "libidinal" usually means sexual or sexually charged. Freud often used the term descriptively to refer to a subjective sense of sexual interest or arousal. Libido also refers to the underlying mental and physical processes that accompany this sense, and in this role it is an important theoretical concept. Freud never offered a formal definition of the term.

Libido did its first major service in Freud's evolving theory of instincts. Freud's theory of motivation was absent until his description of the sexual instincts in the *Three Essays on Sexuality* (1905/1963), when the term was used only twice. Later Freud broadened his thinking to consider sexual energy more generally, and he used the term *libido* to describe a fundamental motivational energy whose specific expression begins in earliest childhood with desires for oral stimulation and proceeds through anal, phallic, and genital motives, each a variety of the broader sexual instinctual energy, libido. Libido could develop, and it could also regress—it could be transformed from more to less mature forms. In obsessional neuroses, for example, phallic sexual drives (desires for genital sexual union) are transformed into impulses of anal cruelty (sadism), while still expressing libidinal desires. Libido could also become "introverted" (turned inward) due to frustration or neurotic conflict, shifting from active engagement with real people to old "imagoes" (images or mental representations) of parents.

Many use the term *libido theory* inaccurately to describe Freud's instinct theory. In fact, libido initially shared the stage with nonsexual ego instincts (reality oriented, self-preservative instincts), and at that time Freud attributed neurosis to conflict between libidinal and ego instincts. For example, the need for sexual release would be opposed by the ego's sense that it would be improper.

Libido theory proper arose from Freud's theoretical work around 1910, as he attempted to account for severe psychopathologies such as schizophrenia and major depression. Prior to this point, Freud believed that the object of the instinct (i.e., the person with whom the need was satisfied) was its least fixed and essential aspect. Objects were critical as means for satisfaction, but any object, including the self, could serve that purpose. The major problem posed by severe pathology is the withdrawal of interest in people in the real world, and this problem required a shift in Freud's emphasis on instinctual desire to the *object* of desire.

The theory Freud developed to deal with this problem posits that in earliest childhood, libido is invested in the self as ego or narcissistic libido. Over time this libido is increasingly invested in other people ("objects"), changing in the process from narcissistic to object libido; in this theory, the object is a defining rather than an incidental property of the instinct. This emphasis on the object later became a point of departure for object relations theories, which share this shift of focus from sexual motivation to the importance of relationships with others. Freud accounted for variations in "object choice" (choice of love objects) by the type of libido involved. Narcissistic object choice, made on the basis of similarity to the self, is due to the use of narcissistic libido to invest in the other. The ego ideal (ideal self) is invested with childhood narcissistic libido and gives some of this libido back to the self when the ideal's standards are met. Being in love involves mostly narcissistic libido, leading to idealization of the loved one and dependency on returned love to feel valued oneself.

A further development in libido theory came with Freud's introduction of the death instinct and of Eros, the life force, both presumed present in every living being. These ideas were little accepted, but they led others to develop the "dual instinct" theory, in which all actual motives are a mixture of libidinal (sexual/loving) and aggressive motives.

In the 1940–1960 period, great efforts were made to extend and rationalize the dual instinct theory to account for the motivation and activities of the ego, such as intellectual pursuits, art, and planning. These efforts relied primarily on Freud's idea of sublimation of libido (known also as desexualization), in which an original libidinal aim (e.g., sexual curiosity) is shifted to other aims (e.g., interest in scientific investigation). *Neutralization* was a term developed to include "deaggressivization" as well as desexualization. Theorists gradually realized that these complex theories were unserviceably remote from clinical data, and they were largely dropped in the 1960s. The issue of libidinal development, however, has remained a key concern for many contemporary psychoanalytic clinicians and theorists (such as Shengold), who follow Freud in arguing that children pass through successive critical stages of sexual and aggressive motivational development that have lasting impact on adult life.

[*See also* Object Relations Theories; Psychosexual Stages; *and the biography of Freud, Sigmund.*]

Bibliography

Compton, A. (1981). On the psychoanalytic theory of instinctual drives: III. The complications of libido and narcissism. *Psychoanalytic Quarterly, 50,* 345–392. A thorough, scholarly examination, part of four papers, of instinct theory and libido.

Fliess, R. (1956). *Erogeneity and libido.* New York: International Universities Press. A rich and full discussion of libidinal and instinctual development.

Freud, S. (1963). *Three essays on the theory of sexuality* (Strachey, Ed. & Trans.). New York: Basic Books. (Original work published 1905)

Nagera, H. (Ed.). (1969). *Basic psychoanalytic concepts on the libido theory.* New York: Basic Books. Traces Freud's instinct theory with annotated descriptions of major concepts.

Shengold, L. (1989). *Soul murder: The effects of childhood abuse and deprivation.* New Haven, CT: Yale University Press. A valuable contemporary use of the libido concept.

Robert L. Hatcher

LICENSURE. The practice of a profession is a privilege conferred by the state or provincial governments that are entrusted with protecting the public welfare. No person has a right to practice psychology or any other profession, although once a profession is recognized, there is a right to be treated fairly and impartially. Connecticut was the first state to license psychologists in 1945 and Missouri was the last in 1977. Psychologists are also licensed in the District of Columbia, Guam, and the Virgin Islands and all Canadian provinces.

Common Features of Psychology Licensing Laws

Licensing laws typically define the scope of practice for the profession and specify the composition of the licensing board, the length of terms and manner of selection of board members, exemptions to the licensing law, the educational or experiential conditions necessary to become licensed, and the disciplinary options available to the board. Generally speaking, licensing laws contain the general framework for the practice of psychology and empower boards to develop regulations or policies that detail how to implement those general principles.

Psychology licensing laws can be divided into title or practice acts. Title acts only restrict the use of the title "psychology," "psychological," or "psychologists." Other persons can perform work of a psychological nature without interference from the psychology licensing board if they avoid using the aforementioned terms. Practice acts restrict the practice of psychology to those who are licensed or who are exempted from the licensing law. Licensing laws commonly exempt psychologically trained professionals who work in academic institutions, under the supervision of psychologists, or in public schools. Some practice acts also exempt psychologically trained professionals who work in publicly funded institutions or who belong to professions with an overlapping scope of practice, such as mental health counselors or marriage and family therapists.

Ensuring Competence

Licensing boards ensure competence by requiring minimal entry-level credentials based upon acceptable academic backgrounds, supervised experience, and the mastery of a basic core of knowledge of psychology. Some states or provinces require an oral examination and/or an additional examination on the state laws and regulations. All states and provinces use the Examination for the Professional Practice of Psychology (EPPP) to assess essential knowledge of psychology.

Most state and many provincial licensing boards require continuing education as a condition of licensure renewal. Boards differ considerably in the number of hours of continuing education required and the types of experiences that qualify as fulfilling the continuing education requirement. Within the next few years, it is anticipated that almost all states and provinces will require continuing education.

Except for a few states and several provinces, all require a doctoral degree as a prerequisite for the independent practice of psychology. In addition to licensing psychologists for independent practice, at least 15 states have a "psychological associate," "psychological technician," "psychological examiner," or similar license for persons trained at less than the doctoral level (Association of State and Provincial Psychology Boards, 1997). The degree of supervision required of these licensees varies from state to state and, in at least some, they can perform assessments without supervision by the psychologist. In addition, five states have restricted licenses that allow certified school psychologists who have less than a doctoral degree to practice without supervision.

The ability to assess competence of prospective psychologists in actual practice is imperfect. Efforts are continually underway to improve the methods of assessing competence. Nevertheless, as a group, persons trained at the doctoral level consistently score significantly higher on the EPPP than persons trained at the master's level. It is logical that this superior performance on the EPPP should translate to superior day-to-day performance as a professional psychologist; however, the evidence for such superiority is not substantial at this time.

Competencies Within the Psychology License

Psychology licensing laws are generic and are written broadly to include the application of psychological principles in a wide range of situations, to a wide range of populations, and to a wide range of disorders, including the diagnosis and treatment of mental and substance abuse disorders. Boards license persons for the overall practice of psychology and do not define which specific techniques, populations, or skills that the particular psychologist is able to perform. Consequently, psychologists may differ considerably in the areas in which they are competent to practice. However, several states have "health service provider" designations to ensure that the individual psychologist is competent to provide health care services. Also, the codes of ethics of the state and provincial licensing boards require psychologists to restrict their practices to areas in which they are competent.

Most psychologists rely on their training programs to define their areas of competence. Nevertheless, some psychologists move from their areas of training into allied areas (e.g., clinical psychologists identifying as neuropsychologists, school psychologists as child clinical psychologists, etc.). In some situations, psychologists are already adequately trained to make the transition.

In other situations, psychologists need to acquire additional proficiencies before they can practice in a new area of psychology.

Whenever embarking in a new area of practice, the general rule is that psychologists should submit themselves to some form of external control until they are ready to practice independently. Also, they should not attempt to move into the independent practices of new areas until they receive verification from external sources that they are competent in the new areas. Many areas of practice have special certificates (biofeedback, treatment of alcohol and other drug disorders, etc.) that show evidence of proficiency. Attending workshops and reading books should be only a preparatory stage to working under the supervision of another professional who is competent in that area of practice.

Frontier Areas of Practice

Recent years have seen psychologists apply psychological principles to new domains of practice (e.g., behavioral medicine, custody evaluations, or divorce/custody mediation) and in new settings (such as in the independent practice of psychology within hospitals). Recent changes in some state laws and regulations have permitted many psychologists to practice within physician oversight in some hospitals. The independent practice of psychology within hospitals did not entail an expansion in the scope of practice of psychology. The professional skills necessary for the ethical and effective professional practice of psychology in a hospital are already part of the scope of practice of psychologists. That does not mean, however, that all psychologists are competent to practice independently within a hospital. Competent practice within hospitals requires a greater knowledge of hospital and medical procedures, protocols, and terminology than is routinely found in the outpatient practice of psychology. Nevertheless, this body of knowledge and skill is found within psychologists' current scope of practice.

There is also an interest among many psychologists, the American Psychological Association (APA), and many state psychological associations to expand the scope of practice of psychology to include the independent prescription of a limited formulary of psychotropic medications. Such an expansion would require a decision by the state or provincial government to expand the scope of practice section of the psychology licensing law. Most licensing laws now explicitly state that the practice of psychology does not constitute the practice of medicine. The impact of any potential prescription privileges expansion on psychology would be extensive and could require changes in the basic curriculum of psychologists and divide the profession into prescribing and nonprescribing psychologists.

Disciplinary Functions of Licensing Boards

State and provincial boards of psychology can discipline psychologists. For a complaint made to a licensing board to be accepted, it is only necessary to show that the psychologist violated the licensing law or provision of the licensing board's regulations or code of ethics. State licensing boards have typically adopted codes of ethics identical or similar to those used by APA or the Canadian Psychological Association (CPA). Licensing boards can mandate supervision or further education for offending psychologists as a condition of continued licensure. If circumstances warrant, they can also restrict or revoke the practitioner's authority to practice. The majority of disciplinary actions occurs because of sexual contact with clients, insurance fraud, or breach of confidentiality. Other disciplinary actions include nonsexual dual relationships, practicing outside areas of competence, failure to comply with informed consent requirements, or failure to explain financial arrangements to clients in advance.

Several licensing boards have impaired professional programs through which impaired psychologists may be exempted from disciplinary actions if they agree to undergo supervision and participate in a rehabilitation program. Currently, impaired professional programs tend to be small and underutilized.

The Association of State and Provincial Psychology Boards (ASPPB)

This is the professional association of state and provincial psychology boards that helps develop the EPPP, shares information on licensing and disciplinary procedures, trains psychology board members, and keeps them abreast of new developments across North America and the world. ASPPB has developed model guidelines for defining doctoral programs and supervising psychologists in training. In addition, it has developed a code of ethics and other guidelines that are often adopted by individual states and provinces.

[See also Ethics; and Prescription Privileges.]

Bibliography

American Psychological Association. (1992). Ethical principles and code of conduct of psychologists. Washington, DC: Author.

Association of State and Provincial Psychology Boards. (1997). Handbook of licensing and certification requirements for psychologists in North America. Montgomery, AL: Author. This volume, which is updated each year, contains licensing requirements for all American states and Canadian provinces.

Canadian Psychological Association. (1991). *Canadian code of ethics for psychologists* (rev.). Ottawa, Ontario: Author. Contains a detailed ethical decision-making format, which makes it distinct from the APA code of conduct.

DeLeon, P., & Wiggins, J. (1996). Prescription privileges for psychologists. *American Psychologist, 51,* 225–229. Succinctly reviews the arguments made in favor of prescription privileges for psychologists.

Robiner, W., Arbisi, P., & Edwall, G. (1994). The basis of the doctoral degree for psychology licensing. *Clinical Psychology Review, 14,* 227–254. Comprehensive review of the literature relating educational level to competency as a psychologist. Despite methodological limitations of existing studies, the authors concluded that the doctoral degree should remain the entry-level degree for practice as a psychologist.

Simon, N., & DeMers, S. (1996). *Professional conduct and discipline in psychology.* Washington, DC: American Psychological Association. Contains a thorough review of the ethical codes and disciplinary functions and procedures for state and provincial licensing.

Stromberg, C., Haggerty, D., Leibenluft, R., McMillan, M., Mishkin, B., Rubin, B., & Trilling, H. (1989). *The psychologists legal handbook.* Washington, DC: National Register of Health Service Providers in Psychology. Reviews a wide range of legal issues for psychologists including a good summary of licensing laws and potential disciplinary actions.

Samuel J. Knapp

LIFE COURSE THEORY. This article presents the life course as a theoretical orientation for the study of human development and aging, a theory that incorporates temporal, contextual, and processual distinctions (Elder, 1998a). In concept, the *life course* refers to age-graded events and social roles in life trajectories that are subject to historical change. Social transitions make up life trajectories, and they derive meaning from them. Change in the life course alters the trajectory of individual development. This interaction constitutes a meeting ground for life course theory and developmental science. Building on advances since the 1960s, life-course theory has uniquely forged a conceptual bridge between developmental and aging processes, the life course, and ongoing changes in society, one based on the premise that age places people in the social structure and in particular birth cohorts.

Clarification of Concepts

The concept of the life cycle generally describes a sequence of life events from birth to death, though it more precisely refers to parenthood stages over the life course, from the birth of a first child to the departure of children from the home to the childbearing of the next generation (O'Rand & Krecker, 1990). This sequence makes reference to a reproductive process in human populations. Within a life cycle of generational succession, children are socialized and attain maturity, give birth to the next generation, grow old, and die. This cycle, commonly known as a family cycle, is repeated from one generation to the next, though only within the framework of a population. Some people do not have children and consequently are not part of an intergenerational life cycle.

Life history most commonly refers either to a method of data collection or to a lifetime chronology of events and activities that typically record information on education, worklife, family, and residence. These records may be generated from information obtained either from archival materials or from interviews with a respondent, as in the use of a life calendar or age-event matrix (Caspi et al., 1996). Life calendars record the age (year and month) at which transitions occur in each activity domain and thus depict the unfolding life course in ways uniquely suited to event-history analyses and the assessment of time-varying causal influences. Life history also refers to self-reported narrations of life, as in Thomas and Znaniecki's famous life history of Wladek in *The Polish Peasant in Europe and America* (1918–1920).

Life span specifies the temporal scope of inquiry, as in life-span developmental psychology. A life-span study extends across a substantial period of life and generally links behavior in two or more life stages. Life-span psychology, as a field of study, gained prominence through a series of conferences at the University of West Virginia beginning in the late 1960s. The approach is defined by a concern with the description of and explanation for age-related biological and biological changes from birth to death.

Life stage is used in varying ways across the disciplines. In both sociology and psychology, stage-based models of social and human development have lost favor to more dynamic accounts in developmental theory and research. In life course theory, social stages remain useful as a context for investigating the mechanisms of development and their explanations. But as a matter of practice, they are seldom a focal point of study.

Emergence of Life Course Theory

Empirical studies of children into the adult years have revealed major limitations in conventional knowledge of human development, including those associated with a child-based model. Three limitations in particular posed challenges that played a major role in the genesis of life course theory (Elder, 1998): (1) replacing child-based, growth-oriented accounts of development with models that apply to development and aging across the life course; (2) thinking about how human lives are organized and evolve over time; (3) relating lives to an ever-changing society, with emphasis on the developmental effects of changing circumstances.

Responses to the first challenge in the 1960s led to the formulation of more life-span concepts of development, especially within the field of life span developmental psychology. Stress has been placed on the relative plasticity and agency of the aging organism, the lifelong interaction of person and social context, and the multidirectionality of life-span development (Lerner, 1991).

The life cycle of human relationships provided one of the first ways of thinking about the organization of human lives. It depicts life organization in terms of social relationships, particularly kin relationships and generational succession. Role sequences chart the pathways of the life cycle, as in the stages of parenting, from the birth of children through their departure from the home to their own childbearing. This life cycle is one of the oldest concepts in the "social relations" tradition of research on lives, along with distinctions of role learning, socialization, self-image, and notions of social exchange.

For many years, the "relationship perspective" offered a useful way of thinking about the connections among lives, though it is limited on matters of temporality. This approach began to converge during the 1960s with newly developing understandings of age and timing to form life course theories that combined the virtues of both theoretical traditions (Riley, Johnson, & Foner, 1972); of linked lives across the life span and generations (an ecology of human development); and of temporality through historical time and age-graded sequences of events and social roles.

The three strands come together in a longitudinal study of Californians from the Oakland growth sample who were born in the early 1920s (Elder, 1974; 1999). The central question concerned the effects of the Great Depression on the lives and development of the Oakland children. An intergenerational perspective seemed appropriate at first but the changefulness of life from the 1920s into the early 1940s raised questions that could not be addressed by this approach. The effect of change depended on many things, including the exposure of youth to the event and their age or life stage at the time of the changes.

The study thus turned to the analytic meanings of age for ways of connecting family and individual experience to historical change, and for identifying pathways across the life course. Life span concepts of development proved useful as the study traced the life course of these Depression children from childhood to the middle years of life. Concepts of life transition, turning point, and life review were employed in tracing

the Depression's impact to the adult life course in different birth cohorts, from young adulthood to later life.

Paradigmatic Principles

The evolution of life course theory is organized around paradigmatic principles that provide distinctive contributions to an understanding of human development and aging. These principles generally guide inquiry on issues of problem identification, model formulation, and research design. They structure a framework of inquiry. Four principles are primary: (1) the interplay of human lives and development with changing times and places; (2) the timing of lives; (3) linked lives; and (4) human agency in choice making and actions (Elder, 1998b).

Lives in Time and Place. This principle asserts that *the life course of individuals is embedded in and shaped by the historical times and places they experience over their lifetime.* Especially in societies undergoing rapid change, a different birth year exposes individuals to different historical worlds, with their constraints and options. Historical effects on life trajectories take the form of a cohort effect when social change differentiates the life course of successive cohorts, such as older and younger men before World War II. History also takes the form of a period effect when the impact of social change is relatively uniform across successive birth cohorts. Birth year and cohort membership locate people in relation to historical forces, but they do not indicate exposure or the process by which historical influences are expressed. Direct study of such change and its influences is essential for identifying the explanatory mechanisms.

The Timing of Lives. The second principle expresses the fundamental bond between age and time; that *the developmental impact of a life transition or event is contingent on when it occurs in a person's life.* The timing of lives refers to the age-grading of events and social roles through social regulation and individual choice, as well as to historical timing and location. The normative concept of social time specifies an appropriate age for events, such as marriage, childbearing, and retirement. Neugarten and Datan (1973) introduced the notion of a social clock by which socially approved age norms are superimposed on the biological timetable, as in the relation between sexual norms and the timing of menarche.

Linked Lives. The third principle distinguishes an older "relationships" or role-theoretical view of human lives. It states that *lives are lived interdependently and that social and historical influences are expressed through this network of shared relationships.* Human lives are typically embedded in social relationships with kin and friends across the life span. Kahn and Antonucci (1980) refer to these lifetime associates as convoys of social integration, support, and obligation. Social relationships also represent a vehicle for transmitting and amplifying the effects of stressful change, as in families under economic stress (Conger & Elder, 1994; Elder, 1974). Linked lives convey negative and positive emotions. The social regulation, structuring, and support of human lives and development occur in part through multiple, interlocking relationships.

Human Agency, Its Options and Constraints. The fourth principle reflects an enduring premise of biographical studies on the constructionist role of individuals in shaping their life course. It states that *individuals construct their own life course through the choices and actions they take within the constraints and opportunities of history and social circumstances.* Concepts of human agency have always been prominent in life history studies (Thomas & Znaniecki, 1918–1920), and they are also prominent in the new wave of life course studies that relate individuals to social groups and institutions. People plan and select options that construct their life course within the constraints of particular worlds, ranging from the totalitarian constraints of China's Cultural Revolution to the liberties of Western democracies.

Conclusion

The emergence of life course theory and its elaboration since the 1960s can be viewed in terms of prominent challenges to developmental studies that questioned traditional empirical work and forms of thought. They include the need for life span concepts of development, a way of thinking about lives over time, and connections that link people's lives to the changes in society. Social theories of relationships and age converged in the 1960s with emerging concepts of life-span development to produce a theoretical orientation to the life course, as defined by principles of historical time and place, the timing of lives, linked or interdependent lives, and human agency. Building upon a wide net of cross-disciplinary scholarship in developmental science, distinctions of time, context, and process have become central to a life course theory of child, adolescent, and human development.

Bibliography

Caspi, A., Moffitt, T. E., Thornton, A., Freedman, D., Amell, J. W., Harrington, H., Smeijers, J., & Silva, P. A. (1996). The life history calendar: A research and clinical assessment method for collecting retrospective event-history data. *International Journal of Methods in Psychiatric Research, 6,* 101–114.

Conger, R. D., & Elder, G. H., Jr. (1994). *Families in troubled times: Adapting to change in rural America.* Hawthorne, NY: Aldine DeGruyter.

Elder, G. H., Jr. (1998a). The life course and human development. In W. Damon (General Ed.), R. M. Lerner (Volume Ed.), *Handbook of child psychology: Vol. 1. Theoretical models of human development* (5th ed., pp. 939–991). New York: Wiley.

Elder, G. H., Jr. (1998b). The life course as developmental theory. *Child Development, 69(1),* 1–12.

Elder, G. H., Jr. (1999). *Children of the Great Depression: Social change in life experience.* Boulder, CO: Westview Press. (Original work published 1974)

Kahn, R. L. & Antonucci, T. C. (1980). Convoys over the life course: Attachment, roles, and social support. In P. B. Baltes & O. G. Brim, Jr. (Eds.), *Life-span development and behavior* (Vol. 3, pp. 253–286). New York: Academic Press.

Lerner, R. M. (1991). Changing organism-context relations as the basic process of development: A developmental contextual perspective. *Developmental Psychology, 27,* 27–32.

Neugarten, B. L., & Datan, N. (1973). Sociological perspectives on the life cycle. In P. B. Baltes & K. W. Schaie (Eds.), *Life-span developmental psychology: Personality and socialization* (pp. 53–69). New York: Academic Press.

O'Rand, A. M., & Krecker, M. L. (1990). Concepts of the life cycle: Their history, meanings and uses in the social sciences. *Annual Review of Sociology, 16,* 241–262.

Riley, M. W., Johnson, M. E., & Foner, A. (Eds.). (1972). *Aging and society: Vol. 3. A sociology of age stratification.* New York: Russell Sage Foundation.

Thomas, W. I. & Znaniecki, F. (1918–1920). *The Polish peasant in Europe and America* (Vols. 1–2). Boston: Badger.

Glen H. Elder, Jr.

LIFE SPAN PSYCHOLOGY THEORY. The theory of life span psychology structures the study of individual development (ontogenesis) from conception into old age. According to life span psychology theory, development is not completed at adulthood but extends across the life course. Across the life span, adaptive processes of acquisition, maintenance, transformation, and attrition in psychological structures and functions take place. As a consequence, the ontogenesis of mind and behavior is lifelong, dynamic, multidimensional, multifunctional, and nonlinear.

Research informed by life span psychology theory is intended to generate knowledge about three components of individual development: (1) interindividual commonalities (regularities) in development; (2) interindividual differences in development; and (3) intraindividual plasticity (malleability) in development. According to life span psychology theory, joint attention to each of these components and the specification of their age-related interplays are the conceptual and methodological foundations of developmental psychology.

On a strategic level, there are two ways to contribute to life span psychology: person centered (holistic) and function centered. The *holistic* approach proceeds from consideration of the person as a system and attempts

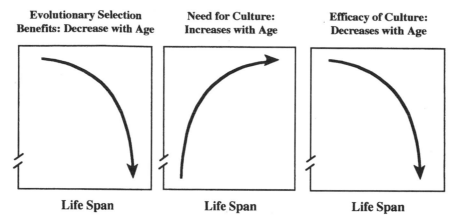

| Evolutionary Selection Benefits: Decrease with Age | Need for Culture: Increases with Age | Efficacy of Culture: Decreases with Age |

LIFE SPAN PSYCHOLOGY THEORY. Figure I. *Theory of life span psychology.* Schematic representation of the average dynamics between biology and culture across the life span.

to generate a knowledge base about life span development by describing and connecting age periods or states of development into one overall pattern of lifetime individual development. An example would be Erikson's psychosocial theory of life span stages. Often, this holistic approach to the life span is identified with life course psychology. The *function-centered* way to contribute to life span psychology is to focus on a category of behavior or a mechanism such as perception, information processing, action control, attachment, identity, personality traits, and to describe the life span changes in the mechanisms and processes associated with the category selected. Life span psychology theory aims at incorporating both approaches to life span ontogenesis into one conceptual framework.

Historical Background

From the beginning, and contrary to the North American tradition, the German conception of developmental psychology pioneered by Johann Nikolaus Tetens covered the entire life span and, in its emergence, was closely tied to philosophy, humanism, and education (Bildung). The Zeitgeist was different when developmental psychology emerged as a specialty in North America and other European countries such as England around the beginning of the twentieth century. At that time, the newly developed fields of genetics and biological evolution were at the forefront of ontogenetic thinking. From biology, with its maturation-based concept of growth, may have sprung the dominant American emphasis in developmental psychology on child psychology and child development. As a consequence, in North American psychology strong bifurcations evolved between child developmentalists, adult developmentalists, and gerontologists.

In recent decades, however, life span approaches have become more prominent in North America for several reasons. First was a concern with life span development in neighboring social-science disciplines, especially sociology. A second factor was the emergence of gerontology as a field of specialization, with its search for the lifelong precursors of aging. A third factor, and a source of rapprochement between child and adult developmentalists, was the aging of several classic longitudinal studies on child development begun in the 1920s and 1930s. In the wake of these developments, the need for better collaboration among all age specialties of developmental scholarship become an imperative of current-day research in developmental psychology.

The Overall Architecture of Life Span Development

Life span psychology theory approaches life span development proceeding from the distal and general to the more proximal and specific. The most general level of analysis concerns the overall biological and cultural architecture of life span development. According to life span psychology theory, the benefits of evolutionary selection decrease with age, the need for culture increases with age, and the efficacy of culture decreases with age (see Figure I).

Evolutionary Selection Benefits Decrease Across the Life Span. The first component of the tripartite argument derives from an evolutionary perspective on the nature of the genome and its age-correlated changes in expressivity and biological potential. During evolution, the older the organism, the less the genome benefited from the genetic advantages associated with evolutionary selection. In other words, the benefits resulting from evolutionary selection display a negative age correlation. Certainly after maturity, and with age, the expressions and mechanisms of the genome lose in functional quality. This general statement holds true even though some indirect positive evolutionary selection benefits are carried into old age (e.g., through grandparenting). The age-associated diminution of evolutionary selection benefits and its implied association with an age-related loss of biological potential is further affected by the fact that in earlier times few people reached old age, and by other aspects of the biology of aging (e.g., wear-and-tear).

Age-Related Increase in Need for Culture. The middle part of Figure 1 summarizes the overall perspective on life span development associated with culture and culture-based processes. Here, culture refers to all the psychological, social, material, and symbolic (knowledge-based) resources that humans have produced over the millennia. Among these cultural resources are cognitive skills, motivational dispositions, socialization strategies, literacy, written documents, physical structures, and the world of economics as well that of medical and physical technology.

The argument for an age-related increase in the "need" for culture has two parts. First, for human ontogenesis to have reached increasingly high levels of functioning, whether in physical or psychological domains, there had to be a conjoint evolutionary increase in the richness and dissemination of the resources and "opportunities" of culture. The second argument for the proposition relates to the biological weakening associated with age. That is, the older we are, the more we need culture-based resources (material, social, economic, psychological) to generate and maintain high levels of functioning. A case in point is that for cognitive efficacy to continue into old age at comparable levels of performance, more cognitive support and training are necessary.

One illustration of the age-related increase in culture is the notion of age-graded developmental tasks proposed by Robert Havighurst. In this view, the life span is constituted by a series of contextualized challenges, or life span goals (e.g., education, work, family, citizenship, retirement, dying and death). To achieve these goals, social institutions and other forms of cultural support are necessary. Currently, a gap exists between the general desirability of these goals and the institutional support structure facilitating their attainment. As emphasized by the life span sociologist Matilda Riley, this gap is especially large for old age. For instance, although spirituality and wisdom are widely accepted goals of late life, the social conditions in support of their achievement are restricted to a small segment of the population.

Age-Related Decrease in Efficiency of Culture. The third cornerstone of the overall nature of life span development is the life span script of a decreasing efficiency of cultural factors and resources. During the second half of life, despite the advantages associated with the developmental acquisition of knowledge-based mental representations, there is an age-associated reduction in the efficiency of cultural factors. The older the adult, the more time and practice it takes to attain the same learning gains. Moreover, at least in some domains of information processing, and when it comes to high levels of performance, older adults may not be able to reach the same levels of functioning as younger adults, even after extensive training and under positive life circumstances.

There are at least three causes for this age-related reduction in cultural efficiency. The first is age-related loss in biological potential. The second can be seen by viewing the life course as in an analogy to a learning curve. In agreement with the experimentally observed reduction of gains in later phases of learning, ontogenetic performance increments become increasingly difficult to achieve when high levels of functioning have been reached, and often require added effort or improvements in technology. The third reason refers to the possibility of age-related increases in negative transfer and costs of specialized knowledge.

The three conditions and trajectories outlined in Figure 1 form a robust and interrelated fabric (architecture) of the life span dynamics between biology and culture. For evolutionary and historical reasons, the ontogenetic structure of the life course displays a kind of unfinished architecture. Whatever the specific content and form of a given psychological theory of life span development, it needs to be consistent with the framework outlined.

Life Span Changes in Relative Resource Allocation

One way to categorize the implications of the overall architecture is to distinguish between three goals of ontogenetic development: growth, maintenance (including resilience), and the regulation of loss. The allocation of available resources for growth decreases with age, whereas investments into maintenance and regulation of loss increase with age. Growth refers to behaviors aimed at reaching higher levels of functioning or adaptive capacity. Maintenance refers to behaviors aimed either at maintaining levels of functioning in the face of a new challenge or at returning to previous levels after a loss. Regulation of loss refers to behaviors that organize adequate functioning at lower levels when maintenance or recovery—for instance because of external or internal losses in resources—is no longer possible.

Life span psychology theory posits that the life span shift in the relative allocation of resources, away from growth toward the goals of maintenance and the regulation of loss, is a critical issue for any theory of life span development. Due in part to this shift, the attainment of positive developmental outcomes is inherently and increasingly tied to recognizing and managing generational turnover as well as managing or becoming reconciled to one's biological losses, finitude, and impending death.

In addition, life span psychology emphasizes the dynamics between the life span trajectories of growth, maintenance, and regulation. The mastery of life often involves conflicts and competition among these three developmental goals. Consider, for example, the interplay between autonomy and dependence in children and older adults. Whereas the primary focus of the first half of life is the maximization of independence and autonomy, the goal-profile changes in old age. The productive and creative use of dependence rather than independence becomes critical. By invoking dependence and support, older people free up resources for use in other domains involving personal efficacy and growth.

The age-related weakening of the biological foundation and the change in the overall life span script associated with growth, maintenance, and regulation of loss does not imply that there is no opportunity for growth at all in the second half of life. Deficits in biological status can also be the foundation for progress; that is, antecedents for positive changes in adaptive capacity. The most radical view of this proposition is contained in the notion of "culture as compensation." Under the influence of cultural-anthropological as well as evolutionary biological arguments, researchers have recognized that suboptimal biological states or imperfections are catalysts for the evolution of culture and for advanced states achieved in human ontogeny.

Metatheoretical Propositions of Life Span Theory

Life span psychology highlights the need to overcome linear, unidimensional, unidirectional, and unifunctional conceptions of development, which had flourished in conjunction with the traditional biological conceptions of growth or physical maturation. In these traditional conceptions, attributes such as qualitative change, ordered sequentiality, irreversibility, and the definition of an end state were critical. Considering evolutionary perspectives, neofunctionalism, and contextualism, life span psychology theory treats developing systems as multidimensional, multifunctional, and dynamic, with different domains and functions developing in a less than fully integrated manner, and with trade-offs between functional advances and discontinuities between age levels being the rule rather than the exception.

Relatedly, development is seen as always being constituted by gains and losses. Important evidence for this view are the diverging life span trajectories proposed and observed for various components of intelligence. For instance, gains in the knowledge-based pragmatics

and losses in the basic mechanics of intelligence coexist during large portions of the life span. The coexistence of gains and losses is further supported by the open systems view of the incomplete biological and cultural architecture of life span development and the multiple ecologies of life, which render it impossible to posit a single end state to development. Given the complex and changing nature of the criteria involved in everyday adaptation, the capacity to move between levels of knowledge and skills rather than to operate at one specific developmental level of functioning appears crucial for effective individual development. Finally, the dynamics between gains and losses are highlighted by the phenomenon of negative transfer associated with the evolution of any form of specialization or expertise, and by the notion of equifinality, which states that the same developmental outcome (e.g., high levels of subjective well-being) can be reached by different means and combination of means. Based on all of these considerations, life span psychology theory rejects the view of development as universal growth as theoretically false and empirically inappropriate.

Another tenet of life span psychology theory deals with the structural composition of the factors that influence and regulate development across the life span. Three sources of influence are distinguished: age-graded, history-graded, and idiosyncratic. Within each source, both biological and cultural causal mechanisms are present. The composition and level of these sources vary across individuals as a function of factors such as genome, gender, social class, and ethnicity. Thus, life span psychology theory portrays life courses as dynamic constellations of age-graded, history-graded, and idiosyncratic influences. As Richard Lerner and Sandra Scarr have emphasized, this includes individuals' own proactive and reactive behaviors and actions.

A Systemic Theory of Life Span Development: Selective Optimization with Compensation

During the 1990s, several efforts at theoretical development in life span psychology emanated from both researchers on childhood and adolescence as well as the community of researchers on aging. Given the emphasis of life span psychology theory on exploring consistency and fertility between levels of analysis, we restrict our presentation to the theory of selective optimization with compensation (SOC theory) developed by Margret Baltes, Paul Baltes, and their colleagues.

A specific example may help to clarify the meaning of the three processes. When the concert pianist Artur Rubinstein, as an 80-year-old, was asked in a television interview how he managed to maintain such a high level of expert piano playing, he hinted at the coordination of three strategies. First, he played fewer pieces (selection); he practiced these pieces more often (optimization); and to counteract his loss in mechanical speed he now used a kind of impression management, such as playing more slowly before fast segments to make the latter appear faster (compensation).

Selective optimization with compensation theory combines the overall framework of life span psychology with process-oriented psychological research and theorizing. It defines successful development as the conjoint maximization of gains (desirable goals or outcomes) and the minimization of losses (undesirable goals or outcomes). The nature of what constitutes gains and losses, and of the dynamic between gains and losses, is conditioned by cultural and personal factors as well as by the position in the lifetime of an individual.

Selection deals with goals or outcomes of development, optimization with the enhancement of means to reach goals, and compensation with the generation of new means (e.g., hearing aids) in order to maintain a given level of goal achievement. According to selective optimization with compensation theory, each developmental process and outcome can be decomposed into aspects of selection, optimization, and compensation.

Selective optimization with compensation theory is both universal and relativistic. In its metatheoretical universality, and without specifying the substantive goals and outcomes of development (which will vary according to theoretical framework, substantive research area, and level of analysis), it postulates that any process of human development involves an orchestration of selection, optimization, and compensation. Selective optimization with compensation theory also states that the coordinated orchestration of these three processes results in desired while minimizing undesirable developmental outcomes.

However, the concrete specification of selective optimization with compensation processes is person-specific and contextually bound. Thus, as the theoretical model is applied to specific domains and contexts of psychological functioning (such as control, autonomy, and professional expertise, or to different cultural contexts), it requires further specification to be derived from the knowledge base of the domain of functioning selected for application and for the context in which this phenomenon is embedded.

Methodological Advances

Metatheory and methodology have been closely intertwined since the very early origins of life span psychology (e.g., Quetelet, 1842; Tetens, 1777), and the search for methods adequate for the study of developmental processes is a continuing part of the agenda of life span psychology. Four examples are provided below. A first methodological development concerns methods to organize and study the temporal flow, antecedents, and correlates of life events including death. Life-course sociologists, in particular, have made major contributions to the advancement of this methodology. Among the relevant methods, models of event-history analysis and associated methods such as hazard rate and survival analysis are especially important.

A second example of methodological innovations involves a strategy to examine the scope and limits of plasticity. This method is similar to efforts in child development to study the zone of proximal development through methods of microgenetic analysis or cognitive engineering. Because of the long time frame of life span ontogenesis, it is difficult to identify the sources and scope of plasticity and its age-related changes. At the same time, the inquiry into what is possible in principle in human development across the life span is important. For instance, cognitive aging researchers want to know whether aging losses in functions reflect experiential practice deficits rather than effects of biological aging. To explore this issue, testing-the-limits research attempts to compress time by providing for high-density developmental experiences in order to identify asymptotes of performance potential (plasticity). These asymptotes, obtained under putatively optimal conditions of support, are expected to estimate the upper range of age-specific developmental potential.

A third example is the use of experimental simulation. The two key features of this method are the search for causal mechanisms through the arrangement of experimental conditions that mimic (simulate) variations in developmental phenomena, and the subsequent evaluation of the evidence in naturalistic settings.

A fourth example for methodological developments closely related to life span psychology theory concerns research designs aimed at discriminating among varieties of environmental change, such as enduring differences between people born at different points in historical time (cohort effects); specific influences of historical events across chronological age (period effects); or generalized and enduring shifts in the environment affecting individuals of all ages and subsequent cohorts (general environmental change).

Conclusion

In developing and refining its multilevel framework life span psychology theory has benefited much from transdisciplinary dialogue, especially with modern developmental biologists but also with sociologists and cultural psychologists. Biologists, for instance, contributed in major ways in moving research away from unilinear, unifunctional, and deterministic models of ontogenesis to a theoretical framework that highlights the contextual, adaptive, probabilistic, and self-organizational dynamic aspects of ontogenesis. Similarly, sociologists and cultural psychologists have demonstrated that the architecture of human development is essentially incomplete because of the multitude of culturally engineered developmental pathways and endpoints. For life span development to extend into later stages of life, the role of adequate institutional and technological support is critical. In this regard, old age is young.

The future of life span psychology theory will depend significantly on the extent to which its metatheoretical and empirical perspectives turn out to be productive not only for the conduct of developmental research, but also for other psychological specialties such as clinical, cognitive, educational, social, personality, and applied psychology. The interconnections with other psychological specialties will be the final testing ground of what life span theory and research has to offer to psychology, as a science and as a profession.

[*See also* Adulthood and Aging; *and* Developmental Psychology.]

Bibliography

Baltes, M. M., & Carstensen, L. L. (1996). The process of successful ageing. *Ageing and Society, 16,* 397–422.

Baltes, P. B. (1997). On the incomplete architecture of human ontogeny: Selection, optimization, and compensation as foundation of developmental theory. *American Psychologist, 52,* 366–380. Includes a succinct summary of the theory of selective optimization with compensation.

Baltes, P. B., Lindenberger, U., & Staudinger, U. (1998). Life span theory in developmental psychology. In W. Damon (Series Ed.) & R. M. Lerner (Vol. Ed.), *Handbook of child psychology: Vol. 1. Theoretical models of human development.* (5th ed., pp. 1029–1143). New York: Wiley. Contains a comprehensive coverage of life span theory, with applications to intellectual functioning and personality.

Baltes, P. B., Reese, H. W., & Nesselroade, J. R. (1988). *Life-span developmental psychology: Introduction to research methods.* Hillsdale, NJ: Erlbaum. (Original work published 1977.) Presents and discusses methodological issues in developmental psychology from a life span perspective.

Dixon, R. A., & Lerner, R. M. (1988). A history of systems in developmental psychology. In M. H. Bornstein & M. E. Lamb (Eds.), *Developmental psychology: An advanced textbook* (2nd ed., pp. 3–50). Hillsdale, NJ: Erlbaum. Locates the life span approach within the various research traditions of developmental psychology.

Elder, G. H., Jr. (1998). The life course and human development. In W. Damon (Series Ed.) & R. M. Lerner (Vol. Ed.), *Handbook of child psychology: Vol. 1. Theoretical models of human development* (5th ed., pp. 939–992), New York: Wiley.

Goulet, L. R., & Baltes, P. B. (Eds.). (1970). *Life-span developmental psychology: Research and theory.* New York: Academic Press.

Labouvie-Vief, G. (1992). Neo-Piagetian perspective on adult cognitive development. In R. J. Sternberg & C. A. Berg (Eds.), *Intellectual development* (pp. 197–228). Cambridge, England: Cambridge University Press.

Lindenberger, U., & Baltes, P. B. (1995). Testing-the-limits and experimental simulation: Two methods to explicate the role of learning in development. *Human Development, 38,* 349–360.

Magnusson, D. (Ed.). (1996). *The life-span development of individuals: Behavioural, neurobiological and psychosocial perspectives.* Cambridge, England: Cambridge University Press.

Nesselroade, J. R. (1991). Interindividual differences in intraindividual change. In L. M. Collins & J. L. Horn (Eds.), *Best methods for the analysis of change* (pp. 92–105). Washington, DC: American Psychological Association.

Neugarten, D. A. (Ed.). (1970). *The meanings of age: Selected papers of Bernice L. Neugarten.* Chicago: University of Chicago Press.

Quetelet, A. (1842). *A treatise on man and the development of his faculties.* Edinburgh, Scotland: Chambers.

Schaie, K. W. (1996). *Adult intellectual development: The Seattle Longitudinal Study.* New York: Cambridge University Press. Summarizes results from the Seattle Longitudinal Study, the most comprehensive longitudinal study on adult intellectual development.

Staudinger, U. M., & Pasupathi, M. (1999). Life-span perspectives on self, personality, and social cognition. In T. Salthouse & F. I. M. Craik (Eds.), *Handbook of aging and cognition* (2nd ed.). Hillsdale, NJ: Erlbaum.

Tetens, J. N. (1777). *Philosophische Versuche über die menschliche Natur und ihre Entwicklung* [Philosophical essays on human nature and its development]. Leipzig, Germany: Weidmanns Erben und Reich. This text is generally regarded as the historical foundation of life span psychology.

Ulman Lindenberger and Paul B. Baltes

LIFE SPAN STAGES. *See the biography of Erikson.*

LIKERT SCALE. Investigators are able to assess people's attitudes toward an issue or outcome through the use of a Likert scale. People indicate their level of agreement with a series of opinion statements, and these ratings are summed to provide a measure of their attitude. For example, a Likert scale that measures attitudes toward genetic testing might require people to rate the extent to which they agree or disagree with statements such as "Genetic testing will result in discrimination against people based on their genes," and "Genetic testing will increase the chances that health problems can be treated early." Because a person's attitude is based on the sum of his or her ratings on individual items, this technique is frequently labeled the method of summated ratings. Rensis Likert, an American experimental psychologist, developed this methodology in 1932 in order to provide investigators with an alternative to the complex tasks that underlie a method for measuring attitudes previously developed by Louis Thurstone.

To construct a Likert scale, investigators must first generate a large set of opinion statements that include items that advocate positions both in favor of and against the particular topic of interest. An initial set of participants would indicate their level of agreement with each statement on a five-point scale that ranges from "strongly disagree" to "strongly agree." Based on these initial ratings, statements are removed that fail to discriminate between people who are thought to hold strongly favorable and strongly unfavorable attitudes (i.e., an item's ratings are not strongly correlated with scores based on the overall scale). Once a final set of opinion statements has been identified, further empirical work is conducted to demonstrate that the items that comprise the scale are reliable and that the scale is a valid measure of the attitude dimension of interest. Differences in the magnitude of respondents' scores are interpreted as reflecting differences in their attitude toward the topic of interest. However, because people's attitudes are based on the sum of their responses to a set of opinion statements, different patterns of responses can result in the same final attitude score.

The basic structure of the Likert scale has been adapted for use in domains across a broad range of areas both inside and outside of psychology. Investigators frequently claim that they have used a Likert scale, but this claim generally indicates that the rating scale that was used is similar in format to that first proposed by Likert and not that the investigators completed the item selection processes originally articulated by Likert.

[See also Attitudes, article on Attitude Measurement; and Scale Development.]

Bibliography

Dawes, R. M., & Smith, T. L. (1985). Attitude and opinion measurement. In G. Lindzey and E. Aronson (Eds.), The handbook of social psychology (3rd ed., Vol. 1, pp. 509–566). New York: Random House.

Eagly, A. H., & Chaiken, S. (1993). The psychology of attitudes. Fort Worth, TX: Harcourt Brace Jovanovich.

Likert, R. (1932). A technique for the measurement of attitudes. Archives of Psychology, 140, 5–53.

Alexander J. Rothman

LINDNER, GUSTAV ADOLF (1828–1887), Czech philosopher and educator. Reflecting the dominance of German in the institutions of higher learning in the Austro-Hungarian empire, most of Lindner's works were written in that language. Following appointments as a high school teacher in Celje (in today's Slovenia) and director of a German high school in Prachatice (in Bohemia), Lindner served from 1872 to 1881 as an effective director of a teacher training institute ("pedagogium") in Kutná Hora, in Bohemia. In 1882 he was nominated full professor (ordinarius) of philosophy and pedagogy at the philosophical faculty of the newly established Czech division of the university in Prague. Due to poor health he stopped lecturing at the school in 1886 and died on 18 October 1887.

Lindner's fame is based on two books: the developmentally oriented *Textbook of Empirical Psychology* (Celje (Cilli), 1858) and a monograph entitled *Ideas for Psychology as a Foundation of Social Science* (Vienna, 1871). The textbook appeared in seven German editions, as well as translations into Greek, Czech, Italian, Croatian, Polish, and English. The English translation, by C. de Garmo, was published in 1890.

Contemporary North American historians of psychology, few of whom are fluent in German, owe warm thanks to the translator, who earned a Ph.D. degree from Halle University, for making available in English a mature works of Herbartian psychology. In the preface Lindner stresses that "Herbart's standpoint was that of empirical psychology." More specifically, such an approach "can and should have regard to those real—not merely verbal—explanations which lie in facts and which can be derived without metaphysical exposition." Such psychology is not only founded on facts but documented by examples. Lindner reinforces these points by citing the statement made by Herbart in the preface to his *Psychology as a Science* (1824–1825): "my basis is as broad as all experience."

Still useful today is Lindner's differentiation between the "old," Aristotelian, and the "new," Herbartian empirical psychology. The "new" psychology deals with the phenomena of consciousness, grouped according to their similarity. Lindner refers to these groups as "types of soul's activity," corresponding, in modern terminology, to mental functions. By contrast, the "old" empirical psychology hypostasized the types of activity into "faculties."

Lindner does not fail to give Herbart credit for showing the limitations of "faculties" as a basic psychological concept; on various occasions Herbart referred to them as "mythological essences." On page 12 Lindner provides a bibliography of the major works of Herbartian psychologists. Furthermore, he supplements it with the works of those who worked in the natural sciences and who furthered the cause of psychology, including H. Lotze, T. Fechner, C. Weber, H. Helmholtz, J. E. Purkinje, and W. Wundt.

One thing is clear: To Lindner psychology is a science, an inductive science. He is not always consistent in his terminology, referring on different occasions to psychology as the "anatomy of consciousness," the "physiology of the soul," even the "physics of the soul." He would probably have argued that all of these approaches are relevant.

Lindner went beyond descriptive "empirical" psychology and noted: "Experiment, which plays so important a part in the field of outer experience, is not to be excluded from psychology" (p. 10). More importantly, Lindner went beyond the psychology of individuals. The three sections of his innovative monograph of 1871 deal, respectively, with society as a social organism (the physiology of society), social psychology—a term that he seems to have introduced—and political psychology. In the introduction (p. 5) Lindner refers to social psychology as a "promising science of the future" ("vielversprechende Zukunftswissenschaft") for which he claims to have provided little more than a "baseline" ("die Grundlinien"), giving ample credit to individuals like Herbart, Herder, Bucle, Lazarus, and Lotze.

Sigmund Freud's biographer Ernest Jones has reported the "remarkably interesting fact" that Lindner's textbook was used at the *gymnasium* (high school) Freud attended, and suggested that it may have been the original source of certain Herbartian concepts—including the "repression" (*Verdrängung*) of ideas—that eventually made their way into psychoanalytic theory (*The Life and Work of Sigmund Freud*, Vol. 1, New York, 1953, p. 376).

[*Many of the people mentioned in this article are the subjects of independent biographical entries.*]

Bibliography

Lindner, G. A. (1885). *Drobné články pedagogické a psychologické z let 1863–1884* [Minor pedagogical and psychological articles from the years 1863 to 1884]. Velké Meziříčí: Library of Pedagogical Classics. Contains a succinct biography and a bibliography of Lindner's publications.

Lindner, G. A. (1890). *Manual of empirical psychology as an inductive science* (by C. DeGarmo, Trans.). Boston: Heath.

Lindner, G. A. (1929). *Myšlenky k psychologii společnosti jako základ společenské vědy* [Ideas for psychology as the foundation of social science]. (J. Král, Trans.). Prague: Czech Academy of Sciences and Arts. Contains an extensive introduction by the translator.

Cach, J., & Dvořák, K. (Eds.). (1970). *G. A. Lindner a jeho odkaz dnešku* [Lindner's bequest to the present]. Prague: State Pedagogical Publishing House. A selection from Lindner's work.

Josef Brožek and Jiří Hoskovec

LINGUISTIC COMPETENCE. *See* Psycholinguistics; *and* Sociolinguistics.

LINGUISTIC DETERMINISM. *See* Psycholinguistics, *article on* Linguistic Determination.

LINGUISTIC PERFORMANCE. *See* Psycholinguistics; *and* Sociolinguistics.

LIPPS, THEODOR (1851–1914), German psychologist. Born at Wallhalben in the Rhineland, Lipps was a pioneer theoretical psychologist broadly trained in philosophy, theology, and the natural sciences before he migrated to psychology. He began his professorial career in Bonn in 1877, moving to Breslau in 1890 and to Munich in 1894, where he founded the Psychological Institute. He was part of an aesthetic tradition in psychology traceable to Fechner and was, during his lifetime, as well known for his work in philosophy, especially in aesthetics, as for his work in psychology. His psychological output spanned 30 years, beginning with comprehensive accounts of the phenomenology of mental life, succeeded by his extensive study of optical illusions, *Raumästhetik und Geometrische-optische Täuschungen* (Aesthetics of Space and Geometric Optical Illusions, 1897) and significant works on hypnosis and autosuggestion, self-perception, will, and humor. Lipps's psychology is preeminently a psychology of consciousness: he described the task of psychology as the explanation of the emergence of consciousness as a system of causal relations between the self, other selves, and the external world in *Leitfaden der Psychologie* (Main Themes of Psychology, Leipzig, 1909). In Lipps's view, the mind is an active organizer of experience according to general laws, many of which have their foundation in aesthetics. In this sense he is a direct precursor of Gestalt ideas of the importance of form and organization in mental life.

Though few American students beyond Herbert C. Sanborn, the translator of Lipps's *Psychological Studies* (1905/1926) and an important early figure in the Vanderbilt University psychology department, took degrees at Munich under Lipps, his influence in America and elsewhere was great. Today, Lipps is most often mentioned in American psychology in connection with empathy. Lipps proposed a concept of empathy in which observers interact emotionally with the world by perceiving structural and dynamic relations in and between objects, internally imitating movements suggested or determined by them, experiencing the corresponding emotions, and then projecting these emotions outward again toward the objects, interjecting the self into the perceived scene. This was one of the earliest and most detailed formulations of empathy to gain prominence in American psychology, and the concept has remained one of the most durable of nineteenth-century psychological ideas, a key element in theories of social cognition and psychotherapy. Lipps's theory of empathy also provided a conceptual starting point for Edith Stein's theories of spiritual empathy (1916/1970). Beyond this, Lipps's psychological ideas have an important place in the work of William James and Sigmund Freud. Citations of Lipps's work on time perception, musical perception, the perception of space and distance, visual illusions, and—significantly, in view of James's commitment to a phenomenological psychology of consciousness—his accounts of the perception of reality and effort occur throughout both volumes of William James's *Principles of Psychology* (New York, 1890). Freud, not usually sympathetic to the academic psychology of his time, found Lipps's ideas congenial with his own. Specifically, Freud and Lipps both agreed on the equal efficacy of the unconscious and the conscious in mental life. This idea can be traced through *The Interpretation of Dreams* (New York, 1900/1965) and *Jokes and Their Relation to the Unconscious* (New York, 1905/1963), in which Lipps's theories of humor also figure prominently, to the last paragraph of the last paper in the *Collected Papers* (New York, 1941/1959). Continuing American interest in Lipps is shown by the republication in a new translation of Lipps's theory of consonance and dissonance, originally published in *Psychological Studies* (*Consonance and Dissonance in Music*, San Marino, CA, 1995).

Bibliography

Freud, S. (1965). *The interpretation of dreams* (J. Strachey, Trans.). New York: Avon Books. (Original work published 1900)

Freud, S. (1963). *Jokes and their relation to the unconscious* (J. Strachey, Trans.). New York: Norton. (Original work published 1905)

Freud, S. (1959). Some elementary lessons in psychoanalysis. In J. Strachey (Ed. & Trans.), *Collected papers* (Vol. 5, pp. 376–382). New York: Basic Books. (Original work published 1938)

James, W. (1890). *The principles of psychology* (Vols. 1–2). New York: Henry Holt.

Lipps, T. (1897). *Raumästhetik und Geometrische-optische Täuschungen* [Aesthetics of space and geometric optical illusions]. Leipzig: J. A. Barth.

Lipps, T. (1926). *Psychological studies* (2nd rev. ed., H. C. Sanborn, Trans.). Baltimore: Williams & Wilkins. (Original work published 1905)

Lipps, T. (1995). *Consonance and dissonance in music* (W. Thomson, Trans.). San Marino, CA: Everett Books. (Original work published 1905)

Lipps, T. (1909). *Leitfaden der Psychologie* [Main themes of psychology] (3rd rev. ed.). Leipzig: Wilhelm Engelmann.

Stein, E. (1970). *On the problem of empathy* (W. Stein, Trans.). The Hague: M. Nijhoff. (Original work published 1916)

David C. Devonis

LITERACY. Literacy is a more general concept than reading or writing, including not only competence with and uses of reading and writing, but also the roles that reading and writing play in the formation and accumulation of archival texts that serve as the primary embodiment of historical culture. Literate, bureaucratic, or document societies are those in which such archival texts play a central authoritative role. Such societies foster literate elites with responsibilities in law, science, and literature. Public education provides the means for democratizing these elite institutions.

Although reading and writing have long been the focus of psychological research, literacy has become part of the intellectual landscape only in the past three decades. The neglect of literacy may be traced to the assumption that writing is simply the visible form of speech, and that the acquisition and use of writing merely reflect changes in patterns of communication. The current interest in literacy arises largely from the fact that literacy not only enables the individual to communicate, but it is also a mode of representation with distinctive intellectual and social implications.

Literacy involves the ability to read and write, but also one's ability to access the documentary resources of a literate society with a measure of competence. Because of these communicative and representational functions, as well as for reasons of power and prestige, literacy holds a prominent place in the political goals of both developed and developing nations as exemplified through universal, compulsory education and in the personal goals of parents and children who see literacy as a means to personal and economic fulfillment.

Writing and Communication

Speech is unquestionably fundamental to the intellectual and social competence of humans, but writing has obvious advantages over speech for communication across space and through time, factors which various media, including the book, the printing press, the telegraph, and computer technologies exploit and extend in various ways. Writing was essential to the formation and operation of the first large-scale societies whether as cities, nations, or empires in ancient China, Sumer, Egypt, and Mesoamerica. The paleographers Hans Nissen, Peter Damerow, and Robert Englund (*Ancient Book-*

keeping: Early Writing and Techniques of Economic Administration in the Ancient Near East, Chicago, 1993) have shown that writing played a critical role in record-keeping in ancient Sumer. Similarly, the historian William Harris (*Ancient Literacy,* Cambridge, MA, 1989) has shown the importance of writing for the codification and publication of law, while the classicist Eric Havelock (*Preface to Plato,* Cambridge, UK, 1963) has shown the impact of writing on the evolution of Western literature. The historian Elizabeth Eisenstein (*The Printing Press as an Agent of Change,* Cambridge, UK, 1979) has shown the importance of the printing press in the accumulation and dissemination of knowledge whether as history or science.

The relation between social and cognitive structures was of much concern to social theorists such as Émile Durkheim (S. Lukes, *Émile Durkheim: His Life and Work,* Markham, ON, 1973). The role that writing has played in the transformation of societies has come into psychology largely through the influence of the Russian psychologist Lev Vygotsky and now makes up an important part of cultural psychology as described by the American psychologists Jerome Bruner (*The Culture of Education,* Cambridge, MA, 1996) and Michael Cole (*Cultural Psychology,* Cambridge, MA, 1996).

Writing and Representation

No one doubts the importance of writing in the accumulation and dispersion of information. Texts and commentaries on texts build a tradition of scholarship. Such accumulations tend to lose their connections with personal authorship and may come to be treated as objects in their own right, as scripture, law, or science. Consequently, writing serves as a mode of representation of what is taken as "known" rather than simply a means of communication between persons. Psychological research on aspects of literacy has focused on three issues: the relation between speech and writing, the acquisition of literacy, and the effects of literate representations on the formation of mind.

Speech and Writing

Although scripts are not designed according to fixed principles, writing systems may be classified according to type, each type bearing a particular relation to the structure of speech. Some writing systems make no direct reference to linguistic form (as in the so-called picture writing of Mesoamerica and North American Indians); some make reference to syntactic structure (as in Proto-Cuneiform); some to word forms (as in Chinese character scripts); some to syllables (as in Linear B in Mycene), and still others to phonemic constituents, consonants, and vowels (as in alphabetic scripts). Each type of script, therefore, relates to language in a somewhat distinctive way. This raises the question as to the precise cognitive relation between graphic and linguis-

tic structure and, in turn, what a learner must grasp in order to work out these relations. It has been generally assumed, on the basis of the writings of Aristotle, Saussure, Bloomfield, and others, that writing is simply the transcription, or the recording, of speech. On that assumption, one already possesses implicit knowledge of the properties of speech and the problem is to work out how the script reflects those properties. A number of writers have argued the reverse, for instance the psycholinguists Donald Shankweiler and Isabelle Liberman ("Misreading: A search for causes," in J. Kavanaugh & I. Mattingly (Eds.), *Language by Ear and Language by Eye: The Relationships between Speech and Writing,* Cambridge, MA, 1972) and more recently the linguist Roy Harris (*The Origin of Writing,* London, 1986). These commentators see the problem as one of analyzing or of becoming conscious of oral speech in terms of the categories offered by the script. In this view, writing systems, rather than transcribing the known, provide models for thinking about speech and language, for bringing aspects of language into consciousness. The properties of speech available for introspection such as words, sentences, syllables, and phonemic segments are the consequence of literacy, of applying written models to oral speech.

Acquisition of Literacy

While the psychological study of reading has focused on issues of word and letter recognition, studies of literacy have focused on the relation between the written and the oral forms of language. From this point of view, a major problem in learning to read is learning to "hear" oral speech in a new way, that is, in a way compatible with the items—words and letters—composing the script. Studies of nonliterate adults by psychologists José Morais, Jesus Alegria, and Alain Content ("The relationships between segmental analysis and alphabetic literacy: An interactive view," *Cahiers de Psychologie Cognitive,* 1987, 7, 415–538), and of prereading children by psychologists Emilia Ferreiro and Ana Teberosky (*Literacy Before Schooling,* Exeter, NH, 1982) indicate that it is exposure to writing systems that leads speakers to think of their spoken language as composed of such categorical elements as discrete phonemes (represented by letters) or discrete words (represented by graphic entities bounded by spaces). The discovery of the alphabetic principle is a discovery about speech as much as it is about writing.

The pedagogy of reading has been dominated by a long and ongoing argument as to the appropriate balance between learning forms as opposed to grasping meanings. Some reading theorists, notably Ken Goodman (*Language and Literacy: The Selected Writings,* Boston, 1982) and Frank Smith (*Understanding Reading,* New York, 1994), emphasize the importance of constructed meanings as the route to graphic recognition.

Others, notably Jeanne Chall (*Learning to Read: The Great Debate*, Fort Worth, TX, 1996) and Marilyn Adams (*Beginning to Read: Thinking and Learning about Print*, Cambridge MA, 1990), emphasize the importance of grasping how the graphic signs represent oral expressions. Standards of achievement have recently come to dominate discussions of pedagogy, although balancing issues of recognition of form with those of meaning and interpretation have not been resolved.

Writing and the Mind

Although the mind as a biological organ is common to all humans, mind as a conscious, conceptual system is, in part, the product of culture. In a modern, bureaucratic culture, mind is closely linked to literacy; however, the nature of the relationship remains the subject of research and theory. Although theories linking forms of writing with levels of culture and thought are to be found in such eighteenth-century writers as Giambattista Vico and Condorcet, modern theory is more clearly traced to anthropologist Lévy-Bruhl's (*Primitive Mentality*, London, 1923) theory of "primitive thought," now widely criticized, and the theories which first appeared in the 1960s by anthropologist Jack Goody, literary theorist Marshall McLuhan, and classicist Eric Havelock, and in the 1980s by literary theorist Walter Ong. These theories contrasted "orality" and "literacy" both as modes of communication and modes of thought. It was argued that writing allowed a particular form of study and contemplation, the formation of logics and dictionaries, a focus on "verbatim" interpretation and memorization with an interpretive bias toward literalism. Historians Michael Clanchy (*From Memory to Written Record*, Oxford, 1993) and Rosalind Thomas (*Literacy and Orality in Ancient Greece*, Cambridge, UK, 1992) have noted the increasing and pervasive reliance on written records and other written documents in many societies. The relations between "orality" and "literacy" continue to be debated, with many researchers, among them the medievalist Mary Carruthers (*The Book of Memory: A Study of Memory in Medieval Culture*, Cambridge, UK, 1990), pointing out the ways in which the oral and the written cooperate in any complex activity and claiming that the contrast between the oral and the written is not as categorical as was once thought. Although writing never replaces speaking, but rather preserves aspects of speech or other information as permanent visible artifacts, these literate artifacts may alter the very linguistic and conceptual practices of a social group, activities which blur the distinction between orality and literacy.

Literate Thought

The technology of greatest importance for understanding conceptual and intellectual advance in the arts and sciences is the availability of appropriate graphic and notational systems. Galileo worked out the relations between time, distance, and velocity in terms of the graphic properties of plane geometry. Advances in the sciences had to await critical developments not only in mathematics but also, as noted by Thomas Sprat (in his seventeenth-century *History of the Royal Society of London*, St. Louis, 1966), the creation of appropriate writing and notational systems. As noted by the psychologist Annette Karmiloff-Smith (*Beyond Modularity: A Developmental Perspective on Cognitive Science*, Cambridge, MA, 1990), conceptual development in children is, in part, the consequence of the invention and acquisition of these systems for representing thought. Not only is the written tradition central to the growth of knowledge in the sciences and arts, it is instrumental to thinking in general as a form of metalinguistic or grammatical and logical analysis. The ability to examine the form and content of an argument is aided by the practice of reflecting on statements. Some writers, for instance Lev Vygotsky and Jack Goody, have characterized this ability as the growth of a technology of mind. Others, like Merlin Donald (*Origins of the Modern Mind*, Cambridge, MA, 1991) and Katherine Nelson (*Language in Cognitive Development: The Emergence of the Mediated Mind*, New York, 1996), view it as an extension of memory. Yet others, like psychologist David Olson (*The World on Paper*, New York, 1994), view this as conceptual change evolving in the tradition of writing and interpreting written texts.

Literacy and Social Development

In spite of the fact that literacy plays such a prominent role in modern societies, it is now recognized that one cannot simply transform a society from a traditional, oral one into a literate one by imposing literacy in the same way as, in an earlier period, one imposed Christianity or Islam. Oral traditions remain in parallel with written ones, although the latter tend to acquire and hold prestige, sometimes undermining existing traditions. As anthropologist Brian Street has shown (*Literacy in Theory and Practice*, New York, 1984), literacy has played many social and personal functions in different cultures at different times, and literacy contributes to a culture to the extent that it proves useful to various textual communities and their members. Rather than being seen simply as a goal, literacy has come to be seen as a means to a number of socially and personally valued ends.

Bibliography

Coulmas, F. (1989). *The writing systems of the world.* Oxford: Basil Blackwell. Explores how various writing systems relate to the languages they depict and how writing effects the development of language.

Faber, A. (1992). Phonemic segmentation as epiphenomenon: Evidence from the history of writing. In P. Dowling, S. D. Lima, & M. Noonan (Eds.), *The linguistics of literacy* (pp. 111–134). Amsterdam: John Benjamins. Reviews evidence of phonemic segmentation ability and the development of the Greek alphabet, theorizing that segmentation ability is a consequence of rather than a precursor to alphabetic writing.

Goody, J. (Ed.). (1968). *Literacy in traditional societies.* Cambridge, U.K.: Cambridge University Press. The first systematic examination of the importance of writing on the development of bureaucratic societies.

McLuhan, M. (1962). *The Gutenberg galaxy,* Toronto: University of Toronto Press. Both brilliant and infuriating, this book, a cult classic, was the first to celebrate the effects of media in general and writing in particular on culture and cognition.

Ong, W. (1982). *Orality and literacy: The technologizing of the word.* London: Methuen. Assesses the intellectual, literary, and social effects of writing in the medieval and early modern periods.

Sampson, G. (1989). *Writing systems.* Stanford, CA: Stanford University Press. A linguistic analysis of the structure of writing systems

Stock, B. (1990). *Listening for the text: On the uses of the past.* Baltimore: John Hopkins. Studies how the growth of interest in language in the Middle Ages forms the background to the contemporary study of oral and literate cultures.

Vygotsky, L. (1986). *Thought and language.* (A. Kozulin, Ed.). Cambridge, MA: MIT Press. A first and most influential attempt to make a theory of mind which reflects the nature of language and other cultural forms including writing.

David R. Olson

LITERATURE. Psychology and literature have been intertwined almost from their beginnings. The 4,000-year-old *Epic of Gilgamesh* is as much concerned with its hero's psychological responses as it is with his godlike powers and fantastic adventures. Homer's *Iliad* and *Odyssey* depict spectacular battles and journeys but also examine the personalities of Achilles, Odysseus, and Penelope. In proposing to ban poets from his ideal republic, Plato had in mind both the persuasive skills of the poets and the psychological weaknesses of their potential audience. In his *Poetics*, Aristotle theorized that the search for knowledge is a major human motive and that we gain pleasure from drama because it brings us increased knowledge of self and others.

Psychological Approaches to Literature

Aristotle's concepts, often interpreted to include emotional catharsis through drama, dominated discussion of the psychology of literary response for two millennia. Further speculation about the psychological effects of literature and the sources of creative imagination, by such writers as Sir Philip Sydney and Samuel Taylor Coleridge, fell far short of a comprehensive theoretical approach and therefore advanced the psychological study of literature little beyond Aristotle.

The psychology of literature was transformed in the early twentieth century by Sigmund Freud. Freud's first contribution to the topic (*The Interpretation of Dreams,* 1900, *Standard edition of the complete psychological works of Sigmund Freud,* vol. 4, London, 1953) was his identification of recurring themes and symbols in dreams and other imaginative products. According to Freud, among the most important of the recurring patterns was one so similar to an ancient literary model (and myth) that he called it by the literary protagonist's name: the Oedipus complex. Freud concluded that the normal childhood development (and then repression) of sexual feelings toward the opposite-sexed parent, accompanied by hostility toward the same-sexed parent, accounts both for this pattern's repeated appearance in literary works from *Oedipus Rex* to *Hamlet* and beyond, and for the powerful emotional impact of such portrayals on most audience members.

Ernest Jones elaborated at length on Freud's analysis of *Hamlet* as Oedipal expression ("The Oedipus complex as an explanation of Hamlet's mystery," *American Journal of Psychology,* 1910). Much subsequent psychoanalytic interpretation of literature has focused on Oedipal and other unconscious emotional patterns, assumed to have been established during the childhoods of writer and audience. In *The Anxiety of Influence* (New York, 1973), Harold Bloom has argued that the very act of creative writing involves Oedipal feelings: The writer unconsciously perceives literary predecessors as parental figures who must be vanquished in order to establish a personal literary identity.

According to both Freud and Jones, William Shakespeare emphasized Oedipal issues in *Hamlet* because of early and contemporaneous events in his own psychological history. Literary critics and biographers have often adopted similar assumptions in developing psychobiographical interpretations of other writers' work. The formalist New Critics of the 1930s and 1940s emphatically rejected such interpretations, as did the "death of the author" deconstructionists of the 1980s. Meanwhile, literary psychobiographers became increasingly sophisticated in their use of Freudian concepts and in their arguments favoring the examination of an author's work in the context of the author's life (see Leon Edel, *Writing Lives,* New York, 1984). Increasingly, they moved beyond strictly Freudian interpretations to use more current psychoanalytic concepts of pre-Oedipal development, ego identity, and narcissism (e.g., David Lynch, *Yeats: The Poetics of the Self,* Chicago, 1979).

Freud himself went well beyond his Oedipal interpretation of *Hamlet* and other specific works in discussing literary creation. He speculated, among other matters, on the psychological functions of literary form and style: for example, that the author attempts to write in an appealing and intriguing form that will yield aesthetic "forepleasure" in order to tempt the reader into absorbing the deeper and potentially disturbing content of the literary work ("Creative writers and day-dreaming," 1908; *Standard edition*, vol. 9, London, 1959). Freud also considered in detail the psychological appeal of "uncanny" elements in literary fantasies, as exemplified by the stories of E. T. A. Hoffman ("The 'uncanny,'" 1919; *Standard edition*, vol. 17, London, 1955).

Jacques Lacan, a French psychoanalyst, combined Freud's ideas concerning the linguistic aspects of literature with Freud's earlier discussions of language in psychoanalytic treatment and with various aspects of philosophical linguistics (*Écrits*, Paris, 1966; *Écrits: A selection*, New York, 1977). Just as the analytic patient's every phrase is bursting with unconscious messages and unresolved conflicts, Lacan said, so the literary artist's every passage is a container for multiple meanings and deep antitheses. Lacan's ideas on how to excavate such contents spread from France to American critical circles, where versions of his "French Freud" approach became central to literary theory in the 1970s and 1980s. In part out of his ideas, a current competitor to Lacanian theory developed: psychoanalytic feminism. Psychoanalytic feminist literary critics rejected certain specifics of Freud's views on feminine psychology (such as penis envy), but eagerly applied his broader concepts concerning the unconscious underpinnings of literature, especially as they may address issues of gender identity. Psychoanalytic feminism, which incorporates ideas from Melanie Klein and other female analysts, remains a strong branch of feminist literary theory, along with such alternatives as Marxist and lesbian feminism.

Although one version or another of Freudian theory has dominated psychological approaches to literature, at times other theories have been employed. The most influential of these is the Jungian archetypal approach, in which literary works are viewed as expressions of core inherited patterns of imagery identified by C. G. Jung and others. Following Jung's own practice, such interpretations tend to emphasize the archetypes rather than the literary works or their authors. However, in examining mature literary productivity, Jungian concepts of midlife personality development may at times be more useful than Freudian concepts of childhood development (e.g., R. Helson, "E. Nesbit's forty-first year," *Imagination, Personality, and Cognition*, 1984–85.)

Contemporary cognitive psychology and neuroscience have so far contributed little to the psychological study of literature. An interesting preliminary effort in this direction is Norman Holland's *Brain of Robert Frost*, which considers the poet as an identity governing a hierarchy of information-processing feedbacks. Perhaps more promising are efforts to apply to literature the script theory of Silvan Tomkins, a blend of concepts about cognitive processes, emotions, and personality structure. Script theory has been suggestively applied to the fiction of Nathaniel Hawthorne by Rae Carlson ("Exemplary lives," *Journal of Personality*, 1988), and other literary applications are in process.

Most research psychologists feel uncomfortable at best with the sorts of qualitative psychological interpretations of literature already discussed. Regarding such efforts as more art than science, some researchers have struggled to develop quantitative approaches to the psychological study of literature. Such efforts are still rather limited, but they have been increasing in number and scope. Among early efforts in this direction were Harold McCurdy's content analyses of the psychological traits displayed by fictional characters, which he then related to biographical information about the characters' creators (e.g., *The Personality of Shakespeare*, New Haven, CT, 1953). Among more recent examples, one of the broadest in scope is Colin Martindale's *The Clockwork Muse* (New York, 1990). Martindale proposed a theory of artistic change over time and provided evidence for it through extensive quantitative analyses of word choice in French and British poetry and in American popular song lyrics.

Using even more complex statistical analyses, Dean Simonton employed data from Shakespeare's plays and sonnets to show significant correlations between the popularity or "greatness" of specific works and such measures as adjective-to-verb ratios and author's age at time of composition ("The creative genius of William Shakespeare," in A. Steptoe [ed.], *Genius and the Mind*, Oxford, 1998). Such quantitative studies are sometimes criticized (especially by researchers who rely on qualitative approaches) for omitting measures of the meaning or emotional content of literary works. But Simonton, for instance, includes assessments of such broad themes as "parental despotism" and "madness or frenzy due to emotional excess" among his successful correlational measures.

Literary Approaches to Psychology

Prior to the twentieth century, creative writers sometimes made use of proto-psychological theories, such as Burton's concept of bodily humors, to delineate literary characters. But Freud's psychoanalytic theories were much more quickly and strongly adopted by creative writers than any theories that had gone before. Soon Oedipal characters abounded in fiction, and characters of all sorts were saddled with Freudian dreams and Freudian slips. Freud himself complained about the formulaic fictional application of his ideas, preferring more subtle evocations of psychoanalytic discoveries.

Such subtle applications were not long in coming.

The fiction of James Joyce and Marcel Proust, the plays of Eugene O'Neill and Tennessee Williams, and the poetry of W. H. Auden and Hilda Doolittle drew heavily on the writers' own observations of human character, but they were all infused with an awareness of the Freudian revolution.

Jungian concepts were welcomed by other writers who were less enthusiastic about Freud. Remarkably, Jack London read Jung's *Psychology of the Unconscious* upon its first American publication in 1916 and incorporated Jungian ideas into his final stories (such as "The Red One," published posthumously in 1918). Over the next decades, few other fiction writers were as adept in their use of archetypal psychology (but see the final chapters of Herbert Read's novel *The Green Child*, London, 1935). In recent decades, more writers have consciously adopted Jungian concepts, perhaps most notably the Canadian novelist Robertson Davies (especially in his Deptford trilogy, beginning with *Fifth Business*, New York, 1970) and the American fantasist Ursula Le Guin (especially in her Earthsea series, beginning with *A Wizard of Earthsea*, New York, 1968).

Other psychological theories have had little apparent impact on creative writers. Beyond B. F. Skinner's own utopian *Walden Two* (New York, 1948), it is hard to find a truly behaviorist novel. Narcissistic personalities abound in latter-twentieth-century fiction, but few if any seem to be based directly on the major theories of narcissism developed by Freud, Heinz Kohut, and Otto Kernberg. Codependent characters have become frequent in popular novels, especially by women authors, but they appear to draw more from the pop psychology writings of Melody Beattie than the original theoretical concepts of Karen Horney. Wilhelm Reich's radical psychoanalytic therapy was incorporated into one of Saul Bellow's best novels, *Henderson the Rain King* (New York, 1959), but Bellow chose to conceal its Reichian origins behind the mask of an African medicine man.

Beyond the incorporation of psychological theories directly into fiction, psychology has influenced literature through the vehicle of the therapist-client relationship. Novels have often depicted such relationships from the outside (F. Scott Fitzgerald's *Tender Is the Night*, New York, 1934), or as told by the client (Italo Svevo's *Confessions of Zeno*, Bologna, 1923, New York, 1930; Philip Roth's *Portnoy's Complaint*, New York, 1969), or from the parallel perspectives of client and therapist (D. M. Thomas's *The White Hotel*, New York, 1981). Novels have been written by former mental patients, fictionalizing their experiences (Hannah Green, *I Never Promised You a Rose Garden*, New York, 1964; Janet Frame, *Owls Do Cry*, New York, 1960), and by therapists fictionalizing their patients (Samuel Shem, *Fine*, New York, 1985; Irvin Yalom, *Lying on the Couch*, New York, 1996). In all these instances and many others, the therapeutic process and related psychological concepts are presented and elaborated, though not always seriously.

Indeed, not all psychotherapy clients come away happy, and not all observers of psychotherapeutic outcomes are positively impressed. Thus, there has also grown up a kind of antitherapy (and sometimes more broadly antipsychology) literature. Its most distinguished practitioner was Vladimir Nabokov, especially in his masterpieces *Lolita* (Paris, 1955; New York, 1958) and *Pale Fire* (New York, 1962). Beyond therapists, other kinds of psychologists have gotten off fairly lightly in fiction. There is, for example, no substantial novel about psychological laboratory researchers, though there is one devastating short story: "The Psychologist Who Wouldn't Do Awful Things to Rats" (1976), by experimental psychologist and science fiction writer Alice Bradley Sheldon (as James Tiptree Jr.; reprinted in *Star Songs of an Old Primate*, New York, 1978).

Conclusion

Aristotle proposed that mimesis, the imitation of life in art, is an essential feature of human psychology. Freud saw the elemental storytelling phenomena of night dreams and daydreams as the original models for creative literature. More recently, such psychologists as Donald Spence (*Narrative Truth and Historical Truth*, New York, 1982) and Dan McAdams (*The Stories We Live By*, New York, 1993) have argued that rendering one's own remembered (or misremembered) life as a story is one of our most valuable means to get through that life in reasonably good shape psychologically. Not surprisingly, writers have also characterized the storyteller's role as central in human psychological functioning (see, for example, Mario Vargas Llosa's novel *The Storyteller*, New York, 1989; Salman Rushdie's novel *Haroun and the Sea of Stories*, London, 1990; and Ursula Le Guin's story collection *A Fisherman of the Inland Sea*, New York, 1994). However preferences among theories may shift, whether in psychology or in literary scholarship, the historically close relationship of psychology and literature is unlikely to diminish. Each field can benefit from greater attention to the other; neither can reasonably ignore the other.

[*See also* Arts Therapy; Creativity; *and* Writing.]

Bibliography

Berman, J. (1985). *The talking cure: Literary representations of psychoanalysis.* New York: New York University Press. Examines numerous stories and novels in which psychotherapy is centrally featured.

Bettelheim, B. (1976). *The uses of enchantment: The meaning and importance of fairy tales.* New York: Knopf. Discusses how a number of classic "fairy tales" (usually literary in their most familiar form) may help children deal with developmental issues. The perspective is psychoanalytic and empathic.

Edel, L. (1982). *Stuff of sleep and dreams: Experiments in literary psychology.* New York: Harper & Row. Brief studies of James Joyce, Virginia Woolf, and other writers; broader consideration of the problems and rewards of psychobiography.

Edel, L. (1985). *Henry James: A life.* New York: Harper & Row. Edel's one-volume condensation and revision of his five-volume psychological biography of James, including new material on James's sexuality or lack thereof. One of the great psychobiographies.

Elms, A. C. (1994). *Uncovering lives: The uneasy alliance of biography and psychology.* Several chapters discuss how creative writing serves important psychological functions for writers. Examples include Vladimir Nabokov, Isaac Asimov, and L. Frank Baum.

Faber, M. D. (Ed.). (1970). *The design within: Psychoanalytic approaches to Shakespeare.* A wide variety of psychoanalytic perspectives on most of Shakespeare's plays, including excerpts from Freud and Jones and critiques of their explications of *Hamlet.* Dated but useful bibliography for further reading.

Guerin, W. L., Labor, E., Morgan, L., Reesman, J. C., & Willingham, J. R. (1992). *A handbook of critical approaches to literature* (3rd ed.) New York: Oxford University Press. Explains the basics of traditional and current literary theories, including several psychological ones; applies each theory to the same literary examples for comparison.

Holland, N. N. (1990). *Holland's guide to psychoanalytic psychology and literature-and-psychology.* New York: Oxford University Press. An outline review of a wide range of approaches to the psychology of literature, including Holland's own reader-response studies. A variety of research aids are listed and annotated.

Murray, H. A. (1981). *Endeavors in psychology* (E. S. Shneidman, Ed.) New York: Harper & Row. Includes several papers from Murray's career-long study of Herman Melville. Especially impressive is the 70-page "Introduction to *Pierre,*" a Jungian elucidation of Melville's most obscure novel.

PsyArt: A hyperlink journal for the psychological study of the arts. This electronic journal, available on the Internet at http://www.clas.ufl.edu/ipsa/journal/index.htm, emphasizes the psychology of literature, although studies of films and other artistic works are also included. Edited by Norman N. Holland.

van Meurs, J. (1991). *Jungian literary criticism, 1920–1980: An annotated, critical bibliography of works in English (with a selection of titles after 1980).* The title says it all. In lieu of a comprehensive text, this bibliography gives a good sense of what Jungian literary criticism is and which works are well done.

Vice, S. (Ed.). (1996). *Psychoanalytic criticism: A reader.* Cambridge, England: Polity Press. Brief examples of Freudian and later psychoanalytic approaches to literature, including fairly readable excerpts from translations of Lacan and other French Freudians.

Alan C. Elms

LOCKE, JOHN (1632–1704), English philosopher. Although he built on traditions previously established by predecessors such as Francis Bacon (1561–1626) and Thomas Hobbes (1588–1679), Locke is widely regarded today as the most important founder of the school of mental philosophy known as British associationism. Locke's *Essay Considering Human Understanding,* the first edition of which appeared in 1690, emphatically rejected Descartes's notion of innate ideas while promoting the empiricist position that the human mind at birth is like a blank slate or "tabula rasa," whose subsequent contents are completely the result of the particular experiences that impinge upon it. The specific term "association of ideas" was not introduced until the *Essay*'s fourth edition in 1700, but that concept had been implicit from the outset in Locke's assertion that the ideas resulting from specific experiences become linked together through factors such as contiguity and similarity to constitute each mind's knowledge of the world. Locke stressed that because of the limited nature of any one person's experience, as well as the accidental nature of many associations, a person's knowledge is inevitably incomplete and imperfect. Impressed by the achievements of scientific contemporaries such as Robert Boyle (1627–1691), Isaac Newton (1642–1727), and the physician Thomas Willis (1621–1675), Locke advocated their observational and experimental methods as a model for minimizing the uncertainty and inaccuracy of knowledge.

Life and Career

Locke was born in the English Somerset town of Wrington on 29 August 1632. He later said he had been born "into a storm," for England then lay on the brink of civil war, and his family strongly supported the parliamentarian roundheads against the royalist cavaliers. As a reward for supporting the victorious side, Locke's father was allowed to send his son to the prestigious Westminster School in London. There, under the supervision of an unusually tolerant schoolmaster, Locke met and befriended fellow students from royalist as well as parliamentarian families and learned firsthand that political arguments virtually always have more than one defensible side. Thus began his lifelong preoccupation with the question of how to decide rationally and peaceably among conflicting political, ideological, or religious views.

At Oxford, Locke pursued the standard, classics-dominated curriculum but also gained firsthand extracurricular knowledge of the power of the newly arising observational and experimental approaches to science. He became friendly with Boyle, then living in Oxford and conducting the famous experiments that led to "Boyle's law" of the pressure of gases. He attended regular meetings hosted by Boyle for scientific discussion, meetings that laid the groundwork for what in 1662, following Boyle's move to London, became the Royal Society. Locke also studied medicine extracurricularly with the physician Willis, a pioneering brain anatomist and proponent of a new, observationally based approach to medicine. Although Locke avoided the classically oriented studies required for a formal degree in medicine, he became a skillful practitioner.

This proved important in 1666, when Locke chanced to perform a minor medical service for an eminent visitor to Oxford, the chancellor of the exchequer Sir Anthony Ashley Cooper (1621–1683). Impressed by Locke's general good sense as well as medical expertise, Cooper invited him to move to London as his personal physician. Locke accepted, and quickly rejoined Boyle and became a fellow of the Royal Society. Besides performing medical services for Cooper (including a risky but life-saving liver operation), Locke became a trusted all-purpose adviser whose influence grew along with the power of his patron. Cooper, who became lord chancellor and was named the first earl of Shaftesbury in 1672, increasingly championed the powers of parliament, and formed the Whigs as Britain's first organized political party to further that cause. This activity gradually incurred the king's wrath, which led Shaftesbury to flee to Holland just before his death in 1683. Locke followed in 1684 and remained in exile until the Glorious Revolution of 1688 placed the English monarchy in the friendlier hands of Queen Mary and her Dutch husband, William of Orange. Soon after his return, Locke published his *Essay* and a related work of political theory, *Two Treatises on Government* (1690). These immediately established his reputation as England's most important philosopher, a reputation he retained until his death in 1704.

Locke's Major Works

Locke's *Essay* was originally inspired by an informal discussion with colleagues in 1671 on the vexed question of whether there was any rational way of deciding among the conflicting claims and beliefs of the many differing religious sects. Locke recalled, "It came into my thoughts that we took a wrong course; and that before we set ourselves upon enquiries of that nature it was necessary to examine our own abilities, and see what objects our understandings were or were not fitted to deal with" (1965, vol. I, p. xxxii). Before squandering further time on inconclusive religious argument, Locke felt it necessary to determine exactly what it was that the human mind was capable of knowing and, equally important, *not* knowing. Locke optimistically thought he could complete this analysis of the mind's capacities in a few days, but in fact it would be nineteen years before he felt ready to publish his conclusions in the *Essay Concerning Human Understanding*.

There Locke described the human mind at birth as a blank slate with the capacity to form and retain ideas

corresponding to its experiences, which can be either sensations derived from the external world, or reflections of the mind's own operations. Early experiences give rise to *simple ideas* such as redness or loudness from sensations, and willing or desiring from reflections. With further experience, simple ideas combine to form *complex ideas*, as when redness, roundness, and sweetness come together in the idea of an apple. Locke noted that one may have complex ideas of "impossible" objects that have not been personally experienced, as long as all of the simple ideas it comprises have been experienced (e.g., anyone can have a complex idea of a two-headed, green cat, as long as the simpler ideas of heads, two-ness, green-ness, and cats have been established). But without prior bases in simple ideas, even the most "obvious" of complex ideas are impossible. In a famous thought experiment suggested by William Molyneux (1656–1696), Locke argued that a congenitally blind person suddenly granted sight would not be able to distinguish a cube from a sphere by the sense of sight alone, even though easily able to make that same distinction by touch. The necessary visual simple ideas would first have to be established.

Greatly concerned about the validity of acquired knowledge about the physical world, Locke followed Galileo and Descartes in distinguishing between the *primary* and *secondary qualities* of objects. He assumed that the primary qualities of solidity, extension, shape, and mobility truly inhere in objects independently of their perception. Secondary qualities, which include normal sensory impressions such as color, smell, and temperature, only arise after the primary qualities of objects have interacted with those of the sensory organs. Knowledge based on secondary qualities is far less certain than that based on primary qualities, as Locke illustrated in a famous example: a bucket of tepid water will simultaneously feel cool to one hand and warm to the other, if they have previously been immersed separately in hot and cold water. The best and most reliable knowledge occurs when secondary qualities are accounted for in terms of the primary qualities responsible for them. For example, the tepid water's "true" temperature is defined by the speed of vibrations of its particles, which are fast relative to a sense organ whose particles have been slowed down by immersion in cold water, and slow to one whose particles have been speeded up by the hot. Analyses such as this, of course, were characteristic of the emerging experimental sciences that Locke admired so much.

Although the *Essay* allowed that reflections—the mind's impressions of its own operations—were a source of ideas and knowledge along with sensations of the external world, Locke's primary concerns and emphases were on the latter. This led to criticism from nativist philosophers such as Gottfried Leibniz (1646–1716), whose *New Essays on Human Understanding* (posthumously published in 1765) emphasized the capacities of the human mind to understand the world in terms of mathematical and logical necessary truths that are innate rather than acquired through experience. Summarizing Locke's position as "there is nothing in the intellect that was not first in the senses," Leibniz insisted on adding a concluding proviso, "except the mind itself."

Ever concerned about the practical implications of his philosophy, Locke sought ways to minimize the limitations of sensory knowledge. To help compensate for the inevitably limited experience and knowledge of any one person, he endorsed the widespread and open exchange of information and ideas in institutions such as scientific societies. His *Two Treatises on Government* extended these values into the political realm. In developing Hobbes's concept of the social contract, Locke produced an argument in favor of participatory democracy and the division of powers that profoundly influenced the framers of the Constitution of the United States. On a more individual level, Locke wrote a cousin long letters offering childrearing advice based on his empiricist principles, denying the importance of innate tendencies in children and arguing that their character may be deliberately shaped by controlling their experiences. These letters formed the basis for Locke's 1693 book, *Some Thoughts Concerning Education*—one of the earliest how-to books for anxious parents.

Prominent British mental philosophers who followed in Locke's tradition included George Berkeley (1685–1753), who applied associationistic principles to the analysis of visual depth perception (while questioning the distinction between primary and secondary qualities); David Hume (1711–1776), who codified the "laws of association" and reduced the concept of causation to the effects of association; David Hartley (1705–1757), who proposed a neurophysiological explanation for association; and the father and son team of James Mill (1773–1836) and John Stuart Mill (1806–1874), who explained the most important individual differences in human intellect and character as the result of differing experiences and associations.

[*Many of the people mentioned in this article are the subjects of independent biographical entries.*]

Bibliography

Cranston, M. (1957). *John Locke: A biography*. London: Longmans.

Fancher, R. E. (1996). *Pioneers of psychology* (3rd ed.). New York: Norton. Chapter 2, "Philosophers of mind," describes and compares the psychological ideas of Locke and Leibniz.

Locke, J. (1960). *Two treatises on government* (P. Laslett, Ed.). Cambridge, England: Cambridge University Press.

Locke, J. (1965). *An essay concerning human understanding* (5th ed.). 2 vols. London: Dent (Original work published 1706)

Locke, J. (1989). *Some thoughts concerning education* (Edited with introduction, notes, and critical apparatus by J. W. Yolton and J. S. Yolton). New York: Oxford University Press.

Russell, B. (1965). *A history of western philosophy*. New York: Simon and Schuster. Devotes three chapters to "Locke's theory of knowledge," "Locke's political philosophy," and "Locke's influence."

Raymond E. Fancher

LOCUS OF CONTROL was the predominant construct in personality research during the 1970s and 1980s. It had originated within Julian Rotter's social learning theory in which behavior is predicted from the value that people have for particular reinforcements, their expectancies about certain behaviors' effects upon the occurrence of reinforcements, and the nature of the given situation. As an example, students' studying behavior would be predicted from knowledge about the value they place on school success, their expectancies that studying enhances the likelihood of success, and the teacher's responsiveness to those efforts. [*See* Social-Cognitive Theory; *and* Expectancy Effects.]

In social learning theory, locus of control is a "generalized expectancy" that pertains to the perception of causal relationships between behaviors and reinforcing experiences. It is similar to a belief or an attitude that persons have about the effectiveness of their behavior to achieve desired outcomes. Persons who become fatalistic, believing that they can do little to change the nature of their experiences, are said to hold generalized expectancies for external control. In contrast, if individuals believe that their experiences reflect their efforts, personal characteristics, and actions, they are said to have developed generalized expectancies of internal control. That is, they assume that their outcomes and experiences are at least partially shaped by their own actions.

Generalized locus of control expectancies have been used to explain the different ways in which people respond to threats and challenges. A more internal locus of control is said to characterize resilient individuals who actively deal with problems in the hope of overcoming them. [*See* Resilience.] A more external locus of control is said to characterize lethargic persons who seem more ready to capitulate, succumbing to inactivity and dysphoria when confronting even small obstacles.

Research with the locus of control construct began formally in the early 1960s and was reviewed in papers by myself in *Psychological Bulletin* and by Julian Rotter in *Psychological Monographs*, published in 1966. Both articles became "citation classics," stimulating a groundswell of subsequent research. The early studies reviewed in these papers demonstrated the effects of control expectancies upon well-known learning phenomena such as extinction and upon social behaviors such as participation in civil rights protests. Individual difference measures of locus of control were presented that had been found to be associated with alertness, information seeking, and a sense of well-being. [See Wellness and Illness.] In each instance, a more internal locus of control, assessed as a personality characteristic, was positively associated with active problem-solving behavior, awareness, resistance to attempts at coercion, and positive affect. [See Thinking, article on Problem Solving.] A more external locus of control was more often found to be associated with passivity, "influenceability," conformity, dysphoria, and diminished ability to cope with stressful life events.

Subsequent research investigations demonstrated the utility of locus of control as a predictor of the ways in which people cope with stress. Reviews of this research indicated that internals often exhibited less emotional reactions to stressful events than externals, which prompted some researchers to question the ways in which control expectancies exerted their effects upon how stress is experienced. One review of pertinent research attested to a link between locus of control expectancies and coping strategies that could account for the moderation of stress effects by locus of control. For example, in a study concerning responses to natural disasters, internals with businesses that had been destroyed by the flooding that accompanied Hurricane Hazel were found to have reestablished themselves more quickly than externals in the 3½ years following the disaster. Differential rates of recovery were attributed to the greater emotionality and less problem-focused coping observed among externals in comparison to internals. [See Emotion.] Analogous findings were obtained among a sizable sample of Israeli soldiers during the 1982 war in Lebanon, indicating nonrecovery from traumas were more common at both two and three years after the war among externals, who had engaged in emotion-focused coping more than had internals. Likewise, among nurses in training, internals were found to have coped more actively with threatening challenges than had externals; they were more likely to have attempted rectifying situations that were deemed controllable, whereas externals most often concentrated upon their emotional responses even when facing what were judged to be controllable difficulties. Finally, in a 4-day simulation of a hostage-taking incident aboard an airplane, investigators found that airline personnel who held external control expectancies became more distressed if they had been taught problem-focused coping methods as opposed to emotion-focused coping strategies. Whereas internals

seemed to have benefited from training in either problem- or emotion-focused coping strategies, externals seemed less able to adopt problem-solving methods for dealing with such a stressful event. It would seem that internals were more versatile than externals in the ways that they dealt with such overwhelming circumstances.

If we extrapolate from these findings, we would expect that groups that have historically been traumatized and deprived of opportunities by external forces would manifest external control expectancies and more emotion-focused than problem-focused coping. Such is the case: members of racial groups and social classes that have been prevented from full participation in society have been found to espouse more external control expectancies than those of more "favored" groups for whom opportunities are more abundant. [See Ethnic and Racial Identity.] This comparative work has been in evidence from the earliest to the latest reviews of locus of control research and was most convincingly presented in a field study by Jessor, Graves, Hanson, and Jessor (1968).

Locus of control was initially assessed by a short measurement device constructed by Julian Rotter and his colleagues. In a 1991 review of currently available assessment methods, I described the psychometric characteristics of 18 different measures designed to assess control beliefs among different groups and for different goals and situations. Research evidence collected with these measures continues, though at a slower pace than was the case during the 1970s through the 1990s, in which locus of control came to be the most prominent personality construct to be investigated in personality psychology.

[See also Behaviorism and Neobehaviorism; Coping; Emotion; Ethnic and Racial Identity; Expectancy Effects; Individual Differences; Learning; Personality; Personality Psychology; Resilience; Social-Cognitive Theory; Thinking, article on Problem Solving; and Wellness and Illness.]

Bibliography

Jessor, R., Graves, T. D., Hanson, R. C., & Jessor, S. L. (1968). Society, personality, and deviant behavior. New York: Holt, Rinehart, & Winston. This book presents the use of social learning theory variables along with cognate variables from sociology and anthropology in predicting the development of pathology in a multicultural community.

Lefcourt, H. M. (1966). Internal versus external control of reinforcement: A review. Psychological Bulletin, 65, 206–220. This is one of the two original review articles that helped to stimulate much of the locus of control research.

Lefcourt, H. M. (Ed.). (1981). Research with the locus of con-

trol construct: Vol. 1. Assessment methods. San Diego, CA: Academic Press.

Lefcourt, H. M. (1982). *Locus of control: Current trends in theory and research* (2nd ed.). Hillsdale, NJ: Erlbaum.

Lefcourt, H. M. (1983). (Ed.). *Research with the locus of control construct: Vol. 2. Development and social problems.* San Diego, CA: Academic Press.

Lefcourt, H. M. (Ed.). (1984). *Research with the locus of control construct: Vol. 3. Extensions and limitations.* San Diego, CA: Academic Press.

Lefcourt, H. M. (1991). Locus of control. In J. P. Robinson, P. R. Shaver, & L. S. Wrightsman (Eds.). *Measures of personality and social psychological attitudes* (2nd ed., pp. 413–499). San Diego, CA: Academic Press.

Lefcourt, H. M., & Davidson, K. (1991). Locus of control and health. In C. R. Snyder & D. R. Forsyth (Eds.), *Handbook of social and clinical psychology* (pp. 246–266). New York: Pergamon Press.

Rotter, J. B. (1954). *Social learning and clinical psychology.* Englewood Cliffs, NJ: Prentice Hall.

Rotter, J. B. (1966). Generalized expectancies for internal versus external control of reinforcement. *Psychological Monographs, 80* (1, Whole No. 609). This is one of the two original review articles that helped to stimulate much of the locus of control research.

Skinner, E. A. (1995). *Perceived control, motivation, and coping.* Thousand Oaks, CA: Sage. Provides an overview of the various control relevant variables, their divergence and convergence.

Herbert M. Lefcourt

LOEB, JACQUES (1859–1924), German biologist. Loeb was born in Mayen, Germany, and emigrated to the United States in 1891. He made several important contributions to psychology. He is perhaps best known for his work on tropisms, or orientation in relation to external stimuli. On the basis of carefully controlled experiments, Loeb showed that an animal's orientation and simple movements were systematically related to several distinct sources of environmental stimulation, including light (heliotropisms), electricity (galvanotropisms), chemicals (chemotropisms), and gravity (geotropisms).

Loeb's methods, based on reactions of the "whole animal" to manipulable variables, differed from the isolated tissue preparations favored by reflexologists of the period. Indeed, for a physiologist, Loeb showed a surprising lack of concern for the physiological underpinnings of tropisms. Partly for these reasons, Loeb's work on tropisms was challenged by zoologists of the period, most notably Herbert Spencer Jennings, who believed that an understanding of physiological mechanisms was essential to a comprehensive evolutionary account. Although Loeb occasionally speculated about underlying mechanisms, he was more interested in bringing his subject matter under experimental control than in

identifying its presumed physiological or evolutionary bases. For Loeb, an appeal to physiological or historical factors diverted attention from variables that could be directly manipulated to predict and control behavior. Loeb came increasingly to view his work in terms of the practical control it afforded over his subject matter, and he actively promoted technological applications of basic science.

These themes were warmly received by early behaviorists struggling to put psychology on firm scientific footing. The behaviorists most influenced by Loeb were John B. Watson, whose graduate studies overlapped with Loeb's tenure at the University of Chicago, and B. F. Skinner, whose early research in the laboratory of the Harvard physiologist W. J. Crozier contained many elements consistent with Loeb's approach to biological problems.

Although Skinner found tropisms too limiting for his purposes, he found much of value in the experimental strategies set forth by Loeb and Crozier. It was while working in Crozier's laboratory that Skinner acquired an appreciation for the organism as a whole, embarking on the study of reflexes (and later, operants) as behavioral rather than physiological facts. Along with Loeb and Crozier, Skinner sought overall quantitative laws relating behavior to its controlling variables while avoiding appeals to hypothetical inner causes. It was also here that Skinner developed an appreciation for within-subject methodology and its emphasis on experimental rather than statistical control. This emphasis on practical control led Skinner, as it had Loeb, to promote technological applications of basic science. Indeed, Skinner became over the years to psychology what Loeb had been to biology a generation earlier—the model of a scientist-engineer, one who sought to understand the world by changing it.

Judged by the space devoted to tropisms in contemporary psychological textbooks, Loeb's impact on psychology might be regarded as negligible at best. This, however, would miss Loeb's most significant contribution to psychology: his insistence that behavior could be pursued as a deterministic science amenable to direct manipulation and control, which served as a rallying cry for subsequent generations of behaviorists.

[*Many of the people mentioned in this article are the subjects of independent biographical entries.*]

Bibliography

Works by Loeb

Loeb, J. (1900). *Comparative physiology of the brain and comparative psychology.* New York: Putnam. Summarizes Loeb's research on animal tropisms and discusses the relationship between tropisms and reflexes.

Loeb, J. (1912). *The mechanistic conception of life.* Chicago: University of Chicago Press. Loeb's most widely cited book. It includes essays written over a 20-year period, summarizing not only his research on tropisms but also his controversial work about artificial parthenogenesis, the development of an unfertilized egg through physicochemical means.

Works about Loeb

Hackenberg, T. D. (1995). Jacques Loeb, B. F. Skinner, and the legacy of prediction and control. *Behavior Analyst, 18,* 225–236. Focuses on specific elements of Loeb's approach to biological problems that reemerged in the work of Skinner.

Pauly, P. J. (1987). *Controlling life: Jacques Loeb and the engineering ideal in biology.* New York: Oxford University Press. The most complete biography of Loeb available. Particularly helpful is the discussion of Loeb's engineering outlook and its impact on subsequent developments in biology and psychology.

Timothy D. Hackenberg

LOGICAL POSITIVISM. *See* Philosophy, *article on* Philosophy of Science.

LOGOTHERAPY was founded by Viktor E. Frankl (1905–1997), a survivor of four concentration camps. The camp experiences reinforced within Frankl his theories about human life. The fundamental thesis of logotherapy is that the striving to find a meaning in life is the primary motivational force in people. Lack of meaning leads to what Frankl termed the "existential vacuum," which becomes a breeding ground for potential neuroses. Gordon W. Allport called logotherapy "the most significant psychological movement of our day" (1963). Joseph Fabry, the foremost expositor of logotherapy in North America, describes logotherapy as "healing through meaning." Logotherapy strives to open up the meaning potential for people to actualize. This approach has lowered recidivism rates in the treatment of delinquency, drug addiction, and alcoholism.

The primary principles of logotherapy are that every person ultimately has freedom of choice, that people "will" rather than being driven to meaning, pursue meaning rather than pleasure or power, and that life has unconditional meaning in all circumstances, including suffering and death.

Logotherapy sees the situation of suffering as the opportunity to actualize values, including "attitudinal" values, meaning the attitude taken to the suffering. Death is seen as a positive reality, for only in the face of death is it meaningful to act. Without death, everything could be postponed forever.

Logotherapy has been influential in fostering a more accepting attitude to the religious quest, including being open to the possibility of a world beyond this world, wherein ultimate meaning unfolds. Many leading thanatologists, including Elizabeth Kubler-Ross, were inspired by Frankl. Guilt is likewise a necessary component of a meaningful life, for if one is never guilty one is never responsible. By virtue of being human, all people are guilty—not guilty from, but guilty "toward" future fulfillment. In realizing one's failings, one is awakened to possibilities waiting to be fulfilled. Logotherapy has been accused of giving too much attention to suffering, but, unfortunately, suffering is an unavoidable part of life, which often challenges one's commitment to living. However, Frankl stressed the importance of living responsibly through fulfilling creative, experiential, and attitudinal values, and actualizing meaning.

Some of the techniques employed by logotherapy are "Dereflection" to counter hyperintention, and "Paradoxical Intention" to address phobias and obsessive-compulsive situations. Logotherapy strives to mobilize the defiant power of the human spirit in addressing the human condition both clinically and meta-clinically. The major logotherapy journals are: *The International Forum for Logotherapy,* the *International Journal of Logotherapy and Existential Analysis,* and *Logoteoria/ -terapia/-actitud.*

Bibliography

Fabry, J. B., Bulka, R. P., & Sahakian, W. S. (Eds.). (1995). *Finding meaning in life: Logotherapy.* Northvale, NJ: Aronson.

Frankl, V. E. (1955–1986). *The doctor and the soul: From psychotherapy to logotherapy.* New York: Vintage Books.

Frankl, V. E. (1963–1992). *Man's search for meaning: An introduction to logotherapy.* New York: Simon & Schuster.

Frankl, V. E. (1978–1988). *The unheard cry for meaning: Psychotherapy and humanism.* New York: Simon & Schuster.

Frankl, V. E. (1997). *Man's search for ultimate meaning.* New York: Insight Books.

Reuven P. Bulka

LOMBROSO, CESARE (1835–1909), Italian psychiatrist and anthropologist. Born into a family of Jewish merchants, Lombroso enrolled in the Faculty of Medicine of the University of Pavia in 1852, and in 1858 he received his medical degree from the university after presenting a study on cretinism.

In 1863, Lombroso was appointed clinical professor for mental illness in Pavia, and in 1864 he published his work *L'uomo di genio* (The Man of Genius), in which he attempted to develop a natural history of genius. In this work, he advanced the thesis that genius and madness are closely related, claiming that the genius is the product of a disequilibrium of the nervous system and is condemned to madness by his intellectual grandeur.

In 1870, while performing an autopsy on an elderly farmer—the "bandit Villella"—Lombroso found "atavistic anomalies . . . corroborating the frequent existence of monstrous regressions, . . . that bring man closer to the inferior animals." He would trace the origin of criminal anthropology to this anatomical discovery, and began, with growing conviction, to formulate his hypothesis that delinquency and an anomalous constitution of the individual are closely related, attributing the primal cause of crime to hereditary flaws. In the first edition (1876) of his main work *L'uomo delinquente in rapporto all'antropologia, alla giurisprudenza e alle discipline economiche* (Anthropological, Legal, and Socio-economical Aspects in the Study of the Criminal), Lombroso emphasized the importance of individual and anthropological elements underlying crime and argued that the criminal needed to be cured rather than punished. In this volume he also proposed a classification for criminals according to a rigid anthropological typology (occasional, habitual, born instinctive or tendential, and passionate).

In 1876, Lombroso became professor of forensic medicine and psychiatry in Turin, and in 1880 he helped found the periodical *L'Archivio di Psichiatria, Antropologia Criminale e Scienze Penali*. Between 1885 and 1887, he was nominated a member of the Consiglio Sanitario (Health Council) of the province of Turin, attended the first conference of anthropology, and received a professorship for forensic medicine at the faculty of law of the University of Turin. A number of published volumes reflect his intense scientific activity and the constant political and social commitment that would lead to his membership in the Italian Workers Socialist Party. In 1896, Lombroso was nominated professor of psychiatry and clinical psychiatry at the University of Turin and published a new edition of *L'uomo delinquente* as well as the volume *Genio e degenerazione* (Genius and Degeneration). In the latter work he partially mitigated the thesis previously advanced in the book *Genio e follia*. He began developing an interest in the forensic implications of hypnotic phenomena and took part in the committee entrusted with the study of hypnosis that declared that hypnotic performances were socially harmful.

In the last period of his life, Lombroso became more politically active. He was elected town councilor in Turin in 1902, an office from which he resigned 2 years later, also leaving the Socialist party. In 1905 he published a treatise on appraisals in forensic medicine (*La perizia medico-legale*), and in 1906 he received a specially created chair in criminal anthropology. Lombroso died on 19 October 1909, leaving his mortal remains to the Criminal Anthropology Museum, which he had founded.

Bibliography

Lombroso, C. (1893). *La donna delinquente, la prostituta e la donna normale* (Fratelli Bocca, Ed.). Turin, Italy:

Lombroso, C. (1894). L'uomodi genio in rapporto alla psichiatria, alla stocia ed all'estetica. Turin: Boccia.

Nino Dazzi

LOMOV, BORIS FYODOROVICH (1927–1989), Soviet and Russian psychologist. Born in Nizhni Novgorod, Russia, and an outstanding Soviet and Russian psychologist and corresponding member of the USSR Academy of Sciences, Lomov founded engineering psychology and the institute of psychology, attached to the USSR Academy of Sciences. Lomov proposed the concept of the active human operator in the multilevel mutual adaptation of man and machine, formulated the category of social interaction (*obschenie*), and developed the principles of a systems approach to psychology. His work has also been influential in general, cognitive, and social psychology.

In 1951, Lomov graduated from the psychology section of the Philosophy Department of Leningrad (St. Petersburg) State University, where, in 1954, he defended his candidate thesis. He belonged to the school of V. M. Bekhterev and B. G. Ananiev, the main feature of which was a multidisciplinary approach to the study of man's mind by taking into account diverse forms of man's relationships with the world. In 1959, he founded the first USSR laboratory of engineering psychology. In 1963, he defended his doctoral dissertation in psychology, and in 1966 became the first dean of the psychology department of Leningrad State University. In 1966, he moved to Moscow and became the chairperson of the department of sociology and psychology in the Academy of National Economy, attached to the USSR Council of Ministers. In 1967, Lomov was elected corresponding member of the USSR Pedagogical Academy. From 1968 to 1983, he was president of the USSR Society of Psychologists. In 1971, he founded the Institute of Psychology within the USSR Academy of Sciences and became its first director. Since 1972 he was a member of the International Union of Psychologists Sciences. Twice he was elected its vice president. In 1976, he became a member of the USSR Academy of Sciences. In 1986, he founded a scientific council devoted to the multidisciplinary study of man. The council was attached to the Presidium of the USSR Academy of Sciences.

Lomov's first works were devoted to the study of sensation and perception (touch and kinaesthetics, and space) in the process of developing and designing skills. The revealed regularities permitted him to demonstrate the importance of mental processes (especially of spacial image) in the process of man's interaction with technology. He founded a new branch of psychology—engineering psychology—which investigates the processes and means of information interaction between man and machine. Its main problem was to analyze the psychological activity of the human operator (sensation, perception, anticipation, and decision-making) in the process of the mutual adaptation of man and the operated system.

By studying the problems of interaction between the active human operator and automatic devices under laboratory conditions simulating various life situations, including space flights, Lomov noticed that the joint activities of operators, or their social interaction (communication), is a very important factor in the multilevel mutual adaptation of man and machine. He argued that the category of object-related activity (*deyatelnost*) cannot explain all the psychological phenomena under observation. He introduced an additional category—social interaction (*obshchenie*)—which covered a special class of relations (subject-subject). Before Lomov, a human operator was viewed as an isolated simple element in the control system. He showed that a human operator is a complex, highly organized system interacting with other operators. This interaction significantly affects not only the operator's perception and anticipation of information, but also the speed, precision, and reliability of the actions of all the other operators involved.

Lomov developed the principles of a systems approach to psychology in general, and assumed that mental phenomena are included in the universal interrelationship of the processes of the material world and the unity of diverse qualities of the living organisms. In this connection, he claimed that the main object of psychological cognition is system genesis of the mind, while the main task of psychological science is revealing the laws of the organizational development of integral mental formations at different levels. At the highest level, man is viewed in the system of social relations and is studied as personality. At the next lower level, man (personality) is analyzed from the point of view of structure and dynamics of properties, in the context of activity, communication, and behavior. The next lower level is characterized by the study of mental processes and states: perception, thinking, memory, emotions, and so forth. At the lowest level, psychological science is related to the biology, or neurophysiology, of mental processes. Thus, Lomov tried to show that psychology is gradually turning into a single central science by integrating many other sciences about man.

Bibliography

Books Written and Edited in Russian

Lomov, B. F. (1963). *Man and technology*. Leningrad: Leningrad University Publishing House.
Lomov, B. F. (1968). *Man in the system of control*. Moscow: Znanie.
Lomov, B. F. (1984). Methodological and theoretical problems of psychology. Moscow: Nauka.
Lomov, B. F. (Ed.). (1972). *Sensory and sensori-motor processes*. Moscow: Pedgogika.
Lomov, B. F. (Ed.). (1977). *Engineering psychology: Theory, methodology, and practical application*. Moscow: Nauka.
Lomov, B. F. (Ed.). (1979). *Psychophysics of sensory systems*. Moscow: Nauka.
Lomov, B. F. (Ed.). (1980). *Psychological problems of mutual adaptation of man and machine in the system of control*. Moscow: Nauka.
Lomov, B. F., & Surkov, E. N. (1980). *Anticipation in the structure of activity*. Moscow: Nauka.
Lomov, B. F., Belyeva, A. V., & Nossulenko, V. N. (1988). *Verbal coding in cognitive processes*. Moscow: Nauka.

Articles Written in English

Lomov, B. F. (1969). Engineering psychology in the USSR. In M. Cole & I. Moltzman (Eds.), *A handbook of contemporary Soviet psychology*. New York, London: Basic Books.
Lomov, B. F. (1970). Man and his working environment. *Soviet Science Review*, 1 (2).
Lomov, B. F. (1984). A system of the science of man. *Social Sciences 3*.
Lomov, B. F. (1988). Cognitive science and the mind-body problem. *International Journal of Social Sciences*, 115, 85–96.

Vladimir M. Roussalov

LONELINESS has long been recognized as a common and distressing human problem, although the scientific investigation of loneliness is a relatively recent development. Earlier in this century, clinical theorists such as Frieda Fromm-Reichmann and Harry Stack Sullivan derived ideas about the nature and causes of loneliness from their work with lonely clients. It was not until the 1970s, however, that research on loneliness began to flourish, stimulated by the publication in 1973 of Robert Weiss's seminal book, *Loneliness: The Experience of Emotional and Social Isolation*, and by the development of psychometrically sound measures to assess loneliness.

Definitions and Measurement

Definitions of loneliness vary. Some theorists, such as Sullivan and Weiss, define loneliness as the emotional distress that results when inherent needs for intimacy and companionship are not met. Other theorists emphasize cognitive processes rather than inherent social needs. Two influential proponents of the cognitive approach, Anne Peplau and Daniel Perlman, define loneliness as the unpleasant experience that results from a perceived discrepancy between a person's desired and actual social relationships. From this perspective, when people judge their existing relationships to be deficient, either in quantity or quality, they experience loneliness. Existential theorists, in contrast, regard loneliness as an inevitable aspect of the human condition and an experience that, even if painful, has the potential to contribute to increased self-awareness and renewal.

Despite these points of difference, most theorists agree that loneliness usually results from deficiencies of some sort in a person's social relationships. In addition, a consensus exists that loneliness is a subjective experience; it cannot be equated simply with being alone. This means that people who have relationships, even those who are married, may describe themselves as lonely, and that people who lack relationships do not always feel lonely. Moreover, although some theorists, such as Clark Moustakas, feel that periods of loneliness and solitude can promote creative renewal, most agree that loneliness is typically an aversive experience.

The emotional distress associated with loneliness may take a variety of forms. Research by Carin Rubinstein and Philip Shaver has documented four common reactions: desperation (feelings of abandonment and helplessness), depression, restless boredom, and self-deprecation. Loneliness has been found to be strongly related to, but nonetheless distinct from, depression and low self-esteem. Other work suggests that loneliness may be characterized by feelings of anxiety and hostility.

Weiss proposed that the distress associated with loneliness will take one of two forms, depending on the particular kind of relationship(s) the lonely person lacks. In his view, people who lack an intimate relationship, such as a relationship with a spouse or romantic partner, will experience emotional loneliness, marked by feelings of utter aloneness and pervasive apprehensiveness. In contrast, people who lack ties to a social group, such as a circle of friends, will experience social loneliness, characterized by feelings of boredom, exclusion, and social marginality. Weiss argued further that each kind of loneliness can be alleviated only by overcoming the relevant relational deficit. Thus, even a highly satisfying relationship with an intimate partner cannot compensate for the absence of group ties, and vice versa.

Lonely people also vary with respect to the duration of their loneliness. For some, loneliness tends to resemble a personality trait, in that it persists over time and across different situations. Such persistent distress has been called chronic loneliness, or trait loneliness. For other people, loneliness is time limited and occurs only in specific social contexts. This has been called situational loneliness, or state loneliness. For example, loneliness is quite common among first-term college freshmen, the understandable result of moving to a new setting and leaving friends and family members behind. For most freshmen, this loneliness is short-lived (or situational) and dissipates as they establish new friendships. For a small group, however, this loneliness represents a continuation of the loneliness experienced in high school, and it persists over the course of the year; this group would be considered chronically lonely. Research by Shaver and his colleagues suggests that chronically lonely individuals tend to be resigned to their loneliness and engage in passive, ineffective coping strategies, such as watching television, sleeping, and overeating.

Researchers have tried to incorporate some of these distinctions in measures of loneliness, although no consensus exists about the optimal way to assess loneliness. The most widely used scale, the UCLA Loneliness Scale (Russell, Peplau, & Cutrona, 1980), contains negatively- and positively-worded items that reflect perceived deficiencies in one's relationships. Some scales, such as the UCLA Scale, intentionally omit the terms *lonely* and *loneliness*, allowing people to receive a score suggestive of a high level of loneliness without labeling themselves as lonely. Other scales, such as the State Versus Trait Loneliness Scale, include one or more items that do involve such explicit self-labeling. The latter scale also attempts to capture the duration of loneliness. Measures of loneliness also differ in the extent to which they assess the particular emotional dimensions of loneliness or the interpersonal domains (e.g., friendships and family relationships) in which difficulties are experienced. Existing measures of loneliness and their conceptual underpinnings have been reviewed by Philip Shaver and Kelly Brennan and by Carol Marangoni and William Ickes.

Causes

Many factors may contribute to the difficulties that some people experience in establishing and maintaining satisfying social relationships. Social inhibition, deficient social skills, or negative social schemas may underlie loneliness for some people. For others, loneliness may be the result of insufficient resources needed to facilitate social interaction or environmental factors that limit opportunities to interact with compatible people. For some people, loneliness arises from a combination of personal vulnerabilities and environmental obstacles.

Individual Characteristics. Lonely people describe themselves as shy and self-conscious in social situations and report difficulty introducing themselves to others, initiating social contact, participating in groups, enjoying themselves at parties, asserting themselves, taking social risks, and resolving interpersonal conflicts. Laboratory studies of acquaintanceship conducted by Warren Jones and others suggest that lonely college students experience difficulty making self-disclosures to their interaction partners, ask fewer questions of their partners, talk more about themselves, change the topic of conversation arbitrarily, and fail to reciprocate eye contact reliably. Lonely older adults have been found to be relatively unskilled at encoding others' expressive nonverbal communications. Jones summarized this evidence as indicating that lonely individuals, compared to nonlonely individuals, tend to be more self-absorbed and less responsive in their interactions with others.

Negative social perceptions have been implicated, as well, as possible causes of loneliness. Lonely individuals report greater cynicism and mistrust toward others than do nonlonely individuals. In Jones's research on acquaintanceship, lonely students evaluated themselves negatively and expected their interaction partners to rate them negatively. The lonely students also rated their partners critically and expressed less desire for future contact, suggesting a possible defensive pattern of rejecting others before being rejected.

Recent work on adult attachment suggests that early experiences in life, particularly interactions with parents, lead to the formation of cognitive schemas, or internalized working models, that represent views of both the self and others. These cognitive schemas include generalized expectations of how other people are likely to relate to the self and, as such, they serve as templates that guide interpersonal motivations, behavior, and emotions throughout life. Negative schemas may contribute to relationship difficulties in adulthood, leading some researchers to suggest that insecure attachment styles are linked to loneliness in adulthood.

Resource Limitations. Initiating and maintaining social ties requires practical resources, such as time and money, in addition to psychological resources. Even something as simple as socializing with others for an evening may entail a variety of expenses, including the costs associated with transportation, meals, entertainment, and perhaps child care. Not surprisingly, levels of loneliness are higher among people with lower incomes and among the unemployed.

Environmental Characteristics. Characteristics of the environment may contribute to loneliness for some people. People tend to form relationships most easily in environments that bring them into contact with others who share similar backgrounds and values. Living or working in settings where one is different from others can limit opportunities to form satisfying relationships. In a classic study of friendships in old age, Zena Blau demonstrated the power of the environment to influence our social lives. She found that the social relationships of widows were influenced by the prevalence of other widows in the local area. In areas where widowhood was uncommon, widows tended to

have fewer social ties. Such regional variations would be difficult to explain in terms of personality or other psychological factors.

Some environments, such as schools and workplaces, also influence the quality of the social interactions that take place. Some settings encourage cooperation and friendliness among participants, whereas others encourage competitiveness and mistrust. In an innovative program of research on what has been called the jigsaw classroom, Elliot Aronson and his colleagues demonstrated that having elementary school children cooperate in teaching pieces of classroom lessons to each other contributed to greater trust and friendliness when compared to children in traditional classrooms. Moreover, these social gains were realized without compromising academic achievement. Thus, settings that encourage people to work together on problem-solving tasks and shared goals may not only promote organizational objectives but also foster friendliness and reduce social isolation.

Demographic Patterns

Demographic factors such as age, gender, marital status, and socioeconomic status may predispose some groups of people to experience greater loneliness than others. Rates of loneliness tend to be highest in adolescence and young adulthood and then decline steadily across the life course, until advanced old age. After age 80 or 85, levels of loneliness appear to increase, perhaps as a result of increased rates of widowhood or poor health in this age group.

Loneliness is also more common among the unmarried than the married. Differences exist among the unmarried as well, with never-married individuals reporting less loneliness than divorced and widowed individuals in a number of studies. Such comparisons highlight the important role that the loss of a primary relationship plays in precipitating loneliness.

Gender differences in loneliness vary across studies, and this variation appears to be linked to the way in which loneliness is measured. When people are asked directly whether they are lonely, women often report greater loneliness. When loneliness is assessed without explicit references to loneliness, men tend to report greater loneliness. One explanation that has been suggested for this measure-specific difference is that men are less willing than women to admit feeling lonely, perhaps because loneliness is more stigmatizing for men. Experimental research by Perlman and others supports this explanation in that hypothetical lonely stimulus figures tend to be evaluated more negatively if they are male than if they are female. Thus, the apparent reluctance of men to disclose their loneliness may be grounded in realistic expectations of rejection by others.

Levels of loneliness are higher among individuals

with lower socioeconomic status, which is probably best explained in terms of resource and environmental factors. In writing about the very poor, Marc Pilisuk noted that "the routine affronts from a noxious and sparse environment" not only threaten health and well-being but also contribute to the breakdown of social ties. Research documenting a link between loneliness and a high level of life stress supports this view.

Relatively little work has examined cross-cultural variations in loneliness, although some social critics argue that cultural values in the United States make Americans susceptible to loneliness. They believe that traditional cultural emphases on individualism, independence, and privacy create conditions that are not conducive to the formation of intimate, interdependent relationships. Other critics suggest that a cultural preoccupation with couple relationships, such as marital relationships or romantic relationships, leads other kinds of social ties to be devalued. Consistent with this latter idea, lonely young adults tend to believe that developing a romantic relationship will help them overcome their loneliness, whereas empirical evidence suggests that the formation of friendships plays a more substantial role in helping young adults overcome loneliness.

[See also Attachment; and Privacy.]

Bibliography

Asher, S. R., Hymel, S., & Renshaw, P. D. (1984). Loneliness in children. *Child Development*, 55, 1456–1464.

Hojat, M., & Crandall, R. (Eds.). (1987). *Loneliness: Theory, research, and applications.* Newbury Park, CA: Sage. (Originally published as a special issue of the *Journal of Social Behavior and Personality*.)

Jones, W. H., & Carver, M. D. (1991). Adjustment and coping implications of loneliness. In C. R. Snyder & D. R. Forsyth (Eds.), *Handbook of social and clinical psychology* (pp. 395–415). New York: Pergamon Press.

Marangoni, C., & Ickes, W. (1989). Loneliness: A theoretical review with implications for measurement. *Journal of Social and Personal Relationships*, 6, 93–128.

Peplau, L. A., & Perlman, D. (Eds.). (1982). *Loneliness: A sourcebook of current theory, research, and therapy* (pp. 135–151). New York: Wiley-Interscience.

Rook, K. S. (1984). Promoting social bonding. *American Psychologist*, 39, 1389–1407.

Russell, D., Peplau, L. A., & Cutrona, C. E. (1980). The revised UCLA Loneliness Scale: Concurrent and discriminant validity evidence. *Journal of Personality and Social Psychology*, 39, 472–480.

Shaver, P. R., & Brennan, K. A. (1991). Measures of depression and loneliness. In J. P. Robinson, P. R. Shaver, & L. S. Wrightsman (Eds.), *Measures of personality and social psychology* (Vol. 1, pp. 195–289). San Diego, CA: Academic Press.

Weiss, R. S. (1973). *Loneliness: The experience of emotional and social isolation.* Cambridge, MA: MIT Press.

Karen S. Rook

LONGITUDINAL RESEARCH is sometimes known as *diachronic research*, which means that the variable of interest is observed in such a way as to uncover changes that occur over successive periods of time. A case in point would be longitudinal research on child development, in which the children are studied repeatedly over a period of time. However, many studies of child development simply examine children of different ages simultaneously, which is known as *cross-sectional research*, and is also sometimes called *synchronic research*, because it takes a slice of time and examines the situation only at one particular point. Problems can arise when cross-sectional research is used to study the life course of some variable of interest, as the results may be limited to the particular slice of time studied. For example, those who were age 40 in 1999 may have had different life experiences at age 10 (in 1969) from those who were 10 years old in 1999.

If the people who are studied can be said to represent a "generation" that has experienced a significant life event (birth, marriage, etc.) during the same period of time, the group or generation is called a *cohort*. Longitudinal research could be used to track several different cohorts to find out, for example, whether a generation gap on some variable is observable. In some studies the researchers are not only interested in measuring one or more cohorts repeatedly through time, but are also interested in making age comparisons on some variable. They may be interested in the period (or calendar date) of measurements as well, though this could complicate the analysis because any combination of two dimensions will then determine the third. [See Cohort Effects.]

Longitudinal data are usually collected prospectively, which means the participants are tracked and measured over time, which is known as a *panel study* by sociologists and economists, but data can also be gotten retrospectively from historical records. For example, a classic prospective study of intellectual abilities was that begun by Lewis Terman and his associates in 1921. [See the biography of Terman.] The investigation tracked the psychosocial and intellectual development of a cohort of over a thousand gifted California boys and girls from preadolescence through adulthood. More recently, using a retrospective approach, Howard S. Friedman et al. have picked up the earlier trail by gathering the death certificates of the participants in Terman's study (*American Psychologist*, 1995, 50, 69–78). Coding the dates and causes of death, these researchers have identified psychosocial and behavioral "risk" factors that were correlated with premature death. For example, they found that the trauma of divorce predicted premature mortality, as did certain personality factors. The findings were interpreted as providing further confirmation of the view in psychology and medicine that a cluster of individual and social factors is critical to longevity.

Not all longitudinal studies follow the participants over that long a period. In another prominent study, Project Talent, the researchers tested 440,000 high-school students in 1960 and then used mailed surveys to find out about the participants' post-high-school education and work experiences. In another example of longitudinal research, Elizabeth W. Morrison focused on the socialization effects of information seeking in 135 staff accountants during their first 6 months of employment (*Journal of Applied Psychology*, 1993, *78*, 173–183). Using data reported by the workers themselves (called self-report data), the researcher found a number of correlations which led her to conclude that the newcomers tended to seek out knowledge and take an active role in adjusting to their environment.

Longitudinal research has come to play a significant role in developmental psychology and medicine. In medical research, for example, an important longitudinal study was inaugurated by the U.S. Public Health Service in 1948—known as the Framingham heart study. Responding to concerns about the soaring coronary disease rate in the United States, this study has followed several thousand residents of Framingham, Massachusetts. The results have increased our understanding of risk factors that predict cardiovascular disease. In 1960, cigarette smoking was first revealed to be a risk factor and in 1961, high blood pressure was found to be another risk factor. The correlational findings in this study have led to randomized clinical trials, which have confirmed the preventive approach to combating heart disease by exercise, not smoking, lowering harmful cholesterol, and reducing stress, blood pressure, and obesity.

[*See also* Nonrandomized Designs.]

Bibliography

Cooley, W. W., & Lohnes, P. R. (1968). *Predicting development of young adults.* Palo Alto, CA: American Institutes for Research. Project Talent, the longitudinal study of a large representative sample that began when the participants were in high school.

Diggle, P. J., Liang, K.-Y., & Zeger, S. L. (1994). *Analysis of longitudinal data.* Oxford, U.K.: Oxford University Press. An advanced text that describes statistical models and methods for the analysis of longitudinal data.

Rosnow, R. L. (1981). *Paradigms in transition: The methodology of social inquiry.* New York: Oxford University Press. Examines the limits and uses of synchronic and diachronic research in the study of behavior.

Rosnow, R. L., & Rosenthal, R. (1999). *Beginning behavioral research: A conceptual primer* (3rd ed.). New York: Prentice Hall. Chapter 8 contains a simplified introduction to longitudinal research, the cohort concept, certain problems of interpretation, and also places this research in the broader context of other nonrandomized research.

Terman, L. M., assisted by Baldwin, B. T., Bronson. E., DeVoss, J. C., Fuller, F., Goodenough, F. L., Kelley, T. L., Lima, M., Marshall, H., Moore, A. H., Raubenheimer, A. S., Ruch, G. M., Wiloughby, R. L., Wyman, J. B., & Yates, D. H. (1925). *Genetic studies of genius: Vol. 1. Mental and physical traits of a thousand gifted children.* Stanford, CA: Stanford University Press. The inaugural volume of Terman's classic longitudinal study of gifted children.

Terman, L. M., & Oden, M. H. (1947). *Genetic studies of genius: Vol. 4. The gifted child grows up.* Stanford, CA: Stanford University Press. The summation volume of Terman's classic research.

U.S. National Heart Institute. (1966). *The Framingham heart study: Habits and coronary heart disease* (Public Health Service Publication No. 1515, Bethesda, MD). Examines the results of this longitudinal study through the mid-1960s.

Ralph L. Rosnow

LONG-TERM POTENTIATION. Virtually all notions about memory hold dear the central notion that learning relies on the modification of synaptic function. In recent years considerable attention has focused on one particular form of use-dependent synaptic plasticity known as long-term potentiation (LTP). LTP was first discovered by Terje Lomo, who observed that repetitive high-frequency electrical stimulations of the pathway from the cortex to the hippocampus resulted in a steeper rise time of the excitatory synaptic potential as well as recruitment of spike activity from a greater number of cells. Moreover, these changes in synaptic and cellular responses to subsequent single shocks lasted several hours, suggesting the possibility of a lasting memory mechanism.

Two key properties of LTP are most notable. First, LTP is *specific* to those synapses activated during stimulation. Other neighboring synapses, even on the same neurons, are not altered. This phenomenon parallels the natural specificity of our memories, and would be a key requirement of any useful cellular memory mechanism. The property of specificity may be key to the storage capacity of brain structures because each cell can participate in the representation of multiple memories composed from distinct subsets of its synaptic inputs.

Second, LTP is *associative*, in that potentiation characteristically occurs across multiple inputs that are stimulated simultaneously. The property of associativity is consistent with Hebb's (1949) postulate that increasing synaptic efficacy requires the repeated activation of a presynaptic element *and* its participation in the success in firing the postsynaptic cell, as indeed occurs in associative LTP when several inputs are simultaneously active. [*See the biography of Hebb.*]

Considerable evidence has now accumulated revealing the cellular and molecular mechanisms that mediate the properties of different forms of LTP, as well as the cousin synaptic plasticity mechanism, called *long-term depression*, in both the hippocampus and the neocortex (Bear, 1996; Bliss & Collingridge, 1993; Madison, Malenka, & Nicoll, 1991; Malenka, 1994).

Is There a Connection Between LTP and Memory?

As Stevens (1996) put it, the mechanism of LTP is so attractive that it would be a shame if LTP turned out not to be a memory device. But there should be no doubt about the fact that LTP is not memory: it is a laboratory phenomenon not observed in nature. The best we can hope for is that LTP and memory share some of their physiological and molecular bases. Evidence from two general strategies has emerged to provide supporting connections between LTP and memory.

Behavioral LTP. One strategy is to determine if learning produces changes in synaptic physiology similar to the increases in synaptic and cellular responses that occur after LTP. LeDoux and colleagues (Rogan, Staubli, & LeDoux, 1997) offered the most compelling evidence to date that these aspects of LTP are a consequence of natural learning. In this case the circuit under study was the pathway from the medial geniculate nucleus of the thalamus to the lateral amygdala nucleus, which is part of the critical circuit for auditory fear conditioning. These investigators found that repeated pairings of auditory stimuli and foot shocks train rats to fear the tones. Furthermore, this learning experience alters evoked sensory responses to the tones in the same way as LTP in that pathway. Thus, in rats with properly timed tone-shock pairings, tones produce evoked potentials of greater slope and amplitude, as does electrical stimulus trains applied to this pathway. No enhancement of field potentials was observed with unpaired tone and foot shock presentations, even though this conditioning control leads to as much of a behavioral response (freezing) as paired presentations, because even the unpaired control rats learn to freeze to the environmental context where shocks are received. Furthermore, this behavioral LTP is enduring,

lasting at least a few days, as long as the behavioral response during extinction trials.

Blocking LTP and Memory. Perhaps the most compelling and straightforward data on a potential connection between the molecular basis of LTP and memory has come from experiments where a drug is used to block LTP and, correspondingly, prevent learning. These studies were based on the observations that induction of the most prominent form of hippocampal LTP is dependent on a specific glutamate receptor, N-methyl-D-aspartate (NMDA), and that drugs such as D-2-amino-5-phosphonovalerate (AP5) selectively block the NMDA receptor and prevent hippocampal LTP while sparing normal synaptic transmission. Thus, to the extent that the role of the NMDA receptor is fully selective to plasticity, one might predict that these drugs would indeed block new learning without affecting nonlearning performance or retention of learning normally accomplished prior to drug treatment.

Consistent with these predictions, some of strongest evidence supporting a connection between LTP and memory has come from demonstrations that drug-induced blockade of hippocampal NMDA receptors prevents hippocampal-dependent spatial learning (Morris, Anderson, Lynch, & Baudry, 1986). Additional experiments showed no effect of AP5 on retention of the same spatial learning when training was accomplished prior to drug treatment. This would be fully predicted because NMDA receptors are viewed as required only for the induction of LTP and not for its maintenance. In addition, targeted genetic manipulations have now shown that knocking out NMDA receptors (McHugh, Blum, Tsien, Tonegawa, & Wilson, 1996) or later stages in the cascade of molecular triggers for maintenance of LTP (e.g., Silva, Paylor, Wehner, & Tonegawa, 1992) also results in severe memory impairments. These studies have also shown some restrictions on the role of NMDA receptor-mediated LTP in spatial memory. Recent experiments have indicated that blocking NMDA-dependent LTP does not necessarily prevent the encoding of a new spatial environment (Bannerman, Good, Butcher, Ramsay, & Morris, 1995). However, NMDA-dependent LTP may be necessary for remembering new episodes within a familiar space (Steele & Morris, 1999).

Bibliography

Bannerman, D. M., Good, M. A., Butcher, S. P., Ramsay, M., & Morris, R. G. M. (1995). Prior experience and N-methyl-D-aspartate receptor blockade dissociate components of spatial learning in the watermaze. *Nature, 378*, 182–186.

Bear, M. F. (1996). A synaptic basis for memory storage in the cerebral cortex. *Proceedings of the National Academy of Science, 93*, 13453–13459.

Bliss, T.V.P., & Collingridge, G. L. (1993). A synaptic model of memory: Long-term potentiation in the hippocampus. *Nature, 361*, 31–39.

Hebb, D. O. (1949). *The organization of behavior.* New York: Wiley.

Madison, D. V., Malenka, R. C., & Nicoll, R. A. (1991). Mechanisms underlying long-term potentiation of synaptic transmission. *Annual Review of Neuroscience, 14*, 379–397.

Malenka, R. C. (1994). Synaptic plasticity in the hippocampus: LTP and LTD. *Cell, 78*, 535–538.

McHugh, T. J., Blum, K. I., Tsien, J. Z., Tonegawa, S., & Wilson, M. A. (1996). Impaired hippocampal representation of space in CA1-specific NMDAR1 knockout mice. *Cell, 87*, 1339–1349.

Morris, R. G. M., Anderson, E., Lynch, G. S., & Baudry, M. (1986). Selective impairment of learning and blockade of long-term potentiation by an N-methyl-D-aspartate receptor antagonist, APS. *Nature, 319*, 774–776.

Rogan, M. T., Staubli, U. V., & LeDoux, J. E. (1997). Fear conditioning induces associative long-term potentiation in the amygdala. *Nature, 390*, 604–607.

Silva, A. J., Paylor, C. F. R., Wehner, J. W., & Tonegawa, S. (1992). Impaired spatial learning in a-calcium-calmodulin kinase II mutant mice. *Science, 257*, 206–211.

Steele, R. J., & Morris, R. G. M. (1999). Delay dependent impairment in matching-to-place task with chronic and intrahippocampal infusion of the NMDA-antagonist D-AP5. *Hippocampus, 9*, 118–136.

Stevens, C. F. (1996). Strengths and weaknesses in memory. *Nature, 381*, 471–472.

Howard Eichenbaum

LORENZ, KONRAD

LORENZ, KONRAD (1903–1989), Austrian ethologist. Lorenz was born in Altenberg, near Vienna, Austria, to Adolf Lorenz and Emma Lecher Lorenz, both medical doctors. Always fascinated with animals, he kept a menagerie at home. His father insisted that he become a physician; Lorenz received his medical degree (1928) from the University of Vienna. Then, studying at Ferdinand Hochstetter's Anatomical Institute at the University, he received his doctorate in zoology in 1933. In 1927, he married Margarethe Gebhart, also a doctor. After serving as an assistant in the Anatomical Institute, Lorenz was a *Privatdozent* (unpaid instructor) at the University of Vienna from 1937 to 1940.

During the 1930s, Lorenz established the major theoretical foundations of classical ethology. His basic insight, shared with predecessors like Oskar Heinroth, Wallace Craig, and Charles Otis Whitman, was that some "instinctive" behavior patterns were fixed in form and just as characteristic of species as organs. He planned to analyze instinctive behavior using comparative techniques.

In several seminal papers, Lorenz set forth the theoretical concerns, findings, investigatory methods, and remaining problems of "his" new science. Many of the details of Lorenz's analyses of behavior from the 1930s have been shown to be incomplete or incorrect. He demonstrated, however, that animal instinctive behavior could be analyzed; documented a repertoire of standard techniques for its comparative study; legitimated the use of behavioral characteristics as a tool in phylogenetic analysis; and posed a number of unsolved research problems.

Lorenz discovered several major concepts still useful for behavior study: (1) the fixed action pattern: an inherited, characteristic, relatively complex movement pattern shared by all members of a species; (2) the releaser or sign stimulus: a specific environmental stimulus, the perception of which is sufficient to cause the performance of a fixed action pattern—an important corollary was that an animal's conspecifics could be the source of many of these stimuli; and (3) imprinting, a rapid, quite stable form of learning in which a social animal's early experiences affect its later social or sexual behavior, apparently without the need for reinforcement. The most famous example is Lorenz himself being followed by a flock of greylag goslings. The birds saw Lorenz, not their parents, immediately upon hatching; they then followed him instead.

The comparative study of human and animal mentation was a dominant theme throughout Lorenz's work. He argued that perceptual and cognitive apparatus could be treated like any other organs that had evolved in response to the environment. Even the "disposition to learn" items crucial to survival could be so explained. Evolutionary psychology and sociobiology are among the contemporary developments that build on these foundations.

During World War II, Lorenz at first benefited from the political circumstances in Germany and Austria. He joined the Nazi party in 1938 and was affiliated with its Race Policy Department. In many of his publications from 1938 to 1943, he associated biology and ethology with the goals of nazism, especially ethnic purification. His animal research was finally funded. In 1940, he was called to the professorship of psychology at the Albertus-University in Koenigsberg, East Prussia (now Kaliningrad, Russia). Whether his Nazi affiliation helped, hindered, or had no effect on this appointment is unclear. Lorenz established an institute for the study of animal behavior and began work with his first graduate student, but after only a year, in October 1941, he was drafted into the German army. He served for about 2 years as a physician in Posen (now Poznan), Poland, where, according to Ute Deichmann (*Biologists Under Hitler*, Cambridge, Mass., 1996), he helped to carry out a psychological testing program to determine mental characteristics of German-Polish "racial mixtures." Then he served in the Second Medical Corps of the 206th Infantry Division and was captured in the Battle of Vitebsk, June 1944.

After being held in various POW camps in the USSR, he was released in December 1947 and returned to Austria in 1948. The postwar situation made research support temporarily impossible, so Lorenz turned to popular writing. His first book of animal behavior stories, *King Solomon's Ring*, was published to great acclaim (Vienna, 1949; New York, 1952). By 1949, international symposia in ethology recommenced. Led by Niko Tinbergen, colleagues welcomed Lorenz in spite of lingering worries concerning his World War II activities, about which he was never explicit.

In the 1950s, critiques of ethology led to a refinement of some key ethological concepts. By the 1960s, classical ethology had ramified into several "schools" of animal behavior study, in Germany, England, Holland, and the United States. Lorenz's work on animal behavior was funded by the Max-Planck Institute (Germany) from 1951 until his retirement in 1973. His institute in Seewiesen, Bavaria, Germany, trained generations of students of animal behavior.

Lorenz's interests in ethology and evolutionary psychology combined with his longstanding concern about human degeneration. He always believed that humanity was in danger from the allegedly deleterious effects of civilization. Lorenz hypothesized varied causes for these effects, successively postulating racial degeneration, uninhibited aggression, and environmental degradation during his career. In *On Aggression* (1966), Lorenz claimed that intraspecies aggression, normally an adaptive phenomenon in animals, has turned deadly in humans because our development of new weapons that can kill at a distance has outrun our innate inhibitions against killing. This popular work incited an international debate on the biological bases of human behavior. In his last years, the German Green party lionized him, since he finally ascribed our species' coming doom to exploitation of the environment.

Lorenz, Niko Tinbergen, and Karl von Frisch were awarded the Nobel Prize in medicine in 1973, for the founding of ethology. At his home in Altenberg, Austria, after his retirement, Lorenz continued his research and writing, producing comprehensive studies of greylag geese, and theoretical studies of animal and human behavior, with support from the Austrian Academy of Sciences, until his death.

Bibliography

Works by Lorenz

Lorenz, K. Z. (1970). Companions as factors in the bird's environment. In *Studies in animal and human behaviour* (2 vols.) (Robert Martin, Trans.). Cambridge, MA: Harvard University Press. (Original work published 1935.) Lorenz's encyclopedic report about releasers/sign stimuli and how members of a species may elicit important behaviors in each other.

Lorenz, K. Z. (1937). Ueber den Begriff der Instinkthandlung. *Folia Biotheoretica 2*, 17–50. Key work in which Lorenz discards the idea that instinctive behaviors are all made up of chain reflexes and accepts that some behaviors are endogenously produced. Unfortunately a translation has never been published.

Lorenz, K. Z. (1957). Comparative study of behavior. In C. H. Schiller (Ed. and Trans.), *Instinctive behaviour: The development of a modern concept*. London: Methuen. (Original work published 1939.) Comprehensive review of the then-current status of ethological theory.

Lorenz, K. Z. (1975). Kant's doctrine of the *a priori* in the light of contemporary biology. In Richard I. Evans (1975), *Konrad Lorenz: The man and his ideas*. New York: Harcourt Brace Jovanovich. (Original work published 1941.) Lorenz's first major treatment of evolutionary psychology, and his best.

Lorenz, K. Z. (1966). *On aggression* (Marjorie Kerr Wilson, Trans.). New York: Harcourt, Brace & World. (Original work published 1963)

Lorenz, K. Z. (1996). *The natural science of the human species: An introduction to comparative behavioral research: "The Russian manuscript" (1944–1948)* (Robert D. Martin, Trans.). Cambridge, MA: MIT Press. Lorenz's voluminous manuscript, written while he was a POW in Russia during World War II. Reviews major contemporary schools of psychology, outlines techniques of comparative behavioral research, discusses key issues in evolutionary psychology, and reviews key historical developments in ethology.

Works about Lorenz

Evans, R. I. (1975). *Konrad Lorenz: The man and his ideas*. New York: Harcourt Brace Jovanovich. Contains several interviews with Lorenz on key ethological concepts, an essay by Donald T. Campbell, "Reintroducing Konrad Lorenz to psychology," translations of four of Lorenz's papers, and a bibliography of Lorenz's works.

Lehrman, D. S. (1953). A critique of Konrad Lorenz's theory of instinctive behavior. *Quarterly Review of Biology, 28*, 337–363. The classic critical paper that brought Lorenz's work to the attention of American students of animal behavior.

Nisbett, A. (1977). *Konrad Lorenz: A biography*. New York: Harcourt Brace Jovanovich. A journalist's account based on extensive interviews with Lorenz.

Thorpe, W. H. (1979). *The origins and rise of ethology*. New York: Praeger. Written by one of the pioneers in the field. The chapter "The establishment of ethology in continental Europe (1910–1950)" discusses Lorenz's work in the context of contemporary psychology and biology, along with the contributions of others.

Theodora J. Kalikow

LOSS. *See* Grief and Loss.

LOTZE, RUDOLF HERMANN (1817–1881), German philosopher, psychologist, and physiologist. Lotze was the leading spirit behind the formation of an experimental psychology that would be primarily empirical (in the philosophical sense) and that would have physiology as its experimental and disciplinary model. As a psychologist, he was best known for a theory of space perception, the idea of local signs. Lotze's goal was best realized by his student Georg E. Müller; two of the three leading figures in the beginning of experimental psychology, Müller and Carl Stumpf, were Lotze's students both for their doctorates and, more important, for their first step into faculty positions (the *Habilitation*). Lotze was later able to make other important moves that helped each to advance in their careers.

Lotze was born the son of a physician who served the Saxon army in Bautzen, in the isolated Sorb region of Saxony. When it came time for him to attend University of Leipzig, he combined his medical study (under Ernst H. Weber and A. W. Volkmann) with extensive studies of philosophy (primarily under Christian Hermann Weisse) and physics (under Gustav T. Fechner). These studies enabled him to complete a dissertation in medicine that had an extensive philosophical component. More important for his future career, he became a member of the Leipzig faculty in both medicine (1839) and philosophy (1840). He was promoted to a lower ranking paid position, *ausserordentlicher Professor* for philosophy, in 1843.

Lotze's book *Allgemeine Pathologie und Therapie als mechanischer Naturwissenschaften* (General Pathology and Therapy as Mechanical Natural Sciences; Leipzig, 1842) points to the reason for his later importance for experimental psychology. This work insisted on mechanistic explanations of medical findings and a rejection of idealistic system building, while accommodating a teleological, almost Hegelian/idealistic, sense of origins, and was to permit him to become accepted during the period of ideological rigidity in Germany that followed the 1848 revolutions. On the basis of the philosophical importance of his Leipzig books, he was selected in 1844 to be the successor, as *Ordinarius* (senior faculty position) for philosophy, of Johann Friedrich Herbart in Göttingen, a position where he remained until just before his death in 1881.

Part of Lotze's importance derives from his ability to take a middle position in the political and philosophical conflicts of the mid-nineteenth century. For many of the German states, philosophy professors needed to be seen as supports of the state and the religious beliefs (usually Lutheran, with varying degrees of orthodoxy) of the government. Although materialism had been stylish in the eighteenth century, the idea of materialism became anathema after the revolution of 1848. Three physiology *Privatdozenten*—Ludwig Büchner, Jakob Moleschott, and Carl Vogt—all lost their positions when they were labeled as materialists. Carl Ludwig was never able to receive a position in Prussia, since he had also been so labeled. In this climate, only a claim to idealist philosophy (thus following Leibniz) legitimized a philosophical position. Lotze's gift was to articulate positions in which a mechanist view of physiology (and ultimately psychology) could be presented, while his ultimate philosophical position was seen to be idealist. Lotze's revision of Weisse's "local signs" also became a source of Hermann Helmholtz's empirical theory of space perception.

Lotze was held in high esteem by Adolph Trendelenburg, who is usually labeled an Aristotelian. Trendelenburg, Hegel's successor, who served as somewhat of an antithesis to Hegel's idealism, sought to have Lotze called to a vacant philosophy chair in Berlin. Although Lotze refused the offer from Berlin, he became close to Trendelenburg's student Franz Brentano, and he became the patron of the careers of two important early students of Brentano, Carl Stumpf and Anton Marty, at a time when Brentano could not sponsor their dissertations.

The importance for early experimental psychology of Lotze's insistence on mechanistic theories of mind (in comparison with Wilhelm Wundt, whose "creative synthesis" was voluntaristic) is severely underestimated. At the time, however, a wide range of psychologists and philosophers saw him as a preeminent representative of an empirical and empiricistic psychology. On the death of Trendelenburg in 1872, Lotze was recognized as the premier philosopher in Germany and was frequently sought out by visiting American students of surprisingly heterogeneous opinions (for example, the idealist Josiah Royce and the experimental psychologist J. McKeen Cattell), who especially valued him for his ideas about psychology. At the same time, starting from his *Medical Psychology* (Leipzig, 1852), he was also an expositor and critic of the psychophysical measurement and parallelism doctrines of his close personal friend Gustav T. Fechner.

Although Lotze's doctrines became important as a justification for the mechanistic movement in German physiology in the 1840s to 1860s, it was only in the 1870s, after the University of Göttingen had become part of the Prussian system, that Lotze's importance dramatically increased. Even though Lotze is not much studied today, he superbly identified the difficulties of rigidly taking either an idealistic or empiricistic position, and in addition to future experimental psychologists, had important students who did not have careers in psychology, including Wilhelm Windelband (philosophy) and Gottlob Frege (logic). He had an important influence on Frege's development of a formal logic, and in the *Microcosmos* (Leipzig, 1856–1864) he published a new version of his psychology.

Lotze seemed to be able to place his students at will in Austrian university positions (for example, Marty in Czernowitz [in present-day Ukraine], 1875; Stumpf in Prague, 1879; Müller in Czernowitz as Marty's replacement in 1880; and Karl Ueberhorst as Müller's replacement in 1881). Lotze was the sponsor of important work for the students who were accepted into the Göttingen faculty in the 1870s and who later were central to experimental psychology (for example, for Stumpf's theory of space and Müller's review and drastic revision of Fechner's psychophysics).

In 1880, encouraged and attracted by Helmholtz and Eduard Zeller, who were then jointly sponsoring the early memory work of Hermann Ebbinghaus, Lotze finally accepted the offer of chairs in both philosophy and physiology at Berlin. In this move, he apparently was able to assure that Müller became his successor and *Ordinarius* in Göttingen. He died of pneumonia in Berlin before he had completed his first semester.

[*Many of the people mentioned in this article are the subjects of independent biographical entries.*]

Bibliography

Gotesky, R. (1967). Rudolf Hermann Lotze. In P. Edwards (Ed.), *The encyclopedia of philosophy* (Vol. 5, pp. 87–89). New York: Macmillan. The standard, somewhat Anglophone, source on Lotze, identifying him as an idealist metaphysician. Although this philosophically oriented treatment deemphasizes Lotze's role in noting the importance of mechanism for science, it includes a clear exposition of the way in which Lotze decoupled mechanism from materialism and thus provided opportunities for a mechanist experimental psychology to come into being. Provides good coverage of Lotze's ideas on psychological topics, although without clearly identifying him as a celebrated psychologist. And the statement that Lotze left no school serves him poorly, since it ignores his role as a teacher of Windelband and Frege, and his influences through G. E. Müller on physiological reductionism in psychology, through Stumpf on Edmund Husserl and the Gestaltists, and through Hans Cornelius on Theodor Adorno and Max Horkheimer.

Häußler, J. N. (1987). Hermann Lotze. In *Neue deutsche Biographie* (Vol. 15, pp. 255–256). Berlin: Duncker & Humblot. The standard authoritative short work on Lotze, containing good descriptions of his importance as a philosopher and his philosophical orientations; especially clear on the significance of his mechanistic doctrines for his philosophy.

Lotze, R. H. (1948). In *Encyclopedia Brittanica* (Vol. 14, pp. 406–407). Chicago: Encyclopedia Brittanica. For nineteenth-century philosopher-psychologists, articles like this from an older encyclopedia (the *Encyclopedia Brittanica* presented much the same article from the 11th edition until the 1960s or so), provide a more appropriate view of the role of such psychologists than recent philosophical discussions that fail to place the discussion in a nineteenth-century context. In addition, the bibliography for this article is full of contemporary and near-contemporary sources that situate Lotze well.

Pastore, N. (1971). *Selective history of theories of visual perception.* New York: Oxford University Press. Probably the most accessible source for understanding Lotze's theory of local signs as a theory of spatial perception.

Stumpf, C. (1919). Errinerung an Franz Brentano [Remembering Franz Brentano]. In O. Kraus (Ed.), *Franz Brentano: Zur Kenntnis seines Lebens und Seiner Lehre* [Franz Brentano: Toward knowing his life and teachings] (pp. 85–149). Munich: Beck. This piece, by one of Lotze's most sympathetic students, is the one work that clearly indicates the intimate connection of Lotze and Brentano in the 1870s. Stumpf appears to have written the piece from his own exhaustive collection of letters, which, however, are not in any single archive.

Woodward, W. R. (in press). *From mechanism to value: Hermann Lotze, physician, philosopher, psychologist (1817–1881).* New York: Cambridge University Press. An extended treatment of Lotze that explicates his unusually complex role in psychology, philosophy, and the culture of his time.

Edward J. Haupt

LOVE. [*This entry comprises two articles. The lead article defines and discusses the nature and conceptions of love, with emphasis on the phenomenon as a social psychological construct. The companion article provides a broad overview on the psychology of religious or spiritual love and devotion. See also* Attraction; Friendship; *and* Intimacy.]

An Overview

Love, as love of family members, seems to be experienced by most humans throughout their lives. Even romantic love is quite common, and has been the focus of the majority of psychological research and theory on love. The value a culture places on romantic love may vary depending on whether the culture has an individualistic or collective orientation. However, anthropological studies have found that some form of romantic love is recognized in virtually every culture studied. Similarly, a recent systematic cross-national study conducted in Japan, Russia, and the United States found majorities of colleges students reporting being "in love" at the moment. Finally, romantic love seems to begin very early. One study surveying schoolchildren of various ethnicities in Hawaii found levels of reported passionate love to be as high among 4- and 5-year-olds as among 18-year-olds.

Systematic research on love has been conducted primarily by social psychologists in North America, usually involving romantic love among heterosexuals, and mainly beginning in the 1980s, with some significant pioneering work in social psychology as early as the late 1960s. The research can be organized into four main topics: (a) what people mean when they use the word *love*, (b) types of love, (c) differences between love and related concepts, and (d) theories of love. There has also been scattered research on other topics, such as the association of personality and love, the appearance of love in animals, and the role of love as an emotion. Finally, there has been a great deal of research on the predictors of romantic attraction and falling in love, which is generally considered under the topic of attraction.

What People Mean When They Use the Word Love

Canadian social psychologist Beverly Fehr (1988) asked college students to list as many characteristics of love as they could think of in a 3-minute period. She then identified 68 distinct features listed by more than one person and had a new group of students rate each for how central it was to the concept of love. In a series of studies using this procedure and others involving memory and linguistic tasks, Fehr demonstrated that the concept of love has a clear prototype structure. This means that there are some features that are consistently central and others that are consistently peripheral, and that people use the prototype to determine whether a particular relationship would or would not be considered to involve love. Other researchers have replicated Fehr's results both in North America and in other parts of the world, using both students and individuals from the general population.

A factor analysis (Aron & Westbay, 1986) of Fehr's 68 features uncovered three underlying dimensions that the researchers labeled (a) intimacy, which mainly includes central features of love, such as feeling free to talk about anything, honesty, openness, and understanding; (b) commitment, which mainly includes love features of intermediate centrality, such as devotion, protectiveness, commitment, putting the other first, and sacrifice; and (c) passion, which mainly includes peripheral features, such as euphoria, excitement, heart rate increases, sex appeal, and sexual passion. These three dimensions approximately correspond to the three components of love in Robert Sternberg's (1986) triangular theory of love, which is based on a review of the way the concept of love has been used in the scientific literature.

Types of Love

Researchers typically distinguish between romantic and other types of love (e.g., parent-child, friendship), and,

as noted earlier, have mostly focused on the former. In their pioneering work on love, social psychologists Ellen Berscheid and Elaine Hatfield [Walster] proposed what has turned out to be a very useful distinction between passionate love, "a state of intense longing for union with another" (Hatfield & Walster, 1978, p. 9), versus companionate love, "an affection we feel for those with whom our lives are deeply entwined" (p. 9). Typically, passionate love begins at a high level and gradually declines over time in a relationship, whereas companionate love may increase gradually over time. However, several studies have found that this pattern is quite variable and that for some people passionate love may remain at very high levels even after decades of marriage.

Another influential typology of love that has been related to a variety of relational experiences and behaviors is a scheme originally proposed by sociologist John Alan Lee (1977) and more thoroughly developed (including constructing the widely used Love Attitudes Scale) by psychologists Clyde and Susan Hendrick (1986). This scheme differentiates among six styles of love: eros (romantic, passionate love), ludus (game-playing, flirtatious love), storge (friendship love), mania (possessive, dependent love), pragma (shopping list, practical love), and agape (all-giving, selfless love).

Differences Between Love and Related Concepts

Researchers also distinguish love from a variety of related concepts. First, love is considered to be more intense than liking and includes some unique features (such as exclusiveness and passion). Social psychologist Zick Rubin (1970), another pioneer in love research, developed loving and liking scales, the former emphasizing "affiliative and dependent need, a predisposition to help, and an orientation of exclusiveness and absorption" (p. 265), and the latter focusing on respect and similarity. In one of Rubin's studies, dating couples were unobtrusively observed during a waiting period; those couples who scored high on Rubin's love scale spent more time gazing into each other's eyes.

Other researchers have examined the link between love and sex. Some have suggested that love is an indirect or secondary expression of sex (including many biologically based theories and some versions of Freudian thinking, whereas others suggest that sex is an indirect or secondary expression of love (such as in Plato's theory and some religious thinking). However, most psychological research treats the two as near coequals, and one theoretical approach (the self-expansion model) treats both as emerging from a single underlying motivational system.

Yet another issue is the relation of love with marriage. Studies of North American college students show that for both women and men, love is overwhelmingly seen as both a prerequisite for marriage and a necessary condition for maintaining a marriage, although in earlier decades this was much less true for women. However, among married couples in North America, studies have found only a modest link between degree of love and marital satisfaction.

Theories of Love

Most research on love has been descriptive or has focused on typologies or aspects of love. However, at least three theoretical approaches have been influential in psychology. First, psychodynamic (Freudian-based) theories traditionally emphasize an unconscious motivation to repeat the early childhood relationship with the parent, with some versions (e.g., Reik, 1944), noting a desire to connect with a person whom one sees (or projects onto) as having one's own ideal traits, resulting in an eventual disillusionment after one comes to see the beloved more realistically.

More recently, psychologists have been influenced by a reworking of psychodynamic thinking in more modern, cognitive terms by British psychoanalyst John Bowlby (1969), who developed attachment theory. The most influential aspect of attachment theory comes from findings of developmental psychology that there are three styles of infants' attachment to their primary caregiver: secure (infant appears confident about the caregiver's supportiveness), avoidant (infant does not seem to expect the caregiver to be responsive), and anxious-ambivalent (infant anxiously monitors the caregiver). Based on these findings, social psychologists Cindy Hazan and Phil Shaver (1987) proposed that these styles manifest themselves in adult love relationships, with secures being comfortable with closeness and mutual dependence, avoidants being uncomfortable with closeness and mutual dependence, and anxious-ambivalents desiring closeness and mutual dependence but often perceiving others as unwilling to reciprocate. A large number of social psychological studies have built on Hazan and Shaver's work to show that these three styles represent different cognitive structures (working models) of expectations about close relationships as well as a consistent pattern of differential emotional and behavioral responses to relationship-relevant circumstances.

A second influential theoretical approach, emerging in part from learning theories, is interdependence theory, developed by social psychologists Harold Kelley and John Thibaut (1978). In this model, attraction to a relationship partner (and ultimately love for this partner) describes the situation in which an individual perceives the relationship as having positive outcomes (benefits minus costs) in relation to her or his basic relationship expectations. (However, this theory emphasizes that whether an individual remains in a particular relationship depends mainly on whether the outcomes exceed those available outside the relationship, as well as issues of how much one has invested in the relationship.) In another aspect of this model, love is understood as referring to the situation in which there has been a transformation of motivation from (a) behaving on the basis of immediate self-interest, to (b) behaving on the basis of broader considerations, including the partner and the relationship. Love thus implies a willingness to accommodate and even to sacrifice for the benefit of the other.

A third influential theoretical approach to love, influenced by both of these approaches as well as others, is the self-expansion model (Aron & Aron, 1997). This model holds that people are motivated to expand the self, including the perspectives, resources, and identities available to the self, and that one way they seek to do so is through close relationships, because in a close relationship, each perceives the other (including the other's perspectives, etc.) to be, to some extent, part of the self. Specifically, love is said to describe the situation in which one perceives a high level of potential expansion to be available from a relationship with a particular person, and the experience of love is most intense when the rate of expansion or perceived potential expansion is very high (such as when entering a new relationship). Some relevant findings based on this model are: individuals process information about close others in similar ways to how they process information about the self (they also confuse self and close others in some contexts); after falling in love, people evidence an increase in the diversity of aspects of the self; the intensity of unreciprocated love is largely accounted for by perceived potential expansion; and love in long-term relationships is increased by participating jointly in activities experienced by the couple as expanding (compared to merely pleasant or enjoyable joint activities).

Bibliography

Aron, A., & Aron, E. N. (1997). Self-expansion motivation and including other in the self. In S. Duck (Ed.), *Handbook of personal relationships: Theory, research, and interventions* (2nd ed., pp. 251–270). Chichester, England: Wiley.

Aron, A., & Westbay, L. (1996). Dimensions of the prototype of love. *Journal of Personality and Social Psychology, 70,* 535–551.

Berscheid, E., & Hatfield [Walster], E. (1978). *Interpersonal attraction* (2nd ed.). Reading, MA: Addison-Wesley.

Bowlby, J. (1969). *Attachment and loss: Vol. 1. Attachment.* New York: Basic Books.

Fehr, B. (1988). Prototype analysis of the concepts of love and commitment. *Journal of Personality and Social Psychology, 55,* 557–579.

Hatfield, E., & Walster, G. (1978). *A new look at love.* Lanham, MD: University Press of America.

Hazan, C., & Shaver, P. (1987). Romantic love conceptualized as an attachment process. *Journal of Personality and Social Psychology, 52,* 511–524.

Hendrick, C., & Hendrick, S. S. (1986). A theory and method of love. *Journal of Personality and Social Psychology, 50,* 392–402.

Kelley, H. H., & Thibaut, J. W. (1978). *Interpersonal relations: A theory of interdependence.* New York: Wiley.

Lee, J. A. (1977). A typology of styles of loving. *Personality and Social Psychology Bulletin, 3,* 173–182.

Reik, T. (1944). *A psychologist looks at love.* New York: Farrar & Rinehart.

Rubin, Z. (1970). Measurement of romantic love. *Journal of Personality and Social Psychology, 16,* 265–273.

Sternberg, R. (1986). A triangular theory of love. *Psychological Review, 93,* 119–135.

Arthur Aron

Spiritual Conceptions of Love

The spiritual traditions of humankind, both Eastern and Western, have historically given love a commanding place within their respective understanding of how human beings are to relate both to one another and to a divine or transcendent reality. Over the long course of this sustained reflection and practice, various spiritual traditions have developed their own religious psychologies. These are often quite intricate and nuanced accounts of the various types of human loving, and of the origins, development, and ultimate goal of human desire.

As psychology separated itself in the nineteenth century from its original grounding in religious and philosophical reflection to assume its present status as a secular social science, these older religious psychologies of love have been challenged in their adequacy. Nevertheless, as psychology matures as a field less reactive to its own religious origins, a creative growing edge has been the identification of points of mutually critical correlation between certain spiritual conceptions of love and an understanding of love derived from a purely psychological investigation. There are recurrent themes across both Eastern and Western spiritual traditions that are also of special relevance to psychology. For instance, what is the relationship of particular life experiences of love and intimacy to the enlarging capacity of an individual to love more comprehensively, inclusively, and selflessly? Is the former a developmental step toward the latter, or are particular human loves, motivated by a desire for reciprocity or gratification, in some essential tension with a wider, more altruistic love? Even when psychology has eschewed the terms of spirituality, it still has had to engage the question of what it is that fundamentally motivates human beings, and what quality of relationship is ultimately both most fulfilling and most possible.

Love in the Jewish and Christian Spiritual Tradition

In the oldest strata of the Hebrew bible, the primary emphasis is upon God's generous and prior love (*hesed*) for human beings, expressed first in the creation and preservation of the world and subsequently in a series of elections, of Abraham, of Moses, and of the Hebrew people at Sinai. The first and most important commandment to the people of Israel, "You shall love the Lord your God with all your heart, and with all your soul, and with all your strength" (Dt. 6.4), is seen as the appropriate human response to the creative and redemptive initiatives of God. The corollary to this commandment, "You shall love your neighbor as yourself" (Lv. 19.18), as well as the other injunctions in Torah to treat both kinsmen and stranger with justice and compassion, are derivative then from this primary covenantal relationship between God and God's chosen people.

Throughout the Hebrew scriptures the privileged metaphors for this experience of divine-human love are all interpersonal. God is imaged as the divine parent, both father and mother, but also lover and suitor. Threading through all of these biblical literatures is the consistent theme of God's persistent, active reaching out toward humankind, extending friendship and a sharing of God's goals and purposes for the created order.

The rabbinic tradition down through the Middle Ages wrestled in various ways with the process by which human beings might in fact come to know, and thus respond, to the loving activity of God. Across all such rabbinic perspectives, however, it is fair to say that the Jewish spiritual tradition has generally not seen human love, including sexual love, as antithetical to the love of God in the way that such a distinction frequently appears in later Christian theological reflection.

The history of Christianity's various conceptions of love has been decisively shaped by the fact that, as a religious movement, it early spread from Palestine into the Greco-Roman world where its core faith experience and central organizing story regarding Jesus as the Christ of God had to be interpreted in the available thought forms of Greek and Roman philosophy.

In the early Christian movement, as traced in the four canonical gospels (Matthew, Mark, Luke, and John) and the canonical epistles, the Hebrew notion of *hesed* is rendered by the Greek *agape* (Latin, *caritas* or charity). This was apparently a deliberate choice over two other Greek terms available to differentiate the manifestations of human love: *eros* (Latin, *amor*), the sexual or carnal love that implies the desire to possess or enjoy an object of beauty or virtue for one's own pleasure and gratifi-cation; and *philia* (Latin, *delectio*), the friendly affection among friends of either gender that generates feelings of altruistic generosity. In the Christian scriptures God's *agape*, the relentlessly loving initiatives of the Creator toward the creature that characterized the Hebrew nar-rative, is fully realized in the person of Jesus and his depth of love culminating in his self-sacrificial death. What Christian spirituality grafts to its Hebrew core is a universalizing thrust in which the appropriate human response to the radically inclusive, indiscriminate, un-conditional, self-emptying love of God is to imitate that love in community (1 Cor. 13.4–7).

The theological, and subsequently psychological, problem that this elevation of *agape* to a moral require-ment creates is how to think about the relationship of such loving to these other human expressions of love, including one's love for oneself, for the objects of erotic desire, and for those who are closest to us in bonds of family and friendship. There is, on the one hand, a point of view traceable through Christian tradition, which holds that self-love or the pursuit of self-interest and the *agapeic* love of God and neighbor are funda-mentally opposed to each other. In modern Christian theology, Lutheran bishop and theologian Anders Ny-gren (1982) argued this position in a highly influential work, *Agape and Eros*. His position was that the self-centered, acquisitive love of human beings in the nat-ural (i.e., "fallen") order is radically disjunctive from the spontaneous, disinterested, and value-conferring love made possible only because of the grace of God's prior love for us. It may be seen that such a theological po-sition has some resonance with the psychological he-donism found in a classical psychoanalytic account of human motivation, Freud's pleasure principle, with the distinctive difference that it holds that such a natural self-interest can be transcended by the grace of God.

Contrasting this position is another tradition that can be found as far back as Thomas Aquinas (1225–1274), which postulated an essential interrelationship and necessary continuity between the love of self and of those closest to one and charity, the love of God and neighbor that is Christianity's loftiest ideal. Modern Ro-man Catholic theologians like Martin D'Arcy (1947) and Protestant thinkers such as Paul Tillich (1954) var-iously developed a kind of "natural theology" that ar-gued that a love of self, and the capacity to give and receive love interpersonally, is the condition of possi-bility for that altruistic and radically generous love that is the highest fulfillment of the human person. The psy-chological perspective on human motivation that is most consonant with such theology would be that rep-resented by the work of Erich Fromm and the object-relations theorists in psychoanalysis, who have held that an attunement to mutuality and the good of the other is from birth fundamental in human persons. [*See the biography of Fromm.*]

Love in the Hindu and Buddhist Spiritual Traditions

The Sanskrit language, and indeed the whole culture of the Indian subcontinent since antiquity, has had a rich and complex set of words and religious imagery to describe the relationship of human and divine love. The most common term is *kama* meaning "wish, desire, or longing," and hence, love or affection. As the Hindu equivalent of the divinely constituted human potenti-ality for erotic pleasure and sensual attachment that the Greeks called *eros, kama* was also seen as a funda-mental energy or life force that animated all living be-ings and had its source in the cosmic fecundity of the gods. The complex development of Hindu spirituality involves myriad experiments in both theory and reli-gious practice to relate *kama* to the equally fundamen-tal human capacity for *sraddha* ("faith, trust, rever-ence") and to the eventual goal of union with the divine.

In the contemplative yogic traditions inspired by the earliest Hindu Scriptures, the Upanishads, union with the transpersonal principle of being, or *brahman*, in-volves ascetic practices that seem to require the mas-tery of human sensuality and an overleaping of the "lesser" forms of human loving. By contrast, the *bhakti*, or devotional yogic traditions associated with the story of the manifestation of the divine in the figure of Krishna (the *Bhagavadgita*), extol the experience of in-tense and unqualified loving devotion to a personal god-head. The parallels between Hindu *bhakti* spirituality and certain Christian and Jewish spiritualities have been frequently noted. One of the general ways in which Hindu religious thinking has related the love of an incarnation of the godhead to the impartial and nondiscriminating love that an individual may develop toward other living beings is by prayer and meditation to cultivate the capacity to see within one's self and within every other person, if not within every sentient being, the spark of divinity or holiness that character-izes them. The practices and political strategies of cre-ative nonviolence (*ahimsa*) developed by Gandhi were rooted in this essential recognition of "the divine within," which has the potential to evoke love and trust.

Whereas Buddhism developed from Hindu culture without explicit reference to a personal divinity, and therefore might be properly called *a*-theistic, it has elab-orated an extensive and sophisticated psychology of the interrelationship of an individual's loving attitudes to-ward himself or herself, toward particular other human persons, and ultimately, toward all other beings. The term within Buddhism, which occupies the place of "love" in the West, is *karuna* or compassion. Within Mahayana ("Great Raft") Buddhism, the idealized embodiment of radical and fully enlightened compassion is the figure of the *bodhisattva* (the one "whose essence is perfected wisdom"). The *bodhisattva* is one who is revered as an infinite and inexhaustible reservoir of compassion or love by virtue of having taken a vow to work for the release from suffering of all beings and to forego his or her own release from the cycle of death and rebirth until that end is attained, or as it was traditionally expressed, "until the grass itself is enlightened."

What the Buddhist spiritual conception of love thus contributes is an understanding of the connection between the capacity for compassion or love and the achievement of wisdom (*bodhi*). For Buddhists, the latter includes seeing clearly into the nature of reality and penetrating the illusions that block the ability to love freely and generously. Principal among these illusions is the individual's anxious clinging to the fiction of being a wholly separate entity—perhaps better, perhaps worse—but in any case essentially different from, and unrelated to, other human beings. Buddhist meditative practices are designed to examine, and over time, deconstruct the habituated patterns of the mind that block the recognition of essential, interdependent, common humanity.

Another traditional meditation, the *mettá* ("loving kindness") meditation found in both Mahayana and Theravada Buddhism involves the recognition that the love one can extend to another person necessarily begins in a loving attitude or intention toward oneself. In this particular practice, an individual focuses upon himself or herself and directs the wish: "May I be safe and happy . . . may I be free from suffering . . . may I gain inner joy." That intention is then very gradually broadened in the meditation to include persons for whom one feels a natural sense of gratitude and affection, those toward whom one is neutral, those who are counted as one's "enemies," and ultimately, as the Buddhist scripture *Sutta Nipata* puts it, "all living beings whatsoever without exception."

The challenge and the promise of the next stage in the dialogue between psychology and spirituality, East and West, will be to note some of the connections described here and further work out the ways in which these two accounts of the vicissitudes of human loving critically complement one another.

Bibliography

D'Arcy, M. C. (1947). *The mind and heart of love: A study in eros and agape.* New York: Henry Holt. A classic treatment from a Roman Catholic and Thomistic perspective of the essential interrelationship of the various manifestations of human loving.

Eckstein, J. (1991). *Metaphysical drift: Love and Judaism.* New York: Peter Langs. Survey from a modern Jewish philosophical perspective of love in the Jewish ethical and philosophical tradition.

Goldstein, J., & Kornfeld, J. (1987). *Seeking the heart of wisdom: The path of insight meditation.* Boston: Shambhala Press. Introduction to Theravada Buddhist practice includes discussions of the way in which meditative practice cultivates loving mind states and works with relationships.

Nygren, A. (1982). *Agape and eros* (P. S. Watson, Trans.) Chicago: University of Chicago Press. This highly influential argument by a Swedish Lutheran bishop for the radical distinction between human self-love (*eros*) and altruistic love (*agape*) inspired prominent American Protestant theologian Reinhold Niebuhr.

O'Flaherty, W. D. (1973). *Asceticism and eroticism in the mythology of Siva.* London: Oxford University Press. Explores, through one Hindu mythic tradition, the interweaving of traditions of both the erotic/sensual and the ascetical.

Sivaram, K. (Ed.). (1989). *Hindu spirituality: Vedas through Vedanta.* New York: Crossroads. Accessible introduction to the many practices and literatures of Hinduism.

Tillich, P. (1954). *Love, power and justice.* New York: Oxford University Press. An examination of the role of love intrapsychically and socially by one of the most significant of modern liberal Protestant thinkers.

Tittman, G. (1959). *What manner of love: The Bible as the love story of God.* New York: Morehouse-Barlow. Although written from a Christian perspective, the text surveys the sources in Hebrew Scripture for seeing the biblical narrative as a drama of a covenantal love affair between God and the people of Israel.

Tsultim Gyseltsen, G. (1997). *Compassion: The key to great awakening.* Boston: Wisdom. Distinguished Tibetan lama presents for Western readers the thought training and the *bodhisattva* practices that cultivate inclusive love and compassion in the Vajrayana (Tibetan) Buddhist tradition.

John McDargh

LURIA, ALEXANDER R. (1902–1977), Russian neuropsychologist. Luria was born in the city of Kazan on the River Volga, where he attended the local university. In 1923, he joined the staff of the Psychological Institute in Moscow. In the 1930s, already a well-known psychologist, Luria entered the Moscow Medical School and was awarded a doctor of medicine degree in 1937. During World War II, Luria was head of psychological services in the brain trauma hospital. After the war, he became a chair of neuropsychology at Moscow University and head of neuropsychological laboratory at the Burdenko Institute of Neurosurgery. In the late 1940s under political pressure, he was forced to resign from the Burdenko Institute. His works of that period are marked by Pavlovian terminology that he was forced to accept. In the late 1950s, Luria regained his influence in academic and clinical institutions. He was among the first who established the working contacts with Western psychologists, including Karl Pribram, Jerome Bruner, Michael Cole, and others. In the 1960s and 1970s, Luria became the most publicized Russian psychologist in English—16 of his books were published in the United States and Great Britain.

Luria's first venture into the field of psychology was inspired by the ideas of Sigmund Freud on the one hand and a study of human reflexes on the other. The young Luria corresponded with Freud and translated some of his papers into Russian. Luria also developed a special methodology that combined an analysis of free associations with a study of motor responses. This so-called combined motor method allowed Luria to obtain objective data on hidden emotional complexes of neurotics, suspected criminals, and students under stress. Although in the early 1930s Luria was forced to renounce his interest in Freudian theory, he still managed to publish the "combined motor method" studies in English (Luria, 1932).

In 1924, Luria started his collaboration with Lev Vygotsky on what would later become the sociocultural theory. According to this theory language and other symbolic systems play a role of psychological mediators helping individuals to master and transform their "natural" processes of perception, attention, and memory into the higher psychological functions. It was further assumed that without the higher order symbolic tools-mediators human thinking is limited by the context of immediate practical experience. An outline of sociocultural theory was published by Vygotsky and Luria as *Essays on the History of Behavior* (Hillsdale, N.J., 1930, 1993). In order to prove empirically the main thesis of the sociocultural theory, Luria and Vygotsky organized an expedition to remote regions of Soviet Central Asia. Luria discovered that people who retained the traditional ways of living solved problems, classified objects, and recalled information differently from their peers who received a few years of formal schooling. For political reasons, Luria was unable to publish these results at that time. Only in the 1970s did they become available (Luria, 1976) and inspire a wide range of studies on the influence of literacy and schooling on cognition.

In the 1930s, Luria turned to the study of disturbed brain functions. This field of research brought him worldwide fame and established him as a leader of Russian neuropsychology (Vocate, 1987). In neuropsychological theory, Luria (1973) advanced the idea of three functional units of brain activity. The first functional unit is responsible for activation and arousal, the second unit receives, processes, and stores information through simultaneous and successive coding. The third unit programs, regulates, and evaluates the results of mental activity. According to Luria, the higher mental functions represent complex functional systems, sociocultural in their development, mediated in their structure, and carried out by a number of jointly working zones of the brain supported by the external tool- and sign-using activities.

In the field of clinical neuropsychology, Luria created a system of flexible, qualitative assessment of brain functions. This system allowed the attribution of a given neuropsychological symptom to an appropriate functional system and further the indication of a brain structure involved in a particular disturbance of this system. Beyond neuropsychology, Luria's methods of assessment of simultaneous and successive information processing contributed to the development of interactive methods of cognitive assessment of children (Das, Nagliery, & Kirby, 1994). In the field of neuropsychological rehabilitation, Luria emphasized vicarious rehabilitation through reconstruction of functional systems. This includes the reactivating of previously subdominant input modalities; the involvement of new input modalities, for example, motor and kinesthetic when visual input is affected; and the creation of new functional systems that can achieve the same behavioral goals by different psychological means.

Luria's lively and engaging writing style and his ability to make clinical cases comprehensible to lay readers made him a best-selling author of popular books.

[*Many of the people mentioned in this article are the subjects of independent biographical entries.*]

Bibliography

Works by Luria

Luria, A. (1932). *The nature of human conflicts*. New York: Liveright.

Luria, A. (1961). *The role of speech in regulation of normal and abnormal behavior*. New York: Pergamon.

Luria, A. (1966). *Higher cortical functions in men*. New York: Basic Books.

Luria, A. (1973). *The working brain*. New York: Basic Books.

Luria, A. (1976). *Cognitive development: Cultural and social foundations*. Cambridge, MA: Harvard University Press.

Luria, A. (1978). *The selected writings*. White Plains, NY: M. E. Sharpe.

Luria, A. (1979). *The making of mind*. Cambridge, MA: Harvard University Press.

Luria, A. (1982). *Language and cognition*. Washington, DC: Winston.

Works about Luria

Das, J. P., Nagliery, J., & Kirby, J. R. (1994). *Assessment of cognitive processes: The PASS theory of intelligence*. Needham Heights, MA: Allyn & Bacon.

Vocate, D. (1987). *Theory of A. R. Luria*. Hillsdale, NJ: Erlbaum.

Alex Kozulin

M

MACH, ERNST (1838–1916), Austrian philosopher, physicist, psychologist, and physiologist. Mach exercized significant influence on several leaders of the generation of scientists that would produce relativity theory in physics, logical positivism in philosophy of science, and both behaviorism and Gestalt theory in psychology. However, almost all of his contributions to physiology and psychology were made during the 1860s and 1870s and had to be rediscovered decades later by other investigators.

He was born in Chirlitz (Chrlice) near Brünn (Brno) in the Habsburg crownland of Moravia (now the Czech Republic). He was educated at home until age 15 by his father, a farmer and renowned tutor, and graduated from the University of Vienna in 1860. He taught mathematics and physics in Graz (1864–1867), experimental physics in Prague (1867–1895), and the history and philosophy of the inductive sciences in Vienna (1895–1898). The latter was the first chair in the history of science in Central Europe and later when reduced to philosophy of science was filled by Moritz Schlick, the founder of the Vienna Circle. Politically, Mach was somewhat to the left, and was a pacifist. He died in Vaterstetten, near Munich, Bavaria, during World War I.

Mach believed that we could know sensations with absolute certainty and that science should be restricted to the most economical description of sensations, which he called "elements." He thought that this methodology of science, largely inspired by Gustav Fechner's *Elements of Psychophysics* (Leipzig, 1860), could be applied equally to physics and psychology. Mach's book *The Science of Mechanics* (Leipzig, 1883) with its epistemological rejection of absolute space and time influenced Albert Einstein, and his works *The Analysis of Sensations* (Jena, 1886) and *Knowledge and Error* (Leipzig, 1905) had a major impact on Rudolf Carnap and Otto Neurath, who helped found logical positivism, and

on John Watson and B. F. Skinner, who helped establish behavioral psychology and make it well known. He also partly anticipated and influenced Ewald Hering, his colleague in Prague, in his major controversies with Hermann von Helmholtz over color theory and nativism.

Mach's own contributions to experimental science were all based on very careful study of sensory appearances. In physics, he is best known for discovering and photographing what are now called Mach shock waves, in physiology for his discovery of the equilibrium function of the inner ear, and in psychophysics for noticing what are now called Mach Bands, inhibitory phenomena that assist the senses to differentiate between different colors more effectively. Later scientists led by Georg von Békésy have discovered that all of the senses appear to use some form of inhibition, which increases sensory differentiation beyond what one would "objectively" expect. Mach's studies in acoustics and optics also contributed to his early discovery (1860s) of Gestalt phenomena, which he fit into his theory of elements but only by silently expanding his definition of the latter term.

The last 18 years of Mach's life were troubled by the aftermath of a stroke that paralyzed the right side of his body and by controversies with many scientific and philosophical opponents including Max Planck among the physicists, Carl Stumpf among psychologists, and eventually even Albert Einstein who did not accept his rejection of atoms, doubts about relativity theory, and his opposition to the existence of the physical world beyond sensations and consciousness. While Mach's attempt to ground methodology of science on epistemology, that is, on a theory of knowledge, would be less successful than he hoped, partly because it would appear too restrictive to many scientists, he is still widely honored for his actual experimental work in physics, psychology, and physiology and as an influential forerunner in theoretical physics.

[Many of the people mentioned in this article are the subjects of independent biographical entries.]

Bibliography

Blackmore, J. T. (1972). *Ernst Mach—His life, work, and influence.* Berkeley & Los Angeles: University of California Press.

Blackmore, J. T. (1992). *Ernst Mach—A deeper look: Documents and new perspectives* (Boston Studies in the Philosophy of Science, Vol. 143). Dordrecht: Kluwer Academic Publishers.

Boring, E. G. (1957). *A history of experimental psychology* (2nd ed.). New York: Appleton-Century-Crofts. This classic work helps relate Mach's contributions to psychology and physiology to their philosophical context and also to the work of his colleagues in those disciplines.

Johnston, W. M. (1972). *The Austrian mind—An intellectual and social history.* Berkeley: University of California Press. This book provides biographical information on Mach, many colleagues and friends, and in general gives extensive background information on turn-of-the-century Vienna, Austria, and the Habsburg Empire.

Ratliff, F. (1965). *Mach bands: Quantitative studies on neural networks in the retina.* San Francisco: Holden-Day. This richly illustrated book on glossy paper is both a specialist's account of the "subjective" phenomena called Mach Bands and a general study of Mach's life and contributions to philosophy, physics, physiology, and psychology. It also includes English translations of Mach's six articles on Mach Bands.

John T. Blackmore

MACHINE DESIGN. Machines have changed the way we view ourselves and our work. They have replaced much of our physical labor with cognitive labor. From the earliest days of their time on earth, humans devised tools to help them accomplish tasks and make their lives easier. For much the same reason, they later learned to devise machines—mechanically, electrically, or electronically operated devices for performing tasks. While the simplest tools may have been mere extensions of appendages designed to increase the reach of the user, or to allow the user to break up the earth more easily to dig a hole, modern machines range from computers to cars to life-support equipment. There are also many complex automated systems made up of integrated machines that accomplish tasks completely from start to finish, requiring no more than supervisory control and monitoring by their human users.

In his book *Human Factors and Systems Engineering* (1996), Alphonse Chapanis discusses machine design as one of the five elements of system design, the other four being personnel selection, personnel training, job design, and environmental design. Among these elements, complex trade-offs exist. For example, the design of the machine in part determines the capabilities that the operator will need, and therefore has implications for personnel selection and personnel training requirements. Similarly, the nature of the environment will determine, in part, how the machine will be designed and the constraints under which it will operate. Thus, machines do not exist in isolation, and cannot be designed successfully as if they did.

Psychology's Role in Machine Design

Psychologists play a key role in machine design through the development of the body of knowledge—human factors—that concern the characteristics, capabilities, and limitations of human beings that are relevant to design. Human factors include knowledge of human perception, information processing, and decision making, as well as data and information about human physical characteristics (anthropometry), capabilities, and limitations (work physiology and biomechanics). Over the course of the history of psychology, many basic human factors principles have been derived from this body of knowledge that can be applied directly to the design of machines. Those professionals who apply the human factors knowledge base and principles to the design of tools, machines, systems, tasks, jobs, and environments are typically designated as human factors psychologists or engineers. If their goals are met, the resulting machines, systems, tasks, and so forth will be safe, effective, easy to use, and acceptable to users.

A System's Life Cycle and the Systems Engineering Process

A machine is part of a system that includes both human and environmental components. As such, it is important to understand both the life cycle of a system as well as the basics involved in the systems engineering process. The life cycle of a system has seven components:

1. Identification of operational need
2. Concept exploration
3. Concept demonstration and validation
4. Full-scale engineering development
5. Production and deployment
6. Operation and maintenance
7. System retirement

In brief, someone identifies an unmet need that may require a new system or a new machine and develops an operational needs statement. This leads to the development of one or more operational concepts for how this need should be met, one of which is selected and pursued during the concept demonstration and validation stage. During this stage, using mock-ups, prototypes, simulations, or other tools, designers demonstrate that the identified need can be met. Once the design concept has been validated, full-scale engineering development takes place and continues until the final product (machine, tool, piece of equipment, etc.) is approved for production. From that point on, the product is produced, deployed, used, maintained, and, finally, retired.

Overlaid on the system life cycle is the systems engineering process. As typically depicted, its first phase, requirements analysis, coincides with the first two stages of the system's life cycle. During this phase, the requirements for the posited system are laid out in sufficient detail so that designers and engineers know exactly what the system must be able to do. The end product of this phase, usually a system requirements document, will drive the system specification that eventually will be developed. In this phase, the role of psychology is to define the users as specifically as possible, and to define those operations that the users will perform using the machine or system. It is extremely important that the characteristics of the users and user actions be designated in such a way that engineers and designers can make use of the information easily during design. For example, hearing loss at the higher frequencies of the audible spectrum may be a characteristic of the user population for a system. To be helpful to the designer or engineer, information about such hearing losses must be translated into a design requirement that specifies the frequency range to be used for auditory information within the system, and/or the decibel level at which speech and/or auditory warnings, for example, will be presented in order to accommodate the users.

The next phase in the systems engineering process is system design, which often is depicted as beginning soon after the need is identified and continuing through full-scale engineering and development. During this phase, human factors professionals have many jobs. They must determine how system or machine functions will be allocated between the human user and the machine or system. These decisions are based on a knowledge of human strengths and weaknesses as compared to machine strengths and weaknesses. For example, most humans are excellent problem solvers relative to a machine but pale in comparison when it comes to doing repetitive, precise, though routine, operations. Once the functions are allocated, interchanges between the human and the machine are specified, and detailed user-task analyses may be conducted. The process of developing user-machine and user-system interfaces begins and is accomplished through a variety of techniques that may range from the use of inexpensive paper prototypes and cardboard mock-ups, through rapid prototyping of more interactive and realistic prototypes, to sophisticated full-scale simulations.

The next phase of systems engineering is system integration and testing, and is often shown to coincide with the full-scale engineering stage of the life cycle and, perhaps, continue into the production and deployment stage. From a human factors perspective, designs are evaluated for usability, effectiveness, safety, and user satisfaction to ensure that system requirements are being met. Following system integration and testing are the last two phases—installation and training, and maintenance and operations—which coincide with the final two phases of the system life cycle.

It is extremely important to note that in reality the systems engineering process does not map to the system life cycle as neatly as it does in most diagrams. Nor are the phases as separate and distinct as typically depicted. The strictly sequential process previously described, often called the waterfall development process, implies that testing doesn't occur until late in the design process, and neither do considerations of training materials and maintainers. If a problem is discovered during testing or concerning maintenance, it will be very costly to fix if systems are designed strictly in accordance with this model. In contrast, systems engineers today recognize that systems engineering is an iterative, or cyclical, process of design-develop-test, in which input from all concerned parties, including marketing, maintenance, public relations, sales, manufacturing, and design is considered throughout the systems engineering process. Problems can be corrected more quickly and cheaply, and communication among everyone involved improves. This form of the systems engineering process is often called concurrent engineering.

The Human Factors Body of Knowledge and the Human-Machine Interface

Throughout the system design process, the focus of the human factors professional will be the user and the human-machine interface. Users often include both operators and maintainers, and the characteristics and requirements of both should be identified to ensure good design. The human-machine interface can be characterized as a feedback loop in which the human provides input to the machine, and the machine responds by providing feedback to the user, who must then sense that feedback, interpret it appropriately, make decisions about next steps, and finally provide further input to the machine. Knowledge from psychology is applied to the design of the human-machine interface.

The human must be capable of sensing information provided by the machine. Thus, the designer must understand the capabilities and limitations of the human sensory systems—vision, hearing, touch, kinesthesia, and, sometimes, taste and smell. In this regard, the body of knowledge related to sensation and perception is critical. For example, knowing the frequency range of normal human hearing, how hearing capabilities change with age, and how the detection of signals is masked in the presence of noise (i.e., signal detection theory) helps designers to develop effective auditory alarm systems for machines. Similarly, knowledge of the nature of normal color vision and anomalous color vision helps the designer to use color effectively in machine displays that must be used by operators who have color deficiencies or are color blind. In addition, knowledge from psychology concerning selective, focused, and divided attention is used by designers to ensure that relevant machine information will draw the user's attention within the context of the task.

Beyond detecting information from the machine, the user must appropriately perceive the input. There are many instances in which perception is quite accurate with respect to what has been presented. However, there are other instances in which the perception of information is woefully inadequate, leading to unfortunate consequences for the user. For example, information about visual illusions is important to machine designers. As an example, one instance of a visual illusion with dire potential consequences for aviators is known as the black-hole effect. A number of accidents have occurred because pilots, under nighttime flying conditions and good weather and making approaches over dark terrain or water, overestimated their altitude on the approach and landed seriously short of the runway. It is the particular combination of environmental and situational conditions that leads to this illusion of increased altitude. Knowledge of this particular illusion can be used to design aircraft displays and training materials that can help pilots avoid succumbing to its effects.

Given that information is sensed accurately, and perceived accurately, it must then be interpreted and processed appropriately. The psychological literature pertaining to learning, memory, and cognition is relevant in this regard. For example, the limitations of working memory have implications for the number of items of information that can be displayed to and processed by a machine operator at any one time. Gestalt organizational principles, such as proximity, continuity, and closure, help designers to lay out machine displays and controls so that the resulting control-and-display element arrangements are compatible with these principles. If operators or other users are expected to do several tasks at once using the machine, then workload and time-sharing issues become important to design. Data from psychological models such as multiple resource theory, discussed in Wickens's *Engineering Psychology and Human Performance* (1984), help to guide machine designers in how to combine display modalities (e.g., visual and auditory) and response modalities (manual and vocal) to facilitate time-sharing and information processing.

The study of human decision making also plays a major role in the design of many machines. For some machines (e.g., many consumer products), decision making may be as simple as deciding whether to switch a device on or off. But in more complex machines, decision making is based on multiple sources of input that must be combined by the operator and synthesized in order for decisions to be made and actions taken. In some systems, the task of information synthesis is sufficiently complex that the organization of displayed information becomes critical, and mechanisms for decision-aiding are necessary. For these machines and systems, knowledge of human problem-solving behavior and capabilities helps to determine the circumstances under which decision-aiding is needed and the form that aid will take.

Finally, once the user has made a decision, he or she must respond to the machine through an action. As is the case with decision making, some machines require only simple actions on the part of the user (the physical action of flipping a switch from on to off, or vice versa). In others, multiple actions may be possible and the user must, for example, choose the correct control from a set and manipulate it in the correct manner. If there are time constraints on the user's actions, reaction time may become an issue. A number of principles from psychology may apply, including stimulus-response compatibility—the idea that user responses should map directly to machine inputs, to the extent possible. A knowledge of population stereotypes for the operation of controls is also important. For example, for a linear control, people expect numbers to increase from left to right, not right to left, and they expect clockwise turns of a rotary control to increase the controlled variable and counterclockwise turns to decrease it.

The physical requirements with respect to user actions are also important. Users must be able to reach controls, have the strength to manipulate them as needed, and have sufficient fine motor control to make delicate machine adjustments. In the design of machines, these issues are often considered to accommodate the operator but are often neglected when it comes to the maintainer, who is also a user. In addition, the needs of users with disabilities have often not been taken into consideration, although in many countries federal legislation is now requiring that this be done. Therefore, data from anthropometry, biomechanics, and work physiology are often critical in the design of machine controls.

Throughout the design of a machine, the designer must focus on optimizing the performance of the user and minimizing human error, or, more important, the consequences of human error. For some machines, the consequences of human error are minor (e.g., if you make a mistake using your VCR remote control, nothing of earthshaking consequence occurs). On the other hand, errors in the design or use of some machines can be catastrophic (e.g., errors in the use of medical equipment can kill patients, and vehicle design errors can kill drivers, aircraft pilots, and passengers). Thus, data and information from psychology tell designers not only what human beings can do but what they can't do and the circumstances in which they are likely to fail. Humans make unintended errors for many reasons, as laid out by James Reason in his book *Human Error* (1990). Their memory fails them, they omit steps in a process, they combine information incorrectly when making decisions, they are subject to biases, they make unwarranted assumptions, and sometimes they simply push the wrong button or press the wrong key. Studies in psychology can help to classify and predict these types of errors, and analyses of machine and system operation can predict their consequences. Designers then use the information to build in safeguards against these consequences, if not the commission of the errors themselves. In addition, there are also errors that occur as the result of a user's willingness to take risks. Data from psychology on the perception of risk, and the assessment of risk in decision making (e.g., utility theory) can be used to predict risk-taking behavior and discourage it through design.

Many of the design principles derived from psychology are embodied in national and international standards for the design of user interfaces. For example, ISO 9241 is an international standard for the design of user interfaces for office work with video display terminals. Similarly, in the United States there are many military standards and handbooks for human-machine interface design; MIL-STD-1472 (Design Criteria Standard—Human Engineering) is one of the best known.

Finally, it should be noted that an important aspect of successfully designing machines is the design of the materials and techniques that instruct the user in how to use the machine effectively and safely. If well designed, simple machines may require little or no training. Complex machines (e.g., a Boeing 747 or a sophisticated medical device like an infusion pump) may require extensive training and periodic retraining of the user. Psychology's body of knowledge related to learning and instruction can assist designers in making decisions, for example, about the degree of fidelity required in an aircraft training simulator, whether part-task or whole-task training should be used in a given situation, and whether training should be embedded within a task context or, by necessity, delivered outside of the task situation.

Tools, Techniques, and Methodologies for Human-Machine Interface Design

Over the years, human factors specialists have developed many tools, techniques, and methodologies to assist them in doing machine and system design work, and have adapted many tools used in other areas of systems engineering. For those designing human-computer interfaces, the GOMS model, developed by Card, Moran, and Newell, has been a significant contribution (1983). GOMS stands for Goals-Operators-Methods-Selection Rules, and is used to model tasks as a means of providing a framework for user interface design. An observational technique often used in the early stages of machine design is contextual inquiry, in which the task performance of current machine or system users is observed in the work context in order to determine where problems exist and what design improvements are needed in a new version of the system. Techniques like link analysis, which analyzes the relationships among controls and displays in a workstation or system, are used to determine the physical layout of the controls and displays in the final design. There are also numerous workload measures and techniques that assist in ensuring that users are neither over- nor undertasked when using a machine or system.

Particularly in critical systems, analyses of errors and safety issues are given priority. Techniques such as THERP (Swain & Guttmann, 1983) are used to predict error rates and human reliability in complex systems. Similarly, Failure Modes and Effects Analysis (FMEA) elucidates the causes and effects of failures, and Fault Tree Analysis (FTA) graphically depicts the sequences of events that lead to failures.

Prototypes, mock-ups, and simulations are frequently used during the design process to evaluate design concepts and to ensure, through usability testing, that the final designs will be effective, safe, and easy to use. These tools range from very simple paper-and-pencil prototypes and "Wizard of Oz" simulations that conceptually represent the actual system but are not operational, to high-fidelity mock-ups and simulations that are operational and very close, both physically and conceptually, to the final products.

Bibliography

Blanchard, B. S. (1991). *System engineering management.* New York: Wiley. Detail-level guidance on the system engineering process and how it is managed.

Card, S. K., Moran, T. P., & Newell, A. (1983). *The psychology of human-computer interaction.* Hillsdale, NJ: Erlbaum. Outlines the GOMS model in detail; one of the better known early texts in the area of human-computer interaction.

Chapanis, A. (1996). *Human factors and systems engineering.* New York: Wiley.

Fleishman, E. A., & Quaintance, M. K. (1984). *Taxonomies of human performance.* Orlando, FL: Academic Press. An excellent resource for those doing task description and task analysis work.

Helander, M. G., Landauer, T. K., & Prabhu, R. V. (Eds.).

(1997). *Handbook of human-computer interaction* (2nd ed.). Amsterdam: Elsevier. At over 1,500 pages, a must-have reference work for anyone working in the area of human-computer interaction.

Nielsen, J. (1993). *Usability engineering*. Boston: AP Professional. Possibly the most cited book on the design and evaluation of software user interfaces.

O'Brien, T. G., & Charlton, S. G. (Eds.). (1996). *Handbook of human-factors testing and evaluation*. Mahwah, NJ: Erlbaum. A detailed guide for conducting and documenting human-factors testing and evaluation.

Reason, J. (1990). *Human error*. New York: Cambridge University Press.

Salvendy, G. (Ed.). (1997). *Handbook of human factors and ergonomics* (2nd ed.). New York: Wiley. What Helander's book is to human-computer interaction, Salvendy's book is to general human factors and ergonomics.

Sanders, M. S., & McCormick, E. J. (1993). *Human factors in engineering and design* (7th ed.). New York: McGraw-Hill. Long the standard college textbook for human-factors engineering.

Smith, W. (1996). *ISO and ANSI ergonomic standards for computer products*. Upper Saddle River, NJ: Prentice Hall. An introduction to the complicated world of national and international standards and guidelines for the ergonomic design of computer hardware and software. Contains numerous design checklists.

Swain, A., & Guttmann, H. (1983). *Handbook of human reliability analysis with emphasis on nuclear power plant applications: Final report* (NUREG/CR-1278). Washington, DC: Nuclear Regulatory Commission. A good introduction to THERP, as applied to the nuclear power industry.

Wickens, C. D. (1992). *Engineering psychology and human performance* (2nd ed.). New York: HarperCollins. An excellent, well-written introduction to engineering psychology, which includes discussions of decision making, memory, attention and perception, workload, manual control, reaction time, and process control and automation.

Daryle Gardner-Bonneau

MAGNETIC RESONANCE IMAGING. *See* Brain Imaging Techniques.

MAINE DE BIRAN. *See* Biran, Maine de.

MAINSTREAMING AND INCLUSION. Three terms, *integration, mainstreaming,* and *inclusion,* have been used to refer to the practice of educating children with and without disabilities together in regular classrooms. Although the terms are often used interchangeably, the underlying philosophies and procedures associated with each are different. *Integration* broadly refers to the practice of actively mixing children with and without disabilities together in the same social, physical, or academic environment. *Mainstreaming* is used to describe the selective placement of children with disabilities in regular education classrooms for some portion of their school day. Inherent in the concept of mainstreaming is the notion that one group (typically developing children) constitutes the "mainstream" into which an otherwise excluded group (children with disabilities) is included. An underlying premise of mainstreaming is that students with disabilities should be able to succeed in the mainstream classroom, where the primary emphasis is on the education of children without disabilities.

Inclusion differs from mainstreaming in important ways. Inclusion means creating an educational environment that is structured to be responsive to the diverse needs of *all* learners. This philosophical difference translates into distinctive practices associated with mainstreaming versus inclusion. For example, mainstreamed students typically spend only part of their day in a regular classroom. In a mainstreaming model, students are "pulled out" of the regular classroom to receive special services. In contrast, inclusion involves complete and active participation of children with disabilities in programs with typically developing children. In inclusive classrooms, support services and adaptations are offered to children in the context of the "mainstream" classroom, rather than in an alternative setting. A common model of inclusion calls for regular and special education teachers to work together to tailor the learning environment and instructional activities to accommodate the needs of students. In effect, a mainstreaming model requires bringing the child to special education services, whereas an inclusion model requires bringing special education services to the child (Fuchs & Fuchs, 1994).

A related characteristic that differentiates mainstreaming from inclusion is the location of the school where students with disabilities receive their education. Mainstreamed students may attend a school not necessarily located in their neighborhood, but specifically designed to provide services for their specific disability. Inclusion, however, means that students with disabilities attend their neighborhood schools with same-age peers. As such, the proportion of students with disabilities included in regular education classrooms reflects the "natural" proportion of children with disabilities in the neighborhood community. Most recently, inclusion has been viewed in a broader context involving *community* inclusion whereby children with disabilities and their family members participate in community-based activities (e.g., recreational) that are similar to those in which children without disabilities and their families participate.

There are two types of evidence underlying the development and implementation of inclusive practices. These are: (1) federal legislation and court decisions related to education and civil rights for people of all ages with disabilities, and (2) an empirical analysis and realization that special education programs have not led to substantial positive outcomes for children with disabilities (Karagiannis, Stainback, & Stainback, 1996).

The requirement of the Individuals with Disabilities Education Act (IDEA) that children with disabilities are educated in the least restrictive environment (LRE) is interpreted to mean that children with special needs must be educated to the maximum extent possible with children who are typically developing (Hasazi, Johnston, Liggett, & Schattman, 1994). Children with disabilities should be included in a regular classroom and provided with special services, accommodations, and supplementary aids necessary to succeed in the classroom. From a civil rights perspective, it has been argued that segregated special education is inherently "unequal" and, as such, a violation of the rights of children with disabilities who are segregated. Thus, there exists a strong legal basis for inclusion of children with disabilities in their home schools, regular education classrooms, and community programs.

The second impetus for inclusion comes from an analysis of outcomes associated with special education services. Despite a steady expansion of special education programs, children who receive special services have not demonstrated the anticipated benefits in terms of academic, social, or cognitive functioning. Educational outcomes for many students with disabilities are discouraging (including lower school completion rates and lower employment records). Two reasons for these poor outcomes are: (1) the unnecessary segregation and labeling of children for special education services, and (2) the ineffective practice of mainstreaming. The unintended effect of mainstreaming children for only part of their day is to give students a fragmented education and a feeling that they belong in neither special nor regular education. Ironically, children with disabilities who are "pulled out" for special services actually lose instructional time while making the transition from special education classes to regular education classes and back. They may also receive instruction with two separate curricula which may not be coordinated to meet their needs. In sum, educational practices that are not inclusive undermine the goal of fully integrating people with disabilities into society. In fact, fewer than 5% of students who enter the special education system ever leave (Roach, 1995).

Although compelling, the legal and philosophical rationales concerning special education should not be the only considerations for inclusion. It is also important to evaluate the benefits or positive outcomes of inclusive practices. Much of the literature that discusses outcomes for students in inclusive settings lacks a strong empirical base (MacMillan, Gresham, & Forness, 1996). The available data do allow some general conclusions, however. Students exhibiting a variety of handicapping conditions perform at least as well as in inclusive settings as they do in segregated settings when appropriate educational experiences and support are provided. There is no conclusive evidence that children with certain handicapping conditions or severity of disability make more or less progress in inclusive classrooms (Alper & Ryndak, 1992; Buysse & Bailey, 1993; Little & Witek, 1996).

Students with disabilities in inclusive classrooms exhibit the greatest gains in social and communication domains. By observing and interacting with typically developing children, children with special needs improve their communication and social skills. Specifically, increased levels of social interaction have been observed and, to a lesser extent, reciprocal friendships between students with and without disabilities (McIntosh, Vaughn, Schumm, Haager, & Lee, 1993). Nonetheless, positive social outcomes occur only when interactions among students are frequent, planned, and directed or monitored by teachers (e.g., as in cooperative learning group situations).

Inclusion may also improve academic learning among children with disabilities. At the least, academic learning does not seem to be negatively affected by participation in an inclusive versus segregated setting (Little & Witek, 1996). Because children with disabilities receive the same curriculum as their same-age peers (modified for their individual learning needs), their academic progress tends to be greater in inclusive than segregated classrooms. Expectations are higher in regular classrooms than in special education classrooms, therefore, students with disabilities are expected to learn more and have high achievement. When students are placed in inclusive settings without necessary modifications, however, they tend to have poorer outcomes than students in segregated special education settings.

There are also benefits for students without disabilities in inclusive classrooms. Through daily exposure to and shared experiences with students with disabilities, typical students learn skills and adopt new values and attitudes toward individuals with disabilities. There is evidence that children learn more about individual differences, are more accepting of students who are different, are more accepting of their own personal limitations, and view classmates with disabilities as models of coping in spite of adversity (Pearman, Huang, Barnhart, & Mellblom, 1992). Similar to benefits for students with disabilities, positive attitudes develop only when appropriate guidance from adults is provided. In terms of academic outcomes, children without disabilities have not been shown to be adversely affected by inclusion.

Finally, parents and teachers also benefit from including children with disabilities in regular education classrooms (Schumm & Vaughn, 1995). Teachers often learn new classroom strategies, acquire better planning skills, and develop competence in individualizing their instruction to meet students' diverse needs. Teachers report that being more flexible and adaptive increases their sense of self-efficacy related to teaching. Parents of students in inclusive settings develop more positive attitudes toward their child with disabilities and a more realistic perspective of their child's accomplishments and challenges. They also feel less socially isolated from the community when their children attend neighborhood schools. They benefit by having the opportunity to meet and interact with other parents with whom they can share common school experiences.

There are several empirically validated "best practices" or "success principles" that promote inclusion for achieving these positive outcomes (Schaffner & Buswell, 1996; Webber, 1997). The first is a *vision* or philosophy that all children belong and can learn in inclusive classrooms, and that diversity among learners strengthens a classroom and offers greater opportunities for learning and development. The second principle is *leadership*—administrators must play active, positive, and supportive roles in the development and implementation of inclusion. The third practice relates to *establishing high standards* for educational outcomes for all students, including those with disabilities. A fourth component is a *sense of community* or belonging to foster self-esteem, pride in individual achievements, mutual respect, and self-worth among all students. Having an *array of services* that are coordinated across and among educational and community professionals is a fifth practice for inclusion. Sixth, inclusive classrooms must be *flexible learning environments* using a variety of grouping procedures, authentic and meaningful learning experiences, and responsive curriculum that is accessible to all students. *Using research-based strategies* is another principle of successful inclusion. There is a growing body of research to document the effectiveness of specific teaching strategies and instructional approaches for diverse learners, including cooperative learning, peer-mediated learning, reciprocal teaching, and curriculum-based monitoring. *Collaboration and cooperation* are also essential for successful inclusion. Inclusive classrooms create natural situations for collaboration among both students and staff. For inclusion to be successful, all school personnel must work together and support each other through professional collaboration. Related to collaboration is the notion of *changing roles and responsibilities* among school staff. For example, the role of teachers may change from being direct instructors to facilitators of learning. Necessary for evaluating the success of inclusion is the development of *new forms of accountability and student assessment* to monitor progress toward important goals, including the use of performance-based assessment practices. Another best practice for inclusion relates to *access*—offering technology and providing necessary modifications to assure full access and participation among all students. The final principle for successful inclusion is *creating partnerships with parents*. In successful inclusive schools, parents are full partners in planning and implementing inclusive strategies.

Clearly, one of the greatest reforms facing education today is the inclusion of children with disabilities in regular education classrooms. This reform has resulted in and will continue to involve expanded roles and new contributions from researchers and practitioners in the field of psychology (Talley & Short, 1996). There are four major areas of contribution. First, determining how to enhance learning and development for all children with special needs requires investigation into the effects of social and psychological variables on individual children. Psychologists will be called upon to contribute the knowledge and methodology for systematic data collection, analysis, and interpretation of findings from research to identify variables that affect performance of students with and without disabilities. Second, inclusion calls for a reevaluation of the purposes and practices of assessment in psychology—specifically, moving away from assessment for classification purposes to assessment for purposes of developing effective interventions. Third, psychologists will have an increasingly important role in working collaboratively with teachers and other school-based and community professionals for improving learning and behavior among students with disabilities. Effective modifications for individual students require the application of knowledge from several areas in psychology—learning theory, behavior analysis, cognitive psychology, curriculum design, and effective teaching. A final contribution of psychology to inclusive education involves the evaluation of outcomes, including knowledge and implementation of appropriate research designs and program evaluation procedures.

[*See also* Exceptional Students.]

Bibliography

Alper, S., & Ryndak, D. L. (1992). Educating students with severe handicaps in regular classes. *The Elementary School Journal, 92,* 373–387.

Buysse, B., & Bailey, D. B. (1993). Behavioral and developmental outcomes in young children with disabilities in integrated and segregated settings: A review of comparative studies. *The Journal of Special Education, 26,* 434–461.

Fuchs, D., & Fuchs, L. S. (1994). Inclusive school movement and radicalization of special education reform. *Exceptional Children, 60,* 294–309.

Hasazi, S. B., Johnston, A. P., Liggett, A. M., & Schattman,

R. A. (1994). A qualitative policy study of the least restrictive environment provision of the Individuals with Disabilities Education Act. *Exceptional Children, 60*, 491–507.

Karagiannis, A., Stainback, W., & Stainback, S. (1996). Rationale for inclusive schooling. In S. Stainback & W. Stainback (Eds.), *Inclusion: A guide for educators* (pp. 3–15). Baltimore, MD: Paul H. Brookes.

Little, S. G., & Witek, J. M. (1996). Inclusion: Considerations from social validity and functional outcome analysis. *Journal of Behavioral Education, 6*, 283–291.

MacMillan, D. L., Gresham, F. M., & Forness, S. R. (1996). Full inclusion: An empirical perspective. *Behavioral Disorders, 12*, 145–159.

McIntosh, R., Vaughn, S., Schumm, J. S., Haager, D., & Lee, O. (1993). Observations of students with learning disabilities in general education classrooms. *Exceptional Children, 60*, 249–261.

Pearman, E. L., Huang, A. M., Barnhart, M. W., & Mellblom, C. (1992). Educating all students in school: Attitudes and beliefs about inclusion. *Education and Training in Mental Retardation, 27*, 176–182.

Roach, V. (1995). *Winning ways: Creating inclusive schools, classrooms, and communities.* Alexandria, VA: National Association of State Boards of Education.

Schaffner, C. B., & Buswell, B. E. (1996). Ten critical elements for creating inclusive and effective school communities. In S. Stainback & W. Stainback (Eds.), *Inclusion: A guide for educators* (pp. 49–65). Baltimore, MD: Paul H. Brookes.

Schumm, J. S., & Vaughn, S. (1995). Getting ready for inclusion: Is the stage set? *Learning Disabilities: Research & Practice, 10*, 169–179.

Talley, R. C., & Short, R. J. (1996). Social reform and the future of school practice: Implications for American psychology. *Professional Psychology: Research and Practice, 27*, 5–13.

Webber, J. (1997). Responsible inclusion: Key components for success. In P. Zionts (Ed.), *Inclusion strategies for students with learning and behavior problems: Perspectives, experiences, and best practices* (pp. 27–55). Austin, TX: Pro-Ed.

Maribeth Gettinger

MALINGERING is defined by the fourth edition of the *Diagnostic and Statistical Manual of Mental Disorders* (*DSM–IV*; Washington, DC, 1994) as the intentional production of false or grossly exaggerated physical or psychological symptoms motivated by external incentives such as avoiding military duty or work, obtaining financial compensation, evading criminal prosecution, or obtaining drugs. The key features of the phenomenon are conscious fabrication or exaggeration of complaints that are produced for the goal of obtaining obviously desirable outcomes. Malingered psychological disturbance has a long history in the lay literature, having been described in *The Iliad*, where Ulysses appears to have feigned madness to avoid the Trojan War, as well as in the Old Testament of the Bible where David feigned insanity to escape persecution. Early modern descriptions of malingering more often involved physical complaints, and appeared in military contexts such as the American Civil War or the mass European wars of the late nineteenth and twentieth centuries. Social insurance systems such as those introduced in Europe in the latter part of the nineteenth century may, however, have been tapped by enterprising individuals thought to be feigning a complex condition quaintly termed "railway spine." Most early papers on malingered mental disorders in the professional literature were presented in the context of case series reports of patients exhibiting apparently fabricated symptoms. However, by the middle part of the twentieth century, more systematic work began. Drawing on Freudian theory which emphasized the importance of the unconscious, psychiatric researchers recognized that hysteria, now known as conversion disorder, was a critical boundary condition conceptually bordering on malingering. In conversion disorder, patients exhibit symptoms involving disorders of voluntary sensory or motor functioning, such as blindness or paralysis, which upon appropriate investigation are shown to have no neurological cause. These often dramatic symptoms are thought to have a psychological cause, albeit one which is not consciously appreciated. Thus, the distinction between malingering and conversion disorder rests on the extent to which the symptoms are consciously versus unconsciously produced. Another interesting boundary condition abutting malingering is factitious disorder. In this syndrome, patients deliberately feign symptoms apparently for the sole purpose of adopting the sick role. The intrapsychic importance in this syndrome of obtaining medical attention is highlighted by the surprising proportion of patients with this condition who have received medical training of some sort (nurses, medical technicians, and so forth) or are related to physicians by blood or marriage. The critical distinction between malingering and factitious disorder hinges on the extent to which the apparent end serves obscure intrapsychic goals (achieving the sick role) versus obvious external goals (financial awards, avoiding work).

Although the *DSM–IV* formulation is superficially appealing, it has been criticized for requiring difficult, if not impossible, clinical distinctions (e.g., discriminating conscious versus unconscious motivation) and resting on an obsolete conceptualization of malingering. Richard Rogers (1997), one of the foremost authorities on malingered mental disorders, has argued that the *DSM-IV* formulation of malingering is unduly moralistic and should be replaced with what he terms an *adaptational model*. In the adaptational model, malingering is essentially seen as behavior produced and maintained by desirable reinforcers. Malingering patients are thought to find themselves in circumstances in which feigning symptoms is the most attractive way to obtain goals. Thus, rather than being an "evil" act of deceiving clinicians, malingering is seen from the perspective of the adaptational model as misleading behavior which is understandable, if not excusable, in the context of the patient's situation.

Malingering is of particular concern to mental health clinicians because of the heavy reliance on self-reported symptoms in the diagnosis of mental disorders. Many manifestations of psychological disorders, such as obsessive thoughts or suspicious ideas, are private events that occur in a patient's subjective experience. Although truthful reports of symptoms by patients are extremely useful in routine clinical practice, in a number of circumstances, self-reports cannot simply be assumed to be accurate. For example, defendants who are accused of committing crimes and who are undergoing psychological examination regarding their mental state at the time of the criminal act (insanity pleas) or being evaluated for competence to assist in their legal defense obviously have potentially powerful incentives to exaggerate or fabricate symptoms. Similarly, plaintiffs in civil proceedings seeking compensation for psychological damage also have potential reinforcers for feigning or embellishing complaints. Although it is thought that only a minority of individuals in these circumstances feign psychological symptoms, it is now generally agreed that in such situations, the accuracy of self-reports must be evaluated.

A variety of methods have been used for evaluating malingering. In one popular approach, scales for detecting feigned symptom reports are embedded within the context of long, multisymptom psychological inventories. Perhaps the best example of this approach is the F scale from the original Minnesota Multiphasic Personality Inventory. The F scale consisted of 64 items selected for a wide range of content and a low endorsement rate in normal individuals. High scores on this scale were thought to be unlikely to result from accurate self-reports of psychopathology because most disorders have a characteristic, restricted range of associated symptoms. Therefore, patients accurately reporting their problems were thought to endorse only a limited subset of the F-scale items. The F scale on the MMPI, as well as the slightly shorter F scale on the revised MMPI-2, have been shown to be very sensitive to feigned psychological symptoms, although it is important to address alternative explanations such as random responding or the presence of severe psychopathology. Similar, although less thoroughly researched, "faking" scales are present on most leading contemporary omnibus personality-psychopathology inventories, including the Millon Clinical Multiaxial Inventory–III, the Personality Assessment Inventory, and the California Personality Inventory. However, diagnosis of

malingering should not be made simply on the basis of high scores on any of these scales. Confirming extratest data are necessary for accurate identification of feigned psychological symptoms.

One clinical phenomenon that illustrates the need for extratest data in evaluating the possibility of malingering is the "cry for help." This occurs when a patient who appears only mildly to moderately disturbed produces highly pathological results on psychological testing. If the patient has no discernible gain from his or her apparently distorted approach to answering psychological test questions, clinicians often interpret this as an attempt to attract clinical attention as opposed to frank malingering. Rather than merely attempting to achieve the sick role, as in factitious disorder, these patients appear to be concerned that their complaints might be overlooked or minimized by busy clinicians and attempt to prevent this by drawing attention to their problems. Distinguishing a "cry for help" from malingering or factitious disorder requires careful consideration of the patient's circumstances and apparent goals in exaggerating their psychological symptoms. It is also easily understood from the standpoint of the adaptational model described earlier.

Another major approach to detecting malingering has involved the use of psychological tests specifically developed to identify feigning. Richard Rogers has published an instrument constructed for assessment of malingering of psychological disorders called the Structured Interview of Reported Symptoms (SIRS). The SIRS utilizes a fixed set of questions employing a variety of strategies, such as endorsement of unlikely symptoms or improbably severe symptoms, to detect feigning. The SIRS has been shown to be effective for detection of feigned mental disorder in a number of studies. Several other tests developed for detection of malingering have been introduced, but little research documenting their effectiveness is available at this writing.

A number of other procedures have been used to detect malingered psychological disorder. In general, research has not supported the effectiveness of approaches dramatized by the media such as drug-assisted interviews (questioning following administration of "truth serum"), the most popular types of polygraph testing ("lie detector tests"), hypnosis, and reliance on clinical impression for the detection of feigned psychological disorders.

Neuropsychological assessment, which involves the use of psychological tests for diagnosis of brain dysfunction, has also become increasingly concerned with the issue of malingering in the context of evaluations for legal purposes. A growing literature in this area documents the sensitivity of neuropsychological test scores to inadequate effort, which may erroneously suggest brain damage. Several procedures, such as the

Digit Memory Test and the Portland Digit Recognition Test, have been shown to be reasonably accurate for the detection of poor motivation during neuropsychological testing and are recommended for routine use during evaluations conducted for legal purposes.

Overall, the development of techniques for the identification of malingering is at a relatively immature stage. Although a few approaches have obtained reasonable support from scientific investigations, more work is clearly needed to develop conceptualizations further and increase diagnostic accuracy. Current evidence suggests that feigning of psychological disorders is a multifaceted phenomenon that should be considered whenever results desirable to an evaluee are contingent on the outcome of an evaluation. Continued research on this problem will eventually bring better understanding of the causes, characteristics, and consequences of malingered psychological symptoms.

Bibliography

Ford, C. (1996). *Lies, lies, lies! The psychology of deceit.* Washington, DC: American Psychiatric Press. Links clinical manifestations of deception with deceit in everyday life.

Lewis, M., & Saarni, C. (Eds.). (1993). *Lying and deception in everyday life.* New York: Guilford Press. Explores the roots of deception in human experience as well as among animals.

Rogers, R. (Ed.). (1997). *Clinical assessment of malingering and deception.* New York: Guilford Press. Provides overview and summary of current literature on assessment of dissimulation in the context of psychological evaluations.

David T. R. Berry

MALPRACTICE. The generic term for legal liability that arises when a standard of professional practice falls below what is acceptable to the profession itself, ordinarily, *malpractice* gives rise to civil liability (money damages), although in rare instances malpractice may result in criminal charges.

The most common legal action for malpractice is in the tort of negligence. The tort of negligence generally involves four elements: (1) the existence of a legal duty; (2) the breach of that duty; (3) an injury recognized by the law; (4) a causal link between the breach of duty and the injury.

Negligence is based on the failure of the defendant (person who caused the harm) to act as a "reasonably prudent person would under the circumstances." In the case of professional malpractice, negligence is generally demonstrated by showing that the professional engaged

in a standard of care that was below that which is reasonably acceptable by the profession. Thus, malpractice is generally what the profession itself would see as "bad practice." It is important to note that the quality of care need not be perfect, but to avoid liability it must not fall below that which a reasonably careful practitioner would provide under the circumstances.

Malpractice liability may also be based on a variety of torts other than negligence, including defamation (libel and slander), invasion of privacy, false imprisonment, and battery. In addition, a number of special statutory provisions may give rise to professional liability. For example, a professional who discriminates against a client based on disability may be liable under the Americans with Disabilities Act, or a practitioner who violates the federal civil rights of a person may be liable under other federal statutes. Some states have made it a crime to engage in certain forms of malpractice. Some states, for example, make it a crime for a psychotherapist to engage in sex with a client, and most states make it a crime to fail to report child abuse.

Psychologists have a number of important defenses against malpractice claims. First, they may claim that the injuries did not result from the negligence of the defendant psychologist. Second, they may state that while the practice was not perfect or ideal, it did not fall so low as to be beneath the standard of care for the profession. They may also claim that there was, in fact, no legally recognizable injury to the client. These are powerful defenses in many cases, because the plaintiff (injured client) has the burden of proving the elements of negligence.

Compared with many other health-care professionals, psychologists and psychiatrists have a relatively low rate of malpractice claims and recovery. This is as a result of several factors, including the reluctance of clients to disclose very personal information during a trial of psychotherapy issues, the fact that many psychological injuries are not obvious, the close personal relationship that clients generally have with psychotherapists, and the traditional reluctance of the law to recognize emotional injuries where there has been no physical injury.

Despite the comparatively low rate of malpractice among psychotherapists, both the number and the size of claims against therapists have been increasing in recent years. In part this reflects the recognition by the law of several new kinds of liability. For example, in most states therapists may be subject to liability for failure to take action to protect or warn the identifiable victims of dangerous clients. Other major areas of liability include the following: engaging in improper sexual contact or other dual relationships with patients or former patients; inappropriate breach of the confidentiality of therapy; the suicide of a patient that was preventable; injuries related to prescription drugs (this is mainly applied to psychiatrists because psychologists do not have prescribing authority); and failure to make proper diagnosis.

The vast majority of mental health malpractice cases arise from clinical practice. Liability may also arise from experimental misconduct, but such cases are rare. Also uncommon is liability arising from such I/O activities as employment test construction. Forensic activities (e.g., testimony in a civil commitment or child custody case) are usually protected by fairly strong immunity from liability, but a therapist who does not act in good faith may be subject to liability.

The current malpractice system has been criticized on many grounds. It is often a very lengthy and expensive process, requires that lay jurors resolve difficult scientific questions, leaves both the plaintiff and the defendant in an emotionally difficult position over an extended period of time, and may result in the release of a substantial amount of very confidential information about the client. For these reasons, a variety of reforms have been proposed as alternatives to the malpractice liability case. For example, some form of arbitration or mediation might be used. To date, however, such reforms have not been adopted widely, and it is reasonable to expect that the current system will continue in the foreseeable future.

[*See also* Liability.]

Bibliography

Jorgenson, L. M., Sutherland, P. K., & Bisbing, S. B. (1995). Transference of liability: Employer liability for sexual misconduct by therapists. *Brooklyn Law Review, 60,* 1421–1481. Reviews the troublesome area of liability based on therapists' improper sexual contact with patients and the degree to which vicarious liability may also make their employers responsible for this misconduct.

Kelley, J. L. (1996). *Psychiatric malpractice: Stories of patients, psychiatrists, and the law.* New Brunswick, NJ: Rutgers University Press. Reviews four different kinds of actual malpractice cases, and considers the roles of mental health professionals, judges, and expert witnesses in these cases.

Perlin, M. L. (1994). *Law and mental disability.* Charlottesville, VA: Michie. Discusses many aspects of mental health professionals' malpractice in chapter 3, "Mental Disability and Tort Law" (pp. 397–498).

Reaves, R. P. & Ogloff, J. R. (1996). Liability for professional misconduct. In L. J. Bass, J. R. Ogloff, S. T. DeMers, C. Peterson, & J. L. Pettifor (Eds.), *Professional conduct and discipline in psychology* (pp. 117–142). Washington, DC: American Psychological Association; Montgomery, AL: Association of State and Provincial Psychology Boards. Considers the situations in which malpractice may arise (e.g., negligence, failure to warn, and breach of confidentiality), as well as criminal liability.

Saccuzzo, D. P. (1997). Liability for failure to supervise adequately mental health assistants, unlicensed practitioners and students. *California Western Law Review, 34,* 115–152. Carefully reviews the malpractice consequences of inadequate supervision in mental health practice.

Shuman, D. W. (1997). The standard of care in medical malpractice claims, clinical practice guidelines, and managed care: Towards a therapeutic harmony? *California Western Law Review, 34,* 99–113. Considers how formal practice guidelines can be used to establish and define professional standards and argues that the standards should be available to the courts for this purpose.

Slawson, P. (1993). Psychiatric malpractice: The low frequency risks. *Medicine & Law, 12,* 673–680. Carefully reviews a large set of data regarding psychiatric malpractice, and concludes that contrary to popular belief, there is a low level of liability related to abandonment, informed consent, ECT ("shock" therapy) and billing.

Smith, S. R. (1991). Mental health malpractice in the 1990s. *Houston Law Review, 28,* 209–283. Discusses the level of malpractice claims against mental health professionals, as well as the modern basis for such claims.

Smith, S. R. (1996). Malpractice liability of mental health professionals and institutions. In B. D. Sales & D. W. Shuman (Eds.), *Law, mental health, and mental disorder* (pp. 76–98). Pacific Grove, CA: Brooks/Cole. Reviews malpractice in psychology generally, from the perspectives both of practitioners and the institutions in which they work. Also criticizes the current tort system's processing of malpractice claims.

Smith, S. R., & Meyer, R. G. (1987). *Law, behavior, and mental health: Policy and practice* (pp. 3–43). New York: New York University Press. Chapter 1, "Ethics, Malpractice, and the Mental Health Professions," provides a detailed discussion of liability issues in mental health practice, including specific areas that give rise to malpractice claims.

Tarasoff v. Regents of the University of California, 551 P.2d 334 (Cal. 1976). This influential case held that mental health professionals could be liable for failing to take steps to protect third parties from their dangerous patients. This is sometimes called the "duty to warn."

Steven R. Smith

MANAGED CARE. The term *managed care* refers to a variety of methods of paying for and managing the delivery of health care that are all designed to control costs through standardization and control of access, utilization, or quality of services (Austad & Berman, 1991). Managed care began as prepaid health care more than 50 years ago, and was designed to provide care for persons who were either too far from physicians or lacked the resources to pay for needed care at all times (Roemer, 1985). The oldest method is the staff-model or group-model health maintenance organization (HMO). These organizations provide all agreed-upon health-care services for a single, fixed monthly fee, by a fixed group of salaried providers. HMOs began after World War II, and include Kaiser-Permanente, Group Health Cooperative of Puget Sound, and the Health Insurance Plan of New York (HIP). The HMO Act of 1973 and the skyrocketing costs of health care in the United States stimulated the growth of alternative models, including preferred provider organizations (PPOs) and network model HMOs. A wide variety of hybrid financing and cost-control systems developed in the 1980s (Stout, Theis, & Oher, 1995), including point-of-service (POS) plans in which patients pay more for nonapproved providers than approved or "in-panel" providers; fixed fees for each case treated (case rates); and fixed fees for each person who identifies a provider as their provider (capitation rates). Psychology is most familiar with the PPO and POS systems and the accompanied case management approach to cost and service delivery control.

Managed care has successfully controlled the costs of medical care in the United States (Levit, Lazenby, & Braden, 1998). In addition, access to care is better under some forms of managed care. Careful review of cases, development of alternatives to costly inpatient care, and development or enhancement of short-term, targeted interventions has improved access and services for many consumers. There are significant questions as to whether managed care can continue to control costs of care, and whether the quality of health care suffers under managed care systems (Wells, Astrachan, Tischler, & Unutzer, 1995). Research efforts are underway to evaluate the impact of cost and care management.

Managed care organizations (MCOs) have used a wide range of specific techniques to control costs and utilization, some of which have received notoriety for their unethical appearance. For example, financial incentives for denying care have been offered to providers. In addition, unreasonable denials of needed care such as emergency room care for chest pain, and contractually precluding providers from providing information to the patient that might reflect negatively on the MCO have been documented. Use of these methods varies widely, but they have received significant attention because of their impact on both consumers and providers. Additional threats to patient care include violations of confidentiality, lack of access to needed care, restricted choice of providers, and nonclinical treatment decision making. Legislative efforts, including a Patient's Bill of Rights, are intended to address these inequities, and maintain a balance between the value and risk of managed care approaches for those needing health-care services.

Bibliography

Austad, C., & Berman, W. H. (Eds.). (1991). *Psychotherapy in managed health care: Optimal use of time and resources.* Washington, DC: American Psychological Association Press. A text providing conceptual models and practical methods for treating patients under the time and utilization constraints of managed care.

Levit, K. R., Lazenby, H. C., & Braden, B. R. (1998). National health spending trends in 1996. National Health Accounts Team. *Health Affairs, 17,* 35–51.

Roemer, M. I. (1985). I. S. Falk, the committee on the costs of health care and the drive for national health insurance. *American Journal of Public Health, 75,* 841–848.

Stout, C. E., Theis, J., & Oher, J. (Eds.). (1995). *The complete guide to managed behavioral care.* New York: Wiley. A recent guide to practicing mental health care under a wide range of managed care systems, including risk management, information systems, and financial systems.

Wells, K. B., Astrachan, B. M., Tischler, G. L., & Unutzer, J. (1995). Issues and approaches in evaluating managed mental health care. *Milbank Quarterly, 73,* 57–75.

William H. Berman

MANAGEMENT. *See* Organizational Management.

MANDATED REPORTING. Every state mandates designated workers (e.g., physicians, psychologists, child care workers, etc.) to report "suspected" child maltreatment, providing civil or criminal penalties for a "willful failure to report," and "good faith" immunity from suit if a report is unfounded. The statutes define child maltreatment and authorize investigations. (State laws differ; each state's laws regarding child abuse reporting, elder abuse reporting, or domestic violence reporting should be consulted.) Many states also have statutes that define elder abuse, permit or require reports, and authorize investigations. Some states have reporting provisions for domestic violence.

The New York Society for the Prevention of Cruelty to Children was chartered in 1875 with power to investigate and assist in the prosecution of child maltreatment, to take children in custody, and to place them in institutions. Child abuse was rediscovered in the early 1960s following research on the "battered child syndrome" (Kempe, Silverman, Steele, Droegemueller, & Silver, 1962). All states passed laws requiring physicians and others who worked with children and families to make reports of suspected child maltreatment to a designated social service or child protection agency, or to the police.

Child Abuse

Child maltreatment includes neglect and physical, emotional, and sexual abuse. Although extreme examples are clear, in the marginal case, legal ambiguity makes the reporting decision a problem. The 1974 Federal Child Abuse Prevention and Treatment Act defined "excessive" corporal punishment as child abuse: What is "excessive"? Those who believe in corporal punishment as discipline argue that state intervention unnecessarily limits parental authority. Neglect is ill-defined: How dirty or how ill-clothed must a child be before the state intervenes? How much is neglect, and how much is a function of poverty? Reports of neglect and abuse are correlated with family income. Emotional neglect is difficult to define, as is sexual abuse. A high percentage of reports from mental health sources are of sexual abuse. Beyond a child's disclosure, there is no psychological syndrome characteristic of sexual abuse. Fondling or oral intercourse may leave no marks; many physical signs of intercourse may be ambiguous.

Because the law requires reports of "reasonable suspicions," and because the consequences of a report are serious for the alleged perpetrator, some professionals adopt strict standards and report fewer cases; others adopt lenient standards, reporting more cases. Some see reporting as a route to obtain services for clients.

Mandated reporting laws allow those in confidential relationships to report suspected child abuse without being subject to action for breaching confidentiality. Reports have grown from 669,000 in 1976 to about 2 million reports on about 3 million children in 1995. Nationally, about 38% of reports are substantiated on investigation; the substantiation rate varies from state to state, and varies by counties within states. Mandated reports are substantiated at a higher rate than those made by the general public. Because not all cases are reported, official reports underestimate the amount of child abuse and neglect in the population.

A report triggers an investigation. Child protection workers or the police are empowered to remove children from their homes in emergencies. If a report is substantiated and a family refuses services, the case may be heard in a specialized dependency court. The judge may order the child's removal from parental custody. Most states have a family preservation policy stating a preference for children to remain in their own homes or to be returned home after removal as soon as parents are rehabilitated. This policy is controversial because of fears for the child's safety. It is also a problem because of our inability to predict accurately the likelihood of future abuse. If rehabilitation fails, parental rights may be terminated and the child released for adoption. If the parent is allegedly mentally retarded or mentally ill, or has been in treatment, mental health professionals may testify at the termination hearing.

Mandated reporting creates an ethical bind: obey the law, but breach confidentiality. Perhaps a third of mental health professionals fail to make a report when they should. Those professionals say that reporting in the particular case does more harm than good; some want to avoid the time involved to respond to investigators or to go to court if the case went forward. About 40% of professionals making a report say reporting is personally stressful. Most professionals working with children and families make at least one report in the course of their careers; some make many.

Arguably, informed consent requires notification of limits of confidentiality before a client enters treatment, but about half of mental health professionals do not initially inform the client of their mandate to report. Some fear informing clients will chill disclosures, thus limiting the ability to protect children. However, fuller informed consent initially may be associated with better outcomes after a report is made.

Effects of Reporting Abuse

About a quarter of clients in treatment drop out after the therapist makes a report; a few continue but with increased resistance. For others, initial anger can be overcome; therapy can continue. For about another quarter, the report may result in an improvement. Fears that therapy will inevitably be spoiled by reporting are not borne out by research. The outcome depends on the relationship the therapist had with the client before the report, and whether the alleged perpetrator was a member of a family in treatment, the client in treatment, or another person not in treatment (e.g., a noncustodial parent). Another factor that influences the effect of a report on the therapeutic relationship is the role of the child protection worker in supporting the therapy, or in relating to the therapist and the client after a report.

We know very little about the outcomes of the child protection intervention. Certainly things are better for those children who are removed from horrible situations. However, whether child protection interventions have any significant impact on less extreme cases remains to be demonstrated. Critics assert that the system is overloaded and top heavy with investigations, but delivers services to relatively few. Some have called for thorough reform of the child protection system to make it more neighborhood and community based and more service oriented.

Elder Abuse

With the increasing number of older Americans, societal concern about the welfare of the elderly has increased. The National Center on Elder Abuse estimated that 735,000 elderly Americans were subject to abuse in their own homes or in nursing homes. The abuse may be physical, emotional, sexual, financial, or the older person may be neglected. About half the laws cover the infliction of mental anguish as well. Some state laws permit the agency to intervene when there is "self-neglect." Forty-four states have adult protective services. Many laws cover individuals 18 or older, but some specify ages 60 or 65. Social workers, physicians, nurses, police officers, dentists, and dental hygienists are designated in statutes as mandated reporters of elder abuse. Mental health professionals and psychologists are included in about a quarter of the laws. Many states permit "any other person" to report as well. The failure of a mandated professional to report is a misdemeanor in many states. Prosecutions for failure to report are more likely when the offense is committed in an institution rather than in the elderly person's home. In some states, the elderly person may recover money damages from the mandated reporter for injuries that followed because of the failure to report.

Reports are made to adult protective service agencies, social service agencies, or to law enforcement. Some states have special investigative units to handle reports of abuse in state or local government operated facilities (e.g., county home). The designated agency initiates an investigation, usually within 48 hours. The investigator may have legal authority to enter the home, and may call upon police; elder abuse offenses are prosecuted in the criminal justice system.

Adult protective services may provide evaluation and assessment of mental competence, psychiatric, psychological, and medical services, or referral as needed. Following a hearing, courts may issue involuntary protective service orders for "endangered" adults. The order may appoint a guardian who manages the elderly person's assets. Mental health professionals may conduct examinations to determine the necessity for the guardianship or its continuation. People have a right to use their property lawfully. When is an elderly person making incompetent decisions, and when is a relative primarily concerned about preserving assets that might pass to him or her as an inheritance? There is little evaluation of adult protective services.

Domestic Violence

Child maltreatment is associated with domestic violence. It may be reportable as child maltreatment if a child witnesses domestic violence even if not physically injured. Advocates claim reporting laws are unfair to victims of domestic violence. Mothers may be charged with endangering the child's welfare for not adequately protecting a child from domestic violence. Reports may increase a woman's risk of further violence. The relationship between domestic violence and child maltreatment is a topic of current research.

One state (California) has a law requiring physicians to report domestic violence to the police. Others permit or require physicians to record suspicions of domestic violence in medical records. Some state laws provide good faith immunity from suit for any person reporting domestic violence to the police. Such laws permit physicians or others in a confidential relationship to report domestic violence concerns without fear of a breach of confidentiality suit. Not much is known about the consequences of mandated reporting for domestic violence, although many have expressed opinions on this controversial subject.

[*See also* Child Abuse and Neglect; Domestic Violence; Elder Abuse and Neglect; *and* Rape.]

Bibliography

Kalichman, S. C. (1993). *Mandated reporting of suspected child abuse: Ethics, law and policy.* Washington, DC: American Psychological Association. This is a comprehensive review of state laws on mandated reporting and research on whether and when mental health professionals and other mandated reporters make reports. It is also a comprehensive source of resources and state agencies involved in child abuse and neglect.

Kempe, C. H., Silverman, F., Steele, B., Droegemueller, W., & Silver, H. (1962). The battered child syndrome. *Journal of the American Medical Association, 181,* 17–24. This article is important historically because it triggered the renewed interest in child abuse and was a factor in stimulating mandated reporting legislation.

Levine, M., Doueck, H. J., Anderson, E. M., Chavez, E. T., Deisz, R. L., George, N. A., Sharma, A., Steinberg, K. L., & Wallach, L. (1995). *The impact of mandated reporting on the therapeutic process.* Thousand Oaks, CA: Sage. This monograph reviews research on the impact of mandated reporting on the psychotherapeutic process. It is based on interviews with therapists who made reports, with child protection workers who investigated reports from mental health sources, and on a national survey of mental health workers who had made mandated reports.

Levine, M., & Levine, A. (1992). *Helping children: A social history.* New York: Oxford University Press. The authors provide a history of the development of services for children in the nineteenth and early twentieth centuries. It includes a chapter on the development of child protective services as well as chapters on the juvenile court, school social work, child and guidance clinics.

National Center on Child Abuse and Neglect. (1996). *Child maltreatment 1994: Reports from the states to the National Center on Child Abuse and Neglect.* 22-10058. Washington, DC: Author. This compilation of statistics from all the states is published periodically. It contains data on child abuse reporting, investigations, and substantiations in all the states.

National Center on Child Abuse and Neglect. (1996). *The third national incidence study of child abuse and neglect (NIS-3).* Washington, DC: Author. This comprehensive report attempts to determine the incidence of child abuse and neglect by examining sources in addition to official reports. It also evaluates changes in rates depending on different definitions of child abuse and neglect, and examines socioeconomic correlates of the incidence of abuse and negelct.

Nelson, B. J. (1984). *Making an issue of child abuse*. Chicago: University of Chicago Press. This monograph describes how national legislation was introduced into the Congress and rapidly spread to all the states. It is useful background for understanding the political context for child abuse reporting legislation

Tatara, T. (1995). *An analysis of state laws addressing elder abuse, neglect and exploitation*. Washington, DC: National Center on Elder Abuse. This is a report of a survey of laws and services throughout the nation. It is an excellent resource for those who are beginning their research in the area of elder abuse.

U. S. Advisory Board on Child Abuse and Neglect. (1993). *Neighbors helping neighbors: A new national strategy for the protection of children*. Washington, DC: Administration for Children and Families. This report contains a major critique of the child protection system, and offers a new plan for child protective services that emphasizes helping over investigation and community based services over centrally provided services and investigation.

Murray Levine

MANIC DEPRESSION. *See* Bipolar Disorder; *and* Mood Disorders.

MARBE, KARL (1869–1953), German experimental and applied psychologist. Marbe was an important, if secondary, leader in the establishment of experimental psychology as a discipline separate from philosophy in Germany. He produced one of the earliest experimental dissertations not written under Wilhelm Wundt, and he taught with Oswald Külpe at Würzburg, where he was an important initiator of and contributor to the imageless thought studies. He was among the first (in Frankfurt, 1905) to be chosen as *Ordinarius* (senior faculty position) in experimental psychology; subsequently, his most important role was the demonstration and use of psychology in applied areas such as apparatus construction, court testimony, and advertising.

Marbe was born in Paris, where his father was active in the export business. His father's illness required a move to Freiburg, where Marbe's parents had been born and where his father then established a business. After his *Abitur* (completion of *Gymnasium*), Marbe made an exceptionally complete round of universities where there was something to be learned from experimental psychologists, going first to his home city of Freiburg (Hugo Münsterberg), then Berlin (E. Zeller, H. Ebbinghaus), Leipzig (Wundt, Külpe), Paris (A. Binet), and Bonn (J. B. Meyer, G. Martius). He settled in Bonn

to produce a dissertation under Meyer, although the experimental work was carried out in the personal laboratory of Götz Martius. His further work there led to his research on the Talbot-Plateau law, which led to his *Habilitation* (becoming a faculty member) in Würzburg, where he played a leading role in the early experiments on imageless thought.

Under Külpe, Marbe initiated the studies that created the "imageless thought" controversy. In 1901, he took the well-standardized Fechner-style studies of comparison of weights and showed that, in many cases, no introspective content about the judgment could be found, a result that posed direct problems for Wundt's voluntaristic psychology. Since Wundt had generally maintained that only studies in which each event was fully available to introspection provided satisfactory material for psychology, such a result raised a clear conflict between Leipzig and Würzburg. With the linguist Albert Thumb, he also initiated the experimental study of analogy in linguistics.

Marbe was chosen, at a relatively young age, to be the first professor (*Ordinarius*) of experimental psychology at the *Handelshochschule* (Graduate School of Commerce) in Frankfurt (to become the university in 1914), and when Oswald Külpe was chosen as *Ordinarius* in Bonn to replace Meyer, Marbe was chosen to replace Külpe in Würzburg, where he remained for the rest of his life. At about the same time as Münsterberg, Marbe (1913a) became one of the first psychologists to write a textbook about the requirements of providing professionally based evidence for courts, and he continued this role throughout his professional life. As he reports in his autobiography, he also spent 5 busy years (1926–1931) as director of the Psychological Institute at the Graduate School of Commerce (*Handelschochschule*) in Nurnberg.

Marbe was important to the organizational life of German psychology. When nonexperimental psychologists attacked the choice of Erich Jaensch to replace Hermann Cohen in Marburg, Marbe (1913b) wrote a pamphlet that surveyed their research and teaching (including whether it incorporated experimental psychology), using these data to show they neither taught experimental psychology nor practiced experimentation and thus to argue that their opinions need not be respected. In 1921, he reiterated the need to separate experimental psychology from philosophy; he was also the first person to follow Georg E. Müller's 23-year tenure as the chair of the German Society for Experimental Psychology, serving from 1927 to 1929.

Marbe's later work in psychology was primarily in applied areas, such as forensic psychology (including work in accident-prone behavior), advertising, and vocational advising. He was thus an important contributor to the expansion of applied psychology positions that took place in the 1920s and 1930s. He never supported the Gestalt movement and militantly opposed studies of occult phenomena, arguing that they were statistical artifacts. He was forced into retirement by the Nazi government in 1934. At the end of the war, he was recalled to his chair, where he taught until his death in Würzburg in 1953. He thus helped to found experimental psychology and became one of the important links between the experimental psychology of pre-Hitler times and later German psychology.

[*Many of the people mentioned in this article are the subjects of independent biographical entries.*]

Bibliography

Works by Marbe

Marbe, K. (1913a). *Grundzüge der forensiche Psychologie* [Fundamentals of forensic psychology]. Munich: Beck. Marbe's early significant work on psychological testimony in court cases. The book relies on the use of experimental methods to examine claims made by witnesses, in order to provide a stronger foundation for evidence.

Marbe, K. (1913b). *Die Aktion gegen die Psychologen* [The assault on the psychologists]. Leipzig, Germany: Tuebner. This pamphlet shows how active Marbe was in supporting the rising organization of experimental psychologists against traditional philosophers led by Paul Natorp who attempted, by petition, to prevent further selection of experimental psychologists for philosophy professorships.

Marbe, K. (1936). Karl Marbe. In C. Murchison (Ed.), *A history of psychology in autobiography* (Vol. 3). Worcester, MA: Clark University Press. A pleasant, chatty, personal account of Marbe's work in psychology. Since he does not point out the success of his work in creating a generation of early applied psychologists, his importance vis-à-vis Münsterberg can easily be overlooked.

Marbe, K. (1964). The psychology of judgements. In J. M. Mandler and G. Mandler (Eds. and Trans.), *Thinking: From association to gestalt*. New York: Wiley. (Original work published 1901.) This selection, which makes short excerpts of Marbe's work available in English, was important in the imageless thought controversy. The book as a whole contains considerable work for which Marbe was a guide and advisor.

Works about Marbe

Elrich, H. (1990). Karl Marbe, Psychologe. In *Neue deutsche Biographie* (Vol. 16, pp. 103–104). Berlin: Duncker & Humblot. The standard short German work on Marbe.

Peters, W. (1953). Karl Marbe. *American Journal of Psychology*, 65, 645–647. This obituary is helpful in that it points out Marbe's political positions and his lack of support for Gestalt psychology (which would not be clear from Mandler and Mandler's book).

Edward J. Haupt

MARGINALIZATION. The concept of *marginalization* was introduced by sociologists, then further developed by anthropologists, and has more recently become an issue for psychologists in their research and practice. Originally Stonequist (1935) proposed that following contact between cultural groups, many individuals in the nondominant group grow up in complex cultural circumstances; as a result, they may develop a particular set of psychological characteristics. The concept of marginalization has thus become employed at two levels: to describe the marginal *situation* of a group; and to describe the marginal *personality* of individuals in that situation (Kerckhoff & McCormick, 1955). The two levels are linked because "living as they do between two cultures, their personalities and careers are interwoven and linked with both systems. They thus mirror in their own personalities aspects of the two cultures, and especially the *relations* of the two cultures" (Stonequist, 1935, p. 3).

The marginal *situation* involves contact between two cultural groups in which one is usually dominant over the other. [*See* Acculturation.] There may be both cultural and "racial" differences between the groups, as well as individuals who trace their ancestry to both groups. For Stonequist (1935) the "general configuration (is) a bi-cultural (or multi-cultural) situation in which members of one cultural group are seeking to adjust themselves to the group which possesses the greater prestige and power" (p. 3). Examples of people in this situation given by Stonequist are Jewish immigrants to the United States, Métis in Canada, and Anglo-Indians in India (who are variously seen as "half caste" or "outcaste").

People in the marginal situation are thought by Stonequist to possess a particular "life cycle": first is a stage of "preparation" in which there is some initial assimilation of the marginal person to the dominant culture; then follows a "crisis" in which conflict, confusion, and estrangement characterize group relations. Finally, there are some more "enduring responses" in which the conflict is resolved either by "passing" into the dominant group (if there are no barriers) or by "swinging about and reaffirming" one's original identity. In the former case, there is assimilation, absorption, and eventual disappearance of the nondominant group; in the latter case there are nativistic and nationalistic movements, perhaps leading eventually to separation between the groups. Whether this "life cycle" is the only one, and whether the two outcomes are the only ones, will be considered below in relation to contemporary research.

The marginal *personality* was thought to be a consequence of living in the marginal situation: the marginal man is "poised in psychological uncertainty between two (or more) social worlds; reflecting in his soul the discords and harmonies, repulsions and attractions of these worlds . . ." (Stonequist, 1937, p. 8). Drawing upon Stonequist's views, Kerckhoff and McCormick (1955, p. 51) developed a "composite personality description" of the marginal man: he has serious doubts about his place in social situations, is unsure of social relationships, is ambivalent, with sudden shifts in mood, and unable to act decisively. Moreover, he is painfully self-conscious, feels lonely, isolated, apathetic, and impotent, and is hypersensitive, critical, apprehensive, gloomy, restless, and generally unhappy. Once again we may ask whether this description is an accurate one, and whether persons finding themselves in a marginal situation inevitably develop and display this personality profile.

Acculturation and Marginalization

At about the same time as marginality theory was evolving in sociology, the related notion of *acculturation* was being developed in anthropology. Both concepts are designed to conceptualize how cultural groups relate to each other, and what the psychological consequences might be for individuals. In an early formulation, "acculturation comprehends those phenomena which result when groups of individuals having different cultures come into continuous first hand contact, with subsequent changes in the original culture patterns of either or both groups" (Redfield, Linton, & Herskovits, 1936, pp. 149–152). In another formulation, acculturation was defined as

> culture change that is initiated by the conjunction of two or more autonomous cultural systems. Acculturative change may be the consequence of direct cultural transmission; it may be derived from noncultural causes, such as ecological or demographic modification induced by an impinging culture; it may be delayed, as with internal adjustments following upon the acceptance of alien traits or patterns; or it may be a reactive adaptation of traditional modes of life. (Social Science Research Council, 1954, p. 974)

In the first definition, acculturation is seen as one aspect of the broader concept of *culture change* (that which results from intercultural contact) and is distinguished from *assimilation* (which may be at times a phase). These are important distinctions for psychological work. In the second, a few extra features are added, including change that is indirect (not cultural, but "ecological"), delayed ("internal adjustments" of both a cultural and psychological character take time), and can be "reactive" (that is, changing toward a more "traditional" way of life, rather than inevitably toward the dominant culture; cf. "swinging about and reaffirming" in the marginality process).

As was the case for marginality theory, the idea

emerged in acculturation theory that individuals who belonged to cultural groups that were experiencing acculturation themselves experienced psychological consequences. This idea was made explicit by Graves (1967), who coined the term *psychological acculturation*. This concept refers to changes in an individual who is a participant in a culture contact situation, being influenced both directly by the external culture and by the changing culture of which the individual is a member. For psychologists, there is a very important reason for keeping these two levels distinct: Not every individual enters into, participates, and changes in the same way; rather substantial individual differences exist.

Psychological Approaches

The entry of marginalization and acculturation theory into psychology began in the 1950s and has had sporadic usage since then. The first studies were by Mann (1958, 1965) with South African "coloreds" and adolescents, who were clearly in a marginal situation. Mann developed a self-report scale to assess psychological marginality, incorporating traits of aggression, suspicion, uncertainty, victimization-rejection, and anxiety. This scale has been widely used in subsequent psychological studies as a benchmark for the presence of feelings of marginality.

Sensing a need for integrating these two concepts (marginalization and acculturation) for purposes of understanding individual psychological consequences of culture contact, Berry (1970, 1974) developed a framework to link them. This framework focuses on individual differences in what are called *acculturation strategies* (Berry, 1984). They are based upon an individual's orientation to two issues that are faced daily in intercultural contact situations. People are known to have a relative preference for maintaining their heritage culture and identity, and a relative preference for having contact with and participating in the larger society along with other ethnocultural groups. These two issues can be responded to on attitudinal dimensions. Generally positive or negative ("yes" or "no" responses) to these issues intersect to define four acculturation strategies. These strategies carry different names, depending on which group (the dominant or nondominant) is being considered. From the point of view of nondominant groups, when individuals do not wish to maintain their cultural identity and seek daily interaction with other cultures, the *assimilation* strategy is defined. In contrast, when individuals place a value on holding onto their original culture, and at the same time wish to avoid interaction with others, then the *separation* alternative is defined. When there is an interest in maintaining their original culture while in daily interactions with other groups, *integration* is the option; here, there is some degree of cultural integrity maintained, while at the same time seeking to participate as an integral part of the larger social network. Finally, when there is little possibility of or interest in cultural maintenance (often for reasons of enforced cultural loss) and little interest in having relations with others (often for reasons of exclusion or discrimination), then *marginalization* is defined.

This fourfold presentation was based on the assumption that nondominant groups and their individual members have the freedom to choose how they want to acculturate. This, of course, is not always the case (Berry, 1974). When the dominant group enforces certain forms of acculturation or constrains the choices of nondominant groups or individuals, then other terms need to be used. Integration can only be "freely" chosen and successfully pursued by nondominant groups when the dominant society is open and inclusive in its orientation toward cultural diversity (Berry, 1984). Thus, a mutual accommodation is required for integration to be attained, involving the acceptance by both groups of the right of all groups to live as culturally different peoples. This strategy requires nondominant groups to adopt the basic values of the larger society, while at the same time the dominant group must be prepared to adapt national institutions (e.g., education, health, labor) to better meet the needs of all groups now living together in the plural society. In this sense, integration is the psychological opposite to marginalization.

Obviously, the integration strategy can only be pursued in societies that are explicitly *multicultural*, in which certain psychological preconditions are established. The preconditions are: the widespread acceptance of the value to a society of cultural diversity (i.e., the presence of a positive "multicultural ideology"); relatively low levels of prejudice (i.e., minimal ethnocentrism, racism, and discrimination); positive mutual attitudes among cultural groups (i.e., no specific intergroup hatreds); and a sense of attachment to or identification with the larger society by all individuals and groups. When these conditions are met, then the marginal situation (and the development of the marginal personality) is not the inevitable consequence of contact between cultural groups as suggested by earlier researchers.

These two basic issues were initially approached from the point of view of the nondominant ethnocultural group only. However, the original anthropological definition clearly established that *both* groups in contact would become acculturated. Hence, the role played by the dominant group in influencing the way in which mutual acculturation would take place was added as a third dimension (Berry, 1974). The addition of this third dimension produced an eightfold framework. For example, assimilation when sought by the acculturating group was termed the *melting pot*, but when demanded by the dominant group, assimilation was called the *pressure cooker*; and when separation was desired by the acculturating group it was termed *rejection*, but when forced by the dominant group it was *segregation*.

Current Issues

From the 1970s until the present, a few researchers in psychology have engaged the concept of marginalization, often in relation to the notion of acculturation. Much of this research has been carried out among indigenous peoples in Australia, Canada, and India and among various immigrant and refugee populations. The general picture is now clear (Berry, 1997). First, the two outcomes proposed by Stonequist are not the only ones: some assimilation (passing) does take place, as does some separation (reaffirmation), but integration is by far the most frequently preferred outcome found in studies, and marginalization is the least preferred. Second, the psychological consequences of marginalization portrayed by Stonequist and others are largely confirmed: for most people, being "poised in psychological uncertainty" indeed is problematic, and is linked to lowered mental health, specifically to increased anxiety and depression.

However, less negative consequences have been proposed for those living in between cultures. Lumsden (1984) has developed the notion of the "liminal" man, in which individuals value positively their independence from ethnic or cultural traditions and seek a more global sense of themselves. Related to this is the idea proposed by Bourhis et al. (1997): some people just don't want to identify with either culture, but prefer to see themselves as individuals; this view suggests that such persons are not necessarily suffering psychologically, but find their well-being as "individualists." Similarly Bennett (1997) has coined the terms *constructive marginal* to refer to people who are "able to construct context intentionally and consciously for the purpose of creating his or her own identity" (p. 5).

It is possible that "individualists" and "constructive marginals" do not differ from those who achieve "integration." Clearly, all three strategies are thought to be positive in terms of psychological well-being, and in some sense they are alternatives to marginalization. Perhaps the three constructs are best seen as varying in the degree to which "cultures" matter to people; for some people, their identities may be less linked to specific cultures or ethnicities and more associated with a universalist, panhuman identity. Such a possibility was not anticipated by Stonequist and others, given their time and place; just as likely, this possibility will evade most of the world's populations, who continue to live in culturally encapsulated contexts, where their daily behaviors and identities are closely tied to their domestic cultures.

Bibliography

Bennett, J. M. (1997). Culture marginality. In M. Paige (Ed.), *Education for intercultural experience* (pp. 1–27). Yarmouth, ME: Intercultural Press.

Berry, J. W. (1970). Marginality, stress and ethnic identification in an acculturated Aboriginal community. *Journal of Cross-Cultural Psychology, 1,* 239–252.

Berry, J. W. (1974). Psychological aspects of cultural pluralism, *Topics in Culture Learning, 2,* 17–22.

Berry, J. W. (1984). Cultural relations in plural societies: Alternatives to segregation and their sociopsychological implications. In M. Brewer & N. Miller (Eds.), *Groups in contact* (pp. 11–27). New York: Academic Press.

Berry, J. W. (1997). Immigration, acculturation and adaptation. *Applied Psychology, 46,* 5–68.

Bourhis, R. et al. (1997). Towards an interactive acculturation model. *International Journal of Psychology,* 369–386.

Graves, T. (1967). Psychological acculturation in a tri-ethnic community. *Southwestern Journal of Anthropology, 23,* 337–350.

Kerckhoff, A., & McCormick, T. (1995). Marginal status and marginal personality. *Social Forces, 34,* 48–55.

Lumsden, D. (1984). *Community mental health in action.* Toronto: Canadian Mental Health Association.

Mann, J. W. (1958). Group relations and the marginal personality. *Human Relations, 11,* 77–92.

Mann, J. W. (1965). Adolescent marginality. *Journal of Genetic Psychology, 106,* 221–235.

Stonequist, E. V. (1935). The problem of marginal man. *American Journal of Sociology, 41,* 1–12.

Stonequist, E. V. (1937). *The marginal man.* New York: Charles Scribner's.

John W. Berry

MARIJUANA, also known in the United States as "grass," "weed," "pot," "reefer," and "dope," comprises the dried leaves and flowering buds of the *Cannabis sativa* plant in the hemp family. Although many constituents can be isolated, marijuana has one major psychoactive ingredient, Δ^9-tetrahydrocannabinol (Δ^9-THC), which binds to the recently identified cannabinoid receptor in the brain to produce its characteristic psychoactive effects (Herkenham, 1995). Δ^9-THC is a very hydrophobic substance which can be extracted in alcohol and purified to a sticky oil. Δ^9-THC has a C_{21} three-ring chemical structure containing a pyran ring, phenolic hydroxyl group, and a linear 5-carbon-atom side chain. The type of structure places Δ^9-THC and other cannabinoids in the phenolic terpene family. Δ^9-THC is concentrated in the resinous portions of the marijuana plant, notably the growing tips and flowering buds. Cultivation and breeding techniques are used to elevate resin levels. Resin stripped from the plant is dried into hashish, a particularly potent form. Marijuana and hashish are smoked, although they can be consumed orally. Pyrolisis (burning) is an effective means of delivery, with rapid absorption into the bloodstream. In scientific studies in humans and animals, marijuana, Δ^9-THC, or synthetic analogs which bind to the cannabinoid receptor are administered by smoking or by oral, intraperitoneal, or intravenous routes of administration.

When marijuana is smoked or Δ^9-THC is injected intravenously, the onset and duration of the subjective experiences parallel the rise and fall of Δ^9-THC in the plasma, where levels peak at 10 to 15 minutes and have a half-life of about 45 minutes. Following oral administration, the peak and fall are considerably longer, lasting hours.

In humans, alterations in thought processes and behavior vary depending on dose, route of administration, setting, and previous experiences of the user. The major effect is a subjective experience termed a *high,* or more colloquially, being *stoned.* The high consists of a loosening of mental associations and fragmentation of thought (Hollister, 1986; Miller, 1984), leading to bizarre or otherwise altered trains of thought and unusual insights. These can be perceived as profound or funny, sometimes causing bouts of laughter. Perceptions of sights, sounds, tastes, and smells are enhanced. Personal detachment from surroundings or self (but without loss of self-control) is common (Tart, 1970). A sense of reverie or dissociation (e.g., floating) can occur, but frank hallucinations do not occur. Feelings of relaxation, pleasantness, or euphoria are common, but these are in part context dependent, and feelings of dysphoria, anxiety, or even panic can occur. Movement feels smooth and well coordinated. A high is typically accompanied or followed by drowsiness and somnolence. Other notable signs are red eye (due to peripheral vasodilatation) and dry mouth. A craving for palatable food can lead to the "munchies." Higher doses are more likely to cause adverse psychological effects (anxiety, paranoia, and panic attacks) and can inhibit movement. Other physical effects are increased heart rate (decreased rate in animals) and decreased blood pressure and body temperature.

The marijuana high is associated with certain kinds of memory deficits. The "stoned" individual can forget the train of thought or might forget episodes that occurred during the high. These can be recalled with special effort. Such deficits have both attentional and short-term memory components. In laboratory tests, Δ^9-THC and other cannabinoid agonist drugs disrupt selective aspects of short-term memory tasks (Miller, 1984), cause memory "intrusions" (Hooker & Jones, 1987), and impair temporal aspects of performance. These effects may be mediated by receptors residing on nerve cells in the hippocampus and cerebral cortex, where mnemonic processing takes place.

Laboratory animals do not self-administer cannabinoids; in fact, some studies show Δ^9-THC to be aversive. Δ^9-THC does elevate extracellular dopamine levels in the striatum in animals, a feature shared with other drugs of abuse associated with craving and dependence (Tanda, Pontieri, & Di Chiara, 1997). However, cannabinoid receptors are not located on dopamine neurons or their terminals, so the effects on dopamine release are indirect. In people, compulsive patterns of marijuana use can occur, and these are treated as addictions. Chronic use does not have pronounced neurophysiological consequences but can indicate a number of psychological problems such as an alienation from family and a failure to address responsibilities and make developmental adjustments.

Tolerance to repeated high-dose cannabinoid administration is observed experimentally (Jones & Benowitz, 1976; Oviedo, Glowa, & Herkenham, 1993). Dependence and craving are minimal and are associated with psychological rather than physiological conditions. Withdrawal following chronic use is subtle, manifested chiefly as a motor agitation (Jones & Benowitz, 1976; Tsou, Patrick & Walker, 1995).

There are virtually no reports of fatal cannabis overdose in humans (Dewey, 1986; Hollister, 1986). The safety reflects the paucity of cannabinoid receptors in the brain stem, specifically in medullary nuclei that control breathing and heart rate.

Cannabinoids have several therapeutic indications. In addition to stimulating appetite, smoked marijuana (and to a lesser extent, oral Δ^9-THC) reduces nausea and vomiting associated with cancer chemotherapy. This combination has made marijuana popular among AIDS patients undergoing AZT chemotherapy who suffer from nausea and wasting. By an unknown mechanism, marijuana lowers intraocular pressure, making it useful for treating glaucoma in some cases. By inhibiting movement, cannabinoids are beneficial for some forms of dystonia and for spasticity associated with multiple sclerosis (Marsden, 1981; Petro & Ellenberger, 1981). The combination of easing muscle tension and inducing drowsiness is appreciated by multiple sclerosis patients who smoke marijuana before bedtime. Finally, cannabinoids are potent antinociceptive agents in animals, and there are some indications that smoked marijuana is useful in blocking pain in people, especially chronic neuropathic-type pain unrelieved by traditional opiate treatments (Herzberg, Eliav, Bennet, & Kopin, 1997; Holdcroft et al., 1997).

[*See also* Drug Abuse.]

Bibliography

Dewey, W. L. (1986). Cannabinoid pharmacology. *Pharmacology Reviews, 38,* 151–178.

Herkenham, M. (1995). Localization of cannabinoid receptors in brain and periphery. In R. G. Pertwee (Ed.), *Cannabinoid receptors* (pp. 145–166). New York: Academic Press.

Herzberg, U., Eliav, E., Bennet, G. J., & Kopin, I. J. (1997). The analgesic effects of $R(+)$-WIN 55,212-2 mesylate, a high affinity cannabinoid agonist, in a rat model of neuropathic pain. *Neuroscience Letters, 221,* 157–160.

Holdcroft, A., Smith, M., Hodgson, H., Smith, B., Newton, M., & Evans, F. (1997). Pain relief with oral cannabinoids in familial Mediterranean fever. *Anesthesia, 52,* 483–486.

Hollister, L. E. (1986). Health aspects of cannabis. *Pharmacology Reviews, 38,* 1–20.

Hooker, W. D., & Jones, R. T. (1987). Increased susceptibility to memory intrusions and the Stroop interference effect during acute marijuana intoxication. *Psychopharmacology, 91,* 20–24.

Jones. R. T., & Benowitz, N. (1976). The 30-day trip—Clinical studies of cannabis tolerance and dependence. In M. C. Braude & S. Szara (Eds.), *The pharmacology of marihuana* (Vol. 2, pp. 627–642). New York: Raven Press.

Marsden, C. D. (1981). Treatment of torsion dystonia. In A. Barbeau (Ed.), *Disorders of movement, current status of modern therapy* (Vol. 8, pp. 81–104). Philadelphia: Lippincott.

Miller, L. L. (1984). Marijuana: Acute effects on human memory. In S. Agurell, W. L. Dewey, & R. E. Willette (Eds.), *The cannabinoids: Chemical, pharmacologic, and therapeutic aspects* (pp. 21–46). New York: Academic Press.

Oviedo, A., Glowa, J., & Herkenham, M. (1993). Chronic cannabinoid administration alters cannabinoid receptor binding in rat brain: A quantitative autoradiographic study. *Brain Research, 616* (1–2), 293–302.

Petro, D. J., & Ellenberger, C. J. (1981). Treatment of human spasticity with Δ^9-tetrahydrocannabinol. *Journal of Clinical Pharmacology, 21,* 413s–416s.

Tanda, G., Pontieri, F. E., & Di Chiara, G. (1997). Cannabinoid and heroin activation of mesolimbic dopamine transmission by a common μ_1 opioid receptor mechanism. *Science, 276,* 2048–2050.

Tart, C. T. (1970). Marijuana intoxication: Common experiences. *Nature, 226,* 701–704.

Tsou, K., Patrick, S. L., & Walker, J. M. (1995). Physical withdrawal in rats tolerant to Δ^9-tetrahydrocannabinol precipitated by a cannabinoid receptor antagonist. *European Journal of Pharmacology 280,* R13–R15.

Miles Herkenham

MARRIAGE. Across countries and cultures, almost all people are involved in a marriage, or a committed, marriagelike, couple relationship at some point in their lives in order to meet needs for affection, companionship, loyalty, and sexual and emotional intimacy. In Western cultures, over 90% of the population marries by age 50, and even of those who choose not to marry, most are involved in committed, marriagelike relationships. With the U.S. divorce rate estimated to be between 40% and 50% and the divorce rate for second marriages projected to be 10% higher than for first marriages, relationship dissolution is also a relatively common occurrence. The desire to be part of a committed relationship is strong even in people with negative past experiences of marriage; 75% of persons who divorce remarry within 3 years of getting divorced (Halford & Markman, 1997).

Changes in Marriage over Time

During the last three to four decades there have been substantial changes in rates of marital dissolution in the United States, Western Europe, Australia, and parts of Asia. These changes covary with a number of social changes, such as the increase in women working outside the home, increased acceptance of divorce, changes in divorce laws, the increased geographical mobility of couples, and reduced contact with extended family. For example, across cultures there is a correlation of about .3 between women working outside the home in one generation and divorce rates in the next. Associated with all these social changes is a transformation in the nature of marriage from relationships in which there were clear gender roles and definitions of power (the so-called traditional marriage) to more gender role–flexible and egalitarian relationships in the 1980s and 1990s (Notarius & Markman, 1993). Not surprisingly, these changes can generate conflict. For example, there may be differences over issues such as whose career is more important, who will be the predominant care giver for the children, or whose opinion will prevail regarding family money matters. Unfortunately, there were no concomitant changes in social institutions to provide couples with the skills to handle such inevitable conflicts, and research has shown that couples who are not able to handle these conflicts and negotiate the challenges in life are at increased risk for marital distress and divorce (Markman, Stanley, & Blumberg, 1994).

In Western culture, most marriages are the result of the partners' having a personal choice in the selection of their spouse. Little research has been conducted on marriages outside Western culture, yet most of the marriages in the world are occurring in these other cultures, and many of them are arranged unions. Data on the success and failure of arranged marriages (apart from divorce statistics, which are low) seem to be virtually nonexistent and are clearly an important part of a research agenda for understanding marriage worldwide. At the same time, as cultural, political, and economic changes are occurring in countries such as Japan, China, and India, alterations in marriage in these lands seem to parallel some aspects of the changes that are taking place in Western countries like the United States, those in Europe, and Australia and New Zealand. For example, recent data from Japan show that divorce rates have increased threefold for couples in the 20- to 29-year age bracket since the mid-1980s, and they appear to be associated with changing expectations about marriage and women working outside the home.

The Impact of Marriage on Individual Well-Being and Children

Marriage is good for the mental and physical health of the spouses (Burman & Margolin, 1992). In a mutually satisfying long-term couple relationship, the partners are protected from the negative effects of life stresses, to some extent, while in distressed relationships partners are more vulnerable to the negative effects of stress. Anxiety and individual maladjustment, including substance abuse or dependency (especially for men) and depression (especially for women), are associated with marital distress. Marital problems often precede the onset of individual problems like excessive drinking and depression and correlate with several health problems, including suppression of the immune system; happy marriages are associated with physical well-being.

With respect to children, growing up in a home with two stable and happy parents is one of the strongest protective factors against a wide variety of mental, physical, educational, and peer-related problems. A high degree of interparental conflict constitutes a major risk of poor mental health both for the parents and the children. Divorce is a risk factor for poor child outcomes, but it is destructive conflict between couples witnessed by their children that, in particular, is most damaging to children (Halford & Markman, 1997).

A positive marital relationship predicts low levels of child behavioral and emotional problems, while marital distress and interparental conflict are associated with significant concurrent and future adjustment problems for children (Emery, 1982). Marital conflict that is more overt, frequent, and intense predicts externalizing as well as internalizing problems, including conduct-related problems, social incompetence, depression, health problems, and poor school performance. Marital conflict is associated with more negative and less effective parenting strategies. However, it is unclear to what extent marital conflict impacts directly on children and to what extent its effects on children are mediated through negative parenting practices (Erel & Burman, 1995; Grych & Fincham, 1990).

Indices of Marital Success

There is no absolute definition of successful couple relationships; the standards by which people judge relationships vary by culture and individual. In the absence of any absolute criterion, relationship satisfaction has been widely used as an index of success. Relationship satisfaction can be defined as an individual partner's complete feelings toward, or evaluation of, their relationship. In psychology, relationship satisfaction usually is operationalized as the score on a global relationship measure. The most widely used measures are two self-report inventories: the Locke Wallace Marital Adjustment Test (MAT) and an expanded revision known as the Dyadic Adjustment Scale (DAS) (Halford & Markman, 1997).

The MAT and DAS, and many similar scales, have been subjected to repeated criticism for confounding relationship satisfaction, measured by items such as, "Overall, how would you rate your marital happiness," with adjustment processes alleged to influence satisfaction, measured by items such as, "How often do you and your partner disagree about finances?" While the collapsing of the constructs of relationship satisfaction and adjustment processes seems conceptually unsound, factor analyses of measures of marital satisfaction consistently show that partners make comprehensive evaluations of their relationships. Partners who are satisfied with their relationships have a positive bias in their reports about their relationships and tend to report that just about anything that could be positive about their relationship is positive.

In addition to satisfaction, a number of other comprehensive relationship characteristics have been proposed as indices of relationship success. Suggestions have included relationship stability, the psychological health and well-being of the partners and any offspring, and the extent to which the relationship buffers the partners against the adverse effects of life stress. Relationship satisfaction is strongly correlated with each of these other characteristics of relationship success. Steps toward separation and divorce usually, though not always, follow periods of deteriorating relationship satisfaction (Gottman, 1993). Relationship success has also been defined in terms of specific characteristics of couple interaction within the relationship. For example, the presence of physical aggression between partners is almost universally perceived as indicative of an unsuccessful relationship.

In contrast, each of the following has been proposed as an index of relationship success: the presence of intimate and self-disclosing communication, effective conflict management, mutual partner support, and shared positive activities. There is a strong association of each of these specific characteristics of couple interaction and complete relationship satisfaction (Halford & Markman, 1997).

In summary, relationship success can be defined relative to numerous criteria. Relationship satisfaction has high face validity as a criterion of success, and the level

of satisfaction is strongly related to other indices of relationship success, such as stability, individual well-being, and a number of characteristics of positive couple interaction. Thus, relationship satisfaction is a good overall index of relationship success.

Predictors of Marital Success

The most basic question in this field of research is why, when virtually all couples begin their relationships very satisfied and very much in love, over half end the relationship in divorce or chronic unhappiness. Relationships within social-learning perspectives suggests that couples begin their relationship happily and that levels of love and attraction are eroded by the negative way partners often treat each other as they negotiate the stress and conflict that inevitably occurs in relationships. Yet, there have been surprisingly few long-term intensive studies on the process of longitudinal change in couples' relationships. Reviews of the existing literature identify two types of factors that increase the risk of marital dissolution: static factors that cannot change as a function of intervention (e.g., divorce history and age) and dynamic factors that can alter how couples handle conflicts.

Consider the important issue of conflict management. Before the wedding day, most couples marrying for the first time have had few significant tests of their ability to handle conflict and negative emotions. Thus, relationship satisfaction is high. Yet research clearly indicates that how couples communicate and handle negative emotion at this stage foretells an important story about their future chances for divorce, stability, unhappiness, and satisfaction. As time progresses, couples increasingly cope with the challenges of life together. This explains in part why so many couples start out happy and committed only to find that their emotional attachment is eroded by the constant force of unresolved and upsetting conflicts that are not handled as a team.

Certain patterns of mismanaged conflict are repeatedly expressed in most couples that are already distressed or headed for divorce. These patterns include how spouses manage their own negative emotions when they are upset and, even more important, when their partner is upset. Couples headed for problems typically show patterns of escalation, withdrawal, and invalidation in such situations. In relationships headed for distress, the presence of the partner over time becomes associated with pain and frustration rather than support or pleasure. This violates basic expectations of having a marriage with a partner who is supportive, caring, and a friend for life. In sharp contrast, research suggests that there are a diversity of ways to have a happy relationship. This is very good news when it comes to designing intervention programs, because interventionists need to educate couples to avoid the destructive ways of handling the varieties of stress and challenge in relationships rather than give advice on how to have a good relationship (Markman, Stanley, & Blumberg, 1994).

Regardless of a couple's ability to handle conflict as a team, individual issues transferred into the relationship from personal and family-of-origin histories, as well as both predictable and unpredictable external stresses, play a role in determining the future relationship outcomes. Predictable life crises that most couples experience include the transition to parenthood, children entering school, and dealing with their own ailing parents. Unpredictable crises include losing a job, major family illnesses, and natural disasters, among others. Individual issues include alcohol and drug problems, and psychopathology such as depression and anxiety disorders.

A major research agenda for the next decade is the application of statistical techniques such as growth curve analyses to change in outcomes over time of couples as a function of conflict management ability, individual factors, and external factors. Outcome measures must be expanded to include not only couples outcomes but child, family, work, and individual mental and physical health outcomes. Research must also be conducted with increasingly diverse samples to increase the range of the socioeconomic status, ethnicity, and cultures of those studied.

Defining the Nature of Relationship Distress

Problems in communication is the most frequently cited specific complaint by couples seeking therapy, cited by up to 90% of distressed couples. Both independent observers and spouses report that communication deficiencies are associated with relationship distress. When discussing problem issues, distressed partners are often hostile, critical, and demand change of each other. Distressed couples seldom actively listen to their partner when discussing problems or offering support and tend to withdraw from problem discussions.

Distressed couples are highly reactive emotionally to their partners' negative behavior and show significantly higher rates of negative reciprocity during interactions than do satisfied couples. In addition to negative reciprocity, relationship distress also is associated with high levels of psycho-physiological arousal during interaction. Such arousal is assumed to be aversive and may explain the higher rates of withdrawal during problem-focused discussions by distressed partners. Both the extent of arousal and the frequency of withdrawal prospectively predict deterioration in marital satisfaction.

Another common complaint of couples seeking relationship therapy is negativity in day-to-day interactions. When partners monitor their spouses' behavior using behavioral checklists, there is a well-replicated finding that daily behaviors correlate with relationship satisfaction. More specifically, relative to satisfied couples, distressed couples report higher rates of negative, displeasing behaviors by their spouse and fewer positive, pleasing behaviors (Birchler et al., 1975). Furthermore, distressed couples tend to reciprocate the behaviors of their spouse on a *quid pro quo* basis. In contrast, satisfied couples' behaviors are less contingent on their partners' preceding behaviors, with satisfied couples tending to be positive regardless of their partners' prior actions.

There also is evidence that distressed couples' perceptions of their partners' behavior are negatively biased. Distressed couples disagree to a greater extent with both objective observers and with each other regarding the occurrence of particular behaviors in their relationship, overestimating the frequency of negative behaviors by their partner. The nature of relationship distress cannot be understood simply in terms of the observed behaviors, but also requires attention to the cognitive appraisal by partners.

Distressed couples have a number of characteristic cognitions about their relationships (Baucom, Epstein, Sayers, & Sher, 1989). Distressed couples selectively attend to and recall their partner's negative behavior. In contrast, satisfied partners tend to overlook negative spousal behaviors, have a realistically positive view of their partners and relationships, and selectively recall positive aspects of the relationship.

Another cognitive characteristic of distressed couples is holding unrealistic beliefs and standards about relationships and partners. More specifically, relative to happy couples, distressed couples are more likely to believe that any form of disagreement is destructive, that change by partners is not possible, and that rigid adherence to traditional gender roles is desirable (Baucom & Epstein, 1990). Distressed couples also report that their relationships often violate standards of how they think their relationship should be. For example, distressed women report that their partners do not share power within the relationship in the manner that the women believe they should, and men believe that their partners should invest more time and energy in the relationship than they do (Baucom et al., 1996).

Distressed couples attribute the causes of relationship problems to stable, internal, negative, and blameworthy characteristics of the partners. For example, a partner arriving home late from work may be perceived by a maritally distressed partner as a "generally selfish person who doesn't care about the family." The same behavior may be attributed by a maritally satisfied partner as the spouse "struggling to keep up with a heavy load at work and being subject to lots of pressure from the boss." The process of attributing much or all of the relationship problems to their partners leaves most people with relationship distress and feeling powerless to improve their relationship (Vanzetti, Notarius, & Neesmith, 1992).

One additional cognitive characteristic of distressed couples is that they anticipate negative outcomes from interaction with their partners. Distressed couples report that prior to a discussion, they expect to be unable to resolve problem issues. In anticipation of a problem-solving discussion, maritally distressed partners show high physiological arousal, exhibit negative affect, and become primed to make negative evaluative judgments about their partner and their relationship. The cognitive characteristics of distressed couples mediate their subsequent behavior toward partners. In unhappy couples, negative thoughts about the partner predict future negative behaviors better than predictions from previous behavior, suggesting that these cognitions are more than just the consequences of negative marital behavior. In other words, relationally distressed partners seem to respond to their subjective perceptions and memories of relationship interactions, and these perceptions and memories are negatively biased.

Promotion of Successful Marriages

Over the past decade, one of the most important developments in the field of marriage has been the development of interventions based on psychological research to promote successful marriages. Perhaps the best-known research effort in this area is the work of PREP (Prevention and Relationship Enhancement Program; Markman, Stanley, & Blumberg, 1994) and variations of PREP in Germany by Hahlweg and his associates, and in Australia by Halford and his associates. In addition, other available programs include Guerney's Relationship Enhancement Program and Miller's Couples Communication Program (see Halford & Markman, 1997, for a review). These empirically based, short-term educational programs are delivered in anywhere from one to six sessions, varying in duration from 6 to 16 hours. Their overall aim is to provide the tools to help couples manage conflict more effectively and to protect and preserve what attracted them to each other in the first place—love, intimacy, sensuality, friendship, and commitment. Some programs also prepare couples to deal with prioritizing and making decisions that enhance their relationship, while at the same time making room for family, personal fitness, work, and other demands on time.

Research on the short- and long-term effects of such programs has been promising. For example, in a long-term follow-up of the German version of the program, PREP intervention couples had a divorce rate of 5%, while control couples who received alternative premarital intervention or no intervention had a divorce rate of 28%. While there are problems in interpreting the results of these studies, including nonrandom assignment in some cases and selection effects, there is no

doubt that the field has made great strides in offering to couples, while they are still happy, the benefits of research and theory that enable them to increase their odds of having a successful marriage (Hahlweg et al., 1998).

One of the challenges facing the field is that many couples are likely to have a successful marriage without needing the intervention. Therefore, more recent efforts have been focused on higher risk couples, for example, those who as children experienced conflict and divorce in their families or whose parents suffered mental or physical health problems. Moreover, programs will benefit to the extent that they are available at low or no cost in community settings with agendas that fit the developmental stage of the couple. The programs should be offered in appropriate settings, and they must be appropriate for the ethnic and cultural background of the couples.

Finally, although research suggests that couples should be able to have a happy marriage by applying the skills and tools reviewed above, such data are not reaching couples. The vast majority of mental health professionals who are practicing therapy with couples are not using these skills and tools in their practice, rather, they are relying on clinical paradigms that seem refractive to contemporary research results. The vast majority of couples who marry will become distressed, stay distressed, or divorce without ever seeing a mental health professional. Thus, we must put these tools directly into the hands of the couples themselves by translating these findings into mass media markets, as well as getting these tools into the hands of professionals such as clergy and health-care providers, from whom couples naturally seek help.

Bibliography

Baucom, D. H., & Epstein, N. (1990). *Cognitive behavioral marital therapy.* New York: Brunner/Mazel.

Baucom, D. H., Epstein, N., Daituo, A. D., Carels, R. A., Rankin, L. A., & Burnett, C. K. (1996). Cognitions in marriage: The relationship between standards and attributions. *Journal of Family Psychology, 10,* 209–222.

Birchler, G. R., Weiss, R. L., & Vincent, J. P. (1975). Multimethod analysis of social reinforcement exchange between maritally distressed and nondistressed spouse and stranger dyads. *Journal of Personality and Social Psychology, 31,* 349–360.

Burman, B., & Margolin, G. (1992). Analysis of the association between marital relationships and health problems: An interactional perspective. *Psychological Bulletin, 112,* 39–63.

Emery, R. E. (1982). Interparental conflict and the children of discord and divorce. *Psychological Bulletin, 92,* 310–330.

Erel, O., & Burman, B. (1995). Interrelatedness of marital

relations and parent-child relations: A meta-analytic review. *Psychological Bulletin, 118,* 108–132.

Gottman, J. M. (1993). A theory of marital dissolution and stability. *Journal of Family Psychology, 7,* 57–75.

Grych, J. H., & Fincham, F. D. (1990). Marital conflict and children's adjustment: A cognitive-contextual framework. *Psychological Bulletin, 108,* 267–290.

Hahlweg, K., Markman, H., Thurmaier, F., Engl, J., & Eckert, V. (1998). Prevention of marital distress: Results of a German prospective longitudinal study. *Journal of Family Psychology, 12*(4), 543–556.

Halford, W. K., & Markman, H. J. (1997). *Clinical handbook of marriage and couples intervention.* Chichester, UK: Wiley.

Markman, H. J., Stanley, S., & Blumber, S. (1994). *Fighting for your marriage: Positive steps for preventing divorce and preserving a lasting love.* San Francisco, CA: Jossey-Bass.

Notarius, C., & Markman, H. J. (1993). *We can work it out: Making sense of marital conflict.* New York: Putnam.

Vanzetti, N. A., Notarius, C. I., & NeeSmith, D. (1992). Specific and generalized expectancies in marital interaction. *Journal of Family Psychology, 6,* 171–183.

Howard Markham, Kim Halford, and Kristin Lindahl

MARRIAGE THERAPY. *See* Couples Therapy.

MARX, KARL (1818–1883), German social and economic theorist. The founder of "scientific socialism," Marx was born in the city of Trier in the Rhineland, and studied law in Bonn and philosophy in Berlin and Jena. He started out in German philosophy when it was overtly metaphysical and included psychology. His doctoral dissertation (1841), on the philosophy of nature in Democritus and Epicurus, found human nature in self-consciousness. Marx left academia for journalism and politics, but scholarly work continued to be his main activity, especially when the defeat of the 1848 revolutions drove him to exile in London, and the International Workingmen's Association (the "First International") collapsed.

By 1845, theorizing about human nature led Marx from metaphysics to social science. The *menschliches Wesen* (human essence) or *Gattungswesen* (generic or generative essence), he reasoned, was "no abstraction inherent in each separate individual" but "the ensemble of social relations," shaped by evolving "modes of production" or socioeconomic systems. Modern capitalism does not embody a universal type of social relations or human nature, as bourgeois economists assume. To overcome that ideological assumption Marx sought a historical sociology of diverse socioeconomic systems with diverse human types. But all past and present types were forms of "alienation" from an authentically

human form, which he held back from describing. It would emerge with the socialist transformation of the future.

Marx only hinted at the authentic human type of the future, since he scorned utopian schemes, and sought *wissenschaftlich* (scholarly or scientific) knowledge. He left unfinished the 1844 manuscript that analyzed alienation and authenticity at length, and "abandoned to the gnawing criticism of the mice" such other manuscripts as the "Sketches" (*Grundrisse*) (1857–1858), which attempted a comprehensive outline of human development. He focused his published scholarship on analysis of the industrial capitalist stage, though continually implying a universal vista. His social science was visionary but truncated, knotted with inward tensions, in contrast to the complacent grandiosity of Auguste Comte or Herbert Spencer. Admirers speak of Marx's dialectics or union of opposites; detractors call it inconsistency. The most obvious cases in point are his joining of socioeconomic determinism with angry moral judgment, and his dismissal of utopian dreaming while forecasting a revolutionary "leap from the realm of necessity into the realm of freedom" (although that famous summation was actually made by Marx's colleague Friedrich Engels).

Such tensions within Marx's thought help to explain its persistent challenge to social scientists. Alienation, for example, is such a common complaint that psychologists may wish to purge the concept of metaphysics, that is, to remove any implicit claim to know the authentic human being that an alienated person is estranged from. But the implicit claim may be inherent in the belief that some human relationships are essentially inhuman. Slavery has been placed in that category, and wage labor will be, Marx argued, as "praxis" leads to an authentically human society. His pejorative concept of ideology is another unavoidable stumbling block within modern thought. Claims to know what is universally human may be a self-deceptive apology for particular class interests, a suspicion that entails agonistic doubts concerning dispassionate reason as the way to knowledge of ourselves. Reason is humbled by "praxis," the historical process by which conscious active beings struggle toward authentic humanity through becoming aware of successive alienations from it.

Marx has often been interpreted as an economic determinist, in part because his political disciples often presented his thought as such, and in part because his youthful philosophizing was mostly unpublished until the midtwentieth century. Academic psychologists paid scant attention to him until the 1920s, when Soviet officials began to insist that all the human sciences must be recast on a Marxist basis. Diverse claims of Marxist psychology resulted, less substantial than decorative, and quite ephemeral, since the ideological bureaucracy that demanded such claims responded to them with despotic caprice. By the mid-1930s it had condemned all, and began to require confession of faith in "Pavlov's doctrine" as the realization of Marxism in psychology, though Pavlov rejected both Marxism and psychology, insisting that his "doctrine" was pure neuroscience.

The most notable examination of Marx's relevance to psychology was L. S. Vygotsky's *The Historical Meaning of the Psychological Crisis*, written in 1927 but kept from publication until 1982. By that time a distorted notion of Vygotsky's views had been fixed in the minds of Soviet and Western psychologists. In actuality he rejected any claim of Marxist psychology. Marx's work, he argued, expresses a *Weltanschauung* or philosophic orientation for psychologists when they reflect upon the incoherent schools and trends that characterize their discipline. "Our science will become Marxist to the degree that it will become true, scientific; and we will work precisely on that, its transformation into a true science, not on its agreement with Marx's theory" (Vygotsky 1982, p. 435). Stalinist ideologists prohibited such frank recognition of the distance between Marx's thought and twentieth-century psychology. They also stifled the "historico-cultural" approach that Vygotsky advocated within psychology.

S. L. Rubinshtein offered Soviet psychologists a different sense of Marx's significance. He had earned a German doctorate in philosophy before the Revolution, and, when Marx's 1844 manuscripts were published (1932), he seized upon them as a program for an eclectic mixture of psychology with philosophy. His vaguely Marxist benediction on diverse psychological schools served a useful function in the Soviet context, but won little interest elsewhere.

In the West Marx's significance for psychology has rarely been discussed by specialists in the discipline, unless one includes Wilhelm Reich and the "Freudian left." Marx's legacy has figured in efforts to rethink the human sciences as a whole, especially by theorists of the Frankfurt School. Their tortured abstractions continue the yearning that Marx shared with the poet Friedrich von Schiller, a longing for scientific knowledge of ourselves that would be fused with expression or creation of ourselves through art or science—or making children or the goods of everyday life, or governments. The fragmentation of knowledge, and the pervasive sense of alienation in social interaction, have mocked that romantic dream so cruelly that a plain statement of it in the 1844 manuscripts is quite startling: "History itself is a *real* part of *natural history*, of the development of nature into man. Natural science will one day incorporate the science of man, just as the science of man will incorporate natural science; there will be a *single* science" (Marx, 1964, p. 164). That yearning, its repression, and the sublimated expression of it in specialized studies, may be the deepest appeal of Marx to twentieth-century scholars.

Bibliography

Works by Marx

Marx and Engels (1975–) *Collected works*, Vols. 1–50. London: Lawrence and Wishart. English translation of Marx-Engels (1960–1968). *Werke* (Vols. 1–39). Berlin: Dietz Verlag.

Marx, K. (1964). *Early writings* (T. B. Bottomore, Ed.). New York: McGraw-Hill. Contains full translation of 1844 manuscripts.

Marx, K. (1973). *Grundrisse: Foundations of the critique of political economy* (M. Nicolaus, Trans. & Foreword). New York: Random House.

Works about Marx

Billing, M. (1982). *Ideology and social psychology*. New York: St. Martin's. See especially chapter 3, "Marx and Ideology."

Joravsky, D. (1989). *Russian psychology: A critical history*. London and New York: Blackwell. Marx is analyzed in chapter 2, Vygotsky and Rubinshtein further on.

McLellan, D. (1974). *Karl Marx: His life and thought*. New York: Harper.

Robinson, P. A. (1969). *The Freudian left*. New York: Harper.

Rubinshtein, S. L. (1959). *Printsipy i puti razvitiia psikhologii*. Moscow: Akademiia Nauk. Analysis of Marx in Part II. In German: (1963) *Entwicklung der Psychologie* [The development of psychology]. Berlin: Akademie Verlag.

Vygotsky, L. S. (1982). In *Sobranie sochinenii* (Vol. 1.). Moscow: Pedagogika. The quotation on p. 435 is badly mistranslated in Vygotsky (1997), *Collected works* (Vol. 3, p. 341). New York: Plenum.

David Joravsky

MASCULINE AND FEMININE CULTURES. The terms *masculine* (masculinity) and *feminine* (femininity) refer to the differences in *social* behavior associated with belonging to one gender rather than the other; they are distinct from *male* and *female*, which refer to the biological differences. Not only individuals but also cultures, in particular at the national level, can be described as "masculine" or "feminine."

I studied the masculinity-femininity distinction at the national level (1980, 1991). I defined the masculinity-femininity dimension as follows: Masculinity may be equated with a society in which men are expected to be assertive, tough, and focused on material success; women are expected to be modest, tender, and concerned with the quality of life. Femininity may be equated with a society in which both men and women are expected to be modest, tender, and concerned with the quality of life.

MASCULINE AND FEMININE CULTURES. Table 1. Masculinity index (MAS) values for 50 countries and 3 regions

Score Rank	Country or Region	MAS Score	Score Rank	Country or Region	MAS Score
1	Japan	95	28	Singapore	48
2	Austria	79	29	Israel	47
3	Venezuela	73	30/31	Indonesia	46
4/5	Italy	70	30/31	West Africa	46
4/5	Switzerland	70	32/33	Turkey	45
6	Mexico	69	32/33	Taiwan	45
7/8	Ireland	68	34	Panama	44
7/8	Jamaica	68	35/36	Iran	43
9/10	Great Britain	66	35/36	France	43
9/10	Germany	66	37/38	Spain	42
11/12	Philippines	64	37/38	Peru	42
11/12	Colombia	64	39	East Africa	41
13/14	South Africa	63	40	Salvador	40
13/14	Ecuador	63	41	South Korea	39
15	United States	62	42	Uruguay	38
16	Australia	61	43	Guatemala	37
17	New Zealand	58	44	Thailand	34
18/19	Greece	57	45	Portugal	31
18/19	Hong Kong	57	46	Chile	28
20/21	Argentina	56	47	Finland	26
20/21	India	56	48/49	Yugoslavia	21
22	Belgium	54	48/49	Costa Rica	21
23	Arab countries	53	50	Denmark	16
24	Canada	52	51	Netherlands	14
25/26	Malaysia	50	52	Norway	8
25/26	Pakistan	50	53	Sweden	5
27	Brazil	49			

(From Hofstede, 1997, p. 84.)

Masculinity-femininity does not primarily concern such visible roles in society as men going out to work and women staying at home to take care of the family. These roles are to a large extent determined by economic factors. Masculinity-femininity concerns first of all the emotional roles in the home to which children are socialized. In masculine societies, men specialize in ego-boosting, women in ego-effacing roles. In feminine societies, the emotional roles are more equally divided, with men especially being also oriented toward ego-effacing goals.

Cultures are a collective, not an individual phenomenon. They belong to anthropology, not to psychology. Their meaning for psychology is that they set the scene on which psychological processes play. They determine, among other things, what is "normal" and "abnormal" behavior in a particular society.

I have presented empirical evidence of differences in culture in survey data from carefully matched samples from each of 40 modern nations (employees in similar jobs in different subsidiaries of the same multinational corporation, IBM). Masculinity-femininity was one of four largely independent dimensions distinguishing national cultures; the other three were Power Distance (unequal versus equal), Uncertainty Avoidance (rigid versus flexible), and Individualism-Collectivism (alone versus together).

A dimension similar to masculinity-femininity was found by Israeli psychologist Shalom H. Schwartz, who surveyed the values of schoolteachers from 23 countries and students from 22 countries. Schwartz identified a national dimension, Mastery, for which the corresponding values (ambitious, capable, choosing own goals, daring, independent, successful) were significantly more important to teachers and students from countries identified by me as masculine, than from those identified as feminine.

At the level of individual personality, masculinity and femininity are usually treated as two separate unipolar dimensions: individuals can be masculine, feminine, both (androgynous) or neither (undifferentiated). At the level of national cultures, however, "more people with masculine values" is statistically so strongly correlated with "fewer people with feminine values," that masculinity-femininity becomes one bipolar dimension.

The masculinity-femininity dimension was originally identified from answers to paper-and-pencil questionnaires about the importance, in an imaginary ideal job,

MASCULINE AND FEMININE CULTURES. Table 2. Key differences between feminine and masculine societies

Feminine	Masculine
General Norm	
Dominant values in society are caring for others and preservation	Dominant values in society are material success and progress
People and relationships important	Money and things important
Everybody is supposed to be modest	Men are supposed to be assertive, ambitious, and tough
Both men and women are allowed to be tender and to be concerned with relationships	Women are supposed to be tender and to take care of relationships
Sympathy for the weak	Sympathy for the strong
Small and slow are beautiful	Big and fast are beautiful
Sexual issues openly discussable	Public discussion of sexual issues taboo
Violence in media taboo	Violence in newspapers and on TV common
In the Family	
Both fathers and mothers deal with facts and feelings	Fathers deal with facts and mothers with feelings
Both boys and girls are allowed to cry but neither should fight	Girls cry, boys don't; boys should fight back when attacked, girls shouldn't fight
In School	
Average student is the norm	Best student is the norm
Failing in school is a minor accident	Failing in school is a disaster
Friendliness in teachers appreciated	Brilliance in teachers appreciated
Boys and girls study same subjects	Boys and girls study different subjects
At Work	
Work in order to live	Live in order to work
Managers use intuition and strive for consensus	Managers expected to be decisive and assertive
Stress on equality, solidarity, and quality of work life	Stress on equity, mutual competition, and performance
Resolution of conflicts by compromise and negotiation	Resolution of conflicts by letting the best "man" win
In Politics	
Welfare society ideal	Performance society ideal
The needy should be helped	The strong should be supported
Permissive society	Corrective society
In wealthy countries: Preservation of the environment should have highest priority	In wealthy countries: Maintenance of economic growth should have highest priority
Government spends more on development assistance, less on armaments	Government spends less on development assistance, more on armaments
More women in elected political positions	Fewer women in elected political positions
In Prevailing Ideas	
Dominant religions stress the complementarity of the sexes	Dominant religions stress the male prerogative
In Christianity, stress on relationships with fellow humans	In Christianity, stress on relationship with God the Father
Women's liberation means that men and women should take equal shares both at home and at work	Women's liberation means that women should be admitted to positions hitherto only occupied by men

(Adapted from Hofstede et al., 1998.)

of different work goals. At the masculine pole, goals were found which enhance the person's ego but do not imply a concern for others (earnings, recognition, advancement, and challenge); at the feminine pole, goals which stress a concern for people, inside or outside the organization (relationship with manager, cooperation, living in a desirable area, and wish for security were found). Scores on masculinity for 40, later 50 countries and three multicountry regions (Arab-speaking countries, East and West Africa) were derived from these answers through a statistical analysis (factor scores in a varimax factor analysis of standardized means, with orthogonal rotation, were brought into a 0 to 100 range by a simple linear transformation). These country scores are listed in Table 1, which shows that masculinity-femininity is unrelated to national wealth; both rich and poor countries are found among the masculine and feminine countries.

For new samples of respondents, masculinity (along with other dimensions of national culture) can be measured with a 20-item questionnaire, the Values Survey Module (VSM 94, published by IRIC). This instrument is only designed *for comparative research using matched samples from different national populations.* It does not produce reliable scores for individuals or for organizations, nor does it allow comparing one single new sample with the scores in Table 1.

Being rooted in different roles and values of the genders, the masculinity-femininity dimension implies much more than the answers on certain "work goals" items. Many other measurable cultural differences among countries are correlated with the masculinity-femininity dimension, both country mean scores for other cross-national surveys and indicators measured at the country level, such as economic or political indexes. These serve as a construct validation for the masculinity-femininity dimension and allow one to put together an integrated picture of what masculinity-femininity stands for, presented in Table 2.

Bibliography

Bem, S. L. (1974). The measurement of psychological androgyny. *Journal of Consulting and Clinical Psychology*, *42*, 155–162. Measuring masculinity and femininity at the *individual*, not the *cultural* level.

Hofstede, G. (1980). *Culture's consequences: International differences in work-related values*. Beverly Hills, CA: Sage. Scholarly reference work on dimensions of national culture. Chapter 6 deals with masculinity-femininity. There is an abridged paperback version (1984), but this does not contain the base data and methodological explanations.

Hofstede, G. (1994). *VSM 94: Values survey module 1994—Manual*. Tilberg, Netherlands: Institute for Research on Intercultural Cooperation (IRIC), Tilberg University. Measuring masculinity-femininity (and other dimensions) at the *national culture* level.

Hofstede, G. (1997). *Cultures and organizations: Software of the mind*. New York: McGraw-Hill. (Original work published 1991.) Popular updating and extension of the 1980 book. Chapter 4 deals with masculinity-femininity.

Hofstede, G., with Arrindell, W. A., Best, D. L., De Mooij, M., Hoppe, M. H., Van de Vliert, E., Van Rossum, J. H. A., Verweij, J., Vunderink, M., & Williams, J. E. (1998). *Masculinity and femininity: The taboo dimension of national cultures*. Thousand Oaks, CA: Sage. Part monograph, part reader on the latest validations of the masculinity-femininity dimension. Part 1 deals with conceptual and methodological issues, Part 2 with gender, Part 3 with sexuality and religion.

Schwartz, S. H. (1994). Beyond individualism and collectivism: New cultural dimensions of values. In U. Kim, H. C. Triandis, C. Kagitçibaşi, S. C. Choi, & G. Yoon (Eds.), *Individualism and collectivism: Theory, method and application* (pp. 85–119). Thousand Oaks, CA: Sage. Describes Schwartz's dimensions of national value systems, including "Mastery" which correlates with masculinity.

Williams, J. E., & Best, D. L. (1990). *Measuring sex stereotypes: A multination study* (Rev. ed.). Newbury Park, CA: Sage. (Original work published 1982.) Compares gender stereotypes among female and male students from thirty countries. Another approach to the study of masculinity and femininity across nations. Some correlations with the Hofstede results.

Williams, J. E., & Best, D. L. (1990). *Sex and psyche: Gender and self viewed cross-culturally*. Newbury Park, CA: Sage. A study of actual and ideal self-descriptions of students from fourteen countries; interpreted in terms of their masculinity and femininity. Some correlations with the Hofstede results.

Geert Hofstede

MASCULINITY. *See* Gender Identity.

MASLOW, ABRAHAM HAROLD (1908–1970), American psychologist. Sometimes called the "father of American humanistic psychology," Maslow was indeed a major figure in the perspective that arose following World War II to counter the impersonal and determinedly objectifying behaviorist emphasis of the most prominent academic and experimental theorists of that time. His move in this way came after more traditional graduate studies and early research, in which he worked with monkeys in Harry Harlow's laboratories.

Maslow's questing spirit confronted him with his own subjective experiences. Rather than ejecting them as some of his professional elders advised, he revived naturalistic/descriptive inquiry. Thus was begun a series of landmark contributions in which he moved beyond a human psychology that was confined to the study of the normal and the subnormal (pathological). Instead he asked what a fully functioning human being might be.

Maslow was part of a broad intellectual circle that was subtly changing many cultural institutions. Among those with whom he studied or was frequently in contact were Erich Fromm, Max Wertheimer, Alfred Adler, Ruth Benedict, Rollo May, and Karen Horney.

In 1941, Maslow published (with the psychoanalyst Bela Mittelmann) *Principles of Abnormal Psychology: The Dynamics of Psychic Illness* (New York). This had a pronounced impact on the field, for it sought to open the subjective aspects of the abnormal in a way that went beyond impersonal nosological description.

Two years later Maslow published an epochal paper, "A Theory of Human Motivation," which was reprinted 23 times over 26 years in the United States and other countries. His view of the mainsprings of human motivation first presented here continued to evolve throughout his life.

Contributing to this perspective was his important depiction of a "hierarchy of needs." This conception opened up the previously held view that all humans are impelled by the same basic—chiefly deficiency—needs no matter what their circumstances. Maslow insisted that when basic survival needs are met, other "higher order" needs are brought into play. These are seekings toward what he termed "self-actualization." That term has been so generally adopted that it has become part of the educated layman's vocabulary—with some loss of the precision that Maslow sought to give it. For Maslow, the concept describes the pull on a person to make his potential actual.

Throughout his career, Maslow returned explicitly or implicitly to this conception. Thus he made repeated contrasts between what he called "D-needs" (that is, deficiency) and "B-needs" (being). Using this dichotomy, he examined motivation, outlooks, cognitions, cultures, life patterns, and similar matters. From his work, these terms have entered into general psychological usage.

The underlying thesis is that those who have satisfied their D-needs and are motivated by B-needs are actualizing the deeper potentials of being human. Such persons he began to call (in a 1950 paper) "self-actualizing people." In doing so, he not only introduced a new term but provided a reference point for countless later follow-up reports and even for more popular usage.

Maslow's Impact on Psychological Theory and Methods

After 1950, Maslow published frequent reports of his explorations of human experiences. What gave a particularly potent thrust to Maslow's thinking and writing was his willingness to go beyond method when the topic he was pursuing could not be contained in the approved modalities of the discipline. In this way, he not only offered fresh conceptions, but he lessened the rigidity of those modalities so that others might similarly grapple with fresh concerns.

Maslow demonstrated again and again his belief that psychological questions of genuine significance should be approached with whatever tools were available—no matter how inadequate initially—and that doing so would lead to developments in the tools as well as in their subject matter.

Where psychology had been developing single valence and quantitative scales of various kinds—general intelligence, social adequacy, academic mastery—Maslow grasped the nettle and proposed broad, nonquantitative, and non-linear dimensions for dealing with whole persons.

His basic "method" was that of naturalistic research. He identified an area for inquiry, then talked to many people, sometimes conducting formal interviews, making "live" observations, many times more informally allowing his "subjects" to express themselves in their own ways. In this pursuit, he would get the views of other observers, read widely, or otherwise amass a body of information, which he would then bring into some order. From there, he devised lists of probable attributes or of tentative implications. At this point, he might recycle the matter through the same processes, or he might essentially leave it to pick for further investigation one or two aspects that intrigued him.

One of Maslow's major contributions was to open up the purview of psychology, bringing into consideration psychological health as well as pathology, extending attention to the religious and transpersonal, identifying and further describing the many implications of the contrast between being states and deficiency states.

Maslow and the Rise of Humanistic Psychology

Maslow readily lent support to the emerging humanistic psychology orientation. For some time, he had been circulating draft papers with a group of colleagues of similar bent. When in 1962, he fostered the initiation of the American Association for Humanistic Psychology and its journal, he declined to hold office but lent abundant and continuing support. The next year the new association convened a landmark conference on the humanistic orientation in psychology, and Maslow was an active member of this meeting, which included many of his associates, for example, Gordon Allport, Jacques Barzun, Charlotte Buhler, Rene DuBos, George Kelly, Rollo May, Gardner Murphy, Henry Murray, Carl Rogers, and Robert White.

Typical of his wide-ranging interests was his acceptance of an appointment at Non-Linear Systems, a manufacturing plant in LaJolla California. This was a remarkable institution with innovative and democratic policies that seemed to him to demonstrate the practical reality of his own views of human nature. At first hesitant, Maslow became totally caught up in studying the program there and found much that validated his belief that, relieved of deficiency-derived constraints, humans could work and relate in a truly synergistic manner.

In 1967, Maslow was nominated for and elected to the presidency of the American Psychological Association. He accepted a fellowship from the Saga Administrative Corporation in California.

Personal Characteristics

Maslow did not simply propose a new conception. Repeatedly, he returned to develop earlier conceptions further—which he did in ten books and numerous articles. He had an almost childlike eagerness to learn about new developments in fields of his interests—encounter groups, psychedelics, employee programs, health care, theology, and so forth.

He was a direct intellectual descendent of William James and, to a lesser degree, of John Dewey. He reinvigorated the tradition of careful and detailed examinations of basic human experiences. In 1966, he published *The Psychology of Science: A Reconnaissance* (New York), a critique of orthodox science.

Maslow's lasting contribution to psychology is his determined reminder of the humanness of human beings. In his view, psychology had become too circumscribed, too suspicious of innovation, of opening new frontiers. While he could be vigorously censorious of what he saw as excesses in the so-called human potential movement of the 1960s and 1970s, he still supported the developing "third force" (after psychoanalysis and behaviorism). This stance won him the support of many younger psychologists but contributed to a measure of estrangement from some of his more established experimentally active colleagues.

[*Many of the people mentioned in this article are the subjects of independent biographical entries.*]

Bibliography

Works by Maslow

Maslow, A. H. (1954, 1970). *Motivation and personality* (Rev. ed.). New York: Harper. A collection of previously published papers that became foundation for his later work.

Maslow, A. H. (1955). Deficiency motivation and growth motivation. In M. R. Jones (Ed.), *Nebraska symposium on motivation: 1955*. Lincoln: University of Nebraska Press.

Maslow, A. H. (1964). *Religions, values, and peak-experiences.* Columbus: Ohio University Press. By equating the religious experience with what he had come to term "peak experience," Maslow broke new ground and brought psychology into an area largely neglected since William James.

Maslow, A. H. (1965). *Eupsychian management: A journal.* Homewood, IL: Richard D. Irwin & Dorsey Press. This collects a variety of notes on topics in which Maslow was interested, particularly deriving from two experiences: his visit to the Non-Linear Systems firm and his observations at the group dynamics laboratory on human relations.

Maslow, A. H. (1968). *Toward a psychology of being* (2nd ed.). New York: Van Nostrand Reinhold. An immensely influential book which did much to encourage the counter-culture movement of the 1960s.

Maslow, A. H. (1971). *The farther reaches of human nature.* New York: Viking.

Works about Maslow

Hoffman, E. (1988). *The right to be human: A biography of Abraham H. Maslow.* Los Angeles: Jeremy P. Tarcher. This is the formal biography. It is rich in detail provided by many of Maslow's students and colleagues. It provides a complete bibliography.

International Study Project & Maslow, B. G. (Mrs. A. H. Maslow). (1972). *Abraham H. Maslow: A memorial volume.* Monterey, CA: Brooks/Cole. Has a complete bibliography of his writing and a valuable collection of his unpublished notes as well as his UCLA presentation (not otherwise available) and eulogies.

Lowry, R. J. (1973). *Abraham H. Maslow: An intellectual portrait.* Monterey, CA: Wadsworth.

Lowry, R. J. (1973). *Dominance, self-esteem, self-actualization: The germinal papers of Abraham H. Maslow.* Monterey, CA: Wadsworth.

Lowry, R. J. (Ed.). (1979). *The journals of A. H. Maslow. Vols. 1–2.* Monterey, CA: Brooks/Cole.

James F. T. Bugental

MASOCHISM. *See* Sexual Masochism.

MATHEMATICAL PSYCHOLOGY. Mathematics has played a role in psychology since its beginning; however, the term *mathematical psychology* does not refer simply to the application of mathematics to psychology. Instead, mathematical psychology was started as a field in the United States in the 1950s by a small group of distinguished scholars who expressed dissatisfaction with the state of theory in experimental psychology at that time. The field grew rapidly with the advent of graduate training programs, handbooks, research monographs, a journal, a professional society, annual meetings, and specialty conferences, all of which continue today. Further, the field has a characteristic approach to experimental and cognitive psychology that has remained fairly constant over the years. In fact, research in mathematical psychology has established new research areas and set the standards for theory construction in others.

Founding and Development

Prior to World War II, experimental psychology was dominated by a behavioristic philosophy that emphasized data gathering more than theorizing, and rigorous formal theories were mostly absent except in areas such as vision and audition. The war effort brought together experimental psychologists and scholars from mathematics and the formal sciences such as engineering, economics, and physics. At that time there was an explosion of new developments in the information sciences, such as automata theory, cybernetics, game theory, information theory, linear systems theory, signal processing, and stochastic processes that seemed ideal for formalizing some subareas of experimental psychology. As a consequence, some experimental psychologists became sophisticated in these new formalisms and some of the scholars in other fields began to work in experimental psychology. It was out of this mix that mathematical psychology evolved.

Mathematical psychology received initial recognition with the publication in the *Psychological Review* of two seminal papers in learning theory by Bush and Mosteller (1951) and Estes (1950) that began the traditions of linear operator and stimulus sampling models, respectively. At that time, learning theory was entrenched at the center of experimental psychology, and these papers presented the first formally rigorous efforts to model detailed data in learning experiments. Many related publications followed soon thereafter. In addition, important theoretical articles and books appeared that initiated the other subareas of mathematical psychology. Included among these are Duncan Luce's choice theory (1959), Tanner's and Swets's theory of signal detection (1954), George Miller's approach to information processing (1956), Clyde Coombs's theory of data (1964), and Patrick Suppes's and Richard C. Atkinson's study of learning in multiperson games (1960).

By 1960 it had become clear to many scholars that it was time to establish a new field called mathematical psychology. The majority of these people were concentrated at the universities of Indiana, Michigan, Pennsylvania, and Stanford, which had already instituted graduate specialties in mathematical psychology, but the field lacked a well-defined literature. This problem was solved by two developments. First, three professors at the University of Pennsylvania edited the *Handbook of Mathematical Psychology* (Luce, Bush, & Galanter, 1963a, 1963b, 1965a), along with a collection of reprinted papers called *Readings in Mathematical Psychology* (Luce, Bush, & Galanter, 1963c, 1965b). The *Handbook* included chapters by many scholars that reviewed and added to each of the aforementioned subareas of mathematical psychology, and the *Readings* reprinted almost all the relevant journal articles.

The second development was the founding of the *Journal of Mathematical Psychology*, whose first volume appeared in 1964 under the editorship of Richard Atkinson. The journal was planned by a small group consisting of Atkinson, Robert R. Bush, Clyde H. Coombs, William K. Estes, R. Duncan Luce, William J. McGill, George A. Miller, and Patrick Suppes, who also constituted the initial board of editors. Following Atkinson, the journal was edited in roughly 5-year terms, and in 1998 it was in its forty-second volume. Furthermore, the journal remains a major international outlet for formal work in the psychological sciences.

The next step was the start of annual meetings in the United States. In 1968, the first Annual Mathematical Psychology Meeting was hosted by Stanford University, with about 50 participants. The meetings have continued at different universities each year, and generally have from 75 to 125 participants. At the ninth annual meeting, a straw vote favored forming an official society, and an organizing committee chaired by Estes developed a set of bylaws that led to the establishment of the Society for Mathematical Psychology. The bylaws state that the purpose of the society is to promote research in mathematical psychology which is "conceived to include, in particular, work of a theoretical character, employing mathematical methods, formal logic, or computer simulation."

Outside the United States, major interest and strength in mathematical psychology developed in Europe in the late 1960s, mostly in Belgium, England, France, Germany, and the Netherlands. In 1971, interested parties decided to initiate an annual European Mathematical Psychology Group (EMPG) meeting. The initial meeting, organized by Jean-Claude Falmagne, was held in Paris; about 30 scholars were invited, and all came. Meetings followed the next year, with a larger group in Nijmegen organized by Edward Roskam. Roskam, along with Jan Drösler of the University of Regensburg, became the mainstays in establishing a con-

tinuing tradition of open EMPG meetings. These have generated a series of edited books, for example, by Doignon and Falmagne (1991). In addition, Europe has a number of active graduate training programs in mathematical psychology.

Research Areas

The research areas in mathematical psychology overlap most topics in experimental and cognitive psychology, especially the basic areas of sensation, perception, and psychophysics and the areas of cognition, such as attention and search, categorization, choice and decision-making, and learning and memory. In addition, there are areas of formal research that are essentially unique to mathematical psychology, such as foundations of measurement (see next section), information-processing models of response time (e.g., Luce, 1986; Townsend & Ashby; 1983), and signal detectability models (see Macmillan & Creelman, 1991).

While the research areas have remained fairly constant since the 1960s, there have been some major changes, especially concerning cognition. For example, in the area of learning and memory there has been a decided shift away from basic models of simple learning situations and toward elaborate models of complex memory phenomena. This trend has been sparked both by empirical discoveries in memory and the use of computational and simulation models such as parallel distributed processing models (Rumelhart & McClelland, 1986) and global memory models, such as Douglas Hintzman's MINERVA, Bennet Murdock's TODAM, and Richard Shiffren's SAM (reviewed in Clark & Grondlund, 1996).

Another example of change has been in the area of categorization. The early work emphasized the acquisition of simple Boolean-based rules defined over stimuli represented by binary valued dimensions. Today, research concerns categorization behavior in its most general form, involving discrete and continuous valued dimensions, complex rules, and detailed patterns of generalization. Ashby (1992) and Estes (1994) are good sources.

There have also been changes in the area of choice and decision making. Early work concerned choice among relatively unstructured sets of alternatives. Today there is an interdisciplinary effort involving mathematical psychologists, experimental economists, and decision scientists to formulate a psychologically adequate foundation for utility theory along with specific models capable of describing both choice behavior and choice times over a wide range of highly structured situations (e.g., part 2 of Marley, 1997). This trend was facilitated by the seminal work of Amos Tversky and his coworkers, and by the creation of the Society for Judgment and Decision-Making.

Another active area is modeling attention and

search behavior. Much of this work uses information-processing language that borrows heavily from operations research; however, there has been an increasing trend to models that have neural underpinnings. A good source is Dosher and Sperling (in press).

There has been less change in research emphasis within mathematical psychology in the basic areas of sensation, perception, and psychophysics. Many of the problems in this area were formulated carefully in the 1960s, and in contrast with the higher process areas, there has been considerable cumulative progress over the years. A good source is *Elements of Psychophysical Theory*, by Jean-Claude Falmagne (1985). There have been changes in the character of formal models in these basic areas, most notably in the areas of computational and neural modeling; however, much of this work is conducted by researchers who are not closely associated with the field of mathematical psychology.

Methods of Theory Formation

Perhaps the most identifying characteristics of mathematical psychology are the approaches it takes to theory building. Three approaches cover most cases: stochastic modeling; the axiomatic method; and the functional-equations approach. In all three cases, the goal is to develop completely rational, formal accounts of psychological phenomena, with empirical consequences.

The main approach to theory building, especially in the cognitive areas, is the formulation of substantive, stochastic models of the data structures of experimental paradigms. This approach was started in the 1950s by the work in learning theory described earlier, and it has continued to influence theory formation in all the empirical areas of mathematical psychology.

There have been two main strategies in stochastic modeling. The first and most frequent is to create models that can fit detailed data patterns that occur across a set of interlinked experimental paradigms. A model then receives a boost if it can reproduce the data to a satisfactory statistical level with a relatively small number of parameters whose values seem psychologically plausible. The hope is that as models compete and evolve to fit data, there will be convergence toward correct psychological theory. Quite naturally, models have evolved into more complex mathematical forms to keep pace with data, and computer simulation is often the only way to evaluate a model. The models in memory and categorization discussed earlier illustrate this trend. The second strategy in stochastic modeling is to create simple models to disentangle and separately measure underlying cognitive capacities in specific experimental paradigms. Such models are theoretically incomplete; however, they are relatively easy to analyze with standard statistical theory. Examples of this strategy are the

models for signal detection described by Macmillan and Creelman (1991) and the multinomial processing tree models reviewed by William Batchelder and David Riefer (1999).

Another approach to theory building in mathematical psychology is the axiomatic method. It proceeds by stating theoretical assumptions in a series of formal statements called axioms. Then, if the axioms are jointly accepted, the theory is derived from the axioms as a body of theorems. The axioms should be judicious, excluding inessential assumptions; and, except for minimal technical concessions to the language of mathematics, each axiom should be empirically testable (falsifiable). Some examples of the successful use of the axiomatic approach are Luce's choice theory (1959), Falmagne's psychophysical modeling (1985), most of the theoretical work on utility and beliefs, and the many applications in the three-volume *Foundations of Measurement* (Krantz et al., 1971; Suppes et al., 1989; and Luce et al., 1990).

The axiomatic approach provides insight into the underpinnings of a theory, and when the theory fails, it may be possible to locate the problem in one of the axioms and make a productive modification. However, not all theories admit to ready axiomatization, and sometimes when an axiom is testable in principle, lacking suitable statistical underpinnings, it may not be testable in practice.

The functional-equations approach to theory construction is closely related to the axiomatic method. To simplify the discussion, suppose that one is seeking a theory to explain the functional relationship of several variables. The theory is formulated as a family of possible functions so that in any particular situation the relationship is given by some member of the family. The functional equations approach attempts to formulate constraints on the functional relationship of various sorts, usually in the form of axioms. Then, using the techniques of functional equations, the family of functions is deduced from the assumed conditions, and it constitutes the theory. The relevant parts of functional equations are covered by Aczél (1987), along with some examples from psychology.

One type of constraint arises when there are trade-offs among the variables that leave the function invariant, for example, when utilities and probabilities trade off in choice among gambles, or when permissible measurement-scale transformations leave the function invariant. Falmagne's *Elements of Psychophysical Theory* and the foundations of measurement literature contain many examples of this type. A second type of constraint occurs when one interrelates two or more ways to measure the same quantity, for example, the measurement of utility in different choice paradigms (e.g., Luce, 1996).

Bibliography

Aczél, J. (1987). *A short course on functional equations based upon recent applications to the social and behavioural sciences.* Boston: Reidel-Kluwer.

Ashby, F. G. (Ed.). (1992). *Multidimensional models of perception and cognition.* Hillsdale, NJ: Erlbaum.

Batchelder, W. H., & Riefer, D. M. (1999). Theoretical and empirical review of multinomial process tree modeling. *Psychonomic Bulletin and Review, 6,* 57–86.

Bush, R. R., & Mosteller, F. (1951). A mathematical model for simple learning. *Psychological Review, 58,* 313–323.

Clark, S. E., & Grondlund, S. D. (1996). Global matching models of recognition memory: How the models match the data. *Psychonomic Bulletin and Review, 3,* 37–60.

Coombs, C. H. (1964). *Theory of data.* New York: Wiley.

Doignon, J.-P., & Falmagne, J.-C. (Eds.). (1991). *Mathematical psychology: Current developments.* New York: Springer-Verlag.

Dosher, B., & Sperling, G. (1998). A century of information processing theory: Vision, attention, and memory. In J. Hochberg & J. E. Cutting (Eds.). *Handbook of perception and cognition at century's end: History, philosophy, theory* (pp. 199–252). New York: Academic Press.

Estes, W. K. (1950). Toward a statistical theory of learning. *Psychological Review, 57,* 94–107.

Estes, W. K. (1994). *Classification and cognition.* New York: Oxford University Press.

Falmagne, J.-C. (1985). *Elements of psychophysical theory.* New York: Oxford University Press.

Krantz, D. H., Luce, R. D., Suppes, P., & Tversky, A. (1971). *Foundations of measurement: Volume 1.* New York: Academic Press.

Luce, R. D. (1959). *Individual choice behavior.* New York: Wiley.

Luce, R. D. (1986). *Response times: Their role in inferring elementary mental organization.* New York: Oxford University Press.

Luce, R. D. (1996). When four distinct ways to measure utility are the same. *Journal of Mathematical Psychology, 40,* 297–317.

Luce, R. D., Bush, R. R., & Galanter, E. (Eds.). (1963–1965). *Handbook of mathematical psychology* (Vols. 1–3). New York: Wiley.

Luce, R. D., Bush, R. R., & Galanter, E. (Eds.). (1963–1965). *Readings in mathematical psychology* (Vols. 1–2). New York: Wiley.

Luce, R. D., Krantz, D. H., Suppes, P., & Tversky, A. (1990). *Foundations of measurement: Volume 3.* San Diego, CA: Academic Press.

Macmillan, N. A., & Creelman, C. D. (1991). *Detection theory: A user's guide.* New York: Cambridge University Press.

Marley, A. A. J. (Ed.). (1997). *Choice, decision, and measurement: Essays in honor of R. Duncan Luce.* Mahwah, NJ: Erlbaum.

Miller, G. A. (1956). The magic number seven, plus or minus two: Some limits on our capacity for processing information. *Psychological Review, 63,* 81–97.

Rumelhart, D. E., & McClelland, J. L. (Eds.). (1986). *Parallel distributed processing. Explorations in the microstructure of cognition, Volume I.* Cambridge, MA: MIT Press.

Suppes, P., & Atkinson, R. C. (1960). *Markov learning models for multiperson interactions.* Stanford, CA: Stanford University Press.

Suppes, P., Krantz, D. H., Luce, R. D., & Tversky, A. (1989). *Foundations of measurement: Volume 2.* New York: Academic Press.

Tanner, W. P., & Swets, J. A. (1954). A decision-making theory of visual detection. *Psychological Review, 61,* 401–409.

Townsend, J. T., & Ashby, F. G. (1983). *The stochastic modeling of elementary psychological processes.* New York: Cambridge University Press.

William H. Batchelder

MATING. *See* Attachment; Intimacy; *and* Marriage.

MATSUMOTO, MATATARO (1865–1943), Japanese educator and experimental-applied psychologist. Matsumoto was born in 1865 at Takasaki in the Kozuke, the present Gumma prefecture. He was the second son of Tasuku Iino, one of the retainers of the Takasaki clan, but when he was 15 years old, he was adopted into the Matsumoto family. He succeeded in entering the Doshisha School in Kyoto and went through the First Higher Middle School in Tokyo. In 1890, he entered the department of philosophy at Tokyo Imperial University, the only university in Japan at that time. He immediately proceeded to graduate work and came under the guidance of Yujiro Motora, Japan's first professor of psychology.

During this time, the American psychologist George T. Ladd came to Japan and delivered a series of lectures. Matsumoto saw him off at the Yokohama wharf and expressed his desire to go abroad to obtain up-to-date knowledge of psychology. With Ladd's support, he entered Yale University on a scholarship as a graduate student and spent a year studying experimental psychology and its research methods under the direction of Edward W. Scripture. The next year, he was appointed as a laboratory assistant at Yale. In 1898, he presented his dissertation, "Experimental Research in Acoustic Space" (published in *Studies from the Yale Psychological Laboratory,* Vol. 5, 1898), for which he received the doctorate in 1899. Ordered by the Japanese Educational Ministry to study psychology in Germany for 2 years, Matsumoto then traveled to Leipzig, where he attended lectures given by Wilhelm Wundt and others at the famous university. After his return to Japan in 1900, he taught at Tokyo Imperial University and went on to establish Japan's first psychology laboratory there in 1903. In 1906, he became professor of psychology at Kyoto Imperial University (Japan's second university), where he founded another laboratory.

Following Motora's sudden death from an illness, Matsumoto succeeded him at Tokyo Imperial University in 1913 and lectured on experimental psychology. Although inspired by Wundt's experimental method, Matsumoto's psychology focused on the bodily expression of mental functions, or what he called mental movement. The most important of the bodily motions were visual movements and those of the upper limbs and vocal organs. Quantitative analysis of these motions would constitute a science—called psychocynematics (Matsumoto, 1914)—that would be intermediate between physiology and psychology and serve as the basis for applied psychology. Matsumoto taught this approach, which paralleled the behaviorism then emerging in America, to more than 125 students, at least 20 of whom went on to obtain a doctorate under him. He and his students applied the psychocynematic approach to a wide range of areas, including vocational guidance, industrial efficiency, aesthetics, child psychology, and military psychology. Matsumoto's role in shaping Japanese psychology remains widely recognized.

After his retirement from Tokyo Imperial University in 1926, Matsumoto founded the *Japanese Journal of Psychology*, the first journal of psychology in Asia and still an important publication. The next year he organized the Japanese Psychological Association. He was elected its first president, a post he continued to hold until his death on 24 December 1943.

[*Many of the people mentioned in this article are the subjects of independent biographical entries.*]

Bibliography

Matsumoto, M. (1914). *Mental works.* Tokyo: Rikugokan.

Matsumoto, M. (1914). *Ten lectures on experimental psychology.* Tokyo: Kodansha.

Matsumoto, M. (1921). Memories of Prof. Ladd. *Psychological Research, 20,* 242–256.

Matsumoto, M. (1923). *Lectures on psychology.* Tokyo: Kaizosha.

Matsumoto, M. (1925). *Psychology of intelligence.* Tokyo: Kaizosha.

Matsumoto, M. (1937). *The history of psychology.* Tokyo: Kaizosha.

Matsumoto, M. (1940). *A record of travel in pursuit of knowledge.* Tokyo: Daiichikoronsha. Autobiographical account of his travels and education in the United States and Germany.

Okamoto, S. (1976). Dr. Matataro Matsumoto: His career and achievements. *Journal of the History of the Behavioral Sciences, 12,* 31–38.

Seiji Kodama

MAX PLANCK INSTITUTE FOR HUMAN DEVELOPMENT AND EDUCATION. A multidisciplinary research institute dedicated to the study of human development and education and their social, historical, and institutional contexts, the Max Planck Institute for Human Development and Education is one of about 70 research institutes that are sponsored by the Max Planck Society for the Advancement of Sciences. The governments of the Federal Republic of Germany and its states provide the core financial support for the Max Planck Society and its institutes.

Total staff at the institute is approximately 110, including 45 scientists. In addition, about 20 scientists hold the status of affiliate research scientist or of predoctoral, postdoctoral, or visiting fellow.

History of the Institute

The institute was founded in 1963 by Hellmut Becker, who was joined in 1964 by Friedrich Edding, Dietrich Goldschmidt, and Saul A. Robinsohn as the first generation of scientific directors. In the first decade, the development of educational research and policy was emphasized. The appointment of a second generation of directors (Wolfgang Edelstein and Peter M. Roeder, 1973) added a commitment to basic research in human development and educational processes.

With the appointment of a third generation of scientific directors (Paul B. Baltes, 1980; Karl Ulrich Mayer, 1983; Jürgen Baumert, 1996), research has increasingly concentrated on questions of basic research associated with the nature of human development, education, and work in a changing society. At the same time, life span developmental and life course research, including the study of human aging, were added as a signature profile of the institute's research program.

The institute is currently organized into four research centers: the Center for Development and Socialization (Wolfgang Edelstein, director), the Center for Educational Research (Jürgen Baumert, director), the Center for Psychology and Human Development (Paul B. Baltes, director), and the Center for Sociology and the Study of the Life Course (Karl Ulrich Mayer, director).

Psychology at the Institute

Although psychological research is represented in all four centers, the Center for Psychology and Human Development contains the highest concentration of researchers using psychological principles, methods, and concepts. Primary research targets in this center are the psychological factors and processes involved in the ontogenesis of learning, mental capacity, motivation, and self-related personal development.

A first major focus is the study of personality and social development. At present, this emphasis comprises the following areas: (1) the study of family-related contextual factors and family transformations, as well as their influence on children and parents; (2) research on goals and beliefs that individuals acquire and use as guiding forces in producing their own and others' development; (3) inquiries into the self as an organized and developing system giving identity and meaning to one's past, current, and future life; and (4) models of successful development. The projects consider a variety of age periods across the human life course to explicate how developmental processes are moderated by social, cognitive, and motivational processes associated with contexts of family, school, and culture.

A second major research focus is the study of cognitive and intellectual development from a life span perspective. Researchers at the institute have developed and tested a dual-process conception of intellectual development that distinguishes between the knowledge-free fluid mechanics and the knowledge-rich crystallized pragmatics of intelligence. Aging declines are likely to occur in the mechanics of intelligence, especially at the limits of functioning. At the same time, continued growth is possible in those selected pragmatic aspects of intellectual functioning, such as wisdom, for which adequate health, support, and practice are present. Recent research has been concerned with individuals' compensatory efforts and skills in counteracting difficulties stemming from age-related decline in the mechanics of intelligence.

A third major research area deals with general questions of theory, method, and history of developmental psychology. Scientists interested in this emphasis include, to varying degrees, most of the center faculty. A concrete example of work in this area is the editing of an annual publication series, *Life-Span Development and Behavior*, originally launched in 1978 by Paul B. Baltes and Orville G. Brim, Jr. This series focuses primarily on contributions from a wide spectrum of the behavioral and social sciences and has as its goal the stimulation and dissemination of programmatic research on the psychology and sociology of the life course.

The organization of international conferences on innovative topics or areas of special interest to institute and center faculty is another regular activity of the center aimed at placing its theoretical work into national and international contexts. In these conferences, various themes of human development are treated from theoretical, methodological, and historical viewpoints. Several books are products of such center conferences.

Interdisciplinary Projects

A certain portion of the center's resources is allocated to interdisciplinary ventures, both within the institute and with colleagues from other institutions. An example of such an interdisciplinary effort is the Berlin Aging Study. In this project, about 35 scientists from two of the four centers of the Max Planck Institute and the Free University of Berlin collaborate to study a representative sample of elderly Berlin residents from the perspective of internal medicine, psychiatry, psychology, and sociology.

Bibliography

Summary of the Institute's Goals and Recent Research Activity

Max Planck Institute for Human Development and Education. (1997). *Annual Report 1995/96*. Berlin, Germany: Author.

Works on the Conceptual Orientation of the Center for Psychology and Human Development

Baltes, P. B. (1987). Theoretical propositions of life-span developmental psychology: On the dynamics between growth and decline. *Developmental Psychology, 23*, 611–626.

Baltes, P. B., Lindenberger, U., & Staudinger, U. M. (1997). Life-span theory in developmental psychology. In W. Damon (Series Ed.) & R. M. Lerner (Vol. Ed.), *Handbook of child psychology: Vol. 1. Theoretical models of human development* (5th ed., pp. 1029–1143). New York: Wiley.

Works on Personality and Social Development

Heckhausen, J., & Schulz, R. (1995). A life-span theory of control. *Psychological Review, 102*, 284–304.

Kreppner, K. (1992). Development in a developing context: Rethinking the family's role for children's development. In L. T. Winegar & J. Valsiner (Eds.), *Children's development within social contexts. Vol. 1. Metatheory and theory* (pp. 161–182). Hillsdale, NJ: Erlbaum.

Oettingen, G., Little, T. D., Lindenberger, U., & Baltes, P. B. (1994). Causality, agency, and control beliefs in East versus West Berlin children: A natural experiment on the role of context. *Journal of Personality and Social Psychology, 66*, 579–595.

Works on Cognitive and Intellectual Development during Adulthood

Baltes, P. B., Smith, J., & Staudinger, U. M. (1992). Wisdom and successful aging. In T. B. Sonderegger (Ed.), *Nebraska symposium on motivation* (Vol. 39, pp. 123–167). Lincoln: University of Nebraska Press.

Lindenberger, U., & Baltes, P. B. (in press). Intellectual functioning in old and very old age: Results from the Berlin Aging Study. *Psychology and Aging*.

Works on Theory, Methodology, and History of Developmental Psychology

Baltes, P. B., & Staudinger, U. M. (Eds.). (1996). *Interactive minds: Life-span perspectives on the social foundation of cognition*. New York: Cambridge University Press.

Heckhausen, J., & Dweck, C. S. (Eds.). (in press). *Life-span perspectives on motivation and control*. New York: Cambridge University Press.

Interdisciplinary Works

Mayer, K. U., & Baltes, P. B. (Eds.). (1996). *Die Berliner Altersstudie* [The Berlin Aging Study]. Berlin: Akademie Verlag.

Peter A. Frensch

MAY, ROLLO (1909–1994), American psychologist and psychoanalyst. May brought together many currents in the body of psychology—scholarship in the classics, training and early devotion to religious studies, psychoanalytic and psychotherapeutic observations and theory, devotion to graphic art, commentary on the mores of our times, and the introduction and adaptation of postwar European existentialism into American philosophy and psychology. Probably, it is the last of these that most distinguishes his contribution. At a 1959 international meeting in Barcelona, Spain, on existential psychology and psychotherapy, it is reported that the postwar Europeans were somewhat patronizing about his "so American" optimism. From our later vantage point, we can see that it was not so much May who changed but the Europeans.

Typically, May kept his own counsel and devoted his great energy to bringing to American psychology and psychotherapy the enlarged view of human nature at which he had arrived. This was particularly forwarded by the publication (with two colleagues, E. Angel and H. Ellenberger) of what is still a landmark book, *Existence: A New Dimension in Psychiatry and Psychology* (New York, 1958).

In 1964, May joined a number of distinguished colleagues—Gordon Allport, Charlotte Bühler, George Kelly, Abraham Maslow, Floyd Matson, Gardner Murphy, Henry Murray, Carl Rogers, and Robert White—in a conference on the newly emerging perspective of humanistic psychology. Subsequently, he frequently lent his support to the further development of this viewpoint.

May's chief institutional affiliation was with the William Alanson White Institute in the 1950s and 1960s. There he served as a training analyst as well as president of the institute. Over the years, he authored or coauthored 9 books, edited or coedited 3 more, and published 34 papers.

May's writing is distinguished by comprehensiveness of survey, lucidity and careful reasoning in exposition, and willingness to venture into areas that carry the reader beyond the conventional. Often he and his thought were also welcomed outside usual psychological precincts—for example, at theological seminaries and conventions of educators, psychiatrists, religious leaders, and other professions.

May's contributions came at a historically important juncture in psychology's affairs. As often happens with major cataclysms, World War II evoked many significant changes in Western culture. Women's roles, relative freedom, and participation in professional and academic life were irrevocably changed. Academic and learned professions were massively democratized, were opened to many who previously might never have entered them, and were broken into many contrasting—often competing—clusters and factions.

May, always basically a classicist, presented a fresh perspective that insisted on the generality and unlimitedness of possibility, responsibility, and guilt. He identified himself chiefly as a psychotherapist or psychoanalyst; yet, outside of his first book, written when he was thirty, he wrote little about the actual processes of the consultation room. Instead, he used case studies as a source for his broader psychological observations. Throughout, his writing infused psychotherapeutic work with a broadened perspective, an implicit humane value system, and a deep respect for the human spirit. In the *Discovery of Being* (New York, 1983, p. 56), he wrote, "The existential approach arose as an indigenous and spontaneous answer to crises in modern culture." In *Man's Search for Himself* (New York, 1953, 1967), May wrote:

> One of the few blessings of living in an age of anxiety is that we are forced to become aware of ourselves. When our society, in its time of upheaval in standards and values, can give us no clear picture of "what we are and what we ought to be," as Matthew Arnold puts it, we are thrown back on the search for ourselves. The painful insecurity on all sides gives us new incentive to ask, Is there perhaps some important source of guidance and strength we have overlooked? (p. 7)

He was not an uninvolved observer. He held that knowledge of the human is not the same as knowledge about things that occur in human form. It is knowing (not "knowing about") humanness from within and in the very essence of its being perceived.

[*Many of the people mentioned in this article are the subjects of independent biographical entries.*]

Bibliography

Works by May

May, R. (1950, 1977). *The meaning of anxiety* (Rev. ed.) New York: Ronald Press. A scholarly yet clinical survey of the concept and implications of anxiety and its therapeutic management.

May, R. (1969, 1973, 1974). *Love and will.* New York: Dell. The most popular of May's books. It brought to the reading public a new conception of basic human psychodynamics.

May, R. (1972). *Power and innocence: A search for the sources of violence.* New York: Norton. A masterful integration of classical and contemporary materials to provide a fertile base for further study and work with these crucial human experiences.

May, R. (1975). *The courage to create.* New York: Norton.

May, R. (1992). In the days of the giants—The steps in therapy to the present day. In J. K. Zeig (Ed.), *The evolution of psychotherapy: The second conference* (pp. 329–333). New York: Brunner/Mazel. A typical May essay linking classical literature to present day matters and graciously acknowledging the contributions of recently deceased colleagues.

Works about May

Bugental, J. F. T. (1965). Introduction. *Journal of Humanistic Psychology,* 5 (2), 180–181. Includes a list of participants in the First Invitational Conference on Humanistic Psychology.

Reeves, C. (1977). *The psychology of Rollo May.* San Francisco: Jossey-Bass. A survey of May's work and views up to approximately 1972. Valuable for including May's own comments on Reeves's presentation.

Schneider, K. J., & May, R. (1995). *The psychology of existence: An integrative, clinical perspective.* Includes reprinting of four of May's papers based on classical literature, three on "philosophical roots" and one case report. Schneider presents his creative therapeutic conception as an extension of May's perspective.

James F. T. Bugental

McCLELLAND, DAVID C (1917–1998), American personality and motivation psychologist. McClelland developed innovative ways of measuring psychological characteristics, and he explored the role of achievement and power motives in personality, social history, and psychophysiology. He graduated from Wesleyan University, where he studied with John McGeoch, and received a doctorate from Yale. His academic career was spent at Wesleyan, Harvard, and Boston universities. Although trained in the rigorous behaviorism of the Clark Hull era at Yale, he became most widely known for his research in personality. A year's teaching at Bryn Mawr during World War II, where he first taught personality, was the catalyst for this transformation (Winter, 1998), which ultimately led him to construct an eclectic, data-based conception of personality as consisting of motives, traits, and schemas (McClelland, 1951).

McClelland combined "experimental" and "personality" approaches by developing (with John W. Atkinson) empirically derived scoring systems for the Thematic Apperception Test (TAT). For example, the scoring systems for achievement motivation or "*n* Achievement" (McClelland, Atkinson, Clark, & Lowell, 1953) was developed by comparing TAT stories of people in whom achievement concerns had been experimentally increased with TAT stories of people in a neu-

tral state (Winter, 1998). This strategy of using experimental arousal to define a measure had been widely used in animal research, but was an innovation in projective testing, where scoring was traditionally based on *a priori* systems derived from clinical intuition or experience. The differences between these two strategies led to continuing psychometric controversy about the experimentally derived scoring methods, focused on issues of reliability (Atkinson, 1982) and the low correlations and differential patterns of validity of projective and questionnaire measures (McClelland, Koestner, & Weinberger, 1989; Spangler, 1992). [*See* Thematic Apperception Test.]

McClelland's students and associates later developed empirically derived scoring systems for the affiliation, intimacy, and power motives and fear of success, as well as a variety of other personality characteristics such as stance of adaptation to the environment, affiliative trust-mistrust, self-definition, and responsibility (Smith, 1992).

McClelland's exploration of the relationship between achievement motivation and economic development, involving content analysis of such archival materials as stories from children's readers and popular literature, was reported in his most widely cited book, *The Achieving Society* (1961). To test the theory, he and his associates developed training courses to increase achievement motivation and thereby promote economic growth (McClelland & Winter, 1969), and they established a behavioral science consulting, training, and research company.

McClelland saw the achievement motive as an example of nontraditional or nonacademic "talent" or competence unrelated to IQ test scores. This perspective led him to criticize traditional intelligence and ability testing (McClelland, 1973, 1994) and to develop alternative methods of measuring competencies important for successful performance in a variety of adult occupational roles and life satisfaction (McClelland, 1998; Winter, McClelland, & Stewart, 1981).

In the 1970s, McClelland turned to the study of power motivation (McClelland, 1975). His approach was characteristically broad. At the macrocosmic level, he used archival data to trace a historical pattern of war being preceded by high levels of power motivation and low levels of affiliation motivation. At the individual level, this same pattern was associated with heavy drinking and impulsive, risk-taking behavior (especially if combined with low activity inhibition or control). At the physiological level, the pattern was associated with increased sympathetic nervous system arousal, decreased efficiency of the immune system, and heightened susceptibility to infectious disease and cardiovascular problems (McClelland, 1989). Toward the end of his career, McClelland explored complex relationships between the arousal of different psychological motives and corresponding changes in hormone levels and other indicators of physiological functioning: for example, power motivation and norepinephrine, affiliation motivation and dopamine, and achievement motivation and arginine vasopressin (McClelland, 1995). [*See* Power Motivation.]

McClelland's background in experimental psychology made him "tough-minded" about "tender-minded" problems. From this philosophy came a unique combination of simplicity and complexity that was one of his most important contributions to personality psychology. On the one hand, he sought to reduce complex phenomena to simple elements that could be scored as present or absent. At the same time, he sought to understand the complex ways in which a large number of "simple" components, drawn from different levels of analysis or even different disciplines, could combine (often in highly interactive, contingent, or nonlinear ways) to produce higher-level psychological processes and life outcomes. Thus, his analyses usually ended with a complex integrative synthesis— of individual personality (1951, p. 591); of the psychosocial substrates of economic development (1961, p. 438); of the motivational dynamics of war, peace, and social reform (1975, p. 347); of relationships between psychological variables and physiological processes; or of the relationship of substitutable competencies to executive performance (1998).

Bibliography

Atkinson, J. W. (1982). Motivational determinants of thematic apperception. In A. J. Stewart (Ed.), *Motivation and society* (pp. 3–40). San Francisco: Jossey-Bass. Discusses psychometric issues of TAT-based measures and contrasts them to classical test theory.

McClelland, D. C. (1951). *Personality*. New York: Holt, Rinehart & Winston. McClelland's basic empirically based conception of personality.

McClelland, D. C. (1961). *The achieving society*. Princeton, NJ: Van Nostrand. Widely cited classic work relating achievement motivation to economic development.

McClelland, D. C. (1964). *The roots of consciousness*. Princeton, NJ: Van Nostrand. Selected papers on a variety of psychological and humanities topics.

McClelland, D. C. (1973). Testing for competence rather than for "intelligence." *American Psychologist, 28*, 1–14. Criticizes traditional intelligence testing and proposes alternative conception and measures of competencies.

McClelland, D. C. (1975). *Power: The inner experience*. New York: Irvington. Wide-ranging series of studies on power motivation.

McClelland, D. C. (1984). *Motives, personality, and society: Selected papers*. New York: Praeger. Selected papers on psychological topics and a brief autobiography.

McClelland, D. C. (1985). *Human motivation*. Glenview, IL: Scott, Foresman. Theoretical statement and empirical research on TAT-based motives.

McClelland, D. C. (1989). Motivational factors in health and disease. *American Psychologist, 44*, 675–683. Summarizes research on power and affiliative motives in relation to physiology and illness.

McClelland, D. C. (1994). The knowledge-testing-educational complex strikes back. *American Psychologist, 49*, 66–69. Further McClelland critique of traditional intelligence testing.

McClelland, D. C. (1995). Achievement motivation in relation to achievement-related recall, performance, and urine flow, a marker associated with release of vasopressin. *Motivation and Emotion, 19*, 59–76. McClelland's final paper on relation of TAT motives to physiological processes.

McClelland, D. C. (1998). Identifying competencies with Behavioral Event Interviews. *Psychological Science, 9*, 331–339. Longitudinal demonstration of the "competency assessment" approach.

McClelland, D. C., Atkinson, J. W., Clark, R. A., & Lowell, E. L. (1953). *The achievement motive*. New York: Appleton-Century-Crofts. Classic work on the first empirically derived TAT motive scoring system.

McClelland, D. C., Koestner, R., & Weinberger, J. (1989). How do self-attributed and implicit motives differ? *Psychological Review, 96*, 690–702. Summarizes differences between TAT-based and questionnaire-based motive variables.

McClelland, D. C., & Winter, D. G. (1969). *Motivating economic achievement*. New York: Free Press. Describes design and results of training courses to increase achievement motivation.

Smith, C. P. (Ed.). (1992). *Motivation and personality: Handbook of thematic content analysis*. New York: Cambridge University Press. Scoring manuals and research documentation on TAT-based scoring systems for motives and other personality characteristics.

Spangler, W. D. (1992). Validity of questionnaire and TAT measures of need for achievement: Two meta-analyses. *Psychological Bulletin, 112*, 140–154. Describes differential validity of TAT-based and questionnaire-based motive variables.

Stewart, A. J. (Ed.). (1982). *Motivation and society: A volume in honor of David C. McClelland*. San Francisco: Jossey-Bass. Festschrift by McClelland students and associates.

Winter, D. G. (1998). "Toward a science of personality psychology:" David McClelland's development of empirically derived TAT measures. *History of Psychology, 1*, 130–153. Recounts history of McClelland's early career and how he came to study personality and the TAT.

Winter, D. G., McClelland, D. C., & Stewart, A. J. (1981). *A new case for the liberal arts*. San Francisco: Jossey-Bass. Identifies several competencies increased by liberal education.

David G. Winter

McCOSH, JAMES (1811–1894), Scottish American philosopher and psychologist. A clergyman educated at

Glasgow and Edinburgh, McCosh was a leader in reconciling Evangelical and Moderate views following the 1843 Disruption of the (Presbyterian) Church of Scotland. McCosh published widely on the reconciliation of science, philosophy and religion, and served as professor of logic and metaphysics in Queen's College, Belfast, Ireland (1852–1868). In 1868, he was called to be president of the College of New Jersey (later Princeton), where he guided Princeton through a period of great growth and change until retiring in 1888.

McCosh believed mind to be composed of faculties—native capacities that unfolded and developed with use and experience—and thought education should be organized to train them. While he always remained committed to education founded on the traditional Western canon and to a hierarchically organized curriculum (language, logic, mathematics, literature, advanced sciences, social sciences, and ethics), McCosh was in close touch with modern debates and changing sciences. He proposed reform of Princeton's curriculum by organizing graduate study and combining required and elective courses to promote study of the new scientific and technical fields. These changes helped the "new" psychology to develop. In debates of national significance, McCosh and Charles Eliot, president of Harvard University, argued the best balance of requirements and electives and the college's role in building moral character.

McCosh was among the last to write a systematic psychology textbook in the Scottish moral philosophy tradition. Like his predecessors (Hutcheson, Reid, Stewart, Hamilton), McCosh attempted to incorporate new scientific knowledge but went beyond them in making perception and knowledge of the thing itself immediate and direct. He argued against the strict sensationalism of John Stuart Mill, and the phenomenology and agnosticism of Immanuel Kant. McCosh's role in recognizing and discussing the "new" psychology has been underestimated. In his first psychological work, *The Intuitions of the Mind, Inductively Investigated* (London, 1860), McCosh included the work of Johannes Müller, David Ferrier, and Alexander Bain. McCosh differed with assumptions of the physiological approach, reserving a place for the spiritual in humans, which would always be beyond description in solely scientific terms. McCosh found great truth in Darwin's theory, and from 1855 on he played an important role in discussing the compatibility of evolutionary theory and Christian belief. He criticized the evolutionist Herbert Spencer for neglecting spiritual powers.

McCosh continued to describe the new scientific work in his texts, *Psychology: The Cognitive Powers* (New York, 1886) and *Psychology: The Emotive Powers; Emotions, Conscience, Will* (New York, 1887), and tried to join it with the older approach in a cohesive philosophy that maintained the role of morals in human interactions. But the movement of the field was toward an individualistic psychology of what could be measured and applied, the concept of "soul" disappeared from science, and American universities soon lost their moral mission. McCosh's student James Mark Baldwin carried McCosh's concern for a philosophically and scientifically linked view of human behavior into the next academic generation.

[*Many of the people mentioned in this article are the subjects of independent biographical entries.*]

Bibliography

Works by McCosh

McCosh, J. (1866). *An examination of Mr. J. S. Mill's philosophy, Being a defence of fundamental truth.* New York: R. Carter.

McCosh, J. (1882). The Scottish philosophy as contrasted with the German. *Princeton Review, 10,* 326–344.

McCosh, J. (1883). *Development: What it can and what it cannot do* (Philosophical Series No. 3). New York: Charles Scribner's Sons.

McCosh, J. (1884). *A criticism of the critical philosophy* (Philosophical Series No. 7). New York: Charles Scribner's Sons.

McCosh, J. (1888). *Twenty years at Princeton College.* New York: Charles Scribner's Sons.

McCosh, J. (1990). *The Scottish philosophy, biographical, expository, critical, from Hutcheson to Hamilton.* Bristol, England: Thommes. (Original work published 1875)

Works about McCosh

Hoeveler, Jr., J. D. (1981). *James McCosh and the Scottish intellectual tradition.* Princeton, NJ: Princeton University Press.

Sloane, W. M. (1896). *The life of James McCosh.* New York: C. Scribner's Sons.

Wertenbaker, T. J. (1996). *Princeton 1746–1896.* Princeton: Princeton University Press. (Original work published 1946)

Karin E. Wetmore

McDOUGALL, WILLIAM (1871–1938), British American psychologist. The history of psychology has not been kind to William McDougall. Current textbooks and research make little or no mention of his work. Yet, during the post–World War I period, he was a significant figure in psychology, with his many works (24 books and 167 articles and notes on physiology, social psychology, philosophy, and social commentary) provoking heated debate. McDougall's championing of unpopular causes, whether instinct, parapsychology, group mind, racial superiority, inheritance of acquired characteristics or purposiveness, guaranteed his visibility and also his unpopularity. [*See* Parapsychology.]

McDougall arrived in America from his native England in 1920 to accept Hugo Münsterberg's vacant chair at Harvard. (Münsterberg was best known for developing the field of applied psychology.) [*See the biography of Münsterberg.*] By this time, McDougall was an established, controversial scholar. Although he had a medical degree from Cambridge University, he was primarily an academician, with his major appointment being in mental philosophy at Oxford University, where he had taught from 1904 to 1920. In 1927, McDougall left Harvard to become a professor of psychology at the recently endowed Duke University. There he continued his scholarly activity and established the first laboratory of parapsychology with the newly hired J. B. Rhine at its head.

The concept most associated with McDougall is instinct. In his *Introduction to Social Psychology* of 1908, McDougall maintained that "the human mind has certain innate or inherited tendencies [instincts] which are the essential springs or motive power of all thought and action." He defined instinct as an inherited or innate disposition that determines perception, feeling, and action. Instincts are purposive and goal directed and thus are not to be mistaken for mechanical reflexes. Instincts are prior to and the basis for the development of learned habits. McDougall subsequently systematized these ideas in his "hormic psychology" (from the Greek word "horme" meaning "urge").

McDougall's views about the inherited bases of behavior provoked intense controversy during the 1920s. One contested issue was what are the human instincts. McDougall usually listed eleven: flight, repulsion, curiosity, pugnacity, self-abasement, self-assertion, parental, reproductive, gregarious, acquisitive, and constructive. There were other lists, however, with the number of instincts ranging as high as 110. Given this lack of agreement, McDougall's opponents claimed that the concept was ambiguous and of limited explanatory value. They pointed out that the number of instincts varied because a new instinct was often coined whenever an explanation was needed. The critics maintained that since instincts were difficult to demarcate from learned habits, there was little reason to invoke this ambiguous, limited explanatory concept.

Beneath these criticisms and their counterarguments was the problematic notion of "purpose." McDougall maintained that it is basic and inherent in the nature of living organisms to be, above all, purposive and goal directed. Purposiveness is a central conscious process, McDougall claimed, that directs behavior and provides action with meaning and significance. Although he believed that purposiveness was an established, obvious aspect of human nature, his opponents viewed it as mysterious and unscientific. Locating purpose in consciousness made it a prime candidate for banishment from psychology by the increasingly ascendent behaviorism movement.

By the early 1930s, the controversy swirling around instinct and purposiveness had died out. Although the issues raised in these debates had not been fully resolved, psychology had shifted its concerns to a more empirical and behavioristic posture. McDougall's eclipse as a significant psychologist was partly a function of this change in theory and strategy. Also contributing to his decline was the lack of empirical support for his research on genetic transmission of acquired characteristics. Few supporters rallied to this unpopular notion as well as the others McDougall championed. His marginalized intellectual position was further increased by his sharp, attacking debating style.

McDougall grappled with the significant issues of inherited bases of behavior and purposiveness, concerns that are still unresolved but are not currently of focal interest. Sociobiology is the closest contemporary area that has resonances with McDougall's perspective, although his position was not influential in this field's development. McDougall's work has left little impression on current psychology except in having forced a needed clarification of some of the field's guiding assumptions.

[*See also* Behaviorism and Neobehaviorism.]

Bibliography

Krantz, D. L., & Allen, D. (1967). The rise and fall of McDougall's instinct doctrine. *Journal of the History of the Behavioral Sciences, 3*, 326–338.

Krantz, D. L., Hall, R., & Allan, D. (1969). William McDougall and the problem of purpose. *Journal of the History of the Behavioral Sciences, 5*, 25–38. Deals extensively with the instinct controversy and the purposive concept.

McDougall, W. (1930). Autobiography. In C. Murchison (Ed.), *A history of psychology in autobiography* (Vol. 1). Worcester, MA: Clark University Press. (Out of print—available in university libraries.) McDougall's self-reflective, often witty, view of his career and work written toward the end of his life.

Robinson, A. L. (1943). *William McDougall, a bibliography.* Durham, NC: Duke University Press. (Out of print—available in university libraries.) A complete bibliography of McDougall writings with a listing of secondary sources.

Watson, J. B., & McDougall, W. (1929). *The battle of behaviorism.* New York: Norton. (Out of print—available in university libraries.) A trenchant debate between two of psychology's major figures that provides insight into the issues and personal styles that separated them.

David L. Krantz

McGEOCH, JOHN A. (1897–1942), experimental psychologist. John A. McGeoch may be considered the "father of verbal learning." While a graduate student at the University of Chicago, Harvey A. Carr trained him in the functionalist tradition. His dissertation *A Study in the Psychology of Testimony* was submitted in 1926. In a career that was as notable for its geographic mobility as its persistent research energy, McGeoch rose through the academic ranks at Washington University in St. Louis and then became professor at the University of Arkansas in 1928 at age 31. A mere 2 years later he became chair at the University of Missouri, and in fairly rapid succession served in the same capacity at Wesleyan University and the University of Iowa. His sudden and unexpected death came from a cerebral hemorrhage.

McGeoch's principal work was published in 1942 as *The Psychology of Human Memory: An Introduction*. It was not originally intended as such: He had been collaborating with Harvey Carr during the 1930s on a multivolume manual covering all published research on human learning. The first draft of the projected manual was nearly completed by 1936, but was delayed for several years due to McGeoch's poor health and frequent moves. Finally, a publisher persuaded McGeoch to release a condensed digest of the intended manual for use as a textbook. McGeoch's lasting impact on the field has come through the comprehensiveness and authority of this book and its revision a decade later by his student, Arthur L. Irion (McGeoch & Irion, 1952). No true competitor was published for decades and although this was to have been only a foretaste of the eventual manual, it has been treated as if it were the manual itself.

McGeoch's reputation has also been based on a theoretical claim and a related body of experimental work. The theoretical claim (McGeoch, 1932) is that the mere passage of time cannot, in principle, be the explanation for anything, as had been claimed for forgetting by the decay or disuse theory of memory. Rather, he said, activities occurring *during that time* must be responsible for forgetting. It follows that the key to understanding forgetting is the understanding of *retroactive inhibition*, the interference created by activities between learning of events and their later retrieval. McGeoch's famous research activities in creating the two-factor interference theory of forgetting respected that same logical agenda.

McGeoch's style in science was to remain close to the data and to shun broad theoretical leaps. His faith was that the psychology of human learning and memory were in a pretheoretical phase, in which the first responsibility was to decide what the data *were* before suggesting elaborate explanations for them. McGeoch imbibed this functionalist perspective from such predecessors as H. A. Carr and J. R. Angell and passed this orientation along to such students as A. W. Melton (an undergraduate at Washington University) and B. J. Underwood (a graduate student at Iowa). The austerity of his book and the programmatic drive of his experiments on retroactive inhibition established McGeoch as an archetype of the careful laboratory approach to human learning and memory. With the more recent ascendancy of cognitive psychology, neither McGeoch's own reputation nor that of verbal learning has survived particularly well. The tradition of verbal learning is even sometimes offered as an example of the sterility of orthodox science.

In the context of McGeoch's total career, such a reputation is a mistake: His dissertation took the form of a series of field studies based on eyewitness testimony using schoolchildren (ages 9 to 14) from the East St. Louis school district. He was also interested, among other things, in the relation between accuracy of memory and intelligence as measured by the Army Alpha test. McGeoch may be among a handful of early pioneers in examining eyewitness testimony in American psychology. Nor was this work on practical aspects of memory isolated; others of his publications in the early years had to do with memory for poetry and the measurement of emotions and the relation between suggestibility and juvenile delinquency. His early career was thus solidly within the functionalist tradition. One is left to speculate that the older McGeoch resorted to traditional standards of laboratory precision and control *because of* his commitment to everyday problems, not to escape from them.

Bibliography

McGeoch, J. A. (1932). Forgetting and the law of disuse. *Psychological Review, 39,* 352–370.

McGeoch, J. A. (1942). *The psychology of human learning.* New York: Longmans, Green.

McGeoch, J. A., & Irion, A. L. (1952). *The psychology of human learning.* New York: Longmans, Green.

Pratt, C. C. (1943). John A. McGeoch: 1897–1942. *American Journal of Psychology, 56,* 134–136.

Wolfle, D. (1943). McGeoch's psychology of human learning: A special review. *Psychological Bulletin, 40,* 350–353.

Robert G. Crowder

MEAD, GEORGE HERBERT (1863–1931), pragmatist and social psychologist. Mead's father, Hiram Mead, held the chair of Sacred Rhetoric and Pastoral Theology at Oberlin College from 1869 until his death in

1881. His mother, Elizabeth Storrs Billings Mead, was the first president of Mount Holyoke College from 1893 to 1900.

Mead entered Oberlin's Preparatory Department in 1876 and Oberlin College in 1879, graduating from the latter in 1883. After a series of makeshift jobs, he experienced a depression that lasted for many years. Mead entered Harvard University in 1887 where he studied with Josiah Royce, the Christian Neo-Hegelian philosopher. Mead switched from a philosophy major to physiological psychology before finishing his degree and going to study in Germany.

Mead studied first in Leipzig, Germany, under Wilhelm Wundt, the physiological and theoretical psychologist, in the winter of 1888–1889. He transferred after one semester to the University of Berlin where he studied under the psychologists Wilhelm Dilthey, Hermann Ebbinghaus, and Friedrich Paulsen, and the socialist Gustav Schmoller. Mead was offered a position in late 1891 to teach philosophy at the University of Michigan in Ann Arbor. He accepted the post and left Berlin without completing his doctorate.

Mead's long depression was resolved finally through his marriage to Helen Castle in 1891 and his new life in Ann Arbor. He was swept into the intellectual life of this department, especially with the professional and personal relationship he established with John Dewey. In 1894, Dewey was offered the chair of the department of philosophy and psychology at the University of Chicago and he argued strongly and successfully that Mead should be hired too.

Mead lived within a vibrant world of friends, family, students, colleagues, community activists, and civic ties in Chicago, which became his home for the rest of his life. This complex and exciting group inspired his life and ideas, including his seminal social philosophy based on social interaction and community.

Mead and Dewey established a school of thought named "Chicago pragmatism" by William James, another psychological pragmatist. This approach, emphasizing process and interpersonal relations, provided a naturalistic and evolutionary interpretation of intellectual activity as problem-oriented and based on scientific methods. It stressed the democratic reconstruction of society through education and other institutions.

Mead's work focused on the genesis of the self and other. He proposed that society and the self were mutually dependent and dynamic. This social process generates the mind, consciousness, intelligence, and the ability to take the role of the other. This distinctive social psychology is called "symbolic interactionism." Mead was also concerned about woman suffrage, access to higher education, and civil rights. He was a friend of and colleague to a number of notable women, including Jane Addams, founder of Hull House. Their

theory and praxis on a gendered social psychology is called "feminist pragmatism."

Although Mead published over 120 articles in his lifetime, his major works were published posthumously. His fame, therefore, grew significantly after his death. His influence continues to increase through the activities of a group based on his ideas, the Society for the Study of Symbolic Interaction. These social psychologists hold two conferences annually and publish a journal, *Symbolic Interaction*, which promotes the development, application, and interpretation of Mead's corpus.

[*Many of the people mentioned in this article are the subjects of independent biographical entries.*]

Bibliography

Mead, G. H. (1934). *Mind, self, and society* (Ed. and Intro. by Charles Morris). Chicago: University of Chicago Press.

Mead, G. M. (1982). *The individual and the social self* (Ed. and Intro. by David L. Miller). Chicago: University of Chicago Press.

Mead, G. M. (1999). *Play, school and society* (Ed. and Intro. by Mary Jo Deegan). New York: Peter Lang.

Mary Jo Deegan

MEAN. *See* Data Analysis.

MEANING OF LIFE. A fundamental and consequential challenge in the human experience is to find life meaningful. Personality, clinical, and social psychologists amongst others have pursued questions regarding the meaning of life. This work encompasses study of how meaning is created (frequently in the context of adversity) as well as examining the impact of having or lacking a sense of life meaning, purpose, and coherence. Understanding life's meaning has also been construed as part of the process of human development; that is, a mark of maturity. Across these formulations, having meaning is viewed as a feature of optimal human functioning, which involves having goals, being engaged, and possessing inner strength in the face of life's obstacles. But to live without meaning is to experience despair, alienation, and confusion. Theoretical and philosophical origins of these perspectives are briefly summarized below, followed by a selective illustration of empirical studies concerned with meaning of life.

Theoretical and Philosophical Origins

How individuals make sense of their lives is a central issue in existential, phenomenological, and humanistic approaches to personality. Existential philosophers (e.g., Kierkegaard, Heidegger, Buber, Sartre, Camus) believed that the creation of meaning in a world that frequently appears senseless, random, or absurd, is the ultimate challenge of human existence. To live authentically requires that one discern meaning, even in a seeming void, and assume responsibility for one's life, described by Sartre as the "fundamental project." Existentialists emphasized that blind following of social customs or convention is not the route to authentic living, nor is the glorification of reason and abstract thought over acknowledging anxiety, loneliness, and irrationality as part of the human condition. A further theme, following from Husserl's phenomenology, is the understanding of subjective experience, free of preconceived notions about it.

Among more psychologically oriented perspectives, Victor Frankl's *Man's Search for Meaning* (Boston, 1992) constitutes a major statement about the power of meaning in the face of horrific human suffering. Written about his 3-year ordeal in a Nazi concentration camp, Frankl (a physician) observed that the capacity to find meaning in the experience was a distinguishing feature between those who survived and those who did not. He translated these insights to clinical psychology with his development of logotherapy, the main goal of which is to help clients find meaning in their adversity and suffering. From a more sociological vantage point, Antonovsky's posed "sense of coherence" (*Unraveling the Mystery of Health*, San Francisco, 1987), or the task of finding life comprehensible, manageable, and meaningful, as a key aspect of human health vis-à-vis the stresses of life.

Humanistic theorists wrote about confrontations with difficulty, although their more optimistic formulations depicted suffering as the route to human growth. Maslow's studies of self-actualizers, for example (*Toward a Psychology of Being*, New York, 1968), emphasized that much important learning in the service of self-development occurred as individuals dealt with tragedies, deaths, and trauma. Rogers's depiction of the fully functioning person (*On Becoming a Person*, Boston, 1961) and Jung's view of individuation (*Man and His Symbols*, New York, 1964) also elaborated the strides forward that come from weathering the storms of life. Allport's characterization of "maturity" (*Pattern and Growth in Personality*, New York, 1961) gave less emphasis to growth through adversity, but gave central importance to having a unifying philosophy of life. This he described as a clear comprehension of life's purpose, a sense of directedness, and intentionality—all essential to achieving a life of meaning.

Scholars explicitly concerned with stages of human development construed the search for meaning as a key part of the unfolding psychosocial crises or challenges of life. For example, Erikson's life-course model (*Childhood and Society*, New York, 1950) postulated "ego integrity" as the key challenge of later life. Those who successfully resolve this task have a sense of integration, meaning, and acceptance of their past lives; those who do not have a sense of despair, regret, and a fear of death. Buhler and Massarik (*The Course of Human Life*, New York, 1968) also described basic life tendencies, which were steps toward personal development that occurred across the life cycle. "Upholding internal order," the most complex of life tendencies, prevailed during the later years. This tendency worked toward the unity of personality as manifest in individuals' goals, ideals, and self-assessments.

In sum, theoretical interest in the meaning of life has been richly elaborated in numerous contexts, including existential philosophy, which emphasized the finding and creating of meaning as a core human responsibility; humanistic perspectives, which elaborate the human potential for growth and fulfillment, the process of which frequently involves confrontations with adversity; and life-span developmental formulations, which define distinct psychosocial challenges across life, with later stages explicitly emphasizing the search for meaning. Many of these conceptualizations have served as guides for empirical studies about meaning and growth. Select examples of these are briefly summarized in the following section.

Empirical Studies of Meaning and Growth

How positive things come to the fore as a result of life's difficulties is illustrated by numerous lines of inquiry, including research on past life traumas in which individuals are encouraged to confront and express emotions about these prior experiences (Pennebaker, 1995). This work shows that when people write their deepest thoughts and feelings about past traumas, they initially experience distress, but within weeks report greater happiness and well-being than comparison groups who write about superficial things. Presumably, putting past difficulties into written form involves a process of coming to terms with the emotional content of the experience as well as an organizing it in cognitive terms. Personal meaning thus emerges from constructing a narrative to explain the trauma.

Related research addresses the growth experiences or meaning that comes from dealing with specific health crises. Spiegel (1993), for example, draws on existential theory to characterize how patients suffering from a terminal illness (breast cancer) found new meaning in life by helping others going through the same dilemma and by gaining insight about what matters and what does not (i.e., trivializing the trivial). Similarly, Folkman and colleagues (Folkman, Chesney, Collette, Boccellari, & Cooke, 1996) examine how caregivers of acquired immune deficiency syndrome

(AIDS) or human immunodeficiency virus (HIV)-infected men cope with the challenges of their situation. A key variable explaining caregiver adjustment is the capacity to find positive meaning in their caregiving. That is, those who view the experience as deeply meaningful exhibit lower levels of depression following the loss of their partner. Their positive meaning comes from multiple sources, including the knowledge that they had provided valuable support and reduced the suffering of a significant other. Linking meaning and growth to human suffering has been the focus of other studies of illness, disability, divorce, and death of a loved one (Emmons, in press). Collectively, these works underscore the gains in personal relationships (deeper, more satisfying connections), improved sense of self (confidence, self-reliance, coping skills), and changed life outlooks (values, goals, and philosophy) that follow in the wake of life adversity.

Largely separate from the above studies is another realm of empirical inquiry also emerging, in part, from the preceding theoretical frameworks, namely, research on people's goals, an area where there has been a revival of interest among personality and social psychologists. Some of these investigators construe goals as key routes through which life purpose and meaning are enacted. Emmons, for example, anchors his studies of "personal strivings" in Allport's writings about teleological orientations of the person (i.e., what she or he is characteristically trying to do). Emmons elaborates the nature of *conflict* that may exist among personally held goals and shows that the inability to resolve chronic conflicts is associated with poorer well-being (negative affect, physical symptoms, visits to health center) (Emmons & King, 1992). The *content* of people's goals has also been elaborated, involving distinctions between motives of achievement, affiliation, and power (Emmons, 1996). Personal goals are differentiated as well in terms of their intrinsic versus extrinsic features. More internal goals (e.g., personal growth, community contribution) have been linked with higher well-being (vitality, self-actualization) than more external goals (e.g., achieving financial success or social recognition). Finally, the *unity* of one's goals is considered a key route to understanding subjective well-being. Meaning in this framework comes from involvement in fulfilling and integrating one's goals into a coherent system (Emmons, 1996).

"Possible selves" (Markus & Nurius, 1986) constitute another avenue of empirical inquiry about goals specifically linked with the self-schema. These include future-oriented conceptions of selves that individuals would like to become, or are afraid of becoming. Delinquent youth, for example, show more feared and undesired future selves, along with fewer positive hoped-for expectations, than do nondelinquent youth (Markus

& Ruvolo, 1989). At the other end of the life course, in multiple inquiries, positive life goals are predictors of health and well-being. Other recent avenues of inquiry regarding goals, life meaning, personal projects, as well as the import of these orientations for counseling and psychotherapy, are summarized in Wong and Fry (1998).

Thus, while earlier psychological perspectives conceived of the person as buffeted about by unconscious motives and drives (psychodynamic theories), or at the mercy of external forces (behavioral accounts), the accounts described above emphasize the proactive features of personhood, with accompanying themes of exercising responsibility for the direction of one's life (the existential message) and implementing goals to realize one's potential (the humanistic message). Related to both, but more explicitly focused on the unfolding time trajectories of such processes, are studies of individual development. Empirical translations of Erikson's final stage of ego integrity (versus despair) show that aged individuals are more likely to view their past lives as meaningful, inevitable, and acceptable, than young adults, or middle-aged individuals (Ryff & Heincke, 1983). Research on Erikson's midlife stage of ego generativity (versus stagnation), emphasizes the meaning that comes from guiding and directing those younger in age. Empirical research documents the prominence of generativity among midlife (and sometimes aged) adults, particularly among women and those with more education (Keyes & Ryff, 1998). This work further shows that those with more generative orientations report higher overall levels of psychological well-being, including assessments of life meaning and purpose.

The overlapping descriptions of positive human functioning in existential, humanistic, and developmental formulations point to core dimensions of human well-being. These include having positive self-regard (self-acceptance), pursuing goals that give life meaning (purpose in life), realizing one's unique potential (personal growth), experiencing deep connection to others (positive relations), managing surrounding demands (environmental mastery), and exercising self-direction (autonomy). Findings from multiple studies, including national surveys, show diverse age trajectories on the various aspects of well-being (Ryff & Singer, 1998a). Environmental mastery and autonomy, for example, consistently show higher profiles among older adults compared to young adults or middle-aged respondents. Purpose in life and personal growth, in contrast, repeatedly show notably lower scores among aged persons relative to the two younger age groups. Self-acceptance and positive relations, in turn, show no significant age differences (or sometimes age increments for the latter). Thus, from a life-course perspective, gains and losses (and stability) in well-being appear to occur from young adulthood through old age (patterns needing replication with longitudinal studies).

Purpose in life and personal growth are aspects of well-being strongly linked with the existential and humanistic theories described earlier. These two dimensions of positive psychological functioning show marked declines in later life as well as lower profiles among individuals with less education and income. Such findings underscore to the social structural contexts within which well-being is realized or thwarted. That older persons, or those with lower socioeconomic (SES) standing, show less meaning, purpose, and growth than younger individuals, or higher SES groups, implicates the limited resources and opportunities that accrue to those in particular locations in the social order. Such observations draw attention to the fact that meaning and growth are not exclusively a function of individual commitment and responsibility; their presence, or absence, in people's lives is also influenced by larger social structural forces.

A final avenue of recent empirical inquiry pertains to the health consequences of meaning, purpose in life, and personal growth (e.g., see prior work of Pennebaker and Emmons). This research reinvokes Victor Frankl's poignant observation that those with a clear sense of meaning have survival advantages, which he speculated may be partially explained by stronger immune systems. Mapping such connections between various aspects of biology (e.g., immune function, stress physiology, neurophysiological reactivity) and core features of quality living (e.g., leading a life of purpose, having quality ties to others) represents a major scientific frontier (Ryff & Singer, 1998b). The study of mind-body interaction, in and of itself, is not new, as a large literature on the negative health consequences of psychological stress can attest. What is novel, however, is the focus on *positive interworkings*, for example, of a life embued with meaning and optimal biological functioning.

[*See also* Quality of Life.]

Bibliography

Emmons, R. A. (in press). *The psychology of ultimate concern*. New York: Guilford Press.

Emmons, R. A., & King, L. A. (1992). Thematic analysis, experience sampling, and personal goals. In C. P. Smith (Ed.), *Motivation and personality: Handbook of thematic content analysis* (pp. 73–86). New York: Cambridge University Press.

Folkman, S., Chesney, M. A., Collette, L., Boccellari, A., & Cooke, M. (1996). Postbereavement depressive mood and its prebereavement predictors in HIV+ and HIV− gay men. *Journal of Personality and Social Psychology, 70,* 336–348.

Keyes, C. L. M., & Ryff, C. D. (1998). Generativity in adult lives: Social structural contours and quality of life consequences. In D. P. McAdams & E. de St. Aubin (Eds.), *Generativity and adult development: How and why we care for the next generation* (pp. 227–263). Washington, DC: American Psychological Association.

Markus, H. R., & Nurius, P. (1986). Possible selves. *American Psychologist, 41,* 954–969.

Markus, H. R., & Ruvolo, A. (1989). Possible selves and motivation. In L. Pervin (Ed.), *Goal concepts in personality and social psychology* (pp. 211–241). New Haven, CT: Yale University Press.

Pennebaker, J. W. (1995). Emotion, disclosure, and health: An overview. In J. W. Pennebaker (Ed.), *Emotion, disclosure, and health*. Washington, DC: American Psychological Association.

Ryff, C. D., & Heincke, S. G. (1983). Subjective organization of personality in adulthood and aging. *Journal of Personality and Social Psychology, 44,* 807–816.

Ryff, C. D., & Singer, B. (1998a). Middle age and well-being. In H. S. Friedman (Ed.), *Encyclopedia of mental health* (pp. 707–719). San Diego, CA: Academic Press.

Ryff, C. D., & Singer, B. (1998b). The contours of positive human health. *Psychological Inquiry, 9,* 1–28.

Spiegel, D. (1993). *Living beyond limits: New help and hope for facing life-threatening illness*. New York: Random House.

Wong, P. T. P., & Fry, P. S. (1998). *The human quest for meaning*. Mahwah, NJ: Erlbaum.

Carol Ryff

MEASURES OF ASSOCIATION. The terms *association* and *correlation* in psychology refers to a relationship between a pair of characteristics measured on the participants within a population, for example, the association of gender with height in adult humans or the correlation of criminal behavior with poverty among U.S. teenagers. A "measure of association" or "correlation coefficient" is some quantification of such an association, usually having a value of zero when there is no association and increasing to a magnitude of one (positive or negative) as the two characteristics become more closely related.

Importance and Role in Psychological Research

Surveys suggest that the most common statistical approach in psychological research is some form of correlation analysis. This is true for several reasons. First, there is great importance attached to observational studies (in which participants are sampled and studied in their natural states) as opposed to experimental studies (in which participants are studied in a controlled laboratory setting as they respond to stimuli provided by the researchers). Correlation approaches tend to be more suitable to observational studies. Second, much of research is directed to attempting to understand the causal relationships between characteristics of participants. There is a long and controversial history concerning how to demonstrate a causal relationship, but demonstration of a correlation between a putative cause and a putative effect is always necessary. Finally, there are some unique specialized applications of correlation of great importance. The reliability (precision, reproducibility) of a measure is often assessed using a test-retest or interobserver correlation coefficient. The validity (accuracy) of a measure for a construct is often assessed using the correlation between the measure and a "gold standard" measure of that construct. Heritability is often assessed by comparing the between-twin correlation for monozygotic versus dizygotic twins.

Historical Development

The roots of correlation lie in the work of Karl Pearson early in the twentieth century. At that time, most statistical methods were based on an assumed normal (bell-shaped) distribution. Not surprisingly, these early approaches assumed that the two characteristics (X and Y) had a bivariate normal distribution, which entailed three fundamental assumptions:

- Normality: Both X and Y individually, and X for each fixed value of Y or Y for each fixed value of X, had normal distributions.
- Linearity: The mean of X for any fixed value of Y is a linear function of Y, with a slope determined by a parameter ρ, called the product–moment or Pearson correlation coefficient.
- Homoscedasticity: The variance of X for any fixed value of Y is a constant equal to $100(1-\rho^2)$ times the overall population variance of X.

The parameter ρ is a number that ranges from -1 to $+1$, with a value of 0 when there is no association between X and Y, with magnitude 1 if one can perfectly predict X from Y and Y from X. From two of the above assumptions come the two common interpretations of a correlation coefficient, one as an indicator of linear association between one variable and another, the other as the percentage of variance in one variable accounted for by the other.

With a sample from the population, one can easily obtain a sample estimate of ρ, Pearson r. The exact sampling distribution of Pearson r, whatever the value of ρ, is known. The percentiles of this distribution are widely available. When ρ is not equal to zero, the exact sampling distribution of r is very complex, but there are two quite accurate and accessible approximations. The older is the variance-stabilizing transformation, called Fisher's z-transformation, $Z(r) = \ln((1 + r)/(1 - r))$, which has approximately a normal distribution with mean $Z(\rho)$ and variance $1/(n - 3)$. The other,

somewhat more accurate, is a standardizing transformation $z(r, \rho) = (r - \rho)/(1 - r\rho)$, which has approximately the same distribution regardless of the value of ρ. Thus the percentiles of $z(r, \rho)$ are the same as those tabled for r when $\rho = 0$. With these approximations, one can structure tests of hypotheses concerning the true value of ρ, perform power calculations for such tests, generate confidence interval estimates, test homogeneity of correlations, and do all the tasks necessary to drawing inferences about correlation from a sample to a population.

Clearly, not all characteristics satisfy the three assumptions above. Many variables of interest (e.g., gender) do not have normal distributions; many associations are nonlinear. The distribution theory of Pearson r is actually remarkably robust to deviations from these assumptions, but not totally so. If Pearson r is used when the assumptions are grossly violated, the results can be misleading. Accordingly, a great deal of effort in the latter part of the twentieth century has been invested in developing correlation coefficients that are more appropriate when the above assumptions do not hold.

Alternative Forms of Correlation Coefficients

Several alternative correlation coefficients to the Pearson r exist.

Intraclass Correlation Coefficient. The most closely related alternative correlation coefficient to the Pearson r is the intraclass r. There is actually a set of coefficients called by this name that impose assumptions over and above the aforementioned three, requiring, for example, that the population means of X and Y, and/or the population variances of X and Y, are equal. When these additional assumptions hold, one can obtain a slightly more precise and powerful estimator of ρ than the Pearson r provides. The intraclass r is usually recommended for assessing reliability or twin-concordance.

The importance of the intraclass r lies not in its precision, which is only slightly greater than that of the Pearson r, but in the fact that this form can be extended to estimate ρ when there are $m > 2$ measures per participant (e.g., $m > 2$ observers for test–retest reliability assessment), where each pairwise correlation coefficient is the same, a situation the Pearson r cannot address.

Rank Correlation Coefficients. When X and Y are measured on an ordinal scale but some of the assumptions do not hold, a rank correlation coefficient is preferable to the Pearson r. To obtain the Spearman r, for example, the observations of X are rank ordered (with tied scores averaged), the observations of Y are rank ordered, and then the Pearson r estimation procedure is applied to the ranks rather than to the raw data. Under quite general circumstances, the sample distribution of the Spearman r is approximated by that of the Pearson r. In fact, if the bivariate normality assumptions hold, the sample value of the Spearman r is approximately that of the Pearson r, and there is very little loss in either precision of estimation or power of tests in using the Spearman r rather than the Pearson r. Any major discrepancy between the two is diagnostic of some serious deviation from the normality assumptions, in which case the Spearman r is preferable to the Pearson r. Another rank-order correlation coefficient is Kendall's tau, which depends on pairwise comparisons rather than on rank ordering.

Kendall's Coefficient of Concordance. As the Spearman r is related to the Pearson r, so is the relation between Kendall's coefficient of concordance and the intraclass r. If each of the $m > 2$ set of observations is rank ordered over participants and the intraclass r formula is applied to the ranks, what results is the average pairwise Spearman r, which is also equal to $(mW - 1)/(m - 1)$, where W is the Kendall's coefficient of concordance.

Biserial Correlation Coefficients. A more extreme deviation from the classic assumptions occurs when X is measured on a binary scale and Y on an ordinal scale (e.g., gender versus height). A correlation coefficient between a binary X and an ordinal Y is called a biserial r, of which there are several forms.

- When it is assumed that the distribution of Y for each of the two values of X (say, 0 and 1) is normal and has equal variance, applying the usual Pearson r formula to the X and Y yields the point-biserial r. Testing that the population value of this coefficient is zero is exactly equivalent to comparing the Y-distribution between those participants with $X = 1$ and those with $X = 0$, using a two-sample t-test. The difficulty with this coefficient is that the equal variance assumption often does not hold.
- An alternative would be the rank biserial r, in which the Spearman r between X and Y is computed (obviously with many ties in the X ranks). This is also a somewhat troublesome choice, since the achievable upper limit of the magnitude of r is now not 1 but much lower depending on the number of ties in the X-ranks.
- A preferable alternative would be the Lord's biserial r, whose numerator is the difference between the mean of Ys when $X = 1$ and the mean of Ys when $X = 0$, and the denominator is the maximum value of that difference obtained by assigning the Xs to the top and bottom of the rank-ordered Ys. This also equals the point-biserial r divided by its maximal value.
- There is also a coefficient, the classical biserial r, now very seldom used, based on the assumption that there exists a pair of variables (X^*, Y) satisfying the bivariate normal assumptions, with $X = 1$ if X^* exceeds some threshold and $X = 1$ otherwise, that is, that X is a dichotomized form of X^*. This biserial r is an estimate of the ρ between X^* and Y, based on the (X, Y) observations.

2 × 2 Association. When both X and Y are binary, the situation becomes even more challenging. Now the observations in a sample can be totally summarized by a 2 × 2 table, and the correlation coefficient sought is some measure of 2 × 2 association. There are literally an infinity of such possible correlation coefficients and dozens that are commonly used.

- The phi coefficient is obtained by assigning values of 1 and 0 to the two possible values of each of X and Y and computing the Pearson r between them. This is a measure with a value of 0 when there is no association, but the achievable limits are determined by the distributions of X and Y. When the probabilities that $X = 1$ and that $Y = 1$ differ widely from each other, the upper achievable limit may be quite close to zero, for example, a maximal value of 0.1 rather than 1.0.
- When it can be assumed that the distributions of X and Y are the same (e.g., in reliability or heritability studies), applying the formula for the intraclass r yields a coefficient called the intraclass kappa. This is very useful in reliability studies with $m > 2$ ratings per participant.
- The odds ratio, or cross product ratio, is another very common measure. If a represents the probabilities that $X = 1$ and $Y = 1$, b that $X = 1$ and $Y = 0$, c that $X = 0$ and $Y = 1$, d that $X = 0$ and $Y = 0$, the odds ratio equals ad/bc. This is a coefficient unlike all others discussed here in that absence of association in this case is indicated by a value of 1 (not 0), negative association ranges from 0 to 1 (not -1 to 0), and positive association ranges from 1 to infinity (not 0 to 1). To avoid misinterpretation, rescaling is sometimes suggested. For example, the gamma coefficient that equals $(OR - 1)/(OR + 1)$ or Yule's index $(OR^{1/2} - 1)/(OR^{1/2} - 1)$ are often used as a rescaled odds ratio.
- Another type of kappa coefficient is obtained when different importance is attached to the two types of discrepancies between X and Y (when $X = 1$ and $Y = 0$ versus $X = 0$ and $Y = 1$): a weighted kappa coefficient. When the two types of discrepancies are considered of equal importance, the coefficient that results is called an unweighted kappa or Cohen's kappa. When the probability that $X = 1$ equals the probability that $Y = 1$, then all weighted kappa coefficients estimate the same population parameter, and that population parameter is the same one estimated by the phi coefficient and by the intraclass kappa coefficient. In general, however, the phi coefficient is the geometric mean of the two most extreme weighted kappa coefficients, and the phi coefficient divided by its maximal value (often also called "attributable risk") equals one of the extreme weighted kappa coefficients.
- If it can be assumed that there is an underlying (X^*, Y^*) satisfying the bivariate normal assumptions and

that X and Y are obtained by dichotomizing X^* and Y^* at a fixed threshold value for each, one can use the 2×2 information to estimate the correlation between X^* and Y^*. This type of correlation coefficient is called the tetrachoric correlation coefficient.

Problems in Application and Interpretation

Any method as widely used as is correlation is likely also to be widely misused. As is apparent, there are many forms of correlation coefficient available for any particular pair of characteristics, and it is not at all assured that the same conclusions will be drawn by researchers using different forms. To avoid this, researchers carefully examine the underlying assumptions justifying each choice and select the one most appropriate to the context in which they propose to use it. Admittedly, not all researchers will make the same choice and draw the same conclusions, but, in reality, choice of coefficient is not the most serious problem in interpreting correlation results.

Very troubling is the miscomputation of correlation coefficients because of inadequate sampling. All the usual correlation coefficient formulas require a representative sample of participants from the population of interest, with X and Y measured on each. If the participants do not constitute a representative sample, although nothing prevents a researcher from computing any sample correlation coefficient, the result might well be misleading.

For example, if one were interested in the correlation between criminal activities and poverty among U.S. teenagers, a random sample of U.S. teenagers might contain only a minority with the characteristics of criminal activity or extreme poverty. The temptation then is to "enrich" the sample, for example, by drawing half of the sample from an inner-city milieu and the other half from a suburb. This then is a stratified sample, not a representative sample, and the value of any r based on such a sample does not necessarily estimate ρ in any population. This is the problem called "Berkson's Fallacy" in epidemiological studies and is the source of many misleading results.

The correlation between X and Y in one population may be quite different from that in another. For example, the correlation between criminal activities and poverty in the inner-city sample may bear no similarity to the correlation in the suburban sample, and both may be quite different from the correlation in the total population of U.S. teenagers, of which each sample is part. In fact, the correlation within every ecological unit might be positive, but the correlation in the total population (including participants in all the ecological units) might be zero or negative. This statistical artifact is called "Simpson's Paradox."

The "ecological fallacy" is yet another related prob-

lem. If, instead of sampling individuals, one samples school districts in the United States, with X and Y measured at the district level, the correlation between X and Y (computed over school districts) is an "ecological correlation," based on sampling and measuring "ecological units," here school districts. This is a valid correlation coefficient among school districts in the population of school districts but bears no necessary similarity to the correlation between X and Y measured on individual participants ("individual correlation") in any population of participants, or to that between X and Y measured on families (another ecological unit) or to that between X and Y measured on cities (yet another ecological unit). Any correlation coefficient is specific to a particular population, and jumping to generalizations beyond the limits of the units or the population sampled often produces misleading conclusions.

Much of psychological research is based on testing the null hypothesis that $\rho = 0$ and finding a "statistically significant" correlation. Of course, "statistical significance" does not mean that the correlation is large or important. With a large enough sample size, the most trivial nonzero correlation can be declared statistically significant. Moreover, very strong correlations may also be found to be not statistically significant because of too small a sample size. For such reasons, it is the magnitude of the correlation and its estimation error that is most important, not whether or not the correlation is statistically significant.

In interpreting the magnitude of correlation, one must consider the problem of attenuation of correlation due to unreliability. Although one might be interested in the constructs of criminal activity and poverty, what one correlates are measures of criminal activity and poverty, neither of which is entirely free of random error of measurement (unreliability). The effect of such unreliability is always to attenuate the magnitude of correlation. The greater the unreliability of one or the other of the two measures, the greater the attenuation of correlation. This is yet another reason that merely reporting that a correlation is not statistically significantly at a level greater than zero can be misleading. Such a situation could arise when the constructs of interest are perfectly correlated but the measures of the construct are extremely unreliable.

However, errors of measurement are not always random, and the interpretation of the magnitude of correlation should also take the possibility of bias in the design into account. For example, one might design a twin study in which the same rater, knowing the zygosity of the twins, rates both twins. In such a study, rater bias might produce a closer correspondence between the twins' ratings than would have been obtained with two different blind raters, and rater expectation effects might lead to a closer correspondence between the ratings of monozygotic twins than between the ratings of dizygotic twins. Then a high heritability coefficient might result even when there is no heritability at all except in the minds of the raters.

Yet with all the problems of sampling, measurement, design, and analysis that can mislead interpretation of correlation, the most consistently troubling one is the unwarranted inference of causality from correlation. To show that X causes Y, one must demonstrate that X is correlated with Y, but that is never enough. In such a case, X may cause Y, Y may cause X, some third factor Z may cause both X and Y, or there may be no direct and meaningful connection between X and Y (pseudocorrelation). Jumping to causal conclusions from a correlational study is the most troublesome and persistent misuse of correlational studies.

In summary, measurement and assessment of association or correlation is one of the most ubiquitous and important research approaches in psychology. There are many unique and potent tools within the approach, but, as is usually the case when there are potent tools, care must be taken to use them well and judiciously.

Helena C. Kraemer

MEASURES OF INTELLIGENCE. [*This entry comprises four articles*:
Intelligence Tests
Biological Theories
Cognitive Theories
Legal Issues
Numerous independent entries related to measures of intelligence are included in the encyclopedia: Determinants of Intelligence; Kaufman Assessment Battery for Children; Peabody Picture Vocabulary Test; Stanford–Binet Intelligence Scale; *and* Wechsler Intelligence Tests.]

Intelligence Tests

Many encyclopedic treatments of mental testing begin with Alfred Binet (1857–1911), which is fitting, given his landmark 1905 contribution of the first test of general mental ability or general intelligence, his 1908 revision, and his 1911 refinement. These instruments spawned the applied mental measurement movement. But a number of antecedents prepared the soil for Binet's contribution to germinate and for the new science of psychometrics to refine what he had achieved. For example, during the prior century, Esquirol distinguished between mental deficiency and mental disorders. Before that, these two conditions were confused and often conflated. Esquirol also stressed that mental deficiencies come in degrees. Subsequently, Gustave Fechner, E. H. Weber, and Wilhelm Wundt demon-

strated that equal intervals of (objective) stimulus intensity do not mirror (subjective) appraisals of "just noticeable differences" in experiential phenomena. The resulting conjoint scaling of physical and psychological phenomena (psychophysics) set the stage for the development of psychometrics, a new psychological specialty predicated on the idea that responses to environmental circumstances are in part a function of individual differences in ability, interests, and personality. Measuring these constructs was, of course, a fallible enterprise. So the limen of psychophysics became the standard error of measurement for psychometric appraisals in differential psychology (the psychology of individual differences).

Before Binet's instrument appeared, Galton, Cattell, and Wissler, among others, were aiming to measure intellect through fundamental psychophysical procedures that indexed the strength of various sensory systems (Thorndike & Lohman, 1990). They were operating under Aristotle's maxim that the mind is in the dark; it is informed to the extent that one's sensory systems bring in clear and reliable information. Using this major premise, ascertaining individual differences in sensory system power became a compelling approach. Yet it was an approach that did not appear to pan out. Binet did something different. He examined complex behavior (e.g., comprehension, judgment, and reasoning) directly. In doing so, his methods could not compare to psychophysical assessments in terms of reliability (internal properties), but he more than made up for this in the validity (external connections) of his assessment procedure. Binet's insight was to use an external criterion to validate his measuring tool. Thus, he pioneered the empirically keyed or external validation approach to scale construction. His external criterion was chronological age, and test items were grouped such that the typical member of each age group was able to achieve 50% correct answers on questions (items) of differential complexity. This reveals, again, connections with psychophysical procedures, which typically calibrate response thresholds for JNDs at 50% accuracy (method of limits, paired comparisons). With Binet's procedure, individual differences in scale scores, or mental age (MA), manifested wide variation around students of similar chronological age (CA). These components were synthesized by Stern to create a ratio of mental development: MA/CA. This was later multiplied by 100 to form what we now know as the intelligence quotient (IQ), namely IQ = MA/CA × 100.

With respect to external criteria, Binet's approach was impressive. Unlike psychophysical assessments of sensory systems, his test forecasted teacher ratings and school performance. And the progressive educational movement in America, coupled with the pragmatic orientation in applied psychology at the turn of the century, served as catalysts for its wide circulation. Early on, two of G. Stanley Hall's students, H. H. Goddard and Lewis M. Terman in particular, cultivated the new enterprise of applied psychological testing. Goddard and Terman specialized at opposite ends of the IQ spectrum (Chapman, 1988; Zenderland, 1998), but both had written and shared similar views about the importance of tailoring curriculum complexity, as well as the rate of its presentation, toward individual differences in mental age. Terman later developed one of the most famous longitudinal studies in all of psychology, exclusively devoted to the intellectually gifted (Chapman, 1988), while Goddard concentrated on the "feeble minded" and directed an institution (Vineland) for training practitioners working with this special population (Zenderland, 1998). Both played key roles in America's military efforts, as they combined forces with Robert M. Yerkes to contribute psychological support in the form of personnel selection during World War I. The armed forces needed an efficient means to screen recruits, many of whom were illiterate. For his dissertation research, Arthur S. Otis, one of Terman's students, had devised a nonverbal test of general intelligence. This work was heavily drawn on to build one of the two group intelligence tests utilized for initial screening and the appropriate placement of recruits: the Army Alpha (for literates) and Beta (for illiterates). The role that mental measurements played in World War I and, subsequently, World War II constitutes one of applied psychology's great success stories. (Even today, an Act of Congress mandates a certain minimum status on the general factor, because training efficiency is compromised prohibitively at IQs <80; see Gottfredson, 1997.)

Following World War I, Terman was one of the first to draw a generalization between the applied utility of military intellectual assessments and problems in America's schools. Terman, a former teacher himself, was aware of the ability range found in homogeneous groupings based on chronological age and became an advocate of homogeneous grouping based on mental age. He felt strongly that, at the extremes (say, beyond two standard deviations either side of IQ's normative mean) the likelihood of encountering special student needs increases exponentially. The more deviant the IQ, the more intense the need. Because holding age fairly constant, as in schooling structured around chronological age placement, results in classes of students with markedly different rates of learning (due to markedly different mental ages), a problem is presented. Optimal rates of curriculum presentation, as well as its complexity, vary in gradation throughout the range of individual differences in general intelligence. With IQ centered on 100 and a standard deviation of 16, IQs extending from the bottom to the top 1% in ability cover an IQ range of approximately 63 to 137. But since IQs are known to go beyond 200, this 74-point span covers

but one third of the possible range. Hollingworth's classic, *Children Over 180 IQ* (1942), provided empirical support for the unique educational needs of this special population, which has since been empirically supported in every decade (Benbow & Stanley, 1996).

While American psychologists were interested primarily in applied applications, according to E. G. Boring, early mental testers were interested in studying "the mind at work." Thus, the theoretical support for a psychologically cohesive dimension of general intelligence came from the other side of the Atlantic. In a groundbreaking publication, Charles Spearman (1904) showed that a dominant dimension (g) appears to run through heterogeneous collections of intellectual tasks (test items). Ostensibly, items aggregated to form such groupings were seen as a hodgepodge. Yet, when such items are all positively correlated and they are summed, the construct relevant aspects of each coalesce through aggregation, whereas their construct irrelevant (uncorrelated or unique) aspects reduce to a miniscule perturbation within the composite. Spearman and Brown formalized this property of aggregation in 1910. The Spearman-Brown Prophecy formula estimates the proportion of common or reliable variance running through a composite: $r_{tt} = kr_{xx} \div 1 + (k - 1)r_{xx}$ (where r_{tt} = common or reliable variance, r_{xx} = average item intercorrelation, and k = number of items). This formula reveals how a collection of items with uniformly light positive intercorrelations (say, averaging $r_{xx} = .15$) can create a composite dominated by common variance. In this example, if fifty items were available, their aggregation would generate an individual-differences measure having 90% common variance (10% random error). Drawing on another connection with psychophysics, the signal-to-noise ratio from signal detection theory underscores the power of aggregation (but in reverse). Although each item on a typical intelligence test is dominated by unwanted "noise," aggregation serves to amass the construct relevant aspect (signal) from each item, while simultaneously attenuating their construct irrelevant aspect (noise) within the composite. Aggregation amplifies the signal and attenuates noise. Using words from Bert Green's "Defense of Measurement" (1978), in psychometrics, "given enough sow's ears you can indeed make a silk purse."

The Nature of IQ and General Intelligence

At the phenotypic level, modern versions of intelligence tests index essentially the same construct uncovered at the turn of the twentieth century by Spearman (1904) contribution, " 'General intelligence,' Objectively determined and measured"—albeit with much more efficiency and precision. While some have bemoaned the stability of this finding as lack of progress, others have stressed that complex human behavior is multiply determined. Yet, given the forecasting efficiency that g has accrued over the years, how much additional forecasting power can be reasonably anticipated from the ability domain? Everyone agrees that many things matter for predicting complex human behavior. We must always remain open to innovative constructs and measures capable of forecasting aspects of criteria that current measures do not tap. There is much room for better prediction, that is, there is much unaccounted criterion variance. In the meantime, however, contemporary representatives at the poles of the applied psychological educational-industrial spectrum, such as Snow (1989) and Campbell (1990), respectively, have underscored the real-world significance of general intelligence by incorporating it in lawlike empirical generalizations:

> Given new evidence and reconsideration of old evidence, [g] can indeed be interpreted as 'ability to learn' as long as it is clear that these terms refer to complex processes and skills and that a somewhat different mix of these constituents may be required in different learning tasks and settings. The old view that mental tests and learning tasks measure distinctly different abilities should be discarded. (Snow, 1989, p. 22)

> General mental ability is a substantively significant determinant of individual differences in job performance for any job that includes information processing tasks. If the measure of performance reflects the information processing components of the job and any of several well-developed standardized measures used to assess general mental ability, then the relationship will be found unless the sample restricts the variances in performance or mental ability to near zero. The exact size of the relationship will be a function of the range of talent in the sample and the degree to which the job requires information processing and verbal cognitive skills. (Campbell, 1990, p. 56)

Modern research on general intelligence has sharpened validity generalizations aimed at forecasting educational outcomes, occupational training, and work performance. But empiricism also has escalated in domains at the periphery of general intelligence's network of external relationships, such as aggression, delinquency and crime, income and poverty. For some benchmarks, general cognitive ability covaries .70 to .80 with academic achievement measures, .40 to .70 with military training assignments, .20 to .60 with work performance (higher values reflect job complexity), .30 to .40 with income, and around .20 with law-abidingness (see Brody, 1992; Gottfredson, 1997; Jensen, 1998, and references therein). An excellent compilation of positive and negative correlates of g is Brand's Table 2 (1987). It documents a variety of light correlations between general intelligence and altruism, sense of humor, practical knowledge, response to psychotherapy, social skills, supermarket shopping ability

(all positive correlates), and impulsivity, accident proneness, delinquency, smoking, racial prejudice, and obesity (all negative correlates), among others. This diverse family of correlates is especially thought-provoking because it reveals how individual differences in general intelligence covary with cascades of primary (direct) and secondary (indirect) effects. Murray's 15-year longitudinal analysis of income differences between biologically related siblings (reared together) who differed on average by twelve IQ points is especially illuminating (1998); it corroborates a handful of studies using a similar control for family environment (Bouchard, 1997)—while not confounding SES with biological relatedness. (For a lucid account of the social significance of general intelligence, see Gottfredson's "Why g matters: The complexity of everyday life," in *Intelligence*. McNemar's *American Psychologist* classic "Lost: Our intelligence? Why?" (1964) is also a must read.)

Empiricism ≠ Policy

The empiricism just described is widely accepted among experts in the field of measurement and individual differences (Carroll, 1993; Gottfredson, 1997; Jensen, 1998; Thorndike & Lohman, 1990). Yet it has been common for empiricism pertaining to general intelligence (and interpretative extrapolations emanating from it) to stimulate contentious debate (Cronbach, 1975). Indeed, psychologists can be found on all sides of the complex set of issues engendered by assessing individual differences in general intelligence (Snyderman & Rothman, 1987). But this is not new, and it is likely to be with us always. Because psychological assessments are frequently used for allocating educational and vocational opportunities, they play a role in implementing social policies. But so far, psychometric data do not (cannot) imply particular policies for test use. Moreover, because different demographic groupings differ in test score and criterion performance, social concern has followed this construct since shortly after Spearman's initial article appeared (cf. Chapman, 1988; Jenkins & Paterson, 1961). Nevertheless, many scientists have been determined to better understand g and the vehicles assessing individual differences on this dimension, because, as indicated (Campbell, 1990; Snow, 1989), by the late 1980s it was becoming clear that general intelligence played a prominent role in outcomes germane to learning and work. This supported Lee Cronbach's evaluation: "The general mental test stands today as the most important technical contribution psychology has made to the practical guidance of human affairs." Robert Thorndike summarized his research findings through the 1980s on cognitive abilities: "The great preponderance of the prediction that is possible from any set of cognitive tests is attributable to the general ability that they share. What I have called 'empirical g' is not merely an interesting psychometric phenomenon, but lies at the heart of the prediction of real-life performances."

Remarks such as these warranted extensive examinations of general intelligence, its measurement, nature, and how best to nurture its development, because powerful scientific tools can be used wisely or unwisely, and their applied use is almost always accompanied by unintended (indirect) effects. So a number of wide-ranging treatments have appeared over the last 2 decades, in part as a function of what this dimension is able to forecast relative to other psychological attributes. For some highlights, John B. Carroll (1993) published his multidecade project, a massive tome entitled *Human Cognitive Abilities*, which included 467 data sets of factor-analytic work dating back to the 1920s. In 1992, *Psychological Science* published a special section, "Ability Testing," as did *Current Directions in Psychological Science* (1993). The National Academy of Sciences published two book-length special reports on the fairness and validity of ability testing (Widgor & Garner, 1982; Hartigan & Widgor, 1989), while the *Journal of Vocational Behavior* launched two special issues, "The g Factor in Employment" and "Fairness in Employment Testing" (Gottfredson, 1986; Gottfredson & Sharf, 1988, respectively). Moreover, Sternberg's two-volume *Encyclopedia of Intelligence* (1994) is an excellent source for systematically examining the landscape of psychological concepts, findings, history, and research about intelligence. Sternberg's *Encyclopedia*, like his *Advances* series, goes well beyond the psychometric assessment of cognitive abilities, as does Detterman's *Current Topics* series.

In 1994, Herrnstein and Murray published a controversial book, *The Bell Curve: Intelligence and Class Structure*. This sharpened the intensity of attention devoted to general intelligence and its assessment. Among other things, Herrnstein and Murray examined the relative predictive power of general intelligence and SES for forecasting a variety of social outcomes (1994). Because of the exchanges this book stimulated, not only within the scholarly community but also in the popular press, the American Psychological Association was moved to form a special task force. Their report, "Intelligence: Knowns and Unknowns," is now available (Neisser et al., 1996). Contemporaneously with the work of this task force, a number of special issues appeared in major psychological outlets. Stephen Ceci served as guest editor for a special issue of *Psychology, Public Policy, and Law* entitled "IQ in Society" (1996), while Robert Sternberg guest edited a special issue of the *American Psychologist*, "Intelligence and Lifelong Learning" (1997). Similarly, for *Intelligence*, Linda S. Gottfredson assembled "Intelligence and Social Policy" (1997), which opened with an editorial, "Mainstream Science on Intelligence," signed by 52 academic scientists working in the general-intelligence arena.

There appears to be a fair amount of agreement among measurement experts. Most believe that measures of general intelligence assess individual differences pertaining to abstract thinking or reasoning, the capacity to acquire knowledge, and problem-solving ability (Brody, 1992; Carroll, 1993; Gottfredson, 1997; Snyderman & Rothman, 1987). Naturally, individual differences in these attributes carry over to facets of life outside academic and vocational arenas, because abstract reasoning, problem-solving, and the rate of learning touch so many aspects of life in general, especially in our computer-driven, information-dense society. The point is that the quoted characteristics listed above fit with correlates of g's nexus of empirical relationships; they are not incompatible with the empirical facts.

Beyond Behavior

Some have suggested that because a fairly comprehensive picture of the forecasting capabilities of general intelligence has been drawn, little is likely to come of examining behavioral aspects of this construct further. Scientists, it is argued, should move beyond behavioral manifestations of g. For example, Jensen has argued that basic research needs to travel down and uncover more fundamental (biological) vertical paths and develop more ultimate (evolutionary) explanations for genuine advances to occur (1998). Recent discussions of purported gains in general intelligence, observed cross-culturally, are important to examine first. But, admittedly, these gains may in part be a function of fundamental biological antecedents.

Flynn Effect

That raw score increases have occurred over time on measures of general intelligence is unquestionably true. During most of this century, observed scores on intelligence tests have been steadily rising cross-culturally. This observation has been labeled the Flynn effect after the investigator who documented its occurrence. Whether these increases reflect genuine gains in general intelligence is, however, less clear-cut. Increases can occur due to increases on a measure's construct relevant or construct irrelevant (nonerror unique) variance, or both. The problem is complex, and it has generated a considerable amount of discussion (Neisser, 1998). Yet, a final answer has not emerged. However, that changes are at least in part due to construct-irrelevant aspects of measuring tools is suggested by the following.

The magnitude of the Flynn effect is positively correlated with the amount of nonerror uniqueness of various measures of g. For example, gains on the Raven Matrices are greater than verbal reasoning composites of heterogeneous verbal tests, which, in turn, are greater than broadly sampled tests of general intelligence (aggregates of heterogeneous collections of numerical, spatial, and verbal problems). The Raven Matrices consist of approximately 50% g variance, whereas heterogeneous collections of cognitive tests aggregated to form a measure of general intelligence approach 85%. (Broad verbal reasoning tests are intermediate.) Complexities are added by considering that test scores have probably increased (especially at the lower end of general intelligence) due to advances in medical care, dietary factors, and educational opportunities. But at the upper end of this dimension, the highly able appear to have suffered some attenuation in their developmental trajectory due to being deprived of appropriate developmental opportunities—a challenging curriculum at the appropriate time (Benbow & Stanley, 1996). Nonetheless, the Flynn effect is definitely a topic deserving of intense study.

Whatever these raw score gains are ultimately attributed to, however, they do not detract from or enhance the construct validity of measures of general intelligence. Mean gains on construct-valid measures do not speak to changes in the associated covariance structure of these instruments (Hunt, 1995). For example, populations at contrasting levels of development typically manifest the same covariance structure with respect to the trait indicators under analysis (Lubinski, 2000). To say that mean changes on an individual difference dimension somehow attenuate the construct validity of measures purporting to assess it does not follow.

Vertical Inquiry

Like other psychological constructs, general intelligence may be studied at different levels of analysis. By pooling studies of a variety of kinship correlates of g (e.g., MZ and DZ twins reared together and apart, and a variety of adoption designs), the heritability of general intelligence in industrialized nations has been estimated to be between 60 and 80% (Bouchard, 1997). Using magnetic resonance imaging (MRI) technology, brain size controlled for body weight covaries in the high .30s with general intelligence (Jensen, 1998, pp. 146–149). Glucose metabolism is related to problem-solving behavior, and the highly gifted appear to engage in more efficient problem-solving behavior that is less energy expensive. Also, highly intellectually gifted individuals evince enhanced right hemispheric functioning. The complexity of electroencephalograph (EEG) waves is positively correlated with g, as are the amplitude and latency of average evoked potential (AEP). Some investigators have suggested that dendritic arborization (the amount of branching) is correlated with g. In addition, a multidisciplinary team appears to have uncovered a DNA marker associated with g.

Proximal and Ultimate Examinations of g

A step beyond the aforementioned proximal associations has been taken on the ultimate basis for their evolutionary development. Bouchard and his colleagues have introduced a revision of experience producing drives (EPD) theory that speaks to the development of human intellectual phenomena. EPD theory-revised is a modification of an earlier formulation by Hayes (1962)—a comparative psychologist and pioneer in the early investigations of language and socialization capabilities of nonhuman primates. The idea is that, like all organisms, humans were designed to do something, and that they have inherited EPDs to facilitate ability and skill acquisition through dispositions that motivate individuals toward particular kinds of experiences and developmental opportunities. Moreover, these evolutionary selective sensitivities can operate in a wide range of functionally equivalent environments (because the environments that children evolved in were highly variable). Bouchard's and his colleagues' formulation also interconnects with contemporary developmental theories on the active role that individuals take in structuring environments for themselves (see Lubinski, 2000, for a review).

Other investigators have contemplated a synthesis of evolutionary psychology with chronometrical procedures for measuring inspection time (Jensen, 1998). Inspection time is a measure of the speed of perceptual discrimination on "simple" elementary cognitive tasks (responses to stimulus configurations that typically take less than 1 second for average adults to perform with essentially zero errors). Theoretically, elementary cognitive tasks aim to index the time course of information processing in the nervous system. A variety of technical measurement issues surround this area of research, but it does appear that the temporal dynamics of performance on elementary cognitive tasks covaries negatively with g (faster processing is associated with higher g levels). Inspection-time measures have been recently used to successfully assess individual differences in cognitive sophistication among nonhuman primates.

The latter is an intriguing line of research. It might constitute a vehicle for comparative psychological inquiry into the biological underpinnings of general cognitive sophistication, comparable with what the sign language modality fostered for language learning in nonhuman primates. This is really not that far-fetched. For some time now, investigators have remarked on the range of individual differences within primate conspecifics. Premack, for example, took this as a matter of course. In his *Behavioral and Brain Sciences* "target article" (1983) (pertaining to individual differences in language versus nonlanguage trained groups of chimpanzees), he noted:

144   MEASURES OF INTELLIGENCE: Intelligence Tests

Although chimpanzees vary in intelligence, we have unfortunately never had any control over this factor, having to accept all animals that are sent to us. We have, therefore, had both gifted and nongifted animals in each group. Sarah is a bright animal by any standards, but so is Jessie, one of the non-language-trained animals. The groups are also comparable at the other end of the continuum, Peony's negative gifts being well matched by those of Luvy. (p. 125)

Individual differences in processing-stimulus equivalency (verbal/symbolic) relationships have been postulated by some experimentalists to be a marker of general intelligence. If such individual differences are ultimately linked to individual differences in CNS microstructure within and between the primate order, and these, in turn, are linked to observations such as Premack's "teacher ratings," all of the ingredients are assimilated for advancing primate comparative psychology. The language-communicative performances now routinely displayed by chimpanzees, and especially pigmy chimpanzees, are truly remarkable. They encompass sign language reports of emotional states and conspecific tutoring. Sue Savage-Rumbaugh has connected these findings with those from child language–development research. Someday, perhaps, primate comparative examinations will provide clues to human individuality. If individual differences in acquiring cognitive skills could be linked to more fundamental biological mechanisms (like the vertical threads already discussed), we might have an especially powerful lens through which to view common phylogenetic processes involved in cognitive development. Research developments on this front will be interesting to follow. Perhaps they might even forestall E. O. Wilson's concern: "Social scientists as a whole have paid little attention to the foundations of human nature, and they have had almost no interest in its deep origins" (1998, p. 184).

Bibliography

Benbow, C. P., & Stanley, J. C. (1996). Inequity in equity: How "equity" can lead to inequity for high-potential students. *Psychology, Public Policy, and Law, 2,* 249–292.

Bouchard, T. J., Jr. (1997). IQ similarity in twins reared apart: Findings and responses to critics. In R. J. Sternberg & E. L. Grigorenko (Eds.), *Intelligence: Heredity and environment* (pp. 126–160). New York: Cambridge University Press.

Brand, C. (1987). The importance of general intelligence. In S. Magil & C. Magil (Eds.), *Arthur Jensen: Consensus and controversy* (pp. 251–265). New York: Falmer Press.

Brody, N. (1992). *Intelligence* (2nd ed.). San Diego, CA: Academic Press.

Campbell, J. P. (1990). The role of theory in industrial and organizational psychology. In M. D. Dunnette & L. M. Hough (Eds.), *Handbook of industrial/organizational psychology* (2nd ed., Vol. 1, pp. 39–74). Palo Alto, CA: Consulting Psychologists Press.

Carroll, J. B. (1993). *Human cognitive abilities: A survey of factor-analytic studies.* Cambridge, UK: Cambridge University Press.

Ceci, S. J. (1996). Special theme: IQ and society. *Psychology, Public Policy, and Law* (Vol. 3–4).

Chapman, P. D. (1988). *Schools as sorters: Lewis M. Terman, applied psychology, and the intelligence testing movement, 1890–1930.* New York: New York University Press.

Gottfredson, L. S. (1997). Intelligence and social policy [Special issue] *Intelligence, 24.*

Herrnstein, R. J., & Murray, C. (1994). *The bell curve: Intelligence and class structure in American life.* New York: Free Press.

Hunt, E. (1995). *Will we be smart enough? A cognitive analysis of the coming workforce.* New York: Russell Sage Foundation.

Jenkins, J. J., & Paterson, D. G. (1961). *Studies in individual differences: The search for intelligence.* New York: Appleton-Century-Crofts.

Jensen, A. R. (1998). *The g factor: The science of mental ability.* Westport, CT: Praeger.

Lubinski, D. (2000). Assessing individual differences in human behavior: "Sinking shafts at a few critical points." *Annual Review of Psychology, 51,* 405–444.

Murray, C. (1998). *Income, inequality, and IQ.* Washington, DC: American Enterprise Institute.

Neisser, U. (1998). *The rising curve: Long-term gains in IQ and related measures.* Washington, DC: American Psychological Association.

Neisser, U., Boodoo, G., Bouchard, T. J., Jr., Boykin, A. W., Brody, N., Ceci, S. J., Halpern, D. F., Loehlin, J. C., Perloff, R., Sternberg, R. J., & Urbina, S. (1996). Intelligence: Knowns and unknowns. *American Psychologist, 51,* 77–101.

Snow, R. E. (1989). Aptitude-treatment interaction as a framework for research on individual differences in learning. In P. L. Ackerman, R. J. Sternberg, & R. G. Glasser (Eds.), *Learning and individual differences: Advances in theory and research* (pp. 13–59). New York: Freeman.

Spearman, C. (1904). "General intelligence," objectively determined and measured. *American Journal of Psychology, 15,* 201–292.

Sternberg, R. J. (Ed). (1994). *Encyclopedia of human intelligence* (Vols. 1–2). New York: Macmillan.

Sternberg, R. J., & Detterman, D. K. (1986). *What is intelligence? Contemporary viewpoints on its nature and definition.* Norwood, NJ: Ablex.

Thorndike, R. M., & Lohman, D. F. (1990). *A century of ability testing.* Chicago: Riverside.

Wilson, E. O. (1998). *Consilience: The unity of knowledge.* New York: Knopf.

Zenderland, L. (1998). *Measuring minds: Henry Goddard and the origins of American intelligence testing.* Cambridge, UK: Cambridge University Press.

David Lubinski

Biological Theories

There is a fairly long history in psychology of attempts to identify the biological bases of human intelligence. Some of these attempts seemed promising at first but either failed to replicate or have not been followed up for one reason or another; others have yielded a more consistent pattern of results. However, at the same time that empirical demonstrations of reliable correlations between intelligence and different biological measures have been reported, theoretical interpretations have generally been less forthcoming. Thus, it is probably safe to say that at this point in time a great deal more is known about *which* biological functions and mechanisms correlate with intelligence than *why* they do.

Head and Brain Size

From early in the twentieth century, numerous researchers have attempted to see whether persons of higher intelligence have larger brains. Early studies used external measures of head size as a proxy for brain size, or measured the brains of deceased individuals; with the more recent advent of computerized axial tomography (CT) and magnetic resonance imaging (MRI), in vivo estimates of brain size are now routinely made.

Since 1906, a total of 53 studies comprising over 50,000 subjects have reported correlations between external head size and different estimates of intelligence. None of the reported correlations is negative; they range from .02 to .54 and average .19. Since the late 1980s, 15 studies comprising 650 subjects have measured brain volumes directly using CT or MRI scans. In these studies, correlations between brain size and intelligence range from .07 to .69 and average .34. These results clearly reveal that larger brains are associated with higher intelligence, but it remains to be seen whether this is attributable to larger brains having a larger number of neurons, a greater myelination of neurons, or other factors.

Brain Electrical Activity

In the 1960s, a number of investigators began to look at relationships between intelligence and the spontaneous electrical activity of the brain. The results of these studies were somewhat inconclusive, prompting other researchers to study various parameters of so-called brain evoked potentials.

As their name implies, evoked potentials refer to the electrical activity of the brain that is caused (or evoked) by some external stimulus (e.g., a light flash or an auditory stimulus such as a beep or a click). Any individual potential typically shows considerable random fluctuations, but over a large number of trials these fluctuations can be smoothed out, yielding an average evoked potential (AEP). Two parameters of AEPs have been studied extensively: their latencies—the speed with which the brain responds to the stimulus, and their amplitude—the amount of electrocortical activity that the stimulus evokes.

In one study (Ertl & Schafer, 1969), several IQ tests—including the Wechsler Intelligence Scale for Children, the Primary Mental Abilities Test, and the Otis—were administered to 573 primary school children. Correlations between IQs and AEPs latencies were primarily negative (ranging from .10 to −.35), indicating that higher IQ scores were associated with shorter, or faster, latencies. Following this report, a number of other AEP-IQ studies were conducted, many of which reported significant correlations between IQ and AEP latencies and/or amplitudes of about the same magnitude as those obtained by Ertl and Schafer. Additional recent studies have provided more fine-grained estimates of different AEP components, many of which show significant and sometimes quite pronounced correlations with measures of intelligence.

Other recent studies have focused on what has become known as the string measure. This measure—essentially, the length of the contour perimeter of the AEP waveform—has yielded variable results. Some studies report substantial correlations between it and intelligence; others reporting nonsignificant correlations or even correlations in the opposite direction to prediction. Recently, some resolution to the inconsistency of the results has been provided, and it has been proposed that both positive and negative correlations between intelligence and string length measures derived from different tasks can be expected, depending upon the attentional demands of the task.

Information-Processing Speed

Since the early work on intelligence of Sir Francis Galton, reaction times and measures of the speed with which individuals can process different kinds of information have been viewed by some as an indirect measure of biological intelligence. Many different tasks have been employed to measure reaction times (RTs), ranging from quite simple tasks, in which subjects press buttons on a response console when they see a light appear, to tasks involving substantially more complex information processing. However, even the most complex RT tests used in intelligence research typically have very low error rates and can be responded to in less than a second.

This apparent simplicity of the tasks notwithstanding, individual RT or speed-of-processing tests show significant correlations (between approximately −.20 and −.40) with scores on standard measures of intelligence, with higher IQ scores being associated with faster, or shorter, RTs. Moreover, when multiple RT measures are employed, studies have reported sizeable multiple correlations between these and IQ scores, ranging from approximately .40 to .75. Results such as these indicate that the speed with which individuals can process different kinds of information may account for as much as 50% of the variance in intelligence. Evidence for the link between RT measures and biology is provided by studies showing both that RT tests have high heritabilities and that the correlation between RTs and intelligence is largely attributable to common genetic effects.

Neural Transmission Speed

Nerve conduction velocity (NCV) refers to the speed with which electrical impulses are transmitted along nerve fibers and across synapses. It has been suggested that individual differences in NCV might be attributable to genetic differences in the structure and amount of a particular type of protein that sets limits on information-processing rates. Given the relationship between information-processing speed and intelligence described above, faster NCV is therefore expected to correlate with higher intelligence.

Although a number of researchers have investigated relationships between NCV, RTs, and IQ (usually measuring NCV in the peripheral rather than in the central nervous system), there has been little agreement in the results. Since 1990, 12 studies have reported IQ-NCV correlations ranging between −.61 and +.62 (a positive correlation is expected) and averaging .15. Studies of males have reported higher IQ-NCV correlations (averaging .21) than studies of females (averaging .06). The reason for this gender difference is unknown, but it has been speculated that it may relate to the increased testosterone levels of males. Age differences have also been reported, and it has been suggested that IQ and NCV may only correlate with one another after a person's NCV has fully matured.

If peripheral system NCVs are estimates of brain neural transmission speed, it might be expected that they would correlate more highly with RTs than with IQ scores, but this has not proven to be the case. One study, for example, reported IQ-NCV correlations of approximately .40 and RT-NCV correlations of approximately −.25. Behavior genetic studies have suggested that even though the IQ-NCV relationship is weak, NCVs have substantial heritabilities and their correlation with IQ is entirely mediated by common genetic factors.

Brain Energy Consumption

Like all physical organs, the active brain consumes energy. Thus, when individuals are engaged in a task that requires cognitive activity, an index of the extent to which their brain is "working" is the rate at which it metabolizes glucose to compensate for its expenditure of energy. Cerebral glucose metabolic rate (CGMR) can

be measured by means of positron emission tomography (PET) scans.

Early PET scan studies involving Alzheimer patients reported high positive correlations of approximately .60 between CGMRs obtained when the patients were at rest and their IQ scores. Other studies have shown that the CGMRs of Alzheimer and other senile dementia patients are markedly lower than those of normal subjects of the same age, whose CGMRs are themselves lower than those of normal young subjects.

When subjects are engaged in some cognitive task before their PET scan, however, a very different pattern of results emerges, with strong negative correlations being reported between CGMRs and intelligence in a number of independent studies. Thus, subjects in these studies who obtain the highest IQ scores consume the least amount of energy.

Taken together, the PET scan studies suggest that when subjects are at rest and can engage in any mental activity they wish, those of higher intelligence will demonstrate increased brain activity. However, when subjects perform an assigned cognitive task, those with higher IQs will be able to accomplish the task with a lower consumption of energy. Persons of higher intelligence may thus be characterized as having greater "brainpower" at their disposal while at the same time being able to use it more efficiently when required to do so. The use of PET scans is an expensive undertaking—a PET scan study of only eight people may cost as much as $20,000—but some researchers believe that this is offset by the tremendous potential of PET studies to yield information about the biological basis of intelligence.

Other Biological Correlates of Intelligence

In addition to the biological measures described, several others have been investigated as possible correlates of intelligence. These include basal metabolic rates, serum calcium levels, regional cerebral blood flow, neuronal myelination, sex hormones, body stature, myopia, serum uric acid levels, vital capacity, and biochemicals (for more information about these, see the bibliography). Attempts have also been made to identify specific genes associated with intelligence (Plomin et al., 1994).

Biological Theories of Intelligence

As early as 1927, Charles Spearman suggested that individual differences in his g (or general intelligence) factor were attributable to differences in people's "mental energy." The relationships between intelligence and such biological measures as nerve conduction velocity, cerebral glucose metabolic rates, averaged evoked potentials, and speed of information-processing have led some authors to propose a similar theory of "neural efficiency" (Vernon, 1993). In this theory, individual differences in the speed and efficiency with which the brain and neural system can execute the information-processing required by cognitive tasks contributes to the success with which the task is performed. Other psychologists, notably Hans Eysenck (1993), have developed a biological theory that focuses on the probability of the error of transmission of impulses across synapses. More error-free processing allows both faster information-processing speed and higher intelligence. Other biologically oriented theories of intelligence include Schafer's theory of neural adaptability and Robinson's arousability theory (1996). The latter, which suggests that differences in arousability exert a sufficiently broad influence on brain functioning to account for the fact that all mental tests are positively intercorrelated, is particularly well explicated and challenging to other biological models.

In general, biological theories tend to focus more on global measures of intelligence and are thus more akin to the Spearman or Burt-Vernon model of intelligence than, say, the Howard Gardner approach. At the same time, psychologists such as Godfrey Thompson, who have criticized Spearman's theory, have also proposed biologically based interpretations of mental ability data. As mentioned, biological theories of intelligence lag well behind empirical demonstrations of correlations between intelligence and biological measures; the latter are sufficiently compelling, however, to suggest that any complete theory of intelligence must take them into account.

Bibliography

Crinella, F. M., & Yu, J. (Eds). (1993). *Thompson, Lashley, and Spearman: Three views of the biological basis of intelligence.* New York: New York Academy of Sciences.

Ertl, J. P. & Schafer, E. W. P. (1969). Brain response correlates of psychometric intelligence. *Nature, 223,* 421–422.

Eysenck, H. (1993). The biological basis of intelligence. In P. A. Vernon (Ed.), *Biological approaches to the study of human intelligence.* Norwood, NJ: Ablex.

Plomin, R., et al., (1994). DNA markers associated with high versus low IQ. The IQ quantitative trait loci (QTL) project. *Behavior Genetics, 34,* 107–118.

Robinson, D. L. (1996). *Brain, mind, and behaviour.* Westport, CT: Praeger Press.

Scarr, S. (1997). The development of individual differences in intelligence and personality. In H. W. Reese & M. D. Franzen (Eds.), *Biological and neuropsychological mechanisms: Life-span developmental psychology.* Mahwah, NJ: Erlbaum.

Schafer, E. W. P. (1982). Neural adaptability: A biological determinant of behavioral intelligence. *International Journal of Neuroscience, 17,* 183–191.

Spearman, C. (1927). *The abilities of man.* New York: Macmillan.

Vernon, P. A. (Ed.). (1993). *Biological approaches to the study of human intelligence.* Norwood, NJ: Ablex.

Philip A. Vernon

Cognitive Theories

The earliest cognitive theories of intelligence grew out of the rationalist tradition in philosophy. One of the best examples was the theory proposed by the British psychologist Charles Spearman in the *Nature of "Intelligence" and the Principles of Cognition* (1923). Spearman, like the American psychologist L. L. Thurstone, believed that factor analyses of correlations among scores on mental tests provided only a first step in developing a theory of intelligence. Understanding intelligence required the identification of general principles of cognition. Spearman proposed that intelligent thinking consisted of three things: the apprehension of experience, the eduction of correlates, and the eduction of relations. *Apprehension* meant the ability to encode the cognitive (knowing), affective (feeling), and conative (willing or motivational) aspects of an event. *Eduction of relations* referred to the ability to infer different types of relationships among elementary ideas. *Eduction of correlates* referred to the ability to apply a relation to an idea (such as inferring "sad" when given the fundament "happy" and the relation "opposite"). Spearman's theory, although in many ways ahead of its time, was firmly rooted in the rationalist tradition. The rise of behaviorism dampened enthusiasm for this sort of speculation about thinking. From the 1930s until the late 1960s, research on intelligence was dominated by debates about the number and organization of dimensions of human intelligence.

Modern cognitive theories of intelligence grew out of the broader cognitive revolution in psychology in the 1960s. The information-processing paradigm provided a new way to conceptualize the action of mental processes; computer simulations derived from such models provided a means to test them; and new methodologies of reaction-time decomposition offered ways to estimate the action of processes as they occurred in human problem solving.

Sources of Task Difficulty

One group of researchers sought to identify those stimulus differences that influenced particular stages or components of task processing, and thus made some items more difficult than others. For example, Herbert Simon and Kenneth Kotovsky developed a computer program that could solve items on a reasoning task called Letter Series. Each item presents a string of letters such as *abcde* _____. The examinee must extrapolate the pattern. Development of a program that could extrapolate patterns required a careful enumeration of the knowledge required to solve problems, the processes that needed to be executed, and stimulus features or sources of difficulty on the task that were associated with each. Other researchers investigated sources of difficulty on subtests of the Wechsler Adult Intelligence Scale and other reasoning, spatial visualization, and perceptual (or clerical) speed tasks. Important sources of difficulty have also been identified for many of the verbal tasks used on intelligence tests (such as verbal analogies, vocabulary, and verbal comprehension), although the difficulty of complex verbal tasks seems to be influenced by many factors that interact in complex ways. The more recent work of the Human Assessment Laboratory in Plymouth, England, has extended this work to the real-time generation of items for computer-based tests. However, the most extensive efforts in this regard is the work Patrick Kyllonen, Raymond Christal, and their colleagues at the Armstrong laboratories on a computer-administered test called the CAM Battery.

Componential Analysis

Some researchers followed the advice of William Estes to view mental tests as cognitive tasks (1974), and attempted to develop process theories of intelligence by studying differences in the thinking exhibited by high and low scorers on these tests, or, more commonly, on experimental tasks modeled after them. For example, Robert Sternberg (1977) sought to model the entire problem-solving sequence—from stimulus presentation to response—and to identify differences in the strategies that subjects used to solve reasoning tasks, the efficiency with which they executed different component processes, or the mode in which they executed those processes (e.g., self-terminating versus exhaustive component execution). This was later called cognitive components methodology. In general, researchers who followed this approach were quite successful in developing models that accounted for much of the variation in average response latencies to different items and, to a lesser extent, in response errors. And some even found differences in strategies used by problem solvers who differ markedly in age or ability profile. For example, young children are more likely than older children to use a self-terminating mode of processing when inferring relationhips among terms in an analogy. Younger and less able children are also more likely to skip crucial processes (such as mapping the A to B relationship onto the C term in an analogy). Conversely, more able young adults exhibit a greater flexibility in problem-solving. More able reasoners also show a much larger working memory capacity for numbers, words, and images—especially on tasks that require the simultaneous storage and manipulation of information in working memory. More successful reasoners also spend more time encoding terms and less time transforming them, and more time performing global planning operations.

Cognitive Correlates

Other researchers started from the laboratories of experimental cognitive psychology and studied how performance on paradigmatic laboratory tasks differed for individuals identified as more able or less able on the basis of psychometric tests. This was later dubbed the cognitive correlates approach. For example, several researchers studied a letter matching task in which subjects are asked to state as quickly as possible whether letters in a pair such as *B b* are physically identical or, in another condition, whether they share the same name. The dependent variable of interest is the difference between these two latencies, which is taken as an estimate of the time required to access a name code in long-term memory. Correlations between this score and measures of verbal intelligence are significant but small (typically around $r = -.3$). Although such component scores may well indicate the action (e.g., duration) of particular mental processes, the subtraction process eliminates individual differences that are consistent across conditions. This means that such scores are typically quite unreliable and, more important, do not represent the main source of individual differences on the task.

Methods of estimating the action of mental processes that do not require subtraction typically show higher correlations with other measures. Inspection-time tasks are one example. In one widely used inspection-time task, the subject must decide which of two parallel lines of markedly different lengths is longer. Stimulus exposure is varied so that the probability of a correct response varies from random responding to perfect accuracy. The subject's score is the stimulus duration that corresponds with a fixed level of accuracy (often 85%). Correlations between this score and psychometric measures of intelligence are typically in the $r = -.4$ to $r = -.5$ range (Deary & Stough, 1996).

Knowledge-Based Theories

Alfred Binet's assumption that aptitude could be cleanly separated from experience has long been recognized as false, especially when attempting to compare children who differ widely in experience. The problem is exacerbated as children mature into adults and their experiential base becomes larger and more diverse. Knowledge-based theories of abilities emphasize the role of knowledge and strategy in explaining the differences between expert and novices in their performance in complex domains, such as physics problem-solving, computer programming, and chess. Robert Glaser and his colleagues have been at the forefront of this effort

(Chi, Glaser, & Farr, 1988). This research suggests that experts differ from novices not so much in the speed or efficiency of elementary cognitive processes, or even in the capacity of working memory, but rather in the extensiveness and organization of their knowledge about that domain. K. Anders Ericsson and Neil Charness (1994) also emphasize the important roles that experience and mentoring play in the development of abilities, especially those abilities developed over many years of dedicated practice and tuned to a high level of proficiency.

Physiological Correlates

Scores on intelligence tests have been found to correlate with a number of indices of brain physiology, most notably brain volume ($r = .3$ to $.4$). Much of the work aimed at mapping cognitive functions onto regions of the brain has helped confirm factor analytic and cognitive theories that hypothesize a variety of different cognitive modules. Differential patterns of brain activity can also help confirm that subjects who differ in experience, ability, or ability profiles solve similar problems in different ways. Estimates of the speed of transmission of neural impulses has also been investigated. For example, measures of neural conductivity (NCV) show a small correlation with intelligence. However, interpretation of the correlation is clouded by the fact that controlling for NCV does not reduce the correlation between simple reaction time and intelligence. Other studies suggest that individuals with higher levels of intelligence show lower levels of brain metabolic activity while solving cognitive tasks. One interpretation is that more intelligent individuals process information more efficiently; alternatively, less intelligent individuals could well be showing higher levels of brain metabolic activity because the problems posed are relatively more difficult for them. In spite of these sorts of interpretive problems, there is much interest among researchers in using modern techniques of brain imaging to study the neurological bases of individual differences in cognition (Jensen, 1998).

Specific Abilities

A broad range of ability constructs represented in trait models of intelligence—including reasoning, verbal, spatial, mathematical, perceptual speed, and working-memory ability—have been investigated using one or more of these methodologies. Several themes dominate this research: First, the ability to maintain information in an active state in working memory while actively processing it is an important source of individual differences in many of the more general ability constructs, particularly reasoning and spatial abilities. Some have modeled this as a capacity difference, others as reflecting differences in attentional resources, and others have emphasized the metacognitive skills involved in

actively managing the trade-off between retention and processing strategies.

Second, the ability to create, retain, and process information in a way that preserves information about the meaning of events seems to underlie the general reasoning abilities that are required by and developed through formal schooling. More specific verbal and spatial abilities seem also to depend on the ability to create and retain particular types of memory codes: analog spatial abilities require that information be coded in a way that preserves information about the configuration of elements in an array; specific verbal abilities (especially knowledge of linguistic conventions, spelling ability, and verbal fluency) require that information be coded in a way that preserves order in a series. John Anderson's (1983) multicode theory of memory conforms well with these findings, as does Alan Baddeley's model of a working-memory system with a phonological loop and a visual-spatial scratch pad (1986).

Third, on many tasks—but especially complex tasks—individuals often solve different problems in different ways. Flexibility in solution strategy appears to be an important source of individual differences, especially on measures of fluid reasoning abilities. Again, this may reflect the action of metacognitive skills in planning or monitoring performance, the automatic application of a rich and "loosely coupled" knowledge base, or the availability of working-memory resources.

Fourth, the speed with which information can be processed is an important source of individual differences on a broad range of tasks. For example, the speed of retrieval of name codes from LTM shows small but significant correlations with verbal ability.

Fifth, the growth of abilities is heavily dependent on growth in knowledge. Some of this knowledge is best modeled as skills; other knowledge is best modeled as conceptual or schematic. Thus, abilities of all sorts have both a process dimension and a content dimension.

Theory-Based Tests

Cognitive theories promise to give us a better understanding of human intelligence at all levels—from cognitive to physiological. These theories have already influenced the measurement of intelligence through the development of ability tests that are well grounded in cognitive theory. Previous efforts to derive tests from theory (such as Raven's attempt to build a test based on Charles Spearman's theory, or J. P. Guilford's attempts to develop tests that fit in particular cells of his structure of intellect model) were based on simple rational models of the domain. The development of general theories of cognition has given researchers a firmer, more elaborate base on which to build.

Theories of intelligence developed in the information-processing paradigm have been criticized for their failure to consider the important roles of affect and context in cognition. Richard Snow, Lyn Corno, and Douglas Jackson reviewed the research on the affective dimension of intelligence in the *Handbook of Educational Psychology* (1996). Snow (1994) has also proposed a way to conceptualize abilities in terms of the extent of the match (or mismatch) between the effectivities an individual brings to a situation and what the situation affords. These and other recent trends are discussed in one or more of the edited volumes noted in the bibliography.

Bibliography

Anders Ericsson, K., & Charness, N. (1994). *American Psychologist, 49*, 725–747.

Anderson, J. (1983). *Architecture of cognition.* New York: Cambridge University Press.

Baddeley, A. (1986). *Working memory.* New York: Oxford University Press.

Chi, M., Glaser, R., & Farr, M. (1988). *The nature of experience.*

Detterman, D. K. (Ed.). (1985–1996). *Current topics in human intelligence* (Vols. 1–5). Greenwich, CT: Ablex.

Deary, I. J., & Stough, C. (1996). *American Psychologist, 51*, 599–608.

Estes, W. (1974). *American Psychologist, 29*, 740–749.

Gustafsson, J.-E., & Undheim, J. O. (1996). Individual differences in cognitive functions. In D. Berliner & R. Calfee (Eds.), *Handbook of educational psychology.* New York: Macmillan.

Jensen, A. R. (1998). *The g factor.* Westport, CT: Praeger.

Lohman, D. F. (1989). Human intelligence: An introduction to advances in theory and research. *Review of Educational Research, 59*, 333–373.

Snow, R. (1994). In R. J. Sternberg & W. Wagner (Eds.), *Mind in context: Interactionist perspectives on human intelligence.* New York: Cambridge University Press.

Snow, R., Corno, L., & Jackson, D. (1996). *Handbook of educational psychology.* New York: Macmillan.

Sternberg, R. J. (1977). *Intelligence, information processing, and analogical reasoning.* Hillsdale, NJ: Erlbaum.

Sternberg, R. J. (1984). *Beyond IQ: A triarchic theory of human intelligence.* New York: Cambridge University Press.

Sternberg, R. J. (1990). *Metaphors of mind.* New York: Cambridge University Press.

Sternberg, R. J. (Ed.). (1982–1996). *Advances in the psychology of human intelligence* (Vols. 1–5). Hillsdale, NJ: Erlbaum.

Sternberg, R. J. (Ed.). (1994). *Encyclopedia of human intelligence.* New York: Macmillan.

Sternberg, R. J. (Ed.). (1994). *Mind in context: Interactionist perspectives on human intelligence.* New York: Cambridge University Press.

David F. Lohman

Legal Issues

Intelligence in its general usage is a virtue, like beauty or kindness or strength. When intelligence is measured, it seems less an exceptional quality of excellence that some human beings have and more a neutral characteristic, like height or weight, that everyone has in some amount. So measuring intelligence may seem to be simply recording a particular individual's quantum of that characteristic—an intelligence quotient (IQ) or some rival quantification. These measured quantities become involved in legal issues because the amount of an individual's intelligence may be important in a vast array of human endeavors. Matters of importance affecting human beings often result in disagreements, and such disagreements often end up in court. The resulting legal dispute may involve controversies about the nature and measurement of intelligence or controversies about the activity that brings intelligence measurements into the legal arena or admixtures of both. What occurs in the legal arena is likely to reflect an ambiguity in which intelligence retains the aura of being a virtue even as, in the foreground of the legal issues presented, it is treated as a neutral measurable characteristic.

A comprehensive yet highly telescoped picture of the field in which measuring intelligence may play an important role in deciding legal issues can be seen by examining two quite distinct dimensions of this subject. The first is the vast array of legal matters potentially influenced by the measurement of intelligence. The second is the interaction through which psychological testing issues become incorporated into and resolved as issues of law.

A Sampling of Legal Issues Affected by the Measurement of Intelligence

Often it is the relative degree of test-demonstrated intelligence that matters in resolving legal issues, as in determining whether a person is competent to stand trial or to manage his or her own affairs; whether a consent to breathe into a breathalyzer or to waive the right not to be interrogated without counsel was voluntary; whether one is fit to be a custodial parent, suffers from a disability covered by insurance, or has the mental capacity to commit a crime. Sometimes, there is an intelligence test cutoff line, which purports to divide identified levels of mental ability. Qualification to participate in a gifted program might be based on a test score that falls above the designated line. Or one child might be assigned to a program for the educable mentally retarded (EMR) based on an IQ that falls below an identified point, while another child might be assigned to a program for the learning disabled (LD) by scoring above the same point.

As these examples illustrate, in some instances it is the legal proceeding itself that brings the measurement of intelligence into play, as in a criminal case for which the defendant's capacity to understand the proceeding is relevant. In other instances, measuring intelligence is independently significant but may become the subject of disagreement and litigation, as in a case involving a dispute about a student's special education classification.

In some cases the legal issue is whether intelligence scores are relevant at all. In constitutional law, being retarded (if not profoundly so) is not relevant in deciding whether a sane defendant may be constitutionally executed, whereas some state statutes preclude the death penalty for an individual retarded to any degree. In other cases, the legal issue focuses on the validity and use of tests, for example, when standardized tests classify disproportionate numbers of minority children for special education or when disproportionate numbers of minority applicants are denied college or graduate school admissions on the basis of achievement or aptitude tests (which are highly correlated with intelligence tests).

Although high test scores resonate with intelligence as a virtue, high scores are not always good for legal purposes. They are if the legal issue is qualification for a "gifted" (or even an LD) education program, but when a state law prohibits capital punishment of retarded defendants, it is the low score that is desired. Sometimes, whether a low score or high score is legally desirable will depend on the perspective of the litigant. A parent might be in court to challenge the correctness of a low score to avoid a stigmatizing, inferior EMR education, whereas school authorities might believe that the low score will enable a student failing in regular classes to transfer into a more appropriate educational setting. The parent-school disagreement might disappear if both agreed that a truly effective educational program would be provided to low scorers (although the parent might still fear the stigmatization associated with the appearance that the student lacks the intelligence virtue).

The Interaction of Legal and Psychological Issues

When measuring intelligence becomes relevant to the outcome of a legal issue, it is rarely because there is a law that straightforwardly defines a legal issue in terms of the measurement of intelligence. For example, under the law, a criminal defendant's right to remain silent without a lawyer may be waived "voluntarily." The defendant's capacity to understand his right is relevant to the "voluntariness" of a waiver, and intelligence test scores may be relevant to determine the capacity to understand.

Characteristically, intelligence test results constitute only one factor among others in deciding an issue of law and may even be legally prohibited from being the sole factor. Psychologists may have views about what these other factors should be and how they should be integrated and assessed along with measures of intelligence. Their views may be taken into account, but they will not control the way the legal issue is conceptualized and decided.

A classic illustration of the specialized way that the law sometimes shapes a problem of general concern is provided by well-known instances of the racially disproportionate distribution of burdens and benefits that are significantly based on intelligence test scores. Under current constitutional law, these discriminatory effects count as racial discrimination only if the use of the test was the result of official action taken with the *intention* to discriminate by race, and proving that intention requires a showing that the official action was taken because of the racial effect and not simply despite certain knowledge that it would occur.

Even when a legal controversy encompasses precisely those questions about measuring intelligence in a particular context that deeply concerns psychologists, those questions are likely to be transformed as they are folded into a legal issue. To determine the admissibility of test measurements into evidence, the long-standing rule under which scientific evidence was admitted if it was "generally accepted" within the relevant scientific community has been replaced by a rule that is meant to be more liberal but gives courts more discretion to evaluate support for the scientific evidence. Under either rule, measures of intelligence will be less likely to be admitted when experts disagree about the nature of intelligence, how to measure it, and how test results should be used. Moreover, the outcome of these disagreements in court may not be identical to their outcome as they are debated in academic journals because a court may be influenced by legally relevant policies and principles of no concern to academic peers. What is presented in court will itself be partly influenced by the culture of the adversary system, in which differences of opinion are exaggerated and accentuated to achieve desired dispositions of legal issues.

Once admitted as evidence, intelligence measures will influence legal outcomes in a manner that is enhanced by the judicial deference that courts are thought to owe to professional opinion interpreting and evaluating such measures. When the experts present conflicting evidence, however, courts must decide between—rather than rely upon—the views comprising professional opinion. In two famously paired cases, the judges came to diametrically opposite conclusions about the claimed cultural bias and invalidity of tests used in making special education classifications, even though the basic issues were the same and the evidence and expert witnesses supporting the claim were virtually identical (*Larry P.* v. *Riles*, 495 F. Supp. 926, N.D.Calif. 1979, *aff'd in part, rev'd in part*, 793 F.2d 969, 9th Cir. 1984; *PASE* v. *Hannon*, 506 F. Supp. 831, N.D. Ill. 1980).

The significance of judicial deference to professional opinion is also diluted by legal rules that govern the standard of proof (preponderance of evidence, clear and convincing evidence, beyond a reasonable doubt), allocate the burden of proof, and require trial court decisions to be affirmed on appeal unless "clearly erroneous." Courts also defer to administrative agencies with responsibility for the enforcement of particular legal policies, and this form of deference may collide with and cancel out deference to professionals. For example, courts that enforce the federal law prohibiting racial discrimination in employment would be expected to defer to professional opinion and to the interpretations of the Equal Employment Opportunity Commission, but when the commission and the American Psychological Association develop inconsistent guidelines concerning the validation of tests for determining employment qualifications, the courts are left in a quandry.

As Victor Rosenblum has commented, judicial deference to both professional opinion and administrative agencies is at its apogee when the two are congruent, but when expert opinion is "diluted by dissonance or dichotomy," hurdles for admissibility go up, deference to scientific opinion goes down, and the judicial treatment of the scientific evidence is likely to be in disarray (1996).

Bibliography

General

Baldus, D. C., & Cole, J. W. L. (1980, with supplements, 1987). *Statistical proof of discrimination*. Colorado Springs: Shepherd's-McGraw-Hill. Exhaustive analysis of the statistical and legal aspects of proving discrimination in courts. Out of print but available in most law libraries; more sophisticated and comprehensive than any other work on the subject.

Bersoff, D. N. (1979). Regarding psychologists testily: Legal regulation of psychological testing in the public schools. *Maryland Law Review, 39*, 27–120. A careful analysis of the use and misuse of psychological testing in several important cases involving tracking and special education.

Ceci, S. J. (Guest Editor). (1996). Special theme: IQ in society. *Psychology, Public Policy, and Law, 2*, 401–645. A collection of articles by psychologists (primarily) and lawyers describing current issues and presenting diverse views related to intelligence testing, public policy, and law.

McCurley, M. J. (1994). Psychological testing and the expert witness. *Practical Lawyer, 7*, 41–59. A thorough analysis of considerations to be evaluated in choosing expert witnesses on psychological testing and questions to be asked in preparing witnesses for friendly direct and hostile cross-examination.

Morison, P., White, S. H., & Feuer, M. J. (Eds.). (1996). *The use of IQ tests in special education decision-making and planning*. Washington, DC: National Academy Press. Summarizes and contains references to working papers presented at two workshops on IQ testing and educational decision-making, sponsored by the Board on Testing and Assessment, the Commission on Behavioral and Social Sciences and Education, the National Research Council.

Cases

Albemarle Paper Co. v. Moody, 422 U.S. 405 (1975). In determining the validity of the test used by employers for making employment decisions, courts were directed to follow "guidelines" of the Equal Employment Opportunity Commission, which, the Supreme Court noted, were influenced by guidelines of the American Psychological Association.

Board of Education of the Hendrick Hudson Central School Dist. v. Rowley, 458 U.S. 176 (1982). In upholding school district refusal to provide a sign language interpreter for a student with only minimal residual hearing, under the Education for All Handicapped Children Act, the Supreme Court admonished lower federal courts not to substitute their judgment on matters of educational policy for those of school authorities.

Daubert v. Merrell Dow Pharmaceuticals, 509 U.S. 579 (1993). Applying Rule 702 of the Federal Rules of Evidence, the Supreme Court held that the longstanding "Frye test," under which scientific evidence was admitted only when generally accepted by the relevant scientific community, was not part of Rule 702, and adopted a test that based admissibility on the trial court's determination that testimony pertained to "scientific knowledge" (explained by the Court to mean derived by the scientific method) and was supported by appropriate validation.

Griggs v. Duke Power Co., 401 U.S. 424 (1971). This case established the requirement that, under federal antidiscrimination employment law (Title VII, Civil Rights Act, 1964), an employer may not use a test that has a discriminatory impact adversely affecting statutorily protected groups, such as members of a particular race, unless the test is properly validated.

School Board of Nassau County v. Arline, 480 U.S. 273 (1987). To determine whether a teacher, who was handicapped under the Federal Rehabilitation Act by reason of having tuberculosis, was qualified for any employment within the school system despite being contagious, the Supreme Court adopted factors proposed by the American Medical Association (an amicus party) and concluded that, in applying these factors, the courts should defer to the reasonable medical judgments of public health officials.

Washington v. Davis, 426 U.S. 229 (1976). This case established that, as a matter of constitutional law, only purposeful discrimination counts as racial discrimination and that an employment test having a disparate racial effect is not required to be validated unless there is a showing that the test was adopted or used for the purpose of discriminating against black applicants.

William G. Buss

MEDIA EFFECTS. Contemporary discussions of media effects are focused on the impact of television on children because television is the most extensively studied medium and children are among the most extensive users of the medium.

However, it is important to note that research questions about the impact of television have their roots in similar questions raised about movies, comics, and radio (e.g., Charters, 1933; Wertham, 1954; Wolfe & Fiske, 1949; Zajonc, 1954). In the case of movies and comics, most studies focused on the effects of violent content on children's values and behaviors. The title of a review of movie research published in 1933, *Boys, Movies, and City Streets* (Cressey & Thrasher, 1933), gives an idea of the concern. In general, these early studies of movies found some relationships between viewing violence and developing aggressive attitudes but cited the need for much more research (Lazarsfeld, 1955; Maccoby, 1951).

The major questions raised about the effects of any medium include concerns about the amount of time spent with the medium, the nature of the content encountered in the medium, and the extent of the effects (i.e., the magnitude, scope, and duration). In the case of television, the initial studies by Wilbur Schramm and his colleagues in the United States and Canada (Schramm, Lyle, & Parker, 1961) and by Hilde Himmelweit and her colleagues in England (Himmelweit, Oppenheim, & Vince, 1958) were focused on the amount of time children spent viewing television and its effects on school performance and reading, as well as influences on other leisure activities and social interaction. The influence of televised violence on aggressive behavior was not as extensively studied in these early investigations, but violence was one of the concerns that led to more extensive later research.

Research on the impact of media, particularly television, has been largely undertaken by scholars in four disciplines: psychology, sociology, communications, and education. In addition to the early survey research by Wilbur Schramm, a communications scholar at Stanford University, and Hilde Himmelweit, a social psychologist at the London School of Economics and Political Science, the other early contributors who shaped the research field were Albert Bandura, a psychologist at Stanford University, and Leonard Berkowitz, a psychologist at the University of Wisconsin. These early researchers and their professional orientations are important because they shaped the nature of the questions asked and the research findings obtained. These differing professional orientations resulted in a differential preference for correlational versus experimental approaches to studying media effects—sociology and communications researchers favored correlational studies, and those in psychology and education favored experimental studies. Experimental studies, largely conducted by psychologists, ask questions about media "effects" or "impact." The correlational studies conducted by sociologists and communications researchers tended to ask questions about media use and the gratification derived from media. This "effects" versus "use" distinction continues in more recent research and gives rise to continuing debates about the extent of media effects.

The history of research on media effects is largely a mid- to late-twentieth-century phenomenon. Research on movies, radio, and comics began in the 1930s, and studies of television began in the 1950s and 1960s. With regard to television, one of the most extensively studied areas of media effects is the impact of televised violence. The initial survey research conducted in the United States and Canada (Schramm et al., 1961) found that children who had high exposure to television and low exposure to print were more aggressive than those with the reverse pattern. Similarly, early experiments conducted with preschool children by Bandura and his colleagues (Bandura, Ross, & Ross, 1961) demonstrated that children imitated or modeled the aggressive behavior that they saw displayed in simulated television programs. Similarly Berkowitz (1962), studying young adults, found that viewing aggressive film portrayals led to heightened aggression.

These early studies of media effects grew out of a common basis of public concern about media violence that has been manifested in a series of hearings and reports by legislative and scientific committees and commissions. For example, the history of concern about television violence began within about a decade from the establishment of television broadcasting in the United States. The first television broadcasting license was issued in 1941, and the first public hearings investigating the impact of televised violence took place in the U.S. Congress in 1952 (*Investigation of radio*, 1952) and 1954 (*Juvenile delinquency*, 1954). Other major investigations and reviews were undertaken by the National Commission on the Causes and Prevention of Violence (Baker & Ball, 1969), the Surgeon General's Scientific Advisory Committee on Television and Social Behavior (1972), and the American Psychological Association's Task Force on Television and Society (Huston et al., 1992). Each of these reports reviewed research and provided interpretative summaries of the effects of television on children and adults. All of these reports concluded that televised violence negatively affected the attitudes, values, and social behavior of viewers. The magnitude of the relationship between media violence and aggression has been estimated by Eron and his colleagues (Donnerstein, Slaby, & Eron, 1994) to be in the range of 20 to 40 and to explain on average about 10% of the variance.

The issue of television violence provides a paradigm for understanding the research and public policy process involved in studying media effects because it reflects the broad range of experimental and correlational studies undertaken by scholars in diverse fields. It has been noted that the early concerns about movies, radio, and comics served as the basis for addressing concerns about the newer medium of television. However, it is equally clear that the research on television occurred at a later stage in the evolution of psychology and other social sciences and therefore benefited from a more diversified and robust research profession. Thus the studies of televised violence evolved from early surveys of viewing patterns and the relationship to ratings or observed behavior in correlational studies (e.g., Himmelweit et al., 1958; Schramm et al., 1961) and the basic experimental studies of Bandura (Bandura et al., 1961) and Berkowitz (1962) to more extensive field studies of television viewing and behavior in natural settings (Friedrich & Stein, 1973). For example, a study by Friedrich and Stein (1973) involved preschool children who were shown either violent or nonviolent programs. The short-term or longer term behavior outcomes were assessed (e.g., children who watched *Batman* and *Superman* cartoons were more aggressive in their preschool settings than those who watched *Mister Rogers's Neighborhood*). In addition, we now have a longitudinal study of more than 20 years' duration that demonstrates a relationship between viewing television violence in childhood and displaying aggressive behavior in midadulthood (Huesmann, Eron, Lefkowitz, & Walder, 1984). Finally, we have moved from the social construction of social behavior in studies of televised violence in the Surgeon General's (1972) study to the neurological correlates of social behavior in brain imaging studies. Functional magnetic resonance imaging (fMRI) is being used to identify areas of the brain that are involved in processing video violence. Initial results of a study of 9- to 13-year-old children suggest that televised violence activates right hemisphere emotional arousal and control (e.g., right prefrontal contact, right amygdala) and enhances long-term memory storage and access because of the emotional content (Murray et al., 1999). Indeed, these brain mapping studies show that children do not differentiate between real-world violence and fictional entertainment violence—the limbic system responds in a similar manner to all violence.

In conclusion, media effects have been studied by scholars in a wide range of social science disciplines, but psychology has provided an integrative force in the study of the individual in the social context. These studies have included correlational investigations that assess the extent to which media exposure is related to attitudes, values, and behavior and experimental studies that provide an understanding of the causal processes. We have learned much about the effects of media (Huston & Wright, 1997; Murray, 1998), from patterns of use to patterns of effects, but there is much yet to learn.

[*See also* Consumer Psychology; *and* Violence and Aggression.]

Bibliography

Baker, R. K., & Ball, S. J. (1969). *Mass media and violence: A staff report to the National Commission on the Causes and Prevention of Violence.* Washington, DC: U.S. Government Printing Office.

Bandura, A., Ross, D., & Ross, S. H. (1961). Imitation of film-mediated aggressive models. *Journal of Abnormal and Social Psychology, 66,* 3–11.

Berkowitz, L. (1962). *Aggression: A social psychological analysis.* New York: Macmillan.

Charters, W. W. (1933). *Motion pictures and youth: A summary.* New York: Macmillan.

Cressey, P. G., & Thrasher, F. M. (1933). *Boys, movies, and city streets.* New York: Macmillan.

Donnerstein, E., Slaby, R. G., & Eron, L. D. (1994). The mass media and youth aggression. In L. D. Eron, J. H. Gentry, & P. Schlegel (Eds.), *Reason to hope: A psychological perspective on violence and youth* (pp. 219–250). Washington, DC: American Psychological Association.

Friedrich, L. K., & Stein, A. H. (1973). Aggressive and prosocial television programs and the natural behavior of preschool children. *Monographs of the Society for Research in Child Development, 38* (4, Serial No. 151).

Himmelweit, H. T., Oppenheim, A. N., & Vince, P. (1958). *Television and the child: An empirical study of the effects of television on the young.* London: Oxford University Press.

Huesmann, L. R., Eron, L. D., Lefkowitz, M. M., & Walder, L. O. (1984). Stability of aggression over time and generations. *Developmental Psychology, 20,* 1120–1134.

Huston, A. C., Donnerstein, E., Fairchild, H., Feshbach, N. D., Katz, P. A., Murray, J. P., Rubinstein, E. A., Wilcox, B. L., & Zuckerman, D. M. (1992). *Big world, small screen: The role of television in American society.* Lincoln: University of Nebraska Press.

Huston, A. C., & Wright, J. C. (1997). Mass media and children's development. In I. E. Siegel & A. Reminger (Eds.), *Handbook of child psychology* (5th ed., pp. 999–1058). New York: Wiley.

Investigation of radio and television programs, hearings, and reports: Hearing before the Committee on Interstate and Foreign Commerce, House of Representatives, 82d Cong., 2d Sess. (1952).

Juvenile delinquency (television programs): Hearing before the Subcommittee to Investigate Juvenile Delinquency of the Senate Committee on the Judiciary, 83d Cong., 2d Sess. (1954).

Lazarsfeld, P. (1955). Why is so little known about the effects of television on children and what can be done? *Public Opinion Quarterly, 19,* 243–251.

Maccoby, E. E. (1951). Television: Its impact on school children. *Public Opinion Quarterly, 15,* 421–444.

Murray, J. P. (1998). Studying television violence: A research agenda for the 21st century. In J. K. Asamen & G. L. Berry (Eds.), *Research paradigms, television, and social behavior* (pp. 369–410). Thousand Oaks, CA: Sage.

Murray, J. P., Liotti, M., Fox, P. T., Ingmundson, P., Mayberg, H. S., Pu, Y., Zamarripa, F., Liu, Y, Woldorff, M. G., & Gao, J-H. (1999). *TV violence and brain activation in children: Effects on attention and long-term memory systems revealed by fMRI.* Unpublished manuscript, Kansas State University.

Schramm, W., Lyle, J., & Parker, E. B. (1961). *Television in the lives of our children.* Stanford, CA: Stanford University Press.

Surgeon General's Scientific Advisory Committee on Television and Social Behavior (1972). *Television and growing up: The impact of televised violence.* Washington, DC: U.S. Government Printing Office.

Wertham, F. (1954). *Seduction of the innocent.* New York: Rinehart.

Wolfe, K. M., & Fiske, M. (1949). Why they read the comics. In P. Lazarsfeld & J. Stanton (Eds.), *Communication research, 1948–49.* New York: Harper.

Zajonc, R. (1954). Some effects of the "space" serials. *Public Opinion Quarterly, 18* (4), 367–374.

John P. Murray

MEDIATION. *See* Negotiation.

MEDICAL TECHNOLOGY DESIGN. Medicine and health care involve topics that are appropriate for study by nearly every specialty within psychology. Notable contributions from psychology have addressed social and cognitive issues related to the design of medical technology.

Social psychological issues pertaining to the design of medical technology particularly are relevant for individuals working in teams in the operating room (OR). The OR team consists of people with diverse, albeit related training: surgical nurses, surgeons, anesthetists, and anesthetic nurses. The actions of one person using complex medical technology can influence the behavior of others. Coordinated performance is of the upmost importance; however, the money spent for training on medical technology in the OR is less than one fifth the cost of the equipment (Helmreich & Schaefer, 1994). Alternatively and perhaps more effectively, team coordination could be enhanced by organizational change based on findings from social psychology.

Cognitive issues are pervasive in the practice of medicine. Clinicians diagnose their patients' conditions from symptoms and select appropriate treatments. Laypersons' perceptions of variations in their physiological

functioning and the decision if and how to treat them also involve cognitive issues (Bogner, 1997). In addition, cognitive issues are involved in providing treatment, especially with technologically sophisticated medical devices. Such treatment typically is provided by trained clinicians in health-care facilities.

Research addressing the use of medical devices usually is prompted by deaths or serious injuries attributed to user error in health-care facilities. Studies conducted by psychologists have addressed issues related to the cognitive impact of the design of medical technology such as syringes of similar appearance preloaded with differing concentrations of lidocaine (Senders, 1994) and alarms for various monitors in the OR that aren't matched to the information needs of the anesthetists (Seagull & Sanderson, in press). These factors increase the likelihood of error.

Physicians have recognized that psychological research and theory are relevant to issues health-care workers confront in their work. The anesthetist's cognitive processes, including the management of medical equipment and the social psychology of the OR, have been studied in simulated OR crises (Gaba, 1994). Surgeons have used cognitive psychology to address errors in laparoscopic surgery. That surgery is performed using a miniature video camera and long-handled instruments inserted into the patient's body through small incisions. The surgeons' actions are guided by video images of the internal surgical site projected on a monitor. Analysis of cognitive issues indicated that cutting the wrong duct resulted from the misperception of discriminating cues from an uncommon set of anatomic factors combined with the constraints of laparoscopic surgery (Gantert et al., 1998).

Collaboration between psychologists and clinicians is evident in most of the literature that addresses psychology-related issues in the design of medical technology. Study findings include errors related to equipment composition and layout in a respiratory intensive care unit (ICU) (Gopher, et al., 1989), and the distracting demands of technology in the operating room (Cook & Woods, 1996). The latter study found that a new highly integrated, microprocessor-based physiological monitoring system used in cardiac surgery created cognitive and physical demands that became most evident at times of high clinician workload. Attempts to use the device effectively included efforts by clinicians to adapt the computer system to their needs as well as clinicians altering their behavior to accommodate computer idiosyncracies.

A number of studies have addressed infusion pump issues. Infusion pumps are computer chip–based devices used to control the rate of flow of medication through a needle or catheter into a person. Design of patient-controlled pumps for pain management and their packaging were found to contribute to error (Brown, Bogner, Parmentier, & Taylor, 1997). Packing material that is not completely removed from every aspect of a pump does not disable it; rather, the unnoticed packaging compromises operation of the pump and results in overinfusion by free flow of the drug. The particular aspects of pump design found to contribute to error include no programming feedback to check drug concentration and pump functioning with misinstalled accessories.

Research in the ICU identified verbal transfer of information between staff members as a source of error (Gopher, et al., 1989). A factor contributing to that error is the abundance of information from various sophisticated patient monitors, the concentration of treatment equipment, and the number of tubes and sensors going in and out of the patient. This plethora of medical technology also exists in other settings with high time-stress—the OR and emergency room (ER). Those settings where the conditions of the patients create demanding cognitive and physical workloads exacerbated by the concentration of uncoordinated, complex sophisticated technology, are those in which the clinicians' functioning is most likely to be impaired by stress and fatigue. Thus, when the stakes are highest, as in the ICU, OR, and ER, the design of medical technology may hinder rather than assist clinicians.

Among the precipitous changes in medicine in the 1990s was the shifting of responsibility for care of all but the most acutely ill patients to home care or self-care. This often involves moving technologically sophisticated treatment and monitoring equipment from the hospital into the home. Thus, complex equipment which when used by health care professionals can contribute to error, is given to lay caregivers whose abilities to use it may be compromised by stress, illness, infirmities of age, or any of a host of other factors. The implications of this are legion.

Design of medical devices often incorporates the newest technological innovations with little regard for their impact on the user. Credit card–sized infusion pumps are available for self-care. Although quite portable, they present problems for laypersons in the delivery of their medication by very complex programming for needle change with no feedback of the completed steps, and confusing warnings. Cognitive information processing issues are evident in medication compliance as well as design of medical technology.

Taking medications, the most widely encountered aspect of home and self-care, has received considerable attention by psychologists. Medications may be prescribed; however, people also take a variety of over-the-counter products. As the number of medications increases, so does the complexity of pill-taking regimens and the possibilities for drug-drug and drug-food interactions. Medications are to be taken at various intervals: some with food, some before or after meals, and others avoiding other medications or foods such as milk. As people age and perhaps as they are affected by side effects of medications, an inverse relationship occurs between the number of medications and the ability to take them as directed. Various memory aids have been developed to assist compliance to medication regimens. These aids include innovations such as electronic devices in pill bottle caps that record the date and time when the cap is removed as well as simple compartmentalized plastic boxes to organize pills.

Psychologists have addressed the issue of cognitive function and medication use in older adults. Although overall recall of details of medication instructions may be higher for younger adults, younger and older adults share similar schemas for actually taking medications (Morrow et al., 1994). Similar research on the use of medical technology might lead to effective instructions for medical devices.

The National Patient Safety Foundation of the American Medical Association has suggested using a systems approach to examine error in health care. This underscores the most pervasive albeit the least apparent, contribution of psychology to the study of health-care issues. The systems approach, which considers the topic for analysis as impacted by an array of interdependent factors, was advocated as a tool for addressing error in medicine, including the design of medical technology (Bogner, 1994). Several questions have been raised concerning the systems approach, one of which was the relationship of part of the system to the whole (Berwick, 1995). That question is familiar to psychologists; heuristic roots of the systems approach appear in the work of two early psychologists. Brunswik (1939/1951) expanded the realm of influence on perception, and by extension, on behavior, by acknowledging distal as well as proximal factors. A precursor to the systems approach, Lewin's field theory understands any event as a resultant of a multitude of interdependent factors (1943/1951).

Although Brunswik focused on perception and Lewin's theory was criticized for not being isomorphic with the field theory of physics, their work provides a mental framework, a mind set, for the application of psychological theory and research in studying the design of medical technology and other health-care issues. By expanding the focus to distal and proximal as well as intrapersonal factors in the life space of individuals and groups in health care, knowledge from psychology can be used prospectively as well as retrospectively to address systems of interpersonal, organizational, and other factors. This approach can further the contribution of psychology by evaluating the design of medical technology for utility and user acceptance, and in general evaluate aspects of health care for safety and effectiveness.

Bibliography

Berwick, D. M. (1995). Improving as science. In D. Blumenthal & A. C. Scheck (Eds.), *Improving clinical practice* (pp. 3–24). San Francisco: Jossey-Bass.

Bogner, M. S. (1994). Human error in medicine: A frontier for change. In M. S. Bogner (Ed.). *Human error in medicine* (pp. 373–383). Hillsdale, NJ: Erlbaum.

Bogner, M. S. (1997). Naturalistic decision making in health care. In C. E. Zsambok & G. Klein (Eds.), *Naturalistic decision making* (pp. 61–69). Mahwah, NJ: Erlbaum.

Brown, S. L., Bogner, M. S., Parmentier, C. M., & Taylor, J. B. (1997). Human error and patient-controlled analgesia pumps. *Journal of Intravenous Nursing, 20,* 311–316.

Brunswik, E. (1951). The conceptual focus of systems. In M. H. Marx (Ed.), *Psychological theory* (pp. 131–143). New York: Macmillan. (Original work published 1939)

Cook, R. I., & Woods, D. D. (1996). Adapting to new technology in the operating room. *Human Factors, 38,* 593–613.

Gaba, D. M. (1994). Human error in dynamic medical domains. In M. S. Bogner (Ed.), *Human error in medicine* (pp. 197–224). Hillsdale, NJ: Erlbaum.

Gantert, W. A., Tendick, F., Bhoyrul, S., Tyrell, D., Fujino, Y., Rangel, S., Patti, M. G., & Way, L. W. (1998). Error analysis in laparoscopic surgery. In M. Bogner et al. (Eds.), *Proceedings of surgical-assist systems,* 3262 (pp. 61–69). Bellingham, WA: The Society of Photo-Optical Instrumentation Engineers.

Gopher, D., Donchin, Y., Olin, M., Badihi, Y., Cohen, G., Bieski, M., Cotev, S. (1989). The nature and causes of human errors in a medical intensive care unit. *In Proceedings of the Human Factors Society 33rd Annual Meeting* (pp. 956–960). Santa Monica, CA: Human Factors Society.

Helmreich, R. L., & Schaefer, H-G. (1994). Team performance in the operating room. In M. S. Bogner (Ed.), *Human error in medicine* (pp. 225–253). Hillsdale, NJ: Erlbaum.

Lewin, K. (1951). Defining the "field at a given time" (1943). In D. Cartwright (Ed.), *Field theory in social science* (pp. 43–59). New York: Harper.

Morrow, D. G., Leirer, V. O., Andrassy, J. M., Tanke, E. D., & Stine-Morrow, E. A. L. (1996). Medication instruction design: Younger and older adult schemas for taking medication. *Human Factors, 38,* 556–573.

Seagull, F. J., & Sanderson, P. M. (in press). Alarms in the operating room: The noise of anesthesia. In M. S. Bogner (Ed.), *Humkan error in health care: A handbook of issues and indications.* Mahwah, NJ: Erlbaum.

Senders, J. W. (1994). Medical errors, and medical accidents. In M. S. Bogner (Ed.), *Human error in medicine* (pp. 159–177). Hillsdale, NJ: Erlbaum.

Marilyn Sue Bogner

MEDITATION. Hundreds of scientific studies have shown that stress impairs psychological, behavioral, and physiological function. Exposure to psychological stress triggers a series of central and peripheral nervous system changes that affect behavior and can produce physiological changes that can cause and exacerbate somatic illness. To counteract these adverse effects, attempts have been made to devise stress management strategies, some of which are related to cognitive restructuring and other therapeutic approaches within the context of Western psychology. Others, such as meditation related approaches, drawn from longstanding Eastern traditions, have also been explored. This article discusses the history of meditation and the relaxation response, the physiology of stress, and the use of meditation and relaxation approaches with medical disorders.

Meditation and the Relaxation Response

Meditation in various forms has been an important part of Eastern religions. Many practitioners believe that it leads to an enlightened perception of reality or to a closer union with God. Until recently, this type of association with the metaphysical has adversely influenced many in Western cultures from accepting the practice of meditation.

Research on meditation within a Western scientific and medical framework began in the early 1970s when Benson and his colleagues began to examine the psychological and physiological components of one form of meditation, transcendental meditation. After studying the cultural, religious, philosophical, and scientific underpinnings, these researchers concluded that various forms of meditation require (1) focusing one's attention on a repetitive word, sound, prayer, phrase, image, or physical activity; and (2) passively returning to this focus when distracted. These two simple steps result in certain predictable physiological changes both within and outside the central nervous system promoting a sense of calm. Benson labeled these effects the "relaxation response," the biological consequence of a wide variety of mental focusing techniques, just one of which is meditation.

The Physiology of Stress

To appreciate the effects of eliciting the relaxation response and its clinical benefits it is necessary to understand the physiology of stress. The counterpart to the relaxation response is the fight-or-flight response, an expression coined by Walter B. Cannon (1941). Cannon reasoned that animals when threatened respond with dilation of the pupils, increases in blood pressure and respiratory rate, increased blood flow to the skeletal muscles, and heightened motor excitability. In man, the fight-or-flight response is elicited by everyday situations that require behavioral adjustment or that are threatening, such as waiting on line or interacting with annoying coworkers.

In contrast to the fight-or-flight response, the relaxation response reduces oxygen consumption, carbon dioxide elimination, heart rate, respiratory rate, and arterial blood lactate—changes consistent with a generalized reduction in sympathetic nervous system activity and distinctly different from the physiologic changes noted during quiet sitting. Chronic stress or tension can contribute to the development and exacerbation of stress-related disorders, whereas regular elicitation of the relaxation response can prevent or reduce the symptoms of stress-related conditions.

Historical References to Practices that Include Components of the Relaxation Response

Prayers and practices that could elicit the relaxation response have been described for millennia. Philosophers have noted that early religious practices often included the repetition of a word or phrase and elimination of distracting thoughts. For example, in the tenth century Fray Francisco de Osuna wrote: "Contemplation requires us to blind ourselves to all that is not God" (p. viii). He urged that one should be deaf and dumb to all else (p. 50) and must "quit all obstacles, keeping your eyes bent on the ground . . ." (pp. 293–294). To achieve this state one could repeat a short, self-composed prayer for one hour in the morning and evening. This exercise was to be taught by a qualified teacher.

In Judaism, similar practices designed to bring about this altered state of consciousness date back to the time of the second temple from the fourth century BCE to the first century CE. They are mentioned in descriptions of merkabalism (Scholem, 1967) one of the earliest forms of Jewish mysticism. In this practice of meditation, the subject would sit with his head between his knees, whisper hymns and songs, and repeat the name of a magic seal.

Meditative practice is also a key feature in Shintoism and Taoism, two traditional religions in Asia. In Shintoism one method of prayer consists of sitting quietly while looking straight ahead at a mirror, breathing in through the nose, holding the breath briefly and breathing out through the mouth. Throughout the exercise, the priest repeats 10 numbers, or sacred words, which are pronounced according to traditional religious teachings (Herbert, 1967, p. 83). In Taoism followers use methods similar to those of Shintoism and concentrate on the concept of nothingness to achieve absolute tranquility (Chang, 1963, p. 167).

Steps in Eliciting the Relaxation Response

In Western cultures numerous secular means of eliciting the relaxation response have been developed including hypnosis, exercise, progressive muscle relaxation, and autogenic training. There appears to be a commonality in the physiological response to all these different methods (Benson and Stuart, 1992). As noted above, two components appear to be essential: mental focusing and a passive attitude toward distracting thoughts. As long as the technique used includes these two basic steps the relaxation response will ensue.

Incorporating elements common to a variety of historical strategies, Benson and his colleagues developed the following set of steps for eliciting the response (Benson, 1996, p. 136):

Step 1. Pick a focus word or short phrase that is firmly rooted in your belief system (e.g., peace, calm, "the Lord is my shepherd," "Shalom").

Step 2. Sit quietly in a comfortable position.

Step 3. Close your eyes.

Step 4. Relax your muscles.

Step 5. Breathe slowly and naturally, and as you do, repeat your focus word, phrase, or prayer silently to yourself as you exhale.

Step 6. Assume a passive attitude. Don't worry about how well you're doing. When other thoughts come to mind, simply say to yourself, "oh, well," and gently return to the repetition.

Step 7. Continue for 10 to 20 minutes.

Step 8. Do not stand up immediately. Continue sitting quietly for a minute or so, allowing other thoughts to return. Then open your eyes and sit for another minute before rising.

Step 9. Practice this technique once or twice daily.

Medical Benefits of the Relaxation Response

Since the early studies of meditation and other related techniques, the relaxation response has been found to be effective in the treatment of many medical disorders including hypertension, chronic pain, insomnia, infertility, in preparation for surgical procedures, and in reducing the side effects of chemotherapy. Frequently, the relaxation response is used in conjunction with nutrition, exercise, and stress management approaches.

In a study of 109 chronic pain patients Caudill et al. (1991) examined the effect of a behavioral group intervention that included relaxation response training. The average duration of pain among the patients was 6.5 years, and the intervention consisted of 90-minute group sessions once a week. After 10 weeks at the completion of the intervention period, participants exhibited a decrease in negative psychological symptoms, including depression, anxiety, and hostility. In addition, the study showed that the intervention resulted in a 36% decrease in clinic use during the first 2 years following the intervention. With the growing interest in the use of nonpharmacologic interventions, the result of this study is particularly pertinent. Interventions incorporating the relaxation response not only facilitated psychological and medical goals but also helped reduce medical utilization and costs. Such interventions can thus have positive economic effects while improving clinical outcomes.

[*See also* Relaxation Training.]

Bibliography

Benson, H. (1975). *The relaxation response.* New York: Morrow.

Benson, H. (1996). *Timeless healing: The power and biology of belief.* New York: Scribner.

Benson, H., Beard, J. F., & Carol, M. P. (1974). The relaxation response. *Psychiatry, 37,* 37–46.

Benson, H., & Stuart, E. M. (1992). *The wellness book.* New York: Simon & Shuster.

Cannon, W. B. (1941). The emergency function of the adrenal medulla in pain and the major emotions. *American Journal of Physiology, 33,* 356.

Caudill, M., Schnable, R., Zuttermeister, P., Bensen, H., & Friedman, R. (1991). Decreased clinic use by chronic pain patients: Response to behavioral medicine intervention. *The Clinical Journal of Pain, 7,* 305–310.

Chang, C. (1963). *Creativity and Taoism.* New York: Julian Press, 1963.

Herbert, J. (1967). *Shinto: At the fountain-head of Japan.* London: Allen & Unwin.

Jacobs, G. D., Benson, H., & Friedman, R. (1993). Home-based central nervous system assessment of a multifactor behavioral intervention for chronic sleep-onset insomnia. *Behavior Therapy, 24,* 159–74.

Osuna, Fray Francisco De. (1931). *The Third Spiritual Alphabet.* London: Benziger.

Scholem, G. G. (1967). *Jewish mysticism.* New York: Schocken Books.

Patricia Myers, Richard Friedman,
and Herbert Benson

MEINONG, ALEXIUS (1853–1920), Austrian philosopher. Meinong was born in Lemberg (Lvov) in the Austrian province of Galicia to a family of minor nobility. He attended *Gymnasium* and university in Vienna from 1862 to 1878. Concentrating at first in history, he turned to philosophy in 1874 under the influence of Franz Brentano, who directed him to the study of David Hume. Meinong became a *Privatdozent* at Vienna in 1878 until receiving an appointment at Graz in 1882. He remained there for the rest of his life, attaining full professorship in 1889.

Meinong considered himself to be an empirical philosopher, which meant for him a fidelity to facts and a commitment to precision and care in argumentation. Psychology was central to his notion of philosophy, for it was through the minute analysis of experience that factuality could be grounded. In the 1880s, Meinong spoke out for the teaching of psychology as part of philosophy in the curriculum for the Austrian *Gymnasium.*

Meinong's contributions to psychology fall into two areas: experimental and phenomenological. He is best known for the former, as he founded the first Austrian laboratory at Graz in 1894. Most of the experimental work there was done by his students, principally Stephan Witasek and Vittorio Benussi. The resulting Graz school was known primarily for its work on Gestalt-qualities, a phenomenon brought to light in 1890 by another student of Brentano and Meinong, Christian von Ehrenfels. The influence of Meinong on the formulations of the Graz school was nevertheless very strong, as he clung tenaciously to the atomistic assumption that complex experiential contents are based upon simple ones. Thus the perception of organized structures involved two levels of contents, the "founding" simple sensations and the "founded" relational and formal contents that bound them together (for example, the Gestalt-qualities). This two-tiered model was controversial already in the 1890s, with other experimentalists such as Hans Cornelius and Friedrich Schumann arriving at results that undermined it. The Graz model eventually gave way to the Gestalt psychology of Max Wertheimer, Wolfgang Köhler, and Kurt Koffka, who nevertheless acknowledged the quality of the Graz experiments, particularly those of Benussi.

The bulk of Meinong's own work was phenomenological, pursuing Brentano's division of experience into act and content, and working out the implications of these descriptions for other philosophical concerns such as ontology and ethics. His writings on these subjects often covered the same territory as did that of Edmund Husserl, particularly the *Logical Investigations* (Halle, 1900–1901) but with characteristic differences of emphasis and result. Meinong's approach was again atomistic, rendering him less sensitive to the dynamic aspects of experience than Husserl but enabling him to develop a more precise vocabulary and syntax to capture the static structures of consciousness. Meinong posited four types of elementary acts: passive cognitive (representations, or *Vorstellungen*), active cognitive (judgments), passive emotional (feelings), and active emotional (desires). He investigated the relationships between fantasy and realistic experiences in this context (for example, his study of assumptions), and located the experience of valuation in the area of feelings and desires (for example, his work on emotional presentation).

[*Many of the people mentioned in this article are the subjects of independent biographical entries.*]

Bibliography

Meinong, A. (1968–1978). *Gesamtausgabe* (7 vols.) (R. Haller, R. Kindinger, R. M. Chisholm, Eds.). Graz: Akademische Druck- u. Verlagsanstalt.

Meinong, A. (1972). *On emotional presentation* (M. L. Schubert Kalsi, Trans.). Evanston, IL: Northwestern University Press.

Meinong, A. (1983). *On assumptions* (J. Heanue, Ed. and Trans.). Berkeley: University of California Press.

Lindenfeld, D. F. (1980). *The transformation of positivism: Alexius Meinong and European thought, 1880–1920.* Berkeley: University of California Press.

Findlay, J. N. (1963). *Meinong's theory of objects and values* (2nd ed.). Oxford, England: Clarendon.

David Lindenfeld

MELTON, ARTHUR (1906–1978), American psychologist. Melton is properly remembered as a pivotal figure in the experimental and theoretical analysis of memory, the creation of applied psychology laboratories, and the development of publications for the American Psychological Association (APA) and the Psychonomic Society. He was a member of the National Academy of Sciences, president of several national organizations, and the winner of APA's Gold Medal Award.

Throughout his career, Melton made seminal contributions to research on memory. Melton and Irwin (1940) published an account of forgetting that invoked two factors: competition and unlearning. This theoretical account set the stage for the study of forgetting for more than a decade. One classic (Melton, 1963) was a reworking of his vice-presidential address to the American Association for the Advancement of Science on the topic of short-term memory. His cogent analyses convinced many that there was no need to postulate structurally separate short-term and long-term memories. The debate on the separation continues, as is evidenced by a special section on short-term memory published in *Memory and Cognition* in 1993. The 1963 paper also introduced psychologists to an analysis of memory as the result of three processes: encoding, storage, and retrieval. This analysis remains the standard approach to understanding memory. In 1970, Melton's research remains the standard approach to understanding memory. In 1970, Melton's research turned to an old but unsolved problem—why it is that distributing repetitions through time facilitates learning compared with massing the same number of repetitions. His discoveries were recognized in the naming of one of the salient effects the Melton lag effect, which holds that increasing the temporal interval between presentations generally increases memory. As with his other seminal papers, Melton (1970) set the tone for research for more than 20 years.

Melton was instrumental in the development of applied psychology laboratories. His interests in applications can be seen in his earliest work on how the placement of artwork in museums affects viewing habits. During World War II, Melton helped to design psychomotor tests used in the selection of pilots, and in 1949 he was called upon by the Air Force to organize the Air Force Personnel Training and Research Center. When Melton moved to the University of Michigan in 1957, he organized the Willow Run Research Laboratories, and with Paul Fitts, combined basic and applied research at the university's Human Performance Center.

Melton had a tremendous influence on publishing in psychology. He was the editor of the *Journal of Experimental Psychology* from 1951 through 1962, when the *Journal* was the most important outlet for experimental work in psychology. He held the highest standards for publication, including standards for experimental design, data analysis, and clarity of writing. He also encouraged authors to publish coherent sets of experiments that made significant progress toward solving problems, a tactic that has become common practice. While Melton was chair of the Council of Editors, APA published the 1957 revision of its *Publication Manual*, which became the bible for professionals and students. Later, Melton served as the chief editorial advisor for APA. This level of service and accomplishment was recognized by APA in the naming of the Arthur W. Melton Library. His high standards extended beyond the laboratory; consequently, he was a effective, inspiring, and demanding teacher.

Bibliography

Works by Melton

Melton, A. W. (1963). Implications of short-term memory for a general theory of memory. *Journal of Verbal Learning and Verbal Behavior, 2,* 1–21.

Melton, A. W. (1970). The situation with respect to the spacing of repetitions and memory. *Journal of Verbal Learning and Verbal Behavior, 9,* 596–606.

Melton, A. W., & Irwin J. M. (1940). The influence of degree of interpolated learning on retroactive inhibition and the overt transfer of specific responses. *American Journal of Psychology, 76,* 173–203.

Works about Melton

Underwood, B. J. (1979). Arthur W. Melton (1906–1978). *American Psychologist, 12,* 1171–1173.

Wickens, D. D., & Wickens, C. D. (1980). Memorial tribute to Arthur W. Melton (1906–1978). *Memory and Cognition, 8,* 305–312.

Arthur M. Glenberg and Robert G. Crowder

MEMORY. [*This entry provides a broad survey of memory. It comprises six articles:*

Many independent entries related to memory are included in the encyclopedia: Forgetting; Implicit Memory; Learning and Memory; Mental Imagery; Recovered Memories; Sensory Stores; *and* Working Memory.]

An Overview

Memory is the general name applied to a wide variety of biological devices by which living organisms acquire, retain, and make use of skills and knowledge. It is present in all higher animals, taking many shapes and forms. Its most advanced level in evolutionary terms is to be found in human beings. The scientific study of memory is over 100 years old.

Although at one time the dominant view was that memory was in some sense a "unitary" capability, today the multiplicity of forms and kinds of memory is widely even if not universally accepted. A major issue has to do with questions such as how, or on what basis, the different forms and kinds are to be classified, and by what criteria their similarities and differences are to be determined. When the bases and criteria used include neuronal substrates of memory, the classification of memory is described in terms of *memory systems*. [*See* Memory Systems.]

Most of our scientific knowledge about memory, as distinguished from casual impressions, has been derived from laboratory studies, but clinical observations of memory pathology and field studies of "everyday memory" have also contributed to it.

A major contrast in the study of memory is that between the input-output method versus the output-only method. In the former, the researcher knows both the input and how it has affected the output, that is, what the rememberer originally witnessed and what she can do, or think, that she could not have done, or thought, in the absence of the input. The input-output method characterizes laboratory studies of memory, in which the learner is given specific training on a certain task, or exposed to some specific stimulus materials, and subsequently tested on the performance of the task, or on the retention of some aspect of the material. The input-output method is also used in studies of *mnemonists*, individuals with apparently exceptional memory abilities. But even ordinary people who have learned to use mnemonic devices can greatly enhance their memory abilities in particular tasks. [*See* Mnemonic Devices; *and* Mnemonists.]

In the output-only method, the input is unknown and the output is used either to make inferences about what the input might have been or as a measure of the individual's memory abilities in relation to that of other members of a particular population.

The output-only method is used in situations in which the observer or examiner does not know what the relevant input into the memory system was, and in which the output is used for making inferences about what that input might have been. An individual's recollections of a past event are widely assumed to be true. Research has shown, however, that the output from memory depends not only on the input but on other equally important factors, and that therefore direct inferences from the output to the input are not always justified. The output-only method is also used to measure the extent of an individual's knowledge of a given kind (e.g., general facts of the world, vocabulary, childhood experiences) where actual input need not be known. Relevant information is derived from psychometric assessments of memory-related abilities (e.g., retrograde amnesia) of individuals and special populations, such as various brain-damaged patient groups, in the study of autobiographical memory, eyewitness testimony in everyday life as well as in the courtroom, in survey research, and similar real-life situations. The output-only method historically came before the input-output method. Indeed, one of the most important contributions made by Ebbinghaus, the father of the modern study of memory, was the adoption of the input-output approach. [*See* Amnesia, Psychometrics, Survey Methodology; *and the biography of Ebbinghaus*.]

The concept of *memory* is closely related to the concept of *learning*, although the relation between the two cannot be precisely specified. There are, however, three senses in which learning and memory may be said to differ. One has to do with the nature of the activity in question: If individuals acquire a new skill or new knowledge slowly and laboriously, they are said to be engaged in "learning"; if acquisition occurs "instantly," individuals are more likely to be thought of as making use of their "memory." Thus people learn to operate a computer and speak a second language; when they remember what kiwi fruit tastes like, or what their new friend is called they rely on their memory. A second sense of separation between learning and memory parallels *acquisition* versus *expression* of skill or knowledge: acquisition is thought of as learning whereas expression of what has been acquired is thought of as memory. A third distinguishing sense has to do with the subdivisions of the biological-psychological domain in which scientists study learning and memory: Some chapters in a textbook, or some entries in an encyclopedia like this one, are classified as learning, others as memory. The reason for doing so lies more in tradition and current fashion than in any disciplined thought, not unlike the reason why some people say "Bordeaux" and others "claret" when they refer to the same bottled liquid.

Learning and memory have been studied in a number of different animals, ranging from insects and worms to human beings. Much of the study of nonhuman species is carried out for its own sake, as a part of comparative psychology, but sometimes investigators use animal memory as a model of human memory. Studies with nonhuman animals prove that language is not a necessary condition for the many sophisticated and refined learning and memory capabilities possessed by organisms, but there is also little doubt that in human beings language and memory greatly influence each other not only in development but also in everyday use.

In real life, memory is ubiquitous, and memory processes permeate all cognition and almost all behavior. To study memory scientifically—according to the traditional recipe of analysis followed by synthesis—researchers break the seamless continuity of memory into tractable entities called memory tasks. A typical memory task begins with encoding, getting information about the witnessed happenings into the memory store, and ends with retrieval—making use of the stored information in one way or another. It is widely accepted that typical memory tasks used in the laboratory, or identified outside it, involve many different kinds of memory and many different kinds of memory processes. [See Cognition.]

A major distinction between memory tasks is based on individuals' conscious awareness of what they are retrieving. If they are aware that they are now remembering an earlier experience, or earlier experiences, they are said to be retrieving information explicitly. If they are not aware that their current behavior has been influenced by a particular past event, their retrieval of the information stored from the event is said to be implicit. An extensively researched form of implicit memory is *perceptual priming*—enhanced facility in identifying and naming perceptual objects. At this time, a distinction cannot be made between explicit and implicit memory in nonverbal people or animals.

Another fundamental division in human memory, one that also cannot be made in studies with animals and other nonverbal individuals, is that between memory and conception, as described by William James in the 1890s, or, as we say today, between episodic memory and remembering on the one hand, and semantic memory and knowing on the other. *Remembering* consists in explicit retrieval of stored information, *knowing* consists in implicit retrieval.

For the first three quarters of a century in the history of the scientific study of memory, most of the knowledge about memory phenomena and underlying processes was gained with purely behavioral or purely cognitive methods. Since the early 1970s, clinical and experimental study of memory disorders induced by brain damage (the neuropsychology of memory), has added significantly to such knowledge. And in the early 1990s, the use of functional neuroimaging techniques, such as positron emission tomography (PET) and functional magnetic resonance imaging (fMRI), has become increasingly popular in the study of memory. These techniques have already provided intriguing and novel insights into the neuroanatomical correlates of memory processes, insights that were not available from the traditional neuropsychological approaches. Although these studies are still in their infancy, it is already clear that they will revolutionize the study of the brain-mind in very much the same manner as the transformations brought about by the telescope and the microscope.

Bibliography

Baddeley, A. D. (1997). *Human memory: Theory and practice.* Hove, East Sussex, UK: Psychology Press. The best traditional, up-to-date textbook of human memory available today, by another giant of today's memory research, who believes that memory lies at the center of all cognition. More technical than Schacter's book, but as lucidly written, it covers laboratory studies of memory as well as memory phenomena in real life.

Schacter, D. L. (1996). *Searching for memory.* New York: Basic Books. A highly acclaimed, easy to read popular book whose contents sweep broadly over the domain of human memory, both normal and abnormal, beautifully written by one of the world's foremost researchers and thinkers on the topic.

Tulving, E., & F. I. M. Craik (Eds.). (2000). *The Oxford handbook of memory.* New York: Oxford University Press. A collection of nearly 40 chapters, written by well-known memory researchers who have themselves contributed greatly to our current knowledge. Contains an extensive bibliography on human memory.

Endel Tulving

Coding Processes

What is meant by coding processes in memory? First, it is clear that all mental processes are represented by neural activities in the brain, and in that sense, there are neural codes that stand for our mental experiences. But cognitive psychologists typically mean something less reductionist than that; when they talk about codes, they are referring to the qualitative nature of the mental representation of an object, a word, an idea, a sound, or other experienced event. Very often, objects and events are represented by several different codes; for example, a concrete noun is likely represented both by a verbal code (including aspects of its semantics and its phonology, etc.) and an imaginal code—what the object looks like (Paivio, 1971). Thus, coding processes are those sensory, perceptual, and higher level cognitive processes whose function is to transform objects and events from the outside world into their coded representations in the mind/brain.

As we will discuss, some ways of representing an event lead to better memory for that event than other possible ways. So, for example, if a person encodes (i.e., processes) a word in terms of its sound or its visual appearance, this will be less beneficial for later memory than encoding it in terms of its meaning or implications. The study of memory encoding thus deals with the different ways in which events can be represented, the consequences for later memory of these different ways, and how the different representations may be achieved. One important distinction in this respect is between stimulus-driven encoding and strategically mediated encoding; for instance, presenting a concept such as "chair" as a picture of a chair, as opposed to the word CHAIR, will drive different encoding operations, and the differences are determined by the physical nature of the stimulus. On the other hand, the same physical object can be encoded in a variety of ways depending on the perceiver's strategic goals; thus, a sentence in a text passage may be read for meaning and comprehension or it may be proofread for spelling errors. These different encoding strategies have different consequences for later memory, even in cases where the reader is not attempting to memorize the material in any sense.

Two further related terms are *decoding* and *recoding*. The concept of decoding obviously refers to changing the coded representation back into its original form. We are therefore dealing here with retrieval processes in a memory context, although the term is not often used in cognitive psychology. On the other hand, recoding is used frequently. The term typically refers to a situation in which some encoded information is changed into a form that is more compact and more meaningful, and so is more easily remembered. For example, the telephone number 244–5646 could be recoded as BIG JOHN using the letters on the telephone dial; the serial number 234199897531, which is quite difficult to remember, could be recoded into three meaningful chunks of 234–1998–97531, which is comparatively easy.

The Information-Processing Framework

Since 1960 or so, cognitive psychologists have found it useful to think of the brain as an information-processing device, and to identify psychological constructs such as memory and attention as components of this complex information-handling system. Within this framework, memory was thought of as a series of stages or stores: first, modality-specific sensory stores,

holding relatively raw sensory information; then a limited-capacity short-term or primary memory; and finally, a permanent and very capacious long-term or secondary memory. In the case of language, information in the sensory stores decays rapidly unless it is selected by attentional processes, and this selection entails recoding processes such that the visual or auditory codes are transformed into short-term memory codes representing the features of heard, seen, or spoken language. Further processing typically recodes the short-term information into semantic or conceptual information that can be retrieved minutes or years later (e.g., What was the long serial number recently presented as an example?).

This information-processing model of memory has been very influential; one of its most successful variants was proposed by Atkinson and Shiffrin (1971) and is still a useful framework. However, the three-store model also has drawbacks: For example, it encourages a rather monolithic view of short-term or primary memory, whereas empirical studies show that the encoding, capacity, and forgetting characteristics of primary memory are anything but stable—they change as a function of materials, people, and tasks. As an alternative, Craik and Lockhart (1972) proposed a levels-of-processing (LOP) view, which suggested that incoming stimuli were processed to different levels or depths in the cognitive system, from shallow sensory levels to deep levels of meaning and implication. In this framework, memory is not information held in a store, but is rather the product of processing operations carried out primarily for the purposes of perception and comprehension: The deeper the processing (determined either by greater attention and effort or by highly meaningful stimuli), the better the subsequent memory. The levels-of-processing view thus stresses the crucial importance of encoding processes for memory. Clearly, retrieval processes are equally important, and a more complete framework would marry the levels-of-processing view of encoding with the transfer-appropriate processing view of retrieval. Once encoding processes have determined the qualitative nature of the stored trace, the optimal retrieval cue will be one whose qualitative nature reflects these same qualitative characteristics (Bransford, Franks, Morris, & Stein, 1979).

The Nature of Codes

When we talk about encoded information, one crucial point is that our mentally encoded knowledge must reflect all aspects of the outside world if the internal mental model is to be useful as a guide to the external environment. Therefore, we must have mental codes that represent smells, tastes, sounds, and touch information, as well as the more commonly studied verbal and pictorial codes. It seems reasonable to assume, in fact, that all sensory modalities first store relatively unprocessed literal copies of the sensory input, and that further processing reveals the associations and implications for action of this sensory information. We can think of the cognitive system as hierarchical, with lower levels representing the surface aspects of stimuli (i.e., shallow levels of processing or sensory stores), which merge into progressively higher levels whose representations become gradually less concerned with the specific sensory details of the current stimulus, and more concerned with general, amodal, categorical, and conceptual aspects of the input. It seems likely that these higher levels of representation can be generated from within more easily than can the lower sensory levels, which in turn are more easily driven by stimuli coming through the senses. It is accepted, however, that normal processing involves some mixture of top-down (conceptually driven) and bottom-up (stimulus-driven) processing, with the mixture depending on such factors as the strength of the perceiver's expectations (which would amplify the top-down component) and the clarity of the sensory input (which would amplify the bottom-up component).

Most memory research has dealt with either language codes or pictorial codes, however. Pictorial or imaginal representations enable us to remember scenes and faces, also to have cognitive maps of spatial layouts—everything from where furniture is in a room to the relative location of states or countries. Most people can form a picture in their mind's eye of familiar objects and locations (i.e., experience mental imagery). Some researchers (e.g., Paivio, 1971) have claimed that the manner in which the brain processes pictures or visual imagery is categorically different from the manner in which the brain processes verbal information. These researchers posited two codes by which information could be represented: an analogue code that preserves the main physical features of the object being represented (e.g., an image of a cat under a table), and a symbolic code that stands for the external event but does not resemble it perceptually (e.g., the sentence, "The cat is under the table"). In support of this dual-code hypothesis, Brooks (1968) showed that visual perception interfered with the production of visual imagery but not with the mental manipulation of words; correspondingly, verbal expression interfered with word processing but not with imagery processing. That is, interference was observed when the same representational system was used for the mental task and additional perceiving or responding.

Other researchers, such as Pylyshyn (1973), subsequently disagreed with this dual-code hypothesis, arguing instead that all information, whether verbal or imaginal, has the same underlying propositional form. That is, information is stored conceptually in a manner indicating the underlying relationship between concepts. Propositional representations are assumed to be more abstract, more fundamental, and more economical to store than are images or words. One possible resolution of this debate is to distinguish more clearly between what is stored and what is experienced. What is stored, after all, is a pattern of neural firing, and this neurological code may perhaps be decoded into several different experimental representations depending on the person's needs at the time. A related point concerns the probability that several codes exist for any given piece of information. For example, in Atkinson and Shiffrin's (1971) three-store model, information in the sensory store has an analogical, short-lived form; in the short-term store, language information is coded in terms of its acoustic or speech-motor features; and in the long-term store, it is coded in terms of its underlying meaning.

Similarly, in Tulving's (1994) memory systems model, there are multiple dissociable memory systems, each with its own unique type of code. For example, information may be encoded perceptually (reflecting the sensory modality in which it was received), procedurally (reflecting knowledge of how to perform cognitive or motor actions), semantically (reflecting general world knowledge, independent of the specific circumstances in which the information was learned), or episodically (representing the specifics of time and place of the event, and how it relates to the individual's life).

Other important concepts in this area are elaboration, organization, and distinctiveness. *Elaboration* refers to the richness or extensiveness of an event's encoding; an example would be noting a person, his or her surroundings, and actions very carefully, as opposed to merely glancing at the person. The general finding (in line with common sense) is that greater degrees of elaboration support higher levels of subsequent memory. *Organization* refers to the linking together of individual representations to form larger units, usually on the basis of their meaning. A list of twenty unrelated nouns is difficult to remember, but if the list is made up of five groups of four related nouns (e.g., tiger, zebra, antelope, elephant; lawyer, dentist, professor, nurse) it is much easier to recollect. The participant organizes the list into five headings (animals, professions, etc.) and then into the specific words under each heading. Some years ago, Bower, Clark, Lesgold, and Winzenz (1969) composed word lists that were highly structured hierarchically (e.g., the top heading "minerals" split into metals and nonmetals; metals split into rare metals, common metals, and alloys; rare metals included platinum, silver, and gold); when they presented such lists in a memory experiment, participants were able to recall all 112 words after just three learning trials. Even when words in a list have no obvious groupings, participants can organize them subjectively (e.g., photograph, tea, settee, daffodils—associated with my mother's living room). In the 1960s, researchers such as George Mandler and Endel Tulving found that measures of subjective organization correlated highly with recall. Finally, *distinctiveness* refers to the situation where an encoded item stands out from its background, much as a brightly colored object stands out perceptually from a drab background. Some theorists have argued that both organization and distinctiveness are important for good recollection (e.g., Hunt & McDaniel, 1993), with organization providing the structured background, and distinctiveness rendering an item salient against this background. An excellent way to encode an event is therefore to process it deeply and elaborately, emphasizing its distinctive characteristics, but also noting how it fits into some well-known piece of structured knowledge.

The Role of Prior Knowledge

The last point is crucial for an understanding of memory-encoding processes. We remember items and events that are readily interpretable in terms of our own specific sets of expertise: A professional mathematician can remember a new equation, a master chess player can remember a board position after studying it for a few seconds, a 10-year-old dinosaur expert can remember some new facts about his or her particular area of expertise. These well-learned, highly structured knowledge systems are known as *schemas*. They are effective for many of the same reasons that a well-organized library is effective: the previously set-up organization provides a precise place for encoding each new acquisition, and the same organization provides the structure to support later retrieval. We know where to look for a particular book, and if it is distinctively large and brightly colored, it will be retrieved all the more easily. Notions of expertise and prior knowledge may explain why both pictures and self-related events are particularly well remembered: We are all experts when it comes to visual perception and in our schematic knowledge of ourselves.

What Makes for a Good Encoding?

By applying the notions discussed previously, we can understand a number of experimental results in the technical literature, and also gain some insight into effective real-world remembering. First, we have to know the goals of the would-be learner. If a person needs to remember a telephone number only long enough to dial it, it is probably best to rehearse it as a speech-motor sequence: this may be the optimal code for the short-term retention of words and numbers. But for long-term remembering, meaningfulness and distinctiveness are the key concepts. Information should be processed deeply (i.e., in terms of meaning) and related to well-structured schematic knowledge, but also processed in terms of its distinctive characteristics. Inter-

estingly, the intention to learn something is not crucial, as long as these good encoding operations are carried out. Craik and Tulving (1975) showed that when participants were asked questions about a series of words, semantic questions (e.g., "Is the word associated with religion?"—PRIEST) led to higher levels of memory in an unexpected later test than did questions relating to rhymes ("Does the word rhyme with yeast?") or to letter structure ("Does the word start with P?").

Other laboratory phenomena such as the generation effect and the spacing effect can also be understood in terms of depth and elaboration. To demonstrate the generation effect, participants either simply read a word or have to carry out some relatively trivial operation (e.g., letter completion or anagram solution) to know what the word is. Thus, related word pairs could be presented and participants asked to name the second words (e.g., boot–SHOE vs. boot–S_OE). Later memory is better for words that were generated rather than read, arguably because generation necessitates a greater involvement of meaning and knowledge of word structure. In the spacing effect, people study a list of words, with some words presented once only, and some twice; the twice-presented words vary in how far apart they are spaced in the list. The finding is that massed repetition (i.e., words presented twice in succession) yields later memory that is barely better than memory for once-presented words, but that memory for twice-presented words gradually increases as the spacing between repetitions increases. The factors underlying this effect are not entirely understood, but they probably include the fact that repeated words are usually recognized as having been encountered previously; longer spacings involve somewhat more difficult and elaborate recognition retrieval operations, and these processes may boost later memory. This point also brings in the notion that *any* cognitive operation can serve as a memory-encoding process, regardless of whether its initial purpose was perception, comprehension, learning, or retrieval. A second factor in the spacing effect is encoding variability; the idea that a somewhat different encoding on the two occasions will elaborate the encoded event to a greater extent, and thus make it more memorable. Greater spacings are likely to be associated with differences in the two encoding operations.

Summary

It seems likely that encoded representations of the outside world are not used exclusively for memory; rather, they primarily represent accrued knowledge that then serves to enable meaningful perception and comprehension of further events. It is also probable that incoming stimuli are represented by several qualitatively different codes ranging from modality-specific sensory codes, through codes representing letters, words, and objects, to abstract codes connecting the current stimulus to prior knowledge. Which code is best for episodic memory will depend crucially on the cues available in the retrieval environment, but the codes that provide the greatest potential for excellent memory (given the appropriate cue) are those that deal with rich, meaningful information within one of the individual's domains of expertise.

[See also Mental Imagery.]

Bibliography

Atkinson, R. C., & Shiffrin, R. M. (1971, August). The control of short-term memory. *Scientific American, 225*, 82–90.

Bower, G. H., Clark, M. C., Lesgold, A. M., & Winzenz, D. (1969). Hierarchical retrieval schemas in recall of categorized word lists. *Journal of Verbal Learning and Verbal Behavior, 8*, 323–343.

Bransford, J. D., Franks, J. J., Morris, C. D., & Stein, B. S. (1979). Some general constraints on learning and memory research. In L. S. Cermak & F. I. M. Craik (Eds.), *Levels of processing in human memory* (pp. 331–354). Hillsdale, NJ: Erlbaum.

Brooks, L. R. (1968). Spatial and verbal components of the act of recall. *Canadian Journal of Psychology, 22*, 349–368.

Craik, F. I. M., & Lockhart, R. S. (1972). Levels of processing: A framework for memory research. *Journal of Verbal Learning and Verbal Behavior, 11*, 671–684.

Craik, F. I. M., & Tulving, E. (1975). Depth of processing and the retention of words in episodic memory. *Journal of Experimental Psychology: General, 104*, 268–294.

Hunt, R. R., & McDaniel, M. A. (1993). The enigma of organization and distinctiveness. *Journal of Memory and Language, 32*, 421–445.

Paivio, A. (1971). *Imagery and verbal processes.* New York: Holt, Rinehart, & Winston.

Pylyshyn, Z. W. (1973). What the mind's eye tells the mind's brain: A critique of mental imagery. *Psychological Bulletin, 80*, 1–24.

Tulving, E. (1994). Organization of memory: Quo vadis? In M. S. Gazzaniga (Ed.), *The cognitive neurosciences* (pp. 839–847). Cambridge, MA: MIT Press/Bradford.

Fergus I. M. Craik and Scott C. Brown

Constructive Processes

Although people believe they remember past experiences accurately, results from hundreds of studies run counter to this intuition. In study after study it has become clear that human memory does not resemble the common metaphors used to describe it. We do not remember by locating and retrieving stored mental objects like a computer hard drive, nor do we watch an event through a camera-like lens in our mind's eye. Even memories for newsbreaking and emotional events are not necessarily accurate, although they may seem vivid.

Immediately after the space shuttle *Challenger* exploded, Neisser and Harsch (1992) asked students to record the activities they were engaged in when they heard the news. Several years later, the same students were asked to recall what they had been doing when they first heard the news. They were surprisingly inaccurate. This indicates that remembering entails more than retrieving a recorded scene from the brain and "playing it back." Rather, the mind actively constructs memory.

Constructive memory refers to an active process of integrating information from multiple sources. Sources of information include perceptions (vision, hearing, etc.), internal thoughts, and interactions with others. Over time, a memory can be reconstructed as new information is integrated with prior information to take the place of forgotten information.

Bartlett (1932) illustrated reconstructive memory by asking people to recall a story they had read. He found that they reconstructed the story so that it differed significantly from what they had originally read. During recall, the participants attempted to resolve ambiguities in the story and omitted significant details. The reconstructed versions became shorter, more stereotypical, and were reduced to a general setting. Bartlett noticed that people changed particular details depending on their beliefs and attitudes.

As a frequently cited example, Bartlett (1932) asked people to recall a folk story about two seal hunters who encounter a war party in canoes and an ensuing war on a neighboring village. During a series of reproductions, most participants dropped out the story title, proper names, numbers, the significance of ghosts, and the canoes. After 2½ years, one person gave the following short and sketchy reproduction:

> Some warriors went to wage war against the ghosts. They fought all day and one of their number was wounded. They returned home in the evening, bearing their sick comrade. As the day drew to a close, he became rapidly worse and the villagers came round him. At sunset he sighed: something black came out of his mouth. He was dead. (Bartlett, 1932, p. 75)

The deletion of certain details cannot be explained by a general failure to encode/store them. Indeed, after a long delay this reproduction still includes the original phrase, "something black came out of his mouth." Some participants easily recalled from the story popular words and phrases, comic words and events, personally relevant details, and other minor details. As the time delay increased, aspects of the story continued to be reconstructed. Participants who were from England changed aspects of the story to make it more familiar, for example, changing "canoe" to "boat" and "paddling" to "rowing." Bartlett concluded that participants unknowingly used their past experiences to construct a coherent story, but at the cost of accuracy. [*See the biography of Bartlett.*]

Mechanisms for Construction and Reconstruction

Describing this phenomenon, Bartlett (1932) borrowed the term *schema* to refer to mental representations of knowledge, which we construct through experience. For example, a schema for grocery shopping might include expectations about the appropriate sequence of events, such as obtaining a cart, selecting items, standing in line, and paying the cashier. However, Bartlett emphasized that schemas are not "lifeless, fixed, and unchangeable memory structures" (p. 33), but that they receive updates from incoming information. Schemas provide a processing advantage by efficiently accessing past experience for present use and flexibly accommodating unique details.

When an experience occurs, our knowledge can direct our attention to particular aspects of it so that our minds are not overloaded by encoding into long-term memory everything that bombards our senses. If we did not filter out some stimuli, a trip to the grocery store would be an overwhelming nightmare of sensory experiences. But typical grocery shopping behavior is relatively automatic: We do not have to rack our brains to remember to pay the cashier. This is made easy because the appropriate sequence of events is constructed in our memories. Although we often fail to encode details we expect, some counterintuitive details stand out that draw our attention and aid recall. For the most part, we behave relatively automatically because of the influence of schemas.

Whereas schemas allow a degree of cognitive efficiency, they can produce inaccuracies by biasing encoding, recall, and recognition. Schematic biases are based on stereotypes, expectations, goals, source misattributions, and the context of recall, both physical and historical.

Stereotypes. Social schemas or stereotypes can lead to biased memory reconstructions. Leichtman and Ceci (1995) told preschool children anecdotes about a prospective visitor's clumsiness. After the man's visit, children in this stereotype condition were more likely to recall falsely that he had behaved clumsily during his visit than did children who were not provided with the clumsy stereotype.

Expectations. The Bartlett (1932) example shows that during encoding and recall, expectations cause us to focus our attention on particular details. Expectations can be based on our implicit theories and attitudes about the world. In autobiographical memory, implicit theories can cause memory reconstruction when, for example, we consult our beliefs about how consistent

peoples' traits are over time (Ross, 1989). For example, studies have shown that people overestimate the positive effects of a learning skills program because they believe the program causes improvement. They therefore underestimate how good their study skills were before they began the program (Conway & Ross, 1984).

Similarly, women's recall of their moods during their menstrual cycle can be biased by their expectancies about their symptoms. In one study, women kept daily records of their physical and emotional symptoms over several weeks (McFarland, Ross, & DeCourville, 1989). Results showed that women who believed their periods to have a greater impact overestimated the negative symptoms during recall. This study shows how cultural biases can strongly influence individual memories by transmitting the theories on which personal memories become reconstructed. We apply our theories not only to ourselves, but also to other people. These influences may help us create a coherent autobiographical story line, but they exact their cost in the reduced accuracy of our memories.

Goals. During encoding we also filter out information, depending on our goal at the time. Studies show that people attend to different details depending on what their goal is. For example, when asked to draw a diagram of your neighborhood for a visiting friend, you might remember landmarks surrounding your house and the location of schools and parks. However, when drawing a diagram of your neighborhood for the city planning commission, you might suddenly remember the location of stoplights, mailboxes, and fire hydrants, which you previously did not remember.

Source Misattributions. In addition to expectancy and goal-related biases, source misattribution is another mechanism for memory reconstruction. Source misattribution refers to the inability to distinguish a memory's true origins by blending information from multiple sources. For example, an event may be familiar to us because we witnessed it on television, but we may misattribute its familiarity to actual experience. Likewise, we may misattribute something we heard to something we saw, or vice versa.

In a classic study of memory reconstruction, Loftus, Miller, and Burns (1978) showed that verbal information can later be integrated into a visual memory. They presented a series of slides that depicted a red car passing through an intersection and striking a pedestrian. A stop sign appeared at the intersection for half of the participants, and a yield sign appeared at the intersection for the other half. Afterward, the experimenters gave half of the students accurate verbal information concerning which sign they had seen, and gave the other half inaccurate information. During the recognition test that followed, students who received inaccurate information were less accurate recognizing which slide they had seen than were students who received accurate information. This study provided evidence that adults can absorb misleading information and use it to recall false details about a staged event that they have witnessed. More recent studies have shown that people also integrate misleading information into events that they have experienced themselves. Young children, particularly preschoolers, have also been shown to incorporate suggestions from others into memory (for a review, see Ceci & Bruck, 1993).

In addition, memory constructions can mingle information from our own thoughts and imaginations with reality. Remembering our third birthday party potentially involves a construction of accurate memory traces, imagined features, details from photographs, and stories repeated by parents and siblings. Once those sources are integrated into a coherent memory of the event, distinguishing reality from fantasy becomes nearly impossible without corroboration.

Context of Recall. Inaccuracies in memory may be due to the physical, social, and historical context of recall. For example, Ceci and Bruck (1993) reviewed evidence that children's memory can be altered by the interviewer's behavior, a form of social context. As an example of a physical context, when Loftus et al. (1978) had students draw diagrams of the car-pedestrian accident they had viewed, more students recalled a stop or yield sign at the intersection when the diagram included a car, which directed their attention to the intersection. Those who drew diagrams without the car present focused their attention on the crosswalk where the accident occurred, and significantly fewer reported seeing a sign. The car drew attention to the intersection and elicited different memories of what had occurred.

In a well-known example of a physical contextual effect, Baddeley (1990) found that words memorized while under water were better recalled when the participants were placed back under water than if they tried to recall them on dry land. Apparently, context is encoded with the content of a memory trace, and therefore, by reinstating it at retrieval, it facilitates the retrieval of the rest of the memory.

Finally, recent research has documented that the period of our lives associated with the largest numbers of retrievals—both accurate and inaccurate—is the so-called transition phase, from early teens to middle twenties (Belli, Schuman, & Jackson, 1997). When adults are asked to recollect memories associated with, say Joseph McCarthy or the Tet offensive, the most accurate ones are from individuals who were in the transition phase of their lives when the event occurred. The same is true of the least accurate memories. For example, respondents who erroneously claimed that Joseph McCarthy was the victim of a Communist witchhunt, rather than the senator who tried to expose Communists, were disproportionately in their transition years when the events in question occurred. Various theories of reconstructive memory have been posited to account for this effect, but there is no consensus.

Are reconstructed memories permanent? What happens to the original memory trace? Is it destroyed and overwritten by the new information, or do the two traces coexist in isolation, or do the two traces blend together and form a unique memory? There is some debate about whether or not false suggestions alter the original memory, or whether it temporarily interferes with recalling the memory (McCloskey & Zaragoza, 1985). Experimental evidence for memory blends between the actual event and misleading postevent information indicates that an original memory trace can be changed, although we cannot assume this happens in every case.

Conclusion

Although inaccuracies based on biased encoding and retrieval offer evidence for the constructive nature of memory, constructive processes do not necessarily lead to false memories. Recognizing a sample of speech as one's native language, recognizing entities in the world as familiar things, recalling autobiographical memories, and many other daily functions entail integrating incoming perceptual information with knowledge already stored in the brain, and the constructed results are typically accurate enough to allow us to survive and thrive.

Communities and cultures rely on long-term memories to glue together a coherent history and identity. These can be socially and cognitively constructed so that the results are less than accurate, and one social group remembers an event differently from another.

Although the constructive and reconstructive nature of memory poses risks for assessing the accuracy of a memory report, it provides critical flexibility to human cognition. This type of memory balances low-effort automatic processes with high-effort conscious recall in a way that economizes our limited cognitive resources to allow humans to experience the present in coherence with the past.

[*See also* Recovered Memories.]

Bibliography

Anderson, S. J., & Conway, M. A. (1997). Representations of autobiographical memories. In M. A. Conway (Ed.), *Cognitive models of memory* (pp. 217–246). Cambridge, MA: MIT Press.

Baddeley, A. (1990). *Human memory: Theory and practice.* Boston: Allyn & Bacon.

Bartlett, F. C. (1932). *Remembering.* Cambridge, England: Cambridge University Press.

Belli, R. F., Schuman, H., & Jackson, B. (1997). Autobiographical misremembering. *Applied Cognitive Psychology*, 11, 187–210.

Ceci, S. J., & Bruck, M. (1993). Suggestibility of the child witness: A historical review and synthesis. *Psychological Bulletin*, 113, 403–439.

Ceci, S. J., Huffman, M. L. C., Smith, E., & Loftus, E. F. (1994). Repeatedly thinking about a non-event: Source misattributions among preschoolers. *Consciousness and Cognition*, 3, 388–407.

Conway, M., & Ross, M. (1984). Getting what you want by revising what you had. *Journal of Personality and Social Psychology*, 47, 738–748.

Leichtman, M. D., & Ceci, S. J. (1995). The effects of stereotypes and suggestions on preschoolers' reports. *Developmental Psychology*, 31, 568–578.

Loftus, E. F., Miller, D. G., & Burns, H. J. (1978). Semantic integration of verbal information into a visual memory. *Journal of Experimental Psychology: Human Learning and Memory*, 4, 19–31.

McCloskey, M., & Zaragoza, M. (1985). Misleading postevent information and memory for events: Arguments and evidence against memory impairment hypotheses. *Journal of Experimental Psychology: General*, 114, 1–16.

McFarland, C., Ross, M., & DeCourville, N. (1989). Women's theories of menstruation and biases in recall of menstrual symptoms. *Journal of Personality and Social Psychology*, 57, 522–531.

Neisser, U., & Harsch, N. (1992). Phantom flashbulbs: False recollections of hearing the news about *Challenger*. In E. Winograd & U. Neisser (Eds.), *Affect and accuracy in recall: Studies of "flashbulb memories"* (pp. 9–31). Cambridge, England: Cambridge University Press.

Ross, M. (1989). Relation of implicit theories to the construction of personal histories. *Psychological Review*, 96, 341–357.

Elizabeth R. Grant and Stephen J. Ceci

Memory Systems

Memory is necessary for carrying out numerous functions that are essential to everyday life: recalling personal experiences, learning facts and conceptual knowledge, recognizing objects and people, and acquiring skills and habits. Scientific thinking about memory was dominated for decades by the assumption that memory is a unitary or monolithic entity. Although the assumption of a unitary memory system has been questioned from time to time, it has been seriously challenged and convincingly refuted: converging lines of evidence from psychology and neuroscience have revealed multiple memory systems that can be dissociated from one another.

Many researchers have distinguished among various types or forms of memory. For instance, recalling someone's name is different from recognizing it, and visual memories differ from auditory memories. Recently, many researchers have distinguished between recollection of everyday experiences, referred to as *explicit memory*, and nonconscious effects of past experiences on subsequent behavior, known as *implicit memory*. However, only some of these distinctions refer to different memory systems. Schacter and Tulving (1994) proposed that a *memory system* (a) is a set of interrelated brain processes that allow one to store and retrieve a specific type or class of information; (b) can be characterized in terms of lists of properties that describe its characteristic mode of operation; and (c) can be dissociated from other systems by converging evidence from psychology and neuroscience.

Five Major Memory Systems

Although concepts of memory systems are still evolving, converging evidence from psychology and neuroscience points toward at least five major systems: episodic memory, semantic memory (together referred to as *declarative memory*), perceptual representation system, procedural memory, and working memory.

Episodic Memory. As Tulving (1983) explained, the episodic memory system is responsible for the explicit recollection of incidents that occurred at a particular time and place in one's personal past. Damage to the medial or inner parts of the temporal lobes, including the hippocampal formation, greatly impairs the acquisition of new episodic memories. Individuals with amnesic syndromes produced by damage to the medial temporal region invariably have serious impairments of episodic memory: they are unable to remember ongoing events in their day-to-day lives, and perform poorly on laboratory tests that require episodic memory.

Regions within the prefrontal cortex play a key role in episodic memory. Although individuals with selective damage to prefrontal regions do not develop a profound amnesia for recent events, they have great difficulty remembering when and where recent events occurred. Damage to the frontal lobes can also yield distortions of episodic memory, in which patients claim to remember events that never occurred.

Recent neuroimaging studies of memory, measuring regional cerebral blood flow using positron emission tomography (PET) and functional magnetic resonance imaging (fMRI), have consistently revealed frontal lobe activation during episodic memory tasks. Right frontal regions have tended to show greater activation than left frontal regions during episodic retrieval, and left frontal regions have tended to show greater activation than right frontal regions during episodic encoding. Hippocampal activations have also been observed during encoding of information into episodic memory and also during retrieval of episodic memories. Somewhat surprisingly, however, quite a few neuroimaging studies have failed to report activation of the hippocampal formation, and researchers are still attempting to understand precisely why hippocampal activation is not always observed. Recent evidence suggests that the hippocampal formation tends to be most active during the actual recollection of that information, whereas prefrontal regions show maximal activation when volunteers make extensive efforts to recall recently presented information. Thus, prefrontal and medial temporal regions both play an important role in episodic memory, although the exact nature of their contributions remains to be determined.

Semantic Memory. Semantic memory refers to general knowledge of facts and concepts that is not linked to any particular time and place. Whereas episodic memory is critical for remembering a specific visit to the city of Paris, for example, semantic memory is important for knowing that Paris is the capital of France. The acquisition of new semantic memories (like the acquisition of new episodic memories) depends on the integrity of the medial temporal lobes. For instance, amnesic individuals have great difficulty acquiring new vocabulary and factual knowledge, although they can acquire large amounts of new semantic knowledge when that information is presented repeatedly.

Squire (1987) argued that the acquisition of new episodic and semantic memories both depend on the integrity of the medial temporal region and, hence, they can be referred to collectively as *declarative memory*. However, episodic and semantic memory can be dissociated from one another. For example, individuals characterized by the syndrome of semantic dementia exhibit poor knowledge of properties of specific objects, yet show generally intact episodic memory. Neuroimaging of such individuals indicates reduced metabolic activity and structural atrophy in the anterior and lateral regions of the temporal lobe, particularly in the left hemisphere. These findings thus suggest that anterolateral regions of temporal neocortex play an important role in the semantic memory system.

Perceptual Representation System. Tulving and Schacter (1990) argued that the perceptual representation system (PRS) plays an important role in the identification of words and objects on the basis of their form and structure. PRS operates at a presemantic level, and is not involved in representing associative or conceptual information, which is the province of semantic memory. They further distinguished among three major PRS subsystems: a visual word form subsystem that handles information concerning the visual features of words; an auditory word form system that handles phonological and acoustic information; and a structural description subsystem that handles information about the relations between parts of an object that specify its global form and structure.

PET scanning studies have revealed that specific regions within extrastriate occipital cortex are involved in processing and representing the visual form of words, whereas regions within temporal and frontal cortices are involved with word meaning. Likewise, evidence from studies of brain-lesioned monkeys and humans, as well as neuroimaging data, suggest that regions near the occipitotemporal junction, such as the inferior temporal gyrus and fusiform gyrus, are involved in representing the global structure of an object.

The PRS also appears to play a prominent role in the phenomenon of *priming*, which refers to changes in one's ability to identify a word or an object from reduced perceptual cues as a consequence of a recent exposure to it. Priming appears to operate nonconsciously, in the sense that people can exhibit effects of priming under conditions in which they lack explicit memory for having studied a word or object. Most importantly, individuals with amnesic syndromes exhibit intact priming across a wide variety of tasks, materials, and situations. These findings indicate that priming does not depend on the medial temporo-diencephalic structures that mediate explicit remembering, and are consistent with the idea that the posterior cortical regions that comprise the PRS are involved in priming. Neuroimaging studies of priming support this idea. Changes in the PRS that arise as a consequence of analyzing perceptual features of words or objects likely constitute the basis of many kinds of priming.

Procedural Memory. Procedural memory refers to the acquisition of skills and habits: knowing *how* rather than knowing *that*. Procedural memories are acquired gradually over time through repetitive practice. Amnesic individuals with a profound inability to remember past experiences explicitly can gradually acquire new perceptual, motor, and cognitive skills, habits that are involved in classification and categorization, and implicit knowledge of sequences or grammatical rules. These results show clearly that the acquisition of procedural knowledge does not depend on the medial temporal lobe structures, which are damaged in amnesic individuals. Likewise, studies with nonhuman animals have demonstrated that amnesic monkeys and rats with lesions in medial temporal structures can acquire new habits at a normal rate.

A variety of studies support the conclusion that procedural memory depends critically on a corticostriatal system. For instance, individuals with Huntington's disease, who are characterized by damage to the basal ganglia, have difficulties acquiring new motor skills despite relatively intact explicit memory: the exact opposite of the pattern exhibited by amnesic individuals (Salmon & Butters, 1995). Recent neuroimaging evidence also implicates the basal ganglia, as well as motor cortex, in procedural learning (see Cabeza & Nyberg, 1997). The cerebellum, too, is involved in some forms of procedural memory: Individuals with cerebellar damage have great difficulty learning how to execute sequences of movements. None of these structures is usually impaired in amnesic individuals, thus further supporting the conclusion that procedural memory depends on a different system than does either episodic or semantic memory.

Working Memory. The memory systems considered so far are all concerned with long-term retention, spanning time periods of minutes, hours, weeks, and years. In contrast, the system known as *working memory* is concerned with short-term retention, operating over periods of seconds. The working memory system is used to hold information on-line in the service of such basic cognitive activities as comprehending, reasoning, and problem solving. The concept of working memory emerged from debates in cognitive psychology during the 1960s concerning short-term versus long-term memory. Studies of amnesic individuals revealed that they maintained intact abilities to remember immediately small strings of digits, despite their difficulties with long-term retention. However, other individuals exhibited the opposite pattern: severely impaired short-term retention of digits and related kinds of verbal information despite a relatively normal ability to acquire new long-term memories. Such individuals typically have lesions in a specific part of the left parietal lobe known as the supramarginal gyrus. Although these findings strengthened the distinction between short-term and long-term memory, they also indicated that information could enter long-term memory even when short-term memory was profoundly impaired.

Baddeley (1986) explained this pattern of findings by postulating a working memory system that consists of three components: a central executive, or limited-capacity work space, and two "slave" subsystems that support it. One subsystem, called the *phonological loop*, allows for rehearsal or recycling of small amounts of speech-based information, but is not necessary for entering information into long-term memory. According to Baddeley, it is this subsystem that is impaired in individuals who exhibit faulty immediate retention yet show normal long-term memory. This idea has received some confirmation from recent neuroimaging research indicating that the supramarginal gyrus is activated when people perform working-memory tasks designed to tap the phonological loop. The second slave subsystem of working memory, named the *visuospatial sketch pad*, was held to be involved in the short-term retention of visual and spatial information. Recent evidence from brain-damaged individuals and PET scans suggests that a variety of regions in the right hemisphere, including visual association cortex, inferior parietal lobule, and inferior prefrontal cortex, are important components of the visuospatial sketch pad.

One emerging point of consensus is that the prefrontal cortex plays a crucial role in working memory. For example, individuals with lesions to the dorsolateral prefrontal cortex are impaired on a task in which they hold in working memory recently presented pictures while attempting to point to new pictures they had not just seen. When healthy volunteers perform the same task, PET scans have revealed areas of increased blood flow within the dorsolateral prefrontal region. Likewise, studies of monkeys by Patricia Goldman-Rakic and her colleagues (Levy & Goldman-Rakic, 1999) have shown that specific neurons within the dorsolateral prefrontal cortex remain active during the delay period of a working memory task in which animals must hold in mind the location of a recently presented object. Studies of both humans and animals support the conclusion that working memory is a distinct system that depends on interactions between areas in the dorsolateral prefrontal area and specific posterior cortical regions.

Concluding Comments

Research concerning memory systems is still at an early stage. The distinctions discussed here will surely be modified as research progresses, and they do not capture all relevant memory phenomena. For example, Ledoux (1996) explained how recent studies of emotional memory have highlighted a special role for the amygdala, which may constitute the anatomical substrate of an additional memory system specifically concerned with emotional experiences. This observation strengthens and expands the fundamental insight of modern cognitive neuroscience that the concept of memory includes a variety of different ways in which the brain adapts and changes as a result of experience.

Bibliography

Baddeley, A. (1986). *Working memory*. New York: Oxford University Press.

Baddeley, A. D., Wilson, B. A., & Watts, F. N. (1995). *Handbook of memory disorders*. New York: Wiley. Brings together a variety of chapters that describe the breakdown of different memory systems in a wide range of neurological and psychiatric conditions.

Cabeza, R., & Nyberg, L. (1997). Imaging cognition: An empirical review of PET studies with normal subjects. *Journal of Cognitive neuroscience, 9*, 1–26. A comprehensive review of studies that use modern brain-imaging techniques (positron emission tomography and functional magnetic resonance imaging) to analyze memory and other cognitive processes.

Graf, P., & Masson, M. E. J. (1993). *Implicit memory: New directions in cognition, development, and neuropsychology*. Hillsdale, NJ: Erlbaum. A variety of articles examines memory systems involved in both implicit and explicit forms of memory in young children, elderly adults, and hospitalized populations.

Ledoux, J. (1996). *The emotional brain*. New York: Simon & Schuster.

Levy, R., & Goldman-Rakic, P. S. (1999). Association of

storage and processing functions in the dorsolateral, prefrontal cortex of the nonhuman primate. *Journal of Neuroscience, 19,* 5147–5148.

Mayes, A. R., & Downes, J. J. (Eds.). (1997). *Theories of organic amnesia.* Sussex, England: Psychology Press. A collection of articles that explore memory systems by examining how they break down in the amnesic syndrome, which is characterized by impairment of the episodic and semantic memory systems.

Roediger, H. L., III, & McDermott, K. B. (1993). Implicit memory in normal human subjects. In H. Spinnler & F. Boller (Eds.), *Handbook of neuropsychology* (Vol. 8, pp. 63–131). Amsterdam: Elsevier. A thorough review of studies that contrast implicit and explicit forms of memory in healthy volunteers.

Salmon, D. P., & Butters, N. (1995). Neurobiology of skill and habit learning. *Current Opinion in Neurobiology, 5,* 184–190. A brief but informative survey of research examining the procedural memory system in brain-damaged individuals and healthy volunteers.

Schacter, D. L. (1996). *Searching for memory: The brain, the mind, and the past.* New York: Basic Books. An accessible overview of modern memory research that emphasizes distinctions among memory systems and their implications for understanding memory in everyday life.

Schacter, D. L., Chiu, C. Y. P., & Ochsner, K. N. (1993). Implicit memory: A selective review. *Annual Review of Neuroscience, 16,* 159–182. A review of memory systems that are involved in priming and other forms of implicit memory, integrating results from brain-damaged and healthy populations.

Schacter, D. L., Coyle, J. T., Fischbach, G. D., Mesulam, M. M., & Sullivan, L. E. (Eds.). (1995). *Memory distortion: How minds, brains, and societies reconstruct the past.* Cambridge, MA: Harvard University Press. Contributions from psychologists, neurobiologists, and historians examine inaccuracy in memory, with particularly relevant chapters by James McClelland, Morris Moscovitch, and Larry Squire exploring how different memory systems may contribute to distorted recollections.

Schacter, D. L., & Tulving, E. (1994). What are the memory systems of 1994? In D. L. Schacter & E. Tulving (Eds.), *Memory Systems 1994* (pp. 1–38). Cambridge, MA: MIT Press.

Smith, E. E., & Jonides, J. (1997). Working memory: A view from neuroimaging. *Cognitive Psychology, 33,* 5–42. A comprehensive summary of studies that have investigated the working memory system using neuroimaging techniques.

Squire, L. R. (1987). *Memory and brain.* New York: Oxford University Press.

Squire, L. R., & Butters, N. (1992). *Neuropsychology of memory.* New York: Guilford Press. Brings together contributions from neuropsychologists and neurobiologists that examine how different memory systems are realized in the brain.

Tulving, E. (1983). *Elements of episodic memory.* New York: Oxford University Press.

Tulving, E., & Schacter, D. L. (1990). Priming and human memory systems. *Science, 247,* 301–306.

Ungerleider, L. G. (1995). Functional brain imaging studies of cortical mechanisms for memory. *Science, 270,* 760–775. A review of studies that have used brain imaging to examine different memory systems.

Daniel L. Schacter

Memory and Aging

The field of psychology focusing on the aging of human memory is a large, diverse, and active one. It is characterized by multiple legitimate theoretical perspectives, research designs, measurement challenges, empirical phenomena, and practical considerations. Neighboring and influential fields include cognitive psychology, life span developmental psychology, social-cognitive psychology, clinical neuropsychology, and the neurosciences.

Rationale and Research Questions in Memory and Aging

Numerous comprehensive reviews have been published (e.g., Bäckman, Small, & Larsson, in press; Craik, Anderson, Kerr, & Li, 1995; Craik & Jennings, 1992; Hultsch & Dixon, 1990; Kausler, 1994; Light, 1992). Although these reviewers maintain divergent perspectives and research priorities, some commonality in rationale and coverage is apparent.

For decades, research in human aging has been concerned with characterizing change in terms of gains (or growth) and losses (or decline). Among the principal foci of this discussion are cognitive processes and skills, especially memory. A tripartite foundation for the continually accelerating research interest in memory and aging has included basic science questions (e.g., what changes and why), practical implications (e.g., can memory be improved), and human interest concerns. The latter refers to a central rationale presented by recent reviewers. With some validity, many adults believe that, whereas memory abilities improve through childhood, they decline with aging (e.g., Ryan, 1992). Because memory is viewed as a functional, if not essential, tool of successful development, researchers and lay adults are profoundly interested in whether their and others' memory abilities decline with aging.

Three traditional sets of research questions are pursued. First, descriptive questions predominate: Does memory performance change with aging? If so, in what directions? Are there differential patterns across individuals, cohorts, or memory variables? Second, explanatory questions are increasingly posed: How and why do observed changes occur? What mechanisms are responsible for universal and differential change? Can explanatory factors ranging from biological, cognitive, and sociocultural be separately and interactively linked to memory aging? Third, intervention questions are of growing interest: To what extent and through what mechanisms may effects of memory aging be altered or ameliorated? Is memory plasticity equivalent in younger and older adults? What are the limits to such plasticity?

Despite formidable research accomplishments, fresh and sophisticated theoretical and methodological approaches are required (e.g., Salthouse, 1991). Four abiding challenges to theoretical progress may be noted. First, much descriptive data are derived from cross-sectional studies of age differences rather than longitudinal studies of age changes. Age-related profiles may vary according to research design (e.g., Hultsch, Hertzog, Dixon, & Small, 1998). Second, the wide range of human memory phenomena has not been exhaustively or evenly explored. Some disparate patterns of aging-related effects have been observed. Third, the phenomena of memory aging may be multiply determined, linked to causal processes and networks operating at different levels of analysis (e.g., biological, sociocultural). Fourth, extant theories may be improved in precision, comprehensiveness, and testability (e.g., Light, 1991).

Selected Research and Theoretical Perspectives

Research on memory and aging reveals provocative patterns of results. Whereas some tasks are associated with robust findings of age-related deficits, other tasks are associated with less pronounced losses or even equivalent performance by younger and older adults. Tasks typically associated with losses include remembering lists of information, expository texts, picture characteristics, spatial locations, and those that tap working memory. Tasks often associated with relatively unimpaired performance include implicit memory, facts and knowledge, and those that reflect familiar situations or include substantial environmental support. What theories have been marshaled to account for the diverse patterns? Two well-developed theoretical models, the memory systems perspective and the memory process perspective, have been especially influential in research on memory and aging.

Memory Systems Perspective. Positing that there are five systems of memory, a central goal of this perspective is to explicate the organization of the systems. A memory system is defined as a set of related processes, linked by common brain mechanisms, information processed, and operational principles (Schacter & Tulving, 1994). *Procedural memory* is reflected in the gradual learning (through practice) of cognitive and behavioral skills. *Perceptual representation* is a system involved in identifying words and objects (viz., implicit memory, priming). *Semantic memory* is expressed

through the acquisition and retention of generic facts, knowledge, and beliefs. The terms, *short-term, primary,* or *working memory,* reflect the fact that some expressions of memory are temporary or still in consciousness. *Episodic memory* refers to memory for personally experienced events or information.

A common expectation is that procedural memory is relatively unaffected by aging. The few age comparative experiments that have been conducted, however, are inconclusive. Current research focuses on whether (a) memory for already acquired skills is affected by aging; (b) the acquisition of new skills is affected by aging; (c) the effects vary by task (e.g., in that speeded skills are more likely to be affected); and (d) neurological and sensory decrements influence procedural memory aging.

Regarding the perceptual representation system, cross-sectional priming research has shown small apparent effects of aging, with older adults less likely than younger adults to show a beneficial effect—and more likely to show a negative effect—of prior presentation (e.g., Howard, 1996). Several qualifications apply. First, age-related deficits may be more likely observed when the task allows for explicit, intentional memory to contaminate implicit memory effects. Second, distinctions are drawn among types of priming processes, including those involving primarily conceptual (e.g., fact completion) versus perceptual (e.g., word stem completion) processes. Age differences may be smaller for some aspects of the latter (e.g., those requiring automatic alterations of perceptual pathways) and larger for the former (e.g., those requiring new conceptual links).

Regarding semantic memory, at least until very late life, older adults typically remember as much information as younger adults on tests of general world knowledge, facts, words, concepts, and associations (cf. crystallized intelligence). In addition, older adults display similar knowledge structures or associative networks. Nevertheless, some studies have suggested that older adults may access such information more slowly and with more frequent blockages than younger adults.

Some aspects of the short-term memory system appear to be relatively well preserved in old age, whereas others show substantial aging-related decline. Because information in primary memory (e.g., ordered repetition of a list of items) is maintained briefly and passively, older adults often perform as well as younger adults. In contrast, because information in working memory must be manipulated or processed more extensively, such tasks are quite sensitive to age differences (e.g., Salthouse, 1991).

The latest developing memory system is the episodic memory system (e.g., memory for words, texts, pictures, and faces). Across multiple experimental manipulations and controls, older adults commonly perform worse than younger adults. Recent research has targeted potential moderating factors, including education, health, lifestyle activities, level of environmental support, biological processes, and ecological relevance of the tasks (e.g., Bäckman et al., in press). To date, no persuasive case has been made that there are systematic exceptions to the rule of decline in episodic memory performance.

In general, a key descriptive question is whether the systems are differentially vulnerable to normal aging. A subsequent explanatory question concerns the extent to which this distribution is robust, coherent, and can be linked to potential explanatory factors (e.g., in the brain mechanisms, information processed, or operational principles underlying the systems). Detailed reviews are available.

Memory Process Perspective. This perspective characterizes memory as an interaction between relatively internal remembering operations, stored experience, and external environmental stimuli and constraints (e.g., Craik et al., 1995). The focus is on identifying the processing operations (rather than memory systems) that are at the source of aging-related decrements. Specifically, memory decrements may be a function of the extent to which difficult, effortful, self-initiated processing is required. Reviews cover research overlapping with that represented in the memory systems perspective. Whereas larger age differences are found for performance on tasks requiring greater self-initiated processing, smaller age differences are found for tasks in which more environmental support is provided. Theoretically, declining resources for effortful self-initiated cognitive processing may account for memory deficits with aging.

Emerging Directions of Research

Although it is hazardous to forecast future developments, some especially promising research directions include: (a) new initiatives incorporating a wider range of correlated and explanatory domains; and (b) novel applications of sophisticated change-oriented research designs.

New Domains. Researchers have considered a broader range of memory domains, neighboring disciplines, and levels of analysis. At a biological level of analysis, recent research on memory correlates of aging-related changes in sensory functioning (e.g., Baltes & Lindenberger, 1997), brain activation patterns (e.g., Bäckman et al., 1997), and neuropsychological conditions (e.g., Moscovitch & Winocur, 1992) have appeared. At a cognitive level, domains such as working memory, information-processing speed, processing resources, and inhibitory control abilities have accounted for age-related variance in memory performance (e.g., Craik et al., 1995; Salthouse, 1991). Novel memory phenomena (e.g., prospective memory) have also been explored. At still another level of analysis, recent progress in examining the role of background characteristics or parallel processes such as gender, health, lifestyle and activities, personality, and metacognition have been reported (e.g., Herlitz, Nilsson, & Bäckman, 1997; Hultsch & Dixon, 1990). Similarly, new efforts to examine performance in conditions representative of those in which older adults typically execute memory tasks (e.g., Hertzog & Dunlosky, 1996), such as in collaborative or interactive situations (e.g., Dixon, 1996), have been marshaled. Further advances will be made by selectively combining these and other factors at a variety of levels.

Developmental Designs. Although the premise of aging research is that the results represent aging-related changes, studies actually examining change directly are relatively rare. Nevertheless, two types of change-structured studies have been conducted, and should be further encouraged. First, longitudinal studies, in which groups of individuals are tested on multiple occasions over time, have proven to be especially useful for charting aging-related changes (description), delineating individual differences in change patterns, and elucidating causal factors (explanation) of memory-aging phenomena (e.g., Hultsch et al., 1998; Zelinski, Gilewski, & Schaie, 1993). Complementary multiple-occasion designs and case studies, in which the focus is on individual-level change and variability, make useful contributions.

Second, intervention studies in which the plasticity of memory is investigated originate in two related concerns. First, memory intervention research addresses (a) whether and how much normal older adults can improve memory performance if given appropriate training or practice; and (b) how differential or generalizable (across tasks and individuals) the effects of intervention are. At present, older adults are capable of impressive memory feats, although the training appears to be relatively domain specific (e.g., Kliegl, Smith, & Baltes, 1989). Second, a complementary focus of intervention research concerns the special case of older adults with impaired memory. Specifically, can training programs be designed to ameliorate the everyday memory performance of older adults who have experienced accelerated memory decline, whether as a function of an accident or a progressive neurological condition? Such research requires multiple occasions of assessment, and often novel assessment techniques. To date, under some limiting conditions, such compensatory interventions are possible (e.g., Dixon & Bäckman, 1995; Wilson & Watson, 1996).

Bibliography

Bäckman, L., Almkvist, O., Andersson, J., Nordberg, A., Winblad, B., Reinick, R., & Långström, B. (1997). Brain activation in young and older adults during implicit and explicit retrieval. *Journal of Cognitive Neuroscience*, 9, 378–391.

Bäckman, L., Small, B. J., & Larsson, M. (in press). Memory. In J. G. Evans, T. F. Williams, B. L. Beattie, J-P. Michel, & G. K. Wilcock (Eds.), *Oxford textbook of geriatric medicine*. Oxford, England: Oxford University Press.

Baltes, P. B., & Lindenberger, U. (1997). Emergence of a powerful connection between sensory and cognitive functions across the adult life span: A new window to the study of aging. *Psychology and Aging, 12*, 12–21.

Craik, F. I. M., Anderson, N. D., Kerr, S. A., & Li, K. Z. H. (1995). Memory changes in normal ageing. In A. D. Baddeley, B. A. Wilson, & F. N. Watts (Eds.), *Handbook of memory disorders* (pp. 211–241). Chichester, England: Wiley.

Craik, F. I. M., & Jennings, J. M. (1992). Human memory. In F. I. M. Craik & T. A. Salthouse (Eds.), *Handbook of aging and cognition* (pp. 51–100). Hillsdale, NJ: Erlbaum.

Dixon, R. A. (1996). Collaborative memory and aging. In D. J. Herrmann, M. K. Johnson, C. L. McEvoy, C. Hertzog, & P. Hertel (Eds.), *Basic and applied memory: Theory in context* (pp. 359–383). Mahwah, NJ: Erlbaum.

Dixon, R. A., & Bäckman, L. (Eds.). (1995). *Compensating for psychological deficits and declines: Managing losses and promoting gains*. Mahwah, NJ: Erlbaum.

Herlitz, A., Nilsson, L-G., & Bäckman, L. (1997). Gender differences in episodic memory. *Memory & Cognition, 25*, 801–811.

Hertzog, C., & Dunlosky, J. (1996). The aging of practical memory: An overview. In D. J. Herrmann, M. K. Johnson, C. L. McEvoy, C. Hertzog, & P. Hertel (Eds.), *Basic and applied memory: Theory in context* (pp. 337–358). Hillsdale, NJ: Erlbaum.

Howard, D. V. (1996). The aging of implicit and explicit memory. In F. Blanchard-Fields & T. M. Hess (Eds.), *Perspectives on cognitive change in adulthood and aging* (pp. 221–254). New York: McGraw-Hill.

Hultsch, D. F., & Dixon, R. A. (1990). Learning and memory in aging. In J. E. Birren & K. W. Schaie (Eds.), *Handbook of the psychology of aging* (3rd ed., pp. 258–274). San Diego, CA: Academic Press.

Hultsch, D. F., Hertzog, C., Dixon, R. A., & Small, B. J. (1998). *Memory change in the aged*. Cambridge, England: Cambridge University Press.

Kausler, D. H. (1994). *Learning and memory in normal aging*. San Diego, CA: Academic Press.

Kliegl, R., Smith, J., & Baltes, P. B. (1989). Testing-the-limits and the study of adult age differences in cognitive plasticity of a mnemonic skill. *Developmental Psychology, 25*, 247–256.

Light, L. L. (1991). Memory and aging: Four hypotheses in search of data. *Annual Review of Psychology, 42*, 333–376.

Light, L. L. (1992). The organization of memory in old age. In F. I. M. Craik & T. A. Salthouse (Eds.), *The handbook of aging and cognition* (pp. 111–165). Hillsdale, NJ: Erlbaum.

Moscovitch, M., & Winocur, G. (1992). The neuropsychology of memory and aging. In F. I. M. Craik & T. A. Salthouse (Eds.), *The handbook of aging and cognition* (pp. 315–372). Hillsdale, NJ: Erlbaum.

Ryan, E. B. (1992). Beliefs about memory changes across the adult life span. *Journal of Gerontology: Psychological Sciences, 47*, 41–46.

Salthouse, T. A. (1991). *Theoretical perspectives on cognitive aging*. Hillsdale, NJ: Erlbaum.

Schacter, D. L. & Tulving, E. (1994). What are the memory systems of 1994? In D. L. Schacter & E. Tulving (Eds.), *Memory systems 1994* (pp. 1–38). Cambridge, MA: MIT Press.

Wilson, B. A., & Watson, P. C. (1996). A practical framework for understanding compensatory behaviour in people with organic memory impairment. *Memory, 4*, 456–486.

Zelinski, E. M., Gilewski, M. J., & Schaie, K. W. (1993). Individual differences in cross-sectional and 3-year longitudinal memory performance across the adult life span. *Psychology and Aging, 8*, 176–186.

Roger A. Dixon

Brain Systems

It now seems clear that various forms and aspects of learning and memory involve particular systems, networks, and circuits in the brain. In the broadest sense, learning can be defined as changes in behavior and awareness as a result of experience, excluding effects of damage, drugs, and so on. Memory is simply the awareness and/or the expression in behavior of what has been learned. A major distinction is made between short-term and long-term memory.

Short-Term Memory

William James first distinguished between short-term memory, which lasts only briefly, and long-term, or relatively permanent, memory. Short-term memory is sometimes termed *working memory*, and generally refers to holding new sequences of digits (e.g., new telephone number) new phrases, new names, and the like, briefly in memory. The magic number, 7 ± 2, describes the novel sequence of digits that can be accurately held in short-term memory for a period of seconds, without rehearsal. In a very real sense, short-term or working memory is equivalent to the contents of consciousness: It is what we are aware of at any given moment in time. Short-term memory not only holds new information, but also information retrieved from long-term or permanent memory. Baddeley (1981) described short-term memory as scratch-pad memory.

It seems clear that the cerebral cortex is the brain substrate for short-term memory. There are several different forms or aspects of short-term memory. Warrington and Weiskrantz (1973) described individuals with selective deficits either in visual short-term memory or in auditory short-term memory; in both types of cases, long-term memory ability was intact. The critical lesions appear to be in posterior visual and auditory association areas.

The prefrontal areas of the cerebral cortex (particularly the region in the sulcus principalis) have been known for many years to be critical for delayed response performance, particularly (for monkeys) for remembering briefly where an object is in space. Recent work suggests that an adjacent area of prefrontal cortex is critical for short-term memory of objects (i.e., what they are; Goldman-Rakic, 1992). Mishkin, Ungerleider, and Macko (1983) identified two visual streams of information flowing from the primary occipital visual region: a ventral stream ending in the anterior temporal lobe cortex concerned with object identification, and a dorsal stream ending in parietal cortex more concerned with object location in space. These two regions are closely interconnected with the prefrontal short-term object and location memory regions, respectively.

Long-Term Memory

The diagram in Figure 1 illustrates a current view of the categories of long-term memory and their putative brain substrates.

Nonassociative Memory. Nonassociative learning and memory refers to changes in already existing responses to stimuli, as in reflex responses, fixed-action patterns, and so forth. The two major phenomena are *habituation*, a decrease in response to repeated stimulation, and *sensitization*, an increase in response to a (usually strong or salient) stimulus.

In the case of habituation of preexisting responses (e.g., reflexes, fixed-action patterns), the brain processes responsible for the behavioral response decrement with repeated stimulation are embedded in the particular stimulus-response circuits that generate the response. It appears that a process of decrease in the probability of transmitter released as a result of repeated stimulation is the underlying synaptic event. Sensitization, on the other hand, involves a process of increased probability of transmitter release at the sensitized synapses (Kandel, 1975; Thompson & Spencer, 1966).

Basic Associative Memory. Basic associative learning involves forming associations between stimuli or between stimuli and responses. The two major categories are *classical* (or Pavlovian) conditioning and instrumental learning. *Classical conditioning* is most generally defined as a procedure by which an experimenter presents participants with stimuli that occur in some prearranged relationship and measures changes in responding to one of them. The conditioned stimulus (CS) typically is paired with, and precedes, the unconditioned stimulus (US). The conditioned stimulus does not elicit the response to be learned before training and the unconditioned stimulus reliably elicits a readily measured response, the reflex or unconditioned response

(UR). Changes in participants' behavior to the conditioned stimulus over the course of training, the conditioned response (CR), reflects associative learning. In order for significant learning to occur, contiguity of conditioned stimulus and unconditioned stimulus, per se, is not sufficient; there must also be a significant contingency of occurrence between the two events. Associatively produced changes in participants' behavior are said to reflect their learning about the causal texture of the environment.

Basic associative memory involves several categories and several corresponding brain systems. For classical conditioning of discrete behavioral responses (e.g., eyeblink, limb flexion) the cerebellar system is essential, and the memory traces appear to be formed and stored in the cerebellum in both humans and other mammals. Classical conditioning of fear (evidenced by freezing or autonomic responses like increased heart rate) critically involves the amygdala. Interestingly, neurons in the hippocampus also become involved in basic associative learning. Under some circumstances all these brain systems can become engaged in basic associative learning. Thus, in classical conditioning, if a sufficiently aversive unconditioned stimulus is used (e.g., shock to the skin around the eye to elicit a strong blink), then the cerebellum is critically engaged (learning the blink response), the amygdala is critically engaged (learned fear), and neurons in the hippocampus are also engaged (Berger, Alger, & Thompson, 1976; Davis 1992; Thompson & Krupa, 1994).

The defining feature of *instrumental learning* is that the behavior of the organism is instrumental in determining the outcome of the situation. Virtually all aspects of learning in nonhuman animals other than classical conditioning can be forced into this category, but such is probably an oversimplification. Basic paradigms range from presenting a conditioned stimulus that signals the opportunity to make a response, for example, press a lever to receive food or avoid shock, to learning a maze for food reward or to escape an aversive situation, to learning to delay a response to receive a reward, and so on. Little is known about the brain substrates of most of these paradigms, particularly for instrumental reward.

Declarative and Procedural Memory. Additional categories of learning have derived largely from work with humans and other primates. This is particularly true of the broad distinction between *declarative* (explicit or "what") memory and *procedural* (implicit or "how") memory, where part of the distinction depends on awareness (declarative) versus nonawareness (procedural). Actually, declarative is a more consistent category. In addition to awareness, it involves very rapid one-trial learning (as in our memories of our life experience) and recognition memory (as in delayed nonmatching to sample in monkeys). Even here, dis-

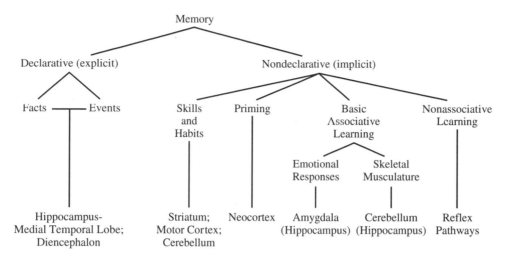

MEMORY: Brain Systems. Figure 1. A view of major categories of memory and the brain structures that seem to be involved.

tinctions are made between *episodic memory* (one's life experiences) and *semantic memory* (one's vocabulary, general knowledge, etc.). It is important to stress that episodic memory of one's past experience is not at all like a video recording. Such memories are dynamic, fragmented, and can be modified by subsequent experience.

On the other hand, procedural is much more of a grab bag category. In addition to nonassociative learning and basic associative learning (classical and instrumental conditioning), it includes priming and motor skills. Priming really refers to the procedure used to measure it, namely, humans are given words to learn, then tested by presenting, for example, the first two letters of the word, the priming stimulus, and asked simply to say any word (with appropriate controls for guessing frequencies, etc.). This aspect of learning can occur without awareness, hence it is placed in the procedural category. *Motor skills* can be included in instrumental learning, particularly for animal studies, but complex motor skills like talking and playing musical instruments are best viewed as a separate category.

The notion of declarative or explicit memory evolved from studies of humans with a particular form of amnesia resulting from bilateral damage to the temporal lobes (HM, a patient with severe declarative amnesia, is the classic original case). The hallmark of this amnesia is the inability to form new verbal-declarative memories (anterograde amnesia). Prior semantic knowledge and ability to form procedural memories (e.g., classical conditioning, motor skills) are intact. Although there is some debate, such individuals do appear to have intact memories for their own life experiences (episodic memory) prior to some period before the brain injury: temporally graded retrograde amnesia. In

both humans and monkeys, the key structures include the hippocampus and related cortical areas in the temporal lobe (Mishkin, 1978; Zola-Morgan & Squire, 1993). A major reason to identify priming (see Figure 1) as a separate procedural aspect of memory is that it appears to be normal in these amnestic individuals. Positron emission tomography (PET) studies in humans, as well as studies of humans with brain damage, have implicated visual areas of the neocortex in visual priming memory.

Similar forms of amnesia can be produced by hippocampal lesions in basic associative learning in lower mammals (e.g., conditioned fear to context in rats; trace conditioning of discrete responses in rabbits; radial arm maze and Morris water maze in rats, etc.). There are other conditions and other forms of brain damage in humans that can yield various aspects of amnesia, for example, Korsakoff's syndrome, Alzheimer's disease, medial thalamic damage. Much remains to be learned.

There is much cause for optimism in the broad field concerned with learning and memory and its neurobiological substrates, although major categories of learning have only been lightly touched upon here. The study of human learning and memory, in particular, has a richness and complexity that cannot be captured in brief definitional articles.

Bibliography

Baddeley, A. D. (1981). A concept of working memory: A view of its current state and probable future development. *Cognition, 10,* 17–23.

Berger, T. W., Alger, B. E., & Thompson, R. F. (1976). Neuronal substrate of classical conditioning in the hippocampus. *Science, 192,* 483–485.

Davis, M. (1992). The role of the amygdala in fear and anxiety. *Annual Review of Neuroscience, 15,* 353–375.

Goldman-Rakic, P. S. (1992). Working memory and the mind. *Scientific American, 267,* 111–117.

Hearst, E. (1975). The classical-instrumental distinction: Reflexes, voluntary behavior, and categories of associative learning. In W. K. Estes (Ed.), *Handbook of learning and cognitive processes* (Vol. 2). Hillsdale NJ: Erlbaum.

James, W. (1890). *The principles of psychology.* New York: Holt.

Kandel, E. R. (1975). *The cerebellar basis of behavior: An introduction to behavioral neurobiology.* New York: Freeman.

Mishkin, M. (1978). Memory in makeup severely impaired by combined but not separate removal of amygdala and hippocampus. *Nature, 273,* 297–298.

Mishkin, M., Ungerleider, L. G., & Macko, K. A. (1983). Object vision and spatial vision: Two cortical pathways. *Trends in Neuroscience, 6,* 414–417.

Rescorla, R. A. (1988). Behavioral studies of Pavlovian conditioning. *Annual Review of Neuroscience, 11,* 329–352.

Schacter, D. L., Chiu, C-Y. P., & Ochsner, K. N. (1993). Implicit memory: A selective review. *Annual Review of Neuroscience, 16,* 159–182.

Thompson, R. F., Donegan, N. H., & Lavond, D. G. (1986). The psychobiology of learning and memory. In R. C. Atkinson, R. J., Hernstein, G. Lindzey, & R. D Luce (Eds). *Steven's handbook of experimental psychology* (2nd ed.). New York: Wiley.

Thompson, R. F., & Krupa, D. J. (1994). Organization of memory traces in the mammalian brain. *Annual Review of Neuroscience, 17,* 519–549.

Thompson, R. F., & Spencer, W. A. (1966). Habituation: A model phenomenon for the study of neuronal substrates of behavior. *Psychological Review, 173,* 16–43.

Warrington, E. K., & Weiskrantz, L. (1973). Analysis of short-term and long-term memory defects in man. In J. A. Deutsch (Ed.), *The physiological basis of memory.* San Diego, CA: Academic Press.

Zola-Morgan, S., & Squire, L. R. (1993). Neuroanatomy of memory. *Annual Review of Neuroscience, 16,* 547–563.

Richard F. Thompson

MEMORY TRACE. *See the overview article on* Memory.

MENARCHE. *See* Menstruation.

MENOPAUSE. Although menopause refers to the cessation of menstruation, a singularly biological event, the experience of menopause encompasses far more than biology. In Western cultures, menopause is often approached with feelings of dread and loss, since traditionally women have been valued for their physical attractiveness and their biological capacity for bearing and raising children.

During the menopausal transition, levels of estrogen and progesterone gradually decrease and levels of follicle stimulating hormone (FSH) and luteinizing hormone (LH) gradually increase. While cyclic fluctuations continue, they become unpredictable and disassociated with fertility. After the menopausal transition and during the postmenstrual years, the ovaries continue to secrete small amounts of estrogen and androgens, and some androgens are converted to estrogen in adipose tissue. The normal hormonal profile of menopause is one of low and stable levels of estrogen, an absence of progesterone, and high and stable levels of FSH and LH. In contrast, surgical removal of the ovaries produces an abrupt menopause, and the hormones secreted by the ovaries after natural menopause are absent.

Midlife changes in women are appropriately studied in several disciplines besides psychology, including medicine, sociology, and anthropology. Each discipline offers its unique perspective. Medicine views midlife changes in women as being due to decreasing levels of estrogen. Psychology attributes transitional difficulties to stress, poor coping responses, and/or personality problems predating menopause. A sociological perspective focuses on changing roles, poverty, physical health, and institutionalized sexism, and anthropologists study midlife developments in the context of a culture's valuation of women, aging, and fertility. In the last decade, there has been a surge of interest in the biological or medical view of menopause, not because the medical perspective is necessarily more valid or more relevant than the other models, but because the medical community and pharmaceutical industry have invested considerable resources in promoting menopause as a medical disorder requiring physician assistance and pharmaceutical remedies.

Research has been conducted within the context of each of these disciplines with surprisingly consistent results. In general, the evidence suggests that hot flashes, slowed sexual arousal, and, to some extent, osteoporosis are caused by the changing hormonal environment of menopause, whereas other physical and psychological complaints, such as heart disease, depression, irritability, fatigue, and wrinkling are due to aging or to historical, cultural, social, and stress factors. Furthermore, many changes and complaints of midlife have multiple causes. For example, the experience of hot flashes during the night may cause insomnia, which, in turn, may cause irritability and depression. Menopause and midlife are also associated with positive changes and benefits. In spite of the potential for new and severe stressors, midlife frequently brings an emerging sense of freedom from caring for children and from conforming to the cultural ideal of womanhood, a freedom likely to improve psychological well-being.

Historically, menopause and the midlife period in women have been assumed to be associated with depression, irritability, and anxiety. However, surveys of psychological problems in women across the life span have found the ages typically associated with child-bearing and childrearing, rather than with menopause, to have the highest incidence of mental health problems. Research suggesting that menopause per se does not increase a woman's vulnerability to mental health problems is rather convincing.

This is not to deny that some middle- and old-aged women at times feel depressed, irritable, and anxious. Middle- and old-aged women are likely to face the type of traumatic stress that is known to increase vulnerability to depression, such as loss of a loved family member or friend. The cumulative effects of chronic stress and the consequences of a lifetime of poverty, loneliness, sexism, racism, and/or poor health may well lead to deteriorating mental health. Traditional psychological and behavioral methods for treating depression, anxiety, and low self-esteem may appropriately be used with middle- and old-aged women, regardless of their menopausal status, who are suffering from these symptoms. Menopause is a natural life transition that conveys benefits as well as difficulties, and associated problems are expected and temporary. Changes in attitudes and attributions likely to improve mental health may occur on an individual level in psychotherapy, on a group level in consciousness-raising groups, on an educational level in the classroom, and/or on a mass-media level.

The most common complaint of menopausal women in the United States is vasomotor instability, or hot flashes. The frequency, intensity, and duration of hot flashes vary greatly among individuals, and they tend to diminish over time, eventually ceasing altogether. Hot flashes have been found to increase under stressful life conditions and, in some women, are exacerbated by high environmental temperatures, caffeine, and/or alcohol. Hot flashes do not usually present a threat to a woman's physical or psychological well-being, but they may be severe enough to cause considerable discomfort or, to some, embarrassment.

Although hormone therapy is effective in treating hot flashes, such treatment is unacceptable to many women because of a preexisting medical condition, undesirable side effects, or a personal disinclination to take drugs. Relaxation training and stress reduction have been successful in reducing the frequency and intensity of hot flashes, as has temperature biofeedback, which is designed to elicit conscious control over the body temperature. Other forms of psychotherapy have been employed, with the goals of modifying attitudes, transforming self-concept, and increasing self-esteem. When successful, these therapies can modify the symbolic meaning of menopause, rendering the hot flashes inconsequential.

Lifestyle changes, including improved diet, increased aerobic exercise, and reduced use of nicotine, caffeine, and alcohol, can also improve the physical and psychological well-being of aging women. Both medicine and psychology now recognize that individuals derive additional benefits from lifestyle changes: overall health, greater self-efficacy and feelings of control, and improved social relationships. Persons of both sexes have difficulty maintaining healthy lifestyles, but women's difficulties are exacerbated by gender stereotypes that define the "perfect woman" as one who is nurturing, dependent, subservient, and self-sacrificing and who does not "lose her figure" as she grows older.

The decision to take or not to take hormone therapy is in itself stressful for menopausal women. The benefits of the therapy are the alleviation of hot flashes, increased lubrication during sexual arousal, and a reduction in the rate of bone loss—the latter true only as long as the woman continues to take medication. The disadvantages are the documented increase in the risk of breast cancer, maintaining or increasing the risk of uterine fibroids, and a continued risk of endometriosis. Although less thoroughly studied, other reported side effects include increased risk of asthma, ovarian cancer, migraine, lupus, and urinary tract infections.

Estrogen therapy (used either for contraception or menopause) may, within a year, use up stores of vitamin B6, increasing a woman's vulnerability to depression. This effect can often be alleviated by taking vitamin B6 supplements. Furthermore, there has been a growing awareness that progesterone may magnify mental health problems. A common complaint of women taking hormones is that, during the progesterone phase of their medication cycle, they experience symptoms similar to those commonly associated with premenstrual syndrome—depression, irritability, anxiety, bloating, and weight gain. For many women, these symptoms are of such severity that they abandon the medication. Thus the decision to avail oneself of hormone therapy or not is not an easy or straightforward one and may be facilitated by informal or formal support and professional help.

[See also Women's Health Issues.]

Bibliography

Coney, S. (1993). *The menopause industry: A guide to medicine's "discovery" of the mid-life woman*. Claremont, CA: Hunter House.

Doress-Worters, P. B., & Siegal, D. L. (1994). *Ourselves, growing older*. New York: Simon & Schuster.

Gannon, L. (1999). *Women and aging: Transcending the myths*. London: Routledge.

Love, S. (1997). *Dr. Susan Love's hormone book: Making informed choices about menopause.* New York: Random House.

Northrup, C. (1994). *Women's bodies, women's wisdom: Creating physical and emotional health and healing.* New York: Bantam Books.

Notelovitz, M., & Tonnessen, D. (1993). *Menopause and midlife health.* New York: St. Martin's Press.

O'Leary Cobb, J. (Ed.). *A friend indeed newsletter.* (Available from the editor, P.O. Box 1710, Champlain, NY 12919.)

Vines, G. (1993). *Raging hormones: Do they rule our lives?* London: Virago Press.

Linda Gannon

MENSTRUATION. A complex physiological component of the reproductive process, menstruation is important for both the individual and the human species. The way in which menstruation is experienced and interpreted is heavily influenced by social and cultural factors. It is amazing how little behavioral research is available for such a pervasive phenomenon, perhaps due to historical taboos regarding the subject.

The phrase the *menstrual cycle* refers to the cycle of events which occur in the woman's reproductive system each month. Ovulation occurs when a mature ovum (an egg cell developed in one of the two ovaries) is released into the Fallopian tubes. If the egg is not fertilized by sperm after approximately 2 weeks in the uterus, a blood flow washes the ovum from the woman's body and the cycle begins again. Given that more than 95% of all menstrual cycles experienced by women range between 23 and 35 days, that the bleeding portion of each cycle lasts from 5 to 7 days, that women continue this process for some 40 years, one can estimate that women engage in this bleeding behavior for a total of about 10 years. By extension, consider the behavioral implications for the commercial sector driven by menstruation. The production and advertising of hygiene products and symptom alleviation is a major industry.

Not all women have the same experiences with menstruation. For example, some women suffer extreme discomfort (dysmenorrhea), of which painful cramps may be just one symptom. Research suggests that depending upon age, perhaps 12 to 26% of women are prevented by various symptoms from engaging in normal activities during menstruation. Further, stress is known to disrupt a woman's typical menstrual pattern. Athletic competition and extreme physical exertion, in combination with dietary factors, may lead to amenorrhea (the absence of periods). Sometimes at the higher levels of competition, in sports such as gymnastics, this disruption of menstruation is desired by participants and their coaches.

Alterations in the pattern of menstruation may also occur for less problematic reasons. Several studies have demonstrated that menstrual synchronization occurs. For example, college students have been found to synchronize their cycles after only 3 months of living together in residence halls. Moreover, this matching of patterns seems to occur even when the women are not cognizant of their friends' cycles. This synchronization is usually attributed to olfactory processes.

The most extensive investigation of the patterns and perceptions of menstruation is that conducted by researchers from the World Health Organization (WHO). They studied more than 5,000 women from 14 cultures in 10 countries. Features of menstruation such as amount of bleeding, activity during the last menstrual period, mood during the last menstrual period, discomfort during the last period, predictability and the characteristics of the blood during the last period were assessed. In addition, these researchers assessed beliefs related to menstruation in four areas: bathing during menstruation; fertility and femininity issues; interpretations and implications of menstruation (ranging from being dirty to being like a sickness, to curtailing sexual activity); and beliefs about not washing one's hair or bathing during menstruation.

Three patterns of experience were reported. First, about one fourth of all women reported low blood loss on the first day, with the duration of bleeding days being quite long. The second group, one half of all women, reported an average first-day bleed, and a quite short period overall. The third group, about one fifth of the women, reported the heaviest first-day blood loss, the heaviest total blood loss, and the longest duration of the bleeding period. It can be noted that variation in the experience of menstruation has been demonstrated to affect decisions such as one's choice of family planning method.

Whereas only *three* patterns were necessary to describe actual experience of bleeding, *nine* patterns (or types) characterized the interpretation of or beliefs about menstruation. Each type represented about 10% of the studied population, with only one type twice as large as the others. In other words, there was tremendous variety in interpretation and beliefs about essentially the same behavior, probably due to differences in socialization.

For the largest group several beliefs were observed: Their femininity would be lost without menstruation; they desired a greater blood loss; and they felt menstruation to be dirty. Another group took the opposite stance toward menstruation, namely, that it is not inherently bad, but they would certainly not mind it if their periods were easier or if they went away. The other seven groups describe almost every other combination of beliefs. It is not known how these different interpretations develop.

In 1987, *premenstrual syndrome* (PMS) was officially listed as a psychiatric disorder. Recent findings call into question its designation as an emotional disorder, suggesting instead that the symptoms of PMS stem from an aberrant effect on the brain of normal changes in blood levels of estrogen and progesterone during menstruation. In other words, there may be an abnormal response to normal hormones and processes. Perhaps future research will lead to chemical agents which might attenuate the problems without interfering with fertility and health processes.

The first appearance of menstruation is termed *menarche*. It typically occurs in the early teens. There is tremendous individual and cultural variation in response to this event, and its interpretation. In some cultures and families, the event is treated as a demonstration that one has achieved the full capabilities of being a woman. Such a "debut" is heralded and celebrated. Other women recall this event as being associated with fear, shame, and guilt, a punishment for wrong doing. ("Who can I tell about this without getting into more trouble?")

Cessation of menstruation is known as *menopause*. It typically occurs when women are in their 50s. Like menstruation, menopause is also subject to individual and cultural variation in attitudes and affect. In some cultures, menopause is associated with cessation of sexual relations with one's spouse, as if the woman's sexual life is at an end once she can no longer conceive a child. Alternatively, the lack of bleeding days is sometimes viewed as an opportunity for sexual spontaneity with one's partner.

Recent research involving a prospective study (Study of Women's Health Across the Nation; SWAN) of almost 4,000 premenopausal women suggests that women in different ethnic groups vary in the degree of reported menopausal symptoms, and in their ability to perform their daily activities as they age. Preliminary findings (reported in 1997 in the *Monitor* published by the American Psychological Association) suggest that (1) different ethnic groups report different kinds and severity of symptoms associated with menopause, (2) up to 20% of women have trouble functioning in daily life but that the proportion varies according to ethnic group, and (3) the medical response to these problems also varies by ethnic group.

Health issues related to menopause are under intense investigation. The SWAN researchers looked at two symptom clusters: *estrogen-related symptoms* (night sweats, hot flashes, vaginal dryness, and urine leakage) and *somatic symptoms* (difficulties sleeping, headaches, a racing heart, and stiffness in the neck, shoulders, and other joints). In addition to ethnic variation in these reported symptoms, it is also clear that cigarette smoking exacerbates these difficulties.

The major health issues associated with menopause involve increased osteoporosis, coronary heart disease, and Alzheimer's disease. Treatment alternatives have included hormone replacement therapy (HRT) and hysterectomy. The SWAN report found ethnic differences in the selection of these two choices with Whites more likely to choose HRT.

Osteoporosis is a debilitating condition in which bone density decreases resulting in a greatly increased risk of bone fractures. It is known to be associated with the menopausal transition and the consequent decline in estrogen levels. Coronary heart disease in women is unusual prior to menopause, but its risk increases sharply in postmenopausal women and is the leading cause of death in women above the age of 60. The likely mechanisms for the effects of lowered estrogen levels on the cardiovascular system include changes in lipids and lipoproteins, glucose and insulin metabolism, body fat distribution, and arterial blood flow. More recently there has been the suggestion that HRT may reduce the risk of Alzheimer's disease and the severity of the associated dementia. The exact role of HRT in Alzheimer's disease remains to be clarified, but the initial evidence indicates that the role of estrogen is worth further study.

The cultural and individual variation in decision making regarding HRT (with or without the benefit of input from health professionals) can also be expected to demonstrate important socialization effects. Partner support is also expected to vary and impact upon decision making and the way in which women interpret this phase of their lives.

[*See also* Women's Health Issues.]

Bibliography

Graham, C. A., & McGrew, W. C. (1980). Menstrual synchrony in female undergraduates living in a coeducational campus. *Psychoneuroendocrinology, 5,* 245–252.

Mahoney, E. R. (1983). *Human sexuality.* New York: McGraw-Hill.

Martin, E. (1988). Medical metaphors of women's bodies: Menstruation and menopause. *International Journal of Health Services, 18,* 237–254.

McFarland, C., Ross, M., & DeCourville, N. (1989). Women's theories of menstruation and biases in recall of menstrual symptoms. *Journal of Personality and Social Psychology, 57,* 522–531.

Severy, L. J., Thapa, S., Askew, I., & Glor, J. (1993). Menstrual experiences and beliefs: A multicountry study of relationships with fertility and fertility regulating methods. *Women & Health, 20,* 1–20.

Snowden, R., & Christian, B. (1983). *Patterns and perceptions of menstruation: A World Health Organization international study.* London: Croom Helm. This work contains an annotated bibliography of 513 relevant references.

World Health Organization (WHO) Task Force. (1981). A

cross-cultural study of menstruation: Implications for contraceptive development and use. *Studies in Family Planning, 12,* 3–16.

Lawrence J. Severy

MENTAL HEALTH CARE. The domain of mental health care is a wide one, covering behavioral and mental disorders as they relate to physical illnesses and conditions, social problems, and biological and psychosocial assessment and intervention. Further, there is the dimension of age, covering the life span from childhood and adolescence through the adult years and into the later years. Add to these complexities the variables of gender, ethnicity, race, and socioeconomic status. Mental health care functions within the larger context of health care delivery and involves scientific and professional disciplines across the fields of knowledge and technology.

Good health care starts with prevention. Unfortunately, the health professions have only recently become more attuned to preventive measures in the area of mental health. Vaccinations for children have been the prototype for prevention, and flu and pneumonia sera are now used with other age groups as well. However, prevention against mental health problems has lagged significantly behind public health methods. Diet, smoking, and other risk-taking behaviors, as with alcohol and other drugs, all have only recently become foci for health measures.

Specifically, in the area of mental health, Pelosi (1996) reported that

> as many as one-third of American adults will suffer from a diagnosable mental disorder at some point in their lives, and an estimated 20% of the population has a mental disorder at any given time. An estimated 12% of the nations' 63 million children and adolescents suffer from one or more mental disorders. Alzheimer's disease affects over 4 million older Americans and at least 15% of the elderly in nursing homes are clinically depressed. . . . In 1990, economic cost of mental disorders, excluding the cost of alcohol abuse, was estimated at $98 billion, and the economic cost of drug abuse was estimated at an additional $66 billion. Despite these enormous expenditures it is estimated that only 10%–30% of individuals in need receive appropriate treatment. (p. 1128)

Before considering the domains of psychological assessment and psychotherapeutic interventions, I should note here that smoking and drug, alcohol, and other substance abuse in the early, formative years of childhood and adolescence are behaviors encouraged by peer pressure, a powerful motivator, in spite of parental and other adult influences.

The roles of psychology in mental health care date back more than a century. Clinical psychology and its roles in assessment, treatment, and research traditionally are ascribed to the occasion of Lightner Witmer's seeing his first patient in March 1896, following the introduction in 1894 of courses for public school teachers at the University of Pennsylvania. Witmer taught one of the courses in 1895–1896. One of his students told of a 14-year-old boy who could not read but otherwise appeared to be normally intelligent. Poor spelling initially seemed to be the pupil's difficulty. Today, we would characterize the student as dyslexic. Witmer described this case in the first volume of the *Psychological Clinic* (Witmer, 1907).

Evaluation and treatment at the "psychological clinic" (a term first used by Witmer in a paper given at the 1896 meeting of the American Psychological Association in Boston) was provided for children and adolescents, with an expanded system of referrals from many sources. It was of historical significance that Witmer's "conception was for a university-quality clinic headed by a psychologist. . . . it would have been totally foreign to both his vision and his personal nature to have worked under physicians . . ." (McReynolds, 1996, p. 239). In the decades since Witmer's pioneering efforts, the American Psychological Association has grown to number more than 76,000 fellows and members, of whom 48% are in divisions associated with mental health care, directly or indirectly. This does not include those social psychologists who have been in or continue to lead research in mental health care.

The wide range of identities of psychologists who contribute to mental health through teaching and training, clinical practice, and research reflects the scope of the field. Though psychological assessment was the early field of involvement and is an extremely active arena for neuropsychologists, the psychotherapies are seen as a major contribution to mental health. The range and scope of psychologists' activities extend from actualizing therapy through transactional analysis in a panoply of more than thirty emphases, arenas, and labels. Thus there are proponents, both psychologists and their patients, who claim varying degrees of success for their particular mode of treatment. Broadly, the range includes, in the more established modalities, psychoanalytically oriented, client-centered, cognitive, and behavioral therapies.

Although the process of psychotherapy is significant to the patient and to the psychotherapist, it is the outcome that is critical for the patient, for the therapist, and for systematic study or research. For nearly a half century, psychotherapy outcome has been studied and debated. Funded by the National Institute of Mental Health, the American Psychological Association held three major conferences between 1958 and 1966 on psychotherapy research, its process, and its outcome (see Rubenstein & Parloff, 1959). VandenBos (1996) summarized the outcome assessment studies. From 1971 through 1994, A. E. Bergin and S. L. Garfield published four editions of their *Handbook of Psychotherapy and Behavior Change*. And, in 1993, M. W. Lipsey and D. B. Wilson reviewed the effectiveness of the psychotherapies in a range of interventions and settings and the behaviors that brought patients to seek and become involved in the treatment process. In the more broadly public domain, *Consumer Reports* (1995) surveyed readers' experiences with psychotherapy and their attitudes toward it. The respondents were asked about their perceptions of their need for and the outcome of their psychotherapeutic experience. This sample of the public's perceptions of psychotherapy and their evaluation of the experience appeared to confirm the data from psychotherapy research. However, not unexpectedly, this report, as with other studies, set off both observations and debate over the study.

Further, as already noted, although clinicians and policy makers talk and write about prevention in the fields of mental health, little is known or practiced, a lack that significantly affects the course of mental illness. From 1990 to 1994, the National Institute of Mental Health held three national meetings of scientists, advocates, and consumers of research (mostly public health officials) and published a report on preventive measures and recommendations, combined with those of the 1994 report of the Institute of Medicine (Muñoz, Mrazek, & Haggerty, 1996). The areas covered included the "preventive intervention research cycle" of risk studies, controlled trials, and implementation. Over the life span there are both risk and protective factors, involving person and environmental risks, individual variations, capacity for change in both arenas and for both change and sustained change, against the background of the community in which the individual functions. It is important to note, for example, that hospitalizations for mental disorders and suicide risks are influenced by the economic state of communities. These complex variables influence not only the introduction of preventive interventions but also whether such interventions can persist and be retained after initiation of the programs. The Institute of Medicine Report (Mrazek & Haggerty, 1994) "identified psychology as the discipline that has most contributed to prevention and preventive research in . . . mental health" (p. 1117).

There are two more areas significant to mental health—the aging of our society and the phenomenon of managed care of interventions in health care. Both are multivariate fields. In the United States, for example, the population has tripled since 1900, a growth associated with immunization and other public health measures, the latter a principal variable related to aging. Life expectancy now is 79 years for women and 73

for men, though the median age is 35. The population of those 65 years and older has grown elevenfold, in contrast to the threefold growth in the general population. And one of the complex phenomena of aging, Alzheimer's disease, is currently diagnosed in nearly 6% of the population aged 60 and older. Further, there are other dementias of the later years, usually with onset after ages 50 to 55. For those patients not in nursing homes, family members, often daughters, are usually their caretakers. In research to understand changes in patients as they age, the initial efforts focused on the aging patient, then on the caregiver; now the focus is on the interaction between patient and caregiver.

Another significant mental health domain is depression, a variable syndrome across the life span. Wells and colleagues have reported the results of their medical outcome study, noting that

> impairment and disability associated with depression is equal to that attributable to cardiovascular disease and greater than that due to other chronic physical disorders such as hypertension, diabetes, and arthritis. Studies using instruments designed for use with older persons. . . . have reported prevalences of 11 to 16 percent. . . . significant depressive symptoms but . . . do not meet diagnostic criteria for major depression. (Wells et al., 1989, p. 917)

To round out this review of psychology's roles in the mental health field, we must consider the effects of managed care and health maintenance organizations (HMOs). The furor over this issue in the past decade suggests a new phenomenon. However, Wolf (1997) points out that "the earliest form of managed care in this country may be traced back more than 150 years, when miners paid a fixed fee to 'camp doctors' to secure medical care" (p. 3). Kaiser health plans have been functioning for more than a half century, beginning with Kaiser Steel's innovation in providing health care for workers in dam construction. The HMO Act of 1973 was passed, "bringing about the opportunity for managing health care and its costs for large populations of patients. Three essential elements emerged from HMO's: fixed monthly payments, utilization review, and quality assurance" (Wolf, 1997, p. 3). Interestingly, "assurance" has been retitled "management" in many plans.

Although HMOs generally are seen as the principal system of health care delivery, there are also preferred provider organizations (PPOs), in which the consumer has some choice of provider, and exclusive provider organizations (EPOs), in which patients may access services only within the EPO network. Point of service (POS) provides the greatest flexibility and choice for the patient. A decade ago, 35 million Americans were enrolled in HMOs, and by 1995 there were over 130 million enrollees. One third of the U.S. population will be enrolled in a POS or HMO in the year 2000. Sixteen managed-care organizations control 75% of the HMO-delivered care, with fewer and larger corporations now in the system.

Wolf (1997) also points out another significant change in health care delivery: "With managed care, more services are delivered in ambulatory care programs, and fewer in inpatient settings. Outpatient care and clinics have come to dominate health care delivery, no longer the focus of treatment is the hospital setting" (p. 8). Some advocates see managed care as a solution to the crisis of funding in what many describe as a national health care crisis. In the field of mental health, only in 1996 was parity achieved with other health care programs, and there still is work to be done. Perhaps it is too soon to expect true parity, as only a few years have passed since formal, legislative action resulted in parity of mental health services with other services.

Bibliography

Bergin, A. E., & Garfield, S. L. (Eds.). (1971). *Handbook of psychotherapy and behavior change: An empirical analysis.* New York: Wiley. This book review psychotherapies and behavioral changes.

Bergin, A. E., & Garfield, S. L. (Eds.). (1994). *Handbook of psychotherapy and behavior change: An empirical analysis* (4th ed.). New York: Wiley.

Garfield, S. L., & Bergin, A. E. (Eds.). (1978). *Handbook of psychotherapy and behavior change: An empirical analysis* (2nd ed.) New York: Wiley. Bergin and Garfield have written, over a span of more than two decades, what are essentially manuals for students and practitioners of psychotherapy.

Garfield, S. L., & Bergin, A. E. (Eds.). (1986). Introduction and historical overview. In S. L. Garfield & A. E. Bergin (Eds.), *Handbook of psychotherapy and behavior change* (3rd ed., pp. 3–22). New York: Wiley.

Lipsey, M. W., & Wilson, D. B. (1993). The efficacy of psychological, educational, and behavioral treatment: Confirmation from meta-analysis. *American Psychologist, 48,* 1181–1209. This is a review of the effectiveness of the psychotherapies, interventions, and settings of treatment and of motives for seeking psychotherapy and becoming involved in the treatment process.

McReynolds, P. (1996). Lightner Witmer: A centennial tribute. *American Psychologist, 51,* 237–240. This historical note reports Witmer's insistence on having a university-quality clinic headed by a psychologist.

Mental health: Does therapy help? (1995, November). *Consumer Reports,* 734–739. This is a survey of *Consumer Reports* readers' experiences with psychotherapy, their attitudes, need for treatment, and perceptions of the outcome of their therapy.

Mrazek, P. J., & Haggerty, R. J. (Eds.). (1994). *Frontiers for preventive intervention research.* Washington, DC: National Academy Press. The editors highlight research designed to focus on prevention studies reported in the Institute of Medicine report.

Muñoz, R. F., Mrazek, P. J., & Haggerty, R. J. (1996). Institute of Medicine report on prevention of mental disorders. *American Psychologist, 51,* 1116–1122. The authors summarize and comment on the Institute of Medicine report on prevention of mental disorders, stressing psychology's role in prevention.

Pelosi, N. (1996). Reducing risks of mental disorders. *American Psychologist, 51,* 1128–1129. The author is a congresswoman who concentrates on efforts in the House for health care, housing, environmental protection, and human rights. She emphasizes the need to focus on the training of researchers in mental health prevention and mental disorders and coordination of federal agencies and departments.

Rubinstein, E. A., & Parloff, M. B. (Eds.). (1959). *Research in psychotherapy* (Vol. 1). Washington, DC: American Psychological Association. The writers report on the first of three major psychotherapy research conferences funded by the National Institute of Mental Health and developed by the American Psychological Association. The conferences were held between 1958 and 1966, a high watermark in studies of outcome assessment of psychotherapy.

VandenBos, G. R. (1996). Outcome assessment of psychotherapy. *American Psychologist, 51,* 1005–1006. The author reviews the conferences on psychotherapy outcome research held between 1958 and 1966 and the 1995 publication of the survey report of mental health services and their outcome by *Consumer Reports.*

Wells, K. B., Stewart, A., Hays, R. D., Burnam, M. A., Rogers, W., Daniels, M., Berry, S., Greenfield, S., & Ware, J. (1989). The functioning and well-being of depressed patients: Results from the Medical Outcome Study. *Journal of the American Medical Association, 262,* 914–919. The writers observe that psychological depression is a major mental health problem, to be ranked with cardiovascular disease and other major chronic physical diseases. They report that, of those elderly patients whose depressive symptoms do not meet the specific criteria for major depression, 11–16% may have major depressive symptoms.

Witmer, L. (1907). Clinical psychology in America. *Psychological Clinic, 1,* 1–9, 53–54. This is a pioneering report on the beginning of clinical psychology.

Wolf, T. M. (1997). Managed care and health maintenance organizations. *Annals of Behavioral Science and Medical Education, 4* (1), 3–10.

Ivan N. Mensh

MENTAL HEALTH LAW came into its own in the United States in the late 1960s and early 1970s. Its roots lie in the civil rights and civil liberties revolution, and in the increased willingness of the courts, including the United States Supreme Court, to recognize the rights of those with little power, such as racial minorities, criminal defendants, prisoners, and mental patients.

It is especially apt to trace the development of mental health law to landmark decisions of the Supreme Court in the area of constitutional criminal procedure. In the early 1960s, the Supreme Court began to overcome its traditional reluctance, grounded in notions of comity (respect for another governmental institution) and federalism (deference to the authority of the states), to require the states to follow its own lead in matters relating to the investigation and adjudication of criminal cases. For example, in 1961, the Supreme Court held that evidence obtained as a result of an unreasonable search and seizure had to be excluded from state criminal proceedings—a rule that had long been the case with respect to the admission of evidence in federal criminal cases. In 1963, the Court held that indigent felony defendants in state criminal trials were entitled to the assistance of appointed counsel. The Court emphasized the importance of liberty, and recognized the importance of affording criminal defendants certain protections so as to guard against the inappropriate forfeiting of liberty. In this period, the Supreme Court engaged in a true revolution in constitutional criminal procedure. It pronounced, with increased specificity, the requirements for conducting constitutional searches and seizures, and, elaborated in great detail the rights of criminal suspects during police custodial interrogations.

The Supreme Court's criminal procedure revolution, and its emphasis on the fundamental nature of liberty and freedom from confinement, laid the groundwork for the development of mental health law. But the bridge to the development of mental health law was made even more apparent by the Court's 1967 decision in In re Gault relating to juvenile delinquency proceedings. Until Gault, proceedings in juvenile court were typically highly informal. Since juvenile courts were developed to protect and rehabilitate troubled youth, rather than to punish them, juveniles were ordinarily not accorded the rights given to adult criminal defendants in criminal proceedings. After all, the reasoning went, if the state is here to help a juvenile, wouldn't the trappings of a criminal proceeding simply serve to frustrate its beneficent mission? Accordingly, juvenile courts traditionally conducted their business without the appointment of assigned counsel for juvenile defendants, and without other protections—such as a privilege against self-incrimination.

The attorneys who brought the Gault case to the United States Supreme Court, however, urged the Court to look at the realities of the rehabilitative ideal rather than merely to its rhetoric. The attorneys emphasized that, in practice, rehabilitation is often far from part-and-parcel of juvenile confinement. And from the perspective of the juvenile, they continued, a loss of liberty is a loss of liberty, regardless of the government's stated purpose or intentions. The Gault Court agreed, and held the right to appointed counsel and the privilege against self-incrimination applicable in juvenile proceedings. In later juvenile delinquency cases, the Supreme Court held the standard of proof to require a "beyond a reasonable doubt" finding, as is the case in criminal matters, but, recognizing some of the differences between juvenile cases and adult criminal cases, the Court refused to require jury trials in juvenile cases.

The stage was thus set for analogical arguments to be made from the criminal juvenile setting to the mental health context. For example, Bruce Ennis, a leading mental health lawyer, argued in his 1971 article entitled "Civil Liberties and Mental Illness" that "if persons are involuntarily to be confined because of mental illness, the standards and procedures for confinement should guarantee no fewer rights than those afforded criminal defendants" (p. 108).

A year later, in 1972, the Supreme Court for the first time considered the extent to which the Constitution places substantive limits on the power of a state to commit an individual to a mental hospital. In Jackson v. Indiana (1972), the Court held that the indefinite commitment of a mentally retarded defendant found to be incompetent to stand trial violated substantive due process. At the least, the Court noted, due process required that the nature and duration of an individual's confinement to a mental hospital must bear a reasonable relation to the purposes of such commitment. When it becomes clear that a criminal defendant committed to a mental hospital because of incompetence to stand trial will not regain competence in the foreseeable future, his continued commitment on this basis becomes impermissible. The Court also held that the defendant was denied equal protection because he was subjected to a more lenient commitment standard and to a more stringent standard of release than standards generally applicable to all others confined to mental institutions who are not charged with a criminal offense.

In that same year, a three-judge federal district court in the landmark case of Lessard v. Schmidt (1972) relied on Gault to invalidate on constitutional grounds much of Wisconsin's civil commitment statute. The court invoked substantive due process to restrict the standards for civil commitment, and procedural due process to expand the procedural protections required prior to commitment, including a hearing with the right to counsel. The Supreme Court later extended these procedural due process protections, holding that the state must carry the burden of persuasion at a civil commitment hearing by clear and convincing evidence, and that a prisoner must be afforded a fairly elaborate due process hearing before transfer to a mental hospital. In the special situation presented when parents commit a minor child to a hospital, the Court held that the evaluation provided by the admitting clinician was sufficient to satisfy due process. Most hospitalizations occur through voluntary rather than involuntary admission, and in 1990 the Court recognized that due process requires an inquiry by the state into the competence of an individual seeking such admission.

The courts have also considered the rights of patients following commitment. In *Wyatt v. Stickney* (1972), an influential federal district court decision recognized that patients had a right to treatment in the state hospital and specified detailed standards and conditions that state hospitals must comply with. While lower courts have recognized a right to treatment, the Supreme Court has avoided deciding the issue. Instead, in 1975 the Court recognized that a patient committed for many years who did not receive treatment was deprived of his constitutional right to liberty. The Court held that a state may not constitutionally confine, without more, a nondangerous mentally ill person who is capable of surviving safely in freedom by himself or with the help of responsible family members or friends. In 1982 the Court held that an individual committed to a mental retardation facility has a right to safe conditions of confinement, freedom from bodily restraint, and minimally adequate habilitation. In considering whether these rights have been violated, however, the Court noted that courts must defer to the professional judgment of clinicians.

A much litigated issue has involved the right of mental patients and criminal offenders to refuse treatment (Winick, 1997). The courts have recognized a qualified right to refuse intrusive treatment. In 1990 the Supreme Court upheld the involuntary administration of medically appropriate antipsychotic medication to a mentally ill prisoner who was dangerous to other inmates and staff when not taking medication. While recognizing that the prisoner had a significant liberty interest in being free of unwanted medication, the Court held that the prison's interest in administering medication outweighed this liberty interest. The Court also held that an administrative rather than a judicial hearing to inquire into the need for such medication would be sufficient as a matter of due process. In 1992 the Court appeared to broaden the right to refuse treatment when it reversed the conviction of a criminal defendant forced to take antipsychotic medication during his trial in the absence of a judicial finding that such medication was necessary to protect others in the jail or to maintain him in a competent state so that he might stand trial.

The courts have placed limits on the way people with mental illness may be dealt with in the criminal process. A criminal defendant may not waive counsel,

plead guilty, or be tried while incompetent; nor may a prisoner who becomes incompetent while on death row be executed. The availability of the insanity defense is largely a matter of state law. The federal courts and all but a few states recognize the defense, most limiting it to cognitive impairment that prevents individuals from distinguishing right from wrong or from understanding the wrongfulness of their conduct (Perlin, 1994b). Defendants acquitted by reason of insanity typically are committed to psychiatric hospitals as long as they remain mentally ill and dangerous. In 1983 the Supreme Court rejected various constitutional challenges to such commitment and accepted that commitment following a defense of insanity could extend beyond the maximum term of imprisonment authorized for the crime had the defendant been convicted. The Court, however, also determined that commitment could not extend beyond the time the insanity acquitee no longer was mentally ill or dangerous. This limitation was reaffirmed in 1992 when the Court treated antisocial personality disorder as an insufficient basis to support continued commitment of an insanity acquittal. In the sex offender context, however, the Court has held that pedophilia is a sufficient predicate for a special sexually violent predator civil commitment scheme.

Traditionally, these issues constituted the "core" (Perlin, 1994a; Wexler, 1981) topics in mental health law—commitment and postcommitment questions regarding the right to receive treatment and to refuse it, the insanity defense, and competence to stand criminal trial. One of the ironies about traditional mental health law is that, despite its subject matter and its major impact on the mentally ill and the professionals who are engaged in the treatment of the mentally ill, the field traditionally was not especially interdisciplinary in its orientation or scholarship. This is presumably attributable to the origins of mental health law in the constitutional-doctrinal arena. As the composition and outlook of the United States Supreme Court changed from the activist approach of the Warren Court era, those involved in mental health law began to explore new directions for development. In the 1990s, the therapeutic jurisprudence perspective (Wexler & Winick, 1991, 1996; Winick, 1997), has sought to make the field truly interdisciplinary, and has sought to bring insights from psychology and the mental health disciplines into the formulation and application of the law.

Therapeutic jurisprudence has been defined as "the study of the role of the law as a therapeutic agent" and as the use of social science to study the extent to which a legal rule or practice promotes the psychological or physical well-being of the people it affects (Wexler & Winick, 1996, p. xvii). Therapeutic jurisprudence focuses on the law's impact on emotional life, and the perspective suggests that the law itself can be seen to function as a kind of therapist or therapeutic agent.

Legal rules, legal procedures, and the roles of legal actors (such as lawyers, judges, and often therapists) constitute social forces that, like it or not, often produce therapeutic or antitherapeutic consequences. Therapeutic jurisprudence proposes that we be sensitive to those consequences, rather than ignore them, and that we ask whether the law's antitherapeutic consequences can be reduced, and its therapeutic consequences enhanced, without subordinating due process and justice values.

Therapeutic jurisprudence does not suggest that therapeutic considerations should trump other considerations; therapeutic considerations are but one category of important considerations, as are autonomy, integrity of the fact-finding process, and community safety. Therapeutic jurisprudence also does not purport to resolve the value questions; instead, it sets the stage for their sharp articulation. In addition, the therapeutic jurisprudence lens generates empirical questions: one may speculate on the therapeutic consequences of various legal arrangements or law reform proposals, but empirical research is often necessary to determine with confidence whether the law actually operates in accordance with the speculative assumption.

The therapeutic jurisprudence perspective grew out of mental health law scholarship, and much therapeutic jurisprudence work therefore continues to concentrate on matters such as civil commitment, the insanity defense, the conditional release of insanity acquittees, incompetency to stand trial, the right to refuse treatment, and the like (Winick, 1997). Recent applications, however, make it clear that the potential of therapeutic jurisprudence extends far beyond traditional mental health law.

Therapeutic jurisprudence today is actually a therapeutic perspective on the law in general, and has been applied to conventional mental health law, as well as to criminal law and procedure, sentencing and corrections law, family and juvenile law, sexual orientation law, health law, disability law, workers' compensation law, personal injury and tort law, labor arbitration law, and even to contract law.

As a field of inquiry, therapeutic jurisprudence brings together a number of topics that have not generally been recognized as related: how the criminal justice system might traumatize sexual battery victims, how workers' compensation schemes might create the moral hazard of prolonging work-related injury, how a fault-based (rather than a no-fault) tort compensation scheme might enhance recovery from personal injury, and how the current law of contracts might operate to reinforce the low self-esteem of disadvantaged contracting parties.

Today, therefore, therapeutic jurisprudence looks broadly at an array of legal issues, and examines the law's role in promoting psychological well-being. Both in terms of mental health and in terms of law, therefore, therapeutic jurisprudence has traveled quite a distance from the traditional core content of mental health law. Indeed, it can be seen as a mental health approach to law in general.

Bibliography

Ennis, B. (1971). Civil liberties and mental illness. *Criminal Law Bulletin, 7,* 101–127.

In re Gault, 387 U.S. 1 (1967).

Jackson v. Indiana, 406 U.S. 715 (1972).

Lessard v. Schmidt, 349 F. Supp. 1078 (E. D. Wis. 1972).

Perlin, M. L. (1994a). *Law and mental disability.* Charlottesville, VA: Michie. A leading treatise on mental disability law in the United States.

Perlin, M. L. (1994b). *The jurisprudence of the insanity defense.* Durham, NC: Carolina Academic Press.

Wexler, D. B. (1981). *Mental health law: Major issues.* New York: Plenum.

Wexler, D. B., & Winick, B. J. (1991). *Essays in therapeutic jurisprudence.* Durham, NC: Carolina Academic Press.

Wexler, D. B., & Winick, B. J. (Eds.). (1996). *Law in a therapeutic key: Developments in therapeutic jurisprudence.* Durham, NC: Carolina Academic Press. The most comprehensive discussion of therapeutic jurisprudence to date.

Winick, B. J. (1997). *The right to refuse mental health treatment.* Washington, DC: American Psychological Association.

David B. Wexler and Bruce J. Winick

MENTAL HOSPITALS. *See* Inpatient Treatment.

MENTAL ILLNESS. *See* Psychopathology.

MENTAL IMAGERY. Imagery is the mental construction of an experience that at least in some respects resembles the experience of perceiving an object or an event, either with or without direct sensory stimulation. The recognition that one can call up a mental "copy" of experiences (such as memory images of specific episodes) or create novel images of events that never happened has long played a central role in notions of thought, memory, and knowledge representation. From the earliest writings onward, the phenomenological experience of mental imagery has been considered important, both theoretically and pragmatically. Theoretical speculations about the origin, function, and representation of mental imagery, many of which parallel debates that continue to this day, can be traced to the writings of Aristotle (circa 350 BCE). Practical work, aimed at using images as a tool, can be traced to the demonstration by Simonides (circa 500 BCE) that, by using imagery, information is fixed in memory.

Philosophical and Early Psychological Inquiries

Aristotle was the most influential of the early philosophers to hold that mental images, as copies of sensory input, are the primary symbols of thinking, with other symbols being secondary and derivative. The Aristotelian position remained essentially unchanged until the mid-seventeenth century, when it was expanded and elaborated by Thomas Hobbes, John Locke, and later British empiricist philosophers such as George Berkeley and David Hume. These writers took a firm stand against the rationalist conception of innate ideas. Although differing in important ways, these philosophers continued to hold to the notion that mental images were the primary symbols of thought and in some cases, as with Hume, were the exact copies of perceptions. Development of the empiricist position involved elaborating the laws of association that governed how simple images combined into complex ones, and how one image can bring another to mind.

The primacy of mental images held by empiricist philosophers carried over to the early days of experimental psychology in the mid-nineteenth century, especially in the method of introspection used by Wilhelm Wundt and his followers, such as Edward Titchener, to study the content of the mind. By the late nineteenth and early twentieth centuries the Wundtian and empiricist approach to imagery was subjected to much criticism. William James made various logical arguments against the notion that images are the reappearance of faint but exact copies of sensation and even against the more basic idea that thought consists of modality-based images. Experiments conducted in Germany at Würzburg, led by Oswald Kulpe, suggested that cognitive activity did not depend on quasi-sensory experience; thought could be imageless. These data indicated that mental images could not be the primary basis for knowledge or thought. Although Wundt, Titchener, and others vigorously attacked the methodology and logic of the Würzburg experiments, those studies, together with the persuasive arguments of the American psychologist J. B. Watson that one could not build a science of psychology on unreliable subjective data, led to half a century in which mental imagery was banished as a respectable topic for serious psychological study.

In parallel to the theoretical development of imagery, investigation of the pragmatic functions of imagery was reestablished by Sir Francis Galton in the 1870s. Galton observed large variability in the degree to which people reported on the use and vividness of images when doing everyday tasks. Attempts to construct individual difference measures of mental imagery continue to this day. Two types of measures are commonly used: those that ask people to report on phenomenological characteristics of evoked images, such as vividness or ease of manipulation, and those that ask participants to do an objective act that presumably depends on mental imagery, such as mentally rotating an object to a new orientation and stating whether the rotated object is the same or different from a physically presented object. Both types of tests are reliable, yet performance on one type of test generally does not correlate well with performance on the other.

Study of Mental Imagery Since 1960

The modern interest in mental imagery grew initially from developments in fields of psychology collateral to the traditional focus of the philosophers and early experimentalists, such as the observation that people deprived of sensory stimulation experienced vivid hallucinations, suggestions in the monitoring of brain activity that visual imagery was associated with an electroencephalogram alpha rhythm, and the finding, during brain surgery, that images of past events were associated with stimulation of the temporal lobes. In clinical settings, asking patients to image became a popular therapeutic intervention. Finally, experiments in human memory and learning, using methodology borrowed from behaviorist approaches to psychology, produced data that seemingly required the need for mental imagery.

The traditional idea that mental imagery facilitates memory can be traced to early mnemonic techniques in which imagery, often bizarre in nature, is associated with enhanced memorability. From the late 1960s onward, the memorial status and consequences of imagery have played a central role in cognitive psychology. Conceptually one can treat the modern interest as consisting of three overlapping phases.

The first phase consisted of rigorous experimental evidence that pointed to the importance of imagery in a wide range of memory tasks and phenomena. Much of this early interest was organized around the dual-coding theory proposed and extensively tested by the Canadian psychologist Allan Paivio. The theory argues for two independent but connected representational and processing systems: an imagery system tied to sensory experience and a verbal system tied to nonsensory experience. Each system has its own characteristics and is evoked under different conditions. Imagery was operationally defined by three factors: stimulus characteristics, imagery instructions, and tests that measure individual differences in images. Each of these variables has been manipulated experimentally, producing a set of robust and reliable findings. One such finding is the concreteness effect, wherein words that refer to concrete referents (e.g., chair) are easier to remember than abstract words for which there are no readily available referents (e.g., truth). A second finding is the instructional effect, which shows that memory can be enhanced even for concrete words if participants are instructed to use mental imagery when studying them for recall. In dual-coding theory these findings are explained by the conjoint effects of using both codes. The dual-coding perspective has been highly influential and has been extended from the study of memory to other cognitive domains, such as problem solving and the processing of language. Nonetheless, whether imagery is required to explain concreteness, instructional, and related effects has been questioned, and, suggestive of the philosophical arguments of James, so has the status of imagery as a primary representational system. Whatever the ultimate resolution of that debate, by the mid-1970s it was generally agreed that imagery was important to cognition and could be studied empirically.

In parallel to the work of Paivio, which concentrated on imagery in permanent memory, the British psychologist Alan Baddeley developed a model of working memory that consists in part of two systems that work in the service of the central executive: a visuospatial module specialized for the maintenance of visual and spatial input and a verbal-articulatory module specialized for the maintenance of verbal auditory input. Using selective interference methodologies, Baddeley has provided evidence for the psychological reality of these modules.

Finally, the American psychologist Stephen Kosslyn developed a computer-based model of imagery in which images are constructed from underlying propositions. Once constructed, the images are functionally autonomous, possessing unique properties, such as the presentation of information in a format that preserves spatial extent and that can be worked on by a set of operations that permit the manipulation of the spatially represented information.

The second phase of research has directly examined some of the presumed characteristics of mental images, especially whether one can discriminate between depictive and propositional accounts of so-called imagery effects. Three lines of research, each of which has roots in the early philosophical literature, have been tested extensively. The first concerns whether mental images are analogous representations isomorphic to perceptual experience. Studies such as those that measure the speed with which a person can mentally rotate objects in memory or scan locations on a memorized map indicate that, analogous to moving in real space, moving in imaginal space takes longer the farther one has to go. The second line of research tests whether similar mechanisms are activated by imaging an object as when the same object is perceived. Tests include having participants do concurrent tasks of perceiving and imagining in the visuospatial modality. Depending on the task, one can successfully predict when facilitation and when interference will occur. Another line of evidence comes from having participants create imaginal conditions that are known to produce illusions when presented in perceptual tasks. Although most participants are unaware of the illusion, often one can create the illusion with imaged stimuli. Neurophysiological evidence has shown many instances also of correspondence between perception and imagery. For instance, there are reports of people who suffer spatial neglect (i.e., who appear unaware of objects or events in part of their visual field) that demonstrate the same neglect for imaged objects. Finally, some studies address the question of whether images are primary representations or secondary, constructed from some more basic symbolic (usually propositionally based) medium. The experimental approach here is to present an ambiguous stimulus (such as a pattern that can be seen as either a rabbit or a duck) that we know from studies of perception can be reinterpreted: If one initially sees the duck pattern, one can, with the stimulus present, reinterpret it as the rabbit. If images are copies of sensory input, then one should be able to reinterpret images as well. However, if images are interpreted constructions from a more basic representation, then one should not be able to reinterpret the image. The data here are mixed, with some early studies indicating a failure to reinterpret and later ones indicating that, with appropriate instructions, imagery reinterpretation can occur.

On balance, the second phase of research has demonstrated that, as suggested so long ago, images seem be related to perceptual experience and to act as depictive representations. This interpretation is not universally accepted, however, and there are many who argue that the positive evidence can be explained by propositional representation, via experimenter demands, or by tacit knowledge held about the task.

The final phase of research has been the attempt to establish more directly the link between imaginal experiences and the neuropsychology underlying the experience. Experiments with patients who have unilateral focal brain damage or are dyslexic have suggested that there are at least two distinct forms of imagery, one supported by left-hemisphere processes and one supported by right-hemisphere processes. The former involves images in which the parts of the image are related by categorical spatial relations (such as "above"), whereas the latter involves images related by metric spatial relations. Other lines of physiological research favoring a perceptual and depictive aspect of imagery include functional magnetic resonance imaging (fMRI) studies indicating that the primary visual cortex (V1) is activated during visual mental imagery, studies that have identified cortical neurons organized to preserve the spatial structure of the information projected on the retina, and studies in which damage to the occipital lobe (including V1) impairs aspects of visual imagery.

Imagery and Psychotherapy

Whatever the underlying representation of imagery, it has long been established that the act of imagery has physiological and therapeutic consequences. Use of imagery is effective in the voluntary control of heart rate, covert activation of voluntary muscles, blood flow, dilation of the pupil, and voluntary movements of the eye. These effects have been employed in various clinical settings to combat specific psychosomatic illnesses, including hypertension, back pain, and the intraocular pressure of glaucoma patients.

Since the early work of Sigmund Freud, the most prominent use of mental imagery has been in the treatment of emotional problems, and imagery can be found as a basic tool in psychoanalysis, cognitive therapy, systematic desensitization, imaginal flooding, and guided affective-imagery therapy. For instance, in Freudian therapy, images are employed for evoking past memories, which, when made available, are then subject to therapeutic intervention. In cognitive therapy, the imagery reported by a client would be used for changing the content of one's thought. In systematic desensitization, clients are asked to image, in a progressive set of steps, scenes that bring a phobic object increasingly closer. Imaging is paired with relaxation until at any stage the image does not produce fear. Although imagery is central to these therapies, the question remains whether something is distinctive about imagery that might contribute to the onset or maintenance of clinical disorders, such as anxiety and depression. Finally, in recent years, an ongoing controversy has arisen about the use of imagery-based therapies in uncovering long-repressed memories of childhood sexual abuse. On one side are those, mainly clinicians, who argue that the techniques are effective and the memories of abuse are real. On the other side are those, mainly memory researchers, who argue that the imagery techniques can contribute to creating false memories of abuse that never actually occurred.

Imagery Play

Some argue that one function of imagery is to serve as a mental space in which ideas can be freely manipulated. For goal-directed problem solving, the evidence is that imagery is used most commonly and effectively during the discovery phase of problem solution and for tasks that are novel and unstructured. The relatively unstructured flow of images is especially noted in the discursive activity of imaginal play. Imaginal, like overt, play occurs in the absence of explicit environmental demands, is relatively unstructured, and is intrinsically motivated.

Both the frequency and the content of imaginal play have been studied, albeit not extensively. Studies of the frequency of imaginal play employ self-report measures to examine the prevalence of imagery play across the life span, comparisons to the frequency of overt play, and difference across different groups. For instance, some data indicate that the usual peaking of imagery play in adolescence is not found with gifted children, who report increasing levels of imagery play as they grow older. Content studies also employ self-report measures, with a commonly reported finding being that there are at least three types of imagery play: disconnected fantasies involving anxieties and worries; those involving achievements, guilt, and self-doubt; and those in which imagery play is an intrinsically pleasurable and creative activity. Distinct literatures exist for specific content, such as the imagery play of depressed people. Studies examining imagery play with sexual content point to the complex interactions of imagery content, biological correlates, and behavioral consequences. For instance, sexual imagery play is associated with level of androgen and is reflected in objective measures of arousal (wherein twice as much arousal occurs to imagined sexual activity than to watching erotica). In general, though, the number of imagery play studies is limited, and further research is required before we can understand fully the genesis, functions, and consequences of imaginal play.

[*See also* Imagination.]

Bibliography

Baddeley, A. (1986). *Working memory*. Oxford, UK: Oxford University Press. Presentation of a model of working memory that includes a visuospatial "slave" system; good review of the relevant literature.

Block, N. (Ed.) (1981). *Imagery*. Cambridge, MA: MIT Press. A compilation of papers by philosophers and psychologists on the epistemological status of imagery.

Finke, R. (1989). *Principles of mental imagery*. Cambridge, MA: MIT Press. A review of literature contrasting depictive and propositional approaches to the empirical literature on imagery effects.

Hampson, P., Marks, D. & Richardson, J. (Eds.). *Imagery: Current developments*. London: Routledge. Fourteen chapters on a range of current research topics.

Holt, R. (1964). Imagery: The return of the ostracized. *American Psychologist, 19*, 254–264.

Jones, L., & River, E. (1997). Current uses of imagery in cognitive and behavioral therapies. In L. VandeCreek, S. Knapp & T. Jackson (Eds.), *Innovations in clinical practice: A source book* (Vol. 15, pp. 423–439). Sarasota, FL: Professional Resource Press.

Kosslyn, S. (1980). *Image and mind.* Cambridge, MA: Harvard University Press. A review of Kosslyn's computer model and related empirical work.

Kosslyn, S. (1994). *Image and brain: The resolution of the imagery debate.* Cambridge, MA: MIT Press. A detailed development of a neurologically based model of imagery, with an exhaustive literature review.

Kunzendorf, R. (Ed.). (1991). *Mental imagery.* New York: Plenum. A compilation of 32 chapters on a wide range of cognitive, creative, and clinical topics.

Leitenberg, H., & Henning, K. (1995). Sexual fantasy. *Psychological Bulletin, 117,* 469–496. An extensive review of the empirical literature on sexual imagery play.

Lusebrink, V. (1990). *Imagery and visual expression in therapy.* New York: Plenum. A review of imagery effects in therapy, mainly those based on art therapy.

Mandler, J., & Mandler, G. (1964). *Thinking: From association to Gestalt.* New York: Wiley. A review of the philosophical and early experimental literature, with selections of writings from influential theorists who have examined the role of imagery.

Paivio, A. (1971). *Imagery and verbal processes.* New York: Holt, Rinehart & Winston. A review of the dual-coding hypothesis and an exhaustive review of relevant research.

Pylyshyn, Z. (1973). What the mind's eye tells the mind's brain: A critique of mental imagery. *Psychological Bulletin, 80,* 1–24. Arguments against a depictive account and for a propositional explanation of imagery effects.

Singer, J. (1975). *The inner world of daydreaming.* New York: Harper. A review of imaginal play, including daydreaming and fantasy, in a wide range of activities.

Albert N. Katz

MENTAL MODELS. In 1983, two books appeared each bearing the title, *Mental Models.* For both, the term *mental model* meant a knowledge structure, like a schema, but more complex, as it not only represents information but also suggests how to process it. The book by Johnson-Laird traced the term to ideas introduced more than forty years earlier by Kenneth Craik (1943). Craik proposed that reasoning proceeded by internal representations and processes that bore structural similarities to external systems. After developing the notion broadly, Johnson-Laird applied the term *mental model* to a description of the mental structures used to solve verbal syllogisms, rather than the rules of logic, which are often violated. According to Johnson-Laird, a mental model contrasts with a propositional representation in being "analogous to the structure of the corresponding state of affairs in the world" (p. 156). A mental model contrasts with an image in being more abstract; an image is seen as a view of a model. The power of a mental model is that it can be inspected to make inferences about some other state of affairs.

The second book of the same title was a collection of papers edited by Gentner and Stevens. There, the term *mental model* was used to characterize conceptual representations of knowledge of primarily physical systems, door bells, calculators, steam plants, electricity, mechanics, navigation. Mental models were seen as configurations of parts or processes causally influencing each other in specified ways. Like a schema, a mental model represents domain-specific knowledge; in contrast to a schema, a mental model incorporates processes that are temporal or causal in nature. Rather than being inspected, such a model is "run" to draw inferences.

A third book appeared in 1983, *Strategies of Discourse Comprehension,* by van Dijk and Kintsch, using a different name for a similar concept. Van Dijk and Kintsch concluded from evidence that comprehension of language cannot be accounted for just by the big three, phonemics, syntax, and semantics. To truly understand discourse, people need to construct a "situation model," a "representation of the events, actions, persons, and in general the situation a text is about" (pp. 11–12). This idea is closely related to a mental model and indeed, the terms have been used interchangeably.

The term *mental model* uses *model* in two different senses: a model as a miniature of a real-world object or system and a model as a theory that generates predictions. There are ambiguities in its use. First, is a mental model meant to be a complete, closed, coherent theory or simply whatever is in a person's mind that allows inferences, however vague, incoherent, shifting, incorrect, inconsistent, and incomplete it may be. Mental models can be conceived of loosely or stringently as models. Next, is a mental model a model of a device or system or a model of a user? Of course, individual researchers may explicitly use the term one way or another, but there is no overall agreement in the field. This is not necessarily bad; it can be argued that many useful terms in psychology (and life) are ambiguous.

Thus, the concept "mental model" has been used in contrast with formal logic, static schemas, and representations of language based on phonemics, syntax, and semantics. These varied beginnings have spawned even more varied research, differing in the questions asked and the tasks examined.

Is There Evidence That People Construct and Use Mental Models?

Yes, people do seem to construct and use mental models, especially if the term is used loosely. The evidence is varied: from reaction times necessary to make different kinds of judgments and inferences, from quality of errors, from explanations and inferences. The contexts are also varied: syllogistic reasoning, discourse comprehension, physical and mechanical systems, and more. Johnson-Laird and others (e.g., Johnson-Laird, 1983; Schaeken, Johnson-Laird, & D'Ydewalle, 1996) have presented convincing evidence that people use mental models to solve a variety of logical, spatial, and temporal reasoning problems. To do so, people seem to put down labeled tokens for the premises in a mental tableau, and then examine the entire set for possible inferences. For some sets of premises, it is possible to construct several different consistent models. According to mental models theory, these are the cases that should be more difficult to solve, and they are. Nevertheless, there are those who argue that mental models are not sufficient for reasoning; in particular, quantifiers and negation are difficult to represent by models (e.g., Braine, 1994; Rips, 1994).

In discourse comprehension, it is clear that readers draw inferences that the language of the text alone does not allow, inferences from mental representations of the situations described by the text (e.g., Taylor & Tversky, 1992; van Dijk & Kintsch, 1983; Zwaan, Magliano, & Graesser, 1995). Because of the objectivity of the independent variables and the naturalness of the dependent measures, much of this work has examined mental models that are spatial. By now, many studies have demonstrated effects of spatial distance and spatial relations on time to make inferences (e.g., for distance, Morrow, Bower, & Greenspan, 1989; for spatial relations, Taylor & Tversky, 1992) though not always (e.g., Gray Wilson, Rinck, McNamara, Bower, & Morrow, 1993). Other kinds of inferences, such as those about causes and character, are also made, presumably from mental or situation models about cause and character (e.g., Zwaan et al., 1995).

Demonstrating the use of mental models for reasoning about physical and mechanical systems has proved to be more complicated. Certainly when they are taught mental models of, say, an imaginary spaceship engine, a calculator or a library system, people learn and use them to solve problems. For some, simple physical systems, people seem to acquire mental models simply from interaction, without explicit instruction, though often the models appear to be incomplete or mixed (e.g., Gentner & Stevens, 1993). The early work on people's understanding of physics showed fascinating systematic errors of, for example, trajectories of moving bodies. It was initially proposed that people drew inferences from mental models, but the wrong ones, those held by earlier generations of physicists. More refined experimentation has revealed that the errors of inference and explanation that people make do not derive from a coherent but incorrect theory but rather from an incoherent set of beliefs (e.g., Kaiser, Proffitt, Whelan, & Hecht, 1992).

What Is the Nature of a Mental Model?

The nature of a mental model depends on the content represented. For space, most research on mental models has shown that they reflect spatial relations and distance categorically (Rinck, Hahnel, Bower, & Glowalla, 1997). Despite the fact that space is continuous, there is little evidence for mental models that are analog or continuous (but see Schwartz & Black, 1996). For mechanical or electronic systems, mental models include the elementary parts and their configuration as well as the causal relations among them (e.g., Gentner & Stevens, 1983). Mental models can be "run" to make causal inferences (Tversky & Kahneman, 1983). For motion, also continuous, there is evidence that mental models are nevertheless discrete, that people conceptualize change by segmenting it into natural units, and represent motion as a sequence of those units, somewhat like comic strips (McCloud, 1993).

What Is a Mental Model Good For?

This question needs to be answered twice, for each of two interpretations. First, are mental models good for users of systems? It is effortful to teach or acquire a mental model for a complex system. The alternative is to learn a set of procedures. For performing routine problems, that seems to be sufficient and efficient; however, for troubleshooting and complex problems, a mental model of a system is helpful if not essential. Second, is the concept "mental model" a useful one for cognitive science? Its widespread use is sufficient answer. Viewed from theories in cognitive science, a mental model is an addition to the catalog of kinds of mental knowledge structures, providing a useful way to talk about inferences and reasoning. Viewed from applications of cognitive science, a mental model is a useful piece of knowledge for users to have in order to reason about complex systems.

Bibliography

Braine, M. D. S. (1994). Mental logic and how to discover it. In J. McNamara & G. E. Reyes (Ed.), *The logical foundations of cognition* (pp. 241–263). Oxford: Oxford University Press.

Byrne, R. M. J., & Johnson-Laird, P. N. (1989). Spatial reasoning. *Journal of Memory and Language, 28,* 564–575.

Craik, K. (1943). *The nature of explanation.* Cambridge, U.K.: Cambridge University Press.

Franklin, N., Tversky, B., & Coon, V. (1992). Switching points of view in spatial mental models acquired from text. *Memory and Cognition, 20,* 507–518.

Garrod, S. C., & Sanford, A. J. (1989). Discourse models as interfaces between language and the spatial world. *Journal of Semantics, 6,* 147–160.

Gentner, D., & Stevens, A. L. (Ed.). (1983). *Mental models.* Hillsdale, NJ: Erlbaum.

Gray Wilson, S., Rinck, M., NcNamara, T. P., Bower, G. H., & Morrow, D. G. (1993). Mental models and narrative comprehension: Some qualifications. *Journal of Memory and Language, 32,* 141–154.

Johnson-Laird, P. N. (1983). *Mental models: Towards a cognitive science of language, inference, and consciousness.* Cambridge, MA: Harvard University Press.

Johnson-Laird, P. N., Byrne, R. M. J., & Schaeken, W. (1992). Propositional reasoning by model. *Psychological Review, 99,* 418–439.

Kaiser, M. K., Proffitt, D. R., Whelan, S. M., & Hecht, H. (1992). Influence of animation on dynamical judgments. *Journal of Experimental Psychology: Human Perception and Performance, 18,* 669–690.

McCloud. S. (1993). *Understanding comics: The invisible art.* New York: HarperCollins.

Morrow, D. G., Bower, G. H., & Greenspan, S. (1989). Updating situation models during narrative comprehension. *Journal of Memory and Language, 28,* 292–312.

Rinck, M., Hahnel, A., Bower, G. H., & Glowalla, U. (1997). The metrics of spatial situation models. *Journal of Experimental Psychology: Learning, Memory, and Cognition, 23,* 622–637.

Rips, L. (1994). *The psychology of proof.* Cambridge, MA: MIT Press.

Schaeken, W., Johnson-Laird, P. N., & D'Ydewalle, G. (1996). Mental models and temporal reasoning. *Cognition, 60,* 205–234.

Schwartz, D. L., & Black, J. B. (1996). Analog imagery in mental model reasoning: Depictive models. *Cognitive Psychology, 30,* 154–219.

Taylor, H. A., & Tversky, B. (1992). Spatial mental models derived from survey and route descriptions. *Journal of Memory and Language, 31,* 261–282.

Taylor, H. A., & Tversky, B. (1996). Perspective in spatial descriptions. *Journal of Memory and Language, 35,* 371–391.

Tversky, A., & Kahneman, D. (1983). Extensional versus intuitive reasoning: The conjunction fallacy in probability judgment. *Psychological Review, 90,* 293–315.

van Dijk, T. A., & Kintsch, W. (1983). *Strategies of discourse comprehension.* New York: Academic Press.

Zwaan, R. A., Magliano, J. P., & Graesser, A. C. (1995). Dimensions of situation model construction in narrative comprehension. *Journal of Experimental Psychology: Learning, Memory, and Cognition, 21,* 386–397.

Barbara Tversky

MENTAL RETARDATION. The definition of mental retardation, according to the latest American Association on Mental Retardation (AAMR) book, is as follows.

Mental retardation refers to substantial limitations in present functioning. It is characterized by significantly sub-average intellectual functioning, existing concurrently with related limitations in two or more of the following applicable adaptive skill areas: communication, self-care, home living, social skills, community use, self-direction, health and safety, functional academics, leisure, and work. Mental retardation manifests before age 18. (Luckasson et al., 1992, p. 1)

There are three aspects of the structure of this definition, represented by a triangle. On one side are capabilities that comprise intelligence and adaptive skills. On another side are environments. These include the environments at home, work, school, and community. Most important, the third side is named functioning. The definition emphasizes the way the individual with mental retardation functions in the presence or absence of support given by the community. Mental retardation is further conceptualized as a state and not a permanent trait of the individual because if a community can provide the support necessary for the individual to function adequately in the society, the individual ceases to be mentally retarded.

One can immediately realize why the definition has problems of acceptance. First of all, by emphasizing functioning and support, it would be difficult to define a person with mental retardation appropriately, as societies differ from each other in terms of support. So also, if capabilities such as intelligence and adaptive skills are only given one third of the importance in defining mental retardation, then the definition presents an indeterminate concept. There were always problems in measuring adaptive skills. Now, in this new definition, only two of the ten adaptive skills listed have to be inadequately developed in order to qualify for the label of mental retardation. However, of importance are the weights placed on the environments and the level of support.

In response to the new definition of mental retardation, the American Psychological Association has edited the *Manual of Diagnosis and Professional Practice in Mental Retardation* (Jacobson & Mulick, 1996). Essentially, it advocates an older definition of mental retardation. Mental retardation (MR) refers to: (a) significant limitations in general intellectual functioning; (b) significant limitations in adaptive functioning that exist concurrently; and (c) onset of intellectual and adaptive limitations before the age of 22 years. Its main difference from the AAMR definition lies in recognizing at least four different levels of mental retardation, in contrast to the AAMR, which recognizes no levels at all. The levels are mild, moderate, severe, and profound, depending on performance on an IQ test and adaptive behavior. Performance on an IQ test below 2 standard deviations defines mild; below 3, moderate; below 4, severe; and below 5, profound. In addition, a borderline level had been recognized in the past, but it is no longer mentioned (Jacobson & Mulick, pp. 13–50). Each level of mental retardation is then described, both in terms of psychological abilities such as language fluency, reading, number skills, and in terms of adaptive skills such as communication, the handling of money, and general self-care skills. Some experts in the field of mental retardation believe that the AAMR definition is more sociopolitical than psychobiological. Furthermore, the new definition is criticized for failing to distinguish between individuals who are learning disabled or who have mild mental retardation from those with intellectual and adaptive behavior handicaps.

It may not be productive to focus on defining mental retardation further. Instead, one should examine the cognitive processes that contribute to the intellectual and adaptive functions of individuals with mental retardation. Familial mental retardation is a category that generally applies to all individuals with intellectual limitation whose IQs are above 50 and a very few of those whose IQs are below 50. This was suggested in 1967 by Zigler, who characterized familial mental retardation as separate from organic mental retardation. The intellectual functions of familial retardation and the development of these functions in childhood are thought to be similar to those of children without mental retardation. Mental age was suggested as a handy way of describing the level of intellectual functioning of individuals with mental retardation. Mental age, in contrast to chronological age, is an approximate guide to placing schoolchildren in instructional programs. A child of 12 who has a mental age of 6 obviously cannot benefit from regular instruction for nonretarded 12-year-olds but is likely to benefit from an instructional curriculum for 6-year-olds. The majority of individuals below the IQ of 50 are likely to have defects in chromosomes or neurological impairment of various kinds. Thus, it was easy to describe familial mental retardation as a delay in development (Zigler, 1967), rather than a defect in brain structures that are supposed to determine intelligence.

The concepts relating to the difference between structure and function have changed in the last 30 years. Neuronal structure in the brain is constantly responding to experience and learning, so much so that experience even in the embryo can change neural structures. In regard to intelligence as measured by IQ tests, recent conceptualizations to be discussed propose multiple components, multiple intelligences, or separate cognitive functions that can be organized in different parts of the brain. Therefore, it is not easy to argue in favor of defect or difference, or to determine mental age from an IQ score.

In concluding this part on the definition of mental retardation, it is apparent that the new American Association for Mental Retardation definition is controversial and does not seem to represent psychological knowledge.

The Alternative Conceptions of Retardation

New concepts of mental abilities assume a close interaction between biological and cultural factors. Interactions determine the course of the development of ba-

sic intellectual functions such as perception, memory, and language. Empirical research supporting the above beliefs have redirected research on mental retardation. In the case of mild mental retardation, similarities in basic cognitive development that were described by Piaget have been observed between people with and without mental retardation. The core difference between them seems to be in learning ability; this is why in Britain, mental retardation is labeled as severe learning difficulty. As more and more research into specific cognitive processes of MRs has been carried out, we are able to understand more about cognitive functions in general. A good example of this is found in research into seeing, hearing, and space and time by O'Connor and Hermelin (1978). From their experiments on spatial and temporal perception of three kinds of children—the deaf, the mentally retarded, and nonretarded hearing children—they concluded that the deaf and the mentally retarded prefer spatial ordering of stimuli to temporal ordering when either kind of ordering is possible. Another example of the unity and differences between the cognitive process of MR and non-MR populations is found in the consistent research of Luria on speech and thought. His research suggests that children with mental retardation have a specific difficulty in regulating their behavior through speech. The development of inner speech is suggested to be the critical factor in regulating behavior in childhood and beyond. Children with MR have difficulty in controlling their behavior by internalized speech (Luria, 1961).

Recent developments in conceptualizing intelligence have also contributed greatly to alternative views of mental retardation. Intelligence is not a global, undifferentiated ability. This is suggested by several contemporary researchers in the area of intelligence (Das, 1984; Gardner, 1983; Sternberg & Spear, 1985). Once it was demonstrated that IQ was inadequate as a measure of intellectual functions (Ceci, 1990), it was easy to reconceptualize intelligence. One new model proposes four major intellectual functions: planning, attention, simultaneous processing, and successive processing (PASS). According to the PASS model, both intellectual limitation and adaptive behavior limitations can be explained in terms of the four processes of planning and judgment, attention and arousal, and simultaneous and successive processing. For example, Down syndrome adolescents were found to be relatively weak in successive processing compared to MR adolescents of other etiologies (Das, Naglieri, & Kirby, 1994). Similarly, it was found that the decline of attentional and planning functions was evident among Down syndrome adults above the age of 40 compared to other MR adults (Das & Mishra, 1995). Thus, the advantages of a new conceptualization of intelligence over a unidimensional concept of IQ are clear.

The current trend of research in understanding

mental retardation is focused on the micro level, that is, on specific differences in cognitive processes of attention, learning, memory, and metamemory (Brooks, Sperber, & McCauley, 1984). At the macro level, there are still overarching theories of intelligent behavior that are found to be useful and prevalent in the field of mental retardation. This has been a continuing trend as information processing theory, neuropsychology, and computer models of intellectual functions have gained prominence in contemporary psychology (Jacobson & Mulick, 1996).

Causes of Mental Retardation

The causes of mental retardation are to be divided into the following kinds, which also determine, to a certain extent, the causes of individual differences in intelligence. If mild mental retardation is regarded as a variation of normal distribution of intelligence in a population, then the cause is probably polygenic inheritance, such as the type that determines skin color or height. There is more to heredity than space permits discussion of here, but it is probably acceptable to say that some individuals who are classified as mildly mentally retarded (IQs between 50 and 70) could be the tail end of the distribution of intelligence, just as short people exist at the tail end of the distribution of height. This would be the explanation favored by Zigler (1967). Contemporary thinkers have moved away from a simple view of heredity. Sophisticated accounts consider not only genes but the expression of genes as the determinant of characteristics such as intelligence.

There are environmental factors that determine intelligence and therefore can causally explain mental retardation. In fact, among the vast number of culturally disadvantaged children who are classified as poor achievers in school, and who can be placed, in terms of IQ, below 1 to 2 standard deviations of the mean of 100, environmentally caused retardation is quite frequent. As mentioned, these include a cultural environment that does not support schooling and literacy, in addition to the basic physical factors such as health and nutrition. But how much of it is due to genetic factors and how much to environmental deprivation would be a very difficult question to answer in view of the changes in concepts of heredity and social-historical conditions that determine mental retardation.

What about those who do not show an improvement in spite of educational and other environmental support and remain below the tenth percentile in measures of school achievement? At this point, a deficit in the general functioning of the brain probably has to be suggested. Luria posited that these children are the truly mentally retarded, as are those who have *abnormal* brain development, manifested in cognitive and motor functions. He argued that we would be doing an injustice to these children by simply designating them as

those with inferior talents or low ability that are variations of *normal* ability (Luria, 1963).

There are several organic causes of mental retardation: disorders of chromosomes, as found in Down syndrome; fragile X syndrome; metabolic disorder; prenatal developmental malformation; the effect of drugs and alcohol; diseases that affect the brain, including syphilis and HIV; severe malnutrition and other physical injuries caused by trauma (child abuse and automobile accidents), and prematurity and growth retardation at the fetal stage. It may be possible to prevent some of the contributing factors to the development of both familial mental retardation and organic mental retardation. Providing better nutrition and environment and active interaction with adults are some of the ways in which cultural familial mental retardation may be ameliorated. Refraining from the use of drugs and preventing infections and injuries that result in mental retardation would be the preventative measures that reduce the incidence of organic mental retardation.

Treatment and Remediation

Treatments for mental retardation as a consequence of physical damage such as toxins, radiation, and infections have been adopted by the medical profession for a long time. However, attempts at increasing intelligence by prescribing drugs, which were quite popular from the 1930s to the 1950s, have been discontinued. There is no drug cure for mental retardation, unless the condition is associated with a disease that can receive recommended medication. For example, vaccinations for rubella and HIV will be effective in preventing mental retardation. Pregnant women are routinely advised to avoid alcohol and tobacco consumption. The availability of good nutrition to the lactating mother and the baby, avoiding exposure to toxic environments including pollution, and adequate primary health care are recommended by the United Nations.

One thing is clear, however. None of the education programs or intervention measures are aimed at curing mental retardation, especially when it is not due to cultural or nutritional disadvantage. The best way to look at the effect of early intervention is in terms of its benefit, which includes profiting from education and preparation for occupation and independent living.

Success in the employability of individuals with mental retardation, which was first assessed many years back, continues to be reported in the scientific literature. Independent living is now the rule rather than an example. The controversy in regard to whether or not we can improve IQ should be left behind.

Mainstreaming in Schools—Does Inclusive Education Work?

There is now general agreement that special classes do not facilitate better learning among children with mental retardation. The recommendation by Lloyd Dunn, one of the early researchers in special education, was to place children with mental retardation in regular classrooms. In the 1970s, the attitude toward normalization began to influence special education. Normalization implied that every child or adult with a mental handicap should lead as normal a life as possible. This meant that children with mental retardation should be placed side by side with children without mental retardation; this will increase their learning opportunities.

Today, a variety of arrangements in the classroom are practiced to make mainstreaming work. The teachers and school administrators get support from the office of their school board. The support includes teams of specialists before the special child is referred to a regular class, collaborative consultation with experts in the school system, cooperative teaching in which teachers of special classes and regular classes teach together, and peer tutoring, in which one or two nonretarded children tutor the child with mental retardation. Where full integration is not carried out, partial integration is practiced. In the final analysis, what counts is the program of instruction in these different kinds of groupings rather than the physical location of the child in a regular class or in a special class. Regular mainstreamed classes are quite common, and although the teachers are reluctant to take too many special needs children, they do manage with the help of teachers' aides. Full inclusion, like its predecessor normalization, has become a political platform for some activists in the field of disability. They argue that there are compelling ethical reasons to include every child, irrespective of the type or degree of handicap, in a regular class. This is acceptable as far as it goes, except that empirical studies ought to be conducted to assess the efficacy of these different arrangements in mainstreaming.

The Aim Is "Normalization"

As support services increase and become easily accessible, mental retardation will not be experienced as a severe handicap. However, both philosophical and empirical questions remain to be answered in mental retardation. The attitude toward a child with mental retardation should be positive, that is, the child should be considered not as inferior but as a special child whose mental and physical adjustments are unique (Vygotsky, 1993). There is no reason to discriminate against people with mild and moderate mental retardation, either in school or at the workplace. To treat them as normal human beings, sharing the learning opportunities and socialization processes afforded by schools, is now legally imposed in some countries, such as the United States. Of course, it is true that adults with mental handicaps, even when fully employed, slide down to the economic status of an ordinary unskilled laborer. The

work experience, though, improves their social skills and at the same time gives them the opportunity to interact with other people. Does it improve their intelligence and adaptive behavior? The IQ of individuals with mental retardation may not be improved because of their integration into the community, but certainly intelligence, as measured in terms of cognitive processes, is challenged and modified because of school attendance and community living. Furthermore, their adaptive skills improve in that they learn to manipulate people and their work environment to their advantage. Schooling, job training, and independent living make demands on their cognitive abilities—they have to plan and evaluate their activities, analyze what is happening around them, and be mindful to control impulsive behavior. These are some of the basic components of intelligence. These are also the unmistakable benefits of eliminating institutionalization. In any case, we do not have to justify why human dignity should be restored to people with mental handicap.

[*See also* Down Syndrome.]

Bibliography

Brooks, P. H., Sperber, R., & McCauley, C. (1984). *Learning and cognition in the mentally retarded.* Hillsdale, NJ: Erlbaum.

Ceci, S. J. (1990). *On intelligence . . . more or less: A bioecological treatise on intellectual development.* Englewood Cliffs, NJ: Prentice Hall.

Das, J. P. (1984). Cognitive deficits in mental retardation: A process approach. In P. H. Brooks, R. Sperber, & C. McCauley (Eds.), *Learning and cognition in the mentally retarded* (pp. 115–128). Hillsdale, NJ: Erlbaum.

Das, J. P., Naglieri, J. A., & Kirby, J. R. (1994). *Assessment of cognitive processes.* Needham Heights, MA: Allyn and Bacon.

Das, J. P., & Mishra, R. K. (1995). Assessment of cognitive decline associated with aging. *Research in Developmental Disabilities, 16(1),* 11–25.

Gardner, H. (1983). *Frames of mind.* New York: Basic Books.

Jacobson, J. W., & Mulick, J. A. (1996). *Manual of diagnosis and professional practice in mental retardation.* Washington, DC: American Psychological Association.

Luckasson R., Coulter, D. L., Polloway, E. A., Reiss, S., Schalock, R. L., Snell, M. E., Spitalnik, D. M., & Stark, J. A. (1992). *Mental retardation: Definition, classification, and systems of supports* (9th ed.). Washington, DC: American Association on Mental Retardation.

Luria, A. R. (1961). *The role of speech in the regulation of normal and abnormal behavior.* London: Pergamon Press.

Luria, A. R. (1963). *The mentally retarded child.* New York: Macmillan.

O'Connor, N., & Hermelin, B. (1978). *Seeing and hearing and space and time.* London: Academic Press.

Sternberg, R. J., & Spear, L. C. (1985). A triarchic theory

of mental retardation. In N. R. Ellis & N. W. Bray (Eds.), *International review of research in mental retardation* (Vol. 13, pp. 301–326). Orlando, FL: Academic Press.

Vygotsky, L. S. (1993). *The collected works of L. S. Vygotsky* (Vol. 2). New York: Plenum Press.

Zigler, E. (1967). Familial mental retardation: A continuing dilemma. *Science, 155,* 292–298.

J. P. Das

MENTAL WORKLOAD. The study of mental load focuses on the "work of the mind"—the cost of mental operations, and the constraints that are imposed by these costs on the ability of a performer to cope with the demands of a task that he or she is given to perform. *Mental operations* is employed as a generic term, to denote all processing activities and transformations that mediate between the presentation of a stimulus for a task, and the generation of a response. Examples are encoding, feature extraction, rehearsal of information, retrieval from memory, categorization, decision making, response selection, and response supervision.

Analysis and measurement of mental load is a topic of focal interest in contemporary basic and applied psychological sciences. It also has deep roots in folk psychology. Listening to people one can often hear statements such as: "You need to put your mind to it, concentrate, invest, devote attention"; "I cannot follow, this is too fast for me"; "The demands are too high." These are few examples of common expressions used by people to describe the demands, or the mental costs of involvement in the performance of a given task. How are these experiences reflected in the scientific study of load?

In the applied sciences the question is often addressed by professionals in the field who are called upon to evaluate the ability of performers to cope with the demands of a task or an engineering system that they need to interact with. It influences design considerations, training programs, and personnel selection batteries. In basic research, the analysis of mental load is the backbone of several theoretical debates focusing on the most adequate conceptual framework and functional model to describe the operation of the human mind. Major issues are energy versus structural limitations on processing and response; scarcity of resources; voluntary allocation of attention and effort as compared to automatic engagement and attention capturing. All can be traced back to the basic issue of the causes of mental load. The definition and assumed nature of mental operations and hence the analysis of their costs, strongly depend on and are bound by the theoretical views held by the analyst. Consequently, while there is a general consensus on the existence of costs and the need to evaluate them, there is a disagreement on their nature and the best ways to measure them.

At present, the mental load of performing a given task, is expressed in terms of one or more of three cost functions: behavioral (the cost of load to performance); subjective (the conscious appraisal of load); and physiological (state variables and specific activations associated with cognitive processes). Each of these functions is accompanied by several sets of measures that have been the subject of extensive empirical and methodological tests. For some tasks, load measures obtained by different methods covary, while in others they dissociate.

Behavioral Indices

Increased costs of mental operations are expected to reduce the efficiency of performance. Behavioral measurement methods attempt to derive an index of load from elements of task performance. The most prevalent approaches are based on analysis of performance levels and interference patterns among two concurrently performed tasks. The two major variants of this paradigm are *secondary task technique* and *performance operating characteristics* (POC) methodology. In the secondary task technique two tasks are performed concurrently. The level of performance on one task (the secondary task) is used to index spare capacity, and by inference, the load imposed on the other task (primary task) with which it is time shared. The convention is to employ a battery of secondary tasks, each designed to emphasize a different process, resulting in a load profile of a task. Performance operating characteristics measure in addition, the influence on performance of varying attention allocation policies. A POC curve depicts all possible, dual-task, performance combinations, arising from splitting efforts in different proportions among concurrently performed tasks.

Subjective Measures

These measures represent the load estimates given by a performer to the mental demands of a task in which he or she is involved. Subjective measures are the most direct mental cost function which is easy to obtain. They reflect the conscious appraisal of an individual of his experience with a task relative to other tasks. This is its strength and weakness, because people are conscious only of a small fraction of their mental operations and their cost. The four most common measurement approaches are rating scales, magnitude estimations, the NASA Task-Load-indeX (TLX), and the U.S. Airforce Subjective Workload Assessment Technique (SWAT). TLX and SWAT provide an integrated measure over several dimensions of subjective load experience.

Physiological Measures

Two classes of physiological cost functions have been associated with the assessment of mental load and efficiency. One includes general arousal and energy modulation measures. The second comprises indices of brain activity corresponding to specific cognitive activities. The basic assumption underlying the use of arousal and energy state measures is that mental effort increases the activation of various bodily systems to support it. A complementary assumption is that metabolic or induced modulations of arousal levels are accompanied by changes in the efficiency of mental operations. Arousal increments have been measured in cardiovascular activation, respiration, brain electrical activity, or parasympathetic manifestations such as pupil dilation. In the class of specific mental activities, cognitive psychophysiology has taken upon itself the task of developing measures of brain activity that can meet the challenge of evaluating cognitive processes in the normal, intact, and functioning organism. Event related brain potentials, magnetic encephalography, functional magnetic resonance imaging, and positron emission tomography are the 4 major measurement techniques that have been applied for this purpose. All have been shown to reflect and be differentially sensitive to cognitive activities.

In summary, the analysis and measurement of mental load is developing and changing as our knowledge and understanding of brain and cognition are enhanced. Notwithstanding, there appears to be emerging an overall view of mental load as a joint product of three determinants: Computational processes, energy modulations, and the control level of resource use.

Bibliography

Gopher, D. (1994). Analysis and measurement of mental workload. In G. d'Ydewalle, P. Eelen, & P. Bertelson (Eds.), *International perspectives on cognitive sciences* (Vol. 2, pp. 265–291). London: Erlbaum.

Gopher, D., & Donchin, E. (1986). Workload: An examination of the concept. In K. Boff & L. Kaufman (Eds.), *Handbook of human perception and performance* (Vol. 2, pp. 1–49). New York: Wiley.

Gopher, D., & Koriat, A. (Eds.). (1999). *Attention and performance XVII: Cognitive regulation of performance: Interaction of theory and application.* Cambridge, MA: MIT Press.

Hancock, P. A., & Meshkati, N. (Eds.) (1988). *Human mental workload.* Amsterdam: North Holland.

Inui, T., & McClelland, J. (1996). *Attention and performance XVI: Information integration in perception and communication.* Cambridge, MA: MIT Press.

O'Donnell, R. D., & Eggemeier, F. T. (1986). Workload assessment methodology. In: K. R. Boff, J. P. Thomas, & L. Kaufman (Eds.). *Handbook of human perception and performance* (pp. 1–49). New York: Wiley.

Daniel Gopher

MENTORING PROGRAMS. Mentoring programs focus on creating one-to-one relationships in which volunteers and protégés meet frequently over a period of several months or years. Mentoring programs are most commonly implemented within business, higher education, and youth settings. Within business settings, mentors are typically recruited from within organizations and paired with more junior employees in an effort to foster the employees' career development. Education-based mentoring programs typically involve the pairing of teachers with students and focus on the development of the students' educational skills and goals. Within youth settings, older individuals are typically paired with youth who are at risk for negative developmental outcomes. Such programs target a wide range of youth (e.g., pregnant teenagers, juvenile offenders, foster children), pairing them with a range of volunteers (e.g., older adults, executives, peer leaders). Most youth mentoring programs offer general support and guidance, whereas some recruit adults to serve very specific, narrowly defined goals.

History

Although some programs (e.g., Big Brothers and Big Sisters) have been in existence for many years, mentoring programs gained considerable popularity in this country in the late 1980s. By the early 1990s, a range of influential organizations had initiated programs, and several foundations were created to stimulate mentoring programs in communities around the country. In addition to launching programs for their own employees, many corporations encouraged employees to "adopt" students from nearby schools. Several states and school systems became actively involved in stimulating mentoring programs (Freedman, 1993).

Central Techniques and Practices

The extent to which mentoring programs include standardized procedures varies considerably. It appears, however, that three practices are critically important to the success of mentoring programs: screening, training, and supervision (Sipe, 1995). The screening process entails the selection of those individuals who are most likely to be successful mentors. The process screens for law-abiding individuals who can consistently meet with their protégés; in addition, there is some evidence to suggest that certain characteristics are preferable to others. For example, mentors who enter programs with an orientation toward building a trusting relationship (as opposed to attempting to immediately "transform" the protégé) tend to be more successful.

Preprogram training increases the likelihood that both the mentors and the protégés will share a common understanding of their roles in the relationship and helps mentors to develop realistic expectations of what they can accomplish. Finally, ongoing supervision and support of matches by program personnel is important for ensuring that pairs meet regularly and develop positive relationships (Sipe, 1995).

Key Assumptions or Theories

Mentoring programs in higher education and employment settings tend to be viewed within the context of adult development. Within this context, Levinson and colleagues (1978) have characterized mentors as teachers, sponsors, counselors, guides, and exemplars and as facilitating the "realization of the Dream" (p. 98) or the positive vision that protégés hold about their futures.

Mentoring programs that are targeted toward youth are often driven by the concept of resilience. Investigators of resilience attempt to understand youth who have adjusted well despite profound, ongoing stress associated with poverty and difficult life circumstances. Researchers have found that resilient children often have at least one nonparent adult in their lives who provided them with consistent emotional support (Garmezy, 1985; Rutter, 1990; Werner, 1995). Mentoring programs are thus seen as addressing the growing need for supportive adults in the lives of vulnerable youth.

Research Findings

Despite widespread enthusiasm for mentoring programs, data on their effectiveness are sparse. Few evaluations of mentoring programs have included comparison groups, statistical controls for initial differences, or follow-up evaluations. Most evaluations in business and academic settings have involved retrospective accounts of informal mentoring relationships. The few evaluations of formal mentoring programs in these settings do, however, yield some promising findings (Murray, 1991).

There is also some evidence to support the viability of mentoring programs in youth settings (DuBois, Hollaway, Cooper, & Valentine, in press). The most comprehensive evaluation of youth mentoring to date is a study of Big Brothers/Big Sisters (BB/BS; Grossman & Tierney, 1998). The study included nearly 1,000 10- to 16-year-olds who applied to a geographically diverse set of BB/BS programs. Control participants were put on a waiting list for 18 months, and treatment youth were matched with mentors. In contrast to the controls, program participants demonstrated significant improvements in peer and parent relationships, attitudes toward completing schoolwork, school attendance, and school performance. Participants also reported comparatively lower levels of substance use and aggressive behavior. These findings highlight the potential benefits of youth mentoring programs. Nonetheless, because many programs provide insufficient infrastructure to achieve adequate mentor screening, training, and supervision, the effectiveness of mentoring programs is presumed to vary widely (Freedman, 1993).

Recurring Issues

As the number of mentoring programs continues to grow, the issue of quality remains a primary concern. The field lacks a basic set of standards to guide the development and monitoring of quality programs and effective relationships (Sipe, 1995). For example, questions regarding the method of training volunteer mentors and the criteria for making successful matches need to be addressed. It will also be important to explore the possible harmful effects of assigned mentoring programs, as failed relationships can lead to considerable hurt and disappointment. Moreover, there remains a need to examine the interface between mentors' and protégés' preexisting social networks and to understand the issues involved in making cross-race matches. Finally, it will be important to identify the underlying processes by which mentors have their positive effects (Rhodes, Grossman, & Resch, in press). Within this context, strategies for facilitating sensitive, high-quality mentoring programs should continue to be identified, implemented, and evaluated.

Bibliography

DuBois, D. L., Hollaway, B. E., Cooper, H., & Valentine, J. C. (in press). Effectiveness of mentoring programs for youth: A meta-analytic review. *American Journal of Community Psychology.*

Freedman, M. (1993). *The kindness of strangers: Adult mentors, urban youth, and the new voluntarism.* San Francisco: Jossey-Bass. Outlines the history and current status of youth mentoring programs in the United States.

Garmezy, N. (1985). Stress resistant children: The search for protective factors. In J. E. Stevenson (Ed.), *Recent research in developmental psychopathology* (pp. 213–233). Oxford, UK: Pergamon Press.

Grossman, J. B., & Tierney, J. P. (1998). Does mentoring work? An impact study of the Big Brothers/Big Sisters program. *Evaluation Review, 22,* 402–425.

Levinson, D., Darrow, C., Klein, E., Lenson, M., & McKee, B. (1978). *The seasons in a man's life.* New York: Knopf.

Murray, M. (1991). *Beyond the myths and magic of mentoring: How to facilitate effective mentoring programs.* San Francisco: Jossey-Bass.

Rhodes, J. E., Ebert, L., & Fischer, K. (1992). Natural mentors: An overlooked resource in the social networks of African-American adolescent mothers. *American Journal of Community Psychology, 20,* 445–462.

Rhodes, J. E., Grossman, J. B., & Resch, N. L. (in press). Agents of change: Pathways through which mentoring relationships influence adolescents' academic adjustments.

Rutter, M. (1990). Psychosocial resilience and protective mechanisms. In J. Rolf, A. S. Masten, D. Cicchetti, K. H. Neuchterlein, & S. Weintraub (Eds.), *Risk and protective factors in the development of psychopathology* (pp. 181–214). New York: Cambridge University Press.

Sipe, C. L. (1995). *Mentoring: A synthesis of P/PV's Research: 1988–1995.* Philadelphia: Public/Private Ventures. Public/Private Ventures has been conducting extensive research on mentoring programs for the past ten years, and this report provides a synthesis of the major findings, as well as summaries of P/PV's report.

Styles, M.B., & Morrow, K. V. (1992). *Understanding how youth and elders form relationships: A study of four linking lifetimes programs.* Philadelphia: Public/Private Ventures.

Werner, E. E. (1995). Resilience in development. *Current Directions in Psychological Science, 4,* 81–85.

Jean Rhodes

MESMER, FRANZ ANTON (1734–1815), German physician. Mesmer, born in the small German town of Iznang near the shores of Lake Constance, studied medicine in Vienna and received his medical degree from the University of Vienna in 1766. Although his doctoral dissertation contained the germ of ideas that would eventually flower into a general theory of disease and healing, those ideas were given more complete expression in Mesmer's most important treatise, *Mémoire sur la découverte du magnétisme animal* (Geneva and Paris, 1779).

The *Mémoire* is widely considered to be a foundational work in the history of Western psychology. Here Mesmer presents his ideas about "animal magnetism," a theory and technique for treating physical illnesses. Having first experimented with magnets to cure diseases, Mesmer came to the conclusion that the human body itself is a magnet and that the physician, using his own body magnetically, could produce more effective cures than conventional medicine. He identified an invisible but purely physical agent that pervades all nature and is the source of life and health in living things. Mesmer believed that this agent, which he called "animal magnetism," operated in the body in the form of a fine "fluid" (the term in use at the time to denote any

subtle substance or influence) and that its natural flow through the organism constituted health, whereas impediments to this flow led to disease. Illness was cured by the direct intervention of the physician himself, who through "magnetic passes" (flowing movements of the hands over the patient's body, usually without touching) could break down the blockages to the free flow of the magnetic fluid and restore healthy functioning.

In 1778 Mesmer moved to Paris and attempted to gain acceptance for his ideas from the medical and political establishment. There he established an office and treatment rooms for the sick. In the course of treatment he made use of various healing aids, including his famous *baquet,* an oaken tub specially designed to store and transmit magnetic fluid to afflicted parts of the body, and "crisis rooms" for people who experienced convulsions. Despite many attestations to the effectiveness of his treatment, he could not gain the official approval he sought. In 1784 two commissions were struck by the king of France to investigate animal magnetism, one of which was headed by Benjamin Franklin, ambassador to France from the United States. Mesmer refused to take part in their investigations, but the commissioners were able to secure the cooperation of, among others, Charles D'Eslon, physician to the Comte d'Artois and an enthusiastic practitioner of animal magnetism. The commissions reported that they found no evidence for a magnetic fluid but did note real effects from treatment by animal magnetic procedures, probably due to the influence of "imagination." Despite the negative findings of the commissions, animal magnetism continued to be used as a healing technique in France. By 1850 it had achieved widespread acceptance in Germany, Italy, England, and the United States, and it would be several more decades before it completely faded from the scene.

Because of his physiological orientation, Mesmer did not himself contribute directly to our understanding of psychology, but some of his followers did. Most notably, in 1784 Armand Marie Jacques de Chastenet (1751–1825), the Marquis de Puységur, took up the practice of animal magnetism and developed it in a direction that would make it truly significant in the history of psychology. Puységur had been taught magnetic healing by Mesmer and in the process of applying the technique discovered that many people, when subjected to magnetic passes, would go into an altered state of consciousness. He called this state "magnetic sleep" or "magnetic somnambulism" (because of its resemblance to the sleepwalking state). Puységur noted five basic characteristics of this state: a sleep-waking kind of consciousness, "rapport" or a special connection between subject and magnetizer, suggestibility, a notable alteration of the personality of the subject, and amnesia for events of that state upon returning to ordinary consciousness. Through his work with magnetic somnambulism, Puységur made possible a new, purely psychological paradigm for thinking about mental disorders, something that would be brought to fruition only much later, with the work of Pierre Janet (1859–1947), Josef Breuer (1842–1925), Jean-Martin Charcot (1825–1893), and other researchers of the 1880s and 1890s who were influenced by the magnetic tradition. Puységur's psychological orientation, as opposed to the purely physiological approach of Mesmer, began a tradition of animal magnetic healing that, 60 years later, would be revised and renamed "hypnotism" by the Manchester physician James Braid (1795–1860).

Bibliography

Bloch, G. (Ed.). (1980). *Mesmerism: A translation of the original scientific and medical writings of F. A. Mesmer.* Los Altos, CA: Kaufman.

Crabtree, A. (1993). *From Mesmer to Freud: Magnetic sleep and the roots of psychological healing.* New Haven, CT: Yale University Press.

Darnton, R. (1968). *Mesmerism and the end of the enlightenment in France.* Cambridge, MA: Harvard University Press.

Ellenberger, H. (1970). *The discovery of the unconscious.* New York: Basic Books.

Gauld, A. (1992). *A history of hypnotism.* Cambridge, England: Cambridge University Press.

Pattie, F. A. (1994). *Mesmer and animal magnetism: A chapter in the history of medicine.* Hamilton, NY: Edmonston.

Adam Crabtree

MESSER, AUGUST (1867–1937), German psychologist and philosopher. Messer studied the act or process of thinking, as opposed to its content, such as the sensations and images associated with thought. In this, he was a follower of Oswald Külpe and the Würzburg school of psychology. He was born in Mainz, in the state of Hesse-Darmstadt. He received a middle-class education, then attended the universities of Giessen, Heidelberg, and Strasbourg. After some teaching in secondary schools, he gained the position of docent in philosophy at the University of Giessen in 1899. He advanced to extraordinary (associate) professor in 1904 and to full professor in 1910. He was married in 1909. The First Congress of Experimental Psychology met at Giessen in 1904. There he heard Külpe from the neighboring University of Würzburg read his paper on *Versuche über Abstraktion* (Experiments on abstraction). In Wilhelm Wundt's laboratory in Leipzig, thought had not been deemed measurable in the laboratory and therefore was considered beyond the scope of experimental psychology. Külpe's research, done with William L. Bryan, later president of both the American Psycho-

logical Association and of Indiana University, raised doubts that sensory impressions were always present in consciousness, since attention to one can result in complete absence in others, thus demonstrating thought without images.

Messer was much impressed by Külpe's approach and spent the next summer with him in Würzburg, where Külpe had assembled a group of experimental psychologists studying thought processes. This "Würzburg school" was joined by Messer and is known particularly for its advocacy of imageless thought, directly challenging Wundt and his Leipzig school. The method used by the group was simple. They tried to analyze the thinking process verbally, leading to individual protocols of introspection describing how they arrived at their solution, sometimes using reaction times. Messer had returned to Giessen, where he pursued his own research on the thought process. The publication in 1906 of "Experimentell-psychologische Untersuchungen über das Denken" (Experimental-psychological Investigations of Thinking) was his first major contribution.

In 1908, Messer published *Empfindung und Denken* (Sensation and Thinking; Leipzig), an attempt to formulate an alternative to sensationalism by an analysis of perception, meaning, attention, abstraction, judgment, and thought. He emphasized the distinction between content and act in thinking, thus following a distinction originally made by Franz Brentano. Further attempts by Messer to explain his position came in his *Psychologie* in 1914 (2nd ed., 1920). Here he tried to reconcile content and acts, such that both could exist side by side. Contents are sensations, images, temporal and spatial relations, and impressions. Acts are knowing, feeling, and willing. Contents and acts were part of intentional experiences. Experiences involved both an unconscious activity and the conscious content of the act. Messer thus was able to combine a psychology of function and of content.

Today, the general principle of cognitive determinants of response has become indispensable. We rely on the notions of set, expectance, attitude formation and change, and cognitive style in theorizing, and in experimentation on perception, learning, memory, attitude formation. Messer's methology, however, and the Würzburg school were swept away with the rise of behaviorism and Gestalt psychology.

Bibliography

Boring, E. G. (1950). *A history of experimental psychology* (2nd ed., pp. 448–456). New York: Appleton-Century-Crofts. The best and most thorough account.

Messer, A. (1906). Experimentell-psychologische Untersuchungen über das Denken. *Archiv für die gesamte Psychologie, 8,* 1–224. Messer's important first paper.

Schmidt, R. (1923). *Philosophie der Gegenwart in Selbstdarstellung* (Vol. 3, pp. 145–176). Messer's autobiography.

Vinacke, W. E. (1952). *The psychology of thinking.* New York: McGraw-Hill. A good reference on thinking.

Helmut E. Adler

META-ANALYSIS is the use of statistical procedures to summarize the results of statistical analyses from multiple, related studies for the purposes of drawing general conclusions. This summary often involves explaining variation in results over studies. Meta-analysis is distinguished from secondary analysis in that the information used in meta-analysis comes from statistical summaries of the data in the original studies and not directly from the raw data themselves. Meta-analysis is a fundamental scientific activity that is widely practiced in all of the empirical sciences (Draper et al., 1993). Since replication of results is a hallmark of the scientific process, some form of research synthesis is essential to determine whether results from different studies replicate and to summarize the bulk of the evidence from replicated studies.

Why Special Methods Are Needed

It is tempting to assume that competent researchers can subjectively interpret the results of several related studies, but this is not usually true. At least two questions arise in the interpretation of replicated results: Is the average effect different from zero and do the studies agree? Neither question can easily be answered satisfactorily by using the outcomes of significance tests alone. It is natural to rely on the proportion of studies that found an effect (the proportion of statistically significant results) to make judgments about the average effect, a process that has been called vote counting. However, as natural as vote counting may seem, it has been shown to have astonishingly low power in most situations and to have power which actually decreases (tending to zero) as more evidence (more studies) are obtained (Hedges & Olkin, 1985). It is also tempting to regard agreement on the outcomes of significance tests as an index of agreement among underlying study findings, but this too is problematic. It can be shown that unless all studies have unrealistically high power, agreement on the outcomes of significance tests will not be impressively high even when all studies have exactly the same underlying effect.

Meta-Analysis as an Aspect of Procedure in Research Synthesis

As in primary research, procedures in research syntheses can influence results. Consequently research synthesists have emphasized the development of methodological standards that are intended to assure the validity of syntheses (Cooper, 1998). The resulting procedures usually have been divided into problem formulation (deciding on constructs and operations); data collection (literature searching, coding of information, calculation of effect size measures, etc.); data evaluation (assessment of study quality and rules for exclusion of studies); and data analysis and interpretation (Cooper & Hedges, 1994). All of these aspects of procedure are important in assuring the validity of research syntheses, but in this article I focus on the last aspect: meta-analysis as an aspect of data analysis and interpretation in research synthesis.

Statistical Procedures in Meta-Analysis

There are two basic types of procedures in meta-analysis: combined significance tests and effect-size analyses. Both are described in detail in Hedges and Olkin (2000). Combined significance tests summarize the exact significance levels (p-values) obtained in the set of studies to be combined. Combined significance tests are well suited to screening studies to determine whether any study found an effect (e.g., Rosenthal & Rubin, 1978), but are poorly suited to assessment of more refined questions about average effects, generalizability, or moderator variables (Becker, 1987; or Cooper & Hedges, 1994, chapter 15).

Effect Sizes

Effect-size analyses are the most widely used meta-analytic procedures. They involve summarizing the results of a study by an index of the magnitude of a relation, such as a standardized mean difference, a correlation coefficient, a proportion responding, or an odds ratio. The reason for using an index of effect size is to make the results of all studies comparable (to put them "on the same scale"). The choice of an effect-size index in a meta-analysis depends on the nature of the experimental design and the outcome measure. Each study provides an estimate (the sample effect size) of its underlying effect-size parameter, and a standard error of estimation as an indication of its uncertainty.

These individual estimates are combined across studies to estimate the average of the underlying effect-size parameters or to characterize the variation across studies in the effect-size parameters. Because some studies have larger sample sizes and produce effect-size estimates with greater precision than others, combining across studies usually involves weighting to give more influence to the estimates with greater precision. The optimal weight is one that is inversely proportional to the variance of the effect-size estimate. Weighting also simplifies the sampling distributions of statistics used in meta-analysis, but contrary to some claims, weighting does not affect bias.

Fixed and Random Effects Models

Two slightly different kinds of procedures are used to combine estimates in meta-analysis. They are called *fixed* and *random effects procedures*. In principle, fixed effects models are intended to make inferences about the effect parameters that are present in the studies that are actually observed. In contrast, random effects models are intended to make inferences about the effect parameters of a putative population of studies from which the observed studies are a random sample.

Consequently, the two types of procedures differ in what variation is taken to be random statistical fluctuation. Both treat as random the sampling variation of estimates about the effect-size parameter within each study. This sampling fluctuation is the only component of random variation in fixed effects models. In contrast, random effects models also treat the variation across studies of effect-size parameters. Thus random effects models have two sources of random variation as random.

Fixed and random effects procedures compute the combined estimate of effect size in similar ways. In each case the combined estimate is the weighted mean and the standard error of the weighted mean is the square root of the reciprocal of the sum of the weights. Because the estimates are normally distributed, confidence intervals can be computed as ranging over a certain number (e.g., 1.96 for 95% confidence intervals) of standard errors above and below the weighted mean. The only difference between fixed and random effects procedures is in how the weights are computed. Fixed effects procedures weight by the reciprocal of the sampling variance of the effect-size estimate. In contrast, random effects procedures weight by the reciprocal of the sum of the sampling error variance and the between-studies variance component. These differences generally lead to larger standard errors, longer confidence intervals, and a smaller likelihood of statistical significance when means are computed by random effects procedures.

Assessing Heterogeneity

Two related omnibus procedures for assessing heterogeneity of study results (study effect-size parameters) are used. One is a test of heterogeneity, which is a formal statistical test of the null hypothesis that all of the underlying effect parameters have exactly the same value. This test uses the weighted sum of squares of the observed effect sizes about the weighted mean, which has the chi-square distribution when all of the effect parameters are equal. The other approach to assessing heterogeneity is to estimate the variance across studies of the underlying effect size parameters (that is, the between-study variance component). This between-study variance component can be estimated from the

weighted sum of squares used in the test of heterogeneity or by subtracting the average of the sampling error variances from the variance of the observed effect sizes. The latter method of computation makes it clear why some writers (e.g., Hunter & Schmidt, 1990) call computation of this variance component "correcting the observed variance (of effect size estimates) for sampling error."

While omnibus procedures are designed to detect *any* variation among effect sizes, they are not optimal for detecting any particular *specific* pattern of variation that can be anticipated. For example, if a specific subset of studies is expected to have effects that differ from the remainder, more powerful tests can be constructed. For example, if the effect is believed to be a linear function of dosage or treatment intensity, a test of that linear relation will be more powerful than a test of generic variation. The problem of detecting specific patterns of variation can be conceived as the problem of determining whether study-level moderator variables are related to effect size.

Three general strategies are used to detect moderator variables. One is based on the evaluation of contrasts, as in the analysis of variance (ANOVA). General procedures for estimating and testing the statistical significance of contrasts among effect sizes are available. The second type of procedure is a generalization of ANOVA for effect sizes, which permits the evaluation (estimation) of the relationship between one or more categorical independent variables and effect size. The third is a generalization of multiple regression analysis for effect sizes, which permits the evaluation (estimation) and testing of the relationship between any categorical or continuous variables and effect size. All three procedures are discussed in Hedges and Olkin (2000) and Cooper and Hedges (1994).

Validity Generalization

A branch of meta-analysis, validity generalization is concerned with the variation of test validity coefficients across validation studies (and coincidently across, sites, jobs, and research designs). In validity generalization, the effect-size index is a test validity. Attention often centers on the degree to which aspects of the research design (such as restriction of range of the test score distribution or measurement error in test and criterion) artifactually influence the validity coefficients. Random effects procedures are usually used to estimate the mean and variance of the test validity parameters net of (or corrected for) the effects of these design artifacts (Hunter & Schmidt, 1990).

Publication Bias

Often called the file-drawer problem, publication bias arises when the chance that the results of a study are observed depends on those study results; for example, when studies that do not find statistically significant results are less likely to be observed (e.g., published or otherwise reported). Publication bias can substantially bias estimates of effect size that are observed and hence can bias meta-analytic results. However, this bias is only large if a substantial fraction of all studies conducted are not included in the meta-analysis. Perhaps the most widely used procedure for detecting publication bias is the funnel plot, a plot of effect size versus sample size (or sampling variance, or standard error). Such a plot will be funnel shaped if there is no publication bias, but will be asymmetric if there is publication bias which could bias results. Such graphs are difficult to interpret if the number of effect sizes is small. A formal test for publication bias which tests the asymmetry of the funnel plot is often useful. More elaborate statistical methods which both estimate the form of publication bias and correct for its effects are also available, and these perform rather well when the number of studies is large (see Hedges & Olkin, 2000, for a discussion of all of these methods).

Model-Based Meta-Analysis

Sometimes the object of a meta-analysis is not just to summarize a simple relation (as in combining effects of a single treatment), but to summarize a set of relations (as in combining estimates of a correlation matrix) to test a more complex multivariate model. These more complex procedures have been called model-based meta-analysis. Methods for combining several correlation matrices and using the combined matrix to estimate and test the statistical significance of standardized regressions have been developed (Becker, 1992). Such methods make it possible to combine information from several studies that estimate similar (but not necessarily identical) path models, estimate other path models involving these variables, and place confidence intervals about the estimates of the path coefficients obtained. These methods have also been used to estimate the generalizability of model-based findings by computing the contribution of variations across studies in procedures or operationalization of constructs on the precision of estimation of regression coefficients (see Cooper & Hedges, 1994, chapter 23).

Bibliography

Becker, B. J. (1987). Applying tests of combined significance in meta-analysis. *Psychological Bulletin, 102,* 164–171. Contrasts what can be learned from combined significance tests and effect-size analyses.

Becker, B. J. (1992). Using the results of replicated studies to estimate linear models. *Journal of Educational Statistics, 17,* 341–362. The seminal paper giving methods for model-based meta-analysis.

Cooper, H. M. (1998). *Synthesizing research: A guide for literature reviews.* Newbury Park, CA: Sage. An excellent introduction to research synthesis as a research strategy.

Cooper, H. M., & Hedges, L. V. (Eds.). (1994). *The handbook of research synthesis.* New York: The Russell Sage Foundation. Contains detailed treatments of both statistical and nonstatistical aspects of research synthesis by leading researchers.

Draper, D., Gaver, D. P., Goel, P. K., Greenhouse, J. B., Hedges, L. V., Morris, C. N., Tucker, J. R., & Waternaux, C. (1993). *Combining information: Statistical issues and opportunities for research.* Washington, DC: American Statistical Association. An examination of meta-analysis as it arises across the behavioral, biological, physical, and social sciences.

Glass, G. V. (1976). Primary, secondary, and meta-analysis of research. *Educational Researcher, 5,* 3–8. The article that first proposed the term *meta-analysis* and argued that more rigorous research reviews were needed in psychology and educational research.

Hedges, L. V., & Olkin, I. (1985). *Statistical methods for meta-analysis.* New York: Academic Press. The standard reference on statistical aspects of meta-analysis of standardization mean differences and correlations, with numerical examples.

Hedges, L. V., & Olkin, I. (2000). *Statistical methods for meta-analysis in the behavioral, medical, and social sciences.* New York: Academic Press. A comprehensive treatment of meta-analysis for all effect size indices, with numerical examples.

Hunter, J. E., & Schmidt, F. L. (1990). *Methods of meta-analysis: Correcting error and bias in research findings.* Beverly Hills, CA: Sage. The standard reference of validity generalization.

Rosenthal, R. (1991). *Meta-analytic procedures for social research.* Newbury Park, CA: Sage. An excellent introduction to meta-analysis.

Rosenthal, R., & Rubin, D. B. (1978). Interpersonal expectancy effects: The first 345 studies. *Behavioral and Brain Sciences, 3,* 377–386. Good example of combined significance tests, with commentary.

Larry V. Hedges

METACOGNITION. *See* Learning Skills.

METAPHYSICS is the branch of philosophy concerned with the ultimate nature of reality. Its name derives from Aristotle's treatment of the subject, which came after (Greek *meta*) that of physics. It typically involves reference to that which is not directly observable. In this sense it is opposed to positivistic science. However, it is now generally accepted that all branches of science employ concepts (such as atoms) which do not refer directly to observable entities, and are concerned to explain phenomena by reference to underlying processes. Psychology is no more the study of behavior per se than is physics the study of meter reading. Theories differ on (1) whether these concepts are regarded as real, existing entities (realism) or merely useful tools to aid prediction (instrumentalism); and (2) how closely related to observables they must be. For example, neobehaviorists distinguished between intervening variables, whose meaning was entirely reducible to observations, and hypothetical constructs which contained surplus meaning over and above observation statements. For example, the meaning of the concept *hunger* might be entirely reducible to its operational definition in terms of hours of food deprivation or refer to some additional internal state.

Ontological, Epistemological, and Conceptual Issues

In discussing the philosophical underpinnings of psychological theories, it is important to distinguish ontological, epistemological, and conceptual issues, which are often intermixed. A particular position, such as behaviorism, typically exists in a variety of forms, though these may tend to co-occur.

Ontology is the study of being, or what can be said to exist. According to *monism*, there is only *one* fundamental reality, while *dualism* posits the existence of two distinct realms, typically mental and physical. Others have argued for a third realm of abstract ideas. (For Plato, these were ideal forms; for the philosopher of science, Karl Popper, they were cultural objects, such as numbers, theories, and books). Somewhat analogously, psychology has different areas of study or subject matter: conscious experience, behavior, and neurophysiology. Different theoretical positions can be distinguished in terms of their focus of attention (e.g., phenomenology, behaviorism, and neuroscience).

Epistemology is the branch of philosophy which deals with methods of acquiring knowledge. Different psychological positions may be distinguished according to the methods adopted (e.g., introspection, behavioral analysis, and neurophysiology).

Conceptual issues are concerned with theoretical analysis—the language used to describe and explain observations. The American philosopher of mind, Daniel Dennett, has distinguished three theoretical stances or different levels of analysis, arguing that it is a pragmatic matter which one is selected. On the *physical stance*, a piece of behavior may be explained by reference to the physical constitution of the organism (e.g., explaining visual perception by reference to the structure of the eye and the brain). This type of explanation has been particularly useful in cases of malfunction (e.g., neuropsychologists explain behavioral dysfunction by reference to brain damage; psychopathological disorders, such as schizophrenia, depression, and Alzheimer's disease, may be explained in terms of brain chemistry). On the *design stance*, processes are explained by reference to a computational program or algorithm capable of generating the behavior. This approach is exemplified by cognitive psychology and artificial intelligence, whether of the traditional symbolic, or connectionist kind. On the *intentional stance*, behavior is explained by invoking mental states such as beliefs, desires, and reasons. The desire might be to have a cup of tea and the belief that boiling a kettle of water is a way of achieving this; these allow the inference that boiling a kettle of water is a reasonable thing to do in the circumstances. The explanation ("justification" or "rationalization") shows why it was reasonable for the agent to perform the action, given certain beliefs and desires. This approach is apparent in the nineteenth-century German tradition of Verstehen and hermeneutics, which argued that the social sciences should pursue empathic understanding rather than the causal prediction of the physical sciences; and "folk psychology"—everyday, commonsense, implicit knowledge which enables the prediction and/or explanation of the behavior of others (and ourselves) by understanding the mental states involved. It is common in much of social and personality psychology, including psychoanalysis (where reasons can be unconscious).

The Mind-Body Problem

The fundamental problem for the philosophy of psychology is that of the relation of the mental to the physical. The nineteenth-century German philosopher, Arthur Schopenhauer, described it as the world knot, insoluble by us, a view shared by the contemporary English philosopher Colin McGinn. The problem is that the two realms appear to be distinctly different but closely related. Mental phenomena consist of sensations and *propositional attitudes*, such as thoughts, beliefs, and desires, which have contents. Physical phenomena have properties such as mass and energy.

A number of features have been suggested as distinguishing the mental and the physical.

The *qualitative character* of phenomenal experience (what philosophers term *qualia*) has been held by many to be distinctive of the mental. Properties such as the redness of vermillion or the sweetness of sugar seem irreducible and distinct from physical properties.

Mental states are thought of as private or *subjective* whereas physical phenomena are public or objective (or at least intersubjective). There is an epistemological difference between the knowledge one has of one's own mental states (e.g., pain) and that of someone else's.

The late nineteenth-century Austrian philosopher Franz Brentano, considered *intentionality* to be the mark of mental. This refers to the directedness or content of propositional attitudes: beliefs and desires are about things, though these may not exist objectively (*intensional inexistence*). Hoping or imagining necessarily involves hoping for or imagining something, even though this may never exist. Cognitive psychologists, adopting the computational model of mind, see this as a way of dealing with representation and meaning.

René Descartes, the seventeenth-century French philosopher and famous dualist, suggested two further distinguishing criteria. He argued that spatial *extension* was distinctive of the physical realm (*res extensa*), whereas thinking was characteristic of the mental (*res cogitans*).

He also believed that the physical realm was subject to or explicable in terms of the *deterministic* laws of the physical or natural sciences; whereas mental phenomena were "free," which would rule out psychological science.

Dualism

According to dualism, a commonsense view, there are two distinct realms of mental and physical phenomena. This poses the problem of the relationship between the two realms. There have been many suggestions as to what this might be.

No one has suggested that mental and physical phenomena are not at least coincidental. The weakest relation is therefore one of correlation, or *psychophysical parallelism* (e.g., two isolated causal systems, as suggested by the seventeenth-century German philosopher, Gottfried Leibniz). The problem for such a view is to explain the apparently fortuitous synchronization between mental and physical events. Leibniz postulated a "preestablished harmony" and was ridiculed by the French eighteenth-century writer Voltaire; Leibniz's contemporary, Nicolas Malebranche, relied on divine intervention. Experiments in physiological psychology which aim merely to localize a function exemplify this approach.

René Descartes suggested *causal interaction*. This accords with the commonsense view that mental causes can have physical effects (e.g., stress causes ulcers, embarrassment causes blushing, thoughts and desires cause actions), and physical causes can have mental effects (e.g., a kick on the shins hurts; visual experiences appear to be the result of physical stimuli). The problem with this view is to determine how there can be causal interaction between two substances defined as distinctly different. Descartes defined mind as nonspatial and nondeterministic but causation depends on physical contiguity and deterministic laws. (His suggestions about the pineal gland, as the place where the interaction was supposed to take place, localize rather than solve the problem.) Furthermore, if the physical cause is sufficient to explain a piece of behavior, how can a mental cause be necessary?

A position which postulates one-way causal interaction is that of *epiphenomenalism*. While attributing reality to mental states, it refuses to allow them causal efficacy. Mental processes are noncausal by-products of physical processes; they are caused by but do not themselves cause physical events. A famous exponent of this view was the nineteenth-century English scientist, T. H. Huxley, who argued that consciousness was like the whistle of a steam engine, a spin-off which had no effect on the working of the machine. Radical behaviorism, which claims that behavior can be explained without recourse to mental events or processes is such a view. Demonstrations by the American psychophysiologist, Benjamin Libet, that electrophysiological responses precede the reported conscious intention to perform a voluntary action, tend to lend credence to such a view. Conscious experience is often the result rather than the cause of behavior. On the other hand, the position is counterintuitive, and untestable: the exclusive efficacy of mental events cannot be demonstrated, since they are always accompanied by physical ones.

Monism

According to monism, there is only *one* basic stuff in the universe. There are two basic forms: idealism and materialism.

Idealism attributes primacy to the mental: the universe is viewed as basically mental. This view has existed in many forms: The early eighteenth-century Irish philosopher, George Berkeley, put forward the doctrine of *immaterialism*, according to which the external world (and physical reality) did not exist: physical objects were merely ideas in our minds. (The Scottish philosopher, David Hume, took the doctrine one step further, in arguing that our minds were merely bundles of sensations and ideas.) The eighteenth-century German philosopher, Immanuel Kant, expounded transcendental idealism: space and time were forms of intuition imposed on reality by the mind.

Transpersonal psychology (*fourth force* psychology, behaviorism, psychoanalysis, and humanistic psychology being first, second, and third forces respectively) aims to study aspects of the psyche or cosmos beyond the personal, ego, or individual, such as spirituality and mystical experiences. It might be considered an example of ontological idealism (or dualism) if it posits a transcendental realm; or epistemological idealism, insofar as it employs the methods of intuition and contemplation.

Current cognitive psychology reflects idealism, in its central claim that reality is dependent on the mind, in contrast to *realism* according to which reality is mind-independent. Idealism underpins the representational theory of mind, advanced by the American philosopher, Jerry Fodor, and the *constructivism* of cognitive psychologists such as Jerome Bruner, Richard Gregory, and Ulric Neisser, who maintain that cognition is an active, constructive process, in contrast to the "realism" of the followers of the American psychologist, J. J. Gibson. For the former group, perception is a top-down, inferential process, involving hypothesis testing and the utilization of past knowledge; for the latter group perception is "direct" and bottom-up, a matter of picking up information from the rich sensory array. For the *constructivists*, information is largely in the head (mind-brain) and perception is error-prone: witness ambiguous figures and visual illusions. For the "direct realists," information is largely in the dynamic environment: the ambient array specifies not only objects but actions they afford us.

The alternative monist position is *materialism* or *physicalism* (the two positions are closely related and the terms are sometimes used interchangeably), which asserts the primacy of the physical. The ontological claim is that everything which exists consists of matter (we may note that our view of what matter is has changed radically in recent times). The conceptual claim is that everything can be explained in terms of the concepts and laws of physics, however currently conceived. The thesis dates back to the pre-Socratic Greek atomist, Democritus, and to Lucretius in the first century BCE. Other notable exponents were Thomas Hobbes and Pierre Gassendi in the seventeenth century. Materialism has been extremely popular amongst scientists but has problems accounting for subjectivity and the qualitative character of the mental.

There have been two notable attempts to eliminate mental concepts in favor of physical ones. Mental states have been defined as equivalent in meaning, and thus theoretically reducible to or replaceable by descriptions in terms of behavior (*behaviorism*), or neurophysiology (*eliminative materialism*).

Behaviorism exists in a variety of forms. In psychology it is primarily an epistemological doctrine, motivated by positivism and a desire for scientific respectability, and put forward originally in 1913 by the American psychologist, J. B. Watson. He prescribed that only objective methods and publicly observable data should be admitted (*methodological behaviorism*). The subject matter of psychology was restricted to behavior, or existence denied to mental states (*metaphysical* or *eliminativist behaviorism*). Concepts were to be restricted to those which could be operationalized: mentalistic explanations were considered unnecessary (B. F. Skinner's *radical behaviorism*) or equivalent in meaning to behavioral or dispositional statements (*analytical* or *logical behaviorism*). It proved difficult to carry out these dispos-

itional analyses, and impossible to explain even relatively simple behavior adequately without recourse to mental states (hence the rise of "cognitivism" and "functionalism").

Eliminative materialism in its current form has been championed by the American philosopher, Paul Churchland, who recommends that commonsense *folk psychological* concepts should replace neurobiological ones, on the grounds that the former are defective as accounts of behavior. It would require a radical revision of our commonsense notions. This is an extreme reductionist theory which appears to ignore and discount the possibility of a scientific psychology.

Ontological Monism but Conceptual Dualism

In recent times the focus of the debate has shifted from ontological discussion about the nature of reality to the conceptual issue of how best to describe the relationship between mental and physical phenomena. Most current theorists adopt some form of ontological monism (generally materialism) but allow conceptual or theoretical dualism; so the same event or process may be described in different ways.

An old version of this position is the double aspect view, espoused by the seventeenth-century Portuguese philosopher, Benedict Spinoza, according to whom mental and physical were two aspects of an underlying, essentially unknowable, neutral substance.

The most popular current views involve some form of *identity*, which holds that the relation between mental and physical is one of constitution.

Mind-brain identity theory claims that mental events are contingently identical to brain states. Mental properties are different in meaning from physical properties but, as a matter of empirical discovery, mental states are found to be identifiable with brain states. The theory was originally motivated by the work of the Canadian neurosurgeon, Wilder Penfield, who elicited autobiographical memories and other behavioral responses by stimulating specific regions of the cortex. One advantage is that, since mental states are identical to brain states, they can be genuinely causal. The truth of the theory depends on the successful demonstration of psychophysical correlations. It is more plausible when applied to sensations than propositional attitudes. The theory is usually considered to be a case of *type-identity*. Thus every instance of a given mental state (e.g., seeing the color green) is claimed to be identical with a specified brain state (e.g., a particular pattern of neural activity in the brain). An objection raised is that this does not allow "multiple" or "variable realizability": the possibility that the same mental state may be realized differently in different individuals or species (e.g., binocular disparity is realized by different structures in the owl and the cat). It also rules out strong artificial intelligence, which attributes mental states to appropriately programmed computers.

Token identity allows multiple realizability. Each instance of a mental state is said to be identical with, in the sense of realized in, some physical state, but there may be no general laws relating types or classes of mental and physical states. On this view, the relation between mental and physical is termed *supervenience*. The mental is dependent on or determined by the physical: any physical change or difference must be reflected in a mental change or difference (but the opposite is not necessarily the case). (Supervenience clarifies physicalism while avoiding a precise specification.) Some have doubted whether it is sufficiently powerful to provide mental causation; and there have been problems providing a physical account of intentionality. The main examples of token identity theories are anomalous monism and functionalism.

Anomalous monism is a doctrine put forward by the American philosopher of mind (formerly a psychologist), Donald Davidson. According to him, laws only apply to events described in a particular way, relative to a particular, conceptual framework. He claims that there are causal laws pertaining to events described physically (and because mental events are identical to physical events, they can be causes) but there are no laws pertaining to events described psychologically (psychology is anomalous, i.e., lacking in laws). This is because he believes that psychological descriptions are to be given in terms of reasons, desires, and beliefs, which involve a radically different conceptual framework. Thus, there can be no psychological or psychophysical laws. But note that this depends on a particular, highly contentious interpretation of the nature of psychological events, as propositional attitudes.

Functionalism is the dominant paradigm and the philosophy underlying current cognitive psychology. On this view, mental states are defined in terms of their causal role, in relation to environmental stimuli (input), other mental states, and behavioral responses (output). For example, a pain might be defined as the state which results from tissue damage, gives rise to distress, and produces attempts to escape it. Description is at the abstract level of process (the *design stance*). Psychology is autonomous with respect to physiology, since mental states are independent of any particular physical embodiment. Functionalism underlies the computational and representational theories of mind, on which cognition consists of computation: mental processes are operations performed on representations, and can be modeled by the manipulation of abstract symbols according to formal rules in a digital computer. The pursuit of artificial intelligence is encouraged. Functionalism has difficulty in accounting for the qualitative character of mental life, since it seems possible to imagine different, functionally indistinguishable, mental states. Whether or not it can account for intentionality and meaning is the subject of current controversy.

[*See also* Philosophy.]

Bibliography

Churchland, P. M. (1988). *Matter and consciousness: A contemporary introduction to the philosophy of mind* (Rev. ed.). Cambridge, MA: MIT Press. A clear, succinct, and sound account of positions on the mind-body problem: dualism, varieties of behaviorism, materialism, functionalism; and discussion of folk psychology, artificial intelligence, and neuroscience, with suggestions for further reading.

Fodor, J. A. (1981). The mind-body problem. *Scientific American, 244*, (1), 124–132. Accessible account of functionalism, by one of its chief exponents, tracing the progression from dualism, radical and logical behaviorism, and identity theory, together with a critical evaluation.

Honderich, T. (1995). *The Oxford companion to philosophy*. Oxford: Oxford University Press. Brief entries on topics and persons in philosophy. The entries on idealism, the mind-body problem, and mental reductionism are particularly recommended.

Horgan, T. (1994). Physicalism 1. In S. Guttenplan (Ed.), *A companion to the philosophy of mind* (pp. 471–479). Oxford: Blackwell. Thorough and comprehensive account of various forms of reductive and nonreductive physicalism (including supervenience, functionalism, identity theory, and eliminativism).

Kim, J. (1994). Supervenience. In S. Guttenplan (Ed.), *A companion to the philosophy of mind* (pp. 575–582). Oxford: Blackwell. Detailed explication of different forms of supervenience by the philosopher largely responsible for its development.

Kim, J., & Sosa, E. (Eds.). (1995). *A companion to metaphysics*. Oxford: Blackwell. Contains entries on several of the positions and terms discussed above.

Loewer, B. (1995). Mind-body problem. In J. Kim & E. Sosa (Eds.), *A companion to metaphysics* (pp. 579–580). Oxford: Blackwell. Overview and classification of positions on the mind-body problem.

Lycan, W. (1994). Functionalism 1. In S. Guttenplan (Ed.), *A companion to the philosophy of mind* (pp. 317–323). Oxford: Blackwell. Good and useful account of functionalism, including its history, varieties, and critique, by one of the most sophisticated exponents of the position.

Lycan, W. (1996). Philosophy of mind. In N. Bunnin & E. P. Tsui-James (Eds.), *The Blackwell companion to philosophy* (pp. 167–197). Oxford: Blackwell. Review article covering the main topics in the philosophy of mind, including dualism, behaviorism, identity theory, varieties of functionalism, artificial intelligence and the computational theory of mind, qualia, intentionality, eliminativism, and folk psychology.

Guttenplan, S. (Ed.). (1994). *A companion to the philosophy of mind*. Oxford: Blackwell. A lengthy orienting essay precedes substantial entries on specific topics, as well as self-profiles by leading philosophers of mind. In some cases two entries are provided on the same topic to illustrate different points of view.

O'Donohue, W., & Kitchener, R. F. (Eds.). (1996). *The philosophy of psychology*. London: Sage. Collection of readings on the philosophy of psychology, including sections on behaviorism and cognitive psychology.

Valentine, E. R. (1992). *Conceptual issues in psychology* (2nd ed.). London: Routledge. Comprehensive text on philosophical psychology and different theoretical approaches to psychology.

Von Eckhardt, B. (1994). Folk psychology 1. In S. Guttenplan (Ed.), *A companion to the philosophy of mind* (pp. 300–307). Oxford: Blackwell. An excellent article on folk psychology, including a taxonomy of positions on its truth, distinguished by giving due weight to scientific psychology.

Elizabeth R. Valentine

METTRIE, JULIEN OFFRAY DE LA. *See* La Mettrie, Julien Offray de.

MEUMANN, ERNST (1862–1915), German experimental educational psychologist and aesthetics researcher. Meumann deserves to be better known as an important founder of experimental educational psychology; it is primarily the shaky connection between pedagogy and educational psychology that makes this poorly known. He was among the first to expand the new experimental psychology to applications in education and served as the German founder to this discipline.

Meumann was born in Uerdingen bei Wesel (near the city of Krefeld), the son of a Lutheran minister. He studied theology and philosophy and completed examinations to become a *Gymnasium* teacher, and a Lutheran minister, although he later seems to have considered himself an atheist. He then completed a philosophical dissertation, describing the positive and negative aspects of traditional (James Mill, Alexander Bain) style studies of psychology through association and reproduction of images, under Edmund Pfleiderer at the University of Tübingen in 1887, receiving the doctorate in 1891. Meumann's study of esthetics can be traced to his art history studies there, based on his secondary doctoral subject, middle and recent art history. The intervening time, much spent with Gustav Störring at Halle, included an attempt to study medicine (through which he might have become a physiologist). Attracted by the chance to experiment and study with Wilhelm Wundt, and later to the salary, he became the second assistant in Wundt's institute in 1893

and completed the work on rhythm for his *Habilitation* (1894); he thus became a member of the Leipzig faculty as a *Privatdozent* (unpaid instructor). When Oswald Külpe was promoted, Meumann became first assistant.

Succeeding rather rapidly, Meumann was selected (1897) to be at Zurich and in 1900, he succeeded Richard Avenarius. While, there, his research radically changed direction, and he adopted the memory research methods of Georg E. Müller to educational problems, published a text (1907) that initiated the discipline of experimental educational psychology, and sponsored the dissertation research of Margaret Keiver Smith. This book shows many of the same distinctions later made between short-term (i.e., immediate memory) and the long-term memory found in his paired-associate studies. In these studies, he emphasized that memorizing produced a generalized transfer, as did a formal discipline—a view that was widely disputed. Meumann also emphasized imagery in the development of memorizing. In developing this field, Meumann associated himself very closely with the German school reform movement of the time.

In 1903, to honor his mentor Wundt, Meumann founded the *Archiv für die gesamte Psychologie*, only the second journal (after the *Zeitschrift*) to have a heterogeneous and distinguished board of consulting editors. After one year, Wundt lost interest in this journal and was replaced by two senior professors, Harald Höffding (Copenhagen) and Friedrich Jodl (Vienna), although Wundt's name remained on the masthead until his death in 1920. Meumann was also part of the founding meeting in 1903 of the *Deutsche gesellschaft für experimentelle Psychologie*, headed by Müller for 23 years. A few years later (1907) he founded the *Zeitschrift für pädagogische Psychologie*, which became a central journal for the study of educational psychology.

After Zurich, Meumann quickly left jobs (at Königsberg, Münster, Halle, and Leipzig) until 1911, when he got a generously supported chair for "public lectures" in the *Kolonialinstitut* in Hamburg (the predecessor of the university there), from which he published his two journals, the *Archiv für die gesamte Psychologie* and the *Zietschrift für pädagogische Psychologie und experimentelle Pädagogik*. From this position, he published a large volume of work on experimental educational psychology as well as a few works on esthetics, cultivated close contacts with teachers and he emphasized the importance of empirical methods for education, including experimentation, controlled observation, and statistical methods. In spite of these important contributions, Meumann seems to have had few dissertation students who had university careers and to have been separate from many other proponents of experimental psychology.

In spite of the onset of World War I, Meumann continued to have easy relations with Americans. He was invited to lecture on merchandising in New York City in 1915. He died suddenly in Hamburg of pneumonia.

[*Many of the people mentioned in this article are the subjects of independent biographical entries.*]

Bibliography

Forster, P. (1993). Meumann, Ernst, Psychologe, Pädagoge [Psychologist, educationalist]. In *Neue deutsche Biographie.* (Vol. 17). Berlin: Duncker & Humblot. The standard German source, with an excellent list of sources.

Meumann, E. (1913). *The psychology of learning: An experimental investigation of the economy and technique of memory* (J. W. Baird, Trans.). New York: Appleton. Although much shorter than his three-volume *Lectures,* this book gives a relatively complete view of Europeans' development of an experimentally based educational psychology in the years before World War I. In particular, it points to his studies of short-term memory and attention, and their effect on long-term memory.

Probst, P. (1991). *Bibliographie Ernst Meumann: mit einer Einleitung zur Biographie.* Herzberg: Traugott Bautz. Presents very little of a narrative biography; the exhaustive source book for further studies of Meumann. Presents his publications, his dissertation students, his translations, his editing work, as well as citations of other authors who make noteworthy citations of his work. In addition, by publishing the self-biographies (*Lebensläufe*) that Meumann had to provide and other official documents, gives a valuable look at the nature of the documents which can be found in German libraries about German figures in any academic discipline.

Stoerring, G. (1923). Ernst Meumann 1862–1915. *American Journal of Psychology, 34,* 271–274. While considerably shorter than Störring's much longer eulogy in Meumann's journal, the *Archiv für die gesamte Psychologie,* this article is an important and accessible source by an author who was both a significant figure in German psychology and a personal friend of Meumann's. In spite of Probst's extensive work, Störring's articles are the only real source for descriptions of Meumann's character and approach to psychology.

Edward J. Haupt

MEXICO. On 27 February 1997, the Mexican Society of Psychology, the Mexican Society of History and Philosophy of Medicine, and the Faculty of Psychology at the National University of Mexico (UNAM), organized a roundtable, "One Hundred Years of Psychology in Mexico." On that occasion it was noted that: "In 1897, a hundred years ago, in a systematic and permanent mode, the teaching of psychology was inaugurated in Mexico" [Molina, in press]. Interestingly, psychology was first taught in the senior year of senior high school, and the course, evolving with the times, remains in the curriculum.

Molina (in press) argues that the only way to understand the role of psychology at any time is to "historicize" it. Ezequiel Chávez, a religious man, the first psychologist in Mexico, took advantage of the differences of opinion between the disciples of Comte and those of the English positivists Spencer and Mills. He did this in the context of the political policies of Porfirio Díaz, the Mexican dictator, and what were then perceived to be the social ills: delinquency, alcoholism, and insanity. Chávez convinced the minister of public instruction, Justo Sierra, to introduce the disciplines of psychology and logic, in the Comtian pyramid of the sciences, which was, during Porfirio Díaz's rule, the basis for public education.

The discipline, *Psicología Experimental* (experimental psychology) was taught then with the goal of stimulating moral and intellectual development, and creating useful and honest students.

Ezequiel Chávez is also credited with the first article written by a psychologist about Mexican psychology (1901).

Valderrana, Colotla, Jurado, and Gallegos (in press) give an account of the viscissitudes of psychology between 1910 and 1938 when Ezequiel Chávez was the dominant figure of the period. He was second only to the Minister of Public Education, Justo Sierra, from 1901 to 1910; Rector (President) of the National University of Mexico in 1913. Chávez's basic interest in psychology, including his essay on the Mexican character, was dictated by its educational significance. Through the efforts of Sierra and Chávez, in 1909 the Mexican Congress founded the Escuela Nacional de Altos Estudios (ENAE) (the National School of Higher Studies), where psychology courses were very important and were taught until the creation of the first academic curriculum of psychology in 1938. The efforts of Sierra and Chávez were essential to the founding by the president of Mexico, Porfirio Díaz, of the new Universidad Nacional de Mexico in 1910, to take the place of the Real y Pontificia Universidad de Mexico, founded in the sixteenth century. Again, the predominance of Chávez determined that James Mark Baldwin, a disciple of Wundt, founder of the psychological laboratory at Princeton University, and editor of the four-volume *Dictionary of Philosophy and Psychology,* should be invited to inaugurate the ENAE with a course in psychosociology. This course was initiated on 18 October 1910.

The unusual climate of enthusiasm for psychology in the first decade of the century was based on the belief that this new discipline could cure all the social ills of Mexico. In 1907 (Valderrama et al., in press) a Sociedad de Estudios Psicológicos (Society for Psychological Studies) was founded, and almost every intellectual figure of the time became members: psychologists, educators, philosophers, criminal lawyers, sociologists, and important literary figures. Psychology, continuing its sensitivity to all other concerns, particularly education, happily survived the difficult economic and political times during the entire Mexican Revolution. It finally became a choice as an academic career in 1938 when Lázaro Cárdenas stabilized the country.

The other extraordinary figure of this period is Enrique Aragón, a neuropsychiatrist, with encyclopedic interests and capacities. At 26 years of age, in 1907, he entered a contest and won the position of "profesor" (teacher) of a psychology course at a senior high school where he remained until his death in 1942. This may have oriented his vocation to psychology because in 1916 he organized the first Laboratory of Psychology in Mexico (Aragón, in Valderrama et al., 1994). The research at this Wundtian laboratory housed and maintained first by the ENAE, was fundamentally demonstrative and instructional. Many students took the courses of psychology which were enhanced by laboratory work.

It is probable that the main impetus for the first applications of psychology were the result of these experiences. Guadalupe Zúñiga and Pablo Boder were Aragón's students and lab assistants. Students who took several courses of psychology and education at the ENAE could, after presenting articles and probably a thesis, receive the degree of "Profesor Académico en Psicología" (Academic psychology teacher). This is the degree obtained by Guadalupe Zúñiga (Zúñiga in Valderrama et al., 1994) in 1921. Since then, until her retirement in 1963 Zúñiga was a tireless advocate and practitioner of applying the knowledge of psychology to the welfare of children and families, as well as to social problems.

David Pablo Boder (in Valderrama et al., 1994) is an intriguing case in the history of Mexican psychology. Born in Russia in 1886, he is said to have studied with Wundt in Leipzig, reaching Mexico around 1920. He helped Aragón in his psychological laboratory, translated and used the Binet–Simon–Terman tests in Mexico, and after seven years, emigrated to the United States. Boder, together with Rafael Santamarina, who had earlier adapted the Binet–Simon test for use in Mexico, and Lucía Montana Hastings, who, in 1929 standardized the Beta and Otis intelligence tests for use in Mexico, are the pioneers of psychological testing in Mexico.

In this early development of psychology in Mexico there are three other contributors who must be mentioned: David Berlanga, José Torres Orozco, and Leopoldo Kiel (Valderrama et al., 1994).

In the first decade of the twentieth century, Berlanga went to Leipzig where he studied with Wilhelm Wundt. Returning in Mexico in late 1911, he founded a journal *El Porvenir Escolar*, where he publicized the work of Wundt and others. While doing this he became active in politics, and was elected representative to the Mexican Congress. He was murdered in 1914, at 28 years of age, it is said, because of his determined opposition to the abuses of Pancho Villa's followers.

José Torres Orozco was a physician, a psychologist, and an educator. In 1918 he discussed the first symptoms of tuberculosis (TB). Writing about the ideas of Freud and neurasthenia, he began to obtain information, through reading and observation, for his original masterpiece, "The Mental State of the TB Patient," which he finished shortly before his death in 1925 at age 35.

Leopoldo Kiel, a Mexican educator at the beginning of the twentieth century, entered the history of psychology because of his radical insistence that for education to succeed, both in the family and at school, it must have a strong psychological base. Kiel is the author of dozens of articles on the impact of psychology on aspects of education, including judgment, abstraction, generalization, memory, and imagination.

Throughout the 1920s and 1930s psychology courses continued to be taught at the ENAE which in 1924 became the Facultad de Filosofía y Letras (Faculty of Philosophy and Letters), that, in 1924, awarded an *Honoris Causa* Doctorate to George Dumas, invited Emil Kraepelin to lecture, and was visited by Pierre Janet, who taught a course on the psychology of feeling, and John Dewey.

The birth of the discipline, inseparable from compelling social and national identity issues, rather than individual problems, continues to influence Mexican psychology today.

The First Academic Career in Psychology

In 1938, Chávez headed a commission that developed the first psychology degree program. It was a six-semester course taught by Chávez and Aragón along with a faculty of distinguished philosophers, and physicians whose avocations were connected with some area of psychology. There was also Oswaldo Robles, a brilliant commentator with clinical interests, who with others developed a course in psychobiography. He published several books on psychology, among them an early criticism of Freud (Robles, Mexico City, 1955), Roberto Solís Quiroga, who dedicated most of his professional life to the special education of handicapped children, and Guillermo Dávila, a competent psychiatrist who taught psychopathology. The staff was strengthened early by Spanish refugees, Eduardo Nicol with his brand of philosophical psychology, Juan Roura Parella, who taught German psychology including Dilthey, Spranger, and Gestalt; Pascual del Roncal who taught Rorschach; Fernando Ocaranza, physician and research physiologist who taught courses on the nervous system, and Matías López and José Gómez Robledo, who taught statistics.

This early program underwent several transformations becoming less academic and more professionally oriented. Then in 1959 the Technical Counsel to the Faculty of Philosophy and Letters approved the new curriculum designed for the professional degree of psychologist or licentiate in psychology. In the early 1960s several large groups of students—on one occasion more than one hundred and their mentors—visited the departments of psychology and educational psychology at the University of Texas during the summer for 2- to 4-week programs of short courses, conferences, workshops, seminars, and visits to professional institutions and centers. These were organized by Wayne Holtzman and many other volunteer members of these departments. In 1966 an internal academic revolution led by students and teachers updated and made more comprehensive the 1959 curriculum. With some minor changes in 1971, the 1966 curriculum remains today.

The Faculty of Psychology

Mexican psychology considers the foundation of the Faculty of Psychology at the National University of Mexico (UNAM), in 1973, and its independence from the Facultad de Filosofía y Letras a transcendent event. Everything indicates that its program of studies and those that preceded it were crucially important for the development of the discipline in the Republic. The first departments or schools of psychology that opened had to be certified by UNAM. Today, it produces from 80 to 90% of all the psychological research in the Republic. Many of the instructors and professors of psychology, particularly in Mexico but also in Latin America and the Caribbean, have been trained at UNAM. The faculty currently occupies several large buildings, and more are planned to keep up with the increase in research and postgraduate studies. Two volumes have been published to account for its achievements and problems in the first and second decades of its charter (García, 1983; Urbina, 1993). In December 1998, an International Committee of Evaluation and Planning reorganized and updated the curriculum for the professional degree, stressing the sociocultural context of behavior and contemplating a "metacurriculum" to include scientific writing, professional ethics, and personal health concerns.

Contemporary Degrees in Psychology

Today in Mexico, as in most of Latin America, before entering the university for an undergraduate degree in psychology, students complete from 11 to 12 years of education, 6 in elementary school (after 1 or 2 pre-

school years) and 6 in secondary and preparatory schools. A professional degree in psychology is conferred after 4 to 5 years of university training. In Mexico, after the founding of the first program in 1938, only four more institutions had opened their doors for training by 1965. As indicated, in 1973 the school of psychology at UNAM was founded, and master's and doctoral degrees are now offered. Two additional years of course work are required for the master's degree. Since 1993 the 2 extra years to qualify for a doctorate are used exclusively for supervised research. Its high quality has gained a grant for UNAM from the National Science Council (CONACyT). Graduate psychological studies at UNAM are considered "Scientific Training of Excellence," and graduate students who are accepted there receive a stipend to carry on with their work.

Training in Mexico is eclectic, and basic, scientific general psychology occupies the first 2 years. Next there are options to either study basic science or to specialize in applied clinical, educational, industrial, or social psychology. A number of credits are obtained in psychological practices and each student must complete a 6-month social service and a research or bibliographic thesis before the exam for the professional degree. In 1983, there were approximately 40,000 students of psychology in the Republic (Díaz-Loving & Valderrama, 1992).

The Profession

The phenomenal growth and the attendant problems for psychology in Mexico have continued, but there is keen awareness of these problems on the part of its leaders. This has led to the publication of an exceptional edited volume (Urbina-Soria, 1989), *El psicólogo, formación, ejercicio profesional y prospectiva* (The psychologist, training, professional practice and prospective). Dozens of established psychologists discuss these issues. For example, Rivera-Sierra and Urbina-Soria (1989) integrate a number of tables that provide insight regarding the complex circumstances of the psychological profession, in one instance combining data from the 82 institutions granting the licenciate or professional degree in psychology in the Republic from 1985 through 1987. The total number of schools in the table is greater than 82 because some indicated that their psychological curriculum included more than one specialty (see Table 1). Thus today there are clinicians, educators, and industrial, labor, organizational, social, child, physiological, and forensic psychologists as well as those doing experimental analysis of behavior. There are also many clinicians utilizing behavioral and cognitive therapies.

Martinez-Fuentes and Urbina-Soria (1989) analyzed 24 studies of the employment situation for professional psychologists and they showed (see Table 2) in order of importance, work undertaken by psychol-

MEXICO. Table 1. Curricular areas for the licenciate (professional degree) in psychology, number of schools, and number of students

Curricular Areas	Number of Schools	1985	1986	1987
Psychology	66	22,443	21,413	24,499
Clinical psychology	9	810	735	744
Educational psychology	11	582	589	1147
Industrial psychology	7	140	130	107
Work psychology	2	270	251	266
Labor psychology	2	226	221	208
Organizational psychology	2	74	79	66
Child psychology	1	227	188	147
Social psychology	6	449	777	965
Psychology of social behavior	1	168	195	
Experimental psychology	1	20	31	19
Psychophysiology	1	2	10	3
Physiological psychology	1	10	10	9
Analysis of behavior	1	104	157	185
Criminological psychology	1	5	4	9
Total	112	25,530	24,790	28,374

Source: Translated with permission from Urbina-Soria (1989, p. 42).

ogists. They included studies which did not specify the particular psychological specialty, and those that indicated the industrial and clinical categories. It is plain that most of the traditional psychological tasks remain important. It is interesting that for the studies not specifying a specialty, proficiency in teaching is considered as important as psychotherapeutic techniques. Indeed, many psychologists, in addition to their practice, teach an introductory psychology course that is part of the senior high-school curriculum throughout the Republic.

The authors of several chapters in Urbina-Soria's 1989 edited work remark that in the future psychology will be called upon to deal with problems beyond those at the interpersonal, individual level. Group dynamics and particularly complex social problems will require substantial psychological intervention; for example, in trauma resulting from natural disasters (earthquakes, flooding, etc.), in the development of behavioral health messages for the mass media, dealing with the effects of violence and poverty; developing a constructive political psychology; increased intervention in the industrial sector; and perhaps a sociotherapy derived from reliable research of Mexican culture that can help to promote the positive characteristics of the Mexican people and eliminate the destructive ones.

Professional Societies and National Journals

In 1951, the Mexican Society of Psychology was founded as a branch of the interamerican Society of Psychology. Its first president was Manuel Falcón Guer-

rero, who was followed by Guillermo Dávila, Rafael Núñez, Rogelio Díaz Guerrero, Angel San Roman, Mario Cicero, Victor Colotia, Juan Jose Sánchez Sosa, and Rosa Korbman de Shein. This society officially represents Mexican psychologists in the International Union of Psychological Science (IUPSyS). It publishes the *Revista Mexicana de Psicologia*. [See Interamerican Society of Psychology; and International Union of Psychological Science.]

Other societies representing special interests have been formed. (1) The Mexican Association of Social Psychology publishes the *Revista de Psicología Social y Personalidad* and holds a biannual congress. At the 1994, 1996, and 1998 congresses it also organized simultaneously the first and second Latin American regional meetings of the International Association for Cross-Cultural Psychology. (2) The Mexican Society of Behavior Analysis publishes the *Revista Mexicana de Análisis de la Conducta* and holds an annual congress. (3) the Asociación Psicoanalítica Mexicana (Mexican Society of Psychoanalysis) publishes the *Revista de Psicoanálisis, Psiquiatría y Psicología*, and holds an annual congress. (4) The Consejo Nacional para la Enseñanza e investigación en Psicología (CNEIP) is a unique organization of faculties and schools of psychology from state and private universities. It publishes the journal *Enseñanza e investigación en Psicología* (Teaching and Research in Psychology) and routinely holds an annual meeting. One of its concerns is to establish a national curriculum for the professional psychology degree and raise teaching and research standards. *Psicología Contemporánea*, an international commercial journal edited

MEXICO. Table 2. Activities demanded of the psychologist in order of importance in 24 studies

Studies That Did Not Specify the Category of Psychology	Studies of Industrial Psychology	Studies of Clinical Psychology	Categories Most Utilized
1. Psychotherapy	Personnel training	Diagnosis and evaluation	Clinical
2. Teaching	Job analysis and evaluation	Psychotherapy	Educational
3. Personnel training	Labor social organization	Research	Labor
4. Vocational and educational counseling	Personnel selection	Personnel selection	Social
5. Planning and personnel development	Planning and personnel development	Vocational and educational counseling	General
6. Testing	Interview	Managing the patient	
7. Diagnosis and evaluation	Testing	Prevention	
8. Personnel selection	Communication	Teaching	
9. Interview	Group dynamics		
10. Special Education			
11. Consulting			
12. Development of didactic materials and programs			
13. Managing the patient			
14. Planning and development programs			

Source: Translated and adapted with permission from Urbina-Soria, 1989, p. 519.

by psychologist Luis Oblitas, which predominantly publishes research work by Spanish-speaking psychologists, has been published since 1994.

Areas of Research

For a developing country, the amount and quality of psychological research in Mexico before 1980 may be considered unique. Hernández-Peón, who died in an automobile accident in 1968, had, besides his internationally recognized contributions (Morgane, 1970), formed a cadre of investigators and they, their students, and other colleagues have continued and multiplied research to this day in neurophysiology, neurobiology, neuropsychology, neuropharmacology, brain potential, and electroencephalography. Most of this work is carried out at the faculties of psychology and medicine at UNAM. Some of the work by this group is referenced in Pick de Weiss and Díaz-Loving (1986).

Another line of systematic research was originated in the 1950s by Rogelio Díaz-Guerrero. He first discovered that a number of sociocultural beliefs of the Mexican family were supported by 80% or more of a good sample of 18-year-olds and those older in Mexico City in 1949. In time these statements became known as historic-sociocultural premises (HSCPs). A number of studies by Díaz-Guerrero and his colleagues and students, in the 1960s and 1970s, ratified the importance of these beliefs in different parts of the Republic. These beliefs cut across ages, sexes, social classes, urban and rural samples, and ethnic groups. Early in the 1970s, factor analyses of the inventories of HSCPs unearthed one cultural factor, labeled Traditionalism. This factor includes obedience and respect for the parents and elders as a determining ingredient. Later several orthogonal factors, among them Affiliative Obedience, Machismo, and Virginity, were found. Concomitantly, many of significant and psychologically important correlations were discovered between the factor scales of HSCPs and cognitive, personality, educational, social, economic, and even political dimensions. By this time it was clear that culture, as embodied in the HSCPs, was a critical determining favor in the psychology of the Mexicans. This led to a theory of personality maintaining that personality emerges from a culture-counterculture dialectic between the information provided by the culture and the individual's biopsychical information in the context of the prevalent information in a given behavioral ecosystem (e.g., Díaz-Guerrero & Pacheco, 1994).

The original interest in culture soon led Díaz-Guerrero and his team to engage in cross-cultural research. There was collaboration with Robert F. Peck on the subject of culture and achievement across seven nations, Charles E. Osgood on cross-cultural universals of affective meaning in 30 nations, Harry C. Triandis on behavioral intentions and family planning in Mexico and the United States, Charles D. Spielberger on cross-cultural anxiety, and a lengthy collaboration with Wayne H. Holtzman on personality development in two cultures. Some of this work is referenced in Díaz-Guerrero (1984) and Pick de Weiss & Díaz-Loving (1986).

In the 1960s, behaviorism entered Mexico with great force. Its four original leaders were Serafín Mercado, Emilio Ribes, Víctor Alcaraz, and Florente López. Using behaviorism as a base, they developed a strong department of psychology at the Universidad Veracruzana in Jalapa, Veracruz. As for the two preceding groups, the amount of research in this area before 1980 cannot be adequately cited in limited space. For an extensive bibliography the reader is referred to Galindo and Worwerg (1985).

It was, among other considerations, this explosion of psychology as a science in Mexico that convinced the Executive Committee of the International Union of Psychological Science (IUPsyS) to have the Sociedad Mexicana de Psicología organize the Twenty-third International Congress in Acapulco. In volumes 1, 2, and 4 of the nine-volume Proceedings of the Congress, (Díaz-Guerrero, Holtzman, Rosenzweig, & Sánchez-Sosa, 1985) there is a foretoken of the areas that were to persist, or to be newly explored, by local research efforts: Biopsychological processes, social, cultural, cross-cultural, and health psychology, and, in all of these, searching for application to social, group, and individual problems.

In the 1980s and 1990s there was a major increase in the number of psychologists doing methodologically valid, often socially conscious, psychological research. Additionally, this research is being done not only in Mexico City with its 18 million inhabitants and several universities, but in state and private universities in several parts of the Republic. The quality and quantity of research is recognized by the National Council of Science and Technology (CONACyT) and a number of psychologists have been nominated investigadores nacionales (national researchers) and receive a monthly stipend to help them with their work.

María Elena Medina-Mora at the Instituto Mexicano de Psiquiatría and Juan José Sánchez-Sosa, Graciela Rodríguez, Benjamín Domínguez, Héctor Ayala, Laura Hernández, and Héctor Lara-Tapia at the Facultad de Psicología UNAM, and their increasing number of colleagues and students, are doing research on addictions, preventive psychology, disaster intervention, and biofeedback for chronic pain. A large number of psychologists are utilizing biofeedback in research or clinical applications. They have formed the Mexican Academy of Biofeedback. Jorge Palacios and his group are using biofeedback with many medical disorders.

Emilio Ribes, now at the University of Guadalajara, Víctor Alcaraz, Feggy Ostrovsky, María Corsi-Cabrera, Carlos Santoyo, and Arturo Bouzas, of UNAM and their colleagues and students are conducting experimental studies on transfer of learning, neurophysiology, and different aspects of cognition, particularly language, often utilizing brain potential techniques. Educational and instructional psychology is another hot topic. Miguel López, Sandra Castañeda, Javier Aguilar, and another large group at UNAM, explore and evaluate learning at the university level through a variety of techniques: computer aided, electroencephalogram, brain potential, etc.

Since 1990, Susan Pick and her group at the Instituto Mexicano de Investigación de Familia y Población (Family and population research institute) have been researching family planning, and, in particular, sex education.

Mieczyslaw Choynowski, a distinguished Polish psychologist, who has worked in Mexico for several decades, is a pioneer in the factorial study of aggression. His sophisticated work was published by the Universidad Pedagógica of the Ministry of Public Education (Choynowski, 1993, Mexico City). This is the best place to acknowledge the stimulating effect upon our discipline, of other foreign, in this case U.S. psychologists, who have taught in Mexico or otherwise helped Mexican psychology: Carl Hereford, Robert Peck, Stark Hathaway, Abraham Maslow, Fred Keller, Ernest Bijou, Roque Méndez, Harmon Hosch, Charles Osgood, Charles Spielberger, Harry Triandis, Herman Witkin, Henry David, Walter Lonner, and especially Wayne Holtzman. Let me also recognize the rise of investigators in the Republic: José Luis Valdéz at the State University of Mexico, Pedro Solís-Cámara at the Center for Biomedic Research in Jalisco, Teresita Castillo-León y Elías Góngora-Coronado, at the Universidad de Yucatán, Rosario Valdéz-Carabeo, Pedro Barrera-Valdivia and Ricardo Blanco-Vega in Chihuahua, José Angel Vera Noriega in Sonora, Rodolfo Espinoza-Fuentes at the Universidad Autónoma de Puebla, Elemi Hernández and Renán García at the Universidad de Tabasco, Héctor Capello at the Universidad Autónoma de Tamaulipas. This trend is increasing as is the number of psychologists doing research in government institutions, banks, private centers, and other settings.

Research is also conducted on acquired immunodeficiency syndrome (AIDS), psychotherapy, psychometric tests, ecological, organizational, community and political psychology, the latter including studies on attitudes toward the revolutionary intent by the EZLN in Chiapas.

But perhaps the most original and significant line of inquiry is in social psychology. At the beginning of the 1980s, a group of younger psychologists, among them Rolando Díaz-Loving, Patricia Andrade-Palos, Sofía

Rivera-Aragón, Mirta Flores-Galaz, Gabina Villagrán, Jorge La Rosa, Celina Girardi, Lucy Reidl, Javier Aguilar, Carlos Bruner, Rosario Silva-Arciniega, Luciana Ramos Lira, and Ruth Mina Estrella scrutinized social and personality dimensions considered universal. Their efforts have ranged from success to failure. The clearest case occurred when Flores-Galaz, Díaz-Loving, and Rivera-Aragón translated and retranslated Rathus's 30-item schedule for assessing assertive behavior. Three hundred fifty university students were tested using the scale. The factor analysis yielded a structure totally different from that found in the United States. In Mexico the first factor was clearly identified as no assertion! The result led Flores-Galaz, under the guidance of Díaz-Loving, to an extensive examination of the possible ways in which Mexicans could be assertive. While she still found nonassertiveness to be prevalent she discovered that in Mexico, U.S.-style assertiveness appears only on highly justified occasions in economic and other settings.

Concurrently, Díaz-Guerrero, aware that this group was utilizing the content of the HSCPs to interpret their unexpected findings, realized that there existed idiosyncratic personality and social dimensions along with the cultural ones. The time was ripe to establish ethnopsychology of personality and cognition. A paper proposing an ethnopsychology with data, postulates, and goals was published (in Díaz-Guerrero & Pacheco, 1994). With the help of Díaz-Loving, a seminar on research in ethnopsychology was established at UNAM. One interesting result was a fact-finding program in collaboration with Melgoza-Enriquez, Avendaño-Sandoval, and I. Reyes Lagunes. One of the postulates of ethnopsychology suggested that personality traits were the result of the previously mentioned culture-counterculture dialectic. If the culture demanded that Mexicans be affiliative-obedient they should develop a trait of flexibility and a trait of abnegation. After developing inventories for these traits and applying them in several populations, the existence of these traits was confirmed. In the case of abnegation a laboratory experiment ratified behavioral abnegation in senior high-school students (Avendaño-Sandoval and Díaz-Guerrero. In Díaz-Guerrero and Pacheco, 1994).

In the last few years the group around Díaz-Loving, another with Díaz-Guerrero, and two more around Reyes-Lagunes and Luis Lara-Tapia, have been conducting ethnopsychological studies, ratifying cultural dimensions, discovering idiosyncratic personality dimensions, and preparing the ground for development of local personality inventories. Starting in 1990, Angel Pacheco and Nydia Lucca, Puerto Rican psychologists, who had also been working on the assumption that culture is all important for psychological development, joined forces with Díaz-Guerrero and have together edited a book with the groundbreaking title of "Etnopsi-

cología, Scientia Nova (Díaz-Guerrero & Pacheco, 1994). In a very recent development, Díaz-Guerrero and Díaz-Loving from Mexico, John Adair from Canada, and Roque Méndez from the United States have begun a cross-cultural study in search of the origin of values.

The old saying "Poor Mexico—so far from God and so close to the United States" was recently modernized by Dr. Luis Lara Tapia to say: ". . . so close to the narco consumers." But this destiny has not befallen Mexican psychology. It owes much of its good points to the devoted collaboration of the American colleagues mentioned here and many others, too many to cite, and probably no less to the growth, since the 1950s of inter-American and international psychology.

The panorama of Mexican psychology, as illustrated throughout this report, is bittersweet. It may be a victim to its own research activity success. Too many young people have been attracted to study the discipline. There are many schools with inadequate staffs and others with too many students per teacher. The battle continues.

Bibliography

Díaz-Guerrero, R. (1966). Mexico. In S. Ross, I. Alexander, H. Basowitz, M. Werber, P. O. Nicholas (Eds.), *International opportunities for advanced training and research in psychology* (pp. 203–209). Washington, DC: American Psychological Association. Provides information on the earliest research efforts in psychology in Mexico. Where and to what extent psychology was taught in the Republic. The earliest professional profile and the requirements and organization for university studies. These last have remained pretty much unchanged.

Díaz-Guerrero, R. (1976). México. In V. S. Sexton & H. Misiak (Eds.), *Psychology around the world* (pp. 280–292). Monterey, CA: Brooks/Cole. A comprehensive work, the first in English by this author. The editors asked him to cut back his extensive bibliography to a few basic references. Contains information on psychology during the three hundred years of Spanish Colonial rule. Also the evolution of the psychology department at the National University (UNAM). The who and what of research in Mexico. The publishing company Trillas launched under the direction of this author, the Bibiloteca Técnica de Psicología, that in time translated in to Spanish over 200 technical books on psychology, mostly American.

Díaz-Guerrero, R. (1984). Contemporary psychology in Mexico. *Annual Review of Psychology, 35,* 83–112. In the second page of this article a printing error elevated from 4,209 to 42,090 students in the psychology program at UNAM. In a later section this becomes clear. The paper covers Mexican psychology from about 1969 to 1983; 194 references.

Díaz-Guerrero, R. (1994). Psychology in Mexico. In R. J. Corsini (Ed.), *Encyclopedia of psychology* (Vol. 3, pp. 206–209). New York: J. Wiley. This is the most recent reference, other than those in Spanish. It was originally prepared for the 1984 edition and was updated with an addendum. It contains a fairly complete listing of individuals doing research in the different categories of psychology.

Díaz-Guerrero, R., & Pacheco, A. M. (1994). *Etnopsicología, Scientia Nova* [Ethnopsychology, a new science]. San Juan, Puerto Rico: Servicios Profesionales y Científicos, Inc. (P.O. Box 22275, University Station, Río Piedras, San Juan, PR 00931-2275.) The theoretical and research foundations of an ethnopsychology as illustrated in the work of a number of Puerto Rican and Mexican psychologists.

Díaz-Loving, R., & Valderrama, P. (1992). Mexico. In V. S. Sexton & J. D. Hogan (Eds.), *International psychology,* (pp. 280–292). Lincoln: University of Nebraska Press. These authors illustrate graphically the mushrooming growth of the discipline in Mexico between 1950 and 1985 (from 1 to 65 schools, from 200 to 40,000 students). They identify student preferences for branches of psychology from 1972 to 1982. They review the situation regarding national journals and professional societies and organizations.

Galindo, E., & Worwerg, M. (1985). La Psicología en México [Psychology in Mexico]. *Ciencia y Desarrollo, 11,* (63), 29–45. An important and comprehensive article. It describes at length the impact of Skinner and behavior modification on Mexican psychology. It is also a good source for contributions to physiological psychology. There is an extensive bibliography.

Garcia Cortés, F. (Ed.). (1983). *Una Década de la Facultad de Psicología, 1973–1983* [A decade of the faculty of psychology]. Mexico.: Facultad de Psicología, UNAM. The most distinguished members of the Psychology Faculty at UNAM collaborated on a comprehensive account of psychology from 1973 to 1983. There are chapters on clinical, educational, experimental, industrial, and psychophysiological psychology. Interesting essays assay the impact of behaviorism, cognitivism, genetic psychology, and psychoanalysis in the curriculum.

Molina, J. (in press). Psicología y Positivismo: La enseñanza de la psicología durante el porfiriato: 1896–1910. [Psychology and positivism: The teaching of psychology during the Porfirio regime]. In A. Treviño (Ed.), *Cien años de la psicología en México* [One hundred years of psychology in Mexico]. Mexico.: Facultad de Psicología, UNAM. The educational and political atmosphere at the birth of modern psychology in Mexico.

Morgane, P. J. (1970). Raúl Hernández Peón (1924–1968). *Physiology and behavior, 5,* 379–388. This is a eulogy with an extensive bibliography of publications by Hernández Peón.

Pick de Weiss, S., & Díaz-Loving, R. (1986). Applied psychology in Mexico. *International Review of Applied Psychology, 35,* 577–598. This is the most complete account available regarding applied psychology in Mexico. There are well over one hundred references.

Ribes, E. (1968). Psychology in Mexico. *American Psychologist. 23,* 565–566.

Ribes, E. (1975). Some recent development in psychology in Mexico. *American Psychologist 30,* 774–776. The first

of these reports by Ribes brought Díaz-Guerrero's (1966) work up to date. Most important is Ribes's description of the inauguration at the University of Veracruz (a state bordering the Gulf of Mexico) of a behaviorally oriented program of psychology, housed in the Faculty of Sciences rather than the Faculty of Philosophy. In the second paper, Ribes reports on the accelerated increase in the number of departments of psychology across the Republic, independent of the faculties of philosophy, the progressive dominance of the behavioral, experimental, and quantitative approaches, and the researchers and types of research prevalent.

Urbina-Soria, J. (Ed.). (1989). *El psicólogo: Formación, ejercicio profesional y prospectiva.* [Psychology: Its formation, professional practice, and future]. Mexico.: Facultad de Psicología, UNAM. This illustrates the excitement of Mexican psychologists about their science and preoccupation with the development of a national curriculum that can best integrate training and practice. The sixty-six chapters in this voluminous work contain a great deal of solid information about psychologists and their practices in Mexico.

Urbina-Soria, J. (Ed.). (1993). *Facultad de Psicología: Testimonios de Veinte Años, 1973–1993.* Mexico.: Facultad de Psicología, UNAM. The editor invited the most active and productive members of the staff (45), to write an article on the birth and evolution of the Faculty of Psychology at UNAM. The information about those twenty years of psychology in Mexico is rich and extensive. One of the articles refers to social psychology which was absent in the account of the first decade.

Valderrama Iturbe, P. (1985). Un Esquema para la Historia de la Psicología en México [A diagram of the history of psychology in Mexico]. *Revista Mexicana de Psicología. 2,* 80–92. The author differentiates five periods in the history of psychology in Mexico. The bibliography contains 59 references, several unique.

Valderrama, P., Colotia, V. A., Gallegos, X., & Jurado, S. (1994). *Evolución de la Psicología en México* [The development of psychology in Mexico]. México, D.F.: El Manual Moderno, S.A. de C.V. The first commercial book published on the history of psychology in Mexico. Each of the significant figures in the early development of scientific psychology is given a chapter, including Morgane's (1970) comprehensive article on Raúl Hernández Peón, translated into Spanish.

Valderrama, P., Colotia, V., Jurado, S., & Gallegos, X. (in press). De la fundación de la universidad a la creación de la maestría en psicología [The founding of the university and the mastery of psychology]. In A. Treviño (Ed.), *Cien años de la psicología en México.* México.: Facultad de Psicología, UNAM. Psychology in Mexico between 1910 and 1938.

Rogelio Díaz-Guerrero

MEYER, ADOLF (1866–1950), American psychiatrist. One of the most influential American psychiatrists during the first half of the twentieth century, Meyer completed his medical studies at the University of Zürich in 1892, where he studied under August Forel, then director of the Swiss Burghölzi mental hospital. That same year, Meyer emigrated from his native Switzerland to the United States. His first position in the United States was as a pathologist for the Illinois Eastern Hospital for the Insane at Kankakee (1893–1895). Here, Meyer attempted to integrate psychiatric research with care for mentally ill patients by educating the staff in the principles of psychiatry. Subsequently, he was appointed pathologist at the Worcester, Massachusetts, State Lunatic Hospital (1895–1901), and director of the Pathological Institute of the New York State Hospitals for the Insane (1902–1909). In both positions, Meyer attempted to raise the level of care for mental patients by teaching asylum physicians and attendants how to take useful records of the behavior of patients. He extensively reorganized record-keeping methods. In 1909, he was appointed the first professor in psychiatry at the Johns Hopkins Medical School and director of the Henry Phipps Psychiatric Clinic; he held both positions until his retirement in 1941.

Meyer's dynamic psychiatry or psychobiology was holistic, pluralistic, and pragmatic. Meyer located the cause of mental disorders in the relation of the individual to his or her environment; mental problems occurred when individuals were unable to face the challenges of life. He considered insufficient the then current neurological research tradition of investigating the brains of deceased mental patients to locate lesions. Meyer also doubted the usefulness of the extensive nosological and diagnostic systems that were common among European psychiatrists at the time; a diagnosis in itself did not improve a patient's condition. He was equally opposed to those who exclusively emphasized psychological factors, most notably psychoanalysts. Meyer integrated all these approaches in his commonsense or psychobiological approach. He emphasized the importance of analyzing each person individually, rather than relying solely on laboratory experimentation, neurological research, or theoretical generalization.

Meyer believed that mental disorder was caused by ineffective habits which had developed as faulty responses to specific situations. Studying the life history of the patient revealed, according to Meyer, the factors that contributed to his or her current condition and could therefore suggest measures that would modify that condition. Meyer demonstrated his approach in his conception of schizophrenia or dementia praecox as it was then known. According to him, dementia praecox was the consequence of a habit disorganization which had led to increasingly ineffective ways of dealing with one's environment. Individuals prone to dementia praecox had shied away from the challenges of life by day-dreaming, rationalization, and inaction, thereby making them increasingly less able to deal with new

situations. In this conception, the differences between normal functioning, neuroses, and psychoses are only a matter of degree; they all appear as more or less serious forms of maladjustment.

Meyer's psychobiology resembled the functionalist psychology as it had been developed by John Dewey and William James, who both emphasized the importance of analyzing human behavior within its context. During his career, Meyer encouraged psychologists to investigate the dynamics and principles underlying individual adjustment. He provided John B. Watson with a laboratory in the Phipps Clinic at Johns Hopkins in the hope that the latter's work would contribute to his dynamic psychiatry. After conducting research on mentally ill patients for a brief period of time, Watson became more interested in animal research. Watson's behaviorism explicitly excluded consciousness from the field of psychology, a move Meyer could only have interpreted as premature and provoked by artificial theoretical reasons. Meyer had corresponded with Edward B. Titchener in an attempt to find common ground; however, in theoretical respects the two remained far apart. During Meyer's career, functionalism in psychology became increasingly marginalized, making a connection between his psychobiology and the discipline of psychology increasingly unlikely. To Meyer's dismay, psychologists increasingly based their research in laboratories rather than in naturalistic settings, which made their work less relevant for dynamic psychiatry. Meyer's influence in psychology can be felt most strongly in those areas that have or have had affinity with psychiatry or that have focused on clinical applications, such as clinical, educational, and developmental psychology.

Bibliography

Leys, R., & Evans, R. B. (Eds.). (1990). *Defining American psychology: The correspondence between Adolf Meyer and Edward Bradford Titchener*. Baltimore, MD: Johns Hopkins University Press.

Meyer, A. (1910). The dynamic interpretation of dementia praecox. *American Journal of Psychology, 21* (2–3), 139–157.

Meyer, A. (1915, September 4). Objective psychology or psychobiology with subordination of the medically useless contrast of mental and physical. *Journal of the American Medical Association, 65*, 860–863.

Meyer, A. (1948). *The commonsense psychiatry of Adolf Meyer: Fifty-two selected papers* (Alfred Lief, Ed.). New York: McGraw-Hill.

Hans Pols

MEYERSON, IGNACE (1888–1983), French psychologist. Ignace Meyerson was born in Poland, which he was forced to leave in 1905 after taking part in the Russian-Polish insurrection. In 1906, he had joined his uncle, the philosopher Emile Meyerson (1859–1933), in Paris. Between 1907 and 1914, he studied medicine and science concurrently; his first work on physiology was published in 1912. Recruited as a doctor during World War I, he was invalided out of the army in 1915 and worked as an intern at the Salpêtrière. At this point, he obtained his degree in philosophy, thus acquiring the combined medical and philosophical qualification characteristic of the first French academic psychologists. In 1919, he became subeditor of the journal of the French Psychological Society, the *Journal de Psychologie Normale et Pathologique*, which had been founded in 1904 by Pierre Janet and Georges Dumas. As a result, he came to serve as secretary of the society. In 1923, he was appointed director of the experimental psychology laboratory of the École Pratique des Hautes Études. In 1926, he published the first French translation of Freud's *Interpretation of Dreams* but subsequently showed little interest in psychoanalysis. From 1927 to 1938, he worked with Paul Guillaume (1876–1962), the main French exponent of *gestaltpsychologie*. Their research concerned the use of tools by apes. During World War II, under the racial laws of the Vichy government, he was dismissed from all his posts. He took refuge in Toulouse, where, with Jean-Pierre Vernant, he coedited the clandestine newspaper of the resistance army of the southwest. After the war, he was restored to his academic posts and continued his teaching duties as director of studies at the École Pratique des Hautes Études until his death.

For 63 years, Ignace Meyerson edited the *Journal de Psychologie Normale et Pathologique*, first with Charles Blondel (1876–1939), then, until 1962, with Paul Guillaume, and finally as sole editor. With *L'Année Pychologique*, this was one of the two most important French journals of psychology. The direction taken by the review under Meyerson's editorship should be noted. His network of friends and intellectual contacts went well beyond the bounds of psychology. He made the journal the forum of a dialogue between psychologists, historians, linguists, aestheticians, anthropologists, and philosophers. He sought to maintain the integrity of psychology while allowing it to benefit from the input of other disciplines. Under his editorship, the journal thus became an invaluable document of the state of French intellectual life before and after World War II.

The key to his interest in such a variety of intellectual fields is to be found in his work *Les Fonctions psychologiques et les oeuvres* (1948), in which he presented the basic tenets of the "historical psychology" thereafter associated with his name. For Ignace Meyerson, the thoughts and acts of human beings were always reflected in perpetually changing human works and institutions in the fields of law, religion, art, the sciences, and technology. All human effort tends toward the production of tools, scientific theories, forms of artistic expression, and so on. These works express the state of the human spirit at a given moment in its history. For Meyerson, the claim that psychological functions are unchangeable is a mere "fixist" prejudice. Humanity is history, and human psychology must for the most part be historical.

His work has remained somewhat peripheral in France to date, given the position occupied by experimental psychology on the one hand and by psychoanalysis on the other.

Bibliography

Meyerson, I. (1948). *Les fonctions psychologiques et les oeuvres*. Paris: Vrin.

Meyerson, I. (1987). *Ecrits 1920–1983. Pour une psychologie historique*. Paris: Presses Universitaires de France.

Vermès, G. (1992). Un rédacteur pour le *Journal de Psychologie Normale et Pathologique* après la Première Guerre Mondiale. In H. Carpintero, E. Lafuente, R. Plas, & L. Sprung, (Eds.), *New studies in the history of psychology and the social sciences* (pp. 353–359). Valencia, Spain: Revista de Historia de la Psicología, Monographs 2.

Régine Plas
Translated from French by Chris Miller

MICHOTTE, ALBERT EDOUARD (1881–1965), Belgian psychologist. Michotte strove to understand adaptive action by doing a wide range of pioneering experimental-phenomenological studies. First, he worked on histology of the nerve cell. Next, he studied logical memory and self-determination. Finally, he turned to phenomenal causality, phenomenal permanence, phenomenal reality, and perception in relation to thought. While he investigated basic psychological processes, Michotte became increasingly aware of social context. Like Wilhelm Wundt, however, he felt that experimentation on basic psychological processes must precede advances in social psychology.

Michotte's early University of Louvain professors, philosopher Désiré Mercier and physiologist Arthur Van Gehuchten, encouraged him to pursue his research interests. Michotte received his doctorate from the University of Louvain in 1900 and later studied for a time with Wilhelm Wundt at Leipzig and Oswald Külpe at Würzburg. He appreciated Kulpe's expanded psychological framework. Like Külpe, Michotte advocated a dynamic conception of psychological activity. He believed that higher mental processes, the search for meaning, and individual differences in needs and values play important parts in adaptive action.

English-speaking scholars are most familiar with Michotte's experimental-phenomenological studies of mechanical causality that clarify commonly experienced adaptive situations. Responding to the approach of an automobile is a case in point. To understand how perception guides adaptation, Michotte designed an experiment and an apparatus that revealed the precise conditions under which perceptual consciousness of mechanical causality occurs. He placed a viewer in front of a large white screen. Through a horizontal slit in the screen, the viewer sees two "rectangles" of different colors that move along the slit. Viewers' judgments enabled Michotte to determine the spatiotemporal conditions that predictably result in causal impressions. In entraining, the first major causal impression, viewers typically report that the first "rectangle" seems to be pushing or carrying the second along. In launching, the second major causal impression, viewers generally say that the first "rectangle" appears to project the second "rectangle" ahead, giving it a push.

R. W. Pickford (*British Journal of Psychology*, 1963, 54, p. 369) appraised Michotte's simple and elegant investigations of impressions of causality as a milestone for twentieth-century psychology. M. D. Vernon (*British Journal of Social and Clinical Psychology*, 1964, 3, p. 75) said of Michotte's perceptual work: "There are few psychologists with the originality of mind, the ingenuity in experimental design and techniques, the psychological insight and the expertise in argument, who could produce a work such as this." In the early 1970s, two psychologists, R. B. Joynson and D. G. Boyle, published papers critical of Michotte's research methodology. His Louvain colleagues, de Montpellier and Nuttin, responded to their claims that Michotte engaged sophisticated colleagues as experimental subjects by citing research with naive subjects that confirmed Michotte's results (*British Journal of Psychology*, 1973, 64, pp. 287–289). American psychologist James Gibson also appreciated Michotte's efforts, finding in them affinities with his own. Michotte's research has relevance for current developments and debates in psychology. His substantive findings, methodological ingenuity, and abiding cordiality toward and interest in other psychologists and their research made his contributions, and the psychological institute he headed at the University of Louvain, recognized far beyond Belgium's borders.

Bibliography

Michotte, A. (1950). The emotions regarded as functional connections. In M. L. Reymert (Ed.), *Feelings and emotions: The Mooseheart Symposium* (pp. 114–126). New York: McGraw-Hill. A resource that bears testimony to Michotte's dynamic conception of psychological activity.

Michotte, A. (1963). *The perception of causality*. New York: Basic Books. A classic that documents Michotte's most celebrated research. Originally published under the title *La perception de la causalite*. In *Études de Psychologie*, 8 (n.d.) 2nd ed., 1954. University of Louvain.

Misiak, H., & Staudt, V. (1954). *Albert Edouard Michotte. Catholics in psychology: A historical survey*. New York: McGraw-Hill, pp. 98–110. Informative account of Michotte's life, contacts with other psychologists, investigations, writings, disciples, and evaluation.

Thinès, G., Costall, A., & Butterworth, C. (Eds.). (1991). *Michotte's experimental phenomenology of perception*. Hillsdale, NJ: Erlbaum. An essential source that contains Michotte's autobiography, major publications in translation, bibliography of primary sources, and helpful commentary.

Eileen A. Gavin

MIDDLE CHILDHOOD. [*This entry provides a general survey of the theories, research, and findings that have informed our knowledge about middle childhood. It comprises five articles:*

Physical and Biological Development
Cognitive Development
Education and Schooling
Social and Emotional Development
Socialization and Social Contexts

For discussions dealing with other stages of development, see Adolescence; Infancy; Early Childhood; *and* Adulthood and Aging.]

Physical and Biological Development

Middle childhood (ages 6 through 11) is a time of relative stability for many biological systems. However, the changes that do occur are of salience for this stage of development.

Physical Growth

Height and weight increase linearly from age 6 to 11. Table 1 shows standing heights for boys and girls. There are small differences in mean height between boys and girls, but at age 9, years boys' and girls' heights are nearly identical.

The rate of growth slowly declines between 6 and 11 years, from about 6 cm to about 5 cm each year. Growth velocity reaches its nadir at the time of onset of physical pubertal development (Department of Health, Education, and Welfare [DHEW], 1973).

Weight also increases linearly in this age range. Table 2 shows weights for boys and girls. On average, weight increases about 3 kg each year between 6 and 11 years of age. There are no significant differences

MIDDLE CHILDHOOD: Physical and Biological Development. Table 1. Standing height (in centimeters) for boys and girls

Sex and Age (years)	Percentile		
	5	50	95
Boys			
6	110.7	118.5	128.0
7	115.6	124.4	134.4
8	120.3	130.0	139.3
9	124.6	135.6	145.4
10	129.3	140.6	151.3
11	134.6	145.8	157.0
Girls			
6	108.3	117.7	126.7
7	113.7	123.6	132.7
8	119.1	129.6	139.3
9	124.4	135.4	147.4
10	129.5	141.0	153.4
11	135.4	147.4	159.7

From Department of Health, Education, and Welfare, 1973, p. 19.

MIDDLE CHILDHOOD: Physical and Biological Development. Table 2. Weight (in kilograms) for boys and girls

Sex and Age (years)	Percentile		
	5	50	95
Boys			
6	17.4	21.6	28.0
7	19.4	24.1	31.5
8	21.5	27.1	36.4
9	23.2	29.7	43.5
10	25.5	32.6	45.0
11	28.6	36.6	53.0
Girls			
6	16.4	21.1	28.0
7	18.7	23.5	31.5
8	20.5	26.7	38.2
9	22.9	29.8	45.6
10	24.9	34.2	49.9
11	28.4	38.2	58.0

From Department of Health, Education, and Welfare, 1973, p. 19.

between boys' and girls' weights in this age range. However, since some girls at ages 10 to 11 years are experiencing physical pubertal development, the range of girls' weights is larger than the range of boys' weights at those ages (DHEW, 1973). It should also be noted that there is considerable variability in children's weight. For instance, the 95th percentile for weight in 6-year-old children approaches the 5th percentile for weight for 11-year-old children. Thus some of the lightest 11-year-olds will have body weights comparable to the heaviest 6-year-olds.

These variations in physical appearance may play a significant role in children's lives. For example, those children whose heights fall in the lower percentiles for age may be perceived as younger than they are. This may affect the manner in which teachers, for example, interact with them. Teacher expectations for younger-looking children may be different from teacher expectations for children whose appearance matches their chronological age.

There has been a substantial increase in the number of immigrant children in the United States in the past several years. It is important to recognize that some of these children come from impoverished backgrounds. Poverty may exert substantial effects on the growth of children (Yip, Kelley, & Trowbridge, 1993). Children from different racial and ethnic backgrounds may also display different patterns of growth from Caucasian Americans (Tanner, 1989).

In addition to height and weight, growth takes place at many other body sites. Differential growth at these other sites (chest, abdomen, hips, hands and feet, etc.) causes changes in various body proportions. There are distinct gender differences in many of these proportions. Boys are larger in measures of hands and feet and torso, whereas girls are larger in buttock and thigh areas during middle childhood.

These variations in body proportions in growing individuals have significant practical implications. The design and manufacture of children's equipment, furniture, and clothing need to take these measures into account. The assumption that children are only "scaled down versions" of adults leads to poorly designed materials. For example, a seat has to be wide enough and long enough to accommodate larger children yet must not be so long as to be of potential discomfort for the shorter child.

Adrenarche

Middle childhood is viewed by most as a period of latency in regard to psychosexual development. Many believe that there are no significant hormonal changes during this phase of life. However, a significant hormonal event occurs between ages 6 and 8. This phenomenon is called adrenarche. Weakly androgenic hormones produced by the adrenal glands are secreted in higher amounts. There is no increase in the other hormones (glucocorticoids or mineralocorticoids), suggesting that there is not a general activation of the adrenal glands. Adrenarche is sometimes accompanied by the appearance of axillary and pubic hair, axillary odor, and increased secretion of sebum (sometimes causing acne). However, in most instances the increased concentration of these hormones in both boys and girls has no significant clinical effects. There seems to be no relation between adrenarche and the onset of true puberty.

Sexual Development

The earliest normal onset of true pubertal physical maturation is eight years in girls and nine years in boys. However, data from 17,077 girls seen in pediatric offices for health maintenance or minor health problems demonstrated that 3 to 5% of White girls and 6 to 15% of African American girls ages 6 and 7 had breast development. One and one half to 2.8% of White girls and 9.5 to 17.7% of African American girls had some pubic hair development. By age 8, 7.7% of White girls had pubic hair and 10.5% had breast development. For African American girls, the figures were 37.8% for breast development and 34.3% for pubic hair (Herman-Giddens et al., 1997). Thus the appearance of these secondary sexual characteristics at earlier ages than previously described, especially in the African American population, must be taken into consideration when considering the diagnosis of sexual precocity. No such data is available for boys. What was previously considered abnormally early development may now have to be redefined. Parents and health care professionals must be prepared to address these phenomena with girls. Since some normal children will experience the onset of puberty during middle childhood, appropriate information about this change should be provided to these children by parents and health care professionals.

Some children in middle childhood do experience early pubertal maturation. Precocious thelarche is the premature development of breast tissue. This not uncommon condition is usually associated with the premature development of an ovarian follicle and the production of estrogen by this follicle. In most instances breast development appears as a swelling beneath the areolae that may be tender. This may persist for several months and then regress, or breast tissue growth may persist and slowly progress over the course of years. There are usually no other indications of a systemic effect of estrogen, in vaginal discharge or bleeding, in development of the labia minora, in growth spurt, or in increased adiposity of hips and thighs. Ovarian or adrenal tumors causing premature thelarche are very rare, but the possibility should be investigated and ruled out.

Precocious pubarche or adrenarche is the premature appearance of sexual hair. The cause of this is unknown in most instances, although congenital virilizing adrenal hyperplasia or tumors of the testis or adrenals must be ruled out by appropriate laboratory tests. There are usually no other indications of a systemic effect of androgens such as growth spurt, enlargement of the testes, increased muscle mass, voice change, and so forth.

True precocious puberty involves early activation of the hypothalamic pituitary gonadal axis. There are usually other indications of systemic effects of all sex steroids. Most of the time there is no identifiable cause, but it is necessary to test for and rule out tumors of the pituitary or hypothalamus. Tumors seem to be a more common cause in males, but with the availability of central nervous system imaging techniques (such as magnetic resonance imaging), small tumors are also being identified more frequently in girls. At one time the main concern of physicians managing this disorder was the possibility that the children, although tall at the beginning of the process, might become short adults because the early onset of pubertal maturation and earlier adolescent growth spurt could cause growth to cease earlier than it would if pubertal onset came later. Thus, many girls were subjected to treatments to slow down the progression of pubertal development. However, when the adult heights of children for whom no treatments were available were compared with the adult heights of treated children, no significant differences were found (Grave, 1996). Treatment for children with true precocious puberty should be related to significant behavioral issues. Girls for whom menstruation poses mechanical and social problems should be considered for treatments designed to stop the occurrence of menses. Boys whose enlarged penis is stimulated by rubbing against clothing, causing frequent erections, or who masturbate should be considered for treatment to supress the concentration of testosterone.

Children with any of these forms of precocious sexual maturation do not seem to experience problems related to reproduction. Some of these children seem more likely to be the victims of sexual abuse.

Girls with true precocious puberty do show earlier engagement (by about 2 years) in sexual behavior during adolescence than girls whose onset of puberty is later (Erhardt & Meyer-Bahlberg, 1986). Those adults who interact with children in this age group who exhibit physical sexual maturation must be cognizant of the potential for misinterpreting the capabilities of children who appear to be more mature than their chronological age.

Neuromuscular Development

Development of the central nervous system is complete from an anatomical perspective by middle childhood. However, new neural networks will develop throughout this stage. This development is manifested primarily through changes in cognition and behaviors. Motor skills are well developed at the onset of middle childhood, but few changes will take place during this period. There seem to be no significant differences between boys and girls until the onset of puberty, when strength increases considerably more in boys than in girls.

Common Health Problems

In middle childhood unintentional injury accounts for 42% of deaths. Twenty-three percent of these unintentional injuries are the result of children being injured as pedestrians, whereas 18% occur to children who are occupants in automobiles. Parents are the most common drivers, and it is their responsibility to ensure that their children are properly secured in their cars with appropriate restraints. In general it seems best to seat child passengers in the rear rather than in the front seats. This recommendation arises in part from the increasing frequency of injuries related to airbags that deploy rapidly and with such force as to injure children seated in front seats. Parents also have the responsibility not to drive when they are intoxicated. Driving while intoxicated is the most common cause of automobile accidents. Other causes of death include drowning (15%), burns and fires (14%), injury related to bicycles (6%), and homicide (6%); other causes account for about 18% of deaths.

Malignant neoplasms (tumors) are the second leading cause of death (12%). The most common cancer is acute lymphocytic leukemia. With recent improvement in treatments, the survival rate for this disorder is quite good. Other less common causes of death include congenital anomalies, suicide, and diseases of the heart (Guyer, Strobine, Venture, MacDorman, & Martin, 1996).

As children enter school, they have increasing contact with other children who may have infectious illnesses. It is not uncommon for children entering school for the first time to have repeated episodes of upper respiratory infections. Children may be almost constantly ill throughout the first year of school.

Immunization programs have almost eliminated the exanthematous diseases (measles, chicken pox, etc.) and other potentially serious diseases such as hepatitis. All children should have completed all of the suggested immunizations by age 5. Detailed information about immunization and childhood infectious diseases can be found in the *Redbook* of the American Academy of Pediatrics (Peter, 1997).

Recurrent episodes of abdominal pain are quite common in middle childhood. These symptoms often lead to extensive medical evaluations by physicians who are not aware of the possibility that the symptoms are often somatic manifestations of psychological distress. Doctors may pursue diagnostic tests and sometimes even perform surgery to establish an organic cause for the symptoms. For example, a child whose mother is chronically ill may develop abdominal pain, which will keep the child from attending school. The child can thus stay at home, monitor the parent, and relieve the anxiety he or she might experience by being at school and worrying about the parent. Symptom management involves recognizing the nature of the symptom and the dynamics involved in its production and providing appropriate psychological intervention while preventing further unproductive medical evaluations.

Nutrition

Most children in mid-childhood do not experience nutritional problems. They should be consuming a well-balanced diet based on the recommendations for adults. The average 6-year-old should be consuming approximately 1,500 Kcal daily, with an increase of approximately 100 Kcal per year. The diet should contain a maximum of 30% of calories from fat, between 15 and 20% of calories from protein, and 50 to 55% of calories from carbohydrate. Intake of cholesterol should not exceed 300 milligrams daily, and salt should be limited to about 1 gm daily. The majority of fat should be polyunsaturated (from plant sources, with the exception of coconut or palm kernel oil) or monounsaturated (olive oil) or from fish. It is clear that the process of atherosclerosis starts in childhood, so restriction of fats as indicated above is important.

Vegetarian diets of the vegan type are likely to be deficient in some nutrients and should only be provided to children under adequate supervision by a nutritionist. A vegetarian diet that includes dairy products and eggs is likely to provide adequate nutrients but is also likely to be high in fat, particularly in saturated fats. It is essential to provide adequate intake of iron, which may be supplied through vegetable sources.

Under most circumstances, adequate micronutrients will be provided by the diet, so supplements of vitamins and minerals are not generally recommended, with the exception that fluoride supplements should be provided.

Obesity is becoming a more frequent problem during childhood, and if it continues into adolescence and adulthood, it will lead to significant health problems, as well as social difficulties. Management of overeating in middle childhood is a family issue, as most children do not comprehend the nature of the problem and the solution. It is thus necessary for all family members to engage in dietary modification if the program for the affected child is to be acceptable to the child and successfully completed. One such program has been successful (Epstein, Valoske, Wing, & McCurley, 1990).

Exercise

There are no standards for frequency or duration of aerobic exercise for children as there are for adults. The President's Council on Physical Fitness and Sports (Clinton, Joyner, & McMillen, 1993) provides some guidance to determine the degree of a child's fitness and describes some components of a program to enhance fitness. However, there seems to be no consideration given to modifying programs to suit the developmental changes that take place at the time of puberty. The second National Children and Youth Fitness Study evaluated fitness in a sample of children in first through fourth grades (Ross & Pate, 1987). In community settings, middle childhood boys and girls participate most frequently in swimming, racing and sprinting, baseball and bicycling, and soccer and playground activities. The findings suggest that current programs may be inadequate to promote lifetime fitness.

School requirements for participation in exercise programs have historically been found lacking in goals and organization. For the most part, exercise takes place during organized community activities such as various leagues (football, soccer, baseball, etc.). These leagues have no regulations that take the physical or cognitive aspects of children's development into consideration. At 10 to 11 years of age some children may well have some pubertal development. This will put them at a significant physical advantage over same-age peers who have not entered puberty. Most organized programs do not take physical or other developmental factors into consideration in determining who will play against whom. This may expose certain children to considerable risks of injury during athletic competition, which is a leading cause of injury in this developmental period. Teams are usually coached by amateur volunteers who may know little about children's development and who are concerned primarily with winning rather than with providing the exercise and satisfying group experiences that children should have.

A summary of the health benefits of exercise for children and an annotated bibliography is available from the International Health, Racquet, and Sportsclub Association (1994). This group suggests that benefits of exercise include improved academic performance and leadership, positive behavior and emotional stability, improved health, and prevention of disease.

Chronic Health Problems

Middle childhood is a time when relatively few chronic diseases appear. Children with cystic fibrosis, rheumatoid arthritis, leukemia and other neoplasms, and congenital heart disease that had onset prior to middle childhood should be supported in their development during middle childhood. They should be allowed and encouraged to take part in the normal tasks of this period of development.

Toward the end of this stage, the number of new cases of diabetes mellitus increases. Although it may seem relatively simple to administer two to three injections of insulin each day to control blood glucose, the regimen imposed is much more complex and places significant restrictions on every aspect of a child's life. At a time when the child is anticipating more independence, parents of children with chronic illness tend to restrict independence and assume more control over the life of the child who has developed chronic illness.

Although some restrictions must be imposed, parents, children, and health care providers must work cooperatively to minimize restrictions (within the bounds of biological constraints) and maximize the continued development of independence that should continue at this stage of life.

Children with any handicapping condition are now "mainstreamed" in as many aspects of their lives as is possible. Children who would have been excluded from public schools in the past are now required to attend, and schools, working in conjunction with parents, must provide adequate facilities and instructional programs.

Bibliography

Clinton, W., Joyner, F. G., & McMillen, T. (1993). *Get fit: A handbook for youth ages 6–17*. (Available from the President's Council on Physical Fitness and Sports, 701 Pennsylvania Avenue NW, Washington, DC 20004). The Council has many publications related to sports participation at all ages, but their approach is generic.

Department of Health, Education, and Welfare. (1973). *Selected body measurements of children 6–11 years* (U.S. Publication No. HSM 73-1605, Series 11, No. 123). Washington, DC: US Government Printing Office. This is part of a large series on many aspects of growth and development. It presents data from a nationally representative sample with little commentary.

Epstein, L. H., Valoske, A., Wing, R. R., & McCurley, J. (1990). Ten-year follow-up of behavioral family-based treatment for obese children. *Journal of the American Medical Association, 264,* 2519–2523. The authors show that weight loss can be safely accomplished in children.

Erhardt, A. A., & Meyer-Bahlberg, H. F. L. (1986). Idiopathic precocious puberty in girls: Long-term effects on adolescent behavior. *Acta Endocrinologica, 279,* 247–253. The authors are well known for their work on gender disorders in children and adolescents.

Grave, G. D., & Cutler, G. B. (1993). *Sexual precocity: Etiology, diagnosis, and management*. New York: Raven Press. This volume contains details of the latest research on all forms of early sexual development. These are proceedings of a conference sponsored by the National Institutes of Health.

Guyer, B., Strobine, D. M., Venture, S. J., MacDorman, M., & Martin, J. A. (1996). Annual summary of vital statistics—1995. *Pediatrics, 98,* 1007–1027. The American Academy of Pediatrics annually publishes vital statistical data summarized from government sources.

Herman-Giddens, M. E., Slora, E. J., Wasserman, R. C., Bourdony, C. J., Bhapker, M. V., Koch, G. G., & Hasemeier, C. M. (1997). Secondary sexual characteristics and menses in young girls seen in office practice: A study from the pediatric research in office settings network. *Pediatrics, 99,* 505–512. This is part of a series of studies done in the offices of pediatricians. There are some methodological problems with research done in offices, but there are no fatal flaws.

International Health, Racquet, and Sportsclub Association. (1994). (Available from HRSA, 263 Summer Street, Boston, MA 02210, 1-800-766-1278). This is a brochure about the benefits of exercise for children, with a brief annotated bibliography.

Peter, G. (Ed.). (1997). *Redbook: Report of the Committee on Infectious Diseases* (24th ed.). Elk Grove Village, IL: American Academy of Pediatrics. This is the bible for information on all infectious disease.

Ross, J. G., & Pate, R. R. (1987, November/December). The National Children and Youth Fitness Study: II. A summary of findings. *Journal of Physical Education, Recreation, and Dance, 58,* 51–56. This has interesting data on the evaluation of fitness in children and adolescents.

Tanner, J. M. (Ed.). (1989). *Auxology 88: Perspectives in the science of growth and development.* London: Smith-Gordon. This contains several papers on differences in growth of children from various racial and ethnic populations. It is a well-written edited volume that presents the latest thinking on a problem that has still not been well described.

Yip, R., Kelley, S., & Trowbridge, F. (1993). Trends and patterns in height and weight status of low-income U.S. children. *Critical Reviews in Food Science and Nutrition, 33,* 409–421. This article presents some interesting effects of socioeconomic status on growth and confirms some common assumptions.

Jordan W. Finkelstein

Cognitive Development

Middle childhood is generally defined as the period from the onset of formal schooling (6–7 years of age) to the beginning of puberty (11–13 years). Although some cognitive processes are near adult levels by the time children reach school age, some important aspects of cognition are still improving. These include changes in how the world is represented, an increasing knowledge base, faster speed of processing, increasing memory abilities, and better metacognition.

Mental Representation: The Advent of Concrete Operations

According to the Swiss theorist Jean Piaget, children enter the stage of concrete operations at about 6 or 7 years of age. During this time, children are able to understand the world in terms of logical rules. In arithmetic, for example, if $5 + 8 = 13$, then $13 - 8$ must equal 5. This is the logical rule of reversibility, which was central to Piaget's theory of concrete operations.

In contrast to younger children, concrete operational children are able to represent part-whole relations properly. For example, in class-inclusion problems, children may be shown pictures of different animals (seven dogs and four cats, for instance), and asked, "Are there more dogs or more animals?" Whereas younger children usually will say that there are more dogs, concrete operational children can represent a subset (dogs) in relation to a superordinate set (animals) to answer the question correctly.

Central to concrete operations is the attainment of the concept of conservation, the realization that an entity remains the same despite changes in its form. Conservation tasks use any substance that can be quantified (e.g., length, number, mass, area, volume). First, the equivalence between two items is established (for example, two balls of clay), then one item is transformed while the child watches (one ball of clay is rolled into a sausage). Finally, the child is asked to judge whether or not the two items are still equivalent and to explain why. Concrete operational children realize that the amount of clay, in this example, has not changed and can provide an appropriate explanation for why this is so (for example, that one could reverse the process or that the decrease in width is compensated for by the increase in length).

Piagetian tasks have been administered in many different countries and cultures to assess whether or not Piaget's stages are universal. The greatest differences in cognition are found between people in schooled and nonschooled (traditional) cultures. As it pertains to middle childhood, children in traditional cultures often attain concrete operational thought at a slower rate. However, differences in how the tasks are presented may have a great influence on the children's performance, such that when children from traditional cultures are tested in their native language, many of the differences disappear.

Basic-Level Abilities

When most of us think about "cognition," we think of higher level forms of problem solving and the use of highly conscious strategies. But of equal importance, and the basis for such "higher level" cognition, are more basic abilities. These include speed of processing, the capacity of short-term memory, and the knowledge base.

Speed of Processing. Over the period of middle childhood, children get faster on a wide range of cognitive tasks, ranging from the very simple (identifying words) to the complex (mental addition); and how fast they process information predicts reasonably well their level of thinking. For example, how quickly children can articulate a series of words affects how many of those words they can store and remember. Much of the change in speed of information processing over middle childhood is apparently due to maturational changes in the brain. However, children who are very knowledgeable about a topic (dinosaurs, for example) process information from that domain more quickly than other information and as a result can often demonstrate more advanced forms of cognition when dealing with information in the realm of their expertise.

Short-Term Memory. Short-term memory (sometimes called *working memory*) refers to the amount of information people can retain for short periods of time (seconds). It is often measured by tests of memory span, in which people must recite back, in exact order, sets of items that had been presented to them at a rate of about one per second. When digits are used, the memory spans of 2-, 5-, 7-, and 9-year-olds are about two, four, five, and six items, respectively. Adults generally have a memory span for digits of about seven items. Cognitive processes, such as problem solving, involve the use of short-term memory in that items must be available for conscious thought and manipulated or reorganized to aid task performance.

Memory span is influenced by speed of processing and knowledge of the to-be-remembered information. For example, Chinese and Japanese children have longer digit spans than American children. The reason for this, however, is not any genetic differences in basic-level processes between the children but differences in how quickly the number words in the different languages can be articulated. It takes less time to articulate the basic number words in Chinese and Japanese than it does in English, and this speed difference translates to an advantage for the Asian children in digit span.

Similarly, children with detailed knowledge of a topic have longer memory spans when dealing with information about that topic than less expert children. For example, chess-expert children have significantly longer memory spans for positions of chess pieces on a chessboard than do chess-novice adults. However, these children perform like 10-year-olds (and less well than the adults) when digits serve as stimuli.

Knowledge Base. As we mentioned in the discussion of speed of processing and working memory, what children know about a particular topic, their knowledge base, will influence substantially how they think. Children's knowledge base expands greatly during middle childhood. Advanced knowledge in a particular domain allows for a greater efficiency of processing in that domain and influences how new information is stored and integrated. Knowledge becomes important not just for basic-level processes but also for higher level cognition, such as the use of strategies or reading. For example, the more background knowledge children have that is pertinent to a story they read or hear, the better their comprehension of that story will be.

Strategies and Problem Solving

Much thinking includes deliberate attempts to solve problems. As children enter school, they demonstrate more sophisticated use of basic problem-solving strategies, and these abilities increase over the course of middle childhood. Strategies are conscious, deliberate, goal-directed operations used to aid task performance, and they are influenced by basic-level processes such as memory span, speed of processing, and knowledge base.

The Development of Strategies. Strategies tend to be domain specific, aiding task performance in a particular area such as mathematics, reading, or memory. Learning and memory strategies become increasingly important as children progress through school. In fact, children learn many strategies in school, and one of the major differences between children in schooled versus nonschooled cultures is their use of deliberate learning strategies. Preschool and early school-age children will often not use a strategy spontaneously (for example, when given a set of pictures to remember, they will not rehearse them), but they can usually be instructed to use simple strategies with corresponding improvements in their performance. However, because of the mental effort that children must use to implement a strategy, children who use a strategy often experience no immediate benefit, a phenomenon termed *utilization deficiency*. By the end of middle childhood, most children are using a wide variety of learning and memory strategies and benefitting from them.

Reasoning. Strategies are used on different types of reasoning problems that require one to make an inference to solve a problem. Simple analogical-reasoning problems (e.g., problems such as "*dog* is to *puppy* as *cat* is to ?") can be solved by preschool children, but such reasoning improves substantially over middle childhood as children gain more knowledge about the things they are asked to reason about. Scientific reasoning involves generating hypotheses about how something in the world works and then systematically testing those hypotheses. Although school-age children can be trained to reason scientifically in some contexts, it is generally a late-developing ability and one that is not easily demonstrated by many adults.

Scientific reasoning and other forms of problem solving can sometimes be enhanced when middle-school-age children work collaboratively as opposed to alone. For example, fourth-grade children who worked on scientific reasoning problems in pairs and talked aloud generated better hypotheses than children who did not talk aloud, presumably because collaboration resulted in the kind of talk between peers that supports learning. Although peer cooperation often results in enhanced learning, parents are usually more effective collaborators than peers.

Math Strategies. Children's mathematical abilities can be viewed as a progression through improved strategy use and factual knowledge. For simple arithmetic, many children begin school using effortful counting strategies. For example, they will use the sum strategy, which involves counting each addend (for the problem $3 + 4 = ?$, saying, "1, 2, 3 . . . 4, 5, 6, 7"). By second grade, most children are also using the min strategy, making only the minimum number of counts (for 3 + 4 = ?, saying, "4 . . . 5, 6, 7"). By fourth or fifth grade, most children can solve simple addition problems quickly by retrieving the correct answer from long-term memory (for 3 + 4 = ?, they know that the answer is 7). This is termed *fact retrieval*. Although the strategies that children use increase in sophistication with age, later ones do not fully replace earlier ones. Rather, as children discover or learn new strategies, they do not totally abandon their older, simpler strategies, but will use them in certain situations. For example, most 10-year-old children can answer the question, "How much is 9 + 2?" quickly by retrieving a single "fact" from long-term memory. Nevertheless, they will sometimes revert to a simpler counting strategy (e.g., thinking to themselves, "9 . . . 10, 11"). Old strategies do not disappear but coexist with newer strategies and compete for use.

Differences in the math performance of males and females have been studied extensively, and significant differences are not usually found until about 10 years of age, when boys show a slight advantage. Gender differences are greatest at the highest ability levels. Interestingly, the magnitude of the gender differences has declined over the past several decades, due in part to increased opportunities for females to take more math classes.

Spatial Cognition

Spatial cognition includes the ability to understand the placement of objects in space with children themselves as the reference point (as when a person is asked to distinguish geographic directions in an unfamiliar locale) and the ability to manipulate visual images in one's mind (as when a person must mentally rotate a visual stimulus to determine if it matches another stimulus or in block design tasks, in which sets of blocks are used to construct models). Children's spatial cognition improves over middle childhood, and reliable gender differences favoring males are found for these tasks. Another type of spatial cognition is object and location memory. Memory for objects and their locations improves with age, and, unlike other spatial cognition tasks, gender differences are found favoring females.

Memory

By early middle childhood, children are able to recall and relate everyday events to others relatively well, although many 6- and 7-year-olds still require specific prompts before they report all the relevant details of an event (e.g., "What happened at recess today? Did you have any tests at school?"). Memory for school-type information (spelling words, history lessons, lines for a play) develops more gradually over middle childhood and requires the use of memory strategies, or *mnemon-*

ics. Two examples of memory strategies are rehearsal, by which children repeat the target information, and organization, by which children combine different items into categories, themes, or other units and recall items from the same category together. Each of these memory strategies increases in use and sophistication over middle childhood and can be improved with instruction.

As with Piagetian tasks, cultural differences are found in the recall performance of children from schooled and nonschooled cultures. Nonschooled children generally perform poorly on memory tasks in which they are asked to remember unrelated pieces of information, and they are less likely to use memory strategies such as rehearsal or organization. The differences do not reflect deficient memory abilities on the part of the nonschooled children but rather are related to the particular context in which they are tested. When tested for event recall or for information from coherent scenes, the recall of nonschooled children is as good as that of schooled children.

Language and Reading

By the time children reach middle childhood, their language skills in terms of basic grammatical structure have developed to a level nearly comparable to that of adults. The skills that continue to develop throughout childhood are vocabulary, knowledge base, and communication skills, including metacommunication (the ability to monitor one's own speech). For example, young school-age children still sometimes have difficulties knowing when they are being understood but are considerably better at this metacommunication skill than preschool children.

Reading is usually considered to be a language skill, but unlike language, which is acquired spontaneously by children without explicit instruction, reading is almost always taught to children, usually in school. This is because, unlike language, which all biologically normal humans acquire, reading is a cultural invention, and, as a result, reading disabilities are quite common.

Many preschool children acquire prereading skills (e.g., knowledge of the alphabet, sounds of letters), but true reading is usually first taught in school, at the beginning of middle childhood. Reading skills develop through childhood so that most children are proficient readers by the time they reach adolescence. The key to proficient reading is the process of automatization, the effortless retrieval of word meaning.

There are many factors associated with reading, and differences in these factors contribute to developmental differences and distinguish normal from disabled readers. One such factor is phonological processing (the process of associating letters to speech sounds and words). Another factor that affects reading is working memory. Younger or less proficient readers have less available mental capacity to store and maintain information in working memory because they devote considerable capacity and time to identifying words and trying to derive meaning. As we noted previously, age differences in knowledge base affect age and individual differences in reading ability. Comprehension monitoring, the ability to monitor one's understanding of the text and to adjust reading strategies accordingly, also increases with age and is deficient in children with reading disabilities. Age and individual differences are also found in the use of reading strategies. Younger children and children with reading disabilities often fail to implement reading strategies in order to improve performance. Boys are much more likely to have reading disabilities than girls, both during middle childhood and later. Gender differences in reading and language processing favoring girls are found even when reading-disabled children are excluded from consideration. However, these differences are small in absolute magnitude and have gotten smaller over the past 25 years.

Metacognition

Metacognition refers to knowledge of one's cognitive abilities. For every type of cognition (attention, memory) there is a corresponding type of metacognition (meta-attention, metamemory). Metacognition develops substantially over middle childhood. Although preschool children are not totally unaware of what they know and how they perform on certain tasks, these abilities increase considerably by 10 or 11 years of age. For example, it is not until about 7 or 8 years that children understand the importance of selective attention (attend only to relevant information and ignore irrelevant information). Similarly, children's understanding of their own memory abilities and their ability to evaluate their performance on memory and problem-solving tasks is relatively poor early in middle childhood but improves substantially by age 11 or 12 years. Also, children are more likely to learn and generalize strategies that are taught to them when there is a significant metacognitive component (that is, an explanation of why the strategy works).

Social Cognition and Perspective Taking

As with other forms of cognition, children's ability to think about social relations increases in middle childhood. Following Bandura's social cognitive theory, children during middle childhood are increasingly able to plan and regulate their social behavior. They are also better able to take the perspective of other people, becoming less egocentric than during the preschool years. This permits them to engage in collaborative learning, which involves two (or more) individuals, with neither being an authority or expert. Rather, collaborative learning occurs in the process of peer interaction,

when two people work together to solve a common problem.

Conclusion

Middle childhood has often been seen as a period in which relatively little of importance goes on (for example, Freud's latency period). For Piaget, middle childhood represented the stage in which children were logical but lacked abstract thought. They had acquired many of the basic cognitive abilities they would need as adults but lacked experience and the ability to think abstractly. Yet, despite the claims of few major changes in the quality of cognition over middle childhood, the thinking of the 11- or 12-year-old is very different from that of the 6- or 7-year-old. By the end of middle childhood, children are able to evaluate their own thinking better (metacognition), are more likely to use learning and memory strategies spontaneously and effectively, and, for children in schooled societies, have mastered the basics of the important technological skills of reading and mathematics. Although they may still lack the reasoning abilities of adolescents and adults, they are well on their way to acquiring the intellectual skills needed to succeed in their culture.

Bibliography

Adams, M. J., Treiman, R., & Pressley, M. (1998). Reading, writing, and literacy. In W. Damon (Series Ed.) & I. E. Sigel & K. A. Renninger (Vol. Eds.), *Handbook of child psychology: Vol. 4. Child psychology in practice* (pp. 275–355). New York: Wiley.

Bandura, A. (1989). Social cognitive theory. In R. Vasta (Ed.), *Annals of child development* (pp. 1–60). Greenwich, CT: JAI Press.

Bjorklund, D. F. (2000). *Children's thinking: Developmental function and individual differences* (3rd ed.). Pacific Grove, CA: Wadsworth.

Bjorklund, D. F., & Schneider, W. (1996). The interaction of knowledge, aptitudes, and strategies in children's memory performance. In H. W. Reese (Ed.), *Advances in child development and behavior* (Vol. 25, pp. 59–89). San Diego, CA: Academic Press.

Ginsburg, H. P., Klein, A., & Starkey, P. (1998). The development of children's mathematical thinking: Connecting research with practice. In W. Damon (Series Ed.) & I. E. Sigel & K. A. Renninger (Vol. Eds.), *Handbook of child psychology: Vol. 4. Child psychology in practice* (pp. 401–476). New York: Wiley.

Goswami, U. (1996). Analogical reasoning and cognitive development. In H. W. Reese (Ed.), *Advances in child development and behavior* (Vol. 26, pp. 92–138). San Diego, CA: Academic Press.

Halpern, D. F. (Ed.). (1995). Psychological and psychobiological perspectives on sex differences in cognition: I. Theory and research [Special issue]. *Learning and Individual Differences, 7.*

Kail, R. (1991). Development of processing speed in childhood and adolescence. In H. W. Reese (Ed.), *Advances in child development and behavior* (Vol. 23. pp. 151–185). San Diego, CA: Academic Press.

Kuhn, D., Amsel, E., & O'Loughlin, M. (1988). *The development of scientific thinking skills.* San Diego, CA: Academic Press.

Rogoff, B. (1998). Cognition as a collaborative process. In W. Damon (Series Ed.) & D. Kuhn & R. S. Siegler (Vol. Eds.), *Handbook of child psychology: Vol. 2. Cognition, language, and perceptual development* (pp. 679–744). New York: Wiley.

Schneider, W., & Pressley, M. (1997). *Memory development between 2 and 20* (2nd ed.). Mahwah, NJ: Erlbaum.

Siegler, R. S. (1996). *Emerging minds: The process of change in children's thinking.* New York: Oxford University Press.

David F. Bjorklund and Kristina Rosenblum

Education and Schooling

Defining what is meant by middle childhood is a matter for discussion, but it is most commonly assumed to encompass the years from 6 to 12, a period that coincides with enrollment in elementary school. Middle childhood is also a time of transition, characterized by a decreasing dependence on adults, growing influence of peers, rapidly developing intellectual potential, and gradual adaptation to group life both in and out of school. What happens during these years provides a base for later development of the child as an individual, as a student, and as a member of society.

Because schooling occupies such a central role during these years, it is not surprising that cognitive aspects of development, including learning to read, to understand mathematics, and to acquire the fundamentals of other school subjects are matters of major concern. These topics, along with discussions of the development of intelligence, motivation, and personal adjustment, account for a major portion of what is known about middle childhood. As a result, there is an unevenness in knowledge about factors related to schooling during this period. Because of the lack of definitive studies, the interpretation of results is often subject to controversy.

Cognitive Development During Middle Childhood

In the framework of cognitive development provided by Piaget, the most influential of cognitive theorists, middle childhood is the period in which the child moves from preoperational thought to a period of concrete operations, a stage that serves as the precursor to formal adult logic. The development of concrete operations is marked by the internalization of mental actions. This means, according to Piaget, that children no longer must rely on concrete actions and experiences but are capable of mental transformations. One example is apparent in studies of conservation. Elementary school children acknowledge that certain properties of an object, such as length, number, and weight, are maintained, or "conserved," even when the appearance of the object is altered. Children at this stage of development also make advances that lead to an understanding of logical classification. From a Piagetian perspective, these cognitive changes have implications, not only for thought but also for moral development and social behavior. Extending Piaget's work, Kohlberg examined children's moral reasoning. In middle childhood moral judgment moves from the self-interest characterized by egocentric thought to a recognition of the perspective of other persons and rule-based interactions.

Despite the far-reaching contributions of Piaget, his theoretical views have been subject to revision, especially his view of stages of development. Research over the past few decades has indicated that, given appropriate modes of presenting information, children are capable of more advanced levels of thought during middle childhood and earlier than Piaget and Kohlberg proposed (Gelman & Baillargeon, 1983).

Other researchers have addressed such issues as problem solving, strategic thinking, and classification from an information-processing perspective (Siegler, 1998). According to this view, children develop a gradually increasing capacity for processing information, which enables them to acquire increasingly complex knowledge and skills. Elementary school children also demonstrate increasingly sophisticated metacognitive skills; that is, the ability to think about their own thought processes. This capability makes it possible, for example, for students to regulate their own learning by reflecting on their understanding and by monitoring and revising their tactics for acquiring information. Self-regulation of learning and thought is a complex process, involving both skill and motivation. As children engage in both formal schooling and informal learning tasks, they gradually develop beliefs about schooling and about themselves as learners. They also build a repertoire of learning strategies as they undergo diverse experiences provided in school and at home.

Closely related to the discussion of cognitive development is a consideration of intelligence. How should intelligence be defined? Efforts to answer this question have generated heated discussions throughout the history of mental testing. Original conceptions of intelligence focused on abilities such as learning, adapting to the environment, and benefiting from experience. The assumption that intelligence is a general ability was quickly challenged by early psychologists, who proposed three types of intelligence—abstract, concrete, and social—characterized by the respective abilities to respond to symbols, things, and persons. The differentiation of intelligence into specific abilities has been extended by other theorists, who defined a wide range of intellectual abilities. The strongest advocates of multiple intelligences have been Howard Gardner (1983), who has described seven basic abilities, and Robert Sternberg (1985), who has described three. When and how the question of general or multiple intelligences will be resolved is not clear, but adopting one view rather than another has important implications for children's schooling, especially for the organization of schools and tracking.

Despite the continuing controversy about the definition of intelligence, there have been few changes in the procedures for measuring intelligence during recent decades. Tests such as the various revisions of the Stanford–Binet still evaluate general intellectual skills. Alternatively, tests such as the Wechsler Intelligence Scale for Children probe different facets of intelligence. Regardless of the approach that is taken, intelligence tests continue to be useful tools, for tests given during middle childhood have substantial relations with students' later academic achievement.

Differences exist, both within and between cultures, in the degree to which people support a "nature" or "nurture" view of intelligence. Dweck (1986), for example, describes two views of intelligence: as a fixed trait (an "entity" view) or as a malleable quality (an "incremental" view). The kinds of schooling that are most appropriate for a child depend on cultural values related to motivation and personal adjustment. Some cultural values dictate that an emphasis should be placed on motivating the child to expend more effort; other cultural values suggest that situations should be created that are the most comfortable and productive for the child. Viewing intelligence as being modifiable by hard work leads to recommending the former, whereas regarding intelligence as the result of innate factors leads to the latter view.

Schooling

Students who enter first grade ready to learn and with a foundation of skill and knowledge are likely to experience academic success; without this foundation students are at risk of poor performance and low achievement. The increasing awareness of individual differences among children of the same chronological age has led to a variety of arrangements to meet these needs, ranging from the manner in which lessons are conducted to the ways in which classrooms are structured to meet the needs of special types of children.

The major mode of instruction in most elementary schools is whole-class instruction, with the teacher being the major source of information and the primary arbiter of what is correct. Whole-class instruction is based on the premise that, although children differ in their rates of learning, they can benefit from being in classes in which there are fast learners and slow learners. In order for this mode of learning and teaching to be effective, teachers must be able to accommodate these differences by altering their modes of teaching in order to meet the different needs of different children.

Some schools may employ whole-class instruction but also follow the pattern of dividing classes into smaller groups for part of the daily lessons. These smaller groups may include children with similar levels of academic skill, or they may be organized to include children of diverse interests, abilities, and backgrounds. Another arrangement involves "pull-out" programs, in which slow learners retain membership in regular classes but are removed from these classes for special instruction with other slow learners for several hours a day.

Regardless of the organizational strategy adopted for classrooms, some schools are more effective in promoting students' progress than are others. Factors such as the quality of teaching, the involvement of parents, the availability of teaching materials and equipment, and the motivation of the children have been suggested as reasons for these differences.

Tracking. "Tracking" or "streaming" involves the separation of children on the basis of their academic ability. Many elementary schools throughout the world employ no form of tracking, but others may separate children into different tracks as early as their fifth year of schooling. If academic ability is believed to be primarily a consequence of innate factors, it is argued that teachers have sufficient information by the later years of elementary school to be able to enroll children in schools that differ in their degree of difficulty or in their type of specialization. If, on the other hand, academic abilities are considered by the society to be more strongly dependent on the child's experience, it may be difficult to make wise decisions until after the child has had many more years in school.

Reading and Mathematics. Although learning to read and to understand mathematics are two of the most important accomplishments expected of children during middle childhood, there remains strong disagreement about the manner in which early instruction in these areas should occur. One position in the area of reading proposes that learning to read is primarily dependent on the child's ability in phonemic segmentation, the ability to "sound out" words. An alternative approach to teaching reading relies on the whole-word method, in which learning to read depends on memorizing the relation between the whole word and its pronunciation. In the first case, reading becomes a matter primarily of analysis of the components of words; in the second, it is a matter of practice and drill. Proponents of a third, "whole language," approach are concerned with the natural integration of reading and writing in the development of literacy (Paris & Cunningham, 1996).

The "cognitive" versus "practice" interpretations carry over into the discussion of mathematics. Some proponents of a cognitive emphasis argue against memorization and practice in favor of an approach that emphasizes the importance of problem solving. Others assume that speed and automaticity are fundamental requisites of effective performance and suggest that such skills can be acquired only through practice. At present, the more analytic, cognitive approach to instruction in both reading and mathematics appears to be increasingly popular, both with parents and with educators.

Because an understanding of mathematics is necessary for understanding science, great emphasis is placed on learning mathematics. During elementary school, wide differences exist among children in their achievement in mathematics, and the differences increase with each year of schooling. Why these differences in achievement begin to increase during middle childhood is a topic of lively debate, one that has not been resolved.

Traditional modes of instruction have been challenged by those promoting a constructivist approach to education. According to this view children must construct their own knowledge, and true learning occurs when they are given the opportunity to do this. Critics point to the inefficiency of this approach and to the greater understanding that occurs with appropriate guidance and feedback by a skilled and sensitive teacher. Alternatively, the constructivist view proposes that effective instruction should rely on involving children in the solution or development of a concept and evaluating the relevance and efficiency of alternative solutions.

Comparative Studies of Academic Achievement. Cross-cultural studies of academic achievement conducted during the past several decades have provided a detailed picture of differences in the academic achievement, primarily in mathematics and science, of students in different cultures. The most recent of these studies is the Third International Mathematics and Science Study (Peak, 1996), the most extensive study of education ever conducted. The results, based on more than 500,000 students from 41 countries, have alarmed many Western educators, parents, and policy makers because students, for the most part, have not demonstrated the knowledge and skill in mathematics and science that should be expected of children at various age levels.

Fourth graders in the United States, however, were among the top performers among the various countries, with scores exceeded only by those of students from Korea. These results are perplexing, for in earlier studies the question was not why U.S. fourth graders performed so well but why a "fourth-grade slump" in motivation and performance appeared. Some writers have proposed that the high mathematics scores of U.S. fourth graders were due to the higher standards for performance recommended by the National Council of Teachers of Mathematics. This interpretation is appealing but lacks convincing supportive data. Whatever the explanation of the U.S. fourth graders' high level of performance in mathematics and science, there is a subsequent decline during the years of secondary school. In explaining this decline, emphasis is placed on the great inclusiveness of topics in U.S. textbooks, inadequate preparation of teachers, disorganized presentation of lessons, and cultural de-emphasis on the importance of schooling in general and of mathematics and science in particular.

Social and Personal Development. In addition to affecting children's cognitive development, schooling makes a major contribution to children's personal and social development through social interaction and the growth of self-esteem.

Social Interactions. Through close interactions with other children and adults, children learn social skills and lay the foundations for their beliefs about themselves and their competencies. The demands placed on elementary school children in being members of a group lead to heightened abilities to delay gratification, cooperate, resolve conflicts, and assume greater social responsibility. In general, children who get along well with their peers and teachers do better in school than do those who have less smooth social interactions.

Self-Esteem and Self-Efficacy. Being required to interact with other persons, being exposed to a variety of new activities and tasks, and being subject to new demands concerning their behavior give children information that is helpful in their developing a better understanding of themselves and how they can progress effectively in school. These demands and experiences of school, in conjunction with the development of cognitive abilities, result in the development of children's beliefs and attitudes about themselves in the social, cognitive, and academic realms.

Children's self-esteem is based on their emotional response to questions about themselves and their sense of self-worth. Self-efficacy concerns children's beliefs about their own abilities, competencies, and likelihood for success. A strong sense of self-efficacy promotes children's achievement and task persistence. Self-esteem, however, is not strongly related to academic performance. Self-efficacy is domain specific such that children can have different beliefs about themselves and their abilities across academic, social, and physical domains.

Individual and Group Differences

Important differences that affect children's educational and school experiences include special needs, gender, socioeconomic status, and ethnicity.

Special Needs. Responding to children with special needs has been a major goal in schooling practices during the past several decades. Prior to the late 1960s, children who were mentally retarded, blind, deaf, or paraplegic or who suffered severe emotional problems were educated apart from their peers in separate institutions or in separate classrooms within public schools. In the past few decades, students with disabilities have been "mainstreamed" into regular classrooms. The Individuals with Disabilities Education Act passed in 1975 guarantees students with disabilities a free and appropriate education, an individual education plan, and an education in the least restrictive environment. In addition to students with obvious disabilities, there are also children with other exceptional needs, including those with learning disabilities or attentional deficits and those who are exceptionally capable.

Gender. Among the fundamental distinctions made in discussing individual differences are differences in motivations, interests, and skills of boys and girls. In the areas of mathematics and science, there is little evidence of gender differences during the middle years of childhood. Thus, during the elementary school years when all students enroll in the same curriculum, girls demonstrate levels of achievement equal to those of boys. By middle school, however, the results of numerous studies indicate that, compared with boys, girls like math and science less, see less relevance for the subjects in their lives, and are less likely to elect courses in these subjects. By the high school years, girls are outperformed by boys in both math and science, whereas in verbal skills and language arts, girls are competitive or even superior to boys. The gender difference in mathematics and science occurs even though males are overrepresented in rates of mental retardation, attentional disorders, dyslexia, stuttering, and delayed speech development (Halpern, 1997). The interpretation given most commonly is that gender differences in mathematics and science result, in part, from a lack of social support for girls in these areas, rather than from some form of innate gender difference in these domains.

Socioeconomic Status. Social and economic differences among families have profound effects on education and schooling during middle childhood. Indeed, one of the most critical problems in contemporary society is the lack of equal opportunity afforded children because of the financial limitations that characterize families of lower socioeconomic status. For a number of reasons, poverty has detrimental effects on children's social and intellectual development (McLoyd, 1998). In addition to such factors as higher risk of low birth weight, greater exposure to lead, and less cognitive stimulation from their parents, children from poor, disadvantaged families do not as often have the opportunity to attend preschools and kindergartens where there are adequate materials and equipment and well-trained teachers. As a consequence, they enter elementary school more poorly prepared than their more fortunate peers.

The risks encountered by young children growing up in disadvantaged circumstances have led to a number of programs designed to promote the physical, emotional, social, and intellectual development of these children. The largest of these is Project Head Start, begun in 1966.

Ethnicity. The socioeconomic status of a family is often linked to a family's ethnicity. Although many immigrant groups have faced problems of social integration, the problems have been especially severe when there are large differences in language or physical and cultural characteristics.

It has been argued that the lack of skills that are useful in a society is more likely a result of failing to acquire these skills than to an intellectual deficit (Ogbu, 1994). For example, persons who voluntarily immigrate to a new culture face fewer problems in subscribing to the values and beliefs of the dominant culture than do immigrants who did not immigrate voluntarily. The latter groups often reject the values and beliefs represented by the dominant culture. Thus, if going to school and doing well in academic subjects are considered to represent values of the dominant society, minority students run the obvious risk of not accepting academic achievement as a goal they wish to pursue.

Outside Influences

Parents, peers, and leisure activities also have important influences on children's educational development.

Parents. The behavior and attitudes of parents can have a significant impact on children's relationship with school and on the child's approach to education. Parents' daily interactions with their children at home take many forms, such as reading or talking to their children, helping them with homework, and providing experiences and resources that facilitate their children's intellectual and academic development. Reading to children has been shown to increase phonemic awareness, as well as being positively related to later reading achievement. In addition to reading, the language used in the home can promote school adaptation. Parents who talk with their children, ask them open-ended questions, and provide clear answers to children's questions prepare their children for the types of interaction that commonly occur in the school environment. Parents can also have a direct effect on their children's schooling by managing their children's school-related activities in the home, such as setting aside time and space for the children to study and supporting their children's schoolwork and school projects.

More subtle and indirect forms of parental influence include the ways parents explain the bases of the successes and failures of their children. Parents who attribute their children's success at school to effort and hard work help their children understand that effort is likely to result in success and lack of effort in problems. This type of explanation for success or problems not only promotes achievement but also increases children's motivation to accept more challenging tasks and to persist in the face of difficulty. On the other hand, parents who attribute outcomes to ability or lack of ability make it much more difficult for children to believe that they have control over the outcomes, and thus children run the risk of decreased motivation.

Children's school achievement can also benefit from positive relations between home and school, such as parents attending school functions, volunteering at school activities, attending parent-teacher conferences, and regularly communicating with the school. Parental involvement demonstrates to the school, teacher, and child commitment and interest in the child's learning and translates into more positive attitudes, higher levels of motivation, and enhanced performance.

Peers. Friends and peer groups constitute a second major outside influence in children's schooling. Although young adolescents are most susceptible to peer pressure, children in middle childhood are also influenced by their peers, and the influence can be either positive or negative. Positive peer influences take the form of valuing education, doing well in school, and studying and working together cooperatively on school assignments. Association with peer groups that devalue education and school success and spending time with peers instead of doing school assignments have been shown to increase the risk of poor school performance.

Television and Media. Children's viewing of television generally has been viewed as a disruption to and a negative influence on children's development. Of special concern is the lack of appropriate television programs for children in the period of middle childhood. The depiction of violence and other types of behavior usually deemed to be unsuitable for young children is often considered to be one of the major impediments to academic progress. Generally, however, research relating amount of television viewing to children's development has yielded only very modest relations between the amount of viewing and children's academic achievement (Huston & Wright, 1997).

Time Use. A second activity in which children spend large amounts of out-of-school time is socializing with other children. Opportunities for social interaction at school are more restricted in some cultures than in those in which children remain at school for longer periods or have greater opportunities at school to engage in social interactions. Children also spend a good deal of time out of school during the summer vacation. In general, children lose ground in their academic performance during the summer; they must spend the first part of each school year reviewing concepts and materials from the previous year. The detrimental effects of being away from school during the summer are not evenly distributed among all students. Children from disadvantaged backgrounds lose more ground than do middle-class and other advantaged children, in part because disadvantaged families experience greater difficulties in providing enriching experiences for their children outside of school. Together with the other factors related to the risk associated with low socioeconomic status, time out of school in the summer further increases the achievement gap between children from different socioeconomic backgrounds.

Conclusion

Perhaps the most notable feature of education and schooling during middle childhood is the presence of change rather than stability. It is a time of increasing potential and of special accomplishments. By the time elementary school is completed, the child has gained the basic competencies that will be necessary later for joining society and obtaining employment. The end of middle childhood is also accompanied by the acquisition of facility in reading, doing mathematics, and understanding the fundamentals of other academic subjects. The rate and degree to which the goals of elementary school are accomplished, however, depend in large part on factors such as the child's gender, the family's socioeconomic status, the culture in which the family lives, and the quality of education to which the child is exposed.

As children begin to move from middle childhood to early adolescence, there is a shift in the organization of schooling from the environment of the elementary school to that of the secondary school. Elementary school students typically spend the day in one classroom with the same teacher and the same group of students, a practice that makes it possible for teachers and students to develop a close relationship and for learning to take place within an ongoing social and academic context. Teachers are expected to have contact with students' parents at regular intervals during the elementary school years, and parental involvement in schooling is at its highest level.

In contrast, the organization of secondary schooling is generally such that students move from class to class, having a new teacher and a new group of students during each class period. The degree of anonymity of students generally increases after elementary school, when teachers become responsible for large numbers of students. Parental involvement in the schools declines, and parent-teacher contact is diminished. The contrast between the needs of the developing adolescent and the school environment typical at this age has been interpreted as a developmental mismatch, potentially contributing to some of the perceived stress of adolescence (Eccles et al., 1993).

Bibliography

Collins, A. W. (Ed.) (1984). *Development during early childhood: The years from six to twelve.* Washington, DC: National Academy Press.

Dweck, C. S. (1986). Motivational processes affecting learning. *American Psychologist, 41,* 1040–1048.

Eccles, J. S., Midgley, C., Wigfield, A., Buchanan, C. M., Reuman, D., Flanagan, C., & MacIver, D. (1993). Development during adolescence: The impact of stage-environment fit on young adolescents' experiences in schools and in families. *American Psychologist, 48,* 90–101.

Gardner, H. (1983). *Frames of mind: The theory of multiple intelligences.* New York: Basic Books.

Gelman, R., & Baillargeon, R. (1983). A review of some Piagetian concepts. In P. H. Mussen (Ed.), *Handbook of child psychology* (4th ed., pp. 167–230). New York: Wiley.

Halpern, D. F. (1997). Sex differences in intelligence. *American Psychologist, 52,* 1091–1101.

Huston, A. C., & Wright, J. C. (1997). Mass media and children's development. In R. M. Lerner (Ed.), *Handbook of child psychology* (5th ed., pp. 999–1058). NJ: Blackwell.

McLoyd, V. C. (1998). Socioeconomic disadvantage and child development. *American Psychologist, 53,* 185–204.

Ogbu, J. U. (1994). Understanding cultural diversity and learning. *Journal for the Education of the Gifted, 17*(4), 354–383.

Paris, S. G., & Cunningham, A. E. (1996). Children becoming students. In D. C. Berliner & C. C. Calfee (Eds.), *Handbook of educational psychology* (pp. 117–147). New York: Simon & Schuster Macmillan.

Peak, L. (1996). *Pursuing excellence: A study of U.S. eighth-grade mathematics and science teaching, learning, curriculum, and achievement in international context.* Washington, DC: U.S. Department of Education, National Center for Educational Statistics.

Siegler, R. (1998). *Children's thinking* (3rd ed.). Upper Saddle River, NJ: Prentice Hall.

Sternberg, R. J. (1985). *Beyond IQ: Toward a triarchic theory of intelligence.* Cambridge, MA: Cambridge University Press.

Harold W. Stevenson, Barbara K. Hofer, and Bruce Randel

Social and Emotional Development

Social and emotional development may be best described as the product of multiple "levels" of determin-istic complexity working all at once. These levels comprise within-individual, within-interaction, within-relationship, and within-group factors (Hinde, 1987, 1995). According to Hinde, events and processes at each level are constrained and influenced by circumstances and processes at other levels. At one level, individual children have somewhat stable temperaments that dispose them to be more or less aroused to social stimuli, or that facilitate or inhibit social approach orientations and emotional expression. Other relevant characteristics include the individual's repertoire of social cognitions, skills, and competencies.

At another level, interactions occur between individuals. When two individuals first meet, they bring with them their physical, dispositional, cognitive, emotional, and social characteristics. Their interactions vary in form and function as a response to fluctuations in the parameters of the social situation, such as the partner's characteristics, social initiations, overtures, and responses. These interactions may be interpreted as being interpersonally positive and rewarding, or, conversely, as unacceptable and unrewarding.

Interactions result in the development of relationships. Relationships are influenced by memories of previous interactions and by expectations of anticipated future interactions. These memories and expectations may influence either of the individuals to avoid (reject), neglect, or approach the other in positive, neutral, or hostile manners. Over the long run, the kinds of relationships that individuals form depend on their history of interactions with the given other, as well as with others in earlier relationships.

Once formed, relationships become embedded in a system that comprises groups, or networks of relationships with more or less clearly defined boundaries (e.g., cliques, teams). As the highest level of social complexity, groups are defined by their constituent relationships and, in this sense, by the types and diversity of interactions that are characteristic of the participants in those relationships.

Individual Development in Middle Childhood

In middle childhood, children begin to develop social cognitive skills and a self-system and start to compare themselves with others.

Social Cognition. Children's interactions and relationships are largely a function of how they think about and view their social worlds. For example, altruistic behavior such as sharing or helping is promoted by the ability to understand that such actions may have positive consequences for the recipient and that failure to demonstrate altruism in situations that require it may have negative consequences for the potential recipient. Further, children come to understand that the failure to help or share with others may have implications for the self—that is, others may grow to dislike the nonaltruistic individual, thereby altering the course of interactions and relationships for the child.

Thus one major accomplishment of the middle-childhood period is the development of mature perspective-taking skills. One of the more comprehensive models of perspective taking emanates from the research of Selman and colleagues (e.g., Selman, 1980). To Selman, perspective taking is a multidimensional, multistage construct that ranges from the very young child's inability to comprehend that any view other than her or his own exists to the adolescent's understanding of how a society or a generalized other would perceive a given person, behavior, relationship, or social situation.

According to Selman (1980), at the onset of middle childhood (approximately 6–8 years) children are able to distinguish between self- and other-centered viewpoints of the same situation; however, at this stage they cannot interpret either their own or the other's actions from the other person's perspective. Importantly, during this period children develop an understanding of others' intentions.

Between 8 and 10 years, children can think that others view them in particular ways. Furthermore, children understand that other people's perspectives of them can have implications for behaviors directed toward them. That is, the child can understand that if others think poorly of her or him, it will influence the types of behaviors directed toward her or him and will have an impact on the types of relationships that can be developed with others.

Children's perspective-taking skills also have an impact on how they think about or arrive at decisions about resolving disputes with others. Again, Selman and colleagues offer insights pertaining to the development of interpersonal negotiation skills during middle childhood (Schultz & Selman, 1989). Interpersonal negotiation skills are "the ways in which individuals in situations of social conflict within ongoing relationships deal with the self and a significant other to gain control over inner and interpersonal disequilibrium" (Schultz & Selman, 1989, p. 123). From interviews about hypothetical situations, one can assess the developmental level of a child's interpersonal negotiating skills (Selman & Schultz, 1990).

For example, an impulsive or aggressive act reflects an undifferentiated egocentric level of perspective taking (Level 0) in which the other is treated as an "object" without personal thoughts or feelings. At Level 1 the other is seen as having needs and thoughts distinct from one's own, but the differentiation is subjective. The child views conflict as being inherently "me versus you" with no coordination or compromise of perspectives. Other-transforming strategies would include the use of direct commands and threats, whereas self-

transforming strategies include weak initiations and quick submissions. Level 2 strategies are self-reflective and reciprocal, revealing a psychological view of the self and other. Other-transforming strategies at this level include attempts to change the other's mind through persuasion (e.g., appeal to feelings of guilt). Self-transforming strategies serve to persuade the self to subordinate one's own goals to those of the other. It is during middle childhood that children achieve this level of interpersonal understanding.

In summary, the ways in which children think about their social worlds become increasingly abstract from early to middle childhood. Young children perceive, think about, and describe social phenomena by referring to appearance, possessions, and behavioral acts; by middle childhood, there is the beginning of a focus on internal (psychological) characteristics, such as the thoughts, feelings, intentions, and opinions of peers.

The Self-System. Just as children's thinking about others becomes less concrete and more abstract in middle childhood, so too do their thoughts about the self. Further, beliefs about their own abilities become more stable and accurate with increasing age. Nevertheless, despite children's new ability to think about themselves in psychological terms, personal characteristics are viewed as immutable and enduring. These views stand in contrast to those of adolescents, who understand that individuals can and do display situational inconsistencies in behavior. In addition to developing a more psychological view of the self, children also acquire an increasingly differentiated sense of self. Thus they distinguish between such areas of competence as the physical, behavioral, social, academic, and athletic (see Harter, 1998, for a review).

Thoughts about the multiple dimensions of the self can have an impact on feelings about the self (self-esteem). Thus, if a child evaluates the self as incompetent in a given area (e.g., social skills), and if that component of the self is viewed as important to the self, then negative self-esteem may result (Harter, 1998).

Social Comparison. Perceptions of the self in relation to others can have a significant bearing on the child's self-esteem. By middle childhood, children's perspective-taking skills allow them to compare their own competencies and relationships with those of others. For example, if a child sees that others in his or her classroom perform better on academic subject matter, he or she may develop a negative self-perception with respect to academic competence. Alternatively, if a child perceives that she or he fares better than peers, a positive view will be ascribed to the "academic self." Similar processes come into play insofar as other significant aspects of middle childhood are concerned, such as athletic and social competencies. Cognitive advances in middle childhood, such as the increased ability to think abstractly, enable children to use a broader range of experiences and observations to make social comparisons. Further, social comparisons are not simply based on recent occurrences; they are also a function of experienced histories of self and other observations.

Clearly, the nature of the social comparison process depends on the ability of children to think about others' strengths and weaknesses. As noted earlier, from ages 7 to 10 years there is a sharp increase in the ability to use psychological constructs to think about the self, others, and the relations between self and others. In later childhood, children begin to draw comparisons between themselves, known others, and perceived, generalized norms (e.g., "David is a lot more shy than other people").

Social Interactions in Middle Childhood

Thus far, we have discussed components of individual development in middle childhood that may have a bearing on how children interact with and relate to others. In this section, we provide a brief review of social interactional development in middle childhood.

By mid-childhood, approximately 30% of all social contact involves peers (the rest being with siblings, parents, and adults); this prevalence of peer interaction may be contrasted with that of preschoolers (10%). Further, peer interaction becomes less closely scrutinized by adults. The contexts within which peers interact also change in middle childhood. Preschool children tend to interact with peers in the home and in day care settings; school-age children come into contact with peers through a wide range of activities, such as sports, traveling to and from school, and "hanging out" (Zarbatany, Hartmann, & Rankin, 1990).

Although the frequency of social interaction increases from early childhood on, certain behaviors are less often displayed during the mid-childhood years. There are, for example, notable declines in the frequencies of pretend and "rough-and-tumble" play. These activities appear to be replaced by games during which children's interactions are coordinated and constrained by mutually agreed-upon social rules and roles. Beyond interactive games, children also engage in prosocial and antisocial exchanges.

Prosocial Behaviors. Researchers have concluded that from early to mid-childhood there appear to be no age-related changes in the prevalence of generosity, helpfulness, or cooperation that children show to peers (e.g., Eisenberg, 1991). Unlike early childhood, during which prosocial behavior is rather inconsistent over time and across contexts, individual differences in the expression of acts of cooperation, kindness, sharing, caring, and helping become comparatively more prevalent and stable by middle childhood (Eisenberg & Fabes, 1998).

Such individual characteristics as temperament, personality, and motivation play a role in the likelihood of prosocial behavioral enactment. For instance, children who approach new people and situations with relative ease are more likely to help others than those who are shy or socially anxious (e.g., Silva, 1992). This is particularly true when a situation involves social initiation rather than requests for assistance (Eisenberg & Fabes, 1998). Although shy children may not initiate as much prosocial behavior as sociable children, they have the skills to engage in other types of prosocial behavior under different circumstances. Indeed, compared to sociable children, shy children may be more likely to behave prosocially under nonsocial circumstances than under situations involving peer contact. Moreover, shy children's motivations for prosocial behavior may differ from those of nonshy children; for example, children who are anxious may act prosocially in order to gain social approval and allay fear of rejection.

Both cognitive and emotion regulation skills contribute to prosocial behavior; however, the presence of these abilities does not necessarily lead to prosocial responses (Eisenberg & Fabes, 1998). Those most likely to engage in spontaneous prosocial behavior are optimally regulated in the sense that they have moderate inhibitory control, good attention regulation, and constructive flexible coping skills (Denham & Burger, 1991; Eisenberg & Fabes, 1992). Conversely, children who display more negative emotionality (e.g., sadness, fear, frustration, anger) tend to exhibit prosocial behavior less frequently.

Two of the most frequently studied prosocial constructs are altruism and empathy. Altruism refers to engaging in behaviors that would benefit another person but do not have selfish interests or self-gain as the motivator. Empathy refers to an affective response that is sensitive or appropriate to another person's situation rather than one's own (Hoffman, 1987). The nature of prosocial behaviors, including the ability to be empathic, is of course directly tied to increasing cognitive ability. For instance, the more advanced a child is at perspective taking, the more likely he or she is to have compassion for another's condition.

In middle childhood, though, empathy tends to be ephemeral and situation specific rather than a lasting global response to other human beings. Moreover, children's empathic behaviors are often a function of concern with others' approval and with the quality of their relationships (Eisenberg & Miller, 1987). With later cognitive sophistication, including abstract thinking and advanced perspective taking, adolescents are more capable of true empathic responses to others.

Antisocial Interactions. There appear to be few overall increases or decreases in the amount of negative interactive behaviors from the early to mid-childhood period. Even though the prevalence of aggressive behavior remains fairly constant, the form of negative behavior appears to change. Insults, derogation, and threats gradually replace physical aggression over this period. Relative to preschoolers, the aggressive behavior of 6- to 12-year-olds is less instrumental (directed toward possessing objects or occupying specific space) and more specifically hostile toward others (Coie & Dodge, 1998). Information regarding the stability of aggression during middle childhood is available for the former types of aggression but not for the hostile, relational types. Physical and verbal aggression are moderately stable phenomena.

Another form of interaction that occurs during middle childhood is bullying and victimization. Bullying refers to acts of verbal and physical aggression by an individual that are directed toward particular peers (i.e., victims). Bullying accounts for a substantial portion of the aggression that occurs in the peer group (Olweus, 1993). What distinguishes bullying from other forms of aggressive behavior is its specificity; that is, bullies direct their behavior toward only certain peers; victims, who comprise approximately 10% of the school population (Olweus, 1993). Research on bullying suggests that the children inclined to engage in this behavior are characterized by strong tendencies toward, and a tolerance for, aggressive behavior as well as relatively weak control over their aggressive impulses.

There is evidence that children who are disproportionately the victims of bullying behavior tend to be anxious, insecure, and isolated from the remainder of the peer group (Olweus, 1993). Victimized children also appear to lack self-confidence, self-esteem, and prosocial skills (Perry, Kusel, & Perry, 1988). Although some researchers (e.g., Olweus, 1993) have reported that the victims of bullies are unlikely to be aggressive themselves, others (e.g., Perry et al., 1988) report that victimized children actually show high levels of aggression.

Peer Relationships in Middle Childhood

Children's conceptions of friendship change during the middle years.

Social Conceptions of Friendship. Friendship refers to a voluntary, reciprocal, mutually regulated, emotionally positive relationship between a child and a peer. Early work on friendship centered on children's understanding of this social relationship. Based on interviews, Bigelow (1977; Bigelow & La Gaipa, 1975) found that children's friendship conceptions at the start of middle childhood (7–8 years) are at a "reward-cost" stage; for example, a friend is someone who is convenient (i.e., who lives nearby), has interesting toys or possessions, and shares similar expectations about play activities. From 10 to 11 years, children go through a "normative" stage in which shared values and rules become important and friends are expected to stick up for

and be loyal to each other. Later, at 11 to 13 years, children's concept of a friend is of an "empathetic" nature: Friends are viewed as sharing similar interests, as being required to make active attempts to understand each other, and as willing to engage in self-disclosure.

The changes in children's abilities to conceptualize friendship may be largely a function of their perspective-taking skills. Thus Selman (e.g., Selman & Schultz, 1990) suggests that by mid-childhood children's discussions of friendship and friendship issues indicate a maturing appreciation that feelings and intentions, not just manifest actions, keep friends together or drive them apart. Children also begin to appreciate that others' thoughts and feelings concerning social events may differ from their own. Nevertheless, these social-cognitive advances are insufficient to move children beyond a unilateral concern with their own, not their partner's, subjective experiences in the relationship. This unilateral perspective eventually subsides, and children begin to express an understanding that both parties in a relationship must coordinate and adjust their needs and actions to one another in mutually satisfying ways. But their cognitive understandings do not include an expectation that friendships can weather specific arguments or negative events. As late childhood/early adolescence begins (around 11 or 12 years), however, most children realize that friendship implies an affective bond having continuity over time, distance, and events.

Features of Friendship. Changes in the understanding of friendship are accompanied by changes in the patterns and nature of involvement in friendships across middle childhood. Children's choices of friends are more stable and more likely to be reciprocated in middle childhood than at earlier ages, although it is not clear that either the stability or reciprocity of friendships increases across the period of middle childhood itself (Berndt & Hoyle, 1985). In addition, the number of selections of close friends that children make has been reported to increase with age until approximately 11 years of age, after which it begins to decline. Moreover, as is commonly observed, children's liking for and friendship involvement with opposite-sex peers drops off precipitously after 7 years of age (Leaper, 1994).

With respect to the features of children's friendships in middle childhood and early adolescence, Newcomb and Bagwell (1995) report that children are more likely to behave in positive ways with friends than nonfriends and to ascribe positive characteristics to their interactions with friends. More important, Newcomb and Bagwell (1995) have shown that the expression of affect varies considerably for pairs of friends and nonfriends during middle childhood and early adolescence. In their interactions with friends (versus nonfriends), children show more affective reciprocity and emotional intensity and enhanced levels of emotional understanding, although these friend-nonfriend differences are greater in early adolescence than in middle childhood. In this regard, friendship is not only a positive relational context, but it also provides opportunities for the expression and regulation of affect (Parker & Gottman, 1989).

One of the few dimensions of interaction in which there are no differences between friends and nonfriends is that of conflict. Research has shown repeatedly that after early childhood, pairs of friends engage in about the same amount of conflict as pairs of nonfriends (e.g., Newcomb & Bagwell, 1995). There is, however, a major difference in the conflict resolution strategies that friends and nonfriends adopt. For example, Newcomb and Bagwell (1995) indicated that friends are more concerned than nonfriends about achieving equitable resolutions to conflicts. Moreover, they are more likely than nonfriends to resolve conflicts in a way that will preserve or promote the continuity of their relationship.

Social Groups in Middle Childhood

Finally, children's likeability or status within the peer group and the formation of social groups are important to consider in middle childhood.

Peer Acceptance and Rejection. The concept of peer acceptance refers to a child's likeability from the peer group's perspective. On the one hand, if a child is nominated as being liked by many class members, he or she is considered popular. On the other hand, if a child receives few such nominations and is named as someone who others "don't like to play with," then he or she is considered to be rejected by the peer group.

Children's appreciation of their own and others' popularity greatly increases during middle childhood. Indeed, children may express much concern and bewilderment over their peer group acceptance or their real or imagined status within the popularity hierarchy. Parker, Rubin, Price, and DeRosier (1995) note that such concern may be partly explained by developmental changes in social comparison processes that accompany entry into middle childhood. Children's concerns about acceptance in the peer group also appear to be related to an increase in the salience and frequency of gossip (Parker & Gottman, 1989), which mainly occurs in the group context of cliques.

Cliques and Gossip. Newly emerging in middle childhood is social participation in stable, polydyadic social groups, or cliques (Crockett, Losoff, & Peterson, 1984). Like friendships, cliques are voluntary and usually comprise same-sex, same-race members (Kinderman, McCollam, & Gibson, 1995); but unlike friendships, cliques range in size from three to nine children. The prevalence of cliques among children younger than 10 years old is not known, but by age 11 years

children report that most of their peer interaction occurs in such groups (Crockett et al., 1984).

Gossip in middle childhood comprises the core attitudes and behaviors that determine group inclusion or exclusion and can basically reaffirm membership in a group (Parker & Gottman, 1989). Much gossip among children at this age involves discussion and debate related to their own interpersonal connections (e.g., whether other children are friends or enemies). Moreover, although some children's gossip involves discussion of others' admirable traits, other gossip unfortunately consists of vilifying third parties. Although there are few sex differences with regard to gossip, there is some evidence that boys who are not close friends utilize gossip to find common ground but girls who are not close friends gossip less than do close girlfriends (Teasley & Parker, 1995).

Conclusion

Conceptualizing social and emotional development within a framework of social levels brings breadth and depth to the understanding and study of such development. Theorists and researchers have expanded our knowledge base by examining socioemotional development and adjustment within individuals, interactions, relationships, and groups. Only in recent years has a research literature emerged on the relations between these levels of social complexity. Yet little effort has been made to explore whether aspects of child temperament, behavioral interaction styles, and friendship quality interact to produce adaptive or maladaptive outcomes. Thus, attention to both within- and between-system linkages seems imperative for a broader understanding of social-emotional development in middle childhood.

Also merited from conceptual and methodological standpoints is the notion that children, relationships, and groups are embedded in larger social ecologies. Different socialization contexts or ecologies (e.g., culture) might provide different norms, values, and definitions of normalcy vis-à-vis social and emotional development. Certainly intra- and cross-cultural studies will enrich our knowledge of social and emotional development in middle childhood. Further enrichment will come from more in-depth examinations of the contributions of home and school environments.

Bibliography

Berndt, T. J., & Hoyle, S. G. (1985). Stability and change in childhood and adolescent friendships. *Developmental Psychology, 21,* 1007–1015.

Bigelow, B. J. (1977). Children's friendship expectations: A cognitive-developmental study. *Child Development, 48,* 246–253.

Bigelow, B. J., & La Gaipa, J. J. (1975). Children's written descriptions of friendship: A multidimensional analysis. *Developmental Psychology, 11*, 857–858.

Coie, J. D., & Dodge, K. A. (1998). Aggression and antisocial behavior. In W. Damon (Series Ed.) & N. Eisenberg (Vol. Ed.), *Handbook of child psychology: Vol. 3. Social, emotional, and personality development* (pp. 779–862). New York: Wiley.

Crockett, L., Losoff, M., & Peterson, A. C. (1984). Perceptions of the peer group and friendship in early adolescence. *Journal of Early Adolescence, 4*, 155–181.

Denham, S. A., & Burger, C. (1991). Observational validation of ratings of preschoolers' social competence and behavior problems. *Child Study Journal, 21*, 185–291.

Eisenberg, N. (1991). Meta-analytic contributions to the literature on prosocial behavior. *Personality and Social Psychology Bulletin, 17*, 273–282.

Eisenberg, N., & Fabes, R. A. (1992). Emotion, regulation, and the development of social competence. In M. S. Clark (Ed.), *Review of personality and social psychology: Vol. 14. Emotion and social behavior* (pp. 119–150). Newbury Park, CA: Sage.

Eisenberg, N., & Fabes, R. A. (1998). Prosocial development. In W. Damon (Series Ed.) & N. Eisenberg (Vol. Ed.), *Handbook of child psychology: Vol. 3 Social, emotional, and personality development* (pp. 701–778). New York: Wiley.

Harter, S. (1998). The development of self-appraisals. In W. Damon (Series Ed.) & N. Eisenberg (Vol. Ed.), *Handbook of child psychology: Vol. 3 Social, emotional, and personality development* (pp. 553–617). New York: Wiley.

Hinde, R. A. (1987). *Individuals, relationships, and culture.* Cambridge, UK: Cambridge University Press.

Hinde, R. A. (1995). A suggested structure for a science of relationships. *Personal Relationships, 2*, 1–15.

Hoffman, M. L. (1987). The contribution of empathy to justice and moral judgement. In N. Eisenberg & J. Strayer (Eds.), *Empathy and its development* (pp. 47–80). Cambridge, UK: Cambridge University Press.

Kinderman, T. A., McCollam, T. L., & Gibson, E., Jr. (1995). Peer networks and students' classroom engagement during childhood and adolescence. In K. Wentzel & J. Juvonen (Eds.), *Social motivation: Understanding children's school adjustment* (pp. 279–312). New York: Cambridge University Press.

Leaper, C. (1994). Exploring the consequences of gender segregation on social relationships. In C. Leaper (Ed.), *Childhood gender segregation: Causes and consequences* (pp. 67–86). San Francisco: Jossey-Bass.

Newcomb, A. F., & Bagwell, C. (1995). Children's friendship relations: A meta-analytic review. *Psychological Bulletin, 117*, 306–347.

Olweus, D. (1993). *Bullying at school: What we know and what we can do.* Oxford, UK: Blackwell.

Parker, J. G., & Gottman, J. M. (1989). Social and emotional development in a relational context: Friendship interaction from early childhood to adolescence. In T. J. Berndt & G. W. Ladd (Eds.), *Peer relations in child development* (pp. 95–131). New York: Wiley.

Parker, J. G., Rubin, K. H., Price, J., & DeRosier, M. E.

(1995). Peer relationships, child development, and adjustment: A developmental psychopathology perspective. In D. Cicchetti & D. Cohen (Eds.), *Developmental psychopathology: Vol. 2. Risk, disorder, and adaptation* (pp. 96–161). New York: Wiley.

Perry, D. G., Kusel, S. J., & Perry, L. C. (1988). Victims of peer aggression. *Developmental Psychology, 24*, 807–814.

Schultz, L. H., & Selman, R. L. (1989). Bridging the gap between interpersonal thought and action in early adolescence: The role of psychodynamic processes. *Development and Psychopathology, 1*, 133–152.

Selman, R. L., & Schultz, L. H. (1990). *Making a friend in youth: Developmental theory and pair therapy.* Chicago: University of Chicago Press.

Silva, F. (1992). Assessing the child and adolescent personality: A decade of research. *Personality and Individual Differences, 13*, 1163–1181.

Teasley, S. D., & Parker, J. G. (1995, March). *The effects of gender, friendship, and popularity on the targets and topics of preadolescents' gossip.* Paper presented at the meeting of the Society for Research in Child Development, Indianapolis, IN.

Kim B. Burgess and Kenneth H. Rubin

Socialization and Social Contexts

Although middle childhood (the years between the ages of 6 and 12) is less clearly set apart developmentally than infancy or adolescence, it is nevertheless a distinctive period. In many cultures, children begin to be absorbed into the world of adults at about 6 or 7, helping to shoulder family responsibilities and fill work roles alongside their elders. In most industrialized countries, however, children of these ages are largely removed from participation in adult society. Middle childhood coincides with the first segment of compulsory education in these countries, so that schooling provides a distinctive social structure that constrains and channels development during this period.

Middle childhood is viewed as part of the continuous process of human development even though the social and emotional lives of children are distinctive during this period. Once thought to be a time of affective quiescence or "latency," it is now apparent that middle childhood is a period of vigorous affectional, relational, and social growth (Collins, 1984). In this essay, we summarize current knowledge concerning childhood socialization in four areas: parent-child relations, sibling relations, peer relations, and institutional experiences.

Parent-Child Relations

Parent-child relations during middle childhood must be viewed in the context of the widening social world that characterizes children's lives during this period.

Normative Trends. Children spend half as much time interacting with their parents after school entrance as before; time spent with other children increases. At the time children enter school they are actually interacting more frequently on a daily basis with other children than with adults, a difference that reaches its peak at ages 8 to 9.

Although interaction with adults declines across middle childhood, children continue to perceive parents as gratifying distinctive social needs (Collins, Harris, & Susman, 1995). Parents, more than any other group of individuals, are identified throughout the period as providing children with affection, instrumental help, reliable alliances, and support for self-worth. Although parents continue to be sources of affection, help, and support, overt manifestations undergo considerable change. For example, physical affection between parents and children declines. Parents and children do not evince emotional outbursts and coercive interactions as frequently in middle as in early childhood, and disciplinary encounters also decline. Other negative emotional displays (e.g., sulking, depressed behavior) increase, and children attribute conflicts with their parents more often to failure in parental competence than they do in earlier years.

Gender differentiates certain aspects of parent-child interaction. Although mothers and children spend more time together than fathers and children, social overtures occur with equal frequency among children toward fathers and mothers and, among parents, toward boys as toward girls. Caregiving occurs more frequently in mother-child interaction than in father-child interaction, as does emotional expression—both positive and negative. Father-child interaction is more robust and physical than mother-child interaction, the same as in early childhood. Both fathers and mothers report increased attention to school performance in middle childhood, and there is little difference between them in this regard.

Control or compliance processes undergo considerable change during middle childhood. Parents use distraction and direct intervention to control the child's misdeeds less frequently; they more often use deprivation of privileges, appeals to self-esteem or responsibility, and guilt induction. These changes are linked in part to changes in parents' attributions about their children's misconduct; parents increasingly regard misbehavior as intentional and their children as capable of self-control. Children also increasingly recognize the superior wisdom and knowledge about the world possessed by their parents.

Taken together, these changes in expectations undergird a general restructuring during middle childhood of arrangements for regulating children's behavior. Rather than relying on direct parental supervision of children's behavior, parents and children together develop a system of complex cooperation and compliance called "coregulation" (Maccoby & Martin, 1983). Discipline is less physical and restraint oriented; simultaneously, it becomes more directed toward developing internal controls. Rather than directly supervising their children, parents now monitor them through periodic reports from the children themselves about their schedules, whereabouts, associates, and activities. Parents communicate their expectations in conversation—not through direct intervention in the child's ongoing behavior. Generally, these changes in parent-child relations constitute a gradual transformation of regulatory responsibilities rather than a "freeing" of the child from parental control. Although this shift from "other regulation" to coregulation in parent-child relations during middle childhood occurs for both sexes, supervision remains closer in most cultures for girls than for boys.

Individual Differences. Among most North American subcultures, child outcomes are most positive when parents practice child-centered modes of discipline, accompanied by clearly communicated demands, parental monitoring, and acceptance of the child. The meager evidence now available from other cultures indicates that optimal child-rearing practices frequently include greater restrictiveness than is considered supportive of development among American families (Collins et al., 1995). Children everywhere are at risk, however, in coercive environments—family situations in which children's aggressive behavior is negatively reinforced through contingent cessation of parent behavior that is noxious to the child. Coercive family processes lead step by step to lowered self-esteem, rejection by other children, and school failure during middle childhood, followed by more serious antisocial behavior and delinquency in adolescence (Patterson, Reid, & Dishion, 1992). These linkages run both ways: Coercive parenting fosters antisocial behavior in children, and, at the same time, aggressive children elicit coercive discipline by parents.

Divorce and remarriage are difficult for children to assimilate, but outcomes in middle childhood depend on circumstances that exist in the relationships network. Longitudinal studies show that, in the first year or two after a divorce, children from one-parent families are absent from school more often, study less effectively, and are more disruptive in the classroom than children from intact families. Risk of being above clinical threshold for both internalizing and externalizing symptoms during middle childhood is about three times greater. Within families that have experienced divorce and/or remarriage, however, children's resilience varies positively with the quality of the child's relationship with the custodial parent and his or her access to the noncustodial parent and negatively with the amount of conflict between parents. Both the social maturity of the child's parents and the supportiveness of their relationships with the child are also correlated with the child's resilience (Hetherington, 1999).

Children born to single teenage mothers are generally at greater risk for both academic and behavior problems in middle childhood than children born to older women. Teenage mothers are likely to be less stimulating and sensitive than older mothers, as well as harsher in their treatment of their children. But these problems are greatly reduced when the teenage mother has returned to school, obtained a job, gotten married, or had no additional children (Furstenberg, Brooks-Gunn, & Morgan, 1987). In a much different situation, "late-timing" childbirth, as compared with "on time" childbirth, seems to result in fathers evincing greater involvement with and sensitivity toward their children and mothers showing greater caretaking responsibility and satisfaction. Whether the children differ, however, has not been established.

Men's and women's employment patterns are associated with differences in caretaking arrangements and responsibilities in middle childhood. In dual-wage-earning families, as compared with those with a single wage earner, fathers are more involved in child care. Maternal employment, however, is not related to children's development. Children of employed mothers do not differ from children of unemployed mothers in social and emotional development, school achievement, or behavior problems during middle childhood (Parke & Buriel, 1997). Attitudes about gender roles differ, however, being more egalitarian among children of employed mothers—especially among girls. Dual-wage-earning families make many different arrangements for care and supervision of their children after school; large numbers of children do not have immediate adult supervision for significant amounts of time. "Latchkey" children are not generally disadvantaged, however, relative to children cared for by mothers, in either social development or academic achievement (Vandell & Corasantini, 1988).

Family economic difficulties are associated with increases in behavior and emotional difficulties in middle childhood—especially depression, loneliness, and lowered self-esteem. Externalizing difficulties are exacerbated among boys and internalizing difficulties among girls. These outcomes are mediated by parental stress and marital conflict, which, in turn, increase coercive discipline and decrease effective monitoring of the children's behavior (Parke & Buriel, 1997).

Sibling Relations

Although family size is smaller in industrialized countries than it was a century ago, more children have siblings than do not.

Normative Trends. Sibling socialization is distinctive as revealed by children's expectations: Both companionship and conflict are regarded as integral features of these relationships in middle childhood; intimacy and support for self-worth are not believed to be provided in sibling relationships as readily as in relationships with friends.

Generally, both children and their parents report sibling relationships to be more positive, egalitarian, and companionable during middle than early childhood, seemingly because fewer conflicts occur that are centered on the mother (Boer & Dunn, 1992). Younger children are more often taught by their siblings than older ones are, imitate them more, and aggress against them less frequently. Caretaking and tutoring are also extended by older to younger siblings more often than the reverse.

Individual Differences. Sibling relations differ according to parents' treatment of their children individually as well as together. Among both mothers and fathers, positive and negative reactions to one sibling are correlated with positivity and negativity, respectively, in relations with the second sibling. When mothers or fathers react more positively to one sibling than to the other (or are believed by the children to behave that way), relationships between the siblings are more hostile than otherwise. Moreover, when children perceive themselves to be less positively treated by their parents than their siblings, social adjustment is likely to be poorer (Boer & Dunn, 1992). For these reasons, family socialization constitutes a "system" rather than a series of disconnected dyadic processes.

The significance of sibling relationships in middle childhood for long-term outcomes is unclear. Direct carryover from sibling relations to friendship relations has not been consistently demonstrated. Coercive sibling relations are linked to aggressiveness and antisocial behavior with peers (Patterson et al., 1992), but otherwise sibling relations do not seem to be direct bridges from family socialization to peer socialization. Good sibling relations may buffer the child from the consequences of poor peer relations, although much more needs to be learned about these so-called compensatory effects.

Peer Relations

Peer relations acquire new significance during middle childhood.

Normative Trends. Although children in industrialized countries attend age-graded schools, children's associates are four times more likely to differ in age by more than one year than to be agemates. Psychological consequences are significant, because prosocial behavior and dependency occur more commonly in cross-age than in same-age interactions, whereas aggression and conflict occur more often with same-age associates (Whiting & Whiting, 1975). Children's companions tend more often to be same-race than other-race, although these patterns vary with school and community conditions. Boys' and girls' "cultures" are segregated throughout middle childhood, although pseudoromantic teasing ("borderwork") is common in cross-sex interaction.

Prosocial behavior in child-child interaction changes during middle childhood in several ways (Eisenberg & Fabes, 1997): (1) its frequency is greater than in early childhood and increases through the school-age years; (2) greater age-related increases occur when situational "demands" are high (e.g., someone is in need) than when they are low; (3) certain forms of prosocial activity (e.g., help giving) emerge for the first time; and (4) children use dispositional attributions (e.g., "kind" and "fair"), situational assessments, and social reasoning more accurately in middle childhood, thus enabling them to better match their actions to the demands of the social situation.

Antisocial behavior also changes during middle childhood (Coie & Dodge, 1997): (1) aggression is displayed less frequently, although a small subset of children become more troublesome and disruptive; (2) person-oriented, hostile aggression becomes more common, whereas instrumental, nonsocial aggression decreases; (3) children are now able to distinguish between intended and "accidental" aggression and to more reliably respond with angry retaliation to the former than to the latter; (4) indirect aggression (e.g., lying and cheating) becomes more common in middle childhood, and bullying becomes a significant issue for the first time. Boys are more aggressive than girls, although girls use "relational aggression" (e.g., excluding others from play, criticizing another's reputation) more than boys do. Still another difference in peer socialization occurring in middle childhood is a steep decline in the frequency of fantasy play (Rubin, Bukowski, & Parker, 1997). Along with rough-and-tumble play, pretend play virtually disappears by adolescence; replacing these activities are games and other more structured pursuits.

Social reputations become more salient during middle childhood and are based on children's experiences with one another (Rubin et al., 1997). Reputations are acquired for aggression and friendliness in this way and lead to being disliked or liked, respectively. Once established, social reputations are relatively stable and affect the attitudes and behavior of other children. Children expect hostility and trouble from children with aggressive reputations, even when provocation is uncertain. Social reputations are related to self- as well as others' attitudes: Both shy and aggressive reputations are associated with low self-esteem.

Friendships become increasingly central in children's social lives during middle childhood (Bukowski, Newcomb, & Hartup, 1996). Although younger children have friends, older children have different expectations of their friends. School-aged children, for example, expect their friends to be loyal, trustworthy, and (in preadolescence) intimate. Friendship networks are a bit smaller and more exclusive among girls than among boys, but boys and girls interact with their friends similarly: As compared with "neutral associates," friends are more interactive, more affectively expressive toward one another, more mutually oriented, more task oriented when the situation calls for it, and more likely to resolve conflicts by compromise and negotiation. Between antisocial children, however, friendships are likely to be more conflict-ridden and contentious than between average youngsters.

Individual Differences. The family system provides children with basic skills for smooth, successful peer relationships. The security of children's earlier relationships with their parents, the provision of opportunities to play with other children in early childhood, social skills training, and monitoring are related to social competence in middle childhood. Parenting skill remains correlated with peer success in middle childhood, although causal chains are difficult to specify. Studies show, however, that coercive parenting, along with poor monitoring, is related to aggression and low academic achievement. These behaviors, in turn, are associated with being disliked by other children (Patterson et al., 1992).

Children with poor peer relations (so-called rejected children) are more aggressive, hostile, and disruptive than those with good peer relations (popular children), have lower self-esteem, and exhibit poorer school performance. One half to two thirds of children who are rejected during one year are not rejected in the next; children who are most consistently rejected, however, are the most antisocial and the most likely to be at risk in subsequent development. For example, boys who are both rejected and aggressive in third grade show increasing antisocial behavior across the transition to adolescence, whereas being either aggressive or rejected (or neither) is associated with decreasing antisocial behavior during this period.

Close friendships in middle childhood are also developmentally significant, enhancing feelings of self-worth and attitudes about interpersonal relationships during adolescence and early adulthood. Friends provide children with "social capital" in difficult life circumstances, for example, in the aftermath of divorce (Hetherington, 1999). Outcomes may be mitigated, however, by the identity of the child's friends and friendship "quality": Supportive friendships between socially skilled individuals predict good subsequent outcomes, but coercive and conflict-ridden friendships, especially between antisocial children, constitute developmental disadvantages (Bukowski et al., 1996).

Institutions and Socialization

Various institutions impinge on children's socialization in middle childhood. Schools are especially significant in industrialized countries, but religious institutions, clubs, sports teams, and other groups also contribute. Quasi institutions such as television, health care systems, and the arts also affect developmental outcome. Except for schools and television, relatively little is known about the consequences of engagement with these institutions.

Schools. Schools vary enormously from one another as socializing agents. Student motivation is best supported by challenging work assignments, mastery expectations, and good emotional support—conditions that are similar to the kind of family environments that enhance social competence (Eccles, Wigfield, & Schiefele, 1997). School characteristics that have relatively little effect on social outcomes are funding, school and class size, classroom structure, and ability groupings.

Teachers have considerable influence on children's behavior in middle childhood through their instructional techniques and the manner in which they evaluate children. Authoritative teaching styles generally have more positive effects than authoritarian or laissez-faire approaches. Parental involvement in school affairs facilitates positive outcomes, although it is not always easy to achieve, especially with disadvantaged students. Cooperative atmospheres have more positive effects on achievement motivation, self-esteem, and peer acceptance than competitive ones, and classroom effects on attitudes toward race and disability depend on the utilization of cooperative goal structures.

Evaluation biases among teachers show that good students are expected to do better and receive disproportionately large amounts of positive performance feedback, whereas expectations and behavior toward poor students are disproportionately negative. These biases, however, may not be simply self-fulfilling prophecies. Students who are expected to do poorly have usually performed poorly previously, and those expected to do well usually have histories of good performance. Other teacher biases relate to gender: Many teachers expect poorer performance from girls than from boys, especially in science and mathematics, and attribute these differences to lower abilities among girls and greater efforts among boys. Generally, parent and teacher expectations, as well as demands, are not as great in the United States as in other countries, particularly China and Japan, conditions that undoubtedly contribute to the lower achievement of American students in many different subject matter areas (Stevenson & Stigler, 1992).

Television. During middle childhood, most children spend more of their free time watching television than doing anything else (3–4 hours per day). Older children watch more television than younger ones, especially boys. Economically disadvantaged youngsters watch three times as much television as their more advantaged counterparts.

Historically, more attention has been paid to the deleterious effects of children's exposure to television than to its positive effects (Huston et al., 1992). Heavy diets of televised violence, in fact, instigate aggression and antisocial behavior, as well as desensitize children to aggression. Stereotyped depictions of men and women, as well as ethnic minorities, are more common on television than they should be, and these affect children's attitudes throughout middle childhood. Commercials frequently instigate unhealthy eating habits. Concomitantly, however, television teaches children much about the world that contributes positively to socialization—about cooperation and prosocial behavior, mastery and achievement, and interpersonal relationships. And, finally, although earlier investigators worried about the effects of television viewing on children's relationships with their families and peers, the weight of the evidence suggests that these effects are relatively minor.

Bibliography

Boer, F., & Dunn, J. (Eds.). (1992). *Children's sibling relationships*. Hillsdale, NJ: Erlbaum.

Bukowski, W. M., Newcomb, A. F., & Hartup, W. W. (Eds.). (1996). *The company they keep: Friendship in childhood and adolescence*. Cambridge, UK: Cambridge University Press.

Coie, J. D., & Dodge, K. A. (1997). Aggression and antisocial behavior. In W. Damon (Series Ed.) & N. Eisenberg (Vol. Ed.), *Handbook of child psychology: Vol. 3, Social, emotional, and personality development* (5th ed., pp. 779–862). New York: Wiley.

Collins, W. A. (Ed.). (1984). *Development during middle childhood: The years from six to twelve*. Washington, DC: National Academy Press.

Collins, W. A., Harris, M. L., & Susman, A. (1995). Parenting during middle childhood. In M. H. Bornstein (Ed.), *Handbook of parenting* (Vol. 1, pp. 65–89). Hillsdale, NJ: Erlbaum.

Eccles, J. S., Wigfield, A., & Schiefele, U. (1997). Motivation to succeed. In W. Damon (Series Ed.) & N. Eisenberg (Vol. Ed.), *Handbook of child psychology: Vol. 3, Social, emotional, and personality development* (5th ed., pp. 1017–1095). New York: Wiley.

Eisenberg, N., & Fabes, R. A. (1997). Prosocial development. In W. Damon (Series Ed.) & N. Eisenberg (Vol. Ed.), *Handbook of child psychology: Vol. 3, Social, emotional, and personality development* (5th ed., pp. 701–778). New York: Wiley.

Furstenberg, F. F., Jr., Brooks-Gunn, J., & Morgan, P. (1987). *Adolescent mothers in later life*. New York: Cambridge University Press.

Hetherington, E. M. (1999). Social capital and the development of youth from nondivorced, divorced, and remarried families. In W. A. Collins & B. Laursen (Eds.), *Minnesota Symposia on Child Psychology: Vol. 30. Relationships as developmental contexts* (pp. 177–209). Hillsdale, NJ: Erlbaum.

Huston, A. C., Donnerstein, E., Fairchild, H., Feshbach, N. D., Katz, P. A., Murray, J. P., Rubinstein, E. A., Wilcox, B. L., & Zuckerman, D. T. (1992). *Big world, small screen: The role of television in American society.* Lincoln: University of Nebraska Press.

Maccoby, E. E., & Martin, J. A. (1983). Socialization in the context of the family: Parent-child interaction. In P. H. Mussen (Series Ed.) & E. M. Hetherington (Vol. Ed.), *Handbook of child psychology: Vol. 4. Socialization, personality, and social development* (4th ed., pp. 1–101). New York: Wiley.

Parke, R. D., & Buriel, R. (1997). Socialization in the family: Ethnic and ecological perspectives. In W. Damon (Series Ed.) & N. Eisenberg (Vol. Ed.), *Handbook of child psychology: Vol. 3, Social, emotional, and personality development* (5th ed., pp. 463–552). New York: Wiley.

Patterson, G. R., Reid, J., & Dishion, T. J. (1992). *Antisocial boys.* Eugene, OR: Castalia.

Rubin, K. H., Bukowski, W. M., & Parker, J. G. (1997). Peer interactions, relationships, and groups. In W. Damon (Series Ed.) & N. Eisenberg (Vol. Ed.), *Handbook of child psychology: Vol. 3, Social, emotional, and personality development,* (5th ed., pp. 619–700). New York: Wiley.

Stevenson, H. W., & Stigler, J. (1992). *The learning gap.* New York: Summit Books.

Vandell, D. L., & Corasantini, M. A. (1988). The relation between third graders' after-school care and social, academic, and emotional functioning. *Child Development,* 59, 868–875.

Whiting, B. B., & Whiting, J. W. M. (1975). *Children of six cultures.* Cambridge, MA: Harvard University Press.

Willard W. Hartup and W. Andrew Collins

MIDWESTERN PSYCHOLOGICAL ASSOCIATION.
See Regional Psychological Associations.

MIGRANTS. Migration has become a global issue. It is estimated that there are 70 to 100 million immigrants and refugees in the world today (United Nations, 1995) who have migrated to other countries as a result of war; political instability; expulsion; economic, social and environmental pressures; population expansion; and poverty. Murphy (1977) differentiated "forced" and "free" migration. Forced or involuntary migration relates to refugees who fled from political, religious, or ethnic persecution, war, and repression with little or no planning, preparation, or choice. This is distinguished from immigrants who voluntarily migrate to another country in search of a better quality of life. Migrants, whether they are voluntary or forced, differ with respect to their countries of origin and destination, their levels of education, skills, and resources, and their reasons for departing from their homelands. Trends have shown that in the late twentieth century the movement of migration has been from developing to more developed countries. For example, in the early 1990s the greatest number of migrants to Western Europe came from less developed countries, with 1 million from Morocco, 1.5 million from Iran, and 2 million from Turkey.

As the growing number of migrants steadily increased, there has been heightened controversy regarding the liberalization or constriction of immigration policies. Some countries, such as Japan, which has less than 1% foreign population, have avoided these debates by maintaining a closed-door policy. Other countries have more liberal policies, such as Australia, with an acceptance rate of two to three times the number of immigrants proportionately to its population as found in Europe. Although policies in most countries change over time according to both internal and external circumstances, current resettlement policies in many countries narrowly focus on the reduction and termination of long-term financial aid and economic responsibility without taking into account the complex needs and issues embodied in the adjustment to a new culture. The priority of attending to food, shelter, serious disease, and sufficient water supplies at the expense of mental health has diminished the importance of psychological well-being, creating the potential for serious long-term problems (Marsella, Bornemann, Ekblad, & Orley, 1994). In fact, the European Regional Mental Health Unit of the World Health Organization urged governments to take vital steps to address migrant mental health.

Given the globalization and dramatic effect of loss, separation, and transition that is inherent in migration, it is imperative for contemporary psychology to address the acculturation and mental health issues encountered by immigrants and refugees.

Theories of Migration

There have been several attempts to conceptualize the relationship between migration and mental health. The first attempt was by Odegaard (1945), who proposed the social selection theory. In this theory, psychological problems were ascribed solely to individual predispositions without consideration of cultural adjustment. Etinger (1959) attributed poor mental health of migrants to a social causation theory whereby psychological difficulties were caused by external stressors, thereby rejecting Odegaard's theory of predisposition. Sixteen years later, Goldlust and Richmond (1974) developed the multivariate model of immigration to explain mental health problems within the context of adaptation. This theory was the first to consider both premigration and postmigration factors, taking into account premigration conditions, individual demographics, and postmigration factors. Researchers have most frequently addressed and generally accepted aspects of this theory as an integrative model.

Acculturation and Psychosocial Adjustment

A correlation has been found between migration and mental health problems, suggesting that migrants encounter adjustment difficulties to the new culture (Bemak, Chung, & Bornemann, 1996). There are four major models of acculturation that include assimilation, biculturalism, rejection, and deculturation and that encompass various factors such as stress, adaptation, and social indicators. Research has found that the bicultural models of adaptation have been the most effective in generating healthy psychological outcomes for refugees and immigrants (e.g., Berry, 1986; Szapocznik & Kurtines, 1980).

Premigration trauma, transition, and postmigration adjustment have been found to have a significant impact on acculturation and have been defined as antecedents of flight, the period of flight, and the process of resettlement as phases of migration that contribute to psychosocial adjustment. Psychological problems from each period must be addressed and resolved in order to minimize mental health risks. Premigration trauma that interferes with adjustment has been characterized as (1) deprivation (e.g., of food and shelter), (2) physical injury and torture, (3) incarceration and reeducation camps, and (4) witnessing of torture and killing. The correlation between poor mental health and these categories has been documented (e.g., Bemak & Chung, 1998; Boothby, 1994; Kinzie, 1993).

Migrants who experience postmigration culture shock, which is typically accompanied by feelings of helplessness and confusion, will also encounter problems in adjustment. Survivor's guilt is another potential barrier to successful adjustment for individuals who are haunted by feelings of guilt derived from escaping dangerous conditions in their home countries and leaving behind family and friends. This separation from family, friends, and community also causes a shift in reference groups (Bemak & Greenberg, 1994) that may be particularly difficult as people move from collectivistic to individualistic cultures.

The first 1 to 2 years of resettlement have been recognized as a crucial time in the adjustment process when refugees must unlearn previous adaptive behaviors that may appear pathological or antisocial in the new society. One model of psychological adjustment developed by Bemak (1989) outlined three phases that serve to establish emotional safety and security: (1) through initial skill development, (2) through the integration of previously learned skills from the country of origin with new skills in the resettlement country, and (3) through the creation of skills and values that foster a realistic acquisition of future goals. Studies have found an association between the phases of postmigration resettlement and mental health. The initial period of psychological well-being and elation has been called euphoric, overcompensation, or incubation and may last from one month to one year. During the second phase, difficulties may manifest and affect psychological well-being. Problems may emerge at different times ranging from 6 months to 7 years.

Psychosocial adjustment to a dramatically new culture rather than to a culture more similar to one's own heritage may be particularly stressful and difficult. Not only must immigrants and refugees learn about the new world, but also what was formerly normative behavior may be unacceptable in host countries. For example, child-rearing methods of discipline such as corporal punishment may be illegal, whereas traditional healing practices such as "coining" or rubbing one's body to let out evil spirits may be perceived as self-mutilation. Other problems may also ensue. There may be marked changes in family roles and dynamics as children acculturate faster than their parents because of greater cultural exposure through school and peers. Children may assume a role as the "cultural bridge" for the family as they become more knowledgeable and comfortable with the dominant culture. There may be other new generational shifts regarding cultural values that cause conflict, such as differences over curfews, dating, decision making, or marriage. Gender roles may also change. Women may be exposed to nontraditional values through work, new friends, or language skills training, which may encourage greater independence and subsequent disruptions in the traditional family structure.

Lack of language proficiency plays an important part in psychosocial adjustment and affects all aspects of the migrant's life, including socioeconomic mobility and employment opportunities and causing overall difficulties in understanding and mastering daily life in a new and strange environment (Chung & Kagawa-Singer, 1993). This deficiency may affect people's ability to acquire new job skills, especially when professional qualifications are not transferable to the resettlement country (Chung & Okazaki, 1991). Furthermore, to compound the difficulties in adjustment, migrants may also experience discrimination by members of the host society, which has been reported to be the most important factor contributing to high levels of anxiety and depression.

Successful acculturation in the postmigration phase is dependent on an individual's ability to integrate his or her culture of origin with that of the resettlement country, as well as an individual's desire and willingness to adapt, ability to identify and create new reference groups, acceptance of the host country's culture, supportiveness of social and family networks, and resolution of past traumatic experiences.

Mental Health Issues

Migrants, particularly refugees, have a higher incidence of psychopathology, depression, posttraumatic stress disorders, anxiety, and psychological problems than the general population of the host country (Kinzie, 1993; Williams & Berry, 1991). During the first half of the twentieth century the predominant mental health disorders for migrants (primarily Europeans) were identified as paranoid reactions with trends of persecution and affective disorders with a high incidence of unipolar depression and anxiety and paranoid schizophrenia. Recent studies have found contemporary problems to be major depression, posttraumatic stress disorder, anxiety, and generalized psychological difficulties (Bemak & Greenberg, 1994; Kinzie, 1993; Marsella, Freidman, & Spain, 1993).

A review of major findings suggested that predictors of psychological distress for migrants include older age (for Vietnamese, Bosnians, Southeast Asian refugees, and Asian immigrants); losing a spouse, being divorced, or being unmarried; and low socioeconomic status, unemployment, and less education.

Cultural Issues in Mental Health

To plan, develop, and offer mental health services for migrants, understanding the cultural context is essential. Clinical diagnoses and interventions must be consistent with the client's fundamental cultural belief systems, values, and healing practices. Kleinman and Good (1985) emphasized the need to understand, accept, and confirm the client's cultural conceptualization of his or her problem. This was done formally when more attention to culture was included in the fourth edition of the American Psychiatric Association's *Diagnostic and Statistical Manual of Mental Disorders (DSM–IV*, 1994), which is the established system of diagnostic classification for mental disorders in the United States. Included in the *DSM–IV* is a glossary of 25 culture-bound syndromes and information about cultural and ethnic dimensions in the clinical presentation of specific disorders.

Despite greater attention to culture, the basis of Western psychology remains focused on a medical model that pathologizes mental health problems while emphasizing the individual in order to facilitate optimum individual functioning and self-development. The emphasis on individualism and autonomy may directly conflict with the cultural context of migrants who frequently come from collectivistic societies in which identity and self are defined and prescribed by family and social networks, underscoring interdependence rather than independence. Furthermore, many migrants may come from societies in which concepts of health integrate mind, body, and spirit, whereas Western psychology clearly delineates each of these as separate entities. Subsequently, for many migrants, Western psychological methodology and practice may be antithetical to basic values and beliefs about healing, family, a sense of community, social networks, the importance of ancestral guidance, spiritual beliefs, and interdependence with living and nonliving forces.

Utilization of Mainstream Mental Health Services

Despite evidence that a disproportionate number of migrants have mental health problems (Struwe, 1994), they have been traditionally unwilling to access mainstream mental health services (Chung & Lin, 1994; Higginbotham, Trevino, & Ray, 1990). This unwillingness may be related to several factors. First, the preferred treatment of choice for more serious mental health problems, after consultations with family members, elders, and social support networks, usually begins with explorations of traditional cultural healing methods, that is, religious or traditional healers. Then, if the traditional healing interventions are unsuccessful, mainstream mental health providers might be contacted by default. This tradition helps explain findings that by the time immigrants and refugees reach mental health services the problem has become acute.

A second reason may relate to the formidable obstacles to accessing mainstream mental health services (Chung & Lin, 1994). The actual facility or provider may be inaccessible, may involve following complicated directions by public transport, or may be situated in an area perceived as dangerous by the migrant. If these barriers are overcome, there may still be the problem of culturally insensitive and inhospitable staff (Bemak, Chung, & Bornemann, 1996). Receptionists and professionals may not understand cultural differences or may be discourteous and inadvertently offensive in their communication.

Finally, there may be language barriers. In this case, bilingual and bicultural workers have been used to assist mental health professionals. It is essential that these workers have a clear understanding of their role and relationship to both the client(s) and professional(s). Issues such as confidentiality, self-disclosure, nonverbal communication, and expectations about translation are delineated.

Clinical Implications

Clinical diagnosis and practice with migrants require unique skills, cultural understanding and awareness, and sensitivity to migration history and acculturation and to the reality of loss and separation from one's past life. It is within this context that mental health professionals must educate migrants about the process and dynamics of psychotherapy, utilize appropriate assessment and intervention methods and techniques that are culturally appropriate, assist clients in mastering the new culture, and incorporate indigenous healing practices that are responsive to the cultural belief systems regarding healing (Bemak, Chung, & Bornemann, 1996).

Bibliography

American Psychiatric Association. (1994). *Diagnostic and statistical manual of mental disorders* (4th ed.). Washington, DC: Author.

Bemak, F. (1989). Cross-cultural family therapy with Southeast Asian refugees. *Journal of Strategic and Systemic Therapies, 8,* 22–27.

Bemak, F., & Chung, R. C.-Y. (1998). Vietnamese Amerasians: Predictors of distress and self-destructive behavior. *Journal of Counseling and Development, 76* (4), 452–458.

Bemak, F., Chung, R. C.-Y., & Bornemann, T. (1996). Counseling and psychotherapy with refugees. In P. Pedersen, J. Draguns, W. Lonner, & J. Trimble (Eds.), *Counseling across cultures* (4th ed., pp. 243–265). Thousand Oaks, CA: Sage.

Bemak, F., & Greenberg, B. (1994). Southeast Asian refugee adolescents: Implications for counseling. *Journal of Multicultural Counseling and Development, 22*(4), 115–124.

Berry, J. W. (1986). The acculturation process and refugee behavior. In C. L. Williams & J. Westermeyer (Eds.), *Refugee mental health in resettlement countries* (pp. 25–37). Washington, DC: Hemisphere.

Boothby, N. (1994). Trauma and violence among refugee children. In A. J. Marsella, T. Bornemann, S. Ekblad, & J. Orley (Eds.), *Amidst peril and pain: The mental health and well-being of the world's refugees* (pp. 239–259). Washington, DC: American Psychological Association.

Chung, R. C.-Y., & Kagawa-Singer, M. (1993). Predictors of psychological distress among Southeast Asian refugees. *Social Science and Medicine, 36*(5), 631–639.

Chung, R. C.-Y., & Lin, K. M. (1994). Helpseeking behavior among Southeast Asian refugees. *Journal of Community Psychology, 22,* 109–120.

Chung, R. C.-Y., & Okazaki, S. (1991). Counseling Americans of Southeast Asian descent: The impact of the refugee experience. In C. C. Lee & B. L. Richardson (Eds.), *Multicultural issues in counseling: New approaches to diversity* (pp. 107–126). Alexandria, VA: American Association for Counseling and Development.

Etinger, L. (1959). The incidence of mental disease among refugees in Norway. *Journal of Mental Science, 105,* 326–338.

Goldlust, J., & Richmond, A. H. (1974). A multivariate model of immigrant adaptation. *International Migration Review, 8,* 193–225.

Higginbotham, J. C., Trevino, F. M., & Ray, L. A. (1990). Utilization of curanderos by Mexican Americans: Prevalence and predictors' findings from HHANES 1982–1984. *Journal of Public Health, 80,* 32–35.

Kinzie, D. (1993). Posttraumatic effects and their treatment among Southeast Asian refugees. In J. Wilson & B. Raphael (Eds.), *International handbook of traumatic stress syndromes* (pp. 311–320). New York: Plenum Press.

Kleinman, A., & Good, B. (1985). *Culture and depression: Studies in the anthropology and cross-cultural psychiatry of affect and disorder.* Berkeley: University of California Press.

Marsella, A. J., Bornemann, T., Ekblad, S., & Orley, J. (Eds.). (1994). *Amidst peril and pain: The mental health and well-being of the world's refugees.* Washington, DC: American Psychological Association.

Marsella, A. J., Friedman, M., & Spain, H. (1993). Ethnocultural aspects of PTSD. *Review of Psychiatry, 12,* 157–181.

Murphy, H. B. (1977). Migration, culture and mental health. *Psychological Medicine, 7,* 677–684.

Odegaard, O. (1945). The distribution of mental diseases in Norway. *Acta Psychiatrica Neurologica, 20,* 247–252.

Struwe, G. (1994). Training health and medical professionals to care for refugees: Issues and methods. In A. J. Marsella, T. Bornemann, S. Ekblad, & J. Orley (Eds.), *Amidst peril and pain: The mental health and well-being of the world's refugees* (pp. 311–324). Washington, DC: American Psychological Association.

Szapocznik, J., & Kurtines, W. (1980). Acculturation, biculturalism, and adjustment among Cuban-Americans. In A. M. Padilla (Ed.), *Recent advances in acculturation research: Theory, models, and some new findings* (pp. 914–931). Boulder, CO: Westview Press.

United Nations. (1995). *Notes for speakers: Social development.* New York: Department of Public Information, United Nations.

Williams, C. L., & Berry, J. W. (1991). Primary prevention of acculturative stress among refugees. *American Psychologist, 46,* 632–641.

Frederic Paul Bemak

MILES, WALTER RICHARD (1885–1978), American experimental psychologist. Miles was born in the Dakota Territories and spent his early years on a farm and attending a one-room schoolhouse, before moving to Oregon at age 8. He began college in the west at Pacific College but completed his undergraduate degree at Earlham College in Indiana in 1908. There his interests in psychological research were sparked by a laboratory course that used Edward B. Titchener's famous manuals. After teaching for a year, Miles went to the University of Iowa, where he earned a doctorate in experimental psychology under Carl E. Seashore in 1913.

Miles's first academic position was at Wesleyan College in Connecticut. There he filled in for Raymond Dodge, who was spending a year at the Carnegie Nutrition Laboratory in Boston, Massachusetts. Dodge became a model of the ideal experimental psychologist for Miles. On Dodge's recommendation, Miles followed him to the Carnegie Laboratory and remained in Boston from 1914 to 1922. While there, Miles completed research on the effects of alcohol and reduced food intake on behavior and completed a war project on gas mask design. In 1922, Lewis Terman asked him to head the psychology laboratory at Stanford University, which he did for a decade. He then returned east to Yale's newly founded Institute of Human Relations, where he rejoined Dodge; Miles remained at Yale from 1932 until his retirement in 1952. He then spent 3 years as visiting professor at the University of Istanbul and another 8 years (1957–1965) as scientific director of the submarine base in New London, Connecticut.

Miles was elected president of the American Psychological Association in 1932 and was elected to the National Academy of Sciences a year later. He was an active member of the Society of Experimental Psychologists, the research society founded by Titchener, earning the society's prestigious Warren medal in 1949. In 1962, the American Psychological Foundation awarded him a gold medal for his lifetime contribution to psychology.

Miles's diverse research career included both applied research and basic laboratory studies in perception and learning. He is best known as an experimental psychologist for creating the platform or elevated maze, on which rats traversed raised runways that lacked side walls. Such mazes enabled researchers to study spatial orientation abilities in rats. He also directed an ongoing series of research projects known collectively as the Stanford Later Maturity Study, one of the earliest systematic attempts to study the effects of aging on perceptual, motor, and cognitive skills. He found that although most skills declined with age, large individual variation occurred, and one fourth of subjects over the age of 70 scored as well as middle-aged adults.

[*Many of the people mentioned in this article are the subjects of independent biographical entries.*]

Bibliography

Miles, W. R. (1930). On the history of research with rats and mazes: A collection of notes. *Journal of General Psychology, 3,* 324–337. Mainly a collection of letters sent to Miles from several of the early pioneers in maze learning research, including Willard Small and Linus Kline of Clark University, concerning the early history of maze learning.

Miles, W. R. (1967). Walter R. Miles. In E. G. Boring & G. Lindzey (Eds.), *A history of psychology in autobiography* (Vol. 5, pp. 143–162). New York: Appleton-Century-Crofts. A reflective autobiographical statement.

Miles, W. R. (1930). The comparative learning of rats on elevated and alley mazes of the same pattern. *Journal of Comparative Psychology, 10,* 237–261. A series of studies comparing traditional alley mazes with Miles's new elevated maze; performance was similar, but rats in the elevated maze completed the maze in less time and with fewer errors.

C. James Goodwin

MILGRAM, STANLEY (1933–1984), American social psychologist. Stanley Milgram was one of the most inventive and controversial social scientists of the second half of the twentieth century. He created a number of highly original research paradigms, and his work became controversial because of his experiments on obedience to authority. The latter revealed that a majority of normal adults would inflict severe punishment in the form of as much as 450 volts of electric shock on an innocent victim at the bidding of a scientific authority. Those experiments would create alterations in some basic assumptions about human nature—that it doesn't take evil or deranged persons to act destructively against innocent human beings—and comprise one of a handful of ethically questionable experiments that led to the formalization of procedures for the protection of human research subjects by the U.S. government.

Stanley Milgram was born on 15 August 1933, in the Bronx, New York, to Samuel and Adele Milgram, Jewish immigrants from Eastern Europe. He was a middle child, preceded by a year and a half by a sister, Marjorie, and followed 5 years later by a brother, Joel. He attended James Monroe High School and then Queens College, receiving a bachelor's degree in political science in 1954.

In the fall of 1954, he entered the Ph.D. degree program in social psychology in the social relations department at Harvard University. Among the faculty there who had a major impact on him and to whom he felt closest was Gordon Allport, who became his mentor, and later, supervised his doctoral dissertation, along with Roger Brown and Jerome Bruner. However, the person whom he considered his major scientific influence was Solomon E. Asch, whom Milgram served as a research and teaching assistant when the former came to Harvard as a visiting lecturer from 1955 to 1956. Milgram's doctoral dissertation, a cross-national comparison of behavioral conformity between Norway and France, used a modification of Asch's experimental paradigm. Milgram spent 1957 and 1958 collecting data in Oslo and then repeated the procedure in Paris in 1958 and 1959. Although both the Norwegian and French participants were responsive to the experimental variations he built into the general procedure—judging which of a pair of acoustic tones was longer—overall the Norwegians showed a higher rate of conformity to a phantom majority than did the French subjects. This was an important study because, as Milgram put it, "It [was] the first attempt to study national characteristics by the direct, experimental assessment of the behavior of two national groups." In 1959 and 1960, Milgram worked for Asch at the Institute for Advanced Study at Princeton University, helping him edit a book on conformity which was never published.

He received his Ph.D. degree in social psychology in

the spring of 1960 and began as an assistant professor of psychology at Yale University in the fall of 1960. That first semester he conducted some pilot studies on obedience with his students in a small-groups class, and then carried out the main experiments, a total of 24 conditions funded by grants from the National Science Foundation, from August 1961 to May 1962. In his obedience experiments, the subject was to teach a learner a series of adjective-noun pairs, punishing him with electric shock for each error. The main prop was an impressive-looking shock machine containing 30 lever switches, each of which when depressed was supposed to deliver increasingly more severe shocks to the learner in 15-volt increments. The rule was that the subject-teacher was to increase the shock one step on each subsequent error by the learner. What the subject did not know was that the shocks were not real and the learner was an actor, who in some conditions feigned increasing expressions of pain with increasing voltages.

In December 1961, Milgram married Alexandra (Sasha) Menkin. After the completion of the obedience experiments, Milgram, together with his students, created the lost-letter technique, an unobtrusive procedure for assessing community attitudes and opinions. It is the most widely used nonreactive measure of attitudes and opinions today. In the fall of 1963, he returned to Harvard as an assistant professor in the social relations department. Here, he continued his work with the lost-letter technique and also devised the small-world method, a behavioral technique for studying social networks. The Milgrams' two children, Michele and Marc, were born during the Harvard years.

After Harvard did not offer him tenure, in the fall of 1967 Milgram accepted the chair of the doctoral program in social psychology at the Graduate Center of the City University of New York (CUNY) at the rank of full professor, skipping the rank of associate professor. While there, he mentored fourteen doctoral students—more than any other member of the psychology faculty. At CUNY, the study of city life became a major focus of his interests, and his article, "The Experience of Living in Cities" (Science, 1970, 167, 1461–1468), played an important role in launching the discipline of urban psychology. In that article, Milgram introduced the concept of stimulus overload as a way to account for behavioral differences between city and town dwellers observed by him and his students. He also conducted other innovative research at CUNY, the most important of which was a unique, massive experiment on the antisocial effects of television, described in the book (with R. Lance Shotland), Television and Anti-Social Behavior: Field Experiments (New York, 1973). He also became increasingly involved in film making, producing together with Harry From, five educational films on various topics in social psychology, including the award-winning The City and the Self. Although he conducted the obedience experiments early in his career, like it or not, they continued to claim his attention for the rest of his life, largely because of the ethical questions they raised.

Milgram died on 20 December 1984, of a heart attack—the fifth in a series which began in May 1980—at the age of 51.

Despite his short life span, he was able to make a number of enduring contributions to psychology. Like few other research endeavors, his obedience studies provided a powerful realization of Kurt Lewin's confidence in the effective use of experimentation to address social problems. In fact, that research remains unparalleled as the most visible and creative example of the use of experimental realism in the service of a question of deep social and moral significance. Furthermore, his example encouraged younger social psychologists to take risks and apply innovative research methods to try to achieve positive social change. And what he considered to be "the most fundamental lesson" to be drawn from his obedience experiments, that "ordinary people, simply doing their jobs, and without any particular hostility on their part, can become agents in a terrible destructive process" (Milgram, 1974, p. 6) has come to serve as the basis for one of the main explanations for the behavior of the perpetrators of the Holocaust. Via his experiments, which invariably focused on situational rather than dispositional determinants, Milgram helped maintain the dominance of situationism as the hallmark of mainstream North American social psychology.

His work was unusually accessible to both public and professional audiences, not only because of the lucidity and often literary quality of his writings, but because in most of his research the outcome behavior was direct, visible, and dichotomous; for example, the subject either did or did not press the next shock-machine switch; viewers of an antisocial film did or did not imitatively steal money from a charity display; finders of a "lost letter" did or did not mail it. And finally, he demonstrated the unexpected power of norms—such as rules of deference to authority—and the difficulty people have in translating their beliefs and intentions into behaviors, even when those behaviors possess a moral dimension.

Bibliography

Works by Milgram

Milgram, S. (1963). Behavioral study of obedience. *Journal of Abnormal and Social Psychology, 67,* 371–378. The first publication by Milgram about his obedience research, describing in vivid detail the method and results of his "remote" condition, in which 65% of his participants were fully obedient.

Milgram, S. (1965). Some conditions of obedience and disobedience to authority. *Human Relations, 18,* 57–76. Most comprehensive report about the obedience series up to that time, it won Milgram the annual Socio-Psychological Prize of the American Association for the Advancement of Science in 1964.

Milgram, S. (1974). *Obedience to authority: An experimental view.* New York: Harper & Row. Milgram's most complete account of his obedience experiments, it contains a description of eighteen experimental conditions, a theoretical explanation of his findings centered on his "agentic state" concept, and his defense against the methodological and ethical criticisms of the work.

Milgram, S. (1992). *The individual in a social world: Essays and experiments* (Rev. ed.). New York: McGraw-Hill. (Original work published 1977.) Contains most of Milgram's publications. Indispensable source for learning about the broad scope of Milgram's research interests.

Works about Milgram

Blass, T. (1991). Understanding behavior in the Milgram obedience experiment: The role of personality, situations, and their interactions. *Journal of Personality and Social Psychology, 60,* 398–413. The only comprehensive literature review of the obedience paradigm.

Blass, T. (1992). The social psychology of Stanley Milgram. In M. P. Zanna (Ed.), *Advances in experimental social psychology* (Vol. 25, p. 227–329). San Diego, CA: Academic Press. An integrative review and systematization of the whole corpus of Milgram's work, distilling from its diversity a set of unifying features.

Blass, T. (1996). Stanley Milgram: A life of inventiveness and controversy. In G. A. Kimble, C. A. Boneau, & M. Wertheimer (Eds.), *Portraits of pioneers in psychology* (Vol. 2, pp. 315–331). The only detailed biography of Milgram to date.

Elms, A. C. (1995). Obedience in retrospect. *Journal of Social Issues, 51*(3), 21–31. Presents the personal perspective of an individual who served as Milgram's research assistant at the beginning of the obedience series during the summer of 1961.

Miller, A. G. (1986). *The obedience experiments: A case study of controversy in social science.* New York: Praeger.

Rochat, F., & Modigliani, A. (1995). The ordinary quality of resistance: From Milgram's laboratory to the village of Le Chambon. *Journal of Social Issues, 51*(3), 195–210. A unique article, because in contrast to most discussions of the obedience experiments, here the emphasis is on defiance of rather than obedience to malevolent authority. Specifically, the authors draw a parallel between the behavior of Milgram's disobedient subjects and the French villagers of Le Chambon, who in defiance of the Nazis' orders, provided a safe haven for thousands of Jews.

Thomas Blass

MILIEU THERAPY. Mental hospitals, psychiatric wards, mental health center inpatient units, and community facilities are all residential treatment settings in the mental health field. They are service sites when the severity of impairment or dangerousness of emotional, behavioral, and mental problems call for a 24-hour environment. Their purpose is to improve functioning so that their clients may return to ordinary community living or to other, less restrictive treatment settings.

Residential facilities furnish a total environment that can exert more influence, for better or worse, than any other setting. The treatment unit, or ward, is the immediate environment. The core of any program lies in the unitwide organizational structure of staff and client responsibilities.

Milieu therapy means treatment by the environment. Two major approaches emerged in the last half of the twentieth century—therapeutic community and social learning approaches. In both, all aspects of the physical and social environment are organized into unitwide psychosocial programs. They focus on individualized reeducation, training, and normalization of functioning with an overriding set of principles and procedures to be followed by all clinical personnel with all clientele. Treatment on these units is by and through their psychosocial programs.

Traditional treatment units, in contrast, are organized like medical hospitals for the physically ill. The environment is merely the place where treatment occurs. Staff administer biomedical interventions—mostly psychotropic drugs since the mid-1950s—and individual and group psychosocial procedures as more or less discrete entities. Programs coordinate the discrete treatments—with no overriding set of psychosocial principles and procedures. The environment provides supportive care. Here treatment is in rather than by or through the unitwide program.

Historically, residential facilities for the "defective" and "insane" were akin to dungeons and torture chambers. At the close of the eighteenth century, Philippe Pinel, a French physician, and William H. Tuke, an English Quaker, were the best known facility directors to advocate humanitarian reform through "moral" treatment. Technical components of later programs were missing, but moral treatment reflected similar concepts for normalization of both environmental and client functioning. That approach dominated progressive practice in the Western world for the first half of the nineteenth century—with recovery rates comparing favorably to modern outcome statistics.

Moral treatment declined from 1850 onward because of ideological and economic factors. Success in conquering many physical diseases led to a somatic defect conception of all problems and an emphasis on nosology. Mental hospitals became large, overcrowded, custodial warehouses for patients awaiting discovery of a cure. Surgery, shock, and other, often bizarre, somatic treatments prevailed. Untrained attendants, the aide culture, and institutionalism became prominent. Twentieth-century exposés and calls for reform regularly reflected conditions reminiscent of the eighteenth century.

The therapeutic community approach represented a return to moral treatment philosophy following World War II. Maxwell Jones, a British social psychiatrist, introduced the concept, and it became so popular by the mid-1960s that most facilities in English-speaking countries claimed to have milieu or therapeutic community units. Descriptions of these programs usually professed popular attitudes and values but without specifying operational procedures—and with no empirical data. Several clinical scientists and practitioners in the 1960s examined evidence and articulated aspects of the approach. Clarifying works were written by John and Elaine Cumming, a psychiatrist-sociologist team, by several social psychiatrists (eg., Kenneth L. Artiss, Marshall Edelson, Alan M. Kraft, Harry A. Wilmer, John K. Wing), and by social and clinical psychologists (e.g., Paul M. Binner, Robert B. Ellsworth, G. W. "Bill" Fairweather, Gordon L. Paul).

These writers explicated the essentials of the milieu/therapeutic community approach. Although no definition enjoys universal acceptance, a requisite is use of unitwide procedures to enlist clientele as agents of change for themselves and their peers. This usually involves high levels of staff-client interaction, group activities, and goal-directed communications for responsible performance, involvement, group cohesiveness, and problem solving. Social pressure is the major source of motivation. Most programs use a governmental structure and downplay the illness model and patient role, although psychotropic drug use ranges from none to routine. Program content varies with the clientele and with the theoretical orientation of program leaders, which ranges from psychodynamic, ego-analytic, or gestalt to rational-emotive or social-interpersonal.

The social learning approach was developed by American clinical and experimental psychologists in the 1960s from laboratory-based principles of learning and performance. Teodoro Ayllon introduced the token economy to extend operant principles to unitwide programs by use of special cards or chips (tokens), vested with reward value. Clients earn, spend, and lose tokens to motivate learning. Ayllon and Nathan H. Azrin reported studies of the first full token economy for female inpatients in 1965, on a closed state hospital ward. Jack H. Atthowe and Leonard Krasner soon followed with an open-ward program for male veterans. More than two dozen facilities in North America, England, and Australia initiated token economies by the end of the decade.

Clinical scientists also extended cognitive, social, and associative learning principles to residential settings, with and without token economies. By the early 1970s, the social learning approach incorporated them from analyses of empirical evidence by a number of clinical psychologists (e.g., Henry E. Adams, Albert Bandura, Richard R. Bootzin, Gerald C. Davidson, Cyril M. Franks, Arnold P. Goldstein, Frederick H. Kanfer, Alan E. Kazdin, Leonard Krasner, Gordon L. Paul, and Leonard P. Ullman) and behavioral psychiatrists (e.g., Robert P. Liberman and Arnold M. Ludwig).

Social learning programs typically use a tiered token economy structure to schedule response-contingent social and material reinforcers for use by all staff with all clientele. Ongoing assessment is required to maintain precision and consistency. Procedures for increasing skills (e.g., modeling, shaping, cognitive training) and for reducing excesses (e.g., graduated exposure, response costs) are used during ordinary activities, as well as in classes, meetings, and therapy groups. Content varies with the clientele, but it regularly incorporates generalization training, ongoing evaluation, and new empirically supported treatments. Most programs downplay the illness model, patient role, and the use of psychotropic drugs.

Empirical evidence shows superior efficacy, effectiveness, and cost efficiency for treatment of chronically and severely disabled clientele with the social learning approach. For less extensively disabled and acutely admitted clientele, both social learning and specific variations of the therapeutic community are better than traditional programs. Comparative studies are needed to establish the relative effectiveness of specific programs. This requires knowledge of what psychosocial programs actually provide and what staff actually do—not just how programs are labeled. New assessment technologies, such as the Computerized TSBC/SRIC Planned-Access Observational Information System (see Mariotto, Paul, & Licht, 1995), can furnish such objective information.

Ideological and economic factors again ruled after the late 1970s. Psychotropic drugs, remedicalization of psychiatry, brain-disease concepts of schizophrenia, and crisis units with community-based care all displaced interest in psychosocial program effectiveness. The census in mental hospitals was reduced by deinstitutionalization, but it increased in prisons and nursing homes and on city streets. Readmission rates tripled, and traditional programs were predominant.

At the close of the twentieth century, economic factors appear to be returning program effectiveness to center stage through managed-care funding. Managed care requires facilities to validate programs and document outcomes. Ultimately, it should force them to use only those that work. Environmental programs are the bedrock of evidence-based practice in residential settings.

Bibliography

Gunderson, J. G., Will, O. A., & Mosher, L. R. (Eds.). (1983). *Principles and practice of milieu therapy.* New York: Aronson. Includes expositions on environmental treatment by major practitioners and clinical scientists. Extensive bibliographies of the milieu/therapeutic community literature.

Johnson, D. L. (Ed.). (1990). *Service needs of the seriously mentally ill: Training implications for psychology.* Washington, DC: American Psychological Association. Report of a national conference. Includes articles on the most promising treatments for the seriously mentally ill, as well as recommendations for implementation and training. Likely available only through university libraries.

Kazdin, A. E. (1982). The token economy: A decade later. *Journal of Applied Behavior Analysis, 15,* 431–445. Update of earlier reviews. Together, they illustrate the wide range of application of token economies with different populations in different settings.

Mariotto, M. J., Paul, G. L., & Licht, M. H. (1995). Assessment in inpatient and residential settings. In J. N. Butcher (Ed.), *Clinical personality assessment: Practical approaches* (pp. 435–459). New York: Oxford University Press. Includes complete references to the development and use of the Computerized TSBC/SRIC Planned-Access Observational Information System. Also illustrative case examples.

Paul, G. L., & Lentz, R. J. (1977). *Psychosocial treatment of chronic mental patients: Milieu vs. social-learning programs.* Cambridge, MA: Harvard University Press. The primary reference for comparative scientific investigation of the major approaches to psychosocial treatment programs in residential settings with severely disabled clientele. Provides details of a 6-year study and comprehensive staff training manuals for social learning and milieu/therapeutic community programs. Also includes thorough discussion of the several legal and regulatory problems in the area, with proposals for change. Currently out of print and available only in university, medical school, and hospital libraries. A revised edition is planned for 1999/2000.

Paul, G. L., & Menditto, A. A. (1992). Effectiveness of inpatient treatment programs for mentally ill adults in public psychiatric facilities. *Applied and Preventive Psychology: Current Scientific Perspectives, 1,* 41–63. Most thorough recent review of the literature. Includes a summary of national statistics, conceptual and research principles needed to interpret the literature, and detailed descriptions of the major approaches to residential treatment.

Paul, G. L., Stuve, P., & Cross, J. V. (1997). Real-world inpatient programs: Shedding some light. *Applied and Preventive Psychology: Current Scientific Perspectives, 6,* 195–206. A critique of residential treatment approaches that the authors view as limited and misleading. Notes the increasing importance of empirically based evidence, with references to this burgeoning literature. Gives the most detailed summary of the contents of the Paul and Lentz (1977) monograph.

Paul, G. L., Stuve, P., & Menditto, A. A. (1997). Social-learning program (with token economy) for adult psychiatric inpatients. *Clinical Psychologist, 50,* 14–17. A concise summary of the treatment program, supportive evidence, and implementation and training sites. Part of the series *Empirically Validated Psychological Treatments,* edited by William C. Sanderson, for a task force of the Division of Clinical Psychology, American Psychological Association.

Ullmann, L. P. (1967). *Institution and outcome: A comparative study of psychiatric hospitals.* New York: Pergamon Press. An excellent exposition on moral treatment and the history of residential facilities. Provides an environmental perspective on the impact of institutions and data on factors influencing the comparative effectiveness of Veterans Administration mental hospitals.

Gordon L. Paul

MILITARY CULTURE refers to the attitudes, beliefs, and behaviors of people in uniformed military service to their countries, who, along with their families, participate in cohesive workplace organizational structures fostering a common "military mind-set." They possess inculcated learned, shared lifestyle expectations, develop camaraderie, esprit de corps, group cohesiveness, and a set of idealistic honorable tenets that make up the glue that hinges military people together with common bonds. Military culture includes a fraternal comradeship in arms, passed on from generation to generation, and has much to do with an array of symbolic unifying identifications associated with the wearing of military uniforms in highly regarded public service.

Military Forces as Organizational Entities

Historically, around the globe, military forces have been constituted by governmental leaders to serve as organizational instruments of defense—of the homeland, a nation's boundaries, and its people—against aggression from neighboring adversaries or enemies. Military organizations also serve governments in power with additional backup forces to augment internal police control of a country's own populace, especially in times of internal civil strife, uprising, or threats of insurrection and turmoil. Some nation-state rulers wear military uniforms in public as a visible sign of power while they govern with absolute authority and rely on loyal uniformed armies as constabulary instruments of control over their own citizenry.

Military forces are used as offensive instruments too. Nation-state rulers employ armies to attack their neighbors and exert the might of one country over another, and in an expansionary way to invade neighboring territories with intent to take over and garner additional lands and peoples as new acquisitions. Powerful conquerors redraw and divide national boundaries by treaties enacted at the end of military conquests.

There are also mercenary military forces, "armies for hire or loan" sponsored to assist with military intervention, to fight not for their own, but for someone else's homeland. Such armies conjure additional aspects of shared military culture unique to their particular circumstances. Established in 1831, the French Foreign Legion enlisted nationals of any country other than France to preserve order in French overseas possessions; its mercenaries fought with distinction in numerous wars and conflicts over the past 150-plus years. To expand their interests in Africa, the Soviets sponsored and sent a mercenary force of Cuban soldiers to intervene in a 1980s civil war in Angola.

Special Characteristics of Military Organizations

Military forces traditionally provided the epitome example of large hierarchical organizations. Indeed, many twentieth-century U.S. and European industrial organizations modeled themselves after the successfully employed hierarchical structure of the military. However, because military missions are substantially different from civilian business requirements, military organizations differ significantly from industry. Consequently, military culture is uniquely different from that of most industrial organizations, and substantially so from most other segments of society.

The core capability and primary role of military organizations is to engage in combat: to conduct war. Images of the military are synonymous with images of combat, defining much of the raison d'etre and setting the basis for much of military culture. Military organizations are made up of assemblages of people, historically, predominantly men, armed with the weapons of the day and who have as their charter a mission to protect, defend, or conquer on behalf of the rulers and/or the citizenry they represent. As institutions comprised primarily of men, military culture has been shaped by men, and thus soldiering has traditionally been viewed as a masculine role, through images of the combat masculine warrior (CMW). Thus, the professions of making war, providing for defense, or engaging in combat have common fraternal goals and purpose in society. They are defined as men's work and are accompanied by a deeply entrenched "cult of masculinity" with masculine norms, values, and lifestyles that pervade military organizations and military culture (see Moskos, 1970; Dunivin, 1994).

Modern military organizations are structured around combat activities—army combat regiments or divisions, air force fighter wings or squadrons, and naval submarines or aircraft carrier battle groups. Military services organize and train themselves around their combat roles, distinguishing between combat arms and support activities (Dunivin, 1994). Configured into classical hierarchical structures, military organizations establish strict vertical command, control, and reporting relationships among the members.

Around the globe, many military forces are lead by a cadre of career military commissioned officers who are appointed to positions of management authority and are responsible to direct the activities of those to be lead, usually conscripts, or the troops (soldiers, sailors, marines, and airmen—uniformed enlisted men and women). Ratios of from 10 to 50 troops per officer are common. Military officers determine the strategic and tactical combat plans, make the major decisions and choices in battle, and point the way for the troops to accomplish military missions. The enlisted troops are traditionally the production-line personnel force of any military organization. The troops are led, directed, and/or managed by their officers while participating under the direct supervision of senior enlisted persons referred to as noncommissioned officers (NCOs). Traditionally, the troops threw the spears, shot the arrows, and fired the muskets, cannons, or other weapons, or engaged in hand-to-hand combat with the enemy. In armored cavalry units, the lieutenant, an officer, was issued a saber with which to point the way; his horse-mounted soldiers were given rifles to shoot at enemies. The troops also cared for the horses, drove most of the vehicles, enacted most of the logistics, and accomplished resupply functions and other combat support work.

Although the roles in some of the world's military forces are becoming less clear-cut with advances in technology, it is still true that the troops are the blue-collar workers of typical military organizations. In most military forces they are predominately young enlisted men (in some countries women as well) in the age range of 18 to 30 years, with compulsory service obligations ranging from about 2 to 4 years. During war, however, terms of military service may be extended indefinitely to meet the needs of the country; for example, some Vietnamese soldiers were indentured for 20 to 25 years of continued warfare from the 1950s to the 1970s. Some military forces consist predominately of volunteers (e.g., the United States in 1973 replaced its conscript army with an "all-volunteer force," a successful 27-year social experiment). The duration of individual service for military volunteers, officers, or enlisted personnel ranges from a term of enlistment of about 3 years up to 25- to 30-year terms, during which career soldiers, "lifers," dedicate most of their productive years to serving their countries.

By military tradition, in most countries there is a clear social and workplace demarcation between the officers and the troops. For centuries, officers in positions of military authority or leadership have been drawn from society's more influential citizenry (gentility or nobility). In some developing nations, many military leaders have been appointed, selected, or voted into their positions of authority because of their social stature or civic influence or have bought positions with money or by granting political favors. The world over, military officers generally have more formal education than their troops, but they do not always possess sufficient military leadership or technical training, nor have all of them been fully inculcated into the military values or cultural system. Officers must gain that through subsequent formal military training or via on-the-job practical experience leading troops in the field.

The large numbers of troops who make up "those who are led" are usually drawn from a cross-section of society, tend to have less formal education than their leaders, and even may be members of ethnic minorities within their country and may therefore have language differences from the officers who lead them (e.g., forces in countries of the former Soviet Union).

Traditionally, all military members are expected to strictly adhere to stringent disciplinary rules, to be willing to follow the directions and orders of those who are leaders by virtue of their position, and to give fierce internal loyalty to senior leaders and to the organization. Soldiers are to do things in strict accordance with established procedures to enact the orderliness and predictability of behavior that becomes necessary for groups to accomplish assigned missions during the inherent chaos anticipated in combat.

In many military societies, it has usually been a contention that officers should not socialize, fraternize, or become emotionally involved with their troops. A certain social-psychological distance is expected. The relationship in the workplace is to be built upon a mutual respect for the role the officer is to play. One day, the officer may be required to direct troops in combat, order them to kill the enemy, and in the process put themselves and others at risk of life and limb. This separateness demands that a good officer exude military technical competence and respectful leadership toward his or her troops so they will follow successfully in combat.

Military Symbolism Contributes to Its Culture

There is great symbolism given to wearing uniform clothing that distinguishes members of a military group from society at large and from other military groups. Rank insignia displayed on their uniforms connotes the job position and status of military personnel. The styles and types of uniform, coats of arms, body armor, distinctive headgear, unit identity sleeve patches, colorful award ribbons, and campaign medals pinned on the chest of military dress uniforms serve as signs of their wearer's degree of commitment and success in participating in military culture. Public military ceremonies and parades, marching honor guards to carry the colors, flags, and battle streamers, the erection of commemorative war memorial monuments, and the dedication of national cemeteries honoring those who defended the homeland are all signs of social recognition of a military culture.

Military Justice

Most military forces employ their own systems of discipline and justice. Often the decision-making authority for military justice is seated in the commander of a military unit itself and is not subject to much scrutiny by outside influences except when governments that empower military commanders anticipate that abuses have occurred and investigate them. The U.S. military system of justice draws from the U.S. Constitution and public law in the form of a disciplinary code called the Uniformed Code of Military Justice (UCMJ). Under the UCMJ, U.S. military laws resemble those of the civilian justice system, but in some arenas, such as governing following military orders and some rules for daily living, they are considerably more strict. The UCMJ consists of a very detailed legal system with punishments and trials by courts-martial. It resembles the eighteenth-century British military court system.

Military Culture and Leadership

Organizational cultures begin with leaders who impose their own values and assumptions on a group. Thus, military leaders create and manage military organizational culture. In Organizational Culture and Leadership (1992), Edgar H. Schein assessed that if the group is successful and the assumptions come to be taken for granted, the evolving culture defines for later members what kinds of leadership are acceptable—and the culture then defines the leadership. The group makes certain assumptions, and when the group encounters adaptive difficulties, as its environment changes, leadership then steps outside the culture to start evolutionary change processes that are more adaptive—the essence and ultimate challenge of military leadership.

Military culture goes back as far as the time when men first banded together in groups for security, defense, and, if necessary, to fight other groups. Leaders of such groups began recruiting new members and gave them a set of uniform clothing, provided them with food rations, crude housing, and especially a set of centrally issued tools or weapons with which to work. Then they inculcated a certain discipline, which included military attitudes, values, behaviors, and expectations in the troops who followed their leaders. Eventually the troops became acculturated to the military culture of the organization.

Military culture is the result of a complex group learning process that is influenced by leader behavior. Customs and rituals that evolve over a particular military organization's history, and the climate and practices that develop around the leaders' handling of people, define a unit's military culture. It refers to the espoused values and credo of each military unit.

Almost 2 years into America's revolution from England (1776), George Washington's Continental Army was made up largely of a loose collection of soldiers mixed from 13 colonial armies. Each group was accomplishing some form of military drill in a combination of French-, British-, and Prussian-style military training. At Benjamin Franklin's invitation, Baron von Steuben, a Prussian army officer, joined Washington at Valley Forge in March 1778 and began helping Washington formally implement uniform military drill and training to instill orderliness, discipline, and unity as the Continental Army prepared to take on the well-trained British army. A year later, Steuben's "Regulations for the Order and Discipline of the Troops of the United States" was enacted (Shilts, 1993). These regulations served as a big influence in determining the tenets of U.S. military culture, which carry over to the present.

A second major contributor to today's U.S. military culture was the Continental Army's adaptation of portions of the eighteenth-century British military officer corps code. The code was based on the code of chivalry of feudal times, a collection of aristocratic principles, values, and traditions encompassing the British officer's concept of honor (Matthews, 1998). The four basic elements of the code were: officers fight for traditional military glory; they are gentlemen; they owe personal loyalty to their commander; and they are members of a cohesive, self-regulating brotherhood (Janowitz, 1960, 1971). General Washington himself indicated that a prerequisite for good officership necessitated men of gentility and character, activated by principles of honor and a spirit of enterprise.

An Honor Code Begets Military Culture

For over two centuries, the influence of the gentlemen's honor code has informed all U.S. military organizations in the system of values that make up the crux of present-day military culture. The U.S. military honor code serves as a positive motivational set of principles for U.S. military officers and enlisted persons alike as they become acculturated to an appeal to patriotism, professional pride, aspirations for excellence, and positive character development.

The U.S. military's officer's code takes on national historical importance and can be fairly labeled the nucleus of the country's military cultural code. General George Washington's high standards of personal honor, discipline, personal sacrifice, leadership, and complete devotion to his mission, formed the foundation of the code. Other great men in our nation's history—generals like Ulysses S. Grant, Robert E. Lee, John J. Pershing, Dwight D. Eisenhower, Douglas MacArthur, Omar N.

Bradley, and more recent counterparts, William C. Westmoreland, Creighton Abrams, H. Norman Schwarzkopf, and Colin Powell—whose names are household words of respect and trust, embraced this code while adding to the code's strength (see Crocker, 1990, p. 31). The U.S. military officer's code can be fairly labeled the nucleus of the country's military cultural code.

Personal loyalty to one's immediate superiors in the military chain of command remains a strongly felt military ideal. Even more so is the notion of loyalty to one's teammates and comrades in arms in the same unit. Unit cohesiveness, that sense of solidarity, of almost filial devotion and loyalty to those who have trained together as members of a team, obligates soldiers to perform to the best of their ability and to fight to the death to protect one another in combat—as U.S. marines are prone to cry, "You don't die for an ideal, you die for your fellow marines!"

In the U.S. military, obedience to authority as a high military ideal pertains to obeying the lawful orders of superiors, but even more so to the subordination of that obedience to allegiance to the U.S. Constitution and the laws that flow therefrom. From this flows the conceptual ideal of civilian control of the military structure, a U.S. expectation that the corporate military organization subjects itself to the directions of constitutionally designated government officials, especially the president of the United States, who is designated as the commander-in-chief.

A statement of U.S. military ideals is provided in the book *Armed Forces Officer* (1988) based on military historian S. L. A. Marshall's writings in 1950 and 1975. It was conceived "to provide a foundation of thought, conduct, standards, and duty for officers," built around the notion that officers are gentlemen who exhibit good moral character, courtesy, and cultivation.

Most officers and enlisted personnel alike, especially those serving a military career, learn to adopt the military cultural high ground in describing their affiliation with the uniformed service they have assimilated for themselves. In 1967, Harold K. Johnson, chief of staff of the U.S. Army, said:

> There is no more important vocation or profession than serving in the defense of the nation—not just any nation, but a nation that is prepared to provide the dignity to man that God intended—our nation. All the benefits that our citizens enjoy exist behind the defense barrier that is manned by the members of the military establishment. No greater honor can be given to any man than the privilege of serving the cause of freedom. (cited in Crocker, 1990, p. 13)

Studies of Military Culture

Research on military culture by that name is relatively dispersed, as the topic is often couched in a swath of behavioral and social science studies examining more specific, perhaps even broader issues (e.g., new leadership paradigms). Only since World War II have behavioral scientists studied in earnest the relationships between military organizations, war, and their effects on society at large. A breakthrough is attributable to Morris Janowitz, an American sociologist, who in his *Professional Soldier: A Social and Political Portrait* (1960) applied sociological concepts to study military organizations in modern societies in new ways. In 1961, Janowitz founded and for 20 years thereafter closely guided the Inter-University Seminar on Armed Forces and Society (IUS) to demonstrate the viability and utility of conducting empirical research on military institutions from a sociological perspective (Burk, 1993). The IUS book *The New Military* (1964) summarized ongoing work of social scientists. By the late 1960s, the IUS broadened its roster of university-based scholars to include multidisciplinary participants from civilian universities and the military in such varied disciplines as political science, psychology, history, and sociology. Hundreds of social scientists around the globe now count themselves as members and participants. The IUS supports empirical research to clarify how trends in civilian society affect military organizations and how military leaders in turn respond and react to these developments (Burk, 1993), including how they adapt social changes to adjustments in military culture. The interdisciplinary journal of the IUS, *Armed Forces and Society*, publishing its twenty-sixth volume in 1999, presents articles from many disciplines and reports a variety of perspectives on military communities in countries around the globe. It serves as an excellent sociopsychological resource on military cultures.

Military Psychology, a bimonthly journal of the American Psychological Association, serves as a secondary source for material related to military culture. For more closely allied U.S. sources, retired and current military leaders routinely publish articles on military leadership, goals, ideals, and values to promulgate present-day military culture to the U.S. forces. Such publications include military service association and trade journals and magazines (e.g., *Military Review, Parameters, Soldiers*, and the Association of the U.S. Army's magazine, *National Defense*), and four weekly newspapers (the *Army Times, Navy Times, Air Force Times*, and the *Defense News*).

Military forces routinely perform pulse-taking self-assessments by collecting psychosocial and command climate surveys, and performing focus group interviews and other studies of their own personnel. They obtain measures of the degree of training readiness, troop morale, unit cohesion, and individual willingness to pursue a military career by reenlisting after initial terms of enlistment are complete. All of these assess topics deemed to contribute to military culture. Service-specific studies are accomplished by in-house military research personnel (e.g., by the U.S. Army Research Institute for Behavioral and Social Sciences, the Naval Personnel R&D Center, the U.S. Army Medical Research and Materiel Command's several laboratories, or the USAF Armstrong laboratory). Sometimes university-based behavioral science contractor teams conduct the surveys.

Military Minorities and Changing Cultural Dynamics

It is the challenge of military leadership to adjust military culture, slightly altering it to adjust to social changes. A part of military culture teaches that soldiers who work together on a common mission tend to develop a working relationship that leads to unit cohesiveness. Troops develop an attitude of being together, having a common unit and individual purpose, and accepting discipline for the common good. Military leadership must adapt social preferences for egalitarianism and diversity in the workplace to its traditional military culture. The challenges listed below are prevalent not only in the U.S. military, but within most other Westernized military forces as well.

In the journal article "Military Culture: Change and Continuity" (1994) K. O. Dunivin points out that for 150-plus years the U.S. military had been a traditional, conservative, homogeneous white male force, with masculine values and norms and exclusionary laws and policies. Previous U.S. laws segregated Blacks in units commanded by White officers, limited the number of servicewomen in uniform, and prohibited women from performing duties aboard combat ships or aircraft. As an extension of such laws, military policies excluded women from combat-related roles, including flying, infantry, armor, and sea duty (Dunivin, 1994). In addition, participation in a homosexual lifestyle was always forbidden, as it violated the combat male warrior image. Such "conduct unbecoming" is punishable under the Uniformed Code of Military Justice.

Some of the most prominent military forces in history incorporated large numbers of troops that were of diverse ethnic backgrounds, and often the mix of them was a makeup different from the officers and NCOs who lead them. This was apparent in the Soviet army, in which minorities and ethnic mixes were of subservient status to the native Russian officers. The U.S. military maintained a separateness of races (Black and White) long after the 1860s and the U.S. Civil War, even until some years after President Truman's 1948 Executive Order 9981, which called for racial equality in the U.S. armed forces and integration of the forces. Racial integration of the U.S. forces was slowly implemented during the early 1950s. During the Korean War, it was still common to witness a White officer and perhaps a White NCO or two in charge of a predominately Black enlisted company in the U.S. Army.

The U.S. military has become the role model for racial integration for the rest of society at large. The military is certainly the first large governmental organization in which Black leaders were placed in charge of White employees and that in wide measure made it work successfully. During the early 1990s, the integration of Blacks to obtain somewhat equal status to that of Whites in the U.S. military improved significantly under the all-volunteer force program. In the late 1990s, it is common to see higher ranking African American military personnel, with nearly full acceptance in the culture, successfully in command and supervisory positions over White and other non-Black military personnel. Indeed, during the mid-to-late 1990s several Black male officers successfully attained the rank of four-star generals. The integration of Hispanic soldiers is now under way with much less fanfare and apparently with slow progress.

Women in Combat?

The U.S. military increased the integration of women into all four branches of the armed forces during the 1980s and 1990s, to a point where in the late 1990s the approximate number of women in the active-duty force numbers ranged from about 12 to 14% of each of the four services. The influx of additional numbers of women was prompted in part by social pressures for equality of job opportunities and by the need to recruit larger numbers of intellectually capable soldiers to operate more technical systems at a time when the available number of post–World War II baby-boom recruits was decreasing.

Because of the fluidity of the modern battlefield and how combat missions have changed, the "battlefront line" has become blurred. Consequently, women dispersed throughout the force are now more likely to find themselves in actual combat whether personnel assignment policies permit it or not. In 1991, Congress repealed laws barring women from duties aboard combat aircraft and ships. In 1994, Les Aspin, the secretary of defense, rescinded exclusionary military policy by directing the services to open assignments on combat aircraft and aboard combat ships to women. As for land combat, it is Defense Department policy that women soldiers are not to be assigned to units below brigade level in which the primary mission is ground combat. Therefore, women are currently barred from assignment to army and Marine Corps direct ground combat units. The prevailing question of women's rights advocates concerns whether or not women should be allowed to compete for front-line infantry positions or any other position for which they are suited, that is, they should be able to compete on the same level as men. They would also advocate retaining high standards, recognizing that not all women would qualify but that some would qualify and therefore should be permitted to compete for those positions.

One combat male warrior contention regarding the inclusion or exclusion of women in traditional men's jobs is that many women would not compete evenly on the basis of the physical strength and endurance requirements for participating in many military jobs and certainly many arduous tasks. As part of the Defense Women's Health Research Program (Institute of Medicine, 1995), some physiological, biomechanical, sports medicine, physical fitness, and occupational medicine specialists (e.g., at the U.S. Army Research Institute of Environmental Medicine) have been conducting women's health and fitness research to resolve some of the concerns. Early research results point out that the selection of some women on the basis of physical abilities, combined with progressive physical- and skill-development training programs, permits some military women to meet the physical strength and endurance requirements expected of most soldiers in many physically demanding jobs. With proper attention to the human-engineering design of military equipment, and materials and procedures to accommodate the particular needs of women, many tools and workplaces can be redesigned to assist most soldiers, but especially to meet the particular needs of military women. An example of this is the design studies of backpack load-carrying equipment to redistribute individual soldier loads and to reconfigure carrying methods for patient litter-carrying devices, which would help the large numbers of women who gravitate to military medical support jobs in the field.

With regard to the deployment of women into combat arenas, the U.S. military had several hundred women in ground combat in Operation Just Cause in Panama in 1989 and deployed well over 40,000 women to the combat zones of the 1991 Persian Gulf War. As for participating in so-called peacekeeping operations, in the early to the mid-1990s, 1,000 American military women worked in Somalia, 1,200 in Haiti, and over 5,000 in Bosnia. Notably, by 1998 three of the four U.S. military services promoted a woman to the flag rank of three stars.

As a result of these changes, the U.S. military is today a more socially diverse force whose military women and minorities perform many nontraditional jobs formerly performed primarily by white men. The services conduct training to sensitize soldiers to racial, ethnic, and women's issues. They work hard to eliminate prejudice in the workplace, and they punish gender harassment and racist and sexist offenders (Dunivin, 1994).

Homosexuals and Military Culture

Another social egalitarian issue in the 1990s that necessitates changes in military culture concerns society's recent trend toward greater acceptance of gays and homosexuals. Thoughtful discussion on all sides of the topic (see Herek, Jobe, & Carney, 1996; Shilts, 1993) at least triggered recognition that homosexuals have served admirably in the U.S. military (albeit closeted) since the Revolutionary War.

In 1993, President Bill Clinton attempted to end the policy of exclusion of lesbians and gay men from military service and to end discrimination on the basis of sexual orientation. He succeeded at least in halting the practice of asking new recruits about their sexual orientation, and he suspended discharge proceedings based solely on sexual orientation. A compromise policy, but still more one of exclusion than inclusion, was reached in 1993, when a "don't ask, don't tell, don't pursue" approach pertaining to sexual orientation was adopted. Under its terms, personnel would not be asked about their sexual orientation and would not be discharged simply for being gay. However, engaging in sexual conduct with a member of the same sex would still constitute grounds for discharge from military service. Obviously this policy has not worked well, because the number of people discharged for being gay increased each year from 1994 to 1998.

As society's egalitarian workplace preferences become clearer, it is likely that military rules and the acceptance of gays within the forces will be as well. This issue is still being worked out, and there is still a struggle ahead on this sensitive topic.

Other Changes Influencing Military Culture

Three additional social changes presently impact military culture: military families, operations other than war, and information management and information technology. Family members (spouses and children of active duty personnel) have always been a big part of military culture, at least in the United States. However, since the advent of an all-volunteer force in the U.S. military in 1973, family issues are even more apparent. In the mid-1990s, almost 40% of U.S. military troops are married. Along with the spouses come accompanying families, some with young children, some being single-parent households and some extended to include aging parents. Considerations of ensuring adequate family housing and family support systems have taken on paramount importance in sustaining U.S. military forces.

Support for military families is especially pertinent during times of high operational tempo (OPTEMPO), when military members are deployed for long periods overseas or away from home. The popular slogan, "The U.S. military takes care of its own," brings with it real

resource, logistics, and personnel assignment challenges for military leadership. Happily, with the assistance of civilian defense leaders and the U.S. Congress, these issues are continually being addressed. As these many families become acculturated, they too have their own impact on military culture, which is continually changing in recognition of the changing force makeup.

The late 1990s brought about a greater frequency of what the U.S. Army presently calls operations other than war (OOW), consisting of some nontraditional military noncombat missions, including peacekeeping, humanitarian and nation-building work, as well as anti–drug running interdiction and antiterrorist missions. If the combat masculine warrior culture is to be preserved, it now must share a softer, almost feminine side of the warrior mentality by helping people in times of need rather than killing them because they are enemies. The sensitivities required are different, and so is the training, adoption, and assimilation into the military culture of new warrior peacemaking approaches to mission accomplishment.

The third consideration is that of information management and information technology, highlighting the rapid advances of the age of electronics and information technologies, as they are adapted to military systems and military life in general. The information explosion offers unique innovative possibilities for the use of high-tech systems on the digitized battlefield. Technological changes could completely revise the techniques for rapid battle-related decision making even by junior military personnel in frontline foxholes and even throughout the chain of military command and control. New paradigms of communication, command, and control are now in the making. These have the potential to dramatically impact military culture in terms of who does what to whom and when on the digitized battlefields to come (Reimer, 1998).

Military Culture Is Alive, Well, and Adaptive

Gradually, social changes become infused into military organizations either by law or new policies or through general assimilation by military members. Military culture, with all its customs and honorable traditions, is therefore alive and well. It adapts where it can and where and when it should. Military culture must serve our citizens who proudly wear their uniforms in service to their nation.

[See also Military Service.]

Bibliography

Burk, J. (1993). Morris Janowitz and the origins of sociological research on armed forces and society. *Armed Forces and Society, 19*(2) 167–185.
Crocker, L. P. (1990). *Army officer's guide* (45th ed.). Har-

risburg, PA: Stackpole Books. A reference manual containing hints on building and living a career as an officer in the U.S. Army.

Dunivin, K. O. (1994). Military culture: Change and continuity. *Armed Forces and Society, 20,* 531–547.

Herek, G. M., Jobe, J. B., & Carney, R. M. (Eds.). (1996). *Out in force: Sexual orientation and the military.* Chicago: University of Chicago Press. Psychological scientists address many issues pertinent to the integration of diversity—blacks, women, and homosexuals—into the U.S. military force structure.

Institute of Medicine. (1995). *Recommendations for research on the health of military women.* Washington, DC: National Academy Press. A National Academy of Sciences committee review the knowledge base in 1995 and make recommendations for military medical research requirements concerning the full integration of women into the U.S. military forces.

Inter-University Seminar on Armed Forces and Society. (1964). *The new military.* New York: Russell Sage Foundation. Summarizes the work of social scientists as it pertains to the military before 1964.

Janowitz, M. (1960, 1971). *The professional soldier: A social and political portrait.* New York: Free Press. A social-psychological portrait of professional soldiering, especially in the United States, which includes coverage of many topics directly related to military culture.

Matthews, L. J. (1998). The evolution of American military ideals. *Military Review, 78*(1) 51–61.

Moskos, C. C. (1970). *The American enlisted man.* New York: Russell Sage. A comprehensive sociopsychological perspective on being an enlisted man in the U.S. military.

Reimer, D. J. (1998). Developing great leaders in turbulent times. *Military Review, 78,* 5–12.

Schein, E. H. (1992). *Organizational culture and leadership* (2nd ed.). San Francisco: Jossey-Bass.

Shilts, R. (1993). *Conduct unbecoming: Gays and lesbians in the U.S. military.* New York: St. Martin's Press. A historical treatise on the involvement of homosexuals in the military, particularly the U.S. military, since the Revolutionary War; comprehensive coverage of pertinent legal issues too.

U.S. Department of the Army. (1960). *Army leadership: Field manual (FM) 22-100, and character development XXI* (draft revision of FM 22-100, 1998). Washington, DC: Author. The U.S. Army bible (doctrine) on leadership. A training manual.

U.S. Department of Defense. (1950, 1975, 1988). *The armed forces officer.* Washington, DC: U.S. Department of Defense. An officer's how-to manual, provided by the Department of Defense.

Gerald P. Krueger

MILITARY PSYCHOLOGY. The domain of military psychology includes selection and classification, training, human factors engineering, organizational (individual and group) behavior, leadership and team effectiveness, social and clinical psychology, and the study of environmental stressors. It also encompasses professional concerns, training requirements, and professional organizations associated with the interests of military psychologists.

Military psychology is described by Driskell and Olmstead (1989) as being "defined neither by a common set of techniques (as is experimental psychology) nor by a common set of problems (as is developmental psychology) but rather by the area or context of application—the military . . . military psychology is the application of psychology to military needs" (p. 43). It represents the use of all psychology disciplines to address organizational (military) needs. The *Handbook of Military Psychology* (Gal & Mangelsdorff, 1991) documents the variety of applications and specialties represented in military psychology. The application of psychological principles within a military environment defines the boundaries of military psychology. Understanding the development, growth, and examination of psychological principles in military settings to meet military requirements is fundamental to recognizing the contributions of military psychology to the evolution of the science and practice of psychology.

As psychology emerged as a discipline in the early twentieth century, American psychologists were curious about mental measurement and the scientific personnel management movement to enhance worker productivity. In 1916, with the war ongoing in Europe, the National Academy of Sciences created the National Research Council to organize support for the national defense of America. With the U.S. entry into World War I in 1917, the United States was faced with assimilating millions of civilians into the armed services. The application of psychological principles to the needs of the military created the discipline of military psychology in the United States.

A committee of psychologists, under the direction of Robert M. Yerkes, then president of the American Psychological Association (APA), met to discuss how psychology could assist in the national defense effort (Yerkes, 1918). The need to quickly classify the intellectual levels of large numbers of troops was the problem (personnel selection and classification of soldier qualifications and abilities). A successful program of group intelligence tests was developed for the armed services: the Army Alpha (for classification of literates) and Army Beta (for classification of illiterates) tests resulted. The assessment procedures led to the appropriate screening, classification, and placement of personnel into military assignments. The principles served as the model for most group intelligence tests developed later for both military and civilian applications.

Other issues addressed by psychologists to support the defense efforts of the United States during World War I included training needs; assessment of opinions, troop morale, and assimilation into the armed services; tests to assess skills such as leadership and flying aptitude; assessment of emotional instability; and measurement of human performance. Psychologists developed tests to group personnel according to ability to learn. Neuropsychiatric patients were evaluated to determine fitness to return to duty. Psychologists contributed to the development of methods and procedures to sustain and improve operational effectiveness. The U.S. military adopted mental measurement procedures to help in manpower management. Psychology's unique contributions to the defense of the nation had been recognized.

With the end of World War I, efforts in military psychology diminished as the armed forces of the world demobilized. During the 1920s and 1930s, there was a lull in the practice of military psychology. At the beginning of World War II, the military reestablished a psychological research program. The Army General Classification Test (AGCT) was developed to replace the earlier Army Alpha test. The AGCT was administered to more than 12 million men during World War II.

In addition to the issues addressed during World War I (personnel selection, classification, placement, training, opinion assessment), new areas emerged, including systems analysis, job analysis and training, combat stress, vocational guidance and rehabilitation, clinical psychology, military leadership, psychological operations and propaganda, group dynamics, human factors engineering, and the effect of environmental factors on human performance. The opinion surveys conducted and analyzed by the research branch of the War Department provided the Army with findings on the attitudes of soldiers to aid in policy formation (Stouffer, Lumsdaine et al., 1949; Stouffer, Suchman, Devinney, Star, & Williams, 1949).

The rapid growth in the size of the armed services during World War II increased interest in leadership and leadership development techniques. Research in leadership was of vital importance; military psychologists were active contributors in the selection, training, and performance assessment of leaders and military performance.

Driskell and Olmstead (1989) report how dominant military psychology was in the psychological literature during the 1940s. More than 2,000 psychologists worked for the military in World War II. "In 1943, fully half of the pages of the *Psychological Bulletin* were devoted to topics of military psychology, and from 1943 to 1945, one in every four psychologists in the country was engaged in military psychology"(p. 45). Psychology was concerned with military issues and research topics. Practical problems that were amenable to solution by psychological research methods were documented in the professional literature. The war years are extensively covered in the Army Air Force volumes (Flana-

gan, 1947), in the *American Soldier* series (Stouffer, Lumsdaine, et al., 1949; Stouffer, Suchman, et al., 1949), and by Bray (1948).

The Division of Military Psychology (Division 19) was organized in 1945–1946 as one of the original divisions of the APA. Its membership and their interests are a microcosm of the spectrum of psychology as a whole (Crawford, 1970). Division 19 is composed of individuals serving in uniform in the armed forces, personnel in the Department of Defense, and those conducting research or consultations with implications for the military and military settings. The common denominator is work associated with the Department of Defense, meeting the needs of the military.

Following World War II, psychological testing became well established in military personnel systems. The research and development capabilities were continued as Congress established the Office of Naval Research in 1946. It was the first federal organization to support scientific research. The Personnel Research Section of the Army Adjutant General's Office evolved into the Army Research Institute for the Behavioral and Social Sciences.

Significant reorganization of the armed services occurred in 1947. The Department of War became the Department of Defense. The Army Air Force became a separate service, the United States Air Force. The Air Force created the Human Resources Research Center in 1949 to continue the work of the Army Air Force Aviation psychology program. The organization merged with others in 1954 to become the Air Force Personnel and Training Research Center, which evolved into the Air Force Human Resources Laboratory. Federal support for research on military topics and applications was encouraged at university and research centers. (For more detailed discussions of military psychology in general, see Driskell & Olmstead, 1989; Gal & Mangelsdorff, 1991; and Wiskoff, 1997.)

Selection and Classification

This area deals with assessment of personnel and prediction of performance in military jobs. Screening and selecting can involve entry-level personnel (both enlisted and officers); appropriate classification and career placement; and selection for special skill positions (such as pilots or special operations). Personnel standards vary as a function of overall military requirements, numbers available, and the quantity and quality of personnel to be considered.

Problems in classifying and assigning personnel led to the development of aptitude tests such as the Armed Forces Qualification Test. Personnel selection and classification requirements are connected to job fields and job performance. Classification has become extremely important as the military of the 1990s takes on new missions (like peace keeping and humanitarian assistance) while reducing the total number of personnel in uniform.

Training

Training aims to develop effective and efficient procedures to educate personnel and to increase operational readiness skills. The areas include acquisition of basic, military, technical, and special skills. Training devices, simulators, and computer-based training procedures are employed to enhance skills acquisition. Realistic training helps to build confidence and unit cohesion and to sustain operational readiness. The armed services train as they expect to function (whether in combat, peace-keeping, or disaster assistance operations). Evaluation of the outcomes of the operations and of efficiency of mission accomplishment helps to determine the effectiveness of training techniques. Criterion-referenced procedures are used to assess team performance and effectiveness.

Human Factors Engineering

Human factors engineering attempts to improve functioning of military systems and equipment by considering the human-machine interface during equipment design. As systems became more complicated, the aims include reducing human operator workload, reducing stressors, adding technology to aid in task performance, and improving decision making. Future directions will be a function of technological changes, cognitive demands, societal changes, and future military requirements.

Organizational (Individual and Group) Behavior

Organizational factors consider the variety of military work settings (in different environmental extremes), acculturation to military service, organizational demands, organizational commitment, training opportunities, socialization, career development, quality of life, family dynamics, morale and cohesion, adjustment and maladjustive behaviors, stresses of military life, variety of operational settings (combat, peace keeping, humanitarian assistance), job demands, leadership opportunities, and transitions. How individual personnel are integrated into military life and back to civilian settings is affected by changes in society at large. The military reflects the society of which it is a part.

Leadership and Team Effectiveness

Military history demonstrates the effects of good or poor leadership (victory or defeat). Skills learned in combat may or may not have applicability during peacetime operations. Leaders need to know what to do at different levels within the organization and how best

to do it. Studies of leadership and command examine the problems of how a leader influences personnel to accomplish assigned tasks and missions. Leadership includes both direct and indirect influences, policy making, systems theory, decision making, strategic management, and personnel management.

Leadership theories have been frequently tested in military settings. Support for varying models has been equivocal, and this result has led to more research efforts. The curricula at all military schools include intensive courses on leadership, group dynamics, situational determinants, and ethics to prepare leaders at all levels of command.

Military personnel perform many of their tasks and functions in units or teams. Processes such as team structure, communications, cohesion, leadership style, and group dynamics may affect group performance. Military leaders need to develop cohesion in their units. How individuals relate to others in an organization may affect accomplishment of their mission and individual survival in combat. One result of armed conflict may be combat stress reactions. Adjustment to the military and the variety of operational settings may be stressful.

Social Psychology

Social psychologists and sociologists contributed significantly to the armed forces during the wartime efforts. During World War II, the research branch of the Army's Information and Education Division conducted numerous attitude surveys and experiments concerning morale and motivation in support of military personnel policies. The *American Soldier* series (Stouffer, Lumsdaine et al., 1949; Stouffer, Suchman et al., 1949) documented the conceptual and methodological contributions of psychologists and social scientists. Some of the findings included the influences of culture and personality in understanding and predicting behavior, the role of attitudes in predicting and controlling behavior, and contributors to morale and motivation in military personnel.

Clinical Psychology

Clinical psychology was not notably active during World War I or the years following. During World War II, practitioners were used for testing and diagnosis of personnel. By the late 1950s, military psychologists moved beyond testing; they became skilled in psychotherapy. Of particular value to the military are forms of brief therapy, neuropsychological evaluation, and treatment. The employment of clinical psychologists was extended to Veterans Administration hospitals, fostering greater acceptance and utilization of this area of applied psychology.

Mental health clinics and outpatient facilities were developed to help uniformed personnel and families adapt to the military. In the 1970s, the military took the lead in the development of programs to control and treat drug and alcohol abuse. Principles of health psychology were applied to increase the physical and psychological wellness of military personnel; the intent was to increase individual readiness and effectiveness. Prevention programs were developed to improve adjustment to the military and reduce demand for health care services. Consultation to military commanders improves individual performance and mental health, as well as organizational effectiveness and unit readiness.

Environmental Stressors

Technological advances have brought more sophisticated machines, weaponry, and physical threats into combat operations. Military personnel are prepared to perform in a variety of special environments, in different climates and situations (with all possible extremes of heat, cold, or altitude). Personnel must adjust to new environments, from underseas to outer space. Acclimatization to the new environment may impair performance. In addition to adapting to military requirements, cultural, social, and political changes may affect accomplishment of the mission.

Military work environments may be noisy, in confined spaces, with high rates of acceleration and vibration, with potentially hazardous substances, which demand protective clothing; the work settings reflect the complete range of environmental extremes. Operations may be conducted for long durations with little time for rest or sleep in harsh (or even toxic) environments. The roles and missions must be assessed to consider the capabilities and limitations of the military personnel in these stressful conditions. Training factors and personnel experiences are moderated by the effects of environmental influences.

Professional Concerns

The U.S. military carries out the nation's political policy directives. The armed services are highly visible and under political and societal pressures. These pressures can have a major impact on military operations. National support for military operations is a critical element in mission planning and execution. In assessing the potential impact of military campaigns, political and societal support for the operations must be considered. This has become more evident as the United States has participated in multinational operations (such as the world wars, the Gulf War, NATO operations, and peacekeeping efforts in Africa, the Middle East, and the former Yugoslavia).

The military serves as a social laboratory for assessing national and societal trends. These have included development of occupational selection and classification categories, development of large-scale screening batteries, increased occupational opportunities for mi-

norities and women, training and utilization of paraprofessionals, health promotion and wellness programs, and crisis intervention and treatment teams. Upward mobility and career development programs for minorities and women were well established in the armed forces before the trends emerged in general society.

Training Requirements

Uniformed psychologists are required to have doctorates from approved training programs. Clinical psychologists must become licensed in a state to practice in the military. The military offers a number of clinical psychology internship programs to train its own future clinicians. Postdoctoral fellowship programs are available as well in neuropsychology and child and health psychology. The Department of Defense conducted a demonstration project to train some psychologists to administer psychopharmaceuticals. The intent was to provide more skills to uniformed clinical psychologists. Joint service internship and fellowship programs are being developed to conserve personnel resources.

Professional Organizations

Military psychology has flourished since World War II. In many nations, the military is the largest single employer of research psychologists. A number of professional organizations conduct programs that attract significant numbers of military personnel. The International Applied Military Psychology Symposium (IAMPS), founded in 1963, provides a biannual forum for the exchange of research information. The Division of Military Psychology, Division 19, of the APA has its own journal, newsletters, and Web site to communicate with its members, who represent the majority of interests in psychology. The history of the Division of Engineering Psychology (Division 21) overlaps that of military psychology in that many of the advances in human factors engineering and ergonomics were developed to meet military requirements. The International Military Testing Association conducts annual conferences to discuss the latest trends in such topics as computer-aided testing, screening, and evaluative methods. The Inter-University Forum on Armed Forces and Society conducts biannual meetings to examine multidisciplinary research on the armed forces.

Future Directions

The military can anticipate engaging in more operations other than war (such as humanitarian assistance and disaster relief), serving as security forces for conflict management (international disputes, cultural differences), participating in multinational operations (peacekeeping, exploration of inner and outer space). Psychology will help military personnel cope with the new operational challenges. Emphasis will be on prevention, health, and wellness programs. There will be more cooperative multiservice training programs, particularly as the service branches consolidate their resources and training assets. There will be more alliances with the Department of Veterans Affairs and civilian mental health resources to combine programs and services. Psychologists prescribing pharmaceutics will add to their clinical skills. Telecommunications will allow for distance assessment, consultation, treatment, and learning opportunities. Psychologists can expect to play an active role in the future of the armed forces in order to maintain operational readiness and psychological fitness of the personnel.

Bibliography

Bray, C. W. (1948). *Psychology and military proficiency: A history of the applied psychology panel of the National Defense Research Committee.* Princeton, NJ: Princeton University Press.

Crawford, M. P. (1970). Military psychology and general psychology. *American Psychologist, 25,* 328–336.

Driskell, J. E., & Olmstead, B. (1989). Psychology and the military. *American Psychologist, 44* (1), 43–54.

Flanagan, J. C. (1947). Research reports of the Army Air Forces Aviation psychology program. *American Psychologist, 2,* 374–375.

Gal, R., & Mangelsdorff, A. D. (Eds.). (1991). *Handbook of military psychology.* Chichester, England: Wiley.

Stouffer, S. A., Lumsdaine, A. A., Lumsdaine, M. H., Williams, R. M., Jr., Smith, M. B., Janis, I. L., Star, S. A., & Cottrell, L. S., Jr. (1949). *Studies in social psychology in World War II. Vol. 2, The American soldier: Combat and its aftermath.* Princeton, NJ: Princeton University Press.

Stouffer, S. A., Suchman, E. A., DeVinney, L. C., Star, S. A., & Williams, R. W., Jr. (1949). *Studies in social psychology in World War II: Vol. 1. The American soldier: Adjustment during Army life.* Princeton, NJ: Princeton University Press.

Wiskoff, M. F. (1997). Defense of a nation: Military psychologists. In R. J. Sternberg (Ed.), *Career paths in psychology: Where your degree can take you* (pp. 245–268). Washington, DC: American Psychological Association.

A. David Mangelsdorff

MILITARY SERVICE. Perhaps more than any other organization in society, the military has been and continues to be at the center of historically important events. The military must deal with difficult, socially disruptive events whether they are wars, peacekeeping operations, or natural disasters. In addition, the military is a crucible in which individual lives and the lives of families are forever changed for better or worse. Military service can be a bridge to the future for a young high-school graduate who enlists to earn money for college or a career disaster for an established physician who is in-

voluntarily called to service and must abandon a medical practice.

Until recently, psychologists lacked an appropriate framework for studying the longer-term human impacts of military service. Military personnel psychology typically devoted itself to studying operational issues of current concern to military personnel communities to the exclusion of examining the longer-term, and sometimes cumulative, impacts of those operations on soldiers, their families, and the military structure and function itself. Life-course theory provides a framework that seems to be particularly well suited to studying the longer-term impacts of military service experiences on people's lives.

The Core Principles of Life-Course Theory

The utility of the life-course approach for studying military service was born in the work of Glen H. Elder, Jr., an American sociologist and developmental scientist, who became interested in the effects of World War II on men who had grown up during the Great Depression. [*See* Life-Course Theory.] Out of this and his continuing work in developmental science, emerged the four major principles of life-course theory. The first of these, *Historical Time and Place,* states that individuals are embedded in and shaped by historically significant events and places they experience during their lifetimes. Because of this, social scientists must consider the historical context of an experience when attempting to describe or explain how an individual's life has been shaped by that experience. This historical context includes the individual's life history of experiences as well as the larger forces of social history. For example, to understand fully the impact of the G.I. Bill on World War II veterans, one must understand how the postwar dissatisfaction of World War I veterans forged the very existence of the G.I. Bill, as well as what impacts the Bill's benefits have had on individual lives.

The second principle, *Timing in Lives,* asserts that the developmental impact of events or critical transitions in a person's life are dependent on when they occur. For example, those who entered military service at an early age during World War II were more likely to benefit from their experience than were those who entered later in life. While wartime service often disrupted lives that were well established, it often facilitated those who entered service before establishing themselves in jobs or marriages.

Linked Lives is the third principle of the life-course approach. This principle holds that lives are lived interdependently and the impacts of events and transitions are expressed through social networks of shared relationships. An example of this principle is the impact of war experiences on the soldier's family as well as on the soldier.

The fourth principle, *Human Agency,* asserts that individuals are active rather than passive in determining the impact of events and transitions on their lives. They construct their lives through the decisions and choices they make within the constraints of the events they experience. For example, not everyone in World War II chose to use the G.I. Bill or to use it in the same way. The decisions people make also shape the experiences they will have. Choosing a branch of the service, for example, will affect the nature of a person's military experience.

A Life-Course Analysis of Combat and Its Aftermath

Perhaps the area in which the life-course approach to studying the effects of military service has made its biggest impact is in understanding the long-term effects of combat on people's lives. When a war is over we often expect combat veterans to resume their former lives as if nothing had changed. Because of this common expectation, many families believe that continued aftereffects of combat are unusual and they may feel isolated as a result. All too soon, combat veterans and their families realize that things will never be quite the same for them again.

Combat veterans are likely to exhibit symptoms indicative of posttraumatic stress disorder (PTSD) or other difficulties in adjusting to postcombat life. Contrary to popular opinion, PTSD is not unique to the Vietnam combat experience. This disorder is a collection of symptoms that accompanies the aftermath of extreme stress, often in life-threatening situations. In prior wars, people suffering from PTSD were said to be shell shocked or suffering from battle fatigue.

Combat veterans suffering from these disorders often have recurring nightmares, are unable or unwilling to talk about their combat experiences, may seem more irritable than before their combat experiences, may have flashbacks, and may have exaggerated responses to loud noises. Many combat veterans suffer from some of these symptoms at one or more points in their postcombat lives; some are never totally free from them. For example, research with World War II and Korean combat veterans found that 21% of soldiers who experienced heavy combat said they still had stress symptoms after age 55. Of these veterans, 29% reported that they still felt guilty about surviving their combat experience, and 68% reported some undesirable, long-lasting aftereffects from combat such as bad memories (Elder & Clipp, 1988).

What about Historical Time and Place and the Combat Experience?

Research has shown that the key variable to understanding a person's reaction to combat stress is the severity of the combat experienced. Directly experiencing killing, death, and dying, particularly of one's com-

rades, has a profound effect on combat veterans (Card, 1983; Elder & Clipp, 1988; Kulka et al., 1990). Although it is difficult to tell for sure, it appears that Vietnam veterans were no more likely to experience PTSD than veterans of previous wars (Fontana & Rosenheck, 1994). Again, the key was the nature of the combat experience.

Research also indicates timing of combat in the life of the soldier can be of critical importance in determining combat stress reactions. Younger, less experienced soldiers are likely to be more negatively affected by combat than are older, more experienced, better-educated soldiers (Kulka et al., 1990).

The linking of lives plays several roles in determining combat stress reactions. Soldiers from cohesive units, where interpersonal relationships among soldiers are very close, who actually see their comrades die, are the most vulnerable to severe, long-lasting combat stress effects. Clearly, the families of combat veterans are also affected by the veteran's postcombat reactions. The combat veteran's reluctance to talk about his or her experiences often adds to the difficulties that families have in living with the veteran's postcombat problems.

Human agency in conjunction with linked lives also plays a role in determining the aftereffects of combat for the veteran. Those who seek out comrades through reunions and veterans' organizations seem to do better in adjusting to the enduring effects of their combat experiences. Very frequently, veterans are able to share their feelings with others who have experienced combat while they often find it difficult to do so with family and friends. It is within the context of such reunions and veterans' organizations that veterans are likely to discover that their postcombat experiences are not strange or unusual, but rather the normal aftermath of the trauma of combat. By attending such veterans' reunions, spouses can often come to understand what their spouses have experienced.

Other Important Life-Course Theory Constructs

Trajectories and transitions are basic concepts in life-course theory. Trajectories are the dynamic paths followed by major components of a person's life. Examples that are important to military personnel as well as to civilians are career, marriage, health, and education. *Transitions* are changes in the directions that trajectories take. Examples of major life transitions are leaving home, entering the military service, entering the workforce, changing jobs, entering college, marriage, and childbirth. Within the military services, critical transitions may include such things as overseas duty, command assignment, attending special schools, and combat duty. *Turning points* are those transitions that are pivotal events in one's life. Turning points represent a significant break with the past and dramatically change the course of one or more of life's trajectories. Turning points can either be abrupt changes in direction, such as those precipitated by experiencing combat, or more gradual changes, such as those precipitated by using the G.I. Bill for education. Examples of military-related turning points are major deployments, wars, selection for Special Forces training, and even the act of entering or leaving the military service itself.

Participation in World War II represented a turning point for many of those who were in the military services. The classic study by Stouffer et al. (1949) of returning World War II veterans, for example, found that 79% felt that service in the Army had significantly changed their lives in some way. Many reported that they were more self-reliant, intellectually broader, and more social than before the war. Vietnam veterans also reported enhanced personal and social development as a result of their military service. However, they also reported delays in educational attainment and occupational deficits in the aftermath of their service.

Elder has suggested that when asked to retrospectively identify turning points in their lives people most frequently cite positive rather than negative events as turning points (G. H. Elder, Jr., personal communication, 1996). At the Army Research Institute, we tested this hypothesis in a study of National Guard and Reserve soldiers who had returned from a voluntary, active duty, peacekeeping deployment to the Sinai desert. We asked these soldiers whether their peacekeeping deployment had been a turning point in their lives. We defined turning points for them as "life events [that] can change the direction and quality of our lives." A little over 60% of the soldiers said that they felt that the Sinai deployment had been a turning point in their lives. Of those who felt it had been a turning point, nearly 86% reported that the turning point had been a positive one. We asked the spouses of the married soldiers the same question and found that 69% of them identified their soldier's deployment as a turning point in their own lives. As with the soldiers, 85% of the spouses said the turning point had been positive.

Military Service as a Bridge in the Life-Course

One of the most interesting applications of life-course theory is to the study of the military as a "bridge" to the future for those who have served. The "bridging hypothesis," says that military service often serves as a bridge from youth to adult life roles and is especially likely to serve that function for disadvantaged youth (Browning, Lopreato, & Poston, 1973). Recall that the early work of Elder and his associates explored the effects of military service during World War II on the lives of those who had experienced the Great Depression. The results of those studies were mixed and depended a great deal on the timing of the World War II experience and, of course, on the degree to which combat had been experienced. In general, those who entered the war at younger ages benefited from the experience. Those that entered at later ages, when careers and families had already been established, did not fare as well, sometimes falling behind in earnings, life satisfaction, and even in physical health. There were some notable exceptions to this pattern.

Physicians who served during World War II often gained greatly from the experience, regardless of age at service. A physician who did not serve in the war probably suffered the disadvantage of not being exposed to the rapid developments in medicine, particularly trauma surgery, which took place during combat (Elder, Pavalko, & Hastings, 1991). Longitudinal work by Sampson and Laub (1996) with World War II veterans has shown that those who had been disadvantaged and even delinquents prior to military service often benefited most from that service, especially those who entered the military earlier in their lives.

Vietnam era veteran studies have corroborated some of the basic findings of studies with World War II veterans, particularly those surrounding the relationship between severity of combat and PTSD symptoms later in life. However, several studies suggest that postservice benefits such as the G.I. Bill have had a much smaller impact on Vietnam era veterans than it did on World War II veterans (Cohen, Segal, & Temme, 1992; Teachman & Call, 1996). Vietnam era veterans may not have gained advantages from these benefits relative to their nonveteran counterparts because similar benefits, such as money for college, were available to nonveterans as well. In addition, military service may actually have hampered the ability of Vietnam era veterans to earn as much as those who did not serve. At least one study claims to have shown that military service had little or no bridging effect for those of lower cognitive abilities (Laurence & Ramsberger, 1991).

Research with active-duty veterans in an all-volunteer era, has reported benefits and costs to the life-course similar to those experienced by veterans who served in previous wars. Consistent with the bridging hypothesis, some of this research indicates that African Americans and women, in particular, have benefited from military service. These benefits tend to show up more as perceived gains in interpersonal skills, self-discipline, and self-confidence than as benefits in the form of better jobs or more pay after military service (Gade, Lakhani, & Kimmel, 1991; Moore, 1996).

The Life-Course and Future Military Human Resource Issues

Life-course as an adult developmental theory seems ideally suited for studying military human resource issues. Unlike civilian employers, the military services are dependent on internal development of leaders. There is no lateral entry of civilians into leadership positions in the military. It comes as no surprise, then, that the development of leaders is one of the critical imperatives for the military services.

As an institution, the military is often at the center of historical events and as a result, historical time and place have great meaning and impact for the lives of service members and their families. The deployments to Bosnia, Macedonia, and Kosovo that engaged the military services during the late 1990s are examples of the impact of world events on those in the military and their families.

The military services, especially the officer corps in each service, are cohort driven. Progress in getting particular jobs, schooling, and being promoted is always gauged in terms of one's entry-level cohort. Being behind your cohort or "year group" in the right assignments or schooling often detracts from future promotions, assignments, and even retirement. Clearly the life-course principles of timing and human agency are very important in understanding the career development of soldiers.

In recent years, the military services have realized how important families, especially spouses, are to the performance and retention of their service members. The principle of linked lives is clearly important to studying military service members and their families. The principle of human agency also comes into play as an important consideration for understanding how military service members and their families manage careers and cope with the impact of world events on their lives.

Perhaps one of the most interesting applications of life-course theory to future military human resource problems lies in the study of the long-term effects of deploying reserve component soldiers for peacekeeping and stability operations. The activation and deployment of reserve component soldiers lends itself well to a life-course analysis. These deployments strongly resemble the mobilization of civilians during wartime in terms of the effects on soldiers' lives and those of their families. Based on life-course research conducted with veterans, one can predict, for example, that deployments will be most disruptive to the life course of older reserve component soldiers. Furthermore, long-term benefits, such as educational attainment and better jobs, will be more likely to accrue to younger soldiers.

In summary, life-course theory offers a rationale as well as methods for studying lives of service members and their families as they move through their military careers. It also offers a systematic way to study the unfolding of the lives of veterans and their families as they make the transition from military service to civilian life due to retirement, completion of a duty tour, or their return from reserve active duty.

[*See also* Military Psychology; *and* Veterans.]

Acknowledgments. The views, opinions, and/or findings contained in this article are solely those of the author and should not be construed as an official U.S. Department of the Army or U.S. Department of Defense position, policy, or decision, unless so designated by other official documentation.

Bibliography

Browning, H. L., Lopreato, S. C., & Poston, D. L. (1973). Income and veteran status: Variations among Mexican Americans, Blacks, and Anglos. *American Sociological Review, 38,* 74–85.

Card, J. J. (1983). *Lives after Vietnam: The personal impact of military service.* Lexington, MA: Lexington Books.

Cohen, J., Segal, D. R., & Temme, L. V. (1992). The impact of education on Vietnam-era veterans' occupational attainment. *Social Science Quarterly, 73,* 397–409.

Elder, G. H., Jr., & Clipp, E. C. (1988). Combat experience, comradeship, and psychological health. In J. P. Wilson. Z. Harel, & B. Kahana (Eds.), *Human adaptation to extreme stress: From the Holocaust to Vietnam* (pp. 131–156). New York: Plenum.

Elder, G. H., Jr., Pavalko, E. K., & Hastings, T. J. (1991). Talent, history, and the fulfillment of promise. *Psychiatry, 54,* 215–231.

Fontana, A. & Rosenheck, R. (1994). Traumatic war stressors and psychiatric symptoms among World War II, Korean, and Vietnam War veterans. *Psychology and Aging, 9,* 27–33.

Gade, P. A., Lakhani, H., & Kimmel, M. (1991). Military Service: A good place to start? *Military Psychology, 3,* 251–267.

Kulka, R. A., Schlenger, W. E., Fairbank, J. A., Hough, R. L., Jordan, K. B., Marmar, C. R., Weiss, D. S., & Grady, D. A. (1990). *Trauma and the Vietnam War generation.* New York: Brunner/Mazel.

Laurence, J. H. & Ramsberger, P. F. (1991). *Low-aptitude men in the military: Who profits who pays?* New York: Praeger.

Moore, B. L. (1996). *To serve my country, to serve my race: The story of the only African American WACs stationed overseas during World War II.* New York: New York University Press.

Sampson, R. J., & Laub, H. (1996). Socioeconomic achievement in the life course of disadvantaged men: Military service as a turning point, circa 1940–1965. *American Sociological Review, 61,* 247–367.

Stouffer, S. A., Lumsdaine, A. A., Lumsdaine, M. H., Williams, R. M., Jr., Smith, M. B., Janis, I. L., Star, S. A., & Cottrell, L. S. Jr. (1949). *The American soldier: Volume 2. Combat and its aftermath.* Princeton, NJ: Princeton University Press.

Teachman, J. D., & Call, V. R. A. (1996). The effect of military service on educational, occupational, and income attainment. *Social Science Research, 25,* 1–31.

Paul A. Gade

MILL, JAMES (1773–1836), British philosopher. Born in Aberdeenshire, Scotland, Mill studied mental philosophy under Dugald Stewart (1753–1828) at the University of Edinburgh before moving to London to work as a freelance journalist. His life was transformed in 1808 when he met Jeremy Bentham (1748–1832) and became a leading proponent of the utilitarian school and its goal of bringing "the greatest good to the greatest number." Mill wrote prolifically on historical, political, and economic topics, as well as two important works for psychologists: an article titled "Education," written in 1815 for the *Encyclopedia Britannica*, and the 1829 book, *Analysis of the Phenomena of the Human Mind*. Both promoted a strongly associationistic psychology, emphasizing the importance of experience and education as the prime determiners of all major mental phenomena.

Mill traced his psychology to the empiricist traditions of John Locke (1632–1704), David Hartley (1705–1757), David Hume (1711–1776), Claude Helvétius (1715–1771), and Étienne de Condillac (1715–1780)—in opposition to the idealist and nativist schools associated with Jean Jacques Rousseau (1712–1778) and Immanuel Kant (1724–1804). Echoing Helvétius, Mill contended that "the great mass of mankind [is] equally susceptible of mental excellence," and therefore "the power of education embraces every thing between the lowest stage of intellectual and moral rudeness, and the highest state . . . of perfection" (1969, p. 69). Like his empiricist predecessors, Mill interpreted the mind at birth as a tabula rasa, devoid of predilections apart from a capacity to retain impressions, or "ideas," of its sensory experiences. Defining "the character of the human mind" as nothing more than "the sequences of its ideas," he saw the goal of education as "to provide for the constant production of certain sequences rather than others" (1969, p. 58).

In a famous chapter of his *Analysis*, "The Association of Ideas," Mill describes how early, simple ideas presumably combine after repeated association to form complex ideas—as when ideas of roundness, sweetness and redness come together in the complex ideas of an apple. Similarly, complex ideas can combine with each other to create what Mill called "duplex ideas": "Brick is one complex idea, mortar is another complex idea; these ideas, with ideas of position and quantity, compose my idea of a wall. . . . In the same manner my complex idea of glass and wood and others compose my duplex idea of a window; and these [and other] duplex ideas, united together, compose my idea of a house. . . . How many more [complex and duplex ideas are united] in the idea called Every Thing?" (Mill, 1967, pp. 115–116). According to Mill's conception, sometimes referred to as "mental compounding," complex and duplex ideas are nothing more than the sum of their simpler components.

Mill emphasized contiguity as the sole principle or law of association causing ideas to become interconnected. He differentiated between experiences occurring simultaneously (contiguously in space) and successively (contiguously in time), arguing that the former lead to complex ideas of objects, the latter to ideas of processes. Although some of his predecessors had regarded association by similarity as an additional law, Mill dismissed this as a special case of contiguity because "we are accustomed to see like things together. When we see a tree, we generally see more than one tree . . . a sheep, more sheep than one; a man, more men than one" (1967, p. 111). Thus for Mill, effective education was simply a matter of insuring that a child be exposed to the proper combinations and sequences of experiences, whose resulting ideas may be expected to combine additively into whatever results one desires. He acknowledged just one complication, because "people in general form a very inadequate conception of all the circumstances which act during the first months, perhaps the first moments, of existence, and of the power of those circumstances in giving permanent qualities to the mind" (1969, p. 70). Accordingly, systematic education must begin at the outset of life.

Mill put his theories into practice in raising his son, John Stuart Mill (1806–1874), who related the extraordinary story of his education in his *Autobiography*. Although John became a famous intellectual prodigy with "an advantage of a quarter of a century over my contemporaries" (J. S. Mill, 1971, p. 20), his training—like his father's theories—paid scant heed to practical or emotional development. Following a severe "mental crisis" in young adulthood, the younger Mill came to view his father's psychology as limited, overly simplified, and doctrinaire. While still endorsing the great general powers of experience and education, John Stuart Mill proposed several refinements to it in his influential editor's annotations to a second edition of his father's *Analysis*, published in 1869. He accepted similarity as a separate law of association, for example, and argued that complex ideas arise following a process he called "mental chemistry" and amount to more than just the sum of their simple components.

[*Many of the people mentioned in this article are the subjects of independent biographical entries.*]

Bibliography

Bain, A. (1882). *James Mill: A biography*. New York: Henry Holt.

Mill, J. (1869). *Analysis of the phenomena of the human mind* (2nd ed.) (Edited with additional notes by John Stuart Mill). London: Longmans, Green, Reader, and Dyer. This edition reprints the original text of the 1829 first edition, with extensive and often critical annotations by Mill's son.

Mill, J. (1969). Education. In W. H. Burston (Ed). *James Mill on Education* (pp. 41–119). Cambridge: Cambridge University Press. (Original work published 1815)

Mill, J. S. (1971). *Autobiography* (Edited by J. Stillinger). London: Oxford University Press. (Original work published 1873)

Packe, M. (1954). *The life of John Stuart Mill.* New York: Macmillan. Although focusing on J. S. Mill, this biography also has much useful information about James Mill and Jeremy Bentham.

Raymond E. Fancher

MILL, JOHN STUART (1806–1874), English philosopher. Mill is most widely remembered as a political and social philosopher, for works such as *Principles of Political Economy* (1848), *On Liberty* (1859), *Utilitarianism* (1863), and *The Subjection of Women* (1869). These works built upon and refined the utilitarian social philosophy Mill had been taught by Jeremy Bentham (1748–1832) and his father James Mill (1773–1836)— a school of thought that denied the existence of any innate or absolute moral agency, and identified the highest ethical goal as "the greatest good for the greatest number." Because of his outspoken support for such causes as universal education and suffrage, women's and minority rights, and the public ownership of natural resources, Mill had a reputation in his own day as a political radical and in posterity as "the patron saint of liberty."

A strongly associationistic psychology provided the conceptual foundation for Mill's political and social views. Outlined in his first published book, *A System of Logic* (1843), this psychology emphasized the preeminent powers of experience and education and represented in some ways the culmination of the school of British associationism traceable to John Locke (1632–1704). It was also partly a product of Mill's own highly unusual background and education.

Mill's Education

Born in London, England, on 20 May 1806, Mill was deliberately reared to be a monument to the power of education. From earliest childhood, he sat daily at the same working table with his father, a prolific journalist and protégé of Bentham. During breaks from his work James tutored John, and with extraordinary effectiveness. At age 3, John started learning Greek with Aesop's *Fables*, and by 8 he had read all of Herodotus, much of Xenophon, and the first six dialogues of Plato in the original. He then started Latin and mathematics and by 12 had mastered virtually the entire classical curriculum, as well as mathematics through the differential calculus. He was also thoroughly trained in prac-

tical scholarship, serving as chief proofreader for his father's monumental *History of India* (1818). At 13, he wrote up notes of lectures on political economy his father had delivered on their daily walks together—notes that served as a first draft for James Mill's *Elements of Political Economy* (1821). Father and son covered the subject of logic in the same way, only this time the notes became the starting points for John's first book, *A System of Logic* (which was not published until 1843). In the meantime, teenaged John served as his father's only constructive critic throughout the composition of *Analysis of the Phenomena of the Human Mind*, a classic account of associationistic psychology that appeared in 1829.

A stern taskmaster who feared his son might develop the trait of "self-conceit," James Mill repeatedly told John that his intellectual accomplishments were completely the result of his unusual education, rather than any innate abilities. John agreed and declared in his autobiography, "I felt that what my father had said regarding my peculiar advantages was exactly the truth and common sense of the matter, and it fixed my opinion and feeling from that time forward" (Mill, 1971, p. 22). As he grew older, John also became acutely aware of certain practical and emotional deficiencies in himself and suffered a severe "mental crisis" as a consequence. Consistent with his environmentalist predilections, he blamed these deficiencies on an education that had excessively stressed the intellectual at the expense of his emotional and practical development. In maturity, he continued to attribute all major variations in human character, whether good or bad, to nurture rather than to nature.

Mill's Psychology

Mill described and defended his approach to psychology most systematically and completely in Book Six of his *System of Logic* (1843), titled "On the Logic of the Moral Sciences." He started with the assumption of his predecessors in the British associationist tradition that the mind at birth is like a blank slate: empty but with a capacity to record memories or ideas of the impressions made on it by experience. Ideas presumably become linked together in varying degrees according to the "laws of association" because of the similarity, contiguity, or intensity of the experiences that produce them. Early experiences give rise to "simple ideas" such as roundness, redness, and sweetness, which may join together after repeated association to form "complex ideas," such as that of an apple. James Mill's *Analysis of the Phenomena of the Human Mind* had hypothesized that complex ideas result from an uncomplicated mental compounding and amount to little more than the sums of their constituent simple ideas. The elder Mill described the idea of a house, for example, as just the sum of the ideas of bricks, mortar, glass, and other components that go into a house's construction. John Mill came to regard this conception as simplistic and argued that complex ideas actually arise following a process he called "mental chemistry." Just as water has qualities very different from those of hydrogen and oxygen added together, so do complex ideas take on emergent properties that transcend the sum of their parts. The notion of a house as a home or a "place to live," for example, goes beyond the sum of its physical components. Mill noted that in the existing state of psychological knowledge these emergent effects of mental chemistry were not easily deducible in advance. Accordingly, psychologists would have to undertake extensive empirical experimentation—systematically subjecting people to many different combinations of simple ideas and observing the myriad ways they fuse into complex ideas—to establish the precise laws of mental chemistry.

Mill believed that once such studies were completed, associational analysis would be able to account for virtually all important psychological phenomena. While conceding that innate factors corresponding to the instincts of animals may play some role in human beings, Mill argued that these effects were surpassingly minor compared to those of experience and association. And further, he argued that psychologists were obliged on purely logical grounds to extend the laws of association as far as they can go before positing anything as innate. Evidence for innate factors logically has to be negative, arising only from the failure of serious attempts to provide experiential explanations. Mill had little doubt that if serious attempts would be made, most of the mental phenomena traditionally regarded as innate would prove to have an experiential basis. The Cartesian "innate idea" of infinity, for example, might be explained by the fact that no one ever actually experiences a point in space or time that does not have others extending before and beyond it; accordingly it becomes impossible to think of any point as not being followed by others. Pangs of conscience, interpreted by some as the promptings of an innate moral sense, were provisionally explained by Mill as the complex associational fusion of the idea of committing an immoral act, with the idea (memory) of the pain suffered in childhood punishments for misbehavior.

Ethology

Mill passionately believed that associationist psychology could account for most of the major individual differences in ability and character and proposed in his *Logic* to develop a new science he called "ethology" to pursue such analyses. (Mill derived this word from the Greek *ethos* for "character," quite independently of a group of French naturalists who coined *éthologie* to denote the

study of animals in their natural habitats. The latter sense of the term prevails today.) Mill freely admitted the existence of distinctive "national characters" and of significant psychological differences between men and women but attributed the origins of these differences to nurture. Presaging his later argument in *The Subjection of Women*, he wrote in the *Logic* that if "at some future, and, it may be hoped, not distant period, equal freedom and an equally independent social position come to be possessed by both [men and women], their differences of character [will be] either removed or totally altered" (Mill, 1973, p. 868).

When he published his *Logic* in 1843, Mill expected to spend the next several years refining his psychology and developing ethology as a new science. In fact, however, his attention became increasingly drawn to more immediate practical and social questions, and he returned to explicitly psychological issues only sporadically (see Bibliography for examples). Nonetheless, his convictions regarding the primacy of nurture pervaded virtually all of his subsequent work and were vigorously summarized in his *Autobiography* (1873) as follows:

> The prevailing tendency to regard all the marked distinctions of human nature as innate, and in the main indelible, and to ignore the irresistible proofs that by far the greater part of those differences, whether between individuals, races, or sexes, are such as not only might, but naturally would be produced by differences in circumstances, is one of the chief hindrances to the rational treatment of great social questions, and one of the greatest stumbling blocks to human improvement. (Mill, 1971, p. 162)

By the latter part of the nineteenth century, Mill's psychology came to be seen as dated and incomplete, partly because he never redefined it in the context of Darwinian evolution. Further, it seemed ill-equipped to accommodate the findings of the new "dynamic psychologies" that emphasized the influence of conscious and unconscious motives on the flow of thought, and the dissociation (as opposed to the positive association) of ideas. Mill's younger friends Alexander Bain (1818–1903) and Herbert Spencer (1820–1903) attempted to remedy these shortcomings of associationist psychology in texts that became standard in England for many years (e.g., Bain, 1899; Spencer, 1881). Mill's concept of mental chemistry anticipated in some ways the findings of the Gestalt psychologists, summarized in their famous dictum "the whole is greater than the sum of its parts." Mill's greatest psychological legacy, however, was undoubtedly his vigorous championing of the nurture side of the nature/nurture controversy, which remains a model for many of his successors today.

[*Many of the people mentioned in this article are the subjects of independent biographical entries.*]

Bibliography

Works by Mill

Mill, J. S. (1971). *Autobiography*, (J. Stillinger, Ed.). London: Oxford University Press.

Mill, J. S. (1973). *A system of logic, ratiocinative, and inductive*, Variorum edition. Toronto: University of Toronto Press.

Mill, J. S. (1978). Bain's psychology. In J. S. Mill, *Essays on philosophy and the classics*. Toronto: University of Toronto Press. (Original work published 1859.) An appreciative review of Bain's elaborations on Mill's approach to psychology.

Mill, J. S. (1979). *An examination of Sir William Hamilton's philosophy*. Toronto: University of Toronto Press. (Original work published 1865.) Contains some of Mill's late psychological theorizing, in the context of a critique of one of England's leading Kantian philosophers.

Works about Mill

August, E. (1975). *John Stuart Mill: A mind at large*. London: Vision Press. Provides succinct summaries of Mill's many interests and contributions.

Bain, A. (1899). *The emotions and the will* (4th ed.). London: Longmans, Green.

Fancher, R. E. (1985). *The intelligence men: Makers of the IQ controversy*. New York: Norton. Chapter 1, "The nature-nurture controversy," contrasts Mill's background and philosophy with that of the arch hereditarian, Francis Galton.

Mill, J. (1869). *Analysis of the phenomena of the human mind* (2nd ed.) (Edited with additional notes by John Stuart Mill). London: Longmans, Green, Reader, and Dyer. James Mill's classic account of associationistic psychology, extensively annotated and sometimes criticized by his son.

Packe, M. (1954). *The life of John Stuart Mill*. New York: Macmillan. A delightful biography, with useful sketches of Jeremy Bentham and James Mill, as well as a full account of Mill's life and work.

Spencer, H. (1881). *The principles of psychology* (3rd ed.). London: Williams and Norgate.

Raymond E. Fancher

MILLER, GEORGE ARMITAGE (1920–), American cognitive psychologist. A leader in cognitive psychology, Miller taught at Harvard, Rockefeller, and Princeton universities. His contributions were recognized through numerous honors including election to the National Academy of Sciences (1962), the American Psychological Association's Distinguished Scientific Contribution Award (1963), and the American Psychological Association presidency (1969).

Miller received his bachelor's degree from the University of Alabama in 1940, majoring in speech therapy, an interest that carried him on to an Alabama master's degree in speech. While engaged in that work, he came to the decision that speaking difficulties should be addressed by clinical psychology. Donald Ramsdell, an Alabama psychology professor, recognized Miller's talents, recruited him into psychology, and arranged for his financial support. In 1942 Ramsdell sent Miller to study clinical psychology in Harvard's summer school, where Miller quickly developed an interest in experimental psychology.

Harvard's distinguished professor Edwin G. Boring spotted Miller's ability for scientific work. After spending one more year at Alabama as an instructor, Miller accepted Boring's offer of a stipend at Harvard and entered graduate school in psychology there. His inclinations toward clinical psychology remained with him, yet his talent for precise scientific research dominated when Harvard appointed him as assistant to S. S. Stevens in Harvard's Psychoacoustic Laboratory. Just then, psychology at Harvard began the move toward a split into two departments: one oriented toward experimentalism, the other toward social relations that encompassed clinical interests. Miller was identified as an experimentalist, and the rivalry between the factions was bitter for him. He tried, with little success, to bridge that gap amidst interdepartmental hostilities. Thus, Miller never fulfilled his initial predilection for clinical psychology, but became a brilliant experimentalist and scientific theorist. His skill for scientific and mathematical rigor stands out in his earliest publications.

Miller found himself, however, at odds with the established vision of what a scientific psychology should be. After an M.I.T. postdoctoral fellowship, he joined Harvard's faculty in experimental psychology. Yet he harbored a determined, if suppressed, view that the scientific style of the utterly dominant behaviorist viewpoint represented shallow and superficial science. That problem was magnified when B. F. Skinner came to Harvard. Miller's thoughts about behaviorism were largely covert in his work for almost two decades until the hegemony of behaviorism weakened.

In his first book, *Language and Communication* (1951), Miller made a serious effort to accommodate the behaviorist approach, for at the time no career in academic psychology seemed possible without that concession. Yet a few years later, he was at work on his cognitive and mentalistic book, *Plans and the Structure of Behavior* (1959), coauthored with Eugene Galanter and Karl Pribram. The book opens with a statement about mental imagery, leaving little doubt that Miller had left behaviorism behind. He then embarked on a program of writings and lectures to introduce the psychological implications of Noam Chomsky's new work in linguistics to scientific psychologists. Chomsky had become one of the most detailed and technical critics of Skinner's behaviorism.

Miller's experimental work spanned the areas of memory, language, and psychophysics. He published influential studies of statistical learning theory, information theory, psycholinguistics, and computer simulation. His best-known study of mental processes appeared in his article "The Magical Number Seven Plus or Minus Two" (1956), which brought to light an old but unappreciated finding: the existence of universal quantitative constants in human mental processes.

In 1960, Miller joined Jerome Bruner to found the Harvard Center for Cognitive Studies, a research institute that supported new streams of thought in American psychology. It launched many careers in psychology by offering lavish postdoctoral fellowships to bright young scientists around the world. The growing involvement of the United States in the Vietnam War eventually led to a cessation of governmental funding for the Center.

In 1967, Miller moved to Rockefeller University to escape the atmosphere of controversy in psychology at Harvard. After his years at Rockefeller, where he studied cognitive development in children, he moved to Princeton for the rest of his career. In these later years, he returned to his first concern, the psychology of language, producing an abundance of research illustrating how the meaning of words is context dependent. In 1976, he published *Language and Perception*, coauthored with Philip Johnson-Laird.

In later publications, Miller became increasingly concerned with defining the proper subject matter of psychology. He arrived at an answer after a long, distinguished career of commitment to rigorous science. *Consciousness*, he claims, constitutes the natural phenomenon that should be the primary object of scientific investigation in this field.

Bibliography

Baars, B. (1986). *The cognitive revolution in psychology*. New York: Guilford Press. Chapter 5 includes a detailed interview with Miller summarizing his career and his views on modern psychology.

Miller, G. A. (1951). *Language and communication*. New York: McGraw-Hill.

Miller, G. A. (1956). The magical number seven, plus or minus two: Some limits on our capacity for processing information. *Psychological Review, 63*, 81–97.

Miller, G. A. (1981). Trends and debates in cognitive psychology. *Cognition, 10*, 215–225. Contains Miller's argument that consciousness forms the "constitutive problem" of psychology.

Miller, G. A. (1989). George A. Miller. In G. Lindzey (Ed.), *A history of psychology in autobiography* (Vol. 8, pp. 391–418). Stanford, CA: Stanford University Press.

Miller, G. A., Galanter, E., & Pribram, K. (1960). *Plans and the structure of behavior*. New York: Holt, Rinehart, & Winston.

Miller, G. A., & Johnson-Laird, P. (1976). *Language and perception*. Cambridge, MA: Belknap Press.

Arthur L. Blumenthal

MILLER, NEAL ELGAR (b. 1909), American psychologist. His long career of experimental research has brought Neal Miller great respect. Although his contributions have been in diverse fields, there are common themes that run throughout his work. One is the importance of solid experimental design in the conduct of experiments. Equally important, however, is the belief that these experiments can be of significance in clinical and other applied settings. Yet another continuing theme is the importance of motivation, especially reward, and the drive reduction hypothesis, for understanding behavior. Throughout his long career, Miller has blended these themes into a set of research programs that has been continuous, innovative, integrative, and effective. In the process he has nurtured many students who went on to develop creative careers.

Miller was born in Milwaukee, Wisconsin, on 3 August 1909. He grew up in the Pacific Northwest, where his father, Irving Miller, was chair of the department of psychology and education at Western Washington State College. Neal Miller decided to concentrate on psychology during 1931, the final year of his undergraduate study at the University of Washington. He went to Stanford University for graduate work and was greatly influenced by Lewis Terman, who interested Miller in a wide range of psychological approaches including those of Sigmund Freud and Clark Hull. After completing a master's degree at Stanford in 1932, Miller moved to Yale University, where he completed his Ph.D. degree in 1935. While at Stanford, Miller had worked with Walter Miles, who took Miller with him to Yale's Institute of Human Relations. There, Miller was exposed to a range of social scientists working on both experimental and clinical problems. He became especially influenced by Hull's experimental approaches. A major theme of Hull's at that time, which became an important theme for Miller, was that much instrumental behavior, such as trial-and-error learning and higher mental processes, could be understood as being governed by the principles that Pavlov had discovered in his work on classical conditioning. Miller became interested in the links between Freudian and Pavlovian theory and did his dissertation on the relation between Freudian repression and Pavlovian inhibition.

Miller then received a Social Sciences Research Council fellowship to study psychoanalysis in Vienna. Advised by Anna Freud, he was accepted for training and analysis under Heinz Hartmann from 1935 to 1936.

Miller then returned to Yale, where he remained with various appointments, for the next 30 years. The ease of interdisciplinary interaction at Yale enabled him to develop various programs in learning theory, the interaction of learning and psychoanalytic theories, physiological psychology, and behavioral medicine.

From 1966 to 1980 Miller served as a professor at Rockefeller University in New York City. He has held several appointments and remained active since his retirement from Rockefeller.

As part of an interdisciplinary group at Yale in the 1930s and thereafter, Miller explored the ways in which learning theory could be brought to bear on problems of human behavior and psychopathology. Discussions in an informal Monday night group led to the development and elaboration of the hypothesis that frustration leads to aggression, and to the book, *Frustration and Aggression* (Dollard, Doob, Miller, Mowrer, & Sears, 1939). This broad treatment of psychological principles, sociological factors, and cross-cultural analyses had a significant impact on the study of aggression.

Much of Miller's early animal research followed from attempts to link Freudian and learning theory concepts. His research on conflict dealt with the interaction of approach and avoidance motivation. Hullian gradients of approach and avoidance, with that for avoidance steeper than that for approach, provided the basis for experimental research with rats, which was aimed at understanding human neuroses, viewed as learned responses related to stress and inner conflict. As predicted, some rats would vacillate at locations where the motives appeared equal. A whole program of research revealed parameters that affect conflict and extended the theoretical and experimental analysis of the phenomena that Freud described as displacement in the context of tendencies to approach and avoid goal stimuli. During this period Miller elaborated his theory of drive reduction that would underlie many of his later formulations.

Working with John Dollard, Miller viewed learning in its social context, leading to their book, *Social Learning and Imitation* (Miller & Dollard, 1941). The core experiments of the work entailed the parameters affecting social learning, as well as the decision as to which individual would be the leader and which the follower. The work was embedded in a theoretical model, a key element of which was the view that thoughts, perceptions, and similar cognitive phenomena had properties similar to overt muscular responses and thus could be learned, elicited by stimuli, serve as cues, and be inhibited by opposing central processes just as could overt responses. This view came to underlie various aspects of Miller's work.

Miller's motivational studies concerned not only appetitive motivations, such as hunger and thirst, but aversive conditioning as well. He did much work elaborating the concept of fear and the manner in which it is conditioned and can motivate behavior.

The culmination of the Yale work on psychoanalysis and learning was Dollard and Miller's (1950) *Personality and Psychotherapy*. The work is an analysis and translation of Freudian ideas into those from the learning laboratory. For example, the principle of reinforcement is substituted for Freud's pleasure principle and repression is interpreted as the inhibition of cue-producing responses related to thinking and reasoning. Conflict, transference, and higher mental processes were similarly analyzed.

Often neglected is important work Miller did as part of the World War II military effort. Among his activities were collaborating with other psychologists in the development of tests to select soldiers with potential for service as pilots, navigators, bombardiers, and officers, developing objective measures of pilot performance, and studies of the effects of various training regimens on flying skill. He worked on the effects of emotional stress, including fear as a drive that could motivate adaptive as well as maladaptive behavior. Miller viewed the success of psychologists in the war effort as a demonstration of the value of their training in scientific research.

The next major turn in Miller's work involved combining a variety of behavioral and physiological techniques to analyze phenomena such as hunger and fear. Miller and his associates used a variety of physiological techniques, including brain lesions, electrical stimulation of the brain, chemical brain stimulation, and electrophysiological recording. This integrated and significant program led to many new findings. Miller found evidence for the concept of hunger as a useful intervening variable. He was able to further dissect hunger, as with the finding that some lesions that cause animals to overeat render them less motivated to work to secure food. Electrical stimulation at some sites elicited eating and drinking that appeared to possess motivational properties similar to those of normal eating. Further research concerned the chemical coding of this behavior in cholinergic and adrenergic systems. Miller became interested in the possibility of eliciting fear responses by electrical brain stimulation in rats and cats and succeeded in demonstrating conditioning motivated by direct brain stimulation, though it proved difficult to separate fear from pain.

Perhaps the crowning accomplishment of Miller's career was his role in the development of the field of behavioral medicine, where he is regarded as a significant founder. In his early research in this field Miller and his associates attempted to condition visceral responses using instrumental procedures in rats paralyzed with curare. Although the initial effects were positive, they proved difficult to replicate in rats. However, other demonstrations in human patients were successful and were pivotal in the development of biofeedback as a clinical procedure. This proved applicable in patients suffering many disorders, including paralyzed individuals and scoliosis patients. The methods have been applied to teaching relaxation, altering unhealthy behaviors, and coping with stress and behavioral toxins. Miller stressed his conception of the brain as the supreme organ of integration of the body and the importance of understanding its hierarchical integrative organization in understanding the functioning of tissues and organs at all levels and for work in behavioral medicine.

Miller remained active throughout the later part of his career. He not only continued work on many of the themes explored earlier, but became a prominent spokesman for many research interests. He advocated the use of solid experimental techniques in the service of important social goals, always counseling "be bold in what you try, but cautious in what you claim" (Miller, 1992a, p. 309). He has been especially prominent in advocating animal research and pointing to the distortions of the literature presented by extreme opponents of animal research in psychology.

Neal Miller is among the most decorated of psychologists. Only a sample of his honors can be given. In 1965 he received the nation's highest scientific award, the National Medal of Science. He received the American Psychological Foundation's Gold Medal (1975), the Warren Medal of the Society of Experimental Psychologists (1964), the Newcomb Cleveland Prize of the American Association for the Advancement of Science (1956), the McAlpin Medal of the Mental Health Association (1978), and numerous similar awards. Miller served as president of the American Psychological Association (1960–1961), the Society for Neuroscience (1971–1972), the Academy of Behavioral Medicine Research (1979–1980), and the Biofeedback Society of America (1984–1985). He was elected to the National Academy of Sciences in 1958. Miller received honorary doctorates from the University of Michigan, the University of Pennsylvania, St. Lawrence University, the University of Uppsala, LaSalle College, and Rutgers University. Miller gave the first American Psychological Association Annual Neal E. Miller Lecture in 1994. The Academy of Behavioral Medicine Research began an annual Neal E. Miller New Investigator Award in 1989.

[*Many of the people mentioned in this article are the subjects of independent biographical entries.*]

Bibliography

Dollard, J., Doob, L. W., Miller, N. E., Mowrer, O. H., & Sears, R. R. (1939). *Frustration and aggression.* New Haven, CT: Yale University Press. Classic elaboration of the hypothesis relating frustration and aggression and also displacement of aggression in a broad psychological, sociological, and anthropological context.

Dollard, J., & Miller, N. E. (1950). *Personality and psychotherapy: An analysis in terms of learning, thinking, and culture.* New York: McGraw-Hill. A classic effort to combine Pavlovian and Hullian learning theory with Freudian psychoanalytic theory.

Miller, N. E. (1951). Learnable drives and rewards. In S. S. Stevens (Ed.), *Handbook of experimental psychology* (pp. 435–472). New York: Wiley. An analysis of the role of learning in the elaboration of drives based on fear, hunger, and other motives.

Miller, N. E. (1954). Fear. In R. H. Williams (Ed.), *Human factors in military operations: Some applications of the social sciences to operations research* (pp. 269–281). Chevy Chase, MD: Johns Hopkins University Press. An application of research on fear to military situations. A nice example of Miller's efforts to integrate laboratory animal research with significant applied problems.

Miller, N. E. (1959). Liberalization of basic S-R concepts: Extensions to conflict behavior, motivation, and social learning. In S. Koch (Ed.), *Psychology: A study of a science, Study 1. Conceptual and systematic. Vol. 2. General systematic formulations, learning, and special processes* (pp. 196–292). New York: McGraw-Hill. Demonstrates broadly the manner in which Miller tries to liberalize basic learning theory to encompass a variety of phenomena including conflict, reinforcement, psychotherapy, motivation, and social learning.

Miller, N. E. (1971). *Neal E. Miller: Selected papers.* Chicago: Aldine. A selection of Miller's important papers from the earlier stages of his career.

Miller, N. E. (1985). The value of behavioral research on animals. *American Psychologist, 40,* 423–440. An eloquent elaboration of Miller's position on the importance of animal research in solving practical clinical problems and of misleading efforts of animal extremists to distort the contributions of animal research.

Miller (1992a). Some trends from the history to the future of behavioral medicine. *Annals of Behavioral Medicine, 14,* 307–309. A nice statement of the interaction between laboratory research and clinical application in behavioral medicine.

Miller, N. E. (1992b). Behavior to brain to health. In F. Samson & G. Adelman (Eds.), *The neurosciences: Paths of discovery* (Vol. 2, pp. 293–305). Boston, MA: Birkauser. An excellent chronological summary of the development of much of Miller's research program with an emphasis on those aspects most related to neuroscience.

Miller, N. E., & Brucker, B. S. (1979). A learned visceral response apparently independent of skeletal ones in patients paralyzed by spinal lesions. In N. Birbaumer & H. D. Kimmel (Eds.), *Biofeedback and self-regulation* (pp. 287–304). Hillsdale, NJ: Erlbaum.

Miller, N. E., & Dollard, J. (1941). *Social learning and imitation.* New Haven, CT: Yale University Press. A study of the processes and implications of social learning in animals and humans.

Donald A. Dewsbury

MILLON CLINICAL MULTIAXIAL INVENTORY.
Since its inception in 1977, the Millon Clinical Multiaxial Inventory (MCMI) has become popular as both a research and a clinical assessment tool. There are three versions—the original MCMI, its revision, the MCMI-II, and the current version, the MCMI-III. Clinicians' surveys indicate that this is one of the three tests most frequently used in clinical assessments.

Initially designed to assess Millon's conceptualization of personality, each version has 175 true/false items and is intended for use only with psychiatric patients. Past versions of this test contained norms for both gender and race; however, the MCMI-III has no minority norms due to the lack of adequate normative samples.

The current version, the MCMI-III, has 24 scales designed to gauge one's similarity to a number of specific categorical prototypes. These scales are arranged into four groups: personality traits, severe personality patterns, clinical syndromes, and severe clinical syndromes. There are also four scales to assess validity and response tendencies.

Scoring involves a complex system of item weightings and unsubstantiated adjustments, despite evidence that these unnecessarily complicate scoring without improving test performance. Scoring may be done manually, with a personal computer and specialized software, or by the test publisher.

The interpretive score used by the MCMI is the BR (base rate) score, which is based on estimates of the prevalence of each characteristic in the population. Each scale's BR scores are anchored on four points: a BR score of 35 defines the median score for a normal or nonpsychiatric population; 60 is the median for a psychiatric population; 75 defines the presence of the characteristic being measured; and 85 is the point at which the characteristic is a prominent attribute for the individual. The use of fixed rather than locally determined BR cutting scores has been criticized, as these scores are optimal only if local base rates are the same as those used to develop the MCMI.

Since the MCMI family of tests is normed for use only with psychiatric patients, use with nonpatients can result in extreme and unrealistic scale elevations.

Test-retest stability for all versions of the MCMI is generally higher for personality style scales than it is for clinical symptom scales, a result that is consistent with the theoretical intent of this instrument. Alpha coefficients are reasonable, ranging from 0.66 for the Compulsive scale to 0.90 for the Major Depression scale. Test-retest correlations show acceptable stability, ranging from 0.82 for the Debasement scale to 0.90 for the Somatoform scale. Scales show low to moderate correlations with clinician ratings, ranging from 0.37 (Alcohol Dependence) to 0.07 (Post-Traumatic Stress Disorder and Dependent Personality Pattern) and −0.07 (Dysthymia). Correlations with similar scales from other personality inventories are quite variable but generally remain in the low to moderate range. Operating characteristics, computed from MCMI-III data in the manual, are poor. For example, positive predictive power (PPP) of the MCMI-III ranged from 0 to 0.32 for personality scales and from 0.15 to 0.58 for clinical symptom scales.

In general, the MCMI fares better when ascertaining personality traits than clinical syndromes, although further validity studies are needed.

Bibliography

Choca, J. P., & Denberg, E. V. (1997). *Interpretive guide to the Millon Clinical Multiaxial Inventory, second edition.* Washington, DC: American Psychological Association. A comprehensive discussion of the development and use of the MCMI tests.

Miller, H., Goldberg, J. O., & Streiner, D. L. (1993). The effects of the modifier and correction indices on MCMI-II profiles. *Journal of Personality Assessment, 60,* 477–485. Discusses the problems of using BR score adjustments.

Millon, T. (1969). *Modern psychopathology: A biosocial approach to maladaptive learning and functioning.* Philadelphia: Saunders. The conceptualization that forms the basis for the MCMI tests.

Millon, T. (1994). *Manual for the MCMI-III.* Minneapolis, MN: National Computer Systems. The basic reference for the most recent version of the MCMI, with norms for the MCMI-III and information and the rationale for the MCMI family of tests.

Millon, T., & Davis, R. D. (1997). The MCMI-III: Present and future directions. *Journal of Personality Assessment, 68,* 69–85. Ideas and suggestions about the further development of the MCMI-III.

Piotrowski, C., & Keller, J. W. (1989). Psychological testing in outpatient mental health facilities: A national study. *Professional Psychology: Research and Practice, 20,* 423–425. Provides information on the frequency of MCMI use.

Retzlaff, P. (1996). MCMI-III diagnostic validity: Bad test or bad validity study. *Journal of Personality Assessment, 66,* 431–437. Describes operating characteristics and problems with MCMI-III validity.

Streiner, D. L., Goldberg, J. O., & Miller, H. R. (1993). MCMI-II item weights: Their lack of effectiveness. *Journal of Personality Assessment, 60,* 471–476. Describes the problems of item weighting.

Widiger, T. A. (1985). Review of the Millon Clinical Multiaxial Inventory. In J. V. Mitchell, Jr. (Ed.), *Ninth mental measurement yearbook* (pp. 986–988). Lincoln, NE: Buros Institute. A review of the initial MCMI.

Harold R. Miller and Darrick M. Jolliffe

MIND-BODY PROBLEM. *See* Philosophy, *article on* Philosophy of Mind.

MINNESOTA MULTIPHASIC PERSONALITY IN-VENTORY. The most widely researched and used personality measure is the Minnesota Multiphasic Personality Inventory (MMPI). The inventory was originally published in 1940 by Starke Hathaway, a psychologist, and J. C. McKinley, a psychiatrist, as a clinical diagnostic aid for appraising emotional problems in psychiatric and medical settings. The MMPI attained broad application across a range of mental health, medical, substance abuse, forensic, and personnel screening settings as a measure of psychological maladjustment in the United States and Canada. In addition, the original MMPI was translated and widely adapted in many non–English-speaking countries around the world (Butcher, *International Adaptations of the MMPI-2*, Minneapolis, 1996).

The MMPI is a true-false questionnaire that consists of a number of psychometric scales, which address emotional and personality problems. A scale is a group of items designed to measure a particular attribute or personality characteristic. The original MMPI clinical scales were developed according to an empirical scale construction strategy sometimes referred to as the criterion keying approach because the items selected for the scales differentiated a defined clinical or criterion sample (such as depressed patients) from a sample of normals. The MMPI content was broad based; items were selected from a number of sources, including clinical cases, textbooks, and previous tests, to address clinical symptoms and personality characteristics. This broad-ranging item pool allowed for a relatively comprehensive psychiatric assessment. Once constructed, the scales also underwent further validation to assure that they assessed accurately in a variety of contexts.

The MMPI scales for an individual are interpreted by comparing each person's scores on the scales against reference samples of normal individuals and patient groups. All of the scales are normalized by converting the raw scores into standard scores, or T-scores. The scale scores are profiled on a graph to make scale comparisons easier.

The traditional clinical scales were designed to assess several important clinical problem areas, including hypochondriasis (Hs scale), depression (D scale), hysteria (Hy scale), psychopathic deviate (Pd scale), paranoid thinking (Pa scale), psychasthenia or anxiety (Pt scale), schizophrenia (Sc scale), With usage, practitioners and researchers came to understand that in clinical settings patients might have more than one scale elevated in the clinical range and found that homogeneous patient groups typically had very similar profile configurations, that is, the same clinical scales as prominent scores in the profile. For example, persons in alcohol treatment programs are typically found to have the D and Pd scores elevated; patients in inpatient psychiatric programs are found to have scales Pa and Sc

elevated in the significant range. These common profile configurations, called profile types or code types, have been widely researched, and the empirical correlates for these scale combinations have become standard elements in MMPI profile interpretation.

After several decades of use, the MMPI underwent a major revision during the 1980s in order to modernize the language in the item pool, to eliminate objectionable item content and outmoded items, to expand the item pool to include a broader range of content, and to develop a new nationally representative normative sample. The revised form for adults, MMPI-2, was published in 1989 and the adolescent version, MMPI-A, was published in 1992 (Butcher & Williams, *Essentials of MMPI-2 Interpretation*, Minneapolis, MN). In addition to developing new norms for the MMPI, a number of new scales were developed in order to address a broader range of clinical problems. The MMPI-2 standardization project employed a nationally representative sample of normal individuals (1,138 men and 1,462 women). The sample was an ethnically balanced representative sample of normals drawn at random from across the United States.

The MMPI-2, 567 true-false questions, assesses symptoms, attitudes, and beliefs that relate to emotional problems and behavior. The original MMPI clinical scales are relatively intact in the revised versions of the instrument in order to maintain continuity between the MMPI-2 and MMPI-A and the original instrument. Validity studies have been conducted on the MMPI-2 scales in order to explore the external correlates of the measures. Validation research by investigators (Graham, Ben-Porath, & McNulty, *MMPI-2 Correlates for Outpatient Mental Health Settings*, Minneapolis, 1999) provides continuing empirical support for the traditional MMPI clinical scales as well as the new MMPI-2 scales.

Any self-report personality instrument is vulnerable to distortion if people taking the test are motivated to deceive or make an effort to present themselves in a manner that is different than they actually are. With the original MMPI, Hathaway and McKinley were aware of uncooperative response sets, such as claiming excessive virtue or exaggerating complaints, and developed validity scales to detect such problems. One important feature of the MMPI-2 is that a number of scales have been developed to evaluate test-taking attitudes that could undermine the assessment. These scales are designed to appraise several invalidating approaches clients might take in responding to items on the test. For example, there are two scales that measure response inconsistency (responding to similar items in different ways). There are three separate scales to evaluate extreme symptom endorsement or symptom exaggeration, such as the original F (infrequency) scale to detect faking. These scales are extremely elevated with persons who falsely claim mental illness. There are three other scales to address overly virtuous or excessively defensive responding, that is, they are designed to detect "fake-good" response sets. Scales L (lie) and K (defensiveness) are examples of measures aimed at appraising test defensiveness. Persons taking the test in settings such as child custody determinations or personnel screening situations tend to present themselves in an overly favorable manner, reducing the credibility of the results. It is important for practitioners to attend carefully to the validity scale pattern to avoid misinterpreting the clinical measures.

There are other scales in the MMPI-2 that differ in construction methodology, psychometric properties, and interpretive strategy: the MMPI-2 content scales (Butcher, Graham, Williams, & Ben-Porath, *The MMPI-2 Content Scales*, Minneapolis, 1990). The content scales are interpreted according to a theoretical approach rather than the empirical correlate approach employed with the traditional clinical scales. The MMPI-2 content scales were derived by first rationally grouping similar items based upon their similar content into a scale. These provisional item groupings were then refined psychometrically by using internal consistency statistics (the alpha coefficient) to eliminate items from the scale that were not central to the construct being measured. Then the provisional scales were validated against external criteria to ensure that they possessed external validity. The MMPI-2 contains a number of content-based measures that address clinical problem areas not addressed by the traditional clinical scales, for example, antisocial personality characteristics (ASP scale), family problems (FAM scale), and negative treatment indicators (TRT scale). The interpretive strategy underlying the use of the MMPI-2 content scales is to consider the scores on each scale as direct communications between the client and the clinician with respect to the problems represented in each item cluster. A high score on the family problems scale, for example, represents the extent to which the client has acknowledged having family relationship problems.

In addition to the traditional clinical scales and the new MMPI-2 content scales, there are several widely used special problem scales, which are designed to address symptom areas not otherwise covered. Three scales to address substance abuse problems have become available. The MacAndrew Alcoholism Scale (MAC-R) and the Addiction Potential Scale (APS) are empirical scales that are focused upon the assessment of alcohol and drug abuse potential; the Addiction Acknowledgment Scale (AAS) was designed to assess the extent to which clients endorse having a problem with alcohol or drugs.

Over the years numerous studies have been conducted to accumulate personality and symptomatic information on patients' behavior for ranges of MMPI scale scores. For example, patients with high depression scale scores have been studied in a variety of clinical settings and their symptoms and behaviors cataloged to document the behavioral correlates of scale score elevations. The descriptive patterns collected in these studies can be applied to other individuals who obtain high scores on the same scale. These cataloged descriptors, often referred to as behavioral correlates, serve as the interpretive basis of MMPI-2 scales and ensure valid and reliable assessments for clients taking the test. One of the most prominent reasons that the MMPI-2 is so widely used in clinical assessment is that it can be interpreted in an objective manner and produces reliable and accurate assessments. The MMPI-2 also lends itself well to computer-based personality assessment (see Eyde, Kowal, & Fishburne, 1991).

Bibliography

Baer, R. A., Wetter, M. W., Nichols, D., Greene, R., & Berry, D. T. (1995). Sensitivity of MMPI-2 validity scales to underreporting of symptoms. *Psychological Assessment, 7,* 419–423.

Ben-Porath, Y. S., McCully, E., & Almagor, M. (1993). Incremental validity of the MMPI-2 content scales in the assessment of personality and psychopathology by self-report. *Journal of Personality Assessment, 61,* 557–575.

Butcher, J. N. (1999). *The MMPI-2: A beginners guide.* Washington, DC: American Psychological Association.

Butcher, J. N., Dahlstrom, W. G., Graham, J. R., Tellegen, A. M., & Kaemmer, B. (1989). *Minnesota Multiphasic Personality Inventory-2 (MMPI-2): Manual for administration and scoring.* Minneapolis, MN: University of Minnesota Press.

Butcher, J. N., Graham, J. R., & Ben-Porath, Y. S. (1995). Methodological problems and issues in MMPI/MMPI-2/MMPI-A research. *Psychological Assessment, 7,* 320–329.

Butcher, J. N., Williams, C. L., Graham, J. R., Tellegen, A., Ben-Porath, Y. S., Archer, R. P., & Kaemmer, B. The validity of computer-based interpretations of the MMPI. (1992). *Manual for administration, scoring, and interpretation of the Minnesota Multiphasic Personality Inventory for Adolescents: MMPI-A.* Minneapolis, MN: University of Minnesota Press.

Eyde, L., Kowal, D., & Fishburne, F. J. (1991). In T. B. Gutkin & S. L. Wise (Eds.), *The computer and the decision making process* (pp. 75–123). Hillsdale, NJ: Erlbaum.

Graham, J. R., Watts, D., & Timbrook, R. (1991). Detecting fake-good and fake-bad MMPI-2 profiles. *Journal of Personality Assessment, 57,* 264–277.

Hathaway, S. R., & McKinley, J. C. (1940). A multiphasic personality schedule (Minnesota): 1. Construction of the schedule. *Journal of Psychology, 10,* 249–254.

Tellegen, A., & Ben-Porath, Y. S. (1992). The new uniform T-scores for the MMPI-2: Rationale, derivation, and appraisal. *Psychological Assessment, 4,* 145–155.

Weed, N. C., Butcher, J. N., Ben-Porath, Y. S, & Mc-Kenna, T. (1992). New measures for assessing alcohol and drug abuse with the MMPI-2: The APS and AAS. *Journal of Personality Assessment, 58,* 389–404.

James N. Butcher

MINORITY PSYCHOLOGY. Psychologists who are people of color and others have contributed in many ways to the development of constructs, research questions and methods, treatment modalities, and assessment measures that are relevant and useful for their own groups. For example, Latino psychologists have argued for the need for Spanish-speaking therapy patients to work with someone who speaks their language. African American psychologists have developed Afrocentric techniques based on African philosophical principles. Native American psychologists have highlighted the importance of recognizing that for many Native Americans, the concept of self is framed from a collective, not an individualistic, perspective. Asian American psychologists have promoted the need to understand more about the immigration experience, and about the need to avoid even "positive" stereotypes about Asian Americans, such as "all Asian Americans are good at math." Psychologists from all four groups have pressured graduate programs, journals, organizations, state licensing boards, and other institutions to make the field less Eurocentric and more relevant and sensitive to people of color. Many European American psychologists are committed to changing training programs and hospital and educational policies that ignore the cultural components of the experiences of people of color.

Hall (1997) asserts that the field of psychology runs the risk of becoming "culturally obsolete" if these changes are not made in the very near future. She cites the chronic need for additional training opportunities and greater promotion of relevant teaching, research, and treatment strategies.

Since its inception, the field of psychology has attended to issues of race and culture in relation to psychological differences between individuals. Historically, African Americans, Latinos, Native Americans, and Asian Americans have been studied by some White psychologists and other scholars, and occasionally by psychologists from other groups with less than favorable, and often damaging and inaccurate results. The conclusions of these reports and studies have often influenced public policy decisions, and they have therefore had serious long-term implications in relation to the lives of people of color. People in these groups, referred to by many as people of color, have often been labeled as deviant, deficient, and pathological, largely because their behaviors, attitudes, and beliefs have varied from those of middle-class, White, Anglo-Saxon, Protestant, heterosexual, able-bodied men and boys who come from families in which both parents live in the same home. The experiences of people of color are dismissed or diminished as "pathological," "inappropriate," "unhealthy," and/or "immoral."

As early as 1906, G. Stanley Hall, known as the father of American psychology, commented on racial differences between African Americans and Whites, arguing that the two groups are so different that they would require completely distinct medical treatments. Historically, scientists and scholars from many disciplines have been interested in and have devoted time and energy to study of the differences between racial groups. They have used their (often scientifically questionable) research to justify many inhumane policies such as slavery, forced sterilization, segregation, and systematically limiting educational, career, housing, and business opportunities. They also tried to erect barriers between people of different races. For example, it was argued that children of African American and White parents could be successfully produced, but that these children could not reproduce (Guthrie, 1976). The last so-called antimiscegenation laws, prohibiting marriage between people of different races, were struck down by the Supreme Court as recently as 1967 in Virginia. The body of literature that has attempted to "document" the presumed inferiority of certain racial groups on a wide variety of traits is known as scientific racism. We might resist referring to this literature as genuinely scientific, opting for a term such as *pseudoscientific racism.* However, this is the term that is widely used, and one must use it to find additional articles and books on this topic.

Led by psychologists who are people of color, psychologists of many races and ethnicities have made efforts to correct the misconceptions that have resulted from earlier racist or culturally insensitive work. While significant progress has been made, future psychologists must continue to strive to study, treat, teach, and represent people of color in ways which are culturally sensitive, reality-based, and nonracist. Furthermore, psychologists must be trained in ways that achieve these goals.

Some psychologists believe that psychological theories should unite people of color throughout the diaspora. While the groups addressed in this article share some characteristics as regards psychological issues, each also has distinct issues related to political and economic status, their history related to American citizenship, the reasons they are in the United States, language, culture, religion, family style, and other areas of concern. It should be clearly understood that there are psychologists who are people of color working in every subdiscipline of psychology, using every treatment modality. It is a mistake to assume that all psychologists who are people of color hold exactly the same views or support the same scholars and theorists.

Definitions of Relevant Concepts

Issues related to class, race, and ethnicity tend to be emotionally charged and can be very difficult to discuss. A number of terms are used in relation to this topic, and these should be defined before we proceed further.

People of Color. There are many different reasons why many psychologists prefer the term *people of color.* It is used, in part, because the large majority of Asian, African American, Native American and Latino people come from or are mixed with racial groups whose skin is more endowed with melanin, and who consequently are readily and immediately visually noticed or identified. Many oppressive actions taken by people in power are initiated based on this readily identifiable physical feature. These actions, sometimes referred to as microaggressions, include being stopped by the police, followed in stores, mistaken at airports and other places of business as skycaps or other employees, treated with indifference and disdain by clerks and others in bureaucracies, and undergoing other daily stressful experiences. Making note of the importance of skin color does not ignore the fact that there are some people in each of these groups whose skin color closely resembles that of Caucasians and that there are Caucasians with darker skin. The term is not intended to offend Caucasians or to imply that they are "people of no color." It is designed as a way of unifying groups of people who have been historically oppressed and disenfranchised based, in part, on their skin color. Many scholars, professionals, politicians, and grass roots organizers believe that with more unity, collaboration, and cooperation among these groups, greater progress could be made regarding progressive changes that could enhance the opportunities and power structure to the benefit of the majority of Americans.

Ethnic Minority. Using the term *ethnic minorities* to describe people of color presents many challenges. First, the term *minority* carries a negative connotation for many, due to the notion of "smaller than" or "less than" inherent in the word. Many psychologists are opposed to labeling people as a minority, particularly when these peoples are not only the majority of the population worldwide, but are expected to make up more than 50% of the population of the United States in the twenty-first century. Certainly, this is already the case in many urban centers. Furthermore, it is noteworthy that there are many "ethnic minorities" among Caucasian Americans who have experienced varying levels of discrimination and prejudice in the United States. Nevertheless, the experiences of visibly different people from the four groups focused on in this article have been different from those of White "ethnic minorities," both quantitatively and qualitatively.

Race. Certainly, there are also many problems with the concept of race. Although it is true that the construct of race is not scientifically supported (Perez Foster, Moskowitz, & Javier, 1996), the fact remains that race and ethnicity have an impact on the lives of people on a daily basis. For example, one is aware of another's race more immediately because often, as noted earlier, it is so visible. In this author's opinion, it is a mistake not to use the term *race* in relation to studying and treating people of color, because in the experience of most people of color, the visual impact of their biologically determined physical features has a tremendous impact on their lives on a routine basis. Many people respond to the visual image created by differences in skin color, hair texture, and nose, eye, and lip shape before they know anything else about an individual. Some other terms are worthy of specific definitions in this context:

Afrocentric psychology—an approach that is based on African philosophical principles and the notion that theories applied to peoples of African descent should be based solely on African philosophical principles.

Black psychology—an approach that argues that the study of the psychology of Black people is a distinct enterprise that should focus on the strengths, social context, and uniqueness of Black people.

Culture—the rules and patterns that govern and determine the lifestyle of a group of people. These include language, religion, family patterns, values, mores, morals, and other issues.

Cultural competence—the belief that people should not only appreciate and recognize other cultural groups but also be able to effectively work with them (Sue, 1998).

Deficit model—a model for studying or treating diverse groups that focuses on the presumed weaknesses and deficits of the less powerful group.

Difference model—a model for studying diverse groups that recognizes that a range of variables results in different behavior, language, attitudes, beliefs, knowledge, and cultural patterns, all of which are valid and should be respected and understood on their own terms and in the socio-political-cultural context in which they occur.

Ethnicity—the nationality and cultural patterns of a group of people.

Ethnocentric—based on and centered around a particular ethnic group. In some instances, it is appropriate to use ethnocentric theories and/or modalities as long as they are being applied only to the group in question and this is clearly understood.

Eurocentric—based on and centered around European (often Western European) philosophical principles.

Psycho-cultural issues—concerns and characteristics that grow out of the complex interplay between psychology and culture.

Race—the biological features of a group of people that are visible and are often used to readily and quickly group them and separate them from others, such as skin color, hair texture, and nose, eye, and lip shape.

Self-determination—to name oneself, define oneself, and speak for oneself, instead of being named, defined, and spoken for by others. In the field of psychology, the importance of groups presenting their own interpretation of their behavior rather than being defined and studied by groups who do not have their best interests at heart.

Additional relevant terms can be found in the body of this article and in many other articles on topics related to culture, race, and the psychology of people of color.

Some believe that focusing too heavily on culture, class, and race moves too far beyond the focus on the individual, which is one of the hallmarks of psychology. They state that a heavy emphasis on culture, economics, politics, and other social issues is more the purview of sociology and anthropology. One can make serious errors in interpreting the psychology of people of color if race, class, ethnicity, and other diverse characteristics are not studied in adequate detail. Furthermore, the psychology of people of color must be understood in connection to the psychology of people in power who benefit economically and politically from theories and behavioral explanations that depict people of color as inferior and deficient. Psychologists who are people of color spend considerable time and energy understanding the psychology of race, racism, and racists, including recent work by Helms and others on the racial identity of White people (Helms & Cook, 1999).

When addressing volatile issues such as these, it is important to avoid generalizations, both about groups as a whole and about individuals within groups. Stylistic variation in language, family style, religious expression, political views, and other issues such as social class, educational, and skin-color differences can cause polarization amongst different groups. A great deal of intragroup conflict and competition can arise as a result of these differences. Sexual orientation can be a highly charged and divisive issue as gays, lesbians, bisexuals, and transgendered people of color fight for equality, respect, and self-determination. As groups compete for scarce resources, tensions run high. Many are striving to build bridges between and amongst these groups by promoting recognition of the collective heritage they share.

In relation to generalization, one must be cognizant of avoiding stereotypes. For example, as they learn about the range of families they treat, therapists must walk the fine line between overgeneralizing about a group's functioning by freely accepting stereotypes and being sensitive to the many variations within and between groups on many family issues. For example, tremendous variations can be found among Native Amer-

ican families of a single ethnic group or nation based on each family's level of acculturation. Acculturation refers to the degree to which members of a cultural group have adopted the values, language, religion, behaviors, and other cultural features of the larger, more dominant group. A conceptual framework for categorizing families can be developed based on language, kin structure, religion, relationship to land, and health habits. These variables directly affect the strategies that families use to solve problems and relate to others, both within and outside of the family.

Many clinicians and theorists take the position that people are essentially the same everywhere, and therefore one can use the same theories or modifications of theories to apply to people from various groups. Others believe that theories designed for one group in a particular sociopolitical, historical, racial, and cultural context cannot effectively be applied to another group (Nobles, 1972). These psychologists believe that it is inappropriate, for example, to apply psychoanalytic concepts that were developed by Freud and others during the late nineteenth century in Vienna to people of color living in the United States in the late twentieth century. Some clinicians have returned to the ancient and early philosophical foundations of their own peoples to design treatment approaches. These spiritual elements are often integrated with psychological treatments to arrive at effective treatments for emotional problems.

When approaching people of color, a multidisciplinary approach is often used. The lines between disciplines are not necessarily rigidly maintained. Holistic approaches that take into account the spiritual, physical, emotional, and intellectual aspects of one's psychological development and functioning are used. For many scholars and practitioners, there is no sharp division between physical and mental health, as in many Western psychological and physical approaches.

In much of the literature on working with people of color, a common thread focuses on the importance of emphasizing the sociocultural and psychocultural contexts in which people live. To ignore the impact of social, economic, cultural, political, and other contextual features would be to possibly seriously misunderstand people of color. Poor health, single-parent family structure, patterns of incarceration, and educational underpreparation are all related, in part, to poverty and limited access to financial, educational, employment, health, housing, and political resources and power. The amount of power a group has and its status in the power hierarchy tremendously affects its level of mental and physical health.

Social class can also be a significant confounding variable in research. Billingsley (1992) points out that although, taken as a whole, African American families are far more likely to be headed by single mothers than are White families, when one controls for social class the differences between Whites and Blacks diminishes. Middle-class Black families, White families, and poor Black and White families have similar family structures. One can find similar patterns in relation to age, geographic location, and religious background.

A major question arises regarding the degree to which a particular feature or characteristic is related to culture as compared to the person's individual personality or a family's unique features. Most scholars agree that individual and family patterns, and social and cultural patterns, interact to produce the variations one sees within and between groups of people of color.

Transracial adoption in the United States is an excellent example of institutional racism at work. Since people of color are less likely to be able to afford to live in their own homes in economically stable neighborhoods, they are often deemed less adequate as parents then their white counterparts. Some psychologists who are people of color have made strong statements in relation to the inappropriateness of transracial adoption (*Journal of Black Psychology*, special issue on transracial adoption, May 1996). It has been argued that adoption agencies often ignore applicants who are people of color in favor of White adoptive parents, based on the assumption that a certain level of economic stability is more important than the racial and cultural identity of the child. Many psychologists assert that the nuances of culture are very subtle and can only be learned in the context of a family of the same cultural background as the child.

Resistance to Considering Race and Culture

Culture and race are more important to some people than to others. It is important to recognize that even some people of color believe that others in their group overemphasize race, culture, and racism, using it to "excuse" maladaptive behaviors. When working with and/or studying people of color, one must get a sense of how each individual relates to his or her race and culture. There can be tremendous variation between individuals based on the degree of acculturation and assimilation, racial identity, Black consciousness (for individuals of African descent), and other issues. It is counterproductive to think that psychologists should ignore culture and race, or give it short shrift, especially in training programs, when this is such an essential part of how people function on a day-to-day basis.

Since there is such great diversity regarding how important a person considers race and culture to be in his or her life, therapists and researchers must be trained to work with those patients for whom it is extremely important in order to avoid the risk of totally misunderstanding the patient's perspective and worldview.

Research on People of Color

One of the major shortcomings of research on people of color has been the tendency to compare Native Americans, African Americans, Latinos, and Asians with Whites as a "comparison group." Furthermore, Asian Americans and Latinos, and Native Americans in particular, have been ignored in favor of studying African Americans in comparison to Caucasians. In most instances, Whites have been used as a standard by which other groups are measured. Any variation from the "standard" of White behavior is considered deviant, deficient, or inadequate and in need of immediate alteration. Again, the myriad reasons for the differences between groups was rarely considered, and the notion that some of the behaviors and attitudes of the less powerful group could be superior or more advantageous is almost never considered. Matsumoto (1994) provides numerous useful examples of the influence of culture on research and statistics.

The Tuskeegee Study

One of the most striking examples of scientific racism is the infamous Tuskeegee study. The study, funded by the federal government through the Public Health Service, involved identifying African American men who were infected with syphilis and withholding treatment from some and offering inadequate treatment to others in order to study the long-term effects of the disease on the subjects (a common misconception is that the men were healthy and were given syphilis). They were offered free "health care," money, burial expenses, and other resources and were led to believe that they were being treated for any illnesses they might have had. Furthermore, an African American nurse was hired to encourage the men to participate in the study. Neither the men nor their wives or other sexual partners knew that they were not being treated. Even after the advent of penicillin, treatment was withheld "in the interest of science." The experiment lasted for over 40 years, ending in the early 1970s. In 1998, President Bill Clinton offered an official apology to the survivors of the experiment. This study exemplifies the degree to which the lives of people of color can be devalued by researchers.

Recent examples, such as the Violence Initiative, which involves studying African American men and boys to attempt to demonstrate the existence of genetic bases for violent behavior, illustrate that this trend has not ended. As a result of the experiences of people of color in relation to research and their exploitation, researchers sometimes find that people of color are reluctant to participate in research and remain suspicious of government agencies and other people in powerful positions. Many psychologists who are people of color and others are acutely aware of this issue and go to great lengths to approach research populations in a respectful, ethical manner, and to eliminate any possible exploitation.

One should not underestimate the impact of research, such as the Tuskeegee study, on the attitudes of people of color about research. The notion that it can be objective or neutral is a myth. Our cultural assumptions guide our research questions, methodologies, and conclusions.

The impact of research in other fields can have an effect on how psychological researchers are received by people of color. Recently, there has been a proliferation of scholarship focusing on the strengths of people of color. It is felt that this is the best way to approach difficult issues rather than to view the behaviors of people of color as deviant or deficient simply because they are different from those of White people.

Understanding Privilege

In a classic article, McIntosh (1992) presents some crucial concerns related to the issue of privilege in the United States. She describes privilege as an invisible "knapsack" that includes road maps, passports, tickets, and visas. These resources, which are often unearned, like the privilege of White skin, have a tremendous impact on the life opportunities and experiences of people in the United States and around the world. Issues of privilege, class, and disability must be a major part of the discourse on the psychology of people of color. McIntosh asserts that privilege can either positively or negatively impact one's life by affecting one's opportunities, access to resources, and the response one receives from the world.

People who are members of privileged, powerful groups often feel threatened when they learn that their own worldview is not supported by everyone. They sometimes challenge and demand that others accept and realize that their way of life is the "right" and "only way," and resist any suggestion that another perspective might be different and equally valid. A tremendous amount of learning can take place by being open to these various psychological adaptations.

Working effectively with people of color means being open to new perspectives, points of view, values, opinions, lifestyles, and beliefs. This does not mean that one will always agree with these varied points of view, but when therapists are unable to even entertain them, the communication of the patient could be cut off and he or she could be invalidated and disaffirmed.

Similarly, in the realms of teaching and research, when one is bound to a single cultural paradigm, one is limited to a narrow range of interpretations and ways of knowing or understanding data and knowledge.

Awareness of one's cultural and racial blinders, biases, and resistances is a first step toward greater openness and sensitivity to a wide range of human experiences.

Many people from privileged groups wonder: How does studying the psychology of people of color benefit me? The benefits are many. In today's society, the likelihood of working in a setting with a homogenous population is very slim, particularly given the predictions that by the year 2000 more than 50% of the U.S. workforce will be made up of people of color. Even rural populations are becoming more diverse. Understanding the many factors that affect the psychology of people of color can increase one's sensitivity to issues that have an impact on all people. For example, knowledge and skills related to the psychology of people of color can apply to gender and the many other ways that people vary, such as physical attractiveness, learning style, family style, religion, and other characteristics.

Psychologists are known for studying individuals. More definitions of psychology are including the notion of the importance of studying behavior in context. This definition of psychology was perhaps first used by Allen and Santrock (*Psychology: The Contents of Behavior*, Madison, Wisc., 1994). Many psychologists believe that although institutional analysis is often seen as the purview of political scientists and sociologists, in order to thoroughly and accurately understand the functioning of people of color, psychologists must study these phenomena as well.

People of color need to be understood from their own perspectives as well as by those who are from other groups. By combining the great wealth of knowledge from the experiences of people from many backgrounds, we can achieve greater understanding of all people. Thus, all people can improve their research, clinical, and teaching skills by increasing their knowledge and understanding of their own group and other groups.

Clinical Issues

In the area of clinical work, as in other areas, if one assumes that groups are completely different from one another, one can be blind to striking similarities. If one is convinced that groups are more similar than different, the striking differences between groups can be overlooked. It is crucial to attend to both similarities and differences in order to gain the fullest understanding of a group. People of color must also acknowledge that they are not immune to cultural biases, prejudices, racism, and other maladaptive attitudes and behaviors. This can be particularly acute when one treats, studies, or teaches people with whom one is very similar. We can overlook important differences as we are empathizing and connecting with many similarities. The key, then, is to balance our focus on similarities and differences and be willing to challenge ourselves to question ourselves even when we feel we know everything there is to know about a group.

When working to understand a group different from one's own, it is useful to also gain a deeper understanding of one's own group's cultural background and history. Given the emotional nature of race and other diversity issues, one must strive to understand his or her own position on these issues in attempting to understand people of color. People often expect others to behave as members of their own group have. For example, I have heard individuals make statements such as: "Since I wouldn't want to talk about my group in the presence of others, I thought he wouldn't want to either." Making assumptions such as these can be dangerous. It is better to ask questions than to make assumptions that may be incorrect. Another example of a broad generalization is the following frequently heard statement: "People of color people don't want to have to speak for their entire group." This may be true of many, but there are many people of color who enjoy and feel quite comfortable sharing their opinions and experiences in mixed or homogeneous settings. These and other generalizations can be useless and even damaging. There are exceptions to every rule.

Many scholars question how individuals trained without a background in the culture of a group of people can effectively treat that group. Others assert that as long as a therapist is sensitive to the differences between himself or herself and the patient, and believes in the fundamental human value of that individual, psychotherapy can be effective. Although one cannot be expected to learn about each culture around the world, practitioners and researchers should take into account the varied lifestyles, values, power relationships, and attitudes of people from different groups and how they can affect their psychological functioning as individuals and members of families and communities.

A popular area of inquiry in relation to the treatment of people of color is whether or not these patients should be seen by someone of their own cultural or racial background. Many patients who are people of color are unwilling to work with counselors or therapists from different racial or cultural groups than their own. They feel that it would be impossible for a therapist of a different race to understand or empathize with them and their experience. They also believe that they could not possibly share their innermost thoughts and feelings with a person of a different race. Many years of being misunderstood, misinterpreted, and discriminated against have had negative repercussions and have taken their toll. These individuals attempt to protect themselves from the possibility of again being damaged in an interracial encounter. Being open to engaging in an open dialogue can have a profound impact.

Teaching. There are cultural and racial implications in every area of psychological inquiry. Some introductory psychology textbooks have begun to include a boxed feature on culture in each chapter or most chapters. As recently as the mid-1980s, culture was rarely mentioned in the introductions of psychology textbooks, and race was essentially confined to discussions of intelligence testing and prejudice. Whitten (1993), Fairchild (1988), Singelis (1998), and others have published works that expand the resources and teaching strategies available to those who wish to address these issues in their courses.

Whitten (1993) noted that when discussing issues related to Black people in college psychology courses, this material should be infused into the curriculum rather than being presented in one unit as a separate issue. At times, diversity issues are presented as boxed features while they are downplayed in the rest of the text. In the past, many texts only discussed issues of race and ethnicity in connection with intelligence and prejudice. Only in the last 10 years has culture or race received more than one or two listings in the popular introductory psychology texts, which tend to be 700 pages long. The first textbook to integrate culture and race throughout was by Allen and Santrock in 1994. Unfortunately, the second edition retreated from its commitment to a heavy emphasis on culture.

Many textbooks have improved their treatment of these issues. The next step is to acknowledge the fact that with regard to all human beings, not just people of color, race and ethnicity are important issues, particularly in the context of the racist, oppressive environments of the United States and other countries around the world.

Training. For people of color, race and ethnicity are issues with which they are confronted virtually every day of their lives. Therefore, it is inappropriate to minimize these issues in psychology training programs. Some training programs remain highly resistant to the notion of integrating information on these issues into their curricula. Unfortunately, this is still the case in many graduate clinical, school, and counseling training programs. This could clearly communicate that these issues are deemed unimportant and/or irrelevant by the faculty. This is not the opinion of most of the people of color that therapists encounter. It is striking that many graduate training programs for psychologists only began to address the issue of culture and other diversity issues about 25 to 30 years ago. Although the American Psychological Association has provided guidelines for training culturally competent counselors and therapists (APA, Office of Ethnic Minority Affairs, 1993), and many other organizations, such as the Association of Black Psychologists, the Asian American Psychological Association, the Native American Psychological Association, and the National Hispanic Psychological Association, have offered training sessions, workshops, and journals and other publications on curriculum, clinical work, and research, many programs still neglect to train their students in cultural competence. In one instance at a training program on the East Coast, one class had not been assigned a single article or book on race, class, or culture during their first 3 years of coursework. This is a travesty of grave proportions. Over 50% of the students will work in internships populated largely by people of color, and they will be ill-equipped to address many of their patients' needs. Research suggests that when people are unaware of, insensitive to, and poorly prepared regarding the cultural background of a group of people, clinical work suffers. Psychologists must be willing to challenge their assumptions about culture and be aware of the impact of their own culture, class, race, and other issues on their views about health, illness, family, power, gender, sexuality, and other issues.

Due to the history of exclusion and discrimination of people of color in higher education in the United States, there is a need for more psychologists who are people of color. Institutional racism and educational inequities contribute to the continuation of this trend.

While many psychologists receive excellent training in working with a "generic human being," White, middle-class, Anglo-Saxon, Protestant, heterosexual, able-bodied men from families where both parents live in the same home are still considered the standard by which all others are measured. Without a consistent, meaningful focus on race, culture, class, and other issues, it is possible to misdiagnose, misinterpret, and overlook important information and material presented by a patient, student, or research participant.

Again, there are many dangers inherent in lumping people of color together. The nuances of each cultural group can be glossed over. This should be kept in mind given the tremendous variation in the history and current status of Native Americans, African Americans, Latinos, and Asian Americans. Furthermore, presenters and authors writing on this topic almost always emphasize the fact that within-group differences can often be greater than between-group differences. It is important to recognize that these groups have some similar experiences and some that are unique to their own group. Yet, public policy has generally revolved around the ways in which people of color are different from White people, not the ways in which they are similar.

Institutional Racism

An important concept to understand when paying attention to the psychology of people of color is institutional racism. This is a construct that is almost never discussed in psychology textbooks at the undergraduate or graduate level. Institutional racism "refers to the established, customary, and respected ways in which society operates to keep the minority in a subordinate position" (Eitzen & Baca Zinn, 1992). Furthermore, it is the systematic discrimination built into policies that results in differential outcomes for various groups. Policies are written in such a way that they are not overtly prejudicial, but differential outcomes may result. Examples are found in the areas of housing, the rates at which mortgages and other loans are granted, admission rates to colleges and graduate school, hiring practices, access to health care, and many other areas. These policies affect opportunities and access to resources based on race. Generally, they are changed only through years of grass roots and other types of organizing and governmental battles.

Institutional racism is different from individual acts of racism perpetrated by a person, such as using a racial epithet or an individual refusing to rent to a person because of his or her race or ethnicity. The experience of these kinds of discrimination, which are often difficult to document and prove, has a profound impact on the psychological functioning of people of color.

Scientific Racism

Early investigations in the area of scientific racism involved a collaboration between psychologists and anthropologists. In his classic book on the history of the treatment of race in psychology and of African Americans in psychology, Guthrie notes:

> Psychology and anthropology were bedfellows during this early age of racism; both searched for, and consequently magnified, the existence of racial differences, mental abilities, and character traits among the peoples of the world. Their zest and zeal reinforced prevailing Western mythologies of racial superiority and the resultant exploitation of non-White peoples. (*Even the Rat Was White*, 1976, p. 3)

Brain size and shape were characteristics that received attention. The shape and size of human brains of various racial groups were used to classify people and draw conclusions about their intelligence. "Since Whites were generally judged to be more intelligent than blacks, the Gall and Spurzheim (1817) line of reasoning eventually led early psychologists to conclude that the skull capacities of Whites were greater than the skull capacities of blacks" (Guthrie, 1976, p. 33). This grew out of the notion that the size of the skull reflected the shape of the brain underneath. In 1824, John Friedrich Blumenbach developed a method for determining whether skulls belonged to "civilized" or "uncivilized" individuals: "The skull was placed between the feet of the observer and after examination from above, classed as oblong, round, and so forth, for the purpose of determining the race to which it belonged" (Guthrie, 1976, p. 33).

These claims were made in an effort to justify discrimination against people of African descent and others based on biological and hereditary differences that explained "deficient" behavior. Others have been affected by the claims of researchers determined to demonstrate the superiority of their own racial group. The Eugenics movement of the late nineteenth century and early twentieth century sought to arrange marriages in order to produce a "superior race." Francis Galton defined eugenics in 1883 as "the study of the agencies under social control that may improve or impair the racial qualities of future generations either physically or mentally" (Guthrie, 1976, p. 78). Laws were passed around the country that sanctioned the sterilization of individuals in mental hospitals and state prisons. Similar laws were passed in a number of European countries. Material on eugenics was included in psychology textbooks and lectures, and it appeared in one popular psychology textbook as late as the 1950s (Guthrie, 1976).

One might ask: "If these ideas are not really scientific and are part of the past, why continue to focus on them?" Unfortunately, there are some scholars who continue to support these ideas, even the notion that brain size and other indicators should be utilized to classify humans into racial groups. There has been an upsurge of racist sentiment around the world. Skinheads, neo-Nazis, Ku Klux Klan members, and, unfortunately, some professionals continue the socially destructive tradition of promoting the belief that Whites are superior to others. As long as scholars and other leaders continue to support racism, anti-Semitism, sexism, classism, heterosexism, and other forms of oppression, these violent acts will continue and those who support them will feel justified in their actions.

Early notions about the racial inferiority of some groups laid the foundation for current policies that continue to discriminate against many people. Those who support scientific racism focus on biological explanations of behavior to the exclusion of social, economic, and cultural explanations. In this way they seek to maintain the existing inequities in society that lead to vast differences in the health, educational, and economic status of some people. The disparities between racial groups are seen as the fault of those groups, due to their inferiority, rather than the result of social barriers to progress. This is known as blaming the victim or victim blaming (Ryan, 1976). Fairchild (1991) points out that people who support scientific racism tend to avoid discussion of the policy implications of their work by hiding behind a "cloak of objectivity" and describing their work as "pure" scientific inquiry. He states, however, that it is important to pay attention to public policy issues. A wide range of policies in the United States continues to affect racial groups differentially. For example, he points out that people once advocated offering sterilization incentives to African American women based on low IQ scores. There are other examples of racist policies that deserve attention:

- In 1991, an African American woman who had been convicted of child abuse was sentenced to use Norplant (the long-term contraceptive implanted in a woman's arm) to prevent future conceptions as a condition to probation (*New York Times*, 15 April 1992). After accepting this judgment, the woman later refused it. In 1992, the decision was declared moot because the woman used cocaine and was sentenced to prison.
- Native American women are also encouraged to use Norplant and are not always informed correctly about some of the risks and problems associated with it (The Native American Women's Health Education Resource Center, 1993).
- Because the culture of Native Americans was seen as inferior to White American culture, children earlier in this century were removed from reservations and sent to boarding schools where they were taught to behave, dress, speak, and think like European Americans (Lomawaima, 1994).

Policies such as these are of concern because they illustrate the degree to which some groups are devalued and disenfranchised. These policies severely limit the rights of less powerful people. Research and intervention by culturally sensitive psychologists can help change these policies.

Educators and mental-health professionals continue to demonstrate bias against some groups of people. These ideas must be challenged so that individuals of all racial groups can reach their potential. A tremendous amount of energy has been used to counter these racist notions. This energy could have been more profitably directed at proactive forms of inquiry. We still have a long way to go before these ideas are put to rest. Psychologists can better spend their time developing creative solutions to social problems rather than struggling to debunk negative myths and stereotypes about less powerful groups of people.

All psychologists must challenge themselves to scrutinize their own attitudes about people of color and the range of issues related to them. Careful evaluation of our own prejudices is an important initial step to overcoming discrimination against people who are different. It is interesting that some individuals who are champions in the fight against one type of discrimination support, consciously or unconsciously, directly or indirectly, discrimination in another area. There are White female feminists who are racist, African American civil rights advocates who are homophobic and/or sexist, and gay men fighting for gay rights who are racist and/or sexist. This makes the struggle to liberate all oppressed people more difficult. Many believe that all forms of discrimination feed on each other and must be eradicated, simultaneously, if possible. By addressing these and other pressing issues in the field, psychology can continue to thrive as a viable, meaningful endeavor rather than becoming "culturally obsolete." By taking advantage of the wide range of resources available, it is possible for psychologists and others to contribute positively to the lives of and scholarship on people of color.

Resources

By joining professional associations, one can learn more about appropriately and usefully applying psychology to particular populations, network with other students and professionals, and indentify a mentor. Most organizations have local, regional, and national conferences where students and others can present papers, and they publish newsletters, journals and books. Some of these organizations are as follows: American Orthopsychiatric Association, American Psychological Association, American Psychological Society, Asian American Psychological Association, Association of Black Psychologists, International Association for Cross-Cultural Psychology, National Black Child Development Institute, National Hispanic Psychologists Association, Society of Indian Psychologists, and World Federation for Mental Health. Scholarships for people of color seeking degrees in psychology can be obtained from organizations such as the Ford Foundation, American Psychological Association, McKnight, and the Association of Black Psychologists. By searching the Web and other databases, other resources can be identified.

Journals covering the field of minority psychology include *Cultural Diversity and Ethnic Minority Psychology*, *Ethnicity and Health*, *Hispanic Journal of Behavioral Sciences*, *Journal of African American Men*, *Journal of Black Psychology*, *Journal of Black Studies*, *Journal of Cross-Cultural Psychology*, *Journal of Ethnic Studies*, *Journal of Multicultural Community Health* (out of print), *Journal of Social Issues*, *New Horizons*, *Journal of the Caribbean Association of Professionals and Scholars*, *Social Science and Medicine*, and *Womanist Theory and Research*.

[*See also* African American Psychology; American Indian Psychology; Asian American Psychology; Ethnic and Racial Identity; *and* Hispanic Psychology.]

Bibliography

American Psychological Association, Office of Ethnic Minority Affairs. (1993). Guidelines for providers of psychological services to ethnic, linguistic, and culturally diverse population. *American Psychologist, 48,* 45–48.

Betancourt, H., & Lopez, S. R. (1993). The study of culture, ethnicity, and race in American Psychology. *American Psychologist, 48,* 629–637.

Billingsley, A. (1992). *Climbing Jacob's ladder: The enduring legacy of African-American families.* New York: Simon & Schuster.

Eitzen, D. S. & Baca Zinn, M. B. (1992). *Social problems.* Boston: Allyn & Bacon.

Fairchild, H. (1988). Curriculum design for Black (African-American) Psychology. In P. A. Bronstein & K. Quina (Eds.), *Teaching a psychology of people: Resources for gender and sociocultural awareness* (pp. 134–141). Washington, DC: American Psychological Association.

Fairchild, H. (1991). Scientific racism: The cloak of objectivity. *Journal of Social Issues, 47*(3), 101–115.

Guthrie, R. (1996). *Even the rat was white.* New York: Harper and Row.

Hall, C. C. I. (1997). Cultural malpractice: The growing obsolescence of psychology with the changing U.S. population. *American Psychologist, 52,* 642–651.

Helms, J. E. & Cook, D. A. (1999). *Using race and culture in counseling and psychotherapy: Theory and process.* Boston: Allyn & Bacon.

Jones, J. (1997). *Prejudice and racism.* San Francisco: McGraw-Hill.

Jones, R. (in press). *Advances in African American psychology* (4th ed.). Cobb and Henry. This is the fourth edition of this text, covering a wide range of topics related to the psychology of African Americans. For a thorough coverage of the development of this field, consult the other editions, some of which are out of print.

La Framboise, T. D., & Low, K. G. (1989). American Indian children and adolescents. In J. T. Gibbs & L. N. Huang (Eds.), *Children of color: Psychological interventions with minority youth* (pp. 114–147). San Francisco, CA: Jossey-Bass.

Lomawaima, K. T. (1994). *They called it prairie light: The story of Chiloco Indian school.* Lincoln: University of Nebraska Press.

Lonner, W. J., & Malpass, R. S. (Eds.). (1994). *Psychology and culture.* Boston: Allyn & Bacon.

Matsumoto, D. (1994). *Cultural influences on research methods and statistics.* Pacific Grove, CA: Brooks/Cole. Provides a concise summary of relevant issues and excellent resources on cultural influences on research dating back to the mid-1970s. A small, affordable text that can be a supplement in almost any psychology course. See also *People: Psychology from a cultural perspective.* Pacific Grove, CA: Brooks/Cole, Matsumoto.

McGoldrick, M., Giordano, J., & Pearce, J. K. (1996). *Ethnicity and family therapy* (2nd ed.). New York: Guilford Press. A rare source of guidelines and suggestions on family therapy which recognizes the need to focus on both race *and* ethnicity, including a broad spectrum of Caucasian ethnic groups.

McIntosh, P. (1992). White privilege and male privilege: A personal account of coming to see correspondences through work in women's studies. In M. L. Anderson & P. Hill Collins (Eds.), *Race, class, and gender: An anthology* (pp. 70–81). Belmont, CA: Wadsworth. A classic and unique article on critical issues surrounding privilege, resources, and power and their relationship to one's everyday functioning.

Monteiro, K. P. (Ed.). (1996). *Ethnicity and psychology: African-, Asian-, Latino-, and Native American psychologies* (Rev. ed.). Dubuque, IA: Kendall Hunt.

Nobles, W. W. (1972). African philosophy: Foundations for Black psychology. In R. Jones (Ed.), *Black psychology* (pp. 18–32). New York: Harper & Row.

Padillo, A. (Ed.). (1995). *Hispanic psychology: Critical issues in theory and research.* Thousand Oaks, CA: Sage.

Perez Foster, R., Moskowitz, M., & Javier, R. A. (Eds.). 1996. *Reaching across boundaries of culture and class: Widening the scope of psychotherapy.* Northvale, NJ: Jason Aronson.

Ryan, W. (1976). *Blaming the victim* (Rev. ed.). New York: Vintage. A classic work on the importance of considering the social, political, and economic limitations placed on some individuals who are then blamed for not overcoming these societal obstacles.

Singelis, T. M. (Ed.). (1998). *Teaching about culture, ethnicity, and diversity.* Thousand Oaks, CA: Sage.

Sue, S. (1982). *The mental health of Asian-Americans.* San Francisco: Jossey-Bass.

Sue, S. (1998). In search of cultural competence in psychotherapy and counseling. *American Psychologist, 53,* 440–448.

Thomas, S. B., & Quinn, S. C. (1991). The Tuskegee Syphilis study, 1932 to 1972: Implications for HIV education programs in the Black community. *American Journal of Public Health, 81*(11), 1498–1505. A clear, concise article which dispels some of the myths of this infamous study.

Trickett, E. J., Watts, R. J., & Berman, D. (1994). *Human diversity: Perspectives on people in context.* San Francisco: Jossey-Bass.

Whitten, L. (1993). Infusing Black psychology into the introductory psychology course. *Teaching of Psychology, 20*(1), 13–21. The third article in the 22-year history of this journal on the importance of exposing undergraduate students to the centrality of race and culture in the field of psychology early in their careers.

Yee, A. H., Fairchild, H. H., Weizmann, F., & Wyatt, G. E. (1993). Addressing psychology's problems with race. *American Psychologist, 48,* 1132–1140.

Lisa Whitten

MMPI-2. *See* Minnesota Multiphasic Personality Inventory.

MNEMONIC DEVICES. Since the beginning of recorded history, people have been dissatisfied with their slowness of learning and their speed of forgetting. To aid memory, procedures called mnemonic ("neh-MON-ic") devices were developed even before ancient Greek and Roman times.

Mnemonic devices are of two general kinds, which I refer to here as macromnemonics and micromnemonics. Macromnemonics are easier to understand and use, but, surprisingly, most historical writing deals with micromnemonics—probably because their successful use enables us to remember almost anything.

Macromnemonics

Macromnemonics are general procedures that we can use to make learning more effective and more efficient. These procedures prescribe not only how, when, and where various kinds of study should take place but also emphasize the importance of the learner's physical, emotional, and mental state. An example of a macromnemonic is the SQ3R technique, which students can use to help to remember the content of textbook chapters. SQ3R stands for survey, question, read, recite, and review. That is, first survey the chapter to find its half dozen most important ideas. Then form a question around each idea. Read about the first idea until you have answered your question. Then recite your answer to the question without looking at the book. Also write down some information related to that idea. Include an example. Do this for each idea. Finally, review the main ideas, the answers to your questions, and added details. During the review, look at your written notes only if you have to.

Micromnemonics

The main idea behind micromnemonics is to relate what you want to learn to something similar that you already know. This is known in learning theory as maximizing proactive facilitation. Often involved in this process are flights of the imagination, which some people enjoy but others feel are frivolous. How can fantasizing help us learn? It turns out that the use of visual imagery is very important in micromnemonics, but the imagery must achieve the activation of old associations and the formation of new ones. Though it may not seem so, these procedures can be surprisingly effective.

Organizational Mnemonics. Over the centuries mnemonists—that is, those individuals who have become skilled at memorizing—have spent much time learning special information whose only purpose is to aid in the memorization of later and more important information. Such information is necessary for the method of loci, from the Latin, meaning the method of locations. This technique was used by Greek and Roman orators to memorize their speeches. Using the method of loci, a person can memorize a long list of words in order. Before using the method of loci one has to first memorize a series of 10 to 1,000 locations. These can be real or imaginary, but they must be practiced to the point where they can be recalled from memory without error and clearly pictured in one's mind. Then, to memorize a list of words, a vivid mental picture is formed of each successive word placed in each of the successive mental locations. Later, when remembering is required, each location is visualized, and the word "placed" there is also automatically visualized and remembered.

The method of loci is simple to describe and amazingly effective when used correctly, but it does require some practice. Consider it more closely. First, there is the necessity of memorizing information to act as mental cues for the more important information. Second, there is emphasis on visual imagery. Not only must good mental pictures be available for each location, but a new image must be made to combine each location with its corresponding list word. For example, you may wish to memorize a grocery list starting with the item of one dozen eggs. If your loci are 50 locations you have created by mentally walking through your house, the first location may be your front door. To memorize the first item, you must combine a visual image of your front door with a visual image of a dozen eggs. Use images with action, interaction, and motion. Picture a dozen eggs smashed against your front door. This emphasis on interaction between the location and the object to be memorized forces you to search your memory for events you experienced in which eggs really did interact with doors. If you remember some similar event, such as your shopping bag breaking as you tried to open your car door, this is an instance of proactive facilitation that enables you to use an existing association. Experiments have shown that many images are related to personal experiences. If you do not remember a specific event of this kind, simply trying to form an image will help you remember. Later you will find that you can remember the grocery items in their correct order by simply visualizing each of your loci.

The method of loci is called an organizational mnemonic because it provides a set of organized mental cues to which to associate new information. Another popular organizational mnemonic that provides ten easily remembered mental cues is based on the rhyme "One is a bun, two is a shoe, three is a tree, four is a door, five is a hive, six are sticks, seven is heaven, eight is a gate, nine is a fishing line, and ten is a hen." Memorize this rhyme and you have ten images in memory that can be used in the same way as loci.

The method of loci and the rhyme "one is a bun" are called multiple-use mnemonics because whatever list of words you associate to them will be replaced when a new list is memorized. This replacement seems to happen automatically, and your memory system seems to enable you to recall the most recent list. Of course, the older lists of words may then be forgotten and no longer cued by the loci.

However, there are also organizational mnemonics that are for single use. The word HOMES is a common mnemonic for remembering the five Great Lakes. Each letter is the first letter of the name of one of the Great Lakes and acts as a cue for the name. Can you remember them?

Substitution Mnemonics. Usually it is easier to write down a grocery list than to memorize it. A more realistic task is memorizing a list of topics from a textbook chapter, as is necessary when using the SQ3R technique. For example, one might want to remember that the five main styles of American domestic architecture in the first half of the nineteenth century were the federal style, the classical revival style, the Greek revival style, the Gothic revival style, and the Italianate style. How can the method of loci be used to memorize these five terms? To do this requires the use of another class of micromnemonics called substitution mnemonics. Our problem with our list of words may be that mental images cannot be easily formed for them. So we substitute for each item an associated word that provides a good visual image. For example, a word associated with the word *federal* is George Washington, the first chief executive of our federal government. So to remember federal, we would form a visual image of George Washington knocking on our front door with his sword. George Washington is a semantic substitute for the federal style of architecture because George Washington is meaningfully associated with the term *federal*. Another substitute for the word *federal* can be a phonetic association to "fed"; for example, the word *bed*. You might form a mental picture of a bed stuck in your front door. For both these examples, when you wish to remember the word list, you would form an image for each of your loci; determine what other objects are in each image, such as George Washington or a bed; and then use the substitute word as a cue for the term you are trying to remember. Then the chain of two associations is used. The locus cues the substitute word in memory, and the substitute word cues the term you need. Imagery is reducing your memory load by utilizing any prior knowledge you might have that can form the basis for these associations.

Although these substitution mnemonics may seem complicated, they are important, because people often try to memorize material that is new to them and not imageable. Hence, substitutions are necessary for associations to take place. Furthermore, substitutions become much easier with practice. A point not often mentioned in books on mnemonics is that a good deal of practice may be necessary to memorize large amounts of information in a relatively short period of time.

Practice is especially important for a substitution procedure called the digit-consonant mnemonic. It is difficult to memorize numbers because meaningful mental pictures of numbers cannot be easily formed. Picturing the digits does not help associate the number with anything in memory. A mnemonist named Gregor von Feinaigle, the eponymous source of the verb "to finagle," developed a substitution system early in the nineteenth century that transforms numbers into imageable words. This system is described in most books on mnemonic devices.

[*See also* Learning Skills.]

Francis S. Bellezza

MNEMONISTS. There are several scientific accounts of people with prodigious memories (mnemonists or memorists). The pioneering work on mnemonists was done by the French psychologist Alfred Binet in 1894. The subsequent scientific literature describes over a dozen people showing skilled memory performance. A comprehensive review of most of these studies can be found in a 1978 chapter by Brown and Deffenbacher in the book *The Exceptional Brain*. The most intensive study of a memorist in recent years is described in *Memory Search by a Memorist*, by Thompson, Cowan, and Frieman (1993).

Studies of exceptional memory performance both describe the processes memorists use and compare them to memory processes used by people with ordinary memory performance. In several papers, Ericsson and his colleagues have suggested three general principles for skilled memory. The three principles they propose are meaningful encoding (the use of preexisting knowledge to store the presented information in memory), retrieval structure (explicitly attaching cues to the encoded material to allow efficient retrieval), and speed-up (a reduction in study time with further practice). They claim that both ordinary people and skilled memorists will show these principles. A brief presentation of some of the data collected on three famous mnemonists (Rajan Mahadevan from India, Alexander Aitken from England, and Shereshevskii from Russia) will demonstrate that the theory proposed by Ericsson and his colleagues is substantially, but not entirely, correct.

Rajan Mahadevan

Rajan may be the most intensely studied mnemonist ever because studies on him were able to take advantage of modern knowledge about memory. Rajan has an exceptional memory for digits but not for other material. In 1981, *The Guinness Book of World Records* reported that Rajan recited the first 31,811 digits of pi from memory.

The investigations by Thompson, Cowan, and Frieman showed that Rajan learned sets of digits more rapidly than other famous memorists. He used a procedure pairing locations and digits to learn the material. He also encoded the digits in chunks (such as a row in a matrix). He explicitly attached cues to the chunks for retrieval. For example, he learned the first column in a matrix as a cue for retrieving each row of the matrix.

Once the material was learned, Rajan's procedure allowed for extremely effective retrieval of information. Working in the first 10,000 decimal digits of pi, he could retrieve a digit at a specified location (e.g., digit 4,765) in an average time of 12 seconds. He had the digits of pi chunked in groups of 10 digits. When he was given the first 5 digits of a 10-digit group in the first 10,000 digits of pi, he could give the next 5 digits in an average time of 7 seconds.

Alexander Aitken

Many psychologists think that Professor Alexander Aitken was the best all-around mnemonist. He was a brilliant mathematician, an excellent mental calculator, an accomplished violinist, and had an extraordinary memory. His primary method for learning was to search out meaningful relationships within the material and with previously learned information.

Although Aitken's memory was prodigious, it was not infallible. For example, in 1936 he correctly recalled 16 3-digit numbers after four presentations. Two days later, he recalled all but one of the numbers and, after an additional presentation, he recalled them all. In 1960, without further study, he recalled 12 of the numbers, but also produced 8 incorrect numbers.

Shereshevskii

A book by Alexsander Luria, *The Mind of a Mnemonist*, has made Shereshevskii the most famous of the mnemonists. Shereshevskii was almost 30 when Luria began his studies and the research continued for almost 30 years. Somewhat surprisingly, Shereshevskii was unaware that his memory was unusual until Luria began his investigations.

Shereshevskii used three basic processes, usually in combination, for remembering verbal material. The first process was to generate rich visual images to represent information. That process was aided by Shereshevskii's synesthesia. Synesthesia is a rather rare condition in which input in one sensory mode (e.g., sound) is also perceived in another sensory mode (e.g., sight). He told Luria, "To this day I can't escape from seeing colors when I hear sounds. What first strikes me is the color of someone's voice." As an example, he once told an individual, "What a crumbly yellow voice you have." The second process was to use familiar locations such as stops on an oft-traveled street to mentally place the images for later retrieval. This procedure is the method of locations developed about 500 BCE. Shereshevskii apparently developed the technique independently. The third process was to create a story with appropriate images to retrieve the information.

With these techniques, Shereshevskii was able to remember any information presented. Luria was unable to find any limit in the amount of material Shereshevskii could recall in this fashion. More surprisingly, there appeared to be no limit to the duration of Shereshevskii's memory. Luria reports a request for recall of a 50-word list given without warning 16 years after presentation of the list. That request, like all the others Luria reports, resulted in successful retrieval of the list.

The Skilled Memory Theory

Consistent with the skilled memory theory, all mnemonists described here attach retrieval cues when learning material to ensure accurate and fast retrieval. Further, with practice, two of the memorists show a reduction in study time. There is no clear evidence available on this point for Aitken. However, it seems likely that he would show a similar effect.

The data from these memorists suggest the skilled memory theory founders on the third principle. All three memorists use procedures for encoding the material that are available to, and used by, people with ordinary memories. But, contrary to the theory, all of them do not encode the material by relating it to preexisting knowledge. Aitken uses that technique and also searches for relationships within the material to be learned. Shereshevskii uses procedures (such as imagery) that would not be considered as relating the material to preexisting knowledge. Rajan does not fit the theory at all. His procedure, pairing locations and digits, cannot be construed as encoding by relation to preexisting knowledge.

Conclusions

Memorists use quite different techniques to remember information. Some of those techniques call into question a portion of the theory of skilled memory. Their memories are unusually good, but the processes they use to remember can all be used by people with ordinary memories. In short, their unusual memories are unusual in the amount they can remember but not in the processes they use to remember.

Bibliography

Brown, E., & Deffenbacher, K. (1975). Forgotten mnemonists. *Journal of the History of the Behavioral Sciences, 11,* 342–349. This article is the first modern review of the early work on memorists.

Brown, E., & Deffenbacher, K. (1978). Superior memory performance and mnemonic encoding. In L. K. Obler & D. Fein (Eds.), *The exceptional brain* (pp. 436–473). New York: Guilford Press. An excellent review of memorists with a complete set of references.

Ericsson, K. A., & Chase, W. G. (1982). Exceptional memory. *American Scientist, 70,* 607–615. This article references some of the early work by Chase and Ericsson and also briefly describes their skilled memory theory.

Hunter, I. M. L. (1977). An exceptional memory. *British Journal of Psychology, 68,* 155–164. This article contains a review of the work on Professor Aitken.

Luria, A. R. (1968). *The mind of a mnemonist.* New York: Basic Books. A very readable book which describes the memorist Shereshevskii.

Obler, L. K., & Fein, D. (1988). *The exceptional brain.* New York: Guilford Press This book contains contributed chapters on many different types of exceptional performance.

Thompson, C. P., Cowan, T. M., & Frieman, J. (1993). *Memory search by a memorist.* New York: Erlbaum. The most complete description of the research on Rajan.

Charles P. Thompson

MOB BEHAVIOR. *See* Crowd Behavior.

MODAL PERSONALITY. *See* Culture, *article on* Cultural Foundations of Human Behavior.

MODELING. *See* Social-Cognitive Theory.

MODERNIZATION. Social and cultural change are continuous processes in all societies (Rogers, 1973). These changes occur at the level of the group (region, nation state, province, or community), and their study resides primarily within the disciplines of anthropology and sociology. As with all such systemic changes there are mutual relationships with psychological factors: individuals who participate in them, or who are influenced by them, also experience psychological changes; and psychological characteristics that are distributed in a population can instigate change in the group (Berry, 1980).

Among the many conceptions of social and cultural change is the notion of *modernization,* which implies change away from some earlier condition (often termed *traditionalism*), toward some new condition that is considered to be a better one (a process that is often termed *development*). There are many assumptions that underlie these concepts, which are considered by many to be inherently ethnocentric (e.g., Mazrui, 1968); however, these difficulties will not be considered here.

Of particular interest is the existence of a psychological counterpart to modernization at the societal level: that of *individual modernity* at the psychological level (Inkeles, 1977). Within this conceptual framework, once again there are mutual relationships: collective changes toward modernization can induce psychological modernity among group members; and psychological factors (such as modernity) can bring about systemic changes in the group as a whole (Inkeles & Smith, 1974). This article will focus on these bidirectional relationships, first by examining the psychological consequences of social and cultural change (considering how modernization influences modernity), and then by discussing how psychological factors may contribute to group-level changes (considering the role that individuals may play in national and international development).

Conceptions of Change

Before delving into these two aspects, though, it is necessary to consider the various conceptualizations of the process and course of social and cultural change. As noted previously, most agree that all societies experience change; but *from* what, and *toward* what, are questions that have not received consensual replies. There are at least three general frameworks that can be used to describe answers (Berry, Poortinga, Segall, & Dasen, 1992). In one there is assumed to be a single root to such attitudes in all changing groups called "traditionalism"; it is further assumed that there is a single outcome of social change called "modernity," and that individuals hold attitudes that lie somewhere on this dimension. Research on overall modernity by Inkeles and Smith (1974) (see below) is an example of this approach. In another approach, different roots are recognized, since acculturating peoples have usually originated in different cultures; however, it is still assumed that there is a single outcome (becoming more modern) to the process. The various scales of Dawson (1967) are examples of this approach (see below). However, the valued goals of acculturation are not necessarily toward modernity or any other single alternative. There can be preference for continuity with one's heritage culture or toward various other kinds of changes. The goal of change as articulated by the dominant society in their policy statements may not be the preferred course among the leaders or individuals in the acculturating group. Hence there is a third framework that considers psychological change to be highly variable in direction and degree, rather than only toward "modernity" (see below).

Psychological Effects of Change

One way to approach these issues is to link them to the concept of *acculturation* (the social and cultural changes that occur as a result of contact between cultural groups), and then to examine the individual changes that result from this process (*psychological acculturation*). These concepts and their relationships have been described (Berry, 1990). [*See* Marginalization.] As noted there, the psychological outcomes are complex: they depend on one's acculturation strategy. That is, the process of acculturation may involve *assimilation* (in which individuals adopt the influence from the dominant cultural group); *separation* (the opposite, in which individuals reject the influence, and instead strive to maintain their heritage culture); *integration* (in which

individuals seek some compromise or balance in order to participate in both cultural groups); or *marginalization* (in which individuals lose psychological contact or involvement in both cultures, and live on the margins of both). Depending on which strategy individuals employ, the psychological changes will be highly variable.

Moreover, they will vary at two levels. First is that of *behavioral shifts*, in which individuals may (or may not) change their overt behaviors, and perhaps the underlying traits. How one dresses, what language one speaks, what values one espouses, or if one changes motives or abilities, are all subject to influence as a result of acculturation and the consequent process of social change. For some individuals, and some behaviors, these shifts will take place rather easily and be accomplished without serious disruption. However, for some individuals and some behaviors, conflicts are likely, creating a second level, that of *acculturative stress*, in which individuals experience psychological disturbances, often in the form of anxiety, depression, or psychosomatic complaints (Berry, 1980, 1990).

The relationships among acculturation strategy, behavioral shifts, and acculturative stress are now rather clear (Berry, 1997). Psychological effects are moderate in degree (behavioral shifts) and minimally stressful with the integration strategy, but the opposite is the case for marginalization; shifts are greatest with assimilation, and least with separation, but these two strategies are both moderately stressful (in between integration and marginalization). A consequence of this complex and variable pattern is that not every individual who is exposed to modernization (in their society) will necessarily become psychologically modernized. A variety of outcomes can be expected, depending on acculturation strategy and the degree of disruption in the lives of individuals. Thus, in answer to the question "Is everyone going modern?" (Stephenson, 1969), the answer is clearly "No"!

To illustrate the empirical research carried out on the psychological effects of modernization, two research programs are outlined, the first of which is the study by Inkeles and Smith (1974). They began with a conception of "modern" that included 24 themes (e.g., public participation, identification with the nation-state, use of mass media) thought to be manifestations of a "general, unified, underlying dimension of modernity" (p. 35), which they termed *overall modernity*. To pursue this question empirically, Inkeles and Smith developed a sampling strategy that encompassed four kinds of people in six developing nations. Since their concern was with modernization, it was important to select countries that were experiencing this kind of change and that had sufficient internal variation to sample from a variety of groups. Those selected were Argentina, Chile, East Pakistan (now Bangladesh), India, Israel, and Nigeria. In each country a sample of about 900 participants was sought that was to be all male, aged 18 to 32, and working in four occupational categories: (1) experienced urban industrial workers; (2) inexperienced urban industrial workers; (3) urban nonindustrial workers; and (4) rural farm workers.

The components of modernity were operationalized by constructing a scale that they refer to as overall modernity (OM). A pool of attitude items was generated from the original themes. Inkles and Smith argue that they have been able "reliably to characterize each individual more or less globally as relatively more modern or traditional by using the general or summary measure," and that the "chief theoretical implication of the combined index is that it establishes the existence of a general quality of the personality which may reasonably be called individual modernity." And, more generally, they conclude, "The modern man is a cross-national, transcultural type who can be identified by our scales whatever the distinctive attitudes with which his culture may otherwise have endowed him."

They conclude that these essentially adult experiences can alter fairly basic attitudes. They base this conclusion both on analysis of OM scores by years of factory experience, and by contrasts between matched urban factory workers and rural agricultural workers. This basic shift they term *modernization* and claim that it has four constituents: The modern man is an informed participant citizen; he has a marked sense of personal efficacy; he is highly independent and autonomous in his relations to traditional sources of influence, especially when he is making basic decisions about how to conduct his personal experiences and ideas; and he is relatively open-minded and cognitively flexible (p. 290).

In the second study, and in some contrast to this absolutist approach, the work of Dawson (1967) was based on the view that the varying starting points of the change process needed to be taken into account. Dawson developed a technique for conceiving of and measuring the traditional-modern dimension using item content from *within* the cultures themselves. In addition to developing this scaling technique for measuring traditional-modern attitudes, Dawson has also developed a theoretical position that attempts to deal with attitudinal conflict and the dynamics of attitudinal change resulting from social change. Dawson argued that traditional concepts must be drawn from the cultural life of the group involved, and that these concepts should sample widely from the culture of the people. In addition, he argues that traditional and Western content should not simply be stated as alternatives, but intermediate attitudinal positions should be phrased to allow compromise attitudes to be exhibited. Finally, Dawson argued that there is some traditional cultural reaffirmation among Western-exposed peoples, and that the scale should not assume linearity but allow for the exhibition of attitudinal reaffirmation.

To meet these requirements, Dawson selected 18 concepts from the culture of Sierra Leone (West Africa) (e.g., on witchcraft, polygamy, gift exchange), and developed four statements about each concept, one each to express a "traditional," "semitraditional," "semi-Western," and "Western" attitude. The concepts were selected with the assistance of anthropologists and local informants.

Dawson then used his scales to test a theory of attitudinal change based upon a generalized theory of consistency or congruence. Dawson considered the problem of "unresolved attitudinal conflict occurring with individuals exposed to a rapidly changing social environment." He noted that "it is a basic premise of this theory that attitudinal inconsistency will be maladaptive to the individual and that this will result in pressures to reduce or eliminate inconsistency." Many attitudes, he considered, would be easily adjusted by moving to a compromise position (i.e., a "semi" item), but others would constitute a real conflict situation, and this is most likely to occur in "traditional high affect attitudes" such as witchcraft.

A technique was developed to estimate the degree of "unresolved attitudinal conflict in the T-W scale"; this technique employed the discrepancy between "traditional" and "Western" responses, and between "semitraditional" and "semi-Western" responses. A score could then be calculated for each individual and each concept. As expected, unresolved attitudinal conflict was highest for those more basic value areas (such as witchcraft and parental authority).

This approach appears to be more sensitive to the cultural origins of social change than that of Inkeles and Smith. However, it retains the common assumption that individuals experiencing social change can be understood psychologically on a single dimension ranging from (various kinds of) traditionalism to (one kind) of modernism. Earlier we saw that at least four kinds of change patterns can be discerned, using the notions of assimilation, integration, separation, and marginalization. These variations are now known (Berry, 1990) to lead to quite different outcomes, not to just one (modernity).

Psychological Influences on Change

To reverse the direction of the discussion, we may ask if the psychological makeup of a population can influence the process of modernization or development. This question was posed early by Sinha (1973) and has remained a focus of research in many developing societies (see Triandis, 1993, and the journal, *Psychology and Developing Societies*, published in India).

The longest established research tradition is that of the role of need for achievement in social and economic change (McClelland, 1961). A basic argument made by McClelland is that economic development cannot be explained without reference to social and psychological variables. In this early search for such variables, he was struck by the apparent role that a motivation to get ahead played in the process of development; and he hypothesized that "achievement motivation is in part responsible for economic development" (p. 36). The interest in studying achievement motivation cross-culturally stems from McClelland's demonstration that there is a pattern of sociocultural antecedents (mainly in socialization) to its development in individuals. Since these socialization antecedents are known to vary cross-culturally, there is a ready-made theoretical scheme for its further analysis. The discovery of the patterning of group differences in achievement orientation (in relation to objective indices of development) was the primary purpose of the McClelland studies. In the 1961 report, historical, modern, and traditional societies were considered at two levels of analysis: the analysis of cultural products (mainly stories) for indicators of achievement motivation, and the analysis of economic development of the society. To an impressive degree McClelland was able to demonstrate, usually with some temporal lag, the covariation of the frequency of achievement themes in the products of a society and economic development. Many other sociocultural factors were considered by McClelland, including the role of religion (the well-known Protestant work ethic thesis).

This early work on achievement orientation has largely come to a halt, despite early promise as a contributor to understanding social change and development. More recently, Kagitcibasi (1995) has advocated a central place for psychological variables in human development and a central role for psychologists in bringing it about. Her focus has been on the importance of early childhood education, family planning, and primary health care, but other factors that require an understanding of human behavior are also relevant to the process (such as motives, abilities, values, and social relationships; see Sinha & Kao, 1988).

A set of specific roles for psychologists involved in development issues has been outlined by Berry et al. (1992). If we define development as the process of individuals and groups moving from some present state to some more valued end state, then psychology can contribute first in understanding the present state. This is the obvious starting point for development and many psychological constructs are relevant to its description: skills (e.g., cognitive, technical, social); attitudes to change; personality characteristics that may assist or prevent change; values concerning maintaining the past (or present) state of affairs; and interests in various change alternatives. That is, constructing a "psycholog-

ical profile" of a population should provide an understanding of the human resources upon which development may take place.

Second is the understanding of the valued end state. Psychological research can draw out the local or indigenous meanings of the concept of development; is it always associated with increased urbanization, industrialization, and organization (as the Western notion of "development" implies), or are there important cultural variations? The valued end state can also be studied by psychologists employing the conventional notions of aspirations, needs, values, and preferences.

Third is the understanding of the process of change. How do people get from the present state to the future valued end state? People have motives, drives, coping mechanisms, and so on, all of which have an established place in psychology. Examining these dynamic factors, including the possibility of increasing their level and the effectiveness of their organization in a population, is an important potential contribution of psychology to national development.

And fourth is the design, implementation, and evaluation of development programs. Psychologists have usually enjoyed a solid training in research methods on human behavior. However, cultural variations in behavior have usually been ignored. As a result of ignoring this human factor, many development programs have ended in failure. A psychology background can also be of immense help in a development team that is attempting to understand whether a particular development program is having its intended effects. In such areas as sampling, interviewing, the use of control groups, the statistical evaluation of change over time (including an informed choice between longitudinal and cross-sectional designs), psychology has a significant contribution to make.

Thus, psychology can contribute substantially to the understanding of "development," in the implementation of development programs, and in their evaluation, both of the intended and the unintended consequences.

Conclusions

Modernization is one conceptualization of the continuous process of social and cultural change. One aspect of this process is development, in which people (both collectively and individually) change from a less to a more desirable condition. What people desire, and how they want to achieve it, are highly variable across cultures and individuals and are not inevitably to be viewed as modernization, Westernization, or development. While originally studied by sociologists, anthropologists, and economists, the change process at the group level is entwined with change at the psychological level, and hence is one that necessarily involves psychological concepts and research. This relationship is mutual and bidirectional: sociocultural change brings about psychological changes that are highly variable; and psychological factors contribute to the process of social on cultural change, and potentially to national development.

Bibliography

Berry, J. W. (Ed.). (1977). Psychological perspectives and cultural change [Special Issue]. *Journal of Cross-Cultural Psychology, 8*, (2).

Berry, J. W. (1980). Social and cultural change. In H. C. Triandis & R. Brislin (Eds.), *Handbook of cross-cultural psychology: Vol. 5, Social* (pp. 211–279). Boston: Allyn & Bacon.

Berry, J. W. (1990). Psychology of acculturation. In J. Berman (Ed.), *Cross-cultural perspectives: Nebraska symposium on motivation* (Vol. 37, pp. 201–234). Lincoln: University of Nebraska Press.

Berry, J. W. (1997). Immigration, acculturation and adaptation. *Applied Psychology, 38*, 5–68.

Berry, J. W., Poortinga, Y. H., Segall, M. H., & Dasen, P. R. (1992). *Cross-cultural psychology: Research and applications*. New York: Cambridge University Press.

Dawson, J. L. M. (1967). Traditional versus Western attitudes in West Africa: The construction, validation and application of a measuring device. *British Journal of Social and Clinical Psychology, 6*, 81–69.

Inkeles, A. (1977). Understanding and misunderstanding individual modernity. *Journal of Cross-Cultural Psychology, 8*, 135–176.

Inkeles, A., & Smith, D. (1974). *Becoming modern*. Cambridge, MA: Harvard University Press.

Kagitcibasi, C. (1995). Is psychology relevant to global human development issues? *American Psychologist, 50*, 293–300.

Mazrui, A. (1968). From social Darwinism to current theories of modernization. *World Politics, 21*, 69–83.

McClelland, D. C. (1961). *The achieving society*. Princeton, NJ: Van Nostrand.

Rogers, E. M. (1973). Social structure and social change. In G. Zaltman (Ed.), *Social change* (pp. 75–78). New York: Wiley.

Sinha, D. (1973). Psychology and problems of developing countries. *Applied Psychology, 22*, 5–28.

Sinha, D., & Kao, H. (Eds.). (1988). *Social values and development*. Newbury Park, CA: Sage.

Stephenson, J. (1969). Is everyone going modern? *American Journal of Sociology, 74*, 265–275.

Triandis, H. C. (Ed.). (1973). Psychological factors relevant to economic development [Special Issue]. *International Journal of Psychology, 8*, (3).

John W. Berry

MONGOLOIDISM. *See* Down Syndrome.

MONTESSORI, MARIA (1870–1952), Italian educator. Born to well-to-do, liberal parents, Montessori was one of the first women to attend medical school in Italy and went on to develop a psychologically based educational system that became known internationally. She attended the University of Rome, where she studied pediatrics and psychiatry and received her doctorate in 1896. A socialist and feminist who grew up in the heady atmosphere of post-reunification Italy, she was a delegate to an international women's conference in Berlin in 1896, where she gave an impassioned speech on the plight of working women.

Montessori became interested in young children's learning and development. By her own account, seeing a poor child in the street playing with a scrap of paper and observing feeble-minded children in an orphanage using crumbs of food as playthings convinced her of the importance of sensory experience and play. She began reading works by Jean-Marc Gaspard Itard and Edouard Seguin, who had developed sensory-motor exercises, and was influenced by the naturalistic pedagogical ideas of Friedrich Froebel, Johann Pestalozzi, and Jean-Jacques Rousseau. After studying anthropology, anthropometry, and criminology with Cesare Lombroso and Guiseppe Sergi, she came to see scientific pedagogy as a means of preventing abnormality, poverty, and crime.

In 1899, Montessori became the director of the Orthophrenic School, a medical-psychological institute, where she worked with abnormal and retarded children. While there she developed a set of sensory teaching materials designed to remediate developmental delays and educational disabilities. She left the school in 1901, after bearing an illegitimate son by a colleague, and returned to the University of Rome to study philosophy and psychology and to lecture in anthropology. She was introduced to Wilhelm Wundt's experimental methods and did observational research in Italian elementary schools. [*See the biography of Wundt.*] The didactic teaching practices she saw there stimulated her to become interested in applying her physiological and environmental theories to normal children.

In 1906, Montessori founded the Casa dei Bambini, or Children's House, where she developed the pedagogical methods that became known as the Montessori system. Located in a settlement house in the Roman slum of San Lorenzo, the school opened in January 1907. It had a homelike atmosphere intended to ameliorate the impoverished family backgrounds from which the children came. She knew poor children were often "perceived as lazy, stubborn, disorderly, disobedient" (*The Discovery of the Child*, Madras, 1946) and thought they could become productive and independent by practicing simple daily activities, such as pouring water and washing dishes, and being given more responsibility for their own learning. Her educational philosophy emphasized self-sufficiency, the unity of work and play, the sensorial basis of learning, and the notion that all children had "absorbent minds."

Her Casa dei Bambini, which soon spread to other cities in Italy and Europe, were carefully structured educational environments. They contained specially designed tactile, visual, auditory, gustatory, and olfactory equipment such as graduated cylinders, bells, taste and smell bottles, sandpaper letters, and number rods, which were introduced in an invariant, supposedly developmental sequence. The overall method, which required intensive teacher preparation from a Montessori-trained instructor, was meant to bring about "the spontaneous progress of the child," as Montessori wrote in 1909 in her first and most influential book, *The Montessori Method* (New York, 1911). She elaborated her ideas in a number of other books, including *Dr. Montessori's Own Handbook* (New York, 1914), *The Advanced Montessori Method* (New York, 1917), *The Secret of Childhood* (Calcutta, 1936), *The Discovery of the Child* (Madras, 1946), and *The Absorbent Mind* (Calcutta, 1949).

Montessori's methods became famous, and Montessori associations and schools were begun around the world. By 1913, when she toured the United States, there were almost 100 Montessori schools in this country. Although supported by the wife of Alexander Graham Bell and others, Montessori's ideas were rejected by American psychologists and educators, especially by William Heard Kilpatrick of Teachers College at Columbia University, who considered them outmoded, unscientific, and rigid. Despite this academic criticism and decline in interest, Montessori's methods spread elsewhere, particularly in India, where she established a training center in 1939. Montessori's pedagogy was reintroduced to the United States in 1958 by Nancy McCormick Rambusch, who founded the American Montessori Society. Since then there have been Montessori Head Start models and continued growth in popularity. Though criticized for being overly structured and insufficiently focused on language and socioemotional development, Montessori's system highlighted sensorial learning and was a precursor of the environmentalistic, constructivist approach to enhancing cognitive development and remediating educational deficits that is influential in developmental psychology and early childhood education today.

Bibliography

Hainstock, E. G. (1997). *The essential Montessori: An introduction to the woman, the writings, the method, and the movement.* New York: Plume. A concise and very useful overview of Montessori's life and ideas, and of the Montessori movement, with excerpts from some of her works.

Kramer, R. (1976). *Maria Montessori: A biography.* New York: Putnam. The first scholarly biography; a well-researched, balanced portrait with detailed discussion and analysis of Montessori's theories, mentality, and the historical context of her work.

Lillard, P. P. (1996). *Montessori today.* New York: Schocken Books. A comprehensive introduction to the Montessori system, with information on its application in the elementary school and at other age levels.

Rambusch, N. M. (1962). *Learning how to learn: An American approach to Montessori.* Baltimore: Helicon Press. The book that reintroduced Montessori to the United States and placed it in perspective with current, progressive approaches to early childhood education.

Standing, E. M. (1957; Rev. ed. 1984). *Maria Montessori: Her life and work.* Fresno, CA: Academy Library Guild. A hagiographical account of her career and methods, written by a friend and disciple.

Barbara Beatty

MOOD. The terms *affect, emotional state,* and *feeling* are often used to describe mood. In popular terminology, we often speak simply of a good or a bad mood or perhaps of feeling depressed or happy, but scientists have studied dozens of feelings as mood variations. Moods are similar to emotions but of longer duration. Thus, whereas an emotional reaction may be over in minutes, a mood can last for hours or days, even months in the case of a serious depression. Also emotions often have identifiable causes, but moods seem to come and go more mysteriously. Life events usually are assumed to cause moods, but recent research suggests that moods are strongly influenced by general biological conditions such as health, sleep, nutrition, physical activity, stress, and even time of day. A good deal of research indicates that moods are cyclical, including differences across the day (circadian), month (menstrual), and year (e.g., seasonal affective disorder). Moods appear to be barometers of both physical and psychological functioning. For example, studies indicate that moods are correlated both with illness and with good physical condition. The relationship of moods to psychological processes is well established. Thus research indicates relationships between mood and such functions as perception, memory, judgment, learning, decision making, processing of persuasive messages, helping behavior, and self-regulation.

Moods are probably controlled by the brain and are associated with its important arousal and limbic systems. The biochemistry of the brain in relation to mood is not well understood, but such neurotransmitters as serotonin, norepinephrine, and dopamine are likely to be involved. Other parts of the body are important as well. For example, skeletal-muscular tension, blood glucose level, and various hormones such as adrenaline and cortisol appear to influence mood. Related to this, there is good evidence of genetic influences on mood. Although scientists agree that moods have physiological and genetic bases, no one is quite sure at this time how they work to produce the subjective experience of mood.

In scientific research, self-reports of current mood state are almost always included. The Profile of Mood State (POMS) is probably the most widely used test of normal mood variations, but there are a number of other well-known adjective checklists with which research participants rate their current mood. Often these ratings are correlated with different psychological functions or used to predict different behaviors. Sometimes experimental procedures are used in which the investigator attempts to manipulate moods and to study their effect. Included here might be systematic suggestion, audiovisual materials (e.g., films, music), exercise, stress, drugs, and even hypnosis. Scientific research on mood is very active. For example, during the 1990s alone more than 5,000 published articles appeared dealing with some aspect of mood, according to PsycINFO, the American Psychological Association database that covers more than 1,300 journals.

Among the latest research are studies about the basic dimensions of mood that may account for the many moods we seem to have. Three well-known two-dimensional models describe moods as part of either positive and negative affect, energetic and tense arousal, or pleasantness and activation. Identifying these core dimensions would allow us to search for common biological and psychological antecedents.

[See also Affect; and Emotion.]

Bibliography

Morris, W. N. (1989). *Mood: The frame of mind.* New York: Springer-Verlag. A book intended for scientific audiences that reviews background issues relating to mood and that seeks to establish the legitimacy of mood as a distinctive hypothetical construct, separable from emotion.

Parkinson, B., Totterdell, P., Briner, R. B., & Reynolds, S. (1996). *Changing moods: The psychology of mood and mood regulation.* London: Longman. A book about people's moods and the way they change over time. It is intended for upper division and graduate students.

Thayer, R. E. (1989). *The biopsychology of mood and arousal.* New York: Oxford University Press. A book intended for scientific audiences in diverse fields that reviews research and theory about normal moods, including theoretical and research issues frequently raised about mood and relationships with cognition, biology, and physiology.

Thayer, R. E. (1996). *The origin of everyday moods: Managing energy, tension, and stress.* New York: Oxford University Press. A reference for general audiences to the origins, influences, and research on self-regulation of normal moods, as well as an analysis of methods of mood management. Also reviews recent research on the biology and physiology of mood.

Wegner, D. M., & Pennebaker, J. W. (Eds.). (1993). *Handbook of mental control.* Englewood Cliffs, NJ: Prentice Hall. A book intended for scientific audiences in which many of the chapters deal with issues and research concerning different aspects of mood and mood regulation.

Robert E. Thayer

MOOD DISORDERS. The term *mood disorders* refers to a number of psychological syndromes in which there is a primary disturbance of mood, with additional cognitive, behavioral, and somatic (physical) symptoms, and interpersonal difficulties. Mood can be defined as a prolonged emotion that colors the person's whole psychological state. Mood disorders were well described as early as the Old Testament. There are currently various systems for classifying mood disorders, all of which take into account whether the mood disturbance is *unipolar*, limited to depression, or *bipolar*, including mania or hypomania as well. In addition, these classification systems take into account how long the mood disturbance persists.

Depression

The term *depression* is commonly understood to mean normal periods of sad or low mood. Depression as a *syndrome*, however, refers to a state of substantial severity, duration, and additional symptoms which are different from normal variations in mood. According to the widely accepted *Diagnostic and Statistical Manual of Mental Disorders* (DSM–IV; APA, 1994), a diagnosis of major depressive disorder requires a mood disturbance of at least two weeks duration involving depressed mood or the loss of interest or pleasure in nearly all activities for most of the day, almost every day. In children, prolonged irritable mood is an alternative way of meeting this criterion. The person must have five or more symptoms including this mood disturbance. The additional symptoms must come from the following list: significant weight loss or gain; insomnia or excessive sleeping nearly every day; psychomotor agitation or retardation; fatigue or lack of energy nearly every day; inability to concentrate; feelings of worthlessness or excessive guilt; recurrent thoughts of death, recurrent suicidal thoughts, or a suicide attempt or plan.

Some features of this definition should be noted. It allows that a person does not have to be sad or blue to be depressed, if the person has lost interest in most activities. This is termed *anhedonia* and involves losing the ability to take pleasure in social relationships, activities, and accomplishments and, in the extreme, even the ability to feel love and affection. Life becomes flat, boring, and unrewarding. Many depressed persons experience both sadness and anhedonia, but some severely depressed persons feel no sadness at all, only an apathy or emptiness. Another feature of this definition is that it requires that the mood disturbance endure every day, much of the day for 2 weeks. Yet persons who meet this definition are typically depressed for 6 to 9 months. A final feature of this definition is that it allows for considerable differences among depressed persons. It is likely that depression is actually a mixture of disorders with similar presentations.

Depression is a recurrent disorder, with periods of remission, but repeated relapses and recurrences. About half of all depressed persons recover within a year, but 30 to 50% of those who recover will be depressed again within 2 years. Few depressed persons have only a single episode in their lives, and the best predictor that someone will get depressed in the future is that they have been depressed in the past. Persons seeking treatment for depression typically spend 20% of their subsequent life depressed.

Melancholia or Endogenous Depression

It had long been thought that there were two kinds of depression, one biological and one tied to life stress. The supposed biological depression, termed *melancholia* or *endogenous depression*, was thought to occur in the absence of stress; to have symptoms such as early morning waking, loss of appetite, and excessive guilt; and to respond better to medication. The other kind of depression, which was less clearly defined, was labeled *nonendogenous* or *neurotic depression*. It is now generally recognized that the absence of life stress does not predict particular symptoms or response to medication. Furthermore, within a given episode of depression, a person may shift from nonendogenous to endogenous symptoms. Melancholic or endogenous may simply represent more severe major depression.

Dysthymia

The term *dysthymia* literally means "ill-humored" and refers to more chronically depressed mood that occurs more days than not for at least 2 years. In addition to chronically depressed mood, two additional depressive symptoms from the list for major depression must be present. In that sense, dysthymia is a milder disorder than major depression. However, because it is so enduring, persons with dysthymia experience considerable impairment in their social life and academic and vocational achievement. Dysthymic persons are also prone to periods of full major depression; when they meet criteria for major depression, they are sometimes labeled as having "double depression." It is then that they often seek treatment, and while their depression

responds well to treatment, they often revert to their chronic dysthymic state without a full recovery. Dysthymia has an early onset for some persons, in childhood or adolescence. Others become dysthymic when they fail to recover completely from an episode of major depression in adulthood.

Bipolar Disorder

Most persons who suffer from mood disorders experience episodes of major depression without any periods of mania or hypomania. This is known as unipolar depression. However, if a depressed person has ever had mania or hypomania in their lifetime, they are classified as having bipolar disorder. Because there is a tendency for bipolar disorder to run in families, it is suspected in persons who have only suffered major depression, but have a family history of bipolar disorder. It is generally agreed that unipolar and bipolar disorders are distinct disorders, with different causal factors, natural histories, and responses to treatment.

The mood disturbance in mania consists of a period of elevated expansive, irritable, or euphoric mood. Persons in a manic state may seem unusually cheerful, but they can be quite irritable, shifting back and forth between euphoria and irritability or rapidly plunging into deep depression. In addition to such a mood disturbance, the person must have three of the following symptoms: grandiosity, decreased need for sleep, pressure to keep talking, flights of ideas, distractibility, increased goal-directed activity, and unwise and impulsive behavior such as buying sprees, sexual indiscretions, or foolish business transactions. Hypomania is a milder form of mania, lasting at least 4 days and with at least three manic symptoms in addition to mood disturbance. The difference between mania and hypomania is that hypomanic symptoms are not sufficiently severe to require hospitalization or result in marked impairment in functioning.

Persons who experience major depression and mania are termed *Bipolar I*, whereas those who experience major depression and hypomania are termed *Bipolar II*. Both forms of the disorder are highly recurrent. For instance, at least 90% of persons who have a manic episode will have at least one more. The course of bipolar disorder varies greatly, but manic episodes frequently precede or follow upon episodes of major depression. Before effective treatment was available, persons with Bipolar I disorder averaged four episodes of depressed or manic disorder in a 10-year period.

Bipolar disorder is associated with creativity, and persons with bipolar disorder are disproportionately represented among writers, performers, and successful businesspeople. However, it is an enormously destructive disorder, personally and socially costly, wreaking havoc in the lives of its sufferers and their family members. Moreover, it is a deadly disorder. Approximately

15% of persons with bipolar mood disorder die by suicide.

Cyclothymia

The term *cyclothymic disorder* describes a chronic fluctuating mood disorder, with repeated periods of both hypomanic and depressive symptoms, but without full-blown major depression or mania. Cyclothymia has an insidious onset, usually in childhood or adolescence. Persons with cyclothymia do not usually seek treatment and they are often unaware of their mood changes or their effects on the people around them. Yet, these mood changes are readily noticed by others and they come to be seen as unpredictable, moody, and unreliable.

Seasonal Variation in Mood Disorders

Many persons with bipolar disorder tend to experience hypomania or mania in the spring and depression in the autumn, although some fit an opposite pattern and still others show no apparent seasonal pattern. Other persons are prone to depression in the late autumn or winter. Often, their episodes of depression are characterized by excessive sleep, overeating, fatigue, and sensitivity to rejection. Some may gain 40 pounds or more in a single season. Seasonal patterns in mood disorders may be tied to changes in the availability of natural light, and the existence of such patterns adds to the weight of evidence that mood disorders are related to disruptions of biological clocks or circadian rhythms.

Mood Disorder and Normal Fluctuations in Mood

Many features found in mood disorders are similar to normal variations in mood, but they differ in a number of important ways. First, mood is only one component of a mood disorder, and changes in sleep, appetite, energy level, and behavior do not typically accompany everyday variations in mood. Second, many sufferers from mood disorder report that their experience differs from the periods of being sad or blue they have experienced at other times in their lives and even from the grief accompanying the loss of a loved one. In his first-person account of depression, *Darkness Visible* (New York, 1990), the American novelist William Styron argues that depression remains nearly incomprehensible to those who have not experienced it in its severe form, even if the everyday blues provide a hint of it. Most normal periods of sad or negative mood are not so relentless as clinical depression. The typical person having a bad day will have a better time next day. Also, a person who is simply sad, rather than clinically depressed, will get some relief in positive events. Even prolonged periods of normal sadness are punctuated by upturns in mood. A third difference between everyday mood changes and mood disorder is their predictive value for the future. Periods of sadness that do not last every day for at least 2 weeks are not indicative of heightened risk of depression, whereas mood disturbance of this duration is likely to predict a future mood disorder. Finally, medications that are effective in the treatment of mood disorders do not have the same effects on normal mood. Antidepressants do not make persons in a normal mood state happier, and medications effective in controlling mania and other aspects of bipolar disorder do not eliminate normal enthusiasm or excitement.

Epidemiology

Depression and other mood disorders are the most common forms of psychopathology. The National Co-Morbidity Study found that 19.3% of the population has a mood disorder in their lifetime, with a rate of 23.9% for women and 14.7% for men. In a 12-month period, 14.1% of women and 8.5% of men will experience a mood disorder. One of the most robust findings in the psychiatric epidemiology literature is that women are twice as likely to suffer depression as men. However, men and women are equally likely to suffer bipolar disorder. Whites are more likely to suffer mood disorders than Blacks, and Hispanics are more likely to suffer mood disorders than non-Hispanic Whites. Yet, the highest rates of lifetime mood disorders are for Black females. Persons with the lowest income and education are more likely to suffer mood disorders than those persons of higher socioeconomic status. Overall, the highest rates for current mood disorders are for females, young adults, and people who lack a college education.

Studies from a number of countries including the United States suggest that rates of depression are increasing and the age of first onset of depression is decreasing with each generation. Depression was once a disorder of middle age, but now the average age of a first episode has dropped to 27 for men and 28 for women, with a marked increase in depression with onset in the early 20s. In the United States, only 1% of Americans born before 1905 had suffered a major depression by age 75. Of those born after 1955, 6% had their first depressive episode by age 24. The causes of this trend are unknown, but are believed to be tied to changing social conditions, including greater disruptions in marital and family relationships.

Social Costs of Mood Disorders

Depression has been called the common cold of mental disorders, but if that is accurate it is because depression is so common, not because it is benign. Mood disorders seriously impair the lives of their sufferers. Comparative studies have found that depressed persons spend more days in bed and spend fewer days functioning at full capacity than persons suffering from chronic illnesses such as hypertension, arthritis, and diabetes. Furthermore, people with mood disorders are 35 times more likely to commit suicide than the rest of the population, and the rate of suicide is particularly high for sufferers from bipolar disorder.

Mood disorders affect one in five families. These disorders tend to be markers for families with a full range of other difficulties including marital conflict, parenting difficulties, adjustment problems in offspring, and more generalized family dysfunction. Over half of married depressed persons presenting for treatment have serious marital problems. Children of parents with mood disorders are at risk for a full range of psychological difficulties themselves, and particularly mood disorders. Studies employing assessment of these children by diagnostic interview find as many as 40% have a psychiatric disorder. While the strength of these associations is strong, it is likely that any single explanation suffices for them. Sufferers from mood disorders have difficulties meeting their responsibilities as spouses and parents, and those who live with them may feel burdened and distressed themselves. Yet, marital and family problems have been shown to play a strong role in a person's vulnerability to mood disorders. Some of the marital and family problems which contribute to a parent being depressed may contribute directly to their children's problems.

Estimates of the overall social costs of mood disorders run high, with conservative estimates of the total economic burden on society exceeding the social costs of coronary heart disease or arthritis. It has been estimated that there is a cost to the U.S. economy of $16 billion a year from direct treatment costs and indirect costs from lost productivity associated with mood disorders. When one takes into account the broader range of social costs such as increased medical care, early mortality, lost days of work, and reduction in quality of life of sufferers of mood disorders and their families, the total cost may be as high as $43 billion. It is estimated that 2 to 4% of total health-care expenditures in the United States are for mood disorders. More than 9 million people in the United States are in treatment for depression at an estimated cost of $1,200 per person per year. However, most people with mood disorders are not receiving treatment, and estimates of the social costs of untreated mood disorders are higher than for its treatment. As an example, it is estimated that without treatment, a woman who develops bipolar disorder at age 25 will lose 14 years of overall productivity and 9 years of life expectancy. The latter figure reflects her risk of suicide. Untreated mood disorders are considered a major public health problem, and sadly enough, effective treatments *are* available.

Theories of Causation

Heredity, biochemistry, and psychological and social factors have been identified as causes of mood disor-

ders. It is generally agreed that the major vulnerability for bipolar disorder is genetically transmitted, whereas there is more of a role for environmental factors for unipolar depression. Nonetheless, both manic and depressive episodes in persons with bipolar disorder are frequently precipitated by stressful life events. Furthermore, hostile criticism from family members predicts relapse among recovered bipolar patients independent of patient medication, baseline symptoms, demographics, and personal history.

The effectiveness of antidepressant medication and their known effects on brain chemicals known as neurotransmitters strongly point to a role for biochemistry in depression. Abnormalities in the hypothalmic-pituitary-adrenal (HPA) axis are commonly found in depression. However, many depressed persons in the community have no identifiable biological abnormality and there is no reliable and valid biochemical test for depression.

Twin and adoption studies support a role for heredity in depression. Yet, while unipolar depression also runs in families, this is not solely a matter of genetics. Early childhood adversity and current social factors such as lack of social support and stressful life events, particularly those involving loss, have also been implicated. Psychodynamic, cognitive-behavioral, and interpersonal theories have all been proposed to explain depression from a psychological perspective. Earlier psychodynamic theories emphasized the role of loss or threatened loss in early childhood, anger turned inward, and ambivalence in close relationships. Contemporary cognitive theories developed by American psychiatrist Aaron T. Beck and American psychologists Martin Seligman, Lyn Abramson, and Christopher Peterson and others emphasize how negative thinking in the form of self-schemas or explanatory style may be activated by stress, resulting in depression. Interpersonal theories developed by British sociologists George Brown and Tirril Harris and American psychologist James Coyne emphasize the role of disruptive life stress and unsupportive relationships, as well as the factor of depressed persons engaging others in their social environments in ways that aggravate their predicament. It is likely that no single set of factors adequately explains the transmission, nature, course, and outcome of mood disorders, and we are far from an adequate comprehensive explanatory framework that can encompass all of the known factors.

Treatment of Mood Disorders

Effective treatments for mood disorders include medication, psychotherapy, and for severe depression, electroconvulsive therapy. It is generally agreed that the treatment and long-term management of bipolar disorders require lithium or another mood stabilizer. Yet among patients who are adequately medicated, family interventions to reduce conflict and improve coping skills can significantly reduce relapse.

A broader range of treatment options can be considered for unipolar depression. For most episodes of depression, antidepressant medication and brief cognitive or interpersonal therapy are on average equally effective. Yet, to date it is not possible to predict reliably which patient will respond to which treatment, and both patients and professionals must be prepared to consider switching approaches when one is not working. The cognitive therapy developed by Aaron T. Beck focuses on the distorted thought processes believed to maintain the mood and behavioral symptoms of depression. The interpersonal therapy developed by Americans Myrna Weissman and Gerald Klerman focuses on understanding and renegotiating the interpersonal relationships of depressed patients. In more severe depression, medication may have an advantage over psychotherapy alone, but a combination of both medication and psychotherapy may be needed to insure both recovery from depression and improvement of social functioning. Electroconvulsive therapy (ECT) is usually reserved for acutely suicidal persons or those with very severe or psychotic depression. Whereas 80 or 90% of severely depressed patients improve with ECT, quick relapse is likely without additional treatment.

[See also Bipolar Disorder; Depression; and Seasonal Affective Disorder.]

Bibliography

American Psychiatric Association (1996). *Diagnostic and statistical manual of mental disorders* (4th ed.). Washington, DC: Author.

Beck, A. T., Rush, A. J., Shaw, B. F., & Emery G. (1979). *Cognitive therapy of depression*. New York: Guilford Press.

Beckham, E. E., & R. Leber, W. R. (1995). *Handbook of depression* (2nd ed.). New York: Guilford Press.

Blazer, D. G., Kessler, R. C., McGonagle, K. A., & Swartz, M. S. (1994). The prevalence and distribution of major depression in a national community sample: The National Comorbidity Survey. *American Journal of Psychiatry, 151*, 979–986.

Brown, G. W., & Harris, T. (1978). *The social origins of depression*. New York: Free Press.

Coyne J. C. (Ed.). (1986). *Essential papers on depression*. New York: New York University Press. Includes many of the classic articles on depression from psychoanalytic, cognitive, behavioral, and interpersonal viewpoints.

Goodwin, F. K., & Jamison, K. R. (1990). *Manic-depressive illness*. New York: Oxford University Press.

Jamison, K. R. (1993). *Touched with fire*. New York: Free Press.

Keller, M. B., Klerman, G. L., Lavori, P. W., Coryell, W., Endicott, J., & Taylor, J. (1984). Long-term outcome of episodes of major depression: clinical and public health significance. *Journal of American Medical Association, 252*, 788–792.

Klerman, G. L., Weissman, M. M., Rounsaville, B. J., & Chevron, E. S. (1984). *Interpersonal therapy for depression*. New York: Basic Books.

Manning, M. (1991). *Undercurrents: A therapist's reckoning with her own depression*. New York: HarperCollins.

Miklowitz, D. J., & Goldstein, M. J. (1997). *Bipolar disorder: A family-focused treatment approach*. New York: Guilford Press.

Rice D. P., & Miller L. S. (1995). The economic burden of affective disorders. *British Journal of Psychiatry 27* (Suppl.) 34–42.

Robins, L. N., & Regier, D. (Eds.). (1991). *Psychiatric disorders in America*. New York: Free Press.

James C. Coyne

MORAL DEVELOPMENT. Theories of moral development ask why and how individuals come to pursue goals that promote the interests of other people, and those of society in general, rather than only acting in their own narrow self-interests. Why do many people give money to charity when they could use it to buy themselves increased material comfort? Why do many people refrain from stealing and cheating when their gains from such behavior could put them at a personal advantage? Why do some people take at times fatal risks for the sake of others when they could live out their lives in safety and comfort by simply ignoring everyone's welfare but their own?

In moral psychology, answers to such questions have diverged along some of the same theoretical lines as those that have marked the rest of the field. Some answers emphasize the importance of natural biological processes, others the role of learning and experience; some theoretical positions focus on cognitive growth, others on social and cultural influences.

Nativist theories have maintained that inborn emotional dispositions, such as empathy, fear, and outrage, provide our species with a natural inclination toward prosocial behavior and away from antisocial behavior (Eisenberg & Fabes, 1998; Kagan, 1984). Learning theories have explained the acquisition of behavioral norms, values, and self-regulatory habits by citing mechanisms of observation, imitation, and reward (Bandura, 1969). Cognitive theories emphasize processes of reasoning and judgment, arguing that moral behavior is often a matter of conscious choice (Kohlberg, 1986; Piaget, 1932/1997; Rest, 1983). Culture theories consider moral behavior to be a legacy of the societal traditions that impose themselves on individuals through inescapable linguistic, visual, interpersonal, and religious messages (Shweder et al., 1998).

For a variety of reasons, none of these theoretical positions has had strong predictive power regarding the problem of individual moral behavior; that is, none has answered the question of which individuals are likely to act morally under particular sets of circumstances. Nativist studies have had more success explaining species-general behaviors than individual-specific behavior. For example, one typical study reports that at a very early age humans generally tend to express outrage over the violation of social norms and expectations (Kagan, 1984); another study shows that human newborns often show positive concern for people and distress at the discomfort of others (Eisenberg & Fabes, 1998).

Research from the learning-theory perspective has concluded that moral behavior is context bound, varying so much from situation to situation that few if any predictions can be made about individuals' moral characteristics. From this perspective, the landmark studies, still frequently cited, were Hartshorne and May's large-scale demonstrations that children's cheating behavior in any situation could not be predicted from their behavior in a previous situation; nor could such behavior be predicted from the children's knowledge of common moral rules such as the Ten Commandments and the Boy Scout Code (Hartshorne & May, 1928–1930).

The cognitive perspective has been tested in a large number of studies by Kohlberg and his colleagues (Kohlberg, 1986; Rest, 1983). Most of these have yielded inconclusive results. For example, one study showed that students who participated in political demonstrations about moral issues such as peace and civil rights were as likely to express Stage 2 (instrumental) as Stage 5 (social contract) judgments (Kohlberg & Candee, 1984). These two reasoning stages reflect wholly disparate value orientations; and even this indeterminate result was weakened by a large degree of variance in the behavior and judgments of these and other subjects in the study.

Culture theorists, like nativist ones, have rarely made predictions concerning the moral behavior of individuals, focusing instead on the morality of entire groups. But, unlike nativists, culture theorists focus not on the entire species but on societies within it, and not on biological dispositions but on collective moral orientations embedded in the daily practices, conventions, narrative scripts, and linguistic codes of those societies (Shweder et al., 1998).

For example, one program of research compares Hindu/Brahmin moral orientations with American ones, demonstrating that from an early age Hindu/Brahmin children learn orientations toward maintaining traditional moral beliefs, respecting defined rules of interpersonal relationships, and helping people in need. American children, in comparison, are more likely to learn orientations toward autonomy, liberty, personal rights, and fairness (Miller & Bershoff, 1992;

Shweder, Miller, & Mahapatra, 1987). Such conclusions are meant to apply to differences among cultural groups rather than among particular individuals.

A conceptually parallel line of theorizing has attempted to contrast moral orientations across genders, claiming that girls at an early age learn an orientation toward caring whereas boys learn an orientation toward rules and justice (Gilligan, 1982). Unlike the predictions made by culture theory, however, gender-based claims have not held up to empirical scrutiny. When educational or occupational levels are controlled, differences between males and females in moral judgment disappear (Walker, 1989). Moreover, as culture theorists point out, evidence indicates that there is far more similarity between male and female moral orientations within any given culture than there is between either male or female orientations across cultures (Miller & Bersoff, 1992).

Recently, in order to address the still unsolved problem of individual moral behavior, a number of theoretical and empirical studies have taken a new tack, determining that it is the relative centrality of a person's moral concerns to his or her sense of self—that is, the person's *moral identity*—which is the best predictor of the person's commitment to moral action. A person's moral identity consists of the person's commitment to pursue moral goals. It defines not merely what the person considers to be the right course of action but also why a person would decide that "*I myself* must take this course." For example, persons of all ages will express the belief that allowing others to starve is morally wrong, but only a subset of these persons will conclude that they themselves must do something to prevent this in particular circumstances such as a famine in Africa (Damon, 1990). The prediction would be that this subset of people, whose moral identity includes a sense of personal responsibility for those particular children, would be those most likely to perform charitable acts on their behalf.

In a review of the empirical literature on moral behavior, Blasi (1993) has argued that moral identity provides a powerful incentive for conduct, because identity engenders a motive to act in accord with one's conception of self. Moral judgment alone cannot provide this motive: it is only when people conceive of themselves, and their life goals, in moral terms that they acquire a strong propensity to act according to their moral judgments. As one identity theorist writes, "if a person sees a value or a way of life as essential to their identity, then they feel that they ought to act accordingly" (Nisan, 1996, p. 78).

People differ in the degree to which they define themselves in terms of moral concerns and aims. An interview study with 80 males and females ranging in age from 16 to 84 found that:

Morality had differing degrees of centrality in people's identities. For some, moral considerations and issues were pervasive in their experience because morality was rooted in the heart of their being; for others, moral issues seemed remote and the maintenance of moral values and standards was not basic to their self-concept and self-esteem. (Walker, Pitts, Hennig, & Matsuba, 1995, p. 398)

Many who study moral development have concluded that such variation may explain differences among people in the propensity to act in ways that they believe to be moral.

In a study of twenty-three adult moral exemplars (people with long, documented histories of performing moral deeds such as charitable and civil rights work), Colby and Damon (1992) found high levels of integration between self and moral concerns. At the same time, the group of moral exemplars showed no signs of elevated moral reasoning on the Kohlberg moral judgment measure. Colby and Damon concluded that sustained moral commitment requires a uniting of self and morality rather than sophisticated abilities in moral reasoning: "People who define themselves in terms of their moral goals are likely to see moral problems in everyday events, and they are also likely to see themselves as necessarily implicated in these problems. From there it is a small step to taking responsibility for the solution" (Colby & Damon, 1992, p. 307).

Similar results have been obtained among populations of youngsters as well. During adolescence, the development of self-understanding normally is marked by a small gradual increase in the use of moral concepts (Damon & Hart, 1988). When asked to describe themselves, most adolescents use a modest sampling of morally tinged adjectives such as "kind," "fair-minded," and "honest." Some adolescents even go so far as to describe themselves *primarily* in terms of systematic moral beliefs and goals (Damon & Hart, 1988; Hart, Yates, Fegley, & Wilson, 1995). Among the adolescents who do so, there is evidence of sustained moral commitment similar to that observed in the Colby and Damon study of adult moral exemplars. Hart and Fegley (1995) found that an exceptionally high proportion of adolescent "care exemplars" (boys and girls who were identified by community members as highly committed to voluntary service) had an understanding of self based upon systematic moral belief systems. Yet these "care exemplars" scored no higher than matched peers on the Kohlberg moral judgment measure. The Hart and Fegley study is noteworthy because it was conducted in an economically deprived urban setting, among an adolescent population often stereotyped as being at high risk in moral terms and criminally inclined.

Antisocial behavior lies at the other end of the moral spectrum from extraordinary altruism. Here, too, there is evidence that identity plays a mediating role. Damon and Hart (1988) reported data from a study that found developmental delays in the self-understanding of delinquent youth, particularly as related to future social pathways. Oyserman and Markus (1990) found that delinquent adolescents were less able than a matched sample of nondelinquents to articulate future possibilities for themselves that reflected positive or negative values, an indicator of still undeveloped moral identity.

How does a young person acquire a positive moral sense? Again, the answer varies according to whether the researcher chooses to focus on moral behavior, moral identity, moral emotions, moral judgment, or moral-cultural traditions. Most psychologists agree that reciprocal social interactions of some form are required for moral growth. Even psychologists who emphasize biological givens such as prosocial emotions acknowledge that these must be elaborated and extended by social feedback if they are to become effective capacities for moral action (Eisenberg & Fabes, 1998).

But the nature of the operative social interactions are in dispute. Those who stress the importance of individual moral judgment (Kohlberg, 1986; Piaget, 1932/1997) believe that interactions that provoke social-cognitive conflict and subsequent intellectual reflection are most likely to trigger moral growth. In support of this position, studies have shown that children's peer debates can generate an increased awareness of fairness and the rights of others (Damon & Killen, 1982). Those who stress the importance of conformity to social tradition believe that close attachment to parental figures, opportunities for appropriate rewards and punishment, and observation of the correct behaviors, lead the child to internalize moral norms. In support of this position, studies have shown that securely attached infants are likely to become more obedient than insecurely attached ones; that finely tuned reinforcement contingencies lead to the acquisition of habits and values, and that children will imitate both moral and immoral acts that capture their attention (Bugental & Goodnow, 1998).

A wave of theorizing in the 1980s and 1990s looked beyond children's immediate peer and family interactions for the source of moral learning. Inspired by writings from the field of sociology, this body of work examined community-level variables such as the degree of consistency between sources of moral influences on the child. For example, in a study of 300 adolescents from 10 American towns and cities, Ianni found high degrees of prosocial behavior and low degrees of antisocial behavior among youngsters from communities that were characterized by widespread consensus in moral standards and expectations for young people (Ianni, 1989). The opposite was true of communities characterized by conflict, divisiveness, and lack of shared standards for the young. Ianni named the set of shared standards that he found in harmonious communities a "youth charter," and he reported that neither the existence of a clear charter nor the moral behavior that it spawned was a function of marker variables such as ethnicity, socioeconomic status, geographic location, or size. The notion of a community youth charter as a facilitator of moral development among the young is being explored in interventions aimed at fostering communication between children, parents, teachers, and other influential adults about shared standards and common values (Damon & Gregory, 1997).

[*See also* Religious Values and Mental Health; *and* Values.]

Bibliography

Bandura, A. (1969). Social learning of moral judgments. *Journal of Personality and Social Psychology, 11,* 275–279.

Blasi, A. (1993). The development of identity: Some implications for moral functioning. In G. Noam & T. Wren (Eds.), *The moral self.* Cambridge, MA: M.I.T. Press.

Bugental, D., & Goodnow, J. (1998). Socialization processes. In W. Damon (Ed.), *Handbook of child psychology* (Vol. 3, pp. 389–462). New York: Wiley.

Colby, A., & Damon, W. (1992). *Some do care: Contemporary lives of moral commitment.* New York: Free Press.

Damon, W. (1990). *The moral child.* New York: Free Press.

Damon, W., & Gregory, A. (1997). The youth charter: Towards the formation of adolescent moral identity. *Journal of Moral Education, 26,* 117–131.

Damon, W., & Hart, D. (1988). *Self-understanding in childhood and adolescence.* New York: Cambridge University Press.

Damon, W., & Killen, M. (1982). Peer interaction and the process of change in children's moral reasoning. *Merrill-Palmer Quarterly, 28,* 347–367.

Eisenberg, N., & Fabes, R. (1998). Prosocial development. In W. Damon (Ed.), *Handbook of child psychology* (Vol. 3). New York: Wiley.

Gilligan, C. (1982). *In a different voice.* Cambridge, MA: Harvard University Press.

Hart D., & Fegley S. (1995), Prosocial behavior and caring in adolescence: Relations to self-understanding and social judgment. *Child Development, 66,* 1346–1359.

Hart, D., Yates, M., Fegley, S., & Wilson, G. (1995). Moral commitment in inner-city adolescents. In M. Killen & D. Hart (Eds.), *Morality in everyday life: Developmental perspectives.* New York: Cambridge University Press.

Ianni, F. (1989). *The structure of experience: A report on American youth today.* New York: Free Press.

Kagan, J. (1984). *The nature of the child.* New York: Basic Books.

Kohlberg, L. (1986). *The psychology of moral development.* New York: Harper & Row.

Kohlberg, L., & Candee, D. (1984). The relationship of moral judgment to moral action. In W. Kurtines & J.

Gewirtz (Eds.), *Morality, moral behavior, and moral development.* New York: Wiley.

Miller, J. G., & Bersoff, D. M. (1992). Culture and moral judgments: How are conflicts between justice and interpersonal responsibilities resolved? *Journal of Personality and Social Psychology, 62,* 541–554.

Nisan, M. (1996). Personal identity and education for the desirable. *Journal of Moral Education, 25,* 75–83.

Oyserman, D., & Markus, H. (1990). Possible selves and delinquency. *Journal of Personality and Social Psychology, 59,* 112–125.

Piaget, J. (1997). *The moral judgment of the child.* New York: Free Press (Original work published 1932)

Rest, J. (1983). Morality. In P. Mussen (Ed.), *Handbook of child psychology* (Vol. 4). New York: Wiley.

Shweder, R., Goodnow, J., Hatano, G., LeVine, R., Markus, H., & Miller, P. (1998). The cultural psychology of development: One mind, many mentalities. In W. Damon (Ed.), *Handbook of child psychology* (Vol. 1). New York: Wiley.

Shweder, R., Mahapatra, M., & Miller, J. (1987). Culture and moral development. In J. Kagan & S. Lamb (Eds.), *The emergence of morality in young children.* Chicago: University of Chicago Press.

Walker, L. (1989). A longitudinal study of moral reasoning. *Child Development, 60,* 157–166.

Walker, L., Pitts, R., Hennig, K., & Matsuba, M. (1995). Reasoning about morality and real-life moral problems. In M. Killen & D. Hart (Eds.), *Morality in everyday life* (pp. 371–407). New York: Cambridge University Press.

William Damon

MORAL DISCOURSE. The psychological low points that bring people to counseling and therapy are typically experienced as negatively moralized. Thus, one person's bitterness over victimization, another's sense of loss from a broken relationship, another's resentment at the apparent onset of dementia in a parent, another's sensitivity to being illegitimate, and another's fear of professional success may all be experientially laced with the negative (and different) moral emotions of guilt, shame, remorse, or regret. As such, the negative moral emotions may have certain distinctive feeling tones, but they also have a cognitive core or base in perceived violations of moral principle. The negative moral feelings that constitute the emotional suffering that drains energy and diminishes agency have moral principles in the background.

Moral philosophers, psychological theorists, and clinical practitioners can all have interests—albeit interests of different kinds—in moral discourse, construed broadly as including moral judgments, moral principles, conceptions of moral agency, and the negative and positive moral emotions. At the most general level, ethical theories study moral discourse in an attempt to characterize and even systematize the structural features of human moral sensibility. The idea here is that just as human beings have certain capacities for intelligence, judgment, and feeling that allow them to know the world and not just react to it, so they also have certain capacities (again, for intelligence, judgment, and feeling) relevant to valuational responses to the world, as reflected in moral action and the sort of appreciation we call aesthetic. The task of the general ethical theories is to illuminate how these capacities work, and part of what there is to study in this connection is moral discourse.

The long-standing general theories that have been found to be important and insightful, for example, those of Aristotle, Kant, or the utilitarians, typically recognize that moral sensibility has a distinctive sort of rationality to it, so that moral valuations are not merely "anything goes" expressions of personal subjectivity. The theories agree that positions on issues of value require defense and justification, even though the theories conflict in certain ways over how these rational processes are to be understood. Thus, if persons disagree in a matter of morality, then rational inquiry must persist, not terminate, and the business of a general ethical theory is to make clear what the logic of moral argumentation actually is, in contrast, say, to economic, political, psychological, or other sorts of argumentation.

Apart from their different accounts of moral argument, the main received theories may be seen to carry among their presuppositions certain conceptual images of what it is to be a moral agent. Thus, the Kantian view prizes the rational nature in persons, which is that juxtaposition of reason and inclination that provides the tension that gives rise to our interest in what we *ought* to do in certain cases, in contrast to what we could do in those cases as a matter of convenience, strong feeling, or self-interest. The utilitarian finds, instead, that morality prizes that form of existence for human beings (and sentient beings generally) that contains as much pleasure and as little pain as circumstances permit, and then treats contributions to making that sort of existence as general as possible as a guideline for decision making between alternative policies or courses of action. Classical Aristotelian theory views persons as sets of dispositions forming character and urges the sort of moral education that helps individuals develop the practical wisdom that consists in good judgment within (and relative to) the communities in which they live.

For many years in the middle of the twentieth century, professional philosophy seemed stalled in explorations of various reductionist theses about the nature of moral judgments, as if critical or positive moral judgments (even those reflecting acts of conscience) were somehow no more than expressions of emotion or manifestations of intuitions that might or might not be common in a community of individuals. During this period ethics was psychologized, and it appeared that professional philosophy mirrored popular culture in the notion that values are somehow noncognitive or subjective. Fortunately, with the publication by John Rawls of *A Theory of Justice* in 1971, this uninteresting period ended. Rawls showed how principles of justice for the basic structure of society have cognitive substance and are open to rational elucidation and critique. Under the pressures of the model provided by Rawls's achievement, philosophical theorists moved again into vigorous discussion of the alternative philosophical portrayals of the makeup of moral agency and the structure of moral sensibility—accompanied now, in fact, by a virtual industry of work in applied or normative ethics wherein topical policy issues (concerning, for example, abortion, capital punishment, physician-assisted suicide, etc.) are engaged.

The current discussion in both ethical theory and applied ethics features explorations of Kantian and utilitarian themes, and is often critical of the latter. At the same time, there is clearly a resurgence of interest in Aristotelian character ethics or virtue ethics, accompanied by increased attention to what contemporary philosophers call moral psychology, and thus to the makeup of the moral self, and especially its moral-emotional experience in the aftermath of moral action. In general, this latter resurgence may be represented as a shifting of attention away from the analysis and justification of candidate moral principles that are, in Kant's phrase, "valid for all rational beings" and toward recognition of the moral force of particulars involved in cases in which moral decisions are called for—particulars such as the relationships between people or the commitments they have to, say, careers or causes in which considerable emotional energy is invested. This shift in attention seems to suggest that morality itself is not just, or only, a system of principles, rules, and policies, but countenances as well as a whole range of other interests and elements in human lives that seem connected not so much to questions of right and wrong as to issues about *meaningfulness* in human lives.

As a result, contemporary moral theory reflects renewed philosophical interest in classical questions about the meaning of life and how to live, as well as interest in the social, historical, and cultural elements of the moral self. Here we move closer to the moral phenomena that actually surface in the one-to-one work of clinicians with clients. The context in which counseling and therapy take place has its way of lifting the reality of an individual's life into view and focusing attention on those particulars, including the stresses and strains connected with them, without the philosophical theorist's preoccupations with generality and objectivity. This is not to say, however, that counseling and therapy do or should proceed independently of moral discourse.

Suppose the clinician faces a client suffering moral-emotional pain. The identity of this pain (is it guilt, or shame, or regret, or remorse, or resentment?) may be unclear to the client suffering it, even though the pain itself is severe. The client's failure to understand the pain (its identity, its causes) may be as difficult for the client to endure as the pain itself. And the failure to understand is not just painful to bear, for the identity of the moralized suffering bears upon how it is to be addressed. If, for example, guilt (as classically understood) is the morally natural aftermath of violations of communitarian principles or rules, and shame is the analogous aftermath of failure to meet one's own standards of quality in some activity or relationship, then *how to proceed* in getting past the moralized suffering must (logically) be different in important respects. How one's pain is identified may guide one's recovery. Indeed, if moral-emotional pain is identified as simply emotional pain, it is then seen in casual terms as psychopathology. As a result, the complex content of moral principles, judgments, and decisions in which the pain is embedded is ignored, and recovery options thereby restricted.

Apart from these cognitive issues, the client's suffering may be complex in further ways that require expression through moral vocabulary. It may seem uncontroversial to the client that his or her pain is grounded in some wrong done to or by him or her, or in his or her failure to perform an expected right action or meet the demands of a central self-defining relationship; and when this is so, the negatively moralized suffering involves for the client the sense that his or her control has failed, sometimes through victimization, and at other times simply gratuitously. The facts of the matter, for the client, leave him or her confused and possibly in self-reproach, so that *autonomy* has been diminished and perhaps lost for all practical purposes.

In these cases, the remote-seeming principles and conceptions of self that are targeted for attention by general ethical theories may be very relevant indeed. The client may be absorbed by negative evaluations of past actions and flooded by regret and remorse, and in some cases may be experiencing despair as well as uncertainty about the future. In these circumstances, perhaps the flat languages of "rights" and "utility," so dominant in the Kantian and utilitarian theories, or even the language of "virtue" and "vice" from the Aristotelian account, may not seem to reach to the urgency of the particular case. But it is a distortion to suppose that moral discourse has been abandoned or left behind. Now the morally relevant features in particular cases—those features that generate moral-emotional pain and diminish prospects for the recovery of energy and self-esteem—are those features of commitment, concern, relationship, and responsibility that lie beneath the surface moral categories provided by the classical theories. Indeed, the questions in clinical practice are not often of the form, What principles do I apply here? but instead of the form, How can I go on from (get past, overcome) this disastrous or grievous mistake in my life? In the clinical context, moral discourse is charged with meaning-of-life urgency and candidate how-to-live strategies. But the discourse in which such urgency and strategies are addressed is nevertheless moral discourse. The *ought* is as alive here as it is anywhere involving decisions and human flourishing, and the risks of bad or unwise choices and prolonged suffering make the rationality of such discourse a precious resource. (For the broader implications of this analysis for developmental and social/personality psychologies, see Flanagan, 1991).

When a low point in one's life is morally negative, and accountability for it is painful to bear, or its identity is simply controversial, then one's self-conception is threatened. One seems to oneself a "bad" person, not what one supposed oneself to be, and one may find oneself pained and confused by this problematic in one's life. The experience of the client immersed in this negativity is unavoidably laced with negative moral emotion, and it seems plain that the activities of the clinician with such a client cannot avoid engaging the normative vocabulary of morality. Indeed, to avoid that vocabulary, or attempt to set it aside, would be to ignore the client.

Of course, when clinician and client work through the client's suffering, the aim is not to devise or establish a new ethical theory. It is rather, in general terms, to develop a recovery strategy for a real person who is suffering in a way that is conceptualized, in important part, in the vocabulary of morality. The task of working out an ethical theory (an adequate form of utilitarianism, for example) is essentially a timeless activity, and when participating in it, one's place in time or history does not matter much. The task of theory is governed by concerns for truth and coherence (among other things), and closure may not be urgent. But the development of an adequate strategy for going on for *this* individual is not similarly timeless in character. It is guided by concerns for the current health, energy, and functioning of the individual (this real person), and closure—or at least practicality—may be very important indeed. The difference in orientation is great: ethical theory means to understand the moral vocabulary and ultimately the general features of moral sensibility; a recovery strategy means to use the moral vocabulary to move an individual beyond a low point toward functionality.

But, of course, a recovery strategy will have a certain structure to it. First, it will recognize and help the sufferer characterize the identity of his or her negatively moralized suffering. This is the point of departure for anything worked out later in the way of a how-to-live strategy, and it is in that way that the reason for the development of a strategy will be attempted. In the end it will also form a test of the strategy since the amelioration of the suffering is what following the strategy is supposed to achieve. So, then, insofar as the suffering is itself conceptualized in the terms of guilt, shame, remorse, or regret, the therapeutic enterprise begins with the power of the moral vocabulary to pick out and identify those aspects of the client's condition that require change.

Second, the clinician and client must work out an interpretation of what it would be to detach from one's life so that the client can achieve some relief from the pain of the negatively moralized suffering. Somehow, therapy must provide the client with the means of standing back from the interpretations of the past and present that are burdened with negative moral emotion. The realization of such detachment is essential if proposals for going on are to be considered genuinely available choices to the client.

A third element in the work of the clinician and client will be the task of sharing a generalized understanding of the nature and makeup of the human condition that the client is enduring. This is, as it were, a metaphysical task embedded in the process of therapy itself, and among its results, in fortunate cases, is the realization on the part of the client that he or she is not alone in the troubling situation that generated the suffering.

A final part of the process of therapy will be straightforwardly normative, and might even be expressed—implicitly if not explicitly—in a number of maxims or policy directives for the client. That is, against the background of the interpretation of the moralized suffering worked out by clinician and client at the beginning, the detachment strategy worked out next, and the general understanding of the human condition that saves the client from isolation, the clinician and client work out a set of how-to-live prescriptions. This set may contain exercises of various sorts: some of these may be quite concrete (bits of self-understanding writing to do, different sorts of relaxation techniques to practice); others may be general or abstract slogans or formulas to keep in mind (e.g., principles that may seem platitudinous in themselves but which come to be helpful or insightful in contexts that are disturbing relative to the moralized suffering in question).

In general, then, the one-to-one work of clinician and client makes use of the vocabulary of morality—moral judgments, moral principles, conceptions of moral agency, interpretations of moral emotions—in an effort to move the client toward an accommodation with the specific problematic in his or her life. The sketch here merely indicates a general structure within which, of course, different particular therapies (behavior therapy, cognitive therapy, psychoanalytic psycho-

therapy, or perhaps some mix of these) may be performed. What the therapy helps the client do is put together his or her own moral autonomy, that is, capacity for choice, with the givens of his or her physical, emotional, and mental being, and all of these together with the contingent external factors in his or her life, so as to secure a level of functionality more adequate to the task of leading a life. Again, the aims are not those of ethical theory—truth and consistency—but instead those of the kind of personal reconciliation with the circumstances of one's life that in ordinary terms we call peace of mind.

Indeed, it is helpful to use the term *peace of mind* to identify the goal of the effort of therapy. In fact, peace of mind is not just a relaxed state of tranquility; it is a condition in which one is *morally* at ease with oneself, which is to say that it is a moralized state of a positive kind. An explanation of peace of mind would, philosophically, make reference to moral principles and respect for them, and to conceptions of self that emphasize the autonomy that informs moral decision making. To have peace of mind is to have a sort of inner calm related importantly to integrity, and it is this condition that is challenged or destroyed by the different sorts of life problems that many people bring to counseling.

By this interpretation, the process of counseling itself is no mere matter of helping a client feel good about himself or herself, but rather a process whereby a client is helped to reach a level of understanding of self that allows peace of mind to occur. Within the structure given here, the ingredients of this process will be different from case to case. The loss of peace of mind in real people takes them down; it results in diminished energy, loss of confidence, and a wariness or fear of decision making. Getting past such a loss need not require forgetting or ignoring the past or the events that generated the moralized suffering; it need not be revisionist regarding the client's history; it need not involve the pretence that past wrongdoing did not occur or was not really wrongdoing. In the end, in fortunate cases, people can be helped to live *with* their pasts, and without blinkering them in ways that land them in self-deception. Peace of mind is not the simple—and impossible—state that one gets to have only if one never did anything wrong and never had anything wrong done to one. It is, instead, a condition one may come to have if one gains a measure of humility, honesty, tolerance, patience, regard for others, and acceptance of human fragility. The moral dimensions of peace of mind are inescapable.

Bibliography

Blum, L. A. (1994). *Moral perception and particularity*. Cambridge, England: Cambridge University Press.

Care, N. S. (1996). *Living with one's past: Personal fates and moral pain.* Lanham, MD: Rowman & Littlefield.

Darwall, S., Gibbard, A., & Railton, P. (Eds.). (1997). *Moral discourse and practice.* New York: Oxford University Press. A collection of essays reviewing the problems under discussion in contemporary ethics; the editors' introduction is comprehensive and detailed.

Deigh, J. (Ed.). (1992). *Ethics and personality.* Chicago: University of Chicago Press. A collection of essays in moral psychology from *Ethics*, a leading philosophy journal in moral theory and social and political philosophy.

Feinberg, J. (1986). *Harm to self.* New York: Oxford University Press. The third volume in a series of four dealing with morality and criminal law; this volume addresses the problem of legal paternalism.

Flanagan, O. (1991). *Varieties of moral personality.* Cambridge, MA: Harvard University Press. Detailed discussion of connections between philosophy and psychology.

Frankfurt, H. G. (1988). *The importance of what we care about.* Cambridge, UK: Cambridge University Press.

Morris, H. (1976). *On guilt and innocence.* Berkeley: University of California Press. Includes detailed discussions of the negative moral emotions of guilt and shame.

Murdoch, I. (1985). *The sovereignty of the good.* London: Ark.

Nagel, T. (1979). *Mortal questions.* Cambridge, UK: Cambridge University Press.

Rawls, J. (1971). *A theory of justice.* Cambridge, MA: Harvard University Press.

Stocker, M., & Hegeman, E. (1996). *Valuing emotions.* Cambridge, UK: Cambridge University Press.

Thomas, L. (1989). *Living morally.* Philadelphia: Temple University Press.

Williams, B. (1981). *Moral luck.* Cambridge, UK: Cambridge University Press.

Wollheim, R. (1984). *The thread of life.* Cambridge, MA: Harvard University Press.

Norman S. Care

MORGAN, CLIFFORD THOMAS (1915–1976), American physiological psychologist and science administrator. Morgan received the Ph.D. degree in 1939 at the University of Rochester. He was an instructor at Harvard University from 1939 to 1943, where he worked closely with Karl Lashley. [*See the biography of Lashley.*] Morgan accepted a position in the biology department at Johns Hopkins in 1943, although he did not begin his duties there until 1946. Meanwhile, he continued affiliation with Harvard while also serving with the government's (U.S. Navy) Systems Research Laboratory in Rhode Island. At Johns Hopkins, he helped reestablish the psychology department and served as its chair (1949–1954). During this time he brought the Systems Research Laboratory to Hopkins. By 1959 Morgan's textbook successes enabled him to seek academic appointments more on his terms (which now meant less involvement in governance and academic minutia). He relocated to the Universities of Wisconsin (1959–1962) and California, Santa Barbara (1962–1964) before resigning to fulfill some textbook commitments. Family matters led to his moving to Austin, Texas, in 1967. An adjunct faculty position with the University of Texas enabled him to teach while avoiding other academic involvement.

Morgan's laboratory research career appears to have spanned the years from about 1943 to 1951, but he gained significant recognition in three areas: the study of audiogenic seizure with its implications for epilepsy, biological motivation, and auditory processing. Essentially, he began to thrive as a textbook author and as a science organizer and administrator. His textbook, *Physiological Psychology* (1943, 1950, 1965; 2nd edition with Eliot Stellar) systematized the field and was highly influential. His *Introduction to Psychology* (1956; with several subsequent editions, some with coauthors such as R. A. King) represented a new approach. Morgan used multiple expert authors (fourteen for the first edition) but retained the cohesion of a single "voice" via his editorial control. He coauthored other textbooks including *Applied Experimental Psychology* (with Alphonse Chapanis and W. R. Garner, 1949). The textbooks gave him financial independence, and he was a generous benefactor at the Universities of Wisconsin and California, Santa Barbara as well as to the Psychonomic Society.

Morgan was an active participant in the meetings in which the Psychonomic Society (originally, tentatively named American Federation of Experimental Psychologists) was conceived (December 1958) and founded (31 December 1959). He wrote the by-laws, which largely set the strong proscience, antiprofessional tone of the society, and he was elected first chair of the Governing Board.

Morgan's experiences as member and subsequently as chair of the American Psychological Association's Publications Board and his experience as the editor who rescued the troubled *Psychological Abstracts* enabled him to found the journals, *Psychonomic Science* (1964), *Psychonomic Monograph Supplements* (1965), *Perception and Psychophysics* (1966), and *Behavior Research Methods & Instrumentation* (1969). He offered these journals to the Psychonomic Society in 1968 together with the managerial establishment and sufficient funds to sustain their operations through the transition years. Until his death, he continued to manage the journals, and during this period, *Animal Learning and Behavior, Memory and Cognition,* and *Physiological Psychology* were founded.

Bibliography

Dewsbury, D. A. (1996). History of the Psychonomic Society II: The journal publishing program. *Psychonomic*

Bulletin and Review, 3, 322–338. The two preceding references include additional information about Morgan's role in the founding of the Psychonomic Society and its journals.

Dewsbury, D. A., & Bolles, R. C. (1995). The founding of the Psychonomic Society. *Psychonomic Bulletin & Review, 2,* 216–233.

Garner, W. R. (1976). Clifford Thomas Morgan: Psychonomic Society's first chairman. *Bulletin of the Psychonomic Society, 8,* 409–415. Informative and insightful address to the Psychonomic Society by a longstanding friend and colleague honoring Morgan after his death.

Stellar, E., & Lindzey, G. (1978). Clifford T. Morgan: 1915–1976. *American Journal of Psychology, 91,* 343–348. Informative and unusually candid reminiscences about Morgan's career divided into the earlier (Stellar) and later (Lindzey) years.

Roger K. Thomas

MORGAN, CONWY LLOYD (1852–1936), British zoologist and comparative psychologist. Born in London, England, Morgan received a doctorate in science. He lectured at the Diocesan College in Rondebosh, South Africa. He returned to England as professor at the University College of Bristol, where he was briefly the first vice chancellor of Bristol University and then professor of psychology and ethics. Morgan also lectured at Clark University in the United States. He became a Fellow of the Royal Society.

In *An Introduction to Comparative Psychology* (London, 1894), Morgan stated that "in no case may we interpret an action as the outcome of the exercise of a higher psychological faculty, if it can be interpreted as the outcome of the exercise of one which stands lower in the psychological scale." This canon was often erroneously identified as the law of parsimony; however, Morgan discussed the function of his canon as one of interpretation (p. 287).

Morgan was a strong advocate of studying comparative psychology using well-controlled experiments. He emphasized the need to observe and accurately record the procedure and the results in order to interpret the findings without bias. He proposed operational definitions in order to prevent misinterpretations, misconceptions, or misunderstandings, as well as replications of experiments for confirmation of the results.

Recordings of a dog's behavior during an experiment gave rise to such terms as "trial and practice" and "trial and failure"; yet it was "trial and error" that was widely accepted (Morgan, *Animal Life and Intelligence,* London, 1889–1890; *Animal Behaviour,* London, 1900; and *The Animal Mind,* London, 1930). Observation on newly hatched chicks pecking at good- and nasty-tasting kernels led to the awareness of differential effects on results.

Nature/nurture, another important topic, was discussed by Morgan. He suggested that instinctive behavior was to a greater or lesser degree congenitally determined. (Currently, it is generally referred to as species-specific behavior.) Morgan felt that nothing was known about the basis of the evolution of behavior from direct observation. And in addition he was an advocate of Pavlovian conditioning to study behavior; and so he focused on conditioning and conditional behavior.

Other areas of Morgan's attention included social situations, such as imitation or observational learning. He also experimented with orphaned chicks and reported on the effects on another hen's social distance.

Among the unresolved topics was migration and its seasonal changes, which he mentioned in several books. Morgan speculated that the underlying basis of behavior might be instinctive (species-specific).

The topics of interest mentioned here represent only a small number of many issues discussed by Morgan. His ideas and contributions to comparative psychology stimulated and inspired young scientists to work in the field of animal behavior.

Bibliography

Adler, L. L. (1973). Contributions of C. Lloyd Morgan to comparative psychology. In E. Tobach, H. E. Adler, & L. L. Adler (Eds.), *Comparative psychology at issue* (Vol. 223, pp. 41–48). New York: The New York Academy of Sciences

Morgan, C. L. (1896). *Habit and instinct.* London, England: Edward Arnold.

Morgan, C. L. (1912). *Instinct and experience.* New York: Macmillan.

Warden, C. J., Jenkins, T. N., & Warner, L. H. (1935). *Comparative psychology* (Vol. 1). New York: Ronald Press.

Leonore Loeb Adler

MORPHEMES. *See* Morphology.

MORPHOLOGY refers to the internal structure of complex words, or sublexical structure. The study of morphology is centrally concerned with how language users store and understand complex words and how they create new ones. Compare the two English words *marry* and *remarry.* There is no way to break the word *marry* down further into meaningful parts, but *remarry* consists of two atomic meaningful parts (each termed a morpheme), and therefore the study of its structure lies within the domain of morphology. It is important to stress that we are talking of meaningful elements of

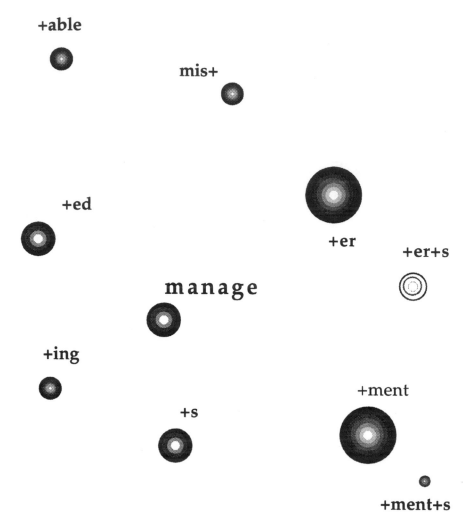

MORPHOLOGY. Figure 1. Lexical entries decomposed into morphological constituents.

sublexical structure. If we look only at sound, then *marry* consists of two syllables and four or five phonemes, but this sublexical structure is purely a matter of sound and has nothing to do with meaning. Work on the role of sound structure in language processing is common, but only recently have psychologists begun to examine morphology as a window to sublexical processing.

The first part of *remarry* is a prefix (*re-*), which means approximately "again"; it is joined together with the second component, the verb *marry*, to form another verb with the predictable meaning of "marry again." The same prefix occurs in many other words (e.g., *reacquaint, redesign, refasten,* and *recalibrate*) and can also be used to form novel words like *redamage* or *retarget*, whose meaning is understood easily by speakers of English. The fact that verbs like *reweep* or *relike* are impossible also tells us that there are restrictions on this prefix. It is the morphologist's job to discover the gen-

eral principles that underlie our ability to form and understand certain complex words, especially those that are novel or unfamiliar (e.g., *reconfine*) but not others (e.g., *relike*). Languages differ greatly in both the complexity and type of their morphology. Some have very little in the way of morphology (e.g., Chinese), while others are famous for their complex morphology (e.g., Navajo). English falls somewhere in the middle, so it is quite common for an English sentence to contain no morphologically complex words.

Affixes (prefixes and suffixes) may also vary quite widely in their productivity—that is, the likelihood that they will be used to form new words. Compare the two English suffixes *-th* and *-ness*, both of which form nouns from adjectives (e.g., *warmth* and *sadness*). The first suffix is completely unproductive in modern English; no new word with this suffix has been added to the language in centuries. The second is highly productive; innovations like *nerdiness* or *emotiveness* are common.

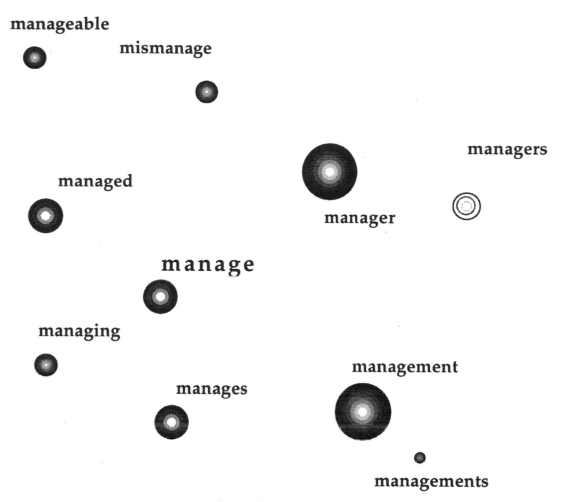

MORPHOLOGY. Figure 2. Lexical entries represented as full forms.

Morphemes are classified into two very basic types: free and bound, the difference between them being that a bound morpheme cannot form a word by itself but must attach to (be bound to) another form. The repeated addition of bound morphemes allows for the formation of fairly complex words by piling one prefix or suffix on another. The word *unmanageableness* contains three bound morphemes and has been built up in stages from *manage* by first adding the suffix *-able* to the base verb *manage*, producing *manageable*, then the prefix *un-* to form *unmanageable*, and finally the suffix *-ness*, resulting in [[*un* [[*manage*]$_V$ *able*]$_A$]$_A$ *ness*]$_N$.

Linguists distinguish derivational morphology from inflectional morphology. Derivational morphology deals with how distinct words are related to one another, inflectional morphology is concerned with the different forms that a word may take, depending on its role in a sentence. English is quite poor inflectionally, but in many other languages (e.g., Swahili or classical Greek) each noun, verb, and adjective will have a large number of inflected forms.

Knowledge about words comprises the mental lexicon. A major research question for psycholinguists is the extent to which morphological knowledge is represented explicitly in the mental lexicon. One point of discussion is whether all word forms or only those that are irregular with respect to either form or meaning are stored in the mental lexicon. If regularity is defined with respect to form, we can ask whether words that undergo a change in spelling (and sometimes pronunciation) are represented differently from words whose base morpheme is always regular. That is, are forms such as *sleep* and *slept* represented differently from forms such as *turn* and *turned*?

Derivation tends to be semantically somewhat unpredictable: *remarry* means simply "marry again," but *review* does not usually mean "view again." If regularity is defined in terms of meaning, we can ask whether inflected and derived forms are represented in the same manner. Similarly, we can ask whether forms must be semantically transparent in order to be represented in the lexicon as morphological relatives. Some theorists express morphological knowledge in terms of lexical representations that are decomposed into constituent morphemes. Other theorists express morphological knowledge in terms of a principle of lexical organization among full forms that are morphological relatives.

In the psycholinguistic literature, a classical task for exploring morphological knowledge is the lexical decision task. Letter strings are presented visually, and skilled readers must decide whether each is a real word. Words are usually presented in pairs, a prime and then a target. Sometimes prime and target are in immediate succession; at other times as many as thirteen intervening items may separate the prime and the target. Decision latencies to the target as a function of the type of prime that preceded it are measured.

Experimental evidence for the lexical representation of morphology is based primarily but not exclusively on visual word recognition and how the pattern of decision latencies in a lexical decision task is influenced by (a) the particular combination of morphological components; (b) the frequency or familiarity of constituent morphemes; or (c) repetition, across successive trials, of a morphological component. For example, in Italian, rejection latencies in a lexical decision task for nonwords composed of illegal combinations of real morphemes (verbal stems and affixes) vary as a function of the type of violation between stem and affix (approximate English analogs would involve illegal past tense verbs like *tooken* or *gived*). Similar effects have been reported as a function of the position of illegal transition in Dutch (analogous to the difference between illegal English words like *manageableize* and *managizing*, where the illegal transition in *manageableize* is between the second and third morpheme, but in *managizing* it is between the first and second). Similarly, in a phoneme monitoring task with Dutch materials, the identification of words that include stems and prefixes is easier than that of words composed of stems without a prefix (English analogs would be *remarry* and *remedy*). Moreover, rejection latencies for Dutch pseudowords are sensitive to the productivity of their morphological components (in English, one would expect *bealness* to be harder to reject than *bealth*).

Typically, targets are faster following morphological relatives (formed from the same base morpheme) than an unrelated word. So *car* would be faster following *cars* than following *card*. This effect is called facilitation due to morphological relatedness. Changes in spelling or pronunciation between a morphologically related prime and target do not reliably diminish the magnitude of facilitation to targets that follow morphologically related primes at long lags with no form change. For example, Serbian forms that undergo palatalization (e.g., *nozi*), forms with letter deletion (e.g., *petku*) and regular forms (e.g., *nogom*) all produced equivalent target latencies (e.g., *noga, petak*). Similar results have been

reported in English for moderately irregular forms (e.g., *slept/sleep*). Equivalent patterns of influence for morphologically related words with differing orthographic and phonological form (e.g., *nozi/noga*) and for words with similar form (e.g., *nogim/noga*) are problematic for any model that assumes that similarity of form alone underlies morphological facilitation.

In addition to being orthographically and phonologically related, two words that are morphologically related tend to be semantically related. Thus, it is possible that, in order to observe facilitation between words formed from the same base morpheme, semantic similarity must be preserved. However, results in Hebrew, Dutch, and Serbian, have found morphological facilitation with semantically opaque as well as transparent morphological relatives. In English, we would expect both *casualty* and *casualness* to provide some facilitation to *casual*.

Some theorists have posited differences in how derivational and inflectional forms are represented in the mental lexicon. Among semantically close relatives, there is some evidence that, at short lags, morphological facilitation is greater following inflectional relatives as compared with derivational relatives (e.g., *dog* and *dogs*, versus *dog* and *doggy*). It is difficult to match semantic similarity across morphological types, but in one study of Serbo-Croatian, the time dimension of an action was manipulated to create inflectional and derivational relatives (something that could not be done with English data). With minimal semantic changes, facilitation for verbal targets was greater following inflectional than derivational relatives.

The segment shifting task, modeled after the reordering of morphemic segments that occurs in spontaneous speech errors, provides further evidence for the psychological reality of the morpheme. In this task, subjects segment and shift a sequence of letters from a source word to a target word (*bright*) and then name the product aloud (*brighten*). Letter sequences (e.g., *en*) from morphologically complex source words such as *harden* (morphemic) and their morphologically simple (nonmorphemic) controls, such as *garden*, are phonemically matched. Whether or not *en* is a morpheme depends on the particular word to which it is affixed. Naming latencies are faster following source words with morphemic letter sequences than their nonmorphemic controls. Similar results have been observed both for English, in which the morphemic status of the shifted sequence was varied and sequences were appended after the base morpheme (linearly concatenated), and for Hebrew, in which the morphological transparency of the root (base morpheme) was varied and one morpheme was infixed inside the other (nonconcatenative) so that the phonological and orthographic integrity of the morphemic constituents was disrupted. It was also the case that productivity influenced segment-shifting times. The effects of productivity have been demonstrated for suffixes as well as for bases that enter into many or few combinations to form words.

In summary, the morphological properties of words play a critical role in word recognition, and morphology cannot be expressed in terms of similarity of form or meaning alone. Psychologists study morphology for what it reveals about how the components of words (their sublexical structure) contribute to word identification and production.

Bibliography

Aronoff, M. (1994). *Morphology by itself*. Cambridge, MA: MIT Press.

Bauer, L. (1983). *English word formation*. Cambridge, UK: Cambridge University Press.

Booij, G., & van Marle, J. (annual). *Yearbook of morphology*. Dordrecht, Netherlands: Kluwer.

Feldman, L. B. (Ed.). (1995). *Morphological aspects of language processing*. Hillsdale, NJ: Erlbaum.

Matthews, P. H. (1991). *Morphology* (2nd ed.). Cambridge, UK: Cambridge University Press.

Sandra, D., & Taft, M. (Eds.). (1994). *Morphological structure, lexical representation, and lexical access*. Hove, UK: Erlbaum.

Spencer, A. (1991). *Morphological theory*. Oxford, UK: Blackwell.

Zwicky, A., & Spencer, A. (Eds.). (1997). *Handbook of morphology*. Oxford, UK: Blackwell.

Mark Aronoff and Laurie B. Feldman

MOTHERING. *See* Parent-Child Relationship; *and* Pregnancy.

MOTION PERCEPTION. Motion provides people with a wealth of information about the world around them, including information about surface structure, distance to objects, the motion of objects in the world, and the motion of the observer through the scene. Motion perception is generally divided into two stages. The first is the perception of the two-dimensional motion of images on the retina. The second is the interpretation of this two-dimensional information to make inferences about the external world.

To perceive motion in the world, the human visual system must interpret a changing pattern of light intensity falling on the retina. Each photoreceptor signals the increase or decrease of light intensity at a single location. To interpret motion across the retina, these signals must be integrated across a portion of the im-

age. The human visual system is remarkably adept at inferring motion from these changes in light intensity. We perceive motion both from the image of a continuously moving object, or from a sequence of discontinuous jumps of the image, known as *apparent motion*. Apparent motion appears smooth and continuous when the time between successive presentations (interstimulus interval) is less than 100 milliseconds and displacement of the image is less than 15 arc minutes (Braddick, *Vision Research*, 1974, *14*, 519–527). The perception of this *short-range* motion stimulus is thought to be mediated by the same neural mechanisms that process continuous motion. Longer interstimulus intervals or larger image displacements produce *long-range* apparent motion, such as that generated by a row of sequentially flashing light bulbs on a sign. The processes that mediate short- and long-range motion perception were long thought to be distinct. However, Cavanagh and Mather argue that they reflect the properties of a single motion system (*Spatial Vision*, 1989, *4*, 103–129).

Our perception of motion as smooth and continuous depends both on the spatial displacement and the interstimulus interval of repeated presentations of an image. As measured by Braddick, the maximum displacement of a random dot field (Dmax) that is seen as coherent motion is 15 arc minutes. However, later studies showed that Dmax varies with dot density, field size, retinal eccentricity, and spatial frequency. Nakayama and Tyler measured the minimum displacement (Dmin) detectable as motion to be 5 arc seconds (*Vision Research*, 1981, *21*, 427–433), although this sensitivity also depends on spatial frequency.

People have a high acuity for discriminating different speeds and directions of motion. A practiced observer can distinguish velocities differing by only 5% (i.e., the Weber fraction is 0.05) for velocities ranging from 3 to 70 degrees per second. This ability is largely independent of variations in the contrast or the temporal frequency of the stimulus (McKee, Silverman, & Nakayama, *Vision Research*, 1985, *26*, 609–629). People can distinguish directions of motion to within about 1 degree (Levinson & Sekuler, *Vision Research*, 1976, *16*, 779–781).

Considerable evidence suggests that the neural pathway that processes motion information is separate from that which processes shape and form. First, the motion pathway can be adapted and shows a *motion after-effect* that is independent of shape and texture. For example, in the waterfall illusion, if one stares at a waterfall for several minutes and then looks at the rock face next to the waterfall, the rocks appear to move upward. This after-effect occurs despite the different surface properties of the waterfall and the cliff. Anatomical and physiological studies of the visual cortex also provide evidence for a distinct motion pathway. The motion

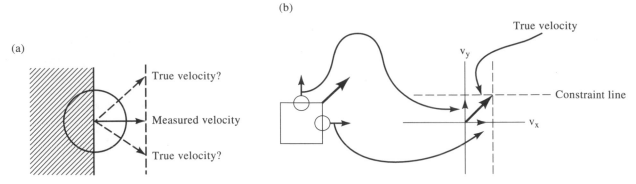

MOTION PERCEPTION. Figure 1. (a): the aperture problem; (b): Intersection of constraints solution to the aperture problem.

pathway, which is found within the dorsal stream of the primate visual cortex, originates in primary visual cortex (V1) which projects to the middle temporal area (MT), which in turn projects to higher cortical areas, such as the middle superior temporal area (MST), (Merigan & Maunsell, *Annual Review of Neuroscience*, 1993, *16*, 369–402). Selective lesions of area MT result in deficits in motion detection in monkeys without affecting sensitivity to contrast (Newsome & Pare, *Journal of Neuroscience*, 1988, *8*, 2201–2211). This suggests that these areas specifically process motion information.

Direction selective neurons found in the primate cortical visual areas V1 and MT process short-range motion stimuli. These cells respond preferentially to objects moving in a particular direction within their receptive field (the region in visual space to which the cell is sensitive). Each cell's activity decreases as the direction of motion deviates from that cell's preferred direction. The primary models of this direction selectivity are the Reichardt or Correlation model, Gradient models (Hildreth & Koch, *Annual Review of Neuroscience*, 1987, *10*, 477–533), and spatiotemporal energy models (Adelson & Bergen, *Journal of the Optical Society of America (A)*, 1985, *2*, 284–289). In the Reichardt model, the response of a cell in one position is multiplied by the delayed response of a neighboring cell. For an object moving in the preferred direction, this delayed multiplication facilitates the total response of the cell. Gradient models measure motion by examining the changes in light intensity across space and time. Spatiotemporal energy models measure the amount of energy at a given spatial and temporal frequency.

While the models described above explain many of the psychophysical results related to human motion perception, they do not explain how humans perceive a type of motion known as *non-Fourier* or *second-order* motion (Chubb & Sperling, *Journal of the Optical Society of America (A)*, 1988, *5*, 1986–2007). One display that produces non-Fourier motion consists of a field of random black-and-white squares with uniform average luminance. Within this field, a region in which the squares change polarity (from black-to-white or vice versa) moves across the display. Observers see this motion clearly, but the motion detectors described above will not register it. There is no current consensus as to how the brain processes this second-order motion.

Cells in areas MT and V1 have spatially limited receptive fields, and thus their measurement of the direction of motion is limited by the *aperture problem*, which results from the fact that only the component of motion that is perpendicular to a straight edge can be measured. This measurement is consistent with a variety of speeds and directions of motion, as diagrammed in Figure 1A. To determine a unique speed and direction of motion for an object, the visual system must integrate these motion estimates across space, either along the borders of an object or within larger regions of the image. Adelson and Movshon (*Nature*, 1982, *300*, 523–525) showed one method for determining the unique direction of motion, as shown in Figure 1B. Each velocity associated with one side of the square defines a "constraint line" in velocity space, which represents all possible velocities of the square. The true velocity lies at the intersection of these constraint lines. To examine how people integrate this motion they used plaid patterns, which consist of the sum of two luminance sinewave gratings oriented along different axes. Each grating moves perpendicular to its orientation axis. Under many conditions, people perceive this as a unified motion of the plaid rather than as two separately moving gratings. The direction of motion perceived tends to be that computed using Adelson and Movshon's intersection of constraint lines. Movshon and colleagues also showed that direction selective cells in V1 respond only to the direction of motion of the individual gratings (or components) that make up the plaid pattern. However, some neurons in the visual area MT appear to respond to the pattern motion as a whole

(Movshon et at., in Chagas, Gattas, & Gross, Eds., *Pattern recognition mechanisms, Pontificae Academiae Scientarum Scripta Varia,* 1985, 45, 117–151).

Once the two-dimensional image motion is determined, the visual system must use this information to infer properties of the external world and the motion of the observer. People perceive the three-dimensional structure of moving objects well. They can interpret the three-dimensional structure of moving silhouettes and they can perceive a three-dimensional structure from a set of randomly positioned dots that move as they would if positioned on the surface of some object, such as a transparent cylinder. Models of this process face a problem in that a single two-dimensional image motion can result from an infinite number of three-dimensional motions. To determine the structure of an object from the two-dimensional image, most models assume that the object is rigid. Ullman (*Perception,* 1984, 13, 255–274) developed a model to determine three-dimensional structure from the motion of points in the image, by gradually constructing a surface over time. At each moment, the model constructs a surface that is consistent with the current positions of the points in the image and that maintains the maximum rigidity between points over time.

Humans can also interpret some nonrigid three-dimensional motions. When viewing only the motion of a few points on a person's limbs, people can identify the action being performed by that person (Johansson, *Perception,* 1971, 6, 367–376). To create these images, light sources are attached to a person's joints and the person is filmed in the dark while walking or riding a bicycle. When observers view one frame of the movie, the lights appear as a jumble of points. When the movie is set in motion, observers immediately recognize the form as a person walking or riding a bicycle. It is not known how the visual system accomplishes this identification of *biological motion.*

The pattern of motion on the retina that is generated when an observer moves through the world provides information about the structure of the scene and about the motion of the observer. For a moving observer who is looking into the distance, the images of nearby surfaces move faster than the images of distant surfaces. For example, when one rides in a car the trees next to the road appear to move rapidly past while the mountains in the distance appear nearly stationary. The difference in the speed of image motion gives the observer an estimate of the relative distance to the surfaces in question. This cue to depth is known as *motion parallax.*

The image motion resulting from observer motion contains information about the direction of observer motion, or *egomotion.* When an observer moves in a straight line, the image motion forms a radial pattern, with each image point moving radially away from a central point. This point, the *focus of expansion,* coincides with the observer's direction of motion, or *heading.* If the observer moves on a curved path, or rotates his or her eyes to track an object in the scene, the motion pattern is more complex, but numerous models have been developed to explain how the brain might compute both the translation (straight line) and rotation parameters of observer motion (see Hildreth & Royden, in Watanabe, Ed., *High Level Visual Motion Processing,* Cambridge, MA, 1998, pp. 269–293). Observer motion parameters are probably processed in the dorsal part of MST (MSTd), because the neurons in this area respond to large-field stimuli that move in patterns, such as expansion or contraction, similar to those seen by a moving observer (Duffy & Wurtz, *Journal of Neurophysiology,* 1991, 65, 1329–1345).

Finally, the visual system must infer the three-dimensional motion of objects that are themselves moving. Psychophysical results show that people judge whether an object will hit them or pass to the left or right of them with discrimination thresholds of less than 0.1 degrees (Regan & Kaushall, *Vision Research,* 1994, 34, 163–177). McBeath and colleagues have presented a theory to explain how moving observers judge three-dimensional object motion accurately enough to run and catch a ball in sports (*Science,* 1995, 268, 569–573). The lateral region of MST (MSTl) probably processes object motion, because the cells in this area respond to small moving spots of light. These cells also likely participate in the maintenance of smooth pursuit eye movements that allow people to track moving objects (Komatsu & Wurtz, *Journal of Neurophysiology,* 1988, 60, 580–602).

Bibliography

Duffy, C. J., & Wurtz, R. H. (1995). Response of monkey MST neurons to optic flow stimuli with shifted centers of motion. *Journal of Neuroscience, 15,* 5192–5208. Response of neurons to the visual patterns seen by moving observers. It is a good source of references to other electrophysiological studies.

Hildreth, E. (1984). *The measurement of visual motion.* Cambridge, MA: MIT Press. This is an extensive look at problems underlying computation of motion and some possible solutions. It is a seminal work in modeling of visual motion perception.

Kandel, E. R., Schwartz, J. H., & Jessel, J. M. (1991). *Principles of neural science* (3rd ed.). New York: Elsevier. This contains a good introduction to central visual pathways and the processing of motion. It gives a good overview of visual processing from retina through cortex.

Lam, D. M., & Gilbert, C. D. (Eds.). (1989). *Neural mechanisms of visual perception.* Houston, TX: Gulf. This contains a selection of articles from some of the top scientists in the field of vision.

Nakayama, K. (1987). Biological image motion processing:

A review. *Vision Research, 25*, 625–660. This gives a detailed discussion of psychophysics and models of motion perception. Some of the more recent models are not discussed as this is an older article.

Royden, C. S., & Hildreth, E. C. (1996). Human heading judgments in the presence of moving objects. *Perception, 6*, 836–856. This gives a brief overview of models and psychophysics of heading in the introduction. It is a good source of other references to heading and ego-motion.

Wandell, B. (1995). *Foundations of vision.* Sunderland, MA: Sinauer. This is a good overview of motion perception. It gives a thorough discussion of the models, experimental results and physiological underpinnings.

Constance S. Royden

MOTIVATION. [*This entry comprises three articles. The first article provides a broad overview of motivation, including a definition of the term and a brief history of the study of motivation in the field of psychology. The second article describes the physiological aspects and key theories and studies of motivation. The third article discusses the various methods and instruments used in the field of psychology for assessing motivation. For discussions that relate to or affect motivation, see* Achievement Motivation; Drive; Goals; *and* Learning and Motivation.]

An Overview

Motivational psychologists ask *why* questions: Why do humans and nonhumans think and act as they do? Given the breadth of this search, variations in the answers are to be expected. Some motivational psychologists seek answers to *why* questions by turning to evolutionary biology, whereas others look to culture. Some motivational psychologists are guided by principles of genetics, others by the rules of learning. Many motivational psychologists impose higher-order thought processes to account for action, whereas others regard living organisms as robots or machines without volition. A few such psychologists answer *why* questions with very general theories that address many behaviors, while others are content with more specific explanations that have little generality. Some theories of motivation are complex with many interrelated variables, while other theories rely on only one central concept. Some motivational theorists primarily embrace experimental methodologies, although others adopt a more clinical or nonexperimental approach. Some in the field of motivation build theoretical networks, while others eschew theory in the search for practical solutions to the many motivational problems in everyday life.

Prior to presenting specific content material, a definition of motivation is in order, as well as some idea of the historical shifts in the field. There is no single agreed-upon phrase that captures the essence of this area of study, but most agree that an analysis of motivation involves the creation of principles to explain why people and animals initiate, choose, or persist in specific actions in specific circumstances. Motivational formulations thus include statements about the needs and goals of the person as well as the incentives in the environment.

A number of trends have been evident in the experimental study of motivation. Initially there was a focus on animal rather than human behavior, and on viscerogenic (e.g., hunger and thirst) rather than on psychogenic (e.g., achievement and affiliative) needs. In addition, the initial formulations in motivation were very general theories to account for a wide array of behavior, while subsequent theories became more circumscribed and limited to a particular motivational domain, such as helping, aggression, or achievement strivings. Finally, the early approaches searched for general laws of behavior that embraced all individuals, whereas more recent formulations often make different predictions for different types of people, thereby incorporating individual differences into their theories.

Why Does a Hungry Organism Search for Food?

The experimental study of motivation, which was grounded in the study of the effects of food and water deprivation, was first linked with the search for what elements drove behavior and was associated with concepts such as *instinct, drive, arousal, need,* and *energization.* Motivational psychologists were concerned with what was necessary to move a resting organism to a state of activity. Guided by the ideas postulated in the 1930s and 1940s by American psychologist Clark Hull, hungry rats were deprived of food, or curious monkeys were placed in rooms without visual stimulation. Then the effects of these need states on a variety of indexes of motivation, including speed of learning and the latency (delay time) and intensity of responses, were examined.

Two concepts were central in guiding this work, and both remain prominent. First was the belief that hedonism is the spring of all motivated action—organisms strive to increase pleasure and to reduce pain. Second was an acceptance of homeostasis, the tendency to reach a state of internal equilibrium. Hence, organisms were expected to display a cyclical response pattern, with motivated action initiated when a departure from equilibrium (for example, brought about by food deprivation) was detected, which then goaded the undertaking of instrumental activities to reduce that state. These activities would bring about equilibrium, which produced pleasure and a state of rest.

This analysis was extended to need systems other than hunger and thirst. For example, Sigmund Freud, the founder of psychoanalysis, contended that instincts involving sexual and aggressive urges propel the person to seek need-satisfying objects to reduce these instinctive needs, thereby returning the individual to a state of equilibrium.

In addition, much motivational research has documented that individuals also prefer their thoughts and social relationships to be in a balanced state, or in a state of cognitive consonance. This work was initiated in the 1960s and 1970s by psychologists Fritz Heider and Leon Festinger. For example, the beliefs that "I like Jane; I like the president; Jane does not like the president" produce an imbalanced state, which gives rise to motivational forces to create balance. Liking Jane or the president less, or persuading Jane of the president's good points could bring about balance. In a similar manner, the understanding that "I smoke and smoking causes cancer" also produces motivational pressure to reduce this dissonance. Consonance could by accomplished by giving up smoking or by disbelieving the evidence that smoking and cancer are linked.

Why Might a Hungry Organism Hunt at Night Rather Than During the Day?

It is now generally accepted that living entities are always active. Motivational psychologists thus are more likely to ask not why behavior is aroused, but rather what determines the direction of activity or of choice. Consider, for example, why an organism might choose to hunt for food during the night rather than when it is light. According to evolutionary biology, behavior is a product of a long evolutionary history and current behaviors are determined by this past history. For example, it might be speculated that at one point in history there were two kinds of mice, those with genetic tendencies to prefer the darkness and others who preferred the light. However, over time, those going out during the day were likely to be killed, whereas those hunting at night tended to live and to reproduce. Thus, only those preferring the night now remain, and this genetic disposition is the dominant determinant of their hunting behavior. Sociobiologists have extended this evolutionary approach to account for the mating and reproductive choices of humans.

A quite different explanation of choice behavior has been offered by expectancy-value theorists such as John Atkinson and Julian Rotter, who greatly influenced motivational psychology between 1955 and 1980. Their conceptual analysis of choice behavior was derived from the formulations of decision theorists and economists. They argue that motivation and choice are determined by the values (incentives) of the goals that are available and by one's perceptions of the probabilities of attaining these goals. That is, choice is guided by what one will get and by the likelihood of getting it. Hence, rather than concentrating on what "energy" is present to activate an organism, expectancy-value theorists believe that the major task of motivational psychology is to discover the determinants of the expectancy of goal attainment and goal value. Again history is important, but in this case it is not the history of the species, but rather the history of a specific organism; for example, the number of times it has hunted successfully during the day as compared to the night, or the goals perceived as available at night as opposed to during the day. These concepts have been used to predict a variety of phenomena, from marriage partners to career choice. Expectancy-value theorists are guided by the metaphor of the organism as a logical decision maker.

Human Motivation

Motivational psychologists hope that the laws of behavior they have posited will account for both human and subhuman behavior. There are, however, a number of motivational phenomena that appear to be uniquely associated with humans, such as the desire to achieve success, the pursuit of life goals, and the wish to be judged as morally good. In addition, the focus on individual differences in needs is also primarily associated with the study of humans. At this time in motivational psychology, investigations using nonhuman populations are primarily conducted by ethologists, with their interest in instinctual behavior, and among other scientific groups paying primary attention to brain and hormonal effects that are invasively studied in the laboratory.

Why Do Individuals Strive to Achieve and What Determines Success?

As already indicated, between 1930 and 1960 the goal of motivational psychologists was indeed grandiose—to develop general theories of behavior that transcend situations and individuals. Over time, this elusive holy grail has been abandoned for the most part. In its place there have emerged concepts, or distinctions, hypothesized to predict a limited set of behaviors. These especially find expression in the domain of achievement motivation, which remains the most active of the content areas within the field of human motivation. It is prominent in part because of its relevance to school-related problems.

Among the most important current constructs in the study of achievement motivation are self-efficacy, intrinsic (versus extrinsic) motivation, mastery and learning (as opposed to ego and performance) goals, causal beliefs, and achievement needs. Self-efficacy is an ability-related construct referring to beliefs about one's ability to perform a task. The stronger the belief in personal ability, the more intense and persistent motivated behavior is expected to be. Intrinsic versus extrinsic motivation relates to the source of the desire to perform a task. It has been contended that motivation is maximized when there is intrinsic motivation to succeed. Mastery (learning) versus ego (performance) goals refer to a distinction regarding what end an individual is pursuing when undertaking a task. Is the individual striving to master that task and improve personal performance, or to do better than others, which emphasizes social comparison and relative ability? This distinction also has been related to beliefs that ability is malleable versus fixed. It has been argued that mastery rather than ego-related goals enhance achievement motivation. Finally, causal beliefs pertain to the perceived reasons that one has succeeded or failed at a task. Ascribing success to oneself increases pride in accomplishment, whereas ascribing one's failure to lack of ability gives rise to shame and withdrawal.

The themes described above are the most dominant in the study of achievement motivation. However, many questions remain about the validity of the conclusions. We are sure that a hungry mouse will initiate attempts to find food and will engage in these activities during the night. But we do not know whether self-efficacy, intrinsic motivation, mastery goals, and/or certain attributions will engage our schoolchildren to undertake and persist at school-related achievement tasks.

Individual Differences

A variety of individual differences in motivation have been examined. The propensities to affiliate, aggress, and attain power have generated much research. However, three other individual-difference variables have been especially prominent in the study of motivation: need for achievement, anxiety, and locus of control. The need for achievement was the first trait to be systematically examined by motivational researchers, starting in the 1940s with the work of David McClelland and his colleagues. It has been contended that individuals high on this trait will undertake achievement activities and particularly prefer tasks of intermediate difficulty. Achievement-related dispositions have been inferred from responses to the Thematic Apperception Test (TAT), a projective assessment instrument in which people are shown pictures and asked to make up stories about them. However, self-report questionnaires also have been used to measure this desire.

Unlike the need for achievement, anxiety is typically conceived as a motivational inhibitor. Anxiety has been construed both as a situation-specific state as well as a general trait producing task-irrelevant thoughts, mental withdrawal, and self-deprecatory ruminations that impede goal-directed performance.

Finally, locus of control is most associated with a classification of individuals proposed by Julian Rotter during the 1960s that describes individuals as attributing the causes of events to factors internal or external to themselves. Believing that one has personal control over events has been related to positive adaptation in stressful circumstances.

Personal Goals Strivings

Striving for a goal requires a continuous inner representation of the goal pursuit. This process, sometimes labeled a *current concern*, directs the individual's perceptions, emotional reactions, thoughts, dreams, and behaviors toward the stimuli associated with the desired goal. Furthermore, the extent and nature of commitments to long-term goals supply meaning to life. The kinds of goals individuals typically strive for are important factors in well-being and health.

Morality and Motivation

Various metaphors have guided thinking in motivational psychology, such as considering the person a machine or a decision maker. Another metaphor conceives of persons as judges who gather evidence in a scientific manner, with the spring of motivated action being not hedonism but rather understanding and mastery. They then evaluate others as good or bad and engage in motivated actions guided by these evaluations. For example, if one in need is perceived as personally responsible for this plight (for example, lacks money because of laziness; is obese because of overeating) then others judge the person unfavorably, tend to be angry, and in turn, withhold help and administer some form of punishment. The judged individuals, in turn, may provide excuses, justifications, or confessions in order to alter their evaluation and their "sentence." Thus, the study of motivation embraces not only self-perception, but also how others are viewed and how these others manage impressions.

In sum, the field of motivation comprises many phenomena, and for this reason there is no one unifying theory or theme. However, there are many pockets of wisdom in diverse areas.

Bibliography

Atkinson, J. W. (1964). *An introduction to motivation.* Princeton, NJ: Van Nostrand.

Dawkins, R. (1976). *The selfish gene.* London: Oxford University Press.

Festinger, L. (1957). *The theory of cognitive dissonance.* Stanford, CA: Stanford University Press.

Heckhausen, H. (1991). *Motivation and action.* New York: Springer.

Heider, F. (1958). *The psychology of interpersonal relations.* New York: Wiley.

Hull, C. L. (1942). *Principles of behavior.* New York: Appleton-Century-Crofts.

Klinger, E. (1998). The search for meaning in evolutionary

perspective and its clinical implications. In P. T. P. Wong & P. S. Fry (Eds.), *The human quest for meaning: Theory, research and application* (pp. 27–50). Mahwah, NJ: Erlbaum.

Lewin, K. (1938). *The conceptual representation and measurement of psychological forces.* Durham, NC: Duke University Press.

Rotter, J. B. (1954). *Social learning and clinical psychology.* Englewood Cliffs, NJ: Prentice Hall.

Weiner, B. (1992). *Human motivation: Metaphors, theories, and research.* Newbury Park, CA: Sage.

Weiner, B. (1995). *Judgments of responsibility: A foundation for a theory of social conduct.* New York: Guilford Press.

Bernard Weiner

Physiological Aspects

Water and food intake often are discussed together, as if they had so many similarities that it was useful to consider them together rather than separately. However, the central controls of water and food intake actually have less in common than is suggested by the superficial resemblance of thirst and hunger, and of the ingestive acts resulting from these strong motivations.

In considering the biological basis of water and food intake, the following general approach has long been taken. Proceeding from the assumption that a critical amount of each nutrient is needed, it was further assumed (and sometimes shown) that this amount is regulated by physiological processes. Moreover, it was assumed that a deficiency of either nutrient creates a specific excitatory stimulus to ingest the needed nutrient and thereby correct its deficiency, and that removal of the deficiency also removes the excitatory stimulus for the motivation to consume it. These points may be summarized in Figure 1.

This simple homeostatic arrangement for the negative feedback control of ingestive behavior is, in fact, too simple; thirst and the control of water intake is much more complex than the schema suggests, whereas hunger and the control of food intake are not adequately represented by the schema.

Thirst

Water deprivation elicits the sensation of thirst when certain brain cells become dehydrated merely 1 to 2% by the osmotic loss of water. Those cells are located in the basal forebrain, just rostral to the third cerebral ventricle. They exist outside the blood-brain barrier and consequently they respond readily to changes in the particulate concentration, or osmolality, of plasma (pOsm). They are not uniquely sensitive to dehydration, unlike the retinal cells that detect photons, but they have unique synaptic connections to other brain neurons that stimulate thirst. When the osmoreceptor cells are impaired, either by experimental lesions or by brain

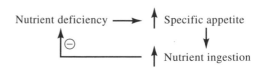

MOTIVATION. Figure 1. Schematic representation of possible mechanism by which ingestive behavior is controlled. In this single-loop negative feedback system, ingestive behavior corrects the nutrient deficiency responsible for the specific appetite that activates and guides the behavior. (–) denotes inhibition.

disease, animals become blind to increases in pOsm and do not experience a normal sense of thirst.

The general schema in Figure 1, with modifications, can be used to summarize this arrangement (see Figure 2).

However, a major problem with this arrangement is that ingested water is not instantly absorbed into the circulation and therefore cannot provide rapid rehydration and negative feedback in the control of water intake. This delay in water absorption allows for the continued consumption of large volumes of water in excess of amounts needed for rehydration. However, ample evidence indicates that such overconsumption of water by dehydrated animals does not occur in many species, which replace water deficits by drinking large volumes of water very rapidly. Thus, some early signal must inhibit thirst. Actually, two signals have been identified: one associated with swallowing and the other associated with osmotic dilution either of intestinal fluid or of blood entering the liver. In support of this conclusion are findings that (1) dehydrated dogs reduce thirst rapidly well before changes in systemic pOsm can be observed; (2) dehydrated rats overdrink water when a pyloric cuff prevents gastric emptying; and (3) dehydrated rats and dogs both overdrink water when visceral sensors have been denervated (and therefore cannot be used to detect early dilutional consequences of water ingestion). Thus, considerations of osmoregulatory

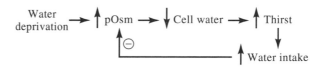

MOTIVATION. Figure 2. Traditional schematic representation of possible mechanism by which water intake is controlled during dehydration. Thirst is stimulated when increased plasma osmolality (pOsm) causes an osmotic loss of water from cerebral osmoreceptor cells, and the induced water intake lowers pOsm to normal levels. (–) denotes inhibition.

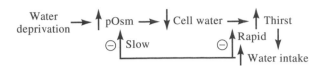

MOTIVATION. Figure 3. Contemporary schematic representation of possible mechanism by which water intake is controlled during dehydration. Thirst is stimulated when increased pOsm causes an osmotic loss of water from cerebral osmoreceptor cells, and the induced water intake rapidly reduces thirst; subsequently, the ingested water is absorbed and lowers pOsm to normal levels. (–) denotes inhibition.

thirst must be further modified in order to include the rapid negative feedback necessary for drinking to occur in amounts appropriate to need.

But even with these modifications our account of thirst is not complete; there are multiple signals of thirst, not just the one resulting from osmoregulatory needs. Animals deprived of drinking water lose water from plasma in addition to water from cells, and the loss of plasma volume (hypovolemia) is itself a stimulus of thirst. Indeed, thirst can be elicited even when no increase in pOsm occurs, as following hemorrhage. Animals detect deficits in blood volume by stretch receptors embedded in the distensible walls of the inferior vena cava (which delivers much of the venous return to the heart) and of the right atrium. The stretch of the vessels is proportional to the volume contained therein, so when blood volumes are low the sensory neurons send an afferent signal of hypovolemia to the caudal brain stem, which then relays that message to the forebrain for stimulation of thirst.

One problem with this arrangement, however, is that ingested water, when absorbed, does not repair the plasma volume deficits that stimulated thirst. Instead, approximately two thirds of the water moves by osmosis into cells. That outcome is desirable when thirst is associated with increased pOsm and cellular dehydration but not when plasma volume is diminished and pOsm is not elevated; then, water consumption only causes osmotic dilution without much correction of hypovolemia. Therefore, it should not be surprising that merely 3 to 5% osmotic dilution provides a potent stimulus for inhibiting thirst even in the presence of marked hypovolemia. This inhibition of hypovolemic thirst by osmotic dilution (Figure 4), may be contrasted with the satiation of osmoregulatory thirst that occurs when appropriate amounts of water are consumed.

The inhibition of water intake despite hypovolemia usefully prevents osmotic dilution from becoming severe, but it does not repair the plasma volume deficits that stimulated thirst in the first place. To restore those volumes, animals must ingest plasma or an equivalently dilute NaCl solution. Having first drunk water due to thirst, they must then consume salt. In fact, rats have been shown to drink water and concentrated NaCl solution in appropriate amounts to create the isotonic NaCl mixture that is ideal for plasma volume restoration. Space does not allow description of the central mechanisms for this control of thirst and salt appetite during hypovolemia, although much of this information is now available.

It is important to note that thirst in response to plasma volume deficits is not eliminated after destruction of the sites in the caudal brain stem that receive neuronal projections from the cardiovascular stretch receptors that detect hypovolemia. This finding indicates that another stimulus of thirst exists during hypovolemia. This signal likely is provided by angiotensin, a peptide hormone formed in the blood after secretion of the enzyme renin from the kidneys. Angiotensin also stimulates salt appetite as well as the hormones that enable the retention of water and sodium in urine, and it is a very potent vasoconstrictor agent as well (thus helping to support blood pressure during hypovolemia). By having so many functionally related actions, angiotensin insures that diverse behavioral and physiological responses to hypovolemia occur simultaneously.

Circulating angiotensin acts in the brain at the subfornical organ, which is located in the dorsal portion of the third cerebral, ventricle and lacks a blood–brain barrier. Surgical destruction of this brain structure eliminates thirst and salt appetite stimulated by angiotensin. However, it does not abolish these dual effects of hypovolemia, which indicates that redundant mechanisms can be used to detect the loss of plasma volume and activate appropriate behavioral responses. Such redundancy should not be surprising given the great significance of adequate blood volume to life.

Hunger

Because the cells of animals cannot long survive depletions of calories, hunger cannot result from nutrient

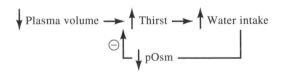

MOTIVATION. Figure 4. Schematic representation of possible mechanism by which water intake is controlled during hypovolomia. Thirst is stimulated by neural input to the brain from cardiac baroreceptors and by humoral input to the brain via the blood-borne hormone angiotensin. The induced water intake lowers pOsm below normal levels, which inhibits thirst and further drinking despite continued plasma volume deficits. (–) denotes inhibition.

shortages. Thus, the depletion-repletion model cannot provide a suitable perspective from which to consider the control of food intake. Instead, the sensation of hunger apparently does not need to be stimulated but is always present, and animals are constantly stimulated to eat unless they have just eaten, in which case the inhibitory effects of satiety generated from the previous meal are still operative. This arrangement presumably evolved because, in the wild, the appearance of food is unpredictable, and animals can take advantage of opportunities to eat whenever they occur. In support of this perspective are laboratory findings that (1) experimenters cannot precipitate eating in satiated rats but can do many things to stop eating by hungry rats; (2) the size of spontaneous meals eaten by laboratory rats are unpredictable, but however much the animals eat in a given meal, meal sizes predict how long they wait until they eat again; and (3) food deprivation does not cause a shortage of caloric nutrients in the circulation (in contrast to evidence of water deficiency during water deprivation). The point here is that food intake appears to be initiated by the gradual disappearance of inhibitory satiety stimuli that were generated by the previous meal, not by the gradual increase in an excitatory hunger stimulus.

Several signals appear to stimulate satiety after a meal. One results from gastric distension, detected by stretch receptors on the walls of the stomach; the bigger the distension, the bigger the inhibition of eating. This afferent signal projects to the caudal brain stem via the gastric branch of the vagus nerve. As expected, animals eat unusually large meals when the gastric vagus is cut or its projection sites in the brain are destroyed. Experiments in rats have revealed that an intestinal hormone secreted during the meal, cholecystokinin, potentiates the gastric vagal signal and produces an exaggerated sensation of satiety related to gastric distension. This signal relates to the bulk of gastric contents, not its nutrient contents, because there are no known detectors of calories in the stomach.

The ingestion of calories, detected in the liver and possibly in the intestines, provides a second satiety signal that is sent to the brain stem by another branch of the vagus nerve. This stimulus appears to develop only in the presence of insulin, a pancreatic hormone secreted when food is consumed. Thus, satiety normally is not lost as the stomach empties, because the gastric signal related to distension is replaced by the postgastric signal related to caloric delivery (except in animals with insulin-deficient diabetes mellitus).

Two other meal-related signals also are known to be potent inhibitors of food intake. One is thirst, resulting, for example, from the presence of relatively large amounts of salt in the food. The other is nausea, as might result from the inadvertent intake of toxins in

MOTIVATION. Figure 5. Schematic representation of possible mechanism by which food intake is controlled. Ingested food provides two signals of inhibition, one reflecting the bulk of the consumed meal and associated with gastric distension, and the other reflecting the chemical content of the meal and associated with neural signals from the intestines, hepatic portal vein, and liver. (–) denotes inhibition.

food. However, these two variables are not relevant to most meals. Excluding them from consideration, Figure 5 summarizes what is known about the control of meals.

Note that an influence of body weight on food intake is not included in this schema. Nonetheless, food intake and body weight have been shown to be closely related. Thus, following a period of food deprivation, food intake is increased until the lost body weight is restored. Similarly, following a period in which food had been consumed in excess, food intake is diminished until the gained body weight is lost.

Changes in body weight largely reflect changes in the storage of calories in adipose tissue. Those stores are diminished during food deprivation, to provide calories needed for cellular function, and they are restored when food intake resumes. Thus, as ingested calories are siphoned off to the adipose tissue, their effects on the liver are diminished, thereby reducing the duration of this postgastric satiety signal. In addition, food empties the stomach more rapidly, thereby reducing the duration of gastric satiety. The opposite effects occur when calorie stores in adipose tissue have been augmented during a period of excessive food intake; both gastric and postgastric satiety signals are prolonged because the rate at which calories are stored in the swollen adipocytes is decreased.

Aside from this indirect influence of body weight on food intake, in recent years a direct inhibitory signal to the brain from adipose tissue has been discovered. This satiety stimulus is a blood-borne protein, leptin, that is secreted from adipose tissue in proportion to adipocyte size; the fatter the animal, the more leptin is secreted, and the less inclination the animal has to eat. Leptin receptors have been found in the hypothalamus, and when they are stimulated food intake is reduced.

The discovery of leptin illuminates genetic obesity in two strains of mice. One strain were born with leptin receptors in their brains but without the capacity to synthesize leptin; the other strain were born without leptin receptors in their brains but with the capacity to synthesize leptin. As might be expected, an intravenous infusion of leptin reduces food intake in the first strain but not in the second.

Summary

Despite the superficial similarity of water and food intakes, the mechanisms by which they are controlled differ greatly from one another. This difference should not be surprising because other fundamental features of water and caloric homeostasis also differ greatly. For example, water consumed in excess is excreted readily in urine, whereas food consumed in excess is stored in liver and adipose tissue. Water deprivation produces cell dehydration and hypovolemia, whereas food deprivation does not compromise cellular metabolism.

Water intake is controlled according to a modified depletion-repletion scheme whereby bodily water loss generates signals that stimulate thirst and water consumption, which repairs dehydration. Two neural signals of thirst have been identified, one associated with increased plasma osmolality and cellular dehydration in brain osmoreceptor cells, and one associated with decreased plasma volume as detected in cardiovascular receptors. A third, humoral signal of thirst, provided by the peptide hormone angiotensin, also arises from the periphery during hypovolemia and acts in the brain. Water intake satiates osmoregulatory thirst but inhibits thirst due to hypovolemia or angiotensin, and salt consumption (also stimulated by hypovolemia and angiotensin) is required to repair plasma volume deficits and thereby satiate thirst. Thus, brain mechanisms respond to excitatory and inhibitory signals, neural and blood borne, that integrate thirst and salt appetite.

In contrast, food intake is not controlled according to a depletion-repletion scheme whereby hunger is generated by caloric deficiencies. In fact, the recruitment of stored calories prevents such deficiencies, and there are no apparent excitatory signals for hunger. Instead, multiple signals for inhibiting food intake have been identified. Some of these satiety signals are nonspecific and disrupt all ingestive behavior (e.g., gastric distension, nausea), whereas others are specific to food ingestion (e.g., postgastric delivery of calories, leptin) or work by stimulating a competing drive (e.g., dehydration stimulates thirst). Thus, brain mechanisms that control food intake respond to inhibitory signals, both neural and blood borne, some of which are related to ingested and stored calories and some that are not.

Bibliography

Fitzsimons, J. T. (1998). Angiotensin, thrist, and sodium appetite. *Physiological Reviews, 78,* 583–686.

Stricker, E. M. (Ed.). (1990). *Handbook of behavioral neurobiology: Vol. 10: Food and fluid intake.* New York: Plenum Press.

Stricker, E. M., & Verbalis, J. G. (1999). Fluid intake and homeostasis. In M. J. Zigmond, F. E. Bloom, S. C. Landis, J. L. Roberts, & L. R. Squire (Eds.), *Fundamental neuroscience* (pp. 1091–1109). San Diego: Academic Press.

Woods, S. C., & Stricker, E. M. (1999). Central control of food intake. In M. J. Zigmond, F. E. Bloom, S. C., Landis, J. L. Roberts, & L. R. Squire (Eds.), *Fundamental neuroscience.* (pp. 1111–1126). San Diego: Academic Press.

Edward M. Stricker

Assessment

Psychologists have long pondered the motivation of human behavior—the *why* of human life. Motivation deals with the direction, persistence, and energization of behavior. Approaches to studying motivation have varied throughout history, from Freudian views of the dynamic unconscious to more contemporary approaches to mastery and self-regulation. These approaches share a concern for the origins of action that can be found in the actor, assuming that human behavior is an expression of some underlying intent.

Generally, motivation has been portrayed as the source of coherence in personality, as the force that brings meaning to apparent anomalies in behavior. Interest in the study of motivation has been a defining feature of personality psychology. Personality and social psychology have long been concerned with the influence of motivation on human thought, emotion, and behavior. A long-standing issue in the personological study of motivation is that of measurement. How can we reliably tell what a person's motives are? The conflict that arises in answering this question is best illustrated in the contradictory views of Henry Murray (1938) and Gordon Allport (1950). Murray held that motives were largely unconscious—that a person had no more insight into his or her motives than an observer. This being the case, motives could only be measured indirectly, through fantasy-based measures. Allport (1950) asserted that if one wanted to know what an individual was trying to do, one should simply ask him or her.

This debate has continued through the years and has given rise to a conception of motivational measures as drawing on two separate underlying systems: implicit motives and explicit motives. The term *implicit motives* applies to the types of needs Murray (1938) referred to. These needs are thought to be primitive, based on universal incentives and childhood experiences (e.g., McClelland, 1985). Implicit motives are measured using imaginative stories. In contrast, explicit motives are largely conscious, cognitively elaborate, and culturally determined (McClelland, Koestner, & Weinberger, 1992) and measured directly via self-report measures such as questionnaires.

Projective Measures

David McClelland, who was a student of Murray's at Harvard University, defined implicit motives as enduring concerns for a particular class of goals, based on a natural incentive, that organize, drive, and select behavior (McClelland, 1985). This definition implies that motives direct attention, cause perseverance in the face of difficulty, and allow the successful choice of strategies in motive relevant tasks. Thus, someone who is high in need for power (the recurrent concern for having impact on one's social environment), would be likely to notice power-relevant information (e.g., a poster for local elections), to persist at a power-relevant task (e.g., continually strive to hold public office), and to succeed, at power-relevant tasks (e.g., to actually be elected to public office more often) than those who are not high in the need for power. Research on implicit motives has focused primarily on three motives: the need for achievement (striving toward excellence), the need for affiliation (striving to make and keep friends), and the need for power.

The original measurement strategy for measuring implicit motives employed projective techniques, such as Morgan and Murray's (1935) Thematic Apperception Test (TAT). These techniques rely on the assumption that, when asked to tell a story about an ambiguous stimulus (such as a picture or ink blot), people will project into their story meaningful psychological information about themselves, such as their needs, unconscious wishes, desires, and conflicts. Thus, the researcher asks an individual to tell an imaginative story about a picture and then analyzes the content of the story for motivational themes. Early in their history, these techniques were attacked for their undeniable subjectivity. After all, interpreting an imaginative story might be just as projective an experience as telling an imaginative story. However, the establishment of standardized scoring systems for implicit motives has greatly reduced the subjectivity of this scoring (Smith, 1992).

The development of the thematic scoring systems for each implicit motive involved a similar procedure. The imaginative stories of individuals who were assumed *a priori* to be high in a motive ("the criterion group") were compared to stories told by individuals who were not assumed to be particularly high in that motive. For instance, a group of individuals who had just been through a socially humiliating experience were expected to have their need for affiliation aroused. Stories by these individuals included images of regaining social approval, positive emotion in interpersonal contexts, or negative emotion in response to being alone. Thus, these images were included in the need-for-affiliation scoring system (Shipley & Veroff, 1952). Similar procedures have led to scoring systems for achievement, power, and intimacy.

In subsequent research, a great deal has been learned about the influence of implicit motives on thought and behavior. For instance, individuals high in a need for achievement tend to set high aspirations, take moderate risks, and enjoy entrepreneurial success (McClelland, 1985). Power-oriented individuals are concerned with attaining status and prestige, choose as friends persons low in power motivation, and are highly promiscuous in heterosexual relationships (McClelland, 1985). People high in the need for affiliation are more people focused. They spend more time visiting friends, writing letters, and making phone calls than do less affiliative individuals.

Questionnaire Measures

Typically, researchers interested in self-reports of motivation have relied on questionnaires to measure these motives. Questionnaire measures tend to have superior reliabilities when compared with projective measures, and these measures are much less time-consuming as well. In addition, these measures tend to be much less controversial than the projective measures. Note however, that according to the implicit explicit motive distinction, questionnaire measures of motivation tap explicit motivation, not the types of unconscious needs described by Murray and McClelland. Importantly, questionnaire and projective measures of motivation tend to be unrelated to each other and have different correlates. In other words, a person may score low on need for achievement in a fantasy-based measure such as the TAT but may report a high degree of achievement orientation when asked directly. In general, research has shown that questionnaire measures tend to predict self-conscious choices, particularly when the motive-relevance of a task has been made clear. On the other hand, projective measures tend to predict spontaneous behaviors that a person performs without being reminded of the motive-relevance of the task (McClelland, et al., 1992). Evidently, self-report measures and thematic measures tap different underlying systems, one cognitive and conscious and the other motivational and unconscious.

Alternative Sources of Motivational Information

Returning to McClelland's (1985) definition of motivation, one can see that although imaginative stories present one way to capture these unconscious motives, there might be other ways as well. If motives exert the kind of pervasive impact on thought and behavior that McClelland's definition implies, then motive-relevant information might be expected to be revealed in a variety of outlets, not simply imaginative stories or even questionnaires. Indeed, researchers have used a variety of materials as motive measures, including essays, speeches, transcribed TV shows, personal documents (such as letters), and interviews. For instance, the match between the motivational imagery in a presidential candidate's announcement speech and the national climate at the time has been shown to predict margin of victory (Winter, 1987). In addition, power motivation expressed in inaugural addresses has been shown to relate to "presidential greatness," to making a large number of important decisions, and to leading the country into war (Winter, 1987).

The range of materials that have been used as measures of motivation continues to broaden. During the 1980s there was a dramatic shift in personality psychology toward the study of human motivation within the context of everyday life and experience. Rather than focusing on broad unconscious motives, researchers became interested in studying the conscious goals that a person might work on in his or her daily life. An important assumption behind the use of measuring motivation through goals is that each person may set and strive for goals in ways that are uniquely individualized—hence the term *personal goals*. These personalized goal approaches provided a new way to look at motivation. For instance, these approaches assumed that the goals that drive behavior are available to awareness. In addition, these approaches acknowledged that in terms of daily life, motivational tendencies are constrained to a particular context. Examples of personalized goal units include current concerns (nonconscious brain processes that persist during every goal pursuit); personal projects (behavior sequences toward a personal goal); life tasks (societally prescribed developmental problems such as starting a family); and personal strivings (typical or characteristic goal themes). Examples of personalized daily goals include "to be a good person," "getting closer to God," "graduating from college," "developing an identity," "to do my best at everything I try to do," "spending more time with my family," and "being a good friend to others."

In contrast to the global implicit motives described earlier, these constructs represent contextualized and circumscribed units to account for human motivation. Current concerns and personal projects are constructs with regard to specific goals, including narrow, short-term goals. In their more general, longer-term forms, they and personal strivings and life tasks have been termed *middle-level* units of analysis for cognitive personality psychology. They are termed *middle level* in that they are typically at a middle level of abstraction in a structural hierarchy, and can be concretized with reference to specific activities and situations and generalized with reference to higher order themes and meanings in life. They represent affectively charged goals and

themes that are central to the person's life while emerging from and determining the nature of the person's transactions with their social worlds. Cantor and Zirkel (1990) have eloquently argued that these middle-level units are cognitive in that they are organized around individuals' beliefs about themselves and their relationships; their autobiographies and identities, and their projects, tasks, and concerns that give meaning to life. They are infused with motivational content, and function as goals to energize and organize purposive behavior.

Assessing Personal Goals

Goals are "personal" in the sense that they are unique to each person. One person's goals are usually qualitatively quite different from those of another. This individualized quality allows researchers to capture the unique flavor of each person's intentions. At the same time, because ratings can be made of these goals on common dimensions, such as how important or difficult the goals are, research can be done at a group level as well. This approach is known as the mixed idiographic-nomothetic assessment method (Klinger, 1995), which has the advantage of tailoring the assessment to each person while still permitting quantitative comparisons between persons. In other words, while each participant produces a unique list of personal goal concerns, each person rates his or her own goals on the same rating scales that others use.

The assessment of personal goals typically occurs in a sequence of three phases. It begins with having respondents freely generate a list of their concerns, tasks, projects, or strivings. In this initial step, the definition of the construct is given, usually with examples, and participants write down as many goals as they can within a specified time period. Following elicitation of the personal goals, respondents are asked to rate each goal on several dimensions. The dimensions used in any one study depend on the specific purposes of the research. Theoretically derived dimensions from the motivational literature include value, expectancy for success, instrumentality, and commitment. These dimensions provide comparable indices that are independent of the content of the goal lists, which by definition are noncomparable between persons. In the third step, a goals matrix is completed in which ratings are made of the extent to which each goal either facilitates or interferes with the pursuit of each of the other goals.

Research on personalized goals has demonstrated how aspects of daily goals impact on daily experience. For instance, working on important but difficult and unrewarding goals is associated with the experience of negative mood (Zirkel & Cantor, 1990). Unpleasant emotional states have been related to ambivalence about one's strivings, as well as conflict between strivings. Pleasant emotional states have been related to the goal characteristics of value, importance, and past fulfillment (Emmons, 1996). Much research on personal goals has tended to focus on the experiential consequences of simply having goals, rather than addressing the moment-to-moment regulation of behavior in the pursuit of the goal. Other research has documented extensive effects on moment-to-moment attention, recall, and thought and dream content (e.g., Klinger, 1995) or processes of intention and self-regulation (Gollwitzer, 1999; Kuhl & Fuhrmann, 1998; Kuhl & Beckmann, 1994).

A few studies have sought to combine middle-level goal units with more classical approaches to motivation. Emmons and McAdams (1991) found that personal goals, coded for motive content, did relate to the corresponding underlying motive. In that study, participants generated 15 strivings in response to the stem "I typically try to——." These strivings were coded for relevance to achievement, affiliation, and power, using a scoring scheme adapted from the scoring procedures used for TAT stories. An individual who was high in the need for power might have the personal goals "to persuade others to my point of view," or "to always get my way." In a similar type of study, King (1995) found that autobiographical memories, wishes, daily goals, and TAT-scored motives were largely unrelated to each other. In that study, the method used to measure a motive was the strongest link between the various motive measures.

In a study of daily events and mood by Emmons (1991), participants completed daily goal lists and also took part in a daily mood study in which participants completed mood forms twice every day for 21 days. On each form they noted the most important events of the day and rated their current mood. Emmons (1991) coded the daily goals for relevance to achievement, power, and affiliation. In addition, the events that were listed each day were categorized for their achievement or interpersonal content. Results showed that having a large number of power-related daily goals was related to poorer subjective well-being. In addition, individuals whose goals were more achievement related tended to respond more strongly to achievement events. In addition, those whose goals were more affiliative tended to be more responsive to interpersonal events. That is, their daily mood was more dependent on the ups and downs of their relationships.

Self-Defining Memories

McAdams (1995) proposed three distinct levels or domains of personality description, with each level containing different constructs and a different focus and accessed through different assessment operations. Level I is comprised of broad, decontextualized trait units,

such as the implicit motives of power, achievement, and affiliation discussed earlier. Level II contains developmental and explicit motivational constructs (goals, plans, strategies) that are contextualized in time, place, and/or role. Constructs at this level are characterized by intentionality and goal-directedness, in comparison to the stylistic and habitual tendencies at Level I. Level III is identity as a life narrative—the internalized and evolving story that lends coherence, unity, and purpose to one's life. We would like to conclude this review by including a motivationally based unit to assess this third level of the person, the self-defining memory.

Self-defining memories (Singer & Salovey, 1993) are a subset of autobiographical memories that are affectively intense, vividly recalled, and repetitively experienced. Self-defining memories differ in levels of generality. Some are single-event memory narratives ("a swimming incident when I was 6 years old at summer camp") and some are summary memory narratives ("senior year of high school"). These serve different affective and motivational functions. Memories combine with personal goals and affect to form a narrative, which provides the individual with continuity and meaning in life. The affective intensity and quality of a personal memory is determined in part by the relevance of that memory to the person's ongoing goal concerns. Personal memories serve an integrating function—they serve to connect the past with the present and future, thus providing narrative coherence. Memories are also motivating—memories of successful goal attainment or conversely of failed efforts to secure a desired outcome, can influence an individual's decision as to what really matters in life and is worth investing in. Singer and Salovey demonstrate that the content of self-defining memories provides valuable insights into motivational functioning of a person.

The interweaving of motivation, cognition, and emotion in naturalistic, self-defined memories has a parallel in controlled laboratory research on emotion as a determiner of motivational effects on cognitive processing (Klinger, 1995). Both point to the pervasive interconnectedness of psychological systems, and the inherent challenges involved in assessing the functioning of one system independently of the others.

Bibliography

Allport, G. (1950). *The nature of personality: Selected papers.* Cambridge, MA: Addison-Wesley. A compilation of some of the most influential papers written by the father of American personality psychology. Includes Allport's approach to motivation.

Cantor, N., & Zirkel, S. (1990). Personality, cognition, and behavior. In L. Pervin (Ed.), *Handbook of personality: Theory and research* (pp. 135–164). New York: Guilford

Press. Reviews research on "middle level" units in personality—conscious goals and tasks. The authors argue for the importance of these middle units as opposed to more broad, high level motives.

Emmons, R. A. (1991). Personal strivings, daily life events, and psychological and physical well-being. *Journal of Personality, 59*, 453–472.

Emmons, R. A. (1997). Motives and goals. In R. Hogan, J. A. Johnson, & S. R. Briggs (Eds.), *Handbook of personality psychology* (pp. 485–512). San Diego, CA: Academic Press. Reviews research with regard to TAT-measured motives, goal approaches to motivation and seeks to integrate these.

Emmons, R. A. (1999). *The psychology of ultimate concerns: Motivation and spirituality in personality.* New York: Guilford Press. Comprehensive review of the "personal striving" concept—an approach to studying goals and personality through what a person is "characteristically trying to do." Includes assessment materials.

Emmons, R. A., & McAdams, D. P. (1991). Personal strivings and motive dispositions: Exploring the links. *Personality and Social Psychology Bulletin, 17*, 648–654. An empirical comparison of TAT-measured motives and motives measured via daily goals.

Gollwitzer, P. M. (1999). Implementation intention: Strong effects of simple plans. *American Psychologist, 54*, 493–503.

Heckhausen, H. (1991). *Motivation and action.* New York: Springer.

King, L. A. (1995). Wishes, motives, goals, and personal memories: Relations and correlates of measures of human motivation. *Journal of Personality, 63*, 985–1007. Empirical comparison of the motive content of wishes, motives, daily goals, and personal memories.

Klinger, E. (1995). Effects of motivation and emotion on thought flow and cognition: Assessment and findings. In P. E. Shrout & S. T. Fiske (Eds.), *Personality research, methods and theory: A festschrift honoring Donald W. Fiske* (pp. 257–270). Hillsdale, NJ: Erlbaum. Describes method and results of research from an "idiothetic" perspective—examining individuality while permitting quantitative comparison. Summarizes important findings with regard to the effects of goals on thought.

Kuhl, J., & Fuhrmann, A. (1998). Decomposing self-regulation and self-control: The volitional components inventory. In H. Heckhausen & C. S. Dweck (Eds.), *Motivation and self-regulation across the life span* (pp. 15–49). New York: Cambridge University Press.

McAdams, D. P. (1993). *Stories we live by.* New York: William Morrow. A contemporary extrapolation of the narrative approach to studying personality. McAdams presents a theory of human identity as life story. Our life stories are products of the unconscious process of creating a unique heroic myth.

McClelland, D. C. (1985). *Human motivation.* Glenview, IL: Scott, Foresman. Recommended for further reading. This book, by the main proponent of the approach, reviews the wide variety of research using the TAT to measure motivation.

McClelland, D. C., Koestner, R., & Weinberger, J. (1992).

How do self-attributed and implicit motives differ? In C. Smith (Ed.). *Motivation and personality: Handbook of thematic content analysis* (pp. 49–72). Cambridge; U.K.: Cambridge University Press. A chapter in the Smith volume that includes the first strong, systematic delineation of implicit and explicit motives.

Morgan, C., & Murray, H. A. (1935). A method for investigating fantasies: The Thermatic Apperception Test. *The Archives of Neurology and Psychiatry, 34*, 289–306.

Murray, H. (1938). *Explorations in personality.* New York: Oxford University Press. A classic in the field of personality and motivation, written by the cocreator of the TAT and a variety of colleagues. This book contains the findings of the in-depth study of 50 college men by the Harvard Psychological Clinic. In content and spirit it represents an example of studying personality "the long way."

Shipley, T. E., Jr., & Veroff, J. A. (1952). A projective measure of need for affiliation. *Journal of Experimental Psychology, 43*, 349–356. The original scoring system for the need for affiliation and how it was developed.

Singer, J. A., & Salovey, P. (1993). *The remembered self.* New York: The Free Press. Through examples from psychological practice, research, life, and literature demonstrates the ways that autobiographical memories reveal important aspects of personality.

Smith, C. P. (1992). *Motivation and personality: Handbook of thematic content analysis.* Cambridge, UK: Cambridge University Press. A complete collection of instructions for scoring a variety of materials for motive content. Includes stimulus materials for the Thematic Apperception Test. Highly recommended.

Winter, D. G. (1987). Leader appeal, leader performance and motive profiles of leaders and followers: A study of American presidents and elections. *Journal of Personality and Social Psychology, 52*, 196–202. Empirical application of TAT scoring of political psychology and presidential speeches.

Laura A. King and Robert A. Emmons

MOTORA, YUJIRO (1858–1913), Japanese psychologist. Motora, the first experimental psychologist in Japan, was born at Sanda at Settsu, the present Hyogo Prefecture. His original family name was Sugita. His father, a follower of Confucianism, died when Yujiro was 15 years old. In 1875, he went to Kyoto and entered the Doshisha, a school that had been established by the Reverend J. H. Nishima, a graduate of Amherst College and Andover Theological Seminary in Massachusetts. Sugita studied English there and eventually became a Congregationalist. In 1878, he went to Tokyo as a teacher in the Gakunosha, which had been established by the Christian educator Sen Tsuda. In 1881, Sugita participated in the founding of the Tokyo Eiwagakko, which is now Aoyama-gakuin University.

Sugita married Yone Motora, adopted his wife's family name, and went to Boston University to study under the professor of philosophy, Borden P. Browne. He then went to Johns Hopkins University to study psychology under its first professor of psychology, G. Stanley Hall. He wrote his important work, "Dermal Sensitiveness to Gradual Pressure Changes" (*American Journal of Psychology*, 1887) under Hall's direction.

After obtaining his degree from Johns Hopkins with a dissertation titled "Exchange Considered as the Principle of Social Life," Motora returned to Japan to lecture on psychophysics at Tokyo Imperial University—at that time the country's only university. In 1890, he was appointed the university's first professor of psychology. The experimental method he taught there was at first misunderstood as materialism, but what he meant to do was to examine hypotheses derived through much philosophical speculation, by experiment. Together with his follower Matataro Matsumoto, he obtained a considerable collection of experimental apparatus.

Motora read a paper, "The Idea of Ego in Eastern Philosophy," at the Seventh International Meeting of Psychology, held in Rome, Italy, in 1905. In this discourse, he referred to Zen, one of the first introductions of that concept to the western world. In 1907, he was dispatched to Europe and America by the Japanese Ministry of Education. In late 1913, he was hospitalized and died at the university hospital, surrounded by his students and graduates. Because of his relatively premature death, he left behind comparatively few who had been intensely influenced by him, but Tanenari Chiba (the psychology of proper consciousness) and Toru Watanabe (psychology of personality) are worthy of special mention.

[*Many of the people mentioned in this article are the subjects of independent biographical entries.*]

Bibliography

Motora, Y. (1890). *Sinrigaku* [Psychology]. Tokyo: Kinkodo Shoseki Kaisha.
Motora, Y. (1909). *Ronbunshu* [The collective works of Motora Yujiro]. Tokyo: Kodansha.
Motora, Y. (1915). *Sinrigaku gatron* [System of psychology]. Tokyo: Teimshuppan Hobunkan.

Seiji Kodama

MOTOR SYSTEM. Current evidence suggests that the earliest vertebrates evolved as active predators from relatively immobile, filter-feeding ancestors. The ability of these early vertebrates to move in a coordinated and goal-directed manner, therefore, represents a funda-mental adaptive breakthrough. As Robert L. Carroll (*Vertebrate Paleontology and Evolution*, New York, 1988) wrote of these ancestral vertebrates, their "most conspicuous structural features are associated with active swimming" (p. 17). They evolved a brain, sense organs concentrated in the head, and the ability to use that brain, their sense organs, and experience to move in relation to objects and places. Of course, not just the vertebrates, but also many invertebrates developed elaborate motor capabilities. But we, not they, descended from mobile ancestral vertebrates, and the organization of our motor system reflects that history.

Spinal Cord

All vertebrates have a dorsally situated nerve cord, the spinal cord, and a system of muscles addressed by pools of motor neurons. Most motor neurons reside in the ventral spinal cord and send axons that terminate directly on muscle fibers on the same side of the body. These synapses excite muscle fibers through cholinergic synapses and form the *final common path* for action. In most vertebrates, muscles are anchored to a rigid skeleton and thus are termed *skeletal muscles*. In early vertebrates, as in many fishes today, skeletal muscles along the long axis of the animal contract to cause the body to bend in their direction. Swimming results from waves of muscle contraction, propagating from head to tail on one side of the body. These waves alternate with comparable contractions on the opposite side of the body. The spinal cord contains the essential circuitry for generating and modulating these patterned rhythmic movements, termed the *central pattern generator*. The vertebrate motor system that supports terrestrial and arboreal locomotion, burrowing, flight, and voluntary limb movements evolved from a system that originally controlled swimming, and many of its most fundamental properties, including central pattern generators, bear witness to that history.

The spinal cord not only contains central pattern generators and motor neurons, but also axons conveying somatosensory information from the periphery and intrinsic (propriospinal) neurons. Various reflexes are subserved by afferent fibers, which make synaptic contact on propriospinal and motor neurons. Intrinsic spinal reflexes are mediated both by sensory fibers that innervate the skin (cutaneous receptors) and those conveying information from deeper tissues (proprioceptors). One important kind of proprioceptor, the muscle spindle afferent, underlies the stretch reflex. Although often said to control muscle length, an alternative view is that the stretch reflex regulates the stiffness of muscles to make the relationship between muscle length and tension more linear over the physiological range. Propriospinal neurons participate in a variety of spinal reflexes, but they are also the targets of axons descending from the brain. Damage to certain propriospinal pathways disrupts goal-directed reaching, at least in domestic cats, showing that they convey descending motor commands in that species. In many primates, however, direct projections from the cerebral cortex to spinal motor neurons also contribute to descending motor control.

The Descending Motor System

The first principle of descending motor control, and one of the most peculiar, is that one side of the brain controls the opposite side of the body. According to A. M. Lassek (*The Pyramidal Tract: Its Status in Medicine.* Springfield, IL, 1954), this principle was recognized by the Hippocratic physicians in the fourth and fifth century BCE. The major descending pathways cross the midline, including those from the cerebral cortex (the corticospinal tract) and red nucleus (rubrospinal tract). Ascending somatosensory pathways similarly respect this principle. Descending motor pathways arise from all levels of the brain, including the cerebral cortex, basal ganglia, cerebellum, and brain stem.

Cerebral Cortex. The cerebral cortex can influence virtually every part of the motor system. Corticofugal projections arise from layer 5 and terminate in the basal ganglia (the corticostriatal projection), red nucleus (the corticorubral projection), superior colliculus (the corticotectal projection), basilar pontine nuclei (the corticopontine projection), brain-stem reticular formation (the corticoreticular projection), and spinal cord (the corticospinal projection). The corticopontine projection provides a major source of information to the cerebellum.

In primates, approximately a dozen functionally distinct cortical fields play a relatively direct role in motor control. The most intensively studied motor area is the primary motor cortex (Figure 1). Along with the rubrospinal tract, the corticospinal projection from primary motor cortex terminates predominantly upon laterally situated motor neurons, which innervate mainly limb muscles in contrast to trunk muscles. Damage to the pyramidal tract, which conveys corticospinal axons to the spinal cord, reduces the flexibility of hand movements, leading to crude grasping movements that do not include individual movements of the digits. Because of this phenomenon, and because corticospinal projections to motor neurons appear to be more prevalent in primate species that have a high degree of manual dexterity, it is often stated that direct connections between cortex and motor neurons control hand movements. However, it is more likely that the pertinent specialization is for generally fine and flexible control of the musculature, and that whatever the motor cortex does it does for the body as a whole. Dorsal and ventral premotor areas (Figure 1) appear to be specialized for sensorially guided movement, such as visually guided limb movements, when the relationship between visual information and the movement is variable. According to this view, these premotor areas also promote flexibility in motor control, although in a different way than does primary motor cortex. Medial premotor areas, such as the supplementary motor area, the presupplementary motor area, and several cingulate motor areas (Figure 1), appear to play their largest role in self-generated movement and in movement sequences.

Basal Ganglia. Much of what is known about basal ganglia function emerges from dysfunction caused by disease. Parkinson's disease, Huntington's disease, and Tourette's syndrome result in large part from dysfunction of basal ganglia. Parkinson's disease causes increased resting muscle tone (rigidity) and involuntary tremor, as well as poverty of willed action (akinesia) and slowness of movement (bradykinesia). Huntington's disease causes numerous motor and cognitive deficits, including involuntary movements around multiple joints (chorea), motor incoordination, and disorders of gait and posture. Tourette's syndrome is particularly intriguing. These patients emit highly inappropriate remarks and have grave difficulty controlling such behavior, despite the "will" to do so. It has also been proposed that obsessive-compulsive disorder, which consists of extraordinary repetition of thoughts and actions, results from basal ganglia dysfunction. Substantial research has been devoted to demonstrating that Parkinson's patients have cognitive deficiencies accompanying their well-known motor abnormalities. Cognitive deficits appear to involve a difficulty in changing the rules by which an action is guided, a deficit described as one of *attentional set*. It has also been suggested that the basal ganglia mediates procedural learning and memory, in contrast to cortical structures, especially those of the medial temporal lobe (including the hippocampus), which are essential for declarative learning and memory. Norman M. White has summarized the evidence for this view (*Current Opinion in Neurobiology*, 1997, 7, 164–169), whereas the present author has presented a critique, based on the primate literature (*Seminars in Neuroscience*, 1996, 8, 39–46).

The mechanisms underlying basal ganglia function and dysfunction have been the subject of intensive investigation in recent years. The pathophysiology of Parkinson's disease is a case in point. Insufficient dopamine, which results from the degeneration of the midbrain's dopaminergic neurons, is the cause of Parkinson's disease. But understanding how dopamine insufficiency leads to rigidity, akinesia, and bradykinesia requires a consideration of the anatomy of the basal ganglia.

Most areas of the cerebral cortex and an important part of the thalamus project to the basal ganglia's input nuclei, collectively termed the *striatum*. The striatum includes the caudate nucleus, the putamen, the nucleus

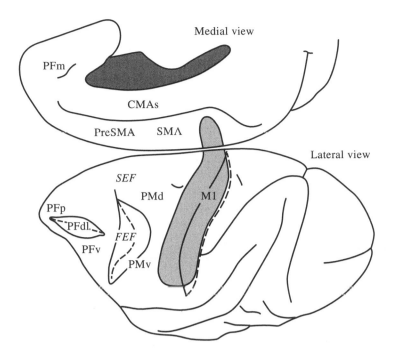

Medial view

PFm

CMAs

PreSMA   SMA

Lateral view

SEF

PMd   M1

PFp

PFdl

FEF

PFv

PMv

MOTOR SYSTEM. Figure 1. Two perspectives of the left hemisphere of a rhesus monkey cerebral cortex. At the top is a medial view, in which dorsal is down and ventral is up. At the bottom, a lateral view, in which dorsal is up. In both parts of the drawing, the frontal cortex is to the left. The shaded region shows the location of the primary motor cortex, and the solidly filled area is the corpus callosum. Abbreviations: M1, primary motor cortex; PMd, dorsal premotor cortex; PMv, ventral premotor cortex; SEF, supplementary eye field; FEF, frontal eye field; PFd, dorsal prefrontal cortex; PFv, ventral prefrontal cortex; PFdl, dorsolateral prefrontal cortex; PFp, polar prefrontal cortex; PFm, medial prefrontal cortex; SMA, supplementary motor area; CMAs, cingulate motor areas. (Modified from Wise, Murray, & Gerfen, 1996.)

accumbens, and other parts of the ventral forebrain. The striatum is the principal target of dopaminergic input from the midbrain and its output neurons are known as the medium spiny neurons. Medium spiny neurons are inhibitory GABAergic neurons that project to the pallidum, which provides the main output from the basal ganglia. The pallidum consists of the globus pallidus and other parts of the ventral forebrain. Pallidal output neurons terminate on thalamic neurons, which in turn project to the cortex. There are other pallidal outputs, such as the pallidal projection to the superior colliculus, which controls eye and head movements.

A key to understanding the pathophysiology of Parkinson's disease is the finding that the striatum projects to the pallidum through two pathways, termed the *direct* and *indirect* pathways. The direct pathway connects the striatal medium spiny cells with pallidothalamic projection neurons, which are also inhibitory GABAergic neurons. As illustrated in Figure 2, the indirect pathways also target pallidothalamic neurons, but do so via the subthalamic nucleus. The indirect pathway arises from different striatal medium spiny neurons and generally opposes direct-pathway mechanisms. Some experts maintain that dopamine affects the direct and indirect pathways oppositely, supporting activity in direct pathway neurons of the striatum but opposing it in indirect pathway neurons. Thus, dopamine deficiency would be expected to decrease activity in the direct pathway and increase it in the indirect pathway. This view remains controversial, but it would explain many of the problems caused by Parkinson's disease.

Diminution of direct pathway activity would undermine thalamic output signals because the inhibitory pallidothalamic cells would be less suppressed. Being less suppressed, they would tend to inhibit thalamic neurons more and reduce the signals being transmitted between thalamus and cortex. Because indirect pathway neurons increase pallidothalamic activity, enhancement of indirect pathway activity by dopamine depletion would have the same effect. According to this view, the generation of smaller output signals, and therefore Parkinson's disease, results from the combination of these factors.

Cerebellum. Traditionally, it has been held that the cerebellum acts as the organ of coordination. However, as with the basal ganglia, some recent research has suggested a cognitive deficit after cerebellar lesions. Changes in cerebellar blood flow have also been attributed to sensory or cognitive function. The idea that the cerebellum subserves cognitive function remains controversial, but is gaining adherents. Nevertheless, the most obvious result of cerebellar dysfunction is motor, rather than cognitive. The view that the cerebellum underlies coordination is consistent with the three basic themes of cerebellar research: one focusing on its role in motor learning (including classical conditioning), a second viewing the cerebellum as an adaptive, feedforward controller of movement parameters, and a third viewing the cerebellum as a feedback controller for responding to interference with movement, including adjustments required by the movement itself. As noted above for the spinal cord, a medial aspect of the cerebellum has been linked to postural support and a lateral aspect to more

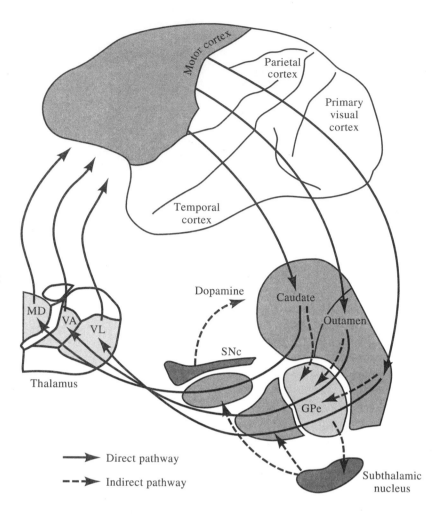

MOTOR SYSTEM. Figure 2. Schematic drawing of selected elements of basal ganglia and cortical circuitry. Three parallel "loops," which consist of recurrent positive feedback networks, are illustrated with solid arrows. The direct pathway through the striatum forms part of these loops. The indirect pathway is illustrated with dashed arrows. Abbreviations: GPe, external segment of the globus pallidus; GPi, internal segment of the globus pallidus; SNr, reticular part of the substantia nigra; SNc, compact part of the substantia nigra. (From Wise, Murray, & Gerfen, 1996. Copyright 1996 by Begell House.)

"voluntary" movement. In accord with this view, vestibular and propriospinal inputs predominate in the medial cerebellum, but inputs to the lateral cerebellum are mainly cortical. While there is some merit to this distinction, it should not be overstated: all limb movements involve an element of postural support. For example, a reaching movement causes *interaction torques* that must be compensated by postural adjustments. Recent studies of the role of the cerebellum in movement have emphasized its role in adapting to influences such as interaction torques. This adaptation is both anticipatory, involving feedforward control, and reactive, involving feedback control. The role of the cerebellum in learning a feedforward model of the motor system, including the motor commands needed to achieve a certain posture or movement, has been an active area of research. All of these, including motor learning and classical conditioning, relate directly or indirectly to coordinating the animal's reflexes and other actions, generating coherent behavior. The view that the cerebellum functions as the organ of coordination may, therefore, be a useful overview of its function.

The mechanism of cerebellar function depends to a large extent on the interaction between cerebellar cortex and the deep cerebellar nuclei. The cortex contains GABAergic Purkinje cells, which inhibit the deep cerebellar nuclei, the site of the cerebellum's output neurons. The cerebellum receives input from a variety of sources, including cortical areas involved in vision, audition, somatic sensation, and motor control. These inputs arrive through mossy fibers, many of which originate in the basilar pontine nuclei. A different input to cerebellum, the climbing fiber, arises from the inferior olivary complex. Cerebellar output is directed to the motor and parietal areas of cortex through the thalamus, as well as to the red nucleus, lateral reticular nucleus, superior colliculus, and spinal cord.

Red Nucleus and Brain Stem. Sources of motor information in the brain stem include the lateral vestibular nucleus (also known as Deiter's nucleus), the red nucleus, brain-stem reticular formation, and the superior colliculus (also known as the optic tectum). These regions give rise to the cerebellospinal, vestibulospinal, rubrospinal, reticulospinal and tectospinal tracts, respectively. Additionally, the brain sends serotonergic, noradrenergic, and dopaminergic projections to the spinal cord. These amines may play a role in initiating and maintaining the activity of central pattern generators. The vestibulospinal system plays an important role in postural adjustments. The superior colliculus is a higher order motor control structure for eye and head movements, subserving orientation toward external stimuli. The brain-stem system for producing eye movement is especially well understood, and its mechanisms are summarized by Michael E. Goldberg and his colleagues in *Principles of Neural Science* (E. Kandel, J. Schwartz, & T. Jessel, Eds. New York, 1991, chapter 43).

Distributed Modules and Network Architectures

Most recent models of the motor system have emphasized its distributed nature. The anatomical interconnections of neocortex with basal ganglia, as well as those between neocortex and cerebellum, have been summarized in terms of parallel, recurrent "circuits," "loops," or "modules" distributed across several structures. Taken together, the direct pathway through the basal ganglia, its cortical inputs, and thalamocortical outputs constitute positive-feedback circuits, which have been termed cortical-basal ganglionic modules (Figure 2). Different cortical areas interact with different, parallel modules comprised of neurons in the striatum, pallidum, and thalamus. The degree of convergence or interaction among these parallel circuits at the corticostriatal and striatopallidal levels remain uncertain, but a strict segregation of information processing among these modules has been proposed. The output from neocortex to cerebellum via the pons, along with the cerebellar projection to thalamocortical neurons, represents similar positive feedback circuits, termed cortical-cerebellar modules. Joyce Kieffer and James C. Houk (*Physiological Reviews*, 1994, *74*, 509–542) have described how cortical-cerebellar modules follow a basic architecture that applies to the cerebellum's output to red nucleus and lateral reticular nucleus, as well.

Motor Learning and Awareness

Some actions are made with full awareness, but others are not. It is well established that the motor system is capable of performing in a highly adaptive and precise manner without the mediation of conscious awareness. For example, in human subjects with blindsight, reasonably accurate pointing can accompany denial of the existence of the visual stimulus at which the subject pointed. One patient, with diffuse cortical damage, can orient her hand in order to put it through a slot, but cannot report the orientation of the same slot. In some respects, the motor system processes information more accurately than the systems of conscious awareness. For example, human subjects can make accurate hand movements that reflect the size of objects they report incorrectly due to illusions. It appears that there is at least some separation between neural networks involved in vision-for-perception and those underlying vision-for-action.

Motor learning and memory include adaptation, skill acquisition, and conditional motor learning. Adaptations involve a variety of changes in motor performance within an operational domain. For example, adapting to a requirement for faster movements within a fixed speed-accuracy trade-off or to displacement of the image of a target on the retina (caused by a prism) does not change the fundamental operating characteristics of the system. By contrast, learning a skill involves obtaining a new capability or attaining an enhanced level of performance, beyond the system's prior operational limits. As noted above, structures in the medial temporal lobe (including the hippocampus) in humans are needed for declarative learning. However, those structures are not necessary and are probably not important for motor adaptation or in the procedural aspects of skill acquisition. Conditional motor learning involves a higher level of flexibility, the ability to map any stimulus that can be detected and discriminated onto any behavior within a learned repertoire. The premotor cortex is necessary for both the learning and retention (including retrieval) of such arbitrary mappings.

Both cerebellum and basal ganglia have been identified as important components of the motor learning system, and the potential mechanisms of motor learning are an important focus of current research into the motor system. An important role for climbing fibers in cerebellum-mediated learning has been a central feature of models of the motor system since the work of David Marr (*Journal of Physiology* [*London*], 1969, *202*, 437–470). The climbing fiber has been proposed to provide a teaching signal for that neuronal network. A similar role has been postulated for dopamine inputs to basal ganglia. As shown in the physiological investigations of dopamine cell activity by Wolfram Schultz and his colleagues (*Science*, 1997, *275*, 1593–1599), these neurons have little modulation of activity when monkeys perform well-practiced tasks, but during the learning of new tasks, they show dramatic increases in such modulation. Moreover, midbrain dopaminergic neurons appear to predict the occurrence of reinforcement, respond to unexpected reinforcement, and are inhibited when an expected reward does not occur. These properties correspond well with those expected of a teaching signal.

Bibliography

Cheney, P. D., Fetz, E. E., & Mewes, K. (1991). Neural mechanisms underlying corticospinal and rubrospinal control of limb movements, *Progress in Brain Research, 87,* 213–252. Review of the physiology of corticospinal and rubrospinal projections, with emphasis on their most direct influences on motor neurons.

Goodale, M. A. (1993). Visual pathways supporting perception and action in the primate cerebral cortex. *Current Opinion in Neurobiology, 3,* 578–585. Brief overview of work showing that the brain system underlying vision-for-perception differs from that subserving vision-for-action.

Grillner, S., Georgopoulos, A. P., & Jordan, L. M. (1997). Selection and initiation of motor behavior. In P. S. G. Stein, S. Grillner, A. I. Selverston, & D. G. Stuart (Eds.), *Neurons, networks, and motor behavior* (pp. 3–20). Cambridge: MIT Press. Overview of motor control in a comprehensive anthology on motor control in the context of computational neuroscience.

He, S.-Q., Dum, R. P., & Strick, P. L. (1993). Topographic organization of corticospinal projections from the frontal lobe: Motor areas on the lateral surface of the hemisphere. *Journal of Neuroscience, 13,* 952–980. Replication and extension of neuroanatomical research showing which cortical areas project to the spinal cord.

He, S.-Q., Dum, R. P., & Strick, P. L. (1995). Topographic organization of corticospinal projections from the frontal lobe: Motor areas on the medial surface of the hemisphere. *Journal of Neuroscience, 15,* 3284–3306.

Houk, J. C., & Wise, S. P. (1995). Distributed modular architectures linking basal ganglia, cerebellum, and cerebral cortex: Their role in planning and controlling action. *Cerebral Cortex, 5,* 95–110. Speculative review of the motor system as a whole, stressing information processing functions at a cellular and systems level, cortical-basal ganglionic loops, and cortical-cerebellar loops.

Middleton, F. A., & Strick, P. L. (1997). New concepts about the organization of basal ganglia output. In J. A. Obeso, M. R. DeLong, C. Ohye, & C. D. Marsden (Eds.) *Advances in neurology: Vol. 74. The basal ganglia and surgical treatment for Parkinson's disease* (pp. 57–68). Philadelphia: Lippincott-Raven. Survey of neuroanatomical research supporting a strict segregation of information processing pathways in cortical-basal ganglionic loops.

Passingham, R. E., Perry, V. H., & Wilkinson, F. (1983). The long-term effect of removal of sensorimotor cortex in infant and adult rhesus monkeys. *Brain, 106,* 675–705. Brain lesion study in monkeys showing that the effects of primary motor cortex damage generally extend beyond movements of the fingers to finely controlled movements.

Preuss, T. M., Stepniewska, I., & Kaas, J. H. (1996). Movement representation in the dorsal and ventral premotor areas of owl monkeys: A microstimulation study. *Journal of Comparative Neurology, 371,* 649–675. Discussion of the literature on the definition of motor cortical fields in a wide variety of primates, including humans.

Wise, S. P., di Pellegrino, G., & Boussaoud, D. (1996). The premotor cortex and nonstandard sensorimotor mapping. *Canadian Journal of Physiology and Pharmacology, 74,* 469–482. Proposes that the premotor cortex functions to enable behaviors other than those involving approach or avoidance of objects and places.

Wise, S. P., Murray, E. A., & Gerfen, C. R. (1996). The frontal cortex—basal ganglia system in primates. *Critical Reviews in Neurobiology, 10,* 317–356.

Steven P. Wise

MOUCHET, ENRIQUE (1886–1977), Argentine psychologist. Mouchet was one of the first leaders of experimental psychology in Argentina during its early development in that country. He was born in 1886 in Rosario (Argentina) and died in Buenos Aires in 1977. His life covered the period in which psychology in Argentina passed through a series of transformations from being a laboratory experimental science to becoming an academic discipline studied in universities, and a recognized profession.

Enrique Mouchet first studied philosophy and literature and graduated in 1910 with a thesis entitled "A Study of the Concept of Identity." He continued his studies in the Faculty of Medicine and graduated in 1914 with a thesis on "An Introduction to the Physiology and Pathology of the Spirit." His career as a psychologist included activities as diverse as research, teaching, writing, and directing academic institutions. He was the director of the Institute of Psychology of the University of Buenos Aires, which was important in the organization and development of psychology as a profession in Argentina.

Horacio Piñero (1869–1918) had established the first laboratory for experimental psychology in Latin America in Buenos Aires in 1898. When he retired from teaching in 1918 due to ill health, Mouchet became his successor, and remained there until his own retirement in 1943. Between 1923 and 1936 he was the dean of the Faculty of Humanities and Educational Science at the Universidad de La Plata and taught psychology in addition to his administrative duties. When in 1930 the Institute of Psychology was founded as part of the Faculty of Philosophy and Letters of the University of Buenos Aires, Mouchet became the director. It was during this time that he carried out most of his research.

Another of the important contributions that he made to Argentine psychology was the reorganization of the Argentine Psychological Society (Sociedad Argentina de Psicología) in 1930. It had been created by José Ingenieros (1877–1925), Piñero, and Rodríguez Etchart in 1908, but had ceased to function in 1914. [*See the biography of Ingenieros.*] The quality of Mouchet's organizational abilities can be seen in the fact that the Society continues to be active more than seventy years after his work reestablishing its existence.

Mouchet also created the first journal of psychology to be published in Spanish, the *Anales del Instituto de*

Psicología de la Facultad de Filosofía y Letras en la Universidad de Buenos Aires. Only three volumes were published in 1935, 1938, and 1941, but Mouchet intended that the *Anales* and the Institute of Psychology would serve to unite psychologists in Latin America. It is important to note that at this time there was no university psychology career in Latin America.

The research carried out by Mouchet can be classified in the following areas: (a) his theory of thought and language; (b) the tactile perception used by the blind; (c) the theory of emotion; and (d) the theory of vital psychology.

Mouchet published many scientific articles in Argentine and in international journals, and many books. His most important works are *El Lenguaje Interior y los Trastornos de la Palabra* [Inner Language and Speech Disturbances] published in 1923; *Percepción, Instinto y Razón* [Perception, Instinct, and Reason], published in 1941; *Tratado de las Pasiones* [Treatise on Passions], 1953; and *Manual de Psicogeriatría* [A Manual of Psychogeriatrics] published in 1966.

Mouchet was not only a distinguished experimental psychologist, he was also a politician. A committed socialist, he served two terms in the Argentine Parliament between 1932 and 1938.

Mouchet can be regarded as one of the most important figures in the first stages of development of experimental psychology both in Argentina and Latin America. His investigations into perception, cognition, and emotion consolidated research in psychology in Argentina. His organizational abilities in the Institute of Psychology and the Argentine Psychological Society and his editorship of *Anales*, helped create the infrastructure necessary for a thriving scientific community. His research work and his numerous publications advanced the knowledge of psychology in his country. Finally, his political work helped apply some of these ideas to improve the standard of life for his countrymen.

Bibliography

Ardila, R. (1993). *Psicologia en America Latina, pasado, presente y futuro* [Psychology in Latin America, past, present, and future]. Mexico: Siglo XXI Editores.

Foradori, I. A. (1941). *Enrique Mouchet, Una vida, una vocacion* [Enrique Mochet, a life, a vocation]. Buenos Aires: Instituto Gonzalez.

Mouchet, E. (1941). *Percepcion, instinto y razon* [Perception, instinct, and reason]. Buenos Aires: Joaquin Gil Editor.

Rubén Ardila

MOWRER, O. HOBART (1907–1982), American psychologist. Born in Unionville, Missouri, 23 June 1907,

Hobart Mowrer served as president of the American Psychological Association (1954), and the American Psychological Foundation (1959 to 1960). Mowrer was a recipient of the Certificate of Merit, University of Missouri (1956); the Distinguished Contribution Award, Illinois Psychological Association (1975), and became a Fellow, American Psychological Association. Mowrer died in June 1982.

Hobart Mowrer is in many ways a psychologist for all seasons. One of the factors that made Mowrer such a maverick in the field is that he managed to bridge the gap between experimental psychology and applied psychology without detriment to either field. He is among the five psychologists most often cited in the literature for their scientific contributions. From the time he retired until his death, Hobart Mowrer remained an active author and speaker in the many areas he contributed to over the years.

Mowrer studied as an undergraduate at the University of Missouri, graduating in 1929. Following this he began his graduate work at Johns Hopkins University. During this time, Mowrer became interested in vestibulo-ocular functions and spatial orientation, and he published extensively on this subject between 1929 and 1934, when he joined the Yale Institute of Human Relations.

In the mid 1940s, Mowrer's work led him into the field of language and learning. One of the results of these studies was one of his most important contributions to the field of language and thought, the *autism theory of speech development*. This theory arose out of Mowrer's work with talking birds (as opposed to rats or other laboratory animals) such as the myna bird. In this theory Mowrer developed the idea of subjective utility as secondary reinforcement in the process of the bird's learning to "talk."

According to Mowrer, the use of certain words or phrases in intimate connection with the process of caring for the birds results in a positive conditioning of the bird; that is, the bird comes to consider them *good sounds*. In the course of its own, at first random vocalizations, the bird will make somewhat similar sounds. Writing in the *Journal of Speech and Hearing Disorders*, Mowrer stated:

> By the principle of generalization, some of the derived satisfaction of pleasure which has become attached to the trainer's sounds will now be experienced when the bird itself makes and hears like sounds; and when this begins to happen the stage is set for the bird's learning to "talk." (Spielberger, 1983, p. 333)

Essentially this means that when the bird hears itself making sounds like the trainer's, it is encouraged to continue making the same sounds. Further, the bird soon learns that he can use these sounds instrumentally, as a means of indicating some need or simply to attract an admiring crowd. Mowrer ascribes such an action to a desire in the bird to be like its trainer, which results from the development of a positive relationship between the bird and the human being.

From this Mowrer extrapolated a theory of language development in human infants. The child first identifies certain sounds as being good because his parents use them in connection with actions that provide the child with pleasure. He begins imitating them and perfecting his imitations; this provides him with a sense of gratification and attracts attention from his parents, which encourages him to continue. Finally he discovers the use of words in communicating, learning to use them to control his parents and other people, and to get what he wants.

In the early 1960s, Mowrer became interested in psychopathology, and this led, through the "back door" as he described it, to an interest in deception and its effects on personality. One of the first pieces he wrote on deception was for the Alcoholics Anonymous newsletter, *The Grapevine* (1962). Mowrer was impressed at the time with the axiom among members of AA that every alcoholic is a "liar" and that he can't get sober until he gets honest.

While Mowrer recognized the role heredity plays in causing mental illness, he felt that the stress created by deception can play an enormous part in triggering otherwise inert physiological troubles. In his paper for *The Grapevine* Mowrer quotes Sir Walter Scott, who says in *Lochinvar*, "Oh what a tangled web we weave, when first we practice to deceive." It is the stress caused by becoming tangled in this web of deception that Mowrer believes is responsible for much of the mental anguish that people suffer. It is not just the deception of others that Mowrer cites too; it is also self-deception.

Few psychologists have contributed more to the advancement of psychology and particularly the psychology of language and thought, than O. Hobart Mowrer. His work has been both imaginative and practical, as well as very often being candid and outspoken in its direction.

Bibliography

Mowrer, O. H. (1934). *The modification of vestibular nystagmus by means of repeated elicitation.* Baltimore, MD: Johns Hopkins University Press.

Mowrer, O. H. (1939). *Frustration and aggression.* New Haven, CT: Yale University Press.

Mowrer, O. H. (1940). *Preparatory set (expectancy)—Some methods of measurement.* Columbus, OH: American Psychological Association.

Mowrer, O. H. (1950). *Learning theory and personality dynamics: Selected papers.* New York: Ronald Press.

Mowrer, O. H. (1953). *Learning theory and research.* New York: Ronald Press.

Mowrer, O. H. (1960a). *Learning theory and the symbolic process.* New York: Wiley.

Mowrer, O. H. (1960b). *Learning theory and behavior.* New York: R. E. Krieger.

Mowrer, O. H. (1961). *The crisis in psychiatry and religion.* Princeton, NJ: Van Nostrand.

Mowrer, O. H. (1962). *The quest for community.* Rockford, IL: Augustana College Library.

Mowrer, O. H. (1964). *The new group therapy.* Princeton, NJ: Van Nostrand.

Mowrer, O. H. (Ed.). (1967). *Morality and mental health.* Chicago: Rand-McNally.

Mowrer, O. H. (Ed.). (1980). *Psychology of language and learning.* New York: Plenum Press.

Mowrer, O. H., & Lamoreaux, R. R. (1942). *Avoidance conditioning and signal duration: A study of secondary motivation and reward.* Evanston, IL: American Psychological Association.

Mowrer, O. H., & Johnson, R. C. (Eds.). (1972). *Conscience, contract, and social reality.* New York: Holt Rinehart.

Spielberger, C. D. (Ed.). (1983). *Leaves from many seasons, Selected papers O. Hobart Mowrer, centennial psychology series.* New York: Praeger.

Robert W. Rieber

MRI. *See* Brain Imaging Techniques.

MÜLLER, GEORG ELIAS (1850–1934), German experimental psychologist and philosopher. Müller was the dominant figure in giving experimental psychology its modern, experimental shape. No other figure combined the creation of conceptual and methodological innovations in several important areas of experimental psychology, the schooling of subsequent leaders and professors, and importance for professional organization to a similar extent; however, the lack of translation of any of his significant works has permitted subsequent generations to overlook the many values of this work and the centrality of his roles.

Müller was born in the small city of Grimma in the then independent country of Saxony as the second son of August Friedrich Müller and Rosalie Zehme in a family steeped in *Neuluthertum* (a revivalist orthodoxy of the mid-nineteenth century), which included an uncle, Constantin von Tischendorff, who was professor of theology at the University of Leipzig. In his *Gymnasium* years (while his father was pastor and religion teacher to the prestigious Grimma *Gymnasium*, Müller broke from the religiosity of his family and made his first steps toward a natural science worldview. He then attended the University of Leipzig, where, in the first semesters, Moritz Wilhelm Drobisch and Gustav Theodor Fechner were his first teachers. After a year at Berlin and a year's service in the war against France, Drobisch sent him to Rudolf Hermann Lotze at the University of Göttingen, who was to sponsor his career.

Müller quickly completed a dissertation that supported mechanistic theories of attention, a dissertation that lacked any data gathered by Müller but used Helmholtz's research to reject voluntaristic arguments. In 1876, Müller went on to become a member of the Göttingen faculty with the preliminary version of the work that later was published as *Die Grundlegung der Psychophysik* (The Founding of Psychophysics; Berlin, 1878) which, living up to its name, modified important aspects of Fechner's work (making the method of constant stimuli central) and set the definitions of American "classical" psychophysics. With little more than this achievement, Müller became Lotze's successor when Lotze moved to Berlin in 1881.

Müller had relatively few obvious achievements (although he did invent the memory drum apparatus for the controlled presentation of syllables) in the first decade of his professorship. His major work during this time proposed a theory of muscular action. While he seems to have begun to carry out psychological experiments in 1879, he received support for the second laboratory in Prussia in 1887 and built it, according to William O. Krohn (*American Journal of Psychology*, 1893, 5, 282–284) into the best research laboratory in Germany. At the close of the decade, he was one of three psychologists named to the editorial board of the newly founded *Zeitschrift für Psychologie und Physiologie der Sinnesorgane*, the first psychological journal in the world to have an editorial board that was both prestigious and inclusive.

In the 1890s, Müller initiated the university career of Friedrich Schumann, and with Schumann, published the standard work on serial anticipation learning, sponsored the dissertation that contained Jost's laws, and wrote a declaration of physiological reductionism as a set of psychophysical axioms (*Zeitschrift für Psychologie und Physiologie der Sinnesorgane*, 1896–1897, *10*, 1–82; *10*, 321–413; *14*, 1–76). He also provided opportunities to study to all but one of the American women students in Germany during this decade (including Christine Ladd-Franklin, Lillien Martin, Margaret Keiver Smith, and Lotte and Laura Steffens). He wrote the standard work, including 44 studies, on paired-associate learning and interference theory (*Zeitschrift für Psychologie und Physiologie der Sinnesorgane*, 1900, Ergänzungsband I, first supplementary volume), and received an honorary doctorate in medicine from the University of Leipzig sponsored by Ewald Hering. It was also during the 1890s that Müller became the conscience of experimental psychology, using his public criticism of Hugo Münsterberg and James McKeen Cattell to insist on a "falsification" standard for experimentation that required a clear realization of alternative theoretical hypotheses for any experimental study as well as a minimization of theorizing.

The subsequent years until the onset of World War I have been described as the golden years of the Göttingen laboratory by Müller's longtime student, David Katz. In these years, Narziss Ach, Joseph Fröbes, Géza Révész, Erich Jaensch, Eleanor Acheson, McCulloch Gamble, Walter Baade, Katz and Katz's future wife, Rosa Heine were among his students, while Edgar Rubin, Charles Spearman, William McDougall, and Raymond Dodge can be counted among the significant resident visitors. During these years, Müller produced the standard summary on psychophysics that guided Edward Bradford Titchener and two of the three books that summarized wide ranging research on memory, cognitive processes, and perception, which went under the name of *Komplextheorie* (sometimes called the constellation theory). This work, in essence, presents a mechanistic theory of the course of ideation based on Johann Friedrich Herbart's doctrines. It included extensive research with Rückle, the memory prodigy, who had come to Müller's attention while Rückle was a doctoral student in mathematics in Göttingen. The year 1903 also saw the founding of the *Deutsche Gesellschaft für experimentelle Psychologie* (DGeP; German Society of Experimental Psychology; now the German Society of Psychology) for which Müller wrote the statutes. This group became the core professional organization of German psychologists and Müller headed it until 1927. In this period, the editors of the *Zeitschrift für Psychologie* were selected almost exclusively from his students.

After World War I, Müller had a few students, who included George Katona, Oswald Kroh, Richard Strohal, and Thorlief Grüner-Hegge (who served as a godfather to American special education at the Wayne County Training School). The DGeP took over the publication of the *Archiv für die gesamte Psychologie*, a journal that had started in 1903 with a board of editors that only included supporters of Wilhelm Wundt.

After his retirement in 1922, Müller turned to the study of color phenomena improving on the theory pioneered by his close friend Ewald Hering, following an interest that dates at least to 1880. He elaborated the two-stage theory in which the first stage comprises the three retinal receptors, the signals of which are transformed into four opponent primary colors. After a preliminary book on color blindness in bees, in 1930, he produced two summary books with a carefully worked out color theory that anticipated the work of Leo Hurvich and Dorothea Jameson in the 1950s.

Müller's critique (*Komplextheorie und Gestalttheorie: Ein beitrag zur Wahrnehmungspsychologie*, Göttingen, 1923) also served as the major associationist counterpoint to Wolfgang Köhler's comprehensive treatment of Gestalt psychology (*Gestalten im ruhem und stationarem Zustand*, Berlin, 1921). Müller argued that many of the effects presented by Gestalt psychologists could be explained by attentional factors and effects much like James J. Gibson's later ideas of affordances.

While Müller never did work that could be considered applied psychology, he sponsored, from the first decade of the century, applied work. He was codirector (with William Stern) of the Institute for Applied Psychology (*Institut für angewandte Psychologie*), which the DGeP sponsored and established in Berlin in 1906.

Müller died in Göttingen, as important parts of the experimental psychology program that he worked so hard to create were being disassembled by the Nazi regime. Nevertheless, his memory was honored by a full issue of the *Zeitschrift für Psychologie*, the journal to which he devoted much of his professional life. The interference theory, which he enunciated with Alfons Pilzecker, continued to influence cognitive studies for at least 30 years after his death.

[*Many of the people mentioned in this article are the subjects of independent biographical entries.*]

Bibliography

Works by Müller

Müller, G. E. (1878). *Zur Grundlegung der Psychophysik. Kritische Beiträge* [On the founding of psychophysics. Critical contributions]. Berlin: T. Grieben. Bibliothek fur Wissenschaft und Literatur, 23. Band. Philosophische Abtheilung. 4. bd. (Habilitation, S. 424; 2. Aufl. Berlin: Hoffmann). This work, described by Fechner as the "greatest service performed for psychophysics," in many ways sets the standards for the later American "classical psychophysics" and includes a comprehensive review of all Weber fraction studies up to that time.

Müller, G. E., & Schumann, F. (1894). Experimentelle Beiträge zur Untersuchungen des Gedächtnisses [Experimental contributions on the investigation of memory]. *Zeitschrift fur Psychologie und Physiologie der Sinnesorgane, 6,* 81–190 and 257–339. This is the first major study of memory after Ebbinghaus's work, completed in 1884 and published in 1885. It redefines the method of choosing syllables which are hereafter called "standard," establishes counterbalancing of vowels across lists, includes experiments on proactive and retroactive transfer, factorial transfer, and rejects Ebbinghaus's finding of the occurrence of remote associations.

Müller, G. E. (1896). Zur Psychophysik der Gesichtsempfindungen. Kapitel 1. *Zeitschrift fur Psychologie und Physiologie der Sinnesorgane, 10,* 1–82 and 321–413. This work expands Fechner's one axiom of psychophysical parallelism to five axioms of physiological reduction and includes the proposal that reversible chemical reactions could account for Hering's four color opponent processes.

Müller, G. E., & Pilzecker, A. (1900). *Experimentelle Beiträge zur Lehre vom Gedächtniss* [Experimental contributions on the theory of memory]. Leipzig: J. A. Barth. (*Zeitschrift für Psychologie*. Ergänzungsband 1) This work, with its 44 experiments, presented a new form of memory drum (Müller had invented the first one in 1887) and set the standards for paired-associate experiments. It is also the source of the major theories of interference, consolidation, and perseveration which were used in American memory research through the 1960s.

Works about Müller

Boring, E. G. (1929, 1950). *A history of experimental psychology.* New York: Appleton-Century-Crofts. Among traditional history of psychology books, this has the most complete description of Müller's life and work. However, unlike Wilhelm Wundt, who has a full chapter to himself, Müller is buried at the end of a chapter on other early experimentalists. In order to use Boring to appreciate the full importance of Müller, it is necessary to use the index entries and to look for the descriptions of Müller's students.

Haupt, E. J. (1997). From whence comes experimental psychology: An alternative family tree. *Cuadernos Argentinos de la Historia de Psicologia, 2,* 53–78. This piece proposes that a coterie of German and Austrian philosophy professors, sponsored by Rudolf Hermann Lotze and Franz Brentano, became the dominant force supporting and sponsoring experimental psychology.

Haupt, E. J. (1998). G. E. Müller as a source of American psychology: The *Zur Grundlegung der Psychophysik* [On the foundation-izing of psychophysics] and *Untersuchung des Gedächtnisses* [Investigation of the memory]. In R. W. Rieber & K. Salzinger (Eds.), *Psychology: Theoretical and historical perspectives* (Rev. ed.). Washington DC: American Psychological Association. This paper presents the argument that Müller was the source of two major streams of American psychology, "classical" psychophysics and syllable-based memory research.

Judd, D. B. (1951). Basic correlates of the visual stimulus. In S. S. Stevens (Ed.), *Handbook of experimental psychology* (pp. 811–867). New York: Wiley. This is the only accessible treatment of Müller's color theory in English. Judd evaluates it as the best of the two-stage theories.

Katz, D. (1935). G. E. Müller. *Acta Psychologica, 1,* 234–240. While this is largely parallel to Katz's obituary in the *American Journal of Psychology*, there are differences of expression which make it superior.

Katz, R. (1972). Rosa Katz. In L. J. Pongratz, W. Traxel, & E. G Wehner (Eds.), *Psychologie in Selbstdarstellung, Bd. 1* [Psychology in self-portrayal, Vol. 1]. (pp. 103–125). Bern: Verlag Hans Huber. This memoir by David Katz's wife, who also did her dissertation under Müller as Rosa Heine, describes some of the less flattering aspects of the hard work that had to be performed for Müller's approval.

Kroh, O. (1935). Georg Elias Müller. Ein Nachruf [Georg Elias Müller. A eulogy]. *Zeitschrift für Psychologie, 134,* 150–190. This is the longest, most complete, and by far most accurate of all the obituaries/eulogies written for Müller.

Edward J. Haupt

MÜLLER, JOHANNES PETER (1801–1859), Prussian anatomist and physiologist. Johannes Müller was born into a Prussian shoemaker's family, in Coblenz, on 14 July 1801. In 1819, he entered the University of Bonn, studying medicine in a romantic milieu. Later, while attending the University of Berlin, Müller experienced a more austere, bench-science style when he studied under anatomist Karl Rudolphi. In 1824, Müller became a lecturer in physiology and comparative anatomy at the University of Bonn, arguing in his inaugural lecture that physiology must include both empirical observation and philosophical insight. During the ensuing period, Müller's work on both human and animal vision, on the compound eyes of insects and crustaceans, and on the functional aspects of sensory tissue caught the attention of the wider scientific community. The discipline of physiology itself was then forming, pulling away from anatomy's influence, and Müller was experiencing an extremely productive time in his life. Müller studied efferent and afferent stimulation of the brain and spinal cord; studied glands, secretions, and genital development, discovering the prenatal female sex organs (i.e., the Müllerian ducts); studied the composition and function of both blood and lymph; studied the retina's image-making properties and the middle ear's auditory properties. Müller confirmed the Bell-Magendie law, conducted comparative neuroanatomical investigations, and added to the understanding of reflex action. In 1833, the University of Berlin invited Müller to succeed Rudolphi. Müller accepted.

In Berlin, Müller's focus turned to animal physiology, specifically as related to structure-function relationships. In Müller's laboratory his assistant, Theodor Schwann, confirmed the cell as the basic anatomical unit in animals. Müller worked to integrate medical insights from basic research and clinical practice and pursued cellular studies that later, through his student Rudolf Virchow, would lead to dramatic advances in pathology. During the 1830s, Müller published what would serve as the founding textbook of physiology, the two-volume *Handbuch der Physiologie des Menschen für Vorlesungen* [A guide to human physiology for lectures] (1834–1840).

Though Müller had expressed several of the *Handbuch*'s concepts in earlier publications, the *Handbuch*'s extensive, systematic presentation became an important conduit for Müller's influence on generations of physiologists. Three of the *Handbuch*'s most important contributions are (1) an epistemological clarification; (2) the doctrine of specific nerve energies; and (3) Müller's version of the "motor-keyboard" conception of action. Edward S. Reed observes (*From Soul to Mind*, New Haven, CT, 1997) that the epistemological clarification reveals the influence of Müller's reading of Spinoza's *Ethics*. Spinoza suggests perception of external objects is simply the reflection of body states. Müller went on to insist specifically that our experience is of neural states rather than of external objects. The nervous system exists in the material world and is influenced by material causes. Given that every material event emerges from relations among causal events, investigators should be able to begin with an event and develop understanding backwards to causal origins. The nervous system mediates between the world and experience, and, by studying both, we can expect to observe in experience reflections of the nervous system's structure-function relationships.

The doctrine of specific nerve energies follows from this clarification, suggesting that the various sensory units within the nervous system each function in response to modality-specific qualities and produce modality-specific experiences: The eye responds no more to sound than the ear to light, and if a sensory system did respond to stimuli other than that for which it was constructed (à la Müller), then the response would occur in the fiber's native experience (e.g., pressing your eye and experiencing light rather than touch).

Müller's version of the motor-keyboard conception of action helped further crystalize the concept's form, prefiguring Alexander Bain's acceptance of that concept as fundamental to psychology. Müller submits that repeated thoughts create "vibration" patterns. As vibrations arise in motor nerves, these currents then play the motor system as hands play a piano keyboard. Repetition leads to control. Later psychological writers adopting a similar account include not only Bain, but also William James, B. F. Skinner, and Jean Piaget.

With his *Handbuch* becoming the standard text in the emerging discipline of physiology, in 1840 Müller began turning his attention to comparative zoology and anatomy, classifying invertebrates, marine vertebrates, and birds. Listing Müller's students reveals his pedagogical influence. These individuals—including Virchow, DuBois-Remond, Helmholtz—produced such major achievements as to eclipse their mentor's own critical contributions. Müller himself experienced cycles of impressive productivity punctuated by serious depressions. Some historians speculate that his death on 28 April 1858, was suicide.

[*Many of the people mentioned in this article are the subjects of independent biographical entries.*]

Bibliography

Boring, E. G. (1950). *A history of experimental psychology* (2nd ed.). New York: Appleton-Century-Crofts. Boring still provides the most accessible account in English of Müller's work.

Fitzek, H. (1997). Johannes Müller and the principle of sensory metamorphosis. In W. G. Bringmann, H. L.

Lück, R. Miller, & C. E. Early (Eds.), *A pictorial history of psychology* (pp. 46–49). Chicago: Quintessence. Describes the psychological significance of Müller's conceptual shift from studying the content of vision to studying the process of vision.

Müller, J. (1826). *Ueber die phantastischen Gesichtserscheinungen. Eine physiologische Untersuchung mit einer physiologischen Urkunde des Aristotles über den Traum* [About the fantastic visions of sight: A physiological investigation with a physiological record of Aristotle about the dream]. Coblenz: J. Hölscher. Apparently Müller's earliest statement in print of the doctrine of specific nerve energies.

Müller, J. (1834–1840). *Handbuch der Physiologie des Menschen für Vorlesungen* (Vols. 1–2). Coblenz: J. Hölscher.

Müller, J. (1838–1842). *Elements of physiology* (Vols. 1–2, W. Baly, Trans.). London: Taylor & Watson. First English translation of the *Handbuch*.

Randall D. Wight

MÜLLER-LYER, FRANZ CARL (1857–1916), German experimental psychologist and sociologist. Müller-Lyer was born in Baden-Baden, Germany, and as a young man studied medicine in Strasbourg, Bonn, and Leipzig, graduating from the University of Strasbourg in 1880. In 1881, he was appointed assistant director of the Strasbourg Psychiatric Clinic, where he remained until 1883. From 1884 to 1888 he studied psychology and sociology at universities in Berlin, Vienna, Paris, and London. During this period he spent time with Emil Du Bois-Reymond and Jean-Martin Charcot, among others. [*See the biography of Charcot.*] In 1888, he established a private practice in Munich, where he remained until his death in 1916. Müller-Lyer's contributions to experimental psychology were made principally in a 5-year period during and immediately after his foreign travels, when he published two papers on psychophysics and in 1889 the paper, "Optical Illusions" (*Perception*, 1981, *10*, 126–146) on the geometric illusion, which bears his name; a second paper on the Müller-Lyer illusion appeared in 1896. After 1894 he turned to sociology and produced a seven-volume study based on a then-current comparative and evolutionary method for social studies.

In the late nineteenth century, optical illusions, with their striking lack of correspondence between stimulus and percept, held great interest as problems of space perception were being investigated. Illusions were held up as "crucial experiments" for much larger general theories of perception, and the Müller-Lyer illusion—the apparent expansion and contraction of extent between outward- and inward-directed pairs of oblique lines—was used as an example in almost all of them. The problem of the degree to which the so-called reti-

nal image "copies" the stimulus became an important theme in Gestalt psychology. In his 1889 paper, Müller-Lyer investigated variables affecting the strength of the illusion and explained the effect by "confluxion": the tendency in perception for the size of the spatial feature to be judged and the features that surround it to flow together. His 1896 paper, "Concerning the Theory of Optical Illusions" (*Perception*, 1981, *10*, 126–146), was devoted to refuting rival explanations and to elaborating additional factors to explain the illusion; he was aware of the complexity of the problem and noted that several factors could be creating the effect simultaneously. Attempts to explain it continue to the present and have produced a large literature.

In contrast to ongoing interest in the Müller-Lyer illusion, his sociology has faded into obscurity. In the manner of social evolutionists, his "phaseological method" described and correlated general successive cultural stages of human societies. Like Marxian historical materialists, he regarded social economy as fundamental in that every great epoch was introduced by extension of natural resources, technical invention, or a new form of labor organization. He regarded a system of stages as a scientific necessity for analysis of the direction of social change and programs to control it. He believed that capitalism, with its exploitation of labor and imperialistic tendencies, should gradually develop into a socialistic system. These writings were translated into several languages, including the artificial language Ido; they were popular among labor groups and idealistic social theorists such as Leonard T. Hobhouse, who supported the translation of Müller-Lyer's works into English. While Müller-Lyer himself was respected as a sociologist, evolutionary cultural theories that imposed a uniform developmental schema on scattered, prescientific ethnographical data generally fell into disrepute during the 1930s and 1940s.

Bibliography

Barnes, H. E., Becker, H., & Becker, F. B. (1940). *Contemporary social theory*, New York: Appleton-Century. Part VI, "Cultural Approach to Problems of Social Development" (pp. 433–569) places evolutionary social theory in the context of the history of social thought 1860–1920.

Boring, E. G. (1942). *Sensation and perception in the history of experimental psychology*. New York: Appleton-Century. While dated, the section on geometrical optical illusions (pp. 238–262) summarizes the history of explanations of the Müller-Lyer illusion and cites primary sources in the debate.

Day, R., & Knuth, H. (1981). The contributions of F. C. Müller-Lyer. *Perception, 10,* 126–146. Includes translations of Müller-Lyer's classic papers on the illusion, biographical sketch, references, and Müller-Lyer's explanations in the light of subsequent research.

Müller-Lyer, F. C. (1920–1924). *Die Entwicklungsstufen der Menschheit* [The developmental stages of the human race]. (7 vols.). Munich, Germany: A. Langen. Müller-Lyer's sociology.

Salomon, G. (1933). F. C. Müller-Lyer. (1933). In E. Seligman (Ed.), *Encyclopaedia of the social sciences* (Vol. 11, pp. 83–84). New York: Macmillan. Müller-Lyer as sociologist.

Barbara Whitney Keyser

MULTICULTURAL COUNSELING. The term multicultural counseling has been used most recently to identify that specialization of counseling psychology that encompasses any situation in which two or more persons with different ways of perceiving and interacting with their social environment are brought together in a helping relationship. Prior to the use of this term, *cross-cultural counseling* and *racial/ethnic minority counseling* were the terms most frequently used. Although all three terms have much in common, they are each reflective of the sociopolitical and academic climate in which they were originally coined.

The term *cross-cultural counseling* came into vogue in the 1960s. This term referred to counseling that involved non-Hispanic White, middle-class, English-speaking counselors working with Black or Hispanic clients. In the 1980s cross-cultural counseling was redefined more broadly as a counseling relationship in which two or more participants differ with respect to cultural background, including values, norms, roles, lifestyle, and methods of communicating. With the advent of the civil rights movement of the 1960s and the increased attention subsequently given to the changing racial/ethnic demographics in the United States, a number of researchers opted to define their work as racial and ethnic minority counseling in general or, when appropriate, to use the actual name of the racial or ethnic group on which their work was focused (e.g., counseling Asian Americans). More recently, a preference for the use of the term multicultural counseling has emerged in an effort to broaden the focus to other groups that might share certain life and/or social developmental experiences with racial and ethnic minority groups (the elderly, women, gays, lesbians, persons with disabilities). Many theorists and researchers are now opting to replace the term *multicultural* with the more inclusive term *diversity counseling*. This comes from the concern that the term multicultural counseling might be perceived as overemphasizing the role of culture while downplaying other psychosocial and developmental factors that might differentiate individuals.

Given the changes in the use of terms and the fact that individual researchers continue to use the term they prefer, persons wanting information relative to multicultural counseling should seek such information under any one of the respective terms.

Historical Perspective

Awareness and interest in multicultural counseling emerged in the counseling profession in the early 1950s. Such interest was piqued by a number of societal changes, including changing demographics, the 1954 Supreme Court decision in *Brown v. Board of Education*, and the civil rights movement of the 1960s. The movement, in particular, served as a catalyst for raising the consciousness of many professionals to the counseling needs of varied powerless, disenfranchised groups, including women, elderly, physically challenged, and other racial/ethnic minority groups. With this increased consciousness, the counseling profession, through its formal organizational structure, began to sensitize and prepare professionals to effectively work in an increasingly multicultural society. Particularly through the encouragement of a number of racial and ethnic minority counseling psychologists, the profession made efforts to address multiculturalism in its ethical principles and standards and initiated efforts to improve the representation of racial and ethnic minorities within its ranks. Finally, steps were taken to identify and develop a process to more adequately include and address the needs of racial and ethnic minorities through research, as well as through the curricula and training experiences required of all psychologists. For a more detailed perspective relative to organizational, research, and training efforts, refer to Ponterotto and Casas (1991).

Although multicultural counseling was originally viewed by the counseling field as a preoccupation of a small number of scholarly pioneers, attention to and interest in multicultural counseling has gradually increased over the years. This increase is documented in the realm of research and publications. The *Journal of Multicultural Counseling and Development*, formerly known as the *Journal of Non-White Concerns in Personnel and Guidance*, and the *Journal of Cross-Cultural Psychology* began publication in the early 1970s. According to Ponterotto and Casas (1991), between 1983 and 1988, 10.2% of the articles published in five major counseling journals focused on multicultural groups. In addition, major counseling journals have dedicated special issues to multicultural counseling topics; some of these are *Counseling Psychologist* (1985, 13, 4); *Journal of Counseling and Development* (1991, 70, 1); and *Career Development Quarterly* (1993, 42, 1). The significant growth and impact of multiculturalism is amply described by Betz and Fitzgerald in the *Annual Review of Psychology*

(Palo Alto, Calif., 1993). The authors assert that the recognition of the profound influence of race, culture, and ethnicity on individuals' life experiences and world-views represents a significant change in the ways that psychologists address their clients, their research, and their training. Their contention underscores the perspective that multiculturalism has the potential to become the "fourth force" in psychology. Such an attainment on the part of multiculturalism is truly remarkable given that only a few years ago in psychology, *Even the Rat Was White* (R. V. Guthrie, New York, 1976).

Research

Early research focused on the relationship between client and counselor demographic differences and attrition, type of service received, and expectations, but did not explicitly focus on cultural variables (i.e., norms, roles, values). This research took an etic or universal perspective (i.e., attempting to fit the client to an existing ethnocentric mold). More recent works focus on the emic or culturally specific perspective. At first, a significant amount of research efforts within the multicultural area were directed to the following topics: racial identity, cultural identity, ethnic identity, acculturation, and counselor-client matching. At this time, multicultural counseling research has extended itself to all areas that fall within the realm of the counseling profession, including development and evaluation of counseling theories, therapeutic practice, career development, psychological assessment, and supervision. With respect to counseling theories, a number of researchers have evaluated the efficacy of existing theories for multicultural individuals with various presenting issues and have taken steps to propose a theory that is specifically earmarked for multicultural groups. Taking a more pragmatic perspective, researchers continue to examine factors related to practice. Such factors include utilization of services, accessibility of services (e.g., home vs. office), use of paraprofessionals, and use of translators with non-English-speaking clients. In the area of career development, major efforts have been directed to issues related to the applicability of career theory and practice to ethnic and racial minority populations. The use of standardized tests across cultures has been examined including factors such as functional and conceptual equivalence, translation, test bias, and norms. In reference to assessment, attention is being directed to examining the purposes of assessment, interpretations of assessment findings, the development of etic and/or emic measures, and procedures for adapting emic measures developed in this country for non-Anglo-American cultural groups. Although there is a paucity of research examining multicultural supervision, the existing research has generally translated all counseling information on the impact of cultural differences within the context of the counseling process into appropriate supervisory practices that can help to nurture a culturally sensitive and skilled counselor. In the expanded multicultural counseling research, special efforts have been made to consider subgroups within racial and ethnic minority populations. Although early writers took a provincial view and were generally concerned with treating respective racial-minority groups as homogeneous entities, since the mid-80s, authors like J. Manuel Casas (e.g., in an article entitled "A Reflection on the Status of Racial/Ethnic Minority Research, *Counseling Psychologist*, 1985, *13*, 581–598), have addressed intragroup variability. This variability incorporates such factors as sexual orientation, racial identity, acculturation, cultural identity, gender, socioeconomic status, age, and disability status.

Training

Because an ever-growing number of counselors and therapists are now confronted with having to work with persons who are different from themselves and because of the general increase in multicultural sensitivity, increased efforts have been extended toward training competent multicultural counselors. Such efforts have included proposing multicultural counseling competencies, identifying those components that researchers believe must be inherent in any training program (i.e., consciousness-raising, cognitive understanding, and affective and skills components), and developing instruments to assess training programs and multicultural counseling competencies. For more information relative to training, refer to Pope-Davis and Coleman (1997). Unfortunately, until now training efforts have fallen short of their objectives. Some researchers even contend that the average new doctoral degree recipient in psychology is only slightly more competent to effectively address the mental health needs of culturally diverse populations than psychologists who completed their training 20 years ago.

Future Directions

It is evident that the field of multicultural counseling has grown significantly in the last 30 years. Some researchers contend that this field represents one of the most vigorous areas of practice-related theory and research today. Given the prevailing needs and changes in society, future research directions could likely include endeavors in the following areas: multiracial identity development, multicultural health counseling, effectiveness of group interventions with multicultural populations, increased prevention and intervention efforts earmarked for youth from multicultural backgrounds, and the use of indigenous models of mental health interventions.

Bibliography

Atkinson, D., & Hackett, G. (1997). *Counseling diverse populations* (2nd ed.). Dubuque, IA: Brown & Benchmark. This book directs the attention of mental health practitioners to the unique experiences and needs of four groups within American society who, along with racial and ethnic groups, share common experiences of oppression: persons with disabilities, elders, women, and gay people.

Dana, R. H. (1993). *Multicultural assessment perspectives for professional psychology.* Boston: Allyn & Bacon. This book meets the need to understand how to apply existing assessment instruments and current research on new assessment instruments to several major cultural groups in American society.

Ivey, A. E, Ivey, M. A., & Simek-Downing, L. (1987). *Counseling and psychotherapy: Integrating skills, theory and practice.* Englewood Cliffs, NJ: Prentice Hall. This text offers its readers a learning tool that is a merger of counseling theories and therapeutic skills, including extensive typescripts to illustrate the actual interview process and the specifics of each theory. Additionally, it includes information on family therapy, multicultural concerns, and feminist concerns.

Lee, C. C., & Richardson, B. L. (Eds.). (1991). *Multicultural issues in counseling: New approaches to diversity.* Alexandria, VA: American Association for Counseling and Development. Each chapter reviews the sociocultural dynamics of a specific racial or ethnic group and discusses the challenge of such dynamics within the context of counseling. The contributors introduce and explore strategies and techniques for addressing these challenges.

Leong, F. T. L. (Ed.). (1995). *Career development and vocational behavior of racial and ethnic minorities.* Hillsdale, NJ: Erlbaum. This book serves as a comprehensive source of knowledge on the career development of racial and ethnic minorities. It is a timely resource for counselors and psychologists who provide career counseling to racial and ethnic minorities and who conduct research on the career development of these diverse groups.

Pedersen, P. B., Draguns, J. G., Lonner, W. J., & Trimble, J. E. (Eds.). (1996). *Counseling across cultures* (4th ed.). Thousand Oaks, CA: Sage. This book examines the cultural context of accurate assessment and appropriate interventions in counseling. This text can serve as a guide for counseling practitioners, a source for researchers and professors, and a resource for students in counseling, psychology, and social work.

Ponterotto, J. G., & Casas, J. M. (1991). *The handbook of racial/ethnic minority counseling research.* Springfield, IL: Thomas. The authors integrate research, theory, and practice devoted to racial and ethnic minorities and racial ethnic minority counseling. This handbook is a comprehensive how-to guide for conducting culturally sensitive, relevant, and meaningful counseling research with American racial and ethnic minority populations.

Ponterotto, J. G., Casas, J. M., Suzuki, L. A., & Alexander, C. M. (Eds.). (1995). *Handbook of multicultural counseling.* Thousand Oaks, CA: Sage. This book offers a compendium of information about recent advances in theory, research, practice, and training for students and professionals in counseling and related disciplines. It covers a variety of topics, including racial and ethnic identity development, multicultural supervision and training, practical strategies for multicultural counseling, multicultural perspectives on assessment, multicultural counseling with children and adolescents, and other critical and emerging topics in multicultural counseling.

Pope-Davis, D. B., & Coleman, H. K. (1997). *Multicultural counseling competencies: Assessment, education and training, and supervision.* Thousand Oaks, CA: Sage. This text is divided into three sections: assessment of multicultural counseling competence, multicultural education and training, and multicultural supervision. It is well grounded in the theory and research of multicultural counseling and can be used as a practical guide for professionals to develop multicultural competence in their faculty, students, curriculum, fieldwork, and supervision.

Sue, D. W. & Sue, D. (1990). *Counseling the culturally different: Theory and practice* (2nd ed.). New York: Wiley. This book covers theoretical and practical issues related to counseling culturally different clients. The authors discuss the political and racial biases inherent in the mental health field and emphasize the need for developing culture-specific communication and helping styles for culturally different clients.

J. Manuel Casas and Carla Victoria Corral

MULTICULTURAL EDUCATION. In the late 1960s, theories and practices of multicultural education entered American schools as a result of the Civil Rights Movement, the 1968 Bilingual Education Act, and the resurgence of progressive education ideas from the 1920s. The catalyst that brought these three movements together was the inequity in education between poor and ethnic minority children and their European American, middle-class peers. This inequitable education was marked by achievement gaps and a cultural deprivation analysis of ability. Initially multicultural education theorists and practitioners focused on correcting the inaccurate portrayals and omissions of ethnic minorities in the curriculum. The emphasis later shifted to equitable and appropriate instructional strategies.

In the early 1990s, as multicultural education gained momentum in the schools, gaps between theorists and practitioners emerged. Theorists moved toward the transformation of schools through culturally pluralistic curricula, instructional strategies, staffing, programming, and policies. Practitioners, on the other hand, seem entrenched in the lifestyle approach which highlighted the histories, heritages, traditions, and customs of ethnic minorities. Unfortunately, this lifestyle approach perpetuated an additive mode (e.g., celebratory months) as opposed to an integrative mode (e.g., multiple perspectives in a thematic unit of study). At the same time that these internal tensions between theorists and practitioners were developing, multicultural education faced external challenges in the form of heated debates in the press and among academicians. The press charged multicultural education with the balkanization of the United States. Academicians like historians Arthur Schlesinger and Diane Ravitch criticized the intellectual rigor of multicultural education. These scholars based their criticisms on several kindergarten through twelfth grade curriculum guidelines and diversity courses in higher education. Schlesinger, Ravitch, and others ignored the large body of research and theoretical works by such multicultural education scholars as James Banks, Geneva Gay, and Christine Bennett. Banks, Gay, and Bennett are some of the founding proponents of multicultural education. Since the 1970s they have been prolific in their theoretical and empirical scholarship. They have also been leaders in articulating the nature and goals of multicultural education.

Nature and Goals of Multicultural Education

James Banks's *Introduction to Multicultural Education* (Boston, 1999) outlines five dimensions of multicultural education: equity pedagogy, empowerment, knowledge construction, content integration, and prejudice reduction. Equity pedagogy involves teachers modifying their teaching to facilitate the academic achievement of culturally diverse students. Empowerment is the deliberate promotion of gender, racial, and social class equity. Knowledge construction means teachers have to facilitate students' understanding of how the implicit cultural assumptions, perspectives, and biases within a discipline influence the ways in which meaning is constructed. In content integration, teachers use culturally diverse examples and content to illustrate key concepts, principles, generalizations, and theories in their subject area. Prejudice-reduction teaching strategies help students to develop more positive attitudes about culturally diverse individuals and groups.

In her book, *At the Essence of Learning: Multicultural Education* (West Lafayette, IN, 1994), Geneva Gay maintains that multicultural education "builds on the assumption that teaching and learning are invariably cultural processes" (p. 3). She presents multicultural translations of general education principles related to human growth and development as well as pedagogy. The principles are organized under the following themes: holistic growth, universal psychological needs and developmental tasks, identity development, individ-

uality and universality, equity and excellence, developmental appropriateness, and teaching the whole child.

In *Comprehensive Multicultural Education: Theory to Practice* (Boston, 1986/1999), Christine Bennett describes multicultural education as a set of knowledges, skills, and attitudes that are integrated to achieve the following goals: (1) build a movement toward achieving educational equity; (2) design and implement curricula to focus on developing knowledge and understanding about cultural differences and the history and contributions of contemporary ethnic groups and nations; (3) facilitate the process by which an individual develops competencies in multiple ways of perceiving, evaluation, believing, and doing; and (4) support the commitment to combat racism and other forms of discrimination.

The following definition of multicultural education is extrapolated from Banks's dimensions, Gay's themes, and Bennett's goals. Multicultural education is an inclusionary, empowering, and transformative approach to teaching and learning that promotes teaching to *and* about cultural diversity. It is designed to encourage acceptance of diversity in others while advocating the maximization of each individual's potential. One aim of multicultural education is equity and excellence for students from all ethnic-racial, gender, and class groups. Achieving unity in diversity is the other aim of multicultural education; it requires an engagement in additional ways of knowing, thinking, and being. In the aforementioned diversity debates of the early 1990s, conservative critics asserted that differences divide, tribalize, and balkanize the United States. This assertion was based on an inability to reconcile unity with diversity because of a worldview that assumes embracing another's understanding of the world means abdicating one's own value system. Unity and diversity are complementary, not oppositional, forces. Diversity can be used to build community. Furthermore, celebration of human commonalities can only occur when human differences are recognized and respected. Inclusionary, empowering, and transformative multiculturalism extends beyond tolerance by emphasizing multivocality as a central force in the construction of a communal "American" identity.

As multicultural education enters the twenty-first century, it is struggling with an internal debate among scholars, researchers, and practitioners regarding the clarity and scope of its focus. While most would agree with the definition presented above, some would find it too restrictive and others would find it too inclusive. The internal debate centers on the following question: What are the boundaries of cultural diversity and multivocality? Even the leading scholars in the field (those who were its founding proponents) are not united in their response to this question. James Banks and Cherry McGee Banks present social class, religion, gender, race-ethnicity, language, and exceptionality as the scope of multicultural education (*Multicultural Education: Issues and Perspectives*, Boston, 1989/1993). Donna Gollnick and Phillip Chinn discuss issues related to differences in social class, race-ethnicity, gender, exceptionality, religion, and age (*Multicultural Education in a Pluralistic Society*, Upper Saddle River, NJ, 1983/1998). Throughout her body of work, Geneva Gay limits the scope of multicultural education to focus on race-ethnicity; she includes gender and social class as they intersect with race and ethnicity. More recently, a few theorists and practitioners have asserted that multicultural education should be inclusive of sexual orientation as a category of cultural diversity.

Multicultural Education and Psychology

Historical trends and the definition of multicultural education presented here most directly connect the field to the cross-cultural, social, and cognitive strands of psychology. Culture is a focal concept in multicultural education. Race-ethnicity (includes language, national origin, region, and religion), gender, and class are the predominant categories of diversity. Culture, race-ethnicity, gender, and social class are also key variables in cross-cultural and social psychology research. Cognitive psychology is concerned with knowledge construction and knowledge transmission. Multicultural education considers these aspects of cognition as they are affected by the social contexts of home, school, and society. Culturally relevant pedagogy and assessment are two strategies for resolving cognitive conflicts that may develop as individuals move between the three environments.

A Concept of Culture

As with most abstract concepts, no one definition of culture is espoused by social scientists, not even anthropologists. In *Culture, Language, and Society* (Menlo Park, CA, 1980), anthropologist Ward Goodenough presents a model of culture that provides a very useful framework for understanding how cultural diversity, from the individual to collective levels, affects teaching and learning. Goodenough contends that culture consists of a set of standards for deciding: (1) what is, (2) what can be, (3) how one feels about it, and (4) how to go about doing it. Grounded in linguistic theory, the model aligns the content of culture with the content of language and describes the ways in which these standards are formulated, accounting for both behavioral and nonbehavioral aspects of human experience. Goodenough's model also locates culture within the individual. As individuals, people use standards to organize their experiences to give them meaning and structure, or a subjective view of the world. This subjective view is the individual's propriospect which is used for perceiving, evaluating, and attributing standards for

others. A group of individuals who share standards is a cultural group. However, a propriospect is an individual's unique view of the world. In Goodenough's model, culture is not a static product, but a dynamic process. Individuals belong to a number of microcultural groups (e.g., African American, middle class, southern, female). In the contexts of our interactions (e.g., schools) we have an opportunity to constantly create culture by way of multiple acculturations. A proactive approach to this process requires an understanding of the propriospects that individuals and the standards that cultural groups bring to the table. Multiculturalists view the United States as a pluralistic society composed of a macroculture (communal American identity) and many microcultures (referred to in cross-cultural psychology as *subcultures*).

Culturally Relevant Pedagogy

Numerous studies have been conducted on the interaction of cultural diversity and learning. Three patterns emerge from these studies: (1) cultural discontinuities appear across the full range of teaching and learning interactions; (2) discontinuities between culturally different students and classroom teachers are especially evident in verbal interactions; and (3) participation structures, learning styles, and intragroup variation are cultural characteristics that contribute to cultural discontinuities. Cultural discontinuities are defined here as mismatches between individual propriospects and/or cultural group standards. Cultural discontinuities adversely affect how students learn; ethnic minority, poverty disadvantaged, and female students have been the most adversely affected in our schools. Equity pedagogy, or culturally relevant teaching and learning, involves teachers modifying their strategies to facilitate the academic achievement of culturally diverse students. Culturally relevant pedagogy promotes cultural synthesis instead of cultural discontinuity by reaffirming cultural competencies brought to school from the home and community contexts. These competencies include cultural identity and learning styles.

The concept of cultural identity is connected to Erik H. Erikson's psychosocial development theory and the symbolic interactionist orientation in social psychology. Erikson was one of the first developmental psychologists to emphasize the effect of society on identity formation (*Identity: Youth in Crisis*, New York, 1968). A basic tenet in symbolic interactionism is the reciprocal relationship between self and society. Identity theory stresses the multiplicity of selves located within an individual, defined by the number of structured relationships (or groups) to which one belongs. In multicultural education, identity development focuses primarily on the microcultural groups related to race-ethnicity, gender, and social class.

There is a substantial body of scholarship related to

ethnic-racial and gender identity development. Cultural identity scholars include psychologists Stephen Bailey, Robert Carter, William E. Cross, Janet E. Helms, and Charles W. Thomas. Multicultural education scholars who examine cultural identity include Geneva Gay and James Banks. Gay has developed a synergetic model of racial-ethnic identity development which uses Goodenough's concept of propriospect to explain how contextual (family, community, school) interpretations of race and ethnicity can positively or negatively affect the development of an individual's sense of ethnic self. The model involves three stages: preencounter, encounter, and postencounter. In Stage 1, the individual is basically a psychological captive who passively conforms to externally defined roles. The individual experiences a conscious confrontation with his or her ethnicity in Stage 2 and responds by rejecting Anglo-conformity (assimilation) and focusing on ethnicity as his or her identity referent. Stage 3 represents the internalization of a positive ethnic self, which consists of defining one's own ethnicity and accepting the right of self and others to be different. Teachers can use an understanding of the relationship between ethnic identity development and learning to develop culturally relevant strategies that will help ethnic minority students realize their full potential (see C. R. Baber, "Ethnic identity development and literacy education," *Reading Psychology: An International Quarterly*, 1992, 13, 91–98).

Since the 1970s numerous studies have examined the nature and salience of cultural identity development. Only recently, however, has the emphasis shifted from a conceptual to empirical study of the relationship between cultural identity formation and student learning; educational anthropologists like Margaret Gibson, Signithia Fordham, and John Ogbu have led this research effort. Multicultural theorists and practitioners need to work together to conduct ethnographic studies of the relationship between cultural identity formation and pedagogy.

The relationship between learning styles and culture, on the other hand, has received a preponderance of attention. Psychologists and educators agree that learning style refers to an individual's consistent preference for approaching learning experiences and involves the cognitive, affective, and physiological dimensions of learning. Multicultural education scholar James Anderson maintains that "for women and people of color many cognitive decisions and processes are influenced by affective considerations that are culturally influenced" (In R. R. Sims & S. J. Sims, Eds., *The Importance of Learning Styles*, Westport, CT, 1995). Manuel Ramirez and Alfredo Casteneda in their seminal work, *Cultural Democracy, Bicognitive Development, and Education* (New York, 1974), found that the interaction of cultural values and socialization behavior affects children's learning styles. Other psychologists and multiculturalists support the conclusions of Anderson, Ramirez, and Casteneda (see the work of Janice Hale-Benson, Valerie Ooka Pang, Barbara Shade, and Karen Swisher, for example).

There are a plethora of instruments available to teachers for ascertaining their students' learning styles. In *Comprehensive Multicultural Education*, Bennett provides a detailed description of four strategies and concomitant instruments for identifying and understanding learning styles: (1) field-independent, field-sensitive; (2) students' need for structure; (3) perceptual modalities, and (4) learning styles inventory. Many of the instruments, however, have been criticized for weaknesses related to construct validity. According to critics the constructs of style (learning preferences) and ability (learning competencies) are often confounded in these instruments. Perhaps multicultural educators, cognitive psychologists, and psychometricians need to collaborate in the development of more valid instruments for assessing learning styles.

Multicultural education scholars caution that although learning styles research provides another important way for understanding and responding to the needs of culturally diverse students, it should be appropriately employed as a means to an end and not the end itself. Summaries of the learning styles of African American, Latino/Latina, and Native American students conclude that individuals from these three ethnic minority groups tend to be field-sensitive learners. Such ethnic group patterns should be the starting point for making pedagogical decisions. Teachers then need to consider other individual differences such as gender and social class. They also need to think about the learning situation or task. For example, a middle-class Latina student may be more field-independent in learning literature, but more field-sensitive in learning mathematics. Multicultural theorists and practitioners need to collaborate in the design and implementation of research projects that (1) examine the effect of learning styles on student achievement and (2) clearly delineate the relationship between learning styles and learning ability.

Culturally Relevant Assessment

Assessment in education has been largely defined by psychological tests and measurements of ability (intelligence, achievement, and aptitude). Up until the 1950s the inherent ethnocentrism and scientific racism of these assessments were not contested. Recently, cognitive psychologists like Howard Gardner and Janet E. Helms have criticized the traditional constructs and measurements of cognitive ability.

Gardner's theory of multiple intelligences expands the concept of intelligence and connects it to culture.

Helms points out (*American Psychologist*, 1992, 47, 1083–1102) the dearth of empirical studies of cultural equivalence in standardized cognitive ability testing. She blames this absence on the lack of alternatives to the statistical approaches to such investigation and the inability of psychologists or psychometricians to recognize and articulate the relevant issues as they affect ethnic minorities. The charge of cultural bias in standardized tests of ability has been refuted by such psychologists as Arthur Jensen. He presents technical arguments that emphasize objective statistical tests of bias and he dismisses cultural bias as a popular, political hypothesis. The cultural bias debate centers primarily on race-ethnicity and social class, virtually ignoring gender in discussions of the adverse effects of standardized testing (see G. Boutte, *Multicultural Education: Raising Consciousness*, Belmont, CA, 1999 for an analysis of gender differences on standardized tests). Although cognitive ability tests are still widely used, they are being interpreted with a higher degree of caution and cultural awareness.

Alternative assessment has been an integral part of the 1990s educational reform movement. This approach deemphasizes standardized testing in favor of strategies more authentic to the context and situation. Gardner's multiple intelligences as well as various learning styles have been used as frameworks for developing authentic assessment strategies including projects, products, and observations. Cognitively guided instruction (CGI), a concept borrowed from research in mathematics education (see the work of mathematics educators Elizabeth Fennema and George W. Bright), can also help teachers assess how students learn by employing a structured interview approach.

Like culture and learning, assessment is a complex, dynamic, and multidimensional process. While there are many resources which demonstrate how to develop and implement culturally relevant teaching strategies (descriptions of some of these are included in the bibliography), few discuss culturally relevant assessment. This gap needs to be remedied by way of empirical studies of the interaction between culture, learning, and assessment. In the meantime multicultural educators (theorists and practitioners) can work together to extrapolate culturally relevant assessment strategies from the scholarship on cultural identity, learning styles, and alternative assessment.

[*See also* Ethnopedagogy.]

Bibliography

Banks, J. A., & Banks, C. M. (Eds.). (1995). *Handbook of research on multicultural education.* New York: Macmillan.

Cole, R. (Ed.). (1995). *Educating everybody's children: Diverse teaching strategies for diverse learners.* Alexandria, VA: Association for Supervision and Curriculum Development. Concise presentation of strategies for increasing the achievement of culturally diverse learners in reading, writing, mathematics, and oral communication.

Davidman, L., & Davidman, P. T. (1997). *Teaching with a multicultural perspective: A practical guide* (2nd ed.). New York: Longman. Offers a clear model for creating effective instruction in culturally diverse middle grades and secondary classrooms. The model is based on a set of field-tested planning questions and is linked to a series of curriculum case studies.

Gay, G., & Baber, W. L. (Eds.). (1987). *Expressively Black: The cultural basis for ethnic identity.* New York: Praeger. A collection of 14 chapters that examines the relationship between African American identity and kinship, leadership, communication, religion, and other cultural values

Kappa Delta Pi. (1994). *Insights on diversity.* West Lafayette, IN: Author. Essays by 45 experts that offer snapshots on the theory and practice of multicultural education concepts including learning styles, aspects of ethnicity, culturally relevant teaching, affirming languages, and so on.

Ladson-Billings, G. (1994). *The dreamkeepers: Successful teachers of African American children.* San Francisco: Jossey-Bass. Useful for teachers, administrators, parents, teacher educators, and researchers who want to understand the complexity of student-teacher interpersonal and pedagogical relationships in attaining equity and excellence in education.

Larkin, J. M., & Sleeter, C. E. (Eds.). (1995). *Developing multicultural teacher education curricula.* Albany, NY: State University of New York Press.

Nieto, S. (1996). *Affirming diversity: The sociopolitical context of multicultural education* (2nd ed.). New York: Longman. Based on an extensive case study research base of 12 high-school students across gender, racial-ethnic, and social class lines. Students' voices are integrated with the author's analysis of the impact of racism, teacher expectations, language, social class, and school structure on learning.

Sleeter, C. E., & Grant, C. A. (1998). *Making choices for multicultural education: Five approaches to race, class, and gender* (3rd ed.). Columbus, OH: Merrill Education. An analysis of the theory and practices of five major approaches to dealing with diversity that have evolved over the almost 30-year history of multicultural education.

Takaki, R. (1993). *A different mirror: A history of multicultural America.* Boston: Little, Brown. A look at 500 years of America's history from the perspective of non-Anglo people, including Native Americans, African Americans, Jews, Irish Americans, Asian Americans, and Latinos.

Tiedt, P. L., & Tiedt, I. M. (1999). *Multicultural teaching: A handbook of activities, information, and resources* (5th ed.). Boston: Allyn & Bacon. Focuses on how to incorporate multicultural content across the curriculum. Provides a knowledge base for extensive studies of gender, Native Americans, African Americans, and Latinos/Latinas.

Ceola Ross Baber

MULTICULTURALISM. *See* Cultural Pluralism.

MULTIMODAL THERAPY (MMT) is a psychotherapeutic approach that places most of its theoretical underpinnings within a broad-based social and cognitive learning theory but draws on effective techniques from many disciplines without necessarily subscribing to their particular suppositions (i.e., it espouses technical, but not theoretical, eclecticism; Lazarus, 1992). MMT is predicated on the assumption that most psychological problems are multifaceted, multidetermined, and multilayered and that comprehensive therapy calls for a careful assessment of seven parameters, or "modalities"—behavior, affect, sensation, imagery, cognition, interpersonal relationships, and biological processes. The most common biological intervention is the use of psychotropic drugs. The first letters from the seven modalities yield the convenient acronym BASIC I.D., although it must be remembered that the D modality represents the entire panoply of medical and biological factors.

The multimodal approach developed mainly from clinical follow-ups that showed a fairly high relapse rate in patients who received "narrow-band" rather than "broad-spectrum" treatment. Addressing the usual A-B-C variables (affect, behavior, cognition), as many systems do, tends to overlook or omit significant sensory, imagery, interpersonal, and biological issues. Untreated excesses and deficits in these areas of human functioning may leave patients vulnerable to backsliding. It is assumed that the more a patient learns in therapy, the less likely he or she is to relapse. In other words, therapeutic breadth is emphasized (Lazarus, 1992, 1997). Over many years, Lazarus's follow-ups have revealed more durable treatment outcomes when the entire BASIC I.D. is assessed and when significant problems in each modality are remedied, but this remains to be demonstrated in controlled outcome studies.

MMT is, in a sense, a misnomer because there is no actual treatment method that is totally distinctive to this approach. There are, however, distinct assessment procedures that tend to facilitate treatment outcomes by pinpointing the selection of appropriate techniques and their best mode of implementation. In MMT, one endeavors to use, whenever possible and applicable, empirically supported methods.

Unique Elements

There is considerable overlap between MMT and cognitive-behavior therapy (CBT), but only MMT clinicians use the following specific procedures:

1. A method called tracking may be used when clients are puzzled by affective reactions: "I don't know why I feel this way"; "I don't know where these feelings are coming from." The client is asked to recount the latest untoward event or incident. He or she is then asked to consider what behaviors, affective responses, images, sensations, and cognitions come to mind. Thus, a client who reported having panic attacks "for no apparent reason" was able to put together the following string of events.

She had initially become aware that her heart was beating faster than usual. This brought to mind an episode when she had passed out after imbibing too much alcohol at a party. This memory or image still occasioned a strong sense of shame. She started thinking that she was going to pass out again, and as she dwelled on her sensations this only intensified and culminated in her feelings of panic. Thus, she exhibited an S-I-C-S-A pattern (sensation, imagery, cognition, sensation, affect). Thereafter, she was asked to take careful note whether any subsequent anxiety or panic attacks followed a similar "firing order." She subsequently confirmed that her two trigger points were usually sensation and imagery. This alerted the therapist to focus on sensory training techniques (e.g., diaphragmatic breathing and deep muscle relaxation) followed immediately by imagery training (e.g., the use of coping imagery and the selection of mental pictures that evoked profound feelings of calm).

2. Second-order BASIC I.D. assessments may be conducted when therapy falters. For example, an unassertive person who is not responding to the usual social skills and assertiveness training methods may be asked to spell out the specific consequences that an assertive modus vivendi might have on his or her behaviors, affective reactions, sensory responses, imagery, and cognitive processes. The interpersonal repercussions would also be examined, and, if relevant, biological factors would be determined. Quite often, this procedure brings to light the reasons behind such factors as noncompliance and poor progress (see Lazarus, 1997).

3. A 35-item Structural Profile Inventory (SPI) yields a quantitative BASIC I.D. diagram depicting a person's degree of activity, emotionality, sensory awareness, imagery potential, cognitive propensities, interpersonal leanings, and biological considerations (Lazarus, 1997). The SPI is particularly useful in couples therapy, where differences in the specific ratings reflect potential areas of friction. Discussion of these disparities with clients can result in constructive steps to un-

derstand and remedy them. Herman (1993) and Landes (1988) have established the reliability and validity of the SPI. Herman has also shown that client-therapist similarity on the SPI is predictive of psychotherapy outcome (1991, 1997).

The BASIC I.D. lends itself to other assessment and treatment tactics that keep the clinician on track and enable him or her to address issues that might otherwise have been glossed over. Lazarus presents these methods in some detail (1997).

Research Findings on Overall Effectiveness

Although it is difficult to study the impact of an entire clinical armamentarium such as MMT, researchers in Holland and Great Britain have nevertheless attempted to do so. Kwee, a Dutch psychologist, obtained encouraging results when conducting a controlled-outcome study using MMT with severe obsessive-compulsive patients, as well as a group of extremely phobic individuals (1984). In a carefully controlled outcome study, Williams, a Scottish psychologist, compared MMT with other treatments in helping children with learning disabilities. He emerged with clear data pointing to the efficacy of MMT in comparison to the other methods (1988).

Research may determine when a more highly focused approach yields better outcomes than a broader MMT process. When treating bulimia nervosa and benign insomnia, a concentrated treatment focus seems to be indicated.

In essence, it should be understood that MMT is a comprehensive orientation that is extremely flexible and ardently strives to match the best and most effective methods with the appropriate treatment style for each individual.

Bibliography

Herman, S. M. (1991). Client therapist similarity on the Multimodal Structural Profile as predictive of psychotherapy outcome. *Psychotherapy Bulletin, 26,* 26–27.

Herman, S. M. (1993). A demonstration of the validity of the Multimodal Structural Profile through a correlation with the Vocational Preference Inventory. *Psychotherapy in Private Practice, 11,* 71–80.

Herman, S. M. (1997). Therapist-client similarity on the Multimodal Structural Profile Inventory as a predictor of early session impact. *Journal of Psychotherapy Practice and Research, 6,* 139–144. In 43 therapist-client pairs, dissimilarity was never associated with higher levels of client satisfaction and rapport, whereas similarity was significantly predictive of better rapport from the very outset.

Kwee, M. G. T. (1984). *Klinishe multimodale gedragtstherapie.* Lisse, The Netherlands: Swets & Zeitlinger. This Dutch book describes the successful application of multimodal therapy to 44 severe obsessive-compulsive patients and 40 extremely phobic individuals in a general psychiatric hospital.

Landes, A. A. (1988). *Assessment of the reliability and validity of the Multimodal Structural Profile Inventory.* Doctoral dissertation, Rutgers University, New Jersey.

Lazarus, A. A. (1992). Multimodal therapy: Technical eclecticism with minimal integration. In J. C. Norcross & M. R. Goldfried (Eds.), *Handbook of psychotherapy integration* (pp. 231–263). New York: Basic Books. Summarizes the basic multimodal approach and spells out the precise advantages, disadvantages, and differences between technical eclecticism and integration.

Lazarus, A. A. (1997). *Brief but comprehensive psychotherapy: The multimodal way.* New York: Springer. Presents the multimodal orientation and shows how one may apply short-term therapy without cutting corners.

Williams, T. (1988). *A multimodal approach to assessment and intervention with children with learning disabilities.* Unpublished doctoral dissertation, University of Glasgow, Scotland.

Arnold A. Lazarus

MULTIPLE INTELLIGENCES. In the human sciences, questions arise about the intellect—what it consists of, how it works, how it develops, how to strengthen it. Addressing these questions invokes a second and ultimately more vexing set of questions. How to measure human intellect? How to ensure that assessments are valid and reliable? Accordingly, scientifically oriented theories of human intelligence are inexorably linked to a model of intellectual assessment of one sort or another.

Recent historical reviews of the scientific study of intelligence show a dominant position, one favoring a general factor of intelligence ("g") and a particular brand of psychometric tests (e.g., IQ tests) to measure it. Beginning with the work of Alfred Binet in the early days of the twentieth century, researchers and educators have focused on a single, flexible form of "general intelligence" thought to operate across the range of tasks and content areas encountered by human beings. This emphasis on general intelligence has been accompanied by a set of measurement tools in the form of intelligence tests (e.g., Stanford–Binet, Otis–Lennon Scales). Patterned after the methodological rigor of "hard sciences" such as physics, intelligence testing involves pencil-and-paper instruments that enable large numbers of individuals to be evaluated inexpensively and in a short period. In the wake of the original IQ tests, a variety of similarly crafted test instruments have been devised to evaluate school performance, employment aptitudes, and other outcomes.

The traditional model of intellect and its assessment have been criticized. A number of researchers have put forth "pluralistic" theories of human intelligence that question the explanatory power of "g" and posit the existence of special-purpose modules that govern thinking in specific content areas, such as mathematical and spatial reasoning (Anderson, 1992; Ceci, 1996; Fodor, 1983; Guilford, 1967; Karmiloff-Smith, 1992; Thurstone, 1938). In addition, psychometric tests have come under scrutiny on questions of validity, especially tests such as the Scholastic Aptitude Test (SAT), that weigh heavily in educational decisions (Gardner, 1998). In particular, questions arise concerning the extent to which tests capture the full range of human abilities in a valid and reliable manner.

Among the more radical of these pluralistic approaches, the theory of multiple intelligences (MI) calls into question both the explanatory value of "g" and the utility of traditional psychometric models of intellectual assessment (Gardner, 1983, 1993, 1998).

Questioning General Intelligence

Around the world, one sees a great many intelligent performances in action. Of course, what passes for intelligent depends on the setting; an intelligent action in, say, New York, may do little good in the Himalayas. Only in a cultural context can intellectual activities be deemed valuable or intelligent. Accordingly, MI puts forth a broad definition of intelligence: a psychobiological potential that can be activated to solve problems or fashion products that are valued in one or more cultural settings (Gardner, 1983, 1993). The term *intelligence* is used as a means of organizing and describing human potentials in relation to the cultural contexts in which they are developed, used, and given meaning.

To examine the full range of intelligent performances of which human beings are capable, Gardner conducted an extensive inventory that departs from traditional theory and research in intelligence (Gardner, 1983). Drawing on diverse sources of empirical evidence (e.g., brain research, studies of exceptional individuals, research on the development of specific cognitive capacities, and cross-cultural investigations of problem-solving), he specified eight criteria that must be met by a candidate intelligence. This analysis yielded a list of eight relatively autonomous intelligences—autonomous in that one cannot predict strength or weakness in one intelligence from strength or weakness in another, and relative in that, in practice, intelligences make use of some of the same processes (e.g., that musical rhythm has mathematical components). According to Gardner, it is unnecessary and misleading to suggest the complete autonomy of intelligences.

Before discussing the criteria and intelligences, however, it is important to note that MI is empirical though not experimental in the usual sense of the term. It is not the kind of theory that can be proved or disproved by a crucial experiment, but it is subject to supporting or invalidating evidence. MI works by establishing a set of criteria for what constitutes an intelligence; additional information, experimental or otherwise, could have an impact on the resulting list of intelligences and the relations that obtain among them.

Eight Criteria of an Intelligence and Sources of Evidence

1. *Potential isolation by brain damage.* Evidence for the autonomy of intelligences is seen in the sparing or breakdown of a capacity after brain damage due to stroke or injury. For example, brain-injured musicians may have impaired speech yet retain the ability to play music; in other cases, language is spared and musical ability is lost (Sergeant, 1993; Hodges, 1996).

2. *The existence of savants, prodigies, and other exceptional individuals.* Studies of special populations also lend support for MI. For example, savants are individuals of low attainment, sometimes classified as retarded, who demonstrate remarkable skills in one isolated ability. They are often skilled in only a small part of a discipline (e.g., some individuals cannot add but they can calculate prime numbers). Findings based on exceptional individuals suggest that the "core operations" of the intelligences (e.g., tonal apprehension in music) may be more autonomous, and some of the ancillary operations (e.g., musical phrasing) are somewhat less autonomous.

3. *Support from experimental psychological tasks.* Research in experimental psychology also points to autonomous intelligences. For example, studies in which subjects are asked to carry out two tasks simultaneously indicate that some abilities operate autonomously while others appear to be linked by the same underlying mental operations (Brooks, 1968). Findings such as these suggest that certain musical, linguistic, and spatial information–processing operations are carried out independently.

4. *Support from psychometric findings.* Psychometric findings also provide support for MI. Gardner has criticized psychometric assessment as taking too narrow a sample of human abilities, but certain abilities within the province of these tests have proven to be autonomous. Factor analyses generally support the existence of two "big group" factors—verbal and spatial.

5. *A distinctive developmental history, along with a definable set of end-state performances.* Another source of evidence for an intelligence is a characteristic developmental trajectory leading from basic and universal manifestations to one or more possible expert end states. For example, spoken language develops quickly and to a high level of competence in normal people. In

contrast, while all normal individuals can count small quantities, few progress to higher mathematics even with formal schooling.

6. *An evolutionary history and evolutionary plausibility.* Evolutionary biology is an additional if more speculative source of evidence for MI. The existence, for example, of bird song suggests the presence of a separate musical intelligence, and there are strong continuities in the spatial abilities of humans and other primates. Other intelligences, such as intrapersonal and linguistic, may be distinctly human.

7. *An identifiable core operation or set of operations.* Each intelligence must have one or more basic information-processing operations or mechanisms that are activated by specific types of input (activated internally or externally). The intelligences are not input systems per se; rather, they are potentials, the presence of which allows individuals to activate forms of thinking appropriate to specific forms of content. Hence, MI is consistent with information-processing accounts of human cognition.

8. *Susceptibility to encoding in a symbol system.* An intelligence must also be susceptible to encoding in a symbol system—a culturally created system of meaning that captures and conveys important forms of information (e.g., language or mathematics). The relationship of a candidate intelligence to a cultural symbol system is no accident. The existence of a core computational capacity anticipates the existence of a symbol system that exploits that capacity. "Symbol systems have evolved in just those cases where there exists a computational capacity ripe for harnessing by culture. A primary characteristic of human intelligence may well be its 'natural' gravitation toward embodiment in a symbol system" (Gardner, 1993, p. 66).

The Eight Intelligences

These criteria and their attendant sources of evidence converge to support a set of eight intelligences, as follows.

1. *Linguistic intelligence* describes the ability to perceive or generate spoken or written language. Linguistic intelligence is exemplified by poets, lawyers, and journalists.
2. *Logical/mathematical intelligence* involves using and appreciating numerical, causal, abstract, or logical relations. It figures heavily in mathematics, science, and engineering.
3. *Spatial intelligence* describes the ability to perceive visual or spatial information, to transform and modify this information, and to recreate visual images even without reference to an original physical stimulus. Spatial intelligence is used in sculpture, architecture, surgery, and navigation.
4. *Musical intelligence* refers to the ability to create, communicate, and understand meanings made out of sound. It can be seen in musicians but also can be discerned outside the musical sphere (e.g., auto mechanics and cardiologists make diagnoses based on careful listening to patterns of sound).
5. *Bodily/kinesthetic intelligence* involves controlling all or part of one's body to solve problems or fashion products. It is used, for example, in athletics, dance, surgery, and dramatic performances.
6. *Interpersonal intelligence* involves the capacity to recognize and make distinctions among the feelings, beliefs, and intentions of other people and use this knowledge to work effectively in the world. Interpersonal intelligence enabled individuals such as Winston Churchill or Mohandas K. Gandhi to communicate with others and succeed in their work.
7. *Intrapersonal intelligence* enables individuals to form a mental model of themselves and to draw on the model to make decisions about viable courses of action. The core operations of intrapersonal intelligence include the capacity to distinguish one's feelings and to anticipate reactions to future courses of action.
8. *Naturalist intelligence* involves the ability to understand and work effectively in the natural world (Gardner, 1998). A recent addition to the list of intelligences, naturalist intelligence is exemplified by biologists, zoologists, and naturalists.

Other intelligences have been proposed, including an "existential" intelligence, concerned with the individual's relation to his or her own consciousness and purpose in the world (Gardner, 1998). Humans are unique in having awareness of their own existence. This evolved potential may have resulted in an autonomous intelligence activated when individuals reflect on the origins and meaning of life. However, because there is no neurobiological evidence relevant to this capacity, it is best to consider this a "candidate" for an intelligence.

Clarifications

Because of their common names, it is inviting to confuse intelligences with domains. As noted, intelligences are psychobiological potentials; in contrast, domains are socially organized areas of expertise. A domain such as mathematics can involve several intelligences (e.g., spatial or linguistic). Similarly, particular intelligences can be used in several domains (note the examples of spatial and bodily kinesthetic intelligence).

MI takes an explicitly developmental view of human abilities. In their initial states, the intelligences are uncommitted potentials for processing particular kinds of information. In the course of development, they are activated and developed—indeed, shaped—by the activities in which the individual participates. These grow out of the surrounding culture and organize how the intelligence will be used and combined.

The intelligences should be conceptualized in two ways. First, they can serve as a taxonomy of the cognitive capabilities of *Homo sapiens*; all normal human beings have these eight sets of intellectual potentials. Second, the intelligences provide a framework for conceptualizing individual differences. By virtue of biology and experience, individuals differ in terms of a current spectrum of intelligences, and no two people are identical.

Questioning Traditional Methods of Intellectual Assessment

The heart of MI is the claim that apparent support for "g" may be an artifact of the procedures and instruments used in cognitive research. Psychometric tests are paper-and-pencil exercises that rely heavily on linguistic and logical-mathematical abilities. Accordingly, individuals who are strong in these areas perform well on tests of general intelligence, and individuals whose gifts lie elsewhere perform more poorly. Of course, schools often place a premium on the mental operations inherent in linguistic and logical-mathematical tasks, and therefore psychometric tests can predict school success with some accuracy. Predicting success outside the classroom has proven more difficult for psychometricians, however. On average, less than one quarter of the variance in job performance is accounted for by scores on cognitive ability tests (Hunter & Hunter, 1984; Wigdor & Garner, 1982). Put the other way, three quarters of the variance in job performance falls outside the skills captured on tests. Clearly, there is more operating in adult success than the academic skills captured on psychometric tests.

Results as such have prompted Gardner to question not just the utility of "g," but the notion of psychometric testing as well. Hence, developing a set of eight assessment instruments—one for each intelligence—is not a useful strategy. To begin with, a single intelligence is an inappropriate unit of analysis for research on normal intellectual development. According to Gardner, single intelligences are visible only in exceptional ("freak") cases, in which mental disease or accident renders an intelligence apart from the rest and allows activity to take place that grows out of a single faculty. Studies of exceptional cases provide a window on the structure of the human intellectual endowment, but they do not present a valid indication of the way the intelligences work when unimpaired individuals combine them in activities in a domain. Complex performances can be understood only by recognizing the combination of intelligences involved. For example, skill in the practice of law cannot be predicted by administering a battery of separate tests, one for each of the intelligences required by the discipline (e.g., linguistic, logical-mathematical, interpersonal). Only an assessment that captures the combination of constituent intelligences can predict who will succeed.

Not only is the single intelligence of limited use as a unit of analysis; certain intelligences are also difficult to test directly. The personal intelligences and musical or bodily expression are not well suited to direct testing. For example, it would be difficult to devise a valid test that captures the lawyer's skill in matters interpersonal (e.g., predicting a jury's response to a particular argument).

A departure from psychometrics as usual, MI calls for a broad shift in assessment practices. Needed are fair intelligence assessments that look directly at an individual's skills instead of through the window of linguistic or logical-mathematical intelligence. In particular, fair intelligence assessment has two requirements. First, procedures should be contextualized (or authentic), assessing individuals in situations that more closely resemble working conditions typical of the domain. For example, a better assessment of the lawyer's work focuses on the activities that practitioners in this domain actually do (e.g., analyzing relevant facts in a case or interacting with clients and colleagues). Second, fair intelligence assessments are ongoing, not of the one-shot variety. Even if tests could be devised to capture, for example, the lawyer's work, a single test administration could not capture long-term aspects of the target performance (e.g., degree of motivation or ability to bring difficult projects to fruition). Only by assessing the individual over time, using multiple measures, can a true measure be taken. The term *performance assessment* is often used to describe such contextualized and ongoing assessment procedures.

Relation of MI to Other Pluralistic Theories of Intelligence

There are some pointed contrasts between MI and other pluralistic models of human intelligence. In particular, MI differs from multifactorial approaches to intellect (e.g., Anderson, 1992; Guilford, 1967; Thurstone, 1938). First of all, these models do not share MI's repudiation of general faculties, such as perception and memory, which may cut across content areas. Multifactorial theories typically intermingle general faculties with those that reflect a content area, such as spatial or linguistic abilities. Second, multifactorial approaches grant a limited role for development, while MI assumes important developmental changes of the intelligences. Third, unlike MI, the multifactorial approach is strictly psychometric—focusing on the correlations among test scores—and thus makes little contact with evolutionary biology or studies of human culture. Finally, the multifactorial approach does not allow the full range of intellectual competences to be considered. Drawn from research methodologies that focus on paper-and-pencil tests or brief interviews, these approaches are precluded from examination of an individual's competence in a number of faculties, such as personal intelligences and musical or bodily expression.

MI is somewhat more consistent with pluralistic theories proposed by Karmiloff-Smith (1992) and Ceci (1996). These models share with MI a skeptical view of the explanatory power of "g," a developmental perspective, and the view that human intellect must be explained in relation to the ambient cultural context. Furthermore, Gardner concurs with Karmiloff-Smith, that at least one strand of development moves in the direction of systems that are increasingly modular (1992). What Gardner has termed later-developing modularity (the development of expertise in domains) is consistent with Karmiloff-Smith's notion of modularization (Torff & Gardner, 1999). At the same time, MI differs from Karmiloff-Smith's model; in particular, MI requires no domain-general processes such as the "representational redescription" posited by Karmiloff-Smith. MI also has much in common with Ceci's bioecological view of intelligence (Ceci, 1996). His model calls for multiple cognitive potentials, as does MI, which goes on to specify a set of intelligences according to explicitly stated criteria.

Educating the Intelligences

MI was put forth as a psychological theory, not an educational one, but the theory has a number of implications for educational practices. To begin with, it is imperative to view the intelligences as means, not ends. The first order of business in education is the goal (or end state) that the culture or community deems important; once specified, it becomes possible to analyze the intelligences that are typically involved and to design vehicles for curriculum and assessment that activate them as they serve the end state. For example, the ability to write clearly is a valued skill, and whereas linguistic intelligence is in the forefront, writing also involves logical-mathematical, interpersonal, and intrapersonal intelligences. An educational scheme should address all these intelligences, not as goals themselves but as the pillars that support the valued target skill—writing ability. In short, the prudent policy involves teaching through (not for) intelligences.

Second, MI calls for educators to provide multiple entry points to learning, that is, offer learners a variety of ways to approach subject matter. For example, learning history by reading a text will be effective for students strong in linguistic intelligence, but other students thrive when the curriculum is expanded to include activities that draw on other intelligences (e.g., drawing maps, writing plays). Providing multiple entry points creates a learning environment favorable to students with diverse profiles of intelligences.

Finally, MI asks educators to reconsider "factory" approaches to education (in which groups of students inevitably engage in the same activity) and instead place greater emphasis on individual-centered instruction. In particular, it can be beneficial to design individually

crafted "bridging activities" for students, especially those at risk for school failure. Bridging activities draw together intelligences in which the student is stronger with the student's weaker areas so that the weaker areas are strengthened through activity sustained by the stronger ones. For example, "dot math" integrates logical-mathematical, spatial, and interpersonal intelligences to enhance math learning for third graders. In dot math, pairs of students solve a set of math problems, with each student completing one of two columns. When completed, the two columns provide the coordinates for dots that students place on a dot grid located on the answer sheet. When students connect the dots, an image (e.g., a dog or boat) emerges. Dot math increases time-on-task in math by bridging from logical-mathematical intelligence to spatial intelligence (fixing the dots and watching the image emerge) and interpersonal intelligence (working in pairs to establish the coordinates).

MI can inspire innovative and effective vehicles for curriculum and instruction, but it is in assessment that the theory's most important educational implications lie. In essence, the theory encourages educators to reconsider the current widespread reliance on standardized tests. These shortchange students by capturing too narrow a range of intelligences and working in a decontextualized and single-administration manner. Moreover, since test scores are so highly prized, there is impetus in schools to boost scores by "teaching for the test," often reducing education to rote memorization of target facts. MI encourages educators to turn to fair intelligence assessments that capture intellectual achievements in context and over time.

Conclusion

A newcomer to the longstanding debate on human intelligence, MI charts new territory by posing a reconfiguration of not only the structure of human intellect, but also its measurement. Distinctive among the pluralistic models of intelligence, MI posits a set of eight intellectual competences based on eight criteria for faculties that constitute a human intelligence. It is also innovative in terms of methods, questioning the utility of psychometric tests and calling for intelligence-fair performance assessments. In the end, it challenges psychologists and educators to account for the full range of human potentials, even those traditionally overlooked and not easily measured.

Bibliography

Anderson, M. (1992) *Intelligence and development. A cognitive theory.* Oxford, UK: Blackwell.
Brooks, L. (1968). Spatial and verbal components of the act of recall. *Canadian Journal of Psychology, 22,* 349–350.

Ceci, S. (1996). *On intelligence . . . more or less.* Cambridge, MA: Harvard University Press.

Gardner, H. (1983). *Frames of mind: The theory of multiple intelligences.* New York: Basic Books.

Gardner, H. (1993). *Multiple intelligences: The theory into practice.* New York: Basic Books.

Gardner, H. (1998). Are there additional intelligences? The case for naturalist, spiritual, and existential intelligences. In J. Kane (Ed.), *Education: Information and transformation.* Englewood Cliffs, NJ: Prentice Hall.

Guilford, J. (1967). *The nature of human intelligence.* New York: McGraw-Hill.

Hodges, D. (1996). Neuromusical research: A review of the literature. In D. Hodges (Ed.), *Handbook of music psychology* (2nd ed., pp. 197–284). San Antonio, TX: IMR Press.

Hunter, J., & Hunter, R. (1984). Validity and utility of alternative predictors of job performance. *Psychological Bulletin, 96,* 72–98.

Karmiloff-Smith, A. (1992). *Beyond modularity.* Cambridge, UK: Cambridge University Press.

Sergent, J. (1993). Music, the brain, and Ravel. *Trends in Neurosciences, 16,* 5.

Thurstone, L. L. (1938). *Primary mental abilities. Psychometric Monographs* (No. 1).

Wigdor, A., & Garner, W. (Eds.). (1982). *Ability testing: Uses, consequences, and controversies.* Washington, DC: National Academy Press.

Torff, B., & Gardner, H. (1999). The vertical mind: The case for multiple intelligences. In M. Anderson (Ed.), *The development of intelligence.* London: University College Press.

Bruce Torff

MULTIPLE PERSONALITY DISORDER. *See* Dissociative Identity Disorder.

MULTIPLE REGRESSION. Multiple regression analysis characterizes the relationship of a set of variables $(X_1, X_2 \cdots X_p)$ to a single variable Y. The Xs are termed *predictors* or *independent variables; Y* is called the *criterion, outcome,* or *dependent variable.* In commonly used regression models predictors may be continuous variables like age or a test score or categorical variables like gender or experimental treatment groups; the dependent variable is continuous. Multiple regression yields an overall correlational measure, R, of the extent of relationship of the set X to the variable Y. Multiple regression also yields estimates of the extent to which each individual X variable contributes to this overall relationship.

Multiple regression analysis is one of the most commonly used data analytic strategies in psychology. Three levels of application of multiple regression are possible, of which the third contributes most to the development of psychology as a basic science: (1) *description,* to provide a statistical summary of the relationship of the Xs to Y; (2) *prediction,* to provide an equation that generates predicted scores on some future outcome (e.g., job performance) based on the observed Xs; and (3) *explanation or theory testing.* In the third application, the sign and magnitude of predicted relationships of Xs to Y can be tested using the actual observed data.

In multiple regression, a *regression equation* is developed that quantitatively summarizes the relationship of the set of Xs to Y:

$$\hat{Y}_i = b_0 + b_1 X_{i1} + b_2 X_{i2} + \cdots + b_p X_{ip} \qquad (1)$$

The equation produces a *predicted score* $\hat{Y}_i$ for case i, which is a linear combination of the Xs. Weights $b_1, b_2, \ldots b_p$ termed *partial regression coefficients,* are assigned to predictors according to a statistical criterion. The *regression constant* b_0 represents the value of $\hat{Y}_i$ when all Xs equal zero. The *residuals* $(Y_i - \hat{Y}_i)$, discrepancies between observed and predicted scores, represent errors in prediction and form the basis of *regression diagnostics* to identify statistical difficulties with regression analysis.

The statistical adequacy of a regression model is evaluated through statistical and graphical examination (*regression graphics*) of the fit of the regression model to the data. The *squared multiple correlation* (R^2), the squared correlation between observed Y and predicted $\hat{Y}$, is a single number summary ranging between 0 and 1, indicating the proportion of variance in the criterion accounted for by the set of predictors.

A predictor set may be divided into two or more conceptually meaningful subsets. *Hierarchical regression analysis* is used to characterize the contribution of a subset B of predictors to prediction over and above another subset A. The *squared multiple partial correlation* ($R^2_{partial}$) then measures the extent to which subset B accounts for residual variance in the criterion not accounted for by subset A.

Multiple regression is a very general and flexible data analytic approach. Predictors may be mixtures of continuous and categorical variables. Relationships of individual predictors to the criterion may be linear or nonlinear. The predictors may have only first order (main) effects on the criterion, as in Equation 1, or they may interact with one another, as in the equation $\hat{Y}_i = b_0 + b_1 X_i + b_2 Z_i + b_3 X_i Z_i$, in which the cross product XZ represents the interaction between X and Z. Although the basic multiple regression model considers only continuous dependent variables, it may be generalized to consider dependent variables that represent binary or ordered categories, counts, or the elapsed time before an event occurs, if ever (*survival analysis*).

Types of Regression Analysis

Ordinary least-squares regression (OLS) is the most common form of multiple regression used in psychology. With a continuous criterion and mixtures of continuous and categorical predictors, the regression coefficients are chosen to minimize the sum of squared *residuals*, $\Sigma(Y_i - \hat{Y}_i)^2$, the OLS criterion. *Robust regression* alternatives to OLS may be used with a continuous criterion when OLS residuals indicate statistical difficulties in the regression analysis. When the dependent variable is not continuous, other alternatives to OLS are used. *Logistic regression* is often used when the dependent variable is binary or otherwise categorical, and predictors are mixtures of continuous and categorical variables. *Poisson regression* may be employed when the dependent variable is a frequency count. *Log linear models* summarize the relationships of a set of categorical predictors to a count of the number of cases in a series of cells defined by the categorical predictors. A special class of these models, *logit models*, summarizes the relationships of a set of categorical predictors to a categorical dependent variable.

In *linear regression*, the regression equation is linear in the coefficients, that is, the regression coefficients enter the regression equation only as multipliers of predictors, as in Equation 1. Equivalently, the predicted score is a linear combination of the Xs. Nonlinear relationships of predictors to the criterion are handled by creating nonlinear functions of the Xs (e.g., log X, X^2), which are used as predictors, as in the *polynomial regression* equation $\hat{Y}_i = b_0 + b_1 X_i + b_2 X_i^2$. *Nonlinear regression* characterizes nonlinear relationships of Xs to Y in equations that are nonlinear in the coefficients, so that predicted scores are generated as nonlinear combinations of the predictors. In psychology, these models historically have been most commonly used to represent growth toward a maximum value (asymptote). For example, the logistic growth model is specified as follows:

$$\hat{Y}_i = \frac{c}{1 + e^{b_0 + b_1 X_i}} \tag{2}$$

Standard regression models assume that the observations are independent of one another, that is, that the data from each case are not contingent on the values of these measures for any other case. Data may be nonindependent because of *clustering*; either because the cases are sampled from common units (e.g., students in a classroom) or because the same individual is measured at repeated times. Extensions of regression analysis, *hierarchical linear models*, or *multilevel models* statistically handle this nonindependence and permit simultaneous examination of the effects of predictors measured at both upper (e.g., classroom) and lower (e.g., student) levels of aggregation. When a large number (e.g., more than one hundred) of observations that are equally spaced over time (temporal time series) are collected on a single unit, *time series analysis* may be performed. Time series analysis permits examination of relationships between independent and dependent variables after proper adjustment for complex patterns of nonindependence in data.

Multiple regression analysis can be extended to the case of sets of both X and Y variables. *Canonical analysis* assesses the extent and form of relationship between a set of Xs and a set of Ys, measured by a series of *canonical correlations*. *Set correlation* serves a similar purpose, with one set designated as a predictor set. *Multivariate multiple regression* refers to a simultaneous series of regressions of a common set of predictors on a series of criteria.

Differences Among Groups

Equation 1 is referred to as the *general linear model*. *Analysis of variance* (ANOVA) is a special case of the general linear model with a single continuous dependent variable Y; predictors are categorical variables that represent factors of a design, as well as functions of the factors, e.g., interactions between factors. *Analysis of covariance* (ANCOVA) extends ANOVA to include a set of predictors that consists of covariates or control variables; in ANCOVA, the effects of the categorical variables are examined over and above the effects of the covariates.

Multivariate analysis of variance (MANOVA) extends ANOVA to the case of multiple criteria $Y_1, Y_2, \cdots Y_q$, with the predictors again categorical variables representing the factorial structure of a design. The impact of the factors on the set of criteria, considered simultaneously, is the focus of MANOVA. *Multivariate analysis of covariance* (MANCOVA) extends MANOVA to include a set of covariates that is controlled when the impact of the factors on the set of criteria is assessed. *Discriminant function analysis* examines whether intact groups of individuals can be distinguished statistically on a set of measures, and can be conceptualized as the prediction of group membership from a set of predictors. Discriminant analysis typically refers to the two group case; *multiple discriminant analysis* refers to three or more groups. Closely aligned with discriminant analysis is *classification analysis*, which examines the extent to which actual group membership can be accounted for by the set of measures.

Structural Equation Modeling

Structural equation modeling (SEM) examines the extent to which a well-formulated theoretical model consisting of explicitly hypothesized relationships among a set of variables is reproduced in the observed data. Structural equation models were earlier called *causal models*. However, SEM can only reject particular models as implausible; it cannot confirm that a particular model is the correct model. These techniques historically also were termed *LISREL models* after the first of several now widely distributed computer programs that permit their estimation.

The SEM model consists of two components. The *measurement model* characterizes the relationships of a series of measured variables to underlying, unobserved *latent constructs* (or factors). The *structural model* (or *path model*) specifies the relationships among the constructs; it typically consists of a concatenated series of regression equations, in which the dependent variables from early equations in the stream become predictors in later equations. In the most rudimentary form of SEM, there is only one measured variable per construct; thus, only the structural model is estimated, an analysis historically termed *path analysis*. The chief potential advantages of the SEM approach are the ability to address measurement error in the observed variables and to specify constraints on the models (e.g., setting regression coefficients equal to a priori values).

Bibliography

Works on Multiple Regression Analysis

Aiken, L. S., & West, S. G. (1991). *Multiple regression: Testing and interpreting interactions.* Newbury Park, CA: Sage. Provides a complete development of methods for specifying, testing, and interpretating interactions among continuous variables and between continuous and categorical variables in multiple regression analysis.

Cohen, J., & Cohen, P. (1983). *Applied multiple regression/correlation analysis for the behavioral sciences* (2nd ed.). Hillsdale, NJ: Erlbaum. The leading reference text in regression analysis in psychology for two decades; includes a complete nonmathematical development of multiple regression, hierarchical regression, treatment of continuous and categorical predictors, statistical power analysis for multiple regression.

Cook, R. D., & Weisberg, S. (1994). *An introduction to regression graphics.* New York: Wiley. Characterizes the use of modern regression graphics to aid in exploring and understanding relationships among variables and to diagnose difficulties in regression analysis; provides intuitive introductions to key plots in common use.

Neter, J., Kutner, M. H., Nachtsheim, C. J., & Wasserman, W. (1996). *Applied linear regression models* (3rd ed.). Chicago, IL: Irwin. Exceptionally thorough, modern reference text in multiple regression analysis, including diagnostic and remedial measures, and introductions to time series, nonlinear regression, logistic and Poisson regression.

Pedhazur, E. J. (1997). *Multiple regression in behavioral research: explanation and prediction.* (3rd ed.). Fort Worth, TX: Harcourt Brace. Standard reference work in multiple regression analysis for psychology and education, newly revised to include topics of current interest, regression diagnostics, logistic regression, multilevel analysis.

Works on Regression with Categorical Variables

Agresti, A. (1996). *An introduction to categorical data analysis.* New York: Wiley. Well-organized overview, covering generalized linear models, including logistic and Poisson regression, loglinear models, logit models; nonmathematical and highly accessible.

Hosmer, D. W., & Lemeshow, S. (1989). *Applied logistic regression.* New York: Wiley. Thorough overview of logistic regression, including interpretation, model building, assessment of fit, introduction to polytomous logistic regression.

Works on Multivariate Analysis

Stevens, J. (1996). *Applied multivariate statistics for the social sciences* (3rd ed.). Mahwah, NJ: Erlbaum. Accessible treatment of multivariate analyses for differences among groups, including multifactor multivariate analysis of variance for nonrepeated and repeated measures, discriminant analysis, plus coverage of other topics in multivariate analysis; provides thorough documentation of multivariate analysis with two leading statistical computer packages.

Tabachnick, B. G., & Fidell, L. S. (1996). *Using multivariate statistics* (3rd ed.). New York: HarperCollins. Extensive, nonmathematically written reference text for the full range of multivariate procedures including multiple regression, canonical analysis, analysis of covariance, MANOVA, MANCOVA, repeated measures, discriminant function analysis, logistic regression, principal components and factor analysis, with an introduction to structural equation modeling; excellent documentation of multivariate analysis with the four leading statistical analysis computer packages.

Works on Structural Equation Modeling

Bollen, K. A. (1989). *Structural equations with latent variables.* New York: Wiley. Standard reference work in structural equation modeling, quite mathematical; covers full complement of topics in SEM.

Loehlin, J. C. (1992). *Latent variable models: An introduction to factor, path, and structrural analysis* (2nd ed.). Hillsdale, NJ: Erlbaum. Broad and accessible introduction to structural equation modeling and factor analysis.

Schumacker, R. E., & Lomax, R. G. (1996). *A beginner's guide to structural equation modeling.* Mahwah, NJ: Erlbaum. Basic introduction to structural equation modeling with computer examples from two leading structural equation modeling software packages.

Leona S. Aiken and Stephen G. West

MULTIPLE TASK PERFORMANCE. The study of multiple task performance, or time-sharing, addresses the issues underlying how well (or poorly) people perform two or more tasks either concurrently, or sequentially, but close together in time. The domain is related to the study of attention, because multiple task performance is often said to require dividing attention between two or more activities. The time-sharing decrement is a critical concept in the study of time-sharing. It is the difference in performance between a task performed alone, and when it is time-shared with one or more additional tasks. When this decrement is zero on both tasks within a time-shared pair, perfect parallel processing is said to take place.

The study of multiple task performance can be categorized into two general areas: one identifies properties of one or both tasks in a time-shared pair that determine the size of the dual task decrement (time-sharing efficiency). The second examines the attention control or workload management strategies that people adopt when they are in a time-sharing overload situation.

Causes of the Dual Task Decrement

Three general factors have been identified that influence the ease or difficulty of time-sharing: automaticity, multiple resources, and task similarity (Wickens, 1992). Automaticity is closely (and reciprocally) related to the difficulty, mental effort, or attention resource demands of a member of a time-shared task pair (Kahneman, 1973). Highly automated tasks are generally those that are well practiced, like walking, and hence can be easily time-shared because they demand few cognitive resources, which can then be allocated to other concurrent activities (like talking or thinking). Tasks that are less automated are more likely to interfere with other activities. Thus, a novice driver for whom steering is not automated is less able than a skilled driver to converse with a passenger.

Human performance does not depend upon a single kind of attention resource, but instead demands various (multiple) resources (Navon & Gopher, 1979; Wickens, 1992). Two tasks that demand more common resources will show larger dual task decrements than two that demand separate resources. There are a variety of different views on what constitutes the important resources, whose multiplicity determines time-sharing efficiency. One view focuses on the stages of information processing, noting that when people try to perform two reaction time tasks at the same time, they are unable to select the response for both tasks simultaneously, even though response selection may be able to proceed in parallel with perceptual processing (Pashler, 1998). This situation may be modeled in terms of separate resources for information encoding, and action selection. Another view focuses on the different resources for perceptual or sensory modalities, noting that access to fo-

veal vision is very limited and cannot easily be time-shared between tasks. Hence we cannot easily read two passages at once. Auditory processing is also a limited resource. Hence we cannot listen to two speakers at once; but with somewhat greater (but not perfect) success, we can listen and read concurrently. A third view focuses on the different resources used for linguistic or verbal processing and for spatial or analog processing, noting the greater success of time-sharing a spatial and verbal task, than two spatial tasks or two verbal ones. This distinction has been closely associated with different systems in working memory, different cerebral hemispheres, and different response modalities (voice versus hands). The use by two different tasks of separate resources does not guarantee perfect parallel processing, but generally produces better time-sharing than when common resources are used.

Features of similarity between the information used for two tasks, or between their stimulus-response mappings, or between their timing, also influence their time-sharing efficiency. It is hard, for example, to rehearse a phone number while listening to the scores of a game, but somewhat easier to rehearse the number while listening to a verbal description. It is easier to tap two similar (harmonically related) rhythms than two different ones.

Attention Control

When humans encounter a multiple task overload, such that the attention demands of a pair of tasks exceed the capacity, they can adopt various *strategies* of attention control (Adams, Tenney, & Pew, 1991). For example, they may choose to protect the more important task of a pair by allocating sufficient resources to it, and allowing a large decrement on the less important task. They may choose to allocate the decrement equally to both; or they may choose to *postpone* the performance of one task entirely, until the other has been completed. Here the study of multiple task performance broadens from that of concurrent performance to a consideration of *sequential* performance, and makes relevant two additional psychological issues. The first of these is understanding how people *switch* attention between tasks. Here evidence suggests that it is more difficult and time-consuming to switch between two very different tasks than between similar ones.

The second issue raised in the study of sequential performance is the question of *scheduling* tasks. How do people choose the order of tasks to perform, that may vary in their time of arrival, importance, and difficulty? While few general conclusions have emerged from research on how people schedule multiple tasks, one clear finding is that more nearly optimal attention control is an important feature that distinguishes better (and more practiced) dual task performers from those who are less skilled (Damos, 1991). Thus the expert driver will not only be able to perform steering at a more automatized level, but will also be able to schedule glances down from the road to the speedometer or rearview mirror, at more nearly optimum times.

Applications

The study of multiple task performance has helped psychologists to understand better the breakdowns in this performance in high workload conditions, like driving a car through heavy traffic, flying an aircraft, taking notes in class, or processing feedback while learning an athletic skill. In some circumstances it has suggested ways in which the design of the task environment or the training program can be altered to bring about greater success in time-sharing, through deployment of multiple resources, or through training to develop automaticity and improve attention control. An important application is in developing measures to assess the resource demand or mental effort required to perform different tasks, the domain of mental workload measurement (Hancock & Meshkati, 1988).

Bibliography

Adams, M. J., Tenney, Y. J., & Pew, R. W. (1991). *Strategic workload and the cognitive management of advanced multitask systems* (State of the Art Report SOAR-CSERIAC 91–6). Dayton, OH: Crew System Ergonomics Information Analysis Center. Describes applied implications of strategies for attention control.

Damos, D. (Ed.). (1991). *Multiple task performance*. London: Taylor & Francis. Contains a set of chapters by different authors on various facets of this topic including automaticity, multiple resources, workload, and attention control.

Hancock, P. A., & Meshkati, N. (Eds.). (1988). *Human mental workload*. Amsterdam: North Holland. A good review of various workload measurement techniques.

Kahneman, D. (1973). *Attention and effort*. Englewood Cliffs, NJ: Prentice Hall. Presents a theoretical overview of the topic.

Navon, D., & Gopher, G. (1979). On the economy of the human processing system. *Psychological Review, 86,* 214–255. Provides the theoretical foundations for the concept of multiple resources.

Parasuraman, R., Davies, R., & Beatty, J. (Eds.). (1984). *Varieties of attention*. New York: Academic Press. Does the same as Damos's book for the related field of attention.

Pashler, H. (1998). *The psychology of attention*. Cambridge, MA: MIT Press. An excellent integration of theoretical research in attention.

Wickens, C. D. (1992). *Engineering psychology and human performance* (2nd ed.). New York: HarperCollins. Contains chapters describing the applied implications of attention, time-sharing, and multiple resources.

Christopher D. Wickens

MÜNSTERBERG, HUGO (1863–1916), German American psychologist. Münsterberg was born in Danzig, Germany, the son of Moritz Münsterberg, a lumber merchant, and Minna Anna Bernhardi, an artist.

According to biographer Matthew Hale, Jr., when Münsterberg died, "he was arguably the best-known psychologist in America and the most prominent member of America's largest minority, the German-Americans" (1980, p. 3). Those two roles—psychologist and spokesperson for Germany—defined Münsterberg's life in America.

Münsterberg entered the University of Leipzig in 1882 to study medicine, but he switched to psychology in the summer of 1883 after taking a course from Wilhelm Wundt, whose Leipzig laboratory, founded in 1879, is frequently acknowledged as the beginning of scientific psychology. Münsterberg worked in the experimental psychology of the laboratory, principally on questions of the will. He completed his doctoral degree with Wundt in 1885. After receiving his medical degree at the University of Heidelberg in 1887, he accepted a position at the University of Freiburg. There he married Selma Oppler on 7 August 1887.

Münsterberg quickly established a reputation based on his opposition to Wundt's ideas about voluntary action, arguing that the will was not directly experienced but was the result of the perception of changes in muscles, joints, and tendons. His research gained considerable attention within German psychology and led to Münsterberg's promotion to associate professor in 1892 at the age of 29. Münsterberg's psychology was also known outside of Germany and was particularly admired by William James, who had met him in 1889 and whose ideas on the experience of emotion were similar to Münsterberg's views on the experience of will. James invited him to come to Harvard University for a 3-year appointment to be director of Harvard's psychology laboratory.

Münsterberg's 3 years at Harvard were very successful. He was an especially popular teacher and was well regarded by his colleagues, although some were dismayed at his flamboyancy and his dogmatism. Harvard offered him a permanent position; however, his goal was a chair in psychology in Germany, and so he returned to Freiburg in 1895, taking a 2-year leave of absence from Harvard and indicating that he would decide between America and Germany by that time. When the professorship in Germany was not forthcoming, Münsterberg returned to Harvard, where he spent the rest of his life. He reasoned that if he could not live his life in Germany, then he would bring the best of Germany to America. What America needed, Münsterberg believed, was Germany's social idealism, and he made that his lifelong project. Toward that end, he began his dual career of psychologist and popular writer.

Münsterberg's first book in English, published

shortly after his return to Harvard, was *Psychology and Life* (Boston, 1899) and consisted of six essays, four of which had already been published in the popular press. He described the purpose of this book as "a scientific synthesis of the ethical idealism with the physiological psychology of our days" (p. vii). The book was well received and established Münsterberg as a psychological expert with the public. Invitations for public lectures, inquiries from the press, and consulting opportunities in business and industry increasingly came his way. Although initially disparaging of applied psychology, Münsterberg became one of its chief promoters, publishing a series of groundbreaking applied books: *On the Witness Stand* (New York, 1908), *Psychotherapy* (New York, 1909), *Psychology and the Teacher* (New York, 1909), *Psychology and Industrial Efficiency* (Boston, 1913), *Psychology and Social Sanity* (New York, 1914), and *Business Psychology* (Chicago, 1915).

In addition to his goals in applied psychology, Münsterberg sought to inform his native Germany of the strengths of American virtues, which he saw as an idealistic commitment to self-fulfillment. These virtues were described in his best known book, *Die Amerikaner* (1903), later translated into English as *The Americans* (New York, 1904), a book that established him as the chief interpreter of American culture to the Germans. However, as noted, Münsterberg was more interested in bringing America the advantages of German *Kultur*. After his return from Germany in 1897, he devoted considerable energies to this task via his writings in newspapers and popular magazines, public speeches, liaisons with political figures, and leadership within the German American community. As tensions in Europe grew in the early twentieth century, Münsterberg became more outspoken on behalf of Germany. He spent a year in Berlin in 1910–1911 to organize and direct the Amerika Institut, an entity of the Prussian Ministry of Education officially founded to improve cultural relations between Germany and the United States but with an obvious political agenda, given the growing tensions between Germany and England.

Münsterberg's actions on behalf of Germany caused serious problems for him with his Harvard colleagues as early as 1907 (although he had been accused of being a secret agent for Germany as early as 1901). Those difficulties escalated yearly. When war broke out in Europe in 1914, Münsterberg increased his political efforts on behalf of Germany, even while reducing his writing for the popular press. His views alienated many of his psychology colleagues and angered much of the American public, where groups called for his deportation. One Harvard alumnus threatened to withdraw a promised gift to Harvard of $10 million unless Münsterberg was dismissed from the faculty.

The last few years of Münsterberg's life were exceptionally stressful; ostracized by many of his colleagues, he withdrew from most campus life and devoted himself to his work on the psychology of motion pictures, *The Photoplay*, published in 1916. On a cold December day in 1916 he walked from his home to Radcliffe College where he was to teach a class. During the lecture he suffered a heart attack and died. He was 53 years old.

Although much of his life in America was filled with controversy over his role as an advocate for German causes, Münsterberg's reputation in psychology today stems from the historical importance of his applied work, particularly his work in business psychology. He is sometimes regarded as the founder of industrial/organizational (I/O) psychology, principally because of his 1912 book, in which treated many of the topics of contemporary I/O psychology and vocational guidance. Yet there were a number of American psychologists (for example, Harlow Gale, Walter Dill Scott, and Harry Hollingworth) already involved in applying the new psychology to the field of business by the time Münsterberg's book appeared. For a time the book was on the bestseller lists. Its import was the role it played in promoting the applications of psychology to business, and there is no doubt that Münsterberg's optimistic outlook for the field and his reputation with the public as an expert psychologist helped sell the American business community on the value of psychological science. The book focused on hiring and training the best worker to do the best work with the best possible outcome. He was especially interested in matching worker abilities to the requirements of the job, which he believed produced satisfied workers and good work output.

Another of Münsterberg's important applied works was his book *On the Witness Stand*, which dealt with topics such as the reliability of eyewitness testimony, the behavior of juries, and lie detection. Today, it is recognized as one of the earliest contributions to the modern fields of psychology and law and forensic psychology.

Münsterberg recognized the role of science in social engineering, and that recognition undergirded his career in applied research. He worked at a time when there was considerable reluctance in the scientific community of psychology to venture into applied work. Münsterberg (1913) wrote:

> The students of mental life evidently had the feeling that quiet, undisturbed research was needed for the new science of psychology in order that a certain maturity might be reached before a contact with the turmoil of practical life would be advisable. The sciences themselves cannot escape injury if their results are forced into the rush of the day before our fundamental ideas have been cleared up, the methods of investigation really tried, and am ample supply of facts collected. But this very justified reluctance becomes a real danger

if it grows into an instinctive fear of coming into contact at all with practical life. . . . For the sciences of the mind . . . the time has come when theory and practice must support each other. (pp. 6–7)

Münsterberg believed in the value of psychological science applied in the public sphere, and he promoted that belief endlessly. Despite the negative public opinion toward him in the last years of his life and the revisionist treatment of his psychological contributions after his death, there is no denying that he was a significant force in the growing professionalization of psychology in the twentieth century.

[*Many of the people mentioned in this article are the subjects of independent biographical entries.*]

Bibliography

Hale, M. Jr., (1980). *Human science and social order: Hugo Münsterberg and the origins of applied psychology.* Philadelphia: Temple University Press. The most complete treatment of the life and work of Münsterberg.

Keller, P. (1979). *States of belonging: German-American intellectuals and the first world war.* Cambridge, MA: Harvard University Press. Contains an extensive account of Münsterberg's political activities as a German in America.

Kucklick, B. (1977). *The rise of American philosophy.* New Haven, CT: Yale University Press. Focuses on the evolution of American philosophy at Harvard University. Chapter 11 treats Münsterberg's philosophical contributions to ethics, social idealism, and values in science.

Münsterberg, H. (1899). *Psychology and life.* Boston: Houghton Mifflin. Münsterberg's essays on psychology and life, physiology, education, art, history, and mysticism.

Münsterberg, H. (1908). *On the witness stand: Essays on psychology and crime.* New York: McClure Co.

Münsterberg, H. (1909). *Psychotherapy.* New York: Moffat, Yard, and Co. One of the earliest American books on psychotherapy, it was important in linking medicine and psychology.

Münsterberg, H. (1913). *Psychology and industrial efficiency.* Boston: Houghton Mifflin.

Münsterberg, M. (1922). *Hugo Münsterberg: His life and work.* New York: Appleton. A biography of Münsterberg written by his daughter, who later deposited her father's papers (more than 6,000 letters) in the Department of Rare Books and Manuscripts of the Boston Public Library.

Ludy T. Benjamin, Jr.

MURCHISON, CARL (1887–1961), American psychologist. Murchison received his doctorate in social psychology in 1923 from Johns Hopkins University. He moved to Clark University in Worcester, Massachusetts,

in June 1923 with the rank of professor, assuming the chair of the psychology department a year later.

Murchison is noted for having rebuilt the psychology department, which had once achieved eminence under its founder, G. Stanley Hall. Within 3 years of his arrival, Clark became a distinguished place for psychology once again and a center where the major rival viewpoints of psychology of the time, structuralism, behaviorism, and Gestalt psychology, were presented. His appointments included John Paul Nafe, an advocate of Edward B. Titchener's structural psychology, the distinguished behaviorist Walter S. Hunter, who accepted the newly established G. Stanley Hall Chair of Genetic Psychology, and Wolfgang Köhler, one of the founders of Gestalt psychology.

In addition to rebuilding the psychology department at Clark, Murchison's work as an editor and publisher is an accomplishment that few others have equaled. Upon Hall's death in 1924, Murchison assumed editorship of the *Pedagogical Seminary*, renaming it the *Journal of Genetic Psychology*. The money from the revamped journal was used to establish *Genetic Psychology Monographs*. At about the same time, he established the *Journal of General Psychology* with Titchener and the *Journal of Social Psychology* with John Dewey. During his last academic year at Clark, in 1935, he founded a fifth journal, the *Journal of Psychology*, as a private venture out of his own home.

In addition to his development of research journals, Murchison was responsible for the editorship of more than 12 handbooks as well as other resource materials. These included handbooks in the fields of experimental, child, and social psychology. Murchison was also editor of the first three volumes of *A History of Psychology in Autobiography* and two volumes of *The Psychological Register*.

Murchison's reputation as a researcher is more limited than his fame in establishing journals and developing resource materials. Early in his years at Clark, he published *Criminal Intelligence* (Worcester, Mass., 1926), and 3 years later *Social Psychology: The Psychology of Political Domination* (Worcester, Mass., 1929). Both books received mixed reviews. Perhaps his most successful publication was his collaboration with Suzanne Langer on the first English translation of Dietrich Tiedemann's 1787 publication, *Beobachtungen über die Entwickelung der Seelenfähigkeiten bei Kindern* (Observations on the Development of Mental Capabilities in Children), widely recognized as the first published psychological diary of development in children (1927, "Tiedemann's observations on the development of the mental facilities of children," *Journal of Genetic Psychology*, 34, pp. 205–230).

Murchison left Clark University in 1936, after a dispute with the administration. He spent the remainder of his life at his home in Provincetown, Massachusetts, where he continued to publish his five journals. While he is not remembered as a theorist or a researcher, he was an organizer of unusual ability. Every one of his five journals is still in existence, and his handbooks formed the basis for many of the contemporary resource books in the field.

[*Many of the people mentioned in this article are the subjects of independent biographical entries.*]

Bibliography

Koelsch, W. (1987). *Clark University: A narrative history.* Worcester, MA: Clark University Press. Contains an analysis of the psychology department under G. Stanley Hall, and Murchison's contributions during the years 1923–1936.

Koelsch, W. (1990). The "magic decade" revisited: Clark psychology in the twenties and thirties. *Journal of the History of the Behavioral Sciences, 26*, 151–175.

Thompson, D. (1996). Carl Murchison. In G. A. Kimble, C. A. Boneau, & M. Wertheimer (Eds.), *Portraits of pioneers in psychology* (Vol. 2, pp. 150–165). Washington, DC: American Psychological Association.

Dennis N. Thompson

MURPHY, GARDNER (1895–1979), American psychologist. Murphy was born in Ohio; after a short period in the South where his father worked for better race relations, Murphy spent most of his formative years in Concord, Massachusetts, with his mother's family in which individualistic and heterodox opinions were encouraged. His formal schooling included the Hotchkiss School (1910–1912), Yale (1912–1916), Harvard (1916–1917), and Columbia (1919–1923). From 1917 to 1919, he saw service with the U.S. Army in World War I in the Yale Mobile Hospital Unit. For 3 years, from 1922 to 1925, Murphy did psychical research at Harvard and taught psychology part-time at Columbia. In 1925, he was offered a full-time position at Columbia, which he accepted. That year he joined the Boston Society for Psychic Research, serving on its council during the society's existence.

Murphy taught at Columbia until 1940, when he left to become chairman of the newly established department of psychology at the City College of New York. With the revitalization of the American Society for Psychical Research in 1941, Murphy became chairman of its research committee, a post he held until he became president in 1965. In 1952, he left CCNY to become director of research at the Menninger Foundation in Topeka, Kansas, where he served until his retirement in 1968. Subsequently, he moved to Washington, D.C., where he gave courses at George Washington University until health problems caused him to cease in 1973.

In K. Clark's 1957 survey of American psychologists, Murphy ranked second only to Sigmund Freud in frequency of listing as the individual most influential in leading the respondents into psychology. [*See the biography of Freud.*] Students' appreciation of him as a teacher, as well as his functioning as an administrator, led to an increase in departmental size. For a number of years, Murphy's department at City College contributed the undergraduate background of more American doctorates in psychology than did any other college. His influence on psychology, rather than on psychologists, is difficult to appraise completely inasmuch as in addition to his many publications (his bibliography includes more than 200 items) he functioned as a "midwife for research" and often stimulated research ideas in others. Attention to his publications provide less ambiguous indices of his influence. His was the first of the history texts for modern psychology and it was sufficiently significant to appear in three editions over the decades from 1929 to 1972. His *Experimental Social Psychology* (New York, 1931, 1937), for which he was honored by Columbia with the Butler medal in 1932, did much to establish the field of social psychology with a broad framework. An early, and very widely used, technique for attitude measurement, the Likert method, initiated with Rensis Likert, was developed as a doctoral dissertation by Likert under Murphy's guidance and as part of his research project, which was reported as *Public Opinion and the Individual* (New York, 1938). His research studies and later books did much to provide a basis and guidance for the development of cognitive psychology. His encouragement of research and the initiation and development of biofeedback was noteworthy and gained him recognition by those in the field. In addition to these numerous specialized fields in which Murphy had significant influence, his theory of personality did much to integrate the general field of psychology as well as to establish a unique perspective within the framework of which many problems, glossed over by others, were illuminated.

Murphy, in his writings and his actions, emphasized the reciprocal relevance of the science of psychology for all humanity. Not only did psychology have significance and application to all people, everywhere, but psychology had to draw on the contributions of all people, everywhere. In his many books, including *Human Nature and Enduring Peace* (1945), *In the Minds of Men* (1953), and *Human Potentialities* (New York, 1958), Murphy successfully sought to bring psychology into the service of resolving the problems of humanity.

Bibliography

Murphy, G. (1947). *Personality: A biosocial approach to origins and structure.* New York: Harper.

Murphy, G. (with Solley, C. M.). (1960). *Development of the perceptual world*. New York: Basic Books.

Murphy, G. (1961). *The challenge of psychical research*. New York: Harper.

Murphy, G. (with Leeds, M.). (1975). *Outgrowing self-deception*. New York: Basic Books.

Murphy, L. B. (Ed.). (1989). *There is more beyond: selected papers of Gardner Murphy*. Jefferson, NC: McFarland.

Murphy, L. B. (1990). *Gardner Murphy: Integrating, expanding, and humanizing psychology*. Jefferson, NC: McFarland.

Eugene L. Hartley

MURRAY, HENRY ALEXANDER (1893–1988), psychologist-physician, biochemist, and Melville scholar. Murray was born on 13 May 1893, in New York City. His father was English, related to the fourth earl of Dunmore, and his mother was an American, the daughter of a wealthy New York financier. The oldest boy and middle of three children, he prepared at Groton Academy and entered Harvard College in 1911, graduating in 1915. By his own account, his biggest interests as an undergraduate remained rowing and social life. The only formal course he ever took in psychology was with Hugo Münsterberg, but he walked out after the first class when he found the material had no relevance to personal experience. In 1916 he married Josephine Lee Rantoul in Beverly Farms, Massachusetts. They moved to New York City, where Murray took an M.D. in 1919 from the College of Physicians and Surgeons and a master's degree from Columbia University in 1920. He followed with a surgical internship at Presbyterian Hospital and then returned to Harvard in 1921 to work for the physical chemist L. J. Henderson on empirical verification of the Hassalbach-Henderson equation. Here, more than a dozen variables in a sample of blood were measured simultaneously at different levels of chemical complexity, a model that Murray would later adapt to the multivariate study of personality as the basis for founding the new field of personology. Also in 1921, his only child, Josephine Lee Murray, was born, who also later became a physician.

From 1922 to 1926, Murray conducted biochemical research for Rockefeller University in New York City, studying aging in live chick embryos. He later said that 1925 was the fateful year that psychology exploded into his personal field of interest. That year he first met Christiana Morgan, a woman who was to become his spiritual partner, collaborator in psychology, and paramour for the next 40 years. On a trip abroad to study at Cambridge University his attention was first drawn under dramatic circumstances to the charismatic writings of Herman Melville. It was also the year that he first met Carl Gustav Jung, the Swiss psychiatrist and founder of analytical psychology, who was to become his lifelong friend and confidante. Also, according to one unconfirmed report, in 1925 Murray first met Sigmund Freud, and allegedly gave him a copy of *Moby-Dick*.

In 1926, Murray was called back to Harvard, and, through the influence of L. J. Henderson, became assistant to Morton Prince, renowned psychopathologist and former colleague of William James. Prince, at the end of his career, had just endowed the Harvard Psychological Clinic in the School of Arts and Sciences, the purpose of which was the scientific study of abnormal and dynamic psychology in a laboratory rather than a medical setting. From 1927 to 1928, Murray held the rank of instructor in abnormal and dynamic psychology, after which he was promoted to assistant professor. In 1928 he also received a Ph.D. in biochemistry from Cambridge University (Trinity College) and, back in the United States, succeeded Prince as director of the Harvard Psychological Clinic, a position which he held until 1937. In that ensuing period, among other events, Murray was B. F. Skinner's first psychology professor (in 1929) and gave Erik Erikson his first job (in 1933). He built up the clinic as a haven for Freudian and Jungian analysis in Boston, launched an entirely new era of personality psychology in the United States, created numerous professional opportunities for women in psychology, and collaborated with Christiana Morgan in creating the Thematic Apperception Test, one of the most successful and widely published of all projective devices in the history of psychology. Also during this period, along with Gardner Lindsey and Gordon Allport, he lent his considerable resources to validating one of the major scoring techniques for the Rorschach Ink Blot Test.

The late 1930s became a controversial period for Murray. In 1938, at the height of the behaviorist domination of experimental psychology, the conversion of the discipline to large sample statistics, and the exclusive study of the white rat, along with 50 collaborators, he published *Explorations in Personality*, which advocated an interdisciplinary team approach to the study of the individual at all levels of experience. Although praised by Allport as more like William James than any other psychologist at Harvard, and vilified by E. G. Boring and Karl Lashley as a mere playboy in soft science, Murray succeeded in winning reappointment, largely on the basis of support from Stanley Cobb in psychiatry and money pledged to Harvard from the Rockefeller Foundation. The compromise, however, was that he was only promoted to associate professor and without tenure. In response, he accepted the terms but resigned as director of the clinic. Thereafter, he turned his full-time attention to writing a psychoanalytic biography of Herman Melville, a single literary case study of his personological system. While this was never completed, through his vast network of colleagues in a number of different disciplines, the biography exerted a profound influence on the subsequent course of Melville scholarship, not the least of which was the introduction of psychoanalysis into American literary criticism.

In the early 1940s, Murray was recruited by the Office of Strategic Services (OSS) to develop tests to select secret agents for overseas work during World War II, and when the war ended he was sent on to China, where he launched a similar program to train members of Chang Kai Shek's army. For his war service he achieved the rank of lieutenant colonel and received the Order of Merit. The report of his training program, built on the theory of organismic and Gestalt psychology, appeared as *Assessment of Men* (OSS Assessment Staff, New York, 1948), produced with the assistance of James Greer Miller and others. Also at this time, he published *A Clinical Study of Sentiments* with Christiana Morgan, a follow-up study of his 1938 research. In 1948, Murray also returned to Harvard as a lecturer, and received tenure in that position. He later said that it was his time of greatest freedom, since he had few formal responsibilities and could concentrate on his own work. Finally, in 1950, he was promoted to full professor of clinical psychology.

In the decade that ensued, Murray immersed himself in elucidation of the Icarus complex, values and vectors of personality structure, myths and mythmaking, and several seminal statements on Melville. He also embarked on a 30-year study of personality in the dyadic encounter, an answer to critics' charges that his early work had been too focused on the individual alone. The basic paradigm developed around the theme of interpersonal stressful disputations, an experimental milieu in which the subject's life values were elicited and then challenged, with measurements of personality variables taken at a variety of different levels. Organized cohorts of Harvard subjects went through the procedure and continued to be tested at periodic intervals for memory of the event up to 25 years afterward. "Aspects of Personality," the major volume reporting the results of this study, was never completed due to the death of his wife in 1962, and a series of strokes Murray suffered in the early 1960s, followed by his retirement from teaching at Harvard.

For the remaining 25 years of his life, Murray continued to work on his projects—publishing a few of the most important kernels from the unfinished Melville biography, keeping up with his students, colleagues, and experimental subjects, and receiving dignitaries, both in psychology and psychiatry and society at large. He married again, to Caroline Fish, a mother of five chil-

dren and an accomplished child psychologist in her own right, who specialized in the treatment of childhood trauma from a Piagetian perspective. Murray also devoted himself to his most passionate causes, such as the antinuclear movement. In addition, he continued to foster the careers of younger psychologists, such as William Runyan and James Anderson, and to revel in the accomplishments of his older students who had carried on developing his line in the scientific study of personality—Sylvan Tomkins, Edwin Schneidman, Robert Holt, Saul Rosenzweig, and others. He died of pneumonia on 23 June 1988, at age 95, at his home in Cambridge, Massachusetts, and was buried in Mt. Auburn Cemetery.

Till the end, Murray believed that the preoccupations of the great American majority—machinery, big business, and party politics—were beyond him. In his twenty-fifth anniversary college report, he declared that he was interested in a host of other things, meaning "theater, literature, social history, music, anthropology, primitive religions, travel, conversation, rum, romanticism, and rebellion." Indeed, his attention was drawn most irretrievably toward the interior world of the person, the creative actualization of our highest possibilities, and the ever-renewing experience of wonder. Ever the statement of his own credo, his motto for the Harvard Psychological Clinic was "Let not him who seeks cease until he finds, and when he finds he shall be astonished."

Bibliography

Works by Murray

Kluckhohn, C., & Murray, H. A. (Eds.). (1948). *Personality in nature, society, and culture.* New York: A. A. Knopf.

Murray, H. A. (1938). *Explorations in personality.* New York: Oxford University Press.

Murray, H. A. (Ed.). (1949). *Pierre, Or, the ambiguities.* New York: Hendricks House.

Murray, H. A. (Ed.). (1960). *Myth and mythmaking.* New York: G. Braziller.

Murray, H. A. (1967). The case of Murr. In E. G. Boring & G. Lindzey (Eds.), *A history of psychology in autobiography* (Vol. 5, pp. 285–310). New York: Appleton-Century Crafts.

Murray, H. A., Morgan, C. D. (1945). *A clinical study of sentiments. Genetics Psychology Monographs, 32,* 3–311.

Schneidman, E. S. (Ed.). (1981). *Endeavors in psychology: Selections from the personology of Henry A. Murray.* New York: Harper & Row.

Works about Murray

Anderson, J. W. (1990). The life of Henry A. Murray, 1893–1988. In A. I. Rabin, R. A. Zucker, R. A. Emmons, & S. Frank (Eds.), *Studying persons and lives* (pp. 304–334). New York: Springer.

Robinson, F. G. (1992). *Love's story told: Life of Henry A. Murray*. Cambridge, MA: Harvard University Press.

Triplet, R. G. (1992). Henry A. Murray: The making of a psychologist. *American Psychologist, 47*, 299–307.

Eugene Taylor

MUSIC. Interest in the psychology of music can be traced back at least to the time of the ancient Greeks. Pythagoras, who lived in the sixth century BCE, is credited with demonstrating experimentally that the perceived pitch of a vibrating string varies inversely with its length, and that certain musical intervals correspond to ratios formed by different lengths of string. Such findings inspired later experimental work on the perception of music. Another strong influence came from Aristoxenus in the fourth century BCE, who argued that musical phenomena should be considered perceptual and cognitive in nature, and that music should be studied as an empirical science.

Because of its historical links with science, music in the Middle Ages and Renaissance was taught as part of what was called the *quadrivium*, the four related studies of astronomy, geometry, arithmetic, and music. As a result, many leading figures of the scientific revolution in the early part of the seventeenth century made important theoretical and empirical contributions to music perception and cognition. These scientists included Galileo (who was also a renowned lutanist and part of a dynasty of musicians), Descartes, Kepler, Mersenne, and Huygens. Mersenne, in particular, made a number of landmark contributions to the subject. For example, he related the sensation of pitch to frequency of vibration, and so explained the relationship between pitch and string length, which had been known since ancient times. He discovered that complex instrument tones consisted of a fundamental together with a series of harmonics, and anticipated later work on timbre by hypothesizing that the sounds of different musical instruments can be characterised by the mixture of harmonics they contain.

At the beginning of the nineteenth century an important mathematical theorem was advanced by Fourier that showed that any curve may be described as the superposition of a number of simple harmonic curves. Fourier's theorem, and its later application by Ohm to sound waves, had a profound influence on thinking about sound and music perception. In addition, a number of technological advances in the nineteenth century enabled scientists to investigate the perception of simple sounds with carefully controlled parameters. These advances included the invention of the siren by Cagniard de Latour and the tonometer by Scheibler. Resonators, which were first described by Helmholtz, enabled the analysis of complex sounds into their component frequencies.

Capitalizing on these developments, scientists began to measure certain fundamental properties of the hearing mechanism. They made determinations of the lowest frequencies that people could hear, and of the smallest differences in pitch or loudness that people could detect. They also explored the cues that people used to localize sounds in space, particularly those based on differences in the amplitude and time of arrival of sound at the two ears.

A particularly important discovery in the nineteenth century was made by Seebeck, who found that the pitch of a harmonic complex tone corresponded to that of its fundamental frequency, even if the fundamental itself was only weakly present in the complex. Seebeck hypothesized correctly that the pitch of the fundamental would be heard even if it was entirely missing from a harmonic series.

Most notable among nineteenth-century scientists who made contributions to sound and music perception was Hermann von Helmholtz, whose treatise *On the Sensations of Tone* was a landmark contribution to the subject. Helmholtz performed experiments on the perception of pitch, consonance and dissonance, timbre, and beats. He also applied his view of perception as unconscious inference to music, and his writings on this subject have inspired much contemporary work on the involvement of higher-level processes in music perception.

In the first half of the twentieth century there was considerable interest in the scaling of sensory and perceptual attributes of sound. For example, the mel scale for pitch was developed by Stevens, Volkman and Newman, and the sone scale for loudness was developed by Stevens and Davis.

Theoretical interest in higher level issues concerning music also developed in the latter part of nineteenth century. The physicist Ernst Mach speculated concerning the perception of melodies that have been transformed in various ways. Gestalt psychologists at the turn of the century, such as Christian von Ehrenfels, Max Wertheimer, Wolfgang Köhler, and Kurt Koffka, made important theoretical contributions to issues concerning musical processing. In particular they proposed a number of principles of perceptual organization, which they applied to the perception both of music and also of visual arrays. These included the principles of proximity, similarity, good continuation, closure, and common fate. However, since they lacked the ability to generate complex musical signals with accuracy and precision, they were unable to perform carefully controlled experiments on these issues.

With the advent of computer technology in the latter part of the twentieth century, psychologists were no longer restricted to narrow signal parameters in their

Pattern

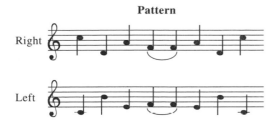

Percept

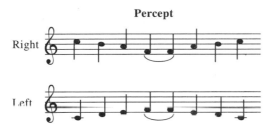

MUSIC. Figure 1. The scale illusion. The upper figure shows the pattern that is presented via headphones, and the lower figure shows the pattern as it is frequently perceived.

investigation of musical phenomena. They were therefore enabled to investigate higher-level questions concerning music perception and cognition using carefully controlled parameters. These include the principles that we employ to abstract musical features and shapes so as to give rise to perceptual equivalences and similarities; the rules that we use to organize components of a musical array into different groupings, the principles whereby we represent music in memory, and so on.

One body of research that arose from the writings of the early Gestalt psychologists concerns the ways in which we form linkages between elements of musical arrays. In particular, the principle of proximity, as applied to pitch, has been the subject of much experimental research. When a series of tones is played in rapid succession, and these tones are drawn from two different pitch ranges, listeners do not perceive a single melodic line, but rather two melodic lines in parallel, one corresponding to the higher tones and the other to the lower ones. Composers have capitalized on this perceptual principle through the use of pseudopolyphony, or compound melodic line. Here a single instrument plays a series of tones at a rapid tempo, and these tones are drawn from different pitch ranges; in consequence the listener experiences two or more melodic lines in parallel.

Under these conditions a number of interesting perceptual phenomena emerge. For example, although temporal relationships are well perceived between tones in the same pitch range, they are poorly perceived between tones in different pitch ranges. Indeed, as shown by the psychologists Bregman and Campbell, if such a passage is played sufficiently rapidly, and the pitch differences involved are sufficiently large, listeners may be unable to identify the orders in which the tones appear. Another interesting effect, discovered by Dowling, occurs when two well-known melodies are played at a rapid tempo, with the notes from each melody appearing in alternation. When the pitch ranges of these melodies overlap heavily, listeners have difficulty in separating them, and therefore in identifying them. However, when the melodies are in different pitch ranges, listeners form perceptual groupings based on pitch, and then readily perceive the two melodies as separate from each other.

Another situation in which pitch proximity has a powerful influence on perception is when two different streams of tones are presented, one to the listeners's left and the other to his or her right. The tones are reorganized perceptually so that the listener perceives two melodies, one corresponding to the higher tones and the other to the lower ones. In addition, the illusion is often created that the higher tones are all coming from one side of space (in righthanders, this is usually the right side) and that the lower tones from the other side of space, regardless of where the tones are indeed coming from (Figure 1). This effect, which is known as the scale illusion, was originally discovered by Deutsch in the laboratory with sounds presented via earphones, and with repeating ascending and descending scales. However, effects of this type have since been shown to occur in certain passages of real music performed in concert halls. One such passage occurs in the final movement of Tchaikovsky's Sixth Symphony, and another occurs at the end of the second movement of Rachmaninoff's Second Suite for Two Pianos.

The early Gestaltists also laid the groundwork for later work concerning musical shape perception. A number of scientists, such as Deutsch, Bharucha, and Gjerdingen, have proposed models for the abstraction of musical features based on pitch. These models take into account the perceptual equivalence of tones that stand in octave relation, the perceptual equivalence of intervals and chords under transposition, as well as higher level perceptual equivalences. Such models have taken the form of neural networks, and several have been subjected to tests in the laboratory.

The writings of music theorists have provided yet another source of input for work on the psychology of music. For example, the eighteenth-century theorist Jean-Philippe Rameau developed an elaborate musical system that was based on the harmonic series together with the principle of octave equivalence. His writings have had a profound influence on the theory of harmony ever since. As a result, the works of many contemporary psychologists are based on Rameau's theoretical assumptions; such work has been concerned with pitch perception, the analysis of musical patterns, the ways in which music is stored in memory, and the use of implicit knowledge concerning the principles underlying the tonal music of our tradition. Empirical studies addressing these issues have been carried out, for example, by Butler, Krumhansl, Bharucha, and Dowling.

The twentieth-century composer and music theorist Arnold Schoenberg proposed a different framework for musical structure, which he used as the basis for the technique of 12-tone composition. He argued that a series of tones, defined as a particular ordering of the 12 tones within the octave, retains its perceptual identity when it is transposed in pitch (transposition), when it is played backwards (retrogression) when its ascending intervals become descending ones, and vice versa (inversion), or when it is transformed by both these operations (retrograde-inversion). In addition, Schoenberg argued that, given the perceptual equivalence of tones that stand in octave relation, a series of tones will be recognized as equivalent when its components are placed in different octaves.

Schoenberg's assumptions have been subjected to a number of experimental investigations. In general, researchers have reported that listeners have difficulty in recognizing tone series that have been transformed in accordance with Schoenberg's rules; this has been found true even for subjects who are very familiar with 12-tone music.

The twentieth-century music theorist Heinrich Schenker has also had a profound influence on work concerning the psychology of music. Schenker emphasized that Western tonal music is structured hierarchically, and he developed a scheme for the representation of music that was similar in certain respects to the hierarchical scheme developed by Noam Chomsky for language. Later in the century, the music theorist Leonard Meyer also proposed an influential hierarchical scheme for music. This differs in many respects from that of Schenker, and also incorporates other principles, such as the Gestalt principles of perceptual organization referred to earlier.

In parallel, psychologists have produced evidence that we tend to encode information in the form of hierarchies when given the opportunity to do so. This has been found true, for example, of visual scenes, linguistic structures, and even artifical serial patterns. Given such considerations, and the evident hierarchical structure of tonal music, a number of mathematical models for the representation of pitch structures in hierarchical form have been proposed, for example by Simon and Sumner, Restle, and Deutsch and Feroe. These models have been the subject of empirical investigation.

Perhaps the most striking input from psychology has

come from demonstrations that listeners do not necessarily perceive music as it is performed; neither do they remember music without systematic distortion. There is much evidence that listeners reorganize the music that they hear, so that the music as it is perceived and remembered may differ substantially from the music as it is notated in a score. Furthermore, striking differences can occur between people in the way they perceive even very simple musical patterns.

The most dramatic evidence for this view comes from a number of musical illusions and paradoxes that were originally discovered by psychologists and later applied to real musical situations. Deutsch's scale illusion, described above, provides one such example. Another illusion, discovered by Shepard, is created with the use of tones that are so configured that their note names are clearly perceived, but that are ambiguous in terms of which octave they are in. Shepard found that when such tones traverse the pitch-class circle clockwise in small steps (Figure 2), they appear to be endlessly rising in pitch. When the tones traverse the circle in counterclockwise direction they are heard as endlessly descending instead. The composer Jean-Claude Risset later produced a number of variants of this illusion using single tones that glided around the pitch class circle so that they appeared to glide endlessly up or down in pitch.

Interestingly, pitch circularity effects approaching these have been intuitively exploited by composers for centuries. Passages involving such pitch circularities occur, for example, in works by Gibbons, J. S. Bach,

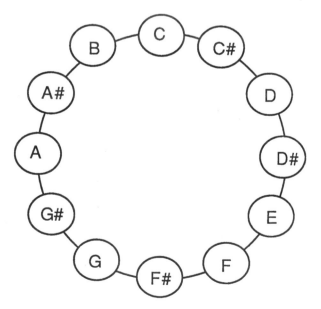

MUSIC. Figure 2. The pitch-class circle. As one moves up a keyboard, one repeatedly traverses this circle of note names, or pitch classes, in a clockwise direction.

Scarlatti, Haydn and Beethoven. In the twentieth century, composers such as Krenek, Berg, Stockhausen, Ligeti, Bartók, and, in particular, Risset have produced convincing circularity effects using both synthesized and natural instrument tones.

The tritone paradox, discovered by Deutsch, also involves tones that have clearly defined pitch classes but that are ambiguous with respect to height. Two such tones are presented that are separated by a half octave (or tritone) and so are diametrically opposed along the pitch-class circle. For example, C might be presented followed by F#, or G# followed by D. When one of these tone pairs is played, a listener might hear an ascending pattern. However, a different listener, on hearing the identical pair of tones, might hear a descending pattern instead. Furthermore, for any one listener the probability that the pattern is heard as ascending or descending depends on the positions of the tones along the pitch-class circle: Tones in one half of the circle are heard as higher and those in the opposite half are heard as lower. However, listeners differ strikingly in terms of which half of the circle is heard as higher and which as lower. As a result, extended passages formed of such tone pairs are heard by different listeners as forming entirely different melodies.

Another group of experiments by psychologists has uncovered certain surprising inabilities to make simple perceptual judgments concerning musical configurations. The experiment by Bregman and Campbell described earlier showed that people can have extreme difficulty in identifying the orders of tones that are presented in a rapid sequence when the tones are drawn from different pitch ranges. A related finding was reported by Warren, Obusek, Farmer, and Warren, who reported that people were unable to identify the order of a rapid series of sounds which differed from each other considerably in timbre.

Psychologists have also used findings from the laboratory to explain certain rules of musical composition that have evolved by trial and error, and for which no formal justification had in the past been presented. Such rules include the law of stepwise progression, which states that successive tones should be related by small pitch differences rather than large ones, and the rule forbidding the crossing of voices in counterpoint. Several of the experimental findings described here provide such laws with rational bases by documenting perceptual effects that occur when they are violated. For example, if the principle of pitch proximity is disregarded, temporal relationships between tones are processed less accurately and spatial illusions may occur.

Other work by psychologists that is of interest to composers concerns the issue of perceptual separation and fusion of simultaneous sounds. A number of studies have shown that tones whose components stand in harmonic relation tend to be fused together perceptually so as to produce a single sound image, whereas inharmonic tones tend to produce multiple sound images. Other studies have shown that components of sounds that begin together tend to be heard as single entities, whereas those that begin to sound at different times tend to be perceptually distinct from each other. Such work has been performed by McAdams, Bregman, De Boer, and Mathews and Pierce, among others. These experiments serve as guides to composers as they aim to achieve various perceptual effects.

Bibliography

Bregman, A. S. (1990). *Auditory scene analysis: The perceptual organization of sound.* Cambridge, MA: MIT Press. Written by an expert psychologist, this book presents a description of theory and research concerning higher-level auditory processing, including music.

Cohen, H. F. (1984). *Quantifying music: The science of music at the first stage of the Scientific Revolution, 1580–1650.* Dordrecht, Netherlands: Reidel.

Deutsch, D. (1992). Paradoxes of musical pitch. *Scientific American, 257,* 88–95. This article describes and discusses a number of musical paradoxes, including the illusion of endlessly ascending pitches and the tritone paradox.

Deutsch, D. (Ed.). (1999). *The psychology of music* (2nd ed.). New York: Academic Press. Written by a number of experts, this book provides the reader with a detailed review of research and theory concerning the psychology of music.

Hunt, F. V. (1978). *Origins in acoustics: The science of sound from antiquity to the age of Newton.* New Haven, CT: Yale University Press. This book, together with the one by Cohen, provides a thorough account of the history of scientific investigation into sound and music.

Meyer, L. B. (1973). *Explaining music: Essays and explorations.* Berkeley: University of California Press. Written by a foremost music theorist, this book provides important linkages between music theory and psychology.

Pierce, J. R. (1983). *The science of musical sound.* New York: Freeman. Written by a foremost scientist, this book gives a very readable overview of our knowledge concerning musical sound and the way it is perceived.

Diana Deutsch

MUSIC PERCEPTION. Psychological research on music perception has a distinguished history, extending from Helmholtz's seminal treatise, through the Gestalt psychologists, psychoacoustics, information processing, to contemporary investigations concerned with cognition and neuropsychology. The research is directed at explicating the psychological mechanisms that underlie the ability to encode and remember sequences of pitches, to organize them into coherent rhythmic and melodic patterns, and recognize musical structures such as scale, harmonic progressions, and distinctive stylistic characteristics. Music theoretic descriptions guide the research by identifying structural regularities in music. The terms defined below apply to Western tonal-harmonic music. This article summarizes research on the perception of pitch and rhythm. In addition, extensive psychological research on music performance addresses performance aspects, such as timing, articulation, and dynamics.

The sensation of musical pitch is logarithmically related to the frequency of the vibrating source and is measured in cycles per second or Hertz (Hz). The range of musical tones is approximately 25 Hz to 4,000 Hz. The psychological dimension of pitch is called "pitch height" and tones with higher frequencies are called "higher." Many musical sounds are harmonic, which means that they contain a number of different frequencies (harmonics). These frequencies are integer multiples of the lowest (or fundamental) frequency of the tone. For example, a piano tone playing middle C (notated C_4) has a fundamental frequency of 262 Hz, and harmonics at frequencies of 524 Hz, 786 Hz, 1048 Hz, and so on. For such tones, the pitch heard corresponds to the fundamental frequency. The harmonics, which have different strengths depending on the musical instrument, contribute to the perception of timbre (also called tone color or quality).

One distinctive aspect of pitch is the special status of intervals. A musical interval consists of two tones. These can be sounded simultaneously as harmonic intervals, or successively as melodic intervals. Intervals used most frequently in music tend to consist of tones with fundamental frequencies that can be expressed as the ratio of relatively small integers. For example, an octave has tones with a 2:1 ratio of fundamental frequencies. Tone separated by octaves have the same name; they are called "octave equivalent." For example, the tone an octave above C_4 is called C_5. A perfect fifth consists of tones with a 3:2 ratio, a perfect fourth a 4:3 ratio, a major third a 5:4 ratio, a minor third a 6:5 ratio, and so on. Intervals with the smallest integers are perceived as most consonant. There is an acoustic basis for this, because when the ratios contain small numbers, most of their harmonics either coincide or are far enough apart not to cause interference. In Western music, the smallest interval used is the minor second (with a ratio of 16:15), also called a semitone; it consists of 100 cents. Intervals retain their perceptual qualities when they are transposed in the musical range as long as the ratio of frequencies is unchanged. For example, the perfect fifth formed by C_4 and G_4 is perceived as the same interval as the perfect fifth that is formed when both tones are shifted up one semitone to $C\sharp_4$ and $G\sharp_4$.

The chromatic scale consists of 12 tones at semitone intervals. They correspond to successive tones on the piano keyboard. The tones of black keys have two names (such as $C\sharp$ and $D\flat$), called enharmonically equivalent. The names of the chromatic scale tones are C, $C\sharp(D\flat)$, D, $D\sharp(E\flat)$, E, F, $F\sharp(G\flat)$, G, $G\sharp(A\flat)$, A, $A\sharp(B\flat)$, and B. Assuming octave equivalence, this forms a circular dimension sometimes called the "chroma circle." Musical scales are subsets of the chromatic scale. The most frequent scale used in Western music is the diatonic scale. It consists of tones with successive intervals (measured in semitones): 2 2 1 2 2 2 1. The C major scale, corresponding to the white keys on the piano, consists of the tones C, D, E, F, G, A, B; the G major scale, which differs from the C major scale by one tone, contains the tones G, A, B, C, D, E, $F\sharp$; the D major scale, which differs from the C major scale by two tones, contains the tones D, E, $F\sharp$, G, A, B, $C\sharp$. Continuing in this fashion gives the cycle of scales called the "circle of fifths." Chords are combinations of scale tones, with the most important harmonies being the chord built on the first scale tone (the tonic triad, I), the fifth scale tone (the dominant chord, V), and the fourth scale tone (the subdominant chord, IV).

Research demonstrates these musical structures have consequences for how tones and sequences of tones are perceived, organized, and remembered. Musically trained listeners perceive pitch categorically as intervals of the musical scale, as shown by results analogous to categorical perception in speech. Musicians, but not nonmusicians, show sharp categorical boundaries and peaks in discrimination functions at category boundaries. This is found for both harmonic and melodic intervals. Different category boundaries are found for non-Western musicians who use other scales. These results indicate that interval categories are learned through musical experience. Both infants and adults show evidence of (partial) octave equivalence; tones at octave intervals are perceived as similar and octave substitutions are sometimes undetected. This has given rise to pitch models in the form of an ascending spiral. Specially constructed tones, called Shepard tones, effectively eliminate octave information by sounding octave-equivalent tones over a wide pitch range. For example, one tone might consist of Cs sounded in 10 octaves, another of C#s sounded in 10 octaves, and so on. When sounded in sequence, they produce the sensation of an unbroken succession of steps, which in fact return to the beginning, as described by the chroma circle.

Pitches and chords presented in musical contexts are hierarchically differentiated in the sense that they are ordered along a continuum of stability or structural significance. In the hierarchy of tones, the tonic (first tone of the diatonic scale) heads the hierarchy, followed by the fifth and third tones of the scale, then the remaining scale tones, and finally the nonscale tones. In the hierarchy of chords, the tonic chord is followed by the dominant and subdominant chords, followed by the other diatonic chords, and finally the nondiatonic chords. The hierarchy is reflected in a number of psychological measures: judgments of how well the tones and chords fit with a musical context, perceived similarity, temporal-order asymmetries, reaction times in judging key membership and tuning, recognition memory, judgments of phrase endings and expectations for continuation, and accuracy of naming tones by listeners with absolute pitch. Style-appropriate tonal hierarchies are perceived in non-Western music, and can be induced perceptually by the distribution of tones in novel styles of music.

Absolute pitch (AP) is defined as the ability to associate sounded pitches with note names without the aid of an external reference pitch. The term *perfect pitch* is sometimes used for this ability, but is misleading because musicians with AP vary in accuracy. Its incidence in the general population is rare, but is considerably higher in samples of musicians. Possessors of AP name pitch rapidly, and without effort or conscious strategy. Absolute pitch is contrasted with relative pitch (RP), the ability to identify specific intervals or to notate music relative to established reference pitch(es). Excellent relative pitch is common among musicians, can be developed through ear training exercises, and is more important in musical practice than AP.

The early-learning hypothesis is the primary focus of recent theorizing about the etiology of AP. The hypothesis states that AP can be learned most easily during a limited period of development, possibly comparable to the critical period for language learning. This hypothesis is supported by a variety of results. AP possessors generally began music lessons earlier than musicians without AP. Among AP possessors, a negative correlation is found between accuracy and age of first music lessons. White-key notes are identified more accurately and rapidly than black-key notes, possibly owing to the preponderance of white-key notes in the early piano repertoire. Confounds between inheritance and environment prevent simple conclusions concerning a possible genetic basis for AP, although some results suggest a genetic basis. In siblings of musicians with AP, the rate of AP is much greater than in siblings of musicians without AP.

Perception of longer sequences of pitches is influenced by knowledge of musical structures as well as Gestalt principles of organization. Gestalt principles are involved in segmenting music (and speech) into separate streams or sources, a process described as "auditory scene analysis." Contour changes are readily detected, but contour-preserving changes conforming to diatonic scale structure are not. Both musicians and nonmusicians are sensitive to transposition distance

around the circle of fifths. Listeners can perceive melodic similarity under a variety of other transformations, including retrograde (playing the tones in reverse order), inversion (inverting the direction of the intervals), syncopation, changed note durations, and other modifications of rhythm. A melodic prototype can be abstracted from transformed versions of it. Melodic expectancies show effects of Gestalt principles of good continuation, similarity, and proximity. Grouping occurs according to pitch range, temporal contiguity, timbral similarity, and spatial location. Phrase endings are signaled by pauses and changes in pitch range (usually descending contours), and even young infants appear to be sensitive to this information. Gestalt principles also operate to segment music into larger-scale units.

Musical pitch and rhythm tend to be studied separately, although similar psychological principles apply to both. In music, a large majority of durations fall into two duration categories: a short duration and a long duration. These tend to be in a 1:2 ratio or, less frequently, a 1:3 ratio. The longer of the two durations usually is in the range of approximately 300 to 900 milliseconds. In Western music, a measure consists of a fixed number of beats, usually two, three, four, or six. The beats in the measure differ in stress, creating a metrical hierarchy. For example, in a measure of four beats, the first beat is the most stressed, followed by the third, followed by the second and fourth beats, and finally the subdivisions of the beats. The meter provides an organizing framework for rhythms, just as the scale does for melodies. Rhythmic patterns typically extend over a number of measures, and consist of groups of groups.

Psychological data show these musical structures affect perception and memory. Listeners tend to perceive durations categorically. In particular, ratios near 1:2 tend to be assimilated to that value, and a sharp category boundary exists between 1:1 and 1:2 duration ratios. Listeners organize patterns by relating them to a regular underlying temporal grid, seeking the simplest possible organization. Beats within measures are perceived as hierarchically organized as described by the theoretical metrical hierarchy. This is found in measures of goodness-of-fit and memory accuracy. Musical structures and Gestalt principles both influence how rhythmic patterns are perceptually organized. When presented with a sequence of identical sounds, listeners tend to group them by twos, fours, or less often threes, depending somewhat on tempo. Elements that are similar in duration, pitch, and timbre tend to be assigned to the same rhythmic groups, and pauses strongly determine segmentation. Tones of long duration are heard as accented as well as tones preceding pauses.

Rhythmic organization can influence the perception of pitch and vice versa. For example, predictable temporal patterns facilitate pitch memory, and memory is better for tones in strong metrical positions. In addition, rhythmic accents can be induced by melody and harmony. Changing the rhythmic pattern impairs melody recognition, and regular pitch patterns determine rhythmic organization. Phrase structure is jointly determined by rhythmic and melodic patterns, and when pitch and rhythmic patterns are out of phase, recall is impaired. However, a number of results, including neurological data, suggest that pitch and rhythm are processed by separate cognitive modules that then combine to yield more complex perceptual representations such as grouping and phrasing.

[*See also* Music; *and* Music Therapy.]

Bibliography

Bregman, A. S. (1990). *Auditory scene analysis*. Cambridge, MA: MIT Press.

Deutsch, D. (Ed.). (1982). *The psychology of music*. New York: Academic Press.

Deutsch, D. (1986). Auditory pattern recognition. In K. R. Boff, L. Kaufmann, & J. P. Thomas (Eds.), *Handbook of perception and human performance: Vol. 2. Cognitive processes and performance*. New York: Wiley.

Deutsch, D. (Ed.). (1999). *The psychology of music* (2nd ed.). New York: Academic Press.

Dowling, W. J., & Harwood, D. L. (1986). *Music cognition*. Orlando, FL: Academic Press.

Francès, R. (1988). *The perception of music* (W. J. Dowling, Trans.). Hillsdale, NJ: Erlbaum. (Original work published 1958, *La perception de la musique*. Paris: J. Vrin)

Handel, S. (1989). *Listening: An introduction to the perception of auditory events*. Cambridge, MA: MIT Press.

Helmholtz, H. L. F. (1954). *On the sensations of tone as a physiological basis for the theory of music* (Rev. ed., A. J. Ellis, Ed. & Trans.). New York: Dover. (Original work published 1885)

Krumhansl, C. L. (1990). *Cognitive foundations of musical pitch*. New York: Oxford University Press.

Krumhansl, C. L. (1991). Music psychology: Tonal structures in perception and memory. *Annual Review of Psychology, 42*, 277–303.

McAdams, S., & Bigand, E. (Eds.). (1993). *Cognitive aspects of human audition*. Oxford: Oxford University Press.

Palmer, C. (1997). Music performance. *Annual Review of Psychology, 48*, 115–138.

Roederer, J. (1994). *The physics and psychophysics of music: An introduction* (3rd ed.). New York: Springer-Verlag.

Sloboda, J. A. (1985). *The musical mind: The cognitive psychology of music*. Oxford: Oxford University Press.

Carol L. Krumhansl

MUSIC THERAPY. An interpersonal process, music therapy emphasizes the maintenance, improvement, or restoration of the client's physical, emotional, social, and/or cognitive health. In this systematic process (involving assessment, treatment, and evaluation), both music and the relationship that develops between the client and music therapist are used to address the client's needs. Although music in and of itself has therapeutic properties (e.g., in enhancing mood), it is important to distinguish between these, which often involve self-help strategies, and music therapy as an applied discipline, which always involves a trained music therapist, a variety of music experiences, and a process which evolves within the context of a relationship.

Music therapy is used with individuals and groups of all ages and a wide range of clinical conditions, including psychiatric, emotional, and behavioral disturbances; developmental and learning disabilities; sensory impairments; communication disorders; substance abuse; physical handicaps; medical problems; aging, abuse, forensics, and socioeconomic disadvantage. There is also a rapidly developing use of music therapy to prevent physical and mental health problems. Clients entering music therapy need no special musical skills or training, as music is adapted to meet their individual needs and abilities.

Treatment Process

Assessment in music therapy often occurs prior to treatment, but may also continue throughout treatment. Assessment involves gathering and analyzing the social, medical, cognitive, perceptual, and emotional aspects of the client's functioning for the purpose of formulating appropriate therapeutic goals. In music therapy, there is also an analysis both of the client's musical history, including the past and present relationship to music, as well as the client's own music making; these may often reveal important information not accessible through other means.

In treatment, the music therapist identifies appropriate intervention strategies by relating the client's needs to the specific requirements of the music therapy experience (Bruscia, 1991). The experiences employed in music therapy clinical work comprise the gamut of possibilities inherent to music and are categorized as follows:

In *receptive* experiences, the client listens to live or recorded music to achieve a variety of clinical goals. Depending on the music selected, the client may experience, for example, relaxation or activation; nurturance or provocation; stimulation of thoughts, feelings, memories, and imagery; calming or excitation of physiological functions; and aesthetic or spiritual states.

In *compositional creative* experiences, the client creates a musical product, often a song or musical piece. In *improvisational creative* experiences, the client spontaneously creates music using the voice and/or instruments, with the therapist providing musical and nonmusical structures. These experiences assist the client in communicating thoughts, feelings, and ideas; developing expressive skills, achieving insight, facilitating interpersonal skills; and in problem solving and decision making.

In *recreative* experiences, the client reproduces music in some manner; for example, learning to play an instrument, rehearsing or performing music, or singing or playing precomposed music (Bruscia, 1991). These experiences help the client to develop perceptual and sensorimotor skills; adhere to structure; commit to a sequential task; participate in a group effort; and be oriented to the present.

In *activity* experiences, the client participates in structured musical activities, games, and musical play. The structure of the activity itself involves, for example, taking turns, responding at appropriate times physically or verbally, and imitating others. It helps the client to achieve designated therapeutic goals, such as developing social, sensorimotor, and perceptual skills, maintaining reality orientation, and increasing adaptive behavior.

Music therapy evaluation involves an analysis of change in the client according to the predetermined therapeutic goals. Changes in the client are often manifest in the client's musical as well as nonmusical behaviors.

Music Therapy Approaches and Levels of Treatment

Due to the breadth of music therapy practice, the theoretical orientation of therapists is often influenced by the needs of their clients. There is no one theoretical orientation that universally underlies the practice of music therapy. The therapist's theoretical orientation, whatever it may be, shapes the goals of treatment, the therapeutic relationship and process, the uses of music, and the assessment and evaluation (Bruscia, 1991).

An overview of this clinical breadth is provided through a categorization of common approaches to music therapy practice (Bruscia, 1991; Dileo-Maranto, 1993) (Table 1).

Levels of Practice

Within each of these approaches, the depth and comprehensiveness of music therapy clinical practice may also be categorized into three levels: supportive, specific, and comprehensive. These are determined by the following: (1) the music therapist's training (entry-level vs. advanced) and clinical experience; (2) the function of music therapy within the client's overall treatment plan; (3) the autonomy with which the therapist implements treatment goals; and (4) the depth and breadth of therapeutic change intended.

At a supportive level of practice, music therapy is employed to supplement other treatment modalities. Moreover, the therapist works interdependently with

MUSIC THERAPY. Table 1. Common approaches to music therapy practice

Approach to Music Therapy	Function of Music Therapy
Behavioral	Music reinforcement used to increase, decrease, shape or provide a cue or prompt for nonmusic behaviors and for behavior management
Educational/developmental	Provides opportunities for the acquisition of nonmusical educational and developmental skills
Rehabilitative	Assists/facilitates restoration of lost abilities and adjustment to condition
Medical	Assists in decreasing the pain and anxiety of illness, hospitalization, and medical procedures and in coping with illness
Recreational	Provides opportunities for the acquisition of leisure and social skills
Psychotherapy	Used to facilitate intra- and interpersonal adjustment. May be used within a number of theoretical orientations
Pastoral	Used to facilitate spiritual awareness and growth
Palliative	Used to minimize pain and optimize quality of life
Preventive	Used to prevent illness and maximize health

other professionals addressing predetermined goals that do not imply in-depth changes in the client's health.

At a specific level of treatment, the music therapist uses music to support other treatment modalities while also addressing several of the client's problems directly; the therapist may facilitate in-depth changes in a limited number of treatment areas.

At a comprehensive level of treatment, the music therapist establishes treatment goals independently, addresses all aspects of the client simultaneously, and works to achieve pervasive changes in the client's health (Dileo-Maranto, 1993).

Treatment Effectiveness

Quantitative research concerning the effectiveness of music therapy as a treatment modality has been conducted since the 1940s, with results often demonstrating its clinical efficacy. A brief and general summary of some of these results with selected clinical populations is presented in Table 2. In addition, the limited number of studies comparing music therapy with other treatment modalities have, in general, underscored its comparable and sometimes superior clinical effects. Also of significance is the recent emphasis on qualitative research methods which are particularly useful in illuminating aspects of the clinical process of music therapy.

History and Professional Information

Music therapy developed as a profession following the Second World War, stimulated by the increasing use of hospital music programs for war veterans and psychiatric patients and the recognition of music's powerful clinical effects. The National Association for Music Therapy, Inc. was founded in 1950. In 1971, a second professional organization, the American Association for Music Therapy, was founded. In 1998, these two organizations merged to form the American Music Therapy Association, Inc. (AMTA) which currently represents over 5,000 professional music therapists and 70 universities offering undergraduate and graduate music therapy training programs. The AMTA provides standards for education and training, professional practice and ethics, holds annual national and regional conferences, and publishes professional clinical and research journals.

Entry-level music therapists in the United States are certified at the bachelor's degree level and are recognized as board certified (MT–BC) after having completed the following: an approved music therapy curriculum, a supervised internship of 1,040 hours, and a national examination administered by an independent agency, the Certification Board for Music Therapy, Inc. Continuing education is required to maintain the MT–BC credential.

The approved undergraduate music therapy curriculum emphasizes the development of competencies in musicianship in addition to clinical and music therapy knowledge and skills. Advanced training in music therapy is offered through a number of graduate programs; institute training is available in specialized methods of music therapy.

Although the music therapy profession in the United States is the oldest and largest worldwide, music therapy is in various stages of development in over 40 countries throughout the world (Dileo-Maranto, 1993). Whereas there may be similarities in music therapy practice in a number of countries by virtue of a shared language or geographical proximity, it is likely that internal cultural, theoretical, and political factors exert even more profound influences than external influences. Thus, each country has developed its own unique approaches to music therapy clinical work; this diversity is both recognized and appreciated. To this

MUSIC THERAPY. Table 2. The clinical process of music therapy

Clinical Population	Selected Treatment Effects
Developmental disabilities, handicapping conditions	*Improvement in:* attention, memory, imitation, perception, discrimination, academic, social & motor skills, speech and communication, affect, impulse control *Decreases in:* inappropriate and stereotypic behaviors
Medical patients	*Decreases in:* anxiety, pain, use of medication and anesthesia, muscle tension, physiological reactivity, stress hormone levels *Improvements in:* mood, relaxation, satisfaction with medical procedure, immune responses
Rehabilitation	*Improvements in:* range of motion, exercise, motor skills, gait, speech, communication skills
Geriatrics	*Improvements in:* reality orientation, communication, motor and social skills, motivation, mood
Acute psychiatry	*Improvements in:* emotional expression, verbal communication, anxiety management, social interaction, self-awareness, and insight

end, the World Federation of Music Therapy, Inc., founded in 1993, seeks to represent and support the efforts of music therapy organizations and therapists internationally through a variety of services, including publications, regular world congresses, and model standards.

[*See also* Music; *and* Music Perception.]

Bibliography

Aigen, K. (1998). *Paths of development in Nordoff-Robbins music therapy*. Phoenixville, PA: Barcelona Books.

Bruscia, K. (1987). *Improvisational models of music therapy*. Springfield, IL: Charles C. Thomas.

Bruscia, K. (1989). *Defining music therapy*. Phoenixville, PA: Barcelona Books.

Bruscia, K. (Ed.). (1991). *Case studies in music therapy*. Phoenixville, PA: Barcelona Books.

Davis, W. B., Gfeller, K. E., & Thaut, M. H. (1992). *An introduction to music therapy: Theory and practice*. Dubuque, IA: Wm. C. Brown.

Dileo-Maranto, C. (Ed.). (1991). *Applications of music in medicine*. Silver Spring, MD: American Music Therapy Association.

Dileo-Maranto, C. (1993). *Music therapy: International perspectives*. Cherry Hill, NJ: Jeffrey Books.

Froehlich, M. A. (Ed.). (1996). *Music therapy with hospitalized children: A creative arts child life approach.* Cherry Hill, NJ: Jeffrey Books.

Priestley, M. (1994). *Essays on analytical music therapy.* Phoenixville, PA: Barcelona Books.

Unkefer, R. (Ed.). (1990). *Music therapy in the treatment of adults with mental disorders: Theoretical bases and clinical interventions.* New York: Schirmer Books.

Cheryl Dileo

MUTUAL-HELP AND SELF-HELP. Throughout history, individuals have joined together with others similar to themselves to cope with the major stresses and challenges of life. In addition, individuals over the years have often drawn upon publicly available information and materials, rather than credentialed experts, in self-guided efforts to cope with life's difficulties. In recent years psychologists have increased their efforts to understand and support these mutual-help and self-help strands of the tapestry of daily life. Special emphasis has been placed on the most salient context in contemporary society in which mutual-help and self-help processes occur—the modern self-help group.

Self-Help Groups

Unlike therapy groups, self-help groups are not led by professionals, do not charge a fee for service, and do not place a limit on the number of members. They are composed of individuals who meet together on a regular basis to help one another cope with a common life problem that brings them together. Since the 1970s, psychologists have become increasingly active in researching and supporting the development of self-help groups, in the United States and abroad. Although mutual help is an integral part of what occurs in these groups, for ease of reference throughout this article the traditional term *self-help group* will be used.

The earliest, biggest, and best-known modern self-help organization is Alcoholics Anonymous, developed in the United States in 1935. [*See* Alcoholics Anonymous.] Beginning in the 1960s and 1970s, and escalating in the 1980s, a rapid increase in the types, number, and visibility of self-help groups occurred. One study in the mid-1980s found a 9% annual growth rate of groups (in the state of New Jersey). This net growth rate resulted from two opposing trends: an average 16.8% of new groups developing per year, and an average 7.8% of groups disbanding per year.

A well-designed survey conducted in the mid-1990s by Kessler, Mickelson, and Zhao indicated that 7.1% of American adults (corresponding to 10 million Americans) had participated in a self-help group during the preceding 12 months, and 18.7% (25 million adults) at some point during their lifetime (*Social Policy*, 1997, *27*, 27–46). Typically, women and Whites are most strongly represented in self-help groups. Exceptions to this pattern are members of AA and other addictions groups, where men and individuals from diverse ethnic backgrounds are present in large numbers. Interestingly, self-help group participants report less support and more conflict in their social networks, and are more likely to have seen a therapist in the past year, than nonparticipants.

Four broad categories of groups can be delineated. *Addiction-compulsion* groups are the most prevalent, and encompass behavioral control problems ranging from alcoholism to gambling to sexual addictions. Most of these groups follow a twelve-step model. [*See* Twelve-Step Programs.] *Illness-disability* self-help groups exist for the entire spectrum of physical and psychiatric illnesses, ranging from cancer to multiple sclerosis to manic-depression to schizophrenia. *Life stress/life transition* groups encompass the various life events which prove stressful in modern society, such as divorce, death of a child, and death of a spouse. Included in this category are groups for family members of an individual with a problem (so-called one-step removed groups), such as family caregivers of Alzheimer's patients and family members of alcoholics. *Disempowered outsider* self-help groups encompass demographically defined subgroups who experience powerlessness, discrimination, or dissatisfaction in society due to their gender, ethnicity, or religion. Women's and men's groups are representative examples in this category. It should be noted that some self-help groups may fit into more than one of the above categories.

Although self-help groups can be most easily differentiated based on the problem facing members, other important distinctions are equally deserving of note. Groups differ in the degree to which they engage in external advocacy to bring about changes in the larger community. Some groups devote extensive energy to causes such as changing laws, gaining increased governmental research or services, or altering professional standards for defining and treating problems. Groups also vary in the extent to which they are linked to larger, external units. Some groups are part of large, national organizations (e.g., Alcoholics Anonymous), others are linked to a local hospital or human services agency, and others simply exist on their own. Additional distinctions of import concern the extent of professional involvement in group operations (none to some), the nature of group leadership (rotated vs. one leader), and the extent of structure (unstructured to highly structured). One important, recent distinction is whether a group is traditional face-to-face, or an online group, a type of group that many believe will grow dramatically in the years ahead.

Self-help groups occupy a unique niche in the community. Although they share some characteristics of human service agencies, in that they explicitly help individuals in need, they clearly differ in extremely important ways. For instance, they provide many benefits which professionals cannot provide, such as friendship, identity, meaningful roles, and a sense of belonging. Self-help groups also share some characteristics of voluntary organizations such as clubs, ethnic associations, churches, and fraternal orders, in that members donate their time and energy in pursuit of shared interests, beliefs, and goals. A distinct difference, however, is the personal problem-focused nature of the interests.

Self-Help Groups' Pathways of Influence

Self-help groups have the potential to influence members through a number of important pathways. *Sense of belonging* represents one salient source of positive influence. Individuals who feel burdened, misunderstood, and alone in their problem or life situation can benefit greatly from belonging to a group of similar others. The message "You are not alone" is a powerful and potentially healing one to individuals suffering life's afflictions. The resulting sense of being understood, of counting, and belonging together constitute a powerful emotional antidote to the pain of isolation.

A second important pathway of self-help group influence is the provision of *adaptive beliefs*. Most groups have a distinctive belief system which, when adopted by members, can serve as a specialized "cognitive antidote" to their troubling problem or life situation. For instance, in the case of Compassionate Friends, a group for bereaved parents, the critical element of the belief system is that any form and any length of grieving for your child is okay—no matter what others might believe about your personal style or length of grieving. In the case of Alcoholics Anonymous, key elements of the belief system are to admit you have a lifelong problem and that you cannot resolve it solely on your own. When self-help group members adopt the belief system of the group, some of the most psychologically disabling aspects of their situation can be ameliorated.

In most self-help groups, members spend a great deal of time sharing information about their life situation, and providing and receiving support. A third powerful pathway of influence involves the positive benefits to individuals of *personal, emotional sharing and support*. The personal sharing allows individuals to relieve pent-up feelings, to clarify the meaning of events, and to reconfirm their sense of resolve and commitment. Furthermore, the empathy, understanding, support, encouragement, guidance, and at times challenge they receive from others can directly contribute to enhanced well-being and/or behavior change. Research in various community settings, including self-help groups, consistently has linked social support to such positive changes.

Role models represent a fourth powerful pathway of self-help group influence. Newer members observe veteran members who have experienced problems or life situations similar to and perhaps even worse than their own. Importantly, these veteran members have mastered or come to terms with their situation and are now doing well. Observing such role models, over time, can provide a strong sense of hope and optimism to individuals whose current life situation seems overwhelming and hopeless. Furthermore, in addition to hope and motivation, observation of the behaviors and lifestyles of veteran members in a group can greatly enlarge the perceived universe of options for newer members whose views may be restricted due to stress and difficulty.

Many members have opportunities to contribute to others in their group, and also to develop friendships with members outside the group meeting *per se*, as time goes on. The opportunity to *contribute meaningfully to others*, and to *expand or rebuild one's social network*, represent additional pathways via which self-help groups enhance individual well-being. Contributing to others can occur as part of the normal group sharing process, or in more formal roles (e.g., group greeter, who welcomes new members; group leader). For its part, friendship development can be particularly important for individuals whose social networks have become weakened or depleted as a result of the new life situation in which they find themselves. A research study conducted by Ken Maton revealed that providing support to others and friendship development were each related to member well-being in various self-help group populations (*American Journal of Community Psychology*, 1988, 16, 53–77).

Provision of *specific coping approaches and practical information* constitutes a final pathway of self-help group influence. At group meetings, members share with each other the means of coping they have found useful over the years for dealing with the various challenges that emerge for their particular problem or life situation. In cases of illness or disability, groups can be a great resource for up-to-date information about potential causes and treatments of a condition. And in some groups, a storehouse of specific coping skills are contained in published manuals, such as AA's *Big Book* and Grow, Inc.'s *Blue Book*. The experiential knowledge that self-help organizations and individual members have gained over the years represents a rich resource for helping individuals cope with difficult problems and life situations.

Research and Action Challenges

Relatively little is known about the effectiveness of self-help groups, in part because it is very difficult to do definitive research in this area. Random assignment of individuals to existing groups versus a control condition is generally not feasible, and finding adequate comparison samples in the community is also difficult. Also, groups are not necessarily willing to accommodate researchers, especially when their research procedures are intrusive. Most of the self-help group outcome research to date has been on behavior control problems such as addictions and compulsions. Findings have generally been positive. Even though firm and rigorous findings on outcome are generally not available, the highly positive anecdotal commentaries provided by most members, and the continued membership growth of groups, provide suggestive evidence that the groups are having some positive impact. What is clearly unknown, however, is the nature and magnitude of positive impact, the relative impact compared to professional or other community resources, the types of individuals who are most or least likely to benefit, and whether some members are harmed by group involvement.

There has been much debate and discussion about the role professionals have played, and should play, in self-help groups. Self-help group leaders and most researchers believe that professionals should be "on tap" and not "on top" of self-help groups. The power and efficacy of self-help groups emerge from the experience, knowledge, and compassion of members. Many believe that mental health professionals would have a negative influence if they attempted to replace peer-based experiential knowledge and mutuality with professionally based technical knowledge and control. There remain, however, important roles for professionals. These include contributing to the development of new types of groups, consulting to existing groups, providing referrals, helping people develop groups if none exist nearby, giving lectures and workshops, and carrying out research into self-help group processes and outcomes.

Self-help clearinghouses exist in many states, and represent an important resource for citizens, groups, and professionals. One of their primary functions is to serve as an information and referral source, providing up-to-date directories of all groups in their jurisdiction, as well as national self-help resources. A second important function is to consult to groups and group leaders. Finally, clearinghouse staff attempt to educate the public and professionals about the nature and availability of groups, and more generally serve as an advocate for the value of the groups. Professionals contribute to clearinghouses in various ways, including day-to-day operations, consultation, and research.

Most research in the self-help group area has focused on group process, member well-being, and attitudes about self-help. Research in these areas remain important, especially if findings can contribute both to theory and to group enhancement. In addition, new areas of research are in need of development. One such area is the impact of groups on the larger society. Little is known about the influence of self-help organizations on community well-being, human service practices, or cultural norms, although such impact likely is important and will increase in magnitude in the years ahead. A second important, and relatively untapped, research area is the relationship between self-help groups and the managed health care system. Research is necessary to examine, for instance, whether as a cost-cutting strategy self-help groups increasingly become used as part of commercialized, for-profit programming, and if the groups become changed in the process.

In pursuing these and related research questions, many self-help researchers have emphasized the need for a diversity of research methods to be employed, given the distinct nature and the inherent complexities of research in this area. Traditional research methods include questionnaire-based research, and outcomes-based research (with viable comparison samples). Nontraditional methods such as qualitative (e.g., ethnography, narrative analysis) and participatory action research represent alternative approaches. The importance of combining qualitative and quantitative methods has also been emphasized.

Other Forms of Mutual Help or Self-Help

Professionally run support groups, self-help materials, and community-based settings are some of the additional community resources available.

Professionally Run Support Groups. In some ways support groups are similar to self-help groups, in that members who share a problem come together to provide help, comfort, and guidance. A primary distinguishing feature, however, is that support groups are led by a professional or agency-based facilitator who does not share the problem of members. In addition, support groups, unlike self-help groups, often last for only a limited, predetermined, number of sessions, and a fee for attendance is sometimes charged. Relatively little research has been carried out on support groups, and little is known about differences between self-help and support groups in terms of group processes, group outcomes, and who attends.

Self-Help Materials. Self-help books, manuals, and cassettes are widely available to help individuals cope with their personal problems. They differ tremendously in focus, quality, availability, and the extent to which they have been based on available scientific knowledge. Interestingly, surveys have shown that self-help therapy materials are often recommended to clients by therapists. However, there is a wide divergence of opinion among psychologists in general as to their value. Critics argue that self-help therapy materials are often unscientific, and may be dangerous. Proponents, on the other hand, point to survey evidence of the generally positive views therapists hold of these materials, and point out that traditional individual and group therapy also can do harm to individuals.

Relatively little empirical research exists on the efficacy of the various types of self-help materials. Rick Marrs carried out a systematic meta-analysis of the existing literature comparing self-help materials to treatment by therapists, and found no overall differences in the extent of impact (*American Journal of Community Psychology*, 1995, 23, 843–870). Susan Curry reviewed the self-help smoking cessation literature and found that self-help smoking cessation interventions result in lower quit rates than more intensive programs (*Journal of Consulting and Clinical Psychology*, 1993, 61, 790–803). Nonetheless, Curry concluded that self-help materials have the potential to have a large public health impact due to their potential for widespread distribution. More generally, the impact of self-help materials likely will be especially strong when they are based on available research, and used in conjunction with media and support group interventions as part of community-wide intervention efforts.

Community-Based Settings. Many Americans belong to one or more community settings in which mutual-help and self-aid are components. Robert Wuthnow's research indicates, for instance, that many members of churches and synagogues take part in small groups (e.g., Bible study, prayer, parenting, worship), in which personal problems are shared, and guidance and support offered (*Sharing the Journey: Support Groups and America's New Quest for Community*, New York, 1994). In addition, members of religious settings are encouraged to participate in personal prayer and other religious activities in their daily lives, which can further serve to buffer stress and enhance personal growth and development.

Citizens also participate in a myriad of other community settings, based on common interests, in which a sharing of personal concerns and mutual-help occurs. These may be organized around age or social roles (teen groups, parenting centers, senior centers), ethnicity (e.g., African American civic associations), hobbies (chess club, sewing-knitting group), sports (bowling leagues, intramural softball), and social action concerns (neighborhood advocacy groups, social movement groups). Unfortunately, relatively little research has focused on the extent of personal sharing and mutual support that occurs in most community-based settings, and the impact on individual and community well-being.

Mutual help and self-help, in their diverse manifestations, constitute important strands in the fabric of contemporary social life. The continued vitality and growth of self-help groups, self-help materials, and community-based settings provide a unique opportunity for psychology to extend and expand its focus beyond traditional helping modalities and perspectives. Although research findings are in short supply, self-help groups and community-based settings appear to represent extremely valuable social resources for behavior change, healing, personal development, prevention, and empowerment. In addition to influencing individual members, they have the potential to contribute to larger changes in the beliefs, values, norms, and practices in the professions and in the larger society. As psychologists' understanding, research base, and capacity to support mutual help and self-help continue to grow, individual and societal well-being should be strengthened accordingly.

Bibliography

Chesler, M. A. (1993). Participatory action research with self-help groups: An alternate paradigm for inquiry and action. *American Journal of Community Psychology*, 19, 757–768. An example of an alternative research paradigm suggested for studying and strengthening self-help groups.

Humphreys, K., & Rappaport, J. (1994). Researching self-help/mutual aid groups and organizations: Many roads, one journey. *Applied & Preventive Psychology*, 3, 217–233. An interesting overview of research on self-help groups which argues that they contribute to identity development, and should not be equated with professional human service organizations.

Jacobs, M. K., & Goodman, G. (1989). Psychology and self-help groups: Predictions on a partnership. *American Psychologist*, 44, 536–545. Reviews current knowledge about self-help groups and considers their interface with the managed health care system.

Jason, L. A., Gruder, C. L., Martino, S., Flay, B. R., Warnecke, R., & Thomas, N. (1987). Work site group meetings and the effectiveness of a televised smoking cessation intervention. *American Journal of Community Psychology*, 15, 57–72. An example of a self-help intervention which combines self-help materials, support groups, and media.

Kurtz, L. F. (1997). *Sage sourcebooks for the human services: Vol. 34. Self-help and support groups: A handbook for practitioners*. Thousand Oaks, CA: Sage. An overview of self-help groups and self-help group research.

Levine, M., & Perkins, D. V. (1997). Self-help groups. In *Principles of community psychology: Perspectives and applications* (2nd ed., pp. 300–337). New York: Oxford University Press. Provides an interesting analysis of various aspects of self-help groups, from a community psychology perspective.

Maton, K. I. (1993). Moving beyond the individual level of analysis in mutual help group research: An ecological paradigm. *Journal of Applied Behavioral Science*, 29, 272–286. Provides a framework for viewing self-help groups as embedded in and contributing to the community and society in which they are situated.

Tebes, J. K., & Kraemer, D. T. (1991). Quantitative and qualitative knowing in mutual support research: Some lessons from the recent history of scientific psychology. *American Journal of Community Psychology, 19,* 739–756. Highlights the importance of combining quantitative and qualitative methods in mutual support research.

White, B. J., & Madara, E. J. (1998). *The self-help sourcebook: Your guide to community and online support groups* (6th ed.). Denville, NJ: American Self-Help Clearinghouse. An accessible and useful listing both of self-help groups in New Jersey, and of national self-help resources.

Kenneth I. Maton

MYERS, CHARLES S. (1873–1946), British experimental and applied psychologist. Myers was born in London. Although his family had been involved in commercial enterprises for at least three generations, he chose to pursue the study of medicine, beginning that program of preparation at Cambridge University in 1891. Myers took his first course in experimental psychology in 1893. At the time, psychology was viewed unsympathetically at Cambridge; the first formal laboratory was not established until 1912. After receiving his undergraduate degree in 1895, Myers pursued the completion of his medical degree for the next 3 years. In 1898, he joined an expedition to the Torres Straits and Borneo and undertook the measurement of various senses (hearing, smell, taste, and so forth) of the indigenous population. He returned to complete his medical thesis and received his degree in 1901.

In 1903, Myers began his career in experimental psychology as an assistant to William H. R. Rivers at Cambridge, progressing to a demonstrator in 1904 and finally a lecturer in 1909. For a short period (1904–1907), he was also a lecturer in psychology at King's College in London. In 1904, Myers joined with James Ward and Rivers to launch the *British Journal of Psychology.* He was an associate editor of the journal from 1911 to 1913 and the sole editor from 1913 until 1923. He was secretary of the British Psychological Society from 1906 to 1910 and was elected to the Royal Society of London in 1915.

In 1909, Myers published the first English-language textbook in experimental psychology. Until then, the only available English language material were laboratory manuals published by Edward B. Titchener and Edmund Clark Sanford. The text was followed shortly by a popular version aimed at the nonprofessional market.

In 1912, Myers was appointed the first director of the psychology laboratory at Cambridge. When World War I broke out, Myers volunteered for service but was rejected because of his age. Undaunted, he traveled to France and offered his services to the British Medical Corps. Over the next several years, he became an expert in the diagnosis and treatment of war-related stress disorders among soldiers, eventually becoming an inspector of treatment facilities. In his spare time, he developed tests for selecting individuals who listened for submarines (called "hydrophonists"). At about the same time, he read a book in industrial psychology by an Australian psychologist, Bernard Muscio. In 1918, he wrote his first textbook in applied psychology, titled *Mind and Work* (London). This was the beginning of his transformation from an academic to an applied psychologist.

Returning to Cambridge after the war, Myers became increasingly frustrated by the unwillingness of his university colleagues to recognize the legitimacy of applied psychology. As a result, in 1921, with the assistance of H. J. Welch, he founded the National Institute of Applied Psychology, leaving the university to become its full-time director in 1922. He was also active in the Industrial Fatigue and Industrial Health Boards and the British Psychological Society. He served as president of the Seventh International Congress of Psychology, which convened at Oxford University in 1923. In addition to editing the journal *Occupational Psychology,* he authored three books in industrial psychology.

As a result of these activities, Myers is widely viewed as one of the founders of applied psychology.

[*Many of the people mentioned in this article are the subjects of independent biographical entries.*]

Bibliography

Myers, C. S. (1909). *A text-book of experimental psychology.* New York: Longmans, Green.

Myers, C. S. (1911). *An introduction to experimental psychology.* Cambridge, UK: Cambridge University Press.

Myers, C. S. (1926). *Industrial psychology in Great Britain.* London: Cape.

Welch, H. J. & Myers, C. S. (1923). *Ten years of industrial psychology; an account of the first decade of the National Institute of Industrial Psychology.* London: Pitman.

Frank J. Landy

MYSTICISM refers to a distinctive experience identifiable by phenomenological and empirical methods. It is an experience of union or presence with a reality perceived to be absolute or ultimate. When the wider reality is identified in personal terms mysticism takes on distinct religious connotations, often identified as a unity with, or sense of, the presence of God. However, if reality is identified in impersonal terms, mysticism is more likely to be perceived as spiritual or even secular. Researchers continue to investigate precisely what the experience of union, or presence might mean, particularly in terms of the theoretical consequences of claims that the empirical ego is diminished or eliminated as a truer or more complete self emerges in identification with a larger reality.

Early investigators of mysticism such as Underhill wrote essentially apologetic treatises, exploring mystical experiences as indicative of the veridicality of a generalized religious worldview. Other more explicitly psychologically oriented investigators such as James Leuba in *The Psychology of Religious Mysticism* (New York, 1925) felt they could provide adequate reductive explanations of mystical experience that would effectively undermine any claims to interpretation of mystical experience as foundational for legitimating a religious worldview. Contemporary scholars are split on whether or not religious experiences in general, and mystical experience in particular, can be used to provide an adequate evidential basis for religious beliefs.

William James in *The Varieties of Religious Experience: A Study of Human Nature* (Cambridge, MA, 1902/1985) made mysticism central to his empirical treatment of the varieties of religious experience. He distinguished between experience and its interpretation, laying the foundation for what has become the highly influential common core thesis. This thesis claims that variations in interpretation mask fundamentally identical experiences. A further assumption is that psychological and social factors influence the interpretation of experience, not the experience itself. Closely associated with his thesis is the controversial claim of causal indifference. This assumes that factors that trigger mystical experiences, including drugs, are irrelevant to the nature of the experience itself. This thesis has been more recently associated with its most strict philosophical defender, Walter Stace. Stace's position has influenced empirical psychology through the widespread use of the Mysticism scale, an empirical measure based directly upon Stace's conceptualization of mysticism.

The common core thesis has stimulated much criticism. Zaehener (1957) has argued that there is only an apparent similarity between drug-induced mystical experiences, and those that are either facilitated by specific traditional religious practices or occur spontaneously. However, empirical research has tended to support the claim that drug-induced experiences are phenomenologically and measurably similar if not identical to other mystical experiences. Differences in interpretation are accounted for by knowledge that the experience was drug induced and by personal and social expectations as to the validity of drugs as triggers of religious experiences.

Both Katz (1978) and Proudfoot (1985) have provided sophisticated conceptual critiques of empirical studies that claim to support the common core thesis. These investigators argue that, mysticism, like all experience, is mediated by such factors as culture, expec-

tations, and personality that inevitably affect the nature of the actual experience, not merely its interpretation. They argue that there can be no unmediated experiences as assumed by the common core theorists. This position has gained wide acceptance among social scientists and philosophers heavily committed to a social constructionist perspective.

The empirical identification of factors influencing mystical experience supports the social constructionist position insofar as expectations, set, and setting factors have clearly been shown to influence the report of mystical experience. However, social constructions influence the interpretation more than the basic experience. Empirical research supports the common core thesis with respect to the report of the constancy of the minimal phenomenological properties of mysticism while supporting the social construction position with respect to the influence of expectations, set and setting on the interpretation of mystical experience.

Most recently, Forman has argued that since a mystical experience of undifferentiated unity is essentially a pure conscious experience, it lacks content and hence is immune from social construction. However, to state what this experience is or means must be mediated through social constructions that social scientists can identify empirically.

Thus, both conceptually and empirically, an experience of union, contact, or presence with a larger reality associated with a change in the typical sense of self has been identified as an unvarying factor among widely varying interpretations of mystical experience. Hence, the social constructions and common core theses can be viewed as complementary rather than mutually exclusive.

There is a consensus among empirical psychologists that the report of mystical experience can be measured and its commonality among healthy individuals has been well established. Survey research in Western societies is consistent in finding that approximately a third of normal populations report mystical experiences. While few, if any, enduring personality traits have been found to be associated with the report of mystical experience, research generally supports that mysticism, as with other religious experiences, is reported frequently by women, and among those generally open to experience regardless of gender. Rigidity and dogmatism tend to be negatively associated with the report of mystical experience and with the evaluation of this experience, especially when it is triggered by less traditional means, such as drugs or sex. The assumption that mystical experiences are rare is unwarranted. Much of the research on mysticism focuses upon texts, often associated with specific religious traditions, producing a bias that links mysticism to religious interpretations. However, it is also true that mysticism is reported outside religious traditions and cannot be considered an inherently religious phenomenon. Still, the centrality of mysticism to the major faith traditions suggest that religions have provided meaningful interpretative schemes for this experience, long treated as pathological by psychologists, despite no strong evidence that mysticism and psychopathology are not causally related. The fact that mystical experience is relatively common and can be adequately measured within normal populations assures that the empirical psychology of religion will be able to more specifically identify factors influencing both the occurrence and interpretation of this experience as research progresses.

[*See also* Peak Experiences; *and* Religious Experience, *article on* Religious Experiences and Practices.]

Bibliography

Forman, R. K. (1997). *The problem of pure consciousness: Mysticism and philosophy.* New York: Oxford University Press. Focuses upon the discussion of contentless mystical states (introvertive mysticism) and argues the case that lacking content, such states cannot be socially constructed.

Hood, R. W. Jr. (1997). The empirical study of mysticism. In B. Spilka & D. N. McIntosch (Eds.), *The psychology of religion: Theoretical approaches* (pp. 222–232). Boulder, CO: Westview. A summary of the empirical study of mysticism focusing largely upon the use of the Mysticism scale derived from Stace's conceptualization of mysticism.

Katz, S. T. (Ed.). (1978). *Mysticism and philosophical analysis.* New York: Oxford University Press. A critical text that argues against Stace's position that there is a common core to mystical experience that is not socially constructed or interpreted.

McGinn, B. (1994). *The foundations of mysticism: Vol. 1. The presence of God: A history of western Christian mysticism.* New York: Crossroad. Volume 1 of a proposed four-volume series, *The Presence of God*, that focuses upon Christian mysticism interpreted in personal terms.

Stace, W. T. (1960). *Mysticism and philosophy.* New York and London: Macmillan. A seminal text that argues for a common core to mystical experiences that is not socially constructed. Introvertive and extravertive mysticisms are discussed.

Proudfoot, W. (1985). *Religious experience.* Berkeley: University of California Press. A currently influential text that argues that there are no unmediated experiences and hence all religious states, mysticism included, are interpretations of experience.

Underhill, E. (1930). *Mysticism: A study in the nature and development of man's spiritual consciousness* (Rev. ed.). London: Methuen. (Original work published 1911.) A seminal and classic tapologetic text describing both mystical experiences and stages of their development.

Zaehner, R. C. (1957). *Mysticism, sacred and profane: An inquiry into some varieties of praeternatural experience.* London: Oxford University Press. A text critical of the claim that all mysticism share a common core. Theistic mysticism is distinguished from other mysticisms, especially those that are drug induced.

Ralph W. Hood, Jr.

MYTH. *See* Religious Symbol, Myth, and Ritual.

N

N=1 DESIGNS. *See* Single-Case Experimental Design.

NARCISSISM. The term *narcissism* was coined by Havelock Ellis in 1898 to refer to a sexual perversion characterized by the taking of the self as a sexual object. Sigmund Freud in his essay "On Narcissism" (London, 1914/1957) broadened the term to include any aspect of thinking and feeling in which the major emphasis was on oneself. Relationships in which the choice of one's partner was based predominantly on one's picture of oneself as one is, as one was as a child, or as one would like to be, were called narcissistic, in contrast to relationships in which the actual qualities of the other were more important. In terms of the self, narcissism refers to any aspect of the complex state of self-esteem, and includes such things as overweening pride, arrogance, and sensitivity to insult. However, in contemporary psychoanalysis, the meaning of the term has been expanded to the point of fuzziness. Perhaps a workable definition is a cognitive, affective, and motivational preoccupation with the self.

Freud, in keeping with the psychoanalytic thinking of his time, thought of the "love of the self" in terms of the libidinal drive. He viewed this as an explanation of the self-centeredness of schizophrenia, dreaming, and hypochondria. He called the earliest stages of infant development, before the infant achieves the ability to differentiate itself from others, the narcissistic stage of development. As psychoanalysis developed, object relation theories, which viewed attachment to other people as the important factor in human motivation, gained prominence. Narcissism was then seen in object-relationship terms. Edith Jacobson in *The Self and the Object World* (New York, 1964), developed the concept of self representations (the images and ideas one has of oneself), and described the intricate interplay of feelings of both love and hate directed toward self representations in the development of self-esteem. Those self representations, which consist of an ideal view of the self and one's view of an ideal love object and ideal relationship, together form a structure in the mind called the "ego ideal." To an important degree, self-esteem is determined by the degree of success one achieves in striving to meet those ideals.

By this time, the term *narcissism* had shed its burden of drive theory and had come to be used almost exclusively to mean self-esteem. The pejorative tone that had invested it began to disappear with the recognition that the term had been used to designate both "good" self-esteem, based on nonconflictual identifications and solid accomplishments, and "bad" self-esteem, based on defensive and compensatory fantasies of grandiosity and the depreciation of others. Attention then turned to clinical aspects of narcissism. In the 1930s, Wilhelm Reich in *Character Analysis* (New York, 1933) described a common solution to feelings of inferiority and inadequacy (disturbances of narcissism or self-esteem) in women, namely, the choice of a partner who had the aggressive and powerful features that the woman herself once desired. In the 1970s, Heinz Kohut focused attention on narcissism in *The Analysis of the Self* (New York, 1971). He proposed a theory of the development and treatment of narcissistic disorders, which while not entirely new, presented an approach that enabled therapists to work with people who had hitherto been deemed untreatable. He viewed narcissism as developing in two structures, which together constituted Freud's ego ideal. The first consisted of the grandiose self, which embraced those self representations which were part of the individual's grandiose fantasies, as, for instance, in young children's normal fantasies that they can do or be anything. The second, the idealized parent imago, was comprised of the internalized idealized pictures of the more or less perfect parents. Together, these structures determine the individual's ideals and ambitions. In people who are relatively healthy, these ideals and ambitions become more realistic over time, and self-esteem derives in part from realistic attempts to attain them. In narcissistic disorders, both these idealized views of what one can be and the person's view of who he is may remain grandiose and unrealistic, leading to a fragile and unrealistic sense of self-esteem.

No matter how well developed self-esteem may be it still requires support from others. Kohut called those who provided such support "selfobjects." Kohut described several specific ways in which narcissistic patients make use of relationships. They may idealize the other person and bask in their perfection, or they may treat the other as important only if the other reflects and supports their own centrality. The relationship can be thought of as narcissistic if the individuality of the other is ignored and the focus in one way or another is on the person himself rather than his partner. In therapy, these modes of relating led to specific types of transference and to specific methods of working with them. This in turn led to the development of the school of self psychology, and has had an enduring effect on broadening the scope of psychotherapy and psychoanalysis. Concomitantly, Otto Kernberg, in *Borderline Conditions and Pathological Narcissism* (New York, 1975) developed an approach to the treatment of pathological narcissism along more traditional lines. Controversy between these two psychotherapeutic approaches to narcissistic disorders continues today.

[*See also* Narcissitic Personality Disorder.]

Bibliography

Kohut, H. (1978). *The search for the self* (P. H. Ornstein, Ed.). New York: International Universities Press.

Moore, E. B., & Fine, B. D. (1990). *Psychoanalytic terms and concepts.* New Haven, CT: Yale University Press.

Moore, E. B., & Fine, B. D. (1990). Narcissism. In *Psychoanalytic terms and concepts* (pp. 124–125). New Haven, CT: Yale University Press.

Morrison, A. P. (1986). *Essential papers on narcissism.* New York: New York University Press.

Pulver, S. E. (1970). Narcissism: The term and the concept. *Journal of the American Psychoanalytic Association, 18,* 319–341.

Sandler, J., Person, E. S., & Fonagy, P. (Eds.). (1991). *Freud's "On narcissism: An introduction."* New Haven, CT: Yale University Press.

Sydney Pulver

NARCISSISTIC PERSONALITY DISORDER is one of the personality disorders included within the American Psychiatric Association's *Diagnostic and Statistical Man-*

ual of Mental Disorders. It is characterized by a chronic and pervasive arrogance and grandiosity, and a persistent need for admiration. Narcissistic persons will often be preoccupied with fantasies of unlimited success, power, brilliance, or beauty. They will believe that they are special and unique, and that they should be associated with or treated by other special, high-status persons. They will often expect or demand especially favorable treatment by others and an automatic compliance with their wishes, requests, and needs. They will often lack feelings of empathy for others, and may even be very exploitative of them. They will believe that others are envious of them, but will often be very envious of those who are receiving benefits or recognition that they feel are more appropriately provided to them (Gunderson, Ronningstam, & Smith, 1995).

Description

The diagnosis of a narcissistic personality disorder was not officially recognized until 1980, when it was included in the third edition of the American Psychiatric Association's *Diagnostic and Statistical Manual of Mental Disorders (DSM–III).* No prior edition of the manual included this diagnosis, and the disorder is still not recognized within the international nomenclature of the World Health Organization (WHO). Narcissistic conflicts and traits, however, have been recognized and researched for some time by psychodynamically oriented clinicians and personality trait researchers. Narcissistic personality disorder is one of the less reliably diagnosed personality disorders, due to the substantial amount of clinical judgment that is necessary to assess for the presence of the diagnostic criteria (e.g., lack of empathy, arrogant attitudes, and need for excessive admiration).

Modesty (versus arrogance) is one of the facets of agreeableness (versus antagonism), a fundamental dimension of personality functioning. Up to 18% of males and 6% of females may be characterized as being excessively immodest or conceited, but only a proportion of these persons would be diagnosed with a narcissistic personality disorder. The disorder is diagnosed more often in males than in females (Widiger & Sanderson, 1997).

As adolescents, they are likely to have been self-centered, assertive, gregarious, dominant, and perhaps arrogant. They will have a high motivation for achievement, and may in fact be quite successful within significant areas of their lives (e.g., career). Their motivation for success and their sustained self-confidence in the face of setbacks may indeed be helpful to their advancements and achievements. However, their relationships with friends and colleagues will often become strained as their exploitation of others for their further success, their need for deferential admiration, and their lack of empathy for the needs and concerns of others, become more evident. Interpersonal relationships may be easy for them to develop, but difficult to sustain, unless the persons are deferential to them or share a mutual need for status and admiration. Occupational success may also be impaired by their difficulty at times in acknowledging or responding appropriately or effectively to normal criticism and setbacks. They will at times simply deny or ignore valid criticism, failing to make appropriate adjustments and simple corrections, or they may explode in anger, rage, and retribution. As parents, they may attempt to live vicariously through the achievements of their children. Their own sense of personal adjustment and self-esteem may be fine as long as they continue to experience or anticipate success. However, they are prone to anxiety disorders when anticipating threats to self-esteem, and mood or substance-related disorders when they experience failure. Some may not experience any maladaptivity until middle age, when they may finally begin to question the excessive priority they have given to achievement and status (Kernberg, 1991).

Etiology and Pathology

The etiology of narcissistic personality disorder is unclear. There have not been any studies on the heritability of the disorder. Theories of etiology have been primarily sociological, psychodynamic, and interpersonal. For example, it has been suggested that Western society has itself become overly self-centered with a decreasing importance given to familial bonds and an increasing importance given to materialism, self-esteem, and self-satisfaction.

Excessive narcissism may also develop in part through a contingent provision of parental attention and affection. The child may learn through the relationship with the parents that a sense of worth, value, or meaning is contingent upon accomplishment or achievement. They are not persons who feel valued for their own sake. However, other theorists suggest that persons with this disorder received an excessive idealization by parental figures, which they incorporated into their self-image.

Conflicts and deficits with respect to self-esteem do appear to be central to the psychopathology of a narcissistic personality disorder. Narcissistic persons may continually seek and obtain signs and symbols of recognition to compensate for feelings of inadequacy. Self-esteem is contingent upon success, accomplishment, or status. Their feelings of insecurity may be masked by an overt indifference or a disdainful devaluation of the opinions of others, but the pathology may still be evident in such cases by the excessive reliance and importance given to status and recognition. Some narcissistic individuals may in fact envy most those persons who are truly indifferent to success and criticism, and who can enjoy a modest, simple, and unassuming life.

The most common form of treatment is psychodynamic psychotherapy, although cognitive-behavioral therapies are being developed.

[*See also* Narcissism.]

Bibliography

American Psychiatric Association. (1980). *Diagnostic and statistical manual of mental disorders* (3rd ed.). Washington, DC: Author.

American Psychiatric Association. (1994). *Diagnostic and statistical manual of mental disorders* (4th ed.). Washington, DC: Author.

Cooper, A. M., & Ronningstam, E. (1992). Narcissistic personality disorder. In A. Tasman & M. B. Riba (Eds.), *Review of psychiatry* (Vol. 11, pp. 80–97). Washington, DC: American Psychiatric Press. Overview of the etiology, pathology, diagnosis, and treatment of narcissistic personality disorder.

Gunderson, J. G., Ronningstam, E., & Smith, L. E. (1995). Narcissistic personality disorder. In W. J. Livesley (Ed.), *The DSM-IV personality disorders* (pp. 201–212). New York: Guilford Press. Overview of issues concerning the diagnosis of narcissistic personality disorder.

Kernberg, O. F. (1991). Narcissistic personality disorder. In R. Michels (Ed.), *Psychiatry* (Vol. 1, pp. 1–12). Philadelphia, PA: Lippincott. Overview of the etiology, pathology, and treatment of narcissistic personality disorder, primarily from a psychodynamic perspective.

Millon, T., Davis, R. D., Millon, C. M., Wenger, A. W., Van Zuilen, M. H., Fuchs, M., & Millon, R. B. (1996). *Disorders of personality. DSM IV and beyond*. New York: Wiley. Overview of DSM–IV personality disorders, including narcissistic personality disorder.

Raskin, R., Novacek, J., & Hogan, R. (1991). Narcissistic self-esteem management. *Journal of Personality and Social Psychology, 60*, 911–918. Illustrative study of narcissistic personality traits.

Widiger, T. A., & Sanderson, C. J. (1997). Personality disorders. In A. Tasman, J. Kay, & J. A. Lieberman (Eds.), *Psychiatry* (Vol. 2, pp. 1291–1317). Philadelphia, PA: Saunders. Overview of the diagnosis, etiology, pathology, and treatment of personality disorders, including narcissistic personality disorder.

Thomas A. Widiger

NARCOLEPSY. The sleep disorder called narcolepsy is a heritable central nervous system disorder with a prevalence of about 0.03 to 0.06% in Western Europe and North America. Descriptions of the disorder appeared as early as 1862. However, Jean Baptiste Edouard Gelineau, in 1876, was first to apply the term *narcolepsy* to a syndrome comprising four key symptoms—the so-called narcolepsy tetrad: sleep attacks, cataplexy, hypnagogic hallucinations, and sleep paralysis (Guilleminault, Dement, & Passouant, 1976). A fifth symptom of narcolepsy that is commonly reported is disturbed nocturnal sleep (Mitler, Aldrich Koob, & Zarcone, 1994). In fact, some patients with narcolepsy come to the attention of the health-care community only with the complaint of insomnia. Typically, narcolepsy emerges in the second decade of life, and symptom severity seems to plateau by the third or fourth decade. In the general population, there is no obvious difference in the prevalence of narcolepsy among males and females.

Narcolepsy is the second most common cause, after sleep apnea, of disabling daytime sleepiness. The narcolepsy patient suffers sudden daytime sleep attacks characterized by episodes of involuntary and unwanted sleep that intrude on waking activity. Narcoleptics also experience abnormally timed components of REM sleep such as paralysis and hallucination. This paralysis depends on the same brain mechanisms that block muscle activity during REM sleep. Episodes of paralysis are involuntary and can occur under two circumstances: (1) cataplexy—sudden muscle weakness leading to partial or complete collapse during amusement or excitement of anticipation, such as when telling a joke or catching a fish; (2) sleep paralysis—an often frightening inability to move just before falling asleep. The hallucinations of narcolepsy are known as hypnagogic hallucinations. These hallucinations also depend on REM sleep mechanisms and come as sometimes benign, sometimes terrifying apparitions just as the patient falls asleep.

Pathophysiology

The pathophysiology of narcolepsy seems to involve dysregulation of wakefulness and sleep rather than a true hypersomnolence. Patients with narcolepsy do not seem to sleep more than normal controls. However, they are prone to fall asleep throughout the day-night cycle—often at inappropriate times. In the 1960s, narcolepsy was shown to be associated with an abnormal tendency to achieve REM sleep shortly after sleep onset. In normals, REM sleep first occurs about 80 to 100 minutes after sleep begins at night. Patients with narcolepsy, however, have sleep-onset REM periods, which are periods of REM sleep occurring immediately at the beginning of sleep or within the first few minutes of the night.

Narcolepsy has also been described in other species, such as canines, equines, and bovines. Canine forms of narcolepsy can be passed genetically from parents to offspring, complete with abnormal sleepiness and cataplexy. Neurochemical and pharmacotherapeutic studies of naturally occurring canine narcoleptics, experimental feline models, and human research suggest that specific brain abnormalities are involved: a widespread underrelease of dopamine and a brain-stem-specific proliferation of muscarinic acetylcholine receptors and hypersensitivity to acetylcholine. These two neuro-chemical abnormalities fit with current understanding of mechanisms that regulate wakefulness, sleep, and REM sleep. Recent studies have determined that loss of function of the gene for the hypocretin 2 receptor is responsible for canine narcolepsy. The extent to which the hypocretin neurotransmittor system is involved with narcolepsy in humans remains to be examined (Lin, Farasco et al., 1999).

In the 1980s, a statistically significant association was first reported between narcolepsy and certain subtypes of the human leukocyte antigens (HLA) DR and DQ, known as DR2 and DQ1 (Honda & Juji, 1988). With progressive refinement in HLA typing, the HLA haplotypes DRB1*1501 and DQB1*0602 now seem to have the strongest association with narcolepsy. The incidence of these particular DR and DQ haplotypes is estimated to be between 12 and 15% in the general Caucasian population. However, in some studies of narcoleptic patients, the incidence of these haplotypes approaches 100%. The HLA DR and DQ findings have generated speculation that narcolepsy, or some forms of narcolepsy, is inherited and that narcolepsy may be an autoimmune disorder, since HLA-DR2 is associated with systemic lupus erythematosus and with a high incidence of drug toxicity in rheumatoid arthritis patients. It may be particularly relevant that HLA-DR2, which is a supertype of HLA-DRB1*1501, is associated with other autoimmune diseases that affect the central nervous system, such as multiple sclerosis and optic neuritis. However, despite considerable research on the human or canine forms of narcolepsy, no abnormal immunological functions have yet been identified.

There are numerous studies indicating that human narcolepsy has a genetic basis. The risk for narcolepsy among the offspring of a patient with narcolepsy is several orders of magnitude greater than the risk observed in the general population (Kryger, Roth, & Dement, 1994). Too few pairs of narcoleptic twins have been studied to estimate the relative degree of concordance between monozygotic and dizygotic twins. At least three pairs of monozygotic twins who are discordant for narcolepsy have also been reported. One pair of monozygotic (identical) twins was found to be concordant for narcolepsy but not for cataplexy. The syndrome of narcolepsy is likely to have a multigenic origin, since it is probable that many genes contribute to sleep induction. More than one locus on the genome may contribute to narcolepsy. In humans, the narcoleptic trait is heritable, although cases of nonfamilial narcolepsy are relatively prevalent. However, in some canine breeds, such as the Doberman pinscher and the Labrador retriever, the narcoleptic trait is passed on in a classical Mendelian fashion, which suggests that a single locus is sufficient to confer the canine form of narcolepsy, as is the case with the abnormalities in the hypocretindreceptor gene.

Because the modern study of narcolepsy involves techniques of neurochemistry, genetics, and immunology, there is great hope that future research on narcolepsy will shed light on fundamental questions about why we sleep and how sleep processes are regulated.

Diagnosis

As originally described by Gelineau, four symptoms are commonly used to define the illness: sleepiness, cataplexy, hypnagogic hallucinations, and sleep paralysis. Objective polysomnographic techniques for diagnosing narcolepsy also exist and are based on the idea that someone who is sleepy will fall asleep quickly and on the discovery that patients with narcolepsy have sleep-onset REM periods. In current practice, the key diagnostic features are an unambiguous history of excessive daytime sleepiness, unambiguous history of attacks of muscle atonia (cataplexy) precipitated by emotion, and/or positive findings on the sleep laboratory test known as the Multiple Sleep Latency Test, which consists of four 20-minute opportunities to nap offered at 2-hour intervals throughout the day. Patients diagnosed with narcolepsy fall asleep quickly, with a mean sleep latency of 8 minutes or less, and will have two or more transitions into REM sleep over the four opportunities to nap. Normal controls, by contrast, will have an average sleep latency of 12 to 14 minutes and show no REM sleep on the Multiple Sleep Latency Test. The certainty of the diagnosis of narcolepsy is decreased if the patient does not have a history of cataplexy, does not show increased tendency to sleep, and does not have REM sleep in sleep laboratory studies. The theoretical relationship between the symptoms of narcolepsy and the polysomnographic finding of sleep-onset REM periods is that, in narcolepsy, the mechanism controlling REM sleep is weakened such that components of REM sleep are manifested abnormally during wakefulness as cataplexy (the motor inhibitory component) and during sleep as sleep-onset REM periods. The current definitions of narcolepsy include signs of abnormal control of REM sleep as a major component of the syndrome.

Treatment

There is no cure as yet for narcolepsy. Stimulant drugs such as the amphetamines were first used to control sleepiness in the 1930s. However, although stimulants such as d-amphetamine, methamphetamine, and methylphenidate are effective in reducing the sleep tendency of patients with narcolepsy, these drugs have little long-term effect on the symptoms of cataplexy, hypnagogic hallucinations, and sleep paralysis. In current practice, the symptoms of narcolepsy are controlled with a two-pronged approach: stimulants to control the abnormal tendency to fall asleep at inappropriate times and drugs such as antidepressants that suppress REM sleep, to control the symptoms of cataplexy, sleep paralysis, and

hypnagogic hallucinations. [See Psychopharmacology.] Even with the chemotherapeutic approach of psychostimulants for somnolence and REM-sleep suppressing drugs for ancillary symptoms, patients with narcolepsy cannot perform on psychomotor tasks or maintain alertness as well as normal controls. Consequently, patients with narcolepsy must face various psychosocial and work-related problems throughout a lifetime of treatment. Patients who take the maximum recommended doses of stimulant medication rarely reach above 70 to 80% of normal control levels on tests of performance and alertness (Miller, Hajdukovic, Erman, & Koziol, 1990).

Although the symptoms of narcolepsy do not worsen greatly with age, they do interact negatively with other age-related problems and medical conditions. As a result, patients with narcolepsy often experience progressive difficulty in meeting economic and social responsibilities throughout their lives. Patients with narcolepsy have the additional burden of having to cope with misinformation in the health-care community about the causes and the involuntary nature of the symptoms of narcolepsy. Common misconceptions are that the symptoms of narcolepsy, such as sleep attacks and cataplexy, are manifestations of denial and avoidance and that symptoms can be controlled with behavioral or psychotherapeutic techniques. There is no credible evidence to support such ideas. However, there is a role for modern psychological intervention in the management of patients with narcolepsy. Such patients often benefit from participation in professionally supervised support groups that focus on coping skills, identification of community resources for assistance with administrative and medical issues related to pharmacotherapy, and general camaraderie (Goswami et al., 1992).

[See also Antidepressants; Arthritis; Autoimmune Diseases; Drugs; Hallucinations; Insomnia; Psychopharmacology; Sleep; Sleep Apnea; Sleep Disorders; and Twins.]

Bibliography

Goswami, M., Pollak, C. P., Cohen, F. L., Thorpy, M. J., Kavey, N. B., & Kutscher, A. H. (Eds.). (1992). *Psychosocial aspects of narcolepsy: Loss, grief and care* (Vol. 5, Nos 3/4). Binghamton, NY: Haworth Press.

Guilleminault, C., Dement, W. C., & Passouant, P. (Eds.). (1976). *Narcolepsy: Vol. 3, Advances in sleep research.* New York: Spectrum.

Honda, Y., & Juji, T. E. (1988). *HLA in narcolepsy.* Heidelberg, Germany: Springer-Verlag.

Kryger, M. H., Roth, T., & Dement, W. C. (1994). *Principles and practice of sleep medicine* (2nd ed.). Toronto, Ontario, Canada: Saunders.

Lin, L., Farasco, J. et al. (1999). The sleep disorder canine narcolepsy is caused by a mutation in the hypocretin (orexin) receptor 2 gene, *Cell 98*, 1–20.

Mitler, M. M., Aldrich, M. S., Koob, G. F., & Zarcone, V. P. (1994). Narcolepsy and its treatment with stimulants. *Sleep, 17*, 352–371.

Mitler, M. M., Hajdukovic, R. M., Erman, M., & Koziol, J. A. (1990). Narcolepsy. *Journal of Clinical Neurophysiology, 7*, 93–118.

Merrill M. Mitler

NARRATIVE PSYCHOLOGY can be variously defined as a broad philosophical development or paradigm shift; an emerging area of theoretical and substantive inquiry; and the application of narrative theory by practitioners and researchers. Each of these ways of understanding narrative psychology can be linked with particular historical developments, issues in academic discourse, and problem-solving efforts in psychology and related disciplines in the social sciences.

The Narrative Turn in the Philosophy of Knowledge

The narrative paradigm of knowledge, which emerged in the 1980s with the *social constructionist movement* and other interpretive approaches to the social sciences (Gergen, 1985), has derived support from the *hermeneutic tradition* in the humanities and the psychology of narrative knowing (Polkinghorne, 1988). [*See* Hermeneutics; *and* Social Constructionism.] In conceptualizing human knowledge in terms of narratives and their interpretation in a social context, implicit assumptions are made about the social nature of the mind as well as the role of language in establishing intersubjective understanding. This constructionist, interpretive view of knowledge departs from the assumptions of objective science which are based on Realist notions of an independent world that exists apart from the knower. It places greater emphasis on the social processes of creating knowledge and validating knowledge claims. Thus, it is consistent with cultural, anthropological, and sociological accounts of science and how knowledge is generated in the human domain.

The shift to a narrative paradigm has coincided with objections to Realist philosophy that is based on untenable assumptions of objectivity in human knowing. Even as philosophers of science granted the mediating role of language in understanding human realities (Greenwood, 1991), however, the ideals of objective science have held strong in mainstream psychology. The preference for logico-scientific ways of knowing is juxtapositioned against narrative knowing as an alternative mode of inquiry (Bruner, 1986). Narrative knowing is premised on the storied nature of human knowledge. This shift to the narrative base of knowledge is reflected

by a continuum of perspectives in the philosophy of knowledge that focus to varying degrees on social, interpretive, and pragmatic practices that are embedded in cultural, sociopolitical, and historical contexts. In this sense, the narrative paradigm has become a second order or meta-level theory about how theoretical accounts are created in human inquiry through social interpretive processes and applications in context.

As a metatheoretical perspective, the narrative paradigm is equated in most circles with the hermeneutic approach that treats knowledge as textual accounts to be interpreted and deconstructed for limiting assumptions or questionable analytical frames. Whether an account is evaluated as having pragmatic validity and social value depends on epistemic and other value judgments made in the hermeneutic process. As a meta-thesis on how to evaluate knowledge, the narrative-hermeneutic approach relies primarily on communal discourse and shared horizons of interpretation. This can present problems with finding common standards and in reaching agreements.

In addition to the philosophical underpinnings of social constructionism, the narrative approach to knowledge also emphasizes the role of the person in self-interpretation, and the assumption of personal agency in enacting story-form knowledge. Consequently, the narrative turn in philosophy has brought about an increased attention to the reflexive or self-referencing and self-directed nature of human knowing. As a philosophy of human nature, the narrative paradigm entails both individual and social ontology to the extent that personal knowing and self-interpretation are expected to interact with intersubjective knowing and social interpretation. Narrative knowledge is a function of the mutual interpretation of self and others in dialogue. The cultural view of psychology accounts for how people appropriate meanings and narrative scripts from their culture in developing individual identities as they interact with the environment (Hoshmand, 1996, 1998). Human beings, as products of culture, are subject to both the possibilities and constraints of social living. Thus, individual ontology or psychological being is coconstituted by social ontology or the nature of human society.

A number of journals, such as *Theory and Psychology* (1996, 6, no. 1) and *Psychological Inquiry* (1996, 7, no. 4), have devoted whole issues to the narrative-hermeneutic perspective. Discussions on the philosophical implications of the narrative perspective can be found in the *Journal of Theoretical and Philosophical Psychology* and in the journal, *New Ideas in Psychology*. Due to its roots in the humanities, narrative study has continued to be the subject of multiple disciplines. For example, the *Journal of Narrative and Life History* included a series of articles (1997, whole Vol. 7) tracing the development of narratology and the changing perspectives in literary theory on a contextualist conception of narrative interpretation. The issues raised in narrative disciplines such as literary study are parallel to those encountered when psychologists and other social scientists engage in interpretive approaches to knowledge.

Issues in Narrative Psychology

A basic tenet of narrative knowledge is that the author of a narrative account and the interpreter or evaluator of the account share a common space of understanding. Shared meaning systems may be appropriated from similar cultural sources or made possible by a shared social and value context. When these conditions are not optimally available, the interlocutors may have difficulty with understanding. The hermeneutic process of searching for interpretive possibilities, while being cognizant of the fact that one's understanding is always limited, also means that assumptions cannot be made about who has ultimate authority in the interpretation of a given text. Although the author of an account has a primary role in its creation, the social, dialogical view of interpretive knowing requires interpretive authority to be shared with others who review the narrated account. This question of authority in interpretation remains the main issue in hermeneutics and all narrative disciplines.

When theoretical accounts are being evaluated for the purpose of knowledge, the issue of judging validity and truth value becomes a problem for the discourse community involved in adjudicating different accounts. One of the underlying issues concerns the representational role of language in establishing truth value. Spence (1982) distinguished between narrative truth that is self-interpreted or socially constructed from historical truth that is constituted by actual events and actions. Although both narrative truths and historical truths are important in the human realm, there is a polarizing tendency in psychology and other social sciences to privilege one type of truth account over another. A continuing debate is seen, for example, in the discussion on the primacy of cognition versus narration (Drury, 1994). The question is raised as to whether causal explanations, in the nature of asserted historical truths based on the realist assumptions of objective science, or hermeneutic accounts, in the nature of narrative truths based on an interpretive paradigm, should be granted. In this case, the narrative approach is placed on the same level as cognitive science as a theoretical perspective and theoretical account to be evaluated.

On the other hand, a narrative-hermeneutic approach can be adopted to evaluate all types of theoretical accounts as narratives. As a philosophy of knowledge or epistemic perspective, the narrative metatheory requires all theoretical accounts to be deconstructed and critiqued in terms of underlying assumptions. This distinction between narrative perspective as theory, and narrative perspective as metatheory, is important in understanding the issues associated with narrative psychology.

A related issue concerns ontological assumptions about nature rather than epistemological assumptions about how we know. Some of the theoretical discussions have been centered around whether narrative psychology is inherently consistent with an individual conception of human nature or with a social ontology (Burkitt, 1996). This is reflected in questions regarding whether personality concepts and developmental theories stemming from a trait conception can be reinterpreted in terms of narrative psychology. As more social conceptions of personality and identity development are derived under the narrative paradigm, there have been opposing arguments for asserting the objective status of causal factors in individual psychology. This polarization between individual and social ontology can be avoided by viewing cognition and culture as coconstituted (Lucariello, 1995) and by seeing narrative as the dialogical organizing principle in the study of culture, mind, and person (Cole & Engestrom, 1995). That the field of psychology has not entirely endorsed this dialectical possibility is reflected in the continuing discussions about contextual versus noncontextual aspects of studying a given phenomenon, and in theorizing about objective nonintentional constraints on psychological life as the limits of a purely interpretive understanding of human nature.

The issue of interpretive authority mentioned above is also closely linked with the issue of voice. The author's voice, which is primary in the construction of a narrative account, should be exercised with a certain degree of freedom. Yet, if expected to interact dialogically with the voices of others, it is subject to social and political constraints. These constraints on voice have implications for power in relationships. Hermans (1996) provides a discussion of the role of dominance in both the interpersonal and intrapersonal processes, and the relevance of collective voices for contemporary psychology. The consideration of voice in dialogical exchange is regarded as crucial to self-organization. Hence, it has both sociopolitical and psychological significance. These complex issues will continue to be encountered by theorists and be addressed by philosophical psychologists.

The Narrative Metaphor in Theory Construction

The narrative turn has brought about great interest in theory development in psychology and the related disciplines. Since Sarbin (1986) introduced the narrative metaphor into psychological theorizing, considerable efforts in theory development have followed. A number of proposals have been made that utilize narrative as a base metaphor for theory construction and theoretical integration. One proposal is for a narrative psychology of human action to serve as a conceptual framework for understanding cultural diversity, psychopathology, and psychotherapeutic practice (Howard, 1991). Another proposal, for an integrative theory of personality development, involves incorporating trait theory, life story, and considerations of culture (McAdams, 1996). This type of conceptual bridging is found also in the proposal to adapt principles from social constructionism, personal construct psychology, and narrative psychology to form an overarching theory for the behavioral sciences (Mancuso, 1996).

The narrative metaphor has stimulated theoretical inquiry into the relationship between the mind and the self in human development. The dialogical self is regarded as an evolving psychological phenomenon that results from self-interpretation in a sociocultural context (Hermens & Kempen, 1993). Narrative structure is conceived to influence accounts of gender and the developing self over the life course (Labouvie-Vief, Orwoll, & Manion, 1995). In the study of human motivation, narrative is used as a theoretical postulate for linking individual psychology with cultural models of motivation (Jansz, 1996). Cultural motives constructed through social interaction are conceived to be translated into personal motivational narratives. In view of the centrality of narrative in human action and identity development through the cultural appropriation of personal motives and life scripts, narrative psychology has been used in developing a conceptual framework for understanding the psychology of moral identity, existential creativity, and commitment (Hoshmand, 1998). Other examples of the conceptual utility of narrative theory can be found in community psychology and therapeutic psychology.

The conceptual fertility of the narrative metaphor has coincided with a movement in psychology and other social sciences to adopt narrative-hermeneutic methods of empirical inquiry that have become available as alternatives to the quantitative research paradigm.

Narrative-Hermeneutic Methods of Inquiry

Developments in the philosophy of science, particularly the challenging of the positivistic tradition, led to new paradigms of research and inquiry in the 1980s and 1990s (Hoshmand, 1994). Whereas quantitative methods of research have been the standard methods in the experimental tradition of psychology, narrative ways of knowing associated with ethnographic, grounded-theory, and phenomenological methods are increasingly in use. These methodological choices share in common a narrative logic of argumentation, rich inductive description, and a process of interpretive analysis that is based on part-to-whole relationships. They are also similar in assuming a collaborative relationship between the researcher or enquirer and the human subject who is the source of self-interpreted meanings, as well as in emphasizing reflexivity on the part of the enquiring person as a participant observer. The fact that these methods focus on narrative data in the form of natural language rather than quantitative data that are statistically transformed, they have been generically referred to as qualitative, interpretive methods.

Although there has been some effort toward teaching narrative-hermeneutic methods of inquiry (Hoshmand, 1989), they are seldom included in standard texts of research design and methodology in psychology. Mainstream journals published by the American Psychological Association (APA) seldom include narrative research or discussions of narrative methods. As an exception, the *Journal of Counseling Psychology* has on occasion included articles on the subject. *The Counseling Psychologist*, which is the journal for the Counseling Psychology Division of APA, has carried discussion articles periodically on qualitative methods, including the narrative-hermeneutic approach. The *Journal of Constructivist Psychology* is most representative of narrative approaches, being open to contributions in personal construct psychology, social constructionism, and narrative psychology. Other sources of information on narrative-hermeneutic methods can be found in the multidisciplinary literature on qualitative research methods, and in books on qualitative methodology and narrative topics such as those published by Sage in the 1990s.

Given the epistemic assumptions of narrative construction and the importance of personal and social context in interpretive methods of knowing, it follows that these methods would be used for substantive inquiry in narrative psychology. Narrative modes of inquiry have contributed to a renewed interest in idiographic approaches, namely, case study and the use of information from personal life history. This is seen in personality research and personological studies. In the years since the *Journal of Personality* devoted a special issue to psychobiography (1998, 56, no. 1), there has been considerable research utilizing biographical case study and narrative methods. The degree of acceptance of these research efforts has been partly a function of how case study methodology is viewed as a scientific tool, and whether the idiographic approach is considered to be capable of contributing to theoretical knowledge. Such issues associated with narrative methods further add to the need for continuing discussion on the nature of reliability and validity in using these methods of inquiry.

From the standpoint of methodological pluralism, narrative-hermeneutic methods are an important part of the research repertoire of psychologists because of their complementary strengths in comparison with quantitative, experimental methods of research. Whereas quantitative, reductionistic (measurement oriented) methods have been used for theory-driven hypothesis testing in experimental research, narrative methods have been helpful in generating hypotheses in discovery research and in building inductive patterns for theory development. Due to the inclusion of context, particularly in connection with case study, these methods have high yields in meaning. For this reason, they are considered to be more suited to understanding human experience. Narrative methods of research have been adopted by those who find traditional experimental methods to be limiting in the study of psychological phenomena that are not amenable to reductionistic ways of knowing that fail to include contextual factors, or quantitative operationalization that fail to capture the essence of what is being studied.

The influence of narrative psychology, with its theoretical and methodological characteristics, has been extended to psychotherapeutic practice. This is partly because there is less of a distance between narrative methods of research and narrative modes of knowing in clinical inquiry. The attitudes and inquiry process adopted by the narrative researcher are similar to those of a practitioner in trying to understand the experience and personal meanings of a client.

Narrative Psychology in Practice

Narrative psychology has appealed to practitioners in counseling and psychotherapeutic practice. Since the notion of therapy as social conversation was advanced (Howard, 1991; McNamee & Gergen, 1992; Martin, 1994), there have been various extensions of this line of thought in the literature on therapeutic psychology. The theoretical rationale for narrative therapy and related issues are presented, for example, in a special section on narrative theory and therapy in the *Journal of Constructivist Psychology* (1994, 7, no. 4).

The narrative approach to psychological practice is characterized by a number of values, including therapist reflexivity, egalitarian attitudes, and empowerment of the client as the author of his or her own experience as narrated and self-interpreted. The social process of facilitating the construction of personal meanings, as well as sensitivity to the political and moral implications of such construction are paramount. It is assumed that people can revise their life scripts and enable new possibilities for living through narrative reconstruction.

Given the similarities between narrative approaches to practice and narrative methods of research and inquiry, narrative epistemology is central to the epistemology of practice. Narrative knowing by story-form self-interpretation, processes of intersubjective exchange, and the discerning of patterns and part-whole

relationships can be regarded as an important means of developing understanding in psychological practice. The philosophical underpinnings of the narrative paradigm have enabled psychological practice to be informed by new models of knowledge that emphasize the intersubjectivity and social embeddedness of practice. Whereas traditional science-based practice was justified by particular philosophical and theoretical foundations, practitioners of postmodern times tend to apply pluralistic approaches that are to be validated pragmatically in action (Polkinghorne, 1992). It is through reflective practice that accounts for the self of the practitioner and the cultural embeddedness of interactions with clients that the knowledge of such practice develops. Case studies and narrative methods of inquiry further enable practitioners to produce and contextualize the knowledge of practice. Hermeneutic analysis can be applied further to evaluate therapeutic narratives and generalized narratives that are evolved from practice.

Just as theoretical accounts as narratives are evaluated for their epistemic value, narrative discourse as a social practice is subject to evaluation for their social, political, and moral implications. Critical theorists and hermeneutic philosophers have examined the narrative discourse and professional practices of psychology for their underlying assumptions and societal implications (Prilleltensky, 1997; Richardson & Woolfolk, 1994). The narrative metaphor and the significance of discourse have stimulated communal attention to the social nature and value of psychological practice. Discourse analysis, as a hermeneutic practice in the social sciences, is being considered by those who believe that the scientific and professional discourse of psychology should be subject to critical analysis in communal evaluation.

The Future of Narrative Psychology

The development of narrative psychology, having coincided with broader philosophical and methodological developments that impacted the social sciences during the 1980s and 1990s, is a phenomenon that has far-reaching implications. Narrative metatheory will continue to be an important perspective in the philosophy of knowledge and in the discussion of how epistemic evaluation of different theoretical accounts should be conducted. It may serve as a framework for theoretical integration in areas such as those currently being considered. The conceptual utility of the narrative metaphor will probably be demonstrated in theory development across diverse areas of psychology. Idiographic case study and personality research that have been stimulated by the development of narrative psychology may yield significant findings on the nature of identity development. To the extent that narrative methods of inquiry based on qualitative, interpretive paradigms are included in the pluralistic methodological repertoire of psychologists, narrative methodology may become a widely used approach in mainstream psychology.

One of the most promising developments associated with narrative psychology is its application in psychotherapeutic practice. Together with scholarly attention to the epistemology of practice, the reflective practice of narrative therapies may offer opportunities for psychologists to study and illuminate the nature of knowing in therapeutic, educational, and other practices.

Another contribution related to narrative psychology is the hermeneutic emphasis on critical deconstruction of both theory and practice. The narrative-hermeneutic approach enables theorists, researchers, and practitioners in psychology and other social sciences to add a critical dimension to their work by questioning the underlying assumptions and being cognizant of the cultural and political context in which their work is embedded. This may help to promote the reflexive evaluation of the professions. Narrative psychology is premised on social discourse and attention to the social processes of establishing the epistemic and social value of research and practice. The rise of narrative psychology may bring about more interest in discourse analysis and the communal processes involved in evaluating the knowledge enterprise and professional practices of psychology.

What remains for psychologists and philosophers to debate is the nature of psychology as a discipline. Narrative psychology favors a cultural view of psychology as an interpretive science and social practice. Social constructionists, critical realists, and pragmatist philosophers will continue to examine the possibility of reconciling the cultural view of psychology with psychology as an objective, experimental science. A broadened perspective may emerge of a less polarized and more complete psychology that can account for our self-interpreting, story-form approach to life as cultural beings, as well as the dialectical interaction of cultural forces with biological and ecological factors in human development.

[See also Epistemology; Hermeneutics; and Philosophy, article on Philosophy of Science.]

Bibliography

Bruner, J. (1986). *Actual minds, possible worlds*. Cambridge, MA: Harvard University Press. Presents a cultural perspective on the nature of the mind, with the distinction between narrative knowing and logicoscientific knowing as two modes of human inquiry.

Burkitt, I. (1996). Social and personal constructs: A division left unresolved: Comment. *Theory and Psychology, 6*, 71–77. Discusses the theoretical and philosophical differences between the individual ontology in personal construct theory and the social ontology in social constructionism.

Cole, M., & Engestrom, Y. (1995). Mind, culture, person: Elements in a cultural psychology: Comment. *Human Development, 38*, 19–24. Comments on the evolution of cultural psychology paradigms, proposing dialogical diversity and collaboration as an integrative approach.

Drury, J. (1994). Cognitive science and hermeneutic explanation: Symbiotic or incompatible frameworks? *Philosophy, Psychiatry, and Psychology, 1*, 41–50. Argues for how cognitive science can serve as an objective, empirical anchor for hermeneutic interpretations in psychoanalysis.

Gergen, K. J. (1985). The social constructionist movement in modern psychology. *American Psychologist, 40*, 266–275. Discusses implications of the new philosophy of science that views knowledge as a social construction and not as an objective representation of the world.

Greenwood, J. D. (1991). *Relations and representations: An introduction to the philosophy of social psychological science*. New York: Routledge.

Hermans, H. J. M. (1996). Voicing the self: From information processing to dialogical interchange. *Psychological Bulletin, 119*, 31–50. Contrasts the narrative metaphor and the computer metaphor of the developing self, emphasizing the role of voice and dialogue in self-organization.

Hermans, H. J. M., & Kempen, H. J. G. (1993). *The dialogical self: Meaning as movement*. San Diego, CA: Academic Press.

Hoshmand, L. T. (1989). Alternate research paradigms: A teaching proposal. *The Counseling Psychologist, 17*, 3–79. Outlines the philosophical assumptions of qualitative research paradigms, including the ethnographic, grounded theory, phenomenological, and narrative-hermeneutic approaches, with a proposal for teaching and curriculum development.

Hoshmand, L. T. (1994). *Orientation to inquiry in a reflective professional psychology*. Albany, NY: State University of New York Press. Provides the historical background for the shift to new philosophies and models of knowledge in psychology, with an emphasis on reflective attention to epistemic development and evaluation of the profession.

Hoshmand, L. T. (1996). Cultural psychology as metatheory. *Journal of Theoretical and Philosophical Psychology, 16*, 30–48. Explains the cultural perspective and how it can serve as an overarching framework for theoretical integration in the semiotic sciences and provide a direction for psychology as a cultural science.

Hoshmand, L. T. (1998). *Creativity and moral vision in psychology: Narratives of identity and commitment in a postmodern age*. Thousand Oaks, CA: Sage. Addresses problems of epistemic and moral relativism by emphasizing practical ethics as demonstrated by a narrative study of professional identity and creative life commitments.

Howard, G. S. (1991). Culture tales: A narrative approach to thinking, cross-cultural psychology, and psychotherapy. *American Psychologist, 46*, 187–197. Argues for a narrative approach to human action, with applications to understanding cultural diversity, that views the development of identity as being a function of life-story construction, psychopathology as instances of life stories gone awry, and psychotherapy as exercises in story repair.

Jansz, J. (1996). Constructed motives. *Theory and Psychology, 6*, 471–484.

Labouvie-Vief, G., Orwoll, L., & Manion, M. (1995). Narratives of mind, gender, and the life course. *Human Development, 38*, 239–257. Reformulates theories of the mind, self, and gender in terms of cultural discourse and the narrative structure of the self.

Lucariello, J. (1995). Mind, culture, person: Elements in a cultural psychology. *Human Development, 38*, 2–18. Examines four views of cognition, culture, and person since the 1960s and proposes an interactive view of culture as intentional worlds constituted by personal agency and practices.

Mancuso, J. C. (1996). Constructionism, personal construct psychology, and narrative psychology. *Theory and Psychology, 6*, 47–70. Discusses the epistemological assumptions shared by social constructionism, personal construct psychology, and narrative psychology.

Martin, J. (1994). *The construction and understanding of psychotherapeutic change.* New York: Teachers College Press. Integrates the narrative understanding of therapeutic change with research on memory and how personal theories are modified through therapeutic conversations.

McAdams, D. P. (1996). What this framework can and cannot do. *Psychological Inquiry, 7*, 378–386. Comments on several critiques of McAdams's proposal for an overarching framework that integrates trait conceptions of personality with the holistic narrative study of lives and identity development.

McNamee, S., & Gergen, K. (Eds.). (1992). *Therapy as social construction.* London: Sage. Presents a number of articles on the application of social constructionist ideas in the therapeutic context.

Polkinghorne, D. E. (1988). *Narrative knowing and the human sciences.* Albany, NY: State University of New York Press. Draws on the narrative traditions in history, literature, and existential-phenomenological philosophy in presenting narrative knowing as an integrative force in the development of human science methodology.

Polkinghorne, D. E. (1992). Postmodern epistemology of practice. In S. Kvale (Ed.), *Psychology and postmodernism* (pp. 146–165). Newbury Park, CA: Sage. Discusses the pluralistic nature of postmodern approaches to knowledge and how it parallels the knowledge of practice in its need for flexibility and pragmatic verification.

Prilleltensky, I. (1997). Values, assumptions, and practices: Assessing the moral implications of psychological discourse and action. *American Psychologist, 52*, 517–535. Presents the critical perspective in deconstructing the assumptions and discussing the moral implications of psychological theory and practice.

Richardson, F. C., & Woolfolk, R. L. (1994). Social theory and values: A hermeneutic perspective. *Theory and Psychology, 4*, 199–226. Provides a philosophical hermeneutic framework for evaluating different approaches to social inquiry, drawing on the ideas of H. G. Gadamer and C. Taylor on issues of cultural values and political power.

Sarbin, T. R. (Ed.). (1986). *Narrative psychology: The storied nature of human conduct.* New York: Praeger. A collection of articles on contextualism, narrative methodology, and theoretical discussions of applications of the narrative approach.

Spence, D. P. (1982). *Narrative truth and historical truth.* New York: Norton.

Lisa Tsoi Hoshmand

NARRATIVE THERAPY is an approach to counseling and psychotherapy that draws on postmodern constructivist ideas to inform its theory and practice. Constructivism holds that persons' lives are constituted by the meanings they ascribe to their experiences. According to narrative therapy theory, people's self-understanding is a constructed meaning scheme that people ascribe to their selves. Narrative therapy also holds that the linguistic form through which people construct the meaning of their lives and the lives of others is narrative, or story. Narratives select from the multitude of one's life actions and happenings and assigns them meaning according to their contribution to their story's theme. In this way, people's narratives about their self provide their lives with a sense of continuity and congruence. The purpose of narrative therapy is to assist clients in becoming aware that often the source of the problem that motivates them to seek therapy is a restrictive self story. Through this awareness clients are able to distance themselves from their restrictive stories and, therefore, to issue forth revised stories that are able to accommodate the full range of their past life events and their preferred future designs.

Narrative therapy developed within the family therapy tradition. Under the influence of therapists associated with the Mental Research Institute of Palo Alto, California, the focus in family therapy has changed from family structures to the meanings or interpretations clients give to life events. One of the techniques that reflects this change is reframing. In reframing, clients are offered alternate interpretations of their situations or other people's behavior. The theory supporting reframing is that the source of people's behavior is the interpreted meanings they give to their own life events and the actions of others. Thus, when clients' interpretations are altered, their behaviors change. Narrative therapy extended the practice of reframing by making use of the view, developed in narrative studies, that people's interpretation or understanding of their selves is brought about by organizing their life events into a narrative, or story. According to this position, one's self is analogous to the meaning that resonates from a text and is not an unchanging essence or object. In addition to extending the idea of reframing, narrative therapy retains, as part of its own practice, other family therapy activities—for example, focusing on clients' strengths and resources, viewing clients as experts on what is best for their own lives, and understanding therapy to be a co-constructive undertaking between clients and therapists.

Family therapists Australian Michael White, who previously had developed the therapeutic technique of externalization, and New Zealander David Epston produced the major theoretical expression in their 1990 book *Narrative Means to Therapeutic Ends*. Their theory makes use of the ideas of the postmodern French philosophers Michel Foucault and Jacques Derrida. From Foucault they drew the idea that the stories that often are employed by people to guide their lives are simply expressions of social assumptions and prejudices. Michael White and David Epston adapted Derrida's technique of deconstruction, which he used to critique philosophic texts, as a method for assisting clients in overcoming the domination that inadequate, socially derived stories have over their lives. In making use of these postmodern ideas, White and Epston altered them to fit with their belief that people have a capacity to make changes in their life stories, and that therapy can assist in making these changes.

In the narrative therapy view, people's familiar and everyday taken-for-granted notion of who they are is constituted by the cultural structures and values in which they are embedded. These cultural patterns are immanent in the language employed for describing, labeling, classifying, and evaluating others and one's self. The stories people internalize give definition to their selves and are framed by the dominant culture's assumptions. For example, in the West, the mainstream story frames establish highly individualistic and gender-distinct specifications for ways of being in the world. People's lives are permeated and produced by the cultural patterns into which they are assimilated. Some people experience the meanings generated by their adopted cultural story as impoverishing for their own lives and the lives of others. The practices in narrative therapy are designed to assist persons to separate from those cultural stories that are permeated by cultural assumptions and into which they were recruited, and to reauthor a self-interpretation that is more open and can displaying the full range of their selfhood.

The general strategy of narrative therapy practice is first, to assist clients in deconstructing their inherently problematic culturally provided identity stories; second, to assist in reconstructing an alternate and preferred interpretation of who they are and who they will be. Separating the narrative therapy into two separate

phases—deconstruction and reconstruction—is a heuristic device; in actual practice narrative therapy fluctuates irregularly between the two phases.

In the deconstructive phase, clients are encouraged to become aware of their self-stories and the cultural assumptions built into them. Through what is termed externalizing conversations, clients are engaged in unmasking and subverting their old, hindering stories and in replacing them with more adequate and preferred stories. Dominating old stories distort clients' views of their selves, and they produce problems in living because of the incongruousness of the story. Externalizing conversations are intended to distance clients from their hindering stories and from the problems they generate. The practice of deconstructing old stories is initiated by encouraging clients to give an account of how the problem generated by their hindering story has affected their view of themselves and their relationships. Clients are then invited to chart the influence that these problems have had on their lives over time. Externalizing conversations also often include an investigation of how clients had been recruited into their dominating and restricting, old stories.

When clients' stories are unmasked through deconstruction, clients become aware that the story that they have internalized manifests the power imbalances supported by their culture. Many problems of living that are experienced by clients are consequences of the culture's structures. In areas such as class, sexual orientation, race, gender, and so forth, culturally structured life stories distribute power to some groups and subjugate others. In living out the dominant stories of one's culture, people often serve to sustain and continue a culture's power imbalances. In the process of deconstructing the stories that have guided their lives, clients' come to realize that their local problems are merely particular instances of the problems inherent in their socially generated stories. The deconstructive phase makes the clients aware that the interpretative story through which they have identified themselves is only one of the possible constructions of their identity. Their operating story is simply the one into which were recruited.

In the second phase of narrative—reauthoring—clients are assisted in reconstructing their self-stories. The understanding that informs reconstructive work is that life experience is richer and more complex than what is called to the fore by their adopted identities. There are always feelings and lived experiences that are not fully encompassed by the dominant story. Narrative therapy holds that many problems for which people seek therapy are a consequence of their self-stories not sufficiently representing their lived experience. There are significant and vital aspects of their experience that contradict their dominant narratives. Two practices— externalizing the problem and recognizing unique outcomes—facilitate the generation of alternate self-stories.

In externalizing the problem, clients are assisted to bring about a linguistic separation of the problem from their personal identity. This move toward separation in expressed in the slogan, The person is not the problem, the problem is the problem. Clients are asked to personify the problem by naming (or drawing) it. For example, a child whose problem is excessive misbehavior might name the problem Mr. Mischief. The therapist then asks questions about Mr. Mischief; for example: How has Mr. Mischief been interfering in your life? When does he try to take control of you? What does he do to produce the mischievous behavior? Dominant stories are often problem saturated and depict a problem as an element within the person's identity. By externalizing their problems, clients are released from the belief that they lack the ability to cope with or gain control over their problems.

The term *unique outcome* is borrowed from the sociologist Goffman, and in narrative therapy it refers to clients' actions that contradict their dominant self-stories. The point of attending to unique outcomes is to make visible life events that had been made invisible by clients' old self-stories. The child in the example would be asked to bring to awareness the experiences in which he had successfully resisted the efforts of Mr. Mischief to take control of his life. The recognition of past unique outcomes penetrates the old, dominant stories and induces changes in the self-story, with the old story's plot revised to incorporate the unique outcomes into its plot. Not all past actions are unique outcomes needs, only those that significantly produced what are understood as preferred outcomes. The work on unique outcomes makes apparent to clients that their dominant stories were too limiting to encompass the full range of their actions. The new, emerging story expands to include those strong actions that resisted the power of the problem.

Both externalizing the problem and recovering unique outcomes serve to separate clients from their previously assumed identity. These processes make it more possible for clients to orient themselves to aspects of their experience that contradicts their previously held interpretations of who they were. Clients then become able to play an active role in how they conceive of their selves. Their reauthoring of their life stories is not a matter of deciding to make themselves into someone else nor is it revisionist history of their past actions. Rather, reauthoring is a process (in part unconscious) of devising, not imposing, a story that is inclusive and complex enough to display the full array of their past actions and serve as a guide for their future ones.

Because narrative therapy focuses on the individuality of each client and resists classification into diagnostic categories, it has looked to case studies and endorsements from therapists for confirmation of its effectiveness. One between-groups study, by White of chronic psychiatric patients, has been published. His finding was that his patients who received narrative therapy stayed in the hospital for an average of 14 days, compared to members of a matched control group receiving standard psychiatric care, who stayed an average of 36 days.

Donald E. Polkinghorne

NATIONAL ACADEMY OF SCIENCES. Chartered in 1863, the National Academy of Sciences (NAS) of the United States of America is an autonomous, private, nonprofit society of distinguished scientists that functions as both an honorific society and an advisory body. Under the terms of its charter, signed on 3 March 1863 by President Abraham Lincoln, the NAS is mandated to advise the federal government on scientific and technological matters whenever called upon.

During its first decades, the NAS drew its membership from the traditional scientific disciplines, mathematics and physics in particular. This followed from its beginnings as a wartime consulting body concerned with evaluating new technologies. Charles Sanders Peirce, a mathematician-logician who had done some early studies of vision, was elected to membership in 1877, but no person who was unmistakably a psychologist was elected to academy membership until 1901, when experimental psychologist James McKeen Cattell was admitted. Because experimental psychology was still a new discipline when Cattell was elected, it was not at that time represented by any of the academy's discipline-based bodies for the classification of members, or standing committees, as they were then called. The closest available representative body was the Standing Committee on Anthropology, and it was to this committee that Cattell was assigned upon his election.

By 1910, the academy recognized that its classification system did not adequately represent the then-current state of science, which was marked by the growth of disciplines, increased interdisciplinary relationships, and burgeoning specialization. Accordingly, in that year a Committee for the Division of the Committees on Anthropology and Biology was put together. Although not a member of this committee, Cattell suggested that the Committee on Anthropology be reorganized as the Committee on Anthropology and Psychology. By Cattell's calculation, the academy membership at that point included three psychologists. Although the committee's original recommendation was to replace the Committee on Anthropology with a Committee on Psychology and Philosophy, its final recommendation, put before the academy's governing council in 1911, conformed to Cattell's suggestion. The recommendation was approved at the academy's annual meeting in 1911.

In its earliest incarnation, the Committee on Anthropology and Psychology (after 1915, the Section on Anthropology and Psychology) represented a diverse grouping of scientists. Besides counting Cattell and Josiah Royce among its members, it included educational philosopher John Dewey and Peirce, the mathematician-logician. This eclecticism in part reflects the fact that over the course of the first 50 years of its history, the academy had elected only three psychologists—Cattell (1901), William James (1903), and Royce (1906). The pace of election of psychologists would not increase until the 1920s, beginning with the election of James Angell in 1920.

With the entry of the United States into World War I in April 1917, the academy once again was in a position to offer its services to a government in need of scientific and technological mobilization for war. In the previous year, the academy had established a new operating arm, called the National Research Council (NRC), which was to serve as the federal government's main body for scientific and technological mobilization. Among the NRC committees set up to deal with war-related matters was a Committee on Psychology, whose chairman, American Psychological Association president Robert M. Yerkes (elected to academy membership in 1923), had suggested the committee's formation. Although Yerkes's committee conducted work in a number of areas, including morale, personnel classification, and the selection of ships' lookouts and airborne observers, it was most notable for having employed the Army Alpha test for conducting group intelligence testing of recruits.

Whatever its immediate merits or subsequent role in later controversies, the testing program played a significant part in realizing scientific psychologists' efforts to obtain general social recognition for their profession. But this did not translate into the attainment of disciplinary autonomy for psychology within the NAS-NRC structure. The 1918 reorganization of the NRC into divisions along disciplinary lines found the psychology committee placed under the Division of Medicine and Related Sciences, and the postwar reorganization of 1919, following the NRC's achievement of permanent status, saw the creation of a Division of Anthropology and Psychology, of which the American Psychological Association (APA) was a member society. The first chairman of this latter division, Walter Van Dyke Bingham of the Carnegie Institute of Technology, was a psychologist, as were three of the five members of its first executive committee.

The new division was intended to undertake interdisciplinary work. Rather than working in areas falling within the spheres of established organizations like the APA, the division was charged with organizing the cooperation of anthropology and psychology with other sciences and, consequently, with taking on projects consistent with that cooperation. Although a number of early project proposals failed to come to fruition, the division was highly active in World War II, having set up an Emergency Committee on Psychology, a Committee on Selection and Training of Aircraft Pilots (later renamed the Committee on Aviation Psychology), and other units working on war-related problems.

Within the academy itself, psychology was still represented in tandem with anthropology in a single section. In 1948 this changed, as the council of the academy, following a poll of the members, decided to separate psychology and anthropology into their own sections. By this time there were 23 psychologists on the membership rolls (representing approximately 5% of total academy membership), in contrast to 9 anthropologists. The decision may therefore be seen as a de facto recognition of the growing importance of psychology as a presence within the academy—an importance measured in terms not only of increased numbers of psychologists among the membership but also of the extensive war work carried out by NRC psychologists both within their division and in such extradivisional units as the NRC executive board's Office of Scientific Personnel. The academy continues to maintain a separate section for psychology, which in 1998 claimed 74 members, or approximately 3% of total academy membership.

Although psychology achieved autonomy in the academy structure, it continued to exist in larger interdisciplinary groupings within the NRC. In 1962 the Division of Anthropology and Psychology was reorganized into the Division of Behavioral Sciences, acknowledging the division's potential for representing a broader scope of work and interests. The first chairman of the new division, Carl Pfaffmann of Brown University, was a psychologist and an academy member since 1959. Subsequent reorganizations of the NRC in 1973 and 1982 placed psychology in cross-disciplinary units focused on broad policy problems, such as those arising from the introduction of new technologies, management techniques, and global changes generally. As a result, NRC studies with a significant psychological components are currently undertaken largely under the auspices of the Commission of Behavioral and Social Sciences and Education, although other study units, most notably those operating under the Institute of Medicine (IoM), may draw on expertise in psychology as well.

In the nearly 100 years since it was first represented in the academy, psychology has gone from a new discipline tenuously situated within the NAS structure to

INSTITUTE OF MENTAL HEALTH 391

a permanent presence within the honorary and advisory organs of the NAS-NRC.

Cochrane, R. C. (1978). *The National Academy of Sciences: The first hundred years, 1863–1963*. Washington, DC: National Academy of Sciences. A general history of the activities and organization of the National Academy of Sciences during its first hundred years. Includes detailed coverage of the National Research Council.

Halpern, J. (1997). The U.S. National Academy of Sciences: In service to science and society. *Proceedings of the National Academy of Sciences, 94*, 1606–1608. Discusses the academy's roles as a membership organization and an advisory body, with focus on current structure and activities.

Sokal, M. M. (Ed.). (1987). *Psychological testing and American society*. New Brunswick, NJ: Rutgers University Press. A collection of papers on the early history of psychological testing. Includes several contributions discussing Yerkes and group intelligence testing in World War I.

Stevens, S. S. (1952). The NAS-NRC and psychology. *American Psychologist, 7*, 119–124. Sometimes impressionistic discussion of psychology in the NAS and NRC through 1952. Touches on the roles and purposes of NAS and NRC.

True, F. W. (Ed.). (1913). *A history of the first half-century of the National Academy of Sciences*. Washington, DC: National Academy of Sciences. Includes detailed discussion of academy founders, early organizational structure, and advisory activities.

Daniel Barbiero

NATIONAL INSTITUTE OF MENTAL HEALTH. The National Mental Health Act, signed into law by President Harry Truman on 3 July 1946, enabled the creation of the National Institute of Mental Health (NIMH). The law provided for research related to understanding the causes of psychiatric disorders; for the development of more effective methods for their prevention, diagnosis, and treatment; for assisting the states in the use of these methods; and for training personnel in matters relating to mental health. Three factors were important in the creation of NIMH: (1) the large number of persons rejected for military service in World War II for mental health reasons, (2) the large number of mental health casualties in the war, and (3) increasing recognition of poor treatment of the mentally ill in state hospitals.

Organizational History

The two major components of NIMH are the extramural programs and activities that deal with grantees and the general public and the intramural research program (IRP), made up of NIMH scientists, support staff, and laboratories on the National Institutes of Health (NIH) campus in Bethesda, Maryland, and considered only briefly in this article. Organizational changes occurred over time in these components and in the location and status of NIMH in the United States Public Health Service (PHS).

From 1946 to 1949 NIMH was part of the Division of Mental Health (DMH) of the PHS, located on the NIH campus. Robert H. Felix, head of DMH, became the first of eight NIMH directors, all psychiatrists. The first NIMH research grant was awarded in July 1947 to psychologist Winthrop Kellogg of Indiana University for work on the basic structure of the learning process. In 1949 the DMH was abolished, and NIMH became the fourth institute of the NIH, uniquely emphasizing, in addition to research, mental health services, clinical training of professionals, and the behavioral and social sciences, distinctions giving NIMH the most checkered organizational history of any institute in NIH. NIMH developed organizational structures to represent the three areas of its broad charter, research, training, and services, adding entities as needed to reflect interests in special problems, populations, or activities.

In 1950 NIMH had fewer than 200 staff members and a budget of $11 million. Incremental growth in all programs during the 1950s sharply increased in the 1960s; when Felix retired in 1964, NIMH had a staff of more than 1200 and a budget of $171 million. Noteworthy accomplishments during this period included the initiation of a psychopharmacology research program (1954) and of research training in the biological and social sciences (1957) and in psychology (1959) and securing funds for construction (1965) and staffing (1967) of a national network of community mental health centers (CMHCs) that would give services the lion's share of the NIMH budget.

Under Stanley F. Yolles (1964–1970), NIMH, then the largest NIH institute, separated from NIH in 1967 as a bureau of PHS, located in Chevy Chase, Maryland. It was given control of St. Elizabeth's federal hospital for the mentally ill. In 1968 NIMH became part of a new agency, the Health Services and Mental Health Administration (HSMHA). Bertram S. Brown was named director in 1970, and NIMH relocated to Rockville, Maryland. NIMH was at its most expansive in the early 1970s, having staff and programs in alcoholism and drug abuse, staff in the ten PHS regional offices, two PHS hospitals, and an experimental field station in Prince George's County, Maryland. President Richard Nixon opposed federal support for training and felt service programs should be administered by the states. He unlawfully impounded funds for several programs in 1973, but his ideas were harbingers of things to come.

HSMHA was abolished in July 1973, and NIMH returned to NIH for a short period. The Alcohol, Drug Abuse, and Mental Health Administration (ADAMHA) was established in September 1973, containing NIMH and its new sister institutes on alcoholism and drug abuse.

Director Herbert Pardes's (1978–1984) major organizational change was to separate program development and management functions from the function of reviewing applications. Although outside experts perform the function of scientific review, they would now operate under review staff as part of a new NIMH review structure rather than under program staff. NIMH reached a high point of support ($569 million) in 1979 and suffered its greatest losses ($232 million) in 1982. The administration of President Ronald Reagan moved the CMHC program to the states under block grants, slashed funds for clinical training, and narrowed and eroded support for social research. Although NIMH had always supported biological research, its early years were characterized by a psychodynamic orientation in clinical research and attention to social factors that coincided with the "Great Society" programs in national government. The CMHCs were intended to be responsive, community-based treatment programs. Influential critics felt that NIMH research support lagged and that biological factors deserved greater attention.

Shervert Frazier's (1984–1986) reorganization in 1985 reflected previous budget decisions and abolished the divisions representing services and training, leaving NIMH with three research and research training divisions (basic, clinical, and applied/services) and a review division to handle a more limited set of functions than those envisioned in the NIMH charter. A tiny AIDS research program initiated in 1983 and directed by psychologist Ellen Stover has gained international recognition and had a budget of $114 million in 1999. Control of St. Elizabeth's Hospital was given to the District of Columbia in 1987. No significant organizational changes occurred during the directorship of Lewis Judd (1988–1991). Under Frederick Goodwin (1992–1994), ADAMHA was abolished in October 1992, and NIMH returned to NIH as a research institute, closing a circle that had begun almost 50 years before. Services research remained in NIMH, but other services-related programs and clinical training, with an exceedingly targeted focus, went to a new agency, the Substance Abuse and Mental Health Services Administration (SAMHSA).

Only a few members of the capable extramural NIMH staff can be noted. John Eberhart (1949–1954), Philip Sapir (1954–1967), and Louis Wienckowski (1967–1983) directed the research enterprise. Key roles were played by Richard Louttit, Lyle Bivens, and David Pearl in behavioral sciences; Martin Katz and Hussain Tuma in clinical research; Jonathan Cole, Nina Schooler, and Jerome Levine in psychopharmacology; Sam Keith in schizophrenia research; Robert Hirschfeld in depression research; Morris Parloff in psychotherapy research; and Morton Silverman and Joyce Lazar in research in prevention. Morton Kramer created the biostatistics program that eventually led to mental health epidemiology under Ben Locke and Darrel Regier. Seymour Vestermark, Neil Waldrop, William Denham, and Sam Silverstein, among others, directed training. Program chiefs included Milton Wittman (social work), Esther Garrison (nursing), Melvin Haas (psychiatry), Stanley Schneider (psychology, clinical and research training), Fred Elmadjian (biological sciences), Kenneth Lutterman (social sciences), and Ralph Simon (pilot and experimental programs). Jerry Carter, Sam Buker, Claudewell Thomas, Steven Sharfstein, Fred Spaner, and Thomas Lalley were associated with services and services research programs. Other notable staff were Joseph Bobbitt (a psychologist who had come with Felix); Elliot Liebow and Maury Lieberman (in metropolitan problems); Bert Boothe (in the scientist development program); Saleem Shah (in the crime and delinquency program); Lucy Ozarin and Charles Windle (in rural mental health programs); Howard Davis (in evaluation research); Delores Parron (in programs affecting women and ethnic minorities); Peter Jensen (in child mental health programs); psychologists Thomas Plaut, Frank Sullivan, Alan Leshner and, currently, Richard Nakamura (all deputy directors of NIMH); Leonard Mitnick, Peter Arnott, and Leonard Lash (research training); and Lorraine Torres and Eleanor Friedenberg (in the review division).

Steven Hyman, director since 1996, restructured the extramural program in September 1997 to address new developments in science and changes in the health-care system. Emphases included basic research in molecular biology, neuroscience, genetics, and behavior; the translation of basic knowledge into clinical applications; research on interventions and outcomes that have an impact on clinical practice; and policy-relevant research and research dissemination. Three new divisions were created: Basic and Clinical Neuroscience, re-titled Neuroscience and Basic Behavioral Science in 1999 (Steven Foote, acting director; Walter Goldschmidts, research training and career development); Mental Disorders, Behavioral Research, and AIDS (Ellen Stover, director of the division and of the Center for Mental Health Research on AIDS; Della Harr, research training); and Services and Intervention Research (Grayson Norquist, director; Kenneth Lutterman, research training). The Division of Extramural Activities, (Jane Steirberg, acting director) handles review but most of its former activities have been integrated into the NIH Center for Scientific Review, formerly the Division of Research

Grants. Two review branches remain in NIMH, one for neuroscience and behavioral science, the other for clinical applications, and they are responsible for the review of treatment research and services research. Both branches are headed by Laurence Stanford. Selected additional staff with general areas of responsibility include Kevin Quinn (behavioral and integrative neuroscience), Steven Moldin (genetics), Linda Brady (molecular and cellular neuroscience), Steven Zaleman (clinical neuroscience), Mary Ellen Oliveri (behavioral science), Doreen Koretz (developmental psychopathology and prevention), Bruce Cuthbert (adult psychopathology and prevention), Peter Muehrer (health and behavioral science), Barry Lebowitz (adult and geriatric treatment and preventive interventions), Benedetto Vitiello (child and adolescent treatment and preventive interventions), Grayson Norquist, acting (services research and clinical epidemiology), Juan Ramos (prevention), Sherman Ragland and Mary Blehar (special populations), Grayson Norquist, acting (rural mental health), and Stephen Koslow (neuroinformatics).

The intramural research program (IRP) gained momentum with Seymour Kety's arrival in 1950 to lead its basic research program. He recruited Robert A. Cohen to oversee clinical research. David Shakow headed the laboratory of psychology, which had almost 80 staff members at one time and which no longer exists. Psychologist John Eberhart was deputy director (1961–1967) and director (1967–1981) of IRP. The IRP has emphasized molecular biological and neuroscience approaches. It has been reviewed by a select outside group of scientists. It lacked a director from 1993 to 1998, when Robert Desimone was appointed. Desimone has a doctorate in neuropsychology and neuroscience and he continues to head the laboratory of neuropsychology. The intent is to revitalize what had been a glory of NIMH research and to capitalize on the ability of IRP to do things that cannot be done elsewhere. The close proximity of basic researchers to a clinical enterprise that is part of NIMH at the NIH clinical center should allow basic and clinical research to inform each other and to make translational research a reality.

Publications

NIMH publishes two quarterlies, the *Psychopharmacology Bulletin* and the *Schizophrenia Bulletin*. The final issue of the *Psychopharmacology Bulletin* is scheduled to appear in the fall of 1999. A third journal, *Psychotherapy and Rehabilitation Research Bulletin*, which had fewer than six issues, is no longer published. NIMH also publishes many volumes of interest to scientists and professionals, as well as mental health material for the general public, some of the latter available in Spanish. The number and scope of publications resulting from NIMH grants is too vast to consider here.

Meetings

The "convening" function of NIMH is a powerful and productive one, allowing expert scientific, professional, and public review and assessment of science, education, services, or policy relevant to mental health. NIMH may convene conferences itself or award a grant to an outside group to do so. Grants to the American Psychological Association, beginning with the Boulder conference in 1949, helped shape training in clinical psychology. The National Advisory Mental Health Council (NAMHC) meets four times a year. Policy sessions are generally open to the public, but grant review portions of these meetings, and those of grant review committees, are not.

Awards

The most prevalent awards are grants, often called awards. Mentored Research Scientist Development and Career Development awards, which originated in NIMH, are made to young investigators of exceptional promise, and more senior versions of these awards support those whose record of scientific productivity, leadership, and influence as mentors is exemplary. Merit awards allow a productive grantee, nominated and critically reviewed by NIMH staff and approved by NAMHC and the director, to receive additional time on a research grant without formal peer review. Grant awards may vary in size, from dissertation grants, B/Start awards for behavioral scientists, and small grants to large awards for several projects in the form of research center grants.

Sponsorship of Discoveries

The major purpose of NIMH is the sponsorship of new knowledge. IRP scientist Julius Axelrod shared a Nobel Prize in 1970 for his elucidation of the mechanisms that allow the brain to regulate the action of neurotransmitters. Roger Sperry, a NIMH awardee, shared a 1981 Nobel Prize for his work on the functional specialization of the cerebral hemispheres. IRP scientist Louis Sokoloff (cerebral glucose metabolism) and grantees Solomon Snyder (opiate receptors and the brain chemistry of pain relief and emotions) and Eric Kandel (mechanisms underlying learning and memory using cell biology techniques) have won Lasker awards. Much recent work of grantees and IRP staff shows promise of clarifying relationships between the brain, behavior, and environment.

Educational and Public Service Activities

The Depression Awareness, Recognition, and Treatment (D/ART) program exemplified NIMH education programs. Designed to reach families, friends, employers, colleagues, and health-care professionals, it emphasized early recognition and treatment and was a collaborative effort with private organizations and citizens. NIMH supports a vast public information and communication enterprise, responding to about 150,000 inquiries and 2,500 media requests yearly. NIMH staff has advisory working relationships with the press, broadcasters, TV producers, and various public service programs to ensure accuracy of mental health information and effectiveness of its communication.

Relationship to the Broader Field of Psychology

NIMH has been the major federal funder of psychological research and, in its halcyon days, the major supporter of training in several fields of psychology (e.g., clinical, developmental, social, experimental, cognitive, personality, biopsychology, school psychology, and methodology). For most of its history psychologists have received the greatest number of NIMH research grants and the largest percentage of research dollars each year. The fields of community psychology, health psychology, psychology and law, ecological psychology, and environmental psychology were developed with NIMH help. Research in family processes and in emotion has been stimulated by consortial postdoctoral training grants. Possibly the most enduring influence on the field resulted from the attention paid in all NIMH training programs to the issue of diversity in psychology in the recruitment and retention of women and ethnic minorities.

Current Facts and Figures

In 1999 NIMH had 819 positions, 522 of them in the IRP. The NIMH budget was $859 million, $711 million in extramural research and training, $113 million in intramural research, and the remainder in staff salaries and other operating expenses. The extramural staff contains scientists representing research areas from molecular biology and genetics to sociology and economics; most of them are psychologists. None of them could function without the help of dedicated support staff. In 1999 the NIMH extramural programs moved into the new NIH Center for Neuroscience building, also in Rockville, Maryland, where it shares space with the National Institute on Drug Abuse and the National Institute of Neurological Disorders and Stroke.

Bibliography

Grob, G. N. (1991). *From asylum to community: Mental health policy in America*. Princeton, NJ: Princeton University Press.

Stanley F. Schneider

NATIONAL MENTAL HEALTH ASSOCIATION. Around the turn of the twentieth century, a young Yale graduate named Clifford W. Beers was hospitalized for manic depression, now known as bipolar disorder. During his stays in public and private hospitals in his home state of Connecticut, Beers became acutely aware of the deficiencies in his care and that of other patients. Despite his own struggle, he chose to investigate the cruel and inhumane treatment he had witnessed and experienced firsthand.

Upon his release, Beers sought to expose and correct the injustices of the system. His autobiography (1908) recounted his harrowing experiences and issued the call to organize a "central organization by which the best ideas in the world may be crystallized and passed along." Beers further wanted this national movement to progress "from reform to cure, from cure to prevention."

In 1909, this vision took shape with the establishment of the National Mental Health Association. Originally known as the National Committee for Mental Hygiene, the organization was committed to addressing broad-based concerns extending beyond the reform of hospitals to other issues, such as child guidance activities. In addition, it set out to establish state and local societies across the nation based on the group that Beers and other reform-minded individuals initially formed in Connecticut.

With the start of World War II, a new mental health advocacy movement began to emerge. Instead of going to battle, conscientious objectors to the war were sent to serve in state mental asylums, where they found appalling conditions for persons with mental illnesses. These experiences led to the creation of a new reform group, the National Mental Health Foundation, the first group to take a position of citizen advocacy.

For several years, the national committee and the foundation worked cooperatively and eventually merged with the Psychiatric Foundation, an offshoot of the American Psychiatric Association, to become a true citizen volunteer-based organization, called the National Association for Mental Health (NAMH). The merger helped to create unprecedented community-based growth through the expansion of state organizations and the formation of local affiliates.

Throughout the 1950s, 1960s, and 1970s, the association continued to expand its reach in communities by providing services to people with mental illnesses and their loved ones, by advocating for better government support, and by reaching out to all Americans through education to dispel the myths and prejudices associated with mental illnesses. In 1979, NAMH changed its name to the National Mental Health Association (NMHA).

In the 1980s and 1990s, NMHA and its affiliates

have become known as convenors and collaborators within the mental health arena. In 1990, the American Mental Health Fund, an organization known for its excellent public education campaigns, merged with NMHA, thereby increasing its strength.

Today, the National Mental Health Association (NMHA) and more than 340 affiliates across the country work to promote mental health, prevent mental disorders, and achieve victory over mental illnesses through advocacy, education, research, and service.

NMHA accomplishes this mission in the following ways:

- Through its advocacy efforts on the national and local levels, NMHA fights for access to appropriate and affordable care, parity in health insurance coverage between mental illnesses and physical ailments, and continued federal funding for research and community programs. In addition, as the nation's first consumer-led organization, NMHA provides leadership in advocating for consumers' rights.
- In its prevention efforts, NMHA helps community agencies locate and implement proven programs that address issues such as teen pregnancy, drug abuse, and violence. The association also convenes coalitions of national and community organizations to coordinate prevention and violence reduction efforts. Prevention programs include the Voices vs. Violence campaign and the Juvenile Justice Initiative.
- NMHA works to increase knowledge, decrease stigma, and promote the availability of treatment through its information center and public education campaigns. The center provides free mental health information to more than 35,000 individuals each year through a toll-free number, message library, fax-on-demand service, and TTY line for the hearing impaired. In addition to distributing educational brochures, the center also provides people with referrals to local support groups, community mental health clinics, and other services. Specific education campaigns include the Campaign on Clinical Depression, National Mental Health Month held each May, the federal Center for Mental Health Services (CMHS) Caring for Every Child's Mental Health: Communities Together campaign, Primary Care Initiative, Anxiety Disorders Education Program, and Partners in CARE, which promotes community-based care for adults with schizophrenia and other serious mental illnesses.
- NMHA's affiliate network provides the grass-roots connections for many services and programs. Affiliates implement national initiatives on the local level and develop individual programs geared to the specific mental health needs of their communities. These programs include support groups, public education campaigns, and rehabilitation, socialization, and housing services.

Over its extensive history, NMHA has enjoyed the leadership efforts of several prominent Americans, including Pearl Bailey, Cliff Robertson, and Rosalynn Carter. The National Mental Health Association is also recognized worldwide for its symbol: the Mental Health Bell. In the early 1950s, NMHA issued a call to asylums across the country for their discarded chains and shackles. During the early days of mental health treatment, asylums often restrained persons with mental illnesses by iron chains and shackles around their ankles and wrists. On 13 April 1953, at the McShane Bell Foundry in Baltimore, Maryland, NMHA melted down these inhumane bindings and recast them into a sign of hope: the Mental Health Bell. Now housed at NMHA headquarters, the 300-pound bell serves as a powerful reminder that the invisible chains of misunderstanding and discrimination continue to bind people with mental illnesses.

The association annually sponsors the Clifford W. Beers Mental Health Conference, which brings together affiliates, consumers, professionals, and other mental health advocates for networking and training. The conference also features the presentation of awards, including the William Styron Award, the Clifford W. Beers Award, and the Tipper Gore "Remember the Children" Volunteer Award. Past NMHA award recipients have included Tipper Gore, Kathy Cronkite, Kay Redfield Jamison, and Jennifer Holiday.

Each month, NMHA publishes its newsletter, the *Bell*, which provides up-to-date news from the association as well as from the whole mental health field.

Bibliography

Beers, C. W. (1953). *A mind that found itself*. Garden City, NY: Doubleday.

Michael M. Faenza

NATIONAL REGISTER OF HEALTH SERVICE PROVIDERS IN PSYCHOLOGY. The Council for the National Register of Health Service Providers was established by the American Board of Professional Psychology (ABPP) in 1974 at the request of the board of directors of the American Psychological Association (APA). Six months later it was independently incorporated. Its publication, the *National Register of Health Service Providers in Psychology*, is a voluntary listing designed to identify psychologists who meet the credentialing requirements for definition as a health service provider. A health service provider in psychology is defined as a psychologist, certified or licensed at the independent-practice level in his or her state, who is duly trained and experienced in the delivery of direct, preventive, assessment, and therapeutic intervention services to individuals whose growth, adjustment, or functioning is impaired or is demonstrably at high risk of impairment.

Recognition of psychologists by statute is typically not by specialty designation, just as physicians, dentists, and lawyers are not licensed in areas of specialty practice. The *National Register of Health Service Providers in Psychology* was created so that various insurers, governmental units, health services, or other organizations and individual consumers could identify psychologists who meet the statutes governing the standards of practice and who have verified training and experience in the health services area. The current criteria for listing in the *National Register* are:

1. Current license, certification, or registration by a state or provincial board of examiners of psychology at the independent-practice level in psychology.
2. A doctoral degree in psychology from a regionally accredited educational institution.
3. Two years of supervised experience in health services in psychology, one year in an organized health service training program and one year at the postdoctoral level.

Collaborative efforts have led to the development of criteria for identifying doctoral programs in psychology for purposes of licensure and credentialing. Those criteria were developed at conferences held in 1976 and 1977 by APA, the National Register, and the American Association of State Psychology Boards (AASPB). The resulting yearly list of doctoral programs was initiated first in 1981 by the National Register and later in 1987 as a joint effort of the National Register and AASPB (now named Association of State and Provincial Psychology Boards).

In 1980 the National Register developed criteria that could be used to identify health service training programs or internships in psychology. The *Guidelines for Defining an Internship or Organized Health Service Training Program in Psychology* were derived from several sources, including applications for listing in the *National Register*. The guidelines, with minor revisions, later became the standards of the Association of Psychology Internship Centers (APIC) and the APA's Criteria for Accreditation of Internship Programs.

In 1982 the board of directors of the National Register approved criteria that would permit dropping from the listing any registrant who had been found guilty of a crime, had been expelled from membership in a state or national psychological association, or had had his or her license revoked, suspended, or restricted. This effort by the National Register and by other professional organizations in psychology represent psychology's concern with the maintenance of standards of conduct and interest in increasing the profession's responsiveness to the public.

From an initial listing of approximately 7,000 registrants in 1975, the list has grown to more than 16,000 psychologists. Typically the *National Register* was published every 2 years, with the yearly edition first published late in 1993.

The publication of "The National Register Survey: The First Comprehensive Study of All Licensed/Certified Psychologists" by Mills, Wellner, and VandenBos (1979) was the first national survey undertaken by the National Register. In 1990, another national survey was initiated. Registrants were asked to describe their practice characteristics and to indicate (1) their highest degree in psychology, (2) the classification of the experience they submitted to the National Register to meet the two-year experience requirement, (3) their current areas of expertise, (4) their theoretical orientations, (5) the age levels and groups they serve, (6) their language fluencies, and (7) their diplomas, licenses, and so forth. Maintenance of an up-to-date database on qualified psychologists is a key mission of the National Register. Check out the Web site for the most current information.

Bibliography

Council for the National Register of Health Service Providers in Psychology. (1975–1999). *National register of health service providers in psychology*. Washington, DC: Author.

Kiesler, C. A., Cummings, N. A., & VandenBos, G. R. (Eds). (1979). *Psychology and national health insurance: A sourcebook*. Washington, DC: American Psychological Association.

Judy E. Hall

NATIONAL SCIENCE FOUNDATION. Since the National Science Foundation (NSF) was established by act of Congress in 1950 as the principal vehicle for support of civilian nonmedical science in the United States, it has supported psychology research. The NSF, a federal agency, in its earliest form consisted of a director and 24 members of the National Science Board, appointed by the president and confirmed by the Senate, who each served for fixed 6-year terms. It is unique in being independent, not a part of any cabinet department. It is unique in that its board, along with the director, constitutes the foundation rather than being an advisory body to it. It is also unique in having a director who serves for a fixed 6-year term and is therefore not subject to the political judgments of each new administration.

Though the staff is now much larger, the organization far more complex, and the budget much larger than at the outset, the formal components of the foundation, the board and the director, remain the same. They are supplemented only by the addition of a deputy director, also appointed by the president and confirmed by the Senate, who is the sole NSF presidential appointee who does not serve a fixed term but serves at the pleasure of the president. After a brief experiment during which they were appointed by the president, the assistant directors in charge of the various directorates of NSF (the level of administration directly below the director and deputy director) are high-level civil servants or the equivalent.

One of the original programs of the NSF was the psychobiology program, part of the Division of Biological and Medical Sciences (BMS), which was intended to cover the natural science aspects of experimental and physiological psychology. Its first program director, psychologist John T. Wilson, went on to a number of higher positions at NSF, culminating in his service as deputy director. He then went on to become provost of the University of Chicago. One of the two grants made by the psychobiology program in its first year was to psychologist William K. Estes, then at Indiana University, along with Cletus J. Burke. This grant led to the well-known research by Estes and Burke on stimulus sampling theory. Estes, now professor emeritus of psychology at Harvard University, continued as an NSF grantee, virtually without interruption and was awarded the 1997 National Medal of Science.

The initial legislation establishing NSF was deliberately ambiguous on the question of the inclusion of the social sciences. However, by the mid-1950s, the legislation was modified to make it explicit that social sciences were part of NSF's mandate. This was significant for psychology, since social psychology was viewed as a social science and had not been supported at NSF until that time. Initially, following the zeitgeist of the late 1950s, social psychology was joined with sociology in a single program. However, the two were finally split into separate programs during the 1960s, becoming part of what was originally the Division of Social Sciences, later the Division of Social and Economic Sciences (SES).

Meanwhile, as scientific psychology was becoming well established in the psychobiology and social psychology programs, NSF got caught up in the concern for social relevance of the late 1960s and established the Research Applied to National Needs (RANN) program, based on the premise that if science can send a man to the moon, it can solve whatever social problem was the current focus of concern. Although applied social science was an extremely visible part of RANN, applied psychology was never more than a very small part of its efforts. There were never more than two psychologists on RANN's staff at any time. Thus, when RANN was discontinued in the very early 1980s, very little applied psychology research had to come to an end.

Richard C. Atkinson, a psychologist then at Stanford University, became deputy director of NSF in 1975; he later went on to become director of NSF, then chancellor of the University of California at San Diego, and eventually president of the entire University of California. Atkinson authored a substantial reorganization of NSF. For the first time, individual directorates, each headed by an NSF assistant director, were devoted to specific areas of science. One of those directorates was the Directorate for Biological, Behavioral, and Social Sciences (BBS). As part of this reorganization, Atkinson created the Division of Behavioral and Neural Sciences (BNS), a bridge between biology and social sciences, and asked Richard T. Louttit, a former National Institutes of Health administrator and psychology department chair at the University of Massachusetts, to direct this new division. The psychobiology program had been split in 1971 into the neurobiology program, which handled research in what would now be called neuroscience, and the psychobiology program, handling animal behavior, cognitive psychology, and perception. These two programs were brought into the new division from BMS, and they immediately became four programs. Research in sensory physiology from the neurobiology program and research in perception from the psychobiology program had been treated in BMS as a "virtual" program; in the new division, it became the sensory physiology and perception program. Cognitive research from the psychobiology program was incorporated into the memory and cognitive processes program. Joining these four programs from BMS were three from the SES: social psychology, which was renamed social and developmental psychology; anthropology; and linguistics, which had been supported in SES for a number of years but only became a program upon moving to BNS.

This arrangement continued relatively unchanged until 1991, when agitation from the behavioral and social science community brought about the split of BBS into two directorates, the Directorate for Biological Sciences (BIO) and the Directorate for Social, Behavioral, and Economic Sciences (SBE). By this time, the neurobiology program had grown into three programs (since then it has become six programs), the psychobiology program had been renamed the animal behavior program, and sensory physiology and perception had lost its perception portfolio and been renamed the sensory systems program. All these programs became a part of the Division of Integrative Biology and Neuroscience in BIO. The other programs from BNS, human cognition and perception (the former memory and cognitive processes program, which had earlier added responsibility for research in perception), social psychology (which had reverted to its original name), anthropology, and linguistics, joined with programs from SES and elsewhere to form the Division of Social, Behavioral, and Economic Research (SBER), initially directed by political scientist Allan Kornberg and later by economist and demographer William P. Butz. SBE, initially headed by sociologist Cora B. Marrett, was headed in 1997 by psychologist Bennett I. Bertenthal.

Other significant individuals in the history of psychology at NSF have been Henry S. Odbert, director of the psychobiology program for 15 years until his retirement in 1973; Fred Stollnitz, director of the psychobiology (later animal behavior) program until 1994 and then program director for cross-directorate activities in IBN; James H. Brown, neurobiology program director and deputy director of BNS and then a division director in BIO; Anne C. Petersen, deputy director of NSF from 1994 to 1996 and then at the Kellogg Foundation; Roland W. Radloff and Jean B. Intermaggio, each a longtime program director for social psychology; Paul G. Chapin, linguist and longtime program director for linguistics; and Joseph L. Young, program director for human cognition and perception from its 1976 inception as the memory and cognitive processes program until early 1997, when he became information director for SBER.

Bibliography

Bush, V. (1990). *Science: The endless frontier.* Washington, DC: National Science Foundation. This publication, commonly known as the Bush Report, first appeared in 1945 as a report to the president from the U.S. Office of Scientific Research and Development. It presented a persuasive case for federal sponsorship of American science and technology in the postwar years, culminating in the founding of the NSF.

England, J. M. (1982). *A patron for pure science: The National Science Foundation's formative years, 1945–1957.* Washington, DC: National Science Foundation.

Schaffter, D. (1969). *The National Science Foundation.* New York: Praeger.

Joseph L. Young

NATION BUILDING. *See* Political Leadership.

NATIVE AMERICAN PSYCHOLOGY. *See* American Indian Psychology.

NATURAL SELECTION. The term *evolution* in the present context refers to change over time in organic struc-

tures. Organic change was suspected by scientists long before Darwin published his classic book in 1859, *On the Origin of Species.* Biologists before Darwin noticed the bewildering variety of species, some of which seemed to contain astonishing structural similarities. Humans, chimpanzees, and orangutans, for example, all had exactly five digits on their hands and feet. The wings of birds seemed similar to the flippers of seals, perhaps suggesting that one was modified from the other. Comparisons among all these species suggested that organic life was not static, as some scientists and theologians argued. Evidence suggesting change over time also came from the fossil record. Bones from older geological strata were different from bones from more recent geological strata. How could these bones be different, scientists reasoned, unless there had been change in organic structure over time?

Another source of evidence for change over time came from comparing the embryological development of different species (Mayr, 1982). Biologists noticed that such development was strikingly similar in species that seemed otherwise very different from one another. This evidence suggested, perhaps, that these species might have descended from the common ancestors many generations earlier. All these pieces of evidence, present before 1859, suggested that life was not static. The biologists who believed that organic structure changed over time called themselves "evolutionists."

Another key observation was evident before Darwin. Many species possessed characteristics that seemed to have a purpose. The long neck of the giraffe seemed well designed to help it to get the higher leaves hanging from the tops of tall trees. The porcupine's quills helped it to fend off predators. The turtle's shell helped it to protect its tender organs from the hostile forces of nature. This apparent functionality, so abundant in nature, also required explanation.

Missing from the evolutionists' accounts before Darwin, however, was a theory to explain how change might take place over time and how such seemingly purposeful structures like the giraffe's long neck and porcupine's sharp quills could have come about. Needed was a *causal mechanism* or *process* to explain these biological phenomena. The theory of such a mechanism was supplied by Charles Darwin and independently by Alfred Russell Wallace.

Darwin's Theory of Natural Selection

Darwin's task was more difficult than it might appear at first. He wanted to explain not only why change takes place over time in life forms, but also to account for the particular ways in which it changes. He wanted to explain how new species emerge (hence the title of his book *On the Origin of Species*), as well as how others vanish. Darwin wanted to explain why the component parts of animals—the long necks of giraffes, the wings of birds, the trunks of elephants—existed in the particular forms that they did. And he wanted to explain the apparent purposive quality of those forms, or why they seem to function to help organisms accomplish specific tasks.

The answers to these puzzles can be traced to a voyage Darwin took after graduating from Cambridge University. He traveled the world as a naturalist on a ship, the *Beagle*, for a 5-year period, from 1832 to 1837. During this voyage, he collected dozens of samples of birds from the Galapagos Islands. Upon returning from his voyage, he discovered that the Galapagos finches, which he had presumed were all of the same species, actually varied so much that they constituted different species. Each island in the Galapagos had a distinct species of finch. Darwin came to believe that these different finches all had a common ancestor, but had diverged from each other due to the local conditions on each island. This geographic variation was probably pivotal to Darwin's conclusion that species are not immutable, but can change over time.

What theory could account for why species change? This was the next challenge. Darwin struggled with several different theories of the origins of change, but rejected all of them because they failed to account for a critical fact: the existence of adaptations. Darwin wanted to account for change, of course, but perhaps even more important he wanted to account for why organisms appeared so well designed for their local environments:

> It was . . . evident that [these others theories] could [not] account for the innumerable cases in which organisms of every kind are beautifully adapted to their habits of life—for instance, a woodpecker or tree-frog to climb trees, or a seed for dispersal by hooks and plumes. I had always been much struck by such adaptations, and until these could be explained it seemed to me almost useless to endeavour to prove by indirect evidence that species have been modified. (Darwin, from his autobiography; cited in Ridley, 1996, p. 9)

A key to the puzzle of adaptations came when Darwin read Malthus's *Essay on the Principle of Population* (1798/1803). This brought home forcefully for Darwin the idea that organisms exist in numbers far more numerous than can survive and reproduce. The result must be a "struggle for existence," in which favorable variations tend to be preserved and unfavorable ones tend to die out. When this process is repeated generation after generation, the end result would be the formation of a new species.

More formally, Darwin's answer to all these puzzles of life was the theory of *natural selection*. Darwin's theory of natural selection has three essential ingredients: *variation*, *inheritance*, and *selection*. Animals vary in all sorts of ways, such as wing length, trunk strength, bone mass, cell structure, fighting ability, defensive ability, and social cunning. This variation is essential for the process of evolution to operate—it provides the "raw materials" for evolution.

Only some of these variations, however, are inherited, that is, passed down reliably from parents to offspring down the generations. Other variations, such as a wing deformity caused by an environmental accident, are not inherited by offspring. Only those variations that are inherited play a role in the evolutionary process.

The third critical ingredient of Darwin's theory is selection. Organisms with some heritable variants leave more offspring *because* those attributes help with the tasks of *survival* or *reproduction*. In an environment in which the primary food source might be nut-bearing trees or bushes, some finches with a particular shape of beak, for example, might be better able to crack nuts and get at their meat than finches with other shapes of beaks. More finches who have the beak better shaped for nut-cracking survive than those with beaks poorly shaped for nut-cracking. Hence those finches with more suitably shaped beaks survive to pass their genes to the next generation.

An organism can survive for many years, however, and still not contribute its inherited qualities to future generations; to do that, it must reproduce. Thus, *differential reproductive success*, because of the possession of heritable variants, is the mechanism of evolution by natural selection. Differential reproductive success is defined by reproductive success *relative* to other individuals. The characteristics of organisms who reproduce more than others, therefore, get passed down to future generations. Because survival is usually necessary for reproduction, survival took on a critical role in Darwin's theory of natural selection.

Indeed, Darwin envisioned two classes of evolved variations—one playing a role in survival and one playing a role in reproduction. Among humans, for example, our sweat glands help us to keep a constant body temperature, and thus help us to survive. Our tastes for sugar and fat help guide us to eat certain foods, and thus help us to survive. Other inherited attributes, however, aid in reproduction. The elaborate songs of some bird species, for example, help them to attract mates, and hence to reproduce, but do nothing to enhance the individual's survival. In summary, differential reproductive success of inherited variants is the crux of Darwin's theory of natural selection. It is useful to think of two classes of characteristics that evolve through this process—those because they help organisms survive and those that help organisms reproduce.

Evolution by natural selection is not forward looking and is not "intentional." The giraffe does not spy the juicy leaves stirring high in the tree and "evolve" a longer neck. Rather, those giraffes that happen to have slightly longer necks than other giraffes have a slight advantage in getting to those leaves. Hence, they survive better and are thus more likely to live to pass on their slightly longer necks to their offspring. Natural selection merely acts on those variants that happen to exist. There is no intentionality about evolution; no looking into the future or foreseeing distant needs.

Another critical feature of natural selection is that it is *gradual*, at least when evaluated by the time-span of a human life. The short-necked ancestors of giraffes did not suddenly evolve long necks overnight, or even in a few dozen generations. It has taken many hundreds, thousands, and in some cases millions of generations for the process of natural selection to gradually shape the organic mechanisms we see today. Of course, some changes occur extremely slowly, others more rapidly. And there can be long periods of no change, followed by a relatively sudden change—a phenomenon known as "punctuated equilibrium." But even these "rapid" changes occur in tiny increments each generation and take hundreds or thousands of years to occur.

Darwin's theory of natural selection offered a powerful theory to account for many of the baffling aspects of life. It accounted for the origin of new species. It accounted for the modification in organic structures over time. It accounted for the apparent purposive quality of the component parts of those structures—(i.e., that they seem "designed" to serve particular functions linked with survival and reproduction).

And perhaps most astonishing to some and appalling to others in 1859, natural selection united, in one bold stroke, all living forms into one grand tree of descent. For the first time in human consciousness, each species was viewed as connected with all other species through a common ancestry. Humans and chimpanzees, for example, share more than 98% of their DNA, and shared a common ancestor perhaps 15 to 20 million years ago. Even more startling is the finding of genetic closeness between a transparent worm, *Caenorhabditis elegans*, and humans. Many human genes turn out to have counterpart genes in this worm, ones that are highly similar in chemical structure. This similarity suggests that they evolved from distant common ancestors. In short, Darwin's theory made it possible to locate humans in the grand chain of life, showing their place in nature and their links with all other living creatures.

Darwin's theory of natural selection, of course, created a storm of controversy in 1859. Lady Ashley, a contemporary of Charles Darwin, remarked upon hearing his theory that humans descended from the apes: "Let's hope it's not true; but if it is true, let's hope that it does not become widely known." In a famous debate at Oxford University, Bishop Wilberforce bitingly asked his rival debater Thomas Huxley whether the "ape" from which Huxley descended was on his grandmother's or grandfather's side of the family.

Even biologists at the time were highly skeptical of Darwin's theory of natural selection for several reasons. One objection was that the theory lacked a coherent theory of inheritance. Darwin himself preferred a "blending" theory of inheritance, in which the offspring are mixtures of their parents, much like pink paint is a mixture of red and white paint. This theory of inheritance is now known to be wrong, as we will see below when we discuss Gregor Mendel. Natural selection could not operate successfully with a blending form of inheritance. So critics were correct in their objections that in 1859 the theory of natural selection lacked a solid theory of heredity.

Another objection was that some biologists could not imagine how the early stages of the evolution of an adaptation could be useful to an organism. How could a partial wing help a bird, since a partial wing is insufficient for flight? How could a partial eye help a reptile, since a partial eye is insufficient for sight? Darwin's theory of natural selection requires that each and every step in the gradual evolution of an adaptation must be advantageous to the organism. Thus, partial wings and eyes must yield an adaptive advantage, even before they evolve to fully developed wings and eyes. The key point is that partial forms can indeed offer adaptive advantages, and so this objection to Darwin's theory was surmountable.

A third objection came from religious creationists, who viewed species as immutable (unchanging) and created by a deity rather than by the slow and painstaking process of evolution by selection. Darwin anticipated this reaction, and even apparently delayed the publication of his theory in part because he was worried about upsetting his wife, who was deeply religious.

The controversy continues to this day. Although Darwin's theory of evolution, with some important modifications, is the unifying and nearly universally accepted theory within the biological sciences, its application to humans, which Darwin clearly envisioned, meets vigorous resistance. But humans are not exempt from the evolutionary process, despite our profound resistance to being analyzed through the same lens used to analyze other species. As we head into the twenty-first century, we finally have the conceptual tools to complete Darwin's revolution and forge an evolutionary psychology of the human species.

Evolutionary psychology is able to take advantage of key theoretical insights and scientific discoveries that were simply not known in Darwin's day. The first among these is the physical basis of inheritance—the gene.

The Modern Synthesis

When Darwin published the *Origin*, he did not know the nature of the mechanism by which "inheritance" occurred. Indeed, as we just discussed, the dominant thinking at the time was that inheritance constituted a sort of "blending" of the two parents, whereby off-spring would be intermediate between the two parents. A short and tall parent, for example, would produce a child of intermediate height, according to the blending theory. But as noted above, the blending theory of inheritance is now known to be incorrect.

Another popular position at the time was Lamarck's theory of the inheritance of acquired characteristics. Lamarck's notion was that an organism could acquire in its own lifetime something useful. For example, a giraffe could acquire a slightly longer neck by repeated efforts to stretch to reach the high leaves. Once acquired, these characteristics were thought to be passed on to the offspring. Whether inheritance involved blending, the inheritance of acquired characteristics, or neither, however, was simply not known in Darwin's day.

Gregor Mendel, an Austrian monk, showed that both views were wrong. Inheritance was "particulate," he argued, and not blended; that is, the qualities of the parents are not blended with each other, but rather are passed on intact to their offspring in distinct packets or genes. Furthermore, the parents already must have the genes to pass on; they cannot be acquired by experience.

Unfortunately for the history of science, Mendel's discovery that inheritance is particulate, which he demonstrated by breeding strains of pea plants, remained unknown to most of the scientific community for some 30 years. Mendel had sent Darwin copies of his papers, but they remained either unread or their significance unnoticed.

Genes are generally defined as the smallest discrete unit that is inherited by offspring intact, without being broken up or blended—this was Mendel's critical insight. *Genotypes*, in contrast, refer to the entire collection of genes within an individual. Genotypes, unlike genes, are not passed down to offspring intact. Rather, in sexually reproducing species such as our own, genotypes are broken up with each generation. Thus, each of us inherits a random half of genes from our mother's genotype and a random half from our father's genotype. The specific genes we inherit from each parent, however, are identical to those of that parent since they get transmitted as a discrete bundle without modification.

The unification of Darwin's theory of evolution by natural selection with the discovery of particulate gene inheritance culminated in a movement in the 1930s and 1940s called the "Modern Synthesis." The Modern Synthesis discarded a number of misconceptions in biology, including Lamarck's theory of the inheritance of acquired characteristics and the blending theory of inheritance. The Modern Synthesis emphatically confirmed the importance of Darwin's theory of natural

selection, but put it on a firmer footing with a well-articulated understanding of the nature of inheritance.

The Inclusive Fitness Refinement of Natural Selection

In the early 1960s, a young graduate student, William D. Hamilton, toiled away on his doctoral dissertation at University College, London. Hamilton proposed a radical new revision of the evolutionary theory of natural selection, which he termed *inclusive fitness theory*. Hamilton reasoned that *classical fitness*—a measure of an individual's direct reproductive success in passing on genes through the production of offspring—was too narrow to describe the process of evolution by selection. He reasoned that natural selection will favor characteristics that cause an organism's genes to be passed on, regardless of whether the organism actually produces the offspring directly. Parental care—investing in your own children—is merely a special case of caring for kin who carry copies of your genes in their bodies. An organism can also increase the reproduction of its genes by helping brothers, sisters, nieces, or nephews to survive and reproduce. All these relatives carry copies of the organism's genes. Hamilton's genius was the recognition that classical fitness was too narrow, and should be broadened to *inclusive fitness* (1964).

Technically, inclusive fitness is not a property of an individual or an organism, but rather a property of its actions or effects. Thus, inclusive fitness can be viewed as the sum of an individual's own reproductive success (classical fitness) plus the effects the individual's actions have on the reproductive success of his or her genetic relatives. For this second component, the effects on relatives must be weighted by the appropriate degree of genetic relatedness to the target organism: for example, 0.50 for brothers and sisters (because they share 50% of their genes with the target organism), 0.25 for grandparents and grandchildren (25% genetic overlap), 0.125 for first cousins (12.5% genetic overlap), and so on.

The inclusive fitness revolution marshaled a new era that may be called "gene's eye thinking." If you were a gene, what would facilitate your survival and reproduction? First, you might try to ensure the well-being of the "vehicle" of body in which you reside (survival). Second, you might try to make many copies of yourself (reproduction). Third, you might want to help the survival and reproduction of vehicles that contain copies of you (inclusive fitness). Genes, of course, do not have thoughts, and none of this occurs with consciousness or intentionally. The key point is that the gene is the fundamental unit of inheritance, the unit that is passed on intact in the process of reproduction. Adaptations arise by the process of inclusive fitness. Genes that have effects that increase their replicative success will replace other genes, producing evolution over time.

Thinking about selection from the perspective of the gene offered a wealth of insights to evolutionary biologists. The theory of inclusive fitness has profound consequences for how we think about the psychology of the family, altruism, helping, the formation of groups, and even aggression. The application of this refined theory of natural selection has given rise to a new field, *evolutionary psychology*, which can be regarded as a fulfillment of Darwin's prophesy. He wrote at the end of his classic book *The Origin of Species*: "In the future I see open fields for far more important researches. Psychology will be securely based on the [new] foundation . . ." (Darwin, 1859, p. 373).

[*See also* Animal Learning and Behavior; Evolutionary Psychology; *and the biography of Darwin.*]

Bibliography

Barkow, J., Cosmides, L., & Tooby, J. (Eds.). (1992). *The adapted mind: Evolutionary psychology and the generation of culture*. New York: Oxford University Press. The most thorough treatment of the application of the theory of natural selection to human behavior, and a description of the foundations of evolutionary psychology.

Darwin, C. (1859). *On the origin of species*. London: John Murray. Monumental treatise that outlines the theory of natural selection and provides extensive empirical documentation from a variety of diverse species.

Dawkins, R. (1976). *The selfish gene*. New York: Oxford University Press. Popular and highly readable account of the current state of the theory of natural selection in its modern formulation as inclusive fitness theory.

Hamilton, W. D. (1964). The genetical evolution of social behaviour. *Journal of Theoretical Biology*, 6, 1–52. The article that proposed the theory of inclusive fitness, a fundamental revision of Darwin's theory of natural selection.

Huxley, J. S. (1942). *Evolution: The modern synthesis*. London: Allen & Unwin. Book summarizing the synthesis of Darwin's theory of natural selection with Mendelian genetics.

Malthus, T. R. (1959). *Essay on the principle of population*. Ann Arbor, MI: University of Michigan Press. (Original work published 1798)

Mayr, E. (1982). *The growth of biological thought*. Cambridge, MA: Harvard University Press.

Ridley, M. (1996). *Evolution* (2nd ed.). Cambridge, MA: Blackwell Science.

David M. Buss

NATURE AND NURTURE THEORIES. [*This entry takes an epistemological approach to the historical developments and major proponents of the nature and nuture theories.*]

It has always been thought that any outcome of the development of individuals (personality, intelligence, physical appearance, abilities, failings) is caused mostly, if not entirely, by either inheritance (genes) or learning (environment). In brief, this is the nature/nurture controversy. This point of view about psychological development has come down to us from the ancients and is still taken in some areas of psychology even though it is now fairly widely known to be faulty (T. D. Johnston, 1987). It is faulty not because genes and environment arc not crucially important (they are), but because it is not possible to specify how much (or which part) of any outcome is caused by genes and how much (or which part) is caused by environment.

Most psychologists now accept that both genes and environment are necessarily involved in all outcomes of individual development. A small group of psychologists, called quantitative (or population) behavior geneticists, accept that genes and environment both play a role in the development of any trait or ability, but they are in the minority in wanting to specify how much of each outcome is determined by inheritance (heredity) and how much by the person's or animal's life experiences (environment). For most traits such as intelligence or personality, behavior geneticists conclude that genes are more important than environment, but knowing that doesn't really tell us anything about how intelligence or personality develops within an individual, nor, since there is a gene-environment interaction, how high or low their intelligence will be, or what kind of personality they will develop. Another problem is that behavior genetics relies on statistical methods that deal with differences in outcomes in populations of individuals that are less and less closely related genetically (identical twins, fraternal twins, siblings, or unrelated persons). They deal with differences *between* individuals in such populations and then wish to generalize their findings to the process of development *within* individuals, which is invalid. For example, if identical twins reared apart show a greater similarity in IQ than fraternal twins reared apart (a between-individual difference), behavior geneticists conclude that genes are more important than environment in the development of intelligence *within* an individual, a conclusion that can't be validly reached because genes and environment interact in the development of individuals. (For detailed discussions of the problems with this approach, see Lerner, 1995; and Wahlsten & Gottlieb, 1997). [*See* Behavioral Genetics.]

Although the fields of behavior genetics and ethology arose independently, the behavior geneticists were supported in their dichotomous nature/nurture approach by the views of classical ethologists such as the Austrian zoologist Konrad Lorenz, one of the founders of ethology, who believed that certain features of behavior are instinctive (determined by genes), while other features of behavior are determined by learning

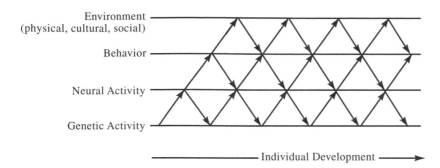

NATURE AND NURTURE THEORIES. Figure 1. Probabilistic epigenesis.

(environmental influences). Lorenz reached this nature/nurture dichotomy by regarding instinctive behavior as being a consequence of the evolution of the species (phylogeny) and learning as arising during the course of individual development (ontogeny). For Lorenz and some of the older ethologists, there were two independent sources of information for behavioral development: phylogeny (evolution of the species) and ontogeny (development of individuals within a species). In this view, phylogeny corresponds to nature and ontogeny to nurture. In well-known critiques by T. C. Schneirla and his student Daniel S. Lehrman, both American comparative psychologists, Lorenz's nature/nurture dichotomy of two sources of information was brought into question by referring to the earlier writings of Zing-Yang Kuo on the usually unknown prenatal experiences that possibly contribute to the development of instinctive behavior (not considered by the ethologists), and by the findings of modern genetics, which show that genes make proteins, not behavior. In the comparative psychologists' view, all behavior is the outcome of genes, neural structures and functions, and the experience of the organism, which is broadly conceived as organism-environment interactions.

In recent years, Gilbert Gottlieb, an American developmental psychobiologist, has built on the work of Kuo, Schneirla, Lehrman, and Ashley Montagu, a British-American anthropologist, to devise a synthetic (integrative) way of thinking about nature/nurture called probabilistic epigenesis, or developmental psychobiological systems theory. While these words are tongue-twisters, Gottlieb's system is fairly easy to understand in its broad outline.

As shown in Figure 1, there are four interdependent levels of analysis that must be considered to understand the development of any individual: genetic activity, neural activity, behavior, and environmental influences. All four levels are coactive and bidirectional; that is, all are more or less simultaneously active and, as indicated by the double-headed arrows, all levels mutually influence each other. During the course of development, you don't have environmental influences on the individual without consequences for behavior, the nervous sys-

tem, and genetic activity, and genetic activity influences neural activity, which influences behavioral development, which, in turn, acts back on the environment. In this view, there are not single causes such as nature or nurture, but, rather, all the factors necessarily act in concert to influence the development of the individual. That is why it is called a systems view of development.

This synthetic way of thinking reflects contemporary approaches to the development of behavior and developmental psychology in that, ideally speaking, it is multidisciplinary, with biologists being interested not only in genes and the nervous system but also in behavior, and psychologists being interested in the biological (genetic and neural) accompaniments to behavioral development. It is in this way that the nature/nurture dichotomy has been overcome—and the nature/nurture controversy resolved—in the 1990s. The future will no doubt see more and more laboratories working not only from genes to behavior but also from the environment to genetic activity to thoroughly understand behavioral and psychological development, thus consolidating the integrative view of nature/nurture (Gottlieb, 1997, and Wahlsten & Gottlieb, 1997, offer evidence of the present-day synthesis of the nature/nurture controversy).

[*See also* Developmental Psychology; *and* Parent-Child Relationship.]

Bibliography

Anastasi, A., & Foley, J. P., Jr. (1948). A proposed reorientation in the heredity-environment controversy. *Psychological Review*, 55, 239–249. The first article of many to say that the correct question to ask to understand any outcome of development is not *how much* but *how*.

Birney, R. C., & Teevan, R. C. (Eds.). (1961). *Instinct: An enduring problem in psychology*. Princeton, NJ: D. Van Nostrand. A collection of representative articles on instinct theory and instinctive behavior from 1890 to 1955.

Boakes, R. (1984). *From Darwin to behaviorism: Psychology and the minds of animals*. Cambridge, UK: Cambridge

University Press. An accessible historical review of the concepts of instinct (nature) and learning (nurture) from Darwin's time to the 1930s.

Gottlieb, G. (1979). Comparative psychology and ethology. In E. Hearst (Ed.), *The first century of experimental psychology* (pp. 147–176). Hillsdale, NJ: Erlbaum. Traces the contrasting modes of thinking of European ethologists and American comparative psychologists on the importance of instinct, experience, and learning in the development of behavior in animals.

Gottlieb, G. (1997). *Synthesizing nature-nurture: Prenatal roots of instinctive behavior.* Mahwah, NJ: Erlbaum. An easily read review of the author's career-long experiments on the development of instinctive behavior in ducklings.

Johnston, T. D. (1987). The persistence of dichotomies in the study of behavioral development. *Developmental Review, 7,* 149–182. Presents examples of nature-nurture thinking in contemporary books and journal articles.

Kuo, Z.-Y. (1976). *The dynamics of behavior development: An epigenetic view* (enlarged ed.). New York: Plenum Press. A saucily written account of the author's career-long experimental and theoretical efforts to undermine the concept of instinct (and, as it turns out, learning).

Lehrman, D. S. (1970). Semantic and conceptual issues in the nature-nurture problem. In L. R. Aronson, E. Tobach, D. S. Lehrman, & J. S. Rosenblatt (Eds.), *Development and evolution of behavior: Essays in memory of T. C. Schneirla* (pp. 17–52). This essay explicitly took on Konrad Lorenz's dichotomous nature/nurture view of the causes of animal behavior and synthesized the concepts based on modern genetics and the developmental biology of the 1960s. It is an advanced article but very well written.

Lerner, R. M. (1995). The limits of biological influence: Behavior genetics as the emperor's new clothes. *Psychological Inquiry, 6,* 145–156. Readily understood criticism of the theory and statistical methods of behavior genetics as applied to human behavior.

Plomin, R. (1989). *Nature and nurture.* Pacific Grove, CA: Brooks/Cole. Describes how contemporary behavior geneticists try to separate the contributions of nature and nurture.

Schneirla, T. C. (1962). Psychology, comparative. In *Encyclopaedia Britannica* (Vol. 18, pp. 690–703). This is a brief account of learning and instinctive behavior written for general readers by the foremost comparative psychologist of his time.

Spalding, D. A. (1954). Instinct. *British Journal of Animal Behaviour, 2,* 2–11. A highly readable reprint of an 1870s paper by an outstanding British animal behaviorist showing how nineteenth-century scientists conceived of experiments to tease out proof of instincts in animals.

Wahlsten, D., & Gottlieb, G. (1997). The invalid separation of effects of nature and nurture: Lessons from animal experimentation. In R. J. Sternberg & E. L. Grigorenko (Eds.), *Intelligence, heredity, and environment* (pp. 163–192). New York: Cambridge University Press. Experimental documentation of why the contributions of na-ture and nurture cannot be independently specified in the development of any individual.

Gilbert Gottlieb

NEAR SENSES. *See* Taste; *and* Touch.

NEGOTIATION. The word *negotiation* refers to a dialogue that occurs between people who attempt to reach agreement on matters where there is a difference of interest. A difference of interest means that the parties believe that they have incompatible preferences among a set of available options. The parties in negotiation (called negotiators or disputants) may be individuals, groups, organizations, or political units, such as nations. Negotiation is an everyday activity and is important in all arenas of social decision-making.

Incompatible Preferences

Clyde Coombs proposed (*American Psychologist*, 1987, 42, 355–363) that incompatible preferences occur in two circumstances: (1) When people want different things but must settle for the same thing: for example, a husband and wife differ on where to spend their vacation; labor and management differ on the plan for medical benefits; or the new member of a start-up company wants 10% ownership but the current owners prefer that she have a salary; and (2) when people want the same thing but must settle for different things: for example, one nation wants the land, and so does another nation; two managers both want the nice corner office but only one can have it. Incompatible preferences can be found in all social arenas, from relations between children on the playground to international relations.

When negotiation occurs, it usually means that the parties are working together to reach agreement. When the negotiation is especially difficult, as when interests are highly divergent, a third party (a mediator) may enter the discussions to help the negotiators reach agreement. When negotiation or mediation fails, alternative routes to agreement may come into play, including decision by a third party (arbitration or adjudication). [*See* Conflict Resolution.] Although agreement is often the stated aim of negotiation, Fred Iklé noted (*How Nations Negotiate*, New York, 1964) that sometimes people enter negotiation to buy time while building the capacity to beat the opponent through other means.

When incompatible preferences exist, the structure of the situation can be described as mixed motive. This means that the situation evokes, at the same time, both competitive and cooperative motives in the parties. The competitive motive arises because the players have opposing preferences for some pairs of options. The cooperative motive arises because the players have similar preferences for other pairs of options. This is seen is Benjamin Franklin's famous statement: "Of course, it is better to strike as good a bargain as one's bargaining position permits. The worst outcome is when, by overreaching greed, no bargain is struck, and a trade that could have been advantageous to both parties does not come off at all"—that is, both parties prefer to agree than disagree, yet, within agreement, each prefers one that favors their own interests over one that favors the other's.

The Elements of Negotiation

Central elements of negotiation include the issues and offers, the outcome, and the negotiation process, which is manifest in the strategies and tactics of negotiation.

Issues and Offers. A key feature of negotiation is the topic under discussion, which can usually be divided into one or more *issues* requiring decisions by the parties. Each issue entails two or more options (also called alternatives). For example, in a negotiation for the purchase of a used car the main issue may be how much money the buyer will give the seller, with the options under consideration being possible prices between $9,000 and $11,000. A secondary issue might be whether a particular package of accessories will be installed in the car, with the options being installation and noninstallation. Issues and options will often reflect the parties interests and underlying needs. These are expressed in the positions taken, that is, in the parties' offers and counteroffers in negotiation.

Roger Fisher and Bill Ury (1981) have argued that focusing on real interests as opposed to the stated positions on issues is the key to good agreement in negotiation. In a similar vein, John Burton wrote (*Global Conflict*, College Park, Md., 1984) that basic human needs like recognition and security lie at the base of all interests and that conflicts cannot be fully resolved unless these needs are brought to the surface. Others have argued that underlying needs are sometimes no more amendable to settlement in negotiation than the surface issues (Pruitt & Carnevale, 1993).

Outcomes. Another important element of negotiation is agreement, the end state of negotiation. Agreement normally requires joint approval, and this reflects the voluntary nature of agreement in negotiation. If either party drops out of the negotiation there is no agreement. No agreement has a value that Roger Fisher and Bill Ury (1981) call the "best alternative to a negotiated agreement," or BATNA. BATNA is usually identical with the *status quo*, that is, the situation that

would have obtained if negotiation had never taken place. No agreement may or may not be a poor outcome for both parties. In some cases, one party may be very much advantaged by the status quo, making no agreement identical to a victory for that party. People who are advantaged by the status quo tend to opt for inaction in negotiation or avoid negotiation altogether.

Howard Raiffa (1982) has written that agreements often are not made when they could have been, and agreements are often not efficient in the sense that other agreements could have been devised that would have been preferred by all parties. Efficient agreements, also called integrative or win-win agreements, are mutually beneficial to the parties. Efficient agreements can often be contrasted with compromises, where the parties follow a simple rule for agreement that ignores their underlying interests. Sometimes agreement is asymmetrical in the sense that one party achieves its own interests to a greater extent than the other party.

In an important contribution, Dean Pruitt (1981) developed a taxonomy of basic types of efficient agreement that can arise from negotiation. Included in this taxonomy are:

1. Expanding the resource, which is an agreement based simply on increasing the available resources so that both sides can get what they want.
2. Bridging, which entails an analysis of the underlying interests for a novel solution for reconciling divergent interests.
3. Logrolling, which is a way to construct win-win agreements by an exchange of concessions on different issues, with each party yielding on issues that are of low priority to itself and high priority to the other party. Such concession exchanges are sometimes called trade-offs.

Strategies and Tactics. It is possible to distinguish strategies that can be used in negotiation. A negotiation strategy is a plan of action specifying broad objectives and a general approach that should be taken to achieve those objectives. Some strategies must be translated into more specific tactics in order to be used. The three main strategies that work toward agreement in negotiation are concession making, contentiousness, and problem solving.

Concession making involves a reduction in demands—changing one's proposal so that it provides less benefit to oneself. Negotiators usually assume that their concessions provide greater benefit to the other party, thereby moving the negotiation toward agreement, an assumption that Leigh Thompson and Reid Hastie (*Organizational Behavior and Human Decision Processes*, 1990, 47, 98–123) showed is not always valid.

Contentiousness involves attempting to persuade the other party to concede or trying to resist similar efforts by the other party. There are many tactics that can be used to implement this strategy, including threats (messages indicating that one will punish the other party if the other fails to conform) and positional commitments (messages indicating that one will not move from a particular position).

Problem solving involves trying to locate and adopt options that satisfy both parties' goals, and is the process associated with the development of integrative, win-win agreements. There are a host of problem-solving tactics, including active listening and providing information about one's own priorities among the issues under discussion.

Models of Negotiation

The analysis of negotiation has generally proceeded in two directions, one emphasizing the causal (thus predictive) relationship among negotiation variables, and the other emphasizing structural accounts.

Causal Models. Causal models of negotiation include models of situation causality, which detail the impact of different social contexts on negotiation process and outcome. Research reviewed by Peter Carnevale and Dean Pruitt (1992) has shown that conditions that reduce the likelihood of using one negotiation strategy increase the likelihood of using the remaining two. If two of the strategies are problematic, the third will be given larger consideration. Thus, time pressure on the negotiators, if it is seen as reducing the effectiveness of contentiousness and problem-solving, will increase concession-making. Some causal models detail the impact of combinations of strategies on negotiation. John Hilty and Peter Carnevale found that combinations of slow and fast concession-making are especially effective in eliciting cooperation, as in the famous "good-cop/bad-cop" strategy (*Organizational Behavior and Human Decision Processes*, 1994, 55, 444–469).

Several studies have examined the impact of cognitive processes on negotiation. Research reviewed by Leigh Thompson (*The Mind and Heart of the Negotiator*, Upper Saddle River, N.J., 1998) has confirmed that information exchange and joint problem-solving are useful ways to achieve win-win agreements. Unfortunately, information exchange and joint problem-solving require a high level of trust in the other party, which is often not available in negotiation. Without trust, negotiators tend to fear that the other party will misuse the information provided; hence they give little of it.

Research has detailed the important role of a broad set of cognitive processes in negotiation. Bill Bottom and Amy Studt (*Organizational Behavior and Human Decision Processes*, 1991, 56, 459–474) reported that negotiations over issues defined as losses produced a greater resistance to making concessions than negoti-

ations over gains. Peter Carnevale and Tahira Probst (*Journal of Personality and Social Psychology*, 1998, 74, 1300–1309) found that conflictual negotiations can produce a general rigidity of cognition that is unrelated to the negotiation issues. Recent work has focused on the important role of emotions. Joe Forgas (*Journal of Personality and Social Psychology*, 1998, 74, 565–577) discovered that positive affect can improve negotiation outcomes.

Many studies support a broad generalization, first advanced by Dean Pruitt (1981) that the most successful problem solving involves a firm but concerned and flexible stance. In this context, firmness means moderate resistance to yielding on one's basic goals, which is needed because one's basic goals must be represented in a viable agreement. The concerned and flexible part is about paying attention to the other party's welfare and being flexible about the means to achieve one's goals so that the other party's perspectives can be brought into the final solution.

Structural Models. Structural models include the description of developmental sequences such as stages or contingent development paths, and mathematical relationships. One important structural account of negotiation derives from game theory, a branch of applied mathematics that details numerical representations of the value of choices made in negotiation. This is seen in Howard Raiffa's work (1982). Another example of a structural account is the model proposed by William Zartman (*Journal of Conflict Resolution*, 1977, 21, 619–638). In complex negotiations, such as in international negotiation, negotiation proceeds in general phases, from diagnosis, to formula, and then to detail. In the formula phase, the parties determine that agreement is possible and desirable and develop a general framework for it. The detail phase addresses the specific issues and reconciliation of positions.

Summary

Psychological research on negotiation is an exciting domain of inquiry that has a long tradition of multidisciplinary and multimethod inquiry; it has relevance and implications for important issues and challenges in everyday life at all levels of society. Scholars in psychology, economics, political science, organizational behavior, law, planning, and so on conduct laboratory studies, field studies, simulations, case studies of actual instances, and surveys in which professional negotiators or mediators are the respondents. This work has tremendous value, especially for fostering greater understanding and awareness of the efficiencies of negotiated agreement and the power of problem solving.

[*See also* Intergroup Relations; Political Decision Making; Thinking, *article on* Problem Solving; *and* Unions.]

Bibliography

Carnevale, P. J., & Pruitt, D. G. (1992). Negotiation and mediation. *Annual Review of Psychology*, 43, 531–582. Research-based monograph on the psychology of negotiation and mediation with an integrated review of motivational and cognitive models.

Druckman, D. (Ed.). (1977). *Negotiations: Social psychological perspectives*. Beverly Hills, CA: Sage. Thirteen essays by scholars in social psychology and political science that defined important theoretical perspectives, with particular relevance to international relations. Regarded as a companion volume to Rubin and Brown (1975).

Fisher, R., Ury, W., & Patton, B. (1991). *Getting to yes* (2nd ed.). New York: Penguin. Pioneering theoretical and practical essay on negotiation with an emphasis on win-win agreements.

Kramer, R., & Messick, D. M. (Eds.). (1995). *Negotiation as a social process*. Newbury Park, CA: Sage. Fourteen chapters by the directors of research projects on negotiation that emphasize organizational and business contexts plus several integrative overviews of the field.

Pruitt, D. G. (1981). *Negotiation behavior*. New York: Academic Press. Comprehensive examination of the dynamics of negotiation based on social psychological theory and research.

Pruitt, D. G., & Carnevale, P. J. (1993). *Negotiation in social conflict*. Pacific Grove, CA: Brooks/Cole. Integration of the research literature on negotiation and mediation.

Raiffa, H. (1982). *The art and science of negotiation*. Cambridge, MA: Harvard University Press. Systematic analysis of negotiation that emphasizes the efficiency of negotiated agreements by blending practical aspects of negotiation with simple mathematical analysis.

Rubin, J. Z., & Brown, B. R. (1975). *The social psychology of bargaining and negotiation*. New York: Academic Press. An early pioneering treatise on social psychological processes of decision-making in mixed-motive settings, with an emphasis on experimental gaming. One of the first integrations of the empirical literature in negotiation.

Walton, R., & McKersie, R. (1965). *A behavioral theory of labor negotiations: An analysis of a social interaction system*. New York: McGraw-Hill. A classic work highly relevant today, based on case studies of labor conflict, that helped define or clarify many important concepts in negotiation, in particular Mary Parker Follett's concept of integrative bargaining.

Peter J. Carnevale

NEIGHBORHOODS. *See* Suburban Communities; *and* Urban Communities.

NEOBEHAVIORISM. *See* Behaviorism and Neobehaviorism.

NEO-FREUDIAN PSYCHOANALYSIS. *See* Psychoanalysis, *articles on* History of the Field *and* Psychoanalytic Psychotherapies.

NEO PERSONALITY INVENTORY. The Revised NEO Personality Inventory (NEO-PI) is a 240-item questionnaire designed to measure the Five-Factor Model (FFM) of personality at the level of both the five broad factors and 30 specific traits that define them. As a general inventory of personality traits in adults, the NEO-PI-R has been used in developmental, educational, and cross-cultural research, and in clinical and industrial-organizational applications. First published in 1985, the NEO-PI draws on recent advances in trait psychology and assessment to offer a contemporary measure of personality.

Both the instrument and the name originated in the recognition that versions of three broad factors, labeled *neuroticism, extraversion,* and *openness to experience,* recurred in analyses of many different personality questionnaires. To measure these factors, six more specific traits (or facets) were identified for each, and eight-item scales were developed to measure each facet. For example, Extraversion is assessed by Warmth, Gregariousness, Assertiveness, Activity, Excitement Seeking, and Positive Emotions facets.

A major advance in personality psychology occurred in the 1980s when several investigators independently concluded that three factors were not sufficient to account for all important personality traits, but that five factors were. The resulting FFM has become a widely accepted representation of personality structure in normal adults. New scales measuring *Agreeableness* and *Conscientiousness* were combined with the earlier scales to create the NEO-PI. As revised in 1992, the NEO-PI is recognized as the most widely used of several measures of the FFM.

The NEO-PI gained prominence through its use in research establishing the reality, pervasiveness, stability, and universality of the traits in the FFM. In the 1970s it was widely believed that traits were cognitive fictions, groundless stereotypes, and myths. But many studies have now shown consensual validation of traits: Knowledgeable observers show substantial agreement in describing how much or little of a given trait an individual has. The biological reality of traits has been documented by twin studies showing that all the factors and facets of the NEO-PI have some genetic basis, and the instrument has been used in recent studies attempting to link personality to specific genes.

The FFM was originally discovered in analyses of natural language trait adjectives, meaning that all five of the factors are commonly used in everyday descriptions of self and others. But the five factors are not merely folk descriptions: Studies relating the NEO-PI to most other personality inventories have shown that almost every trait identified by personality psychologists is correlated with neuroticism, extraversion, openness, agreeableness, or conscientiousness. For example, tolerance of ambiguity, need for variety, thin mental boundaries, Jungian intuition, and xenophilia (love of foreign countries and cultures) are all related to Openness to Experience. The traits measured by the NEO-PI pervade personality psychology.

Personality traits are supposed to be enduring dispositions; longitudinal studies of the NEO-PI showing retest correlations near 0.80 for intervals as long as 7 years confirm that they are. Finally, studies in men and women, younger and older adults, and White and non-White samples suggest that the FFM is a human universal. Perhaps the most persuasive evidence of its universality comes from studies using translations of the NEO-PI into Dutch, French, German, Russian, Croatian, Portuguese, Spanish, Italian, Hebrew, Japanese, Chinese, Korean, and Filipino, which all yield the same five factors.

The NEO-PI-R was developed using contemporary principles of scale construction. Items are generally brief and clearly related to the construct they are designed to assess, because it has been shown that obvious items are more valid than subtle items. Roughly equal numbers of positively and negatively phrased items are used, so that any effects of acquiescence response set (the tendency to agree with items indiscriminately) are minimized. There is no item overlap among facets or among domains, and no filler items are included that needlessly lengthen the inventory. From a pool of rationally developed items, factor analyses were used to select items with maximum convergent and discriminant properties.

One of the major innovations of the NEO-PI-R is that it is published in two forms. In addition to the usual self-report version (Form S), there are observer rating versions (Form R) for men and women. Substantial correlations between self-reports and observer ratings using these two forms have provided important evidence on the reality of traits; use of Form R also allows valid personality assessment of individuals who are unable or unwilling to give accurate self-reports. It has been used, for example, to understand personality changes in patients with Alzheimer's disease by obtaining caregiver ratings, and to create personality profiles of all U.S. presidents based on the judgments of professional historians. When both Form S and Form R are available on the same individual (as in marital counseling), statistics have been developed to pinpoint areas of agreement and disagreement for further discussion.

A number of features have been developed to facilitate use of the instrument. Separate norms and profile sheets are available for adults and college age men and women. A short, 60-item version, the NEO Five-Factor Inventory (NEO-FFI) allows quick assessment of the five factors. Computer programs are available to administer and score the inventory and to provide an interpretive report with sections giving global and detailed description of personality; implications for coping and defense, somatic complaints, interpersonal behavior, cognitive processes, and needs and motives; and clinical hypotheses about possible personality disorders. The inventory has been published in Spanish for use by Hispanic Americans, and a score of translations into other languages are available through license.

Over 500 publications and scientific presentations have reported data from the NEO-PI. Researchers have used it to show links between personality and creativity, happiness, moral development, and coronary disease. Industrial-organizational psychologists have begun to use it in personnel selection and career development. Clinical psychologists and counselors use it to understand the client and select the most appropriate forms of intervention. As a comprehensive, contemporary measure of personality, the NEO-PI has a multitude of possible uses.

Bibliography

Block, J. (1995). A contrarian view of the five-factor approach to personality description. *Psychological Bulletin, 117*, 187–215. Presents a critical perspective on the Five-Factor Model, followed by exchanges with proponents.

Costa, P. T., Jr., & McCrae, R. R. (1992). Four ways five factors are basic. *Personality and Individual Differences, 13*, 653–665.

Costa, P. T., Jr., & McCrae, R. R. (1992). *Revised NEO personality inventory (NEO-PI-R) and NEO five-factor inventory (NEO-FFI) professional manual.* Odessa, FL: Psychological Assessment Resources. The basic source on the instrument, it includes details on its development, validation, and use.

Costa, P. T., Jr., & McCrae, R. R. (1995). Domains and facets: Hierarchical personality assessment using the Revised NEO Personality Inventory. *Journal of Personality Assessment, 64*, 21–50.

Costa, P. T., Jr., & Widiger, T. A. (Eds.). (1994). *Personality disorders and the five-factor model of personality.* Washington, DC: American Psychological Association. Includes theoretical, empirical, and clinical studies interpreting personality disorders in terms of the factors and facets of the NEO-PI.

Jang, K. L., McCrae, R. R., Angleitner, A., Riemann, R., & Livesley, W. J. (1998). Heritability of facet-level traits in a cross-cultural twin sample: Support for a hierarchical model of personality. *Journal of Personality and Social Psychology, 74*, 156–1565.

McCrae, R. R. (1992). The five-factor model: Issues and applications [Special issue]. *Journal of Personality, 60* (2). Illustrates applications of the NEO-PI in understanding psychopathology, health psychology, and emotions.

McCrae, R. R., & Costa, P. T., Jr. (1989). Reinterpreting the Myers-Briggs Type Indicator from the perspective of the five-factor model of personality. *Journal of Personality, 57,* 17–40. An example of the research relating the NEO-PI to other personality measures.

McCrae, R. R., & Costa, P. T., Jr. (1990). *Personality in adulthood.* New York: Guilford Press. Summarizes evidence on the stability of personality.

McCrae, R. R., & Costa, P. T., Jr. (1997). Personality trait structure as a human universal. *American Psychologist, 52,* 509–516.

Wiggins, J. S. (Ed.). (1996). *The five-factor model of personality: Theoretical perspectives.* New York: Guilford Press. Five different theoretical perspectives are offered, including that on which the NEO-PI is based.

Paul T. Costa, Jr. and Robert R. McCrae

NERVOUS SYSTEM. *See* Brain; Cognitive Electrophysiology; Neuron; *and* Synapse.

NETHERLANDS. Like most European countries, well before the twentieth century the Netherlands also had its share of savants who had been intrigued by the why and how of human behavior. These were sometimes scholars, like Erasmus, Spinoza, Heemsterhuis, and Bilderdijk, who approached the issue from a philosophical or ethical perspective. Sometimes they were natural or life scientists, like Huygens, Boerhave, and Donders, who concentrated more on physical and physiological preconditions and determinants. Nevertheless, before 1900 a comprehensive theory of psychology, or any systematic research toward one, was conspicuously absent.

The nineteenth century was a period of important economic and societal development, the consequence of exciting advances in science and technology. Many improvements in agriculture and health care, technological innovations, and especially industrialization—that is, large-scale manufacture for a mass market—were due in part to this scientific progress. There was wide expectation at the start of the twentieth century that it would now be time for improvements in social relations, welfare, childrearing, and education. Insights into this field would be the responsibility of the behavioral sciences, founded principally on psychology. This optimistic attitude was most clearly expressed by the founder of psychology as an independent discipline, the Groningen professor Gerard Heymans, in his 1909 rectorial address, "The Next Century of Psychology."

Initially, psychology and pedagogics took a comparatively modest position within the domain of Dutch science. As in Germany, then the model for many Dutch academic aspirations, both studies were subsumed within the faculty of philosophy and had leaned somewhat toward philosophy. This was the case until just after the First World War.

Gradually, three tendencies which were spreading through Europe began to be felt in the Netherlands. First, following the views of the father of psychology, Wilhelm Wundt, the importance of experimental methods was recognized. Second, there was curiosity about individual differences and their measurement, stimulated by the work of Stern, Galton, McKeen Cattell, and Pearson. Third, there was growing interest in the practical application of psychological insights. The significance of these applications in psychiatry had already been demonstrated by the French psychiatrists Esquirol and Seguin and their German colleagues Kraepelin and Ebbinghaus; in business life, by Münsterberg and Moede; and in education, by the diagnostic testing carried out by Binet and Simon in Paris.

However, the strongest influence on the practical application of psychology came from the United States, where industrial, clinical, and educational psychology had all undergone rapid development, especially after World War I. The successful selection research, which had been carried out by the U.S. Army, and involved large-scale testing using written tests, certainly contributed to this picture. Psychology in the United States had also been more scientifically oriented from the start, and it had been accorded scientific status much earlier than in Europe. Remarkably, then, we see that European psychology, after having been exported to the United States, grew into an independent, acknowledged discipline much more quickly there than it did in Europe, and in turn took on a pioneering role when it returned to Europe.

Early Developments

Dutch psychology gradually took root during the years between the two world wars (Eisenga, 1978). When the University of Groningen decided to inaugurate a chair of psychology in 1919 (awarded to H. J. F. W. Brugmans), many other universities followed suit. Utrecht nominated F. J. M. A. Roels as professor of psychology in 1922, and in 1929 J. Waterink was made professor of psychology and education at the Vrije Universiteit (Free University) in Amsterdam. In 1931 the Catholic University of Nijmegen nominated F. J. Th. Rutten; in 1933 the University of Amsterdam nominated G. Révész, and the Tilburg College of Economics nominated J. E. de Quay. That the Netherlands was acting with its usual pragmatism is borne out by the fact that almost all these appointments included a responsibility to study and practice applied psychology. The appointees took this responsibility seriously, and many translated it into the development of departments for industrial selection and school and vocational choice. Various university research institutes were set up (including the Psychotechnical Laboratory at the Vrije Universiteit, the Institute for Applied Psychology [GITP] at Nijmegen, and the Institute for Psychotechnics—Stichting voor Psychotechniek—at Utrecht), some of which would later become independent consultancy and advisory bureaus. Today, they remain among the most prominent institutes of applied psychology in the Netherlands.

Nonetheless, despite this manifest interest in its practical application, the Netherlands was not yet ready to develop an "American" kind of psychology. There were two reasons for this. The first has to do with a specifically Dutch phenomenon, that of *verzuiling*, a kind of social and religious divisionism; the second has to do with the field's abidingly philosophical orientation.

First, *verzuiling* (literally, "pillarization") describes a tendency which characterized the Netherlands in the early twentieth century and which strongly determined its societal character. Almost all aspects of social life were guided and formally arranged along lines dictated by religious and political convictions. The edifice of Dutch society was built on three main pillars of belief: Protestant, Roman Catholic, and secular. Naturally, the last of these categories has also been subject to a further doctrinal division between liberal conservatives and social democrats, but if one looks at the Dutch infrastructure—its schools, colleges and universities, its cultural and political alliances, its employers's and employees's organizations, its societies, associations and sports clubs, in fact, organizations touching every aspect of an individual's public life—then the description "thoroughgoing religious and political compartmentalization" can certainly be applied to the pre–World War II Netherlands.

The same applied equally to university courses and to professional practice in psychology. There were Protestant, Roman Catholic, and secular school and careers advice centers, teacher training institutes, recruitment and selection bureaus, mental health organizations, and, of course, educational courses in psychology and educational theory. In this "battle of the pillars," the more scientific arguments were sometimes accorded second place; certainly, the more religious groups vigorously resisted scientific concepts of psychology that had little room for a prescientific, though in their eyes no less important, philosophy of life.

Second, there is the affinity of Dutch psychology to the humanities in the first half of the twentieth century. Although the psychological investigation of individual differences in the Netherlands—for example, for

selection or vocational advice purposes—was initially carried out using a variety of laboratory tests drawn from the classical repertoire of such experimental tests, opposition to these techniques quickly arose. Remarkably, this opposition came not from empirical researchers criticizing the low validity of these and similar test assessments with respect to real-life criteria, but from theoreticians who saw the tests as being too simplistic and analytical. In their view, this approach failed to recognize people as complex, individual entities. They adhered to the paradigm put forward by Gestalt psychology and personalism, in which much more was expected of the (often intuitively working) psychologist than the merely mechanical drawing of conclusions from aptitude and reaction time tests. Observation, interview, the qualitative analysis of test performance, and, later, projective tests and graphology, it was argued, offered much richer psychological insights than did objective tests and experimental methods.

This interpretive and personalistic approach found support in philosophical schools of thought, often originating in German-speaking countries, such as existentialism, phenomenology, and (within psychology) characterology and diverse typologies. It was most influentially represented by the University of Utrecht, with such professors as F. J. J. Buitendijk, M. J. Langeveld, D. J. van Lennep, and H. J. van den Berg. Here, personal encounters and individually oriented diagnostics took the place of experiments and quantification; qualitative interpretation replaced objective measurement. This approach was suited not only to a more humanistic philosophy of life, but also to those whose concepts of psychology and pedagogics were more religiously constituted. They certainly found it easier to identify with such philosophical precepts than with an approach founded on positivism and natural science. This applied to both Protestants and Roman Catholics.

This paradigmatic choice also affected psychological practice, which consisted largely of testing and test-based diagnostics, whether this concerned clinical practice, training or vocational advice, or industrial applications, of which personnel selection was by far the most important aspect. The "clinical method," which was later to be forcefully disputed by Meehl (1954), dominated practically the entire domain of assessment and diagnostics, and it would be 10 or 15 years after World War II before a sea change took place.

Expansion

After the Second World War, the Netherlands, like many European countries, underwent a period of marked growth and expansion which lasted for several decades. People experienced a new sense of *élan*, a feeling of togetherness and harmony, and a sense of their collective responsibility for the country's reconstruction after the ravages of war. The interests of different parties were strongly aligned, and fundamental societal conflicts were all but absent.

The world of psychology, too, shared in the general euphoria. Interest in the study grew strongly, as did societal demand for psychological consultancy and advice. While only a few hundred students followed the newly independent university courses in psychology that were offered in 1945, under the supervision of one or at most two professors per university, by 1960 this had grown to 1,600 students, and the six universities which ran full-fledged psychology courses (Amsterdam, the Gemeente Universiteit and the Vrije Universiteit, Groningen, Leiden, Nijmegen, and Utrecht) each had at least half-a-dozen psychology professors and lecturers. In 1961, psychology studies were brought by law into a separate psychology department within the social sciences faculty, and the content of the curriculum was also made more systematic and more comparable between different universities.

Amsterdam Professor H. C. J. Duijker's 1959 article "Nomenclature and Systematics in Psychology" probably made a greater contribution to this national integration program than any other single factor. Duijker first distinguished between four "basic theories," of psychological functions, the person, development, and social behavior, while noting that a fifth, methodology, is an indispensable supporting subject. The other usual "psychologies" are mostly directed toward research into specific application areas; this applies to industrial, clinical, educational, forensic, and other branches of psychology. In most modern psychology studies in the Netherlands, this division has given rise to a curriculum structure in which students concentrate on these four basic theories plus methodology during the first two years, and then specialize in a practical application. This usually means choosing between one of three main domains: work and organization, school and childrearing, or health and sickness (including pathology and clinical psychology). Naturally, students may also opt to graduate in an experimental or theoretical area.

The practice of psychology, too, was subject to increased systematization and professionalization. The Nederlands Instituut van Praktizeerende Psychologen (Dutch Institute of Psychology Practioners; NIPP), which was set up in 1938 to represent the interests of practicing psychologists, systematically investigated such matters as the links between psychology training and professional practice, professional ethics, psychologist titles and their protection, and methodological issues including the quality of tests. Many prominent psychology professors chaired the NIPP over the years, but many important initiatives were stimulated by Professor S. D. Fokkema, who was its secretary for many years (1959–1967). NIPP "sections" were created; the first of these brought together the industrial psychologists, always among the best-organized members. Other sections—clinical, vocational, child, and educational psychology—quickly followed. In order also to be able to represent psychologists working in research and at universities, the word *practicing* was dropped from the association's name, in 1960. Also that year, a professional code of practice was accepted. This code would eventually be replaced by a second version in 1976 and a third version in 1994.

Between 1960 and 1980 Dutch psychology underwent two profound shocks, though of a very different nature. The first was the transition from a humanitarian, intuitive, "encounter"-type psychology to a quantitative, experimental, empirical psychology; in the 1960s almost all Dutch universities replaced their existing phenomenological and holistic approach with a more scientific, positivistic approach, as a result of an unmistakable American influence. This also had important repercussions for professional practice, much of which was based on the application of test methods. Objectivity, reliability, and validity became more important test criteria than the issue of whether tests generated the kind of qualitative information which could be used for a rich description of an individual. The universities were the first to change allegiance. A book whose influence it is difficult to overestimate in this respect is A. D. de Groot's *Methodology* which appeared in 1961, but important work was also carried out by J. Linschoten (especially with his critical and influential 1964 book *Idols of Psychology*), B. J. Kouwer (both of the Utrecht school, but propagandists for an experimental and quantitative psychology) and J. P. van de Geer. Critical comment from within the NIP's Test Research Committee (TRC), which, particularly in the early days, housed many of the Netherlands' methodology focused professors, and a book written by the erstwhile secretary of this TRC, P. J. D. Drenth, *The Psychological Test* (1966), which became required reading at most Dutch universities, also contributed toward the growing debate. Still, practice proved more intractable than theory; many professional psychologists and consultancy bureaus continued to put their faith in the intuitive and qualitative methods. It was not until the 1980s, when university psychometricians reappraised methods such as observation and interview (as used in assessment centers, for instance) and issues such as situational selection and the person-job fit, and when professional practice developed a serious interest in the importance of scientific evaluation (with many consultancy bureaus setting up with their own research departments), before a measure of equilibrium between theory and practice would return.

The second shock was brought about by the critical social movement that took shape among students and many young intellectuals in the Netherlands in the late 1960s and the beginning of the 1970s; these, either following the example of or together with their counterparts elsewhere in Europe, opposed the role of the scientific establishment in maintaining the social *status quo*—and this included psychology. Largely motivated by ideals based on the Marxist concept of class struggle, and encouraged by widespread social antipathy toward the Western, and particularly American, power politics which had culminated in the Vietnam War, their protests brought about large-scale unrest and, in places, revolutionary changes in traditional procedures and traditions. Universities and faculties in the Netherlands were reorganized and democratized; the social science faculties, which comprised the psychology departments, were often in the forefront of these changes. Partly under student influence, the curriculum content was modified so as to include a more proactive stance on social issues. Student interest in industrial psychology ("the servant of the military-industrial complex") fell sharply. Even clinical psychology ("facilitating adaptation to the existing order") suffered. By the same token, more interest was shown in social and political psychology and the practical issues of trade union work and the protest movement itself.

Although this movement had less radical outcomes in the Netherlands than were seen in several other European countries, it certainly had its effects (see also Van Strien, 1988). The far-reaching democratization of university management structures that was introduced in 1971 was subjected to some legal reversal only as late as 1997. Concepts such as openness, autonomy, and emancipation, participation (both in the workplace and political spheres), and the development of individual social rights—central elements in the NIPP's ethical code as revised in 1976, and important values in the practical work of today's professional psychologists—would have been accepted less readily in the absence of this movement. We also have to appreciate the more critical consideration of the question which has been asked since then: In whose interests is a psychologist's work carried out; whose values does he or she adopt; and what loyalties does he or she owe to clients and to the system (society, the institute, the company), particularly when these come into mutual conflict?

Established and Recognized

The oil crisis of the 1970s, the economic recession of the 1980s, and the upturn in the country's economy in the 1990s all had important consequences for Dutch psychology. First, a "no-nonsense" mentality gained ground, particularly among young people and students: a study course should be useful, and should provide adequate preparation for the world of work. Workplace psychology, organizational psychology, economic psychology, and social psychology (now unfettered by the ideological legacy of the 1970s) once again became more popular. New areas of interest were growing, such issues around working parents and childrearing, stress and burnout, the psychology of industrial design, architectural psychology, environmental psychology, forensic psychology, gender studies, information processing and computer use, and new technologies; these are giving psychology graduates an unprecedented range of options for professional practice.

The study of psychology has become more popular than ever, and continues to attract large numbers of new students. In 1996 and 1997 more than 2,000 first-year psychology students registered with Dutch universities. At present, besides the aforementioned Amsterdam universities (the University of Amsterdam and the Vrije Universiteit) and those in Groningen, Leiden, Nijmegen, and Utrecht, the universities of Tilburg and Maastricht also offer full degree courses in psychology, and the subject can also be studied through the Open University, which was inaugurated in Heerlen in 1984. Important course options in psychology are also available at the technical universities of Delft, Eindhoven, and Twente and at the Erasmus University in Rotterdam.

Dutch psychology has been responsible for several important scientific developments and these have earned the country an acknowledged seat in the international forum. Scientific productivity at Dutch university faculties and research institutes is generally high, and their work compares favorably with the work done in other countries, as a national research review by an international review committee showed in 1993. New developments in psychological research, such as the areas of neuropsychology, cognitive information processing and artificial intelligence, psycholinguistics, biological psychology, genetics, emotions, attachment in child development and education, social cognition and language acquisition, cross-cultural psychology, and many more have led to the creation of chairs and institutes and to the foundation of collaborative networks, many of them international in scope, which have put the Netherlands clearly on the map. Dutch journals have provided an impulse to qualitative improvements in the field by improving review procedures and tightening up norms. The journals include *Nederlands Tijdschrift voor Psychologie en haar Toepassingen* (Netherlands Journal for Psychology and Its Applications) which was founded in 1946, and is the most important psychology journal in the Netherlands, and also *Acta Psychologica, Tijdschrift voor Onderwijsresearch* (Journal for Educational Research), *Gedrag en Organisatie* (Behavior and Organization), *Paedagogische Studiën* (Pedagogical Studies), and even the in-house journal of the NIP, *De Psycholoog* (The Psychologist). The Council for Scientific Psychological Research, which was set up in 1975, was recognized as a foundation within the national science research organization (NWO) in 1981. This acknowledgment of the scientific nature of modern Dutch psychology is borne out by the fact that of the 200 members of the prestigious Royal Netherlands Academy of Arts and Sciences, who are elected on the basis of scientific excellence, no fewer than 7 are psychologists (in the order of their nomination: W. J. M. Levelt, P. J. D. Drenth, J. A. Michon, W. K. B. Hofstee, W. A, Wagenaar, G. J. Mellenbergh, and A. F. Sanders [A. D. de Groot and N. H. Frijda are now retired members]. One of these (Drenth) also served as president of the academy from 1990 to 1996.

The Dutch are natural organizers and Dutch psychologists continue to sit on many of the executive committees of international psychological associations and many other European organizations. They participate in many of the editorial boards of international psychological publications and journals. They are often present in quite large numbers at international psychology conferences, and are also frequently involved in their organization; for instance in 1989 the Netherlands originated the successful series of biennial European psychology congresses.

Today, the emancipation of Dutch psychology is more or less complete; it has successfully accrued both a national and an international reputation. Whether it has succeeded in achieving the optimistic ambitions it set itself at the start of the twentieth century with regard to the betterment of society and the improvement of its members' welfare, in other words, whether psychology has been able to contribute significantly toward the advancement of truth, human dignity, and compassion, is another matter. These goals could be held up as an ideal to strive toward, but if we look at the world around us, it certainly cannot be claimed that these ambitions have been achieved in the twentieth century. If we were more modest, however, we would confine ourselves to Frijda's (1992) observation made in his valedictory address: "the world may not become a better place thanks to psychology, but it certainly becomes inferior without it—more stupid, more vulgar, and more vulnerable to tyranny."

Bibliography

Drenth, P. J. D. (1969). De psychologische test [The psychological test]. Arnhem: Van Loghum Slaterus.

Duijker, H. C. J. (1959). Nomenclatuur en systematiek der psychologie [Nomenclature and systematics in psychology]. Nederlands Tijdschrift voor de Psychologie, 14, 176–217.

Eisenga, L. K. A. (1978). Geschiedenis van de Nederlandse psychologie [History of Dutch psychology]. Deventer: Van Loghum Slaterus.

Frijda, N. H. (1992). Heeft de psychologie wel zin? [Does psychology make sense?]. Valedictory address, University of Amsterdam.

Groot, A. D. de (1961). Methodologie; grondslagen van onder-
zoek en denken in de gedragswetenschappen [Methodology; fundamentals of research and thinking in behavioral sciences]. Den Haag: Mouton.

Heijmans, G. (1909). De toekomstige eeuw der psychologie [The next century of psychology]. Rector's address, University of Groningen.

Linschoten, J. (1964). Idolen van de psychologie [Idols of psychology]. Utrecht: Bijleveld.

Meehl, P. E. (1954). Clinical versus statistical prediction. Minneapolis: University of Minnesota Press.

NIP(P). (1989). Beroepsethiek voor de psychologie [Professional ethics for psychologists]. Amsterdam: NIP. (Original work published 1961)

Strien, P. J. van. (1988). De ontwikkeling van de A&O-psychologie in Nederland [The development of work and organizational psychology in the Netherlands). In P. J. D. Drenth, H. Thierry, & Ch. J. de Wolff (Eds.), Nieuw handboek arbeids en organisatiepsychologie (pp. 1.4.1–1.4.49). [New handbook of work and organizational psychology]. Deventer: Van Loghum Slaterus.

Pieter J. D. Drenth

NEUROMUSCULAR DISORDERS (NDs) primarily affect anterior motor horn cells in the brain stem, spinal cord, peripheral nerves, neuromuscular junctions, and muscle fibers. Symptoms and signs of NDs include muscular atrophy or hypertrophy, muscle weakness, rapid fatigue, myalgia, and muscle cramps. The diagnosis is usually based on detection of high levels of serum enzyme concentrations (mainly creatin kinase), EMG (to differentiate neurogenic/primary lesions and myopathies), muscle biopsy, CT, MRT, and gene defect localization.

Treatment of genetically determined NDs is limited to symptomatic relief and aims at maintaining and reinforcing functional capacity. Symptomatic physical therapy focuses on the stabilization and strengthening of functional muscles; optimization of functionality, blood circulation, metabolism, delay of malfunction like contracture of the joints and scoliosis, and the maintenance of the orthostasis and adequate oxygen supply. In addition, the accompanying symptoms of ND, like pains, insomnia, decubitus, ischialgies, osteoporosis, and circulatory problems need treatment. At times orthopedic measures (passive fixation, wheelchair, walking aids, etc.), surgical interventions (i.e., with scoliosis), and supplementary food intake (gastric tube, etc.) are needed.

The adequate psychological care and counseling of patients and their families are required to deal with the special psychological and behavioral issues associated with NDs. In order to achieve maximum compliance and combat depression, an atmosphere should be created in which supportive family, genetic, and vocational counseling, along with information on latest research and advances in the field and patient experiences, can be exchanged.

Effective psychological treatment could be provided by behavior therapy, which focuses on the emotional state and behavior of the patient. Functional analysis of specific antecedent, mediational, and consequent variables that currently maintain the patient's (mis-) behavior is mandatory. Time-limited therapy is recommended, with emphasis on restructuring certain maladaptive cognitions, including the patient's expectancies of self-efficacy and probable outcome, through direct verbal persuasion and logical analysis, assertion training, modeling, and self-control techniques (e.g., relaxation training and self-monitoring evaluation and instruction). Explicit strategies designed to facilitate generalization and maintenance of treatment-induced improvement and to ensure the utilization of newly acquired self-control skills has good effects on problem behavior and illness management. The loss of health and motor functions in those with NDs may lead to a major reduction in social reinforcement (the loss of a job or partner). To avoid depression, therapy should be emphasized to strengthen the patient's ability to secure alternative sources of reinforcement. It should convince the patient that in every state of the disease there is at least a minimum of control over aversive consequences and symptoms.

Due to the fading of voluntary motor function, communication may become seriously impaired in patients with NDs, as well as their ability to manipulate their environment. Even if the disease progresses to a "locked-in" state, with tetraplegia and paralysis of the facial muscles, verbal interaction with the totally paralyzed can be provided through a technique by which subjects learn to control their brain responses. Based on previous studies and longtime experience with slow cortical potentials (SCPs), medical psychologists have developed an EEG-based brain-computer interface, the thought translation device. Within a 2-second rhythm, differences between a baseline interval and an active control interval of SCPs are transformed into vertical or horizontal cursor movements on a computer screen, producing either cortical negativity or positivity. The learned cortical skill enables the patients to select letters or words in a language supporting program (LSP). In addition, they can operate an environment control unit performing the distinct brain response in a defined order to turn on an alarm clock, call the care giver, switch a light, TV set, or radio on and off, and perform other functions. Fast and stable SCP self-control can be achieved with operant training and without mediation of any muscle activity.

Biofeedback is used to help patients correctly perceive both their visceral responses and skeletal musculature responses. Biofeedback therapy has been her-

alded as a potential means of obtaining clinically significant changes in many NDs. The value of EMG feedback in muscle reeducation and control over involuntary movements (spasm) is generally accepted. It also showed encouraging results in the rehabilitation of both upper and lower motor neuron dysfunction. Cases of muscular weakness—wasting, hypotonia, lost tendon stretch reflexes, muscular fasciculation, contractures, trophic changes, and degeneration—can be treated with EMG feedback. Significant reduction in the severity of muscular-skeletal pain and affective distress could be maintained.

Posture biofeedback, designed to achieve a permanent body posture correction, turned out to be highly effective in scoliosis and kyphosis patients. Significant reductions can be achieved both in spinal curvature and signs of Scheuermann's disease.

Relaxation, useful for treating anxiety, tension, and fears, is especially effective for patients with NDs. Biofeedback can be applied to reduce the levels of stress and tension that stimulate muscle contraction. In many of the NDs, psychological stress induces subsequent worsening of the disease. With relaxation skills, the patient learns to remain relatively calm in face of anxiety-evoking situations.

Classification

John Walton (*Neuro Muscular Diseases News Bulletin*, 1991, 9–10) differentiated four classes of neuromuscular disorders as follows.

Motor neuron diseases (the official classification of the World Federation of Neurology lists numerous different forms of such spinal muscular atrophy) are degenerative disorders of either lower (peripheral) or both the upper (central) and lower motor neurons. Common symptoms are muscular atrophies, paresis, fasciculations, and absent tendon reflexes. Their heredity (autosomally recessive) is mostly evident.

There are three forms of hereditary spinal muscular atrophies. Following the introduction of EMG after World War II, Kugelberg-Welander noted physiologic evidence of denervation in adolescents with proximal limb weakness. This condition is therefore called Kugelberg-Welander syndrome, or spinal muscular atrophy (type 3) with an incidence of 1 out of 75,000 and a highly variable course. The onset of the disease starts at age 2 to 17 (with a mean of 9), with a higher risk for males. Spinal muscular atrophy (type 2) is a special intermediate class with similar symptoms but later onset in life. Infantile spinal muscular atrophy (type 1 Werdnig-Hoffmann syndrome) appears in 1 out of 25,000 newborns, with symptoms evident at birth or soon thereafter but always manifest before the age of 4 months. Type 1 is described as generalized muscular hypotonus. Tendon reflexes are absent, and spontanous movement is reduced. The rapid progression with amplifying paresis often leads to death within the first 18 months of a baby's life.

The type Aran-Duchenne is the most frequent nuclear atrophy, with first symptoms at the ages of 20 to 45 (with a mean of 30). After some years, symmetric atrophies of the hand muscles cause thenaratrophy and convulsions. The chronic, slow course over decades is not life threatening as long as there are no bulbar signs.

The term *motor neuron disease* is used to describe an adult disease, amyotrophic lateral sclerosis (ALS, Lou Gehrig's disease or Charcot disease), of unknown cause and pathogenesis (no identified consistent risk factors), in which upper motor neurons (hyperactive tendon reflexes, Hoffmann signs, Babinski signs or clonus), and lower motor neurons (weakness, wasting, fasciculation) are affected. ALS is found worldwide, with roughly the same prevalence (50×10^{-6}; mean 4.1 per 100,000). Despite time, place, and racial, sociocultural, and climatic differences in surveyed communities (annual incidence rates: 1.0 per 100,000) values are remarkably even. Heredity is only seen in 5 to 20% of cases (familial ALS). Primary symptoms are convulsions, followed by paresis and atrophies. A characteristic sign is spastic tension and increase of spontanous muscle reflexes. Depending on the parts of body that show the weakness first, ALS is classified in three types. In 50% of the patients hands and lower limbs are affected first, usually asymmetrically. In the pereonal type (approximately 20%), the disease starts laterally in a lower limb, with paresis of the lifting toe and foot. The oropharynx (bulbar) type of ALS is composed of slurred speech or dysarthria and difficulty swallowing. Usually there is no change in the emotional responses or personality of the patient and no dementia, even though it has been reported that some patients develop an impairment of cognitive function of the frontal lobes. The lacking inhibition of voluntary facial muscles may lead to pathological facial expression (involuntary laughing and crying). Emotional support in ALS is vitally important for the major decisions concerning tracheostomy and percutaneous gastrostomy for nutrition. Many patients on ventilatory support are found to report a high quality of life (no depression, no hopelessness, and psychological well-being, even on a ventilator). Psychological distress can be reduced through integrated interdisciplinary care that requires a broad psychological approach to patient management. The course of ALS is progressive without remissions. Since there is no effective drug therapy, treatment is symptomatic, as in most NDs. Physical therapy can maintain functions as long as possible. Death results from respiratory failure, aspiration pneumonitis, and pulmonary embolism in about 50% of patients. The mean duration of symptoms is 4 years; 20% live longer than 5 years. After tracheostomy, patients stay alive although totally paralyzed, locked in. ALS has its onset in middle and late life, and there is a male predominance (a gender ratio of 1.5 males to 1.0 females).

Polyneuropathy and peripheral neuropathy result from diffuse lesions of the peripheral nerves, usually manifested by distal limb muscles weakness, sensory loss, and autonomic dysfunction. Symptoms include acral (distal) pain, paresthesias, and loss of tendon reflexes. The chronic form progresses over weeks and months with little remission. The acute, fast-ascending course shows a complete paralysis of the proximal and distal muscles within a few hours or days (Landry's paralysis). The motor and/or sensory axons or the myelin sheaths may be predominantly affected, or the neuropathy may be mixed, axonal, or demyelinating. In severe polyneuropathy, the patient may become tetraplegic and respirator dependent.

The most common hereditary peroneal muscular atrophy is the Charcot-Marie-Thooth syndrome (hereditary motor and sensory neuropathy, HMSN 1 and HMSN 2). At first, patients realize problems walking and deformations of the feet, and then atrophies and paresis of the peroneal muscles and distal parts of the arm. There are also sensory and nociceptive disturbances accompanied by balance problems. Nerve conduction velocities are clearly reduced, and peripheral nerves are demyelinated. Intellectual functions stay unaffected. Although the disorder may start early (between the first and fifth decade of life) the development of symptoms is slow and benign over many years, in some cases until old age. The HMSN III syndrome (hypertrophic neuritis dejerine-scottas) is the more extreme form, with faster progression and early immobility. Other syndromes include *amyloiosis, morbus refsum, and neuropathy with hereditary ataxy.*

The term *neuritis* is typically reserved for inflammatory disorders of nerves resulting from infection or autoimmunological factors. The most frequent acquired inflammatory demyelinating polyneuropathies with acute onset of peripheral and cranial nerve dysfunction, with an incidence of 0.6 to 1.9 per 100,000, is the Guillain-Barré syndrome and its variants. It consists of an autoimmune response against peripheral nerve tissues, striking the autonomic nervous system (disregulated blood pressure, cardiopathy). This syndrome, with unknown etiology, shows rapidly progressive symmetric (limb) weakness, loss of tendon reflexes, facial displegia, respiratory paresis, and impaired sensation in hands and feet. It displays in a characteristic history of symmetric motor or sensorimotor neuropathy after viral illness, delivery, or surgery. Symptoms are most severe and rapidly progressive within 1 week of onset but may progress for 3 weeks or more (subacute). Recovery is slow and incomplete for many months. Death is uncommon but may follow aspiration pneumonia, embolism, infection, or autonomic dysfunction. For the involved psychological and behavioral factors, EMG biofeedback therapy is known to be exceptionally helpful.

The most complex of *disorders of the neuromuscular junction* is the Myasthenic syndrome. Myasthenia gravis (MG/pseudoparalytica) is an autoimmune disorder with a prevalence of 4 to 7 per 100,000, caused by a defect of neuromuscular transmission due to an antibody-mediated attack against the postsynaptic end-plate of the muscle (acetylcholine receptors, AChR). The overt pathology of myasthenia is found primarily in the thymus gland. MG may begin at any age but is most common in the second to fourth decades of life. About 12% of infants born to myasthenic mothers have a syndrome characterized by impaired sucking, a weak cry, and limp limbs. Some cases are drug induced. Initial symptoms are ptosis and abnormal weakness (exhaustion and rapid tiring after physical or psychic effort) with progredient spread on proximal, and later distal muscle groups. Respiratory insufficiency and paralysis may lead to death when intercostal muscles are affected. The characteristic decremental response to repetitive stimulation of the motor nerve reflects the failure of end-plate potentials (about 20% of normal). Early research and recent findings on psychological aspects in the differential diagnosis of MG document the role of psychological factors in the pathogenesis, manifestation, and course of MG, its effects on the patient's personality and interpersonal relations, illness-related stress experiences, and coping strategies. Psychotherapeutic interventions and stress-reduction therapy (biofeedback) is necessary. Immune-suppressive medication and corticosteroids lead to remission in 80% of cases.

The ocular type, with the predominance of symptoms in the eye muscle, is found in 90% of myasthenia patients. At the next stage (the facio-pharyngeale type), paresis is also seen in bulbar parts and distal muscles. Ten percent of patients show an acute distribution with implication of the respiratory system and the risk of rapid progredience and high mortality. The Lambert-Eaton-myasthenic syndrome (LEMS), a disease of adults, is an autoimmune reaction of peripheral cholinergic synapses often following a small carcinoma of the lung.

In the fourth class of NDs, the *myopathies*, the symptoms are mainly due to a dysfunction of the muscle, whereas there is no evidence of causal denervation. Dystrophies are frequently observed myopathies as diagnosed by clinical, histologic, and EMG criteria. They are inherited, all symptoms are due to progressive weakness, and there are no histologic abnormalities besides the degeneration and regeneration of the muscle, and no signs of denervation or sensory loss.

Progressive muscular dystrophies are a group of inherited, subacute or chronic, degenerative disorders (weakness and atrophic signs, typical EMG) of the voluntary muscles. As in most of the other NDs, treatment and management is only symptomatic. Psychological and behavioral factors play a critical role in the onset of muscular dystrophies. Exogenous stressors or traumatic life events often trigger the first symptoms. Psychological problems and conflicts can aggravate the condition and course. As dystrophies are mainly disorders of early life, children are characterized by retardation of their intellectual development, which might be a consequence of their overprotective parents. Later on, depressive symptoms and a passive and hopeless attitude may dominate. Therapy of depression, biofeedback, relaxation therapies, and techniques to reduce fear are required.

Duchenne is the most frequent muscular dystrophy of childhood, with an incidence of 1 per 3,500 newborn boys. Together with the rarer type Becker (incidence of 1 per 30,000), which has a benign course and slower progression, the malignant Duchenne type is inherited as an X-linked recessive trait, although usually females are not concerned but carry the gene.

The symptoms start with delayed walking. Since the child cannot raise his knees properly, there is little forward progression. Soon toe walking, waddling gait, and lumbar lordosis are evident. The condition progresses to overt difficulties walking, climbing stairs, and rising. A state called climbing up oneself is later seen. Arms and hands are affected as the disease progresses. Between the ages of 9 and 12 a child needs a wheelchair. At this stage scoliosis becomes serious; contractures at elbows and knees contribute to disability. Ninety percent of the patients show dilatative cardiomyopathy, restricted cardial performance, and abnormal ECG. By the age of 20, respiration failure may lead to death or mechanical ventilation. Since precise diagnostics allow predicition of the course of the disease, prophylactic operations are carried out. The diagnosis of Duchenne dystrophy is usually evident from clinical features. Fasciculation, limb weakness, calf hypertrophy, EMG evidence, and excessive high serum enzyme levels and dystrophin analysis identify the disorder. Besides physiotherapy, treating scoliosis with biofeedback therapy is the noninvasive treatment of choice.

Particular psychotherapeutic intervention is needed to support coping with anger, fear, and depression related to the short life expectancy. The eventual inability to walk and obesity in puberty cause dramatic psychosocial problems for the boys, their care givers, and families.

Myotonic muscular dystrophy is a nonlethal disorder of adult life. As the penetrance of the gene is almost 100%, it has a high prevalence of about 5 per 100,000 throughout the world. This multisystem disease includes a dystrophy of unique distribution, myotonia, cardiopathy, ocular cataracts and endocrinopathy. Even though cerebral symptoms are not common, patients often lack vitality and show emotional indifference.

Polymyositis is one of many inflammatory NDs. Within weeks or months, muscle weakness starts proximally, then spreads cranially, involving bulbar parts and ultimately reaching distal muscles. Muscles ache and swell, fever and gastrointestinal problems occur, together with characteristic dermatomyositis (inflammatory alteration of the skin). The course is intermittent, but 50% the patients with acute polymyositis die within one year.

Multiple sclerosis (MS) is akin to NDs but is actually not classified as such. Rather, it is categorized as an organic nerve disorder of which no "classic" form exists. Its etiology is unknown, but its susceptibility is inherited. The prevalence is subdivided in high-prevalence areas (in 30:100,000 Northern and Western countries), medium-prevalence areas (5 to 30:100,000 in Africa, the Middle East, and Asia) and low-prevalence areas (like Japan and South America, with less than 5:100,000). An environmental factor is obviously critically important in pathogenesis and autoimmune mechanisms. MS could be precipitated by a viral infection or by trauma. The age at onset shows unimodal distribution, with a peak between ages 20 and 30 years. Young adult women are 1.4 to 3.1 times more often affected than men. This chronic disease displays multiple areas of (CNS) white matter inflammation, demyelination, and glial scarring (sclerosis), commonly involving the optic chiasm, brain stem, cerebellum, and spinal cord. As in NDs, no known cure exists. Acute attacks are to be treated, and symptomatic therapy is important (with antispastic drugs, pain management, bladder management, decubitus, and ulcer prevention), but the cerebellar symptoms are generally resistant to therapy.

Although (older) models of a "predisposition in personality type" are no longer accepted, it should be noted that in 70 to 80% of patients the outbreak of the first symptoms or a dramatic worsening arise following psychological stress. There are several psychopathological symptoms evident in MS that, together with the uncertainty of long-term prognosis, complicate management: emotional lability, forced laughing and crying, mental symptoms like depression, aphasia and cognitive loss, and psychosis and dementia. Patients show affective expressions that do not match their inner feelings, together with an inability to convey their actual emotions. The most prominent psychological disorder in MS is major depression, with a fourteenfold elevated risk to suicidal behavior. Psychotherapeutic awareness should therefore focus at first

on treating depressive symptoms with antidepressive medication if needed. Biofeedback is highly useful in MS for muscular relaxation, the treatment of spastics, and emotional stress reduction.

Bibliography

Neuromuscular Disorders

Carter, G. T., Abresch, R. T., Fowler, W. M., Johnson, E. R., Kilmer, D. D., & McDonald, C. M. (1995). Profiles of neuromuscular diseases: Hereditary motor and sensory neuropathy, types I and II. *American Journal of Physical and Medical Rehabilitation, 74*(Suppl. 5), 140–149.

Johnson, E. R., Abresch, R. T., Carter, G. T., Kilmer, D. D., Fowler, W. M., Sigford, B. J., & Wanlass, R. L. (1995). Profiles of neuromuscular diseases: Myotonic dystrophy. *American Journal of Physical and Medical Rehabilitation, 74*(Suppl. 5), 104–116.

Kilmer, D. D., Abresch, R. T., McCrory, M. A., Carter, G. T., Fowler, W. M., Johnson, E. R., & McDonald, C. M. (1995). Profiles of neuromuscular diseases: Facioscapulohumeral muscular distrophy. *American Journal of Physical and Medical Rehabilitation, 74*(Suppl. 5), 131–139.

Lissoni, A. (1995). Tracheostomy and mechanical ventilation in ventilatory failure of patients with neuromuscular diseases. *Monaldi Archives of Chest Diseases, 50*(3), 232–234.

McDonald, C. M., Abresch, R. T., Carter, G. T., Fowler, W. M., Johnson, E. R., & Kilmer, D. D. (1995). Profiles of neuromuscular diseases: Becker's muscular distrophy. *American Journal of Physical and Medical Rehabilitation, 74*(Suppl. 5), 93–103.

Rowland, L. P. (Ed.). (1995). *Merritt's textbook of neurology* (9th ed.). Baltimore, MD: Williams & Wilkins.

Psychological Factors Involved in Neuromuscular Diseases

Bain, L. (1996). Neurodegenerative diseases: Sustaining hope. *Professional Nurse, 11*(8), 515–516.

Bardach, J. L. (1995). Psychosocial considerations in the sexual rehabilitation of individuals with neuromuscular diseases. *Semin-Neurol., 15*(1), 65–71.

Grant, I. (1986). Neuropsychosocial and psychiatric disturbances in multiple sclerosis. In W. I. McDonald & D. H. Silberberg (Eds.), *Multiple sclerosis* (pp. 134–152). London: Butterworths.

Mang, S. Weiss, H., & Schalke, B. (1993). Psychosomatic and somatopsychic aspects of myasthenia gravis: A critical review of the literature. *Zeitschrift fur Klinische Psychologie, Psychopathologie, und Psychotherapie, 41*(1), 69–86.

McDonald, E. R., Hillel, A., & Wiedenfeld, S. A. (1996). Evaluation of the psychological status of ventilatory-supported patients with ALS/MND. *Palliative Medicine, 10*(1), 35–41.

Peyser, J. M., Edwards, K. R., & Poser, C. M. (1980). Psychological profiles in patients with multiple sclerosis. *Arch Neurol, 37,* 437–440.

Viemero, V. (1991). The effects of somatic disability or progressive illness on psychological and social well-being. Eighteenth European Conference on Psychosomatic Research (Helsinki, Finland, 1990). *Psychotherapy and Psychosomatics, 55*(2–4), 120–125.

Warren, S., Greenhill, S., & Warren, K. G. (1982). Emotional stress and the development of multiple sclerosis. *Journal of Chronic Diseases, 35,* 861–865.

Worthington, A. (1996). Psychological aspects of motor neurone disease: A review. *Clinical Rehabilitation, 10*(3), 185–194.

Self-Regulation of the Brain and Communication

Birbaumer, N. (1999). Slow cortical potentials (SCP): Behavioral effects of operant control. *Neuroscientist, 15,* 74–78.

Birbaumer, N., Ghanayim, N., Hinterberger, T., Iverson, I., Kotchoubey, B., Perelmouter, J., Taub, E., & Flor, H. (1999). A spelling device for the paralysed. *Nature, 398,* 297–298.

Elbert, T., Rockstroh, B., Lutzenberg, W., & Birbaumer, N. (Eds.). (1994). *Self-regulation of the brain and behavior.* New York: Springer.

Kübler, A., Kotochoubey, B., Hinterberger, T., Ghanayim, N., Perelmouter, J., Schauer, M., Fritsch, C., Taub, E., & Birbaumer, N. (1998). A thought translation device for brain computer communication. *Studia Psicologia, 140,* 17–30.

EMG Biofeedback

Birbaumer, N., (1967). Biofeedback training: A critical view of its critical application and some possible future directions. *European Journal of Behavioral Analysis and Modification, 4,* 235–251.

Birbaumer, N., Flor, H., Cevey, B., Dworkin, B., & Miller, N. E. (1994). Behavioral treatment of sciolosis and kyphosis. *Journal of Psychosomatic Research, 38*(6), 623–628.

Brach, J. S., Van Swearingen, J. M., Lenert, J., & Johnson, P. C. (1997). Facial neuromuscular retraining for oral synkinesis. *Plastic and Reconstructive Surgery, 99*(7), 1922–1931.

Carlson, J. G., & Seifert, A. R. (Eds.). (1991). *International perspectives on self-regulation and health.* New York: Plenum Press.

Carlson, J. G., Seifert, A. R., & Birbaumer, N. (Eds.). (1994). *Clinical and applied psychophysiology.* New York: Plenum Press.

Cohen, B. A., Crouch, R. H., & Thompson, S. N. (1997). EMG biofeedback as a therapeutic adjunct in Guillain-Barré syndrome. *Archives of Physical and Medical Rehabilitation, 58*(12), 582.

Haag, G. (1990). Biofeedback training in psychosomatic and neuromuscular disorders. In B. Diehl & J. M. Miller (Eds.), *Neuromuscular disorders* (pp. 411–417). Berlin: Springer.

Miller, N. E. (1978). Biofeedback and visceral learning. *Annual Review of Psychology, 29,* 373–404.

Schwartz, M. S. (Ed.). (1995). *Biofeedback: A practitioner's guide* (2nd ed.). New York: Guilford Press.

Wentworth, R. I. (1988). *Symptom reduction through clinical biofeedback.* New York: Human Sciences Press.

Margarete Schauer and Niels Birbaumer

NEURON. The nervous system contains two major types of cells: neurons and glia. The primary function of glia (also called glial cells) is to support and protect neurons. Neurons communicate with each other and with some other types of cells outside the nervous system. Some serve as sensory receptors, detecting environmental stimuli and thus providing information required for perception. Others monitor various characteristics of the body, such as temperature, blood pressure, and presence of available nutrients and thus provide information required for maintenance of homeostasis. The activity of all skeletal muscles and some glands (endocrine glands such as the adrenal medulla and exocrine glands such as the salivary gland) are controlled by neurons. In addition, neurons control smooth muscles in organs such as the intestines, blood vessels, and the urogenital system.

The main part of a neuron, the soma, includes the nucleus, which contains the chromosomes. Attached to the soma of most neurons are several treelike dendrites and a single axon, which often branches extensively. Dendrites receive information from other neurons; axons transmit information to other neurons. The axon is a long hollow tube filled with a jellylike fluid. Most axons are insulated from other axons by the myelin sheath, produced by glial cells. Each branch of an axon ends in a terminal button that forms part of a synapse, the junction through which information is passed from one neuron to another. The neuron that transmits information through a synapse is called the presynaptic neuron; the neuron that receives this information is called the postsynaptic neuron (see Figure 1).

The message carried by an axon is called an action potential. Although an action potential involves an electrical charge, it is a biological processes, not a simple transmission of electricity. An action potential consists of a brief impulse that travels at speeds up to 120 m/sec (265 mph). The membrane of an axon contains an electrical charge called the membrane potential. When at rest, the outside of the membrane is positively charged. This charge is maintained by sodium transporters, special protein molecules embedded in the membrane that transport positively charged sodium ions out of the axon. These transporters consume a major part of the brain's supply of energy. When a neuron is stimulated, one or more action potentials are triggered in the axon. Each action potential consists of the entry of a small quantity of sodium ions, which produces a brief reversal in the electrical charge.

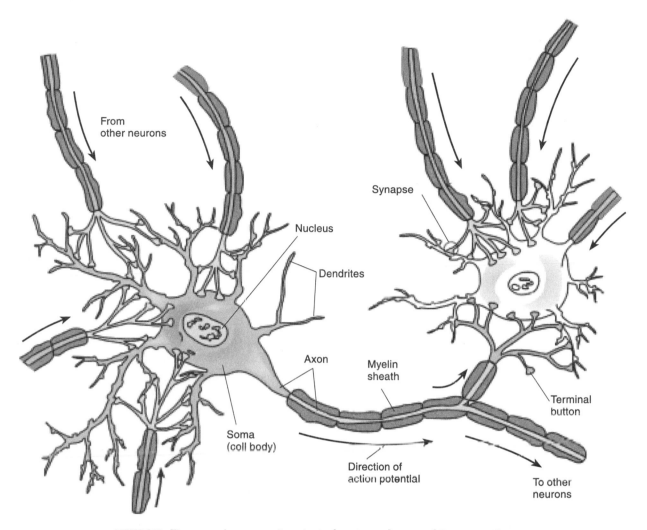

NEURON. Figure 1. A neuron, its principal parts, and some of its connections with other neurons. The arrows represent the directions of the flow of information. (Adapted from Carlson, 1998.)

Action potentials begin at the junction of the axon with the soma and travel down each of the branches to the terminal buttons. Each action potential lasts for approximately 2 milliseconds, after which the outside of the axon recovers its positive charge. Once an action potential is triggered in the axon of a given neuron, it is transmitted, undiminished in size, through all the branches to the terminal buttons. This observation has been called the all-or-none law.

When an action potential reaches a terminal button, it triggers the release of a small quantity of a chemical called a neurotransmitter. Different types of neurons release different neurotransmitters through their terminal buttons, and these chemicals have different effects on the postsynaptic neurons. The effects fall into two categories: excitatory and inhibitory. Excitatory effects increase the rate at which action potentials occur in the axon of the postsynaptic neuron; inhibitory effects decrease this rate. [See Synapse.]

Although an individual action potential obeys the all-or-none law, axons can transmit information about variables that can assume a range of values by varying their rate of firing. For example, by varying their rates of firing, axons that transmit visual information can represent changes in brightness or hue, and axons that control a muscle can produce weak or strong contractions.

Sensory neurons receive information from the environment. Specialized dendrites of sensory neurons in the skin detect stimuli that impart mechanical energy, such as those that stretch or vibrate parts of the skin. Other sensory neurons in the skin are sensitive to changes in temperature. Photoreceptors in the retina of the eye contain chemicals that detect the presence of light. Gustatory neurons on the tongue and olfactory neurons in the mucous membrane inside the nose are sensitive to particular chemicals dissolved in saliva or contained in the air we breathe. Information from all sensory neurons is transmitted to the central nervous system through synaptic connections with other neurons.

Neurons that control movements of muscles or secretions of glands do so by means of synaptic connections with the cells of these organs. The contraction of muscles is controlled by motor neurons, whose axons form synapses with muscle fibers, the individual cells of which muscles are composed. When an action potential reaches the terminal buttons of a motor neuron, the muscle fibers with which they form synapses receive an excitatory message that causes them to contract. Similarly, the terminal buttons of neurons that control glands stimulate the cells of these organs to secrete their products.

The brain contains several billions of neurons, which exchange information through synapses. Just as complex electronic circuits can be constructed of simple elements such as transistors, capacitors, and resistors, the complex circuits that are found in the nervous system consist of arrangements of interconnected neurons. Some neurons have short axons and communicate with other nearby neurons; presumably, these neurons form circuits that analyze information received from other circuits of neurons. Other neurons have long axons and communicate with circuits of neurons located some distance away; presumably, these neurons transmit the results of the analysis performed by a particular neural circuit to other neural circuits, which perform further analyses. Research indicates that neural circuits are not static; they can be altered by means of changes in the strength of individual synaptic connections. Most neuroscientists believe that such changes are responsible for the formation of memories.

[See also Brain; and Synapse.]

Bibliography

Bear, M. F., Connors, B. W., & Paradiso, M. A. (1996). *Neuroscience: Exploring the brain*. Baltimore: Williams & Wilkins.

Carlson, N. R. (1998). *Physiology of behavior* (6th ed.). Boston: Allyn & Bacon.

Hall, A. (1992). *An introduction to molecular neurobiology*. Sunderland, MA: Sinauer.

Kandel, E. R., Schwartz, J. H., & Jessell, T. M. (1992). *Principles of neural science* (3rd ed.). Norwalk, CT: Appleton & Lange.

Nicholls, J. G., Martin, A. R., Wallace, B. G., & Kuffler, S. W. (1992). *From neuron to brain* (3rd ed.). Sunderland, MA: Sinauer.

Rosenzweig, M. R., Leiman, A. L., & Breedlove, S. M. (1996). *Biological psychology*. Sunderland, MA: Sinauer.

Neil Carlson

NEUROPSYCHOLOGY. [*This entry comprises three articles*: Theories; Testing; *and* Interventions. *For discussions related to neuropsychology, see* Biological Psychology; Health Psychology; *and* Psychoneuroimmunology.]

Theories

Current scientific knowledge is a product of past experimental and theoretical efforts, and the field of neuropsychology is no exception. In fact, modern neuropsychological research continues to address many of the questions that established the field. For example, it is still unclear how memory is organized within the brain, or how brain systems interact to mediate attention. Considerable progress has been made in addressing these and other of brain-behavior relationships.

The search for biological explanations of human mental abilities began in antiquity with the search for the location of the soul, which was thought to house all ideation (Gross, 1987). But by the second century CE, the Greek anatomist Galen (130–200 CE) and others had provided empirical evidence that the brain was the center of the nervous system and responsible for sensation, movement, and thought. For many centuries after this realization, the religious idea that the soul was a fluid and dynamic spiritual force prevailed, and so the fluid-filled ventricles of the brain were considered the source of cognitive abilities (Zola-Morgan, 1995).

Evidence against ventricular localization gradually accumulated from the fifteenth through the eighteenth centuries. During this time, the efforts of Leonardo da Vinci (1472–1519), the anatomists Andreas Vesalius (1514–1564) and Thomas Willis (1621–1675), and medical professor Joseph Baader (1723–1773) contributed to the idea that intellectual functions were attributable to brain matter and not the ventricles. Baader in particular gathered clinical descriptions of patients and their brain damage (Zola-Morgan, 1995).

Shortly after the turn of the nineteenth century, the anatomist and physiologist Franz Joseph Gall (1757–1828) published his doctrine of organology, which was the first systematic view of localization of brain functions. Based on his brilliant and unique anatomical observations, he formulated the theory that discrete regions of the brain were responsible for specific human mental characteristics. Further, he reasoned that variations in the shape of the skull would reflect variations in the size of underlying brain regions. Thus, skull contours should correlate with the expression of specific mental functions (Gross, 1987; Zola-Morgan, 1995).

Gall's work was criticized on religious, political, and scientific fronts, most notably by the famous French experimental physiologist Pierre Flourens (1794–1867), who argued that the cerebral hemispheres, like the soul, were physiologically homogenous and indivisible in terms of function. He further believed that specific mental functions required the communal action of the entire cerebrum, an idea commonly referred to as equipotentiality (Harrington, 1991). Although the ideas of Flourens prevailed for some time, the efforts of late nineteenth-century scientists such as the neurologist Paul Broca (1824–1880), Fritsch (1838–1927), and neurologist Carl Wernicke (1848–1904) supported revised versions of Gall's localization proposal (Clendening, 1942; McHenry, 1969).

Nonetheless, the debate over localization continued into the twentieth century. By this time, experimental psychology was replacing its introspective methods with objective and quantifiable behavioral tests. Also, the publication of Darwin's (1809–1882) theories of evolution and natural selection stirred a change in thinking about the similarity between animal and human behavior. As a result, interest in the use of animal models for human behavior expanded (Donegan & Thompson, 1991).

It was in this context that psychologist Karl Lashley (1890–1958) joined the localization debate in the early twentieth century. Lashley began his explorations into the neural correlates of psychological constructs as a student of James Watson (1878–1958) working primarily on conditioned reflexes. For this, they relied heavily on concepts formulated by the Russian scientists Ivan Petrovich Pavlov (1849–1936) and Vladimir Mikhailovich Bekhterev (1857–1927). Lashley's interest in tracing the biological pathway of the conditioned reflex led him into a collaboration with Sheppard Franz (1874–1933) at St. Elizabeth's Hospital in Washington D.C., where Franz had been working on the recovery of function following brain damage in both humans and animals. The collaboration resulted in a significant publication in 1917 (Lashley and Franz, 1917) that described the remarkable resistance of well-learned behaviors to variously sized ablations of the frontal lobes in rats. They argued that this evidence could not be explained by a theory of localization (Beach, Hebb, Morgan, & Nissen, 1960; Donegan & Thompson, 1991; Horton & Wedding, 1984; Orbach, 1982).

Following his work with Franz, Lashley began a long research program into the location of the memory trace, or engram, within the cortex. He continued to use the lesion method in both rats and primates coupled with tests for retention of learned behaviors, such as simple maze navigation or visual discrimination. He reasoned that if the memory for a particular learned behavior were localized within the cortex, it should be possible to destroy that memory with selective ablations. In this respect, he was employing improved methodologies to replicate with rats and monkeys what Flourens had accomplished with birds and physiologist Friedrich Goltz had accomplished with dogs. And, like these predecessors, his collection of data revealed the equipotential nature of cortex. In his pivotal work, *Brain Mechanisms and Intelligence* (1929), he formulated two laws concerning the relationship between the cortex and learned behaviors. First, his law of mass action stated that the degree of impairment to learned behaviors is proportional to the amount of cortex removed. Second, according to his law of multipotentiality, every single part of the cortex participated in multiple functions (Beach et al., 1960; Donegan & Thompson, 1991; Horton & Wedding, 1984; Orbach, 1982).

Lashley concluded that no single region of the cortex was responsible for the retention of individual learned behaviors. Current views of the brain emphasize its high degree of anatomical specificity and specialization of function. These modern views are not entirely incompatible with Lashley's ideas in the sense that his notion of functional equivalence could apply within any of the specialized areas of the cortex that have been and will likely continue to be discovered. A more integrated theory proposed by the English neurologist Hughlings Jackson (1835–1911), at the time, allowed for an alternate, and perhaps more biologically plausible explanation of Lashley's data. Though Jackson's works were completed before the turn of the century, his significant publications were not widely available until shortly after the publication of Lashley's classic text. Based on his work with epileptic patients, Jackson essentially postulated that each mental function is represented at three different levels: the brain stem and spinal cord, the sensory and motor cortices, and the association and frontal cortices. According to Jackson, attempts to obliterate memories or functions by cortical ablation would fail regardless of the style of cortical storage, since only one of three representations had been removed (Horton & Wedding, 1984).

Perhaps the most integrated neuropsychological theory to date appeared with the publication of *The Organization of Behavior* (New York, 1949), by Donald O. Hebb (1904–1985), one of Lashley's former students. Besides attacking the current theories relating brain and behavior for their lack of breadth and their ignorance of internal mental processes, Hebb proposed an interdisciplinary theory of his own which accounted for a diversity of data. He asserted that neural memories develop with frequent exposure to experience, which in turn alters the morphology or metabolism of connections between nerve cells. Hebb suggested that experience had the effect of developing and strengthening assemblies of cells spanning the diencephalon and telencephalon develop, and that single cells may be members of multiple assemblies. This theory accounted for Lashley's idea of a distributed memory trace and reconciled, to some degree, the arguments of localizationists (Horton & Wedding, 1984; Klein, 1980).

A few years before Hebb's publication, the physiological psychologist Ward Halstead had outlined a different approach for relating the brain and cognitive functions. He set out to investigate the mechanisms of what he called biological intelligence by giving 13 different psychological tests to brain-damaged patients. After correlating the test results with the locations of damage he was able to statistically isolate mental functions that he felt relied on the integrity of the cerebrum. Though some of his conclusions are now considered false, he is respected as the first individual to use an impairment index derived from a neuropsychological test battery to explore brain-behavior relationships. This ultimately enhanced the opportunities for nonclinicians to assess brain-damaged patients for experimental purposes (Hartlage & DeFilippis, 1983; Horton & Wedding, 1984).

Halstead's student, the psychologist Ralph Reitan, founded a neuropsychology laboratory with neurologist Robert Heimburger in the early 1950s to validate and expand Halstead's efforts. Reitan was successful in strengthening the relationship between Halstead's impairment index and neurological criteria. Additionally, he developed modified versions of the Halstead test battery for use on children and young adults (Hartlage & DeFilippis, 1983; Horton & Wedding, 1984).

Further valuable modifications of what is now referred to as the Halstead–Reitan Test Battery were made by a number of individuals, including Kurt Goldstein (1878–1965). Versions of the Halstead–Reitan Battery are still in common use today and provide a valuable link between psychological abilities and the brain sites most involved in their expression (Hartlage & DeFilippis, 1983; Horton & Wedding, 1984).

The efforts of the early neuropsychologists described here, as well as others not profiled, have contributed significantly to recent developments in neuropsychological research. For example, neuropsychological assessment techniques have been critical for neurobiological investigations of age-related cognitive decline. Test batteries like the Halstead–Reitan Battery have localized brain areas preferentially altered during the course of normal aging, such as regions of the frontal and temporal lobes. The use of neuropsychological tests in human and animal aging studies has also demonstrated that there is substantial variation in cognitive and behavioral ability in aged populations. Specifically,

chronological age is not always a reliable predictor of performance, and investigators have begun dividing aged populations into subgroups based on test performance, rather than simply chronological age (Gallagher & Rapp, 1997; Zola-Morgan, 1993, for discussions of strategies for studying age-related effects on cognition).

Although this brief review has included only a subset of individuals involved in the the development of ideas about localization of function and the search for brain-behavior relationships, their careers are representative of the rich and exciting field of neuropsychology. Additionally, the results of their efforts are clearly evident in current themes of neuropsychological research.

[*Many of the people mentioned in this article are the subjects of independent biographical entries.*]

Bibliography

Beach, F. A., Hebb, D. O., Morgan, C. T., & Nissen, H. W. (Eds.). (1960). *The neuropsychology of Lashley: Selected papers of K. S. Lashley.* New York: McGraw-Hill.

Clendening, L. (1942). *Source book of medical history.* New York: Dover.

Donegan, N. H., & Thompson, R. F. (1991). The search for the engram. In J. L. Martinez & R. P. Kesner (Eds.), *Learning and memory: A biological view* (pp. 3–58). San Diego, CA: Academic Press.

Gallagher, M., & Rapp, P. R. (1997). The use of animal models to study the effects of aging on cognition. *Annual Review of Psychology, 48,* 339–370.

Gross, C. G. (1987). Phrenology. In G. Adelman (Ed.), *Encyclopedia of neuroscience* (pp. 948–950). Boston: Birkhauser.

Harrington, A. (1991). Beyond phrenology: Localization theory in the modern era. In P. Corsi (Ed.), *The enchanted loom* (pp. 207–215). New York: Oxford University Press.

Hartlage, L. C., & DeFilippis, N. A. (1983). History of neuropsychological assessment. In C. J. Golden & P. J. Vicente (Eds.), *Foundations of clinical neuropsychology* (pp. 23–59). New York: Plenum Press.

Horton, A. M., Jr., & Wedding, D. (1984). *Clinical and behavioral neuropsychology: An introduction.* New York: Praeger Scientific.

Klein, R. M. (1980). D. O. Hebb: An appreciation. In P. W. Jusczyk & R. M. Klein (Eds.), *The nature of thought: Essays in honor of D. O. Hebb* (pp. 1–18). Hillsdale, NJ: Erlbaum.

Lashley, K. S., & Franz, S. I. (1917). The effects of cerebral destruction upon habit-formation and retention in the albino rat. *Psychobiology, 1,* 71–139.

McHenry, L. C., Jr. (1969). *Garrison's history of neurology* (Rev. ed.). Springfield, IL: Thomas.

Milner, B., Squire, L. R., & Kandel, E. R. (1998). Cognitive neuroscience and the study of memory. *Neuron, 20,* 445–468.

Orbach, J. (1982). The legacy of *"Brain Mechanisms and*

Intelligence." In J. Orbach (Ed.), *Neuropsychology after Lashley* (pp. 1–20). Hillsdale, NJ: Erlbaum.

Squire, L. R. (1987). *Memory and brain.* New York: Oxford University Press.

Zola-Morgan, S. (1993). A perspective on behavioral studies in aged monkeys. *Neurobiology of Aging, 14,* 647–648.

Zola-Morgan, S. (1995). Localization of brain function: The legacy of Franz Joseph Gall (1758–1828). *Annual Review of Neuroscience, 18,* 359–383.

Stuart M. Zola and James D. Brady

Testing

A 75-year-old retired executive tells his primary physician that he has become increasingly forgetful. He has also been feeling depressed over his health and memory problems. He is referred to a neurologist, who conducts a neurological examination, magnetic resonance imaging (MRI) brain scan, and electroencephalograph (EEG) study. The results are normal for his age. The neurologist refers the patient to a neuropsychologist, who administers a comprehensive set of cognitive and motor tests. The patient's IQ is in the Superior range, but his scores on tests of delayed free-recall and recognition memory are severely impaired. The patient also displays mild deficits in word-finding skills and novel problem-solving abilities. His profile of cognitive strengths and weaknesses is consistent with a progressive dementia rather than with cognitive difficulties related to depression. Follow-up neuropsychological testing conducted one year later confirms the presence of progressive cognitive decline typical of Alzheimer's disease.

In recent years, the field of neuropsychology has been embraced by medicine in general and neurology and psychiatry in particular. Many patients with microscopic lesions located in specific brain regions that mediate vital cognitive functions are found to be "normal" using the most advanced medical technology available, such as MRI brain scans. The patient discussed above illustrates this point. However, it is the neuropsychological evaluation that, with its rigorous testing of multiple cognitive and motor domains, can often identify whether or not general brain regions have likely been compromised by a neurological disorder.

A Brief History of Neuropsychological Testing

In the past, if a patient was thought to have brain damage, he or she typically was referred to a neurologist. The primary focus of the neurological examination involves testing of reflexes and senses, both of which are mediated by the sensorimotor cortex and connecting pathways. There are, however, vast regions of the brain that, when damaged, do not alter sensorimotor functions. Instead, pathology to these regions may affect higher-level cognitive skills. When the brain damage is subtle to moderate, the decline in cognitive functions also may be mild to moderate. Neurologists and other physicians often conduct a "mental status exam," which is a very cursory assessment of higher-level thinking, such as asking the patient to remember three words. Such brief, nonstandardized exams usually are capable of identifying patients with severe brain damage, but they frequently fail to identify patients with mild to moderate neurocognitive dysfunction.

Enter the psychologist. Since the early 1900s, psychologists have been armed with powerful methodologies for rigorously measuring subtle differences in higher-level thinking. The fields of psychometrics and IQ testing, two of the greatest contributions in the history of psychology, have provided clinicians with the means for reliably measuring the level of intellectual and cognitive functions that a child or adult has acquired. In the hands of the neuropsychologist, these methodologies offered the ideal procedures for gauging even subtle declines in intellectual and cognitive functions in the dysfunctional brain.

The heroes of the neuropsychology story were a handful of psychologists in the 1940s, 1950s, and 1960s who, before there was a field of clinical neuropsychology, had the vision to see the tremendous utility of adapting psychometric tests to the assessment of cognitive dysfunction in brain-damaged patients. These early leaders included, among others, Arthur Benton, Harold Goodglass, Ward Halstead, Edith Kaplan, Alexander Luria, Brenda Milner, André Rey, Elizabeth Warrington, David Wechsler, and Ralph Reitan. The pioneering efforts of these and other psychologists launched a field that has earned the respect of the entire medical and scientific community.

The Basic Premise of Neuropsychological Testing

Since the early 1960s, there has been a burgeoning of research demonstrating that different brain regions mediate distinct cognitive and motor processes. Examples of some classic brain-behavior relationships for most people include the following: the posterior region of the left frontal lobe plays a vital role for adding grammar to language production; the superior gyrus of the left temporal lobe is a key region for infusing meaning into language; the right parietal lobe is critical for global spatial orientation; the mesial temporal/hippocampal regions are responsible for transferring information from short-term memory into long-term memory; and the frontal lobes are essential for higher-level cognitive skills, such as problem solving and abstract thinking.

As a general rule, cognitive and motor functions tend to fall within the normal bell curve in an individual with a healthy brain, with some relative strengths and weaknesses. However, when one or more regions of the brain have been damaged by injury or disease, the cognitive and motor functions mediated by those regions often will become significantly impaired. Accordingly, the clinical neuropsychologist will typically administer to a patient with known or suspected brain damage 30 to 40 different tests assessing language skills, math abilities, spatial functions, new learning and memory, problem solving, abstract thinking, and other cognitive and motor skills. In past research, these tests were administered to large numbers of neurologically intact individuals and to patients with different types of brain damage; the neuropsychologist uses these normative and clinical data to draw conclusions about whether the patient's raw scores on the tests fall within the expected or impaired ranges. This determination is not an exact science, since many neurologically normal individuals will have some test scores that fall in the impaired range, and some brain-damaged patients, especially if they are bright to begin with, may have few scores in the impaired range. Nevertheless, by examining the patient's profile of cognitive and motor strengths and weaknesses, the neuropsychologist can begin to make inferences about the integrity of different brain regions and to formulate hypotheses about the presence or absence of different neurological disorders.

What Comprises a Neuropsychological Evaluation?

The typical neuropsychological evaluation takes 6 to 8 hours. For most teenagers and adults, the examination can be completed in one day, with ample breaks. For younger children, older adults, or patients whose endurance has been significantly compromised by a neurological, medical, or psychiatric disorder, the examination can be conducted across two half-days.

In the morning and early afternoon hours, when patients usually are more alert, they are administered the cognitive and motor tests. As noted above, it is not uncommon for 30 to 40 different tests to be administered to a patient. Some neuropsychologists administer the tests themselves, whereas others employ a trained psychological technician to administer the tests; both approaches are acceptable in the field, since the tests have standardized administration procedures. Some of the cognitive tests are similar to those that students take in school (e.g., math, vocabulary, reading), but others are unfamiliar to most people (e.g., fluently saying words that start with a particular letter; sorting cards according to conceptual rules). The neuropsychological tests assess a wide range of cognitive and motor domains, including:

• Attention
• Language skills
• Mathematics abilities
• Visual-spatial skills
• New learning and memory

• Memory for previously learned facts
• Higher-level cognitive skills, such as abstract thinking, novel problem solving, planning, and flexibility of thinking
• Motor speed and fine-motor dexterity

In this era of managed care, many patients are first given neuropsychological screening exams, which usually vary from 30 minutes to 3 hours in duration. If a patient exhibits some evidence of cognitive impairment on the screening exam, then more extensive neuropsychological testing may be conducted.

Selection of Tests. Neuropsychologists typically select tests that have (1) empirically documented reliability and validity; (2) adequate normative data; and (3) empirically demonstrated clinical utility in identifying neurocognitive deficits in brain-damaged patients. Some neuropsychologists use a "battery approach," meaning that they will administer *all* tests or subtests that comprise a particular battery or scale (e.g., all subtests of the Wechsler Memory Scale–III). Other neuropsychologists use an "eclectic approach," meaning that they will pick and choose only certain tests or subtests from different batteries or scales (e.g., many psychologists administer only two subtests of the Wechsler Memory Scale–III: Logical Memory and Visual Reproduction). In addition, some neuropsychologists adopt a "fixed approach," meaning that they try to give the exact same tests to all patients, whereas other neuropsychologists use a "flexible approach," meaning that they will tailor the selection of tests administered to each patient based on the patient's presenting problems and referral question. These different approaches are all acceptable in the field, provided that the major domains of cognitive, motor, and behavioral functions are adequately covered by the tests selected.

Table 1 lists a number of tests that are commonly used by neuropsychologists to assess cognitive and motor functions in children and adults.

The Clinical Interview. A critical part of the neuropsychological evaluation is the clinical interview. Many factors beyond brain damage per se can affect performance on rigorous psychometric tests of cognitive and motor skills, and these factors must be systematically explored in the interview. Some of these factors include early developmental problems (e.g., prenatal exposure to alcohol or other teratogenic agents; pregnancy and delivery complications; delays in achieving developmental milestones as an infant or toddler); cultural factors (e.g., English as a second language; being raised in another country); educational history (e.g., level and type of education obtained; history of learning disability); occupational history; history of medical illnesses that are risk factors for brain dysfunction (e.g., hypertension, diabetes); history of head injury or loss of consciousness; past and current psychiatric disorders; past and current alcohol and

NEUROPSYCHOLOGY: Testing. Table 1. Examples of commonly used neuropsychological tests

Domain	Representative test
Intellectual functions	Wechsler Adult Intelligence Scale–III
Learning and memory functions	Benton Visual Retention Test
	California Verbal Learning Test–II
	Rey Osterrieth Complex Figure Test
	Rey Auditory Verbal Learning Test
	Warrington Recognition Memory Test
	Wechsler Memory Scale–III
Visuospatial abilities	Block Design subtest (WAIS–III)
	Hooper Visual Organizational Test
	Judgment of Line Orientation
	Rey Osterrieth Complex Figure Test
Language	Boston Diagnostic Aphasia Exam
	Boston Naming Test
	Tests of Verbal Fluency
	Token Test
	Vocabulary Subtest (WAIS–III)
Executive functions, abstraction ability	Category Test
	Delis-Kaplan Executive Function Scale
	Similarities subtest (WAIS–III)
	Stroop Color-Word Interference Test
	Trail Making Test
	Verbal Fluency Tests
	Wisconsin Card Sorting Test
Attention	Digit Span Subtest (WAIS–III)
	Digit Vigilance Test
	Spatial Span (WMS–III)
Motor functions	Finger Tapping Test
	Grooved Pegboard Test
	Grip Strength (Hand Dynamometer)
	Tactual Performance Test
Emotional/behavioral functions	Beck Depression Inventory
	Hamilton Depression Scale
	Millon Clinical Personality Inventory
	Minnesota Multiphasic Personality Inventory–II
Screening instruments	Mattis Dementia Rating Scale
	Mini Mental Status Exam
	MicroCog
Academic achievement	Wechsler Individual Achievement Test
	Wide Range Achievement Test–III

Tests designed for assessment of children and adolescents

Domain	Representative test
Intellectual functions	Cognitive Assessment System
	Peabody Picture Vocabulary Test–III
	Wechsler Intelligence Scale for Children–III
	Woodcock-Johnson Tests of Cognitive Ability
Specific neuropsychological domains	California Verbal Learning Test–Children's Version
	Children's Memory Scale
	NEPSY Neuropsychological Battery
	Wide Range Assessment of Memory and Learning
	WISC–III as a Neuropsychological Instrument
Emotional/behavioral functions	Child Behavior Checklist
	Personality Inventory for Children

drug abuse; current medication usage; current emotional state; current physical state, including headaches and other pain symptoms; and family history of medical and psychiatric disorders (e.g., a family history of Alzheimer's disease is a serious risk factor for this devastating disorder). Based on information gathered in the clinical interview, the neuropsychologist attempts to identify which risk factors may be present in a patient and how they may affect the patient's performances on the cognitive and motor tests.

Another step in the clinical interview is to ask the patient, and family members if they are available, about their perceptions of the patient's cognitive complaints, the onset of the problems, and whether or not the problems have changed over time. Sometimes this information can be helpful in evaluating, for instance, whether a patient's cognitive difficulties started abruptly, as with a stroke, or gradually, as in Alzheimer's disease. However, the perceptions of cognitive difficulties by patients and their family members often fail to correlate with objective test results. For example, depressed patients sometimes report severe memory difficulties when their actual scores on objective tests of memory may be normal or near normal.

Test-Taking Effort. Scores on difficult cognitive and motor tests are valid only if the patient exerts adequate effort in taking them. An important part of the neuropsychological evaluation is the assessment of the patient's *motivation* to perform well on the tests. Some patients exert minimal effort on neuropsychologist tests for secondary gain. For example, an inmate may purposefully perform poorly on memory tests to support his or her claim of amnesia for the accused crime. As another example, a patient involved in litigation related to a car accident may claim that he or she suffered a brain injury in the accident. When this patient undergoes a neuropsychological evaluation, he or she may fail to exert adequate effort on the tests with the hopes of looking "brain damaged" and obtaining a large settlement.

Neuropsychologists have developed a number of tools for evaluating a patient's test-taking effort, including specific cognitive "malingering" tests, analysis of typical and atypical profiles of neurocognitive dysfunction, consistency of test findings and score profiles across repeat evaluations, and examination of whether or not a patient's low scores on the neuropsychological tests are consistent with how he or she is functioning in everyday life. Even with these procedures, however, it is sometimes difficult to identify a clever patient who is feigning cognitive difficulties, especially if he or she does so to a mild degree (more blatant forms of exaggeration are easier to detect). It is unfortunate that, as reported in the literature, some patients have admitted to having been "coached" by their attorneys prior to their neuropsychological evaluations as to which tests

are designed to detect malingering. This coaching creates the need for neuropsychologists to employ different methods for the detection of inadequate effort, and to stay one step ahead of public knowledge by developing new effort-testing techniques.

Premorbid Level of Cognitive Functioning. The most common reason that patients are referred for a neuropsychological evaluation is to determine whether or not they have *acquired* brain damage from some neurological insult, and, if so, whether or not they have experienced a *decline* in their level of cognitive functioning from a premorbid (preexisting) state. However, inferences about declines in cognitive functioning must include estimates of the patient's level of cognitive functioning *before* the onset of the insult. Neuropsychologists employ several techniques for estimating premorbid level of cognitive functioning. These techniques include:

- Testing overlearned cognitive skills that tend to be resilient to the effects of more diffuse brain damage and that correlate robustly with IQ (e.g., tests of reading or vocabulary level are good predictors of premorbid Verbal IQ);
- Developing normative test data that are corrected not only for age but also for education level, a powerful predictor of premorbid IQ;
- Using regression analyses based on key demographic variables such as education and occupation levels to derive formulas for estimating premorbid IQ;
- Obtaining prior standardized achievement test scores from the patient's school records, since these scores correlate robustly with an individual's Verbal IQ as an adult.

The estimation of a premorbid level of cognitive function is a difficult task, and each patient must be considered individually. For instance, while education level is a powerful predictor of premorbid IQ for *groups* of people, it may be inaccurate for a particular individual. As an example, some individuals with average IQs are extremely motivated and achieve high levels of education typical of people with superior IQs. In contrast, some extremely bright people drop out of school early for hardship or other reasons. For these types of individuals, estimations of premorbid IQ based on education level would be misleading. As a general rule, prior scholastic achievement or IQ test scores that are obtained from the patient's school records are the best method for estimating a person's premorbid level of intellectual functioning; however, for the vast majority of patients evaluated, these test data are not available to the neuropsychologist.

Scoring and Analysis of Test Performance. After the neuropsychological tests have been administered, raw scores are computed for each test and converted to standardized scores. Most neuropsychological tests have normative data that are corrected for age, since age effects at both ends of the developmental spectrum can profoundly influence cognition. Some tests also are corrected for gender and education level, when these demographic variables are found to be significant predictors of test performance (Heaton, Grant, & Matthew, 1991).

In addition to analyzing test performance by computing *quantitative* scores, many neuropsychologists also examine test performance for *qualitative* features that may be pathognomonic of brain dysfunction. For instance, a patient may speak primarily in content words and omit the little grammatical words of language (e.g., the patient says, "Hospital . . . Monday" when trying to say that he came into the hospital on Monday). This qualitative feature of the patient's language, when seen consistently, is pathognomonic of a type of language disorder called Broca's aphasia, and likely reflects a brain injury in the posterior region of the left frontal lobe. As another example, a patient may omit most details and features from the left side of his drawings (see Figure 1); this neurobehavioral syndrome, known as left hemi-inattention, typically occurs following a brain injury in the posterior region of the right hemisphere.

Emotional, Behavioral, and Personality Testing. The neuropsychological evaluation typically goes beyond the assessment of cognitive and motor skills, and also includes psychometric testing of emotional, behavioral, and personality functioning. Many neuropsychologists administer tests such as the Minnesota Multiphasic Personality Inventory-2 (MMPI-2) or the Beck Depression Inventory as part of their standard evaluation, given that the patient has the cognitive capacity to take them. These tests assist the neuropsychologist in determining whether or not a patient has a psychiatric disturbance, which, in turn, may be affecting his or her performance on the neuropsychological tests. Most practicing neuropsychologists obtain their doctoral degrees in clinical psychology before receiving specialized training in neuropsychology, and this training enables them to conduct general psychodiagnostic assessments as part of their neuropsychological evaluations.

Final Interpretations and Recommendations. The heart of the neuropsychological evaluation, and the most difficult part, is drawing final conclusions about the presence, nature, extent, and causes of a patient's cognitive, motor, and behavioral difficulties and, if necessary, formulating recommendations for helping the patient. Just because a patient obtains test scores that fall in the impaired range does not mean that he or she has brain damage.

The first step in the interpretation process is to determine whether or not a patient's test scores are valid (using techniques discussed above) and internally consistent (e.g., if a patient has a word-finding deficit, then

he or she should exhibit difficulty on any task that places extensive demands on precise naming ability). If the test scores appear valid and consistent, the neuropsychologist then attempts to characterize the patient's *profile* of cognitive-motor strengths and weaknesses. Based on an estimate of the patient's premorbid level of cognitive functioning, the neuropsychologist opines whether or not the patient's weaknesses represent acquired problems. Next, the neuropsychologist, drawing upon his or her knowledge of brain-behavior relationships, tries to decide whether the patient's profile of cognitive-motor strengths and weaknesses is typical of particular types and locations of brain dysfunction. The neuropsychologist then must weigh all of the patient's risk factors for acquired brain damage, such as a recent head trauma or stroke; history of medical illnesses that may compromise brain functioning; history of serious psychiatric disorder; past alcohol or drug abuse; or a family history of a genetically based neurological disorder (e.g., Alzheimer's disease). In considering these different risk factors, the neuropsychologist tries to determine whether the patient's cognitive-motor profile is more likely to be associated with one risk factor than another, or with multiple risk factors.

Before a final conclusion can be reached about the presence of neurocognitive dysfunction, the neuropsychologist must rule out all possible explanations for the patient's low test scores that go beyond brain damage per se, such as developmental, educational, and cultural factors; current medications; current emotional and physical state; and level of motivation to perform well on the tests. In addition, the neuropsychologist must conduct a psychodiagnostic evaluation to determine whether or not the patient has a psychiatric disorder and, if so, whether this disorder is contributing to the patient's cognitive difficulties. After integrating, analyzing, and synthesizing this extensive and varied body of information, the neuropsychologist is then in a position to proffer his final impressions about the presence or absence of brain dysfunction and its sequelae. If the neuropsychological data strongly implicate a neurological disorder, such as Alzheimer's disease, then it falls within the neuropsychologist's expertise to make those diagnoses.

At the end of the report, the neuropsychologist will typically offer his or her recommendations for the patient. Common areas of recommendations include:

- Additional neurological, medical, or psychiatric examinations, consultations, or procedures;
- Speech therapy or cognitive rehabilitation;
- Individual or family psychotherapy or other behavioral interventions;
- Educational interventions and programs (especially for children and young adults);
- Vocational testing and counseling;
- Social work consultation to address the patient's liv-

NEUROPSYCHOLOGY: Testing. Figure 1. A patient who suffered a stroke in the posterior (back) region of the right side of his brain was asked to copy a daisy (see left). His drawing (see right) illustrates a classic deficit known as left hemi-inattention. Patients with this deficit often fail to process visual information presented in the left side of space.

ing situation and the need for various levels of assistance and supervision with activities of daily living;

• Repeat neuropsychological evaluation in the future to determine the status of the patient's cognitive functioning over time.

When feasible, the neuropsychologist often will meet with the patient and his or her family to discuss the findings of the evaluation and the need for the various recommended interventions.

Repeat Neuropsychological Testing

The readministration of the same or similar neuropsychological tests to a patient at a later time can serve several clinically useful purposes. As an example, for patients suspected of having a *progressive* dementing process, such as Alzheimer's disease, the first neuropsychological testing provides baseline data. The repeat testing, which usually is done 9 to 12 months later, affords an objective measure of whether or not the patient exhibits a decline in cognitive functions typical of a progressive disease. Some neuropsychological tests may show practice effects on repeat testing, which is an improvement in performance from having taken the same or similar tests before. However, the inexorable progression of a disorder like Alzheimer's disease typi-

cally overrides any improvement in scores related to practice effects.

Repeat testing also is helpful for charting the recovery of neurocognitive functions over time following a brain insult, such as a stroke or head trauma. The brain recovers relatively slowly from such disorders as a traumatic brain injury, with a one-year time period often used as the benchmark for the vast majority of the recovery to have occurred. By comparing a patient's test scores obtained a few months after an injury with those obtained a year or more postinjury, the neuropsychologist, after factoring in practice effects, can provide objective data about the patient's recovery process. Other functions of repeat testing include (1) monitoring improvement in cognitive functions following various interventions, such as cognitive rehabilitation and pharmacological treatment; and (2) determining the validity of a patient's test scores by examining the consistency of his or her profile of cognitive and motor strengths and weaknesses over time.

Common Referral Questions for Adults

Adult patients typically are referred for a neuropsychological evaluation by neurologists, neurosurgeons, clinical psychologists, psychiatrists, physicians, speech pathologists, other health professionals, and attorneys.

The following examples of consult questions illustrate some of the reasons why adult patients undergo neuropsychological testing:

- To assist in evaluating whether or not a patient with increasing cognitive difficulties, as reported by the patient, family members, or health professionals, has an insidious neurological disorder. Examples of these disorders include multiple sclerosis, brain tumor, idiopathic hydrocephalus, white matter ischemic changes, and Alzheimer's disease.
- To evaluate whether a patient who has had a known risk factor for brain damage does, in fact, exhibit cognitive-motor deficits or emotional-behavioral changes consistent with brain dysfunction. Examples of these risk factors include head trauma; chronic alcohol or drug abuse; certain medical illnesses (e.g., hypertension, diabetes, kidney failure, HIV infection); certain psychiatric disorders (e.g., schizophrenia); and exposure to neurotoxic agents.
- To assess the presence, nature, and degree of cognitive-motor deficits and emotional-behavioral changes in patients with *known* brain pathology. These patients are referred after it has been determined, usually from the neurological examination and neuroimaging, that they have had, for instance, a cerebral vascular accident, brain tumor, structural brain damage following a head trauma, Parkinson's disease, or probable Alzheimer's disease. The question for these patients is not whether they have brain damage, but rather the presence, nature, and extent of cognitive, motor, and behavioral sequelae of the brain dysfunction.
- To assist neurosurgeons in several ways, such as (1) evaluating whether a patient with intractable seizures and in need of resection of the epileptogenic focus has language skills localized in this general brain region (this testing usually involves a Wada procedure, where one cerebral hemisphere is anesthetized at a time); (2) conducting pre- and post-surgery evaluations to determine whether or not a neurosurgical procedure (e.g., insertion of a shunt into a brain ventricle to relieve hydrocephalus; resection of a brain tumor) alters cognitive-motor functions for better or worse; and (3) to reevaluate cognitive functions over time in a hydrocephalus patient who has received a shunt in order determine if the shunt has continued normal functioning.
- To provide recommendations regarding the patient's capacity to return to work or to receive vocational retraining in a new occupation that would be best suited for the patient, given his or her profile of cognitive strengths and weaknesses.
- To offer recommendations for cognitive rehabilitation (e.g., teaching the patient memory compensatory strategies).
- To assist in determining whether a patient with brain dysfunction has the cognitive, motor, and behavioral capacity to perform important activities of daily living (e.g., drive a car, handle finances, prepare meals, live independently, comply with medication regimens, care for self).
- To make recommendations regarding the best living situation for the patient in light of his or her cognitive, motor, and behavioral deficits (e.g., independent, semisupervised, or nursing-home placement).

Common Referral Questions for Children

Neuropsychological evaluations are generally more difficult to conduct for children than adults. Just as children differ in their physical growth rates, they also differ in the development of their cognitive and motor functions. It is sometimes difficult to determine whether a "cognitive deficit" in a child represents a permanent impairment or simply a lag or delay in the development of that ability. In addition, the classic brain-behavior relationships that have been documented in adults do not always apply to children, making it difficult to localize cognitive deficits to particular brain regions. Finally, some children present with pronounced attention problems, hyperactivity, or other behavioral disturbances that make it difficult for the child to focus on the psychometric tests and provide valid test responses.

Despite the challenges facing child neuropsychology, this area of practice has become one of the fastest growing disciplines within the field. Referrals for child neuropsychological evaluations usually are made by pediatricians, pediatric neurologists, clinical psychologists, speech therapists, educators, and sometimes parents. Many of the referral questions for children are similar to those for adults, such as assessing whether the apparent onset of new cognitive difficulties reflects an insidious neurological disorder (e.g., brain tumor); evaluating whether a known risk factor for brain damage (e.g., head trauma, lead exposure) has, in fact, resulted in cognitive, motor, or behavioral dysfunction; and assessing the presence, nature, and degree of cognitive, motor, and behavioral changes in patients with known brain pathology (e.g., childhood seizure disorder). The following are examples of other specific reasons why children are referred for neuropsychological testing:

- To determine whether a child who is struggling academically in school has a learning disability. Neuropsychological research has documented different types of learning disabilities (e.g., verbal versus nonverbal) that may reflect neurodevelopmental abnormalities in distinct brain regions.
- To assess whether or not a child whose mother abused alcohol or drugs or consumed other teratogenic agents during her pregnancy (e.g., certain medications) exhibits cognitive, motor, or behavioral deficits suggestive of prenatal brain damage (e.g., fetal alcohol syndrome).
- To assist educators in developing the best educational

program for a child based on the child's profile of cognitive and behavioral strengths and weaknesses.

• To document recovery of function in a child who has suffered a traumatic brain injury and to provide recommendations for cognitive remediation and educational assistance.

Conclusions

Clinical neuropsychology has become one of the fastest growing disciplines in psychology. Not only does neuropsychological testing provide a wealth of clinical services for neurological, medical, and psychiatric patients, it also enhances our scientific understanding of one of the great mysteries of life, namely, the mediation of mind by brain.

Bibliography

Benton, A. L. (1980). Psychological testing for brain damage. In H. I. Kaplan, A. M. Freedman, & B. J. Badock (Eds.), *Comprehensive textbook of psychiatry*. Baltimore: Williams & Wilkins.

Delis, D. C. (1989). Neuropsychological assessment of learning and memory. In F. Boller & J. Graftman (Eds.), *Handbook of neuropsychology* (Vol. 3, pp. 3–33). New York: Elsevier.

Goodglass, H., & Kaplan, E. (1983). *The assessment of aphasia and related disorders*. Philadelphia: Lea & Febiger.

Grant, I., & Adams, K. (Eds.). (1996). *Neuropsychological assessment of neuropsychiatric disorders* (2nd ed.). New York: Oxford University Press.

Heaton, R. K., Grant, I., & Matthew, C. G. (1991). *Comprehensive norms for an expanded Halstead–Reitan Battery*. Odessa, FL: Psychological Assessment Resources.

Heilman, K., & Valenstein, E. (Eds.). (1993). *Clinical neuropsychology* (3rd ed.). New York: Oxford University Press.

Kaplan, E., Fein, D., Morris, R., & Delis, D. C. (1991). *WAIS–R as a neuropsychological instrument*. New York: Psychological Corporation.

Lezak, M. D. (1995). *Neuropsychological assessment* (3rd ed.). New York: Oxford University Press.

Luria, A. R. (1980). *Higher cortical functions in man* (2nd ed.). New York: Basic Books.

Reynolds C. R., & Fletcher-Janzen, E. (Eds.). (1997). *Handbook of clinical child neuropsychology*. New York: Plenum Press.

Spreen, O., & Strauss, E. (1998). *A compendium of neuropsychological tests: Administration, norms, and commentary* (2nd ed.). New York: Oxford University Press.

Squire, L., & Butters, N. (Eds.). (1992). *Neuropsychology of memory* (2nd ed.). New York: Guilford Press.

Dean C. Delis and Mark Jacobson

Interventions

Neurological insult can result in a range of impairments and disabilities that can seriously disrupt an individual's ability to function independently in everyday life. In some cases, deficits are confined to a single cognitive function such as language, attention, or memory, or even to a specific component of one of these functions; in other cases, deficits are more global, affecting an individual's personality and emotional life as well as various aspects of cognition. When impairments are broad reaching, as they are likely to be in cases of severe traumatic brain injury, for example, a holistic approach to treatment is sometimes proposed, in which emotional, social, and motivational disturbances are treated concurrently with cognitive problems. More commonly, however, neuropsychological interventions target a single cognitive dysfunction.

Four approaches to rehabilitation are outlined below along with examples of their application in the domains of memory, language, and attention. The first two approaches focus on the repair or optimal use of damaged cognitive processes in an attempt to restore function to premorbid levels and modes of functioning. These approaches are indirect, targeting the underlying causes of cognitive dysfunction rather than behavior itself. The second two approaches are used when neural or cognitive damage is deemed irreparable and alternate ways of accomplishing cognitive tasks are sought. These approaches intervene directly at the behavioral rather than at the causal level in order to achieve specific functional outcomes.

Restoration of Damaged Function

The underlying assumption of this perspective is that patients' cognitive abilities can be restored through stimulation and exercise or through relearning of cognitive skills that were lost as a result of brain damage. The focus of this approach is either on restoration of global function within a cognitive domain such as memory or language or on repair of specific subcomponents within these domains. Training regimens invariably involve extensive repetitive practice of cognitive processes or basic skills, often with tasks or materials that have little real-world relevance, in the hope that such practice will strengthen the damaged mechanisms and provide generalizable improvements in the targeted areas. Contrary to this hypothesis, however, the effects of practice are often highly specific, accruing only to the material or task being practiced and not generalizing to other related tasks or to real-world situations. For example, in the memory domain, amnesic patients may spend long hours trying to remember arbitrary lists of words, digits, shapes, pictures, or locations, and although they may learn these particular materials after many repetitions, their ability to learn and remember other new information remains largely unchanged. Similarly, in the language domain, stimulation therapies designed to elicit linguistic responses in aphasic patients through intensive and repeated auditory or multimodal presentations may be effective in a constrained laboratory or clinical context but fail to produce changes in everyday language usage. The method is somewhat more promising for treatment of attentional dysfunction, but findings here too have been inconsistent. Some studies have found generalization to untrained tasks, others have failed to show transfer except to highly similar materials, and few have demonstrated maintenance of training effects in real-world tasks.

The main problem with the restoration approach is that there is little evidence that *general* function can be restored through exercise or stimulation. Although practice is essential for the learning of *specific* information or the reacquisition of specific skills, it appears not to confer general benefits within a particular cognitive domain. Practice, therefore, might be best directed at specific functional tasks that can directly impact real-world competence. The restoration approach also sometimes suffers from a lack of a strong theoretical rationale. At a cognitive level, interventions are often not motivated by any particular cognitive theories or models, and although the approach implicitly assumes changes at the neural level, mechanisms remain unspecified.

Optimization of Residual Function

An alternative way to view the rehabilitation process is as a means of making optimal use of residual function. This approach assumes that sufficient cognitive function remains following brain trauma to support retraining or relearning of specific processes or skills that were used premorbidly. The success of methods developed within this framework depends at least in part on how well cognitive theories or models are able to specify the component processes involved in normal function so that the target of the intervention can be clearly formulated. Training usually takes the form of extensive practice in the use of the damaged component so that it can ultimately be employed as efficiently as possible. In effect, the brain is being retrained to perform a specific function in much the same way as it did prior to trauma. This approach differs from the one outlined above in specificity and in theoretical motivation. Whereas the general restorative remedies are usually atheoretical and aimed at obtaining broad, general improvements in a cognitive domain, the optimization approach targets specific component processes of a cognitive task, which are determined according to theoretical models.

This approach has been particularly popular in the treatment of language disorders, where models of normal cognitive function are better specified than in other cognitive domains. For example, anomia (i.e., difficulty in word finding) may occur as a result of impairments in any one of several components of the language system—the semantic lexicon, the phonological output lexicon, or access to phonology from semantics—and will be treated differently depending on where in the system the cause of the problem is thought to occur. Once a careful assessment of a patient has been carried out and the deficit has been located within the model of normal language functioning, treatment can be directed at the specific causal component. These theoretically derived techniques have been found to be more effective than the general stimulation methods described above, both in improving function on the specific training materials as well as demonstrating generalization to untrained items in some cases. Real-world benefits in functional communication, however, are rarely observed.

Models of normal attentional functioning are much less well elaborated than the language models and so theoretically motivated restorative treatments are somewhat more broadly conceived. Still they are often focused at the component process level and treatment may be applied independently to sustained, selective, and focused attentional processes. Specific positive effects of attention training have been observed along with some generalization to untrained tasks and materials. The expected broad-ranging transfer to other cognitive domains and to real-world contexts, however, has seldom been obtained.

One of the most commonly used remedial techniques for memory impairment involves training in the use of mnemonic strategies. Consistent with the notion that mnemonic strategy training relies on the use of residual memory function, such training has been found to benefit only those patients with mild to moderate memory disorders. Patients with extensive brain damage and severe memory impairments tend not to be able to learn or apply the strategies effectively. The more moderately impaired patients who are capable of learning the techniques and employing them successfully when instructed to do so still tend not to use them spontaneously. So even though mnemonic benefits are observed in the laboratory or clinic, real-life gains are minimal. Despite this failure of generalization, mnemonic strategies can be useful in helping people learn specific pieces of information that are applicable in their daily lives.

Compensation for Lost Function

When brain damage is extensive and cognitive problems are severe, the likelihood of restoration of normal function is remote. In these cases, interventions are often directed toward alleviating functional problems in ways that do not require neural or cognitive changes but can be achieved through the provision of external supports or environmental restructurings. In the rehabilitation of memory disorders, these methods, which are often used along with other training techniques, may include relatively simple environmental changes such as labels on cupboards and instructions on appliances, as well as aids requiring more active participation of the individual such as notebooks and alarm watches, pocket and microcomputers, and paging systems. Many of these have been incorporated effectively into the everyday lives of memory-impaired patients, although extensive training in their use is usually required. Computer technologies have also affected rehabilitation of aphasic disorders where they have been used to provide both visual and auditory cues for word-finding difficulties. Other nonverbal communication strategies such as the use of writing or gesture and the learning of visual symbol systems have also proven to be effective compensatory devices for some patients with expressive language impairments.

Substitution of Intact Function

This approach, like the compensation approach just described, assumes that the cognitive and neural mechanisms required for normal cognitive function cannot be restored or improved, but that other intact processes can be recruited to act as substitutes. The idea here is that there may be alternate ways—cognitive and/or neural—to perform any given task or to achieve a particular functional outcome. The goal of treatment is to find these alternatives and make them efficient.

A recent application of this principle in the memory domain takes advantage of the finding that implicit memory processes (those that occur without conscious awareness) are intact in amnesic patients even though consciously controlled explicit memory processes are impaired. New training techniques, which may take advantage of preserved implicit memory, have enabled memory-impaired patients to learn considerable amounts of new information, including people's names, job skills, and aspects of home management. Using a system of cues and prompts that help them to retrieve newly acquired knowledge automatically and without error, patients have been able to learn even very complex skills such as word processing, despite having no knowledge of the learning episodes. Although this alternative learning method is slow relative to normal, it nevertheless enables behavior that would not be possible through normal means.

The substitution approach has also had some success in the treatment of attentional dysfunction. For example, patients suffering from unilateral spatial neglect resulting from right hemisphere damage have been trained to cue themselves verbally to attend to the left side of space. This intervention takes advantage of an intact phasic alertness system and a preserved left hemisphere language system. Conversely, in the rehabilitation of language disorders, which reflect left hemisphere damage, treatments have been devised that rely largely on preserved right hemisphere function. For ex-

ample, melodic intonation therapy for aphasic patients may engage the intact right hemisphere through the use of melody and rhythm and thereby activate latent right hemisphere language functions. Further, pragmatic approaches to language training, which focus more directly on real world communication, often try to build on patients' intact knowledge of nonverbal (i.e., right hemisphere) strategies and conversational roles to foster effective communication.

The success of the substitution approach depends on careful assessment of patient strengths as well as weaknesses, and on solid theoretical accounts of the processes involved in cognitive performance. Rehabilitation is usually focused on enhancing a specific functional behavior directly, and so generalization is not assumed or required for success. Interventions often take place in relevant real-world settings rather than in artificial laboratory or clinical environments and training is directed toward learning to perform cognitive tasks in novel ways rather than toward the relearning of old ways. This approach has gained support as a result of findings from functional neuroimaging studies suggesting that the brain can compensate for impaired functioning in one area by using a homologous area in the other hemisphere or another brain region not normally involved in the behavior.

Conclusion

Rehabilitation methodologies have expanded considerably in recent years as theoretical models of normal cognitive function have become more elaborated, and advances in cognitive neuroscience and neuroimaging technologies have revealed new information about the structure, function, and plasticity of the human brain. To ensure further progress, we need to continue to explore basic learning principles and mechanisms, which are clearly important for all kinds of rehabilitation, and to find effective ways of dealing with problems of generalization so that real-world functional gains are achieved. At the same time, continued cross-disciplinary interaction whereby knowledge about brain-behavior relations is used to support and inform neuropsychological interventions seems likely to be a productive direction for future research.

Bibliography

There are numerous individual articles on neuropsychological interventions in each cognitive domain. Below is a listing of individual and edited books on cognitive rehabilitation, some providing general overviews across cognitive domains and others dealing with different approaches within a particular cognitive area. The journal *Neuropsychological Rehabilitation* publishes articles of interest bimonthly and from time to time produces special issues devoted to a single topic.

Baddeley, A. D., Wilson, B. A., & Watts, F. N. (Eds.). (1995). *Handbook of memory disorders*. Chichester, UK: Wiley. This book includes chapters on different kinds of memory disorders and on assessment issues as well as eight chapters on memory rehabilitation.

Berndt, R. S., & Mitchum, C. C. (Eds.). (1995). Cognitive neuropsychological approaches to the treatment of language disorders. [Special issue]. *Neuropsychological Rehabilitation, 5*.

Boake, C. (Ed.). (1996). Historical aspects of neuropsychological rehabilitation. [Special Issue]. *Neuropsychological Rehabilitation 6*, 241–343. Historical antecedents to some current approaches to rehabilitation.

Luria, A. R. (1963). *Restoration of function after brain injury*. New York: Macmillan. A classic.

Mapou, R. L., & Mateer, C. A. (Eds.). (1996). Attention and memory. [Special Issue]. *Journal of Head Trauma Rehabilitation, 11*, 1–95.

Meier, M. J., Benton, A., & Diller, L. (Eds.). (1987). *Neuropsychological rehabilitation*. New York: Guilford Press. Covers a range of topics including assessment and methodological issues and a section on neuropsychological rehabilitation programs internationally.

Paradis, M. (Ed.). (1993). *Foundations of aphasia rehabilitation*. New York: Pergamon Press. A variety of approaches to aphasia rehabilitation.

Riddoch, M., & Humphreys, G. (Eds.). (1994). *Cognitive neuropsychology and cognitive rehabilitation*. Hillsdale, NJ: Erlbaum.

Seron, X., & Deloche, G. (Eds.). (1989). *Cognitive approaches in neuropsychological rehabilitation*. Hillsdale, NJ: Erlbaum. An overview of rehabilitation methods across cognitive domains from the cognitive neuropsychological perspective.

Sohlberg, M. M., & Mateer, C. A. (1989). *Introduction to cognitive rehabilitation*. New York: Guilford Press. An introductory overview of rehabilitation methods in a range of cognitive domains with particular emphasis on the process approach.

Elizabeth L. Glisky

NEUROSCIENCE can be broadly defined as the study of the structure and function of nervous tissue. From an anthropocentric point of view, it is regarded as primarily the study of the human, primate, or at least mammalian brain. However, numerous examples have amply demonstrated the intellectual and practical rewards of investigations of nervous tissue in other species, as well as the study of spinal cord and of peripheral nerves in mammals. Because nervous tissue, especially the brain, involves complexities of organization, cellular differentiation, and intercellular communication not observed in other organs, neuroscience encompasses an extensive and ever expanding variety of anatomical, physiological, biochemical, molecular, behavioral, genetic, computational, and other approaches.

Historical Considerations

It has been only a few decades since the term *neuroscience* was coined, and it was not used to formally designate academic departmental entities until the early 1970s. Neuroscience emerged by melding together what were previously distinct (sub)disciplines, such as neuroanatomy and neurophysiology. For example, neuroanatomy was formerly a subdiscipline of anatomy, both in terms of academic departmental affiliations and in terms of technical approaches. An analogous situation prevailed for neurophysiology. However, as specialized knowledge of the anatomy and physiology of nervous tissue began to rapidly expand, it became clear to investigators in these subdisciplines that they had more in common with each other than they did with their colleagues in more traditional academic departments. Soon, significant momentum to form "interdisciplinary" programs and departments was generated. At present, in most domains of neuroscience, the term *multidisciplinary* has become such a commonplace that it has lost its meaning. Physiological, anatomical, biochemical, and behavioral approaches are routinely amalgamated within departments and even within individual laboratories. Many of the major success stories of neuroscience have been those that have brought to bear multiple approaches to a particular problem.

In the relatively brief interval since its emergence, neuroscience has expanded enormously. Within the scientific life span of a single generation of investigators, this field has exploded from a very limited enterprise, where the practitioners, primary literature, and fundamental progress of the entire field could be tracked by a single (albeit energetic) individual. Now, even with computer assistance, that was not envisioned in the 1970s, investigators are challenged to track developments within relatively circumscribed subdivisions of neuroscience.

At present, neuroscience is, in both the intellectual and professional sense, a multidisciplinary community of scientific inquiries involving all levels of biological complexity, from the molecular to the organismic, even the multiorganismic. It might be argued that this multifaceted, rapidly expanding discipline has yet to assume an entirely cohesive or relatively stable identity. Since the 1970s, novel techniques have permitted the development of new dimensions of knowledge about brain structure and function that would have astounded cynics (or even skeptics) who were "present at the creation." The vastly increased knowledge in these few decades has not so much provided explanations of how the brain operates as it has begun to elaborate how immensely intricate are the mechanisms available to the brain to perform its functions. Compounding the complexity produced by ever accumulating new knowledge is the fact that new developments at any given level of analysis almost immediately require adjustment (and usually, added complexity) at other levels of analysis. The discovery of novel neurotransmitter molecules (or receptor subtypes) requires added complexity at the cellular level of analysis because the contents of individual neurons must be further specified. This, in turn, requires additional complexity at the level of neural circuitry analysis in that projections that were thought to consist of homogenous neuronal phenotypes must now be subdivided on the basis of transmitter specificity. A major development since the mid-1980s has been the evolving appreciation of the complexity of the computations that can be performed by individual neurons. This has resulted from the description of membrane events that are exceedingly complex in their time courses and often have multifaceted conditional dependencies related to other membrane events.

At present, the explosive growth of neuroscience continues. Technical developments, interacting with an ever expanding core of knowledge, are yielding massive amounts of data concerning brain structure and physiology. Neuroscience is being challenged to archive, analyze, and interpret this vast amount of information.

The Relationship of Neuroscience to Psychology

The domains of "neuroscience" and "psychology" overlap extensively. These disciplines are two areas of emphasis or perspective within a seamless biological system of brain-behavior interactions. These two areas share such an extensive, permeable, fuzzy interface, it is not surprising that "behavioral neuroscience" has come to encompass an enormous array of approaches involving, most commonly, the simultaneous assessment or manipulation of both behavioral and neuroscience variables. The term *neuropsychology* has not become commonly used for this endeavor because its use continues to be primarily reserved for the study of the impact of brain lesions on behavior. The terms *physiological psychology*, *psychobiology*, and *behavioral neuroscience* have varied in their prominence and in how they are defined, as particular aspects of this subdiscipline have been more or less emphasized. *Physiological psychology*, the academic and scientific origin of much of neuroscience, was the preferred term when efforts were focused on obtaining relatively preliminary knowledge about potential brain substrates of behaviors that had already been intensively studied at the psychological level. *Behavioral neuroscience* has now become a prominent term because technology, as well as knowledge of neurocircuitry and neural function, has developed to the stage where it is possible to characterize the specific neural circuitry and mechanisms underlying behavioral propensities or capacities.

Cognitive neuroscience is a rapidly expanding subdivision of behavioral neuroscience that encompasses learning, memory, reasoning, attention, perception, and other "higher" processes in the behavioral-psychological realm while simultaneously incorporating electrophysiological and imaging measures to assess brain circuitry on the neuroscience side.

The endeavors of neuroscience, behavioral neuroscience, and psychology are inevitably mutually reinforcing. The mechanisms, and thus the organization, of behavior are embedded in the operations of the brain. Unfortunately for behavioral neuroscience, it may be that the brain operations underlying behavior, especially complex behaviors such as cognition, will be those most resistant to characterization and clear understanding. This is because these brain functions quite probably involve the simultaneous operation of numerous distributed, at times parallel, systems. Thus, there is a technical issue of how to measure, repeatedly, over a behaviorally relevant time span, in a physiologically interpretable way, the operation of several distributed neural systems. This involves very large data sets, and thus there is also a significant problem in terms of storing, analyzing, and comparing with other data sets, the immense number of measures that result.

Behaviors are emergent properties, often goal directed and guided by ongoing, repeated interactions between the behavior, the environment, sensory information, and the results of motor output. A wide variety of situation-dependent measures will be necessary in order to accurately attribute behavioral outcomes to specific aspects of brain function.

Neuroscience and Behavioral Pathologies

The complexity of brain-behavior relationships is impressively evident in the arena of psychiatric disorders. These disorders are often readily perceived at the behavioral level, but they are refractory to satisfactory diagnosis, presumably because of the current near-total reliance on behavioral signs. Although neuroscience knowledge about these disorders is limited, many of them are now commonly viewed as brain-based disorders for which biological treatments are being sought. Currently, both behavioral and pharmacological treatments are used, but it is clear that for major disorders, such as depression and schizophrenia, pharmacological treatments are potent, although not perfectly targeted. These clinical problems bring into focus the profound interdependence of neuroscientific and psychological conceptualizations of brain-behavior systems.

The Future of Neuroscience

Protoneuroscientists came together for scientific and professional interaction because expanding knowledge in biology as a whole, and in the "neuro" sciences in particular, determined that interactions between anatomists studying the brain and physiologists studying the brain were more immediate and relevant than their interactions with anatomists or physiologists studying other tissues or organs. These fruitful intraneuroscience interactions, combined with vigorous borrowing of information and techniques from other disciplines such as basic molecular and cellular biology as well as physics, have led to explosive developments in neuroscience. The current status of the discipline, that of a huge, unwieldy, heterogeneous enterprise, raises issues of fractionation rather than unification. This may be especially relevant when viewing the extremes of the field in terms of levels of analysis. For example, does fascination with the precision and power of genetic tools and analyses threaten the integrity and vitality of cognitive and behavioral neuroscience endeavors? Will there be a reactive "Balkanization" of neuroscience subdisciplines? Answers to such questions are obviously highly speculative, but certain previous developments in the field provide examples of the integrative pressures that will probably continue to serve as "glue" to hold even the far ends of neuroscience together. One example is the issue of clinical problems originating in the brain. Mental illnesses, such as schizophrenia and affective disorders, clearly raise issues that span the spectrum from molecular pharmacology to behavioral assessment. It appears that future advances will depend upon the combination, perhaps within individual research programs, of the best of behavioral, neural systems, and molecular approaches. A common focus on a disease entity by investigators working at a variety of levels of analysis, with a broad armamentarium of methods, appears to offer the best hope of real progress with such disorders. This common focus serves as a unifying force across large areas of neuroscience. Another example is that of functional *in vivo* brain imaging. The implementation of these revolutionary methods has been interdisciplinary in the sense that it has depended upon the integration of physicists into neuroscience research teams. Furthermore, the imaging methods have been integrative in that they have provided information relevant to many levels of neuroscientific inquiry, from cerebral blood flow to receptor binding, to neuronal circuitry, to cognitive behavior and mental illness.

A crucial issue for the future of neuroscience is how complex "explanations" of behaviors and diseases reveal themselves to be. To most practitioners, it appears very unlikely that complex disorders, such as those now characterized as mental illnesses, will turn out to result from a simple genetic or other molecular disturbance that then produces, in any simple way, the behaviors that have been used to diagnose the disorder. Particular developments in pharmacology or genetics have at times made it appear that a comprehensive, coherent "explanation" of a complex behavior or behavioral disorder would involve a "single-gene, single-protein, single-brain system, single-behavior" scenario. The ever increasing complexity that has been described for brain structure, circuitry, and physiology makes it all but certain that such explanations will be vastly oversimplified and perhaps not even useful, except as initial, heuristic hypotheses.

Neuroscience is largely still at a stage of description, and the field is characterized by an explosion of data and observations that have become overwhelming. As other sciences have matured, there have been developments that have led to principles of organization or unified mechanisms of action that have provided elegant explanations or characterizations that synthesize huge amounts of data, permitting "simple" descriptions, predictions, and explanations of a variety of phenomena. Neuroscience does not seem to be on the verge of such a development.

Special Contributions of Neuroscience to Behavioral Science

Obviously, despite the intimate relationship between brain and behavior, behavior can be studied at its own level, with the discernment of regularities, antecedent conditions, pathologies, developmental sequences, and patterns of organization all being obvious and desirable products of this endeavor. Much of neuroscience and much of psychology can, and do, develop along parallel lines with modest interaction. Even as these fields become more highly developed, and neuroscience begins to provide causal, in addition to correlative, scenarios for simple and eventually complex behaviors, the intrinsic relationships between these fields of study may not be clear. However, there are specific contributions that can be made by neuroscience that may substantially hasten and enrich descriptions and understanding of behavior. These contributions include (1) dissociations of normally co-occurring behaviors or capabilities by brain damage or pharmacological manipulation, revealing potentially dissociable components of an apparently unitary behavior; (2) characterizations of brain status that predict which of many possible responses to a particular environmental input will actually occur, permitting predictions about behavior and its antecedent conditions that cannot be made on the basis of behavioral observations alone; (3) determination of the biological correlates of behavioral traits that can help independently classify subjects with regard to individual differences in behaviors.

[*See also* Society for Neuroscience.]

Bibliography

Adelman, G. (Ed.). (1987). *Encyclopedia of neuroscience* (2 vols.). Boston, MA: Birkhaeuser. An extensive encyclopedia, composed of individually authored articles dealing with a vast array of neuroscience topics.

Brazier, M. A. B. (1988). *A history of neurophysiology in the nineteenth century*. New York: Raven Press. An account of the pioneering, fascinating work that set the stage for "modern" neuroscience.

Churchland, P. S. (1986). *Neurophilosophy: Toward a unified science of the mind-brain*. Cambridge, MA: MIT Press. A philosopher examines the mind-body issue and the nature of explanation in the context of modern neuroscience.

Churchland, P. S., & Sejnowski, T. J. (1992). *The computational brain*. Cambridge, MA: MIT Press. Examines the importance of modeling efforts in understanding brain mechanisms.

Gazzaniga, M. S., Ivry, R., & Mangun, G. R. (1998). *Cognitive neuroscience: The biology of the mind*. New York: Norton. A textbook overview of this rapidly growing, major area of contemporary neuroscience.

Gross, C. G. (1987). Neuroscience, early history of. In G. Adelman (Ed.), *Encyclopedia of neuroscience* (pp. 843–846). Boston, MA: Birkhauser. A brief review of the early development of neuroscience.

Gross, C. G. (in press). History of localization of function in the cerebral cortex. In *Encyclopedia of the cognitive sciences*. Cambridge, MA: MIT Press. Addresses the history of one of the most persistent and fundamental questions in neuroscience.

Kandel, E. R., Schwartz, J. H., & Jessell, T. M. (1991). *Principles of neural science* (3rd ed.). New York: Elsevier Science. A comprehensive textbook with extensive, from-the-ground-up coverage of the major areas of neuroscience.

Kandel, E. R., Schwartz, J. H., & Jessell, T. M. (Eds.). (1995). *Essentials of neural science and behavior*. Norwalk, CT: Appleton & Lange. An extensive treatment of brain-behavior interactions.

Squire, L. R. (Ed.) (1996). *The history of neuroscience in autobiography* (Vol. 1). Orlando, FL: Academic Press/Society for Neuroscience. Autobiographies of eminent neuroscientists.

Squire, L. R. (Ed.). (1998). *The history of of neuroscience in autobiography* (Vol. 2). Orlando, FL: Academic Press/Society for Neuroscience. Autobiographies of eminent neuroscientists.

Stephen L. Foote

NEUROTICISM. *See* Personality Traits.

NEWCOMB, THEODORE MEAD (1903–1984), American social psychologist. Newcomb was born and raised in Ohio, the son of a Congregational minister. He completed his undergraduate education at Oberlin College in Ohio, and then studied at Union Theological Seminary in New York City and subsequently at Columbia University. Excited by the courses at Columbia, he left theology for psychology, working with Goodwin Watson and Gardner Murphy. Newcomb received his doctorate in 1929 and accepted an assistant professorship for one year at Lehigh University in Pennsylvania, followed by four years (1930–1934) at Western Reserve University in Cleveland, Ohio. He was married to Mary Shipherd in 1931 and they had three children. In 1934, Newcomb joined the faculty of Bennington College in Vermont. He remained there for 7 years, moving to the sociology department of the University of Michigan in 1941. Subsequently, he was also appointed to the psychology department at the University of Michigan. He remained at Michigan until his death.

Newcomb had a major influence in the development of social psychology, particularly emphasizing the interdisciplinary nature of the field. The central theme throughout Newcomb's career was the need to integrate behavioral concepts from both psychology and sociology into social psychology, emphasizing the social nature of the field.

In 1947, Newcomb, Robert Angell, and Donald Marquis founded the doctoral program in social psychology at the University of Michigan. For 20 years, this joint interdisciplinary program granted over 200 doctorates, thus developing the field of social psychology. Newcomb provided the leadership that brought and held this program together and made the University of Michigan one of the leading centers in social psychology. [*See* Social Psychology.]

In 1947, Newcomb and Eugene Hartley edited a book (*Readings in Social Psychology*, New York), comprising research and theory from psychology, sociology, and anthropology. This book along with Newcomb's 1950 textbook, *Social Psychology* (New York), were very influential in establishing the research and theoretical base for an interdisciplinary social psychology.

Newcomb's research studies focused primarily on social relations in a real setting. His study of Bennington College students between 1936 and 1940 investigated the changes in attitudes and values in students as they completed their education. The study *Personality and Social Change: Attitude Formation in a Student Community* was cited widely and has been assigned in graduate and undergraduate courses for more than 50 years. Newcomb anchored these attitude changes in the social context of norms, reference group membership, leadership, and friendship patterns.

Interest in the Bennington study led to two follow-up studies of the original cohort of students: one conducted 25 years later and the last 50 years later. In each of these studies, the continuities and discontinuities in the values, interpersonal associations, and political orientations of these women were assessed.

In the 1950s, Newcomb developed a balance theory of two-person interaction based on the consistency of the attitudes of the individuals toward each other and a common object. Newcomb's theory was unique in that it was concerned with balance in the interpersonal system and not just with individual internal consistency. He tested this theory in a 2-year field study of emerging friendship patterns among initial strangers living in the same house (*The Acquaintance Process*, New York, 1961).

Newcomb's contribution to psychology was his abiding contention that there is a set of phenomena that is best described as neither psychological nor sociological but as social psychological.

Bibliography

Alwin, D. F., Cohen, R. L., and Newcomb, T. M. (1991). *Political attitudes over the life-span: The Bennington women after fifty years.* Madison, WI: University of Wisconsin Press. A follow-up 50 years later and a comparison of their attitudes to those of other university women their age.

Jackson, T. T., & Campbell, K. E. (1984). Interview with Professor Theodore Newcomb. *Contemporary Social Psychology, 10,* 3–16.

Murphy, G., Murphy, L., & Newcomb, T. M. (1937). *Experimental social psychology* (Rev. ed.). New York: Harper. This early handbook established the research base for social psychology. Newcomb edited about one third of the book, including the section on attitudes.

Newcomb, T. M. (1943). *Personality and social change: Attitude formation in a student community.* New York: Holt, Rinehart & Winston. The classic study of student change.

Newcomb, T. M. (1974). In G. Lindzey (Ed.), *A history of psychology in autobiography* (Vol. 6, pp. 367–391). Englewood Cliffs, NJ: Prentice Hall. An autobiographical account detailing major contributions to social psychology and social issues, as well as an analysis of personal influences on his career.

Newcomb, T. M., & Feldman, K. (1969). *Impact of college on students* (Vols. 1–2). San Francisco: Jossey-Bass. A critical review of research dealing with the impact of colleges upon their students.

Newcomb, T. M., Koenig, K. E., Flack, R., & Warwick, D. P. (1967). *Persistence and change: Bennington College and its students after twenty-five years.* New York: Wiley. Twenty-five-year follow-up of the 1930s cohort and a study of the students in 1959–1962, Bennington College.

Kathryn Koenig

NEWELL, ALLEN (1927–1992), American cognitive psychologist and computer scientist. Newell made profound contributions to psychology, especially through the invention and empirical testing of symbolic information processing theories of human thinking. One of the founding fathers of artificial intelligence and cognitive science, his work continues to exercise a major influence on these developing fields.

Born in San Francisco, the son of Robert R. Newell, a distinguished radiologist at the Stanford Medical School, and Jeanette LeValley Newell, Newell attended San Francisco public schools and served in the U.S. Navy just after World War II, assisting in mapping radiation intensities at the Eniwetok A-bomb tests, an experience that helped awaken his interest in science. After earning a bachelor of science degree in physics at Stanford University in 1949, he spent a postgraduate year studying mathematics at Princeton University. Then a desire to work on less abstract matters led him to a position with a group studying air defense crews at the Rand "think tank" in Santa Monica, California, and gave him early contact with the new electronic digital computers and their potential for nonnumerical symbol processing.

Newell and two collaborators, J. C. Shaw and H. A. Simon, were among the first to conceive that computers might solve nonnumerical problems by selective heuristic search, much as people do (if using quite different "hardware"). Needing flexible associative memory structures for such computation, they invented in 1956 the first list processing languages (the IPLs), whose successors, especially John McCarthy's LISP, are indispensable tools for cognitive simulation at the symbolic level.

The research was carried out at Rand and at Carnegie Institute of Technology (after 1965, Carnegie Mellon University), where Newell enrolled in 1955 to pursue a doctorate in the business school, with a thesis on heuristic programming. Over the next few years, he and his colleagues used the IPLs to create some of the first computer simulations of human thinking, including the Logic Theorist (1956), the General Problem Solver (1960), and the NSS chess program (1958). They introduced fundamental ideas that remain at the core of cognitive theory, including heuristic search, means-ends analysis, planning, adaptive production systems, and problem spaces. To test how well these computer simulations accounted for human behavior, the group reintroduced thinking-aloud protocols (which had been largely banned from psychology as "introspective"), improving the methods for gathering and analyzing them.

Newell joined the faculty of Carnegie in 1961 as a full professor, retaining this position until his early death in 1992. In 1972, he and Simon published *Human Problem Solving* (Englewood Cliffs, N.J.), summarizing their psychological research, which showed how empirically testable (and tested) theories of complex human thought processes could be constructed.

To generalize the simulations and endow them with a more realistic control structure, Newell focused increasingly on a cognitive architecture that would provide a framework for veridical general cognitive theories. The Soar system, developed with Paul Rosenbloom and John Laird, is a substantial extension of the General Problem Solver that operates in multiple problem spaces and has powerful learning capabilities. Dozens of investigators are now using Soar as the architecture for simulations of human thinking. Soar and psychological theory were the subject of Newell's last book, *Unified Theories of Cognition* (Cambridge, Mass., 1990), based on his William James Lectures at Harvard. He argued persuasively, supported empirically by the systems he built and tested, for the importance of broad, operational theories to bring coherence into the welter of very specific experiments and experimental paradigms that, he thought, characterized contemporary psychology.

Over his career, a good deal of Newell's productive effort went into what he called his "diversions," many on important topics in computer science outside psychology, but several that produced important contributions to psychology. He served as chair of the committee that monitored the research in computer speech recognition sponsored by the Advanced Research Projects Agency (ARPA). Another such "diversion" was research with S. Card and T. P. Moran (*The Psychology of Human-Computer Interaction*, Hillsdale, N.J., 1983) that reinvigorated human factors studies, extending them to complex cognitive processes and stimulating the new subfield of human-computer interaction within psychology.

In addition to his scientific work, Newell served as president of both the American Association for Artificial Intelligence and the Cognitive Science Society and as an advisor to several agencies of the federal government. He played a leading role in bringing modern information processing psychology as well as computer networking to Carnegie Mellon University.

Bibliography

Newell, A., Shaw, J. C., & Simon, H. A. (1958). Chess-playing programs and the problem of complexity. *IBM Journal of Research and Development, 2*, 230–335.

Newell, A., Shaw, J. C., & Simon, H. A. (1960). Report on a general problem solving program. *Proceedings of the International Conference on Information Processing*, 256–264.

Newell, A., & Simon, H. A. (1956). The logic theory machine: A complex information processing system. *IRE Transactions on Information Theory, IT-2*, (No. 3), 61–79.

Herbert A. Simon

NEW ENGLAND PSYCHOLOGICAL ASSOCIATION. *See* Regional Psychological Associations.

NEWTON, ISAAC (1642–1727), English natural philosopher and mathematician. Born in Woolsthorpe, Lincolnshire, and educated at King's School, Grantham, Newton graduated from Trinity College, Cambridge University, in 1665. Early in his career, Newton made breakthroughs in the theory of optics and dynamics, and in mathematics. He became Lucasian Professor at Trinity College in 1669. His difficult personality led him into many disputes, even as his many talents led, for example, to his appointment as master of the mint in 1699 and to election to Parliament in 1701.

His epochal *Principia Mathematica* of 1687 used three simple laws of motion (Newton's Laws) to derive the principles of motion of all moving bodies. By showing that planetary motions could be predicted and explained, Newton integrated physical laws and observational astronomy and gave impetus to the spread of scientific thinking. In the same work, he demonstrated the value of a new mathematical approach to the representation of changing quantities. He is thus remembered (with Gottfried Leibniz) as the coinventor of calculus.

In optics, Newton used a prism to separate sunlight into colored bands, and to resynthesize these into the original whitish yellow light, showing that color was a property of light, not of objects. He speculated that color perception was due to "vibrations" of differing intensities in retinal pathways. Favoring the view that light consisted of particles, Newton could not account for all optical phenomena; thus his corpuscular view was challenged by Christian Huygens's wave theory. Even so, Newton's *Opticks* (1704) served as a model of insightful experimentation, and his speculations on light, vision, force, and the existence of atoms were important for the development of psychology.

In mathematics, calculus today relies on the notation of Leibniz rather than Newton's cumbersome approach; even so, the *Principia* represents its first powerful application. Among many examples within psychology, Gustave Fechner used calculus to develop psychophysics, while Fisher relied upon it to formulate statistical principles. In current psychology, calculus is essential for some dynamic theories of human cognition (for example, neural networks) and in some studies of sensation, perception, memory, and motor action.

Historically, Newton's *Principia* inspired grand psychological theories, for example, by John Locke. He was frequently referenced by eighteenth- and nineteenth-century psychological thinkers, such as Reid, Hartley, and Jonathan Edwards. In the twentieth century, Newton's use of axioms as starting points for formal theory (imitated unsuccessfully by Hull) has been an ideal for many psychological theorists.

As a philosopher of science, Newton is important for his comments on scientific method. In the *Principia*, he stated that he would not entertain hypotheses about the nature of gravity. Yet he was not averse to speculation, as the *Opticks* clearly reveals. Actually, Newton was careful to place speculation in context; for his optical work, he lacked a unified theory and therefore explored all possible explanations. But in his more developed theory of motion, he avoided speculation. Instead, he presupposed the existence of gravitational force ("action at a distance"), showing *how* gravity worked rather than *what* gravity was. He thus was one of the first to recognize that scientific claims may be limited in scope and dependent on otherwise unverifiable foundations.

Newton's mechanics is a deterministic system, that is, it rests upon interrelated laws capable of generating complex phenomena. It is not a mechanistic, "push-pull" account, in which one event causes another, which in turn causes a further event, and so on. There is no strict separation of cause and effect; instead, a continuous "dance" of dynamic events is unified by deterministic laws. Some psychological systems manifest a similar character, for example, Simon's account of problem solving, James Gibson's "ecological" approach to perception, and recent connectionist theories. Such examples suggest that Newton will continue to serve as a model of science for psychology.

Bibliography

Newton, I. (1952). *Opticks, or, a treatise of the reflections, refractions, inflections and colours of light* (4th ed.). New York: Dover. (Reprinted from *Optiks*, 1931, London: for William Innys) (Original work published 1730.) The most readable of Newton's works, although perhaps best approached with the interpretive assistance of, for example, Sepper's book (1994).

Newton, I. (1999). *The Principia: Mathematical principles of natural philosophy* (3rd ed.) (I. B. Cohen & A. Whitman, Trans.). Berkeley: University of California Press. (Original work published 1687). An extremely demanding book, but well worth browsing for Newton's comments on scientific thinking. This edition has a very useful introduction and reading guide by I. B. Cohen.

Sepper, D. L. (1994). *Newton's optical writings: A guided study*. New Brunswick, NJ: Rutgers University Press. Helpful commentary, diagrams, and reprints from Newton's earlier writings enable a deep understanding of his experimental work in optics.

Shapere, D. (1967). Newton, Isaac; Newtonian mechanics and mechanical explanation. In P. Edwards (Ed.), *Encyclopedia of philosophy* (Vol. 5, pp. 489–496). New York: Macmillan. Excellent brief summary by a philosopher of science.

Tweney, R. D. (1997). Jonathan Edwards and determinism. *Journal of the History of the Behavioral Sciences, 33*, 365–380. Contains an exposition of Newton's determinism and describes the psychological system developed by the American Puritan thinker Jonathan Edwards to account for human thought and action.

Westfall, R. S. (1980). *Never at rest: A biography of Isaac Newton*. Cambridge, UK: Cambridge University Press. Outstanding scientific biography by a historian of science, covering all aspects of Newton's life and works.

Ryan D. Tweney

NEW ZEALAND. The population of New Zealand, numbering 3.7 million, lives in a country 1,200 miles long and 150 miles wide, separated by mountains of up to 12,000 feet, swift rivers, and thick rain forest. Consequently, its nineteenth-century White settlers established several communities that remain relatively distinct to this day. Each of the six major communities developed a university, and psychology is taught at all six.

Currently 72% of New Zealanders are of European descent, 15% are indigenous Maori, 5% Pacific Island Polynesian, and 4% Asian. However, until 1945, over 90% of the population was of not just European but of overwhelmingly British descent. Consequently, the original four universities (Otago, founded in 1850; Canterbury, 1873; Auckland, 1882; and Wellington, 1899) followed the British model and taught psychology in their departments of philosophy as mental and moral science. The marking of examination papers in English universities strengthened the British influence.

The acceptance of psychology as a subject was made more difficult by a requirement that new courses be unanimously accepted by all four campuses. Despite this difficulty, Thomas (later Sir Thomas) Hunter, appointed to teach philosophy at Wellington in 1904, established Australasia's first psychology laboratory after spending 1906–1907 visiting Titchener at Cornell University, Rivers, Myers, and McDougall at Cambridge University, and Wundt at the University of Leipzig in 1906–1907. Research cited in his teaching included that of Dewey, Mead, Thorndike, Woodworth, and Watson.

New Zealand's second major stream of psychology teaching started with Clarence Beeby at Canterbury University, Christchurch, in 1923 in the Department of Education. Freud, Terman, Spearman, Thorndike, and Piaget were among the theorists covered. Beeby developed an interest in industrial psychology, and his student Ralph Winterbourn carried on the vocational guidance aspect of the field in training educational psychologists, culminating in his establishment of the first postgraduate diploma in educational psychology at the University of Auckland in 1960. Meanwhile, Beeby expanded his interests to criminology and the education of children with special needs, and education departments at Otago and Wellington universities also taught educational psychology. The New Zealand Council for Educational Research was established in 1934 and has researched and monitored the development of educational psychology ever since. The industrial psychology department of the Department of Scientific and Industrial Research (DSIR) and the Vocational Guidance Service of the Education Department followed in 1942 and 1943, respectively. Psychology was also established at Auckland in 1922 and at Otago in 1930, although it remained part of moral and mental philosophy.

Psychology played a role in personnel selection and allocation during World War II, with the air force establishing a selection and assessment corps to serve all three armed services. This developed into the Defences Science Corps, which serves all three services to the present day.

New Zealand has evolved from a pioneer society based on Western European individualistic, democratic, and capitalist social mores. Its White majority has been increasingly influenced by the collectivist mores of its indigenous Polynesian people, the Maori. Living in a temperate climate with magnificently varied scenery, New Zealand's 3.7 million people have developed a reputation for being friendly, independent, environmentally sensitive, and lovers of sports and of the outdoors, even though 80% are urban dwellers. Being 1,200 miles from the nearest other country, they also travel often and widely. With literacy at 99%, New Zealanders read more books and magazines than people in most other countries. Although the concept of the welfare state that was pioneered in the 1890s and developed in the 1930s has undergone considerable revision, the tradition of "helping others to help themselves" still persists. All this leads to an emphasis on applied, socially oriented psychology.

Research Traditions in New Zealand

Earnest Beaglehole was appointed to the first chair in psychology at the Victoria University of Wellington in 1948. He called himself an "ethnopsychologist," reflecting his dedication to a cross-cultural viewpoint. He and his students went on to conduct extensive research into the psychology of the indigenous people of New Zealand, the Polynesian Maori, and their relationship with the White majority well before such research became popular in the 1960s. Research on small groups and on coping with disasters such as earthquakes and airplane crashes, as well as support of social worker training, have also been important issues.

Researchers at Auckland have pursued the experimental study of learning, especially with animals. Corballis is prominent among a strong neuropsychology team for his work on the split brain. Serving the world's largest Polynesian urban population, Auckland also features the psychology of the indigenous Maori. A strong clinical program, publication of New Zealand's first social psychology textbook, and the education department's postgraduate diploma in educational psychology are also important developments.

Canterbury University in Christchurch combines experimental and social approaches, focusing especially on cognition, as well as on criminology and on industrial/organizational, clinical, and social psychology, while maintaining an interest in the links between philosophy and psychology through the work of Ken Strongman.

Otago University in Dunedin was for many years the site of the country's only medical school, so it focused on neurological, physiological, and clinical psychology. A strong current of research into epilepsy, notably the "kindling" phenomenon, initiated by Goddard, continues despite his untimely death in 1989. Cognition and perception are also emphasized.

The two youngest universities, Massey at Palmerston North, founded in 1960, and Waikato in Hamilton, founded in 1964, both included psychology departments when they were founded. Both departments teach a range of topics, but L. B. Brown and then George Shouksmith at Massey University emphasized industrial and organizational psychology, as well as developing a special interest in topics as diverse as social work, rehabilitation after disablement, and air-crew ergonomics. Clinical psychology is strong, and health psychology is a growing field.

The psychology department at the University of Waikato, headed by Beaglehole's student James Ritchie, focused on cross-cultural and social psychology but soon developed interests in clinical, community, and industrial/organizational psychology. A laboratory for the study of domestic animal behavior adjacent to New Zealand's largest agricultural research institute has been very productive, and since 1993 an extensive research program on perception and road safety was developed. Maori make up 25% of the student roll at Waikato, a percentage that is reflected in its teaching and research.

Clinical psychology in New Zealand developed only slowly, with British-style psychiatry dominating the field for decades and clinical psychology only gradually becoming accepted. Beaglehole's critical review of mental health services in 1950 antagonized medical-model psychiatry. However, fully accepted postgraduate diplomas in clinical psychology have been offered at all six universities since the late 1960s and are very popular, with entry to the programs being highly competitive. Most are based on behavior modification and produce clinicians focused on community care. Postgraduate qualifications in industrial/organizational psychology are offered on three campuses and in community psychology at Waikato.

Key Societies, Associations, and Institutions

A branch of the British Psychological Society established in 1947 evolved into the independent New Zealand Psychological Society (NZPsS) in 1968. Originally a largely academic group, its main activities were to run an annual conference and to publish the *New Zealand Journal of Psychology*. Since 1981, however, it has increasingly become a professional association of practicing psychologists, with academics making up about 25% of its membership. Groups representing educational and clinical psychologists are affiliating with the parent NZPsS.

The practice of psychology is regulated by the Psychologists Board, a statutory body responsible for certification and disciplining of psychologists. The initiative for registration came in the early 1960s from the then New Zealand branch of the British Psychological Society. This proved unpopular with the British society, which was seeking Royal Charter, so the registration issue was a factor in the formation of the New Zealand Psychological Society. This new society generated the draft legislation that eventually became the Psychologists Act, which was passed by Parliament in 1981.

The NZPsS publishes the *New Zealand Journal of Psychology* and the *Psychologists' Bulletin*. However, New Zealand research is also widely reported overseas, especially in the *Australian Journal of Psychology*, as well as in all prominent specialty journals. Textbooks focusing on New Zealand and Australian research have recently appeared, notably in social psychology.

Current Status and Future Direction

Today psychology is one of the most popular subjects taught at all six universities. Doctoral programs based on the British thesis-only model are offered by all six, and each has an active faculty (ranging in size from 20 to 30 tenured members) conducting and publishing research in a variety of fields. Since the passing of the Psychologists Act in 1981, psychology has also become widely accepted in the community. Increasingly, psychology is recognized by government and business as necessary for dealing with human problems as machines take over basic production and human labor is devoted to social support. Consequently, more than 1,000 psychologists now hold annual practicing licenses, and this number continues to increase. Government departments, such as at the Departments of Health, Education, Justice, Children and Young Persons' Service, Social Welfare, and Defence are prominent employers, although increasingly they contract their work out to psychologists who also practice privately. However, private practitioners make up the single largest category and are increasing rapidly, currently numbering more than 400. Industrial/organizational work is also expanding, but it has far to go before it can match the opportunities available in larger industrial societies. The Registration Act is under revision to tighten definition and control, and qualifications in clinical, community, and industrial/organizational psychology are being upgraded, with applied doctorates being offered

on some campuses. Psychology is becoming increasingly accepted by business, medicine, education, justice, and other areas as able to play a vital role in service development. Its future is bright, and demand for education and training in psychology, already strong, continues to increase.

Bibliography

Beeby, C. E. (1979). Psychology in New Zealand fifty years ago. In R. St. George (Ed.), *The beginnings of psychology in New Zealand: A collection of historical documents and recollections.* (Delta Research Monograph No. 2, pp. 1–6.) Palmerston North, New Zealand: Massey University, Department of Education.

Brown, L. B., & Fuchs, A. H. (1971). Early experimental psychology in New Zealand: The Hunter–Titchener letters. *Journal of the History of the Behavioral Sciences, 7,* 10–22.

Hearnshaw, L. S. (1965). Psychology in New Zealand: A report. *Bulletin of the British Psychological Society, 18,* 17–24.

Hunter, T. (1952). The development of psychology in New Zealand. *Quarterly Bulletin of the British Psychological Society, 3,* 101–111.

Ritchie, J. E. (1979). Earnest Beaglehole at Victoria: A personal memoir. In R. St. George (Ed.), *The beginnings of psychology in New Zealand: A collection of historical documents and recollections.* (Delta Research Monograph No. 2, pp. 61–67.) Palmerston North; New Zealand: Massey University, Department of Education.

Shouksmith, G. (1997). First steps towards structured clinical psychology training in New Zealand. *Bulletin of the New Zealand Psychological Society, 92,* 22–24.

St. George, R. (Ed.). (1979). *The beginnings of psychology in New Zealand: A collection of historical documents and recollections.* (Delta Research Monograph No. 2.) Palmerston North; New Zealand: Massey University, Department of Education.

St. George, R. (1987). Psychology in New Zealand: A history and commentary. In G. H. Blowers & A. M. Turtle (Eds.), *Psychology moving East: The status of Western psychology in Asia and Oceania.* Boulder, CO: Westview.

St. George, R. (1990). Legacies of empire for psychology in New Zealand. *Journal of the History of the Behavioral Sciences, 26,* 359–365.

Statistics New Zealand (1997). *1996 Census of population and dwellings: National summary.* Wellington, NZ: Statistics New Zealand.

Sutch, M. S. (1972). Psychological and guidance services. In S. J. Havill & D. R. Mitchell (Eds.), *Issues in New Zealand special education* (pp. 203–208, 212–213). Auckland; New Zealand: Hodder & Stoughton.

Taylor, A. J. W. (1997). Collegiate psychology in New Zealand: The early days of the Society. *Bulletin of the New Zealand Psychological Society, 92,* 14–17.

Winterbourn, R. (1953). A review of psychology in New Zealand. *Australian Journal of Psychology, 5,* 17–27.

Michael D. Hills

NIETZSCHE, FRIEDRICH W. (1844–1900), German philosopher. Few writers in the history of Western thought have sparked as much controversy and diversity of interpretation as Friedrich Nietzsche. Today, Nietzsche is considered one of the most influential philosophers in the past 200 years and is seen as one of the intellectual grandfathers of postmodernism. Although he frequently referred to himself as a "psychologist," this was before the term took on its present experimental connotations. Contemporary psychology has typically not regarded him as a psychologist.

Nietzsche's philosophy touches on practically all aspects of human existence but focuses primarily on the problem of human values (for example, morality and ethics). Nietzsche did not present his ideas in terms of structured "theories" or "systems," making an understanding of his work as a whole rather difficult. He wrote mainly in aphorisms; they are often—intentionally—ambiguous and bombastic and do not provide a clear or immediate explanation of his ideas. To follow his own suggestion, to understand Nietzsche, it is best to read his major works in chronological order.

Nietzsche was both a critic of contemporary morality (especially Christianity) and a prophet bearing a new vision of humanity, whereby morality moves "beyond good and evil." One of Nietzsche's most controversial ideas, often called "perspectivism" (or "relativism"), emphasized that there is no objective, context-independent truth. All knowledge is dependent upon a human act of interpretation, which always carries with it social and personal meanings and values. This view of knowledge is not unique to Nietzsche and has more recently been advanced within psychology by proponents of "social construction."

Nietzsche's perspectivism leads to one of his most important concepts, the "transvaluation of values." Nietzsche believed that the world itself is intrinsically "value-less" or amoral, yet people are unable to exist without values. It is, therefore, we ourselves who create values. Thus, his famous announcement that "God is dead" symbolized his rejection of preordained moral laws and pointed to human activity as the actual source of morality.

Other central concepts in Nietzsche's philosophy are the "overman" (or somewhat less accurately, the "superman"), the "will to power," and the "eternal return." Each of these are deliberately vague and were not meant to be understood in isolation but as a part of Nietzsche's whole vision. This vision involved questioning the moral and ethical conventions of society, an enlightened and creative "will" that continually redefined and reshaped one's own values and identity, and a person who in so doing was able to live finding fulfilment because of, rather than in spite of, the inherent ambiguity and lack of certainty in the world.

Many of Nietzsche's concepts and ideas were precursors to those of Sigmund Freud and the field of psychoanalysis. [See the biography of Freud.] Nietzsche very accurately anticipated Freud in several key areas: a view of the unconscious that is instinctual and conflict-ridden and is a repository of undesirable or unpleasant material; defense mechanisms, such as repression, projection, and sublimation; the concept of over-determination; the significance of aggressive and self-destructive drives; the ancestral origins of conscience and guilt; and dreams as manifestations of the unconscious. After reviewing a number of these points, Walter Kaufmann, in his series *Discovering the Mind* (New York, 1980), went so far as to call Nietzsche the "first depth psychologist." In fact, Freud used Nietzsche's term for the unconscious ("das Es") in his own theory, which was later rendered as the Latin "id" by Freud's English translators. Nietzsche has also been closely associated with the existentialist movement, and his ideas have had an impact on a number of existential psychologists, such as Rollo May. [See the biography of May.]

The controversy surrounding Nietzsche's work was increased by an erroneous connection between it and the Nazi party during and after World War II. During World War II, Hitler and the Nazis perverted Nietzsche's ideas—a move that was tragically endorsed by Nietzsche's sister—into a pseudo-philosophical foundation for their anti-Semitic hatred and practices. This view of Nietzsche was accepted until the 1960s when Kaufmann disproved Nietzsche's supposed anti-Semitism and his reputation as a proto-Nazi.

By late 1888, Nietzsche had begun to show signs of delusions and the insanity that would later envelop him. In January 1889, he collapsed in the street, never to recover fully, and later that year he was taken to an asylum. Nietzsche deteriorated mentally and physically over the next 10 years. He died on 25 August 1900 from the effects of general paresis, probably brought about by syphilis. Some have mistaken Nietzeche's bold hyperbole for the ravings of a madman, but most Nietzsche scholars now agree that his occasional literary excesses should not be taken as signs of psychosis.

Bibliography

Aschheim, S. (1992). *The Nietzsche legacy in Germany: 1890–1990.* Berkeley: University of California Press. For those wanting a thorough, detailed account of the various interpretations of Nietzsche in Germany (including that of the Nazis).

Kaufmann, W. (1974). *Nietzsche: Philosopher, psychologist, antichrist.* Princeton: Princeton University Press. Still one of the best introductions to Nietzsche available.

Megill, A. (1985). *Prophets of extremity.* Berkeley: University of California Press. An excellent overview of Nietzsche in what is a sophisticated but clear introduction to postmodern thought (also looks at Heidegger and Derrida).

Nehamas, A. (1985). *Nietzsche: Life as literature.* Cambridge: Harvard University Press. Nietzsche's aesthetics and the question of truth are discussed.

Nietzsche, F. (1961). *Thus spoke Zarathustra* (R. J. Hollingdale, Ed. and Trans.). New York: Penguin. (Original work published 1885.) Probably Nietzsche's single most important work.

Nietzsche, F. (1967). *The will to power* (W. Kaufmann, Ed. and W. Kaufmann and R. J. Hollingdale, Trans.). New York: Random House. (Original work published 1901.) Not a complete work, but a collection from Nietzsche's notebooks, published posthumously, and dealing at length with the "transvaluation of values."

Nietzsche, F. (1968). *The basic writings of Nietzsche* (W. Kaufmann, Ed. and Trans.). New York: Random House. A collection of some of Nietzsche's most important works including: *The birth of tragedy, Beyond good and evil, On the genealogy of morals, The case of Wagner,* and his last work, *Ecce homo.* A good, inexpensive way to begin reading Nietzsche.

Nietzsche, F. (1968). *Twilight of the idols/The Antichrist* (R. J. Hollingdale, Ed. and Trans.). New York: Penguin. (Original work published 1889.) Nietzsche's renowned attack on Christianity and Western metaphysics in general. Better for the experienced Nietzsche reader.

Nietzsche, F. (1974). *The gay science* (W. Kaufmann, Trans.). New York: Random House. (Original work published 1882; second edition published 1887.) Contains Nietzsche's famous declaration, "God is dead."

Solomon, R. (Ed.). (1973). *Nietzsche: A collection of critical essays.* Notre Dame, IN: University of Notre Dame Press. Several excellent essays on Nietzsche from Kaufmann, Danto, Jaspers, Heidegger, and others. Mitchell Ginsberg also gives a good summary of the overlap between Nietzsche and psychoanalysis.

Scott Greer

NIGHTMARES. A *nightmare* is usually defined as a "frightening dream." In everyday speech, the term is also used to describe dreams in which sadness, despair, or disgust is the predominant emotion. In the *Diagnostic and Statistical Manual of Mental Disorders* of the American Psychiatric Association (1994), frequent distressing nightmares are defined as nightmare disorder. Nightmares are also listed as a symptom of posttraumatic stress disorder.

Nightmares are often confused with night terrors because both conditions involve sudden anxious awakenings from sleep. However, nightmares can be distinguished from night terrors by the following features:

1. Nightmares are dreams, contain visual imagery and a narrative structure, and typically occur during rapid-eye movement (REM) sleep. Night terrors are not dreams and typically occur during slow-wave sleep.

2. Nightmares tend to occur during the second half of the night, when REM sleep is most common. Night terrors usually occur in the first hours of the night, when slow-wave sleep is most common.

3. A person awakening from a nightmare is usually alert and oriented to his or her surroundings. A person awakening from a night terror is usually confused and disoriented for several minutes afterward.

Nightmares are common in the general population. For example, it is estimated that college students have 20 to 25 nightmares per year. The occurrence of nightmares is unrelated to gender. However, there does appear to be a relationship to age: Nightmare frequency decreases somewhat over the life span, and the elderly report much less distress from nightmares than do younger persons. There is some evidence to suggest that nightmares may be especially common among children under 6 years of age. However, night terrors and nighttime fears are also relatively common in this age group and may account for many cases labeled as nightmares.

Nightmares can be produced by several medications, including reserpine, levodopa, beta blockers, digoxin, monoamine oxidase inhibitors, cholinesterase inhibitors, and nitrazepam. In addition, nightmares can occur during withdrawal from psychoactive substances that inhibit REM sleep, such as alcohol, benzodiazepenes, barbiturates, and amphetamines.

Nightmares are more common among persons who have experienced recent psychological distress. In particular, an unusually stressful experience, or a traumatic event such as rape, combat, or natural disaster, may cause an increase in nightmares, especially nightmares about the stressful event. In such cases the nightmares usually return to normal levels within 6 months. Increases in nightmare frequency have also been reported during depressive episodes and the prodromal phase of schizophrenia. The theory that nightmares can be caused by indigestion was popular in the nineteenth century, but has not been supported by research evidence. Similarly, the popular modern belief that nightmares can be caused by a scary movie or a TV show is supported only by anecdotal evidence and may be untrue.

Some individuals report experiencing chronic distress from nightmares. However, nightmare distress is only moderately related to nightmare frequency, and in some cases the distress caused by nightmares may be due to their content rather than their number. Several studies suggest that lifetime nightmare sufferers may exhibit generally elevated levels of psychopathology. Hartmann (1984) has also argued that chronic nightmare sufferers have "thin psychological boundaries," an openness to experience that he believes to be related to both creativity and psychopathology.

An especially distressing type of nightmare involves false awakenings, in which the individual dreams that he or she has awakened in the same room where he or she fell asleep. Bizarre and frightening nightmare experiences may then follow. Nightmares of this type tend to be unusually vivid and lifelike, and the dreamer may have difficulty believing afterward that they were "just a dream." Little is known about these nightmares, although they typically seem to occur at sleep onset or at the very end of the night.

Two treatments for chronic nightmares have been shown to be effective in controlled studies. The first is systematic desensitization. In this approach, the therapist and client construct a hierarchy of nightmare events, ranked from least to most disturbing, and then follow the common protocol for systematic desensitization. The second treatment is imagery rehearsal. In this approach, the client is asked to "rewrite" the plot of a nightmare to make it more positive, then visualize it in its new, more positive form. As may be seen, both systematic desensitization and imagery rehearsal involve imaginal exposure to nightmare events.

Some individuals report that their nightmares occur at the very end of the night (as in false awakenings). Such nightmares can sometimes be eliminated simply by limiting sleep to 8 hours and giving up the pleasure of "sleeping in" in the morning.

[*See also* Dreams; Night Terrors; *and* Sleep Disorders.]

Bibliography

American Psychiatric Association. (1994). *Diagnostic and statistical manual of mental orders* (4th ed.). Washington, DC: Author.

Belicki, K. (1992). Nightmare frequency versus nightmare distress: Relations to psychopathology and cognitive style. *Journal of Abnormal Psychology, 101,* 592–597.

Ferber, R. (1985). *Solve your child's sleep problems.* New York: Simon & Schuster.

Hartmann, E. (1984). *The nightmare.* New York: Basic Books.

Hunt, H. T. (1989). *The multiplicity of dreams.* New Haven, CT: Yale University Press.

Krakow, B., Kellner, R., Pathak, D., & Lambert, L. (1995). Imagery rehearsal treatment for chronic nightmares. *Behaviour Research and Therapy, 33,* 837–843.

Miller, W. R., & DiPilato, M. (1983). Treatment of nightmares via relaxation and desensitization: A controlled evaluation. *Journal of Consulting and Clinical Psychology, 51,* 870–877.

Salvio, M. A., Wood, J. M., Schwartz, J., & Eichling, P. S. (1992). Nightmare prevalence in the healthy elderly. *Psychology and Aging, 7,* 324–325.

Wood, J. M., & Bootzin, R. R. (1990). The prevalence of nightmares and their independence from anxiety. *Journal of Abnormal Psychology, 99,* 64–68.

Wood, J. M., Bootzin, R. R., Rosenhan, D., Nolen-Hoeksema, S., & Jourden, F. (1992). Effects of the 1989 San Francisco earthquake on frequency and content of nightmares. *Journal of Abnormal Psychology, 101,* 219–224.

James M. Wood and Christiane Herber

NIGHT TERRORS. A night terror episode is characterized by sudden bolting out of sleep screaming, with a behavior that is a manifestation of intense fear. A night terror episode, also known as a sleep terror, is associated with autonomic arousal, including tachicardia, fast breathing, sweating, increased skin conductance, and increased muscle tone. During a night terror episode an individual will often have incoherent speech, and although the eyes might be open, the individual will typically be nonresponsive to external stimuli. If awakened from a night terror episode an individual will act disoriented and confused. Complete amnesia to these episodes is common, but sometimes there is fragmented recollection of a frightening event.

Classification

The International Classification of Sleep Disorders identifies sleep terrors as an arousal disorder, a subclass of the parasomnias that also includes confusional arousals and sleepwalking. It is common for an individual to experience more than one arousal disorder and to have a family history of arousal disorders. Laboratory sleep studies consistently demonstrate that each of the three arousal disorders typically occurs during the first third of the sleep period as partial arousal from slow-wave sleep. A partial arousal is distinct from both wakefulness and sleep. Normal sleep is characterized by multiple transitions between the sleep stages as well as transitions from sleep to wakefulness. It has been hypothesized that night terrors, and the arousal disorders in general, are a result of an impairment in arousal from sleep. Because arousal thresholds from slow-wave sleep are high, it is not surprising that an impairment of the arousal mechanism is manifested during this stage of deep sleep as a failure to completely arouse from sleep.

Prevalence and Developmental Course

Although lifetime incidence of night terror is not uncommon (estimated at approximately 20% of the population), frequent night terrors occur in a small proportion of the population, with a prevalence of 1 to 3%

during childhood and less than 1% during adulthood (mostly before age 30). When the onset of night terrors is during the first decade of life, the disorder tends to spontaneously remit during adolescence, paralleling the developmental decrease in the amount of slow-wave sleep. Night terrors are also more prevalent in males than in females.

Although sleep terrors rarely result in injuries to self or others, the incident is often embarrassing to the patient. Children with night terrors are embarrassed to spend the night away from home. Adults with the disorder often seek help when they plan a trip. Family members (and patients) tend to be concerned about the patient's mental health. In reality, the prevalence of psychiatric disorders among children with night terrors is comparable to that of the general pediatric population. In contrast, there appears to be higher incidence of psychiatric disorders among adults with night terrors compared with the general adult population.

Precipitating and Exacerbating Factors

For individuals with a biological predisposition, they can be precipitated or worsened during periods of insufficient sleep, when the increase in sleep debt leads to greater amounts of slow-wave sleep and the likelihood of a partial arousal increases. The most common causes of sleep deprivation are self or environmentally imposed sleep restrictions. In Western cultures, individuals who need more than average amounts of sleep are at a particularly high risk for sleep deprivation, as are preschoolers whose naps have been prematurely terminated. In addition, some sleep disorders, such as sleep apnea or periodic limb movement of sleep, are associated with fragmented nonrestorative sleep that increases sleep debt. Other factors that may precipitate or worsen sleep terrors include fever, stress, and use of central nervous sytem (CNS) depressants (e.g., alcohol or presciption medications that are CNS depressants).

Differential Diagnosis

Several sleep-related phenomena need to be distinguished from night terrors. These include nightmares, nocturnal panic attacks, REM behavior disorder, and sleep-related epilepsy. Unlike sleep terrors, nightmares and REM behavior disorders occur during REM sleep, and as a result occur primarily during the latter half of sleep. In addition, the cognition associated with a night terror lacks the vividness, details, and storylike features of nightmares. Instead, following a sleep terror, individuals are more likely to describe their experience in nonspecific terms, such as "It is going to get me." On the other hand, the fear associated with a nocturnal panic episode is usually a vague fear of impeding

doom that is usually not associated with a specific fearful imagery and not accompanied by a scream. Unlike sleep terrors, nocturnal panic episodes typically occur during the transition between stages 2 and 3. Finally, nocturnal seizures share some important clinical features with sleep terrors. These include the difficulty to arouse during the event, confusion upon arousal, and the fact that nocturnal seizures occur more frequently during non-REM sleep. An important clinical feature distinguishing the two is the daytime sleepiness that is present following nocturnal seizures and absent following sleep terrors. A conclusive differential diagnosis between the two can be done using a sleep study. When the clinical presentation suggests the possibility of a seizure disorder, an all-night sleep study can assist the differential diagnosis. Sleep terrors are not associated with daytime EEG abnormalities.

Treatment

One of the most important components of nonpharmacological treatments of sleep terrors is the prevention of sleep deprivation through the restructuring of the sleep-wake schedule. This is seldom an easy task because it often necessitates changes in daytime activity schedules to accommodate a nap and/or to allow for a longer sleep period. Identification of a psychological stressor and the introduction of stress management and stress reduction interventions, including relaxation techniques, is another important component of treatment. A third component, scheduled awakenings, is used primarily when sleep terrors occur nightly. Its first step is monitoring the temporal placement of the sleep terror episodes. This is usually done by an individual who lives with the patient. If these episodes follow a recognizable pattern, then a schedule of awakening is set in which the patient is awakened about 10 minutes prior to the anticipated time of an episode. The awakening can be done by another person or by using an external devise such as an alarm clock. If no temporal pattern of the episodes emerges, then the patient can be awakened at the first signs of autonomic arousal during sleep. Of course, this necessitates the involvement of another person who is willing to monitor the patient. Finally, informing the patients and their family about night terrors often corrects misperception and reduces worry and concern. Providing a safe sleep environment becomes important when night terrors are associated with high-risk behaviors. Pharmacological interventions, seldom indicated for children, include hypnotic medications and other medications that suppress slow-wave sleep (e.g., tricyclic antidepressants). One concern with the long-term use of pharmacological agents with children is the potential negative effects on the child's development. Short-term use of hypnotic medication is particularly helpful for adults during periods of time in which they sleep in an environment other than their own.

[*See also* Dreams; Nightmares; *and* Sleep Disorders.]

Bibliography

Rosen, G., Mahowald, M. W., & Ferber, R. (1995). Sleep-walking, confusional arousals, and sleep terrors in the child. In R. Ferber & M. Kryger (Eds.), *Principles and practices of sleep medicine in the child* (pp. 99–106). Philadelphia: Saunders.

Rachel Manber

NISSEN, HENRY WIEGHORST (1901–1958), American comparative psychologist. Born to a German American family in Chicago, Illinois, Henry Nissen received a bachelor's degree in English from the University of Illinois in Champaign-Urbana in 1923. With the death of his father, a bookkeeper, and the subsequent strain in family finances, he had to take time off from his education to work before attending graduate school. Nissen eventually studied with Carl Warden at Columbia University, completing a Ph.D. degree in 1929 for work in which he measured drives in rats using a Columbia Obstruction Box apparatus. [*See the biography of Warden.*]

Nissen spent most of the rest of his career in research with great apes in association with Robert Yerkes and his colleagues at Yale University and the Yerkes Laboratories of Primate Biology in Orange Park, Florida. He was the assistant director of the Yerkes Laboratories from 1939 until 1955 and the director from 1955 until his death.

Nissen worked in varying capacities, becoming the world's leading expert on the biology and behavior of chimpanzees. He conducted a pioneering field study in French Guinea, in 1929, concluding that the acquisition of resources was relatively easy for the animals and that much of their energy was devoted to emotional expression and social interactions. Despite various illnesses that affected his career efforts, Nissen was closely involved in day-to-day work with captive animals at the Yerkes Laboratories and developed an unusual touch in working with them.

Nissen's psychology was strongly based in the study of motivation. He thought that sequences of behavior are composed of clusters of independent acts, each with its own motivation. Comparative studies, he believed, had to be started with complete descriptions of the units from which complex behavior is built. However, he thought that it is the complex psychological units, not the behavioral elements, that manifest purpose and relate to the adaptations of animals to their environments.

There was a strong developmental flavor to Nissen's efforts. He treated the nature-nurture distinction as a continuum, rather than a dichotomy, and advocated careful, systematic developmental studies. Beginning in 1939 Nissen conducted a long-term normative study of the physical and psychobiological growth of chimpanzees. The study was later expanded to analyze the effects of different environmental conditions on development. Rearing chimpanzees with restricted social interactions resulted in disturbances of sexual and other behaviors.

Nissen conducted a variety of studies of learning in chimpanzees, generally using complex tasks such as the delayed response problem and delayed alternation. He concluded that his subjects showed some evidence of symbolic processes, but only of a rudimentary kind. He further believed that they showed evidence of intentions, expectations, and satisfactions, but that such concepts, though useful in designing experiments, had no place in formal psychology.

Nissen was a shy and self-effacing man who was more concerned with developing a firmly grounded comparative psychology than in promoting his accomplishments. Although he laid the foundation for much subsequent comparative psychology, his work is rarely cited today. Nevertheless, he was honored in his time, for example, by election to the National Academy of Sciences.

Bibliography

Carmichael, L. (1965). Henry Wieghorst Nissen, February 5, 1901–April 27, 1958. *Biographical memoirs, National Academy of Sciences of the United States of America* (Vol. 38, pp. 205–222). New York: Columbia University Press.

Dewsbury, D. A. (1997). Henry W. Nissen: Quiet comparative psychologist. In G. A. Kimble, C. A. Boneau, & M. Wertheimer (Eds.), *Portraits of pioneers in psychology* (Vol. 3, pp. 229–242). Washington, DC: APA Books. 1998.

Nissen, H. W. (1931). A field study of the chimpanzee. *Comparative Psychology Monographs, 8* (No. 36).

Nissen, H. W. (1951). Phylogenetic comparison. In S. S. Stevens (Ed.), *Handbook of experimental psychology* (pp. 347–386). New York: Wiley.

Nissen, H. W. (1958). Axes of behavioral comparison. In A. Roe & G. G. Simpson (Eds.), *Behavior and evolution* (pp. 183–205). New Haven, CT: Yale University Press.

Riesen, A. H. (1958). Henry Wieghorst Nissen: 1901–1958. *American Journal of Psychology, 71,* 795–798.

Riesen, A. H. (1971). Nissen's observations on the development of sexual behavior in captive-born, nursery-reared chimpanzees. In G. H. Bourne (Ed.), *The chimpanzee* (Vol. 4, pp. 1–18). Basel: Karger.

Donald A. Dewsbury

**NOMOTHETIC AND IDIOGRAPHIC ORIENTA-
TIONS.** The distinction between nomothetic and idiographic approaches to the pursuit of knowledge was formulated by the German philosopher Wilhelm Windelband in *Geschichte und Naturwissenschaft* (History and Natural Science, Strassburg, 1894). Windelband noted that any object can be viewed in either of two ways: as a representative of a class, manifesting the properties of that class, and reacting in accordance with all laws governing the class; or as an individual entity with features distinguishing it from the general class. The purpose of the distinction, in this original formulation, was to distinguish between the characteristic perspectives of natural science and history. Windelband regarded this distinction between nomothetic and idiographic perspectives as applicable to all scientific disciplines, and he saw the two perspectives as simultaneously incommensurate. The idiographic approach is *not* the assessment of individual values of variables included in the general laws of nomothetic science. Nevertheless, Windelband regarded nomothetic and idiographic orientations as complementary approaches if adopted alternately.

In most sciences, and in most areas of psychology, the nomothetic orientation is dominant. Whether the unit of analysis is a subatomic particle, a mountain range, or the social behavior of the chimpanzee, the scientific orientation is usually aimed toward the search for general mechanisms and laws. But when the unit of analysis is a person, the idiographic approach promises an understanding of the unique, individual characteristics of that person; a kind of understanding that is different from knowledge of the general laws that govern the behavior of persons. In those areas of psychology where the person is the unit of analysis (e.g., personality, developmental, or clinical psychology), the idiographic approach has appeal.

Gordon Allport's *Personality: A Psychological Interpretation* (New York, 1937) introduced Windelband's terms to American psychologists, and the landmark status of this text served to keep the issue of idiographic and nomothetic perspectives a part of the conceptual framework of personality psychology through successive generations of readers, to the present. A central theme in Allport's work is that the nomothetic perspective, though admittedly useful for many purposes, cannot provide an account of human individuality. At the core of Allport's argument is the observation that "personality" refers to processes occurring within an individual, and that research and theory built on variables summarizing individual differences can offer little insight into such processes. Vigorous debate followed Allport's championing of idiographic approaches. Holt's 1962 article, "Individuality and Generalization in the Psychology of Personality" (*Journal of Personality, 30*, 377–404), urged that further discussion be discontinued because the idiographic-nomothetic distinction added little of substance to either theoretical or empirical endeavors, and explicit discussion of the topic subsequently waned and nomotheticism continued to dominate psychological research. Lamiell (1987) has suggested that Allport's characterization of idiographic analysis as akin to procedures in art and literature and beyond the reach of scientific methods contributed to the failure of Allport's point of view.

The nomothetic approach of contemporary psychology might be idealized as including a major focus on how psychological processes work in the typical individual (i.e., general psychological laws), with individual variation constituting "noise" in this systematic investigation. A subsidiary focus (the study of individual differences) seeks to understand this variation as specific values of variables included in the general laws. Experimental, quasi-experimental, and correlational methods utilizing human participants, animal subjects, and tissue samples characterize this approach. In virtually all cases, multiple individuals are studied.

Contemporary idiographic psychology includes a spectrum of alternatives to the predominant nomothetic orientation. Some fully endorse a version of Windelband's original dichotomy to argue for the intrinsic merits of both perspectives while noting the relative imbalance in actual practice (e.g., Runyan, 1982). Single-subject methods, especially narrative life history, are used to illuminate specific, unique features in the attributes of individuals selected for study due to their historical importance, theoretical relevance, or compelling human interest. Other strands of idiographic psychology ignore or reject Windelband's incommensurability claim. Lamiell (1987), for example, alters the entire epistemological framework so that an "idiothetic" integration of idiographic and nomothetic orientations is achieved. Runyan follows Allport in accepting Windelband's claim of incommensurability between idiographic and nomothetic views; Lamiel rejects this.

For a variety of reasons, contemporary proponents of idiographic and nomothetic perspectives have adopted a more pluralistic stance; and are less likely to be engaged in vigorous arguments with one another about fundamental scientific values. In this sense, Holt's view has carried the day. It must be noted that this pluralism was long a component of the worldview of those identified with the idiographic orientation, who long recognized the value of nomotheticism. This view is clearly articulated in Kluckhohn and Murray's (1953) observation that each person is like all people in some ways, like some people in other ways, and in some ways fully unique. Champions of the idiographic approach sought to promote their orientation to the status of equal. Nomotheticists did not reciprocate: Little of value was attributed to the idiographic perspective.

This lack of contemporary debate does not mean that the issues are settled. Rather, in the course of this long-standing argument, there seems to have developed a recognition that Windelband's initial dichotomy can be construed as a challenge: How shall psychology formulate general laws of behavior and universal mechanisms while simultaneously being attuned to the unique, individuating characteristics of each person? Many adherents of both nomothetic and idiographic perspectives actively seek to solve this problem, and progress in achieving this end has made this issue much less contentious.

This progress is apparent in methodological, empirical, and theoretical domains; and both idiographers and nomotheticists have contributed. Statistical procedures (e.g., hierarchical linear modeling) have evolved to permit consideration of the individual within the larger aggregate. Insight into long-standing empirical problems (e.g., the person-situation controversy) arising in nomothetic psychology has been obtained by invoking idiographic considerations (e.g., Bem & Allen, 1974), and theoretical frameworks for integrating idiographic and nomothetic concepts are beginning to appear (e.g., McAdams, 1995). Nomotheticists' reservations that idiographic perspectives cannot aid in the formulation of general laws and mechanisms are refuted by recent counterexamples, including script theory (Tomkins, 1987), which is both closely tied to individual experience but broadly applicable to persons in general.

Perhaps the most recalcitrant issue within the spectrum of argument subsumed by these orientations to knowledge is the utility of narrative methodologies. Idiographic psychology understands the narrative as a fundamental form of psychological data and the appropriate means of representing psychological theory (Barresi & Juckes, 1997). Nomothetic psychology seeks to quickly transform narrative data (when obtained at all) to quantitative indicators; and sees the narrative representation of theory as a temporary substitute for a fully quantified science. Controversy surrounding the relative merits of quantitative and qualitative methods in psychology is, in principle, separable from the idiographic-nomothetic distinction; but the idiographic psychology of today is the narrative understanding of individual lives. It is this endeavor that fully distinguishes it from a pluralistic nomothetic psychology which has yet to discover how to use such accounts to further its own scientific ends. The duality of interests among practitioners of the human sciences, as depicted by Windelband, will likely endure in psychology. For a science, the formulation of general laws and mechanisms underlying psychological processes is paramount; for a human science, the search for understanding of ourselves and those around us will always lead to a particular interest in the specifics of time, place, and person that constitute unique individuality.

Bibliography

Barresi, J. & Juckes, T. J. (1997). Personology and the narrative interpretation of lives. *Journal of Personality, 65,* 693–719. An up-to-date survey of narrative methods employed by idiographic psychology.

Bem, D. J., & Allen, A. (1974). On predicting some of the people some of the time: The search for cross-situational consistencies in behavior. *Psychological Review, 81,* 506–520. In this now classic study, quasi-idiographic methods were used to help resolve an enduring controversy concerning the cross-situational consistency of behavior.

Kluckhohn, C., & Murray, H. A. (1953). Personality formation: The determinants. In C. Kluckhohn, H. A. Murray, & D. Schneider (Eds.), *Personality in nature, society, and culture.* New York: Knopf.

Lamiell, J. T. (1987). *The psychology of personality: An epistemological inquiry.* New York: Columbia University Press. The entire philosophic foundation leading to the idiographic-nomothetic distinction is reexamined and found wanting. Lamiell's "idiothetic" perspective argues for a radical change in psychological theory, method, and measurement.

McAdams, D. P. (1995). What do we know when we know a person. *Journal of Personality, 63,* 365–396. The often abstruse difference between idiographic and nomothetic orientations is vivified by placing it in the context of everyday social interaction, and further elaborated by linking this analysis to different kinds, or levels, of understanding.

Runyan, W. M. (1984). *Life histories and psychobiography: Explorations in theory and method.* New York: Oxford University Press. This volume provides an articulate description and justification for narrative life history in psychology.

Tomkins, S. S. (1987). Script theory. In J. Aronoff, A. I. Rabin, & R. A. Zucker (Eds.), *The emergence of personality* (pp. 147–215). New York: Springer.

Daniel J. Ozer

NON-DIRECTIVE THERAPY. *See* Client-Centered Therapy.

NONHUMAN COMMUNICATION. Understanding nonhuman communication is important for psychologists. Understanding the diversity of communication modalities provides an understanding of the sensory and perceptual processes that extend beyond the limitations of human sensory abilities. Understanding how nonhuman species use communication to manage their social interactions suggests mechanisms for improving human social communication. Models of the ontogeny of communication developed from nonhuman species have had direct relevance to theories of language development. Recent research illustrating the complexity of communication in both natural systems of nonhuman animals as well as in training animals in the use of language analogues suggests that the communication of humans and nonhumans share important evolutionary continuities.

Modalities

Human language is vocal, and much research on nonhuman species has focused on vocal communication. The development of tape recording and sound spectrographic equipment for preserving and analyzing human speech led to extensive studies of auditory communication in other species. The auditory stimulus can be defined precisely in terms of frequency, amplitude, and temporal pattern, and synthetic sounds can be created to test the perception of signals. Bird song has been the most studied phenomenon, with documentation of song structure and complexity, the mechanisms of vocal production, both brain structures and peripheral mechanisms, and mechanisms of perception. Vocal communication in insects and nonhuman primates has also received extensive attention. Communication extends beyond the human auditory range. Elephants and whales use very low frequency infrasound to communicate over long distances, and bats and many rodents use high-frequency ultrasound to communicate with high resolution over short distances.

Visual communication has received less study than vocal signals. Visual signals are less easily described than auditory signals, and only recently, with the advent of computer graphics, has it been possible to manipulate or synthesize visual signals. Color, shape, movement, and contrast are all critical features of visual signals.

Chemical signals are even less accessible to human observers, but many insects use chemical signals to locate mates, deter predators, mark trails, and communicate membership in social groups. Many mammals use chemical signals to mark territories, attract mates, indicate fear or alarm, communicate reproductive status, and even manipulate reproduction in other group members. For example, marmosets and tamarins, small neotropical monkeys, use odors to suppress ovulation in subordinate females, and human female axillary odors can shift menstrual cycle length in other women.

Several species of fish use electrical pulses produced by specialized muscles to communicate in murky waters. Several frogs and kangaroo rats use seismic signals produced by thumping their legs on the ground.

Evolution of Signal Structure

Within each modality, environmental and social variables shape signal structure. For many small birds and primates, the alarm calls given upon detecting a predator are high-pitched whistles with little frequency modulation and slowly rising and falling amplitude ramps. These features minimize psychophysical features for sound localization. In contrast, calls used to attract group members to attack a predator are lower pitched, short, and with much frequency modulation, features that allow other group members to locate the caller easily. Both alarm calls and mobbing calls are often similar across several species living in the same area. Signals used for mate attraction also are structured to be highly conspicuous, but in contrast to mobbing calls provide highly specific information about the identity of the signaler. The songs of birds and the territorial calls of many nonhuman primates often can be discriminated by species, subspecies, sex, reproductive condition and individual. Each of these variables provides information that might be useful to the decision-making of a potential mate. So robust are species' and subspecies' distinctive features that signal structure has been a valuable trait in deriving the phylogeny and taxonomy of several species.

Animals communicating threat or aggression often use signals that provide exaggerated views of their size: a low-frequency growl or bark makes the signaler seem larger than reality, and fluffing feathers or piloerecting hair creates a larger-than-life visual image. In contrast, a submissive or retreating animal is likely to make itself appear smaller through higher pitched sounds or sleeking its feathers or hair.

Environmental variables constrain signal structure: Low-frequency sounds travel around environmental obstacles but allow for less signal complexity and spatial resolution. In forest environments there appears to be a frequency "window" where sound travels farthest, and many forest animals utilize this frequency for long distance calls. Sounds travel farther at dawn due to atmospheric conditions that create an acoustic lens reflecting sound downward toward the ground; thus it is not surprising that most birds and many monkeys sing or call mainly at dawn. For example, the pygmy marmoset, the world's smallest monkey, calls at a frequency range that is above the frequency of most environmental noise and beyond the most sensitive hearing range of its major predators. These monkeys also adjust the structure of their contact calls according to how far they are from other group members, producing calls that are increasingly easy to localize the farther they are from other group members.

Visual signals are most useful when animals are close to each other, live in open areas, and are active in daylight, whereas vocal signals are more common in forest-dwelling or nocturnal animals. Chemical signals have a unique advantage in being active long after the communicator has moved away from the scent, providing an ideal means of avoiding detection by predators. Odors of low molecular weight are more volatile and diffuse farther, but can provide less specific and detailed information than large molecular weight odors that do not diffuse far. Many olfactory signals combine chemicals of different volatility so that distant recipients can be attracted by small molecules to the source of the more complex odors that convey more precise information.

Models of Development

Studies of vocal development, particularly of bird song, have influenced views of child language development. Four competing views of song learning have been dominant. Age-based learning argues that exposure to song must occur within a critical or sensitive period and that the tutoring that a bird experiences must fit within a perceptual template that limits the range of what can be learned. Action-based learning argues that an organism at birth has the potential for producing many different sounds, but that social interactions select certain sounds that will remain in the repertoire while others will be extinguished. Social-based learning argues that there is neither a sensitive period nor a selective attrition of signals and that communication signals are constantly shaped by the responses of current social companions. A final model is that communication is genetically based, with little or no subsequent modification. Examples in support of each model can be found in different species, suggesting that the differing ecological and social variables affecting each species may constrain the type of development seen. Highly precocious species may have a genetically based song, sedentary species may develop age-based learning of song, and migrating species or species that change social group membership frequently may show action-based or socially based learning.

Less evidence has been adduced for vocal learning in mammals, but recent demonstrations of vocal modification in species as diverse as bats, dolphins, kangaroo rats, and nonhuman primates suggest a potential for vocal learning. Interestingly, the most mobile mammals, dolphins and bats, demonstrate the clearest plasticity of vocal development.

Most research has focused on the development of production of signals, but there are two equally important aspects of communication: comprehension and appropriate usage. There appears to be greater plasticity in comprehension than production, with several demonstrations that mammals can learn to understand the signals of other species. Appropriate social models may be necessary for learning how and when to use signals appropriately.

Complexity

The relative complexity of communication becomes important in using nonhuman animal communication as a basis for understanding how human language evolved. Some have argued that nonhuman animal signals are limited in number. However, close analyses of nonhuman primate vocalizations have found subtle variation analogous to the subtle variation among human phonemes. Thus, calls that seem similar to a human ear have been parsed into several discrete variants, each of which is a different context. Even when discrete call types cannot be found, complexity can be coded through continuous gradations along a continuum of signal structure. Many animal communication systems have more complex repertoires than might seem apparent on first observation.

Historically, much of what animals communicate about was thought to be mainly emotive or motivational: hunger, sex, fear, threat. Several studies on nonhuman primates and birds have indicated the ability to communicate about specific referents. Thus, many species have different alarm calls for aerial versus terrestrial predators; vervet monkeys communicate even more precisely about the presence of eagles, leopards, and snakes. Playback studies demonstrate that monkeys "understand" that a specific call represents a specific type of predator. A variety of animals have specialized signals to indicate that food has been discovered. In macaques, variations in screams given by infants communicate to mothers information about the rank and degree of threat posed by an opponent of the infant.

The structures of many signals follow simple grammatical rules. In black-capped chickadees, the "chickadee" call has four notes that follow one of two patterns: A to D or B to C to D. Less than 0.03% of the calls recorded violate either of these rules. Many neotropical primate species produce complex sequences of calls made up of components and are used individually as well. In some cases these sequences preserve the meanings of the individual calls, analogous to forming phrases or sentences from individual words.

Many examples suggest that animal signals are not simply reflexive, but are responsive to social and environmental conditions. Thus, chickens do not produce alarm calls to predators unless other chickens are nearby, and cocks do not produce food calls in the presence of rival cocks, but only in the presence of a hen. Some monkeys demonstrate an understanding of the social structure of their groups, such as indicating which infants belong to which mothers, and discriminating the calls of one's matriline compared with other, rival matrilines. Deliberate deception has been demonstrated in the communication of some species of great apes.

Great apes and other species trained to use language analogues, such as computer-based arbitrary symbols, can learn to use a large number of symbols to communicate about objects, locations, and motivation. Demonstrations of counting, the ability to parse arbitrary symbols into components, and to understand the knowledge of companions have illustrated how cognitive complexity can be illuminated through studies of communication.

Coordination of Communication

Many animals carefully coordinate communication by duetting or turn-taking. In many tropical songbirds and several species of monogamous primates, duets are produced between mates. The close coordination of these duets with little silent space between the calls of one individual and another suggest close social interactions in which the precise timing of calling can be learned. These duets are thought to serve the dual function of repelling potential intruders that might disrupt the pair bond and to reinforce the social relationship between pair mates, though not all examples of duetting can be so easily explained. Some species show antiphonal calling between more than two individuals, which suggests turn-taking with a clear sequence of callers. Thus, each individual calls once before others call twice. Such turn-taking could be used to identify all members of a group and coordinate group movement in areas where visual contact between group members is difficult.

Animals may mark changes in social relationships within groups by altering signals to match those of companions. When birds form new flocks, several individuals will frequently converge on a specific call type or song type. Starlings within a group that have a close affiliation as measured by time spent in close proximity tend to share song types with each other. Bats and primates that join new groups will alter call structure to converge with new social companions. In squirrel monkeys, a specific call has been found that is exchanged only between females that have a close social relationship, and duetting or turn-taking have been observed.

Bibliography

Bradbury, J. W., & Vehrencamp, S. L. (1998). *Principles of animal communication.* Sunderland, MA: Sinauer. An integrative text on communication emphasizing the physics and physiology of signal propagation and reception, the evolution of cooperative communication, and how communication is influenced when sender and recipient do not share the same interests.

Catchpole, C. K., & Slater, P. J. B. (1995). *Bird song: Biological themes and variations.* Cambridge, UK: Cambridge University Press. An introduction to the structure, function, and ontogeny of bird song written for a general audience, with excellent illustrations.

Cheney, D. L., & Seyfarth, R. M. (1990). *How monkeys see the world.* Chicago: University of Chicago Press. An excellent monograph summarizing the authors' research on the complex vocal communication and social cognition abilities of vervet monkeys. Several excellent models for experimentation in field conditions are described, as are some of the curious limitations of understanding by the monkeys.

Hailman, J. P. (1978). *Optical signals.* Bloomington: Indiana University Press. The only comprehensive volume on visual communication, illustrating how visual signals are produced and perceived, using psychophysical principles.

Hauser, M. D. (1996). *The evolution of communication.* Cambridge, MA: MIT Press. A comprehensive text on communication providing a levels of analysis approach: neurophysiological, ontogenetic, functional, and psychological, with emphasis on evolutionary principles that could lead from animal communication to human language. Primary focus on audition and vision.

King, B. J. (1994). *The information continuum: Evolution of social information transfer in monkeys apes and hominids* Santa Fe, NM: SAR Press. Discusses differences in information transfer between monkeys and apes and suggests a continuity of information transfer processes from monkeys through hominids to modern humans.

Kroodsma, D. E., & Miller, E. H., Jr. (Eds.). (1996). *Ecology and evolution of acoustic communication in birds.* Ithaca, NY: Cornell University Press. An edited volume of up-to-date research on all aspects of how birds communicate: ecological and evolutionary aspects, perception of calls, ontogeny, neural control of vocal production, use of communication in mate attraction, mate choice, aggression, and affiliation.

Snowdon, C. T. (1990). Language capacities of nonhuman animals. *Yearbook of Physical Anthropology, 33,* 215–243. A review article that summarizes research on language analogue studies (signing and computer training) and then reviews aspects of natural communication in nonhuman species that might be related to language: ontogeny, syntax, referential or symbolic signals, audience effects, deception, perception, and neurological parallels.

Snowdon, C. T., & Hausberger, M. (Eds.). (1997). *Social influences on vocal development.* Cambridge, UK: Cambridge University Press. Chapters by scientists studying bird songs and other vocalizations, dolphins, nonhuman primates, and children demonstrating the role of social influences in vocal development and showing a general continuity of vocal development across many taxa.

Charles T. Snowdon

NONHUMAN INTELLIGENCE. Although animals have always been recognized as remarkable for their variety, beauty, adaptations, and behavior, at the dawn of the twentieth century most people characterized animals by a single mental attribute: dumbness. Even today the Cartesian view that animals are senseless "beast-machines" probably is more commonly believed than is Darwin's postulate that organisms are continuous with humans on biological and psychological dimensions. G. J. Romanes attempted to provide scientific evidence for the intelligence of nonhuman animals, first by collecting and reporting anecdotes in an 1882 book called *Animal Intelligence*. This effort, and more specifically the anecdotal method he used, was so ridiculed that the whole concept of animal intelligence was discredited. One of his critics was the American psychologist Edward L. Thorndike, who meticulously and colorfully documented in a series of books and articles—including a book of his own called *Animal Intelligence* (1911)—the mindless trial-and-error behavior of animals in problem boxes. Thorndike concluded that animal learning basically was the gradual establishment of bonds between stimuli and responses formed by the consequences of their successes and mistakes. This conservative and objectivistic attitude was the basis of the school of behaviorism founded by John B. Watson and supported by the later behaviorists, including B. F. Skinner, Clark L. Hull, Edwin R. Guthrie, and Kenneth W. Spence, all of whom rejected rationality as a parameter of behavior, both human and animal.

During the heyday of behaviorism, opposing views, although rare, were also influential. Robert M. Yerkes unabashedly discussed primate intelligence in his book *The Mental Life of Monkeys and Apes* (New York, 1916), reflecting a comparative perspective that included learning, intelligence, and the mental lives of apes, monkeys, mice, rats, frogs, crabs, turtles, dogs, cats, pigs, and even earthworms. During World War I, Wolfgang Köhler, a cofounder of the school of Gestalt psychology, studied chimpanzees' problem-solving and concluded that it could be insightful rather than just trial and error; that is, apes were able to solve novel problems by reasoning and creativity, not simply by trial and error, as held by Thorndike. In the decades that followed, the avowed behaviorist Edward C. Tolman created a cognitive framework that he called purposive behaviorism to account for maze learning by rats. He ascribed learning to the perception of relationships, called cognitive maps, between stimuli such as those that differentiate between routes to the goal of a complex maze.

The key issue that divided Tolman and Köhler from Thorndike and his followers was how to account for the observed performances of animals. Thorndike pictured the animal as like a machine that generated a series of random responses until one was successful in that a "satisfying state of affairs" ensued. The response was hence "stamped in," or learned, and the probability that the responses would recur in that situation in the future was increased. Clearly this view credits animals with little or no intelligence. Tolman and Köhler viewed organisms as thinking beings that, given the opportunity, would evaluate situations and choose responses that were likely to satisfy a purpose or achieve a goal. Such organisms could learn passively as well as actively, through observing the performances and successes or failures of others.

Harry F. Harlow provided a bridge between these contrasting perspectives in 1949 with his research on learning set, or "learning to learn." Harlow studied changes in learning proficiency by monkeys over long series of problems. Initially their learning was essentially like that of Thorndike's trial-and-error improvement—slow and arduous. With experience, however, the monkeys became increasingly skilled and learned new problems with apparent insight—quickly and nearly errorlessly. Thus, Harlow defined the course (i.e., the operations) whereby certain protracted experiences provide for the emergence of insightful, one-trial learning, even of novel problems of a kind that, initially, required gradual trial-and-error learning.

Meanwhile, European scientists emphasized biology, genetics, and development in founding the science of ethology (the description of animal behavior in the natural environment, as contrasted with "psychology," in which animal behavior is studied using laboratory or field experiments that involve the manipulation and control of variables that influence behavior). The ingenious studies of Konrad Lorenz and Niko Tinbergen yielded the concept of species-specific or instinctual behaviors that are unlearned and adaptive (e.g., courtship routines and imprinting) and that appear at the first opportunity. However, the right experience at a critical time might be necessary in order for the response to become adaptive; for example, goslings learned to follow their mothers only if they saw them during this critical period. If they, instead, saw and followed Lorenz first, they "imprinted" on him as though he were their mother.

Ethologists generally discounted or ignored the types of learning phenomena that psychologists considered to be important indices of animal intelligence. Thus, despite difficulties in establishing productive communication between stimulus-response behaviorists, cognitivists, and ethologists, it is now almost universally accepted that nature and nurture interact to produce the complex behavioral adaptations of both humans and other animals. The biological preparedness of many forms of wildlife to learn rapidly to avoid certain tastes associated with toxins and poisons is a case in point. As the result of a single experience, memory traces for new tastes can be maintained by special networks for many hours to become specifically associated as conditional stimuli "to be avoided" in the future. Hence, bait shyness manifested by predators, after ingesting poisoned meat left in fields by farmers to control predation on their herds by wolves, is the product of an interaction between biology and learning mechanisms. Critics of the manuscript submitted for publication rejected it—the data simply didn't fit within the frameworks of learning that then held sway.

What appeared to be contradictions between the results of early experiments now appear to be the results of disparate paradigms and subjects used in studies of behavior. For example, Gestalt psychologists, among whom Köhler was prominent, argued that Thorndike's puzzle boxes reduced his animals to trial-and-error behavior because the animals were not allowed to see the relationship between means and ends, whereas Köhler's chimpanzees could see these relationships, and hence had the opportunity to manifest insightful learning. Unquestionably, some animal species are less adroit at learning than others, notwithstanding the obvious fact that they are well adapted to their niches. But even the most facile learners can be made to appear relatively "unsmart" if given either a very simple task or given one so difficult or obscure that it cannot be mastered. On the other hand, many animals (but especially those with large, complex brains) can demonstrate impressive intelligence, problem-solving, and even language competence when they are given appropriate training and opportunities to benefit from experience so as to master rules and principles for generalized competence in solving problems in ways not unlike those of humans.

Intelligence

Intelligence is a construct that references special kinds of highly adaptive behaviors. Generally, intelligence is imputed to facile, efficient, and clever learned or acquired behaviors and skills. There are other behaviors, however, that also are facile, efficient, and clever but that are clearly not learned. They are instincts, and are primarily predicated by genetics. How each kind of these ingenious behaviors should be defined and measured is subject to continuing debate. Here biological smartness will be differentiated from psychological intelligence as the point of departure in defining animal intelligence.

Biological smartness is used here to reference behaviors that are highly adaptive yet primarily dictated by genetics and maturation within the ecological niches appropriate to various species. Various species' patterns of migration, reproduction, foraging, communicating, and so forth are familiar markers and serve as examples of biological smartness. They are instinctive behaviors and/or response patterns that characterize various species. They may require specific age-linked experiences that are generally assured in the species' natural niches. There are still other kinds of behavioral systems that, while less specifically guaranteed by biology and genetics, equally distinguish species. Thus, gorilla in-

fants find it relatively easy to learn gorilla ways, but not those of leopards. Similarly, the challenge of becoming a competent gorilla is beyond the capacity of a chimpanzee or orangutan or human child who, in turn, have their own genotypes that direct their general styles of behaving and learning. Although biologically predicted behaviors clearly fulfill many species' needs "smartly," their parameters are quite different from those of the next more commonly defined type of intelligence.

Psychological intelligence contrasts with biological smartness in that it is not instinctive. We regard psychological intelligence as the potential to learn quickly and to solve problems creatively. To do so entails the capacity to transfer learning of the past in ways that gain an leveraged advantage for the individual as it encounters new contexts, problems, and challenges. Because differences exist both within and between species in psychological intelligence, it is not divorced from biology. Psychological intelligence clearly is related to learning, memory, the speed of information processing, problem solving, and language. Although it might be viewed as having a core that is global or "general," it appears best to view it as having several more specific dimensions—for example, social, verbal, or performance intelligence.

It is only reasonable that we as humans are curious about whether animals are intelligent in ways that characterize our own intelligence, but it is also important to remember that our intelligence has an evolutionary history. Thus, some animals, notably the apes, might have certain dimensions of intelligence that are similar to ours, though limited. Indeed they do. But it is very important to acknowledge that animal intelligence is organized to service their own adaptations in highly varied ecological niches. They can be highly intelligent in ways that are quite unlike ours. We have yet to identify their kinds of intelligence satisfactorily so as to measure our human abilities against their standards. By eventually doing so, however, the risks of anthropocentricity will be minimized.

It is not surprising that the many issues that rage in debate on the topic of human intelligence are also critical for studies of animal intelligence: How can one measure animal intelligence in equitable ways for valid comparison between individuals or species? What are the different kinds of intelligence, or qualitatively different ways in which intelligence can be manifested? What is the relationship between intelligence and brain? How are different dimensions of intelligence subject to early environment and rearing variables?

Attempts to quantify differences in animal intelligence have frequently focused on variations in the ability to learn. Learning can take various forms, some of which we view as reflections of more intelligence than others. Basic forms of Pavlovian and operant conditioning are so ubiquitous—observed in organisms like flatworms (*Aplysia*) as readily as in humans—that "readiness to be conditioned" cannot serve as a meaningful dimension along which to evaluate the intelligence of animals. Efforts to quantify intelligence based on learning rate or asymptote are similarly unreliable. More complex processes and behaviors permit more promising methods for discriminating different levels of intelligence in animals, as they do in humans.

We believe that a highly defensible way of assessing intelligence across animal species is based on the ability to transfer measured amounts of prior learning to new contexts. Thus, rather than comparing the speed with which chimpanzees versus rhesus monkeys versus capuchins, for example, learn a new problem (e.g., that a treat is hidden beneath a red triangle but not beneath a black cube), each animal first learns or achieves a level of performance accuracy defined by specified criteria (e.g., until the animals are correct on two thirds of the trials). Transfer-of-learning test trials are then given in a slightly altered context; for example, the valences of objects comprising a problem are reversed (e.g., the treat is hidden beneath the black object but not the red one). One can then measure how well the animals will transfer their learning to a limited number of test trials. The ratio of performance (i.e., percentage of correct choices) on reversal trials to prereversal or acquisition trials, obtained from a series of problems so administered, is known as the transfer index. It is based on learning set procedures. Transfer index values have been obtained for a variety of animal species, particularly those in the primate order. In general, transfer index values increase as one compares from prosimians to New World monkeys to Old World monkeys to lesser apes to great apes.

Additionally, transfer index methodology, first formulated by Duane Rumbaugh in 1969, allows assessment of the direction and degree of the transfer of learning. Continuing the example, would capuchin monkeys be more or less likely to transfer their learning (i.e., to look for rewards under the black rather than the red object) if they had learned the original relationship to 84% accuracy instead of 67%? Would chimpanzees be better or worse at transferring their learning if the prereversal criterion were similarly shifted from 67% to 84%? The direction of transfer refers to whether reversal learning is impaired or improved as the prereversal criterion is raised. If increasing the criterion improves the transfer of learning, the transfer is said to be positive. If making the acquisition criterion more stringent impairs subsequent reversal performance, the transfer is said to be negative.

Examination of the direction and degree of the transfer of learning across primate species reveals systematic species differences in intelligence. The prosimians, relatively small and primitive, tend to manifest very negative transfer. Small New World monkeys, like capuchins, typically show slightly less but still negative transfer. In this situation, Old World monkeys transfer their learning from strongly negative (particularly true of the small talapoin) to strongly positive (as with the relatively large rhesus monkey). By contrast, all of the great apes (chimpanzee, bonobo, gorilla, and orangutan—all larger than monkeys) are generally highly positive transferers of learning.

It is important to emphasize that the transition from negative to positive transfer of learning represents a qualitative shift, not just a quantitative one, in animal intelligence. It allows for small amounts of learning to be highly or even extraordinarily adaptative to the interests of solving novel problems in new contexts—a characteristic that perhaps everyone agrees is a manifestation of psychological intelligence. That shift is germane to the emergence of the remarkable levels of intelligence achieved by primates, and notably by the great apes and humans. That qualitative shift, or direction of transferred learning, in relation to the evolution of primate brain size and complexity within the primates order, serves as a prime example of Henry Nissen's (1951) mid-century perspective regarding the interactive productivity of interacting continua through the course of evolution. He anticipated that "quantitative complication may become so great that it produces, in effect, qualitative differences with new, 'emergent' properties." He agreed with Novikoff that "each level of organization possesses unique properties of structure and behavior which, though dependent on the properties of the constituent elements, appear only when these elements are combined in the new system. Knowledge of the laws of the lower level is necessary for a full understanding of the higher level; yet the unique properties of the phenomena at the higher level cannot be predicted, a priori, from the laws of the lower level" (Novikoff, 1945). For intelligence at the human level to be fully understood, it is important that it be pursued within a comparative neuropsychological framework.

Hallmarks of Animal Intelligence

There are, of course, other methods appropriate to studies of animal intelligence. The common theme for these indices of intelligence is emergent processes because they permit operational definitions of different levels and kinds of intelligence beyond those afforded by basic respondent and operant conditioning. Emergent behaviors are not reducible to respondent and operant behaviors, are not specifically reinforced during discrete trial-training procedures, nor are they conditioned to specific conditioned, discriminative stimuli. Rather, they take form and emerge when stimulated by new contexts, and they involve new patterns of behavior that appear to be based on principles or rules. This is not to say that emergent behaviors must lack well-defined antecedents, as we saw in Harlow's learning-to-learn paradigm. For example, contemporary behaviorist Murray Sidman has tracked the emergence of novel relations (i.e., transitivity and equivalence) between stimuli, responses, rewards, and all combinations of these.

Relational Learning. Consider again the transfer index procedure and findings. Are the animals learning a series of stimulus-response associations such as "lifting a particular red object results in a treat"? Or are they learning a rule-like relation or strategy such as "if a treat is beneath a particular type of object, look there next trial; otherwise, shift to the other object"? The capacity to learn relationally or mediationally can be assessed with a variation of the learning-and-reversal procedure. Among primate species, only humans, apes, and macaques (if given extraordinary learning histories) have demonstrated the capacity for mediational learning. Other primates are predisposed or constrained to learn associatively, that is, through stimulus-stimulus or stimulus-response associations. Humans and apes, of course, also learn associatively. However, at least under some circumstances, they can break the bonds of associative learning and extract the more general, rule-like relations that emerge from experience.

Processing Speed. For humans, measures of mental speed (i.e., responding and solving tasks) correlate with intelligence. Relatively fast decision or inspection times are generally associated with high scores on intelligence tests. Comparable correlations have been reported for nonhuman primates, with smarter rhesus monkeys (as indicated by a high transfer of learning, as described above) making faster decisions than those made by less intelligent individuals. The speed-intelligence correlations for monkey data are about the same magnitude as have been reported for humans. Curiously, however, decision times exhibited for nonhuman primates on a variety of tests are reliably faster than those for humans on comparable tests, suggesting the question, "If thinking faster means being smarter, why are humans slower than monkeys?"

Developmental Hallmarks. Jean Piaget formulated a framework for discussing the development of human intelligence, and numerous scientists (including Piaget himself) have applied this model to animal intelligence. Studies of object manipulation and permanence, numerical and inferential reasoning, and tool construction and use have revealed various degrees of intelligent behavior by animals. For example, chimpanzees can imitate the actions of others, such as by playing with a novel tool in a way demonstrated in their presence and generalizing to other ways of using the tool, or even modifying it when these methods are demonstrated. The evidence for true imitation by monkey species is far less compelling, perhaps suggesting that they can learn to produce a single behavior but not to generalize to other contexts. Researchers have concluded that many other species, including birds, rats, and dolphins, can imitate, although the evidence is not equally compelling for all of these species. Other examples of behaviors that illustrate Piagetian hallmarks of intelligence include the ability of pigeons to make transitive inferences, of rats and primates to circumvent novel obstacles in navigation (e.g., detour problem-solving), and of capuchins and bonobos to use tools. Bonobos will, in fact, skillfully knap flint so as to make "stone knives" (Figure 1). Once a satisfactory shard of stone is produced they will use the tool to cut rope or leather so as to gain access to a treat or other object. This skill requires coordination of goal-directed object manipulation and representation of the characteristics of effective stone tools.

Self-Knowledge. For humans, "what you know" is frequently less important than "knowing what you know." That is, an important hallmark of intelligence is the awareness of what one does or does not remember, can or cannot accomplish, is or is not confident about. Some scientists have studied animals' capacity for metacognition (cognition about cognition). Humans, dolphins, and macaques have been shown to monitor their levels of certainty and to respond adaptively to subjective uncertainty. Rats showed a different pattern of behavior, responding to objective stimulus cues with no evidence of self-monitoring.

A different kind of self-knowledge that has been extensively studied is self- or mirror-recognition. It seems clear that some species like chimpanzees can readily recognize their own reflection in a mirror or television screen, and will use the reflected image to explore parts of their bodies that cannot be viewed directly. In contrast, rhesus monkeys and many other primate species respond to their reflections as if they were other members of their species. These animals (like dogs and cats) show no evidence of recognizing themselves in the mirror; rather, they will display and grimace or even race behind the mirror to interact with the unfamiliar conspecific.

Control. The ability to perceive choices and control over one's circumstances is an important hallmark of intelligence. The perception of control distinguishes organisms that respond in a passive way to the bombardment of environmental stimuli from those who actively seek the predictable relations that emerge from experience. The perception of choices and control reduces stress and reliably improves task performance by humans, apes, and monkeys. Doubtless, further investigation will reveal other animals who manifest this emergent hallmark of intelligence.

Social-Cognitive Hallmarks. Some researchers investigate intelligence in terms of the ability to understand what other animals know. Studies of so-called

NONHUMAN INTELLIGENCE. Figure 1. Kanzi (*Pan paniscus*) has helped us to better understand the interaction between genetics and environment. Quite unexpectedly, he came to understand human speech and the meanings of word lexigrams. Without formal training, he became competent in their social communicative use. He could decode the syntax of novel spoken sentences of request, including the meaning of embedded phrases, equal to or better than a precocious 2½-year-old child in controlled tasks. He also could benefit complexly and richly from observations, to wit he has become a skilled flint knapper. He rotates the cobble to strike at edges that will, more likely than others, produce a chip with a sharp edge. That edge is then used promptly, if appropriate to the challenge, to cut cables of nylon and leather to open containers holding incentives that otherwise could not be accessed. Perhaps more than any other nonhuman primate, Kanzi's accomplishments and the processes by which he has achieved them have served to complete the bridge of psychological continuity postulated by Darwin in the nineteenth century.

theory of mind are designed to determine whether animals can make accurate inferences and attributions about the knowledge, motives, or intentions of others. Chimpanzees, for example, will attend to cues about the location of hidden food items if the hints are provided by someone who saw the concealment, but ignore cues given by someone who was not in the room when the food was hidden. Monkeys, in contrast, appear to be uninfluenced by the "guesser" and the "knower." This suggests that chimpanzees but not monkeys attribute unique knowledge to individuals who have unique perceptions or experience relevant to the situation.

Deception. Deception is a special class of social cognition, requiring both an animal's ability to infer what other organisms know (or do not know) and also that animal's intention by its actions to mislead or manipulate other organisms. Examples of deceit are common in nature, and many scientists have systematically studied and organized these examples. For the present discussion, it should be sufficient to summarize by noting that the complexity with which an organism deceives is indicative of the level of sensorimotor intelligence characteristic of that animal. Some hold that social deception has been a major factor in primate brain evolution.

Numerical Cognition. One of the most active areas of comparative research in recent years focuses on animals' representation of and response to quantities, numerical stimuli, and simple problems of summation. A very nice hierarchy of numerical competence can be described, spanning from relatively basic abilities such as selecting the larger of two arrays of quantities to relatively complex enumeration or counting skills, complete with evidence of ordinality, cardinality, and abstraction. The numerical competencies of a diverse array of animals have been studied using many different tasks or paradigms. At this point, several conservative conclusions seem defensible. Many (and perhaps all) animals are sensitive to quantity as a basic attribute of stimuli, and will respond differentially to the numerousness of stimuli. Dolphins, monkeys, and apes (at a minimum) can learn to respond appropriately to arbitrary symbols on the basis of the number of objects (e.g., reinforcers) that each symbol represents. Convergent evidence has similarly been provided from different laboratories and paradigms to indicate that chimpanzees, at a minimum, can learn to count relatively small numbers of objects (six to eight, possibly more). It appears certain that these number-related skills will serve as valuable hallmarks for animal intelligence.

Language. Perhaps no competency defines—and facilitates—intelligence as much as language. During the last four decades, there have been a number of serious programmatic research programs to discern whether chimpanzees, bonobos, orangutans, gorillas, dolphins, sea lions, or parrots have the capacity for any aspect of human language. Of course, these animals are not human. They do not have brains as large or complex as humans, nor do they naturally experience language-rich environments as humans do. No one should expect that their language capacity would equal our own. Thus, the question is not, Do animals have full capacity for all dimensions of human language? but rather, What dimensions of language might animals be capable of acquiring and what are the conditions under which they do so?

Animals are capable of learning arbitrary symbols as names or labels, or things, persons, activities, foods, drinks, and places. They also are capable of asking for any of the foregoing items or to visit specific places just for the interest value of doing so. They can think in terms of arbitrary symbols in that they can, for instance, select an object by touch given its arbitrary name, or vice versa; they can coordinate their social behaviors and share foods and tools with precision; they can announce intended actions and choices; and they can attend to diverse dimensions or attributes of items and give the quantity of them. Language-competent chimpanzees also are able to classify word lexigrams (i.e., geographic patterns on a keyboard) for a variety of foods and tools known to them through use of two other lexigrams, one for "food" and another for "tool." Their performance on even the first test trials was nearly errorless and served to define their capacity for basic semantics or word meaning. They also make appropriate comments on events and the environment and report the actions of others. Each of these and other related accomplishments by apes is clearly within the language domain.

Perhaps the most surprising and important fact is that both the bonobo (a rare form of chimpanzee) and the common chimpanzee spontaneously learn the meanings of word lexigrams and how to use them, and also come to comprehend human speech if reared from birth in an environment in which speech and word lexigrams are used in a coordinated manner by the care givers with the infant apes so as to describe what has happened, to explain what is or about to happen, and to describe items and events of interest to the ape. In controlled tests, the emergence of their capacity for speech comprehension, even for novel sentences of request, awaits maturation, and hence remains silent, up to age three or more years. The evidence indicates that the complex structuring of cognition and its operations transpires during protracted years of ape and human development and is based on perceptions of reliable predictive relationships among stimuli and the various events of each day, rather than operant conditioning histories.

The same is true for bonobos' and chimpanzees' comprehension and use of lexigrams. As is true and characteristic of the course of language acquisition for the human child, comprehension of word lexigrams and gestures precedes skill for their competent use in expressing language. Here, too, their productive competence includes simple rules of grammar, which includes rules of their own innovation.

Intelligence and Brain. Current and future research will reveal whether apes' brains function similarly to ours as they learn, solve problems, and comprehend human speech. Such studies, essentially noninvasive and the same as used with humans, are in progress and promise to reveal by the millennium whether the planum temporale, now known to be elaborated in the left hemisphere of the chimpanzee brain in a manner homologous to the human brain, serves to facilitate speech comprehension for chimpanzees just as it is thought to do for humans.

The methods and paradigms of neuropsychology may complement the study of animal intelligence in other ways. Significantly, emergents appear more readily when species' brain complexity is high and early environmental conditions provide the opportunity for behavioral interaction. Brain complexity is in some manner related to the brain's mean absolute size and cytoarchitectonics. The former of these is the more accessible measurement and has been shown to correlate reliably ($\rho = .79$) to 12 primate species' abilities to transfer small increments of learning to altered test situations, consistent with the transfer index methods described above. When the transfer of training was measured as a function of the amount learned, the performance of the smaller-bodied and smaller-brained prosimians and New World monkeys was profoundly compromised, whereas that same increase in the level of learning profoundly enhanced the transfer of learning for the larger-brained monkeys and great apes. There is a similar probabilistic shift from basic stimulus-response associative learning to relational learning (i.e., principle or rule learning) as one goes from prosimians to monkeys to apes, a progression that entails enhancement of species' differences in brain size and complexity. Whether this relationship holds true within other orders of mammals is not known, though much literature attests to the advanced intelligence of complex-brained mammals such as whales, dolphins, sea lions, and elephants.

Summary

Progress within psychology in this century includes affirmation of the principle that all behavior is a reflection of interactions between nature and nurture (i.e., heredity and environment). That principle holds true in our assessment of animal intelligence if we define it in terms of the ability to learn with facility, the ability to transfer learning to a leveraged advantage, the capacity to benefit from enriched early rearing, and to achieve specific hallmark behaviors—even to the end of coming to understand human speech and novel sentences of request. Recognition of each species' singular adaptation to its niche does not prevent the comparison of species' general intellectual capacities for acquiring skills and knowledge and for using this information in ways that are emergent, insightful, and, in some cases, symbolic and communicative.

Darwin would be pleased to know of data that, at the turn of the millennium, support the principles of both biological and psychological continuity that he articulated in the nineteenth century. His postulates anticipated that at least some animals would be found to be highly intelligent. He was correct.

Acknowledgments. Preparation of the manuscript supported by the NICHD (06016) and the College of Arts and Sciences at Georgia State University.

Bibliography

Blum, D. (1984). *The monkey wars.* New York: Oxford University Press. A Pulitzer Prize–winning book that portrays informed views and attitudes held by scientists and lay persons regarding many research questions, methods, and arguments about research on animal intelligence and behavior.

Boysen, S. T., & Capaldi, E. J. (Eds.). (1993). *The development of numerical competence: Animal and human models.* Hillsdale, NJ: Erlbaum. Contains recent reviews from most of the scientists in the field of numerical cognition by animals, and provides historical perspective and theoretical frameworks for understanding the many studies in this literature.

Calvin, W. H. (1996). *How brains think: Evolving intelligence, then and now.* New York: Basic Books. The turning of scientific ideas and data led this theoretical neurophysiologist to important new perspectives that consider important steps in the evolution of intelligence in our ancestors. Creativity might have its foundation in Darwinian-type contests within the brain. Throwing skills, language, musical skills, and evolutionary pressures are some of the several topics of this book considered in relation to the evolution of intelligence.

Corballis, M. (Ed.). (1998). *The descent of mind.* New York: Oxford University Press.

Deacon, T. (1998). *The symbolic species.* New York: Norton. Reviews brain and neuroscientific data, and builds a comprehensive perspective of the evolution of human intelligence and language.

Dewsbury, D. A. (1984). *Comparative psychology in the twentieth century.* Hutchinson Ross. Reviews significant figures, events, and issues in the history of research on animal intelligence.

Domjan, M. (1993). *The principles of learning and behavior.* Pacific Grove, CA: Brookes/Cole. A comprehensive treatise and review of conditioning and learning processes that serve behavior.

Fobes, J. L., & King, J. E. (1982). Measuring primate learning abilities. In J. L. Fobes & J. E. King (Eds.), *Primate behavior* (pp. 289–326). Reviews early efforts to quantify and compare animal intelligence, particularly those based on differences in learning or transfer rate, within a book that contains many excellent summaries of research on primate behavior.

Gould, J. (1982). *Ethology: The mechanisms and evolution of behavior.* New York: Norton.

Kalat, J. (1998). *Biological psychology.* Pacific Grove, CA: Brooks/Cole. An important text and presentation of basic biopsychological topics that include the organization, evolution, and ontogeny of the nervous system. Perceptual mechanisms and those of learning and conditioning in relation to human competence are clearly explicated. A fine review of biological psychology at the turn of the millennium.

Krasnegor, N. A., Lyon, G. R., & Goldman-Rakic, S. (Eds.). (1997). *Development of the prefrontal cortex—Evolution, neurobiology, and behavior.* Baltimore, MD: Brookes. Contains chapters about brain development and evolution, the evolution of intelligence and creativity, and brain-behavior relationships. Of particular relevance to the present discussion are chapters by Harry J. Jerison, Patricia Goldman-Rakic and colleagues, Duane Rumbaugh, and Karl H. Pribram.

Mackintosh, N. J. (Ed.). (1994). *Animal behavior and cognition.* New York: Academic Press. Contains chapters on a wide variety of learning, perceptual, and comparative psychological topics.

Masterson, R. B., Bitterman, M. E., Campbell, C. B. G., & Hotton, N. (Eds.). (1976). *Evolution of brain and behavior in vertebrates.* Hillsdale, NJ: Erlbaum. A comparative perspective of learning, brain evolution, and neuroanatomy.

Matsuzawa, T. *The perceptual world of a chimpanzee.* Project number: 63510057. Inuyama, Aichi, 484 Japan.

Mitchell, R. W., & Thompson, N. S. (Eds.). (1986). *Deception: perspectives on human and nonhuman deceit.* Albany: State University of New York Press. A collection of studies on deception, offering perspectives from comparative psychology, developmental psychology, philosophy, and ethology.

Nissen, H. W. (1951). Phylogenetic comparison. In S. S. Stevens (Ed.), *Handbook of experimental psychology* (pp. 347–386). New York: Wiley. A seminal chapter on comparative psychology in a valuable collection of mid-century knowledge and theory regarding instinct, learning and learning theories, sensory processes, and psychobiological research.

Novikoff, A. B. (1945). The concept of integrative levels and biology. *Science, 101,* 209–215.

Parker, S. T., & Gibson, K. R. (Eds.). (1990). *Language and* intelligence in monkeys and apes: Comparative developmental perspectives. Cambridge, UK: Cambridge University Press. A bio-anthropological treatment of intelligence and its relation to language.

Roitblat, H. L., Bever, T., & Terrace, H. (Eds.) (1984). Animal cognition. Hillsdale, NJ: Erlbaum. An edited volume of developments in animal cognition from a comparative perspective; an outstanding source for state-of-the-art reviews of learning, memory, language, concept formation, and other aspects of cognition that are related to animal intelligence.

Romanes, G. J. (1883). Animal intelligence. London: Keegan, Paul, & French.

Rumbaugh, D. M., Washburn, D. A., & Hillix, W. A. (1996). Respondents, operants, and emergents: Toward an integrated perspective on behavior. In K. Pribram & J. King (Eds.), Learning as a self-organizing process (pp. 57–73). Hillsdale, NJ: Erlbaum. Introduces a third class of behavior (emergents) to Skinner's famous division operants and respondents. It is in these emergent behaviors that the hallmarks of psychological intelligence are found.

Savage-Rumbaugh, E. S., Murphy, J., Sevcik, R., Brakke, K., Williams S. L., & Rumbaugh, D. M. (1993). Language comprehension in ape and child. Monographs of the Society for Research in Human Development, 58(3–4, Serial No. 233). Describes an extensive experiment on the comprehension of novel sentences by Kanzi, a bonobo, and a human child, and reveals for the first time that an ape can understand human speech at a level comparable to that of a 2½-year-old human.

Savage-Rumbaugh, E. S., & Lewin, R. (1994). Kanzi: The ape at the brink of the human mind. New York: Wiley. A detailed account of the bonobo Kanzi and his spontaneously coming to understand human speech and knap flint to make sharp-edged chips.

Savage-Rumbaugh, E. S., Shanker, S., & Taylor, T. (1998). Apes, language, and the human mind. New York: Oxford University Press. Perspectives of scholars who research questions on the acquisition of language, with apes as subjects, in relation to philosophy and linguistics.

Thomas, R. K. (1996). Investigating cognitive abilities in animals: Unrealized potential. Cognitive Brain Research, 3, 157–166. Presents a heuristic and integrated hierarchy of animal learning.

Thorndike, E. L. (1911). Animal intelligence: Experimental studies. New York: Macmillan.

Toth, N., & Schick, K. (1993). Early stone industries and inferences regarding language and cognition. New York: Cambridge University Press.

Vauclair, J. (1996). Animal cognition: An introduction to modern comparative psychology. Cambridge, MA: Harvard University Press. Includes reviews of the literatures on developmental hallmarks, tool use, and theory of mind.

Weiskrantz, L. (Ed.). (1985). Animal intelligence. London: Clarendon Press. Contains chapters basic to varied views, approaches, topics, and methods used to assess animal intelligence from rats to apes.

Yerkes, R. (1916). The mental life of monkeys and apes. New York: Holt.

Duane Rumbaugh and David A. Washburn

NONPARAMETRIC STATISTICS. Many statistical methods are based on the assumption that observations are generated from a specific class of distributions characterized by one or more parameters. For discrete or categorical data, often such distributions can be justified under random sampling, the simplest example being the binomial. For continuous data, the best known example of a parametric class of distributions is the class of normal distributions, each distribution being completely determined by two parameters, its mean and its variance. Nonparametric methods are designed to make inferences about a distribution, or to compare two or more distributions, without assuming that observations are generated from a particular class of parametric distributions. Some books include methods designed explicitly for categorical data under the term nonparametric methods (Conover, 1980), whereas other books restrict the term to situations in which observations are generated from some continuous distribution (Hettmansperger, 1984). Typically, nonparametric methods are based on the ranks of the observations. Often the term rank-based is used as a synonym for nonparametric.

Some books make no distinction between nonparametric and distribution free methods, but various authorities (such as Kendall & Buckland, 1982, or Staudte & Sheather, 1990) make it clear that a distinction should be made. A distribution-free method refers to some hypothesis testing procedure by which, under random sampling, the probability of a type I error can be determined exactly. Most nonparametric methods are not distribution free. For example, Fligner and Policello (1981) report the probability of a type I error for the Mann–Whitney (MW) test when sampling from various distributions. When testing at the .05 level, the actual probability of a type I error ranges between .049 and .093, with sample sizes of 25 and 20 for the two groups. In contrast, the Kolmogorov–Smirnov test is distribution free; the exact probability of a type I error can be determined under random sampling regardless of the distributions associated with the groups.

One reason for using nonparametric methods is maintaining relatively high power under nonnormality. All methods for comparing means, such as the ANOVA F test and related multiple comparison procedures, can have very poor power under arbitrarily small departures from normality (e.g., Staudte & Sheather, 1990; Wilcox, 1996, 1997). However, rank-based methods are not always optimal for achieving high power, and they can be unsatisfactory when there is interest in comparing measures of location such as the mean or median.

To elaborate, consider two independent groups, and let p be the probability that a randomly sampled observation from the first group is less than a randomly sampled observation from the second. If there are no differences between the groups, meaning that they have identical distributions, then $p = \frac{1}{2}$. The MW test is based on a direct estimate of p and provides a test of H_0: $p = \frac{1}{2}$. When distributions are symmetric, the test is sensitive to differences between the means, and under normality its power is only slightly less than that of the t test. For example, Fligner and Policello (1981) consider three normal distributions in which the t test has power 0.218, 0.583, and 0.878. The MW test has power 0.198, 0.506, and 0.851. When sampling from a symmetric distribution that is only slightly different from normal (a mixed normal), the power of the t test drops to 0.121, 0.235, and 0.344, but the MW test has power 0.185, 0.455, and 0.801. However, for skewed distributions, situations arise in which the MW test has substantially less power—it is testing a hypothesis about p, not the difference between the means—but there are also situations in which its power is again substantially higher. That is, neither method dominates the other in terms of power, and each can be sensitive to different features of the data.

As an illustration, consider the data in Wilcox (1997, p. 182) taken from a study on the effects of consuming alcohol. Comparing the mean of Group 1 to the mean of Group 2 using the Time 3 observations yields a significance level of 0.43. If we apply Mee's method, a modern analog of the MW test (see Wilcox, 1996, 1997), we reject the null hypothesis at the 0.05 level. That is, it rejects H_0: $p = \frac{1}{2}$, but it does not provide a confidence interval for the difference between the means or any other measure of location that might be of interest. (The data are highly skewed.) Another argument for Mee's method is that it provides reasonably good control over the probability of a type I error for a broader range of situations than conventional methods for comparing means.

Another general reason for using nonparametric methods is that they provide a perspective on how groups differ that is not offered by methods based on comparing measures of location. Included are global comparisons of distributions that can be informative beyond methods based on p or on means. For example, Wilcox (1997) illustrates Doksum's shift function with data from a study on the effects of ozone on weight gain in rats. The shift function reveals that there is a differential effect depending on the initial weight of the rat. Lighter weight rats, prior to exposure to ozone, tend to lose weight, but heavier weight rats show no effect.

The heaviest rats actually seem to gain more weight in an ozone environment. This is not to say that comparing measures of location is an unsatisfactory approach to comparing groups, but that nonparametric methods help provide a deeper understanding of how groups differ.

A third argument for using nonparametric methods is that psychological data are inherently ordinal (Cliff, 1996). Cliff argues that ordinal methods are preferable because of the possibility that conclusions from a metric analysis of ordinal data could be changed, even reversed, under ordinal transformations. He also argues that in many instances, what is desired is an ordinal comparison of groups, such as making inferences about p. If this is the case, ordinal methods are preferable because they deal directly with this goal.

There have been many important developments in recent years that have great practical value, such as improvements on the Kruskal–Wallis and Friedman tests (e.g., Wilcox, 1996). A simple way of extending rank-based methods to a one-way or higher design is to replace observations by their ranks and apply a method designed for means. This strategy gives reasonable results in some cases but fails miserably in others (e.g., Marden & Muyot, 1995). Extensions of nonparametric methods to regression have been proposed, but certain practical problems remain. For a recent treatment of robust nonparametric methods, see Hettmansperger and McKean (1997).

Bibliography

Cliff, N. (1996). *Ordinal methods for behavioral data analysis.* Mahwah, NJ: Erlbaum.

Conover, W. J. (1980). *Practical nonparametric statistics.* New York: Wiley.

Fligner, M. A., & Policello, G. E., II. (1981). Robust rank procedures for the Behrens-Fisher problem. *Journal of the American Statistical Association, 76,* 162–168.

Hettmansperger, T. P. (1984). *Statistical inference based on ranks.* New York: Wiley.

Hettmansperger, T. P., & McKean, J. W. (1997). *Robust nonparametric statistics.* London: Arnold.

Kendall, M. G., & Buckland, W. R. (1982). *A dictionary of statistical terms.* New York: Longman.

Marden, J. I., & Muyot, M. E. (1995). Rank tests for main and interaction effects in analysis of variance. *Journal of the American Statistical Association, 90,* 1388–1398.

Staudte, R. G., & Sheather, S. J. (1990). *Robust estimation and testing.* New York: Wiley.

Wilcox, R. R. (1996). *Statistics for the social sciences.* San Diego, CA: Academic Press.

Wilcox, R. R. (1997). *Introduction to robust estimation and hypothesis testing.* San Diego, CA: Academic Press.

Rand Wilcox

NONRANDOMIZED DESIGNS. Nonrandomized designs have two features. First, they are typically used to study causal questions; and second, the researcher does *not* assign units to conditions on a random basis (e.g., by toss of a coin or using a table of random numbers). The absence of randomization is crucial. When properly implemented, randomized designs are presumed to yield unbiased estimates of treatment effects; nonrandomized designs do not have this desirable property. Unfortunately, it is not always possible to randomize; for example, ethical constraints may preclude withholding treatment from needy people based solely on chance; those who administer treatment may refuse to honor randomization; or questions about program effectiveness may arise only after treatment has been implemented so that randomization is impossible. Consequently, the use of nonrandomized designs is frequent and inevitable in practice, and an extensive literature has emerged that describes and evaluates these designs. In this literature, the term *quasi-experiment* is usually synonymous with nonrandomized design; and the terms *observational study* and *nonexperimental design* are often synonymous, as well.

The range of nonrandomized designs is large, including but not limited to (1) *nonequivalent control group designs* in which the outcomes of two or more treatment or comparison conditions are studied but the experimenter does not control assignment to conditions; (2) *interrupted time series* designs in which many consecutive observations (prototypically about one hundred) over time are available on an outcome of interest, and treatment is introduced in the midst of those observations in hopes of demonstrating its impact on the outcome; (3) *regression discontinuity* designs in which the experimenter uses a cutoff score on a measured variable to determine eligibility for treatment, and an effect is observed if the regression line for the treatment group is discontinuous from that of the comparison group; (4) *single-case* designs in which one participant is repeatedly observed over time (usually on fewer occasions than in time series designs) while the scheduling and kind of treatment is manipulated to demonstrate that the treatment controls the outcome; (5) *case-control* designs in which a group that has an outcome of interest is compared retrospectively to a group without that outcome to see if they differ in exposure to possible causes; and sometimes (6) *correlational* designs in which observations on possible treatments and possible outcomes are observed simultaneously, often with a survey, to see if they are related to each other. Some of these designs are inherently *longitudinal* (e.g., time series, single case designs), that is, they observe participants over time; and others can be made longitudinal by adding more time points before or after treatment. [*See* Longitudinal Research.]

Randomized designs emerged with the work of R. A. Fisher in the 1920s, but nonrandomized designs have a far longer history. For example, around 1850 epidemiologists used case-control methods to identify contaminated water supplies as the cause of a cholera epidemic in London; and the idea of using a nonrandomized control group emerged even earlier. Modern work on nonrandomized designs has been associated with four main developments. The most important development in psychology and many other social sciences is the work of Donald T. Campbell and his associates, especially his classic works with Julian C. Stanley (*Experimental and Quasi-Experimental Designs for Research*, Chicago, 1963) and Thomas D. Cook (*Quasi-experimentation: Design and Analysis Issues for Field Settings*, Chicago, 1979). Campbell's work had three important features. First, he coined the term *quasi-experiment* and described or invented a large number of these designs. Second, he developed a validity typology to use in evaluating inferences from such designs. The typology now includes four validity types and a set of threats to each type, where those threats are common reasons why researchers may be wrong about the inferences they draw from nonrandomized experiments. [*See* Validity.] *Statistical conclusion validity* concerns inferences derived from statistical evidence about covariation between presumed cause and effect; and examples of threats to statistical conclusion validity include low statistical power, violations of assumptions of statistical tests, and inaccurate estimates of effect size. *Internal validity* concerns inferences that the presumed treatment A caused the presumed outcome B; and examples of threats to internal validity include history (extraneous events that happened when treatment occurred that could also cause the effect); maturation (natural growth processes that could also have caused an observed change); and selection (differences between groups before treatment may be the cause of differences observed after treatment). *Construct validity* concerns inferences about higher-order constructs that research operations represent; and examples of threats to construct validity include expectancy effects whereby participants' guesses about the purpose of the experiment cause them to perceive a different treatment construct than the researcher intended, and mono-operation bias in which researchers use only one measure that reflects a construct imperfectly or incorrectly. *External validity* concerns inferences about generalizing a causal relationship to units, treatments, observations, settings, and times that were *not* the constructs studied in the original design; and threats to external validity include various interactions of the treatment with other features of the design that produce effects that would not otherwise be observed, and failures to detect those interactions.

The third feature of Campbell's approach was his advocacy of using design features rather than statistics to rule out these threats to validity. Design features are things an experimenter can manipulate (e.g., assignment methods including matching and stratifying, the number and scheduling of treatments and measures, the kind of comparison group) either to prevent a threat from occurring or to diagnose its presence and potential impact on study results. Campbell advocated using design to prevent threats rather than to attempt the more difficult task of trying to adjust threats statistically after they have already occurred. [*See the biography of Donald T. Campbell.*]

The other three important modern developments in nonrandomized designs pertain to those statistical adjustments. One is the work of statisticians such as Paul W. Holland, Paul R. Rosenbaum, and Donald B. Rubin on statistical models for nonrandomized designs. The statistical model emphasizes the need for some measure of what would have happened to treatment participants had they not been given treatment (the counterfactual), and focuses on methods that can approximate that counterfactual when randomization is not possible. A central method in this approach is the propensity score, the predicted probability of group membership obtained from using logistic regression of actual group membership on predictors of outcome or of how participants got into treatment. Matching, stratifying, or covarying on the propensity score can balance groups on those predictors, improving causal inference by creating a better counterfactual. However, propensity scores cannot balance groups for unobserved variables, so hidden bias may remain. Hence these statisticians have developed sensitivity analyses to measure the amount of that hidden bias that would be necessary to change the effect in important ways. Both propensity score analysis and sensitivity analysis should be more widely used in nonrandomized designs, although they do not solve the fundamental problem of selection bias.

The second statistical development has been pursued mostly by economists, especially James Heckman and his colleagues, under the rubric of selection bias modeling. Their aim is to remove the hidden bias that remains in effect estimates from nonrandomized experiments by modeling the selection process into nonrandomly formed groups. These models are widely used in the analysis of nonrandomized designs in economics and occasionally in other disciplines. In principle the statistical models are exciting, but in practice this ambitious program of research has been less successful. A series of studies in the 1980s and 1990s found that estimates of treatment effects from selection bias models did not match results from randomized experiments. Heckman responded with various adjustments to these models, and with proposed tests for their appropriate application, but so far results have been only slightly more encouraging. Most recently, Heckman has improved results somewhat by combining his approach with the propensity score approach. Although selection bias models cannot be recommended for widespread adoption, this topic is developing rapidly and serious scholars must attend to it. For example, several other economists such as Charles F. Manski have developed useful econometrically based sensitivity analyses. Along with Heckman's incorporation of propensity scores, this may promise some future convergence in the statistical and econometric literatures.

The fourth development is the use of structural equation modeling (SEM) to model causal relationships in nonrandomized designs. As with selection bias models, SEM has been only partly successful. The capacity of SEM to model latent variables reduces problems of bias caused by unreliability of measurement; but its capacity to generate unbiased estimates of treatment effects is hamstrung by the same lack of knowledge of selection that has so far thwarted selection bias models.

As the above examples suggest, many researchers are studying nonrandomized designs as a research topic in its own right. Other examples include studies of whether threats to validity actually occur regularly in nonrandomized designs, of how to measure the plausibility of such threats, and of the kinds of nonrandomized control groups that more or less closely approximate results from randomized controls. This empirical program promises to revitalize the theory and practice of nonrandomized designs.

[*See also* Experiments; *and* Randomized Single-Case Experimental Design.]

Bibliography

Cook, T. D., & Campbell, D. T. (1979). *Quasi-experimentation: Design and analysis issues for field settings.* Chicago: Rand-McNally. A revision of this major reference work is currently near completion.

Cook, T. D. (1991). Clarifying the warrant for generalized causal inferences in quasi-experimentation. In M. W. McLaughlin & D. C. Phillips (Eds.), *Evaluation and education: At quarter-century* (pp. 115–144). Chicago: National Society for the Study of Education. More current than Cook and Campbell, it also describes a theory for generalizing results from single and multiple experiments.

Holland, P. W. (1986). Statistics and causal inference. *Journal of the American Statistical Association, 81,* 945–970. Describes "Rubin's model," the one most often used in conceptualizing nonrandomized designs in the statistical literature.

Winship, C., & Mare, R. D. (1992). Models for sample selection bias. *Annual Review of Sociology, 18,* 327–350. A comprehensive review of econometric selection bias modeling to 1992; the reader is urged to consult the current literature in this rapidly developing area.

Rosenbaum, P. R. (1995). *Observational studies.* New York:

Springer-Verlag. The most comprehensive of recent statistical treatments of propensity scores, sensitivity analyses, and other issues in nonrandomized designs.

Schlesselman, J. J. (1982). *Case-control studies: Design, conduct, analysis.* New York: Oxford University Press. An excellent introduction to the case-control method from epidemiology.

William R. Shadish

NONVERBAL COMMUNICATION refers to the expression and perception of nonlinguistic signals between people. The core assumption is that people cannot *not* communicate since human communication is a multichannel process that includes a good deal more than words. Early on, some proposed that most communication in face-to-face encounters takes place in the nonverbal realm. That idea, now generally regarded as an overstatement, nonetheless has led psychologists and other communication scholars to substantiate the idea that nonverbal communication serves numerous social-psychological functions.

Nonverbal communication subsumes several categories of human expressiveness such as facial displays (including eye contact and gaze behavior), gesture and body movement, posture and body orientation, touch, human spacing and territorial behavior, and vocal and paralinguistic behavior. Some explications also include physical attractiveness, babyfacedness, and other physical attributes, odor, and features such as hair, clothing, and adornment. These latter aspects, however, are less frequently included under the nonverbal communication rubric since they are more static than messages sent and received in ongoing interactions.

Although Darwin is often seen as initiating the scientific study of nonverbal behavior with *The Expression of the Emotions in Man and Animals* in 1872, social scientific work in this area began in earnest in the mid-twentieth century. Birdwhistell (1970), an anthropologist, coined the term *kinesics* for the study of communication via body movement; Hall (1959), also an anthropologist, instigated study of interpersonal space and human territorial behavior which has become known as the study of *proxemics*; Goffman (1959), a sociologist, carved out the field of *face-to-face interaction* which describes how nonverbal behavior affects and reflects interpersonal dynamics; and Ekman began his studies on the psychological import of *affect displays* (Ekman & Friesen, 1969).

For psychologists, nonverbal communication has been used to understand processes at several levels of psychological analysis: the individual, the interpersonal, and the structural. Individual differences in some personality traits are reflected in characteristic nonverbal behaviors as are some psychopathological conditions. In fact, personality psychologists and psychotherapists have long speculated that a person's nonverbal behavior disclosed aspects of disposition or character that a person cannot or will not reveal in words. Early on, Allport and Vernon (1933) provided detailed descriptions of how personality is revealed in expressive style. More recently, the aim has been directed toward documenting relationships between interpersonal traits and particular patterns of nonverbal behavior. For example, extroverts tend to engage in more eye contact, to adopt smaller spacing, and to display more facial expressivity than those who are less extroverted. There are also individual differences in social skills associated with nonverbal behavior, such as the ability to accurately perceive and interpret the nonverbal cues of others, a trait usually referred to as *nonverbal sensitivity*. Nonverbal cues have also been used diagnostically to assess and differentiate psychopathological conditions such as depression and schizophrenia.

Also at the individual level of analysis, a substantial body of work has focused on documenting the relationship between particular emotions and particular facial expressions. Several investigators, following in Darwin's footsteps, have proposed that there is a direct biological link between the triggering of basic emotions and the subsequent display of particular facial expressions (Ekman, 1972). However, controversy continues as to how universally or culturally variant these relationships are (Russell, 1994).

At an interpersonal level of analysis, nonverbal communication is useful for understanding various dyadic and group processes. According to one view, nonverbal behaviors are instructive about three key dimensions of interpersonal relationships: immediacy (i.e., how positive or close individuals feel toward others), status (i.e., whether individuals have higher, equal, or lower standing with respect to others), and responsiveness (i.e., how active and focused an individual's communication is; Mehrabian, 1969).

With respect to immediacy, research has explored the role that nonverbal behaviors play in reflecting the quality of attachment between infants and caretakers. Developmental researchers, for example, have described the degree to which the body movements of infants are temporally synchronized with those of various caregivers. Among adults, a frequently explored topic is the role that nonverbal behaviors play in communicating attraction-aversion and in creating and reflecting interpersonal rapport. There are indications, for example, that nonverbal synchrony or the degree to which participants adopt similar body movements or postures reflects the extent to which those individuals are in accord with one another (LaFrance, 1979). Evidence also shows that when people like each other, they tend to adopt smaller interpersonal spaces and more direct body orientation, engage in more eye contact, show more positive facial expressions, and use more gestures.

As to status, nonverbal behaviors have been found to reflect differences in social power. For instance, Dovidio and his colleagues have shown that people with higher power are more likely to show visual dominance (Dovidio, Ellyson, Keating, Heltman, & Brown, 1988). Specifically, visual dominance describes the ratio of how much a person looks at the other while speaking compared to how much he or she looks while listening. People higher in power or dominance look about the same whether they are listening or speaking, while those lower in power or dominance look more while listening than while speaking.

There are other nonverbal indicators of status differences between people. Specifically, it appears that those with higher status or power have more options than lower power people with respect to the nonverbal behaviors they display. For example, a person with higher power may look or not at a lower status person, may approach very closely or maintain some considerable distance, may smile or not depending on how positive he or she feels, or may adopt a very relaxed or decorous posture with respect to a lower power other. In contrast, lower power people in the company of their superiors appear to adopt a more predictable and narrower range of nonverbal behavior.

Finally, the responsiveness dimension of interpersonal relationships appears to be cued by nonverbal behaviors. Specifically, people are more nonverbally expressive when they are in the company of other people and especially when they are attempting to influence others. There are also indications that some nonverbal behaviors such as gaze direction are useful in the communication of a particular kind of responsiveness, namely sexual interest or flirtatiousness.

Nonverbal behaviors have also been implicated in those interpersonal encounters when people engaged in deception or when perceivers believe that they are being deceived, although the jury is still out as to whether there are any cues that reliably indicate when someone is lying. Freud, for example, argued that were one to pay close attention to nonverbal behavior, one would be convinced that nobody can keep a secret. Indeed, a substantial line of research within nonverbal communication has focused on the processes involved in deception; asking, for example, whether people who lie reveal that they are doing so via changes in facial display, vocal intonation, gaze aversion, and gesture (DePaulo & Friedman, 1998). A related question is whether perceivers are able to detect deception in others when they have visual and/or vocal access to persons who are actually being deceptive or who are believed to be engaged in deception. As to the former question, the conclusion is that changes in facial expressions do not reliably denote the presence of deceit.

Nor can perceivers rely on particular cues to consistently signal that a person is lying (DePaulo & Friedman, 1998).

Interpersonal interactions also involve a significant component of self-presentation which is typically accomplished through the deliberate use of nonverbal behaviors. There are occasions, for instance, where people aim to have others see them in particular ways, such as being credible or modest or competent, even though it appears that perceivers are inclined to take these presentations at face value. According to DePaulo (1992), success at regulating nonverbal behaviors to promote particular self-portrayals depends on knowledge, skill, practice, experience, confidence, and motivation.

At a more structural level, nonverbal communication has proved useful in understanding how occasions of social interaction are organized. The idea here is that participants draw on known repertoires of verbal and nonverbal behaviors in order to be able successfully to carry out a host of interpersonal transactions such as greetings and farewells, signaling listening or managing speaker-listener conversational turn taking, and conveying and accepting apologies, compliments, and the like. Social rituals such as these appear to be automatic as does much of nonverbal behavior. They also occur mostly out of awareness, but close study of how people negotiate the myriad and mundane interpersonal encounters of everyday life suggest that people are exquisitely knowledgeable about and sensitive to the placement of the right nonverbal cues in the right place.

Questions of how various groups differ nonverbally speaking are also structural in the sense that gender, ethnic, cultural, class, and age groups are thought to display characteristic patterns of nonverbal behavior. Such inquiries have inspired debate about the degree to which nonverbal behaviors are influenced by innate versus cultural factors.

Gender has proven to be a fertile ground for the investigation of group differences in nonverbal behaviors. The evidence indicates that women are more facially and vocally expressive than men, that they signal more social engagement with others via such behaviors as smiling and gazing, and that they are more sensitive to the nonverbal cues of others than are men (Deaux & LaFrance, 1998). Nonetheless, the reasons for these differences are in dispute. Evolutionary psychologists tend to argue that the observed differences are due to genetic differences between the sexes; that is, women are more nonverbally expressive because it behooves the female to be especially demonstrative given her role as primary caregiver. Developmental psychologists, on the other hand, are more likely to point to evidence that suggests that females and males learn how to display gender-appropriate nonverbal behavior. Social psychologists point to differences in social roles, social expectations, and social status to explain why the nonverbal behavior of men differs from that of women.

Cultural variations have been described for many types of nonverbal behavior. For example, researchers have distinguished between "contact" and "noncontact" groups with the former showing smaller interpersonal distances, more direct body orientation, and more touching and eye contact. More generally, it appears that there are characteristic expressive and gestural patterns associated with speaking different verbal languages, so that, for example, speakers of French or Italian or Japanese have distinctive ways of moving their hands and faces while engaged in conversation.

Nonverbal communication researchers have, to date, given a great deal of attention to facial expressions, seeing in them a singular locus for the communication of emotion. For those who display them, facial expressions have been shown to contribute to the activation and regulation of emotion experiences as well as eliciting emotional states in expressors themselves, a phenomenon known as the *facial feedback hypothesis*. The facial feedback hypothesis maintains that facial expressions such as smiling or grimacing are not merely readouts of underlying affect but can themselves bring about or at least modify experienced emotion by those who show them. In fact, Darwin suggested that facial feedback (sensations created by the movements of expressive behavior) activate or contribute to the activation of emotion feelings. A number of experiments have provided substantial evidence that intentional management of facial expression contributes to the regulation (and perhaps activation) of emotion experiences. Most evidence is related not to specific emotional feelings but to the broad classes of positive and negative states of emotion. Studies of motivated, self-initiated expressive behaviors have shown that, if people can control their facial expression during moments of pain, there will be less arousal of the autonomic nervous system and diminution of the pain experience.

Facial expressions of emotion communicate something about internal states to others as well as activating emotions in others, a process that can help account for empathy and sensitivity. There has been the suggestion, for example, that perceivers of facial expressions sometimes engage in "facial mimicry" which is associated with feeling what the expressor is feeling. The social communication function of emotion expressions is most evident in infancy. Long before infants have command of language, they can send a wide variety of messages through their facial expressions. Virtually all the muscles necessary for facial expression of basic emotions are present at birth. Through the use of an objective, anatomically based system for coding the separate facial muscle movements, it has been found that neonates have the ability to smile and to facially express pain, interest, and disgust. Babies as young as 3 to 4 weeks can display a social smile; other emotions come somewhat later. Sadness and anger are shown usually by about 2 months; and fear by 6 or 7 months. Informal observations suggest that expressions indicative of shyness appear by about 4 months and expressions of guilt by about 2 years.

It is also apparent that very young children are responsive to the facial expressions of others. Research has shown that, when mothers display sadness expressions, their infants also demonstrate more sadness expressions and decrease their exploratory play. Infants under 2 years of age respond to their mother's real or simulated expressions of sadness or distress by making efforts to show sympathy and provide help. And research has shown that infants will cross a modified "visual cliff" (an apparatus consisting of a glass floor that gives the illusion of a drop-off) if their mother stands on the opposite side and smiles, but none cross if she expresses fear. In addition, infants cry in response to other infants' cries but not to a computer-generated sound that simulates crying.

Microanalysis of facial movements from video records have shown that small changes in particular constellations of facial muscles reveal important psychological processes. For example, facial expressions can differentiate between distressed and nondistressed couples, reveal the extent to which people really find sexist humor amusing, distinguish embarrassment from shame, and reflect different reactions to female than to male leaders among other processes.

Gaze behavior has been studied for several reasons. First, eye behavior is often one part of a whole facial display, such as the downward gaze that accompanies feelings of embarrassment. People also look more at those with whom they seek contact or engagement, and eye contact or mutual gaze is thought to say something about the degree to which people are actually involved with one another, either positively or negatively. As noted above, the timing of looking relative to talking has also been found to be important. In addition, studies indicate that eye behavior plays an important role in regulating various aspects of conversation, such as monitoring attention or seeking responses or negotiating the exchange of speaker and listener roles.

Body movements and gestures can also be communicative. First, there are speech-independent gestures known as emblems which can be translated into a few words quite easily and are often used as a substitute for words. For example, in North America, the joining of the thumb and index finger on one hand with the other fingers upright means that things are "OK." Typically, the meaning of emblems are culturally specific. Next, there are speech-related gestures, often referred to as *illustrators* which accompany the verbal stream. Illustrators can anticipate, supplement, or complete verbal description by depicting metaphorical as well as literal relationships; they can accent and emphasize verbal points; and they can deliberately or inadvertently contradict verbal statements. The latter have sometimes been termed *leakage cues* or *clues to deception*. Other illustrators, sometimes referred to as *interaction gestures*, assist in directing the flow of conversation and effecting processes of inclusion or exclusion. And the presence of gestures by speakers tend to have the effect of forestalling verbal intrusion by listeners.

There are also body movements that are directed toward oneself. These gestures, sometimes referred to as self-adapters, include self-touching behaviors like stroking oneself or twirling one's hair. Researchers have hypothesized that self-touching behaviors occur in situations in which people are experiencing psychological discomfort.

The literal distances that people adopt vis-à-vis each other, sometimes known as territoriality, appear to change depending on individual proclivities, interpersonal context, and cultural differences. Although people tend to move closer to those with whom they want more involvement, the behavior can sometimes trigger feelings of being invaded. Many studies have shown that too close approach by strangers is often met with withdrawal either by moving away or by other nonverbal signs of rejection, such as hostile glances and turning or leaning away. These observations led to the more general idea that depending upon the nature of the interpersonal relationship at hand, there is an appropriate level of nonverbal immediacy. According to the intimacy-equilibrium hypothesis, too close or too distant interactions will be met with a corresponding correction in nonverbal behavior. So if one person is perceived to be looking too much or standing too close, the target can respond by orienting their eyes or their bodies away from the intrusive other.

Lastly, vocal cues like loudness, pitch, and tempo, and voice characteristics like breathiness, nasality, and raspiness lead perceivers, not always wisely, to assume that they are indicators of personality. Although some personality characteristics may be associated with particular vocal attributes, the research tends for the most part to show that there is greater agreement among perceivers as to what vocal characteristics go with what traits than there is actual accuracy. However, evidence does suggest that various emotional states are associated with distinctive vocal patterns. For instance, elation is associated with higher average frequency, greater frequency range and variability, higher loudness, and faster rate.

In sum, nonverbal communication subsumes many different channels and is used in the service of many psychological and social functions. It is also highly variable across place and group with the consequence that there is no one-to-one correspondence between any nonverbal cue and any specific psychological disposition or state. Nonetheless, human beings use a substantial array of nonverbal behaviors for communicating intended and unintended messages.

[*See also* Sign Languages.]

Bibliography

Allport, G. W., & Vernon, P. E. (1933). *Studies in expressive movement.* New York: Macmillan.

Birdwhistell, R. L. (1970). *Kinesics and context: Essays on body motion communication.* Philadelphia: University of Pennsylvania Press.

Darwin, C. (1872). *The expression of the emotions in man and animals.* London: John Murray.

Deaux, K., & LaFrance, M. (1998). Gender. In D. T. Gilbert, S. T. Fiske, & G. Lindzey (Eds.), *The handbook of social psychology* (4th ed., Vol. 1, pp. 788–827). New York: McGraw-Hill.

DePaulo, B. M., & Friedman, H. S. (1998). Nonverbal communication. In D. T. Gilbert, S. T. Fiske, & G. Lindzey (Eds.), *The handbook of social psychology* (4th ed., Vol. 2, pp. 3–40). New York: McGraw-Hill.

Dovidio, J. F., Ellyson, S. L., Keating, C. F., Heltman, K., & Brown, C. E. (1988). The relationship of social power to visual displays of dominance between men and women. *Journal of Personality and Social Psychology, 54,* 233–242.

Ekman, P. (1972). Universals and cultural differences in facial expressions of emotion. In J. K. Cole (Ed.), *Nebraska symposium on motivation, 1971* (pp. 207–283). Lincoln: University of Nebraska Press.

Ekman, P., & Friesen, W. V. (1969). The repertoire of nonverbal behavior: Categories, origins, usage and coding. *Semiotica, 1,* 49–98.

Freud, S. (1959). *Collected papers.* New York: Basic Books.

Goffman, E. (1959). *The presentation of self in everyday life.* Garden City, NY: Doubleday Anchor.

LaFrance, M. (1979). Nonverbal synchrony and rapport: Analysis by the cross lag panel technique. *Social Psychology Quarterly, 42,* 66–71.

Mehrabian, A. (1969). Significance of posture and position in the communication of attitude and status relationships. *Psychological Bulletin, 71,* 359–372.

Russell, J. A. (1994). Is there universal recognition of emotion from facial expression? A review of the cross-cultural studies. *Psychological Bulletin, 115,* 102–141.

Marianne LaFrance

NON-WESTERN THERAPIES. Non-Western alternatives to talk therapy include many different means of restoring a client's healthy balance. The label *Western* reflects more of a political than geographic reality in the counseling literature, with many Westernized influences in non-Western geographic areas and vice versa. It is an oversimplification to polarize Western and non-

Western therapies. The term *Westernized methods* refers to methods derived from research in Europe and the United States and disseminated elsewhere in what John Berry et al. (*Cross-Cultural Psychology*, Cambridge, UK, 1992) call "scientific acculturation." Western cultures are described as more idiocentric, emphasizing competition, self-confidence, and freedom, whereas the contrasting cultures are more allocentric, emphasizing communal responsibility, social usefulness, and acceptance of authority. Approximately 33% of Americans, 50% in Europe, and 80% of people worldwide regularly use some kind of complementary or alternative health treatment, frequently originating in non-Western cultures (Micozzi, 1996). Kleinman (*Rethinking Psychiatry*, New York, 1988) suggests that new and important approaches to psychiatric diagnosis and treatment are being developed in non-Western cultures that will significantly influence all international health programs.

Western and non-Western approaches are complementary to one another as psychology increasingly includes attention to non-Western therapies. There are several assumptions which distinguish non-Western therapies (Nakamura, 1964). (1) Self, the substance of individuality, and the reality of belonging to an absolute cosmic self are intimately related. Illness is related to a lack of balance in the cosmos as much as to physical ailments. (2) Asian theories of personality generally deemphasize individualism and emphasize social relationships. Collectivism more than individualism describes the majority of world cultures. (3) Interdependence or even dependency relationships in Hindu and Chinese cultures are valued as healthy. Independency is much more dysfunctional in a collectivist culture. (4) Experience rather than logic can serve as the basis for interpreting psychological phenomena. Subjectivity as well as objectivity are perceived as psychologically valid approaches to data. Sheikh and Sheikh (1989) and Scotton, Chinen, and Battista (1996) provide the best review of non-Western therapies.

1. Ayurvedic therapies from India combine the word for *life, vitality, health,* and *longevity (āyus)* with the word for *science* or *knowledge (veda)*, and focus on promoting a comprehensive and spiritual notion of health and life rather than healing or curing any specific illness. Ayurvedic treatments are combined with conventional therapies more frequently in Europe than in the United States. Health is treated as more than the absence of disease and involves a spiritual reciprocity between mind and body. Western-based research has documented the efficacy of Ayurvedic therapies.

2. Yoga has a history of thousands of years as a viable therapy based on the Sanskrit root *yuj* meaning to yoke or bind the body-mind-soul to God. Yoga has its main source in the *Bhagavad Gita* in understanding the connection of the individual to the cosmos. Research on yoga has demonstrated benefits in lowering blood pressure and stress levels through meditation, personality change, and therapeutic self-discovery.

3. Chinese therapies include an elegant array of therapies based on the concepts of the *Tao* or "the way," *Ch'i*, or "the energy-force," and *Yin/Yang*, or the "balance of opposites." The various systems of Chinese therapies are grounded in religion and philosophy by the mystical union with God or the cosmos and nature. The *Tao* describes those patterns that lead toward harmony. The *Ch'i* describes a system of pathways called meridians in the body through which energy flows. The *Yin/Yang* describes the balance of paradoxes, each essential to the other.

4. Buddhist therapy is based on the absence of a separate self, impermanence of all things, and the fact of sorrow. People suffer by desiring and striving to possess things that are impermanent. The cure is to reach a higher state of being to eliminate delusion, attachment, and desire in the interrelationship of mind and body. Elements of cognitive restructuring, behavioral techniques, and insight-oriented methods are involved in the healing process.

5. Sufism is the mystical aspect of Islam that exists inside the person. The outward dimension, *sharia*, is like the circumference of a circle, with the inner truth, *haqiqa*, being the circle's center, and the path, *tariqa*, to that center going beyond rituals to ultimate peace and health. The Sufi's goal is to enable people to live simple, harmonious, and happy lives. Jung's analytical psychology and Freud's interpretation of the fragmented person are similar but more objective in their emphasis than the Sufi, who seek to go beyond the limited understanding of objective knowledge.

6. Japanese therapies of Zen Buddhism, *Naikan*, and *Morita* therapy focus on "constructive living" and their aim is for people to become more "natural." Morita was the professor of psychiatry at Jikei University School of Medicine in Tokyo who developed principles of Zen Buddhist psychology. Yoshimoto was a successful businessman who became a lay priest at the famous shrine at Nara and developed *Naikan* therapies in the Jodo Shinshu Buddhist psychology. *Morita* therapy is a way to accept and embrace our feelings rather than ignore them or attempt to escape from them. *Naikan* therapy emphasizes how many good things we have received from others and the inadequacy of our repayment.

7. Shamanism is a family of therapies involving altered states of consciousness where a person experiences their spiritual being in order to heal themselves or others. Shamanism is found from Siberia and the Native American cultures to Africa and Australia, going back perhaps 25,000 years in South Africa. The focus of healing is through spirit travel, soul flights, or soul journeys, which distinguishes shamans from priests, mediums, or medicine men. These altered states include psychological, social, and physiological approaches to

modify consciousness as perhaps the world's earliest technology.

8. The *Kabbalah* of Jewish mysticism was developed by the Zohar schools of Spain and Provence in the thirteenth and fourteenth centuries, by the Cordoverian and Lurianic schools in Safed in the sixteenth century, and by the classical Hasidism of the late eighteenth century. The Kabbalah describes a three-world cosmology with the body in the world of *Assiyyah*—sensation, action, and behavior; *Ru'aHh* (the breath or spirit) involving feeling, images, values, and myths aimed at purification of emotions; and *B'ruttah*, or creation in the world of thinking and philosophy. The *Kabbalah* brings people to inner states through levels of reality and by maintaining careful balance in a personal encounter.

9. Native American healers recognize four main causes of illness: offending the spirits or breaking taboos, intrusion of a spirit into the body, soul loss, or witchcraft. Illness can be a divine retribution for breaking a taboo or offending divine powers, requiring that the patient be purified with song, prayers, and rituals. In the same way, removing objects or spirits from the body by a healer restores health. When the soul is separated from the body or possessed by harmful powers, it must be brought back to energize the patient, and sometimes the shaman must travel to the land of the dead to bring the soul back. Finally witchcraft causes illness by projecting toxic substances into the patient. Elements of dissociative reaction, depression, compulsive disorder, and paranoia are present.

10. African healing, as described by Airhihenbuwa (1995), is based in cultural values and is available, acceptable, and affordable. Even today, African divinities, diviners, and healers continue to be popular in a religious or psychosocial dimension of health that goes beyond medical care. Beliefs include symbolic representations of tribal realities, illness resulting from hot/cold imbalance, dislocation of internal organs, impure blood, unclean air, moral transgression, interpersonal struggle, and conflict with the spirit world. Health depends on both balance within the individual and between the individual and the environment or cosmos. Similarities with allopathic medicine are evident.

A great variety of other non-Western systems exist: Christian mysticism, homeopathy, osteopathy, chiropractic, herbalism, healing touch, naturopathic medicine, *Qigong*, Curanderismo, and Tibetan medicine, among the many. Each of these systems are divided into a great variety of different traditions. However, many of the same patterns of spiritual reality, mind-body relationships, balance, and subjective reality run through many if not all the non-Western therapies.

Micozzi (1996) describes the characteristics of complementary and alternative medicine as a new ecology of health; the central ideas of biomedicine have made tremendous advances in therapies and medicine. "However, the resulting biomedical system is not always able to account for and use many observations in the realms of clinical and personal experience, natural law, and human spirituality" (p. 3). Micozzi goes on to document the scientific research supporting non-Western therapies in biomedical terms.

Bibliography

Airhihenbuwa, C. O. (1995). *Health and culture: Beyond the Western paradigm*. Thousand Oaks, CA: Sage.

Micozzi, M. S. (1996). *Fundamentals of complementary and alternative medicine*. New York: Churchill Livingstone.

Nakamura, H. (1964). *Ways of thinking of Eastern peoples: India, China, Tibet, Japan*. Honolulu: University of Hawaii Press.

Pedersen, P. (1997). *Culture-centered counseling interventions: Striving for accuracy*. Thousand Oaks, CA: Sage.

Scotton, B. W., Chinen, A. B., & Battista, J. R. (1996). *Textbook of transpersonal psychiatry and psychology*. New York: Basic Books.

Sheikh, A. A., & Sheikh, K. S. (1989). *Healing East and West: Ancient wisdom and modern psychology*. New York: Wiley.

Paul Pedersen

NORMS are cognitive representations of what is typical, average, or appropriate. They serve as standards for comparative judgment. All judgments of quantity and extent or quality and value are made with reference to norms. Norms are both descriptive and prescriptive, that is, they characterize both what an object, event, person, or experience *is* like and what it *ought to be* like.

Norms are not static representations, stored in memory, but are constructed on-line, as needed. As Daniel Kahneman and Dale Miller proposed (Kahneman & Miller, 1986), each occasion of comparative judgment brings into existence its own frame of reference, and thus involves the construction of a norm specific to that occasion. For example, the norm used to evaluate one's salary will depend on whether one is prompted to think about it by a bounced check, a sizable raise, knowledge of a well-paid colleague's salary, or a wish to buy a new home. Each of these triggering events calls to mind representations of how well particular others are paid, how well one has been paid in the past, how well one might be paid in other jobs, and how well one wishes one were paid. The representations evoked by a specific set of circumstances combine to yield the norm that is used in that particular evaluation of one's salary. Because the evoked representations vary with context, so, too, does the resulting norm. Moreover, because these norms are constructed from whatever representations come to mind, any factor that increases the accessibility of a particular representation will enhance its contribution to the norm. This definition of norms as on-line constructions contrasts sharply with sociological notions of norms as stable and enduring properties of groups.

Psychologists have proposed a number of distinctions between types of norms that differ in their antecedents and/or consequences. One especially useful distinction, proposed by Robert Cialdini and his colleagues (Cialdini, Kallgren, & Reno, 1991), contrasts descriptive and injunctive norms. Descriptive norms are defined by how people actually behave; injunctive norms are defined by how people believe one should behave. Although both of these norms are influential, the specific nature and mechanism of their influence differ considerably.

Social psychologists have shown particular interest in those norms that characterize social groups or emerge out of social interaction—so-called social norms. Much research has demonstrated the powerful influence that social norms exert on individuals' thoughts, feelings, and actions. These demonstrations have taken three general forms. First, some studies have shown how readily collections of people form norms, especially under circumstances in which reality is ambiguous. Muzafer Sherif (1936) demonstrated this fact most persuasively in his studies of the social formation of perceptual norms. In these studies, participants were placed in a completely darkened room and shown a pinpoint of light. They were asked to state aloud the distance the light moved on each trial. In fact, the light did not move; it only appeared to move in erratic and random ways (a phenomenon known as the autokinetic effect). Tested in isolation, participants gradually developed a personal norm for the movement, defined by a narrow range within which their judgments consistently fell. Brought together in twos and threes, their estimates converged on a social norm, which persisted even when they again made their judgments in isolation. Subsequent studies using this paradigm showed that the effect of the social norm on individual judgments persisted for up to a year, and that even artificial norms, created with the aid of experimental confederates, were transmitted across several generations of naive participants.

Second, a number of studies have shown that norms exert more of an influence on judgments than other variables that one would expect to dominate them. Solomon Asch (1956) provided the best-known demonstrations of this point. His studies pit social norms against objective reality. Groups of students participated in a visual discrimination task, in which they were presented with a target line and a set of three comparison lines, and were asked to state aloud which of the three comparison lines matched the target. Each group contained one naive participant and one to eight confederates; the naive participant always responded second to last. On 12 of the 18 trials, the confederates unanimously gave an unambiguously incorrect response. The surprising finding was that naive participants went along with the group—and went against the evidence from their own senses—on fully one third of these trials. This percentage held across most experimental conditions, except when there was only one confederate or when the confederates were not unanimous in their incorrect response.

Third, studies of social norms have highlighted the range of phenomena in which norms play a role. For example, they have shown that social norms influence people's private attitudes and emotions. In one famous study, Theodore Newcomb (1943) showed that the sociopolitical attitudes of Bennington College students became steadily more liberal with time spent in that strongly liberal environment. Moreover, adherence to the norms had a strong influence on sociometric choices: The most popular students were those with the most liberal attitudes. Social norms also exert a powerful influence on behavior. Especially striking are a number of demonstrations of the role of norms in producing deleterious behaviors, including the failure of bystanders to intervene in emergency situations, the tendency for college students to drink excessively, and the binge-eating patterns of sorority members. In group contexts, social norms produce more polarized judgments following group discussion. They also tend to highlight distinctions between groups, enhancing in-group solidarity and exaggerating intergroup differences. These many, varied demonstrations attest to the pervasive influence of social norms.

Bibliography

Asch, S. E. (1956). Studies of independence and conformity: A minority of one against a unanimous majority. *Psychological Monographs: General and Applied, 70,* 1–170.

Cialdini, R. B., Kallgren, C. A., & Reno, R. R. (1991). A focus theory of normative conduct: A theoretical refinement and reevaluation of the role of norms in human behavior. In M. P. Zanna (Ed.), *Advances in experimental social psychology* (Vol. 24, pp. 201–234). Orlando, FL: Academic Press.

Festinger, L., Schachter, S., & Back, K. (1950). *Social pressures in informal groups.* New York: Harper & Row. Reports on a classic study of the formation and influence of social norms in groups of students living in a housing project.

Fishbein, M., & Ajzen, I. (1975). *Belief, attitude, intention, and behavior: An introduction to theory and research.* Reading, MA: Addison-Wesley. Presents a comprehensive theory of the influence of norms and attitudes on behavior. This theory has proven extremely useful in research on health-related behaviors.

Kahneman, D., & Miller, D. T. (1986). Norm theory: Comparing reality to its alternatives. *Psychological Review,* 93, 136–153.

Miller, D. T., & Prentice, D. A. (1996). The construction of social norms and standards. In E. T. Higgins & A. W. Kruglanski (Eds.), *Social psychology: Handbook of basic principles* (pp. 799–829). New York: Guilford Press. Provides a recent review of various literatures pertaining to the formation of social norms.

Newcomb, T. M. (1943). *Personality and social change.* New York: Holt, Rinehart & Winston.

Sherif, M. (1936). *The psychology of social norms.* New York: Harper.

Turner, J. C. (1991). *Social influence.* Pacific Grove, CA: Brooks/Cole. Provides an excellent review of the literature on social norms and social influence processes.

Deborah A. Prentice

NORTH AFRICA. [*This entry includes discussions on five North African countries: Algeria, Egypt, Libya, Morocco, and Tunisia.*]

Algeria

Psychology could hardly be expected to develop in Algeria during the long colonial period from 1848 to 1962. Indeed, psychological research up until independence was restricted to what was taught at the bachelor's degree level in connection with philosophy, except for the teacher training school curriculum, which was entirely French in character.

In general, education and training in Algeria during the colonial era were basically aimed at providing middle-level administrative staff at best. There was often resistance to the educational system in many places and in several ways. There were also attempts to set up a different, national educational system. In spite of this situation, and in addition to the contributions of the baccalaureate system, there were some practical psychological applications in health institutions as well as anthropological and clinical analyses which crossed to neighboring countries (Tunisia and Morocco). Once Algeria gained independence, interest in psychology took a more practical turn, especially in the field of educational psychology. Primary and secondary teacher training schools were set up to meet the country's needs. There was also a major increase in the number of universities (25 by 1990).

Thanks to the educational plans it introduced, especially to remedy the lack of experience and training among teachers, the 1980 to 1984 report contributed to promoting interest in psychology. This led to the establishment of Al-ma'had at-tarbawi al-watani (the National Educational Institute) which began publishing educational books and pamphlets for teachers using psychological principles.

There was a common-core syllabus for Algerian universities, which combined social sciences and philosophy, with a 2-year study period leading to further specialization, including a 2-year psychology program.

Psychological studies in the Algerian higher education system are characterized by the existence of institutions which supervise educational and research programs, including psychology institutes at the universities of Algiers, Oran, and Canstantine.

The psychological specialties in Algerian institutes are similar to those in European and other Western countries in general, except in the area of educational psychology, where the syllabus emphasizes the social and intellectual heritage, including the contributions of Ibn Khaldun and other Islamic scholars.

In addition to Algerian faculty members, there are Arab professors (mostly Egyptians) who contribute, through the Arabization trend, to the early inception of universities and institutes. However, a large share of the merit for the development of psychology goes to the Algerian students who went abroad for further studies and research.

Some of those students went to Arab countries (Egypt and Syria) while others headed for Europe and North America. As a result, a certain variety of trends and schools characterizes the psychological field in Algeria. Algerian psychology researchers are interested in a variety of social, industrial, and anthropological fields in addition to educational and clinical topics. Similarly, the question of immigration receives special interest in Algerian psychological research projects.

Periodicals which tackle educational psychology issues are published by some institutions at the local and national level, including *Al-majalla al-jazaa'iriyya li-'ilm an-nafs wa 'uluum at-tarbiyya* (*The Algerian Magazine of Psychology and Educational Sciences*), which was first published in the early 1970s. Algerian psychologists take part in international conferences held outside Algeria at the Maghreb, Arab, and international levels.

Bibliography

About the Article

Boughazi, T. (1992, October). *Binaa' al-mandhuuma at-tarbawiyya fil-jazaa'ir* [Magazine of education sciences], 3 [Rabat].

Meziane, M. (1993). *Tahweel al-ma'rifa an-nafsiyya ila ad-duwwal ghair al-musanna'a* [Proceedings of the first international psychology symposium in Morocco], 'Ilm an-nafs wa qadaayaa al-mujtama' al-muaasir. Rabat: College of Arts and the Humanities.

Readings on the Colonial Period

Faci, M. (1931, April). Mémoires d'un instituteur algérien d'origine indigène [Memoirs of an indigenous Algerian bureaucrat]. *La Voix des Humbles*, 98.

Marchand, M. (1956). *Hygiène affective de l'éducateur* [The mental health of the educator]. Paris: P.U.F.

Egypt

The early beginnings of psychological study in Egypt can be traced back to the late nineteenth century. There were contributions by some of the eminent figures of the Egyptian renaissance who first came in contact with the West through scientific expeditions, as was the case with Rafa'a Tahtaawi (1875). However, this period's stock of knowledge merely reflected a general scholarly ambition basically linked to education though some articles that addressed subjects which are directly related to psychology, if only from a formal viewpoint, such as imagination and hypnotism.

In the early twentieth century, some articles were published in periodicals such as *Majallat attarbiya al-Hadeetha* (The Modern Education Magazine) and tackled more interesting psychological issues such as intelligence tests. The contributions of the educationist Ismaa'll Qabani represent a landmark in the history of psychology in Egypt, especially his fine translation of *Test de Stanford–Binet d'intelligence* (Stanford Binet test; 1928).

Credit for the development of psychology in Egypt goes to European professors, especially French ones, who came to teach in Egypt, the most famous of whom was the Swiss Eduoard Claparède. The development of psychological study was also partly achieved through the contributions of Egyptian students who went to Europe in the 1930s and studied under major psychologists in France and England before returning to Egypt to teach and conduct university research. Among these is Abdulaziz al-Qudi, who studied under Charles Edward Spearman (1934) and Yusuf Murad, who studied under P. Guillaume in France (1940). The dissertations of these psychologists concerned such topics as intelligence, skills, and related questions in the light of the scientific level reached in psychological studies at that time. Other researchers were interested in nervous and affective areas, notably Mustapha Zyour, a professor and psychiatrist, who studied under Froment in France (1941).

Egypt is one of the first African and Arab-Islamic nations where psychology was taught separately from other philosophical or sociological subjects. This has been the case since 1950, at Ain Shams University (this autonomy of psychology occurred in Anglo-Saxon countries in 1930, in the former Soviet Union in 1966, and in Iran in 1964).

Egyptian universities award all types of scientific degrees, starting with a bachelor's degree (four years after the baccalaureate), and also a master's degree and a Ph.D. degree. There are also psychology laboratories in professional and experimental departments, and many test devices and instruments are locally manufactured. There are various studies and productions in the area of adaptation and standardization as well as psychological tests.

Outside academic circles, there are practical clinical, pathological, and industrial applications of psychology in health and industrial institutions. Similarly, psychological counsellors play an important role in many public institutions.

One of the most active associations is the Al-jam'iyya al-masriyya lid-diraasaat an-nafsiyya (Egyptian Association of Psychological Studies). It publishes a quarterly journal, *Diraasaat Nafsiyyah* (Psychological Studies); its editor-in-chief is Dr. Abdulkader Taha Farag. The association holds an annual conference and is one of the main founding associations of Al-ittihad al-arabi li-'ilm an-nafs (Arab Psychology Federation).

Bibliography

About the Article

(1971–1972). *Bulletin de Psychologie (L'Enseignement de la Psychologie)*, 25, 294. [Paris].

(1965). *Hay'at uddiraasaat al arabiya fil jaami'a al amirikiyah, Nashaat al-'Arab fil 'ulum al-ijtimaa'iya fi mi'at 'aam*. Beirut.

Meziane, A. (1982). *Bidaayat addiraasaat annafsiya fil 'aalam al-'arabi, 1.* Rabat.

Wahba, M. (1994). *Yussuf Murad wal-mazhab attakaamuli, Al-hay'a al-misriya al-'aamma li kitaab*. Cairo.

Readings

Malika, K. L. (1965). *Qiraa'aat fi 'ilm annafs al-ijtimaa'i fil 'aalam al-'arabi* (Vols. 1–3). *Addar al qawmiya littibaa'a wan-nashr*. Cairo.

Libya

The first signs of interest in psychology in Libya appeared as education and educational institutions began to spread throughout the country. This trend was itself linked to the level of urbanization achieved within Libyan society. Up until the Italian invasion (1911), there were two main cities, Tripoli and Benghazi, and several small cities along the coastline and inland.

In the 1940s, two high schools were set up in Tripoli and Benghazi under the British administration. Interest in psychology during that period was basically related to the preparation of an educational curriculum and the relation between psychology, the social sciences, and humanities. These two high schools soon played a key role in paving the way for the establishment of intermediate teacher training schools. Educational psychology was the first application of psychology because of its practical aspects. The development of secondary education in the 1950s in terms of the number of educational institutions, the schooling period, especially for ages 12 to 17, and the award of a general high-school diploma were important factors in prompting more decisive interest in psychology as well as the necessity to train sufficient numbers of teachers and hire others from Arab countries (mostly from Egypt).

In high schools, psychology was part of the curriculum and included an introduction to the most important psychological theories and schools in addition to topics such as perception, development, instincts, and impulse.

Between 1950 and 1960, there was a qualitative interest in psychology as Libyan society entered the oil era and witnessed the advent of graduate education. Thus, Benghazi University was set up in 1956 for the main purpose of training teachers for secondary education institutions. Psychology as a subject was taught in all sections and departments of the Arts College of Benghazi University.

Ten years later, in 1966, the higher teacher training college (Kulliyyat al-mu'allimeen al-'ulyaa) was set up only to be named, in 1968, the education college (Kulliyat at-Tarbiyya'). Thus, educational psychology became a full-fledged subject with all the basic topics in addition to practical educational methods.

Most university teachers during this period were Egyptians. There were also some Iraqis and a few Libyan figures, such as Dr. Omar At-Toumi Shebani. The same situation was experienced in the then newly established universities, including Qar-Younes University, in which a specialized education and psychology department was founded (Qism at-tarbiyya wa 'ilm an-nafs). This department became autonomous in 1981 and offered a bachelor's degree in psychology, then 10 years later a master's degree. Most Libyan students pursuing doctoral studies continued to go abroad, to Arab and Islamic countries (mostly Egypt and Morocco), but also to Europe, the United States, and Canada.

Many Libyan students who came back from abroad with advanced psychological training opted for the teaching profession and for university research along with other colleagues from Arab countries. In addition to the educational sector, researchers addressed various other psychological areas, including certain innovative and specialized fields such as intelligence, disability, and gifted people. Numerous research works were also conducted to compare certain aspects of intelligence and behavior between Libyans and non-Libyans. As the number of universities increased, so did the psychology departments and educational research centers.

Bibliography

About the Article

Attir, M. (1994). *Ittijaahaat at-tahaddur fil mujtama' al-leebi, Al muassasa al-'arabiya lin-nashr wal-ibdaa'*. Rabat: Arab Foundation for Publishing and Creativity.
Statistics of education in Islamic countries. Islamic Educational Scientific and Cultural Organization. (1989). Rabat: Islamic Educational Scientific and Cultural Organization.

Readings

Al Markaz al-watani lil-buhuuth at-ta'leemiyya wat-tarbawiyyah (National Center for Pedagogical and Educational Research). (1994). Symposium on Ri'aayat al-mawhubeen (Caring for gifted people), Tripoli (1992). Rabat: Al-muassasa al-'arabiyya lin-nashr wal-ibdaa (Arab Foundation for Publishing and Creativity).
Shebani, B. L. (1984). *Correlates of life satisfaction among older Libyans and Americans*. Doctoral dissertation, University of Florida, Gainesville. See a summary in the proceedings of the international symposium on psychology held in Morocco, "Psychology and Current Social Issues." (College of Arts and the Humanities). Rabat: 'Kulliyyat al-aadaab wal 'uluum al-insaaniyyah'.

Morocco

The advent of psychology in Morocco is linked to the emergence of the modern educational system, especially in the 1940s and 1950s. Some writings by French sociologists and anthropologists, which were aimed at investigating the Moroccan personality, can be viewed as informal and indirect psychological studies. There is a direct relationship between the various types of teacher-training institutions set up during the colonial period, especially after the country's independence (1956), and the emergence of psychology.

Some short books were published to assist teachers. These publications, which were of a theoretical and educational nature, were written by Moroccan authors who relied on Egyptian psychological references of varying degrees of importance, while other publications were written by French educational officials, before independence and shortly after it, in their capacity as experts and educationists.

In the 1950s, some publications came out and were mostly written by Moroccan education inspectors who essentially based their writings on their practical experience as well as on their readings, mostly in Arabic (Egyptian publications), and other publications were translated into Arabic. Most of these writings lacked a specific character.

Concurrently, there were scientific applications of psychology in various fields, including clinical and medical psychology in some health institutions and specialized child centers. In addition to what was generally applied in health centers, some experts relied in their practical work on tests such as "test du bonhomme" (Draw-a-Man test) and Koch's "test de l'arbre" (tree test). Psychotechnical applications exist in some industrial units, including tests used for the selection of staff members in light of skill and muscular coordination. These tests are administered by technicians, as is the case in Office Chérifien des Phosphates (OCP), Carnaud factories for the manufacturing of tin for preserved food (such as sardines and fruits).

The proliferation of higher educational institutions, in particular, constituted a turning point in the development of psychology in Morocco. Thus, psychology held its rightful place, as of the 1960s, as one of the mandatory subjects for the four-year bachelor degree program in philosophy, with one full year devoted to the study of psychology and leading to the award of a diploma. Similarly, the teacher training institutions known as Centres Pédagogiques Régionaux (CPR) and Écoles Normales Supérieures (ENS) continued to make substantial progress in technical and educational training as well as in research work.

In the mid-1970s, an important step was made with respect to the autonomy of psychology although the latter remained at least formally in the department of philosophy and social sciences. In fact, the department is made up of three specialized sections, the study period in each one of them in the bachelor degree program is three years, plus one combined year.

Training and research in philosophy, social sciences, and psychology departments of all Moroccan colleges span all educational levels: bachelor's, master's, and doctoral degrees (the latter is now called the national doctoral degree as of 1997).

Although educational psychology seems to predominate, research work and publishing activities tackle numerous other fields of interest which are just as important, including social psychology, clinical psychology, and psychometry.

There is, however, a lack of specialization in physiological, industrial, and experimental psychology as the tendency to set up laboratories has not yet fully taken shape. Tentative laboratories exist in the psychology departments of the College of Arts in Rabat (Mohamed V University) and the one in Fez (Sidi Mohamed Ben Abdallah University). There are also periodicals, the most important of which are concerned with educational psychology and are published by the College of Education Sciences (Mohamed V University) and Mu'assasat at-takween at-tarbawi (Educational Training Institution).

Psychology in Morocco seems to be quite a diversified field, reflecting the different schools, specializations, and reference sources of Moroccan researchers. Most of those researchers were trained in European, Canadian, and American universities, in addition to those who attended Arab universities (mainly in Egypt).

There are also researchers who studied under Egyptian professors in Morocco in the late 1970s.

Many psychological events are held in Morocco. Chief among these was the first international psychology symposium in Morocco, which was held in the College of Arts in Rabat in 1990. In 1991, the Jam'iyyah al-maghribiyya lid-diraasaat an-nafsiyya (Moroccan Association for Psychological Studies) was set up to serve as a national association grouping psychology researchers. With headquarters in the Rabat College of Arts, the association is now a member of the International Federation of Psychology.

Bibliography

About the Article

Aharchaou, A. (1994). *Waaqi' at-tarbiyya as-seekulu|iyya fil-watan al-'arabi, Al markaz ath-thaqaafi al-'arabi.* Casablanca.

Rabi, M. (1996–1997). *Majaalaat 'ilm an-nafs, ishkaalaat al-mawduu' wal-manhaj, daleel al-'uluum al-ijtimaa'iyya, Al-ma'had al-jami'i lil-bahth al-'ilmi* (C.U.R.S). Rabat.

Readings

Bourgeois, P. (1959–1960). *L'Univers de l'ecolier marocain* [The world of Moroccan scholarship]. (Vols. 1–5). Rabat: *'Ilm an-nafs wa qadaayaa al-mujtamu' ul-mu'aasir* [First international psychology symposium]. Rabat: College of Arts and the Humanities.

Tunisia

Psychology was taught in Tunisia as a baccalaureate subject as was the case in the French system. This situation lasted until the mid-1950s and the early independence years. Then, psychology began to acquire greater significance in teaching and training programs as the number of specialized institutions and training centers started to grow.

Naturally, clinical psychology was practiced in health centers, and this aspect of psychology was further consolidated with the return of Tunisian graduates who studied in European colleges and institutes (mostly in France). Mannuba Hospital is one of the most renowned institutions in clinical psychology. However, research and study in the field of psychology is basically linked to the existence of higher specialized Tunisian colleges and schools for educational training and research.

The 1988 to 1990 report on education in Tunisia, which was submitted to the Geneva-based Centre International des Études (CIE), can be regarded as a turning point in terms of research, training, and teaching orientations, which also had an impact on the field of psychology.

Most of the achievements in psychological study,

and especially in research, are related to the activities of educational institutions, such as the Kulliyyat al-aadaab (9 April) in Tunis, Al-ma'had al-'aali littarbiyya wat-takween al-mustamir, Ecole Normale supérieure, and Markaz ad-diraasaat wal-abhaath al-iqtisaadiyya, in spite of these institutions' different orientations and the diverse reasons for which they were established.

Psychological research in Tunisia covers most classical topics. However, certain issues receive particular attention, including the following:

Differential studies in various fields (masculine-femine differences), but more particularly in the workplace, in relationships, and in roles.

Sexuality and its relation to identity: this is clearly a specific field of interest, especially through the question of identity and sexuality for instance. Research in this domain is conducted on the basis of psychological analysis. It is characterized by a substantial measure of adaptability to Tunisian realities, unlike the markedly colonial character it had when it crossed from occupied Algeria to Tunisia (and also to Morocco). These differential studies are also supported by some purely sociological studies and research works as well as sociopsychological studies by some researchers such as Abdelwahab Bouhaddiya.

Various conferences and symposia are held in Tunisia, such as the First Arab Conference on Psychology, held in Tunis in July 1987; and the international symposium on "L'Apport de Piaget aux études pédagogiques et didactiques," held in April 1996 under ISEFC patronage. Since the 1980s, there have been some publications in the field such as *Revue tunisienne des sciences de l'éducation* (Tunisian Review of the Educational Sciences).

Bibliography

About the Article

Institut des Recherches sur le Maghreb, Correspondances, 41, June 1996.

Psychologie différentielle des sexes (1986). Université de Tunis, Centre de Recherches Economiques et Sociales (C.E.R.E.S), Série Psychologique No. 3, Tunis.

Readings

Ben Regeb, M. (1995). *Migration, psychopathologies et psycholinguistique.* Tunis: *Alif, les Editions de la Méditerranée, Faculté des Sciences Humaines et Sociales.*

M'barek Rabi
Translated from Arabic by Aziz Zellou

NORTHERN IRELAND. Psychology emerged as a distinctive discipline in Northern Ireland from a background in education and philosophy. The first university department of psychology was created in 1958 at Queen's University Belfast under Professor George Seth. In response to the need to provide psychological services, postgraduate programs in clinical, educational, and occupational psychology were started at Queen's during the 1960s.

Currently, psychology is taught to both undergraduates and postgraduates at four university campuses in Northern Ireland—at Queen's University in Belfast and the three campuses of the University of Ulster established in the 1970s at Coleraine, Jordanstown, and Magee. The scientific underpinnings of the discipline are emphasized in all degree programs, students studying a range of methodologies and statistical techniques. In order to meet the accreditation requirements of the British Psychological Society (the professional body in the United Kingdom), students must study the core areas—cognitive, social, developmental, and biological psychology as well as individual differences and personality. Undergraduate degrees take either 3 or 4 years to complete and, at all four campuses, have an applied focus. This is particularly so at the Jordanstown campus where the application of psychological knowledge is strongly emphasized, students in their third year completing an 18-week placement in agencies such as hospitals, rehabilitation units, or applied research centers.

Psychology is a popular subject with a high demand for undergraduate places, particularly from women—a consistent trend in most United Kingdom psychology departments. Students from both Catholic and Protestant communities study together at all campuses and are joined by increasing numbers from the Republic of Ireland. This cultural diversity results in healthy cross-cultural perspectives during undergraduate study.

Obtaining a first degree in psychology is not sufficient to practice as a psychologist in Northern Ireland, which requires an additional postgraduate qualification in a specific area. Postgraduate psychology programs are available at all campuses, in clinical psychology (doctorate), educational psychology (master's), and occupational psychology (master's) at Queen's Belfast and a more general master's program in applied psychology can be taken at the University of Ulster at Jordanstown. Students study for doctoral degrees by research at all four campuses. Entry into postgraduate study is extremely competitive and only a minority (20% approximately) of students with bachelor's degrees in psychology continue their studies to postgraduate level.

The majority of psychologists in Northern Ireland work in clinical settings (the National Health Service), in education (local education authorities), as occupational psychologists in both the public and private sectors (although very few work in private practice), and in universities as teachers and researchers. Emergent areas of the discipline (with a consequent demand for professional employment) are in counseling, sport, and health psychology.

Psychology is not yet a legally registered profession in the United Kingdom (or in the Republic of Ireland), although there are discussions ongoing with government on this question. However, the majority of psychologists in Northern Ireland are members of the British Psychological Society (BPS) and work under a Code of Professional Conduct. They participate fully in the scientific and professional activities of the BPS both at a national level and locally through the Northern Ireland Branch. The Northern Ireland Branch is very active: it holds scientific meetings and provides opportunities for professional development including an annual conference and a local newsletter. A monthly news bulletin, *The Psychologist*, is distributed to all BPS members keeping them abreast of wider developments and forthcoming national and international meetings and conferences. Cooperation between Northern Ireland and Republic of Ireland psychologists is strong, many also being members of the sister association, the Psychological Society of Ireland. The *Irish Journal of Psychology*, published by the Psychological Society of Ireland, is an important publication outlet for researchers from both Northern Ireland and the Republic (see examples of special issues of the journal in the bibliography).

For the past 30 years, Northern Ireland has been a community in conflict. This has presented considerable challenges to both professional and research psychologists. It is not surprising that a distinctive research theme to emerge has been on the question of national identity, the nature of intergroup conflict, and the effects of violence on children (Cairns, 1987; Cairns & Darby, 1998; Trew, 1994; Weinreich, 1997). The signing of the Northern Ireland political agreement in the late 1990s brought an era in which new psychological questions will arise. Examples include resettlement into the community of people imprisoned for offenses committed in sectarian causes, the emotional reaction of victims, and the significance of linguistic and other symbols in the maintenance of ethnic identity.

In general, psychological research in Northern Ireland has both applied and interdisciplinary emphases. For example, psychologists work with members of other professions in such areas as fetal development and low birthweight babies (Hepper, 1997); children's understanding of the global environment (Wylie, Sheehy, McGuinness, & Orchard, 1998); the psychology of sport (Kremer & Scully, 1992; Kremer, Trew, & Ogle, 1997). Other interdisciplinary and cross-cultural research with wide application is also pursued (Weinreich, 1997).

In summary, both the scientific and professional practice of psychology in Northern Ireland is relatively healthy. Demand for studying the discipline is high at universities and there are well-established study programs at both undergraduate and postgraduate levels. Psychology at the predegree level is not widespread in Northern Ireland but secondary schools and further education colleges are starting to provide appropriate syllabuses to meet existing demand. While employment of psychologists is buoyant largely in the public sector, significant opportunities for expansion remain in the private sector. The research ethos is well placed to respond to interdisciplinary developments and applied psychology opportunities.

[*See also* England; *and* Republic of Ireland.]

Bibliography

Brown, K. & McGuinness, C. (Eds.). (1995). Celebrating 150 years of Queen's colleges in Ireland. [Special issue] *The Irish Journal of Psychology, 16*(4), 269–435. Contains 14 papers on current research being undertaken by psychologists in Ireland. The issue celebrates 150 years of the "original" Queen's colleges in Ireland which are Queen's University Belfast, University College Cork, and University College Galway.

Cairns, E. (1987). *Caught in crossfire: Children and the Northern Ireland conflict.* Syracuse, NY: Syracuse University Press.

Cairns, E. (Ed.). (1992). [Special issue on Northern Ireland]. *The Psychologist, 5*(8), 341–358. Seven papers provide an overview of psychological research relating to the Northern Ireland troubles. Topics include identity and intergroup conflict (Trew, Weinreich), violence, stress, and psychological disorder (Cairns, Wilson, McWhirter), and education (Gallagher, Harbison).

Cairns, E. & Darby, J. (1998). The conflict in Northern Ireland: Causes, consequences, and controls. *American Psychologist, 53,* 754–760.

Gallagher, A. G. & Tierney, K. (Eds.). (1996). Psychology and the environment. [Special issue] *The Irish Journal of Psychology, 17*(4), 295–372. Contains papers on communication failure and environmental issues (Sheehy, Harvey) and on children's cognitions about the global environment (Sheehy, Wylie, McGuinness).

Halliday, A., & Coyle, K. (Eds.). (1994). The Irish psyche. [Special issue] *The Irish Journal of Psychology, 15*(2,3), 243–507. Contains 17 papers related to aspects of life in Ireland including papers on identity from a Northern Ireland perspective (Trew), terrorism (Heskins), and promoting peace (Cairns).

Hepper, P. G. (1997). Memory in utero? *Developmental Medicine and Child Neurology, 39,* 343–346.

Kremer, J., & Scully, D. (1994). *Psychology in sport.* London: Taylor & Francis.

Kremer, J., Trew, K., & Ogle, S. (1997). *Young people's involvement in sport.* London: Routledge. A collection of papers which analyze the nature and extent of sport involvement of 7–16-year-olds in Northern Ireland.

Leslie, J. C. (Ed.). (1996). Contemporary ethical issues for psychologists. [Special issue] *The Irish Journal of Psychology, 17,* 87–190.

Trew, K. (1994). What it means to be Irish from a Northern perspective. *The Irish Journal of Psychology, 15,* 288–299.

Weinreich, P. (1997). Enculturation of a semi-alien: Journeying in the construction and reconstruction of identity. In M. H. Bond (Ed.), *Working at the interface of cultures: Eighteen lives in the social sciences* (pp. 154–165). London: Routledge. Applications of identity structure analysis in a variety of interdisciplinary and cross-cultural settings.

Wylie, J., Sheehy, N., McGuinness, C., & Orchard, G. (1998). Children's thinking about air pollution: A systems theory analysis. *Environmental Education Research, 4,* 117–137.

Mehroo Northover and Carol McGuinness

NORWAY. The first Norwegian scholarly treatise in psychology was written by Niels Treschow in 1803 as a high-school textbook. It was later expanded into a broader and more philosophical work on "Human nature, particularly its spiritual side." Treschow was an eclectic philosopher, equally influenced by Continental rationalists and British empiricists, who in 1813 became the first professor of philosophy at the newly founded university in Christiania (Oslo).

Treschow referred to his subject as anthropology rather than psychology. The first book entitled *Psychology* was written by the Hegelian philosopher Marcus J. Monrad in 1850. Monrad's idealistic and rather abstract psychological text was required, but usually undigested reading for several generations of students entering the university, where Monrad held a dominating position until the end of the century. His colleague in the 1890s, John Mourly Vold, acquired some fame (including a favorable review by Freud), for experimental studies of dreams.

The "new" psychology was introduced in Norway between 1890 and 1910 by the next generation of philosophers (Løchen, Aars, and Aall) who had been visiting experimental laboratories on the continent. Anathon Aall (1867–1942) founded the Institute of Psychology at the University of Oslo in 1909, which began with nothing more than a small collection of instruments and books, stored away in a basement room belonging to the department of physiology. Aall conducted experimental studies of memory, and claimed to have discovered a "new law of memory": the influence of temporal set upon retention. Aall remained professor of philosophy, but wrote textbooks on general psychology (1926) and social psychology (1938).

The first doctorate in psychology was awarded in 1913 to a woman, Helga Eng (1875–1966), for her dissertation on *Abstract Concepts in Children's Speech and Thought.* Eng did psychophysiological experiments on emotions in children (1921), and published a book on children's drawings (1926). She founded the first psychotechnic institute in 1925, and the Pedagogical Research Institute at the university, where she was appointed the first professor of pedagogics (1938).

Besides Aall and Eng, only a handful of scholars did empirical research in psychology in the 20-year period between 1909, when the Psychological Institute was established, and 1928, when the first master's degrees in psychology were awarded. These were: M. L. Reymert, known for his early studies on the ideals of children and youth; Th. Grüner-Hegge, who did memory research; Th. Schjelderup-Ebbe, who in the 1920s acquired world fame for his discoveries of dominance hierarchies in the social life of animals; and H. Schjelderup, with psychophysical studies on vision.

Harald Schjelderup (1895–1974) became in 1922 Løchen's successor as a very young professor of philosophy. In 1928, his professorship was changed to psychology. For 30 years, he remained the first and only professor of psychology in this country. Schjelderup was a broad-minded and well-respected scholar who tried to integrate, or at least balance, traditional experimental psychology, learning theories, and psychoanalysis, as documented by his 1927 textbook of psychology. This book, and its successor, appearing in 1957, were standard introductory texts for all students entering university for 50 years. Schjelderup had early become fascinated by the new perspectives for psychological understanding opened by the psychoanalytic method. He studied psychoanalysis in Vienna, Berlin, and Zürich in the 1920s, and returned with great enthusiasm about the importance of the analytic method and analytic phenomena, but a more skeptical attitude toward analytic concepts and theories. Schjelderup played a main role in introducing psychoanalysis in Norway and also in making it academically respectable. His own psychoanalytic writings from the 1930s and 1940s were modern for the age, foreshadowing later developments in ego psychology and object relation theory. He also was a pioneer in the study of long-term effects of psychoanalytic treatment.

In the 1930s Norway became a temporary residence for prominent refugees from Nazi Germany, notably Charlotte Bühler, Otto Fenichel, and Wilhelm Reich. Reich stayed in Norway for four years, and his theories of sexual economy and life energy became the subject of heated public and professional debates. Strongly inspired by Reich, body-oriented therapists like Ola Raknes and Nic Waal continued to exert an influence on new generations of psychotherapists and child psychologists still forming a strand of the Norwegian psychological landscape.

After World War II, Norwegian psychology gathered

its main impulses from the United States rather than from German psychology, partly through Fulbright fellowships which enabled an exchange of research scholars for shorter and longer visits to both countries. In 1948, a new professional degree in psychology (Cand. Psychol.) was introduced at the University of Oslo, leading to the development of a professional program designed to qualify candidates mainly for clinical and applied positions outside of university (1956).

Besides Schjelderup, the most prominent figures in Norwegian psychology in the 1950s and 1960s were child psychologist Åse Gruda Skard (1905–1985), best known for her popular works on child rearing and practical child psychology; Per Saugstad (b. 1920) who became the main inspiration for a generation of experimental psychologists that still occupies central positions at Norwegian universities; and Ragnar Rommetveit (b. 1924), who played a central role in the establishment of postwar European social psychology, before turning to psycholinguistics. Jan Smedslund (b. 1929) began his career doing experimental studies in cognitive and developmental psychology, inspired by Brunswik and Piaget, but became generally critical about the value of empirical research. Saugstad, Rommetveit, and Smedslund were all concerned about the possibilities and limitations of scientific knowledge in psychology, a debate originating in this country in the writings and teachings of philosopher Arne Næss, who also took an active interest in psychological research. Kjell Raaheim (b. 1930) did pioneering research in problem solving and its relation to experience, intelligence, and creativity.

Between 1946 and 1971 three new universities were established in Norway, which eventually developed their own psychology departments: Bergen (1964), Trondheim (1967), and Tromsø (1983). A full professional program leading to Cand. psychol. degree was introduced in Bergen in 1969, particularly because of the efforts of the entrepreneurial professor Bjørn Christiansen (1927–1987), who also was the architect behind the establishment of a separate Faculty of Psychology in 1980, with Hallgrim Kløve as its first dean. At the other three universities, the psychology departments are part of the faculties of social science. Today, the department in Oslo and the faculty in Bergen each employ 50 to 60 faculty members at the associate and full professor levels. The departments in Tromsø and Trondheim are of about half this size.

Professional programs of psychology were opened at the University of Tromsø in 1991 and at the Norwegian University of Science and Technology in Trondheim in 1995. Currently, 212 new students are accepted into the 5-year programs at the four universities each year. The 5-year programs follow a first year of introductory psychology (admission to the professional program being based on introductory grades). Graduate programs

leading to doctorates in psychology (Dr. Psychol.) were first introduced in Bergen and Oslo in 1986.

Scientific journals in psychology are *Nordisk psykologi*, established 1949, for publications in Scandinavian languages, and *Scandinavian Journal of Psychology*, established 1959, for English-language articles. Both journals were the result of cooperation between the psychological associations in the Nordic countries. Since 1964 the Norwegian Psychological Association issues its own journal, *Tidsskrift for Norsk Psykologforening*, which includes research articles (with English abstracts). But today, most Norwegian psychological research is published in international journals appropriate for the area of research.

The Norwegian Psychological Association (NPF) was founded in 1934 with only a dozen members. By 1960 there were 270 psychologists in Norway, which grew to 500 in 1970, and to 1,300 in 1980. Today there are more than 3,000 psychologists (around 2,750 NPF members), or 68 psychologists per 100,000 inhabitants. These figures will continue to grow rapidly for several years, as the number of psychologists retiring from the profession is still much lower than the number of new graduates.

Since 1973, psychologists have to be legally licensed. Licensing requires a Cand. psychol. degree (or its equivalent). This requirement is circular, demanding a broad background of scientific and practical training (including supervised internship) to be built into the degree. Thus university education in psychology has become fairly standardized, with restricted opportunities for individual concentration around selected themes. This may have been detrimental for recruitment to research, but has probably strengthened the general position of psychologists in the labor market. After graduation, it is possible to take one of four routes toward specialization: community psychology, work and organizational psychology, clinical psychology with intensive psychotherapy, and clinical psychology (with several subspecialities), each requiring a minimum of 5 years' professional work.

About half of all Norwegian psychologists are working as clinical psychologists in adult, children, and youth psychiatric clinics, drug abuse clinics, somatic and mental hospitals, or in private practice. Approximately 25% are employed by school authorities, mainly engaged in psychological and educational counseling of children and youth. Research and higher education employ about 15%, whereas the remaining 10% are working in various applied settings, for instance as organizational psychologists or in public administration.

Norwegian clinical psychologists, especially those trained in Oslo, have been exposed more strongly to psychodynamic than to other psychotherapeutic approaches, but also systemic, cognitive, and behavioral approaches have become widespread in recent years. A survey (H. Hjorth, unpublished study, University of Oslo) shows a dynamic orientation to be more popular with psychiatrists than with psychologists, who consider themselves more eclectic.

Psychological research is conducted primarily in the universities, but also in some cross-disciplinary, applied research centers. It is difficult to discern a particular national research tradition or profile. The four psychology departments have all been developed to cover a broad spectrum of theoretical and applied topics, encouraging diversity rather than specific thematic concentrations.

Perhaps the most prominent research groups are to be found at the department of biological and medical psychology in Bergen, centered around cognitive neuropsychologist Kenneth Hugdahl, physiological psychologist Holger Ursin, and pioneer in clinical neuropsychology Hallgrim Kløve.

The Norwegian population is relatively easily mapped, and well suited for family studies and epidemiological research, which has resulted in several high-quality studies of the heritability of psychopathology (Kringlen, Torgersen), as well as studies of trends in various health-related issues (HEMIL-center in Bergen, NOVA and the National Institute of Public Health in Oslo).

A third strong area has been psychotherapy research, originating in the Schjelderup tradition, with Bjørn Killingmo (Oslo) as a major spokesman for the advancement of psychodynamic theory, and Odd E. Havik (Bergen) as the architect of a recent major project aimed at assessing effects of therapist and patient characteristics on psychotherapeutic outcomes.

The five most extensively cited Norwegian psychologists in the period from 1992 to 1997 (according to ISI databases) are: Dan Olweus, at the University of Bergen, for large-scale studies on aggression and bullying among schoolchildren; Svenn Torgersen (Oslo), for studies of personality and anxiety disorders; Kenneth Hugdahl (Bergen), for experimental studies of hemispheric differences; Holger Ursin (Bergen) for psychophysiological studies of stress; and Jan Smedslund (Oslo) for his analysis of psychological concepts implicit in ordinary language.

Norwegian psychology is still in a very expansive stage, enjoying a rapid growth in academic as well as in applied settings. It is increasingly internationally oriented, not so much toward Scandinavia (apart for some Swedish contacts and influences), as toward the English-speaking scientific community (most university books and scholarly publications are in English). This trend has been reinforced in recent years through the import of foreign scholars to university positions, especially in Trondheim and Tromsø. There has recently been some concern about recruitment to areas of basic

research, and about the need to develop new professional roles supplementing that of the traditional clinical psychologist. There is still no scarcity of jobs; since the 1970s, there has been virtually no unemployment for psychologists, though that picture may change.

Bibliography

Bjørgen, I. A. (Ed.). (1989). *Basic issues in psychology: A Scandinavian contribution*. Bergen: Sigma forlag. Essays chiefly written by Norwegian psychologists honoring Per Saugstad, professor in experimental psychology at the University of Oslo.

Holter, P. A., Magnussen, S., & Sandsberg, S. (Eds.). (1984). *Norsk psykologi i 50 år* [Norwegian psychology over 50 years]. Oslo: Universitetsforlaget. Published for the fiftieth anniversary of the Norwegian Psychological Association. Contains overview chapters on the development of selected applied and research areas.

Kaufmann, G., Helstrup, T., & Teigen, K. H. (Eds.). (1995). *Problem solving and cognitive processes: A festschrift in honour of Kjell Raaheim*. Bergen: Fagbokforlaget. Essays chiefly written by Norwegian psychologists honoring Kjell Raaheim, professor in cognitive psychology at the University of Bergen.

Moustgaard, I. K., Pedersen, J. M., & Teigen, K. H. (Eds.). (1987). *Seculum primum*. København: Dansk psykologisk forlag. Selected discussions on the history of psychology in Scandinavia, published at the one hundredth anniversary of the Psychological Laboratory in Copenhagen.

Myklebust, J. P., & Ommundsen, R. (Eds.). (1987). *Psykologiprofesjonen mot år 2000* [The psychology profession toward the year 2000]. Oslo: Universitetsforlaget. Memorial volume for professor Bjørn Christiansen (1927–1987), founder of the professional program in psychology at the University of Bergen.

Skard, Å. G. (Ed.). (1959). *Psykologi og psykologar i Norge* [Psychology and psychologists in Norway]. Oslo: Universitetsforlaget. Published for the fiftieth anniversary of the Institute of Psychology in Oslo. Contains extensive autobiographical entries of all important psychologists educated before World War II.

Skard, Å. G. (1976). Norway. In V. S. Sexton & H. Misiak (Eds.), *Psychology around the world* (pp. 317–328). Monterey, CA: Brooks/Cole.

Teigen, K. H. (1996). Psykologi. In N. R. Hansen, J. Goksøyr, L. M. Irgens, K. B. Helle, T. I. Bertelsen, R. K. Lie, A. Nernæs, K. A. Selvig, F. W. Thue, S. Bagge, & K. H. Teigen, *Universitetet i Bergens historie* (Vol. 2, pp. 706–742). Bergen: Universitetet i Bergen. The history of psychology at the University of Bergen, published at the university's fiftieth anniversary.

Ursin, H. (1987). Norway. In A. R. Gilgen & C. K. Gilgen (Eds.), *International handbook of psychology* (pp. 347–367). London: Aldwych Press.

Karl Halvor Teigen

NTL INSTITUTE FOR APPLIED BEHAVIORAL SCIENCE. In 1946, at a conference on intergroup relations held in New Britain, Connecticut, social psychologist Kurt Lewin and a number of his colleagues, including Leland P. Bradford, Kenneth Benne, and Ronald Lippitt, observed the discussion groups as part of their research into group dynamics. In the evenings, Lewin's research group met to discuss their observations of the days' events. Some members of the conference asked if they could observe the researchers' discussions and found themselves in some disagreement with the observations of the psychologists. A lively exchange ensued, which Lewin and his colleagues saw as a powerful learning experience in itself about the way groups function and how individuals function in them. This suggested that a workshop could be created in which the participants were invited to study their own and their groups' processes in order to learn about leadership and membership roles in a group. Thus what is now called a human interaction laboratory, with the "T-group" as its centerpiece, was born.

A new organization, the National Training Laboratories (NTL), with Bradford as president was created, and the first summer program was held on the campus of Gould Academy in Bethel, Maine, in the summer of 1947. This first summer program, supported by a grant from the Office of Naval Research, with the National Education Association acting as the sponsoring organization for NTL, lasted for 3 weeks and consisted of theory presentations, T-group sessions, and structured experiences, all aimed at exploring group processes.

Every summer since then, summer training laboratory programs have been held in Bethel, and the success of the work can be seen in the fact that NTL currently offers such programs throughout the year and at locations all around the country. Programs related to the basic human interaction laboratory include management workshops, in which the application of group dynamic principles to management and leadership are the focus; a variety of "personal growth laboratories," pioneered by John and Joyce Weir, which focus on individual and personal learning about groups; and programs designed to train professionals in the skills of experiential education. Key issues in most of NTL's programs include explorations of race and gender, management and membership issues, and the development of effective work groups.

NTL's membership includes approximately 450 individuals who come from a wide variety of occupations, including teaching, consulting, psychological practice, and management. Its board of directors is elected by the membership and provides overall policy guidance. The day-to-day administrative work of the organization is the responsibility of the central office staff at NTL's headquarters in Alexandria, Virginia. The president

and chief executive officer, currently Lennox E. Joseph, is elected by the board. Various committees of members deal with issues of membership, creation of new programs, publications, and planning.

NTL publishes the *Journal for Applied Behavioral Sciences* and a number of books in human relations training and organizational development.

Sherman Kingsbury

NUCLEAR FAMILIES. *See* Family Psychology.

NULL HYPOTHESIS. *See* Data Analysis; *and* Hypothesis Testing.

NURSING HOMES. *See* Elder Care.

NUTRITION. The term *nutrition* refers to the science that describes the associations between food, health, and disease. Nutritional status is determined from anthropometric measurements, biochemical indices, clinical observations, and dietary intake data. A combination of several of these is definitive and is the "gold standard" for determining nutritional status. Dietary intake is important because it is among the earliest signs of malnutrition and therefore needs to be included in screening or assessment of nutritional status. It is also important for developing dietary recommendations. No single indicator suffices either for diagnosing all forms of malnutrition or for shaping dietary interventions. Dietary evaluation involves the interpretation of the information on dietary intake with other information to reach appropriate conclusions about nutritional status.

There are many forms of malnutrition. They include starvation (insufficient amounts of the energy providing nutrients), protein calorie malnutrition (deficits of protein and/or energy in varying degrees), other nutrient deficiencies (vitamins, minerals, or essential fatty acids), excess energy intakes (giving rise to excess body fat or obesity), imbalance of macro- or micronutrients (such as too much saturated fat or cholesterol), and toxicities (alcohol or other nutrients). Malnutrition may occur due to lack of a nutrient or nutrients in the diet (primary malnutrition), toxicity, or diseases that secondarily alter intake, absorption, metabolism, or excretion of nutrients (secondary malnutrition).

Role of Nutrition in Mental and Physical Health

When intakes are grossly inadequate, dietary deficiency diseases result. Several of these, such as pellagra, beriberi, iodide deficiency disease, and protein-calorie malnutrition, have profound effects on mental health. These are now rare in the United States and in most Western countries, but some are still common in many parts of the world and retard mental development. Protein calorie malnutrition, when it is chronic, severe, and occurs under the age of 2 years, is associated with decreased achievement on IQ tests later in childhood. It is also associated with immediate alterations in affect, such as apathy and crankiness. Micronutrient deficiencies also affect mental development. Iodide deficiency disease when it occurs in pregnancy can cause permanent mental retardation (cretinism) as well as disorders in hearing and gait. Iron deficiency anemia, especially when it occurs early in infancy and is chronic, is associated with immediate as well as later deficits in attention and achievement on some tests. Severe vitamin A deficiency, when it reaches the stage of xerophthalmia, is associated with nutritional blindness, providing a sensory deficit that inhibits learning.

A recent link between diet and mental and physical development is the apparent effect of diets very low or devoid of folic acid during the periconceptional period on the prevalence of neural tube defects, a serious and potentially fatal defect in organogenesis that may cause profound mental retardation or death (anencephaly) or physical handicap (spina bifida). To protect against low intakes, cereals in the United States are now fortified with folic acid, and for women at high risk, folic acid supplements are also recommended in the periconceptional period.

Toxic amounts of food constituents can also give rise to ill health. Chronic alcohol abuse during pregnancy is associated with increased prevalence of fetal alcohol syndrome, with potentially irreversible effects on mental development and IQ deficits later in childhood. Fetal alcohol effects of a lesser degree include low birth weight, which may increase risks of poor physical health as well as mental development. In adults, chronic alcoholism is often accompanied by malnutrition and deficiencies of several of the B vitamins, including folic acid. A combination of chronic alcoholism and thiamin deficiency appears to be associated with the Wernike-Korsikoff syndrome, and with loss of recent memory, so severe that institutionalization may be needed. Finally, vitamin B-12 deficiency arising either primarily due to disease or secondarily to pernicious anemia, or to malabsorption due to atrophic gastritis and bacterial overgrowth of the small intestine, can give rise to forgetfulness and, if long continued, irreversible changes in mentation owing to degeneration of the spinal cord.

Another type of toxicity results from chronic megadoses (e.g., several orders of magnitude higher than the levels recommended by the Food and Nutrition Board of the National Academy of Science in the Recommended Dietary Allowances) of vitamin B-6. Such treatments have been inappropriately advocated for carpal tunnel syndrome, premenstrual syndrome, and occasionally for mental retardation. A reversible peripheral neuropathy is associated with these doses. Lead is another substance that, if present in high amounts in food, water, air, or elsewhere in the environment, can adversely affect mental development. In addition to these effects on mental health, the physical effects of malnutrition of all sorts are well defined.

Diet as an Adjunct to Psychotherapy

Dietary therapy is essential in several conditions that are primarily psychological or psychiatric in origin. Anorexia nervosa, both the bulimarectic (bingeing and purging) and classical (starvation-like) forms of the disorder are accompanied by protein calorie malnutrition, and some changes in affect are due to starvation alone. It does little good to commence with psychotherapy if the undernutrition is not treated. Some symptoms disappear with realimentation; then the underlying disturbances must then be treated with psychotherapy.

In bulimia (bingeing), and bingeing/purging behaviors, dietary therapy is also helpful as an adjunct to psychotherapy. The patient often benefits from a structured eating pattern and plan.

Diet is helpful in treatment of addictive disorders, such as alcoholism and drug abuse, if they are chronic and the patient is in a nutritionally debilitated state. Many recovered addicts are convinced that large amounts of supplemental vitamins or avoidance of sugar will help decrease cravings, although they do not; what is needed is a good diet.

Elderly persons who are depressed and isolated may lose large amounts of weight and need dietary counseling and therapy to regain it. Patients with manic-depressive disorder and certain other disorders are often undernourished and fail to eat. They may need special nutritional measures to rehabilitate them. During treatment some patients with emotional or character disorders are prescribed drugs that either alter body weight or may give rise to drug-nutrient interactions. Such medications include lithium, Prozac, benzodiazepam, other antidepressants, and other drugs such as Prolixin for schizophrenic symptoms. Admonitions about use of alcohol by persons on such drugs are often in order. Individuals on Prolixin, lithium, and Thorazine often gain very large amounts of weight and require dietary counseling for weight control.

Dietary therapy, with the "Feingold diet" low in food dyes, especially tartrazine, and salicylates for attention deficit/hyperactivity disorder has not proven to have reliable positive effects in the majority of studies to date. Special diets, including megadoses of various vitamins and gluten-free or low-sugar diets have also been claimed to be useful in improving behavior and mental performance in children with Down syndrome and autistic disorders. There is virtually no evidence that such diets have any positive effects; efforts are better spent on conventional educational and psychological therapies.

Elimination diets that eliminate whole food groups to treat chronic fatigue syndrome have not been shown to be useful in controlled randomized clinical trials.

Diet in Treatment of Obesity

The only ways to lose excess body fat are to eat less food and/or increase energy output. All psychotherapy of obesity affects body fatness by modifying one or both of these factors. A hypocaloric diet (e.g., a diet which is lower in food energy than the individual is used to eating when his or her weight is stable) may be explicit (such as prescription of a reducing diet) or may be implicit (as by administration of a medication that decreases hunger and thereby decreases energy intake). Since most Americans do not or cannot increase their energy outputs enough each day to create the deficit of 500 calories daily needed to lose a pound a week, it is essential that the weight reduction phase involve some degree of caloric restriction as well. There must be a caloric deficit: The notion that "healthy eating" alone is enough will not suffice, although of course an eating plan, such as the U.S. Department of Agriculture's food pyramid is important to ensure dietary adequacy. Anorectic agents that alter hunger or satiety are also useful in some cases. To the extent that behavior modification techniques decrease energy intake or increase energy output, such as restricting eating to certain environments, conscious recording of food intake in diaries or records, or development of strategies for social and other situations that are likely to be associated with unbridled food consumption, these are all to the good. However, psychotherapy alone is not sufficient and is adjunctive. Counseling by a registered dietitian, or membership in a nonprofit or commercial weight control group, use of prepackaged foods for those who can afford it, and recourse to structured programs of physical activity and exercise, can help the patient adhere to a low calorie diet. Physical activity, exercise, and behavioral modification are all components of a sound weight control program.

Diet in Treatment of Diabetes

Psychotherapy is adjunctive and diet, physical activity/ exercise, and pharmacologic treatment are primary in the treatment of diabetes mellitus. The most common form of diabetes is type II, adult onset or noninsulin dependent diabetes mellitus (NIDDM), which is common among the obese. A hypocaloric diet and a more physically active life alone can often decrease symptoms in the obese and normalize the underlying biochemical deficit in insulin metabolism if sufficient weight is lost. Often an oral hypoglycemic agent is also helpful.

In the rarer form of diabetes, insulin dependent diabetes mellitus (IDDM), exogenously administered insulin, dietary intake of energy and other nutrients that affect blood sugar, and physical activity/exercise are all essential for keeping blood sugar within reasonable limits without the radical swings that give rise to symptoms and accelerate the cardiovascular and other sequellae of the disease. Since persons with diabetes vary in their comorbidities, their sensitivity to diet and other factors, it is important that they receive dietary counseling from a registered dietitian or another health professional, who is well versed in clinical nutrition.

Key Assumptions and Theories

Human nutrition's tenets are shared by nutritional scientists throughout the world. All agree that human beings within the same age and sex group under the same environmental conditions need the same kinds and amounts of nutrients. Differences in nutrient requirements in different parts of the world result chiefly from variations in environmental conditions; genetic differences are small but can also be important hereditary lactose intolerance is one example. It is also recognized that all human beings need food energy, but not too much; human beings under the same environmental conditions have no means of excreting excess food energy and it is stored as fat. The body's response to insufficient food energy in the diet is first to decrease nonobligatory physical activity and resting metabolism. When these adjustments do not suffice, body fat and lean body mass are mobilized and burned for energy, and eventually starvation and death ensue.

In addition to getting sufficient nutrients it is also important to make sure that intakes are balanced and varied. It is now apparent that many chronic degenerative diseases including coronary artery disease, NIDDM, and certain forms of cancers (breast and prostate) may be influenced in part by dietary intake and it can have a favorable impact upon decreasing complications. It is also clear that food-borne diseases also cause illness; appropriate animal husbandry, food preparation, and handling can reduce food safety risks.

Food and drink clearly affect mood. Alcohol intake is the most obvious example. There are also other associations between food, mental health, and well-being, although the effects are not usually as dramatic.

Research Findings

Nutritional science continues to increase as our knowledge of genetics, molecular biology, biochemistry, and the physiology of plants and animals expands and clarifies. The Food and Nutrition Board of the Institute of Medicine, National Academy of Sciences in Washington, D.C., periodically reviews information on diet and health and issues reports on the state of nutritional research as it affects the nutritional status of the nation. The U.S. Department of Agriculture, the U.S. Department of Health and Human Services, and certain other branches of government (Defense, Education) fund and produce research, as do state land grant colleges of agriculture and human ecology, and certain private foundations.

Controversies

Major controversies today include the appropriate role of food versus dietary supplements for obtaining nutrients. A growing area of controversy is the safety and efficacy of botanical and other supplements. The upper safety levels of most nutrients are not known because little scientific effort has been devoted to examining these effects and systematic reports of side effects are not available. Another controversial question is the extent to which substances in food other than nutrients (such as flavonoids, fiber, etc.) have beneficial or prejudicial effects on health. Currently there is much interest in phytochemicals—substances found only in plants. The most appropriate amounts, types, and routes for nourishing very small infants and very ill people by special feeding routes (enteral and parenteral) are being debated. The safety and efficacy of various dietary measures for preventing or treating chronic degenerative diseases is also being examined; while all scientists agree that prevention is better than cure, there is debate about the extent to which diet contributes to and dietary changes can reverse various chronic degenerative diseases and conditions. A final contentious issue is the extent to which good nutrition is related to positive health outcomes and quality of life, and how best to measure these factors.

Overall Effectiveness

Some medical nutritional therapies involve the direct provision of food. These modalities include total parenteral nutrition with nutrients provided intravenously, enteral alimentation by nasogastric or other tubes to the gut, or regular oral intake of foods in hospitals and institutional settings. Other therapies are indirect. They involve the provision of dietary counseling to encourage free-living people to enable them to make dietary changes on their own. Direct provision of therapeutic diets is more effective but is rarely possible for more than a few days or weeks in most cases. Dietary coun-

seling's effectiveness varies depending on the nutritional problem that is present (single nutrient or multiple deficiencies), the patient (motivation, ability to change one's eating environment, economic resources), and the skill of the counselor. Just as psychotherapy should not be practiced by untrained individuals, medical nutrition therapy is safest and most effective when the therapist is appropriately trained. Such training includes a B.S. registration in dietetics (R.D.), or better still, an advanced degree in clinical human nutrition (e.g., M.S. or Ph.D.), preferably coupled with the R.D., or an M.D., with specific advanced clinical training in clinical nutrition. Unfortunately, the term *nutritionist* implies no specific education or relevant clinical training, and therefore does not provide a sufficient credential.

Conclusion

We are what we eat. Nutrition, inasmuch as it affects both physical and mental health, is a vital factor to keep in mind in dealing with psychological issues.

[*See also* Determinants of Intelligence, *article on* Nutrition and Intelligence.]

Bibliography

Committee on Dietary Allowances and Food and Nutrition Board. (1989). *Recommended dietary allowances* (10th ed.). Washington, DC: National Academy Press.

Committee on Diet & Health. (1989). *Diet & health: Recommendation to reduce chronic disease risk*. Washington, DC: National Academy Press.

Marriott, B. M. (Ed.) & Committee on Military Nutrition Research. (1994). *Food components to enhance performance*. Washington, DC: National Academy Press.

Marriott, B. R. (Ed.) & Committee for Military Nutrition Research. (1993). *Not eating enough*. Washington, DC: Institute of Medicine/National Academy Press.

Marriott, B. R., & Grumpstrup-Scott, J. (Eds.). (1992). *Body composition and physical performance*. Washington, DC: National Academy Press.

Shils, M. E., Olsen, J. A., Shibe, M., & Ross, K. (Eds.). (In press). *Modern nutrition in health and disease* (Vols. 1–2). Philadelphia: Lea & Febiger.

Thomas, P. R. (Ed.). (1995). *Weighing the options*. Washington, DC: National Academy Press.

U.S. Department of Health & Human Sciences/Public Health Science. (1990). *Healthy people 2000*. Washington, DC: U.S. Government Printing Office.

Woteki, C. R., & Thomas, P. R. (Eds.). (1992). *Eat for life: The FNB guide to reducing your risk of chronic disease*. Washington, DC: National Academy Press.

Johanna Dwyer

OBEDIENCE. To follow orders from a person with higher status within a defined hierarchical social system or chain of command (e.g., military, government, corporation, family) is to be obedient. Obedience to authority, a particularly explicit form of social influence, may reflect diverse motives (e.g., willingly obeying laws, respecting the expertise or achievements of authorities, or fearing the consequences of disobedience; Tyler, 1990).

For psychologists, the most influential analysis of obedience is that of Stanley Milgram, who conducted a 3-year programmatic series of experiments at Yale University in the early 1960s (Miller, Collins, & Brief, 1995). Milgram was concerned with a particularly compelling occurrence of destructive obedience to authority, namely the Holocaust:

> Gas chambers were built, death camps were guarded, daily quotas of corpses were produced with the same efficiency as the manufacture of appliances. These inhumane policies may have originated in the mind of a single person, but they could only be carried out on a massive scale if a very large number of persons obeyed orders. (Milgram, 1963, p. 371)

Milgram asked a simple question: "If X tells Y to hurt Z, under what conditions will Y carry out the command of X and under what conditions will he refuse?" (1965, p. 57), and devised an ingenious method to answer it. Adult participants, having volunteered for a study of memory and learning, were told, upon arriving at Milgram's laboratory, that the experiment would deal with the effects of punishment. Two individuals (one an accomplice) were assigned by what appeared to be a random draw to be either the "teacher" (the true participant) or "learner." The learner was then positioned with (bogus) electronic wiring to receive shocks from the teacher. The learner made (upon a prearranged schedule) errors on a memory task for which

punishment was to be administered by means of a shock generator consisting of 30 switches at 15-volt increments. Beginning at the first switch, participants who remained in the experiment to its completion were ultimately ordered to inflict the most intense punishment (450 volts). No shocks were in fact administered, although the learner went through a series of simulated (on tape) vocalizations of distress and demands to be released.

The experiment escalated over its course to a situation involving an intense moral conflict for the participant—incessant demands from the experimenter to continue shocking the learner and mounting pleas from the learner to be released. The experimenter ignored the learner's plight other than assuring participants that no permanent harm would occur, and ordered that all punishments be administered. Resistance from participants was met by increasingly strident prods, including, "You have no other choice, you must continue." Those refusing to continue were finally excused. Evidence suggests that this scenario was highly believable for a majority of participants (Miller, 1986). A thorough debriefing was conducted following each session.

The baseline condition situated the learner in an adjoining room. At the 300-volt level, the learner could be heard pounding on the wall. *Obedience* was defined as administering *all* of the required shocks. An unexpectedly high rate of obedience (65%) was observed in the initial study. This contrasts sharply with the extremely low predictions of obedience made when people are given a description of Milgram's experiment (Miller, 1986). This intuitive (mis)understanding of destructive obedience reflects a pervasive tendency to attribute dispositional causes (sadism, aggressiveness) for behavior actually controlled by powerful situational constraints. Milgram's findings suggest that destructive obedience is well within the behavioral repertoire of *most* people regardless of their personality or moral virtue. Authority, in many circumstances, may thus supersede matters of conscience or empathy. The co-occurrence of high rates of destructive obedience and the severe tension observed in many of Milgram's research participants have made the Milgram experiments the center of an ethical controversy regarding risks imposed upon participants (Baumrind, 1964; Milgram, 1964; Miller, 1986).

Obedience was shown to be strongly determined by specific, at times subtle, elements of the situation. Increasing the physical distance between the participant and learner increased the obedience rate. Obedience dropped sharply when the experimenter was not physically present but issued orders by phone. Relocating the study to an urban office building (as contrasted with the university setting) had no significant impact on obedience. Women serving as participants produced an obedience rate identical to that of male participants in the baseline experiment.

Milgram's basic findings have been observed in a variety of other research contexts. Harmful obedience has been observed with children (Shanab & Yahya, 1977) as well as women in the "teacher" role, and in a hospital context with nurses as unsuspecting participants (Miller, 1986). An informative study was conducted in the Netherlands, in which participants were ordered to inflict verbal harassment (instead of physical punishment) upon a peer (accomplice) working on an employment-interview exam. High rates of obedience were observed (over 90%), even higher than Milgram's baseline result, but also the sharply reduced obedience in the "rebellious peers" and "experimenter absent" variations (Meeus & Raaijmakers, 1986). Recent evidence also suggests that regardless of personal values, people may conform to the preferences of an authority in the context of ethical decision making (e.g., a management decision to market a potentially dangerous drug), whereas without such constraints, decisions are based on personal values (Brief, Dukerich, & Duran, 1991). Given the behavior observed in the relatively temporary conditions of the laboratory setting, one appreciates the vastly stronger pressures for destructive obedience in organizational contexts where the constraints upon subordinates are much greater (Darley, 1992).

Milgram identified three major dynamics to the process of obedience. A *sociocultural* perspective suggests that we learn to obey authorities (e.g., parents, teachers, police, doctors) and expect to encounter legitimate, trustworthy authority in innumerable contexts. This is particularly true with respect to institutions with powerful cultural or symbolic value (e.g., religion, education, science, medicine, the military, government). The people who volunteered to participate in Milgram's scientific study thus entered the laboratory with a history of rewarded obedience and a presumption that a trust-

worthy, credible authority would meet them. In contrast to the experimental situation, it should be noted that settings for obedience in the more ordinary lives of people may well be extremely protracted and involve stronger pressures and consequences for the individual. There is, for example, the phenomenon of whistle-blowing, as a result of which extraordinary costs are paid by individuals who have challenged authority within the context of their organization and disclose corrupt or immoral practices to outside sources (Miceli & Near, 1992).

Once participants are situated in the experiment, *binding factors* become operative. Diverse cues create psychological barriers to disobedience (e.g., the experimenter's austere manner, his uniform, the learner's willingness to receive punishment, the participants having volunteered to be in the study). The *gradual* increase in punishment levels ordered by the experimenter is of particular importance. Self-perception theory (Bern, 1972) can explain relatively powerful behavioral consequences if an individual can be initially induced to perform seemingly inconsequential acts that virtually anyone would agree to perform. Cognitive dissonance theory (Festinger, 1957) also suggests that disobedience might be particularly difficult if it is viewed as inconsistent with the individual's previous behavior and emotional investment. Milgram also suggested the importance of a seemingly trivial norm of "etiquette," namely, that some individuals might find it embarrassing or impolite to challenge authority, to "make a scene." The power of authority is thus intricately linked to psychological transitions occurring over time in terms of the progressively more intense harm ultimately committed, and in terms of the difficulty many people have in defining malevolent authority as truly illegitimate and taking decisive action in defying that authority. Many persons, in their past, have never disobeyed authorities in any context remotely similar to the Milgram laboratory. It is, in short, an extremely difficult thing to do.

The concept of binding factors links Milgram's findings to destructive obedience in other real-world contexts. People become enmeshed in bureaucratic scenarios in which unethical, immoral, perhaps genocidal policies are set into motion by authorities, policies which are invariably preceded by a number of intermediate, seemingly minor violations. It is the slow, often subtle *progression* toward destructive obedience that is crucial in helping to understand how ordinary individuals, without initial malice, can ultimately commit actions of undeniable evil (Baumeister, 1997; Darley, 1992; Kelman & Hamilton, 1989).

Finally, the issue of *responsibility* is given a central role in Milgram's theoretical analysis, specifically his concept of the agentic shift. The subordinate does not accept personal responsibility for his or her actions, but allocates this responsibility to an individual higher in the organization. One prototype of the agentic shift is the military chain of command. This was seen in the Nuremberg trials, where many high-ranking Nazi defendants disavowed personal responsibility in the context of following orders. The denial of personal responsibility for actions committed under authority does not, of course, necessarily absolve subordinates of responsibility for the consequences of their actions. Military law, for example, requires that immoral orders be disobeyed (Kelman & Hamilton, 1989). Nevertheless, an important psychological consequence of being in a subordinate role is that people can justify their destructive actions by attributing responsibility to superiors. It is also difficult, in many situations, to evaluate, very precisely, the morality or legitimacy of orders prior to obeying them.

One should not, however, overlook the *disobedience* observed in Milgram's research. In the baseline study, 35% of the participants defied the experimenter at some point, and there were marked individual differences within many of the experimental variations. One should not minimize the role of personality factors. A number of such variables, related to authoritarianism, political orientation, and moral development, may play a role (Kelman & Hamilton, 1989), particularly in interactions with situational factors (Blass, 1991).

Conclusions

Many individuals are capable of committing destructive acts when these are authorized, behaviors which they would never commit (nor think themselves capable of committing) without such influence. Furthermore, we are unlikely to recognize our susceptibility to such influence. Rather, we attribute the actions of those we observe in such situations to their defective moral character—not realizing that we, too, would likely engage in similar actions in the same situation. These circumstances need not require the massive trappings of military or governmental authority. The seemingly benign context of a university laboratory is shown to contain more than sufficient social-psychological force for the occurrence of destructive obedience.

[*See also the biography of Milgram*].

Bibliography

Baumeister, R. F. (1997). *Evil: Inside human violence and cruelty*. New York: W. H. Freeman.

Baumrind, D. (1964). Some thoughts on the ethics of research: After reading Milgram's "Behavioral study of obedience." *American Psychologist, 19,* 421–423.

Bem, D. J. (1972). Self-perception theory. In L. Berkowitz (Ed.), *Advances in experimental social psychology* (Vol. 6, pp. 1–62). New York: Academic Press.

Blass, T. (1991). Understanding behavior in the Milgram obedience experiment: The role of personality, situations, and their interactions. *Journal of Personality and Social Psychology, 60,* 398–413.

Brief, A. P., Dukerich, J. M., & Doran, L. I. (1991). Resolving ethical dilemmas in management: Experimental investigations of values, accountability, and choice. *Journal of Applied Social Psychology, 21,* 380–396.

Darley, J. M. (1992). Social organization for the production of evil. *Psychological Inquiry, 3,* 199–218.

Festinger, L. (1957). *A theory of cognitive dissonance.* Stanford, CA: Stanford University Press.

Kelman, H. C., & Hamilton, V. L. (1989). *Crimes of obedience: Toward a social psychology of authority and responsibility.* New Haven, CT: Yale University Press.

Meeus, W., & Raaijmakers, Q. (1986). Administrative obedience: Carrying out orders to use psychological-administrative violence. *European Journal of Social Psychology, 16,* 311–324.

Miceli, M. P., & Near, J. P. (1992). *Blowing the whistle: The organizational and legal implications for companies and employees.* New York: Lexington Books.

Milgram, S. (1963). Behavioral study of obedience. *Journal of Abnormal and Social Psychology, 67,* 371–378.

Milgram, S. (1964). Issues in the study of obedience: A reply to Baumrind. *American Psychologist, 19,* 848–852.

Milgram, S. (1965). Some conditions of obedience and disobedience to authority. *Human Relations, 18,* 57–76.

Milgram, S. (1974). *Obedience to authority: An experimental view.* New York: Harper & Row.

Miller, A. G. (1986). *The obedience experiments: A case study of controversy in social science.* New York: Praeger.

Miller, A. G., Collins, B. E., & Brief, D. E. (1995). Perspectives on obedience to authority: The legacy of the Milgram experiments. [Special issue]. *Journal of Social Issues, 51*(3).

Shanab, M. E., & Yahya, K. A. (1979). A behavioral study of obedience in children. *Journal of Personality and Social Psychology, 35,* 530–536.

Tyler, T. R. (1990). *Why people obey the law.* New Haven, CT: Yale University Press.

Arthur G. Miller

OBESITY is a condition that is characterized by excessive accumulation of fat in the body. Traditionally, overweight has been defined in terms of tables of "ideal" or "desirable" body weight, but today the Body Mass Index (BMI=kg/m^2) is used, with overweight defined as a BMI of 25 to 29.9 and obesity as a BMI of more than 30.

Unlike many "real" diseases and like hypertension, obesity represents one arm of a distribution curve of body weight, with no physiologically defined cut-off point.

Obesity is one of the most pervasive public health problems in the United States today. About 20% of Americans are obese and more than 50% are overweight, with somewhat higher values for women than for men. Furthermore, the prevalence is increasing.

What causes obesity? In one sense the answer is simple—consuming more calories than are expended as energy. In another sense the answer is elusive. The causes of obesity are to be found in the regulation of body weight (which is primarily the regulation of body fat), and we still have only an imperfect understanding of this regulation. Surprisingly, body weight is regulated in obese persons as well as in those of normal weight, with an error in caloric balance of less than 0.0017% per year. So why are people obese? The causes are attributed to an elevation of the set point at which weight is regulated, an elevation with both genetic and environmental determinants.

Causes

The causes of obesity include genetic, environmental, and the interaction of genes and environment.

Genetic Determinants. Recent twin and adoption studies have established that there is a strong genetic influence on human obesity with about one third of the variation in body weight ascribed to genetic factors. The children of obese parents are far more likely to be obese than are the children of thin parents.

Environmental Determinants. The fact that genetic influences may account for no more than one third of the variation in body weight means that the environment exerts an enormous influence. The extent of this influence is demonstrated by the dramatic increase in the prevalence of obesity during the 1990s.

One environmental determinant is socioeconomic status, and there is a strong inverse relationship between socioeconomic status and obesity, particularly among women. Longitudinal studies have shown further that growing up in a lower-class environment is a powerful risk factor for the development of obesity.

These social determinants operate via both energy intake and energy expenditure. Increased food intake clearly plays a major role; the recent introduction of the doubly labeled water method has shown conclusively that obese persons have an increased food intake.

The second environmental factor promoting obesity is sedentary lifestyle. Physical inactivity contributes to a positive energy balance by at least three mechanisms: by decreasing caloric expenditure from activity, by failing to oppose the fall in metabolic rate that is associated with caloric restriction, and by impairing the control of food intake.

Genes and Environment. The current view of the relationship between genetic and environmental determinants of obesity is that they are not antagonists. It is not a question of genes *or* environment or of genes *versus* environment but of genes *and* environment; neither acts alone to determine the clinical outcome. This outcome is determined instead by the combination of genetic vulnerability and adverse environmental events.

Obesity has traditionally been viewed as a disorder with strong psychological determinants, but current thinking limits these determinants to two specific eating disorders. They are binge eating disorder and night eating syndrome. Binge eating disorder is characterized by the consumption of large amounts of food in a short period of time together with a subjective sense of loss of control during the binge and distress following it. Unlike patients with bulimia nervosa, these patients do not engage in compensatory behaviors such as vomiting or laxative abuse in order to prevent the weight gain following a binge and the binge, accordingly, contributes to excessive food intake. Persons with binge eating disorder manifest increased levels of psychopathology and as many as 50% of them suffer from depression (compared to 5% of obese persons who do not binge). Binge eating disorder increases in prevalence with increasing body weight and afflicts about 10 to 20% of persons entering treatment programs for obesity.

The night eating syndrome, characterized by morning anorexia, evening hyperphagia, and insomnia, appears to be a manifestation of an altered circadian rhythm, precipitated by stressful life circumstances. It, too, increases in prevalence with increasing body weight and may afflict as many as 10% of persons entering treatment programs for obesity.

Consequences

The serious health hazards of obesity are currently receiving increasing attention as part of the movement to view obesity as a "disease" rather than as a biological variant. McGinnis and Foege (1993) have recently estimated that 280,000 deaths per year in the United States are attributable to "overnutrition," making it second only to smoking as a preventable cause of death. This influence is exerted via increased prevalence and severity of diabetes, hypertension, sleep apnea, and coronary heart disease.

According to the early, psychogenic theory of obesity, the disorder was caused by deep psychological problems, but in recent years this view has changed dramatically, and while emotional problems specific to obese persons do exist, they are now seen not as a cause of the obesity, but as a consequence of the stigma associated with obesity. In addition to the eating disorders noted above, a major emotional problem specific to obesity is disparagement of the body image. Persons with this disturbance feel that their bodies are grotesque and loathsome and that others view them with hostility and contempt. The problem occurs most commonly in middle-class White women in whom the prevalence of obesity is low and the sanctions against it high, and only among those who have been obese since childhood.

Treatment

The major indication for the treatment of obesity is obesity-related medical disorders. The majority of obese persons seeking treatment, however, are women with no medical complications. For the former, modest weight loss (reduction of body weight of no more than 5 to 10%) will greatly improve weight-related disorders and is indicated. For the latter, the injunction must be *primum non nocere*—do no harm—even if it means focusing on psychological problems rather than on weight loss.

In 1995, the Institute of Medicine of the National Academy of Sciences divided methods of treatment into three categories: (1) do-it-yourself programs that include diet books and self-help approaches, such as Overeaters Anonymous; (2) nonclinical (i.e., commercial) programs such as Weight Watchers and Jenny Craig; and (3) clinical programs that provide medical care and aggressive measures such as very-low-calorie diets (VLCDs), drug therapy, and surgery. The first and second categories rely heavily upon behavioral treatment.

Behavior Therapy. As applied to obesity, behavior therapy refers to a set of principles and techniques for the modification of eating and exercise habits. This approach is goal oriented; the objectives and methods of treatment are clearly specified in weekly homework assignments that patients discuss with their counselors each week. The techniques are used to facilitate patients' adherence to any one of a number of dietary regimens. Patients are usually asked to consume their customary foods but to reduce their caloric intake by 500 to 700 calories per day and their consumption of fat to no more than 30% of total calories. In the initial weeks, patients keep daily records of the types and amounts of foods that they eat. Later, record keeping is expanded to include information about times, places, and feelings associated with eating.

Patients are asked to increase their physical activity by a variety of changes in lifestyle, such as walking more, using stairs rather than escalators, and reducing their dependence on energy-saving devices such as extension phones and remote control devices. Most patients also adopt a structured exercise program, such as walking or swimming, but are cautioned not to make the program so strenuous as to be punishing.

The behavioral approach is most effective when delivered in groups of 10 to 12 persons in which participants discuss their weekly homework assignments. Individual treatment may also yield adequate weight loss, although it does not provide the emotional support of group care. A favorable outcome is facilitated in either case by the use of a structured treatment manual, such as Brownell's LEARN Program for Weight Control.

Patients treated by group behavior therapy lose an average of 8 kilograms in 15 to 20 weeks, equal to a loss of 0.5 kilograms (1 pound) a week. Longer therapy produces larger losses, but they rarely exceed 15 kilograms, even with 52 weeks of treatment. When patients stop treatment, they regain approximately one third of their weight loss in the year after therapy, and more thereafter. Relapse prevention measures have been introduced to cope with this problem, so far with inconclusive results. Continuing contact, however, in the form of group meetings, telephone calls, and postcards has helped to minimize weight regain. Furthermore, persons who engage in regular physical activity are the most likely to maintain their reduced weights for reasons that are still unclear.

Childhood Obesity. Landmark studies by Epstein have revealed an unexpectedly favorable outcome for the behavioral treatment of obese children. Ten years after brief treatment in groups with their parents, the extent of their remaining overweight was significantly less than that of control groups. This effect of treatment can be considered a form of secondary prevention. It stands in striking contrast to the failure of primary prevention of obesity. Community-based programs have either had no effect or, at best, have slightly slowed the secular trend toward an increase in obesity.

Medication. We stand at the threshold of a major new emphasis on the treatment of obesity with medication. This development arises from controlled clinical trials that demonstrate weight losses of 10% of body weight within 6 months and, a major attraction, maintenance of these losses for as long as 2 years. When medication is discontinued, however, weight is promptly regained. For this reason there is a growing consensus that medication should be used on a long-term basis or not at all.

Surgery. Reduction of the stomach volume is the treatment of choice for severely obese persons—those more than 100 pounds or 100% overweight. It produces major health benefits, including the only documented evidence of reduction in mortality from obesity. The psychologist can play an important part in preparing patients for surgery and in supporting them afterward.

[*See also* Behavior Therapy; Eating Disorders; and Nutrition.]

Bibliography

Brownell, K. D. (1990). *The LEARN program for weight control.* Dallas: Brownell-Hager.

Epstein, L. H. (1996). Family-based behavioural intervention for obese children. *International Journal of Obesity & Related Metabolic Disorders, 20* (Suppl. 1), S14–S21.

McGinnis, J. M., & Foege, W. H. (1993). Actual causes of death in the United States. *Journal of the American Medical Association, 270,* 2207–2212.

National Academy of Sciences, Institute of Medicine. (1995). *Weighing the options: Criteria for evaluating weight-management programs.* Washington, DC: National Academy Press.

Albert Stunkard and Petra Platte

OBJECT RELATIONS THEORY. Perhaps *the* major tradition of psychoanalytic thought since the 1940s, *object relations theory* is a term used on several different levels of abstraction and in several different contexts.

Originally, object relations referred to the dimension of Freud's concept of drive that pertains to the target of the drive, the object employed by the drive in seeking its "aim" of tension reduction. By 1897 Freud had decided that he had granted too much importance (in his theory of infantile seduction) to the impact of actual people on psychic development and neurotic etiology. It is not other people in the form of seducers that are the problem, he decided; the problem is inborn instincts or desires. By emphasizing instincts, universal primal fantasies, and the body, subsequent drive theory relegated "objects" to a secondary (Freud's term was *accidental*) status.

In the 1940s, in the decade following Freud's death, the pendulum swung back the other way, and object relations were granted increasingly central importance in psychoanalytic theorizing. This trend emerged in its purest form in the work of W. R. D. Fairbairn, who presented his object relations theory quite pointedly and clearly as a comprehensive alternative to Freud's drive theory. Fairbairn suggested that Freud's grounding of his theory of mind in the instinctual *impulse* as the basic unit was both wrong on scientific grounds and counterproductive on clinical grounds. Freud regarded the basic motivational thrust that generates mind to be pleasure seeking, using objects (people) as a means for pleasurable tension reduction. Fairbairn, however, regarded the basic motivational thrust that generates mind or personality to be object seeking, the need to establish and maintain connections with others. Fairbairn thereby reversed the means-end relationship at the center of Freud's theory. For Freud, object relations are a means for pleasure seeking; for Fairbairn, pleasure seeking (and sometimes pain seeking) are a means for object relating.

Another major, pure form of object relations theory was proposed by John Bowlby in connection with *attachment theory.* The impetus for Bowlby's innovations came from his work with childhood deprivations, leading him to posit a direct, primary, instinctual bond between infant and mother that is not mediated through the mother's role as a need-gratifying object (as it is understood within Freudian drive theory). Bowlby worked closely with Harry Harlow and other primatologists and ethologists. Bowlby's challenge to classical Freudian drive theory is a direct analogue of Harlow's challenge to classical American stimulus-response theory (where the mother is also understood to accrue value through her role as a secondary reinforcer of more basic needs). Because he replaced Freud's assumption of the motivational primacy of sexual and aggressive drives with the motivational and structural primacy of attachment, Bowlby was excoriated by psychoanalytic critics. Attachment theory has had a long, rich development, amply supported by an array of broad research programs, most of which have been from outside psychoanalysis proper.

Within psychoanalysis itself, the most influential object relations theorist was Donald Winnicott, who came to psychoanalysis through pediatrics, and, like Fairbairn and Bowlby, placed great emphasis on a basic connection between child and mother that was not derivative of sexual or aggressive drives. Winnicott was most centrally interested in the development of a personal sense of self and of psychopathology involving a "false self," that is, a compliant adaptation to the standards and expectations of others. He suggested that a robust personal self develops only through the provision by caregivers of a safe and responsive human ("holding") environment through which the child comes to experience himself as real and alive.

Winnicott's work has come to have a profound impact on psychoanalysis. Unlike Fairbairn, he was careful not to challenge traditional drive theory directly, and consequently found greater acceptance within the mainstream literature. Freud had depicted the analytic relationship in terms of battle metaphors (the rationality of the analyst's interpretations pitted against the infantilism and primitivism of the patient's fantasy-driven neurosis). Winnicott, however, provided new metaphors that created a view of the analytic relationship in terms of maternal provisions healing developmental deficits. The content of interpretations generating insight became less important than the experience of being (metaphorically) held, responded to, and durably surviving. Under the influence of the pediatrician Winnicott, psychoanalysis became kinder and gentler.

Sometimes the term *object relations theory* is also employed in reference to the contributions of Melanie Klein and her intellectual descendants, but this is an object relations theory of a different sort. Klein actually provided the basic lexicon of the terms in which later object relations theory was written. In groundbreaking innovations from the 1920s through the 1950s, Klein introduced such concepts as "internal objects" and "part objects." Internal objects are fantasies of significant others that are experienced as internalized "presences" within the mind (like the "voice" of one's mother); part objects are developmentally primitive internal objects like the mother's breast. Klein also described cycles of introjection and projection through which external objects (people) become established as internal presences and internal presences are relocated in the external world. Fairbairn, Bowlby, and Winnicott were all supervised and taught by Klein herself or prominent Kleinians and drew on Kleinian concepts as a springboard for their own contributions. But Klein and the Kleinians always worked very hard to present their work as extensions of Freudian drive theory. In fact, the Kleinians embraced some of the most problematic features of classical drive theory (such as the death instinct) that had been abandoned by the majority of mainstream Freudians. So, Kleinian theory has remained a psychoanalytic school unto itself. Contemporary Kleinian theory (influenced mostly, after Klein, by Wilfred Bion's contributions) has incorporated many of the concepts developed by Fairbairn and Winnicott (generally without attribution), moving Kleinian theory further from its original grounding in classical drive theory.

Because the theoretical tradition of object relations theories was not the work of a single theorist propagated in a systematic fashion, but rather an intellectual climate developed in different ways by several major theorists, object relations concepts and clinical approaches have been put to many different kinds of uses both by subsequent theorists and clinicians. For example, a Winnicott-based tradition of theorizing, including Masud Khan and Christopher Bollas, puts a different spin on some of Freud's fundamental ideas. For Freud, fantasy was essentially a defensive, compensatory retreat from actual frustration; for Winnicott, fantasy is linked with the imagination and creative sources of personal subjectivity. For Freud, at the core of the individual was the "seething cauldron" of the id's instinctual impulses; for Winnicott, at the core of the individual is a deeply private, unknowable, "incognito" self.

Object relations theory has been paired by other authors with self psychology, developed initially by Heinz Kohut, whose formulations bear a remarkable resemblance to concepts introduced by Winnicott. Other authors, notably Jessica Benjamin, have drawn on Winnicott's principles in an exploration of gender in the development of self. Thomas Ogden has developed a rich, integrative synthesis of concepts drawn from Winnicott, Klein, and traditional Freudian theory. Ogden stresses the creative, generative nature of fantasies in states of reverie in both analyst and analysand, and the interpenetrability of the minds of the two participants in the analytic process. And Otto Kernberg, who has been one of the most influential proponents of object

relations theories, has developed his own synthesis of some of Fairbairn's concepts with many Kleinian principles, all grounded in the framework provided by traditional Freudian theory. Kernberg theorizes with a classical cast, blending together the relational account of early development introduced by object relations theories with the traditional Freudian emphasis on the sexual and aggressive drives.

In American psychoanalysis there has been a great interest in the convergence between British object relations theories (e.g., Winnicott, Fairbairn) and the interpersonal psychoanalysis developed in the United States by Harry Stack Sullivan, Erich Fromm, and Clara Thompson. Grounded in the philosophy of pragmatism, interpersonalists stressed the importance of primary relations with other people, but eschewed theorizing about intrapsychic structures or internal presences. One might say that interpersonal psychoanalysis contained within it an implicit but unrealized object relations theory, and that, constrained by its traditional Freudian origins, object relations theory contained within it an implicit but unrealized interpersonal theory. Both traditions prioritized relations with significant others, but explored them in different domains. In the 1980s there began to develop considerable interest in the convergence of these two currents, often linked with the term *relational psychoanalysis*, which bridges object relations and interpersonal relations (Greenberg & Mitchell, 1983; Mitchell, 1988; Mitchell & Aron, 1999).

Psychoanalytic object relations theories have also maintained an important presence in the great blossoming of research in infancy and early childhood in their emphasis on the notion of a primary relatedness between infants and their caregivers. In both the theoretical and clinical realms, object relations theories are associated with a refocusing from the classical centrality of the Oedipus complex to earlier, more fundamental ties between child and parent.

Because the term has such a diverse array of referents, it is difficult to pinpoint the specific impact and implications of object relations theories within contemporary psychoanalysis. In the broadest terms, it has been part of the sweeping shift in theory away from Freud's drive-based, classical model in the direction of privileging relationships with others, real and imagined, past and present. It has also been part of the equally sweeping shift in clinical practice away from the classical, remote, interpretation-giving analyst in the direction of an analytic relationship which stresses emotional contact, human relatedness, and authentic engagement in the here-and-now.

However, because there are so many facets and so many controversies within this cluster of theories, their clinical application is enormously variable. For example, some clinicians use object relations concepts within a phase-specific developmental framework, regarding the analyst as involved with repair of early developmental failures. Others (I. Z. Hoffman, S. Mitchell) use object relations concepts in connection with a focus on the dialectic between old and new relational patterns as they are reenacted, unfold, and are transformed in interactions between patient and therapist. Some writers (e.g., C. Bollas) use object relations concepts in an essentially "one-person" framework, in which the significant other (e.g., the mother or the analyst) functions as the medium within which the subject (e.g., child or patient) finds herself. Other writers (e.g., T. Ogden) use object relations concepts in a more "two-person" framework, in which subjectivity is understood as always inseparable from the personal relations between patient and analyst and the material of analysis is always a dyadic, collaborative product of two minds.

[See also Psychoanalysis, article on Theories.]

Bibliography

Benjamin, J. (1988). The bonds of love: Psychoanalysis, feminism, and the problem of domination. New York: Pantheon.

Bowlby, J. (1969). Attachment and loss: Vol. 1. Attachment. New York: Basic Books.

Fairbairn, W. R. D. (1952). An object-relations theory of the personality. New York: Basic Books.

Greenberg, J., & Mitchell, S. (1983). Object relations in psychoanalytic theory. Cambridge, MA: Harvard University Press.

Grosskurth, P. (1983). Melanie Klein: Her world and her work. New York: Knopf.

Guntrip, H. (1969). Schizoid phenomena, object relations and the self. New York: Basic Books.

Hoffman, I. Z. (1999). Ritual and spontaneity in the psychoanalytic process. Hillsdale, NJ: Analytic Press.

Kernberg, O. (1976). Object relations theory and clinical psychoanalysis. New York: Aronson.

Mitchell, S. (1988). Relational concepts in psychoanalysis: An integration. Cambridge, MA: Harvard University Press.

Mitchell, S., & Aron, L. (Eds.). (1999). Relational psychoanalysis: The emergence of a tradition. Hillsdale, NJ: Analytic Press.

Racker, H. (1968). Transference and countertransference. New York: International Universities Press.

Winnicott, D. (1958). Through paediatrics to psychoanalysis. London: Hogarth Press.

Stephen A. Mitchell

OBSERVATIONAL LEARNING. *See* Learning; *and* Social-Cognitive Theory.

OBSESSIVE-COMPULSIVE DISORDER (OCD) is one of the most chronic and debilitating of the anxiety dis-

orders (American Psychiatric Association, *Diagnostic and Statistical Manual of Mental Disorders*, 1994). Although obsessive thoughts and compulsive behaviors occur frequently in everyday life, OCD is diagnosed when these symptoms occupy a significant amount of time, create intense distress, or interfere with life functioning.

Diagnosis and Phenomenology

OCD is characterized by the presence of obsessions and/or compulsions that usually are perceived by the patient as excessive or unreasonable (*DSM–IV*, 1994). Patients who fail to acknowledge the irrationality of their symptoms are characterized with overvalued ideation. To qualify for diagnosis, symptoms must create significant distress or interfere with life function, and they must not be the result of another psychiatric disorder, substance use, or a general medical condition.

Obsessions are characterized as any recurrent, intrusive thought, image, or urge that is unwanted and cannot be controlled. Individuals with OCD must acknowledge that the obsessions are a product of their own minds (i.e., not inserted by an external force), and they generally try to suppress or ignore the thoughts. The most typical obsessions involve themes of contamination, dirt, or illness (e.g., fearing that one will contract or transmit a disease) and doubts about the performance of certain actions (e.g., an excessive preoccupation that one has neglected to turn off a home appliance). Other common themes include aggression, sexual ideation, symmetry, and religious issues.

Compulsions are defined as purposeful, repetitive behaviors or mental activities that are performed in a ritualistic or stereotypic way, generally with the function of reducing anxiety associated with obsessions. Common compulsive behaviors include repetitive cleaning or washing, checking, ordering, repeating, and hoarding. Repetitive mental activity can also serve a compulsive function when it is designed to reduce the anxiety associated with an obsession (e.g., repeating a prayer a certain number of times may reduce the anxiety associated with "forbidden" sexual or religious thoughts).

In the majority of cases, both obsessions and compulsions are reported in OCD. Significant disturbance in occupational and interpersonal functioning is generally reported, given the excessive amount of time per day frequently spent engaged in repetitive thoughts and behaviors. The nature of OCD is generally consistent across the life span, and similar symptoms have been reported by patients with diverse cultural and ethnic backgrounds. The disorder is also frequently accompanied by high levels of depression and generalized anxiety, with many patients reporting symptoms consistent with a coexistent anxiety or affective disorder. Etiological theories have posited the roles of genetic, neurochemical, neuroanatomical, and behavioral variables in the onset and maintenance of OCD.

In recent years, a number of disorders currently categorized as distinct from OCD have been proposed as possible variants of the syndrome. Known as the obsessive-compulsive spectrum disorders (OCSDs), these disorders are thought to share features with OCD in a range of domains, including phenomenology, comorbidity, family history, clinical course, treatment response, and possible neurochemical mediation (e.g., Jenike, 1989; McElroy, Phillips, & Keck, 1994). Disorders represented in the proposed OCSD category include the eating disorders, somatiform disorders, and impulse control disorders. However, the validity and utility of this categorization have not been determined.

Assessment

A thorough assessment of OCD involves the use of clinical interviews, self-report questionnaires, self-monitoring procedures, and behavioral observation (Steketee, 1993; Turner & Beidel, 1988). Many standardized assessment tools are available to improve the reliability and validity of diagnostic and clinical decision-making. In particular, the Anxiety Disorders Interview Schedule, a semistructured clinical interview, results in highly reliable diagnoses of OCD. The Yale-Brown Obsessive-Compulsive Scale (YBOCS) is a clinician-rated instrument designed to provide a quantitative rating of OCD symptom severity. The YBOCS has excellent psychometric properties and is routinely used to document treatment response in both experimental trials and clinical practice. Well-validated self-report questionnaires for the assessment of OCD include the Maudsley Obsessive Compulsive Inventory, the Leyton Obsessional Inventory, and the Padua Inventory. The use of these standardized clinician-rated and self-report measures is often complemented by self-monitoring procedures that assist patients in recording the nature, frequency, and duration of OCD symptoms. A variety of behavioral observation techniques are also used to evaluate the nature and severity of OCD behaviors in real-life settings (e.g., at the patient's home or in other settings where the ritualistic behaviors occur most often). In general, the clear diagnostic criteria and range of available assessment tools make diagnosing OCD and assessing its severity a relatively straightforward task for experienced clinicians.

Epidemiology

OCD has a lifetime prevalence rate of 1.9 to 3.0% (Karno, Golding, Sorenson, & Burnam, 1988). Onset of the disorder is generally in late adolescence or early adulthood, although OCD also can occur in very young children. The age of onset appears to be younger for males than for females (Rasmussen & Eisen, 1990).

Overall, gender distribution of the disorder is relatively even, although some studies have suggested a slightly higher incidence of OCD among women than men. The gender distribution is more skewed, however, when patients are classified according to primary type of rituals, with women more likely than men to report excessive washing behaviors. The incidence of OCD appears to be distributed relatively evenly across racial groups (Karno, Golding, Sorenson & Burnham, 1988), although minority patients are significantly less likely to present for psychiatric treatment (Hatch, Friedman, & Paradis, 1996).

The onset of OCD often seems to occur during or after a period of life stress (e.g., childbirth or change in occupational or marital status). However, data in this regard are contradictory, given that this type of information is generally collected in a retrospective fashion. Nonetheless, the course of the disorder is chronic, with exacerbations of symptoms during periods of stress. As supported by extremely low placebo response rates in controlled clinical trials, OCD only infrequently remits without active psychiatric treatment.

Treatment

Based on a significant body of research, two primary modes of treatment for OCD are recommended: pharmacotherapy with serotonergic reuptake inhibitors (SRIs) and a method of behavior therapy known as exposure and response prevention (ERP). Outcome data in these two domains are reviewed below (for more details, see Stanley & Turner, 1995).

Pharmacotherapy

The majority of literature regarding drug treatment for OCD has focused on the SRIs, with the largest body of work investigating the effects of clomipramine (CMI). The use of CMI is clearly superior to a placebo, with approximately 50% of patients who complete treatment judged to have a meaningful reduction in symptom severity. When patients who refuse or drop out of treatment are considered, response rates to CMI range from 30 to 40%. Similar rates of response have been demonstrated following treatment with more selective SRIs, including fluvoxamine, fluoxetine, paroxetine, and sertraline. In all cases, active medications have produced significantly greater symptom reduction than a placebo. Although meta-analyses comparing results across separate placebo-controlled trials suggested an inverse relationship between serotonin selectivity and treatment response, recent direct comparisons of CMI and the more selective SRIs have demonstrated no significant differences in response rates to these medications.

Of particular note in the drug treatment literature is the extremely low placebo response rate generally reported. In addition, preliminary studies have shown high relapse rates when medication is discontinued, although it appears that with reduced doses of effective compounds, patients can maintain treatment gains long-term.

Behavior Therapy

Based on a large body of empirical work, the behavioral treatment of choice for OCD is exposure response prevention (ERP). This approach consists of two components: exposure to stimuli that provoke obsessions; and prevention of ritualistic responses designed to reduce associated anxiety. Exposure sessions can be conducted in an imaginal fashion, with patients asked to visualize feared stimuli and consequences (e.g., imagining a family member becoming ill as a result of contamination passed on by the patient), or in an *in vivo* manner, with patients asked to confront feared stimuli in real life (e.g., touching a "contaminated" object and then touching a family member's clothing). Empirical data do not clearly support the utility of one of these strategies over the other, although clinical recommendations generally involve using the approach that best evokes the feared consequences (Stanley & Averill, 1998). Exposure procedures also can be conducted in a gradual or rapid fashion, and the degree of therapist involvement is sometimes varied, based on symptom severity and the patient's ability to conduct exposure sessions independently. A recent meta-analysis, however, suggested that therapist-supervised exposure is more effective than patient-controlled exposure (Abramowitz, 1996). Complete response prevention, which involves instructions to discontinue all rituals, also appears to be more effective than partial discontinuation of compulsive behavior (Abramowitz, 1996).

In general, 80 to 90% of patients who complete ERP demonstrate notable reduction in symptom severity after approximately 20 sessions. When dropout and refuser rates are considered, approximately 60% of patients can be expected to respond to ERP. Long-term follow-up data suggest that patients generally maintain treatment gains following ERP, although recent studies have begun to examine the efficacy of various relapse prevention strategies.

[*See also* Obsessive-Compulsive Personality Disorder.]

Bibliography

Abramowitz, J. S. (1996). Variants of exposure and response prevention in the treatment of obsessive-compulsive disorder: A meta-analysis. *Behavior Therapy*, *27*, 583–600.

American Psychiatric Association. (1994). *Diagnostic and statistical manual of mental disorders* (4th ed.). Washington, DC: Author.

Hatch, M. L., Friedman, S., & Paradis, C. M. (1996). Behavioral treatment of obsessive-compulsive disorder in African Americans. *Cognitive and Behavioral Practice*, *3*, 303–315.

Jenike, M. A. (1989). Obsessive-compulsive and related disorders: A hidden epidemic. *New England Journal of Medicine*, *321*, 539–541.

Jenike, M. A., Baer, L., & Minichiello, W. E. (1990). *Obsessive-compulsive disorders: Theory and management* (2nd ed.). Chicago: Year Book Medical.

Karno, M., Golding, J., Sorenson, S., & Burnam, M. A. (1988). The epidemiology of obsessive-compulsive disorder in five U.S. communities. *Archives of General Psychiatry*, *45*, 1094–1099.

McElroy, S. L., Phillips, K. A., & Keck, P. E. (1994). Obsessive-compulsive spectrum disorder. *Journal of Clinical Psychiatry*, *55* (Suppl.), 33–51.

Rachman, S. J., & Hodgson, R. S. (1980). *Obsessions and compulsions*. Englewood Cliffs, NJ: Prentice Hall.

Rasmussen, S. A., & Eisen, J. L. (1990). Epidemiology of obsessive-compulsive disorder. *Journal of Clinical Psychiatry*, *51*, 20–23.

Stanley, M. A., & Averill, P. M. (1998). Psychosocial treatment: Clinical applications. In R. P. Swinson, M. M. Antony, S. Rachman, & M. A. Richter (Eds.), *Obsessive-compulsive disorder: Theory, research, and treatment* (pp. 277–297). New York: Guilford Press.

Stanley, M. A., & Turner, S. M. (1995). Current status of pharmacological and behavioral treatment of obsessive-compulsive disorder. *Behavior Therapy*, *26*, 163–186.

Steketee, G. S. (1993). *Treatment of obsessive-compulsive disorder*. New York: Guilford Press.

Swinson, R. P., Antony, M. M., Rachman, S., & Richter, M. A. (1998). *Obsessive-compulsive disorder: Theory, research, and treatment*. New York: Guilford Press.

Turner, S. M., & Beidel, D. C. (1988). *Treating obsessive-compulsive disorder*. New York: Pergamon Press.

Zohar, J., Insel, T., & Rasmussen, S. (1991). *The psychobiology of obsessive-compulsive disorder*. New York: Springer.

Melinda A. Stanley

OBSESSIVE-COMPULSIVE PERSONALITY DISORDER. Individuals who are orderly, perfectionistic, punctual, detail-oriented, work-focused, frugal, and morally scrupulous are often referred to as obsessive-compulsive. Depending on how many such traits are manifest and their intensity, the term may be applied either to individuals with normal-range personality styles or to those with a personality disorder. No sharp boundary separates normality and abnormality in personality functioning. However, individuals diagnosable with the disorders are, in addition, likely to be stubborn, rigid, and inflexible and to use the traits listed as a means of exerting control over others. The obsessive-compulsive personality disorder is one of twelve Axis II personality disorders recognized by the American Psychiatric Association (APA), and should be distinguished from the obsessive-compulsive clinical syndrome described on Axis I. The former features a constellation of covariant personality traits, while the latter is an anxiety disorder featuring ego-dystonic obsessive and intrusive thoughts and compulsive or ritualistic behaviors.

Historically, the obsessive-compulsive personality has its strongest links to the psychoanalytic tradition. Freud's brief 1908 essay "Character and Anal Eroticism" introduced the type through his psychosexual model of erogenous zones. In psychoanalytic theory, character types reflect fixations at particular stages of personality development; the anal character is fixated at the anal stage. Such individuals are supposedly orderly, parsimonious, and obstinate, with the latter possibly amounting "to defiance, with which irascibility and vindictiveness may easily be associated" (p. 83). According to Freud's framework, the primary task during the anal stage is toilet training. This task requires parental supervision, and children acquire their personality characteristics through the parents' reaction to this developmental inevitability. If the parents are disgusted, children learn that cleanliness and orderliness are highly important; if the parents are demanding, children may assert their own autonomy by holding their feces, acquiring stubborn and stingy traits. In 1913, Freud distinguished between obsessive and compulsive neurotic symptoms as a failure to repress prohibited impulses and thoughts and the anal character, in which these impulses were successfully sublimated, that is, transformed into a more adaptive expression. Later analysts, such as Karl Abraham and Wilhelm Reich, came to include indecisiveness as an additional primary feature.

The ambivalence of the obsessive-compulsive, presaged by Freud in 1908, has become an enduring feature of the construct. Other analysts elaborated Freud's portrayal by noting that anal characters displayed a split in their behavior, assuming responsibility and persevering with assigned tasks, but also procrastinating until the last moment. Likewise, Rado (1959) framed the dual nature of anal character as a struggle between obedience and defiance. Thus, the superficially compliant, obedient, and scrupulous nature of these personalities often conceals a deeply hidden hostility. While narcissistic, antisocial, dependent, and histrionic personalities have a consistent, albeit imbalance interpersonal style, the negativistic (passive-aggressive) and obsessive-compulsive personalities are riddled by a deep and intrinsic ambivalence that they can neither escape nor resolve. In one sense, their conformity to established conventions and behavioral standards suggests the dependent personality. In another sense, however, they churn with defiance, anger, and rebelliousness reminiscent of the antisocial or sadistic. Fearing social disapproval or condemnation, their hostility is expressed indirectly by holding others to standards that make almost anyone appear flawed, while behaving "flawlessly" themselves.

As the history of psychology has progressed, domains other than the psychodynamic have moved to the forefront. Modern theorists have formulated the disorder from a variety of perspectives. From an interpersonal view, Leary (1957) saw such "hypernormal" individuals as wishing to present themselves as mature and reasonable, avoiding weakness and unconventionality. Similarly, Benjamin (1993) stressed the fear of making a mistake or being viewed as imperfect, while being critical of oneself but implicitly blaming and controlling toward others. From a cognitive standpoint, Beck and Freeman (1990) saw the rigidity and perfectionism of the obsessive-compulsive as being driven by dichotomous black-or-white thinking that precludes balanced appraisals of the self and others. By thinking in "shoulds" and "musts," obsessive-compulsives magnify and catastrophize, an information-processing style through which minor errors or foibles becomes exaggerated into major faults and transgressions. Working from a biopsychosocial framework, Millon (1996) described the passive-ambivalent type, emphasizing restrained affectivity (emotionally controlled, grim, cheerless), cognitive constriction (narrow-minded, methodical, pedantic), conscientious self-image (practical, prudent, moralistic), and interpersonal respectfulness (ingratiating with superiors, formal and legalistic with subordinates). Millon and Davis (1996) discussed four obsessive-compulsive subtypes. The puritanical compulsive is austere, self-righteous, highly controlled, but deeply conflicted about conformity to authority and convention. The bureaucratic compulsive feels strengthened by traditional values, associations, and organizations, and works within "the system" to enforce official rules and regulations on careless and disrespectful transgressors. The parsimonious compulsive is miserly and hoarding, holding tightly to possessions as material symbol of security. Finally, as a mixture of the obsessive-compulsive and passive-aggressive personalities, the bedeviled compulsive highlights the ambivalence of these two main types, being indecisive, procrastinating, and uncertain.

The obsessive-compulsive shares certain characteristics with other personality disorders. Both the obsessive-compulsive and the narcissist may be committed to the attainment of perfection. However, the obsessive-compulsive fears that this standard cannot be maintained and is excessively self-critical of small lapses. In contrast, the narcissist usually believes it has already been achieved and ignores minor faults. Both the schizoid and the obsessive-compulsive may be excessively formal. However, the schizoid lacks the capacity to experience deep emotions and attachments, while obsessive-compulsive stifles this capacity through devotion to the work ethic. Both the avoidant and the obsessive-compulsive experience social anxiety and may appear self-critical and fearful of the judgments of others. However, the avoidant responds with social isolation, while the obsessive-compulsive responds with rigid conformity and hidden reactive hostility.

The prevalence of obsessive-compulsive personality disorder is difficult to estimate precisely. The *Diagnostic and Statistical Manual of Mental Disorders* (American Psychiatric Association, 1994) conceptualizes the personality disorders through the so-called medical or disease model. Here, the presence of a certain number of diagnostic criteria lead to a diagnosis, while one less results in no diagnosis or an ascription of obsessive-compulsive traits. Such diagnostic boundaries do not exist in nature and make exact prevalence and incidence figures somewhat arbitrary. Nevertheless, the *DSM–IV* suggests that the disorder appears to be twice as prevalent in males as in females, with a 1% prevalence in the community and 3 to 10% in those presenting to mental health clinics (1994).

[*See also* Obsessive-Compulsive Disorder.]

Bibliography

American Psychiatric Association. (1994). *Diagnostic and statistical manual of mental disorders* (4th ed.). Washington, DC: Author. Contains diagnostic descriptions of personality disorders used by mental health officials in the United States.

Beck, A. T., & Freeman, A. (1990). *Cognitive therapy of personality disorders.* New York: Guilford Press. A comprehensive description of the cognitive basis of many of the personality disorders, considered a standard reference for personality disorders.

Benjamin, L. S. (1993). *Interpersonal diagnosis and treatment of personality disorders.* New York: Guilford Press. A comprehensive description of the interpersonal dynamics of the personality disorders, developed from the author's Structured Analysis of Social Behavior model.

Freud, S. (1908/1925). Character and anal eroticism. In *Collected papers* (Vol. 2). London: Hogarth Press. (Original work published 1908.) This seminal essay introduced the anal character, the psychoanalytic parallel to the modern obsessive-compulsive personality.

Leary, T. (1957). *Interpersonal diagnosis of personality.* New York: Ronald Press. With this book, Leary formalized much of Sullivan's thought and laid the foundation for the interpersonal circumplex model of personality and its disorders.

Millon, T. (1969). *Modern psychopathology: A biosocial approach to maladaptive learning and functioning.* Philadelphia: Saunders. A seminal text offering descriptions of many of the modern personality disorders from a biosocial framework.

Millon, T., & Davis, R. D. (1996). *Disorders of personality: DSM–IV and beyond* (2nd ed.). New York: Wiley-Interscience. The classic reference in the field of personality disorders, offering detailed discussion of the fourteen personality disorders recognized by the American Psychiatric Association since 1980, as well as discussions of possible subtypes of these disorders.

Theodore Millon

OCD. *See* Obsessive-Compulsive Disorder.

OEDIPAL STAGE. *See* Psychosexual Stages.

OEDIPUS COMPLEX. In classical Freudian psychoanalysis, the Oedipus complex refers to a constellation of wishes, fears, and defenses woven into an unconscious fantasy regarded as essential to the development of the normal personality, as well as playing a central role in neurotic psychopathology. The child's sexual instinct, so it is thought, reaches the developmental stage in which the external genitals are experienced as the paramount site of erotic pleasure between the ages of 3 and 6, the phallic, or Oedipal, phase. Simultaneously, cognitive skills and the emerging capacity for genuine interpersonal relations converge to produce a situation in which the child feels passionate sexual longings toward one or the other of its parents, along with jealous rivalry with the other parent and consequent fear of retaliation on the part of the rival parent.

In the paradigmatic case, the child has erotic longings for the parent of the opposite sex and feels hostility, including death wishes, toward the parent of the same sex. In the so-called negative Oedipus complex the situation is reversed, with the child feeling erotic love for the same sex parent and rivalry with the opposite sex parent. Innate bisexuality ensures that elements of both will be present, though with differing salience. Even in the typical positive Oedipus complex, affection toward the rival parent, and rage at the loved parent for preferring the rival parent, result in complicated, ambivalent feelings toward both. It is the negative complex that is more often implicated in the development of neurosis and other forms of psychopathology, because it comes into conflict with conscious ideals, moral values, and self-images.

In the normal case, the intense strivings of the Oedipus complex are abandoned for a variety of reasons; among these are the immaturity of the child's genitals and their perceived incommensurability with those of the parents; the child's inadequate conceptual grasp of sex, conception, and birth; the boundaries normally set and maintained by the parents; and the perceived threat of the risk of catastrophic punishment, usually taking the form, in unconscious fantasy, of castration or genital mutilation, abandonment, or annihilation by the parent or parents. In the wake of the failure of the Oedipal project, the child identifies with the former rival parent and internalizes an image of him or her as the basis of the regulating and sanctioning agency of the psyche, the superego.

In cases in which there have actually been boundary violations with parents, or in which the child perceives itself as an Oedipal victor—that is, one whom the desired parent really does prefer to the rival parent—the superego may inflict unusually harsh retribution in the form of debilitating guilt, inability to enjoy sexual love, self-sabotage, and/or crippling inhibitions based on fear of success and of the perceived danger that one's own wishes and ambitions will lead to dreadful punishment or retaliation.

In cases where the transition through the Oedipus complex has not been accomplished smoothly, a typical outcome is regression to a pregenital mode of libidinal organization, in which oral, anal, narcissistic, sado-masochistic, or other forms of eroticism may be preferred to genital object love. Therefore, Oedipal neurotic pathology may, in its outward appearance, take the form of a set of characteristic defenses against pregenital erotic impulses that may not seem very "Oedipal" on the surface, even though the aggravating unconscious conflict may be a fear of retribution for unconscious incestuous longings and aggressive wishes directed at loved ones.

Freud and his immediate followers believed that the problems and conflicts in the Oedipus complex were to be found at the core of every case of neurosis; it was consequently also known as the nuclear complex. In the later development of psychoanalytic theory and practice, the centrality of the Oedipus complex receded somewhat. The foremost reason was the increasing recognition of the importance, both in normal development and in the origin of psychopathology, of pre-Oedipal dynamics pertaining to the early close relationship between the child and its mother, dating from an age before genuinely interpersonal relations can be adequately imagined or understood. At the same time, Oedipal relations came to be seen differently, in that the father was often regarded not so much as a jealous rival and potential dispenser of punitive retaliation (for boys) or a sexual oject (for girls), but rather as a necessary third party helping the child in its separation from embeddedness in a symbiotic merger with the mother. Conflicts that appeared Oedipal in the classical sense came to be seen more as the result of earlier failures in pre-Oedipal self-other relations rather than as the primary sources of neurotic conflict themselves. Although its role as the nuclear core of all neurosis has been diminished,

the Oedipus complex's centrality in normal development and in the relationship of the individual to society remains firm.

The widespread appearance of Oedipal themes in art, literature, religious symbolism, and other expressive forms of Western culture has been amply demonstrated many times over; this is consistent with the ubiquitous evidence of Oedipal material in the psychoanalytic treatment of Western patients, whether or not it is the locus of core psychopathology. Early in the history of psychoanalysis the question was raised whether the Oedipus complex was peculiar to modern Western society, with its focus on the nuclear family, or whether it might not be absent or take very different forms in societies with divergent forms of family organization. While no consensus on this subject exists, a substantial empirical case by now exists for the presence of Oedipal dynamics in a wide range of diverse sociocultural settings, albeit with divergent surface manifestations.

Thus, for example, in many cultures characterized by hierarchically ranked men's societies, boys are forcibly separated from the domestic realm, subjected to harsh initiations, and gradually elevated to senior masculine status in rituals marked by conflict between the generations. In many matrilineal societies, on the other hand, the locus of male-male conflict may take the form of strained relations between a young man and his maternal uncle while the father plays a more nurturant role. At the same time, the strongest incest taboo may be displaced from mother to sister, as occurs in the famous Trobriand case discussed by the anthropologist Bronislaw Malinowski.

The Oedipus complex today should not be understood as pathological in itself, but rather as a necessary phase of human psychological and social growth. In many societies, including our own, Oedipal themes are the basis for important aspects of myth, religion, art, literature, and fantasy. As Freud recognized, in adverse cases of individual development, the Oedipus complex can also frequently be a key site of pathogenic neurotic conflict.

[See also Psychoanalysis, *article on* Theories.]

Bibliography

Freud, S. (1909). Analysis of a phobia in a five-year-old boy. In *The standard edition of the complete psychological works of Sigmund Freud* (J. Strachey et al., Trans.). (Vol. 10, pp. 1–150). London: Hogarth Press. The first empirical observation and clinical treatment of an infantile neurosis involving Oedipal dynamics.

Freud, S. (1910). A special type of object choice made by men. In *The standard edition of the complete psychological works of Sigmund Freud* (J. Strachey et al., Trans.). (Vol. 11, 163–176). London: Hogarth Press. Freud's first published use of the term *Oedipus complex* with particular reference to male sexuality.

Freud, S. (1925). Some psychical consequences of the anatomical distinction between the sexes. In *The standard edition of the complete psychological works of Sigmund Freud* (J. Strachey et al., Trans.). (Vol. 19, pp. 241–260). London: Hogarth Press. One of the best known of Freud's classical theoretical accounts of the different Oedipal dynamics in men and women.

Johnson, A. W., & Price-Williams, D. (1996). *Oedipus ubiquitous: The family complex in world folk literature.* Stanford, CA: Stanford University Press. A comprehensive survey demonstrating the presence of Oedipal tales in societies throughout the world.

Loewald, H. W. (1979). The waning of the Oedipus complex. *Journal of the American Psychoanalytic Association, 27,* 751–775. Marks a theoretical shift away from the view of the Oedipus complex as the universal nucleus of neurosis in contemporary psychoanalysis.

Paul, R. A. (1996). *Moses and civilization: The meaning behind Freud's myth.* New Haven, CT: Yale University Press. Demonstrates the centrality of Oedipal themes in the foundational myths of the Western Judeo-Christian tradition.

Pollock, G. H. (1988). Oedipus: The myth, the developmental stage, the universal theme, the conflict, and the complex. In G. H. Pollock & J. M. Ross (Eds.), *The Oedipus papers* (pp. 339–372). Madison, CT: International Universities Press. A comprehensive contemporary overview of the subject.

Simon, B. (1991). Is the Oedipus complex still the cornerstone of psychoanalysis? *Journal of the American Psychoanalytic Association, 39,* 641–668. An authoritative contemporary evaluation of the place of the Oedipus complex in psychoanalysis today.

Simon, B., & Blass, R. B. (1991). The development and vicissitudes of Freud's ideas on the Oedipus complex. In J. Neu (Ed.), *The Cambridge companion to Freud* (pp. 161–174). Cambridge, UK: Cambridge University Press. A thorough historical study of the changing conceptualizations of the Oedipus complex across Freud's five-decade career.

Spiro, M. E. (1982). *Oedipus in the Trobriands.* Chicago: University of Chicago Press. Demonstrates the presence of the Oedipus complex in the matrilineal Pacific island society long considered the classic example showing the absence of Oedipal dynamics in a non-Western society with a different family system.

Stephens, W. N. (1962). *The Oedipus complex: Cross-cultural evidence.* New York: Free Press. A rigorous empirical study employing the cross-cultural comparative method that tests the hypothesis that the Oedipus complex is universal and finds it to be confirmed.

Robert A. Paul

OGDEN, ROBERT MORRIS (1877–1959), American psychologist and educator. Ogden was born on 6 July 1877, the son of James Sherman Ogden and Beulah Maria Carter, in Binghamton, New York. While studying engineering at Cornell University, he was influenced by E. B. Titchener (1867–1927) and finished by obtaining his B.Sc. degree in psychology in 1901. Following the fashion of the time, he went to study psychology in Germany, choosing to work with O. Külpe (1862–1915) at Würzburg. Although most of Külpe's colleagues were using introspection to examine the processes of adult thinking and reasoning, Ogden obtained his Ph.D. degree there in 1903 with an experimental study on reading speed. He then held successive positions as assistant to Max F. Meyer (1873–1967) at the University of Missouri (1903–1905), as assistant, associate, and then full professor of philosophy and psychology at the University of Tennessee (1905–1914), and as professor and chair of the department of psychology at the University of Kansas (1914–1916), where his interests became more focused on education. He was appointed as professor and chair of the department of education at his alma mater, Cornell University, and stayed there until his retirement in 1945. In 1939 he had transferred to the psychology department; he had also acted as Dean of the College of Arts and Sciences (1923–1945). He died of cancer on 2 March 1959, leaving a son, two daughters, and eleven grandchildren by his marriage to Nellie Dorsey, which had taken place in 1903.

In 1909, during a return visit to Würzburg, he had served as a subject in experiments on thinking and not only came to believe that "imageless thought" was a useful concept in psychology, but extensively reviewed the ongoing controversy about it (Ogden, 1911). But contemporaneously, J. B. Watson (1878–1958) was using this controversy and others to illustrate his point that introspection was more likely to lead to disagreement than to agreement in psychology (Watson, 1913, p. 163, footnote). Ogden nevertheless integrated imageless thought into a textbook, *An Introduction to General Psychology* (New York, 1914).

His period at Cornell included the publication of three books, *Hearing* (New York, 1924), *Psychology and Education* (New York, 1926), and *Psychology of Art* (New York, 1938). He was also cooperating editor of *Psychological Bulletin* (1909–1929) and of *American Journal of Psychology* (1926–1959), in which journal he published a valuable review of Külpe's contributions to psychology (Ogden, 1951). But he is best remembered for having played a major role in introducing Gestalt psychology to North America (Henle, 1984); he arranged for visits to Cornell by Koffka in 1924 to 1925, Köhler in 1926 and 1928, and by K. Lewin from 1933 to 1935. He also translated Koffka's book on child psychology, *The Growth of the Mind* (New York, 1925); and he persuaded Koffka to write the first article in English on Gestalt principles (Koffka, 1922).

His book on hearing included a theory that judgments about tones, vowel sounds ("vocables"), and noise were, in each case, determined by the values of five perceptual attributes, namely, pitch, brightness, intensity, duration, and volume. His book on education discussed the application of Koffka's Gestalt theory of "configurationalism" to education and also to the study of sensations, emotions, and learning. His book on art incorporated some mention of Gestalt views, for example, on the role of symmetry in art, but was more devoted to aesthetic theory than to perception.

[*Many of the people mentioned in this article are the subjects of independent biographical entries.*]

Bibliography

Dallenbach, K. M. (1959). Robert Morris Ogden: 1877–1959. *American Journal of Psychology, 72,* 472–477. This obituary is a useful source for the details of Ogden's life and work.

Henle, M. (1984). Robert M. Ogden and Gestalt psychology in America. *Journal of the History of the Behavioral Sciences, 20,* 9–19. This scholarly article, based on primary sources such as correspondence, reveals the dedication with which Ogden pursued his goal of introducing English-speaking psychologists to the Gestalt movement.

Koffka, K. (1922). Perception, an introduction to the Gestalt-theorie. *Psychological Bulletin, 19,* 531–585. It is sometimes claimed that Ogden did not quite succeed in winning Americans over to Gestalt psychology because this article, although excellent on perception, was not followed up by a later article by Koffka on the applications of Gestalt theory to memory.

Ogden, R. M. (1911). Imageless thought: Résumé and critique. *Psychological Bulletin, 8,* 183–197. Ogden discusses not only the answers by members of the Würzburg school to the question of whether "imageless thought" exists, but also those of A. Binet and R. S. Woodworth (who thought it did) and E. B. Titchener (who thought it did not). Most of these answers were based on introspection.

Ogden, R. M. (1951). Oswald Külpe and the Würzburg school. *American Journal of Psychology, 64,* 4–19. Ogden shows how Külpe, over the course of his lifetime, developed a systematic philosophical theory of realism that he believed should underlie any theory of psychology.

Watson, J. B. (1913). Psychology as the behaviorist views it. *Psychological Review, 20,* 158–177. Ogden (1951, p. 18) said that this article did much to cause the evaporation of interest in introspection as a psychological method. But he himself turned to Gestalt psychology rather than to behaviorism, in part because he believed that human conscious experience is indeed a valid topic for investigation by psychologists, a belief criticized by Watson.

Watson, R. I. (1974). *Eminent contributors to psychology* (Vol. 1, p. 117; Vol. 2, pp. 794–795). New York: Springer. See bibliography of Ogden's work.

David J. Murray

OLDS, JAMES (1922–1976), American biological psychologist. James Olds discovered the presence of pleasure centers in the brain, one of the most important discoveries in the history of psychology. He also pioneered the development of techniques to record the activity of individual brain cells in awake, freely behaving animals.

After receiving his Ph.D. degree from Harvard, under Richard Solomon, he became a postdoctoral fellow at Donald Hebb's laboratory at McGill University, where he and Peter Milner intended to study the recently discovered arousing effects of electrical stimulation of the midbrain reticular formation. While testing his first animal, Olds noticed that the animal behaved as if it "enjoyed" the stimulation. He used the stimulation to reward the animal for moving to any location on the testing table. Histology revealed that the electrode was not in the midbrain, but in the septal area of the forebrain. Olds and Milner then showed that rats would press a lever in order to receive electrical brain stimulation to the septal area, and their report on this became the most cited paper in the field of psychology for the next two decades (Olds & Milner, 1954).

Olds and Milner were not the first to use electrical brain stimulation to study brain-behavior relationships. However, because their report stimulated such a flurry of research, they are credited with producing a paradigm shift in the study of the biological mechanisms of behavior. Following their research, brain stimulation became a standard method for investigating brain-behavior relationships.

After leaving Hebb's laboratory at McGill in 1955, Olds became a research associate in the laboratory of H. W. Magoun and D. B. Lindsley at the University of California, Los Angeles (UCLA). He moved to the University of Michigan in 1958, where he and his wife, Marianna, and their students addressed a number of important questions about the nature of rewarding brain stimulation and its implications for motivation and reinforcement. They mapped the brain for the locations where electrical brain stimulation produced different degrees of reward and showed that the reward produced by electrical stimulation could far exceed the reward produced by natural biological motivation. The rats would even cross an electrified grid floor to receive the stimulation. They studied the relationship between rewarding brain stimulation and various hormonal conditions and natural biological motivational behaviors, such as feeding, drinking, and sex, and found significant interactions between the motivational state of the animal and the rewarding effects of electrical stimulation, which produced maximal reward in the lateral hypothalamus, a region traversed by the medial forebrain bundle. Lesions in this region had been previously shown to interfere with consummatory behaviors, such as feeding, drinking, sex, and nest building. Stimulation of the sites that produced consummatory behaviors was also generally rewarding. This research radically altered the way we think about motivation, reward, reinforcement, and addiction.

In the early 1960s Olds began investigating methods for recording the activity of individual brain cells in awake, freely behaving animals. Although techniques were available for recording multiple unit activity from small populations of neurons, the techniques available for recording single-cell activity were not suited for recording in awake, freely behaving animals. He discovered that large, blunt, soft, wire electrodes could record from individual neurons in awake, freely behaving animals for reasonable periods of time. This was a monumental task, because the cellular signals were of very low amplitude, the background noise level was generally very high, and it was often difficult to distinguish between brain cellular activity and movement artifact in freely behaving animals.

His laboratory produced an impressive series of studies on the effects of motivational and arousal state on cellular activity in various brain regions, as well as regional differences in cellular activity during learning. He was the first to show changes in single brain cell activity during learning in freely behaving animals. In 1969 Olds moved to the California Institute of Technology, where his research focused on isolating those parts of the brain that were critical for learning. His laboratory was very productive, discovering a number of phenomena, including the observation that the earliest conditioned changes in brain activity often occurred in sensory pathways.

Olds received many awards and honors during his career, including the Hofheimer Award from the American Psychiatric Association in 1958, the Warren Medal from the Society of Experimental Psychologists in 1962, and the Newcomb Cleveland Prize of the American Association for the Advancement of Science in 1956. He also received the Distinguished Scientist Award from the American Psychological Association in 1967, and the Kittay Prize from the Kittay Scientific Foundation in 1976, and was elected to the National Academy of Sciences. Tragically, Olds died while swimming off Newport Beach, California, in 1976 at the age of 54.

Bibliography

American Psychological Association. (1967). Distinguished scientific awards: 1967. *The American Psychologist, 22,* 1135–1138. Includes Olds's citation for the Distinguished Scientific Contribution Award, a brief biography, and a complete list of his scientific publications from 1953 until 1967.

Olds, J. (1975). Mapping the mind unto the brain. In F. G. Worden, J. P. Swazey, & G. Adelman, (Eds.), *The neurosciences: Paths of discovery* (pp. 375–400). Cambridge, MA: MIT Press. This autobiographical chapter provides a very personal account of the development of his ideas and of his career. This volume includes autobiographical chapters by many of the most distinguished neuroscientists of that time.

Olds, J. (1977). *Drives and reinforcements: Behavioral studies of hypothalamic functions.* New York: Raven Press. An excellent, comprehensive statement of Olds's ideas concerning brain mechanisms of motivation, reinforcement, and reward, with a fascinating foreword by Neal Miller, one of the leading animal psychologists of the time.

Olds, J., & Milner, P. (1954). Positive reinforcement produced by electrical stimulation of septal area and other regions of rat brain. *Journal of Comparative and Physiological Psychology, 47,* 419–427. The original journal article reporting that electrical stimulation of specific brain regions was rewarding. It was the most cited article in the American psychological literature for over two decades.

Phillip J. Best

OLFACTION. *See* Smell.

OPERANT CONDITIONING. [*This entry comprises two articles. The lead article provides a broad overview and defines and describes the process of operant conditioning. The companion article discusses the Skinner box and its development, purpose, and use, including a review of the most current thinking regarding the apparatus. See also the biography of Skinner.*]

An Overview

The term *operant conditioning* refers to the process by which the consequences of an action affect the likelihood that the action will occur again; that is, it refers to one of the processes by which experience alters subsequent behavior. Consequences may make behavior more likely to occur in the future (*reinforcement*), or less likely in the future (*punishment*). Operant conditioning functions to produce behavior that appears purposive or voluntary in character.

The scientific study of operant conditioning began with the use of "puzzle boxes" (Thorndike, 1898). Hungry cats were placed in boxes equipped with various trip mechanisms that would allow the animals to escape and gain access to food. When a cat was trapped repeatedly, the amount of time it took to escape decreased, indicating that the cat operated the trip mechanism more rapidly. Experiments like these led to the formulation of the Law of Effect (Thorndike, 1898), which in its most general form states that behavior can be influenced by its consequences.

Refinements for the study of operant behavior, and substantial theoretical developments for understanding it, were developed largely by B. F. Skinner (1938). Important among these innovations was the development of experimental apparatus for the study of operant behavior. The operant-conditioning chamber (or Skinner box, as it is often called by those who do not specialize in the study of such behavior) consists generally of a small space, with extraneous sounds and light blocked out, equipped with a device that can be moved (e.g., a small lever for a rodent) and a method for delivering consequences (e.g., a device that dispenses small amounts of food). In Skinner's earliest experiments individual, mildly food-deprived rats were placed in such apparatus and allowed to explore. If the rat pressed the lever, a pellet of food was delivered immediately. Subsequently the rat pressed the lever frequently; that is, its initially low probability of pressing the lever was replaced by a high probability. This change in the rat's behavior is called *operant conditioning*, and several features of the procedure and the resulting change in behavior are worthy of note.

First, the behavioral process that produces the increased probability is called *reinforcement*, and the consequence itself is called a *reinforcer*. The arrangement wherein a food pellet follows each lever press is called a *contingency of reinforcement*. The action, e.g., the lever press in this example, that is increased in probability is typically called a response (although it apparently occurs in response to nothing in particular). Thus, a contingency is arranged between a response and a reinforcer. Operant conditioning can be viewed as analogous to natural selection (Skinner, 1981). Just as successful variations in organisms survive and become more prevalent across generations, so do successful forms of behavior in a creature's lifetime. Also, as is the case in interpreting the complexity and diversity of biological organisms, complexity of behavior can be interpreted as arising from the repeated, cumulative operation of simple selection.

Careful consideration reveals that each repetition of action in an operant conditioning process is actually an instance from an *operant class* (Skinner, 1938). For example, because no two lever presses are exactly alike with respect to all details (e.g., force, extent, limbs used,

placement of parts of paws, etc.), what increases in subsequent probability is the likelihood that the lever is pressed, not the particular form of the behavior that accomplishes that end. Operants, therefore, are defined by what they accomplish rather than their appearance (i.e., their function rather than their form). Catania (1973) elaborated on this feature of operants by distinguishing between descriptive and functional operants. The descriptive definition of an operant describes what the operant must accomplish, i.e., the physical parameters of what each instance of the operant must achieve in order to be eligible for reinforcement. In the simplified case of a rat pressing a lever, the descriptive definition indicates the minimum force with which the lever must be pressed and the distance it must travel. Any action on the part of the rat that accomplishes moving the lever in accord with those criteria counts as an eligible instance. The functional operant, by contrast, includes only those forms of behavior that become more probable after reinforcement. For example, presses of the lever that are insufficient in force to move it may increase in probability, whereas certain forms, like diving onto the lever and hitting with the nose, may show no increase in probability.

That operants are identified by their function has led to important perspectives in cases of maladaptive behavior. For example, behavior such as vomiting and self-injury that usually would be thought of as "involuntary" has been shown to be operant behavior in some cases (Iwata, Dorsey, Slifer, Bauman, & Richman, 1982; Wolf, Birnbrauer, Williams, & Lawler, 1966). Such discoveries allowed arrangement of new consequences to reduce the frequency of the maladaptive behavior.

Reinforcement is most effective if it is immediate, and less effective if there is a delay between the action and the delivery of the reinforcer. Behavior, however, can be effectively conditioned with delayed reinforcement (Lattal & Gleeson, 1990), but conditioning proceeds slowly and response probability cannot be increased to as great a degree as that seen with immediate reinforcement.

The experimental setup devised by Skinner allows the action of interest (e.g., the lever press) to occur at any time. This arrangement is referred to as a *free-operant* situation, and may be contrasted with other arrangements in which performance of the measured behavior does not leave the subject in position to execute it again immediately (e.g., going out a door, which requires that the room be reentered before it can be exited again). These latter arrangements are called discrete-trial operant-conditioning procedures.

The most commonly used measure of performance in experiments with free operants is response frequency, or rate. Response rate is assumed to reflect response probability. Rate of response is a measure that that can be obtained for any activity. Rate of behavior can be illustrated in the slope of *cumulative records*. A cumulative record of the occurrence of some activity is produced by having a pen that moves at a constant speed from left to right also move up a fixed amount each time the behavior of interest occurs. A graph is formed that shows the cumulated total number of instances of the operant over time.

Operants may be very tiny actions, or aggregates of several actions. For example, the contraction of a single muscle fiber can serve as an operant (e.g., Laurenti-Lions, Gallego, Chambille, Vardon, & Jacquemin, 1985). Similarly, an action as complex as imitating the action of another person has been shown to operant behavior (Baer, Peterson, & Sherman, 1967). Interestingly, in the case of contraction of single muscle fibers serving as operants, the human subjects in those experiments were unable to describe what they did that resulted in presentation of reinforcers. That is, the operant conditioning was unconscious.

Concern with the identification of consequences that can serve as reinforcers has been an enduring theoretical and research issue. Obviously, not all consequences can serve effectively as reinforcers, and those that do may not do so at all times. For practical purposes, once one discovers a reinforcer for one operant class it usually will be effective as reinforcement for another operant class; there are, however, exceptions. The most recent general developments in attempts to identify reinforcers in advance of their demonstrated effectiveness as reinforcers have focused on what behavior the reinforcer itself allows (cf. Timberlake & Allison, 1974). For example, presentation of a food pellet allows one to eat. In a wide variety of cases, depriving a creature of the opportunity to engage in some activity will make the opportunity to engage in that behavior effective as reinforcement for some other behavior. In the case described for the rat whose lever presses result in food presentation, depriving the rat of the opportunity to eat is necessary for presentation of food to serve as reinforcement. More generally, depriving the rat of doing anything it normally does will result in making the opportunity to engage in that behavior effective as reinforcement.

Deprivation is one example of what have come to be called *establishing operations* (Michael, 1982), circumstances that temporarily alter the effectiveness of consequences and evoke behavior formerly reinforced by those consequences. Consider, for example, a situation in which one is repairing a bicycle. It may become apparent that a screwdriver is needed to accomplish the next step: It is evident a screw must be removed. At that point, the screw appearing is an establishing operation that turns access to a screwdriver into a reinforcer. Thus behavior that has previously been effective in getting screwdrivers, for example, looking in the tool-box or asking an assistant to hand over a screwdriver, will become more likely. The effects of establishing operations are typically temporary. Once a rat has eaten, food will not be effective as reinforcement for a while, and once the screw is removed from the bicycle the screwdriver is no longer needed.

When presentation of some event as a consequence of behavior makes that behavior more likely in the future, the process is called *positive reinforcement*. When removal of a stimulus (e.g., a loud noise) or situation as a consequence of behavior increases the subsequent probability of that behavior, the process is called *negative reinforcement*. Some stimuli (like food for a hungry animal or painful stimuli) function as reinforcers without any special training. Such events are called primary, or unconditioned, reinforcers. Other stimuli (e.g., money) can serve as reinforcers only after special learning has taken place. These stimuli are called conditioned reinforcers.

Operant conditioning not only can increase the frequency of behavior that originally occurs at a low frequency, it also can be used to produce entirely new forms of behavior through *shaping*, which is accomplished by reinforcing successive approximations to the desired final form of behavior. For example, to induce a pigeon to peck a lighted disk on a wall, one can initially make reinforcement depend on movement toward the wall. Once the pigeon approaches the wall, reinforcement can then be made to depend on small head movements toward the disk. The criterion for reinforcement can then be gradually altered to require ever larger head movements, and so on until the disk is pecked.

Once an operant has been established with reinforcement its rate can be maintained at high levels by delivering reinforcement after some rather than all instances (intermittent reinforcement). When each instance produces reinforcement, the procedure is called *continuous reinforcement*. There are virtually limitless ways in which intermittent (or partial) reinforcement can be arranged, and such arrangements usually are called *schedules of reinforcement* (cf. Ferster & Skinner 1957; Zeiler, 1984). Common schedules are those that base reinforcement on the number of instances (ratio schedules) or that require that some amount of time must pass before a response can result in reinforcement (interval schedules). Reinforcement schedules exert great influence over the rate and temporal patterns of operants through time. One of the important functions of schedules of reinforcement is to establish very large, temporally extended samples of behavior with very little reinforcement. For example, thousands of responses per hour can be maintained under a schedule in which every two hundredth response, on average, is followed by reinforcement (Ferster & Skinner, 1957).

The discontinuation of reinforcement is called *ex-*

tinction, and the effect is that the rate of response eventually returns to its original level. A cumulative record of a response undergoing extinction is negatively accelerated and is called an *extinction curve*. One important effect of intermittent reinforcement is that it can greatly slow the decline in response rate produced by extinction: It increases the persistence of behavior when reinforcement is not available. This result is often called the *partial-reinforcement-extinction effect*.

Reinforcement and extinction can be employed in tandem to produce *response differentiation* or *stimulus discrimination*. In the case of response differentiation, some forms (or *topographies*) of behavior are eligible for reinforcement and others are not. For example, suppose lever presses with force exceeding some minimum amount are established through operant conditioning. Next, the minimum force required is doubled so that some of the previously effective presses no longer are, that is, they are subjected to extinction. The usual result is that the frequency of presses that meet the new criterion increases and the frequency of those that no longer are effective decreases (cf. Herrick, Myers, & Korotkin, 1959). Shaping is a special case of response differentiation in which the criteria for reinforcement change systematically. In the case of stimulus discrimination, whether instances of an operant class can be reinforced depends on the presence or absence of an external stimulus. For example, a rat's lever presses can result in food presentation when a light is on, but not when it is off. Arranging such a circumstance usually results in the probability of the lever press being high when the light is on and low when it is off. When that occurs, the light is called a *discriminative stimulus* (S^D) that sets the occasion for the lever press to be reinforced, and the response is said to be under *stimulus control*. When an operant is under stimulus control it is said to be a *discriminated operant*, and to exemplify the effects of a *three-term contingency*. The three terms are the S^D, the action (or response), and the reinforcer, sometimes summarized as the antecedent condition, the behavior, and the consequence (ABC). All operants can be conceptualized as illustrating effects of three-term contingencies.

Once a stimulus has been established as an S^D it can serve additional functions. One of the most important is that it can serve as a conditioned reinforcer. This is easily illustrated by its use in establishing a sequence of actions called a *behavioral chain*. For example, if illumination of a light has been established as an S^D for pressing a lever then one can arrange a circumstance in which when a tone is on, sniffing a hole will result in illumination of the light, in the presence of which a lever press can result in food presentation. Onset of the light will serve as effective reinforcement for sniffing the hole. The sequence can then be lengthened by making onset of the tone depend on some other action, like

pulling a string, so that the behavioral chain would become: pull string→tone on, sniff hole→light on, press lever→get food. In this sequence, the tone and the light each serve two functions. They serve as discriminative stimuli, tone for the sniff and light for the lever press, and as conditioned reinforcers, tone for the pull and light for the sniff. They are called conditioned reinforcers because their effectiveness as reinforcers is conditional on the experience with the three-term contingencies.

After a stimulus has been established as a discriminative stimulus for some action, other stimuli that are similar to that stimulus may also come to evoke the same action. This phenomenon is called *stimulus generalization*. For example, a monkey might be exposed to a contingency in which presses on a panel with a vertical line on it are reinforced and presses on the panel when it has a horizontal line on it are not. The usual result of such experience is that a discrimination will form, that is, the monkey presses when the vertical line is on the panel and does not when the horizontal line appears. If a line that deviates 10° from vertical is presented, the monkey, never having seen that line before, is likely to press the panel. If a line that deviates 70° from vertical is displayed the monkey is less likely to press, but perhaps more likely to press than when the horizontal line is presented. Such an outcome would illustrate a *gradient of generalization*.

Separate contingencies for independent operants can be arranged. Such arrangements allow the study of concurrent operants. A great deal of experimental attention has been given to the study of concurrent operants in which each operant is maintained by a schedule of reinforcement. In these "choice" situations a very common result is that the relative frequency of emission of the two operants is well predicted by the relative frequency of reinforcement for them. For example, if the reinforcement schedule for one of the operants provides consequences twice as often as for the other operant, then the first operant will occur more frequently. In many circumstances, the relative frequency of an operant is close to the relative frequency of reinforcement for it. This regularity is known as the *matching law* (Davison & McCarthy, 1988; Herrnstein, 1970).

There are two general classes of procedures to study negative reinforcement. The simpler of the two is *escape* conditioning in which a stimulus (e.g., an irritating loud noise) is presented, and some action (e.g., a lever press) terminates it for some period of time. If such a contingency results in an increase in the frequency of the action, negative reinforcement has been observed, and the stimulus is called an *aversive stimulus*. In the case of negative reinforcement, the establishing operation is not deprivation but rather the presentation of an aversive stimulus.

The more complicated set of procedures to study

negative reinforcement comprise those called *avoidance contingencies*. In these arrangements, instances of an operant class postpone or prevent the delivery of an aversive stimulus. In a commonly used procedure (Sidman, 1953) brief electric shocks are scheduled to occur at fixed temporal intervals (e.g., every 20 seconds). If the subject makes the specified response (e.g., pushes a button), the possibility of shock delivery is postponed by some amount of time (e.g., 20 seconds). Thus, each button press yields 20 seconds of "safety" from the time of the press, so if the button is pressed more frequently than once every 20 seconds no shocks will be delivered. Avoidance contingencies are effective in increasing the probability of behavior and therefore offer a puzzle. There is no immediate consequence of an effective avoidance response, yet conditioning can proceed quite rapidly.

A widely used procedure that appears to involve avoidance conditioning is called *passive avoidance*. In these procedures a two-chamber apparatus is used, one part is dark and the other part brightly lit. Subjects, frequently mice, are placed in the brightly lit side. Bright light is aversive for mice, so they go to the dark side as an escape activity. When they reach the dark side however, electric shock to the feet is delivered. Upon subsequent exposure to the apparatus, a mouse will be slower in moving to the dark part of the apparatus. This procedure is probably better categorized as illustrating the process of punishment. [*See* Punishment.]

Bibliography

Baer, D. M., Peterson, R. F., & Sherman, J. A. (1967). The development of imitation by reinforcing behavioral similarity to a model. *Journal of the Experimental Analysis of Behavior, 10*, 405–416.

Catania, A. C. (1973). The concept of the operant in the analysis of behavior. *Behaviorism, 1*, 103–116.

Davison, M., & McCarthy, D. (1988). *The matching law.* Hillsdale, NJ: Erlbaum.

Ferster, C. B., & Skinner, B. F. (1957). *Schedules of reinforcement.* New York: Appleton-Century-Crofts.

Herrick, R. M., Myers, J. L., & Korotkin, A. L. (1959). Changes in S^D and $S^\triangle$ rates during the development of an operant discrimination. *Journal of Comparative and Physiological Psychology, 52*, 359–364.

Herrnstein, R. J. (1970). On the law of effect. *Journal of the Experimental Analysis of Behavior, 13*, 243–266.

Iwata, B. I., Dorsey, M. F., Slifer, K. J., Bauman, K. E., & Richman, G. S. (1982). Toward a functional analysis of self injury. *Analysis and Intervention in Developmental Disabilities, 2*, 3–20.

Lattal, K. A., & Gleeson, S. (1990). Response acquisition with delayed reinforcement. *Journal of Experimental Psychology: Animal Behavior Processes, 16*, 27–39.

Laurenti-Lions, L., Gallego, J., Chambille, B., Vardon, G., & Jacquemin, C. (1985). Control of myoelectrical responses through reinforcement. *Journal of the Experimental Analysis of Behavior, 44*, 185–193.

Michael, J. (1982). Distinguishing between discriminative and motivational functions of stimuli. *Journal of the Experimental Analysis of Behavior, 37*, 149–155.

Sidman, M. (1953). Two temporal parameters in the maintenance of avoidance behavior by the white rat. *Journal of Comparative and Physiological Psychology, 46*, 253–261.

Skinner, B. F. (1938). *The behavior of organisms: An experimental analysis.* New York: Appleton-Century-Crofts.

Skinner, B. F. (1981). Selection by consequences. *Science, 213*, 501–504.

Thorndike, E. L. (1898). Animal intelligence: An experimental study of the associative processes in animals. *Psychological Review Monograph Supplements, 2* (No. 4).

Timberlake, W., & Allison, J. (1974). Response deprivation: An empirical approach to instrumental performance. *Psychological Review, 81*, 146–164.

Wolf, M. M., Birnbrauer, J. S., Williams, T., & Lawler, J. (1966). A note on the apparent extinction of the vomiting behavior of a retarded child. In L. P. Krasner & L. Ullman (Eds.), *Case studies in behavior modification* (pp. 364–366). New York: Holt, Rinehart, & Winston.

Zeiler, M. D. (1984). The sleeping giant: Reinforcement schedules. *Journal of the Experimental Analysis of Behavior, 42*, 485–493.

M. N. Branch

Operant Conditioning Chamber

A device invented by B. F. Skinner in the 1930s, originally for animal experimentation, in which stimuli, responses, and consequences of behavior could be specified, isolated, and thereby studied precisely. The device became known colloquially both in and outside psychology as the Skinner Box after being thus described by Clark Hull, but Skinner himself expressed displeasure with the label. The chamber is a ubiquitous feature in psychology laboratories devoted to studies of operant behavior, Pavlovian conditioning, animal psychophysics, memory, cognition, and pharmacological and physiological variables that affect behavior. Skinner's early chambers, illustrated in Figure 1, were designed for rats but analogous chambers have been used in the study of most species of interest to psychologists, including humans.

Although the size and configuration of the chamber differs depending on the species and the variables under study, most chambers share several features (Ator, 1991; Ferster, 1953). Chambers typically are separated by a vertical panel into a work area, where the subject is located, and a service area, where control and recording devices attached to the vertical panel are maintained by the experimenter. These attached devices of-

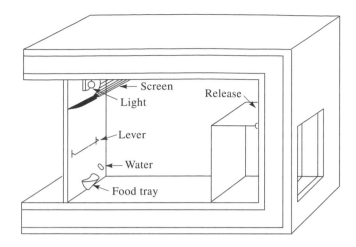

OPERANT CONDITIONING: Operant Conditioning Chamber. Figure 1. Diagram of an operant conditioning chamber for a rat. Contemporary versions usually do not include a screen over the light nor a "release" antechamber. Dimensions are not given for this chamber, but a typical contemporary chamber for rats is approximately 25 centimeters long by 22 centimeters wide by 20 centimeters high. (From Skinner, 1938, p. 49. Copyright 1938 by the B. F. Skinner Foundation.)

ten include: a response-defining and measuring device, or operandum (Skinner, 1962); lights, speakers, or other devices for generating stimuli; and one or more devices for delivering consequences such as food, water, or electric shock. The range of events that can be programmed as antecedent stimuli and as consequences in the chamber are limited only by the investigator's ingenuity. For example, Henton (1969) studied olfactory sensitivity of pigeons by infusing odors into the chamber, and Van Hemel (1972) created a device for delivering live mice to mouse-killing rats to assess the reinforcing properties of mice killing.

The chamber proper is isolated from such extraneous variables as lights and ambient noise by enclosing it in a sound-attenuating shell. Adequate ventilation is ensured by an exhaust fan in the wall of the shell. Visual access to the organism in the chamber is provided through "peep holes" or closed-circuit television. The chamber typically is interfaced via connecting cables to a computer that is programmed to arrange presentations of antecedent stimuli and consequences and to record responses.

Nonhuman animals are either allowed to move freely about within the chamber or, often with primates, physically restrained within the chamber. Human subjects typically are seated at a console and asked to remain seated during the experimental session. In some cases, the animal actually lives in the chamber throughout the experiment, but more commonly animals are placed in the chamber for time-limited experimental sessions but permanently housed elsewhere.

Specific chamber features may affect behavior. For example, key-peck response rates of pigeons are higher in chambers with less floor space (Skuban & Richardson, 1975). The typical chamber is a cube, but one early chamber for rats was cylindrical (Heron & Skinner, 1939), and Skinner (1938) suggested that such a cylin-

drical chamber for pigeons might modulate competing exploratory behavior typical in conventional cube-shaped chambers.

Bibliography

Ator, N. A. (1991). Subjects and instrumentation. In I. Iversen & K. A. Lattal (Eds.), *Techniques in the behavioral and neural sciences: Experimental analysis of behavior, part 1* (pp. 1–62). Amsterdam: Elsevier. A contemporary review of operant conditioning chambers and associated apparatus.

Ferster, C. B. (1953). The use of the free operant in the analysis of behavior. *Psychological Bulletin, 50,* 263–274. A discussion of operant conditioning chambers and associated apparatus and methods by the scientist who, aside from B. F. Skinner, probably contributed the most to the development of behavioral research apparatus.

Henton, W. W. (1969). Conditioned suppression to odorous stimuli in pigeons. *Journal of the Experimental Analysis of Behavior, 12,* 175–185.

Heron, W. T., & Skinner, B. F. (1939). An apparatus for the study of animal behavior. *Psychological Record, 3,* 166–176. A detailed description of an early apparatus for use with animals.

Skinner, B. F. (1938). *Behavior of organisms.* New York: Appleton Century. Skinner's scholarly and highly original book that is rich in apparatus, research methods, and behavioral data.

Skinner, B. F. (1962). Operandum. *Journal of the Experimental Analysis of Behavior, 5,* 224.

Skinner, B. F. (1986). Some thoughts about the future. *Journal of the Experimental Analysis of Behavior, 45,* 229–235.

Skuban, W. E., & Richardson, W. K. (1975). The effect of the size of the test environment on behavior under two temporally defined schedules. *Journal of the Experimental Analysis of Behavior, 23,* 271–275.

Van Hemel, P. (1972). Aggression as a reinforcer: Operant behavior in the mouse-killing rat. *Journal of the Experimental Analysis of Behavior, 17,* 237–245.

Kennon A. Lattal

OPERATIONALISM. *See* Philosophy, *article on* Philosophy of Science.

OPIATES are drugs derived from opium and include morphine, codeine, their semisynthetic congeners, and derivatives of thebaine, another constituent of opium. The term *opioid* is more inclusive, designating all drugs with morphine-like activity, naturally occurring and synthetic opioid peptides, and antagonists. At one time the term *narcotic* referred to any drug that produced sleep, but it then became associated with strong opiate analgesics. It is now used in the legal context to refer to a wide variety of abused substances.

The word opium is derived from the Greek name for juice. Opium powder is obtained from the air-dried, milky exudate of unripe seed capsules of the oriental poppy *Papaver somniferum.* This poppy had its origin in Asia Minor but is now grown in countries with similar climates throughout the world. Opium contains more than 20 active alkaloids, but the main constituents are the phenanthrenes morphine (10 to 10.5% by weight), named after Morpheus, the Greek god of dreams, and codeine (0.5% by weight). Thebaine (0.2% opium by weight) has little analgesic activity, but several important opiates are derived from it (e.g., oxycodon, buprenorphine, and the antagonist naloxone). Semisynthetic derivatives of morphine or codeine include diacetyl morphine (heroin), hydromorphone (Dilaudid), oxycodone (Numorphan, OxyContin), and hydrocodone used in conjunction with other ingredients in antitussive (e.g., Duratuss HD) and analgesic-antipyretic mixtures (e.g., Lortab, Vicodin, Vicoprofen). Synthetic opiate analgesics such as meperidine (Demerol), and methadone (Roxane) have different chemical structures than morphine but produce similar behavioral and physiological effects.

Opium has been used for centuries in the Middle East. The earliest written reference to the psychological effects of opium was a Sumerian idiogram dated about 4000 BCE and translated as "joy plant" (McKim, 1997). Opium was used by the oral route medicinally for pain relief and to control dysentery. Opium smoking for its euphoric effects was popularized in China in the 1600s. As its popularity increased through Europe, opium found its way into elixirs, salves, syrups, and many other formulations and was used to treat nearly every disorder and disease.

Morphine was isolated from opium in 1806, and the discovery of other opiates soon followed. The use of opiates rather than opium preparations began to spread throughout the medical world in the middle of the nineteenth century. Shortly afterward, the invention of the hypodermic syringe led to the intravenous use of opiates, which are not well absorbed from the gastrointestinal tract and need to be inhaled or injected for their full effect. The increasing use of intravenous opiates for clinical management of pain as well as recreational use led to the search for opiates free of addictive potential and opiate antagonists such as naloxone (Narcan) for the treatment of acute opiate toxicity due to clinical overdosage, accidental overdosage in addicts, and suicide attempts.

Studies in animals and humans show that morphine exerts its primary effects on the central nervous system and organs containing smooth muscle. The pharmacological effects of opiates are diverse and include analgesia, drowsiness, alterations in mood (euphoria), respiratory depression, decreased gastrointestinal motility, alterations in the endocrine and autonomic nervous systems, nausea, vomiting, and miosis.

In humans, rapid intravenous injection of an opiate produces a brief, intense "rush," "kick," or "thrill," consisting of a warm flushing of the skin and sensations in the lower abdomen described by addicts as similar or greater in intensity and quality to sexual orgasm. The euphoria is associated with feelings of well-being, inner satisfaction, and a reduction in anger, anxiety, and depression. As use continues, tolerance to the euphoric effects of opiates develops and there is a shift to unpleasant mood states and increased psychiatric symptoms. In a study of adult male heroin addicts, the initial euphoric effects of intravenous heroin were replaced over a period of days by unpleasant feelings, relieved for only a brief period ranging from 30 to 60 minutes after each injection (Meyer & Mirin, 1979). In addition to the deterioration in mood, a decrease in physical activity and an increase in aggressive behavior and social isolation were observed. These effects were diminished when the subjects were maintained on methadone, a long-lasting opiate used in the treatment of opiate addiction. The effects of opiates on mood also differ, depending on whether the drug is given to an experienced user or a naive subject. A classic study has shown that former addicts are more likely to experience positive feelings after opiates, whereas first-time users report sedation, mental clouding, and feelings of sickness or nausea (Lasagana, Felsinger, & Beecher, 1955).

In humans, compulsive use of low to moderate doses of opiates does not appear to interfere with work performance, intellectual and physical abilities, or health.

As long as users have access to a cheap, reliable source of opiates, it is possible to pursue careers and maintain a normal life. Thus, the current approach to the treatment of addiction to opiates, primarily heroin, is maintenance therapy with opiates such as methadone (Roxane, Dolophine) or LAAM (l-alpha-acetylmethadol), which can be administered orally and are able to suppress physical withdrawal symptoms for a period of 24 hours or more.

The development of tolerance and physical dependence with repeated use is a characteristic feature of all opiates. Tolerance of the euphoric effects of opiates (especially heroin) develops rapidly, so addicts need to increase their dose to reexperience the elusive "high." Tolerance also develops to the sedative, analgesic, respiratory-depressant, and emetic effects of opiates but does not develop equally or at the same rate and depends in part on the pattern of use. Constipation, insomnia, some degree of miosis, excessive sweating, and diminished sex drive and sexual function can persist in addicts even after several years of methadone maintenance, but tolerance never develops to the respiratory depressant effects.

Opiates exert their actions via interaction with three major classes of opioid receptors—mu, delta, and kappa—that have been identified in the central and peripheral nervous systems of animals and humans, and cloned from rodent and human cDNAs (Mansour, Khachaturian, Lewis, Akil, & Watson, 1988). In addition, three types of endogenous opioid peptides—enkephalins, dynorphins, and beta-endorphins—which are derived from distinct precursor molecules (proenkephalin, prodynorphin, and pro-opiomelanocortin, respectively) have been identified in the central and peripheral nervous systems. Opioid peptides are collectively referred to as endorphins. Enzymatic processing of the precursors gives rise to peptides that vary in length, opioid-receptor selectivity, and potency. Opioid peptides are present in the brain, peripheral tissues, and plasma in animals and humans and appear to function as neurotransmitters or neuromodulators.

Experimental studies of transgenic mice deficient in the precursor molecules for opioid peptides will help to clarify the physiological roles of enkephalins, dynorphins, and endorphins. The profiles of opiate interactions with opioid receptors in humans has been inferred from clinical observations and extrapolations of pharmacological effects in animals. Attempts to identify the functional effects of opioid receptors and opioid peptides have been established by targeted disruption or knockout approaches in mice. Transgenic mice with targeted disruption of the mu, delta, or kappa opioid receptor suggest that the reinforcing, analgesic, behavioral, and neuroendocrine effects of opiates are mediated primarily by mu receptors (Kieffer, 1999). Future studies will define the role of delta and kappa opioid receptors in the regulation of pain and emotions.

In humans, the prominent psychological, emotional, and clinically useful actions of opiates are mediated through interaction with the mu receptor. Consequences of mu receptor activation include euphoria, analgesia, reduced gastrointestinal motility, respiratory depression, and miosis.

In humans, drugs that interact with the kappa receptor produce a syndrome that is comprised of perceptual changes, cognitive alterations, dysphoria, pseudohallucinations, and a variable sedative component with decrements in performance and an overall deterioration of well-being. The constellation of disturbances in thought and body image induced by kappa opiates has been referred to as psychotomimetic (disoriented and/or depersonalized feelings), although they differ from those seen in true psychoses in that the subjects are typically aware that the effects are drug-induced (Pfeiffer, Brantl, Herz, & Emrich, 1986). Opiates such as pentazocine, nalorphine, and nalbuphine produce analgesia by activating kappa receptors in the spinal cord. The analgesia is not diminished in animals tolerant to morphine-like mu agonists, suggesting that there is a distinct separation of the functional effects of mu and kappa opiates. Kappa opiates also produce less intense miosis and respiratory depression than mu opiates.

The consequences of activating delta receptors in humans is not clear, in part due to the lack of selective drugs that can enter into the brain. In animals, delta agonists produce analgesia and positive reinforcing effects. The development of selective agonists may help clarify the physiological role of delta receptors in humans.

Opiates have several therapeutic indications. They are used primarily as potent analgesics reducing the emotional response to pain as well as producing analgesia. Morphine remains the major drug for the treatment of moderate to severe pain (Foley, 1993). Morphine, codeine, and meperidine (Demerol) are used to induce analgesia, tranquility, and even euphoria in managing the pain associated with terminal illnesses and cancer. Oral codeine or oxycodone are combined with nonsteroidal anti-inflammatories (e.g., Percocet, Percodan) to manage mild to moderate postoperative pain. Opiates are used as antitussive agents for cough suppression (e.g., codeine) and to alleviate the dypsnea associated with left ventricular failure and pulmonary edema. Loperamide (Imodium) and diphenoxylate (Lomotil) are used for inducing constipation in ileostomy or colostomy and treating exhausting diarrheas and dysenteries due to a number of causes. Opiates such as fentanyl (Sublimaze) and its congeners are used as primary anesthetic agents in certain surgical procedures, as well as intrathecally, epidurally, and for postoperative pain.

[*See also* Drug Abuse.]

Bibliography

Foley, K. M. (1993). Opiate analgesics in clinical pain management. In A. Herz (Ed.), *Handbook of experimental pharmacology* (Vol. 104, pp. 697–743). Berlin: Springer-Verlag.

Kieffer, B. L. (1999). Opioids: First lessons from knockout mice. *Trends in Pharmacological Sciences, 20,* 19–26.

Lasagana, L., Felsinger, J. M., & Beecher, H. K. (1955). Drug-induced mood changes in man. *Journal of the American Medical Association, 157,* 1006–1020.

Mansour, A., Khachaturian, H., Lewis, M. E., Akil, H., & Watson, S. J. (1988). Anatomy of CNS opioid receptors. *Trends in Neurosciences, 11,* 308–314.

McKim, W. A. (1997). *Drugs and behavior: An introduction to behavioral pharmacology* (3rd ed.). Upper Saddle River, NJ: Prentice Hall.

Meyer, R. E., & Mirin, S. M. (1979). *The heroin stimulus.* New York: Plenum Press.

Pfeiffer, A., Brantl, V., Herz, A., & Emrich, H. M. (1986). Psychotomimesis mediated by kappa opiate receptors. *Science, 233,* 774–776.

Linda Brady

OPINION. *See* Attitudes; *and* Survey Methodology.

OPPOSITIONAL DEFIANT DISORDER was introduced as a psychiatric diagnosis (first called oppositional disorder) in 1980 (American Psychiatric Association, *Diagnostic and Statistical Manual of Mental Disorders,* 1980), with the criteria and the diagnostic label changed in 1987 to oppositional defiant disorder (ODD). According to the *DSM–IV,* oppositional defiant disorder (ODD) is characterized by "a recurrent pattern of negativistic, defiant, disobedient, and hostile behavior toward authority figures" (APA, 1994, p. 91). The diagnosis requires the presence of at least four out of eight behaviors, which include losing one's temper, arguing with adults, defiance or refusal to comply with adult requests, deliberately annoying others, blaming others for one's mistakes or misbehavior, being easily annoyed, appearing angry and resentful, and behaving in a spiteful or vindictive manner. ODD is not diagnosed if symptomatic behaviors occur exclusively during a psychotic or mood disorder, or if criteria for antisocial personality disorder (if the individual is 18 years or older) or conduct disorder (CD) are met. Without this latter exclusionary criteria, almost all children diagnosed with CD would also qualify for a diagnosis of ODD.

ODD occurs in 2 to 16% of children (*DSM–IV,* APA, 1994), with two to three times as many boys as girls being diagnosed with ODD (Andersen, Williams, McGee, & Silva, 1987). The prevalence of ODD decreases at adolescence, while the prevalence of CD increases.

According to psychometric standards, the reliability for the diagnosis is moderately low. Based upon *DSM–IV* field trials (Lahey, Loeber, Quay, Frick, & Grimm, 1992), agreement between clinicians' independent diagnoses (kappa = 0.59) and test-retest reliability (kappa = 0.54) indicated little or no increase in reliability over earlier diagnostic criteria.

The status of ODD as a psychiatric diagnosis has been controversial since its inception and has included concerns about whether it is sufficiently distinct from normal oppositional behavior (Rey, 1993), especially in the preschool years. *DSM–IV* seeks to differentiate ODD from normative oppositionality by requiring not only that behaviors occur "more frequently than is typically observed in individuals of comparable age and developmental level" (APA, 1994, pp. 93–94), but also that these behaviors "cause significant impairment in social, academic or occupational functioning" (APA, 1994, pp. 93–94). The clinician has to decide, however, what constitutes more frequent than normal oppositional behavior, since guidelines have not been empirically determined.

Debate surrounding ODD has also centered on whether the diagnosis represents a distinct disorder or only a mild form of conduct disorder. The validity of ODD as a distinct diagnosis has been supported by factor analytic studies showing a high rate of internal consistency among ODD symptoms and evidence that ODD and CD follow a different developmental course. ODD behaviors occur, on average, at a younger age than CD behaviors, with the average age of onset being 6 years for ODD and 9 years for CD (Loeber, Lahey, & Thomas, 1991). Although a very high percentage of youth (80 to 90%) diagnosed with childhood-onset CD were previously diagnosed as ODD, this is not true for adolescent-onset CD (Frick et al., 1991; Lahey, Loeber, Quay, Frick, & Grimm, 1992). The majority of children diagnosed with ODD do not develop conduct disorder as they grow older. Among ODD youth followed over a 3-year period, 25% were later diagnosed as CD, 52% retained the diagnosis of ODD, and another 20 to 25% received no diagnosis (Lahey Loeber, Quay, Frick, & Grimm, 1992). Although critics voice concern that some young children with transitory symptoms are labeled unnecessarily, proponents of the ODD diagnosis (Loeber, Lahey, & Thomas, 1991) believe that it is important for the early identification and treatment of children who are at risk for continued aggressive and antisocial behavior.

Substantial overlap exists among youngsters diagnosed with Attention Deficit Hyperactivity Disorder (ADHD) and either ODD or CD, but they remain separate problem areas (Waldman & Lilienfield, 1991). The co-occurrence of ODD and ADHD contributes to the risk of childhood onset CD, particularly among youngsters with an early onset of ODD, many ODD symptoms or other comorbid psychiatric disorders, and a high rate of antisocial disorders among family members (Biederman et al., 1996). Children diagnosed with ADHD and either ODD or CD are at risk for academic failure, peer rejection, antisocial activity, and later negative life outcomes (Hinshaw & Anderson, 1996).

Individual, familial, and broader contextual factors and their transactional interplay have been implicated as complex casual influences in the etiology of ODD (Hinshaw & Anderson, 1996). Social cognition, including the child's perception and evaluation of the social world, constitutes an individual factor through which psychobiological and family factors may effect antisocial behavior. For example, aggressive youngsters often attribute hostile intent to unclear peer interactions, have difficulty in generating assertive solutions to conflictual situations, expect that aggressive behavior will be rewarded, and overlook pertinent social cues (Crick & Dodge, 1994). Familial factors associated with the risk for ODD include parental psychopathology, a history of antisocial activity, substance abuse, poor quality attachment, marital disruption, and ineffective parenting practices (Barkley, 1997). Among contextual factors, exposure to community violence has been shown to place children at risk for aggression (Guerra, Huesmann, Tolan, Van Acker, & Eron, 1995), supporting the need for community-based prevention efforts. Community violence may also indirectly impact children through its effects on parents.

The observation that family interactions of many oppositional children are characterized by coercive interactions (Patterson, 1982), in conjunction with harsh and inconsistent parental disciplinary methods (Patterson, 1982) and negative child temperamental characteristics (Loeber, 1988) has contributed to the design of behaviorally oriented parent training programs (e.g., Barkley, 1997; Patterson, 1982). Although childhood oppositional problems are particularly resistant to treatment, research indicates that parent-training programs are among the most frequent and effective, especially when intervention occurs early (Dishion & Patterson, 1992). Providing parents with additional education and counseling aimed at reducing marital conflict and strengthening parental beliefs about behavior management may also increase effectiveness (Hanish, Tolan, & Guerra, 1996). Cognitive-behavioral interventions, including social-skills training, teaching problem-solving skills, and anger management programs, have also achieved substantial success (Kronenberger & Meyer, 1996).

[*See also* Disruptive Behavior Disorders.]

Bibliography

American Psychiatric Association. (1980). *Diagnostic and statistical manual of mental disorders* (3rd ed.). Washington, DC: Author.

American Psychiatric Association. (1994). *Diagnostic and statistical manual of mental disorders* (4th ed.). Washington, DC: Author.

Anderson, J. C., Williams, S., McGee, R., & Silva, P. A. (1987). DSM–III disorders in preadolescent children. *Archives of General Psychiatry, 44,* 69–78.

Barkley, R. A. (1997). *Defiant children: A clinician's manual for assessment and parent training* (2nd ed.). New York: Guilford Press. A useful manual for clinicians involved in designing behaviorally oriented parent training programs for aggressive youth.

Biederman, J., Faraone, S. V., Millberger, S., Curtis, S., Chen, L., Marrs, A., Ouellette, C., Moore, P., & Spencer, T. (1996). Predictors of persistence and remission of ADHD into adolescence: Results from a four-year prospective follow up study. *Journal of the American Academy of Child and Adolescent Psychiatry, 35,* 343–351.

Crick, N. R., & Dodge, K. A. (1994). A review and reformulation of social information processing mechanisms in children's social adjustment. *Psychological Bulletin, 115,* 74–101.

Dishion, T. J., & Patterson, G. R. (1992). Age effects in parent training outcome. *Behavior Therapy, 23,* 719–729.

Frick, P. J., Lahey, B. B., Loeber, R., Stouthamer-Loeber, M., Green, S., Hart, E. L., & Christ, A. G. (1991). Oppositional defiant disorders and conduct disorders in boys: Patterns of behavioral covariation. *Journal of Clinical Child Psychology, 20,* 292–208.

Guerra, N. G., Huesmann, L. R., Tolan, P. H., Van Acker, R., & Eron, L. D. (1995). Stressful events and individual beliefs as correlates of economic disadvantage and aggression among urban children. *Journal of Consulting and Clinical Psychology, 63,* 518–528.

Hanish, L. D., Tolan, P. H., & Guerra, N. G. (1996). Treatment of oppositional defiant disorder. In M. A. Reinecke, F. M. Dattilio, & A. Freeman (Eds.), *Cognitive therapy with children and adolescents* (pp. 62–78). New York: Guilford Press.

Hinshaw, S. P., & Anderson, C. A. (1996). Conduct and oppositional defiant disorders. In E. J. Mash & R. A. Barkley (Eds.), *Child psychopathology* (pp. 113–149). New York: Guilford Press.

Kronenberger, W. G., & Meyer, R. G. (1996). *The child clinician's handbook.* Needham Heights, MA: Allyn & Bacon.

Lahey, B. B., Loeber, R., Quay, H. C., Frick, P. J., & Grimm,

J. (1992). Oppositional defiant and conduct disorders: Issues to be resolved for *DSM–IV. Journal of the American Academy of Child and Adolescent Psychiatry, 31,* 539–546. Identifies critical issues in the diagnosis of oppositional defiant disorder.

Loeber, R. (1988). Natural histories of conduct problems, delinquency, and associated substance use. In B. B. Lahey & A. E. Kazdin (Eds.), *Advances in clinical child psychology* (Vol. 11, pp. 73–124). New York: Plenum Press.

Loeber, R., Lahey, B. B., & Thomas, C. (1991). Diagnostic conundrum of oppositional defiant disorder and conduct disorder. *Journal of Abnormal Psychology, 100,* 379–390. Describes issues in differential diagnosis of ODD and CD.

Patterson, G. R. (1982). *Coercive family process.* Eugene, OR: Castalia. A classic work identifying interactional processes in families of aggressive children. Subsequent work by Patterson and his colleagues has contributed greatly to knowledge about families of aggressive children.

Rey, J. M. (1993). Oppositional defiant disorder. *American Journal of Psychiatry, 150,* 1769–1778.

Waldman, I. D., & Lilienfeld, S. O. (1991). Diagnostic efficiency of symptoms for oppositional defiant disorder and attention-deficit hyperactivity disorder. *Journal of Consulting and Clinical Psychology, 59,* 732–738.

Maureen E. Kenny